INVESTMENTS

SEVENTH EDITION

FRANK K. REILLY
Bernard J. Hank Professor
University of Notre Dame

EDGAR A. NORTON
Illinois State University

THOMSON

SOUTH-WESTERN

Australia · Canada · Mexico · Singapore · Spain · United Kingdom · United States

THOMSON

SOUTH-WESTERN

Investments, Seventh Edition
Frank K. Reilly and Edgar A. Norton

VP/Editorial Director:
Jack W. Calhoun

VP/Editor-in-Chief:
Dave Shaut

Executive Editor:
Scott Person

Senior Developmental Editor:
Elizabeth Thomson

Marketing Manager:
Heather MacMaster

Production Editor:
Tamborah Moore

Manager of Technology, Editorial:
Vicky True

Technology Project Editor:
John Barans

Web Coordinator:
Karen Schaffer

Senior Manufacturing Coordinator:
Sandee Milewski

Production House:
Lachina Publishing Services

Printer:
Transcontinental Printing
Louiseville, Quebec, CANADA

Art Director:
Chris Miller

Internal Designer:
Imbue Design

Cover Designer:
Imbue Design

Cover Photo:
Getty Images

Library of Congress Control Number:
2004118204

For more information about our
products, contact us at:

Thomson Learning Academic
Resource Center

1-800-423-0563

Thomson Higher Education
5191 Natorp Boulevard
Mason, OH 45040
USA

Asia (including India)
Thomson Learning
5 Shenton Way
#01-01 UIC Building
Singapore 068808

Australia/New Zealand
Thomson Learning Australia
102 Dodds Street
Southbank, Victoria 3006
Australia

Canada
Thomson Nelson
1120 Birchmount Road
Toronto, Ontario
M1K 5G4
Canada

Latin America
Thomson Learning
Seneca, 53
Colonia Polanco
11560 Mexico
D.F. Mexico

UK/Europe/Middle East/Africa
Thomson Learning
High Holborn House
50/51 Bedford Row
London WC1R 4LR
United Kingdom

Spain (including Portugal)
Thomson Paraninfo
Calle Magallanes, 25
28015 Madrid, Spain

To my best friend and wife,
Therese,
and the greatest gifts and
sources of our happiness,
Frank K. III, Charlotte, and Lauren
Clarence R. II, Michelle, and Sophie
Therese B. and Denise
Edgar B., Michele, Kayleigh, and Madison J. T.
—F.K.R.

To Dad and to the Memory of Mom;
to my best friend and wife, Becky,
and our gifts from God, Matthew and Amy
—E.A.N.

BRIEF CONTENTS

C O N T E N T S

The pleasure of authoring a textbook comes from writing about a subject that one enjoys and finds exciting. As authors, we hope that we can pass on to the reader not only knowledge but also the excitement we feel for the subject. In addition, writing about investments brings an added stimulant because the subject can affect the reader during his or her entire business career and beyond. We hope what readers derive from this course will help them enjoy better lives so that they will have learned how to manage their financial resources properly.

Throughout the book, a number of key points are emphasized:

1. Developed markets are nearly informationally efficient. That means news and its effect on investments are quickly reflected in asset prices. It is difficult to "beat the market averages" after taking differences in the risks between investments into account, which leads us to our second key point . . .

2. There is a tradeoff between expected return and risk. Because markets tend to be efficient, higher returns are expected to occur only if an investor takes on additional risk. Risk and expected return are directly related. However, it is likely inappropriate for an investor to take on higher and higher risks in the hopes of earning higher returns because of our third key point . . .

3. Investors need to invest at a risk level that is consistent with their risk preferences and constraints. Investors should take—and manage—prudent risks to maximize their after-tax returns in an effort to meet their financial goals. Taxes have a tremendous impact on investment returns, and investors must consider their effect. But investments need to be made based on one's risk preferences and financial goals. If a financial goal appears to be unattainable, an investor should think carefully before committing to higher-risk investments.

4. Investors need to consider investing across different asset classes, industries, and country borders to take advantage of growing opportunities in the global marketplace. As portfolio theory shows, one may be able to invest in a diversified portfolio of high-risk assets with little or no increase in the risk of the overall portfolio.

The purpose of this book is to help you understand how to manage your money so that you will derive the maximum benefit from what you earn. To accomplish this purpose, you need to learn about the investment alternatives available today, and, more importantly, you must develop a way of analyzing and thinking about investments that will remain with you in the years ahead when new and different opportunities become available.

Because of its dual purpose, the book mixes description and theory. The descriptive material discusses available investment instruments and considers the purpose and operation of capital markets in the United States and around the world. The theoretical portion details how you should evaluate current investments and future opportunities so that you can construct a portfolio of investments that will satisfy your risk–return objectives.

Preparing this seventh edition has been both exciting and challenging for two reasons. First, many changes have occurred in the securities markets during the last few years in terms of theory, empirical research, financial instruments, and trading practices. Second, as mentioned in prior editions, capital markets continue to become global and more integrated; cross-border investments are commonplace. New markets are being created or are opening around the world. Consequently, very early in the book (in Chapter 3) we present a compelling case for global investing. Subsequently, to ensure that you are prepared to function in this new global environment, almost every chapter discusses how investment practice or theory is influenced by the globalization of investments and capital markets. This completely integrated treatment will ensure that you leave this course with a global mind-set on investments that will serve you during the twenty-first century.

Intended Market

This book is addressed to both undergraduate and graduate students who want an in-depth discussion of investments and portfolio management. The presentation of the material is intended to be rigorous without being overly quantitative. A proper discussion of the modern developments in investments and portfolio theory must be rigorous. The summary results of numerous empirical studies reflect our personal belief that it is essential for theories to be exposed to the real world and be judged on the basis of how well they help us understand and explain reality. We also share insights from practitioners to show how theory is practically applied. To help prepare students for a possible career in investment analysis and portfolio management, this book draws on the body of knowledge and readings recommended for those preparing for the Chartered Financial Analyst (CFA®) exams. Many end-of-chapter questions and problems are drawn from previous CFA® exams.

Major Changes and Additions in the SEVENTH Edition

Every edition contains changes in writing and content, which we will review shortly. First, we want to mention several exciting additions to the Reilly/Norton *Investments* package.

- Thomson ONE is a professional analytical package used by professionals worldwide. Our text allows students to access Thomson ONE: Business School Edition. Students will find information on firms, including financial statement comparisons with competitors, stock price information, and indexes for comparing firm performance against the market or sector. Thomson ONE: Business School Edition is a great package for hands-on learning that rivals or exceeds those offered by other textbook publishers. We feature Thomson ONE: Business School Edition exercises in several end-of-chapter problem sets.
- Stock Navigator allows students to use real, time-delayed market information to simulate real-world stock-portfolio performance. Students can buy and sell securities in a time-dependent educational environment, without the high cost of mistakes in the real environment.
- Interactive e-Lectures reinforce key concepts through Flash-animated tutorials and interactive simulations. Students can review key concepts from the chapters on their own time, at their own pace, through the tutorial, and simulations allow students to manipulate charts, graphs, tables, and other calculations to dynamically reinforce concepts such as time value of money, standard deviation, bond valuation, and more. Interactive e-Lectures are highlighted throughout the text and are available on the Reilly/Norton Xtra! Web site. Instructors may have access to this site bundled with the textbook, or students may purchase access at http://reillyxtra.swlearning.com.

This edition has a number of changes suggested by reviewers that include expansion, reduction, and revision.

In terms of expansion, we've increased the number of chapters from 20 to 21. The new chapter—Chapter 11, "An Introduction to Valuation"—focuses solely on valuation techniques for bonds and stocks: time value of money concepts applied to bonds and several dividend discount models and relative pricing models (P/E, P/B, etc.) applied to stocks. This expansion allows the subsequent fixed-income and equity chapters to focus on variables that are important to valuation without the need to teach valuation concepts, too. The chapter can be taught in class or assigned, as background or review reading.

Over time, as the investments world has gained complexity, this book has added information on market changes, new instruments, techniques, and relevant academic studies. Still the seventh edition has joined the "dieting craze" by carefully reducing or rewriting content to slim down the size of the text without deleting important material.

Most chapters have undergone major revisions to keep them fresh, in terms of both content as well as new data and examples. The order of the chapters in this edition has been rearranged to better reflect how many users teach the subject of investments, particularly equity analysis. A firm grounding in investment principles, our four key points, and the investment environment is provided in Chapters 1 through 7. Portfolio concepts, theories, and practices in efficient markets are reviewed in Chapters 8 through 10.

The valuation section of the text begins with the new Chapter 11, which is followed by applications to fixed-income analysis in Chapter 12. Chapters relevant to stock analysis follow each other sequentially (Chapters 13 through 16).

We introduce the various kinds of derivative securities in Chapter 17 and show applications of forwards, futures, and options. Chapter 18 continues our discussion of derivatives, highlighting their valuation and several advanced uses in fixed-income and equity markets. The final part of the text ties valuation, portfolio theory, management, and derivatives together in a discussion of equity-portfolio management, fixed-income portfolio management, and various performance evaluation tools and methods.

Our text was among the first investment texts to reflect the growing use of the World Wide Web as a learning tool and a source of information. We continue this tradition as each chapter contains an annotated list of Web sites that relate to the chapter's topic. We go one step further to expose students to the practice of investments—all chapters have Web exercises to help the student learn the many investments-related resources available on the Internet. Further, virtually all chapters have spreadsheet exercises that offer students the opportunity to perform various analyses applying electronic spreadsheets to the chapter's topic.

A consistent industry and company example is used in the equity valuation–oriented chapters. We review the financial statements of Walgreens, analyze influences on the retail drugstore industry and the firm, and estimate the intrinsic value of Walgreens stock employing two valuation techniques and several specific valuation models.

The text has been thoroughly updated. In addition to chapter revisions, this edition includes numerous new questions and problems, many from Chartered Financial Analyst exams. By chapter, some specific changes include the following:

Chapter 1   Focuses more effectively on the text's themes with examples. We've updated our discussions of the importance of ethics in the investments profession, job opportunities, and professional designations such as the CFA® and CFP™.

Chapter 2   Focuses on reviewing the relationship between risk and return and how to measure them using ex-post data for domestic investments. The risk–return tradeoff is illustrated with capital market history data, including an elementary construction of the capital market line.

Chapter 3   Shows how to compute returns for overseas investments and illustrates the effect of varying exchange rates on investor returns. New or revised features include the implications of rising inter-market correlations and a revised discussion of global securities, including the rapidly growing asset-backed securities sector.

Chapter 4   Has been revised to incorporate information on the mutual fund scandals and recent research on mutual fund expenses and performance.

Chapter 5   Focuses on the portfolio management process and the role of and the need for an investment policy statement with special consideration of the individual investor. We revised the section illustrating the latest research on the effect of asset allocation on overall portfolio performance.

Chapter 6   Was heavily rewritten to delete some material that is no longer relevant. In its place, there are major additions related to the emerging organization and functioning of the secondary equity market caused by the rapid growth of electronic trading and, specifically, electronic communication networks (ECNs) that have gained significant market share from formal stock exchanges.

Chapter 7   Because security-market indexes have a growing role in portfolio performance as benchmarks, we updated the changing composition of these indexes. In addition, we examine several new international indexes and alternative "style" indexes.

Chapter 8   Demonstrates the portfolio model using recent data for stocks, bonds, and cash, tying this presentation back to the asset allocation chapter.

Chapter 9   Includes an expanded discussion of multifactor asset pricing models, including complete examples that employ microeconomic and macroeconomic variables and detailed demonstration of an estimate.

Chapter 10   Beyond an update of the voluminous research on the topic of the efficient market hypothesis (EMH)—including several new anomalies—there is an updated and expanded discussion involving behavioral finance that considers major findings that are at odds with the EMH and points out the implications of these findings.

Chapter 11   Is a new chapter that introduces the basic approaches and techniques of asset valuation for all assets. Thus, this chapter lays the groundwork for subsequent chapters on the analysis of fixed-income securities and the specific valuation of equities.

Chapter 12   Includes an expanded discussion of duration and convexity, two very relevant valuation concepts for bonds.

Chapter 13   Has been revised to focus on the main economic and industry analysis themes that influence security analysis. We continue to use an expectational framework for supporting investment decisions and monitoring their results.

Chapter 14   Contains an expanded discussion on alternative cash flow measures that are widely used in valuation, including EBITDA, which we do not advocate. Given the widespread use of operating leases, we demonstrate how to capitalize lease payments and show the significant impact this has on financial risk measures.

Chapter 15   Highlights the concepts of a true growth company and a real growth stock. It is specifically noted that the stock of a growth company may not be a growth stock. It is emphasized that a real growth stock is an undervalued stock that can be from any type of company. The chapter subsequently contains detailed demonstrations of the several valuation models that provide the basis for identifying real growth stocks.

Chapter 16   Has been condensed with an emphasis on maintaining the overall reasoning behind technical analysis and new examples of technical analysis applied to bonds, yields, and foreign securities in addition to common stocks.

Chapter 17   Is the introductory chapter on derivatives; it has been moved toward the end of the text so instructors can focus on bonds and stocks before introducing derivative securities. Using payoff profiles to illustrate return patterns, this introductory chapter focuses on derivative basics and applications rather than institutional detail.

Chapter 18   Picks up where Chapter 17 leaves off with advanced discussions and applications of derivatives. A notable addition is a discussion of the binomial option-pricing model prior to the introduction of the Black–Scholes option-pricing model.

Chapter 19   Has been revised to focus on passive and active equity-portfolio management strategies. We continue to emphasize recent research on equity styles and the need for tax-efficient investment strategies with examples and data.

Chapter 20   Reviews bond-portfolio management techniques (passive, active, and matched-funding) and demonstrates the use of derivatives in portfolio management.

Chapter 21   Reviews several methods of evaluating performance, including information ratios and M^2 or risk-adjusted performance measures. We include discussions of attribution analysis and performance evaluation methods for fixed-income portfolios.

Supplements

The *Instructor's Manual/Test Bank,* prepared by Murli Rajan of the University of Scranton, contains the following aids for each chapter: an overview of the chapter; answers to all of the questions and problems; and a Test Bank of multiple-choice questions.

A *Computerized Test Bank* is also free to instructors and contains all the test questions found in the printed *Test Bank.* The computerized Test Bank program, ExamView, has many features that facilitate exam preparation: random question selection; key-word searches; adding and editing of test items; conversion of multiple-choice questions into short-answer questions; and creation of customized exams by question scrambling.

Spreadsheet Templates, created by Paul Bursik of St. Norbert College in Microsoft Excel, are available for students. At the end of most chapters, there are several spreadsheet exercises that instructors may assign in order for students to apply and extend some of the problems covered in the chapter. For many of these exercises, spreadsheet templates have been prepared to offer students varying degrees of assistance with the problem. There are also templates prepared as financial calculators for some recurring types of problems such as time value of money and valuation.

Lecture Presentation Software, also created by Paul Bursik, has been developed to cover all the essential concepts in each chapter. These slides, created in Microsoft PowerPoint, are designed to enhance the lecture experience as well as complement the text through examples and illustrations.

A *Web page* can be accessed through http://reilly.swlearning.com that will provide up-to-date teaching and learning aids for instructors and students. The site provides students and instructors with access to the PowerPoint presentations, Excel Spreadsheet Models, and Internet applications and exercises. Instructors also may access the Instructor's Manual.

South-Western will provide complimentary supplements or supplement packages to those adopters qualified under our adoption policy. Please contact your local sales representative to learn how you may qualify.

Acknowledgments

So many people have helped us in so many ways that we hesitate to list them, fearing we may miss someone. Accepting this risk, we will begin with the University of Notre Dame and Illinois State University for their direct support. Professor Reilly would also like to thank the Bernard J. Hank family, who have endowed the Chair that helped bring him back to Notre Dame and has provided support for his work.

We would like to thank the following reviewers for this edition:

Charles Gahala, Benedictine University
Gunita Grover, Villanova University
David D. Hemley, Eastern New Mexico University
Jonathan Ohn, Wagner College
Debbie Psihountas, Webster University

Greg T. Smersh, University of Florida
P. V. Viswanath, Pace University
Richard Warr, North Carolina State University
Edward Zajicek, Kalamazoo College

We were fortunate to have the following excellent reviewers for earlier editions:

Robert Angell, East Carolina University
George Aragon, Boston College
Brian Belt, University of Missouri–Kansas City
Omar M. Benkato, Ball State University
Arand Bhattacharya, University of Cincinnati
Carol Billingham, Central Michigan University
Susan Block, University of California–Santa Barbara
Gerald A. Blum, Babson College
Robert J. Brown, Harrisburg, Pennsylvania
Dosoung Choi, University of Tennessee
John Clinebell, University of Northern Colorado
Susan Coleman, University of Hartford
James P. D'Mello, Western Michigan University
Eugene F. Drzycimski, University of Wisconsin–Oshkosh
John Dunkelberg, Wake Forest University
Eric Emory, Sacred Heart University
Thomas Eyssell, University of Missouri–St. Louis
James Feller, Middle Tennessee State University
Eurico Ferreira, Clemson University
Michael Ferri, John Carroll University
Joseph E. Finnerty, University of Illinois
Harry Friedman, New York University
R. H. Gilmer, University of Mississippi
Stephen Goldstein, University of South Carolina
Steven Goldstein, Robinson-Humphrey/American Express
Keshav Gupta, Oklahoma State University

James Haltiner, College of William and Mary
Sally A. Hamilton, Santa Clara University
Ronald Hoffmeister, Arizona State University
Ron Hutchins, Eastern Michigan University
A. James Ifflander, Arizona State University
Stan Jacobs, Central Washington University
Kwang Jun, Michigan State University
George Kelley, Erie Community College
Ladd Kochman, Kennesaw State College
Jaroslaw Komarynsky, Northern Illinois University
Tim Krehbiel, Oklahoma State University
Kartono Liano, Mississippi State University
Danny Litt, Century Software Systems/UCLA
Miles Livingston, University of Florida
Christopher Ma, Texas Tech University
John A. MacDonald, Clarkson University
Stephen Mann, University of South Carolina
Jeffrey A. Manzi, Ohio University
George Mason, University of Hartford
John Matthys, DePaul University
Stewart Mayhew, University of Georgia
Michael McBain, Marquette University
Dennis McConnell, University of Maine
Francis J. McGrath, Iona College
Jeanette Medewitz, University of Nebraska–Omaha
Jacob Michaelsen, University of California–Santa Cruz
Nicholas Michas, Northern Illinois University
Edward M. Miller, University of New Orleans

Lalatendu Misra, University of Texas–San Antonio

Michael Murray, LaCrosse, Wisconsin

Raj A. Padmaraj, Bowling Green State University

John Peavy, Southern Methodist University

George Philippatos, University of Tennessee

Aaron L. Phillips, The American University

George Pinches, University of Kansas

Rose Prasad, Central Michigan University

George A. Racette, University of Oregon

Murli Rajan, University of Scranton

Bruce Robin, Old Dominion University

James Rosenfeld, Emory University

Stanley D. Ryals, Investment Counsel, Inc.

Katrina F. Sherrerd, CFA Institute

Frederic Shipley, DePaul University

Ravi Shukla, Syracuse University

Douglas Southard, Virginia Polytechnic Institute

Tommy Stamland, University of Wyoming

Harold Stevenson, Arizona State University

Kishore Tandon, City University of New York–Baruch College

Donald Thompson, Georgia State University

David E. Upton, Virginia Commonwealth University

Robert Van Ness, Kansas State University

E. Theodore Veit, Rollins College

Bruce Wardrep, East Carolina University

Toni Whited, University of Iowa

Rolf Wubbels, New York University

Ata Yesilyaprak, Alcorn State University

Valuable comments and suggestions have come from former graduate students at the University of Illinois: Wenchi Kao, DePaul University; and especially David Wright, University of Wisconsin–Parkside, a frequent co-author who has provided consistent support. Once more, we were blessed with bright, dedicated research assistants when we needed them the most. This includes Neal Capecci, Brandon Grinwis, Marouan Selmi, who were careful, dependable, and creative.

Current and former colleagues have been very helpful: Rob Battalio, Yu-Chi Chang, Michael Hemler, Jerry Langley, Bill Nichols, Norlin Rueschhoff, University of Notre Dame; and John M. Wachowicz, University of Tennessee. As always, some of the best insights and most stimulating comments came during vigorous walks with our very good friend, Jim Gentry of the University of Illinois.

We are convinced that professors who want to write a book that is academically respectable, relevant, as well as realistic require help from the "real world." We have been fortunate to develop relationships with a number of individuals (including a growing number of former students) whom we consider our contacts with reality.

We especially want to thank Robert Conway of Goldman Sachs & Company for suggesting several years ago that the book should reflect the rapidly evolving global market. This important advice has had a profound effect on this book over time.

The following individuals have graciously provided important insights and material:

Sharon Athey, Brown Brothers Harriman

Joseph C. Bencivenga, Bankers Trust

David G. Booth, Dimensional Fund Advisors, Inc.

Gary Brinson, UBS Brinson

Dwight Churchill, Fidelity Management Research

Abby Joseph Cohen, Goldman Sachs & Co.

Robert Conway, Goldman Sachs & Co.

Robert J. Davis, Crimson Capital Co.

Robert J. Davis, Jr., Goldman Sachs & Co.

Philip Delaney, Jr., Northern Trust Bank

Sam Eisenstadt, Value Line

Frank Fabozzi, *Journal of Portfolio Management*

Kenneth Fisher, *Forbes*

John J. Flanagan, Jr., Lawrence, O'Donnell, Marcus & Co.

Martin S. Fridson, FridsonVision, LLC

Khalid Ghayur, Morgan Stanley

William J. Hank, Moore Financial Corporation

Rick Hans, Walgreen Corporation
Lea B. Hansen, Greenwich Associates
Joanne Hill, Goldman Sachs & Co.
John W. Jordan II, The Jordan Company
Andrew Kalotay, Kalotay Associates
Luke Knecht, Dresdner RCM Capital Management
Mark Kritzman, Windham Capital Management
Martin Leibowitz, Morgan Stanley
Douglas R. Lempereur, Templeton Investment Counsel, Inc.
Robert Levine, Nomura Securities
George W. Long, Long Investment Management, Ltd.
John Maginn, Maginn Associates
Scott Malpass, University of Notre Dame
Jack Malvey, Lehman Brothers
Dominic Marshall, Benson Associates
Frank Martin, Martin Capital Management
Todd Martin, Martin Capital Management
Joseph McAlinden, Morgan Stanley
Richard McCabe, Merrill Lynch Pierce Fenner & Smith
Michael McCowin, Wisconsin Investment Board
Terrence J. McGlinn, McGlinn Capital Markets
Mitch Merin, Morgan Stanley
Kenneth R. Meyer, Lincoln Capital Management
Brian Moore, U.S. Gypsum Corp.

Salvatore Muoio, SM Investors, LP
Gabrielle Napolitano, Goldman Sachs & Co.
David Nelms, Morgan Stanley
George Noyes, Standish, Ayer & Wood
Ian Rossa O'Reilly, Wood Gundy, Inc.
Philip J. Purcell III, Morgan Stanley
Jack Pycik, Consultant
John C. Rudolf, Summit Capital Management
Guy Rutherford, Morgan Stanley
Ron Ryan, Asset Liability Management
Mark Rypzinski, Henry & Co.
Sean St. Clair, Lehman Brothers
Brian Singer, UBS Global Asset Management
Clay Singleton, Rollins College
William Smith, Morgan Stanley
Fred H. Speece, Jr., Speece, Thorson Capital Group
William M. Stephens, Husic Capital Management
James Stork, Uitermarkt & Associates
William M. Wadden, Long Ship Capital Management
Sushil Wadhwani, Goldman Sachs & Co.
Jeffrey M. Weingarten, Goldman Sachs & Co.
Robert Wilmouth, National Futures Association
Richard S. Wilson, Ryan Labs, Inc.

We continue to benefit from the help and consideration of the dedicated people who are or have been associated with the CFA Institute: Tom Bowman, Whit Broome, Bob Johnson, Bob Luck, Katie Sherrerd, Jan Squires, and Donald Tuttle.

Professor Reilly would like to thank his assistant, Rachel Karnafel, who had the unenviable task of keeping his office and his life in some sort of order during this project.

As always, our greatest gratitude is to our families—past, present, and future. Our parents gave us life and helped us understand love and how to give it. Most important are our wives, who provide love, understanding, and support throughout the day and night. We thank God for our children and grandchildren, who ensure that our lives are full of love, laughs, and excitement.

Frank K. Reilly
NOTRE DAME, INDIANA

Edgar A. Norton, Jr.
NORMAL, ILLINOIS

About the Authors

Frank K. Reilly is the Bernard J. Hank Professor of Finance, and former dean of the Mendoza College of Business, at the University of Notre Dame. Holding degrees from the University of Notre Dame (B.B.A.), Northwestern University (M.B.A.), and the University of Chicago (Ph.D.), Professor Reilly has taught at the University of Illinois, the University of Kansas, and the University of Wyoming in addition to the University of Notre Dame. He has several years of experience as a senior securities analyst, as well as experience in stock-and-bond trading. Having earned the right to use the Chartered Financial Analyst (CFA) designation, he has been a member of the Council of Examiners, the Council on Education and Research, and the grading committee, and was Chairman of the Board of Trustees of the Institute of Chartered Financial Analysts and Chairman of the Board of the Association of Investment Management and Research (AIMR), now CFA Institute. Professor Reilly has been president of the Financial Management Association, the Midwest Business Administration Association, the Eastern Finance Association, the Academy of Financial Services, and the Midwest Finance Association. He is or has been on the board of directors of the First Interstate Bank of Wisconsin, Norwest Bank of Indiana, the Investment Analysts Society of Chicago, UBS Brinson Global Funds (Chairman), Fort Dearborn Income Securities (Chairman), Discover Bank, NIBCO, Inc., International Board of Certified Financial Planners, Battery Park High Yield Bond Fund, Inc., and Morgan Stanley Trust FSB.

As the author of more than 100 articles, monographs, and papers, Professor Reilly has had his work appear in numerous publications, including *Journal of Finance, Journal of Financial and Quantitative Analysis, Journal of Accounting Research, Financial Management, Financial Analysts Journal, Journal of Fixed Income,* and *Journal of Portfolio Management.* In addition to *Investments,* Seventh Edition, Professor Reilly is the co-author of another textbook, *Investment Analysis and Portfolio Management,* Eighth Edition (South-Western, 2006) with Keith C. Brown.

Professor Reilly was named on the list of *Outstanding Educators in America* and has received the University of Illinois Alumni Association Graduate Teaching Award, the Outstanding Educator Award from the M.B.A. class at the University of Illinois, and the Outstanding Teacher Award from the M.B.A. class and the Senior Class at Notre Dame. He also received from the Association of Investment Management and Research (AIMR) both the C. Stewart Sheppard Award for his contribution to the educational mission of the Association and the Daniel J. Forrestal III Leadership Award for Professional Ethics and Standards of Investment Practice. He was part of the inaugural group selected as a Fellow of the Financial Management Association International. He is editor of *Readings and Issues in Investments, Ethics and the Investment Industry,* and *High Yield Bonds: Analysis and Risk Assessment,* and is or has been a member of the editorial boards of *Financial Management, The Financial Review, International Review of Economics and Finance, Journal of Financial Education, Quarterly Review of Economics and Finance,* and the *European Journal of Finance.* He is included in the *Who's Who in Finance and Industry, Who's Who in America, Who's Who in American Education,* and *Who's Who in the World.*

Edgar A. Norton, Jr. is professor of finance and associate dean for the College of Business at Illinois State University. He holds a double major in computer science and economics from Rensselaer Polytechnic Institute, where he graduated magna cum laude. Professor Norton received his M.S. and Ph.D. from the University of Illinois at Urbana-Champaign. Having earned the right to use the Chartered Financial Analyst (CFA) designation, he regularly receives certificates of achievement, signifying his continual development in the field of investments. Professor Norton has served as a grader for Chartered Financial Analyst exams, as a curriculum consultant for the Chartered Financial Analyst equity specialization program, and on the CFA Institute's Council of Examiners. He has taught at Fairleigh Dickinson University, Liberty University, and Northwest Missouri State University. He has served on the Board of Directors and as President of the Midwest Finance Association.

Professor Norton has authored or co-authored more than 30 papers that have been published in journals and conference proceedings, as well as presented at international, national, and regional conferences. His papers have been published in journals such as *Financial Review, Academy of Management Executive, Journal of the Midwest Finance Association, Journal of Business Venturing, Journal of Business Ethics, Journal of Small Business Finance, Journal of Business Research, Small Business Economics,* and *Journal of Small Business Management.* He co-authored a paper that received an Award of Excellence at the 36th International Council of Small Business World Conference, held in Vienna, Austria. He is co-author of several books, including *Finance: An Introduction to Institutions, Investments, and Management; Foundations of Financial Management;* and *Economic Justice in Perspective: A Book of Readings.* Professor Norton has been listed in *Who's Who in the East, Who's Who in American Education,* and *Who's Who Among Young American Professionals.*

INVESTMENTS

SEVENTH EDITION

1   The Investment Setting

The field of investments is an interesting area of study. Everybody knows at least a little about financial markets—from news about the stock market to what the interest rates are at the local bank. Successful investment strategies require discipline, patience, and a good grounding in the foundational concepts of finance in general and investing in particular. "Get rich quick" sales pitches from spam email will not do much to help your financial situation.

In the introductory chapter of our text we lay the groundwork for the fruitful study of investing theory and practice. An important component of this chapter is the main themes or foundational truths of the investment world:

- There is a tradeoff between risk and expected return. Higher risk investments should offer higher levels of expected return. Or to phrase it a different way, a low risk or conservative investment should not offer large expected returns.

- It is difficult to find undervalued stocks and bonds. In most developed countries, financial market prices reflect known information about the economy and company. Although stock market prices may sometimes be higher or lower than justified for a particular company, such discrepancies are difficult to find.

- Focus on what you can keep, not what you earn from your investments. Taxes, fees, and investment expenses can reduce an investor's return by one-third or more. Investors need to be aware of the eroding effect of fees and expenses, as well as taxes on income and capital gains, on their returns.

- Diversify, or spread out, your investment assets. For a long-term investor, placing all funds in a bank CD is as unwise as putting all funds in a single stock. We will learn about the principles of diversification and the benefits of placing funds in a variety of assets and securities, not just in your home market but internationally, too.

In addition to reviewing these and other investment fundamentals, we review the importance of ethics to investment practitioners. We highlight two professional certifications, CFA® and CFP™, and discuss different kinds of jobs and career paths available in the field of investments.

The Investment Setting

I n this initial chapter we discuss several topics basic to the subsequent chapters, beginning with the definition of the term *investment* and the concept of the required rate of return. Individuals as well as institutional investors such as pension funds, insurance companies, and endowments invest in stocks, bonds, CDs, real estate, and other investment vehicles to meet future goals. These goals may include income, capital preservation, capital appreciation, needs, or a combination of these.

We also describe several major themes about which every investor needs to be aware. First, there is a tradeoff between risk and expected return; a "great return, no risk" investment is very likely neither. Second, asset prices (such as stock and bond prices) in developed financial markets—such as those in the United States, Canada, Australia, and much of Europe and Asia—almost always reflect all that is known about an economy and the issuing firm. In other words, is difficult to consistently find undervalued stocks. Third, the success of an investment can only be determined after the effects of commissions, fees, and taxes have been considered. Finally, smart investors will diversify by investing in several different industries, in several different asset types, and even across national boundaries. We will continually come back to these themes as we incorporate them in later chapters.

Why Invest?

The answer to the question "Why invest?" is similar to the answers to "Why go to college?" or "Why study for a professional designation?" You spend time and money earning a college degree or professional designation because you expect to earn more in salary and benefits over your working career, gain additional opportunities for advancement, and enjoy life more. You are investing in yourself now, trading current time and funds in anticipation of a future return on that investment.

So it is with the use of money. We can do two things with our funds: spend them on current consumption (food, clothing, shelter, transportation) or save them with plans to spend them some time in the future. This tradeoff of *present* consumption for a higher level of *future* consumption is the reason for savings. What you do with the savings to make them increase over time is *investment*.

INVESTMENT DEFINED

An *investment* is the current commitment of resources for a period of time in the expectation of receiving future resources that will compensate the investor for (1) the time the resources are committed, (2) the expected rate of inflation, and (3) the *risk*—the uncertainty of the future payments. The investor is trading a *known* (or reasonably certain) amount of resources (e.g., money) today for *expected* future resources (e.g., a lump sum of cash or income stream) that will be greater than the current outlay.[1] A key word here is "expected." Many investments contain risks, so the actual future payments may be higher or lower than expected. For example, you may buy shares of common stock expecting to earn a positive return. But the value of the shares could fall, due perhaps to an overall decline in the stock market or because future investors are not willing to pay such a high price for the stock.

THE TIME VALUE OF MONEY

Those who give up immediate possession of savings (that is, defer consumption) expect to receive in the future a greater amount than they gave up. Conversely, those who consume more than their current income (that is, borrow) must be willing to pay back in the future more than they borrowed. An important principle in finance is this concept of the *time value of money*: a dollar today is worth more to us than the same dollar in the future. There are three reasons why money has a time value:

1. ***Pure or real risk-free interest rate*** We expect a reward for postponing spending. Otherwise there is no incentive to save. We want to be rewarded with additional dollars at a future time even on a no-risk investment when there is zero inflation. The return in such an environment is the *pure or real risk-free interest rate*.
2. ***Inflation protection*** We would rather have a dollar today than a dollar in the future since inflation will reduce the purchasing power of the dollar in the future.
3. ***Risk*** We would rather have a dollar today since the promise of a dollar in the future may be broken; there is always the possibility of nonpayment or reduced payment.

REASONS FOR INVESTING

Individuals invest funds for many different reasons. Some invest during their working years to provide a retirement fund from which they can withdraw after they stop working. Others invest to obtain funds for their children's future education, a down payment on a new car or house, or annual vacation trips. Organizations also invest for various reasons. For example, pension funds invest so payouts can be made to retired workers. Endowment funds invest to provide income for university operating expenses or scholarships. Life insurance companies invest policyholders' premiums to provide adequate funds when policies are cashed out or when benefits need to be paid.

---

[1]Items that do not qualify as investments include gambling (the expected future return is less than the amount paid); property insurance (as protection against loss it is a good risk management tool but does not offer a greater expected return than the premiums paid); and consumer durables, such as a car or computer which are wasting assets; they may last several years but decrease in value over time).

All invest with one or more of three basic needs in mind:

Income   Investments are made now in the hopes of providing future income. Usually investors want income to begin in the immediate future (such as when an annuity or a bond is purchased).

Capital preservation   Investments are made to preserve capital, or the original value. These are generally conservative investments. The investor simply wants the money set aside with the assurance that the funds will be available, with no risk of loss in purchasing power, at a future point in time. As such, the term *capital preservation,* though used by many, is misleading. Since the investor actually wants to preserve the *real* value of the invested capital, the nominal value of the investment should increase at a pace consistent with inflation trends.

Capital appreciation   Investments are made so that funds will appreciate, or grow in value, to meet a future need such as retirement or children's college education. The aim is to have the value of the invested money grow at a faster rate than inflation so there is a positive real return after the effects of taxes and inflation. Typically, investments made for capital appreciation include some risk exposure to get the desired returns. As we have stated, risk can affect returns either in a positive (returns are higher than expected) or negative (returns are lower than expected) way.

Key Issues in Investing

Before going much further, let's review the reality of the investing world. Many students go into an investments class believing that they will learn the secrets of successful investing for an early, prosperous retirement through stock picking. But in the real world, successful stock picking is rare. Therefore, the insights we give in this book for successful investing lead to a slow-and-steady "tortoise" strategy rather than get-rich-quick "hare"-brained schemes. The rapid rise and decline of the Nasdaq market and high-tech stocks in 2000–2002 should convince anyone that what goes up does come down, even in the stock market. In the following overview, we discuss concepts that every successful investor should keep in mind. We will elaborate on these four basic themes throughout the book.

THERE IS A TRADEOFF BETWEEN RISK AND EXPECTED RETURN

Would you invest in a risky asset with the expectation of earning a 5 percent return if you could instead invest in a safe, risk-free asset with a 6.5 percent return? Probably not; there's little reason why someone would put their money at risk with the expectation of earning a lower return than expected from a no-risk option. If there were such a situation, it would not endure. Investors' funds would flood the market to purchase the safe asset while selling the risky asset. Supply and demand then would adjust the prices and expected returns for these assets. The price changes would continue until the safe asset had an appropriate (low) expected return and the risky asset an appropriate (higher) expected return.

The relationship between prices and expected returns may not be clear to some at this early point in the book. The return on an investment arises from the difference between its price (when purchased) and its expected price in the future. Let's consider two assets, Risky and Safe, each with an expected value of $100 in one year. Risky's current price is $95.24 (so its expected return is about 5 percent if the price rises over time to $100). Safe is priced at $93.90 (so its expected return is about 6.5 percent.). Attracted by Safe's low risk and higher return, investors will buy Safe, which will increase its price, and sell Risky, which

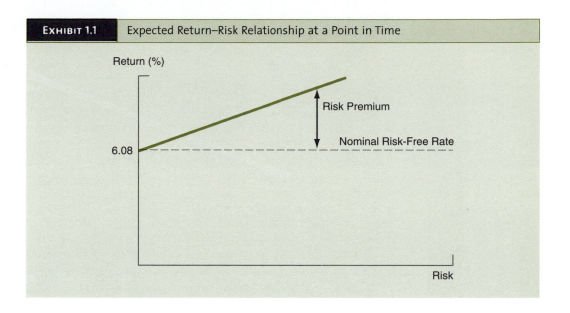

| EXHIBIT 1.1 | Expected Return–Risk Relationship at a Point in Time |

will depress its price. Suppose equilibrium is reached with Safe priced at $96 (offering an expected return of $100/$96 − 1 = 0.0417 or 4.17 percent) and Risk priced at $94 (offering an expected return of $100/$94 − 1 or 6.38 percent). The adjustment in current market prices have also adjusted the assets' expected returns.

Investors' decisions to buy and sell assets will always correct mispricing. Investors require an expected return commensurate with their perceptions of the asset's risk; higher-risk assets should always offer higher expected returns. Thus, we can say that *risk drives expected returns.* Exhibit 1.1 shows the upward-sloping relationship between expected return and risk. An asset's risk is determined by the market environment (such as expectations about interest rates, exchange rates, inflation, company sales and earnings, and international conflicts) and the asset's characteristics (Does it offer fixed cash flows [like a bond or bank CD]? Highly variable cash flows and price [like common stock]? What is the financial condition of the issuing firm?) Given investors' perceptions about an asset's risk, the market sets the expected return level commensurate with the risk.

The expected return on an asset is based on the nominal risk-free interest rate and a risk premium as follows:

Expected return

1.1

$$= (1 + \text{Nominal Risk-Free Interest Rate})(1 + \text{Risk Premium}) - 1$$

The *nominal risk-free interest rate* is the basic interest rate that incorporates the effects of expected inflation. A *risk premium* is the extra expected return (above the nominal risk-free rate) required by investors as an incentive to place their funds at risk. For example, a nominal risk-free rate of 6.08 percent and a 3 percent risk premium lead investors to expect a return of (1 + 0.0608)(1 + 0.03) − 1 = 9.26 percent. The nominal risk-free rate will be the same for all investments in any economy since it is based on growth opportunities and expected inflation in the economy. We usually use short-term government debt, such as U.S. Treasury bills, as a measure of the nominal risk-free rate in a country's market. Since the market's perception of risk determines the size of the risk premium and the risk premium determines the expected return, we see that risk perceptions determine expected

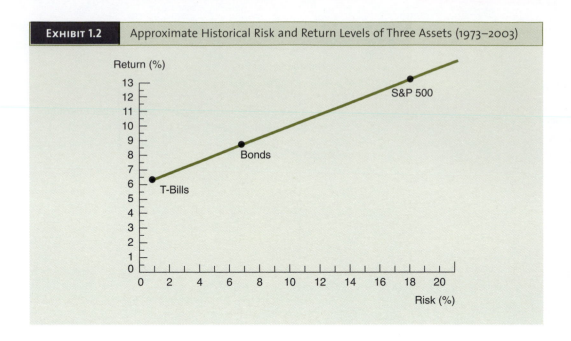

EXHIBIT 1.2   Approximate Historical Risk and Return Levels of Three Assets (1973–2003)

returns on an asset. Exhibit 1.2 shows the historical risk and return levels of three assets, showing that higher-risk investments (common stocks) have earned higher returns than lower-risk investments (corporate bonds and Treasury bills).

DEVELOPED FINANCIAL MARKETS ARE NEARLY EFFICIENT

A market is *internally efficient* if transactions costs of trading in the market are low. But in finance, the term *efficient* typically has a different meaning. When we say a market is efficient, we mean the market is *externally or informationally efficient*. That means that new information is quickly reflected into asset prices; so quickly, in fact, that by the time we hear and react to the new information the markets have already assimilated the information and the price has adjusted to it. In other words, we cannot use current news or recent price movements to try to determine future asset price moves. Future asset price changes will be determined by future news and any differences between actual news and what the market expected. For example, if the financial markets expect the Fed to increase interest rates by a quarter-point (0.25 percent) prices will not change much when the Fed does so; the market had already "priced in" this news. But should the Fed instead increase rates by a half-point (0.50 percent), this unexpected news will likely create a larger change in prices.

We are not arguing that bond, stock, and other asset markets are totally efficient. Some appear to be more efficient than others; we will discuss this more fully in Chapter 10. But just as you occasionally may find a quarter or a $10 bill lying on the sidewalk, there may be times when a security analyst will find a stock that is apparently priced too low (and is a "buy" candidate) or too high (and is a "sell" candidate).

As an example of market efficiency and the difficulty in consistently "beating the market," let's compare returns earned on the investment strategies of professionals to that of the overall stock market. Let's look at a study using the Wilshire 5000 stock market index. The Wilshire 5000 attempts to measure the returns on the overall U.S. stock market. As its name implies, it tracks the performance of a group of 5,000 different stocks. How do professionals do when their return performance is compared to the return of the Wilshire 5000 index?

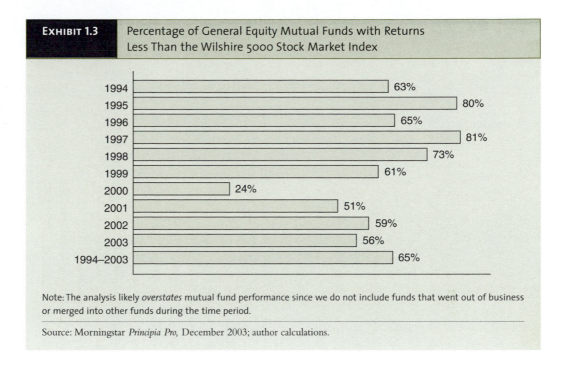

EXHIBIT 1.3 Percentage of General Equity Mutual Funds with Returns Less Than the Wilshire 5000 Stock Market Index

Year	Percentage
1994	63%
1995	80%
1996	65%
1997	81%
1998	73%
1999	61%
2000	24%
2001	51%
2002	59%
2003	56%
1994–2003	65%

Note: The analysis likely *overstates* mutual fund performance since we do not include funds that went out of business or merged into other funds during the time period.

Source: Morningstar *Principia Pro,* December 2003; author calculations.

As seen in Exhibit 1.3, not too well. The graph shows, for the entire 1994–2003 decade and for each year of the decade, the percentage of equity (or stock) mutual funds that had lower returns than the Wilshire 5000 index. A percentage higher than 50 percent means that the index outperformed (earned higher returns than) most of the mutual funds; a percentage under 50 percent, as in 2000, means that most mutual funds outperformed the index. For the ten years shown, 65 percent of equity mutual funds earned lower returns than the Wilshire 5000 index. Or to put it another way, over these ten years only about one-third of equity mutual funds earned higher returns than the index. This is evidence of the efficiency of the stock market; it is difficult, even for well-trained investment professionals, to consistently outperform an appropriate market index. This explains the popularity of index investing, wherein individuals and institutions do not try to outperform the markets but instead buy securities that replicate an index. The old adage "if you can't beat 'em, join 'em" works in investing.

FOCUS ON AFTER-TAX RETURNS, NET OF EXPENSES

It is not how much you *earn* by investing but how much you actually *receive* and *keep* that is important. For example, interest income from municipal bonds (bonds issued by state and local governments that meet certain criteria) is exempt from federal income tax, whereas interest income on corporate bonds is not. Dividends from stock investments are taxable as income, but capital gains (or losses) from price changes are not taxable until the investor realizes the gain or loss by selling the asset.

Some investors will have funds in tax-deferred accounts such as IRAs (individual retirement accounts), pension plans such as 401(k) plans, or insurance products such as variable annuities. Such investment strategies are tax-deferred; no taxes are paid on investment gains until money is withdrawn from the account. In such cases, investors may have been able to keep the returns earned on their investments.

EXHIBIT 1.4	Comparing Tax-Deferred and Taxable Investment Growth

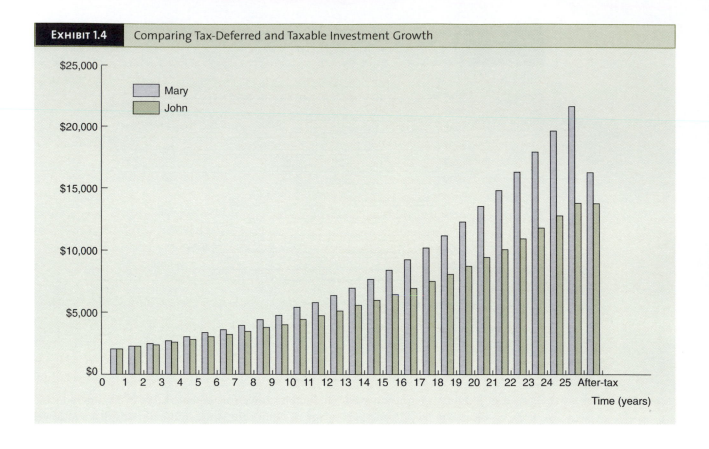

But other investments, particularly those in accounts that are not tax-deferred, may earn after-tax returns well below the advertised returns. We show an example in Exhibit 1.4. Mary and John pay taxes at an average rate of 25 percent. They each invest in a mutual fund account that earns over time an average annual 10 percent return on a pre-tax basis. An investor's average annual return could be only 8 percent after income and capital gains taxes. Mary's money is invested in the fund through a tax-deferred IRA; after twenty-five years, her $2,000 regular IRA investment will have become $21,669.41 [$2,000 × $(1.10)^{25}$]. If she takes all the funds out of the IRA in a lump sum and pays taxes on them (an unlikely event), she will have $16,252 after taxes (assuming the 25 percent tax rate).[2] John, who invested in the fund through a taxable account, will have only $13,697 [$2,000 × $(1.08)^{25}$] after twenty-five years. This shows that investors should take full advantage of any tax-deferred investing they can.

Expenses are another concern. Commissions on securities trading[3] and mutual fund purchases lower the net returns received by investors. And when investors give their money to a professional advisor, mutual fund, or annuity, there will be expenses related to record-

---

[2]She will pay taxes on the value of the withdrawal: Tax = 0.25(21,669.41) = $5,417.35. Thus, her net proceeds are 21,669.41 − $5,417.35 = $16,252.06.

[3]For research on how frequent trading can result in lower returns, see Brad M. Barber and Terrance Odean, "Trading is Hazardous to Your Wealth: The Common Stock Investment Performance of Individual Investors," *Journal of Finance,* vol. 55, no. 2 (April 2000): 73–806.

keeping, trading commissions, and money management fees. Such expenses can have large impacts. For example, suppose $2,000 invested in a tax-deferred IRA account over twenty-five years in a low-expense fund gives an investor a net average annual return of 10 percent and a portfolio value of $21,669. A higher-expense investment could reduce the net average annual return to only 8 percent and the portfolio's value to only $13,697.

Higher expenses are similar to a hidden tax on the investor.[4] All else equal, a lower-expense investment is preferable to a higher-expense investment. Similarly, a tax-efficient investment strategy is preferable to one that ignores the tax consequences. The bottom line is: taxes and expenses can have a large impact on your ability to meet your investment goals.

DIVERSIFY, DIVERSIFY, DIVERSIFY: ACROSS ASSETS, INDUSTRIES, AND EVEN COUNTRIES

The idea behind diversification is "don't put all your eggs into one basket." If you drop the basket, all your eggs will break. Similarly, placing your savings in only a handful of companies or industries could lead to financial disaster. A recent example of this is the nearly 80 percent decline in the Nasdaq market index from March 2000 to October 2002. This index, with many high-tech company stocks, took a nosedive as earnings and other worries arose about the high-tech sector in 2000.

But this does not mean that you should place funds only in safe and secure investments. Earning 2–4 percent on a bank certificate of deposit is safe, but it violates prudent investment thinking for all but the most risk-averse or short-term–oriented investors. Higher return possibilities over time are much greater when investments are placed in several different asset classes.

Diversification works because at times some investments will do well while others are performing poorly and vice versa. Investors should spread funds across several different investments to prevent overexposure to any one investment.

We show one example of the benefits of diversification in Exhibit 1.5. In strategy 1, $10,000 invested in one asset at an average annual rate of 7 percent gives us $54,274.33 in our account after twenty-five years. In strategy 2, we divide our $10,000 initial investment into five subaccounts, investing $2,000 in each one. One of the investments turns out to be a total failure and we lose the entire $2,000 invested. The second investment earns no return at all; twenty-five years later we still have $2,000 in that account. The third subaccount earns a meager 5 percent annual average return over the twenty-five years. The fourth and fifth subaccounts perform better, one earning 10 percent and the other 12 percent on an average annual basis. Then, even though some accounts performed poorly, our total investment grows to $64,442.25 over twenty-five years, a gain of more than $10,000 over the single-basket strategy.

For maximum diversification benefits, investors should invest not only in various asset classes (such as stocks and bonds) and industries but also across country borders, particularly as "country borders" become blurred in a business sense. For example, is DaimlerChrysler a German or an American company? Such cross-border mergers and acquisitions have increased dramatically in the past fifteen years. Firms such as Ford or Coca-Cola may have U.S. headquarters, but much of their product sales and revenue streams are from beyond U.S. borders. Some studies have found that a firm's industry sector has more to do with its

---

[4]The 2 percentage point spread in expenses is not unrealistic. A review of Morningstar equity fund data will reveal some funds with low expenses (0.25 percent expense ratios) and others with expense ratios exceeding 2.50 percent. The median ratio in 2004 was 1.44.

EXHIBIT 1.5	Diversification Illustration

INVEST $10,000 OVER 25 YEARS

Investment Strategy 1: All Funds in One Asset		Investment Strategy 2: Invest Equally in Five Different Assets	
Number of assets	1	Number of assets	5
Initial investment	$10,000	Amount invested per asset	$2,000
Number of years	25	Number of years	25
		Five asset returns (annual):	
Annual asset return	7%	Asset 1 return	−100%
		Asset 2 return	0%
		Asset 3 return	5%
		Asset 4 return	10%
		Asset 5 return	12%
		Total accumulation at end of time frame:	
		Asset 1	$0.00
		Asset 2	$2,000.00
		Asset 3	$6,772.71
		Asset 4	$21,669.41
Total accumulation at end of time frame:		Asset 5	$34,000.13
Total funds	$54,274.33	Total funds	$64,442.25

stock market performance than does a "country" effect.[5] So, why should U.S.-based investors prefer Motorola (U.S.) over Nokia (Finland) or Ericsson (Sweden) as a cellular phone investment? Although foreign investing may be problematic for individual investors, professionally managed international mutual funds and other means of foreign investing can remove many of the difficulties.

In short, investors need to look for good investments everywhere in the global economy. We will discuss this in more detail in Chapter 3.

The Financial Environment

Investments in securities arise in economies that have developed mechanisms for transferring funds from those who have excess funds to those who need funds. The sector with surplus cash to invest is typically the household sector. The savings of individuals are funneled through financial institutions to businesses, other individuals, and governments who have cash deficits and need to access capital. Both surplus and deficit units look for the best value: Surplus units (investors) seek the highest return within their risk preferences while deficit units (security issuers) seek the lowest-cost financing with reasonable terms. Capital

---

[5]Stefano Cavaglia, Christopher Brightman, and Michael Aked, "The Importance of Industry Factors," *Financial Analysts Journal,* vol. 56, no. 5 (September–October 2000): 41–54; Phyllis Feinberg, "Importance of Sectors Grows for International Investors," *Pensions and Investments* (November 27, 2000): 56.

markets allow individuals to use savings productively to assist the allocation of funds in the economy. Applying savings toward production activities helps to create jobs and provide goods and services needed by consumers, businesses, and governments. In turn, the markets provide a return to the savers.

Savers can choose from two basic types of investments for an investment portfolio: real assets and financial assets. Real assets are, for the most part, tangible assets. That is, we can see them and their effects. Examples include real estate, buildings, equipment, and so forth. Financial assets have been developed to represent claims on real assets. Such claims may represent ownership claims (shares of common stock), debt claims (trade credit, bank loans, bonds, notes), or even claims based on the value of other financial assets (for example, the value of a convertible bond may be affected by the share price of the stock into which the bond may be converted; other examples include futures and options contracts).

There are a number of ways to invest in financial assets or securities: directly, indirectly, or through derivatives.

Direct investment   Direct investment occurs when one buys shares of common stock or bonds.

Indirect investment   Indirect investment occurs when one purchases securities that themselves represent claims on other securities. For example, investors deposit funds in a bank or credit union or buy mutual fund shares; this money is pooled with that of other investors to make loans and to purchase stocks and bonds. Similarly, premiums paid on whole or universal life insurance are invested by the life insurance firm in other assets and securities. Pension funds also invest money contributed by the employer and employee.

Derivatives   Futures and options contracts are two popular types of derivatives. The value of derivative securities depends on (or is derived from) the value of an underlying security. For example, the value of options on a firm's stock depend on the current stock price. Derivatives have built-in leverage, meaning relatively small investments in derivative securities can control large sums of wealth. Derivative securities are purchased to hedge (or reduce) the risk in investment positions or speculate (or increase) one's risk exposure.[6] For example, an investor who owns stock but wants to protect the value of his portfolio against a short-term market decline can do so by using derivative securities. Similarly, an investor who believes a market is poised for an upswing can increase her exposure to the asset (and its risk) by using derivatives. We will cover the topic of derivatives more thoroughly in Chapters 17 and 18.

Where do people invest? Exhibit 1.6 shows the results of the *Survey of Consumer Finances,* a study done periodically by the Federal Reserve Board. Whether it was a result of aging baby boomers, smarter investing, or the effects of a rising stock market, people placed a greater portion of their financial assets in equities and longer-term investments such as retirement accounts over the years of the survey.

Market Participants

The financial environment is a complex system of markets, institutions, laws, relationships, securities, and funding sources. Households are the major source of investment funds in the

---

[6]The "rogue trading" strategies of Nick Leeson led to the collapse of Barings because of the leverage effects of his unauthorized derivative trading. The downfall of Long-Term Capital Management was exacerbated by the high amounts of leverage they used in their derivatives trading strategies. Derivatives have many useful purposes, which we examine in Chapter 17. But inappropriate trading of any investment vehicle can result in high-risk positions and large losses.

EXHIBIT 1.6	Where U.S. Households Invest Their Financial Assets: Percentage of Financial Assets Held in Various Forms				
Type of Financial Asset	1989	1992	1995	1998	2001
Transaction accounts	19.1%	17.5%	14.0%	11.4%	11.5%
Certificates of deposit	10.2	8.1	5.7	4.3	3.1
Savings bonds	1.5	1.1	1.3	0.7	0.7
Bonds	10.2	8.4	6.3	4.3	4.6
Stocks	15.0	16.5	15.7	22.7	21.6
Mutual funds (excluding money market funds)	5.3	7.7	12.7	12.5	12.2
Retirement accounts	21.5	25.5	27.9	27.5	28.4
Cash value of life insurance	6.0	6.0	7.2	6.4	5.3
Other financial assets	11.4	9.2	9.3	10.3	10.6
Total	100.0	100.0	100.0	100.0	100.0
Financial assets as a percentage of total household assets	30.4	31.5	36.6	40.6	42.0

Source: A. M. Aizcorbe, A. B. Kennickell, and K. B. Moore, *Recent Changes in U.S. Family Finances: Results from the 1998 and 2001 Survey of Consumer Finances,* Federal Reserve Board of Governors, Washington, DC, 2003.

U.S. economy. Household wealth invested in financial assets is double the household wealth invested in tangible assets such as real estate Although many may not directly invest in securities such as stocks and bonds, most invest indirectly by placing their money in financial intermediaries such as banks, pension funds, life insurance firms, or mutual funds. In 2004, U.S. households owned $45.1 trillion more than they owed in liabilities.

Households are the net savers in the U.S. economy; firms are net borrowers. Firms access both the money market (for short-term loans maturing in less than one year) and capital markets (for debt maturing in more than one year and for equity). Money market borrowing is to finance short-term needs such as inventory; capital markets are tapped for major equipment purchases, building programs, acquisitions, and to finance research and development (R&D). The federal government is also a net borrower, with outstanding borrowing comprised of U.S. Treasury securities. State and local governments can be net borrowers or net lenders, depending on the status of the local economy and the amount of tax revenues coming into their coffers.

Borrowers issue stocks and bonds with the assistance of investment bankers. Some well-known investment banking firms include Merrill Lynch, Goldman Sachs, and Smith Barney. Investment bankers use their knowledge and networks among financial institutions and investors to negotiate the type of security, the size of the issue, the price, and other terms with the issuer. Many times they commit their own capital funds to purchase the issue for immediate distribution or resell to other investment bankers, financial institutions (such as pension funds and insurance companies), and wealthy individuals. Such transactions, when a firm or government sells securities to raise money, are known as *primary market transactions*. The participants in the primary market who gather funds from savers and channel them to borrowers are the *financial intermediaries*. They help increase the operational efficiency of the financial markets. But whether an insurance company, pension fund, or mutual fund purchases the securities, the primary source of the financing is households.

When the securities are sold in the primary market, they are purchased by investors who will likely want to sell them at a future point in time. When investors trade among themselves, they are buying and selling securities in the *secondary market*. At times a *broker,* who brings the buyer and seller together, a *dealer,* who trades securities from his own account, or an electronic order-matching service may assist the transaction. We'll discuss security trading in more detail in Chapter 6.

Investment Strategies

There are many financial assets in which to invest and many security analysis and portfolio management strategies from which to choose. Each investment analyst must determine his or her own strengths and use them to optimally manage a portfolio and discover value in the securities markets.

The overall collection of assets owned by an individual or institution is called a *portfolio*. Since a good portfolio contains securities from one or more asset classes (stocks, bonds, mortgages, and so on), each investor must decide on an appropriate asset allocation, that is, what percentage of the portfolio should be in each asset class. The asset allocation decision has a large bearing on the expected return and risk of the portfolio. Once the asset allocation is determined, the security selection process begins—deciding which specific securities will be purchased for the portfolio. Once made, the asset allocation and security selection decisions are not permanent; markets change, expectations change, the circumstances surrounding the portfolio and the client change. Thus the asset allocation and the securities comprising the portfolio will be monitored and revised on a periodic basis. How one determines an asset allocation decision and security selection strategy depends on one's investing philosophy; that is, should an investor pursue an active investment management role or a passive one? Exhibit 1.7 lists various possibilities under each philosophy.

A manager with an active asset allocation decision philosophy uses market timing to try to increase the portfolio's allocation in the asset classes believed to be the most likely to perform best over the next period. She will have broad discretion regarding an asset's allocation within (sometimes large) predetermined ranges. A manager with a passive asset allocation philosophy will work with the client (or the portfolio's investment policy committee) to determine a target allocation and a range within which the allocation may vary. For example, in a target allocation of 60 percent stocks/40 percent bonds, the equity range may be 55–65 percent and the bond range may be 35–45 percent. Should a well-performing stock market push the asset allocation from 60 percent stocks to 65 percent stocks, the

Exhibit 1.7	Investment Philosophies	
	Asset Allocation Decision	**Security Selection Decision**
Active	Market timing	Stock picking by top-down or bottom-up approach
Passive	Maintain predetermined allocation with periodic rebalancing	Try to track a well-known market index

manager will sell some stocks and buy some additional bonds to adjust the asset allocation back to the 60/40 mix. Generally, the allowable ranges will be narrower for a passive manager than for an active one.

A manager with an active security selection philosophy will try to identify and purchase securities that will likely do well over the coming period of time and sell securities that are expected to underperform or do poorly compared to the market. Such managers typically have either a "top-down" or "bottom-up" approach to security analysis. Top-down adherents examine the overall economic picture to determine which sectors are expected to perform well and which are expected to perform poorly over the next year. Bottom-up stock pickers focus on individual firms with good management, a good strategy, and a good product that will likely gain market share and increase the firm's earnings in the future.

A passive manager has a simpler security selection task: Once an asset allocation has been determined, he will invest the funds to track, as closely as possible, a selected market index such as the S&P 500 stock index or the Lehman Brothers bond index. Such managers believe the securities markets are 100 percent efficient, so as the saying goes, "if you can't beat 'em, join 'em." They follow the indexes rather than try to earn above-average returns for a given risk level by security selection.

A manager can be active in one decision and passive in another. For example, a manager who believes she can forecast when the stock market will outperform the bond market (and vice versa) but does not have skill in selecting specific securities may be active in the asset allocation decision but will implement the strategy by investing in indexes. Or a manager with perceived stock-picking strengths may abide by a consistent asset allocation but manage the portfolio by actively analyzing and selecting the securities to include in it.

Ethics and Job Opportunities in Investments

An important component of the financial markets are the laws and regulations governing them. Without regulatory bodies and laws, the financial markets and securities trading would be hampered. Regulations dealing with deposit insurance in banks, the required discussion of risks in a new security prospectus, laws forbidding corporate "insiders" to use their privileged information for private gain, and requirements for fair dealings by brokers and dealers when trading for clients work to increase the public's sense of trust and confidence in the financial markets. Individuals who deal with clients must be registered in the state in which they work as well as with the Securities and Exchange Commission (SEC).

Regulations often arise from past abuses or problems. For example, the Securities Act of 1933 and the Securities Exchange Act of 1934 resulted from the circumstances surrounding the stock market crash of 1929. More recently, the Sarbanes–Oxley Act of 2002 arose from corporate accounting scandals. The oversight supposedly provided by corporate boards and external auditors failed in some companies; false financial statements hid the companies' true condition. Once the scandals were uncovered, corporate failure, bankruptcy, job losses, pension losses, and criminal charges involved companies such as Enron, Worldcom, Tyco, Arthur Andersen, HealthSouth, Kmart and Qwest.

Unfortunately, others entrusted with people's savings also have been found less than worthy. Several mutual fund firms and investment banks have been accused of wrongdoing in recent years. Stock analysts in investment banking firms wrote false and optimistic research reports, hoping to attract or to keep clients. Others allocated shares of "hot" or popular IPOs to top executives of client firms. Persons and firms involved in such unethical

EXHIBIT 1.8	Ethical Standards in Investment Professional Certifications

Chartered Financial Analyst (CFA®) **Standards of Professional Conduct**	**Certified Financial Planner (CFP™)** **Code of Ethics and Professional Responsibility**
Standard I: Fundamental Responsibilities Standard II: Relationships with and Responsibilities to the Profession Standard III: Relationships with and Responsibilities to the Employer Standard IV: Relationships with and Responsibilities to Clients and Prospects Standard V: Relationships with and Responsibilities to the Investing Public For additional details, see *http://www.cfainstitute.org*.	These Principles of the Code express the professional recognition of its responsibilities to the public, to clients, to colleagues, and to employers. They apply to all CFP designees and provide guidance to them in the performance of their professional services. Principle 1: Integrity Principle 2: Objectivity Principle 3: Competence Principle 4: Fairness Principle 5: Confidentiality Principle 6: Professionalism Principle 7: Diligence For additional details, see *http://www.cfp.net*.

dealings include Frank Quattrone of CSFB, Jack Grubman of (what was then) Salomon Smith Barney, and Henry Blodgett of Merrill Lynch.[7]

In addition, some mutual fund firms allowed illegal late trading. Late trading occurs when a client submits an order for mutual fund shares *after* the 4 P.M. close of the financial market and is allowed to purchase shares at the 4 P.M. price instead of the following day's closing price. Late trading can be advantageous if, for example, news occurs shortly after 4 P.M. that will affect the market. Of special note is the ability of late traders to purchase shares of, say, funds that specialize in European stocks. A rising U.S. market may bode well for good performance overseas the next day. Late traders who buy European fund shares after the close on the U.S. markets could capture profits if the European market rises the next day. This is an example of market timing—mutual funds allow certain investors to purchase large amounts of fund shares one day, knowing the shares would be sold the following day, even though the fund's stated regulations prohibit such activity.

To help avoid such problems and maintain the professionalism and ethics of the investments field, professional designations have been developed. Very few persons with the CFA® or CFP™ designations were involved in these scandals because of the ethics training that is part of these programs. Persons who receive the designations, by passing exams and having a requisite amount of work experience, show they have a certain level of expertise in their field and have agreed to abide by a code of ethics and professional standards in their dealings with clients and their employer. An overview of expected behaviors for holders of two investment professional certifications is given in Exhibit 1.8.

Ethics is an important concern in investments professions since practitioners advise clients and handle large sums of money. Virtually any career path within the investments field has federal or state regulations on behavior in addition to those required from an earned professional designation. Following is a brief discussion of some specific investments positions with various financial institutions. Additional information about investments

---

[7]For a list of corporate scandals, see *http://cbs.marketwatch.com/news/features/scandal_sheet.asp*.

careers can be found at this book's Web site and the Web pages of financial firms (such as *http://www.ml.com, http://www.smithbarney.com,* and *http://www.agedwards.com*).

1. *Registered Representative with a Brokerage Firm*   Also referred to as a *broker,* the registered representative is involved in the sale of stocks, bonds, options, commodities, and other investment instruments to individuals or institutions. If you decide to buy or sell stock, you call your broker at the investment firm where you have an account, and he or she arranges the purchase or sale. If you are a regular customer, your broker may call you and suggest that you buy or sell some stock; if you agree, he or she will arrange it. This position has evolved in recent years and now focuses more on client financial planning and less on earning commissions by generating trades.

2. *Investment Analyst*   Investment analysts (or security analysts) become experts in an industry and the companies within the industry. For example, as an employee of Merrill Lynch, you might make an analysis of the computer industry and all the major companies within the industry and then prepare a report outlining your purchase and sell recommendations. Then registered representatives at Merrill Lynch offices all over the country would use this report.

    Alternatively, if your firm is an investment banking firm that underwrites new stock or bond issues, you may analyze the industry and companies within the industry regarding a potential securities issue your firm will underwrite in order to determine its needs and to provide suggestions regarding the characteristics of the issue. In addition, investment bankers are often involved in finding merger partners for their clients and helping negotiate terms. As an analyst you would help determine how much the potential merger firm is worth as well as reasonable terms for the merger.

    There are two basic classifications of investment analysts: buy-side and sell-side. A buy-side analyst works for a portfolio manager and sifts through economic data, industry forecasts, and firm financials to recommend securities for purchase by the manager. Buy-side analysts typically work for banks, money managers, mutual funds, insurance firms, pension funds, and endowments. A sell-side analyst works to identify potentially attractive investments for the firm's brokers and sales force to recommend to clients. As such, sell-side analysts work mainly for brokers and investment banking firms.

3. *Portfolio Manager*   The financial firms we have mentioned (banks, investment counselors, mutual funds, insurance companies) employ portfolio managers in addition to analysts. Portfolio managers are responsible for gathering information and recommendations from the analysts. On the basis of the information, the recommendations, and the overall needs of the portfolio, they make final decisions about the securities in the portfolio.

4. *Financial Planner*   Because most individuals do not have the time or the desire to learn about stocks, bonds, and all the other components of a properly constructed portfolio, recent years have brought significant growth in the number of individuals and firms that provide assistance in personal financial planning. Based on what a client reveals about his or her current assets, goals, needs, and constraints, the financial planner provides a blueprint of how much that client should invest and in what financial instruments. Thus, financial planners help create appropriate financial plans for clients, analyze individual securities, and construct and monitor portfolios that fulfill the clients' financial plans.

5. *Corporations: Treasury Management and Investor Relations*   Corporations receive and spend huge sums of cash over the course of a year. Firms must accumulate cash for future dividend and tax payments, acquisitions, or other future use. Thus, corporations hire treasury, or portfolio, managers to invest the firm's excess cash in marketable securities to earn returns with low risk. The investor relations staff is the liaison between investors and the

EXHIBIT 1.9	Median Compensation Levels
INVESTMENT PROFESSIONALS EMPLOYED AT:	**COMPENSATION LEVEL**
Mutual funds	$157,000
Investment counseling firms and securities brokers/dealers	$150,000
Insurance companies	$149,500
Banks	$123,000
Endowments/foundations	$118,000
Pension consulting firms	$101,000
Securities broker/dealer	$144,390
Portfolio manager, domestic equities	$142,210
Portfolio manager, global equities	$160,000
Portfolio manager, domestic bonds	$165,000
Portfolio manager, global bonds	$176,105

Source: CFA Institute.

corporations. Stock and bond analysts (as well as individual investors) use the investor relations staff to obtain financial data and information such as the firm's interpretations of its recent performance or its reasons for higher or lower earnings. The investor relations staff has access to the firm's top officers so they can communicate the firm's message to the financial markets.

THE IMPORTANCE OF PROFESSIONAL DESIGNATIONS

Anyone considering a career in investment analysis or portfolio management should attempt to become a Chartered Financial Analyst (CFA®), a professional designation similar to the CPA in accounting. Financial institutions around the world hold this designation in high regard and many require, or at least encourage, their analysts and portfolio managers to earn it.[8] The program and its requirements are described in an appendix at the back of the book. A CFA charterholder will likely work in an institutional setting, but many work in personal financial planning, too. With their expertise in analyzing investments, they will be equipped to recommend specific securities for purchase by their clients.

Alternatively, individuals interested in being a financial planner should consider becoming a Certified Financial Planner (CFP™), which is likewise a respected professional designation. A personal financial planner must consider insurance, tax and estate planning, and the investment goals of their clients, and the rigorous training and ethical standards of the CFP designation will prepare one to do so.

The earnings potential in investment analysis and financial planning is lucrative for those willing to work hard, although compensation levels will raise and fall based on financial market performance; many analysts and portfolio managers receive a bonus as well as salary. Exhibit 1.9 shows the median compensation levels from a 2003 survey of investment management professionals. This same survey showed the value of the CFA designation: Charterholders had a median compensation 21 percent higher than non–charterholders.

[8]Rod Newing, "Increasing the Importance of 'the Gold Standard,'" *Financial Times,* June 23, 2003, special report "Financial Training," page 4.

Summary

The purpose of this chapter was to provide background for subsequent chapters. To achieve that goal, we covered several topics:

- We discussed why individuals save part of their income and why they decide to invest their savings. We defined investment as the current commitment of these savings for a period of time to derive a rate of return that compensates for the time involved, the expected rate of inflation, and the uncertainty.

- We considered that investors commit current resources to achieve financial goals concerning income, capital preservation, capital appreciation, or some combination of these.

- We reviewed the four major themes of the text, important not only to investors but also to those who work in the investments field. The four themes are: the tradeoff between expected return and risk; the consequences of investing in markets that are nearly infor-

mationally efficient; the need to manage a portfolio to maximize net after-tax returns for a given level of risk; and the need to diversify across different assets and countries.

- We discussed three ways to invest in a financial asset: directly, indirectly, or through derivative securities whose value is dependent on the value of underlying securities.

- We examined the paramount role of financial intermediaries in gathering funds from savers (typically households) and channeling those funds to deficit units such as governments and businesses needing debt and equity financing.

- We saw that the most important decision in constructing a portfolio is the asset allocation decision; the securities selection decision is secondary. In making these decisions, managers may take either an active or a passive approach. Active managers will try to time markets

Investments Online

Many Internet sites seek to assist the novice investor. Because they cover the basics, have helpful links to other Internet sites, and sometimes allow users to calculate items of interest (rates of return, the size of investment necessary to meet a certain goal, and so on), these sites are useful for the experienced investor, too.

http://www.finpipe.com The Financial Pipeline is an excellent financial education site for those just starting to learn about investments or who need a quick refresher. The site contains information and links on a variety of investment topics such as bonds, stocks, strategy, retirement, and consumer finance.

http://www.investorguide.com This is another site offering a plethora of information useful to both novice and seasoned investors. It contains links to pages with market summaries, news research, and much more, including a glossary of investment terms. Basic investment education issues are taught in their "University" section. There are links to a number of personal financial help pages, including sites dealing with home

or car buying, retirement, loans, and insurance as well as to a number of calculator functions to help users make financial decisions.

Many representatives of the financial press have Internet sites:

http://online.wsj.com *The Wall Street Journal*

http://news.ft.com *Financial Times*

http://www.economist.com *The Economist* magazine

http://www.fortune.com *Fortune* magazine

http://money.cnn.com *Money* magazine

http://www.forbes.com *Forbes* magazine

http://www.worth.com *Worth* magazine

http://www.smartmoney.com *Smart Money* magazine

http://online.barrons.com *Barron's* newspaper

by shifting funds between asset classes and by selecting specific securities to purchase. Passive managers will stay with a set asset allocation, rebalance it periodically as the allocation strays from its target, and invest in order to track, rather than try to beat, an index in each asset class.

- Finally, we considered ethics, job opportunities, and professional designations in the investments field.

Because financial advisors deal with personal client information and invest large sums of money, ethics and a trusting relationship are important. Major investments certifications have strong ethics components, and state and federal regulators maintain registration requirements for financial advisors. Many career opportunities exist in the investments field, and for some the pay can be quite lucrative.

QUESTIONS

1. Define investment. What is the overall purpose for investing?
2. As a student, are you saving or borrowing? Why? Even if you are borrowing, are you investing? How? What future returns do you expect on your investment?
3. Divide a person's life from ages twenty to seventy into ten-year segments and discuss the likely saving or borrowing patterns during each of these periods.
4. Discuss why you would expect the saving–borrowing pattern to differ by occupation (for example, for a doctor versus a plumber).
5. What is meant by the phrase "time value of money"?
6. If an economy's nominal risk-free rate of return is 6 percent and the risk premium on a certain asset is 3 percent, should an investor's required rate of return be 9 percent? Why or why not?
7. What will happen if a risky asset has an expected return of 7 percent while a safe asset has an expected return of 8 percent? Explain.
8. Why is the phrase "risk drives expected returns" true?
9. How does operational efficiency in a market differ from informational efficiency?
10. How are investment expenses similar to a tax to the investor?
11. Why would we want to diversify even if we identified a "sure thing" investment?
12. What is the major source of funds for investing in the U.S. economy?
13. What is the role of financial intermediaries in the functioning of the investment sector?
14. How does a broker differ from a dealer?
15. How do an active and a passive investment manager differ in the asset allocation decision? The security selection decision?
16. How might a manager be active in setting the asset allocation but passive in security selection? How might a manager be passive in the asset allocation decision but active in security selection?
17. Why are ethical considerations so important to the functioning of the financial sector?

PROBLEMS

1. What would be the required rate of return on an investment in an economy with a 7 percent nominal risk-free rate of return, expected inflation of 4 percent, and a risk premium of 4 percent? What would you expect $1,000 invested at this rate to grow to after ten years? Twenty years?
2. Compute the required rate of return under the following scenarios:
   a. Nominal risk-free rate = 11 percent, risk premium = 2 percent
   b. Nominal risk-free rate = 12 percent, risk premium = 3 percent
   c. Nominal risk-free rate = 6 percent, risk premium = 5 percent
3. The return on a tax-deferred account averages 8 percent over twenty years. The initial investment is $10,000. Compare the investor's after-tax value of his portfolio if (a) he removes the savings all at once and his tax bracket at the time is 25 percent; (b) an equivalent portfolio earns 8 percent pre-tax in a taxable account; the assumed tax rate on all annual investment returns is 25 percent.
4. Use the situation in Problem 3, only now assume in part (b) that tax-efficient investing allows the investor to earn 7 percent after-tax. How does the portfolio value compare with the after-tax value of the portfolio in part (a)?

WEB EXERCISES

1. Visit the Web site for the CFA Institute, *http://www .cfainstitute.org*. What are the requirements for earning the Chartered Financial Analyst (CFA) designation?
2. Visit the Web site for the Certified Financial Planning Board (*http://www.cfp.net*). What must candidates do before they can earn the CFP mark?

3. Visit the Web site of several investment banks and brokerage houses. Based on the job descriptions and skill needs of available positions, what knowledge, skills, and abilities do you need to develop to obtain one of these positions?

SPREADSHEET EXERCISES

1. Construct a spreadsheet to replicate the analysis of Exhibit 1.5. That is, assume $10,000 is invested in a single asset that returns 7 percent annually for twenty-five years and $2,000 is placed in five different investments, earning returns of −100 percent, 0 percent, 5 percent, 10 percent, and 12 percent, respectively, over the twenty-five-year time frame. For each of the questions below, begin with the original scenario presented in Exhibit 1.5.
   a. Experiment with the return on the fifth asset. How low can the return go and still have the diversified portfolio earn a higher return than the single-asset portfolio?
   b. What happens to the value of the diversified portfolio if the first two investments are both a total loss?
   c. Suppose the single-asset portfolio earns a return of 8 percent annually. How does the return of the single-asset portfolio compare with that of the five-asset portfolio? How does it compare if the single-asset portfolio earns a 6 percent annual return?
   d. Assume that asset 1 of the diversified portfolio remains a total loss (−100 percent return) and asset 2 earns no return. Make a table showing how sensitive the portfolio returns are to a 1 percentage point change in the return of each of the other three assets. That is, how is the diversified portfolio's value affected if the return on asset 3 is 4 percent or 6 percent? If the return on asset 4 is 9 percent or 11 percent? If the return on asset 5 is 11 percent or 13 percent? How does the total portfolio value change if each of the three assets' returns are 1 percentage point lower than in Exhibit 1.5? If they are 1 percentage point higher?
   e. Using the sensitivity analysis of parts (c) and (d), explain how the two portfolios differ in their sensitivity to different returns on their assets. What are the implications of this for choosing between a single-asset portfolio and a diversified portfolio?

REFERENCES

There are many books available for the beginning investor. Several interesting ones that have remained popular over the years include:

Bogle, John C. *Bogle on Mutual Funds.* Burr Ridge, IL: Richard D. Irwin, Inc., 1994.

Lynch, Peter, with John Rothschild. *One Up on Wall Street.* New York: Simon and Schuster, 1989.

Lynch, Peter, with John Rothschild. *Beating the Street.* New York: Simon and Schuster, 1993.

Malkiel, Burton. *A Random Walk Down Wall Street,* 7th edition. New York: W. W. Norton & Co., 2004.

THOMSON ONE
Business School Edition

1. Read *A Guide to Using Thomson One: Business School Edition* by Rosemary Carlson which was shrink-wrapped with your text. Thomson One: Business School Edition is a special version of a powerful data and analytical package used by many investment professionals. It will be useful to you in this and other classes you are taking this semester.

2. Follow the directions in section III "How do I find general overview information for a firm?" for Amazon (stock symbol: AMZN) and Wal-Mart (WMT), two firms in the retail industry (or try two firms in an industry of your choice). On what stock markets are the firms traded? How do their growth rates in sales and earnings compare? How have their stocks performed over the past few months? Are stock analysts recommending investors buy or sell each of the two firm's stocks?

GLOSSARY

Broker Assists the purchase and sale of securities by bringing together buyers and sellers.

Dealer Facilitates primary and secondary market trading by buying and selling securities from his own account.

Externally or informationally efficient When a market's prices move quickly and in an unbiased manner to new information.

Financial intermediaries Institutions that gather funds from savers and channel them to borrowers, such as banks, credit unions, and investment banks.

Internally efficient When a market's mechanisms allow trading to occur at minimum cost.

Investment The current commitment of resources for a period of time in the expectation of receiving future resources that will compensate the investor for the time the resources are committed, the expected rate of inflation, and the uncertainty of future payments.

Nominal risk-free interest rate The basic interest rate that incorporates the effects of expected inflation.

Portfolio The overall collection of assets owned by an investor.

Primary market transactions When a firm or government sells securities to raise money.

Pure or real risk-free interest rate The basic interest rate with no accommodation for inflation or uncertainty.

Risk The uncertainty that an investment will earn its expected rate of return.

Risk premium The extra expected return above the nominal risk-free rate that investors require to commit funds in a risky investment.

Secondary market The name for markets where investors trade among themselves.

Time value of money The principle that a dollar today is worth more to us than the same dollar in the future.

PART

2

The Investment Environment

The chapters in this section will provide a background for your study of investments. After you read these chapters you will be able to answer the following questions:

- How do we measure the returns and risks for investments?
- Why should we diversify investments?
- Why should we diversify globally?
- What investments are available?
- Why are mutual funds ideal investment vehicles for individuals?
- What factors should be considered when selecting among numerous mutual funds?
- What factors should be considered and what steps should be taken when making asset allocation decisions?
- What is the function of and how do securities markets operate?
- How and why are securities markets around the world changing?
- What are the major uses of and differences among security-market indexes?

Because a major goal of investing is balancing risk and return, it is crucial to understand how to properly measure these components. We discuss this in Chapter 2. We also consider what factors determine the required rate of return on an investment.

In Chapter 3 we deal with one of the fundamental tenets of prudent investing—diversification. Beyond traditional diversification, we make a strong case for global investing and provide examples of historical risk-return results that demonstrate the concepts discussed.

For good reasons, individual investors put a substantial percentage of their savings in mutual funds. Because of the importance of funds to investors, Chapter 4 is dedicated to what they are, the advantages they provide, how to determine which ones to invest in, and a review of historical investment results.

It is well documented and widely acknowledged that the secret to success is an effective asset allocation strategy. In Chapter 5 we lay out the process and the specific steps to accomplish this critical task.

In Chapter 6 we examine how securities markets work in general, and then specifically focus on the functioning of primary and secondary stock-and-bond markets. In addition, we consider the globalization of existing markets, the development of new capital markets, and the rapid changes in securities markets.

Investors, market analysts, and financial theorists often gauge the behavior of securities markets by evaluating changes in various market indexes and determine portfolio performance by comparing a portfolio's results to an appropriate benchmark. In Chapter 7 we examine and compare a number of domestic and global stock- and bond-market indexes available for these purposes.

Overall, this section provides the framework for understanding various securities, how to allocate among alternative asset classes, the markets where they are bought and sold, the indexes that reflect their performance, and how to manage an investment portfolio.

CHAPTER 2

Return and Risk Basics

In this chapter we will answer the following questions:

What are the sources of investment returns?

How can returns be measured?

What is risk and how can we measure risk?

What are the components of an investment's required return to investors and why might they change over time?

One purpose of this book is to help you choose wisely among different investments. To do so, you must estimate and evaluate the expected return–risk tradeoffs for the various investments available. Therefore, you need to know how to accurately measure the rate of return and the risk involved. To meet this need, we examine the sources of returns on investments and how to measure *historical* rates of return and risk. We consider the historical measures because this book and other publications provide numerous examples of historical average rates of return and risk measures for various assets, and understanding these presentations is important. In addition, these historical results are often used by investors to estimate the *expected* rates of return and risk for an asset class. We discuss expected rates of return and risk in Chapter 8.

The simplest return measure is the historical rate of return on an individual investment over its holding period, the time period the investment is held. We first review the two sources of investment return, income and price changes. Next, we consider how to measure the *average* historical rate of return for an individual investment over a number of time periods. We then examine risk: what is it and how to measure it. Finally, we take a conceptual look at risk and return and review the components of an asset's required rate of return and their influences.

An Example of Return and Risk

Exhibit 2.1 presents historical data on returns and risk on several assets. Returns are important since they represent growth in wealth and (if they exceed the inflation rate) growth in purchasing power. But rates of return are not constant; they vary over time. The variability of the rate of return is one way to measure risk.

Exhibit 2.1	Summary Statistics of Annual Returns, 1984–2003, U.S. Securities		
	Geometric Mean (%)*	Arithmetic Mean (%)*	Standard Deviation (%)
Large company stocks (S&P 500)	13.33	14.74	17.92
Small company stocks (S&P SmallCap 600)	10.82	12.86	21.21
Government bonds (Lehman Brothers)	9.07	9.20	5.33
Corporate bonds (Lehman Brothers)	10.07	10.24	5.99
Intermediate-term corporate bonds (Lehman Brothers)	9.25	9.34	4.37
Intermediate-term government bonds (Lehman Brothers)	8.43	8.50	3.84
30-day Treasury bill	5.23	5.23	0.64
U.S. inflation	3.01	3.01	0.81

*We will describe how each of these is calculated and why they differ in value in a later section.

If we were to graph the data in Exhibit 2.1, the points would not all lie on a straight line but we would see an upward-sloping relationship. We expect to receive higher returns from taking on higher risks and these data show that, at least among these assets in the United States, that expectation has generally been met. Riskier stocks have higher levels of average return than safer bonds and Treasury bills.

Types of Returns

What types of returns can investors earn on their investments? First, recall from Chapter 1 why investments are made: to generate income, to appreciate capital (grow in value), or to preserve capital (maintain value in the face of inflation). These investment goals shed light on the two sources of investment returns:

Income   The investment periodically generates cash for the investor in the form of interest, dividends, or rent. Examples of income-generating investments include bank certificates of deposit (CDs), bonds, dividend-paying stocks, and some real-estate investments.

Changes in price or value   Over time, the value or market price of an investment asset could rise or fall. If the price of the asset rises above what we paid, we have a *capital gain*. For example, we may purchase land for $30,000 and sell it later for $40,000, giving a $10,000 capital gain. Of course, prices can move down, too. Should the price fall below what we paid, we have a *capital loss*. If we had invested $10,000 in ProFunds Ultra OTC in March 2000, our investment would have been worth about $530 in April 2001—a capital loss of $9,470.

The total dollar return on an investment over time is

2.1   **Total Dollar Return = Income + Price Change**

Investors seeking capital appreciation focus on the price change component of total return (capital gains). Those seeking to generate income focus primarily on the income component (although securities can be sold and then accumulated capital gains used to provide funds for spending). Investors seeking to preserve capital are concerned with combined effects of income and price changes.

HOLDING PERIOD MEASURES

The amount of time an investment is owned is the *holding period*. The percentage return from income and price changes during this time is called the *holding period return (HPR)* and is found by dividing the dollar return by the initial purchase price of the investment. The HPR can be expressed in either decimal form (for example, 0.15) or as a percentage (15%):

2.2 $$\text{Holding Period Return (HPR)} = \frac{\text{Income + Price Change}}{\text{Purchase Price}}$$

For example, suppose an investor purchases 100 shares of Walgreens stock for $2,318.75. A year later, the investor receives a total of $13.50 in dividends for the shares (income) and the market price of 100 shares of Walgreens stock had risen $3,287.50 (price change). The investor's total dollar return is:

$$\$13.50 + (\$3,287.50 - \$2,318.75) = \$982.25$$

The holding period return is $982.25/$2,318.75 = 0.4236 or 42.36 percent.[1]

Note that a holding period can be any length of time. If an asset is purchased today and sold next week, the holding period is just a few days. If shares of stock are purchased as a present for your newborn daughter and not sold until she retires at age 60, the holding period is many years.

ANNUALIZING A HOLDING PERIOD RETURN

Sometimes we may want to compare the performance of investments with different holding periods. Suppose we have owned one investment for four years, another for ten years, a third for six months, and a fourth for two and a half years. To measure and compare the performance of these investments over time, we can standardize on *annual* holding period returns. For holding periods more or less than a year, we adjust the calculation to *annualize* the return. If the holding period is less than one year, we assume the return over that holding period will continue for the entire year. If the holding period is more than one year, we determine the average yearly return that would give us the holding period return we have earned. The annualized holding period return is calculated using the HPR in decimal form by

2.3 $$\text{Annualized HPR} = (1 + \text{Holding Period Return})^{1/n} - 1$$

where n is the number of years in the holding period.

Suppose we have the four assets shown in the table.

Asset	HPR (percent)	HPR (decimal)	Length of Holding Period
Stock A	825	8.25	10 years
Mutual Fund B	90	0.90	4 years
High-Yield Bond C	5	0.05	4 months
Real Estate D	−12	−0.12	2.5 years

---

[1]This calculation could have been done on a per-share basis: The total dollar return per share was $0.135 + ($32.875 − $23.1875) = $9.8225. The holding period return was $9.8225/$23.1875 = 42.36%.

EXHIBIT 2.2	Holding Period Returns and Return Relatives		
	HPR (percent)	HPR (decimal)	Return Relative
Stock A	825	8.25	9.25
Mutual Fund B	90.0	0.90	1.90
High-Yield Bond C	5.0	0.05	1.05
Real Estate D	−12.0	−0.12	0.88

Applying equation 2.3 to each of these, we compute the annualized holding period returns.

Stock A: $(1 + 8.25)^{1/10} - 1 = 0.2491$ or 24.91%
Mutual Fund B: $(1 + 0.90)^{1/4} - 1 = 0.1741$ or 17.41%
High-Yield Bond C:[2] $(1 + 0.05)^{1/(4/12)} - 1 = 0.1576$ or 15.76%
Real Estate D: $[1 + (-0.12)]^{1/2.5} - 1 = -0.0499$ or −4.99%

The term (1 + Holding Period Return), called the *return relative,* is equal to the sum of the income from an investment and the value of the investment divided by the asset's purchase price:

2.4

$$\textbf{Return Relative} = \frac{\textbf{Income + Ending Value of an Investment}}{\textbf{Purchase Price}}$$

In other words, the return relative is the sum of the cash flows received by the investor during the holding period if the asset were sold today divided by the asset's purchase price. The return relative[3] is equal to 1 + HPR. Thus, equation 2.3 can be rewritten as

2.5

$$\textbf{Annualized HPR = (Return Relative)}^{1/n} - 1$$

Exhibit 2.2 presents the holding period returns and return relatives for our four-asset example.[4]

---

[2]Since the holding period is four months, *n,* the number of years is 4/12. Had the holding period been expressed in terms of weeks, to determine the number of years we would divide by 52; if it had been expressed in days, we would divide by 365. If the holding period is less than one year, the exponent $1/n$ becomes a number larger than 1.

[3]Substituting the definition of the holding period return from equation 2.2, we have

1 + HPR = 1 + (Income + Price Change)/Purchase Price

The price change is equal to the difference between the ending value and purchase price of the asset:

1 + HPR = 1 + [Income + (Ending Value − Purchase Price)]/Purchase Price

Simplifying, we obtain

1 + HPR = 1 + [(Income + Ending Value)/Purchase Price] − Purchase Price/Purchase Price

which equals

1 + HPR = 1 + (Income + Ending Value)/(Purchase Price) − 1 = (Income + Ending Value)/Purchase Price

which is the definition of the return relative.

[4]Though they may seem esoteric now, return relatives are used to determine compound returns over time. Return relatives for a one-year holding period can be multiplied together to determine the return relative of a longer holding period.

Measures of Historical Rates of Return

Interactive e-lectures

For more explanation and an animated example of measuring returns, go to: **http://reillyxtra.swlearning.com.**

Thus far we have taken a conceptual view of the sources of investment returns and some holding period return calculations. We have learned the basics of computing returns over an investor's holding period and annualizing them to allow comparisons over a common time frame. Now, since we often will have monthly, quarterly, or annual data on income and market values, let's consider how to determine the *mean or average rate of return* for an investment over some period of time.

The first step in computing historical summary measures is to compute periodic rates of return. To do so, we usually compute for each year the one-year holding period return for each asset; from this we develop a series of annual returns. Exhibit 2.3 shows such a set of calculations involving prices and dividends from Walgreens stock. For every year since 1994 at the end of August (which is the end of Walgreens' fiscal year), we have recorded the stock price and the total dividends per share from the previous twelve months. Then we computed a year-by-year holding period return based on the dividends and change in price.

Given a set of annual rates of return for an individual investment, there are two summary measures of return performance: the arithmetic mean return and the geometric mean return. To find the *arithmetic mean return (R_A)*, the sum (Σ) of annual holding period returns is divided by the number of years (n) as follows:

2.6

$$R_A = \frac{\Sigma\,\text{HPR}}{n}$$

where

Σ HPR = the sum of annual holding period returns or annual returns

To illustrate, let's find the arithmetic mean return for Walgreens stock for this time period.

EXHIBIT 2.3	Share Price and Dividends from Walgreens

(Stock prices and dividends are adjusted for stock splits.)

Year	Ending Stock Price	Dividends	Annual Holding Period Return (decimal)	Annual Holding Period Return (percent)	Return Relative
2004	$35.65	0.172	0.100	10.0	1.100
2003	32.57	0.157	−0.058	−5.8	0.942
2002	34.74	0.144	0.001	0.1	1.001
2001	34.86	0.140	0.064	6.4	1.064
2000	32.89	0.135	0.424	42.4	1.424
1999	23.19	0.130	0.215	21.5	1.215
1998	19.19	0.130	0.434	43.4	1.434
1997	13.47	0.125	0.654	65.4	1.654
1996	8.22	0.110	0.359	35.9	1.359
1995	6.13	0.110	0.328	32.8	1.328
1994	4.7				

$$R_A = \frac{\Sigma \, HPR}{n}$$

$$= \frac{32.8 + 35.9 + 65.4 + 43.4 + 21.5 + 42.4 + 6.4 + 0.1 + (-5.8) + 10.0}{10}$$

$$= \frac{252.1\%}{10}$$

$$= 25.2\%$$

To find the *geometric mean return* (R_G), we find the nth root of the product (symbolized mathematically by Π) of the return relatives $(1 + HPR)$ for n years, minus 1.

2.7 $$R_G = [\Pi \ (\textbf{Return Relatives})]^{1/n} - 1$$

where

Π = the product of the return relatives as follows
(Return Relative$_1$) (Return Relative$_2$) $\cdots$ (Return Relative$_n$)
or $(1 + HPR_1)(1 + HPR_2) \cdots (1 + HPR_n)$

Computing the geometric mean return for the Walgreens stock, we have

$$R_G = [\Pi \ (\textbf{Return Relatives})]^{1/n} - 1$$

$$= [(1.328)(1.359)(1.654)(1.434)(1.215)(1.424)(1.064)(1.001)(0.942)(1.100)]^{1/10} - 1$$

$$= (8.172)^{1/10} - 1 = 0.234 \text{ or } 23.4\%$$

Investors are typically concerned with long-term performance when comparing alternative investments. The geometric mean return is considered a superior measure of the long-term mean rate of return because it indicates the compound annual rate of return based on the ending value of the investment versus its beginning value.[5] In the context of the Walgreens data, this means that $1 invested in Walgreens stock in August 1994 would have grown to $8.17 in value (with dividends reinvested) by August 2004. The product of the return relatives, 8.172, represents how a $1 investment would have grown over the time period under study.[6]

Although arithmetic mean return provides a good indication of the rate of return for an investment during any one year, it has an upward bias when measuring an asset's long-term performance. Consider, for example, a security that increases in price from $10 to $20 during year 1 and drops back to $10 during year 2. The annual holding period returns would be:

Year	Beginning Value	Ending Value	HPR (decimal)	HPR (percent)	Return Relative
1	10	20	1.00	100	2.00
2	20	10	−0.50	−50	0.50

[5]The astute student may wonder if we should compute the internal rate of return (IRR) for the investment. Our time-zero cost is −4.7, the 1994 stock price. We receive cash flows (dividends) each year through 2004; the year 2004 cash flow is the sum of that year's dividend and stock price. The IRR of this cash flow stream is 23.74 percent. This differs from the geometric mean return of 23.4 percent. Why does this difference occur and why is the geometric mean return preferred over the IRR of the investment? A quick answer (the answers are discussed fully in the Chapter 21 appendix) is: the IRR calculation is sensitive to the size of the cash flows whereas the geometric mean rate of return is not.

[6]The product of the return relatives is known as the *cumulative wealth index*. It indicates the wealth generated by each dollar invested at the beginning of the time frame.

This would give an arithmetic mean rate of return of

$$\frac{(100\%) + (-50\%)}{2} = \frac{50\%}{2} = 25\%$$

The geometric mean rate of return would be

$$[(2.00)(0.50)]^{1/2} - 1 = (1.00)^{1/2} - 1 = 0.00 \text{ or } 0\%$$

This answer of a 0 percent rate of return accurately measures the fact that there was no change in wealth from this investment.

An actual example of this is the ProFund Ultra OTC mutual fund, which lost 94.7 percent of its value during the March 2000–April 2001 time period and then rose by 95.6 percent in May 2001. A simple arithmetic mean would lead the naive investor to believe his investment had broken even: $(-94.7 + 95.6)/2 = 0.45$ percent arithmetic mean return. But investors looking at their account statements (and readers of this book) would know that March 2000 investors still face a substantial loss: A $1,000 investment in March 2000 was worth about $103.67 in May 2001.[7]

When rates of return are the same for all years, the geometric mean return will equal the arithmetic mean return. If the rates of return vary over the years, the geometric mean return will always be lower. The difference between the two mean values will depend on the year-to-year changes in the rates of return: Larger annual changes in the rates of return (that is, more volatility) will result in a greater difference.[8]

An awareness of both methods of computing mean rates of return is important. Most published accounts of investment performance or descriptions of financial research use both measures, as do most studies dealing with long-run historical rates of return (as we saw in exhibit 2.1). We will also use both throughout this book.

EFFECTS OF REINVESTING

Equation 2.1 presents the total dollar return on an investment as the sum of the income generated by an investment and its capital gain or loss. With that information, we can compute a holding period return (equation 2.2). In these calculations, we assumed that any income received is spent. However, many investors—especially those with long time horizons or little need for current income—will be able to reinvest the income they receive from dividends, interest, or rent. The reinvested income then generates additional income through compounding. This occurs, for example, when the principal and interest in a bank CD is rolled over, or continuously reinvested, upon maturity or when a company allows shareholders to automatically reinvest dividends in the firm's stock. The return from reinvesting income can become substantial over time.

Suppose we place $10,000 in a bond that pays annual interest of 9 percent indefinitely. The bond will generate income of $900, or 9 percent of the invested amount, each year. If we spend the $900 interest income each year rather than reinvesting it, only the $10,000 principal will earn interest each year. When only the initial principal earns interest, it is said to earn *simple interest*. Under simple interest, our principal remains at $10,000 and next year the investor will receive another $900 in interest income.

---

[7]The story of a large percentage loss followed by a large percentage gain can be seen in Karen Damato, "Doing the Math: Tech Investors' Road to Recovery Is Long," *The Wall Street Journal*, May 18, 2001, p. C1.

[8]As an approximation, the geometric mean return and the arithmetic mean return are related as follows: $(1 + R_G)^2 = (1 + R_A)^2 - \sigma^2$, where all the numbers are in decimal form.

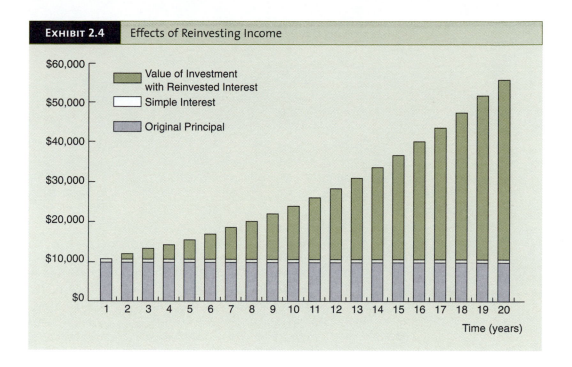

EXHIBIT 2.4 | Effects of Reinvesting Income

But what happens if the interest income is reinvested in the same bond with the same 9 percent interest? If the interest is reinvested, prior years' interest payments will themselves earn interest indefinitely. In our example, the initial investment of $10,000 becomes $10,900 in one year, which will generate 0.09 × $10,900 or $981 in interest income. $900 of this interest income is from the initial $10,000 investment; the extra $81 is 9 percent interest on the first year's interest of $900. This is called *compounding*. When interest returns are reinvested and added to the principal, the investment earns *compounded interest,* or more generally, *compounded returns.*

With simple interest, in the tenth year the interest payment is still $900 and the amount invested is still $10,000. But with compounding, we receive $1,955 in interest income in year 10 and our invested funds total $23,674. As Exhibit 2.4 graphically shows, compounded returns are obviously preferable.

Exhibit 2.5 elaborates on the effects of reinvesting income in this example over ten years. As we have seen, if we spend the interest each year, the annual interest income remains constant at $900 each year. But with reinvesting the interest income rises from $900 in year 1 to $1955 in year 10. Reinvesting each year's interest has had two effects. First, the amount invested has grown from $10,000 to $23,674 at the end of year 10. Second, more income is earned over the ten years: Total interest income *without* reinvesting is $9,000 (9% × $10,000 × 10 years); total interest income *with* reinvesting is $13,674.

The total wealth at the end of ten years can be broken down as follows:

Source of Funds	Amount	Percentage of Total
Original principal	$10,000	42.24%
Interest (simple)	$9,000	38.02%
Interest-on-interest	$4,674	19.74%
Total wealth	$23,674	

EXHIBIT 2.5	Benefit of Reinvesting Income at 9 Percent									
Year	1	2	3	4	5	6	7	8	9	10
Original principal	$10,000	$10,000	$10,000	$10,000	$10,000	$10,000	$10,000	$10,000	$10,000	$10,000
Simple interest	$900	$900	$900	$900	$900	$900	$900	$900	$900	$900
IF INCOME IS REINVESTED										
Interest with reinvestment	$900	$981	$1,069	$1,166	$1,270	$1,385	$1,509	$1,645	$1,793	$1,955
Wealth in the investment	$10,900	$11,881	$12,950	$14,116	$15,386	$16,771	$18,280	$19,926	$21,719	$23,674
TOTALS										
Cumulative interest-on-interest	$0	$81	$250	$516	$886	$1,371	$1,980	$2,726	$3,619	$4,674
Cumulative simple interest	$900	$1,800	$2,700	$3,600	$4,500	$5,400	$6,300	$7,200	$8,100	$9,000
Cumulative total interest	$900	$1,881	$2,950	$4,116	$5,386	$6,771	$8,280	$9,926	$11,719	$13,674

The interest-on-interest return represents 34.2 percent of the total amount of interest earned on the bond over the ten years ($4,674/$13,674). Further calculations on a spreadsheet will show that at the end of fifteen years the interest-on-interest represents 35.5 percent of the total wealth; after twenty years it represents over 50 percent of our wealth in the bond.

From this discussion, we can see that if the situation permits, we should always reinvest cash flows. The benefits of *not* spending investment income increase over time and with the return that can be earned on the reinvested funds.

One final note: when funds are continually reinvested, wealth accumulates as income and price changes compound. The average annual return on such an investment is easily computed using a variation of equation 2.5. The annualized average return is

2.8
$$\text{Annualized Average Return} = \left(\frac{\text{Ending Wealth}}{\text{Initial Investment}} \right)^{1/n} - 1$$

For example, an original investment of $1,000 that compounds over twenty years to $5,000 has earned an annualized average return of ($5,000/$1,000)$^{1/20}$ −1 or 8.38 percent.[9]

Defining Risk

An inherent factor of investment returns is uncertainty or risk. *Risk* is the chance of not meeting one's investment goals because of return uncertainty over time. To put it another way, risk arises from the expected volatility in asset returns over time. Unless we invest for only short holding periods or place our funds in a short-term fixed-rate bank CD or a short-term Treasury bill, we will face uncertain returns from investments. For a working person, poor returns or overly conservative investments could mean insufficient funds for retirement. For a pension fund, poor returns could mean not being able to pay retirees their promised pensions. From this perspective, even a "safe" investment such as bank CDs could

[9]The ending value of investment represents the total compounded returns earned from the initial investment, or (initial investment + compounded returns). Thus, the return relative equals (initial investment + compounded returns)/initial investment). Following equation 2.5, the annualized return is the return relative raised to the power of $1/n$, minus 1.

be considered risky in that it does not offer the return potential over time that, for example, a twenty-something investor needs to meet an early retirement goal.

We have seen that there are three sources of investment returns:

1. Income
2. Price changes
3. Reinvestment of income or price changes (compounding)

We can say, then, that investment risk must arise from variability in one or more of these return sources. Thus, sources of risk in any one investment may cause:

1. fluctuations in expected income (caused, for example, by varying dividends, missed interest payments, or unoccupied rental housing)
2. fluctuations in the expected future price of the asset (caused, for example, by changing economic conditions or asset-specific circumstances)
3. fluctuations in the amount available for reinvestment and fluctuations in returns earned from reinvestment (caused, for example, by changes in tax rates, interest rates, or asset returns).

We can classify risk sources as either systematic or asset- (or issuer-) specific. *Systematic risk* affects the economic or financial "system," hence the name; its effect is pervasive throughout the economy. Examples of systematic risk include changes in interest rates, the economic growth rate, changes in taxes, actions by the Federal Reserve Board, changes in exchange rates, and major military actions.

Asset-specific risk, also called *unsystematic risk,* deals with the characteristics of a type of asset or security issuer (such as a company or government) rather than broad economic factors. Examples of unsystematic risk include poor management decisions, labor strikes, deterioration of product or service quality, and the rise of new competitors. How varying sales revenues affect a firm's earnings and its ability to pay its debts will depend on a number of firm-specific factors such as how sensitive expenses are to changing sales and how much debt a firm has. For example, *business risk* is the uncertainty of income flows and asset prices caused by the nature of a firm's business. The less certain the income flows of the firm, the less certain the income flows to the investor. For example, the retail food industry typically experiences more stable sales and earnings over time and thus has lower business risk than the auto industry, where sales and earnings fluctuate substantially. *Financial risk* is the uncertainty introduced by the method by which the firm finances its assets. If a firm uses only common stock to finance its assets, it incurs only business risk. If instead a firm borrows money to finance its assets, it must pay fixed financing charges (in the form of interest to creditors) prior to providing income to the common stockholders, which increases the stockholders' uncertainty of returns.

Investors also may face *liquidity risk,* the possibility of not being able to sell an asset for fair market value. When an investor acquires an asset, he or she expects that the investment will mature (as with a bond) or that it could be sold to someone else. In either case, the investor expects to be able to convert the security into cash and use the proceeds for current consumption or other investments. The more difficult it is to make this conversion, the greater the liquidity risk. A U.S. Treasury bill has almost no liquidity risk because it can be bought or sold in minutes at a price almost identical to the quoted price. In contrast, a work of art, an antique, a parcel of real estate in a remote area, and thinly traded securities (that is, securities for which there is little trading activity) carry high liquidity risk. Foreign securities, depending on the country and the liquidity of its stock and bond markets, could also have high liquidity risk.

Measuring Risk

The historical risk of an asset can be measured by the variability of its returns over time around its arithmetic mean. Some quantitative measures of this variability are the variance, standard deviation, and coefficient of variation. All these measures use deviations of periodic returns from the mean return, that is, $R_t - R_A$, where, as before, R_A denotes the arithmetic mean return over some time frame and R_t the return over a specific time interval t. Note that the sum of the deviations, $\Sigma(R_t - R_A)$, is always zero.

The *variance, σ^2*, from a sample of data is computed by summing the squared deviations and dividing by $n - 1$:[10]

2.9

$$\sigma^2 = \frac{\Sigma\,(R_t - R_A)^2}{n - 1}$$

As an example, let's use the Walgreens data from Exhibit 2.3 and the arithmetic mean return we computed from that data, 25.2 percent, to compute the variance. The following spreadsheet shows the calculations.

Year	Annual Return	Minus the Arithmetic Mean	Equals the Deviation	Squared Deviations
2004	10.00%	−25.20%	−15.20%	231.04%
2003	−5.80	−25.20	−31.00	961.00
2002	0.10	−25.20	−25.10	630.01
2001	6.40	−25.20	−18.80	353.44
2000	42.40	−25.20	17.20	295.84
1999	21.50	−25.20	−3.70	13.69
1998	43.40	−25.20	18.20	331.24
1997	65.40	−25.20	40.20	1616.04
1996	35.90	−25.20	10.70	114.49
1995	32.80	−25.20	7.60	57.76

Sum (of squared deviations): $4604.55\%^2$

Variance =   Sum/9   = $511.62\%^2$

Thus, over this time frame, the Walgreens stock had a variance of 511.62 percent squared.

Squaring the deviations can make variance difficult to interpret. What do units like percent squared tell an investor about a stock's risk? Because of this difficulty, analysts often prefer to use the *standard deviation, σ*, which is simply the square root of the variance:

2.10

$$\sigma = \sqrt{\sigma^2}$$

The standard deviation formula gives units of measurement that match those of the return data. Taking the square root of the variance of 511.62 for the Walgreens stock gives a standard deviation of 22.62 percent.

Interactive e-lectures

For more explanation and an animated example of standard deviation, go to: http://reillyxtra .swlearning.com.

---

[10]The reader may recall from a prior course in statistics that when a sample is drawn from a population, dividing by $n - 1$ observations instead of n observations provides a more accurate estimate of the variance and standard deviation characteristics of the population.

EXHIBIT 2.6 The Normal Curve

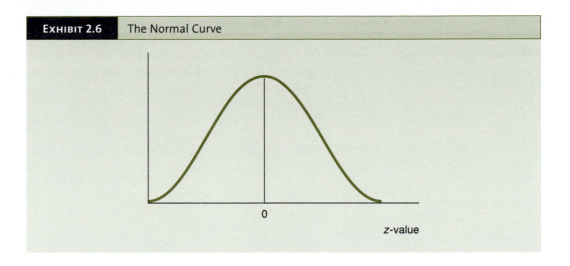

0

z-value

The standard deviation also can be given a statistical interpretation to help give the investor an intuitive feel for the possible range of returns that can occur *if the investor believes the future will resemble the past.* As shown in Exhibit 2.6, *if* the underlying distribution of returns is continuous and approximately normal (that is, bell-shaped), then we expect 68 percent of actual periodic returns to fall within 1 standard deviation of the mean, that is $R_A \pm 1\sigma$. About 95 percent of observed returns will fall within 2 standard deviations of the mean: $R_A \pm 2\sigma$. Actual returns should fall within 3 standard deviations of the mean, $R_A \pm 3\sigma$, about 99 percent of the time. Thus, if we know the mean and standard deviation, we can estimate a rough range for expected returns over time.

If returns are normally distributed, we can use statistical tables to estimate the probability of earning a range of returns. If we compute the *z*-statistic,

2.11
$$z = \frac{\text{Target Return} - R_A}{\sigma}$$

We can use knowledge about the *z*-distribution to estimate the probability of earning a return above a given target, below a given target, or even in-between two target returns. For example, using the Walgreens data, we can estimate the probability of investors earning a return below 0 percent in any one year if Walgreens stock returns are normally distributed and if future returns are expected to resemble those in the past:

$$z = \frac{\text{Target Return} - R_A}{\sigma} = \frac{0\% - 25.2\%}{22.62\%} = -1.114$$

From a table of standard normal probabilities, we find that the probability of a *z*-value less than or equal to −1.114 is 13.3 percent.

Another measure of variability, the coefficient of variation, allows us to make comparisons because it controls for the size of the mean. The *coefficient of variation (CV)* is a measure of risk per unit of return and is computed as

2.12
$$CV = \frac{\sigma}{R_A}$$

A higher coefficient of variation indicates more risk per unit of return. The Walgreens coefficient of variation is 22.62 percent/25.2 percent, which equals 0.898.

Let's look at an example of the potential use of the coefficient of variation. Consider the following two investments.

	Real Estate Index	Growth Stock Index
Mean Return	10.6%	15.5%
Standard Deviation	14.9%	17.6%

From these absolute measures of risk, the growth stock index appears to be riskier because it has a larger standard deviation. However, the CV figures show that the real estate index is riskier since it has more risk per unit of return:

$$CV_{\text{real estate index}} = \frac{14.9\%}{10.6\%} = 1.41$$

$$CV_{\text{growth stock index}} = \frac{17.6\%}{15.5\%} = 1.14$$

According to the coefficient of variation, the growth stock index has less volatility, relative to its mean return, than does the real estate index. Although the growth stock index has a larger standard deviation, it also has a higher average return, so the net effect is a lower coefficient of variation.

Determinants of Required Rates of Return

We have examined how we can use historical data to estimate measures of return and risk. In this section we will examine conceptually the influences that affect an asset's required rate of return—that is, the minimum expected return that an asset should offer investors given its risk level. Specifically, the *required rate of return* for an asset should compensate investors for (1) the pure time value of money, called the real risk-free rate, during the period of investment, (2) the expected rate of inflation during the period, and (3) the investment's risk. The combined influences of (1) and (2) determine the nominal risk-free rate of return. To determine an appropriate return for risky assets, a risk premium is added to the nominal risk-free rate.

Short-term Treasury bill rates provide the best real-world example of a nominal risk-free rate of return; differences in spreads between T-bills and longer-term government securities and corporate securities reflect both the risk of the longer-term assets and investors' changing perceptions of risk. Widening spreads indicate a "flight to quality" as investors, concerned about inflation or future economic trends, sell other assets and purchase safe securities. Spreads will narrow when investors are optimistic and more willing to take on risk. The data in Exhibit 2.7 show that investors were more willing to take risks in 1995 and 1997 (Baa–Aaa return difference was narrow) and were more concerned with risk in 1990–1991 and 2002–2003.

THE REAL RISK-FREE RATE

The *real risk-free rate (real RFR)* is the pure time value of money; it measures the change in purchasing power over time. It assumes no inflation and no uncertainty about future flows. An investor in an inflation-free economy who knew with certainty what cash flows he or she would receive at what time would demand the real risk-free rate on an investment.

EXHIBIT 2.7	Yields on Different Types of Bonds													
Type of Bond	1990	1991	1992	1993	1994	1995	1996	1997	1998	1999	2000	2001	2002	2003
Three-month Treasury bill	7.51%	5.42%	3.45%	3.02%	4.29%	5.51%	5.02%	5.07%	4.81%	4.66%	5.85%	3.45%	1.62%	1.02%
U.S. long-term bond*	8.61	8.14	7.67	6.59	7.37	6.88	6.71	6.61	5.58	5.87	5.94	5.49	. . .	. . .
Aaa corporate bonds	9.32	8.77	8.14	7.22	7.96	7.59	7.37	7.26	6.53	7.04	7.62	7.08	6.49	5.67
Baa corporate bonds	10.36	9.80	8.98	7.93	8.62	8.20	8.05	7.86	7.22	7.87	8.36	7.95	7.80	6.77
Baa–Aaa return difference	1.04	1.03	0.84	0.71	0.66	0.61	0.68	0.60	0.69	0.83	0.74	0.87	1.31	1.10
Inflation rate	5.40	4.21	3.01	2.99	2.56	2.83	2.95	2.29	1.56	2.21	3.36	2.85	1.58	2.28
Ex-post real risk-free rate	2.00	1.16	0.43	0.03	1.69	2.61	2.01	2.72	3.20	2.40	2.41	0.58	0.04	−1.23

*The U.S. Treasury stopped issuing 30-year bonds in 2001.

Source: *Economic Report of the President, 2004* (Washington, DC: U.S. Government Printing Office, various issues).

Two factors, one subjective and one objective, influence this rate. The subjective factor is the time preference of individuals for the consumption of income. If there is a greater desire to spend now, the real RFR will increase in order to attract savings. If the desire is to spend less, the real RFR will decrease as it will be easier to attract savings. Time preferences vary among individuals, and the market creates a composite rate that includes the preferences of all investors.

The objective factor that influences the real risk-free rate is the set of investment opportunities available in the economy. In turn, the investment opportunities are determined by the long-run real growth rate of the economy. A rapidly growing economy produces more opportunities to invest funds and experience positive rates of return. In such a situation, an increase in demand for capital causes the price of capital to rise, all else constant. Thus, a *positive* relationship exists between the real growth rate in the economy and the real RFR.

FACTORS INFLUENCING THE NOMINAL RISK-FREE RATE

Most observed returns are nominal, not real rates. Nominal rates of interest are determined by real rates of interest plus factors that will affect the level of interest rates that prevail in the market, such as inflation expectations and conditions in the capital markets.

Expected Rate of Inflation If investors expect the price level to increase during the investment period, they will require the rate of return to include compensation for the expected rate of inflation. An investor's nominal required rate of return in current dollars on a risk-free investment should be

> 2.13   **Nominal RFR = (1 + Real RFR) × (1 + Expected Inflation Rate) − 1**

For instance, assume that you require a 4 percent real rate of return on a risk-free investment, but you expect prices to increase by 3 percent during the investment period. In this case, your required rate of return on a risk-free security will be 7.12 percent [(1.04 × 1.03) − 1].

Rearranging equation 2.13, we can calculate the real risk-free rate of return on an investment as follows:

2.14 $$\text{Real RFR} = \frac{1 + \text{Nominal Risk-Free Rate of Return}}{1 + \text{Inflation Rate}} - 1$$

The last line in Exhibit 2.7 shows estimates of the real risk-free rate using equation 2.14 based on short-term Treasury bill and inflation rates that existed during 1990–2003. The significant changes in T-bill returns during this period were caused in large part by changes in the year-to-year real risk-free rate. Analysis shows that the correlation between the year-to-year changes in the T-bill rate and the inflation rate is 0.629; the correlation between the year-to-year changes in the T-bill rate and the real rate is 0.776. The estimate of the negative real rate in 2003 occurs due to the very low T-bill rates as the Fed used monetary policy to stimulate the economy. Currently, the return on Treasury Inflation-Protected Securities, or TIPS, offers a market-based estimate of the real risk-free rate. The payout to investors in TIPS is indexed to inflation so the yield at which they trade is an estimate of the real risk-free rate.

Conditions in the Capital Market   The purpose of capital markets is to bring investors with savings together with companies or governments who need capital to expand or to finance budget deficits. The cost of funds at any time (the interest rate) is the price that equates the current supply and demand for capital. A change in the relative ease or tightness in the capital market is a short-run phenomenon caused by a temporary disequilibrium in the supply and demand of capital. For example, a disequilibrium could be caused by an unexpected change in monetary policy such as a change in the growth rate of the money supply. A decrease in the growth rate of the money supply (a tightening in monetary policy) will reduce the supply of capital and increase interest rates. In turn, this increase in rates will cause an increase in savings and a decrease in the demand for capital by corporations or individuals. These changes will bring rates back to the long-run equilibrium, which is based on the long-run growth rate of the economy.

RISK PREMIUM

The nominal risk-free rate is a base for determining all other required rates of return. We learned in Chapter 1 that risk drives expected returns. Most investors require higher rates of return on investments to compensate for any uncertainty; this increase in the required rate of return over the nominal risk-free rate is the *risk premium*. Assets with different levels of risk have different risk premiums; the product of the nominal risk-free rate and the risk premium determines the required rate of return for an asset at a point in time:

2.15   **Required Return = (1 + Nominal RFR) × (1 + Risk Premium) − 1**

If the nominal risk-free rate is 7.12 percent and the risk premium on common stock is 5 percent, the required return on stock is (1 + 0.0712) × (1 + 0.05) − 1 or 12.48 percent. We develop the methods for estimating risk premiums in Chapter 9.

RELATIONSHIP BETWEEN RISK AND RETURN

Exhibit 2.8 is a graph of the expected relationship between risk and return. For the sake of illustration, we include only two assets on the graph: short-term bills (an approximation for the nominal risk-free rate) and the S&P 500 common stock index. The graph shows that investors increase their required rates of return as perceived risk (uncertainty) increases.[11]

---

[11]We expect the relationship between expected return and risk to be linear; we will discuss why this is so in Chapter 9.

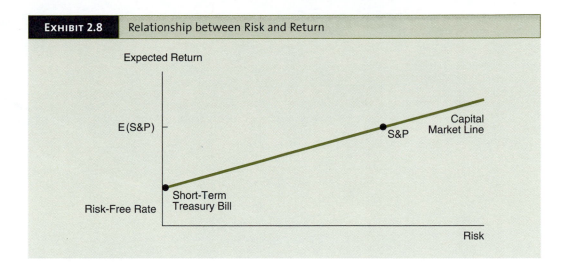

EXHIBIT 2.8 Relationship between Risk and Return

The line that reflects the combination of risk and expected return available on different investments at a point in time is the *capital market line (CML)*.[12] Investors would select investments that are consistent with their risk preferences; some consider only low-risk investments, others welcome high-risk investments, and still others want a diversified portfolio with some of each.

Beginning with an initial capital market line, three changes can occur. First, individual investments can change positions on the CML because of changes in the perceived risk of the investments. For example, increased use of debt financing by corporate America will increase firms' financial risk and move point "S&P" to the right along the CML.

Second, the slope of the CML can change because of a change in the attitudes of investors toward risk; that is, investors can change the returns they require per unit of risk. (We saw an example of varying return spreads over time in Exhibit 2.7.) During times of optimism, risk premiums will narrow; they widen during times of economic distress or uncertainty. This change in the risk premium implies a change in the slope of the capital market line. Exhibit 2.9 shows such a change due to an increase in risk premiums. A change in the slope of the CML affects required rates of return for all risky assets; no matter where an investment is on the original CML, its required rate of return will change even though the asset's individual risk characteristics may remain unchanged. This is seen in the new expected return for the S&P portfolio, $E(S\&P)_{new\ risk\ premium}$.

Third, the CML can experience a parallel shift due to a change in the real RFR or the expected rate of inflation—that is, a change in the nominal RFR. The CML shifts when there are changes in one of the following factors: (1) expected real growth in the economy, (2) capital market conditions (including investors' time preferences), or (3) the expected rate of inflation. For example, an increase in expected real growth, temporary tightness in the capital market, or an increase in the expected rate of inflation will cause the CML to experience a parallel shift upward, as in Exhibit 2.10. The parallel shift occurs because these changes affect all investments no matter what their levels of risk. Note that the expected return on the S&P increases from its original position to $E(S\&P)_{shift}$.

---

[12]This concept should be familiar to students who have had previous coursework in corporate finance. We develop the concept of the capital market line more rigorously in Chapter 9.

EXHIBIT 2.9	Change in Risk Premium

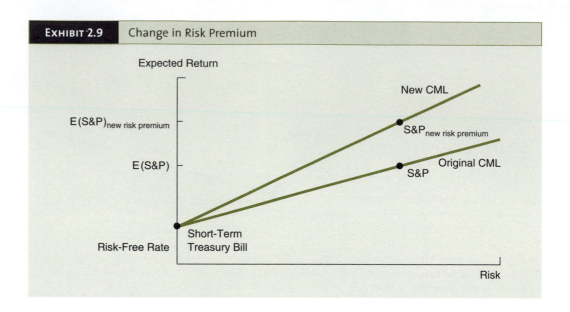

EXHIBIT 2.10	Capital Market Conditions, Expected Inflation, and the Capital Market Line

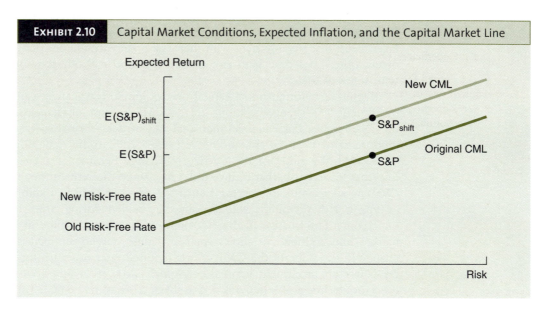

SUMMARY OF CHANGES IN THE REQUIRED RATE OF RETURN

The relationship between risk and the required rate of return for an investment can change in three ways:

1. A movement *along* the CML demonstrates a change in the risk characteristics of a specific investment, such as a change in its business, financial, or systematic risk. This change affects only the individual investment.
2. A change in the *slope* of the CML occurs in response to a change in the attitudes of investors toward risk. Such a change demonstrates that investors want either higher or lower rates of return for the same risk. A change in the risk premium will affect all risky investments.

3. A *parallel shift* in the CML reflects a change in expected real growth, in capital market conditions (such as ease or tightness of money), or a change in the expected rate of inflation. Again, such a change will affect all investments.

Summary

The purpose of this chapter is to provide further background that can be used in subsequent chapters. To achieve that goal, we covered several topics:

- We examined types of returns and ways to measure historical returns. We used annual holding period returns to compute two measures of mean return (arithmetic and geometric) and applied these to a historical series for an individual investment and to a portfolio of investments during a period of time. We saw that, over time, a major source of return to investors is the reinvestment of income and gains from investments.

- We defined risk and examined its sources and how it can be measured by the variance, standard deviation, and the coefficient of variation.

- We examined the specific factors that determine the required rate of return: (a) the real risk-free rate, which is based on the real rate of growth in the economy, (b) the nominal risk-free rate, which is influenced by capital market conditions and the expected rate of inflation, and (c) a risk premium, which is a function of factors such as business risk or the systematic risk of the asset relative to the market portfolio.

- We discussed the risk–return combinations available on various investments at a point in time (illustrated by the CML) and the three factors that can cause changes in this relationship. We saw first that a change in the inherent risk of an investment will cause a movement along the CML. Second, a change in investors' attitudes toward risk and thus a change in the market risk premium will cause a change in the slope of the CML. Finally, a change in expected real growth, in capital market conditions, or in the expected rate of inflation will cause a parallel shift of the CML.

Armed with this understanding of risk and return, we are prepared to consider the global investment environment and the asset allocation decision. These are the subjects of Chapters 3, 4, and 5.

Investments Online

Some of the following Web sites help us make basic investment decisions; others provide more detail into the topics of risk, return, and investing.

http://www.moneyadvisor.com This site has a calculator feature to help make decisions such as whether to buy or lease a car. Other calculations and information can answer questions about loans, mortgages, insurance, tax, college, and saving goals. The site also includes several "just for fun" calculations. For example, by answering several questions you can compute your body mass ratio and compare it to the ideal.

www.aaii.com This is the home page for the American Association of Individual Investors, a group dealing with investor education. Educational topics include mutual funds, stocks, bonds, dealing with a broker, and portfolio management issues. It offers a number of features for both the beginning and experienced investor.

Some other sites that may be of interest can be found at:

http://fisher.osu.edu/fin/osudata.htm and
http://fisher.osu.edu/fin/journal/jofsites.htm, both of which have links to numerous finance sites.

QUESTIONS

1. *The Wall Street Journal* reported that the yield on common stocks is about 2 percent, whereas a study at the University of Chicago contends that the annual rate of return on common stocks since 1926 has averaged about 11 percent. Reconcile these statements.

2. What are the three sources of return on an investment? Which is likely to be the largest source of return on a bond after a few years if reinvestment occurs? After many years?

3. If it is suitable to an investor's goals, why is it preferable to reinvest gains from investing rather than spending them?

4. Discuss the three components of an investor's required rate of return on an investment.

5. Discuss the two major factors that determine the nominal risk-free rate. Explain which of these factors would be more volatile over the business cycle.

6. Briefly discuss the factors that influence the risk premium of an investment.

7. You own stock in the Gentry Company, and you read in the financial press that a recent bond offering has raised the firm's debt/equity ratio from 35 percent to 55 percent. Discuss the effect of this change on the variability of the firm's net income stream, other factors being constant. Discuss how this change would affect your required rate of return on the common stock of the Gentry Company.

8. Draw a properly labeled graph of the capital market line (CML) and indicate where you would expect the following investments to fall along that line. Discuss your reasoning.
   a. Common stock of large firms
   b. U.S. government bonds
   c. United Kingdom government bonds
   d. Low-grade corporate bonds
   e. Common stock of a Japanese firm

9. Explain why you would change your nominal required rate of return if you expected the rate of inflation to go from zero (no inflation) to 7 percent. Give an example of what would happen if you did not change your required rate of return under these conditions.

10. Suppose the long-run growth rate of the economy increased by 1 percent and the expected rate of inflation increased by 4 percent. What would happen to the required rates of return on government bonds and common stocks? Show graphically how the effects of these changes would differ between these two investments.

11. You see in *The Wall Street Journal* that the yield spread between Baa corporate bonds and Aaa corporate bonds has gone from 350 basis points (3.5 percent) to 200 basis points (2 percent). Show graphically the effect of this change on the CML and discuss its effect on the required rate of return for common stocks.

12. Give an example of a liquid investment and an illiquid investment. Discuss why you consider each of them to be liquid or illiquid. All else equal, which one should have the higher risk premium?

PROBLEMS

1. On February 1, you bought some stock for $34 a share and a year later you sold it for $39 a share. During the year, you received a cash dividend of $1.50 a share. Compute your HPR and return relative on this investment.

2. On August 15, you purchased some stock at $65 a share and a year later you sold it for $61 a share. During the year, you received dividends of $3 a share. Compute your HPR and return relative on this investment.

3. At the beginning of last year, you invested $4,000 in eighty shares of the Chang Corporation. During the year Chang paid dividends of $5 per share. At the end of the year, you sold the eighty shares for $59 a share. Compute your total HPR on these shares and indicate how much was due to the price change and how much was due to the dividend income.

4. The rates of return you computed in Problems 1, 2, and 3 are nominal rates of return. Assuming that the rate of inflation during the year was 4 percent, compute the real rates of return on these investments. Compute the real rates of return if the rate of inflation was 8 percent.

5. Find the annualized returns for the following set of investments.

Asset HPR		Holding Period
A	10%	8 months
B	−6	15 months
C	8	2 years
D	15	3 years
E	5	18 weeks

6. The following are annual rates of return for U.S. government T-bills and United Kingdom common stocks.

Year	U.S. Government T-Bills	United Kingdom Common Stock
1	6.3%	15.0%
2	8.1	−4.3
3	7.6	37.4
4	9.0	19.2
5	8.5	−10.6

a. Compute the arithmetic mean rate of return and standard deviation of rates of return for the two series.

b. Discuss these two investments in terms of their arithmetic mean rates of return, standard deviation, and coefficient of variation.

c. Compute the geometric mean rate of return for each of these investments. Compare the arithmetic mean return and geometric mean return for each investment and discuss this difference between mean returns as related to the standard deviation of each series.

7. During the past five years, you owned two stocks that had the following annual rates of return.

Year	Stock T	Stock B
1	19%	8%
2	8	3
3	−12	−9
4	−3	2
5	15	4

a. Compute the arithmetic mean annual rate of return for each stock. Which is most desirable by this measure?

b. Compute the standard deviation of the annual rate of return for each stock. By this measure, which is the preferable stock?

c. Compute the coefficient of variation for each stock. By this relative measure of risk, which stock is preferable?

d. Compute the geometric mean rate of return for each stock. Discuss the difference between the arithmetic mean return and the geometric mean return for each stock. Relate the differences in the mean returns to the standard deviation of the return for each stock.

8. Compute the average Treasury bill rate using the data in Exhibit 2.7. Find the variance and standard deviation of the returns.

9. During the past year, you had a portfolio that contained U.S. government T-bills, long-term government bonds, and common stocks. The rates of return on each asset were as follows:

U.S. government T-bills	5.50%
U.S. government long-term bonds	7.50
U.S. common stocks	11.60

During the year, the consumer price index, which measures the rate of inflation, went from 160 to 170 (1982–1984 = 100). Compute the rate of inflation during this year. Compute the real rates of return on each of the investments in your portfolio based on the inflation rate.

10. You read in *Business Week* that a panel of economists has estimated that the long-run real growth rate of the U.S. economy over the next five-year period will average 3 percent. In addition, a bank newsletter estimates that the average annual rate of inflation during this five-year period will be about 4 percent. What nominal rate of return would you expect on U.S. government T-bills during this period?

11. What would your required rate of return be on common stocks if you wanted a 5 percent risk premium to own common stocks given what you know from Problem 10? If common stock investors became more risk averse, what would happen to the required rate of return on common stocks? What would be the impact on stock prices?

12. Assume that the consensus required rate of return on common stocks is 14 percent. In addition, you read in *Fortune* that the expected rate of inflation is 5 percent and the estimated long-term real growth rate of the economy is 3 percent. What interest rate would you expect on U.S. government T-bills? What is the approximate risk premium for common stocks implied by these data?

WEB EXERCISES

1. Where on the Web can you find data on historical financial market returns and interest rates?

2. Go to *http://finance.yahoo.com,* click on Stock Research, then Historical Quotes. Obtain monthly stock price and dividend data for the past three years for Microsoft (MSFT), ExxonMobil (XOM), Walgreens (WAG), McDonald's (MCD), and The Gap (GPS). Download each firm's data into a spreadsheet and compute the monthly average arithmetic return, geometric return, standard deviation, and coefficient of variation. Which stock has offered the highest monthly return? Based on the measures you computed, which is riskiest?

3. Find the Economic Report of the President on the Internet and download statistical table B.95 on common stock prices and yields. Using the values of the S&P 500 index and the dividend yield (the ratio of dividends to stock prices) develop an annual estimate of S&P 500 stock returns. Compute average return and risk measures for the past five, ten, and thirty years.

SPREADSHEET EXERCISES

1. Construct a spreadsheet to compute annualized returns from data on holding period returns and the length of the holding period.
2. Using the spreadsheet format in Exhibit 2.5, see how the interest-on-interest component of returns changes with different interest rates and different time periods. How much of the total return is interest-on-interest when:
   a. the interest rate is 4 percent and the time period is fifteen years?
   b. the interest rate is 10 percent and the time period is twelve years?
   c. the interest rate is 7 percent and the time period is twenty-five years?
3. Using the spreadsheet for Exhibit 2.3, (a) enter data on stock prices and dividends from another company, *or* (b) update Exhibit 2.3 using more recent Walgreens stock data (available from the Walgreens Web site, *www.walgreens.com*). Use the spreadsheet to find the arithmetic mean return, geometric mean return, and standard deviation of stock returns for your stock.
4. Using the NORMDIST function in Excel and assuming the stock returns for the company you chose in Exercise 3 are normally distributed, find the probability of the return falling (a) below 0 percent; (b) below −5 percent; (c) below +5 percent; (d) above 10 percent; (e) above 0 percent.

REFERENCES

A book that presents an interesting perspective of risk through history is:

Bernstein, Peter L. *Against the Gods: The Remarkable Story of Risk.* New York: John Wiley and Sons, Inc., 1996

A book that is required reading in the Chartered Financial Analyst® program and that includes additional background on the topics of risk and statistical analysis is the following:

Defusco, Richard A., Dennis W. McLeavey, Jerald E. Pinto, and David E. Runkle. *Quantitative Methods for Investment Analysis.* Charlottesville, VA: CFA Institute, 2001.

Glossary

Arithmetic mean return (R_A) A measure of mean return equal to the sum of annual holding period returns divided by the number of years.

Business risk Uncertainty due to the nature of a firm's business that affects the variability of sales and earnings.

Capital market line (CML) The line that reflects the combination of risk and return of different investments.

Coefficient of variation (CV) A measure of relative variability that indicates risk per unit of return. In general, it is equal to the standard deviation divided by the mean value.

Financial risk Uncertainty due to the method by which a firm finances its assets.

Geometric mean return (R_G) The nth root of the product of the annual holding period returns for n years, minus 1.

Holding period The amount of time an investment is owned.

Holding period return (HPR) The total return from an investment for a given period of time, stated as a percentage.

Liquidity risk Uncertainty due to the ability to buy or sell an investment in the secondary market.

Mean or average rate of return The average of an investment's returns over an extended period of time.

Real risk-free rate (real RFR) The basic interest rate with no accommodation for inflation or uncertainty; the pure time value of money.

Required rate of return The return that compensates investors for their time, the expected rate of inflation, and the uncertainty of the return.

Return relative Equals 1 plus the holding period return.

Risk The uncertainty that an investment will earn its expected rate of return.

Risk premium The increase over the nominal risk-free rate that investors demand as compensation for an investment's uncertainty.

Standard deviation A measure of variability equal to the square root of the variance.

Systematic risk The portion of an individual asset's total variance that is attributable to the variability of the total market portfolio.

Unsystematic risk Asset-specific risk that deals with the characteristics of a type of asset or security issuer rather than broad economic factors.

Variance A measure of variability equal to the sum of the squares of a return's deviation from the mean, divided by $n - 1$.

Selecting Investments
in a Global Market

In this chapter we will answer the following questions:

Why should investors have a global perspective regarding their investments?

What has happened to the relative size of the U.S. and foreign stock and bond markets?

How can investors compute returns on investments outside of their home country?

What additional advantage is there to diversifying in international markets beyond the benefits of domestic diversification?

What securities are available? What are their cash flow and risk properties?

What are the historical return and risk characteristics of the major investment instruments?

What is the relationship among the returns for foreign and domestic investment instruments? What is the implication of these relationships for portfolio diversification?

I n the global investment market of today, there are four basic types of financial assets: debt, equity, derivatives, and managed investments. The first three are direct investments; that is, an investor can trade these securities himself. In the fourth, an investor pools funds with others, and professional managers make the decisions and trade securities (Examples of managed investments include mutual funds and hedge funds.) These four types of investments are called *financial assets* because they represent lending or ownership claims on productive assets, such as those of a firm or government. (Real property [such as homes or land] and collectibles [such as coins, stamps, or antiques] are known as *real assets.*)

In this chapter we give an overview of the investment alternatives in the global market. This is essential background for Chapter 5, where we discuss the asset allocation decision, and for later chapters when we analyze individual investments such as bonds, common stock, and other securities in depth. It is also important for chapters in which we consider how to construct and evaluate investment portfolios. A major goal of this text is to help you understand and evaluate the risk–return characteristics of investment portfolios, and an appreciation of the various security types is the starting point for such an analysis.

This chapter is divided into four main sections. First, we show how changing exchange rates affect returns on international investments. Second, we make a case of global investing, examining several reasons investors should include foreign as well as domestic securities in their portfolios. Third, we discuss the main features and cash flow patterns of securities in both the domestic and global markets. We will see how the varying risk–return characteristics of the alternative investments suit the preferences of different investors and issuers. Finally, we assess the historical risk and return performance of several investment instruments from around the world and examine the relationship among the returns for many of these securities. These relationships provide further support for global investing.

Computing Returns on Foreign Investments

From the perspective of a U.S. investor, a return of, say, 12 percent on a foreign investment does not mean that the value of the investment has risen by 12 percent. There are two forces affecting returns from foreign investments. One is the return earned in the other country; the other is the change in the exchange rate between the two countries. The *exchange rate* is the price of one currency in terms of another. And as with most prices, exchange rates will fluctuate over time. For example, the U.S. dollar may get stronger (able to buy more units of other currencies) or weaker (able to buy fewer units of other currencies). Thus, depending on what happens to exchange rates during the holding period, the returns from foreign investments may increase or decrease when the returns are translated into the U.S. dollar. This is called *exchange rate risk*. In general, the relationship between home country returns and foreign returns is given by

3.1   **(1 + Home Country Return)**

$$= \textbf{(1 + Foreign Return)} \left(\frac{\textbf{Current Exchange Rate}}{\textbf{Initial Exchange Rate}} \right)$$

Since a return relative is equal to (1 + Holding Period Return), we can restate this equation as

3.2   **(Home Country Return Relative)**

$$= \textbf{(Foreign Country Return Relative)} \left(\frac{\textbf{Current Exchange Rate}}{\textbf{Initial Exchange Rate}} \right)$$

where the exchange rate is defined as the home currency per unit of foreign currency, such as U.S dollar per peso or U.S. dollar per euro for a U.S. investor.

Exhibit 3.1 shows an example. In part (a), a U.S. investor converts dollars to pesos at an initial exchange rate of $0.20 per peso to invest in shares of a Mexican stock that earns a 12 percent holding period return during the year. During that year, the peso strengthens relative to the dollar (rising from $0.20 per peso to $0.22 per peso). When the stock is sold and the pesos are converted back to dollars, each peso can purchase more dollars. As a result, the U.S. investor earns a larger (23.2 percent) return than the 12 percent earned by a Mexican investor.

Part (b) shows a similar situation from the perspective of a Mexican investor buying shares in the United States. He converts pesos into dollars at an exchange rate of $1 = 5.00 pesos (note that this is the reciprocal of 1 peso = $0.20; 1/0.20 = 5.00) and invests in a U.S. stock that earns a 12 percent holding period return during the year. But since the peso strengthened during the year, he only receives 4.55 pesos (the reciprocal of 1 peso = $0.22; 1/0.22 = 4.55) for every dollar he converts back into his home currency. Thus, his home-country percentage return is only 1.82 percent; translating the funds back into pesos hurt his overall return.

From this example we see that a strengthening foreign currency (weakening home currency) is good from the home-country investor's perspective but a strengthening home currency (weakening foreign currency) can lead to lower returns. As we will discuss in later chapters, there are tools, called options contracts and futures contracts, that investors can use to reduce the risk of fluctuating exchange rates from foreign investments.

EXHIBIT 3.1	Converting a Foreign Rate of Return to a Home Currency Return

(a) Dollar is the home currency; invest funds in Mexico

Initial exchange rate	$0.20 per peso
Exchange rate one year later	$0.22 per peso
Investment return	12% in peso terms Return relative = 1.12
Return relative (U.S.)	= return relative in pesos × (current dollars per peso/ initial dollars per peso)
	= 1.12 × ($0.22/$0.20) = 1.232
U.S.-based rate of return	= 0.232 or 23.2%

(b) Peso is the home currency; invest funds in the U.S.

Initial exchange rate	5.00 per dollar
Exchange rate one year later	4.55 per peso
Investment return	12% in dollar terms Return relative = 1.12
Return relative (Mexico)	= return relative in dollars × (current pesos per dollar/ initial pesos per dollar)
	= 1.12 × (4.55 / 5.00) = 1.0182
Mexico-based rate of return	= 0.0182 or 1.82%

The Case for Global Investments

Today, a call to a broker gives you access to a wide range of securities sold throughout the world. With relative ease you can purchase General Motors or Toyota stock, U.S. Treasury or Japanese government bonds, a mutual fund that invests in U.S. biotechnology companies, a global growth stock fund, or a German stock fund, or options on a U.S. stock index, just to name a few of the innumerable investments available.

But besides the ease of investing in global securities, there are four interrelated reasons why U.S. investors should consider global investment portfolios:

1. **Broaden horizons.** When investors compare the absolute and relative sizes of U.S. and foreign markets for stocks and bonds, they see that ignoring foreign markets reduces their choices to less than 50 percent of available investment opportunities. Because more opportunities broaden the range of risk–return choices, it makes sense to include foreign securities.
2. **Return enhancement.** The rates of return available on non-U.S. securities often have substantially exceeded those on U.S. securities. The higher returns on non-U.S. equities can be justified by the higher growth rates for the countries where they are issued. These superior results prevail even when the returns are risk-adjusted.
3. **Risk reduction via diversification.** One of the major tenets of investment theory is that investors should diversify, or spread the risk of, their portfolio. U.S. securities markets' performance will be related to the condition of the U.S. economy. Although the global business community is getting smaller, firms in other countries will be affected by conditions in their home country. As long as all markets and economies do not move together, portfolio risk may be reduced by diversifying.
4. **Global economy.** Due to growing levels of international trade and freer flows of capital, firms are no longer restricted to their "home market." Exports compete for consumer purchases overseas as imports compete with domestically produced goods. Since competition is

on a global scale in a growing number of industries, the search for attractive investments in a given sector or industry may lead to a firm whose headquarters is in a foreign country.

Let's analyze these reasons to demonstrate the advantages of foreign financial markets for U.S. investors and to assess the benefits and risks of trading in these markets.

RELATIVE SIZE OF U.S. FINANCIAL MARKETS

Ignoring foreign investment means choosing to ignore over half the world's investable capital market. Exhibit 3.2 shows the breakdown of securities available in world capital markets in 1969 and 2003. Not only has the overall value of all securities increased dramatically (from $2.4 trillion to $70.9 trillion), the composition has also changed. For example, the table shows that U.S. dollar bond and equity securities made up 53 percent of the total value of all securities in 1969 versus 28.4 percent for nondollar bonds and equity. By 2003, U.S. bonds and equities accounted for 45.4 percent of the total securities market versus 44.1 percent for nondollar bonds and stocks. Thus, the U.S. proportion of the combined stock and bond market declined from 65 percent of the total in 1969 to about 50 percent in 2003.

Exhibit 3.3 focuses on the equity markets from another data source. In terms of market capitalization (number of shares multiplied by their value), the U.S. equity markets comprised about 43 percent of the world's equity markets in 2004. In other words, more than half of the available equity investment opportunities lie outside U.S. borders.

Another consideration is market efficiency, that is, the degree to which securities are fairly priced given information that is known about their issuers. Developed countries—such as the United States, Japan, and most European countries—have well-developed capital markets, good information flows, and many analysts examining their stocks and bonds. This is not always the case for developing and emerging economies. Astute analysis may allow an investor to find securities that are attractively priced relative to their prospects.

RATES OF RETURN ON U.S. AND FOREIGN SECURITIES

An examination of the rates of return on U.S. and foreign securities demonstrates that many non–U.S. securities provide superior rates of return.

EXHIBIT 3.2	Total Investable Capital Market, 1969 versus 2003		
1969		**2003**	
U.S. equity	30.70%	U.S. equity	18.50%
Japan equity	1.60	Emerging-markets equity	1.20
All other equity	11.20	All other equity	15.10
U.S. real estate	11.60	U.S. real estate	5.40
Cash equivalents	6.90	Cash equivalents	6.90
Dollar bonds	22.30	Dollar bonds	25.70
Japan bonds	1.30	Emerging-markets bonds	2.30
All other bonds	14.30	All other bonds	25.50
Private markets	0.10	Private markets	0.30
		High-yield bonds	1.20
Market value: $2.4 trillion		Market value: $70.9 trillion	

Source: Brinson Partners, Inc., Chicago, Illinois.

Exhibit 3.3	Market Capitalization of World Equity Exchanges, 2004	
	(USD millions)	
United States	14,266,023.1	43.0%
Japan	4,904,617.0	14.8
U.K.	2,460,064.0	7.4
Euronext	2,076,410.2	6.3
Germany	1,079,026.2	3.3
Canada	888,677.7	2.7
Switzerland	727,103.0	2.2
Spain	726,243.4	2.2
Hong Kong	714,597.4	2.2
Italy	614,841.6	1.9
Australia	585,431.0	1.8
Rest of the world	4,110,784.3	12.4
Total Capitalization	33,153,818.9	100.0%

Source: World Federation of Stock Exchanges, http://www.world-exchanges.org.

Global Bond-Market Returns   Exhibit 3.4 reports annual compound rates of return for several major international bond markets for 1985–2003. The returns have been converted to U.S dollar returns, so the exhibit shows mean annual returns and standard deviations that a U.S.-based investor would receive. An analysis of the returns in Exhibit 3.4 indicates that the performance of the U.S. bond market ranked fourth out of the six countries. Part of the reason for the better performance in dollar terms of the non-U.S. markets is that the dollar generally weakened during this time frame, giving U.S. investors a boost to their foreign returns, similar to the effect shown in Exhibit 3.1.

Global Equity-Market Returns   Exhibit 3.5 shows the annual returns in local currencies and in U.S. dollars for thirty-four major equity markets from 1997 through 2003. In spite of the U.S. market's seemingly stellar performance in the latter half of the 1990s, its average

Exhibit 3.4	Long-Term Government Bond Annual Rates of Return, 1985–2003		
Returns expressed in terms of U.S. dollars			
	Geometric Mean (%)	Arithmetic Mean (%)	Standard Deviation (%)
Canada	11.75	12.42	12.37
France	14.61	15.62	15.49
Germany	8.86	9.70	13.79
Japan	9.58	10.84	17.06
United Kingdom	13.33	14.52	16.71
United States	10.83	11.33	10.54

Source: Citigroup.

EXHIBIT 3.5 Annual Returns in U.S.-Dollar Terms

PERFORMANCE OF DOW JONES GLOBAL INDEXES

Country	Year 2003 U.S.-Dollar Returns	Rank	Year 2002 U.S.-Dollar Returns	Rank	Year 2001 U.S.-Dollar Returns	Rank	Year 2000 U.S.-Dollar Returns	Rank	Year 1999 U.S.-Dollar Returns	Rank	Year 1998 U.S.-Dollar Returns	Rank	Year 1997 U.S.-Dollar Returns	Rank
U.S.	28.44%	31	−23.32%	28	−13.09%	12	−10.15%	11	18.90%	21	26.78%	13	31.69%	7
Australia	45.95%	15	−3.06%	7	−1.30%	8	−10.03%	10	20.53%	20	5.40%	19	−10.31%	21
Austria	58.26%	9	21.16%	3	0.05%	7	−15.40%	17	−6.97%	30	−3.00%	22	−1.72%	19
Belgium	40.78%	18	−9.48%	10	−13.30%	13	−13.95%	13	−17.29%	34	62.73%	4	11.85%	14
Brazil	131.40%	2	−36.16%	34	−23.85%	23	−10.25%	12	50.99%	10	−46.19%	33		
Canada	51.54%	11	−12.56%	15	−20.09%	18	0.85%	6	42.98%	11	−5.10%	24	13.44%	13
Chile	83.53%	4	−14.32%	16	−4.08%	10	−17.61%	20	32.91%	17	−28.50%	28		
Denmark	49.35%	14	−14.54%	17	−23.21%	20	22.23%	1	5.38%	26	3.26%	20	34.05%	6
Finland	17.33%	34	−29.68%	31	−37.83%	33	−15.23%	16	153.14%	1	94.63%	2	11.53%	16
France	39.11%	20	−20.47%	24	−23.44%	22	−7.89%	8	32.18%	18	40.26%	7	22.67%	10
Germany	61.33%	7	−32.36%	33	−24.25%	24	−15.96%	18	20.87%	19	28.38%	12	21.20%	11
Greece	65.08%	6	−27.79%	29			−42.09%	29	39.30%	15	86.24%	3	39.27%	3
Hong Kong	38.69%	21	−19.90%	23	−20.52%	19	−14.96%	15	73.20%	5	−10.34%	25	−25.06%	24
Indonesia	65.95%	5	30.27%	2	−18.57%	16	−56.44%	33	77.31%	4	−41.94%	32	−63.25%	28
Ireland	44.26%	16	−21.38%	25	−3.50%	9	7.38%	4	−13.24%	33	38.05%	8	24.05%	9
Italy	38.35%	23	−10.33%	12	−28.23%	29	−5.46%	7	6.45%	25	50.57%	5	36.95%	5
Japan	37.61%	24	−9.36%	9	−29.47%	31	−31.15%	27	67.26%	7	5.42%	18	−26.39%	25
Malaysia	26.19%	32	−6.05%	8	3.52%	6	−20.81%	23	42.30%	12	−2.19%	21	−70.03%	30
Mexico	31.46%	28	−15.17%	19	19.06%	2	−22.25%	24	91.01%	3	−38.16%	31	54.21%	1
Netherlands	25.27%	33	−22.46%	27	−23.29%	21	−8.03%	9	7.24%	24	29.95%	11	24.19%	8
New Zealand	50.85%	12	16.63%	5	6.28%	4	−31.62%	28	9.27%	23	−23.57%	27	−17.98%	23
Norway	40.62%	19	−11.37%	13	−25.36%	27	2.43%	5	33.29%	16	−31.87%	30	6.55%	18
Philippines	49.62%	13	−19.04%	22	−27.33%	28	−43.70%	30	2.59%	28	14.47%	15	−62.36%	27
Portugal	38.53%	22	−15.79%	20	−24.47%	25	−20.45%	22	−7.17%	31	30.91%	10	51.04%	2
Singapore	36.27%	26	−9.82%	11	−19.91%	17	−23.75%	25	56.18%	9	−4.82%	23	−37.83%	26
South Africa	41.78%	17	43.60%	1	−24.81%	26	−19.20%	21	64.35%	8	−31.43%	29	−11.52%	22
South Korea	31.45%	29	4.88%	6	45.29%	1	−58.77%	34	110.63%	2	117.12%	1	−68.68%	29
Spain	55.59%	10	−14.77%	18	−13.44%	14	−25.29%	26	4.58%	27	48.09%	6	10.46%	17
Sweden	60.06%	8	−30.83%	32	−30.34%	32	−17.15%	19	70.72%	6	6.23%	17	11.56%	15
Switzerland	33.14%	27	−11.86%	14	−29.26%	30	16.21%	2	−6.70%	29	21.13%	14	38.36%	4
Taiwan	36.63%	25	−22.44%	26	11.51%	3	−45.43%	31	42.30%	13	−19.45%	26	−4.73%	20
Thailand	138.70%	1	17.75%	4	4.62%	5	−50.96%	32	39.46%	14	31.89%	9	−75.83%	31
U.K.	28.54%	30	−17.26%	21	−16.58%	15	−14.60%	14	14.26%	22	13.40%	16	17.79%	12
Venezuela	119.88%	3	−28.27%	30	−11.67%	11	11.93%	3	−12.57%	32	−55.46%	34		

Source: *The Wall Street Journal*, various issues, and author calculations.

rank in U.S. dollar returns in 1997–2003 was 17.5 out of thirty-four countries. Its performance was well behind the returns of some stock markets in these years.

These results for equity and bond markets around the world indicate that investors who limit themselves to the U.S. market may well experience rates of return below those in many other countries.

RISK DIVERSIFICATION

Interactive e-lectures

For more explanation and an animated example of correlation, go to: **http://reillyxtra .swlearning.com.**

Wise investors will create diversified portfolios to reduce the variability of returns over time. A properly chosen asset will provide a more stable rate of return for the total portfolio, giving a lower standard deviation and therefore less risk.

The way to measure whether two investments will contribute to diversifying a portfolio is to compute the correlation coefficient between their rates of return over time. Correlation coefficients can range from +1.00 to −1.00. A correlation of +1.00 means that the rates of return for these two investments tend to move together; if one asset rises 10 percent, the other may rise 8 percent; if the first asset falls 20 percent, the other may fall 16 percent. In contrast, a correlation coefficient of −1.00 means that the rates of return for two investments move exactly opposite of one another. When one asset is experiencing above-average rates of return, the other is suffering similar but below-average rates of return. This negative correlation stabilizes the rates of return over time, reducing the standard deviation of the portfolio rates of return and hence the risk of the portfolio. Therefore, the wise investor looks for an investment with either *low positive, zero,* or, ideally, *negative correlation* with the other investments in the portfolio. This is why diversifying with uncorrelated foreign securities can substantially reduce portfolio risk.

Global Bond-Portfolio Risk Exhibit 3.6 lists the correlation coefficients between rates of return for bonds in the United States and bonds in the major foreign markets in U.S. dollar terms from 1985 through 2003. Except for the United States' closest trading partner (Canada), most correlation coefficients are moderate. However, these correlations still mean that U.S. investors could substantially reduce risk through global diversification of bond portfolios. A U.S. investor who bought bonds in any market except Canada would substantially reduce the standard deviation of the well-diversified portfolio.

Why do these correlation coefficients for returns between U.S. bonds and those of various foreign countries differ? The answer is that the international trade patterns, economic growth, fiscal policies, and monetary policies of the countries differ. For example, the U.S. and Canadian economies are closely related because of their geographic proximity, similar domestic economic policies, and the extensive trade between these countries. Each is the other's largest trading partner. In contrast, the United States has less trade with Japan, and the fiscal and monetary policies of the two countries differ dramatically. For example, the U.S. economy was growing during much of the 1990s while the Japanese economy was in recession.

Global Equity-Portfolio Risk The correlation of world equity markets resembles that of bond markets, except that the correlations are slightly higher.[1] Exhibit 3.7 lists the correlation coefficients between monthly equity returns of each country and the U.S. market (in terms of U.S. dollar returns) for the 1985–2003 period. Note that eight of the eleven correlations exceed 0.50, and the average correlation is 0.55. These relatively modest correlations

---

[1] A reason for this is that bond returns are greatly influenced by interest rate movements. Many factors will affect stock market returns, but if the world economy is growing and conditions are favorable for trade (as they were in the 1990s), it is not surprising that the stock-market correlations are higher than those for the bond market.

EXHIBIT 3.6	Correlation Coefficients between U.S.-Dollar Rates of Return on Bonds in the U.S. and Major Foreign Markets, 1985–2003

Country	Correlation Coefficient
Canada	0.6514
France	0.4775
Germany	0.5698
Japan	0.1949
United Kingdom	0.3910
Average	0.4569

EXHIBIT 3.7	Correlation Coefficients between U.S.-Dollar Rates of Return on Stocks in the U.S. and Major Foreign Markets, 1985–2003

Country	Correlation Coefficient
Australia	0.4792
Canada	0.7689
France	0.5816
Germany	0.5412
Italy	0.3671
Japan	0.3109
Netherlands	0.6636
Spain	0.5459
Sweden	0.5745
Switzerland	0.5337
United Kingdom	0.6401
Average	0.5461

Source: Data from MSCI.

between U.S. stocks and foreign stocks have similar implications to those derived for bonds: Investors can reduce the overall risk of their stock portfolios by including foreign stocks.

Exhibit 3.8 demonstrates the impact of international equity diversification. The upper (darker) curve demonstrates that as you increase the number of randomly selected securities in a portfolio, the standard deviation will decline due to the benefits of diversification *within your own country*. This is referred to as *domestic diversification*. After a certain number of securities (thirty to forty), the curve will flatten out at a risk level that reflects the basic market risk (that is, the portfolio will diversify away all unsystematic risk and will contain only systematic risk) for the domestic economy. The lower (lighter) curve illustrates the benefits of international diversification. This curve demonstrates that adding foreign securities to a U.S. portfolio enables an investor to experience lower overall risk because the non-U.S. securities are not correlated with the U.S. economy or stock market, allowing the investor to eliminate

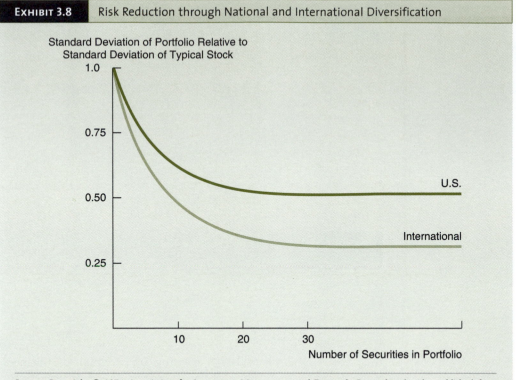

EXHIBIT 3.8   Risk Reduction through National and International Diversification

Standard Deviation of Portfolio Relative to
Standard Deviation of Typical Stock

U.S.

International

Number of Securities in Portfolio

Source: Copyright © 1974, Association for Investment Management and Research. Reproduced and republished from "Why Not Diversify Internationally Rather than Domestically" by B.H. Solnik in *Financial Analysts Journal* (July–August 1974): 48–54, with permission from CFA Institute.

some of the basic market risks of the U.S. economy. The world's level of systematic risk, because of cross-country diversification benefits, is less than that of any one country.

To see how this works, consider, for example, the effect of inflation and interest rates on U.S. securities. As discussed in Chapter 2, all U.S. securities will be affected by these variables. In contrast, a Japanese stock is mainly affected by what happens in the Japanese economy and typically will not be affected by changes in U.S. variables. Thus, adding a Japanese stock to a U.S. stock portfolio should reduce portfolio risk.

Are Country Correlations Rising over Time?   Several studies have found higher correlations between the equity market returns of countries over time. Higher correlations will decrease the risk-reducing benefits of diversifying across countries. Of particular interest is that in times of economic or market distress (such as the 1987 market crash or the aftermath of the September 11th terrorist attacks), equity markets have very high correlations as they decline in value.[2] Among the equity markets listed in Exhibit 3.7, the average correlation over

[2]This finding of rising correlations is consistent with that of more formal studies, such as Mark Barnes, Anthony Bercel, and Steven Rothman, "Global Equities: Do Countries Still Matter?" PanAgora Asset Management White Paper, 2000; Anonymous, "Equity Portfolio Management: The Dominance of Industry Factors," *Quarterly Focus,* UBS Asset Management, September 30, 2000; Roger G. Ibbotson and Charles H. Wang, "Global Asset Allocation: Philosophy, Process, and Performance," *Journal of Investing* (Spring 2000): 39–51. In this last paper, the authors found that the average correlation across eighteen developed equity markets rose from 0.40 over 1970–1998 to 0.50 over 1994–1998.

the 1985–2003 time period is 0.55 using U.S.-dollar-based returns. If we focused on the 1995–2003 time frame, we would see an average correlation of nearly 0.68. With freer trade and better policy coordination (with the advent of trading zones in the European Community, North America, and the Pacific Rim), it is not surprising that economic and financial links are drawing economies closer over time. But, like a sample mean, a correlation is a sample statistic that will vary between samples. In other words, the correlation measure will differ based on time frames and sampling frequency (daily, weekly, monthly, or annual). Thus an upward trend in correlation between the U.S. and other financial markets could arise from simple "noise" in the data.[3]

But if the "true" correlations between markets are indeed rising, what are the implications regarding the benefits of global investing? First, there is still the diversification benefit from seeking investments in other countries. Second, greater diversification benefits exist from seeking investments in emerging economies, whose growth potential in all likelihood exceeds that of developed nations. Third, as the following section on global competition shows, "country" markets are losing some prominence with investors and stock analysts looking for good industry investments. For example, GM, Honda, DaimlerChrysler, and Peugeot are all part of the global auto industry. Although the performance of each of their stocks is mostly related to their home-country sales, it depends on global sales, too.

GLOBAL COMPETITION

Even as the importance of national boundaries has become less important for trade over time, researchers still find that investing across countries enhances diversification benefits. But evidence is mounting that investing across countries *and* industries leads to even greater benefits. Whereas country effects have weaker benefits for diversification, industry effects are helping to bolster the case for global portfolios.[4] This is clearly seen in Exhibit 3.9. Diversifying across countries leads to benefits similar to those seen in Exhibit 3.8. But further risk reduction occurs by diversifying across both countries and industries. Thus, the global investor benefits most from diversifying across different industries in different countries.

Country effects dominate—and are the primary tool for diversification—for smaller firms and for those operating in more localized or heterogeneous industries (such as health care and retailing). However, industry and sector diversification have the greatest impact for larger firms or for those in homogeneous industries (such as oil, autos, and technology).

One poor means for diversifying globally is to invest in U.S.-based multinationals. Many studies have shown that such firms—such as Coca-Cola, Caterpillar, and Ford—have returns that are much more highly correlated with the U.S. stock market than with global

---

[3]At least two papers argue that changes in correlations between countries could be due to random variation. See K. Forbes and R. Rigobon, "No Contagion, Only Interdependence: Measuring Stock Market Co-movements," *Journal of Finance* (October 2002); and M. Loretan and W. B. English, "Evaluating 'Correlation Breakdowns' During Periods of Market Volatility," in *International Financial Markets and the Implications for Monetary and Financial Stability,* Bank of International Settlements, Switzerland, 2000.

[4]Some studies showing the benefits of global diversification across industries include Leila Heckman, Singanallur Narayanan, and Sandeep A. Patel, "Country and Industry Importance in European Returns," *Journal of Investing,* vol. 10, no. 1 (Spring 2001): 27–34; Sean P. Baca, Brian L. Garbe, and Richard A. Weiss, "The Rise of Sector Effects in Major Equity Markets," *Financial Analysts Journal,* vol. 56, no. 5 (September–October 2000): 34–40; Roger G. Ibbotson and Charles H. Wang, "Global Asset Allocation: Philosophy, Process, and Performance," *Journal of Investing* (Spring 2000): 39–51, Richard A. Weiss, "Global Sector Rotation: New Look at an Old Idea," *Financial Analysts Journal,* vol. 54, no. 3 (May–June 1998): 6–8.

EXHIBIT 3.9	Risk Reduction Benefits of Diversifying across Countries and Industries

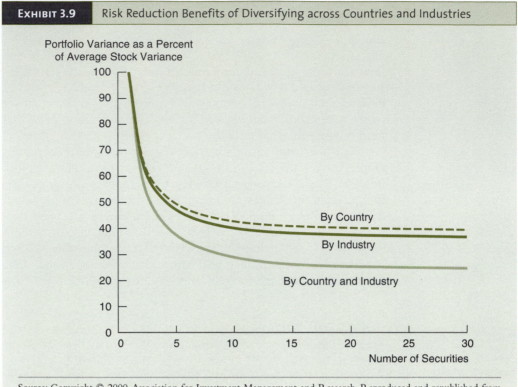

markets. Because of this, there is little global portfolio risk-reduction benefit for a U.S.-based investor buying shares in such firms.[5]

SUMMARY ON GLOBAL INVESTING

At this point, we have considered the relative size of the market for non-U.S. bonds and stocks and found that it has grown in size and importance. We have also examined the rates of return for foreign bond and stock investments and determined that, in many instances, their rates of return are attractive to those participating in the U.S. market. Our analysis of the correlation between rates of return on U.S. and foreign bonds and stocks indicated a consistent pattern of moderate and low positive correlations, which can lead to beneficial diversification effects. In addition, global competition in some industries makes it important to search worldwide for the best investments. For the U.S.-based investor, industry influences are gaining importance for global diversification. Therefore, we conclude that due to the relatively high rates of return on foreign securities combined with low correlation coefficients, adding foreign stocks and bonds to a U.S. portfolio *will almost certainly reduce the risk of the portfolio and can possibly increase its average return.*

---

[5]See Stephen E. Christophe and Richard W. McEnally, "U.S. Multinationals as Vehicles for International Diversification," *Journal of Investing,* vol. 9, no. 4 (Winter 2000): 67–75; Bertrand Jacquillat and Bruno Solnik, "Multinationals Are Poor Tools for International Diversification," *Journal of Portfolio Management* (Winter 1978): 8–12.

Global Investment Choices

Investments can be grouped into two basic categories: *money market* and *capital market.* Money market securities mature in one year or less and typically are used in low-risk, low-return strategies in which investors want to "park" temporary cash balances. Capital market securities mature in more than one year and include bonds and stocks. Securities can also be divided into the categories of debt, in which the issuer is a borrower and the security holder is the lender, and equity, in which the security holder owns a part or share of an asset or organization.

There are literally hundreds of variations of money market, capital market, debt, and equity securities. Each type of security meets the specific needs of some segment of the financial market. Securities differ one from another in the following ways:

- **Timing of cash flows.** Securities may distribute cash flows to investors monthly (mortgage-backed securities, some annuities), quarterly (stock dividends), semiannually (corporate bonds), annually (Eurobonds) or at maturity (zero coupon bonds, CDs, most money market securities).
- **Maturity.** The spectrum of money and capital market securities have a variety of times to maturity. But some offer maturities that can be shortened by the investor (puttable bonds, convertible preferred stock), shortened by the issuer (callable stock, some types of convertible bonds and preferred stock), shortened by the cash flow patterns of the issuer (e.g., maturities on mortgage-backed securities depend on how rapidly homeowners pre-pay or refinance their mortgages), or lengthened by the issuer or investor (notes or preferred stock with resetable interest rates or dividends; extendable notes).
- **Source of cash flows to the investor.** Cash flows to the investor can arise from the productivity of underlying real assets (many stocks, corporate bonds); governmental taxing authority (Treasury securities, municipal general obligation bonds, tax anticipation notes); specific revenue sources (revenue bonds issues by water authorities or turnpike authorities); or the organization's ability to raise cash (literally borrowing from one to pay another [commercial paper, debtor-in-possession financing]).
- **Risk of cash flows to the investor.** Securities differ on the basis of the stability and predictability of the periodic cash flows to the investor and to the stability of their price or maturity value. Fixed-coupon-rate corporate bonds pay a constant cash flow every six months. Variable-rate or reset-coupon bonds pay a coupon that varies depending on market conditions. The risk to the bondholder of actually receiving cash flows on a timely basis is measured in part by the bond rating and by the collateral—specific assets—that is supporting the bond issue. Future prices or maturity values may be fairly certain (in the case of Treasury bonds) or very uncertain (in the case of common stock or complex mortgage-backed securities).

To meet the needs of the variety of issuers and investors who desire different combinations of the foregoing security characteristics, a vast array of securities have been developed. We begin our brief overview with a survey of *fixed-income investments,* which have contractually mandated payment schedules.[6]

---

[6]In our discussion of both money market and capital market investments, we assume the student has been introduced to the basics of such in previous course work. Many books have been written on the details of financial market securities. In the discussion that follows, we leave many of the details to those books.

MONEY MARKET SECURITIES

You might not think of a *savings account* as a fixed-income investment, yet an individual who deposits funds in a savings account at a bank or credit union is really lending money to the institution. These investments are generally considered to be convenient, liquid, and, because almost all are insured, low-risk. Consequently, their rates of return are generally low compared with other alternatives.

For investors with more funds who are willing to give up liquidity, banks developed the *certificate of deposit (CD),* which requires a minimum deposit (typically $500 or more) and has a fixed duration (usually three months, six months, one year, or longer). The promised rates on CDs are higher than those for savings accounts, and the rate increases with the size and the duration of the deposit. An investor who wants to cash in a CD prior to its stated expiration date must pay a heavy penalty in the form of a much lower interest rate. A secondary or resale market exists among institutions for large-denomination ($100,000 or more) CDs; these are called *negotiable CDs.*

Investors with larger sums of money ($10,000 or more) can invest in Treasury bills (T-bills), which are short-term obligations of the U.S. government sold in weekly auctions with maturities of 7, 13, 28, 91, or 182 days. Exhibit 3.10 shows the results of an auction in mid-2004. The discount rate is calculated using a 360-day year:

3.3a
$$\text{Discount Rate} = \left(\frac{\text{Par Value} - \text{Price}}{\text{Par Value}} \right) \times \left(\frac{360}{\text{Maturity of the Bill in Days}} \right)$$

If we know the discount rate, we can estimate the price by rearranging equation 3.3a:

3.3b

$$\text{Price} = \text{Par Value} - \text{Discount Rate} \times \frac{\text{Maturing of the Bill in Days}}{360} \times \text{Par Value}$$

For the 91-day T-bill, using the price of $99.666 and a par of $100, we compute the discount rate as

$$\text{Discount Rate} = \left(\frac{\$100 - \$99.666}{\$100} \right) \times \left(\frac{360}{91} \right) = 0.01321 \text{ or } 1.321\%$$

This differs slightly from the discount rate shown in the exhibit because the prices and interest rates in the table are rounded to three decimal places.

The investment rate (sometimes called the bond equivalent rate) is computed using a 365-day year (366 in leap years) and divides by the price rather than the par value:

EXHIBIT 3.10	Treasury Bills Weekly Auction Results					
Term	Issue Date	Maturity Date	Discount Rate (%)	Investment Rate(%)	Price per $100	CUSIP*
7-day	07–08–2004	07–15–2004	1.160	1.200	99.977	912795QT1
91-day	07–08–2004	10–07–2004	1.320	1.344	99.666	912795RF0
182-day	07–08–2004	01–06–2005	1.630	1.666	99.176	912795RU7

*A unique identifier for each T-bill issued.

3.4a

$$\text{Investment Rate} = \left(\frac{\text{Par Value} - \text{Price}}{\text{Price}}\right) \times \left(\frac{365}{\text{Maturity of the Bill in Days}}\right)$$

If we know the investment rate, we can estimate the price by rearranging equation 3.4a:

3.4b $$\text{Price} = \text{Par Value}/\left[1 + \text{Investment Rate} \times \left(\frac{\text{Maturity of the Bill in Days}}{365}\right)\right]$$

Using the information for the 91-day T-bill, we use equation 3.4a to compute the price at the investment rate of 1.344 percent:

$$\text{Price} = \$100/\left[1 + 0.01344 \times \left(\frac{91}{365}\right)\right] = \$99.666 \text{ to three decimal places}$$

Two other important money market securities are Eurodollars deposits and Eurodollar CDs. *Eurodollars* are dollar-denominated deposits placed in overseas banks. Despite the "euro" prefix, such deposits do not have to be in European banks; they can be in Asian banks or foreign branches of American banks. Eurodollars are short-term (typically six-months or less) and form the basis for short-term lending to institutions and corporations seeking U.S. dollar loans. Because the funds are in overseas banks, they escape regulation by the Fed.

A final word on two important short-term interest rates. The federal funds rate is the interest rate at which U.S. banks borrow from one another. Similarly, the LIBOR (London Interbank Offer Rate) is the rate at which large London banks borrow from one another. LIBOR is important in short-term international borrowing and lending; quoted interest rates are often expressed as LIBOR plus 1/2 percent or LIBOR plus 2 percent, much like the prime rate is used in U.S markets.

CAPITAL MARKET INSTRUMENTS

Capital market instruments fall into five general categories: (1) U.S. Treasury securities, (2) U.S. government agency securities, (3) municipal bonds, (4) corporate bonds, and (5) asset-backed securities.

U.S. Treasury Securities All government securities issued by the U.S. Treasury are fixed-income instruments. They may be bills, notes, or bonds, depending on their times to maturity. U.S. government obligations are highly liquid and essentially risk-free; there is little chance of default.

A typical price quote in the financial pages for Treasury bonds will appear as follows:

Rate	Maturity, Mo/Yr	Bid	Asked	Chg.	Asked Yld
9	Nov 18	146:01	146:04	−7	4.95

The coupon rate for this bond is 9 percent of par value, meaning that a $1,000 par value bond will pay $90 of interest annually in two semiannual payments of $45. The bond matures in November of 2018. Treasury bond prices are expressed as percentages of par value in 32nds of a point. The bid price, to be received by investors wanting to sell bonds, is $146\frac{1}{32}$ percent of par, or $1,460.3125. The ask price, to be paid by investors wanting to purchase bonds, is $146\frac{4}{32}$ of par, or $1,461.25. The bid–ask spread represents the dealer profit, or $0.9375 per $1000 par value bond. Spreads are often an indicator of investment liquidity. The decline in price from the previous day was $\frac{7}{32}$ of a percentage point. The yield to maturity, based on the ask price, is 4.95 percent. This number will slightly understate the true yield to maturity. It is obtained by computing the semiannual yield—given the coupon payments, ask price, and par value—and then doubling it. To be exact, we would compound the semiannual yield over two half-year periods. That is, if the reported Asked Yield is 4.95 percent, the computed semiannual yield is 4.95/2 or 2.475 percent. Compounding this over two semiannual periods, a truer estimate of the yield to maturity is $(1 + 0.02475)^2 - 1$, which is 5.01 percent.

If the bond quote has an "n" after the maturity month and year, it is a Treasury note; if it has an "i," it is an inflation-indexed issue. Inflation-indexed bonds are known by the acronyms TIPS (Treasury Inflation-Protected Securities) or TIIS (Treasury Inflation-Indexed Securities). The coupon rate on such a bond remains constant over its life but the par value increases by the inflation rate. For example, suppose a TIPS bond has a coupon rate of 2.5 percent, a par value of $10,000, and during the year inflation is 3 percent. The par value will rise to $10,300 and the coupon payment (which equals 2.5 percent of the par value) will rise from a total annual payment of $250 to $257.50. Thus both par value and total coupon payment for the year rise by the 3 percent rate of inflation.

U.S. Government Agency Securities   Agency securities are sold by various agencies of the government to support specific programs, but they are not direct obligations of the Treasury. Examples of agencies that issue these bonds include the Federal National Mortgage Association (FNMA or Fannie Mae), which sells bonds and uses the proceeds to purchase mortgages from lending institutions. Other agencies are the Government National Mortgage Association (GNMA or Ginnie Mae), Banks for Cooperatives, Federal Land Banks (FLBs), and the Federal Housing Administration (FHA).

These securities have developed secondary markets for trading and are fairly liquid. Because the Treasury does not officially guarantee them, they are not risk free (although it is inconceivable that the government would allow them to default). With slightly higher default risk and less market liquidity than Treasury bonds, they typically provide slightly higher returns than Treasury issues.

Municipal Bonds   Municipal bonds are issued by local government entities as either general obligation or revenue bonds. A *general obligation bond (GO)* is backed by the full taxing power of the municipality, whereas a *revenue bond* pays the interest from revenue generated by specific projects (e.g., the revenue to pay the interest on sewer bonds comes from water taxes).

Municipal bonds differ from other fixed-income securities in that their interest payments are exempt from federal taxes. In addition, their interest is exempt from state tax in the state that issued the bond, if the investor is a resident of that state. For this reason, municipal bonds are popular with investors in high tax brackets. To illustrate, we can compute the equivalent taxable yield on a municipal bond as:

3.5

$$\text{Equivalent Taxable Yield} = \frac{\text{Yield on the Municipal}}{1 - \text{Marginal Tax Rate}}$$

Thus a municipal bond offering a tax-exempt yield of 6.0 percent to an investor with a 35 percent marginal tax rate has an equivalent taxable yield of

$$\text{Equivalent Taxable Yield} = \frac{6.0\%}{1 - 0.35} = 9.23\%$$

In other words, unless a taxable bond of similar risk offers a taxable yield of at least 9.23 percent, the investor will prefer the municipal bond.

Corporate Bonds Corporate bonds are fixed-income securities issued by industrial corporations, public utility corporations, or railroads to raise funds to invest in plant, equipment, or working capital. They can be broken down by issuer, in terms of credit quality (measured by the credit ratings assigned on the basis of probability of default), in terms of maturity (short-term, intermediate-term, or long-term), or based on some component of the indenture (sinking fund or call feature). Some of their features are summarized in Exhibit 3.11.

A typical corporate bond quote in the financial pages will appear as follows:

Company (Ticker)	Coupon	Maturity	Last Price	Last Yield	Est Spread	UST	Est $ Vol (000's)
Ford Motor (F)	7.450	Jul. 16, 2031	94.624	7.936	273	30	88,175

The ticker symbol (F) refers to Ford's common stock. The coupon rate of the Ford Motor bond is 7.450 percent of par. Most corporate bonds have a par value of $1,000, so this bond pays interest of $0.07450 \times 1,000 = \$74.50$ per year or $37.25 every six months. The bond matures and the par value will be paid on July 16, 2031. The "Last Price" reports the closing price of the bond expressed as a percentage of par value. Here, a closing price 94.624 represents a price of $946.24.

A commonly used term that is simple to compute is the current yield of a bond. We calculate current yield by dividing the annual coupon interest by the current price. This bond's current yield is $74.50/$946.24 = 7.87 percent. However, the current yield does not adequately represent the return on a bond investment since it considers income return

EXHIBIT 3.11	Some Features of Corporate Bonds

Security

Senior	Has first claim on specified assets.
Mortgage bonds	Backed by specific assets such as land and buildings.
Equipment trust certificates	Mortgage bonds secured by "rolling stock" such as railroad cars, airplanes.
Debenture	Unsecured debt.
Subordinated debenture	Claim on income and property is junior, or subordinate, to debenture holders.

Maturity

Call provision	Bond can be redeemed by issuer prior to maturity; investor receives par value plus a call premium equal to one year's coupon interest; bond is typically called after market interest rates have fallen significantly.
Put provision	Investor can force the issuer to repurchase the bond at par; typically allowed only in situations where the bond's credit risk has markedly increased.
Convertible	Investor can convert the bond into a prespecified number of common-stock shares.
Extendable	Term of bond can be extended at the investor's option.

Income

Fixed coupon rate	Bond pays a fixed coupon over its life.
Floating- or variable-rate note	Coupon payments fluctuate based on movement in a prespecified market rate such as LIBOR or T-bill rates.
Zero coupon	Bond pays no interest; investor's return is the difference between the bond's purchase price and its par at maturity.

only and ignores price changes. The yield to maturity, 7.936 percent, is a better measure of investor return and is shown by the "Last Yield." This measure represents an estimate of the investor's return on the bond if it was purchased today and held to maturity.

The "Estimated Spread" is the difference between the yield to maturity on the Ford bond and a similar maturity U.S. Treasury bond. Here, the spread is 273 basis points, or 2.73 percent (1 basis point represents 0.01 percentage points) more than that of a thirty-year Treasury bond, as seen by the number under the "UST" column. Since the Ford bond has a yield to maturity of 7.936 percent, the thirty-year Treasury bond must have a yield to maturity of about $7.936 - 2.73 = 5.21$ percent.

"Vol" represents actual bond trading volume in thousands of dollars for this Ford bond. The market value (quantity traded times last price) of the trading volume is $88,175,000. With a last price of $946.24, the approximate number of bonds traded is $88,175,000/ $946.24 = 93,185.

Bond Ratings   Bond ratings are an integral part of the bond market because most corporate and municipal bonds are rated by one or more of the rating agencies. The exceptions, known as *nonrated bonds,* are either very small or from certain industries, such as bank issues. The three major rating agencies are (1) Fitch Investors Service, (2) Moody's, and (3) Standard & Poor's (S&P).

The primary concern in bond credit analysis is whether the firm can service its debt in a timely manner over the life of a given issue. Consequently, the rating agencies consider expectations over the life of the issue along with the historical and current financial position of the company.[7] Letter ratings ranging from AAA (Aaa) to D depict the agencies' view of the default risk of an obligation. Exhibit 3.12 describes the various ratings assigned by the major services. Except for slight variations, the meaning and interpretation of the designations are basically the same. Fitch and S&P modify their ratings with $+$ and $-$ signs; Moody's uses numbers (1-2-3). (For example, an A+ bond is at the top of the A-rated group.)

The top four ratings—AAA (or Aaa), AA (or Aa), A, and BBB (or Baa)—are generally considered *investment-grade securities.* The BB- and B-rated obligations are known as *speculative bonds* (or high-yield or junk bonds). The C categories are generally either income obligations or revenue bonds, many of which are trading flat (which means the issuer is in arrears on interest payments). D-rated issues are in outright default, and the ratings indicate the bonds' relative salvage values.

Asset-Backed Securities   An asset-backed security is a special type of bond backed by a collection of income-generating securities such as mortgages, car loans, or even claims on royalties from music. One such bond is the GNMA (Ginnie Mae) pass-through certificate, a government agency obligation of the Government National Mortgage Association.[8] These bonds represent an interest in a pool of federally insured mortgages. The bondholders receive monthly payments from Ginnie Mae that include both principal and interest

[7]For a detailed listing of both rating classes and factors considered in assigning ratings, see "Bond Ratings" and "Bond Rating Outlines," in *The Financial Analysts Handbook,* 2nd ed., edited by Sumner N. Levine (Homewood, IL: Dow Jones–Irwin, 1988), pp. 1102–1138.

[8]For a further discussion of mortgage-backed securities, see *Mortgage-Backed Bond and Pass-Through Symposium,* Charlottesville, VA (Financial Analysts Research Foundation, 1980); Andrew S. Carron, "Collateralized Mortgage Obligations," in *The Handbook of Fixed-Income Securities,* 5th ed., edited by Frank J. Fabozzi (Chicago: Irwin, 1997); and Amy F. Lipton, "Evolution of the Mortgage Securities Market," in *Fixed Income Management: Techniques and Practices,* edited by Dwight R. Churchill (Charlottesville, VA: Association for Investment Management and Research, 1994), pp. 26–30.

EXHIBIT 3.12	Bond Ratings				
	Duff and Phelps	Fitch	Moody's	Standard & Poor's	Definition
High Grade	AAA	AAA	Aaa	AAA	The highest rating assigned to a debt instrument, indicating an extremely strong capacity to pay principal and interest. Bonds in this category are often referred to as *gilt-edge securities*.
	AA	AA	Aa	AA	High-quality bonds by all standards with strong capacity to pay principal and interest. These bonds are rated lower primarily because the margins of protection are less strong than those for Aaa and AAA bonds.
Medium Grade	A	A	A	A	These bonds possess many favorable investment attributes, but elements may suggest a susceptibility to impairment given adverse economic changes.
	BBB	BBB	Baa	BBB	Bonds regarded as having adequate capacity to pay principal and interest, but certain protective elements may be lacking in the event of adverse economic conditions that could lead to a weakened capacity for payment.
Speculative	BB	BB	Ba	BB	Bonds regarded as having only moderate protection of principal and interest payments during both good and bad times.
	B	B	B	B	Bonds that generally lack characteristics of other desirable investments. Assurance of interest and principal payments over any long period of time may be small.
Default	CCC	CCC	Caa	CCC	Poor-quality issues that may be in default or in danger of default.
	CC	CC	Ca	CC	Highly speculative issues that are often in default or possess other marked short-comings.
	C	C			The lowest-rated class of bonds. These issues can be regarded as extremely poor in investment quality.
		C		C	Rating given to income bonds on which no interest is being paid.
		DDD		D	Issues in default with principal or interest payments in arrears. Such bonds are extremely speculative and should be valued only on the basis of their value in liquidation or reorganization.
		DD			
		D			

Source: *Bond Guide* (New York: Standard & Poor's Corporation, monthly), *Bond Record* (New York: Moody's Investors Services, Inc, monthly), *Rating Register* (New York: Fitch Investors Service, Inc., monthly).

because the agency "passes through" mortgage payments made by the original borrower to Ginnie Mae.

The coupons on these pass-through certificates are related to the interest charged on the pool of mortgages. The portion of the cash flow that represents the repayment of the principal is tax-free, but the interest income is subject to federal, state, and local taxes. The issues have minimum denominations of $25,000 with maturities of twenty-five to thirty years but an average life of only twelve years due to prepayments. Prepayments can occur when homeowners pay off their mortgages when they sell their homes or when they refinance their homes when mortgage interest rates decline (as they did in 1992, 1993, 1997, and 2001–2003). Therefore, unlike most bond issues, the monthly payment is not fixed. In fact, the monthly payment is *extremely* uncertain because prepayments can vary dramatically over time as interest rates change. Thus a major disadvantage of GNMA issues is that they can be seriously depleted by prepayments, which means that their maturities are uncertain.

Another type of asset-backed security is the *collateralized mortgage obligation (CMO)*, developed to offset some of the problems existing in traditional mortgage pass-throughs.[9] CMOs attempt to stabilize and increase the predictability of cash flows to investors by issuing several classes of bonds against a pool of mortgages. For example, for a CMO issue with four classes of bonds,[10] the first three (class A, B, and C) pay interest at their stated rates but the fourth is an *accrual bond* (also referred to as a *Z bond*). All of the mortgage pool's cash flows are used to pay interest on the A, B, and C classes of bonds. All mortgage principal payments are directed first to the shortest-maturity class A bonds until they are completely retired, then to the class B bonds until they are retired, and last to the class C bonds until they are paid off.

During the early periods, the accrual bonds (class Z bonds) pay no interest; the interest accrues as additional principal. After the A, B, and C bonds have been retired, all remaining cash flows are used to pay off the accrued interest, to pay any current interest, and then to retire the Z bonds. This prioritized sequential pattern means that the class A bonds are fairly short term and each subsequent class is a little longer term. The class Z bond, which is a long-term bond, functions like a zero coupon bond for the initial years.

Ginnie Maes and CMOs are but two of a rapidly expanding set of asset-backed securities. The process of securitizing debt allows financial institutions to bundle various types of loans and sell portions of this portfolio of loans to individual investors. This practice increases the liquidity of these individual debt instruments, whether they are individual mortgages, car loans, or credit card debt. For example, *certificates for automobile receivables (CARs)* are securities collateralized by loans made to individuals to finance the purchase of cars.

INTERNATIONAL BOND INVESTING

There are several bond instruments available to U.S. investors who want to build a global portfolio. A *Eurobond* is an international bond denominated in a currency not native to the country where it is issued. Specific kinds of Eurobonds include Eurodollar bonds, Euroyen bonds, Eurodeutschemark bonds, and Eurosterling bonds. A Eurodollar bond is denominated in U.S. dollars and sold outside the United States to non-U.S. investors. If it appears that investors are looking for foreign currency bonds, a U.S. corporation can issue a Euroyen bond in London.

A *Yankee bond* is sold in the United States and denominated in U.S. dollars, but it is issued by foreign corporations or governments. This allows a U.S. citizen to buy the bond of a foreign firm or government but receive all payments in U.S. dollars, eliminating exchange rate risk. Similar bonds are issued in other countries, including the Bulldog Market, which involves sterling-denominated bonds issued in the United Kingdom by non-

---

[9]For a detailed discussion, see Andrew S. Carron, "Collateralized Mortgage Obligations," in *The Handbook of Fixed-Income Securities,* 5th ed., edited by Frank Fabozzi (Chicago: Irwin, 1997).

[10]The four-class CMO was the typical configuration during the 1980s and is used here for demonstration purposes. CMOs are now being issued with eighteen to twenty classes. More advanced CMOs, referred to as REMICs, provide greater certainty regarding the cash flow patterns for various components of the pool. For a discussion of REMICs, see Andrew S. Carron, "Understanding CMOs, REMICs, and Other Mortgage Derivatives," *Fixed Income Research* (New York: The First Boston Corp., 1992).

British firms, or the Samurai Market, which involves yen-denominated bonds issued in Japan by non-Japanese firms.

An *international domestic bond* is sold by an issuer within its own country in that country's currency. An example would be a bond denominated in yen sold by Nippon Steel in Japan. A U.S. investor acquiring such a bond would receive maximum diversification, but would incur exchange rate risk.

PREFERRED STOCK

Preferred stock is a fixed-income security with a yearly payment stipulated as either a coupon (for example, 5 percent of the face value) or a stated dollar amount (for example, $5 preferred). Preferred stock differs from bonds in that its payment is a dividend and therefore not legally binding. For each period, the firm's board of directors must vote to pay it, similar to a common-stock dividend. Thus, even if the firm earned enough money to pay the preferred-stock dividend, the board of directors could vote to withhold it. Because most preferred stock is cumulative, the unpaid dividends would accumulate to be paid in full at a later time.

EQUITY INSTRUMENTS

Equity instruments differ from fixed-income securities in that their returns are not contractual. As a result, returns can be much better or much worse than those from a bond. Common stock is the most popular equity instrument.

Common stock represents *ownership* of a firm. Thus, owners of a firm's common stock share in the firm's successes and failures. If—like Wal-Mart stores, McDonald's, Microsoft, or Intel—the company prospers over time, the investor receives high rates of return and can become wealthy. In contrast, if a firm loses money or goes bankrupt, the investor could do the same. Thus, common stock is a more risky investment than a fixed-income security.

A typical stock listing in the financial pages will appear as follows:

52 weeks								
Hi	Lo	Stock (Sym)	Div	Yld. %	PE	Vol 100s	Close	Net Chg
35.06	24.75	McDonald's (MCD)	.23	.8	19	32732	27.20	+0.18

McDonald's stock symbol is MCD; its high and low price over the previous fifty-two weeks were $35.06 and $24.75, respectively. Note that unlike bonds, stocks are traded in decimals; their prices show the dollar-and-cents value of a share. Based on its last quarterly dividend, McDonald's is paying dividends at an annual rate of 23¢ per share, a dividend yield of $0.23/$27.20 or 0.8 percent, rounded to one decimal place. "Close" represents the closing price for the stock; "PE" is the price/earnings ratio. Since the PE, 19, is rounded to the nearest integer, we can estimate McDonald's earnings per share: since 19 = price/eps = $27.20/eps, earnings will be approximately $1.43 per share. During the trading day shown, the volume (or shares traded) was 3,273,200. "Chg" shows that the stock price increased by 18¢ over the previous day's closing price.

For the investor creating a global portfolio, there are several popular ways to acquire foreign common stock:

1. Purchase or sale of American Depository Receipts (ADRs)
2. Direct purchase or sale of foreign shares listed on a U.S. or foreign stock exchange
3. Purchase or sale of international or global mutual funds

The easiest way to acquire foreign shares directly is through *American Depository Receipts (ADRs)*. Issued by a U.S. bank, these certificates represent indirect ownership of a certain number of shares of a specific foreign firm on deposit in a bank in the firm's home country. ADRs are convenient because the investor buys and sells them in U.S. dollars and receives all dividends in U.S. dollars. This means that the price and returns reflect both the domestic returns for the stock and the exchange rate effect. Also, the price of an ADR can reflect the fact that it represents multiple shares—for example, an ADR can be for five or ten shares of the foreign stock. ADRs can be issued at the discretion of a bank, based on the demand for the stock. The shareholder absorbs the additional handling costs of an ADR through higher transfer expenses, which are deducted from dividend payments.

ADRs are quite popular in the United States because of their diversification benefits. By 2003 there were about 2,000 depositary receipt programs available to investors. In 2003, the most popularly traded ADRs included Nokia (Finland), Vadafone (U.K.), Ericsson (Sweden), Royal Dutch Petroleum (Netherlands), and BP (U.K.).

Buying shares directly on a foreign market is another, less convenient, way to invest globally. The most difficult and complicated foreign equity transaction is one that takes place in the country where the firm is located because it must be carried out in the foreign currency and the shares must then be transferred to the United States. This routine can be cumbersome. A second alternative is a transaction on a foreign stock exchange outside the country where the securities originated. For example, if an investor acquired shares of a French auto company listed on the London Stock Exchange (LSE), the shares would be denominated in pounds and the transfer would be swift if the broker has a membership on the LSE.

Finally, one can purchase foreign stocks listed on the NYSE, AMEX, or Nasdaq. The procedure is similar to buying a U.S. stock, but only a limited number of foreign firms qualify for—and are willing to accept—the cost of listing. Still, this number is growing. At the end of 2001, more than 100 foreign firms (mostly Canadian) were directly listed on the NYSE, in addition to the firms that were available through ADRs.

For the small investor, mutual funds are a good avenue for foreign investing. The alternatives range from *global funds,* which invest in both U.S. stocks and foreign stocks, to *international funds,* which invest almost wholly outside the United States. International funds can (1) diversify across many countries, (2) concentrate in a certain segment of the world (for example, Europe, South America, or the Pacific basin), (3) concentrate in a specific country (for example, the Japan Fund, the Germany Fund, the Italy Fund, or the Korea Fund), or (4) concentrate in specific market types (for example, emerging markets, which would include stocks from countries such as Thailand, Indonesia, India, and China).

DERIVATIVES

In addition to common-stock investments, one can also invest in derivative securities, which *derive* their value from an underlying security. The underlying security can be shares of common stock, the value of an index, an interest rate, or an exchange rate. In the following discussion, we focus on derivatives of common stocks.

One kind of derivative security is an *option*—the right to buy or sell common stock at a specified price for a stated period of time. A *call option* is an option to buy the common stock of a company within a certain period at a specified price called the *strike price*. A call option is not issued by the company but by another investor who is willing to assume the other side of the transaction. Call options are generally valid for less than a year. The holder of a *put option* has the right to sell a given stock at a specified price during a designated time period. Put options are useful to investors who expect a stock price to decline during the specified period or to investors who own the stock and want protection from a price decline.

Another derivatives instrument is a *futures contract*. This agreement provides for the future exchange of a particular asset at a specified delivery date (usually within nine months) in exchange for a specified payment at the time of delivery. Although the full payment is not made until the delivery date, a good-faith deposit, the *margin,* is made to protect the seller. This is typically about 10 percent of the value of the contract.

Popular financial futures contracts include those on instruments such as T-bills, Treasury bonds, and Eurobonds. For example, one can buy or sell a futures contract that promises future delivery of $100,000 of Treasury bonds at a set price and yield. The major exchanges for financial futures are the Chicago Mercantile Exchange (CME) and the Chicago Board of Trade (CBOT). These futures contracts allow individual investors, bond-portfolio managers, and corporate financial managers to protect themselves against volatile interest rates. Certain currency futures allow individual investors or portfolio managers to speculate on or to protect against changes in currency exchange rates. Finally, futures contracts pertain to stock market series such as the S&P 500, the FTSE index (London), and the Nikkei Average on the Tokyo Stock Exchange.

MANAGED INVESTMENTS

Managed investments pool funds from individuals and invest the funds according to stated guidelines. Examples of such indirect investments are investment companies, hedge funds, venture capital pools, and real estate investment trusts.

Investment Companies   An *investment company* sells shares in itself and uses the proceeds of this sale to acquire bonds, stocks, or other investment instruments. As a result, an investor who acquires shares in an investment company is a partial owner of the investment company's portfolio of stocks or bonds. Open-end investment companies, better known as mutual funds, have a fluctuating number of shares since investors purchase and redeem shares directly from the company. Major types of mutual funds include money market, bond, common stock, and balanced funds. *Money market funds* are investment companies that acquire high-quality, short-term investments such as T-bills, high-grade commercial paper (public short-term loans) from various corporations, and large CDs from the major money center banks. Bond funds generally invest in various long-term government, corporate, or municipal bonds. They differ by the type and quality of the bonds included in the portfolio as assessed by various rating services. Numerous common-stock funds invest to achieve various investment objectives, which can include aggressive growth, income, precious metal investments, and international stocks. Such funds offer smaller investors the benefits of diversification and professional management. Balanced funds invest in a combination of various bonds and stocks, depending on their stated objectives.

Hedge Funds   A typical hedge fund is a partnership. A general partner (which could be an individual or a firm) commits capital, makes trading decisions, and runs the day-to-day operations of the fund. Limited partners invest capital in the fund. Hedge funds have a variety of strategies. Some invest aggressively in stocks, even borrowing money to buy shares. Others invest in concentrated positions in distressed securities (that is, firms that are at or near bankruptcy). Still others invest to generate income, focus on emerging markets, or take advantage of macroeconomic policy shifts. According to the Hedge Fund Association, about $875 billion was invested in over 8,000 hedge funds in 2004. As compensation and as a performance incentive, the general partner receives an administrative fee of 1 percent of the fund's assets each year and 20 percent of the net profits of the partnership.

Venture Capital   Venture capital is the process of raising and investing funds in small, private, high-growth-potential companies with the goal of achieving positive risk-adjusted returns when exiting the investment. The firms receiving venture capital funds are typically start-up firms or privately held firms with an attractive idea and some sales who need capital to fund further expansion. Venture capitalists get a return on their investment by exiting the investment (1) when a firm does an initial public offering (IPO) by selling shares of common stock to the public, (2) when the firm is bought out by another firm, or (3) when the firm is merged with another firm. The investments are high risk with high return potential. The basic structure of a venture capital pool is similar to that of a hedge fund. A general partner enlists investors, earns a 1 percent administrative fee, and receives 20 percent of the net profits. Limited partners invest funds in the venture capital pool.

Real Estate Investment Trusts (REITs)   Most investors view real estate as an interesting and profitable investment alternative but believe that it is only available to a small group of experts with a lot of capital to invest. In reality, some feasible real estate investments through REITs require neither detailed expertise nor large capital commitments. A *real estate investment trust (REIT)* is an investment fund similar to a stock or bond mutual fund, except that the money provided by the investors is invested in property and buildings.

There are several types of REITs. Construction and development trusts lend money to builders during the initial construction of a building. Mortgage trusts provide the long-term financing for properties once construction is completed. Equity trusts own various income-producing properties (such as office buildings, shopping centers, or apartment houses) so an investor who buys shares in an equity REIT is buying part of a portfolio of these properties. Thus, although REITs are subject to cyclical risks depending on the economic environment, they offer small investors several ways to participate in real estate investments.[11]

We will discuss many of the common investment alternatives we have described in this section in more detail when we consider how to evaluate them for investment purposes. Keep in mind that new investment instruments are constantly being developed. You can keep abreast of these by reading business newspapers and magazines.

Historical Rates of Return and Risk

In this section we present data on historical rates of return and risk measures for several of the investments we have discussed. This background on their historical return–risk performance should give us some feel for the return and risk characteristics we might expect in the future. First we examine U.S data; then we examine the return and risk of global assets.

T-Bills, Bonds, and Stocks

In Exhibit 3.13 we present the annual geometric mean, annual arithmetic mean, and standard deviation of annual returns for 1980–2003 for a series of six assets. We use large-capitalization stocks (represented by the S&P 500 index), small-capitalization stocks (represented by the Russell 2000 index), corporate bonds, long-term government bonds, intermediate-term government bonds (all represented by Lehman Brothers indexes), T-bills (based on a Citigroup index), and we include the U.S. inflation rate. As discussed in Chapter 2, the geometric means of the rates of return are always lower than the arithmetic means, and the difference between these two mean values increases with the standard deviation of returns. As

---

[11]For a review of studies that have examined returns on real estate, see C. F. Myer and James Webb, "Return Properties of Equity REITs, Common Stocks, and Commercial Real Estate: A Comparison," *Journal of Real Estate Research* 8, no. 1 (1993): 87–106; Stephen Ross and Randall Zisler, "Risk and Return in Real Estate," *Journal of Real Estate Financial Economics* 4, no. 2 (1991): 175–190; and William Goetzmann and Roger Ibbotson, "The Performance of Real Estate as an Asset Class," *Journal of Applied Corporate Finance* 3, no. 1 (Spring 1990): 65–76. For an analysis of the diversification possibilities, see Susan Hudson-Wilson and Bernard L. Elbaum, "Diversification Benefits for Investors in Real Estate," *Journal of Portfolio Management* 21, no. 3 (Spring 1995): 92–99.

EXHIBIT 3.13	Basic and Derived Series: 1980–2003			
		Geometric Mean (%)	Arithmetic Mean (%)	Standard Deviation (%)
BASIC SERIES				
Large-cap stocks (S&P 500)		13.64	15.03	17.87
Small-cap stocks (Russell 2000)		12.21	14.45	22.50
Corporate bonds (Lehman Brothers Corporate Bond)		10.36	10.66	8.25
Long-term government bonds (Lehman Brothers Long-Term Gov't Bond)		10.74	11.39	12.20
Intermediate-term government bond (Lehman Brothers Intermediate-Term Gov't Bond)		9.11	9.22	5.01
T-bills (Citigroup U.S. Domestic 3-Month T-Bill)		6.45	6.46	0.94
U.S. inflation		3.71	3.72	1.08
INFLATION-ADJUSTED BASIC SERIES				
Large-cap stocks		9.57	10.94	17.40
Small-cap stocks		8.19	10.39	21.88
Corporate bonds		6.41	6.71	8.15
Long-term government bond		6.77	7.43	11.98
Intermediate-term government bond		5.26	5.38	5.11
3-month T-bill		2.64	2.65	0.97
DERIVED SERIES				
Equity risk premium		6.75%	8.57	
Small-stock risk premium		−1.26%	−0.58	
Horizon premium		4.03%	4.93	
Default premium		1.15%	1.44	

expected, higher-risk assets generally had higher returns over the 1980–2003 time frame. An exception is the behavior of small stocks, which had higher risk and slightly lower returns than large stocks during this 24-year period.

We adjusted each return series by the annual inflation rate to estimate their real returns. Real returns were estimated each year as follows:

$$\textbf{Annual Real Return} = \frac{\textbf{1 + Annual Nominal Return}}{\textbf{(1 + Annual Inflation Rate)}} > \textbf{1}$$

We computed the averages and standard deviations based on these annual calculations. During this period, large-cap stocks earned an average real compound return of 9.57 percent. Bonds performed well on an after-inflation basis because of the decline in interest rates during this period.

The four derived series shown in Exhibit 3.13 were computed from data in other series and focus on four different types of risk premiums. First is the *equity risk premium,* the difference in the rate of return that investors receive from investing in large-cap stocks rather than in risk-free U.S. Treasury bills. On average, investors earned 8.57 percent more each year by investing in large-cap stocks than T-bills. The *small-stock risk premium,* defined as the return on small-cap stocks minus the return on large-cap stocks, is negative over the time frame shown. The *horizon premium* is the difference in the rate of return received from investing in long-term government bonds rather than short-term U.S. Treasury bills. Investors earned a compounded return of 4.03 percent more per year by investing in the longer-term riskier bonds. Finally, the *default premium* is the difference between the rates of return on corporate bonds and government bonds. As previously discussed, corporate bonds have default or credit risk as measured by the bond ratings; government securities have zero default risk. Since the typical maturity of corporate bonds is similar to that of intermediate-term government bonds, we computed this series using the Lehman Brothers corporate index and the intermediate-term bond index. On average, investors earned slightly more than 1 percent more by taking on default risk.

WORLD PORTFOLIO PERFORMANCE

Now let's expand our analysis from domestic to global securities. Specifically, for the period from 1980 to 2003 we will examine the performance of stocks, bonds, short-term securities, real estate, and commodities in the United States, Canada, Europe, Japan, and the emerging markets. Exhibit 3.14 shows the geometric and arithmetic mean annual rates of

EXHIBIT 3.14	Summary Risk-Return Results for Various Capital Market Assets, 1980–2003			
	Geometric Mean (%)	Arithmetic Mean (%)	Standard Deviation (%)	Coefficient of Variation
STOCKS				
S&P 500	13.64	15.03	17.87	1.19
Wilshire 5000	13.17	14.62	18.16	1.24
Russell 1000	13.42	14.83	17.98	1.21
Russell 2000	12.21	14.45	22.50	1.56
Russell 3000	13.28	14.71	18.05	1.23
S&P/IFCG Emerging Composite	9.82	12.75	25.75	2.02
MSCI EAFE	11.12	12.80	19.61	1.53
S&P/Toronto Stock Exch 60	9.16	10.64	17.94	1.69
MSCI Germany	10.05	12.72	24.58	1.93
MSCI Japan	5.01	6.95	20.59	2.96
MSCI World	11.91	13.16	16.80	1.28
BONDS				
Lehman Brothers Government Bond	9.56	9.74	6.33	0.65
Lehman Brothers Corporate Bond	10.36	10.66	8.25	0.77
Lehman Brothers Aggregate Bond	9.79	10.00	6.81	0.68
Lehman Brothers Hi-Yield Bond	9.90	10.21	8.25	0.81
Merrill Lynch World Government Bond	9.02	9.26	7.21	0.78
Merrill Lynch World (except U.S.) Gov't Bond	9.92	10.49	11.30	1.08
OTHER				
Wilshire Real Estate	11.25	12.43	16.27	1.31
Goldman Sachs Commodity	8.15	9.68	18.62	1.92
Citigroup U.S. domestic 3-month T-bill	6.45	6.46	0.94	0.15
U.S. inflation	3.71	3.72	1.08	0.29

return, the standard deviations of returns, and the coefficients of variation for a variety of asset classes.

Asset Return and Risk   The results in Exhibit 3.14 generally confirm the expected relationship between annual rates of return and the risk of these securities. The riskier stocks generally had higher rates of return and standard deviations than bonds, which in turn had higher returns and standard deviations than short-term government securities.

Relative Asset Risk   In the coefficients of variation (CV), which measure relative variability of risk per unit of return, we see a wide range of values. The T-bill had the lowest CV. Japanese stocks had the highest CV because of their large standard deviation and relatively low returns during this period. The CVs for stocks ranged from 1.19 to 2.96, with U.S. stocks toward the lower end of this range. Finally, the MSCI World Stock index had a rather low CV (1.28), demonstrating the benefits of global diversification. The graph in Exhibit 3.15 shows the positively sloped relationship among these historical risk and return measures.

Correlations among Asset Returns   Exhibit 3.16 shows the correlation coefficients among these same U.S. and world assets. The first column shows that U.S. equity returns, as measured by the S&P 500, have a reasonably high correlation with Canadian stocks (0.791). Lower correlations exist between the U.S. market and emerging-market stocks (0.480) and Japanese stocks (0.373). U.S. equities have negative correlation with world (except U.S.) government bonds (−0.023 when measured by the S&P 500, −0.040 when the Wilshire 5000 is used). Correlations among the emerging-market returns and the equity assets (both U.S. and non-U.S.) were consistently around 0.500, while many bond returns were negatively correlated with emerging-market stock returns. Similarly, the other equity indexes,

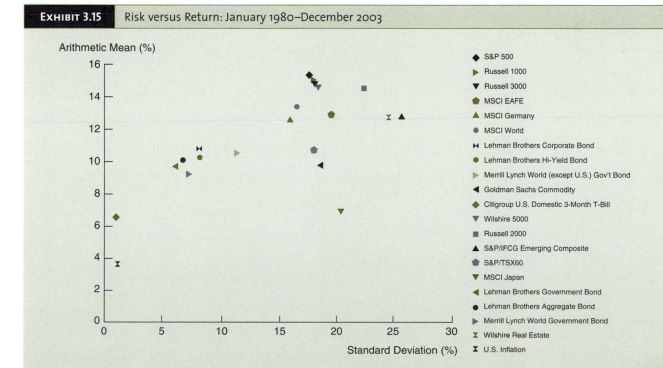

EXHIBIT 3.15   Risk versus Return: January 1980–December 2003

Exhibit 3.16	Correlations among Global Capital Market Assets, 1980–2003				
	S&P 500	Wilshire 5000	S&P/IFCG Emerging Mkts	MSCI EAFE	MSCI World
Stocks					
S&P 500	1.000	0.986	0.480	0.566	0.843
Wilshire 5000	0.986	1.000	0.508	0.573	0.840
Russell 1000	0.997	0.994	0.487	0.564	0.839
Russell 2000	0.799	0.878	0.511	0.506	0.703
Russell 3000	0.992	0.998	0.497	0.567	0.839
S&P/IFCG Emerging Composite	0.480	0.508	1.000	0.457	0.515
MSCI EAFE	0.566	0.573	0.457	1.000	0.913
S&P/Toronto Stock Exch 60	0.791	0.809	0.542	0.597	0.746
MSCI Germany	0.566	0.570	0.498	0.523	0.601
MSCI Japan	0.373	0.384	0.400	0.745	0.662
MSCI World	0.843	0.840	0.515	0.913	1.000
Bonds					
Lehman Brothers Government Bond	0.169	0.149	−0.214	0.122	0.150
Lehman Brothers Corporate Bond	0.274	0.264	−0.095	0.182	0.243
Lehman Brothers Aggregate Bond	0.223	0.207	−0.170	0.158	0.200
Lehman Brothers Hi-Yield Bond	0.502	0.534	0.336	0.341	0.448
Merrill Lynch World Government Bond	0.018	−0.006	−0.191	0.374	0.253
Merrill Lynch World (except U.S.) Gov't Bond	−0.023	−0.040	−0.148	0.440	0.287
Other					
Wilshire Real Estate	0.564	0.605	0.341	0.384	0.511
Goldman Sachs Commodity	0.024	0.039	0.040	0.090	0.068
Citigroup U.S. Domestic 3-Month T-Bill	0.002	−0.011	−0.048	−0.035	−0.025
U.S. inflation	−0.116	−0.122	−0.024	−0.164	−0.156

namely EAFE (measuring returns in European, Australia, and Far East stock markets) and Morgan Stanley's World stock index showed higher correlations with equity returns, lower correlations with bond returns, and lower still correlations with commodities and short-term U.S. government securities. Recall that such information can be used to build a diversified portfolio by combining those assets with low-positive or negative correlations.

Summary

- Investors who want the broadest range of choices in investments must consider foreign stocks and bonds in addition to domestic financial assets. Many foreign securities offer investors higher risk-adjusted returns than domestic securities. In addition, the low-positive or negative correlations between foreign and U.S. securities makes foreign securities ideal for building a diversified portfolio.

- Foreign bonds (or stocks) are considered riskier than domestic bonds (or stocks) because of the unavoidable uncertainty due to exchange rate risk and country risk.

- Studies on the historical rates of return for common stocks and other investment alternatives (including bonds, commodities, real estate, and foreign securities) point toward two generalizations:
    1. A positive relationship typically holds between the rate of return earned on an asset and the variability of its historical rate of return. This is expected in a world of risk-averse investors who require higher rates of return to compensate for more uncertainty.
    2. The correlation among rates of return for selected U.S. and foreign stocks and bonds can be quite low. This confirms the advantage of global diversification.

- Many direct investments, such as a variety of domestic and foreign stocks and bonds, are available for investors. In addition, investment companies allow investors to buy investments indirectly. These can be important to investors who want to take advantage of professional management but also want instant diversification with a limited amount of funds.

QUESTIONS

1. What are the advantages of investing in the common stock rather than the corporate bonds of a company? Compare the certainty of returns for a bond with those for a common stock. Draw a line graph to demonstrate the pattern of returns you would envision for each of these assets over time.
2. Discuss four factors that cause U.S. investors to consider including global securities in their portfolios.
3. Discuss why international diversification reduces portfolio risk. Specifically, why would you expect low correlation in the rates of return for domestic and foreign securities?
4. Discuss why you would expect a *difference* in the correlation of returns between securities from the United States and those from other countries (for example, Japan, Canada, South Africa).
5. Discuss whether you would expect any *change* in the correlations between U.S. stocks and the stocks for different countries. For example, should the correlation between U.S. and Japanese stock returns change over time?

Investments Online

As this chapter describes, the variety of financial products is huge and potentially confusing to the novice (not to mention the experienced professional) investor. Two good rules of investing are (1) stick to your risk tolerance (many people will try to sell instruments that may not be appropriate for the typical investor) and (2) do not invest in something if you do not understand it. The Web sites mentioned in Chapters 1 and 2 provide useful information on a variety of investments. Following are a few others that may be of interest.

http://www.site-by-site.com This site features global financial news including market information and economic reports for a variety of countries with developed, developing, and emerging markets. Some company research is available on this site, as is information on worldwide derivatives markets.

http://www.moneycafe.com MoneyCafe offers information on personal and commercial financial products and services, in addition to news, interest rate updates, and stock price quotes.

http://www.emgmkts.com The Emerging Markets Companion home page contains information on emerging markets in Asia, Latin America, Africa, and Eastern Europe. Available information and links includes news, prices, market information, and research.

http://www.law.duke.edu/globalmark Duke University's Global Capital Markets Center includes information and studies on a variety of financial market topics, most written from a legal perspective.

http://www.lebenthal.com Lebenthal is a firm specializing in municipal bond sales to individual investors. Their site contains a variety of research and information about municipal bonds.

http://search.sothebys.com The Sotheby's Inc. site contains auction updates and information on collectibles, Internet resources, and featured upcoming sales.

6. Will growing international trade increase or decrease the correlation between stock markets in different countries? Explain.

7. How does a strengthening U.S. dollar affect returns to a U.S.-based investor? A weakening U.S. dollar?

8. When you invest in Japanese or German bonds, what major additional risks must you consider besides yield changes within the country?

9. Some investors believe that international investing introduces additional risks. Discuss these risks and how they can affect a return. Give an example.

10. Why are correlations between stock markets in different countries rising over time?

11. Should investors diversify across countries? Industries? Both? Explain.

12. What alternatives to direct investment in foreign stocks are available to investors?

13. Why might an individual in a high tax bracket consider investing in a municipal bond rather than a straight corporate bond, even though the promised yield on the municipal bond is lower?

14. You can acquire convertible bonds from a rapidly growing company or from a utility. Speculate on which convertible bond would have the lower yield and discuss the reason for this difference.

15. What advantage to an investor does a CMO have over a Ginnie Mae pass-through?

16. Briefly describe two indenture provisions that can affect the maturity of a bond.

17. What factors determine whether a bond is senior or junior? Give examples of each type.

18. Explain the differences in taxation of income from municipal bonds and income from U.S. Treasury bonds and corporate bonds.

19. How does a bond's indenture affect its bond rating?

20. What is the purpose of bond ratings? What are they supposed to indicate?

21. Discuss the difference between a foreign bond (for example, a Samurai) and a Eurobond (such as a Euroyen issue).

22. Which bond should have the higher initial offering price (no calculations needed)?
    a. A fifteen-year zero coupon bond with a yield to maturity (YTM) of 12 percent
    b. A twenty-year zero coupon bond with a YTM of 10 percent.

23. Define *derivative security*. Give two examples of this type of security.

24. Why would an investor have need of a call option? A put option?

25. You have a fairly large portfolio of U.S. stocks and bonds. At a social gathering, a financial planner suggests that you diversify your portfolio by investing in gold. What information would you need to evaluate this suggestion?

26. See Question 25. Another financial planner at this social gathering suggests that you diversify your portfolio by investing in non-U.S. bonds. Discuss whether the correlation results in Exhibit 3.16 support this suggestion.

27. *CFA Examination Level I*
Chris Smith of XYZ Pension Plan has historically invested in the stocks of only U.S.-domiciled companies. Recently, he has decided to add international exposure to the plan portfolio.

Identify and briefly discuss *three* potential problems that Smith may confront in selecting international stocks that he did not face in choosing U.S. stocks. (6 minutes)

28. *CFA Examination Level III*
TMP has been experiencing increasing demand from its institutional clients for information and assistance related to international investment management. Recognizing that this is an area of growing importance, the firm has hired an experienced analyst/portfolio manager specializing in international equities and market strategy. His first assignment is to represent TMP before a client company's investment committee to discuss the possibility of changing their present "U.S. securities only" investment approach to one including international investments. He is told that the committee wants a presentation that fully and objectively examines the basic, substantive considerations on which the committee should focus its attention, including both theory and evidence. The company's pension plan has no legal or other barriers to adoption of an international approach, and no non-U.S. pension liabilities currently exist.
    a. Identify and briefly discuss *three* reasons for adding international securities to the pension portfolio and *three* problems associated with such an approach. (8 minutes)
    b. Assume that the committee has adopted a policy to include international securities in its pension portfolio. Identify and briefly discuss *three* additional *policy-level* investment decisions the committee must make *before* management selection and actual implementation can begin. (12 minutes)

PROBLEMS

1. Elizabeth, a U.S. investor, buys several stocks that trade in Europe. Michael, a European investor, purchases several U.S.-traded stocks. Over the past year, Elizabeth's European portfolio gained 7 percent. Michael's portfolio of U.S stocks fell 5 percent. At the beginning of the past year the dollar/euro exchange rate was $1.05/€; at the end of the year the dollar/euro exchange rate was $1.15/€.

a. What was Elizabeth's percentage return in terms of the dollar?

b. What was Michael's percentage return in terms of the euro?

2. Compute the return to a U.S. investor from each of the following investments.

PERCENTAGE CHANGE IN TERMS OF:

Country	Local Returns	Exchange Rate ($/unit of foreign currency)
Russia	10.5%	−18.6%
U.K.	5.1	12.3
Germany	−12.5	14.3
Japan	−12.8	−4.5

CFA

3. *CFA Examination (Adapted)*

The following information is available concerning the historical risk and return relationships in the U.S. capital markets.

U.S. Capital Markets Total Annual Returns

Investment Category	Arithmetic Mean	Geometric Mean	Standard Deviation of Return[a]
Common stocks	10.28%	8.81%	16.9%
Treasury bills	6.54	6.49	3.2
Long-term government bonds	6.10	5.91	6.4
Long-term corporate bonds	5.75	5.35	9.6
Real estate	9.49	9.44	3.5

[a]Based on arithmetic mean.

a. Explain why the geometric and arithmetic mean returns are not equal and whether one or the other may be more useful for investment decision making. (5 minutes)

b. For the time period indicated, rank these investments on a risk-adjusted basis from most to least desirable. Explain your rationale. (6 minutes)

c. Assume the returns in these series are normally distributed.
   i. Calculate the range of returns that an investor would have expected to achieve 95 percent of the time from holding common stocks. (4 minutes)
   ii. Suppose an investor holds real estate for this time period. Determine the probability of at least breaking even on this investment. (5 minutes)

d. Assume you are holding a portfolio composed entirely of real estate. Discuss the justification, if any, for adopting a mixed asset portfolio by adding long-term government bonds. (5 minutes)

4. An investor in the 28 percent tax bracket is trying to decide which of two bonds to purchase. One is a corporate bond carrying an 8 percent coupon and selling at par. The other is a municipal bond with a $5\frac{1}{2}$ percent coupon, and it, too, sells at par. Assuming all other relevant factors are equal, which bond should the investor select?

5. An 8.4 percent coupon bond issued by the state of Indiana sells for $1,000. What coupon rate on a corporate bond selling at its $1,000 par value would produce the same after-tax return to the investor as this municipal bond if the investor is in

a. the 15 percent marginal tax bracket?
b. the 25 percent marginal tax bracket?
c. the 35 percent marginal tax bracket?

6. Consider the following bond quote for a $1,000 par value bond.

Company (Ticker)	Coupon	Maturity	Last Price
General Motors (GM)	8.375	Jul. 15, 2033	104.508

Last Yield	Est Spread	UST	Est $ Vol (000s)
7.974	276	30	70,928

a. What is the annual dollar coupon amount investors will receive?
b. How many bonds were traded during the day?
c. In dollars, what is the bond's price at the end of trading?
d. What is an estimate for the yield on a thirty-year Treasury bond?

7. Consider the following bond quote for a $1,000 par value bond.

Company (Ticker)	Coupon	Maturity	Last Price
Viacom (VIA)	7.700	Jul. 30, 2010	115.107

Last Yield	Est Spread	UST	Est $ Vol (000s)
4.791	118	5	39,697

a. When will the bond mature?
b. What is the current yield of the bond?
c. What semiannual coupon will investors receive?
d. In dollars, what is the bond's price at the end of trading?
e. What is the approximate yield to maturity on a five-year Treasury security?

8. Consider the following bond quote.

Rate	Maturity Mo/Yr	Bid	Asked	Chg.	Asked Yld
$5\frac{1}{2}$	Feb 08n	108:15	108:18	−7	3.94

a. What kind of bond is quoted?

b. What is the amount of the spread? What does the size of the spread tell you about the liquidity and amount of trading of this bond issue?

c. What is the price that would be paid by someone wanting to buy this bond? Someone wanting to sell?

d. What is a more correct yield-to-maturity estimate of this bond?

9. Consider the following stock quote.

52 weeks

Hi	Lo	Stock (Sym)
37.69	20.50	AnyCorp (ANYP)

Div	Yld. %	PE	Vol (100s)	Last	Net Chg
1.04	3.5	15	989	29.87	−0.23

a. What was the stock's last quarterly dividend?

b. How many shares were traded?

c. If an investor owned 200 shares, what would be the change in the value of her holdings given the change in price from the previous day?

d. Estimate the firm's earnings per share.

10. Consider the following stock quote.

52 weeks

Hi	Lo	Stock (Sym)
39.56	23.43	SomeCorp (SOMC)

Div	Yld. %	PE	Vol (100s)	Last	Net Chg
.36	1.1	18	15944	31.76	+0.26

a. If someone purchased the stock at its lowest price in the past year, what is their holding period return? Assume the dividend payment has remained constant over the year.

b. If someone purchased the stock at its highest price in the past year, what is their holding period return? Assume the dividend payment has remained constant over the year.

c. Verify that the dividend yield percentage is correct.

d. What was the closing price of the previous trading day?

e. Estimate the firm's earnings per share.

11. Using a recent edition of *Barron's,* examine the weekly percentage change in the stock price indexes for Japan, Germany, Italy, and the United States. For each of three weeks, which foreign series moved most closely with the U.S. series? Which series diverged most from the U.S. series? Discuss these results as they relate to global diversification.

12. You are given the following long-run annual rates of return for several investment instruments.

U.S. government T-bills	4.50%
Large-cap common stock	12.50%
Long-term corporate bonds	5.80%
Long-term government bonds	5.10%
Small-cap common stock	14.60%

a. On the basis of these returns, compute the following:
   i. The common-stock (equity) risk premium
   ii. The small-stock risk premium
   iii. The horizon (maturity) premium
   iv. The default premium

b. The annual rate of inflation during this period was 4 percent. Compute the real rate of return on these investment alternatives.

WEB EXERCISES

1. Using a source of international statistics, compare the percentage change in the following economic data for Japan, Germany, Canada, and the United States for a recent year. What were the differences, and which country or countries differed most from the United States?
   a. Aggregate output (GDP)
   b. Inflation
   c. Money supply growth

2. Using published sources (for example, *The Wall Street Journal, Barron's, Federal Reserve Bulletin*), look up the exchange rate for U.S. dollars with Japanese yen for each of the past ten years (you can use an average for the year or a specific time period each year). Based on these exchange rates, compute and discuss the yearly exchange rate effect on an investment in Japanese stocks by a U.S. investor. Discuss the impact of this exchange rate effect on the risk of Japanese stocks for a U.S. investor.

3. Visit *http://www.adrbny.com,* one of the more comprehensive Web sites for ADRs. What are the most frequently traded ADRs? How does this compare to the list mentioned in this chapter? What are the five largest countries whose firms have depository receipts?

4. What is the status of the world's financial markets? Some investment banks and brokerage houses, such as Smith Barney (*http://www.smithbarney.com*), Merrill Lynch (*http://www.ml.com*), or Morgan Stanley Capital International (*http://www.msci.com*), offer stock, bond, and global market research on their Web sites. Visit these three sites and report on the information they contain.

SPREADSHEET EXERCISES

1. Construct a table showing the taxable equivalent yields on corporate bonds using the current U.S. tax brackets (available from the IRS Web site) on municipal bond yields ranging from 4 percent to 10 percent, in half-point increments.

2. a. Construct a spreadsheet to compute U.S. dollar returns if the local currency return is known and the change in the exchange rate is known.
   b. Construct a spreadsheet that will compute the missing item if any two of U.S. dollar return, local currency return, and change in exchange rate are known.

3. Using the data from Exhibit 3.5, construct a table showing:
   a. The arithmetic and geometric mean returns for each country over the 1997–2003 time frame.
   b. The correlation between the U.S. dollar returns, based on (i) returns and (ii) relative ranks.

4. Using the data from Exhibit 3.5,
   a. Compute the mean return and standard deviation of each country's markets, in U.S.-dollar terms, across 1997–2003. Using this information, what is the mean return and standard deviation across all thirty-four countries?
   b. Randomly choose pairs of countries to form seventeen different two-country portfolios. Assuming equally weighted portfolios, compute the mean return and standard deviation of each portfolio's returns. Across all seventeen portfolios, what is the mean return and standard deviation?
   c. Randomly choose countries to form ten pairs of five-country portfolios. Assuming equally weighted portfolios, compute the mean return and standard deviation of each portfolio's returns. Across all ten portfolios, what is the mean return and standard deviation?
   d. Compare and contrast the mean return and risk for a one-country, two-country, and five-country portfolio.

5. Using the data in Exhibit 3.5, compute the correlation coefficients between the U.S. market's return and the U.S.-dollar returns of each of the other countries. Which countries offered U.S. investors the greatest risk-reduction benefits?

REFERENCES

Cavaglia, Stefano, Jeffrey Diermeier, Vadim Moroz, and Sonia De Zordo. "Investing in Global Equities." *Journal of Portfolio Management* (Spring 2004): 88–94.

Hopkins, Peter J. B., and C. Hayes Miller. *Country, Sector, and Company Factors in Global Equity Portfolios.* Charlottesville, VA: Research Foundation of Association for Investment Management and Research, 2001.

Reilly, Frank K., and David J. Wright. "Analysis of Risk-Adjusted Performance of Global Market Assets." *Journal of Portfolio Management* (Spring 2004): 63–77.

Rosenberg, Michael R. "International Fixed-Income Investing: Theory and Practice." In *The Handbook of Fixed-Income Securities,* 5th ed., edited by Frank J. Fabozzi. Chicago: Irwin Professional Publishing, 1997.

Solnik, Bruno, and Dennis McLeavey. *International Investments.* 5th ed. Boston: Pearson Addison-Wesley, 2004.

Squires, Jan, ed., *Global Bond Management.* Charlottesville, VA: Association for Investment Management and Research, 1997.

Steward, Christopher, and Adam Greshin. "International Bond Markets and Instruments." In *The Handbook of Fixed-Income Securities,* 5th ed., edited by Frank J. Fabozzi. Chicago: Irwin Professional Publishing, 1997.

THOMSON ONE
Business School Edition

1. Compare the performance of several country markets. Using the "index" tab, do a search on FTSE. You will obtain a list of many FTSE indexes. Select at least three from different countries or regions (such as Eurobloc, Americas, and Japan). How have their stock markets been performing of late?

2. Some indexes are presented in both U.S. dollar terms and in terms of other currencies. Compare the performance of the DJ Euro STOXX index in terms of euros and the U.S. dollar. Find one other index that will allow a comparision between two difference currencies and discuss their relative performance.

GLOSSARY

American Depository Receipts (ADRs) Certificates of ownership issued by a U.S. bank that represent indirect ownership of a certain number of shares of a specific foreign firm. Shares are held on deposit in a bank in the firm's home country.

Call option An option to buy a firm's common stock within a certain period at a specified price called the *strike price.*

Call provisions Specify when and how a firm can issue a call for bonds outstanding prior to their maturity.

Capital market instrument A fixed-income investment that trades in the secondary market.

Certificate for automobile receivables (CAR) An asset-backed security backed by pools of loans to an individual for financing an automobile purchase.

Certificate of deposit (CD) An instrument issued by banks and S&Ls that requires minimum deposits for specified terms and that pays higher rates of interest than savings accounts.

Collateralized mortgage obligation (CMO) A debt security, based on a pool of mortgage loans, that provides a relatively stable stream of payments for a relatively predictable term.

Collateral trust bond A mortgage bond wherein the assets backing the bond are financial assets like stocks and bonds.

Common stock An equity investment that represents ownership of a firm, with full participation in its success or failure. The firm's directors must approve dividend payments.

Convertible bond A bond with the added feature that the bondholder has the option to turn the bond back to the firm in exchange for a specified number of common shares of the firm.

Debentures Bonds that promise payments of interest and principal but pledge no specific assets. Holders have first claim on the issuer's income and unpledged assets.

Equipment trust certificates Mortgage bonds that are secured by specific pieces of transportation equipment like boxcars and planes.

Eurobond An international bond denominated in a currency not native to the country in which it is issued.

Exchange rate risk Uncertainty due to fluctuating exchange rates when investing in foreign securities.

Fixed-income investments Loans from investors to firms or governments, with contractually mandated payment schedules.

Futures contract An agreement that provides for the future exchange of a particular asset at a specified delivery date in exchange for a specified payment at the time of delivery.

General obligation bond (GO) A municipal bond backed by the full taxing power of the municipality.

Income bonds Debentures that stipulate interest payments only if the issuer earns the income to make the payments by specified dates.

Indenture The legal agreement that lists the obligations of the issuer of a bond to the bondholder including payment schedules, call provisions, and sinking funds.

International domestic bond A bond issued by a foreign firm, denominated in the firm's native currency, and sold within its own country.

Investment company A firm that sells shares of the company and uses the proceeds to buy stock, bonds, or other financial instruments.

Money market fund An investment company that holds portfolios of high-quality, short-term securities like T-bills. High liquidity and superior returns make this a good alternative to bank savings accounts.

Mortgage bonds Bonds that pledge specific assets such as buildings and equipment. The proceeds from the sale of these assets are used to pay off bondholders in case of bankruptcy.

Option The right to buy or sell a firm's common stock at a specified price for a stated period of time.

Preferred stock An equity investment that stipulates a dividend payment either as a coupon or a stated dollar amount. The firm's board of directors may withhold payments.

Put options An option to sell a firm's common stock within a certain period at a specified price.

Real estate investment trust (REIT) An investment fund that holds portfolios of real estate investment.

Revenue bond A municipal bond backed by revenue generated by specific municipal projects.

Savings account A money market security wherein an individual loans money to a bank or credit union through a liquid, low-risk, low-interest account.

Senior (secured) bonds The most senior bonds in a firm's capital structure. They have a first claim on specific assets of the firm in case of bankruptcy.

Subordinated bonds Debentures that, in case of default, entitle holders to claims on the issuer's assets only after the claims of holders of senior debentures and mortgage bonds are satisfied.

Yankee bond A bond sold in the United States and denominated in U.S. dollars but issued by a foreign firm or government.

Zero coupon bond A bond sold at a discount from par value that promises no interest payment during the life of the bond, only the payment of the par value (principal) at maturity.

Mutual Funds and Other Managed Investments

F rom the last chapter we know that mutual funds pool the savings of many investors to purchase securities with a general investment goal in mind. Mutual funds are gaining in popularity with individual investors. As of 2004, investors had nearly $7.5 trillion invested in mutual funds, and there were more mutual funds (about 9,700 according to one industry group) than there were stocks on the New York Stock Exchange. About half of all U.S. households own shares in at least one mutual fund. Since 1990, total mutual fund assets have increased 600 percent and the assets of mutual funds that invest in stocks have increased twentyfold.[1]

In this chapter we examine the advantages for the individual investor of using mutual funds, the different types of mutual funds, sources of information about mutual funds, and what studies have shown about mutual fund performance over time. We conclude with a review of other investments that at first glance may look like mutual funds but are not; these investments include closed-end investment companies, exchange-traded funds, and variable annuities.

What Is a Mutual Fund?

A *mutual fund* is an investment company that invests a pool of funds belonging to many individuals in a portfolio of investments such as stocks and bonds. Each individual in the pool owns a percentage of the investment company's total portfolio. As an example, a mutual fund might sell 10 million shares to the public at $10 a share for a total of $100 million. If this fund emphasized blue-chip stocks, the manager would invest the proceeds of the sale ($100 million less any commissions) in the stock of such companies as ExxonMobil, Microsoft, Wal-mart, General Motors, and General Electric.

---

[1]Eric M. Engen and Andreas Lehnert, "Mutual Funds and the U.S. Equity Market," *Federal Reserve Bulletin* (December 2000): 797–812.

The value of the mutual fund shares depends on the value of the portfolio of stocks. With no further transactions, if the market value of the stocks in the portfolio of our example increases to $105 million (net of any liabilities[2]), then each original share of the investment company would be worth $10.50 ($105 million/10 million shares). This per-share value, or *net asset value (NAV),* equals the total market value of all its assets, net of liabilities, divided by the number of fund shares outstanding:

4.1

$$\text{Net Asset Value} = \frac{\textbf{Market Value of Assets} - \textbf{Liabilities}}{\textbf{Number of Shares Outstanding}}$$

The management of the portfolio as well as most other administrative duties are handled by a separate *investment management company* hired by the board of directors of the mutual fund. Many management companies start numerous funds with different characteristics. Well-known companies such as Fidelity, Vanguard, and T. Rowe Price offer dozens of different funds under the name of the management company. The variety of funds allows the management group to appeal to many investors with different risk–return preferences. In addition, fund companies usually allow investors to switch among funds within the company at low or no cost as economic or personal conditions change. This "fund family" concept promotes flexibility and increases the total capital the investment firm manages. Fidelity Investments, the nation's largest investment company, offers more than two hundred mutual funds.

Mutual funds are more formally known as *open-end investment companies*. They are called "open-end" since they are prepared to sell additional shares of the fund to any who want to invest in it. Similarly, the mutual fund will redeem, or give investors the value of their shares (less any fees), whenever an investor wants to sell. A lesser-known type of investment company is the *closed-end investment company*. It is "closed-end" because once the company sells an initial offering of shares it neither issues additional shares nor redeems the shares. Investors who want to buy or sell closed-end investment company shares after the initial offering must trade through a broker, much like trading shares of stock in any publicly listed company.

WHY INVEST USING MUTUAL FUNDS?

The rising popularity of mutual funds is due to the attractive features they offer individual investors. Small investors can use the mutual fund organization to manage their day-to-day investment affairs, receiving many services previously relegated to large institutional investors. Specifically, advantages of using mutual funds include:

1. **Liquidity.** Investors buy and sell shares directly from the mutual fund. Such trades are priced at the NAV at the close of trading on the day (or sometimes the day after) the order arrives at the fund.
2. **Diversification.** Money invested in the fund is automatically diversified across all the fund's investments. Thus a small investor can get ownership in a diversified portfolio for as little as $500 (or less), depending on the fund's minimum investment requirements.
3. **Professional management and record-keeping.** The mutual fund's professional managers access research on economic and company trends to judge what securities to purchase

---

[2]Liabilities may include money borrowed to purchase additional securities (this is known as trading on *margin* and will be discussed in detail in Chapter 6) or payables for management fees and for securities purchased but not yet paid for. The amount of liabilities is usually quite small compared to the total assets of a mutual fund. For example, in 2004 Fidelity Magellan Fund had liabilities equal to 0.70 percent of assets. Vanguard's Asset Allocation Fund had liabilities of less than 0.4 percent of assets.

and when to trade them. The fund will keep track of all fund share purchases as well as income and capital gains (or losses) from the fund's investments.

4. **Choice and flexibility.** Fund families offer a wide variety of funds to meet the investment goals of diverse individuals. Fund families allow fund investors no-cost or very low-cost switching from one fund to another.

5. **Indexing.** An investor who believes that markets are reasonably efficient can select mutual fund investments in "index" funds, which are especially designed and managed to track a broad market index such as the S&P 500 for stocks or the Lehman Brothers Aggregate Bond Index for bonds.

Interactive e-lectures
For more explanation and an animated example of mutual funds, go to: http://reillyxtra .swlearning.com

With these advantages, it is hard to imagine that mutual funds have drawbacks, but they do. For a small investor the following points may seem minor, but they can cause difficulties:

1. **Portfolio turnover.** Most mutual funds do not buy and hold securities; they actively trade them based on price changes and the outlook for market sectors (technology, health care, telecom, consumer goods, etc.). Such active trading, which may lead to complete turnover of a portfolio every twelve months (or sooner), can lead to high trading costs and brokerage commissions, which in turn can lower fund returns.

2. **Control over taxation.** Because of the securities they select and portfolio turnover, the fund will receive income from its investments and realized capital gains (and losses) that are passed on to the fund's shareholders. Every year, the income and realized capital gains/losses are reported to investors and the IRS. Thus, an investor who thought he had sufficient money set aside to pay the year's taxes may be surprised by unexpected capital gains tax liabilities. Such an event can be financially painful if securities prices (and fund NAVs) fall after beginning-of-year capital gains are realized. Such a scenario in 2000 left some shareholders with a capital gains tax bill but fund shares that had declined in value, in some cases, by 30 percent or more by year-end.

SOURCES OF RETURN

There are three sources of return for mutual fund investors. First, there is income from the fund's investments (such as bond interest or stock dividends). Second, as mentioned above, there may be realized capital gains or losses when the fund's managers sell securities. Third, changes in the fund's NAV can result in a capital gain or loss when the shares are redeemed. Only in the third situation does the investor have some control.

Most mutual funds allow investors to choose either to receive distributions in cash or to have the income and capital gains reinvested in additional shares. We can use this data to calculate the return on a mutual fund investment. Recall our calculation of holding period returns in Chapter 2; Equation 2.2, repeated here, states that

4.2 $$\text{Holding Period Return (HPR)} = \frac{\text{Income} + \text{Price Change}}{\text{Purchase Price}}$$

In the case of mutual funds, the "Income" in the equation includes both kinds of distributions, income and capital gain. The "Price Change" refers to the change in net asset value over the time frame. For a mutual fund, the holding period return is

4.3 $$\text{HPR} = \frac{\text{Income Distribution} + \text{Capital Gains Distribution} + \text{Ending NAV} - \text{Beginning NAV}}{\text{Beginning NAV}}$$

Data on distributions and net asset values can be obtained from a fund's prospectus, which, by law, an investor must receive before committing funds. A *prospectus* provides information about the fund's objectives, historical and forecast expenses, historical returns, investment strategy, and risks, as well as information about how to buy and sell fund shares and when dividends and capital gains are distributed to fund shareholders. As we shall soon examine, not all the money placed in a mutual fund is invested and earns returns. Some is used to pay the expenses of marketing the funds, hiring investment advisers, and paying commissions.

TYPES OF INVESTMENT COMPANIES BASED ON PORTFOLIO OBJECTIVES

Mutual funds can be classified in a variety of ways. One is to classify them by the type of security in which they invest. Exhibit 4.1 uses a Lipper Inc.'s classification scheme based on

---

EXHIBIT 4.1   Types of Mutual Funds

MUTUAL-FUND OBJECTIVES

Categories compiled by The Wall Street Journal, based on classifications by Lipper Inc.

STOCK FUNDS

Emerging Markets (EM): Funds that invest in emerging-market equity securities, where the "emerging market" is defined by a country's GNP per capita and other economic measures.

Equity Income (EI): Funds that seek high current income and growth of income through investment in equities.

European Region (EU): Funds that invest in markets or operations concentrated in the European region.

Global Stock (GL): Funds that invest in securities traded outside of the U.S. and may own U.S. securities as well.

Gold Oriented (AU): Funds that invest in gold mines, gold-oriented mining finance houses, gold coins or bullion.

Health/Biotech (HB): Funds that invest in companies related to health care, medicine and biotechnology.

International Stock (IL) (non-U.S.): Canadian; International; International Small Cap.

Latin American (LT): Funds that invest in markets or operations concentrated in the Latin American region.

Large-Cap Growth (LG): Funds that invest in large companies with long-term earnings that are expected to grow significantly faster than the earnings of stocks in major indexes. Funds normally have above-average price-to-earnings ratios, price-to-book ratios and three-year earnings growth.

Large-Cap Core (LC): Funds that invest in large companies, with wide latitude in the type of shares they buy. On average, the price-to-earnings ratios, price-to-book ratios, and three-year earnings growth are in line with those of the U.S. diversified large-cap funds' universe average.

Large-Cap Value (LV): Funds that invest in large companies that are considered undervalued relative to major stock indexes based on price-to-earnings ratios, price-to-book ratios or other factors.

Midcap Growth (MG): Funds that invest in midsize companies with long-term earnings that are expected to grow significantly faster than the earnings of stocks in major indexes. Funds normally have above-average price-to-earnings ratios, price-to-book ratios and three-year earnings growth.

Midcap Core (MC): Funds that invest in midsize companies, with wide latitude in the type of shares they buy. On average, the price-to-earnings ratios, price-to-book ratios, and three-year earnings growth are in line with those of the U.S. diversified midcap funds' universe average.

Midcap Value (MV): Funds that invest in midsize companies that are considered undervalued relative to major stock indexes based on price-to-earnings ratios, price-to-book ratios or other factors.

Multicap Growth (XG): Funds that invest in companies of various sizes, with long-term earnings that are expected to grow significantly faster than the earnings of stocks in major indexes. Funds normally have above-average price-to-earnings ratios, price-to-book ratios, and three-year earnings growth.

Multicap Core (XC): Funds that invest in companies of various sizes with average price-to-earnings ratios, price-to-book ratios and earnings growth.

Multicap Value (XV): Funds that invest in companies of various size, normally those that are considered undervalued relative to major stock indexes based on price-to-earnings ratios, price-to-book ratios or other factors.

Natural Resources (NR): Funds that invest in natural-resource stocks.

Pacific Region (PR): Funds that invest in China Region; Japan; Pacific Ex-Japan; Pacific Region.

Science & Technology (TK): Funds that invest in science and technology stocks. Includes telecommunication stocks.

Sector (SE): Funds that invest in financial services; real estate; specialty & miscellaneous.

S&P 500 Index (SP): Funds that are passively managed and are designed to replicate the performance of the Standard & Poor's 500-stock Index on a reinvested basis.

Small-Cap Growth (SG): Funds that invest in small companies with long-term earnings that are expected to grow significantly faster than the earnings of stocks in major indexes. Funds normally have above-average price-to-earnings ratios, price-to-book ratios, and three-year earnings growth.

Small-Cap Core (SC): Funds that invest in small companies, with wide latitude in the type of shares they buy. On average, the price-to-earnings ratios, price-to-book ratios, and three-year earnings growth are in line with those of the U.S. diversified small-cap funds' universe average.

Small-Cap Value (SV): Funds that invest in small companies that are considered undervalued relative to major stock indexes based on price-to-earnings ratios, price-to-book ratios or other factors.

Specialty Equity (SQ): Funds that invest in all market-capitalization ranges, with no restrictions for any one range. May have strategies that are distinctly different from other diversified stock funds.

Utility (UT): Funds that invest in utility stocks.

TAXABLE BOND FUNDS

Short-Term Bond (SB): Ultra-short Obligation; Short Investment Grade Debt; Short-Intermediate Investment Grade Debt.

Short-Term U.S. (SU): Short U.S. Treasury; Short U.S. Government; Short-Intermediate U.S. Government debt.

Intermediate Bond (IB): Funds that invest in investment-grade debt issues (rated in the top four grades) with dollar-weighted average maturities of five to 10 years.

Intermediate U.S. (IG): Intermediate U.S. Government; Intermediate U.S. Treasury.

Long-Term Bond (AB): Funds that invest in corporate- and government-debt issues in the top grades.

Long-Term U.S. (LU): General U.S. Government; General U.S. Treasury; Target Maturity.

General U.S. Taxable (GT): Funds that invest in general bonds.

High-Yield Taxable (HC): Funds that aim for high current yields from fixed-income securities and tend to invest in lower-grade debt.

Mortgage (MT): Adjustable Rate Mortgage; GNMA; U.S. Mortgage.

World Bond (WB): Emerging Markets Debt; Global Income; International Income; Short World Multi-Market Income.

MUNICIPAL DEBT FUNDS

Short-Term Muni (SM): California Short-Intermediate Muni Debt; Other States Short-Intermediate Muni Debt; Short-Intermediate Muni Debt; Short Muni Debt.

Intermediate Muni (IM): Intermediate-term Muni Debt including single states.

General Muni (GM): Funds investing in muni-debt issues in the top-four credit ratings.

Single-State Municipal (SS): Funds that invest in debt of individual states.

High-Yield Municipal (HM): Funds that invest in lower-rated muni debt.

Insured Muni (NM): California Insured Muni Debt; Florida Insured Muni Debt; Insured Muni Debt; New York Insured Muni Debt.

STOCK & BOND FUNDS

Balanced (BL): Primary objective is to conserve principal, by maintaining a balanced portfolio of both stocks and bonds.

Stock/Bond Blend (MP): Multipurpose funds such as Balanced Target Maturity; Convertible Securities; Flexible Income; Flexible Portfolio; Global Flexible and Income funds, that invest in both stocks and bonds.

Note: *The Wall Street Journal* records money market mutual funds in listings separate from other mutual funds, so these are not mentioned here.

Source: *The Wall Street Journal*, July 6, 2004, p. R13. Copyright © 2004 Dow Jones. Reprinted by permission of Copyright Clearance Center.

four broad categories (stock, taxable bond, municipal debt, and stock-and-bond funds) and forty-five subcategories. The trade organization for investment companies, the Investment Company Institute, uses four broad categories (equity, hybrid, bond, and money market) and thirteen subcategories. Morningstar, a popular source of mutual fund information, uses four broad categories (domestic stock, international stock, taxable bond, and municipal bond) and forty-eight subcategories. These asset categories include a variety of funds, from those that invest in the broad asset market to those that invest in narrow segments, and from those that invest aggressively to those that have a conservative focus. Let's briefly review the variety of funds.

Common-Stock Funds   With over $3.8 trillion in assets (as of 2004), stock funds are the most popular type of mutual fund. Some funds invest almost solely in common stocks, whereas others invest in preferred stocks and bonds. Within the category of common-stock funds, there are wide differences in emphasis, including funds that focus on growth companies; small-cap stocks; or companies in specific industries, sectors, or even geographic areas. International equity funds invest only in non-U.S. securities; global equity funds invest worldwide, both in U.S. and non-U.S. stocks. Conservative equity funds have equity income as their primary objective; more aggressive funds include some of the sector funds, small-company funds, and those whose main objective is capital appreciation. Index funds also are available.

Taxable Bond Funds   Bond funds generally seek to generate current income with minimal risk, although several aggressive bond funds exist. Investors can choose funds that invest in a certain segment of the yield curve (short-, intermediate-, or long-term maturities), in different sectors (governments, corporates, mortgage-backed, or high-yield), or in funds that focus on domestic or global securities. Management strategies of these funds can range from buy-and-hold to extensive trading in an attempt to earn high total returns (income plus capital gains). Index funds also are available.

Municipal Bond Funds   These funds provide investors with monthly interest payments that are exempt from federal income taxes, although some of the interest may be subject to state and local taxes. To avoid the state tax, some municipal bond funds concentrate on bonds from specific states; for example, the New York Municipal Bond Fund allows New York residents to avoid most state taxes on the interest income. As with taxable bonds, investors can find funds that concentrate on short-, intermediate-, or long-term bonds.

Stock-and-Bond Funds   These are known by a variety of names, such as balanced funds, blended funds, or flexible funds. Their objective is to maximize return or income by combining common stock with fixed-income securities including government bonds, corporate bonds, convertible bonds, or preferred stock. The ratio of stocks to fixed-income securities will vary by fund, as stated in each fund's prospectus.

Money Market Funds   With about $2 trillion in assets, money market funds are second only to stock funds in size. Money market funds attempt to provide current income, safety of principal, and liquidity by investing in a diversified portfolio of short-term securities such as Treasury bills, bank CDs, bank acceptances, and commercial paper. They typically have no up-front costs and, unlike bank CDs, impose no penalty for withdrawal at any time. They typically allow holders to write checks against their account. Their NAV is constant at $1; any income earned is returned to the investor or is reinvested in additional shares. Notably, money invested in money market mutual funds is *not* government insured.[3] Yields on money market mutual funds generally exceed those of interest-bearing bank checking accounts.

INNOVATIONS

In the recent past, two innovations arose in the mutual fund industry: life-stage funds and mutual fund "supermarkets." Life-stage funds allocate investors' money among three to five mutual cash, bond, and stock funds that reflect expert views of how money should be allocated across asset classes given the objectives and constraints of an "average" thirty-, forty-, fifty-, or sixty-year-old, or from the perspective of someone who wants to withdraw his or her funds ten, twenty, or thirty (or more) years in the future. Such funds are useful in that they can allocate assets for investors automatically. However, since some life-stage funds have higher expenses than their component parts, investors may be able to save money by allocating investment dollars themselves among stock, bond, and cash funds.[4]

Fund "supermarkets" are somewhat more controversial. Offered by firms such as Charles Schwab, Fidelity Investments, and brokerage houses such as Merrill Lynch and Citigroup, the supermarket allows investors one-stop fund shopping. They can invest in a broad array of funds, not just the sponsoring firm's "in-house" funds. Investors can transfer money from one firm's fund to another firm's without paying fees that would ordinarily occur. But such convenience comes at a price: In addition to paying regular mutual fund fees (to be described in the following section), supermarkets require the funds to pay twenty-five to forty cents for every $100 (or 0.25–0.40 percent) invested through the supermarket; some require an additional up-front fee when a new fund joins the supermarket.[5]

The Prospectus

The mutual fund prospectus is a valuable information and research source for mutual fund investors. It should be reviewed prior to committing funds to a mutual fund. Thanks to the

---

[3]Known as breaking the buck (that is, dipping below the $1 NAV), losses can occur if overly aggressive managers invest funds in risky assets such as derivative securities or low-rated commercial paper of an issuer that later defaults. This happened in 1994 to Community Bankers U.S. Government Money Market Fund, a money market fund catering to large institutions and corporations, when its shares fell to 94 cents. Mutual fund families have at times pumped money into their money market fund to cover such losses to protect their investors and the reputation of their funds. Stricter SEC regulations following a commercial paper panic in the early 1990s have helped to reduce risk in money market mutual funds. Despite this, a default in 1997 on commercial paper issued by Mercury Finance Company caused Strong Capital Management to purchase Mercury's paper from three of its money market funds to prevent the loss on the defaulted paper from causing the funds to break the buck. California's energy crisis in 2001 caused a commercial paper default by Southern California Edison and Pacific Gas and Electric. At least five fund families (including Scudder Kemper Investments and Dreyfus Founders) had to purchase defaulted commercial paper from their money funds to prevent them from breaking the buck. See Lewis Braham, "Money Market Funds Enter the Danger Zone," *Business Week,* April 9, 2001, p. 86; Julie Creswel and Robert McGough, "Money-Market Funds Nearly 'Break the Buck,'" *The Wall Street Journal,* February 4, 1997, C1; and Charles Gasparino, "Mercury Lights Up Money-Fund Flaw," *The Wall Street Journal,* February 7, 1997, C25.

[4]But if they do so, investors will need to periodically rebalance their allocations themselves. Exceptional good or poor performance in a fund will make the portfolio's asset allocation differ from the investor's desired allocation. Such rebalancing occurs automatically in a life-stage fund. More will be said about asset allocation in Chapter 5.

[5] Terri Cullen, "Big Brokers Adopt Supermarket Approach," *The Wall Street Journal,* July 31, 2000, p. C27; Ellen E. Schultz and Vanessa O'Connell, "No Free Lunch: 'Supermarket' Fees Lift Costs," *The Wall Street Journal,* September 18, 1996, pp. C1, C25; and David Whitford, "The Mutual Fund Revolution: Is It Good for You?" *Fortune* (February 3, 1997): 136–140.

Securities and Exchange Commission's regulations requiring "plain English," the prospectus is now easier to read. A prospectus will contain information about:

- The fund's investment objective (total return, income, etc.).
- Investment strategies, or the type of securities in which the fund will invest as it tries to meet its objective.
- Principal risks faced by investors in the fund (effects of up and down markets, changing interest rates, changing exchange rates, etc.).
- Recent investment performance. An SEC-mandated table must be included to show the mutual fund's performance over the most recent one-, five-, and ten-year periods in comparison to an appropriate market index return and an average return for mutual funds with similar objectives. The table must show the effects of any load (up-front commissions) that would be paid by an investor at the beginning of these three time periods. For example, part (a) of Exhibit 4.2 shows the investment performance information on two of the largest (in terms of assets) mutual funds: Fidelity Magellan, which invests in stocks with a goal of capital appreciation, and Vanguard 500 Index Fund, which seeks to track the S&P 500 stock-market index.
- Fees and expenses. The fees and expenses must be shown in an SEC-mandated format. (See part (b) of Exhibit 4.2). This important table indicates how much of the fund's returns are never seen by the investor as money is paid for commissions, costs of managing the fund, advertising costs, and other operating expenses. In addition, the SEC requires a separate table to show the hypothetical costs of the fees and expenses. (See part (c) of Exhibit 4.2). This table shows the fees and expenses that would be paid following a $10,000 investment in the fund assuming a 5 percent annual return and no change in expenses over one-, three-, five-, and ten-year time periods. (We will discuss the fees and expenses in more detail shortly).
- Other useful information. The prospectus will detail how to buy and sell (redeem) shares in the fund, along with Internet addresses, street addresses, and phone numbers for contacting the fund. Minimum investment requirements are listed, although many times lower minimums are allowed for IRA accounts or if the investor promises to make regular purchases of additional shares over time. Another important piece of information in the prospectus is the distribution dates for dividends and capital gains. A common mistake for investors with taxable accounts is to purchase shares of a mutual fund just before the distribution date. Suppose an investor purchases 400 fund shares at $25 per share for a total investment of $10,000. The next day, a distribution of $2 is paid, reducing the NAV to $23 (ignoring market price changes). The investment is still worth $10,000 ($23 × 400 shares = $9200 plus 400 shares × $2 cash distribution = $800 in distributions), but under IRS regulations the investor owes tax on the $800 distribution (even if it is reinvested automatically) even though it seems to represent funds just invested.

MUTUAL FUND COSTS

Mutual funds offer liquidity, diversification, and professional management to the small investor. But such services are not free. In this section we discuss some of the expenses associated with mutual fund investing.

Load   Some mutual funds charge a *load,* or commission, when an investor buys the fund. The stated purpose of the load is to pay a commission to the financial planner or broker selling the fund. The offering price for a share of a load fund equals the NAV plus a *sales charge,* which can be as high as 8.5 percent of the NAV. If a fund has an 8 percent sales

EXHIBIT 4.2	Average Annual Total Returns, Fees, and Expenses

(a) RETURNS FOR YEARS ENDED DECEMBER 31, 2003

	Past 1 Year	Past 5 Years	Past 10 Years
Fidelity Magellan			
Return before taxes	24.82%	−1.08%	9.17%
Return after taxes on distributions	24.67	−1.84	7.48
Return after taxes on distributions and sale of fund shares	16.32	−1.15	7.17
S&P 500 (reflects no deduction for fees, expenses, or taxes)	28.69	−0.57	11.07
Lipper Growth Funds average (reflects no deduction for sales charges or taxes)	29.63	−0.66	8.66

	Past 1 Year	Past 5 Years	Past 10 Years
Vanguard 500 Index Fund			
Return before taxes	28.50%	−0.63%	10.99%
Return after taxes on distributions	28.20	−1.09	10.24
Return after taxes on distributions and sale of fund shares	18.86	−0.78	9.33
S&P 500 (reflects no deduction for fees, expenses, or taxes)	28.69	−0.57	11.07
Lipper Growth Funds average (reflects no deduction for sales charges or taxes)	29.63	−0.66	8.66

(b) FEES

	Fidelity	Vanguard
Shareholder fees (paid by the investor)		
Sales charge (load) on purchases	None	None
Sales charge (load) on reinvested dividends	None	None
Deferred sales charge on redemptions	None	None
Annual fund operating expenses		
Management fee	0.50%	0.16%
Distribution and service (12b-1) fee	None	None
Other expenses	0.20%	0.02%
Total annual fund operating expenses	0.70%	0.18%

(c) EXPENSES

Hypothetical expenses from investing ($10,000 initial investment, 5% assumed annual return, operating expenses remain constant) over the following time periods:

	Fidelity	Vanguard
1 year	$72	$18
3 years	$224	$58
5 years	$390	$101
10 years	$871	$230

charge, an individual who invests $1,000 will receive shares that are worth $920, with $80 paid as a commission. A *no-load* imposes no initial sales charge and sells shares at the NAV. Between the full-load fund and the pure no-load fund are several variations. One is the *low-load*, which imposes a low front-end sales charge, typically about 3 percent. Investors with large amounts to invest may be able to purchase shares with a smaller load. For example, a fund with a 3 percent load may charge the full 3 percent on investments under $250,000, 2 percent on investments between $250,000 and $499,999, 1 percent on those between $500,000 and $999,999, and no load on those of $1 million or more.

12b-1 Fees   These fees, named after the SEC rule that originated them, permit funds to deduct as much as 0.75 percent of average net assets *per year* to cover distribution costs such as advertising, commissions paid to brokers, and general marketing expenses.[6] Thus, rather than have investors pay a front-end load, under 12b-1 fees a fund collects money to pay marketing expenses over time.

Deferred Sales Load   This fee is also called a *redemption charge* or a *rear-end load*. With a deferred sales load, investors pay when they sell or redeem their shares instead of when they purchase them. Often these sales charges are steep—5 to 7 percent—if shares are sold within a year of their purchase, but the charges decline over time, usually at a rate of one percentage point a year. Thus, an investor who holds the shares for a long period of time may pay no deferred sales charge.

It is important to note that none of these sales charges—loads, 12b-1 fees, or deferred sales charges—relate to the fund's performance. Their sole purpose is to finance commissions, 1-800 phone numbers and Web sites, supermarket fees, and advertising material (print, radio, and TV).

The details regarding a fund's charges are found in the fund's prospectus. As a marketing tool, some load mutual funds offer investors a choice regarding how commissions and marketing expenses can be paid by offering "A," "B," or "C" fund shares. Class A shares pay the usual front-end load charge and low annual expenses. Class B shares do not have an initial load, but have an annual 12b-1 charge and a deferred sales charge for shareholders selling after only a few years. After a specified number of years, during which the equivalent of the front-end load fee has been paid, the class B shares convert into class A shares, which means only annual expenses are paid. Class C shares have no front-end load or redemption charge, but they do have a 12b-1 fee that is never canceled.

Sophisticated investors will compare the impact of front-end loads versus 12b-1 fees over their investment horizon to determine which is the less expensive alternative. Typically, investors who anticipate redeeming their investment in the near future are better off with a 12b-1 fee. Due to the cumulative nature of 12b-1 fees, long-term investors who plan to buy a fund's shares and hold them into the foreseeable future may be better off paying only a front-end load.

Exhibit 4.3 presents a scenario in which we assume

- a 5% annual return,
- a 5 percent front-end load for class A shares,
- a 5 percent deferred sales charge for class B shares that is eliminated after five years (and an annual fee that shrinks from 1 percent to 0.25 percent over five years), and
- a 1 percent 12b-1 fee for class C shares.

With these return and expense assumptions, we see that investors are better off paying the front-end load (class A) if they expect to hold the shares twelve years or longer. Shorter-term investors benefit from paying the 1 percent 12b-1 fee (class C). Class B shares become attractive after sufficient time has passed to eliminate the deferred sales charge and are the best choice for intermediate-term investors.

---

[6]Under SEC rules, mutual funds can charge no more than 0.75 percent for 12b-1 fees and 0.25 percent in "service" fees, which are used to compensate brokers for maintaining records of your investments. Prior to these SEC ceilings, many funds charged up to 1.25 percent for 12b-1 fees.

EXHIBIT 4.3	Comparison of Returns on Class A, B, and C Shares over Time

Initial investment	$10,000
Annual return	5%
Decline rate of DSC deferred sales charge	1.00% per year
Class B fees decline to	0.25%
after	5 years

	Class A Shares	Class B Shares	Class C Shares
Load	5.00%	0.00%	0.00%
12b-1 fee	0.00%	0.00%	1.00%
Other fees	0.00%	1.00%	0.00%
Deferred sales charge	0.00%	5.00%	0.00%

Value If Sold at End of Year

	Class A Shares	Class B Shares	Class C Shares	Preferred Class
1	$9,975.00	$9,875.25	$10,395.00	C
2	$10,473.75	$10,389.10	$10,805.60	C
3	$10,997.44	$10,945.03	$11,232.42	C
4	$11,547.31	$11,546.90	$11,676.10	C
5	$12,124.67	$12,198.96	$12,137.31	B
6	$12,730.91	$12,905.95	$12,616.73	B
7	$13,367.45	$13,517.37	$13,115.10	B
8	$14,035.83	$14,157.76	$13,633.14	B
9	$14,737.62	$14,828.48	$14,171.65	B
10	$15,474.50	$15,530.98	$14,731.43	B
11	$16,248.22	$16,266.76	$15,313.32	B
12	$17,060.64	$17,037.40	$15,918.20	A
13	$17,913.67	$17,844.54	$16,546.97	A
14	$18,809.35	$18,689.93	$17,200.57	A
15	$19,749.82	$19,575.36	$17,880.00	A
16	$20,737.31	$20,502.75	$18,586.26	A
17	$21,774.17	$21,474.06	$19,320.41	A
18	$22,862.88	$22,491.40	$20,083.57	A
19	$24,006.03	$23,556.93	$20,876.87	A
20	$25,206.33	$24,672.94	$21,701.51	A

Management Fees   The major duties of the investment management company are invest-ment research, portfolio management, and administrative duties such as issuing securities and handling redemptions and dividends. For these management and operational duties, the management company charges an annual management fee. Some mutual funds (such as Fidelity Magellan) have a management fee that is adjusted up or down by a preset formula to reward (or punish) the fund's managers if the fund earns returns higher (or lower) than a target index (the S&P 500 in the case of Fidelity.)

Expense Ratio   The fund's expenses are the sum of its management fees, 12b-1 fees, and other expenses. Operating expenses are paid out of each fund's assets and therefore lower the fund's returns to shareholders. The expense ratio represents the fund's annual expenses expressed as a percentage of the fund's assets.

A fund's expense ratio will depend on the fund's objectives and management philosophy. All else equal, a passively managed index fund has a lower expense ratio than an actively managed fund; an aggressive growth equity fund generally has a higher expense ratio than a more conservative equity income fund. (For example, see Exhibit 4.2.)

A charge against shareholder return that does not appear in the expense ratio is the cost of commissions paid by the fund to trade securities. Information on trading commissions is not easily found; investors must examine the fund's *Statement of Additional Information,* which is available upon request as well as on fund Web sites. At times the cost of trading does not significantly add to the overall expenses; for example, in 2004 Magellan's expense ratio would rise from 0.70 percent of net assets to 0.73 percent if commissions were included. For some other funds, trading commissions can effectively double the reported expense ratio. For example, in early 2004 the expense ratio of the Van Eck International Investors Gold Fund (A shares) would rise from 1.965 percent of net assets to 5.817 percent if commissions were included.[7] One reason for high trading commissions is high portfolio turnover.

Portfolio Turnover Another cost from investing in mutual funds does not explicitly appear in the prospectus, but its effect is reflected in shareholder returns. As must any investor, the mutual fund's managers pay commissions whenever they purchase or sell securities. In the prospectus, mutual funds must report portfolio turnover. A portfolio turnover of 100 percent implies that, on average, the securities owned by the mutual fund are "turned over" once—were bought and sold once—during the year. In other words, on average, all securities owned in January were sold and replaced by another set of securities by December. If we take the portfolio turnover rate, divide it by 100, and then divide 12 by the resulting number, we can determine the *average holding period* for securities in the portfolio:

4.4 $$\text{Average Holding Period for Fund Securities} = \frac{12 \text{ Months}}{(\text{Portfolio Turnover}/100)}$$

For example, the average holding period for a portfolio with a turnover is 125 percent is

$$\frac{12 \text{ Months}}{(125/100)} = 9.6 \text{ Months}$$

If the portfolio turnover is 33 percent, the average holding period is

$$\frac{12 \text{ Months}}{(33/100)} = 36.36 \text{ Months, or about 3 Years}$$

Some funds report portfolio turnover rates of 150 percent, 200 percent, or higher. Because commissions are paid with every stock or bond purchase and sale, higher turnover rates result in higher brokerage commissions, and, all else equal, lower net returns to the investor. A fund's turnover rates are higher when the purpose of the fund is to aggressively seek capital gains, when the financial markets are particularly volatile, or when the fund experiences unusually high cash inflows and outflows from sales and redemptions of mutual fund shares.

[7]John Hechinger, "Deciphering Funds' Hidden Costs," *The Wall Street Journal,* March 17, 2004, pp. D1, D2.

Other Sources of Information about Mutual Funds

Because of the wide variety of funds available, it is wise to examine the performance of various funds over time to understand each one's goals and management philosophies. Daily and monthly information for numerous open-end funds appear in *The Wall Street Journal. Barron's* publishes quarterly updates on the performance of various funds during the previous ten years. *Forbes* issues an annual survey of mutual funds. *Business Week* publishes a "Mutual Fund Scoreboard" containing information on performance (both risk-adjusted performance and total return), sales charges (including those for 12b-1 plans), expenses, portfolio yield and maturity, and telephone numbers for all the funds.

A major source of comprehensive historical information is an annual publication issued by Arthur Wiesenberger Services entitled *Investment Companies Yearbook,* which contains detailed profiles of the 600 most well-known funds. Each profile includes a brief history, investment objectives and portfolio analysis, statistical history, special services available, personnel, advisers and distributors, sales charges, and a chart of the value of a hypothetical $10,000 investment over ten years. The Wiesenberger book also contains a summary list with annual rates of return and price volatility measures for a number of funds not profiled.

Morningstar's popular *Morningstar Mutual Funds* evaluates the performance of more than 1,300 open-end mutual funds and provides an informative one-page sheet on each fund. This sheet provides up-to-date information about a fund and its performance, as well as a short analysis of the fund by one of Morningstar's analysts. Morningstar popularized the use of 3 × 3 style boxes, as shown in Exhibit 4.4. Equity securities are classified according to market-capitalization size (small, medium, and large) and style value (generally, low P/E ratios), growth (high P/E), or blend. The fund is then categorized according to the preponderance of style/size characteristics of its holdings. For example, in Exhibit 4.4, Fidelity Magellan is shown as a large blend. Similarly, a fund's bond holdings are classified according to time to maturity and credit quality. Thus Vanguard's High-Yield Corporate Bond fund is shown as investing in intermediate-term, low-quality bonds.

Tax analysis is gaining importance as a way to evaluate funds. Funds generating much income—or generating capital gains through frequent trading—increase the taxable income of the fund's shareholders. Thus many information sources include estimates of a fund's tax efficiency, based on a typical investor's income tax bracket and capital gains tax rates. One

EXHIBIT 4.4	Style Boxes for Mutual Funds

EQUITY: FIDELITY MAGELLAN FUND   **FIXED INCOME: VANGUARD HIGH-YIELD CORPORATE BOND FUND**

popular measure of tax efficiency first estimates the fund's tax-adjusted return, that is, the return an investor would earn after paying taxes on the fund's income and capital gain distributions.[8] Then the fund's tax efficiency is simply the after-tax or tax-adjusted return divided by the pre-tax return:

$$
\boxed{4.5} \qquad \textbf{Tax Efficiency} = \frac{\textbf{Tax-Adjusted Return}}{\textbf{Pre-Tax Return}}
$$

The higher the tax efficiency percentage, the more beneficial for the fund's taxable investors.

Performance of Investment Companies

Many studies have examined the historical performance of mutual funds because these funds reflect the performance of professional money managers. The basic result of these studies supports the concept of efficient markets: It is difficult for mutual funds to consistently outperform their benchmark indexes after taking risk differences into account. Numerous studies, both in the academic and popular press, have found below-average returns on actively managed equity and bond funds over varying periods of time. Studies also indicate that, after controlling for other mutual fund characteristics, funds with lower expense ratios earn, on average, higher returns, as do funds with lower portfolio turnover ratios.

MUTUAL FUND RISK AND RETURN PERFORMANCE

An investor considering buying a fund needs to know whether the fund's performance is consistent with its stated objective. For example, does the performance of a balanced fund reflect less risk and lower return than an aggressive growth fund? To answer such questions, several studies have examined the relationship between funds' stated objectives and their measures of return, risk, and investment style (large-cap, small-cap, value, growth).

Return Performance Numerous studies on equity mutual fund performance have generally agreed on the following findings: On a risk-adjusted basis, equity mutual funds outperform indexes based on *gross* returns (that is, ignoring expenses). But once the expenses of investing and managing the fund are considered, mutual funds earn *net* returns that are lower than the market average. Similar results have been found for international equity mutual funds and for bond mutual funds.[9]

The average equity fund has an expense ratio of 1.52 percent whereas the average equity index fund's expense ratio is 0.75 percent (one of the lowest-expense index funds

---

[8]Morningstar's tax calculation assumes that all income and short-term capital gain distributions are taxed at a federal tax rate of 39.6 percent at the time of distribution. Long-term capital gains are taxed at a 20 percent rate. The after-tax portion is then reinvested in the fund. State and local taxes are ignored. A specific individual investor's marginal tax rate and tax situation will determine the investor's after-tax return.

[9]Ravi Shukla, "The Value of Active Portfolio Management," *Journal of Economics and Business* 56 (July 2004): 331–346; Russ Wermers, "Mutual Fund Performance: An Empirical Decomposition into Stock-Picking Talent, Style, Transactions, Costs, and Expenses," *Journal of Finance* 55, no. 4 (August 2000): 1655-1694; Kent Daniel, Mark Grinblatt, Sheridan Titman, and Russ Wermers, "Measuring Mutual Fund Performance with Characteristic-Based Benchmarks," *Journal of Finance* 52, no. 3 (July 1999): 1035–1058; Christopher R. Blake, Edwin J. Elton, and Martin J. Gruber, "The Performance of Bond Mutual Funds," *Journal of Business* 66, no. 3 (July 1993): 371–403; Warren Bailey and Joseph Lim, "Evaluating the Diversification Benefits of the New Country Funds," *Journal of Portfolio Management* 18, no. 3 (Spring 1992): 74–80; Robert E. Cumby and Jack D. Glen, "Evaluating the Performance of International Mutual Funds," *Journal of Finance* 45, no. 2 (June 1990): 497–522; and Bruce N. Lehmann and David M. Modest, "Mutual Fund Performance Evaluations: A Comparison of Benchmarks and Benchmark Comparisons," *Journal of Finance* 42, no. 2 (June 1987): 233–265.

has an expense ratio of only 0.18 percent). This means the average equity fund has to earn gross returns that are $1.52 - 0.75 = 0.77$ percentage points above the index fund just to earn the same net return as the index fund after subtracting expenses. Studies have shown that it is difficult for active managers to do this on a risk-adjusted basis. One study found that although the stocks held by actively managed funds outperform their indexes by 1.3 percentage points, these gains are more than negated by 1.6 percentage points of expenses and transactions costs. That is why indexing of both equities and bond funds has attracted an increasing number of investors and their money.

These studies deal with averages—can some well-performing funds maintain consistently good performance over time? The evidence is mixed. Some studies indicate that in the short-run (one to three years) there may be some consistency in returns among top- and bottom-ranked performers,[10] but other studies show that mutual funds advertising good return records are likely to have poorer performance in subsequent years.[11] Consistently good performance is just not evident over longer time periods.

Several influences could explain why funds with good short-term records then experience average or below-average performance. First, they could be victims of their own success. Good returns attract investors' money, and such large inflows of cash are difficult to invest wisely and quickly, and thus may harm future returns. In addition, continued superior performance requires the fund manager to continually identify new securities with good return potential. As a result, larger funds own many different securities (sometimes hundreds or thousands), each representing only a small part of the overall portfolio. By owning so many securities, the fund is essentially buying the market so their returns will match the market over time. As a result, they become a de facto index fund with active management fees.

Second, a fund may have an attractive short-term record because of one or two exceptionally good (or exceptionally lucky) years. But occasional blips on a fund's record are no guarantee of future skill (or luck), so future returns are more modest than the past record may predict.

Finally, investment styles do go in and out of favor. For example, mutual funds focusing on large stocks did well in the 1980s; funds focusing on small stocks outperformed in the early 1990s; funds emphasizing growth stocks outperformed in the late 1990s; and value-oriented funds did well after the turn of the century. This implies that mutual funds with good short-term performance records may have done well simply because their particular style of investing was in favor. Over the next several years, some other style may offer better returns. Even in academic studies that incorporate style analysis in their examination of mutual fund returns, researchers have generally found that above-average risk-adjusted returns do not persist over time in equity or fixed income mutual funds.[12] In addition, little evidence has been found of managers' ability to time different styles and switch to a style coming into favor as another is going out.[13]

---

[10]Andrew Clark, "How Well Do Expenses and Net Returns Predict Future Performance?" Lipper Research Study, May 3, 2004; Ian McDonald, "What Helps to Find Fund Winners?" *The Wall Street Journal,* May 3, 2004, pp. R1, R8; Darryll Hendricks, Jayendu Patel, and Richard Zeckhauser, "Hot Hands in Mutual Funds: Short-Run Persistence of Relative Performance, 1974–1988," *Journal of Finance* 48, no. 1 (March 1993): 93–130.

[11]Prem C. Jain and Joanna Shuang Wu, "Truth in Mutual Fund Advertising: Evidence on Future Performance and Fund Flows," *Journal of Finance* 55, no. 2 (April 2000): 937–958.

[12]R. N. Kahn and A. Rudd, "Does Historical Performance Predict Future Performance?" *Financial Analysts Journal* (November–December 1995): 43–52.

[13]Kent Daniel, Mark Grinblatt, Sheridan Titman, and Russ Wermers, "Measuring Mutual Fund Performance with Characteristic-Based Benchmarks," *Journal of Finance* (July 1997): 1035–1058.

Risk Performance   Although return performance is not historically consistent, risk apparently is. In one study, most funds in the top 25 percent in terms of risk over one five-year period were still high-risk in a subsequent five-year period. When ranked by risk in the subsequent period, 63 percent remained in the top quartile and 93 percent remained in the top half.[14] Several studies have examined the relationship between funds' stated objectives and their measures of risk and return. Results show a positive relationship between the funds' stated objectives and risk measures, with risk measures increasing as objectives become more aggressive. The studies have also found a positive relationship between return and risk.[15] Thus, it is worthwhile for investors to seek mutual funds with objectives and risk levels similar to their own risk tolerance.

Style Consistency   If an investor buys a fund thinking it will follow, for example, a growth strategy, can the investor be sure that will happen? The financial press often features articles about funds that have gone astray by advertising one investment philosophy while pursuing another.[16] Such *style drift* occurs in 20–30 percent of equity mutual funds in any one year period.[17] Some legitimate style drift can be explained, for example, by the successful stock selection of a small-cap stock fund manager, whose best selections will increase in market value and after a while will no longer be considered small. But style drift in search of the latest investment fad (e.g., tech stocks in the late 1990s) or toward a better-performing style is not in the fund shareholder's best interest. It can hurt the diversification of the fund shareholder's overall portfolio if all funds start to drift to the same style. In addition, some evidence suggests that style-shifting funds earn lower returns than do style-consistent funds[18.]

FEES AND EXPENSES

As we stated earlier, front-end loads, deferred sales charges, and 12b-1 fees are related to marketing expenses; they are not compensation for fund-manager expertise or investment success. In studies that have compared the risk-adjusted performance of load and no-load funds, the result is clear: The average load fund offers investors no better performance than the average no-load fund and may even earn, on average, lower returns.[19]

Expenses differences, however, should directly translate into return differences for fund investors. Studies for equity mutual funds find that after controlling for risk and investment style, funds with lower expense ratios tend to earn higher returns, although the evidence is not unanimous.[20] For example, Exhibit 4.5 summarizes a study that divided mutual funds

---

[14]Robert McGough, "Heeding Risk-Adjusted Returns May Pay," *The Wall Street Journal,* August 7, 1998, p. C23.

[15]John D. Martin, Arthur J. Keown Jr., and James L. Farrell, "Do Fund Objectives Affect Diversification Policies?" *Journal of Portfolio Management* 8, no. 2 (Winter 1982): 19–28.

[16]Laura Saunders Egodigwe and Bridget O'Brian, "Some Funds Find Losing Their Balance in Favor of Stocks Reaps Huge Rewards," *The Wall Street Journal,* February 18, 2000, p. C1; Pui-Wing Tam, "Excuse Me Sir! But There Are Tech Stocks in My Bond Fund," *The Wall Street Journal,* February 14, 2000, p. C1.

[17]George R. Arrington, "Chasing Performance Through Style Drift," *Journal of Investing,* 9, no. 2 (Summer 2000): 13–17.

[18]Daniel C. Indro, Christine X. Jiang, Michael Y. Hu, and Wayne Y. Lee, "Mutual Fund Performance: A Question of Style," *Journal of Investing,* 7, no. 2 (Summer 1998): 46–53.

[19]See, for example, Mark M. Carhart, "On Persistence in Mutual Fund Performance," *Journal of Finance* 52, no. 1 (March 1997): 57–82; Jonathan Clements, "Taking the First Step in Picking Your Fund," *The Wall Street Journal,* July 22, 1991, pp. C1, C21.

[20]Studies finding a *positive* relationship between excess returns over an index and expense ratios include Andrew Clark, "How Well Do Expenses and Net Returns Predict Future Performance?" Lipper Research Study, May 3, 2004; and Ravi Shukla, "The Value of Active Portfolio Management," *Journal of Economics and Business* 56 (July 2004): 331–346.

Exhibit 4.5	Equity Fund Expense Ratios and Fund Returns, 1993–1998

Fund Type and Expense Quartile	Average Annual Expense Ratio	Average Five-Year Return	Difference between 1st and 4th Quartile Expense Ratio	Difference between 1st and 4th Quartile Return
Large-Cap				
1	0.64%	20.70%	−1.55%	3.03%
2	1.07	19.72		
3	1.50	18.54		
4	2.19	17.67		
Mid-Cap				
1	0.85%	15.56%	−1.51%	2.34%
2	1.25	15.40		
3	1.69	14.65		
4	2.36	13.22		
Small-Cap				
1	0.89%	12.84%	−1.52%	2.62%
2	1.32	12.44		
3	1.71	12.71		
4	2.41	10.22		
Foreign Stock				
1	0.90%	8.92%	−1.67%	2.90%
2	1.46	7.76		
3	1.90	6.08		
4	2.57	6.02		

Source: Jonathan Clements, "Hint: Managers Are Only as Smart as the Expenses They Charge," *The Wall Street Journal,* July 6, 1999, pp. R1, R10. Copyright © 1999 Dow Jones. Reprinted by permission of Copyright Clearance Center.

into quartiles based on their expense ratio. For different types of equity funds, the table shows the average expense ratio and five-year average returns for each quartile. Except for small-cap funds, the relationship between expenses and returns is inverse; that is, as expenses rise from quartile to quartile, average returns fall. Lower-expense funds appear to earn markedly superior returns.[21]

This is true for bond mutual funds, too. Exhibit 4.6 shows the results of a study that divided bond funds into different expense categories. The results are clear: Funds with lower expenses had higher average returns than high-expense bond funds. The study's analysis shows there is almost a one-to-one inverse relationship between expenses and

---

[21]Among the academic research studies supporting this perspective are William Reichenstein "Bond Fund Returns and Expenses: A Study of Bond Market Efficiency," *Journal of Investing* (Winter 1999): 8–16; D. C. Indro, C. X. Jiang, M.Y. Hu, and W.Y. Lee, "Mutual Fund Performance: Does Fund Size Matter?" *Financial Analysts Journal* 55, no. 3 (May–June 1999): 74-87; John C. Bogle, "The Implications of Style Analysis for Mutual Fund Performance Evaluation," *Journal of Portfolio Management* 24, no. 4 (Summer 1998): 34–42; Mark M. Carhart, "On Persistence in Mutual Fund Performance," *Journal of Finance,* 52, no. 1 (March 1997): 57–82.

EXHIBIT 4.6	Bond Fund Expense Ratios and Fund Returns			
Fund Type and Expense Category	1998 Expense Ratio Category Average	Average Five-Year Return 1993–1998	Difference between High and Low Expense Ratio	Difference between High and Low Return
High-grade short-term				
Low	0.40%	5.77%	−0.94%	0.95%
High	1.34	4.82		
High-grade intermediate-term				
Low	0.51	6.78	−0.83	0.97
High	1.34	5.81		
High-grade long-term				
Low	0.48	8.41	−0.86	2.06
High	1.34	6.35		
Medium-grade short-term				
Low	0.55	5.55	−0.65	0.39
High	1.20	5.16		
Medium-grade intermediate-term				
Low	0.62	6.69	−1.19	1.02
High	1.81	5.67		
Medium-grade long-term				
Low	0.70	6.67	−1.00	0.75
High	1.70	5.92		
Low-grade intermediate-term				
Low	0.73	8.04	−0.96	1.62
High	1.69	6.42		

Source: William Reichenstein, "Bond Fund Returns and Expenses: A Study of Bond Market Efficiency," *Journal of Investing* (Winter 1999): 8–16. Reprinted by permission of Institutional Investor.

returns; for every one-percentage-point increase in the expense ratio, the average return falls one percentage point.[22]

Data on average expense ratios for different kinds of funds are available from the previously mentioned sources of information on mutual funds. Exhibit 4.7 lists average expense ratios for the nine equity styles in Morningstar's 3 × 3 style box and domestic bond funds. The exhibit also includes the average expense ratio for index funds for each style and the difference between the two. This difference represents the extra return, over and above the index return, that the actively managed fund has to earn just to compensate for its extra expenses. In a world of nearly efficient markets, that is a tough barrier to overcome.

As we have seen, mutual fund portfolio turnover also affects shareholders' returns. Over half of domestic stock mutual funds have turnover ratios exceeding 75 percent. Because trading increases costs (such as brokerage commissions, an "unseen expense" to most fund investors), funds with lower portfolio turnover have higher average returns than those with

---

[22]William Reichenstein, "Bond Fund Returns and Expenses: A Study of Bond Market Efficiency," *Journal of Investing* (Winter 1999): 8–16.

EXHIBIT 4.7	Expense Ratios of Actively Managed Funds versus Index Funds		
Type of Fund	Actively Managed Average Expense Ratio	Index Fund Average Expense Ratio	Difference in Expense Ratios Active − Index
EQUITY			
Large growth	1.57%	0.58%	0.99%
Midcap growth	1.66	0.40	1.26
Small growth	1.79	0.69	1.10
Large blend	1.27	0.68	0.59
Midcap blend	1.50	0.72	0.78
Small blend	1.58	0.86	0.72
Large value	1.42	0.96	0.46
Midcap value	1.52	0.25	1.27
Small value	1.53	0.64	0.89
International	1.86	0.93	0.93
BOND			
Domestic	1.12%	0.48%	0.64%

Source: Morningstar Principia Pro, June 2004; author calculations.

higher turnover.[23] If high portfolio turnover is more likely for an aggressive risk-taking mutual fund, the difference in average returns on a risk-adjusted basis is apt to be even greater.

TAXES

Portfolio turnover in a mutual fund has another implication for investors: It affects their tax obligations.[24] Higher portfolio turnover leads to higher levels of realized capital gains for fund shareholders. A year-end statement from a mutual fund showing a large capital gain distribution can wreak havoc on a carefully planned strategy that sought to minimize taxes.

All else equal, high turnover funds will generate more realized capital gains and more realized short-term capital gains than low-turnover funds. Thus, if both funds have the same pre-tax return, investors in the low-turnover fund will likely have a higher after-tax return. Some studies estimate that a high-turnover fund needs to earn 2–3 percent more than a low-turnover fund to have the same after-tax return, a difficult feat in nearly efficient

---

[23]See Mark M. Carhart, "On Persistence in Mutual Fund Performance," *Journal of Finance* 52, no. 1 (March 1997): 57–82. A study by Wermers' argues that high-turnover funds have higher net returns than low-turnover funds but his finding may result from how he tracked fund portfolios at the beginning of each quarter. See his article and the discussion following it, Russ Wermers, "Mutual Fund Performance: An Empirical Decomposition into Stock-Picking Talent, Style, Transactions Costs, and Expenses," *Journal of Finance* 55, no. 4 (August 2000): 1655–1695; and Tobias J. Moskowitz, "Discussion," *Journal of Finance* 55, no. 4 (August 2000): 1695–1703.

[24]This is not the case for mutual funds that are part of a tax-deferred investment plan, such as an individual retirement account (IRA) or 401(k) plan.

EXHIBIT 4.8	Comparing Tax Implications of Two Portfolios

Investor wants to allocate 40 percent in bonds, 60 percent in equities.

Tax-Wise Portfolio	**Tax-Ugly Portfolio**
40% municipal bonds	40% taxable bonds
32% index of U.S. large-cap stocks	50% actively managed U.S. stocks
12% international stocks	5% international stocks
6% emerging-market stocks	5% U.S. small-cap stocks
5% U.S. small-cap growth stocks	
5% U.S. small-cap value stocks	
PRE-TAX RETURN: 8.6%	PRE-TAX RETURN: 9.0%
AFTER-TAX RETURN: 6.5%	AFTER-TAX RETURN: 5.8%

Source: "Which Is Your Portfolio?" *Fortune* (March 18, 1996): 88. Copyright © 1996 Time Inc. Reprinted by permission. All rights reserved.

markets.[25] Index funds, where active trading is discouraged and turnovers are traditionally low, will likely have higher tax efficiency than most actively managed funds.

Exhibit 4.8 illustrates the importance of tax-wise investing for taxable investors. For IRAs and other tax-deferred accounts, focusing on pre-tax returns is appropriate and the Tax-Ugly Portfolio is the preferred choice; its pre-tax expected return is 9.0 percent versus the Tax-Wise Portfolio's pre-tax expected return of 8.6 percent (assuming the portfolios' risks are similar). But the story changes for a taxable account. The Tax-Wise Portfolio's emphasis on tax–exempt income (municipal bonds), passive investing (large-cap stock index), and capital gains potential (international stocks, emerging-market stocks, and small-cap stocks) lowers the tax bill. For this type of investment, the Tax-Wise Portfolio's estimated after-tax return of 6.5 percent is preferred to the Tax-Ugly Portfolio's 5.8 percent.

SOME SUGGESTED MUTUAL FUND INVESTMENT STRATEGIES

We have learned much in this chapter about what drives mutual fund performance. Based on this, we offer the following suggestions for investing in mutual funds.

1. Choose only those mutual funds consistent with your objectives and constraints, including your tax situation.
2. Consider index funds for a large portion of your fund portfolio. Your index funds will never be featured as the quarter's or the year's top performer, but over longer periods of time they will outperform most actively managed funds. A variety of equity, bond, and international no-load funds that seek to replicate both broad and narrow indexes are available for the small investor.
3. Whenever possible, invest in no-load funds, particularly those that do not have front-end loads, deferred sales charges, and 12b-1 fees. Information sources discussed earlier can help you identify these funds. Given funds' investment objectives, invest in funds with below-average expense ratios and below-average turnover ratios.

---

[25]Robert D. Arnott, Andrew L. Berkin, and Jia Ye, "How Well Have Taxable Investors Been Served in the 1980s and 1990s?" *Journal of Portfolio Management* 26, no. 4 (Summer 2000): 84–93; and Robert H. Jeffrey and Robert D. Arnott, "Is Your Alpha Big Enough to Cover Its Taxes?" *Journal of Portfolio Management* 19, no. 3 (Spring 1993): 15–25.

4. Invest at least 10 percent to 20 percent of your mutual fund portfolio in international or global funds to diversify and participate in the high return potential of non-U.S. securities.
5. Own mutual funds in several asset classes to diversify and participate in the different investment cycles. For example, purchase shares in both value- and growth-oriented equity funds, in large- and small-cap funds, and in high-grade and low-grade bond funds.
6. If you want to actively manage your mutual fund portfolio, consider investing in the past year's "hot" funds. (Remember that investment styles do come in and out of favor.)
7. Do not attempt to time the market by aggressively entering and exiting the stock market. Timing strategies appear to add little value, and they can increase risk considerably.
8. To help avoid market timing, use a dollar-cost-average strategy of investing a set dollar amount every month. Most mutual funds have plans that accept regular deposits; many will assist you in making arrangements to automatically withdraw funds from a bank account.
9. Many mutual funds distribute capital gains around December; to avoid paying taxes on capital gains shortly after you have purchased a fund's shares, read the prospectus and avoid investing money shortly before the capital gains distribution dates.
10. Do not own too many funds. Diversifying holdings across too many actively managed funds leads to performance that will likely follow the indexes but at the cost of active management.

WHEN TO SELL A FUND'S SHARES

Careful research can help identify appropriate index and actively managed funds to meet your needs. If, however, an investment choice sours, when should you sell a mutual fund investment and reinvest the proceeds elsewhere?

Generally, when your objectives and constraints change, it may be appropriate to rebalance or rearrange your portfolio. As people age, asset allocation gradually shifts from equities to bonds. As big bills—such as a child's college tuition—approach, funds are transferred into short-term, low-risk investments. Aside from such policy changes, the following considerations should help you determine when it may be time to sell a fund's shares.

Two warnings. First, beware of the "quick trigger," which occurs when disappointing short-term performance leads investors to sell their shares and switch to another fund. Remember that selling one fund and buying another can increase costs (load fees) and generate tax obligations, which is our second warning. Be aware of any capital gains tax obligations based on increases in your shares' net asset value. If you purchased the shares some time ago and are now thinking of selling, the difference between the purchase price and the selling price has tax implications. Disappointing current performance on a fund that has performed well over a longer period of time may require that you pay a large capital gains tax if you sell the shares.

With those warnings, the following are some events that may cause you to sell your shares. First, it may be time to sell when the fund's portfolio manager changes and the new manager lacks an attractive track record. Typically, when the manager of a fund leaves, the investment company will attempt to replace him or her with a manager who has successfully run another fund within the fund family. If a successful fund manager is replaced by an unknown, it may be time to reduce or close out your position in the fund. (The Securities and Exchange Commission requires mutual funds to identify their managers in their prospectus. However, if investment decisions are made by committee, a single manager need not be named; in fact, none of the committee members need to be publicly disclosed.) Of course, sometimes a fund manager is replaced because of poor performance. In such cases, do not bail out. There is evidence that on average the new manager will improve the risk-adjusted performance.[26]

Second, it may be time to sell when the fund's portfolio manager changes his or her investment style. Changes in a fund can occur when an experienced manager appears to be straying from a past successful investment pattern. This may be a sign of a panicking manager. Also beware of managers who abandon their investment style because it is cyclically out of favor. Recall that value-oriented mutual funds generally underperformed the overall market during the late 1990s, but managers who stuck with this investment style earned better returns after the turn of the century. Several sources are available for informing fund investors about managerial style changes—for instance, the fund's quarterly report or comments from the manager in sources such as *Morningstar*. The Morningstar 3×3 style boxes are especially helpful, as discussed earlier in this chapter.

Third, a fund that is becoming too large or is growing too rapidly may signal inferior future performance. As we discussed, it is difficult to wisely invest continuously large cash infusions from investors. Also, large funds may start to look and act like index funds.

Fourth, it may be time to sell a fund when it underperforms similar funds for three or more years. The key word here is "similar." For example, the performance of a small-cap fund should be compared to other small-cap funds, not to the S&P 500.

Circumstances differ over time and between investors. Because of this, we have avoided recommending specific conditions for selling a fund's shares. The signals we have mentioned need to be balanced with the investor's objectives and any capital gains that might be realized if shares in a taxable account are sold.

MUTUAL FUND SCANDALS

Unfortunately, the idea that mutual funds are the champion of small investors was tarnished in 2003. When New York Attorney General Eliot Spitzer and the SEC launched their investigations, they uncovered mutual fund practices that benefited the fund managers and hurt longer-term shareholders. The result of their findings: hefty fines for those breaking regulations, embarrassing headlines for guilty fund families, and new regulations for the industry to help protect the interests of shareholders. Some of the wrongdoings included market timing, late trading, and miscalculating load fees.

In a market timing scheme, large investors purchase big quantities of fund shares in one day in anticipation of a major price increase. After the price jump occurs, they sell the shares. Many times market timing is coupled with late trading, when the fund allows large investors to purchase shares after the 4 P.M. close of the New York Stock Exchange. Why did fund managers allow large investors to do this—even in cases when the rules of the fund prohibited it? Typically, the large investors had agreed to invest money in other accounts as well, helping to increase the amount of assets managed by the funds and therefore increasing fees they could collect. It was a simple matter of the funds choosing to enrich themselves rather than watching over the needs of their shareholders.

Market timing and late trading is unfair to smaller fund investors as it dilutes their returns. A large sum of cash deposited in the fund late in the day may not be able to be quickly fully invested. Here's a simple example. Suppose twenty investors hold one share each in a mutual fund investing in Asian stocks. The fund holds stocks worth $2,000 so the NAV is $100 and each investor owns $100 of the fund. Based on news she hears while the NYSE is open, a market timer believes the Asian market will rise tomorrow so she buys

---

[26]John G. Gallo and Larry J. Lockwood, "Fund Management Changes and Equity Style Shifts," *Financial Analysts Journal* 55, no. 5 (September–October 1999): 44–52.

one share for $100 just before—or after—the order deadline. The NAV remains $100 per share. But the late purchase does not allow the fund managers to invest her $100 in the market, so the fund's holdings are $2,000 worth of stocks and $100 in cash, for a total value of $2,100.

The next day, the expected price rise occurs in the Asian markets and the fund's stocks increase 10 percent in value. The fund's holdings are now $2,000 + 10 percent + $100 cash or $2,300. The NAV of the fund has risen to $2,300/21 to $109.52. The market timer sells at the day's close, netting a profit of 9.52 percent for a one-day trade. However, the fund's longer-term shareholders have had their returns diluted. Rather than rising 10 percent with the Asian markets, their fund's NAV only rose 9.52 percent. The market timer's cash deposit caused an unfair "drag" on the performance of the longer-term fund shareholders while she gained from the shareholders' previously invested money.

In addition to late trading and market timing, some mutual funds were accused of encouraging shareholders to purchase class B shares when class A shares would have been more cost-effective to the investor. Another problem was that some front-end commissions were miscalculated. Although many funds offer "breakpoints" at which large investments pay a smaller front-end load, some large investors were not given the lower load charge they deserved. Finally, there is the questionable practice of *soft dollar commissions* in which the cost of trading is bundled with the cost of research or software. Fund managers benefit from paying soft dollar commissions because the commissions are charged against fund shareholders (thus lowering their returns) while the fund managers use the stock research or software for free. In 2004 several funds announced they would no longer pay soft dollar commissions, preferring to pay for research separately from a management account rather than via brokerage commissions.

Among the rule changes implemented to combat such fraud, the SEC now requires that mutual fund companies have a chief compliance officer who reports to the fund's board of directors. The compliance officer will review all personal trading done by fund managers, ensure the accuracy of information submitted to regulators and investors, oversee compliance to government regulations and to the fund's own policies, and report any wrongdoing or questionable practices to the board rather than management.

A Review of Other Managed Investments

There is an old saying, "if it looks like a duck, walks like a duck, and quacks like a duck, it must be a duck." However, in investments it may be a decoy. Several investments have some characteristics of mutual funds but differ in important ways. Exhibit 4.9 summarizes the characteristics of a number of such investments.

CLOSED-END INVESTMENT COMPANIES

Investment companies begin like any other company—someone sells an issue of common stock to a group of investors. A closed-end investment company (typically referred to as a *closed-end fund*) differs from an open-end investment company (often referred to as a *mutual fund*) in the way each operates *after* the initial public offering. Shares of a closed-end investment company trade like any other public corporation. Investors go through a broker to trade shares on exchanges and the market price of the fund's shares is determined by supply and demand. As of 2004 there were nearly 600 closed-end funds with assets of over $225 billion. Over three-quarters of the closed-end funds invest in bonds; the remainder are equity

Exhibit 4.9	Comparing Characteristics of Managed Funds			
	Mutual Fund	**Closed-End Investment Company**	**Exchange-Traded Funds**	**Variable Annuity**
Liquidity	Yes; buy, sell from mutual fund	Perhaps; depends on market liquidity. Frequently price is less than NAV	Perhaps; depends on market liquidity	Poor
Diversification	Yes, offers partial ownership in a pool of securities	Yes, offers partial ownership in a pool of securities	Yes, shares represent a diversified basket of securities	Yes, annuity claim represents ownership in a pool of securities
Choice of Investment Objective	Yes	Yes	Yes	Yes
Professional Management	Yes	Yes	Replicates a market index	Yes
Flexibility	Yes; exchange privileges allow investors to shift money among the family of funds	No	No	Limited
Accessibility	Frequently via Internet, phone, otherwise via a broker; some offer check-writing services, automatic deposits and withdrawals	Limited; some funds offer automatic reinvestment of dividends and capital gains	Via broker	Via Internet, phone, broker
Insurance Coverage	No	No	No	Yes; offers death benefit equal to amount invested (less prior withdrawals)
Tax Deferral	Only if part of an IRA or 401(k) plan	Only if part of an IRA or 401(k) plan	Only if part of an IRA or 401(k) plan	All income and capital gains grow tax-deferred
Lifetime Income Payout	No, income stops when fund balance is zero	No, income stops when fund balance is zero	Income only as long as shares are held	Guaranteed payout
Taxation of Benefits	Income at income tax rates, capital gains at appropriate capital gains rate	Income at income tax rates, capital gains at appropriate capital gains rate	Income at income tax rates, capital gains at appropriate capital gains rate	All benefits taxed at income tax rates
Expenses	Low-to-medium	Low-to-medium	Low, but broker commissions on trades	High

funds. There are closed-end funds that invest in stocks, specialized sectors (such as precious metals (Dundee Precious Metals), utilities (Gabelli Utility), and health (H&Q Health), global equity markets (Templeton Emerging Markets), single-country markets (such as Austria, Chile, and China), convertible securities (Calamos Convertibles), bonds (including government, mortgages, high-yield, and world), and municipal securities (including funds focused on investors in high-tax-rate states such as California and New York).

The closed-end investment company's net asset value (NAV) is computed twice daily based on prevailing market prices for the securities in the portfolio. The NAV and the market price of a closed-end fund are almost never the same. Over the long run, the market prices of these shares have historically been from 5 to 20 percent below the NAV (that is, they sell at a discount to NAV). It is still a mystery why closed-end funds typically sell at a discount to their net asset value. Some studies find evidence that the size of the discount changes according to the level of the fund's undistributed capital gains, which are taxable to the investor. Others argue that, because small investors typically purchase closed-end investment company shares, the relative size of the discount or premium measures small-investor optimism or pessimism of the market. The analysis of these discounts remains a major research topic of modern finance.[27]

The uncertainty about discounts is both a blessing and a bane to investors. Some investors view the discounts favorably, because they can purchase a portfolio of assets for less than market value. A closed-end fund investor can earn attractive returns two ways: (1) when the fund performs well and (2) when the discount to NAV narrows and the shares can be sold for a capital gain despite lackluster investment manager performance.

Another attractive feature of closed-end funds is that for many investors they are the only means of diversifying into certain foreign markets. For example, emerging markets are risky and the risk of buying a few shares of a few stocks—with the concomitant difficulties of settlement, taxes, and so on—makes investing in such markets unattractive to many. But if a closed-end investment company focuses on such a market, the small investor can use the professionally managed fund to obtain such diversification. In fact, closed-end funds are the *only* means whereby investors can have a stake in markets such as Russia, Turkey, Mexico, and a variety of other small and emerging markets.

EXCHANGE-TRADED FUNDS (ETFs)

First issued in 1993, exchange-traded funds (ETFs) had attracted over $160 billion of investor's money by 2004. An ETF is like a closed-end fund in that shares are purchased on an exchange and represent ownership in a basket of securities. But unlike an actively managed closed-end fund, the ETF is passively managed to mirror an index. Whereas index mutual fund shares are purchased or redeemed by investors once a day, the ETF trades throughout the day. ETFs can focus on broad indexes such as the S&P 500 (SPDRs), investment styles such as value and growth (iShares S&P 500/Barra Growth Index Fund), sectors such as energy (SPDR Energy), countries (iShares MSCI-Taiwan) or regions (iShares MSCI-EAFE). Unlike closed-end funds whose market price can deviate substantially from NAV, exchange-traded funds offer a unique method for keeping their market

---

[27]Studies throughout the years include Robert Ferguson and Dean Leistikow, "Valuing Active Managers, Fees, and Fund Discounts," *Financial Analysts Journal* 57, no. 3 (May–June 2001): 52-62; Michael Barclay, Clifford Holderness, and Jeffrey Pontiff, "Private Benefits from Block Ownership and Discounts on Closed-End Funds," *Journal of Financial Economics* 33, no. 3 (June 1993): 263–292; and Charles Lee, Andrei Shleifer, and Richard Thaler, "Investor Sentiment and the Closed-End Fund Puzzle," *Journal of Finance* 46, no. 1 (March 1991): 76–110. For a discussion of bond funds, see Malcolm Richards, Donald Fraser, and John Groth, "The Attractions of Closed-End Bond Funds," *Journal of Portfolio Management* 8, no. 2 (Winter 1982): 56–61.

price close to NAV: Large institutional investors can assemble baskets of the underlying stocks and exchange them for ETF shares if the ETF is selling at a price above its NAV. Similarly, if the ETF is selling at a price below NAV, institutional investors can buy ETF shares and convert them to the underlying securities. Expenses are usually low on ETFs; the SPDR 500, which replicates the S&P 500 index, has an expense ratio of 0.17 percent compared to the low-cost Vanguard Index 500 fund's expense ratio of 0.18 percent and the average stock mutual funds' ratio of about 1.52 percent.

One drawback of ETF shares is that although their expenses are low, they can only be purchased and sold on exchanges. Thus, since brokerage commissions will increase the cost of trading ETFs, they are not a good vehicle if frequent purchases are planned, such as from monthly savings. Also, some ETFs do not frequently trade, so it may be difficult at times to quickly purchase or exit an investment.

Nonetheless, ETFs have proven to be popular. Virtually nonexistent a few years ago, assets in ETFs have risen from nearly $7 billion in 1997 to $80 billion in early 2002 to over $160 billion in 2004, nearly three-quarters the size of their much-older closed-end fund cousin.

VARIABLE ANNUITIES

Another mutual fund look-alike is the variable annuity, a security offered by insurance companies and subsidiaries of a few mutual fund companies. A *variable annuity* offers investors the choice of several funds in which to invest; the invested funds grow tax-deferred over time. Unlike some tax-deferred retirement plans, there are no upper limits on what an investor can place in the variable annuity. A variable annuity is an insurance product since in the case of death a benefit is paid that is at least equal to the initial investment less any withdrawals. Upon the investor's retirement, the annuity will pay an income stream as long as the policyholder lives, so a long-lived annuitant can end up earning a nice return on the invested funds.

One disadvantage of an annuity is its higher costs. In addition to expenses and fees for managing the fund, investors pay a mortality fee for the insurance protection and promise of a life-long annuity. Because of this, total annual expenses usually exceed 2 percent on stock and bond funds, as seen in Exhibit 4.10. This far exceeds the average expense ratios of most mutual funds.

EXHIBIT 4.10	Annuity Expenses
Type of Fund	**Average Total Expense**
Aggressive growth	2.37%
Balanced	2.37
Corporate bond	2.06
Government bond, general	2.13
Growth	2.36
Growth and income	2.16
High-yield bond	2.22
International bond	2.48
International stock	2.40
Money market	1.91
Specialty fund	3.00
U.S. diversified equity average	2.31
Fixed-income average	2.08

Source: *The Wall Street Journal,* July 6, 2004, p. R9. Copyright © 2004 Dow Jones. Reprinted by permission of Copyright Clearance Center.

Another disadvantage is that, since the annuity pays an income stream, all investment gains, even those arising from capital gains, are taxed at higher rates. Also, although some switching of accounts is allowed, variable annuity families offer fewer investment options than do mutual fund families.

Summary

- A mutual fund is an investment company that pools money from many sources and invests it in a collection of individual securities such as stocks, bonds, and other publicly traded securities. Mutual funds can be classified as closed-end or open-end; the latter can include either load or no-load funds. Since a wide variety of mutual funds are available, there is one to match almost any investment objective or combination of objectives.

Investments Online

As mutual funds have grown in popularity as a means to gain instant diversification and professional management, so have the number of Web sites devoted to some aspect of mutual fund investing. Any of the major fund companies (Fidelity, T. Rowe Price, Vanguard, Scudder, and so on) will have interesting Web sites to visit. Here are some others:

http://www.morningstar.com Morningstar is a leading provider of mutual fund information. The site features much information and many links of interest to mutual fund investors. Items on the Web site include news, analysis, personal investor case studies, columns by several Morningstar writers, and an interview with a fund manager. Past articles are available in an archive. The site also features sections dealing with learning, planning, and researching about mutual funds. A mutual fund screen allows users to find funds from Morningstar's database that meet certain investment category, return, rating, and volatility criteria. The site contains information about ETFs, including comparison with mutual funds and informative articles.

http://www.wiesenberger.com/ The home page of Wiesenberger (part of Thomson Financial) offers an overview of their firm's various investment products. Both closed-end and open-end investment company data, analysis, and software can be purchased, hard copy or on-line, from this firm.

http://www.brill.com Brill's Mutual Funds Interactive[SM] Web site offers basic information about mutual fund investing:

quotes of fund prices, charts, and market commentary. Its education features include discussions of investing topics, the different types of mutual funds, a Q&A section, and a manager profile.

http://www.mfea.com The home page for the Mutual Fund Education Alliance is a good place to start to learn more about mutual funds. This site, called the Mutual Fund Investor's Center, offers a great deal of information. The News Center features information, economic analysis, and market commentary from mutual fund analysts. The Fund Center allows users to research, track, and customize their own fund portfolio. Investors can search by a specific fund's name or search for funds that have certain characteristics, including investment category, level of 12b-1 fee, expense ratio, sales charge, and so on. Investors can also discover the three top-performing funds year-to-date in different investment categories and find the lowest-cost fund by investment category. The site also has links to various fund families.

http://www.investorguide.com/funds.html The InvestorGuide Web site was reviewed in Chapter 1. This page from that Web site focuses on mutual fund investing and has links to a variety of related sites. Topics include learning about mutual funds, getting performance data and ratings, screening mutual funds, and obtaining a mutual fund prospectus.

http://www.ishares.com and **http://www.spdrindex.com** These two sites feature exchange-traded funds.

- The mutual fund prospectus contains much useful information about the fund, such as the investment objective, investment strategies and style, risk and return data, fees and expenses, and other details. The prospectus, as well as other sources of information regarding the fund (such as periodicals, various financial publications, and Web sites), should be carefully examined before a fund is chosen.

- Numerous studies have examined the historical performance of mutual funds. Most studies have found that fewer than half the funds matched the risk-adjusted net returns of the aggregate market. The results with gross returns generally indicated average risk-adjusted returns slightly above the market's, with about half of the funds outperforming the market.

- The performances of actively managed mutual funds are hurt somewhat by their higher expenses and brokerage commissions from high portfolio turnover. Several studies have found that index funds are above-average long-term performers among mutual funds, in part because their passive investment strategy limits their expenses and portfolio turnover.

- Investors should not necessarily invest in mutual funds with above-average long-term performance records without first doing some research. The fund's superior performance may be because the fund's investment style (for example, small-cap stocks) had been in favor in recent years. Or, a good five-year or ten-year record may have been from just one or two years of outstanding returns and may not be repeatable in the future.

- The returns received by the average individual investor on investments managed by mutual funds may be inferior to the average results for a specific U.S. or international market. However, the benefits of services such as diversification, reinvestment, and recordkeeping provided by these investment companies make mutual funds an important alternative to investing in individual stocks and bonds in the United States or worldwide.

- Recent scandals involving mutual fund firms will result in an industry more focused on making decisions with its shareholders in mind.

- It is important to know the differences between mutual funds and their look-alikes—closed-end investment companies, exchange-traded funds, and variable annuities—so the correct investment choice can be made.

QUESTIONS

1. How is the net asset value of a mutual fund computed?
2. Discuss the difference between a mutual fund and a closed-end investment company.
3. What two prices are provided for a closed-end investment company? What is the typical relationship between these prices?
4. What is the difference between a load fund and a no-load fund?
5. What are the differences between a common-stock fund and a balanced fund? How would you expect their risk and return characteristics to compare?
6. Why might you buy a money market fund? What would you want from this investment?
7. Should you care about how well a mutual fund is diversified? Why or why not?
8. Discuss why the stability of a risk measure for a mutual fund is important to an investor. Are mutual funds' risk measures generally stable?
9. Should the performance of mutual funds be judged on the basis of return alone or on a risk-adjusted basis? Discuss why, using examples.
10. Define the net return and gross return for a mutual fund and discuss how to compute each.
11. As an investor in a mutual fund, discuss why net and gross returns are relevant to you.
12. As an investigator evaluating how well mutual fund managers select undervalued stocks or project market returns, discuss whether net or gross returns are more relevant.
13. Based on numerous tests of mutual fund performance, you are convinced that less than half of the funds do better than a naive buy-and-hold policy. Does this mean you should forget about investing in mutual funds? Why or why not?
14. You are told that fund X experienced above-average performance over the past two years. Do you think it will continue to do so over the next two years? Why or why not?
15. You are told that fund Y experienced consistently above-average performance over the past six years. Do you think it will continue to do so over the next six years? Why or why not?
16. You see advertisements for two mutual funds indicating that they have investment objectives consistent with yours.
   a. How can you get a quick view of these two funds' performance over the past two or three years?

b. Where would you find more in-depth information on the funds, including addresses so you can write for prospectuses?

17. Why would an individual investor consider purchasing shares of a mutual fund?

18. Why would an individual investor consider purchasing shares of a closed-end fund?

19. Why should index funds be a part of most investors' mutual fund investment strategy?

20. Why might a fund with a good one- or two-year performance record be a better investment selection than one with a good five-year performance record?

21. What are some characteristics investors should look for in a mutual fund before investing?

22. A mutual fund that you own performed well over several years but has had below-average returns this year. What factors should you consider before selling your fund shares?

23. Consider each of the events below separately. Explain why (or why not) each is an indicator that it is time to sell your position in a mutual fund.

a. There is a change in the fund's manager.

b. A small-cap fund has underperformed the S&P 500 for three years in a row.

c. According to Morningstar, the fund's style has changed from mid-cap value to small-cap growth.

24. How do market timing and late trading harm mutual fund investors?

25. Define breakpoints and soft dollar commissions.

26. What is an exchange-traded fund? How is it similar to an index mutual fund?

27. What are the differences between an exchange-traded fund and a closed-end investment company?

28. What is a variable annuity? What advantages does it offer investors over mutual funds? What are its disadvantages?

PROBLEMS

1. Suppose ABC Mutual Fund had no liabilities and owned only four stocks as follows:

Stock	Shares	Price	Market Value
W	1,000	12	$12,000
X	1,200	15	$18,000
Y	1,500	22	$33,000
Z	800	16	$12,800
			$75,800

The fund began by selling $50,000 of stock at $8 per share. What is its NAV?

2. You are considering investing $1,000 in a load fund that charges a fee of 8 percent, and you expect your investment to earn 15 percent over the next year. Alternatively, you could invest in a no-load fund with similar risk that charges a 1 percent redemption fee. You estimate that this no-load fund will earn 12 percent. Given your expectations, which is the better investment and by how much?

3. In *Barron's*, look up the NAVs and market prices for five closed-end funds. Compute the difference between the two values for each fund. How many are selling at a premium to NAV? How many are selling at a discount to NAV? What is the overall average premium or discount? How does this compare to the Herzfeld chart (published in *Barron's*), which tracks the average discount on these funds over time?

4. Find the annual returns for the following mutual fund data on distributions and NAV.

Selected Per-Share Data	YEARS ENDED DECEMBER 31				
	2004	2003	2002	2001	2000
Net asset value, beginning of period	$143.26	$129.75	$108.82	$80.20	$87.52
Less distributions					
From net investment income	−0.27	−0.73	−0.67	−1.25	−1.1
From net realized gain	−4.69	−11.39	−5.15	−5.21	−12.85
Total distributions	−4.96	−12.12	−5.82	−6.46	−13.95
Net asset value, end of period	$104.50	$143.26	$129.75	$108.82	$80.20

5. Find the annual returns for the following mutual fund data on distributions and NAV.

Selected Per-Share Data	YEARS ENDED DECEMBER 31				
	2004	2003	2002	2001	2000
Net asset value, beginning of period	$121.86	$135.33	$113.95	$90.07	$69.17
Net investment income	0.60	1.29	1.370	1.33	1.31

(continued)

Selected Per-Share Data	YEARS ENDED DECEMBER 31				
	2004	2003	2002	2001	2000
Net realized and unrealized gain (loss) on investments	−8.87	−13.46	22.415	24.30	21.50
Total from investment operations less distributions	−8.27	−12.17	23.785	25.63	22.81
Dividends from net investment income	−0.57	−1.30	−1.410	−1.33	−1.32
Distributions from realized capital gains	—	—	−0.995	−0.42	−0.59
Total distributions	−0.57	−1.30	−2.405	−1.75	−1.91
Net asset value, end of period	$113.02	$121.86	$135.33	$113.95	$90.07

6. Compute the offer prices for the following mutual funds.

Fund	NAV	Load Fee
HBJ	$19.67	8%
ICFB	$41.23	3%
EAN	$17.59	6%
FKR	$75.90	NL

7. Given the following fees and return expectations for each pair, which fund in each pair is the better investment?

	E(Return)	Load	12b-1 Fee	Deferred Sales Charge	Number of years to Be Held
PAIR I					
a.	10%	3%	1.00%	0%	5
b.	9%	6%	0.25%	0%	5
PAIR II					
a.	13%	6%	0%	0%	8
b.	15%	NL	1%	0%	8
PAIR III					
a.	8%	0%	1%	6% (reduces by 1% per year)	3
b.	10%	6%	0%	0%	3

8. Compute the average holding periods (annual) that correspond to the following portfolio turnover ratios.
   a. 100%
   b. 50%
   c. 15%
   d. 135%
   e. 175%

WEB EXERCISES

1. Compare and contrast the expenses, portfolio turnover, returns, and top ten stock holdings of two different mutual funds with the same investment objective.
2. Locate the Web sites of two mutual fund supermarkets and describe the services they offer to investors.
3. Report on the services and information available on the Morningstar Web site. Explain how Morningstar computes a mutual fund's return and risk and how Morningstar uses these measures to determine a fund's "star" rating.
4. What is a real estate investment trust (REIT)? How does it differ from a mutual fund and closed-end investment company?

SPREADSHEET EXERCISES

1. Graph the relationship between turnover and average holding period. When is the effect of increasing portfolio turnover largest on a fund in terms of realizing taxable gains?
2. Assume an initial investment of $10,000 in the "average" active fund and the index fund in each of the fund categories listed in Exhibit 4.7. Assume both funds earn 10 percent before expenses. Using the expense data in that table, what is the dollar difference in returns between the active fund and its corresponding index fund after five years? Ten years? Recalculate the dollar difference if the index fund earns 10 percent before expenses and the active fund earns 12 percent before expenses.
3. Use a spreadsheet to find the correlation between the stock fund expense ratios and average five-year returns in each fund category in Exhibit 4.5. Find the correlation between the high/low expense ratio difference and the high/low return difference in Exhibit 4.6.
4. From a fund prospectus or Morningstar table, develop a spreadsheet showing a fund's NAV, total return, income return (in dollars), and capital gain return (in dollars) over five or more years. Compute the fund's after-tax return in each year assuming an income tax rate of 35 percent and a capital gains tax rate of 18 percent. What is the fund's tax efficiency ratio over that time frame?

References

In addition to the references in the footnotes, here are some examples of useful reading on mutual funds:

Bogle, John C. "Selecting Equity Mutual Funds." *Journal of Portfolio Management* (Winter 1992): 94–100.

Bogle, John C. *Bogle on Mutual Funds.* Burr Ridge, IL: Irwin Professional Publishing, 1994.

The Investment Company Institute, the industry trade association for investment companies, publishes helpful pamphlets and an annual book on the mutual fund industry. Many of its brochures are available at little or no cost for classroom purposes from Investment Company Institute, 1401 H Street NW, Washington, DC, 20005 or on the Internet at *http://www.ici.org.*

Glossary

Closed-end investment company An investment company that issues only a limited number of shares, which it does not redeem (buy back). Instead, closed-end shares are traded in securities markets at prices determined by supply and demand.

Investment management company A company, separate from the investment company, that manages the portfolio and performs administrative functions.

Load *See* Sales charge.

Low-load fund A mutual fund that imposes a moderate front-end sales charge when the investor buys the fund, typically about 3 to 4 percent.

Mutual fund An investment company that pools money from shareholders and invests it in a variety of securities, including stocks, bonds, and money market securities. A mutual fund ordinarily stands ready to buy back (redeem) its shares at their current net asset value, which depends on the market value of the fund's portfolio of securities at the time. Mutual funds generally continuously offer new shares to investors.

Net asset value (NAV) The market value of an investment company's assets (securities, cash, and any accrued earnings) after deducting liabilities, divided by the number of shares outstanding.

No-load fund A mutual fund that sells its shares at net asset value without adding sales charges.

Open-end investment company The more formal name for a mutual fund, which derives from the fact that it continuously offers new shares to investors and redeems them (buys them back) on demand.

Prospectus A booklet that describes a mutual fund and offers its shares for sale. It contains information required by the Securities and Exchange Commission on such subjects as the fund's investment objective and policies, services, investment restrictions, officers and directors, procedures for buying or redeeming shares, charges, and financial statements.

Sales charge An amount charged to purchase shares in most mutual funds that are sold by brokers or other members of a sales force. Typical charges range from 4 to 8.5 percent of the initial investment. The charge is added to the net asset value per share to determine the offering price. *See also* No-load fund.

Variable annuity A contract under which an annuity is purchased with a fixed amount of money that is converted into a varying number of accumulation units. At retirement, the annuitant is paid a fixed number of monthly units, which are converted into varying amounts of money. The value of both accumulation and annuity units varies with the performance of a portfolio of equity securities.

Investment Policy Statements and Asset Allocation Issues

F rom your study of previous chapters, you should be convinced that *risk drives expected return*. Therefore, the practice of investing funds and managing portfolios should focus primarily on managing risk rather than on managing returns.

In this chapter we examine some of the practical implications of risk management in the context of asset allocation. *Asset allocation* is the process of deciding how to distribute an investor's wealth among asset classes, sectors, and countries for investment purposes. An *asset class* is comprised of securities that have similar characteristics, attributes, and risk–return relationships. A broad asset class such as "bonds" can be divided into smaller asset classes, such as Treasury bonds, corporate bonds, and high-yield bonds. We know that, in the long run, the highest compounded returns will most likely accrue to those investors with larger exposures to risky assets. Although there are no shortcuts or guarantees to investment success, maintaining a reasonable and disciplined approach to investing will increase the likelihood of investment success over time.

The asset allocation decision is not an isolated choice; rather, it is a component of a portfolio management process. In this chapter we present an overview of the four-step portfolio management process. As we will see, the first step in the process is to develop an investment policy statement, or plan, that will guide all future decisions. Much of an asset allocation strategy depends on the investor's policy statement. The policy statement includes the investor's goals or objectives, constraints, and investment guidelines.

To help illustrate this process, most of our examples are in the context of an individual investor; however, the concepts we introduce here—investment objectives, constraints, benchmarks, and so on—apply to any investor, individual or institutional. We will review studies that show the importance of the asset allocation decision and discuss the need for investor education, an important issue for individuals as well as companies who offer retirement or other savings plans to their employees. We conclude by examining asset allocation strategies across national borders to show the effect of market environment and culture on investing patterns in different countries.

Managing Risk

Investors have four ways to manage the risks confronting their wealth. One is the *risk-avoidance* strategy, in which investors avoid any reasonable risk of nominal loss of wealth by investing in securities such as FDIC-insured bank CDs and Treasury bills. This is a poor strategy for investing an *entire* portfolio except in the most extreme scenarios. However, it is an acceptable strategy for *part* of the portfolio if cash for a house down payment, car purchase, college tuition bill, or the like will be needed soon.

A *risk-anticipation* strategy assumes risk will occur and tries to position part of the portfolio to protect against it. Such is the case of having a cash reserve for large unexpected bills. In addition to providing a safety cushion, a cash reserve reduces the likelihood of being forced to sell investments at inopportune times to cover unexpected expenses. Most experts recommend a cash reserve of about six months' worth of living expenses. Though called a "cash" reserve, the funds should not actually be in cash; rather, they should be in investments easily converted to cash with little chance of a loss in value—such as money market mutual funds or bank accounts. Purchasing insurance to protect real assets, oneself, or one's family is another component of a risk-anticipation strategy. In fact, certain types of insurance should be a component of any financial plan. Life insurance protects loved ones against financial hardship should death occur before financial goals are met. Experts suggest life insurance coverage should be seven to ten times an individual's annual salary if a family depends on the person for income.[1] Other types of insurance coverage provide protection against other uncertainties. Health insurance helps to pay medical bills. Disability insurance provides continuing income should one become unable to work. Automobile and home (or rental) insurance provide protection against accidents and damage to cars or residences.

A third risk management strategy is *risk transfer,* or "spreading the risk." Insurance plays a role here, too, in that a person can anticipate risk and try to minimize its potential impact by transferring the adverse consequences of risk to someone else. But an investment portfolio can gain from risk-transfer strategies as well. Risk can be transferred from investors who are not willing to bear it to investors who are. This is the role of derivative securities such as futures contracts and options contracts, which we will discuss more fully in Chapters 17 and 18. Just as a farmer can hedge by using futures contracts to lock in a price for his crop well before it is harvested, investors can use derivatives and hedging strategies to protect their portfolios against unfortunate financial scenarios.

Risk reduction, the fourth risk management strategy, includes several aspects of investing that we discuss in later chapters. For example, as we mentioned in Chapter 1, investors

---

[1]Individuals can choose among several basic life insurance contracts. *Term life insurance* provides only a death benefit; depending on the contract, the premium to purchase insurance may change every renewal period. Term insurance is the least expensive life insurance to purchase, although the premium will rise as you age to reflect the increased probability of death. *Universal* and *variable life policies,* although technically different from each other, are similar in that they each provide both a death benefit and a savings plan to the insured. The premium paid on such policies exceeds the cost to the insurance company of providing the death benefit alone; the excess premium is invested in a number of investment vehicles chosen by the insured. The policy's cash value grows over time, in part based on the size of the excess premium and in part on the performance of the underlying investment funds. Insurance companies may restrict the ability to withdraw funds from these policies before the policyholder reaches a certain age.

should diversify across several different types of assets and even countries. The risk of a diversified portfolio is typically less than that of a single risky asset—higher returns in some securities offset lower returns in others over time.[2] Investors reduce risk by doing security analysis (or by hiring professionals such as mutual fund managers to do so) to discover and purchase a diversified set of creditworthy bonds and stocks with apparent upward price potential.

Whether an investor wants to avoid, anticipate, transfer, or reduce risks, each investor must continually determine and manage the risk exposure that is prudent for him or her. Investors' personal financial situations will change over time, as will their risk preferences.

Individual Investor Life Cycle

Financial plans and investment needs are as different as each individual. Investment needs change over a person's life cycle. How individuals structure their financial plan should be related to their age, financial status, future plans, needs, and risk preferences.

LIFE-CYCLE INVESTMENT STRATEGIES

Assuming basic insurance and cash reserve needs are met, individuals can start a serious investment program with their savings. Because of changes in their net worth and risk tolerance, individuals' investment strategies will change over their lifetime. Although each individual's needs and preferences are different, some general traits affect most investors over the life cycle. Let's look at the four life-cycle phases shown in Exhibit 5.1.

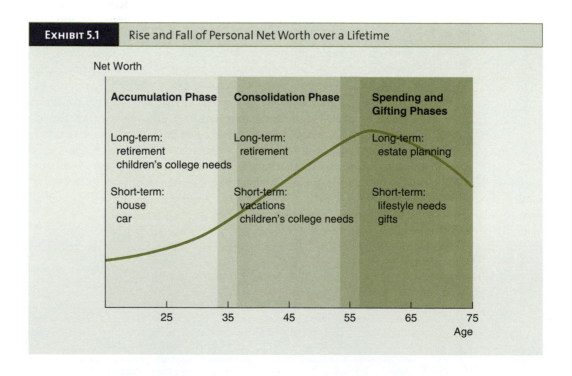

EXHIBIT 5.1 Rise and Fall of Personal Net Worth over a Lifetime

[2]We discuss portfolio diversification in more detail in Chapter 8.

Accumulation Phase   Individuals in the early-to-middle years of their working careers are in the *accumulation phase*. As the name implies, they are attempting to accumulate assets to satisfy fairly immediate needs (for example, a down payment for a house) or longer-term goals (children's college education, retirement). Typically, their net worth is small, and debt from car purchases or their own college education may be heavy. As a result of a long investment time horizon and their earning ability, individuals in the accumulation phase are willing to make moderately high-risk investments in the hopes of making above-average nominal returns over time.

Here we must emphasize the wisdom of investing early and regularly in one's life. Funds invested in early life-cycle phases, with returns compounding over time, will reap financial benefits during later phases. Exhibit 5.2 shows growth from an initial $10,000 investment over twenty, thirty, and forty years at assumed annual returns of 7 and 8 percent. The middle-aged person who invests $10,000 "when they can afford it" will only reap the benefits of compounding for twenty years or so before retirement. The younger person who saves will reap the much higher benefits of funds invested for thirty or forty years. Regularly investing $2,000 a year reaps large benefits over time, as well. A person who has invested a total of $90,000—an initial $10,000 investment followed by $2,000 annual investments over forty years—will have over half a million dollars accumulated from the 7 percent return. If the funds are invested more aggressively and earn the 8 percent return, the accumulation will be nearly three-quarters of a million dollars.

Consolidation Phase   Individuals in the *consolidation phase* are typically past the midpoint of their careers, have paid off much or all of their outstanding debts, and perhaps have paid, or have the assets to pay, their children's college bills. Earnings exceed expenses, so the excess can be invested to provide for future retirement or estate-planning needs. The typical investment horizon is still long (twenty to thirty years), so moderate-to-higher risk investments remain attractive. Some will have concerns about capital preservation and will not want to take large risks that may put their current nest egg in jeopardy. The long-term benefits of compounding will be of some help, but, as we mentioned, the biggest benefits come when investing begins early in life.

Spending Phase   The *spending phase* typically begins when individuals retire. Living expenses are covered by Social Security income and income from prior investments, including employer pension plans. Because their earning years have concluded (although

Exhibit 5.2	Benefits of Investing Early		
		Value of an Initial $10,000 Investment	Value of Investing $2,000 Annually	Value of the Initial Investment Plus the Annual Investment
Interest rate	7.0%			
Twenty years		$38,696.84	$81,990.98	$120,687.83
Thirty years		$76,122.55	$188,921.57	$265,044.12
Forty years		$149,744.58	$399,270.22	$549,014.80
Interest rate	8.0%			
Twenty years		$46,609.57	$91,523.93	$138,133.50
Thirty years		$100,626.57	$226,566.42	$327,192.99
Forty years		$217,245.21	$518,113.04	$735,358.25

some retirees take part-time positions or do consulting work), they seek greater protection of their capital. At the same time, they must balance their desire to preserve the nominal value of their savings with the need to protect themselves against a decline in its *real* value because of inflation. The average sixty-five-year-old person in the United States has a life expectancy of about twenty more years. Thus, although their overall portfolio may be less risky than in the consolidation phase, they still need to have some risky growth investments, such as common stocks, for inflation protection.

The transition into the spending phase requires a sometimes difficult change in mindset; throughout our working life we are trying to save; suddenly we can spend. We tend to think that if we spend less, say 4 percent of our accumulated funds annually instead of 5, 6, or 7 percent, our wealth will last far longer. But a bear market early in our retirement can greatly reduce our accumulated funds. Fortunately, there are planning tools that can give a realistic view of what can happen to our retirement funds should markets fall early in our retirement years; this insight can assist in budgeting and planning to minimize the chance of spending (or losing) all the saved retirement funds. Annuities, which transfer risk from the individual to the annuity firm (most likely an insurance company), are another possibility. With an annuity, the recipient receives a guaranteed, lifelong stream of income. Options can allow for the annuity to continue until both a husband and wife die.[3]

Gifting Phase   The *gifting phase* is similar to, and may be concurrent with, the spending phase. In this stage, individuals believe they have sufficient income and assets to cover their expenses while maintaining a reserve for uncertainties. Excess assets can provide financial assistance to relatives or friends, establish charitable trusts, or fund trusts that provide an estate-planning tool to minimize estate taxes.

The Portfolio Management Process

Good portfolio management considers the life-cycle phases just discussed and is a continual process. Once the funds are initially invested according to the plan, the portfolio must be monitored and updated according to the investor's changing needs.

The first step, as seen in Exhibit 5.3, is for the investor to construct a *policy statement*, either alone or with the assistance of an investment adviser. The policy statement is a road map; in it investors specify the types of risks they are willing to take and their investment goals and constraints. All investment decisions are based on the policy statement to ensure they are appropriate for the investor. We will examine the process of constructing a policy statement later in this chapter. Because investor needs change over time, the policy statement must be periodically reviewed and updated.

The process of investing seeks to peer into the future and determine strategies that offer the best possibility of meeting the policy statement guidelines. Thus, the second step is for the investor (or advisor) to study current financial and economic conditions to forecast future trends. The investor's needs (as reflected in the policy statement) *and* the financial market expectations will jointly determine investment strategy. Economies are dynamic; they are affected by numerous industry struggles, politics, changing demographics, and social attitudes. Thus, the portfolio will require constant monitoring, rebalancing, and updating to reflect such changes in financial market expectations. (We take a closer look at the process of evaluating and forecasting economic trends in Chapter 13.)

---

[3]See, e.g., Christopher Farrell, "A Better Way to Size Up Your Nest Egg," *Business Week* (January 22, 2001): 100–101; Jonathan Clements, "Retirement Models That Let Reality Bite," *The Wall Street Journal,* February 20, 2001, page C1.

EXHIBIT 5.3	The Portfolio Management Process

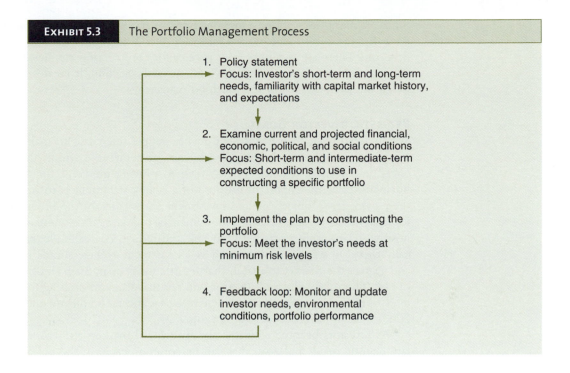

1. Policy statement
   Focus: Investor's short-term and long-term needs, familiarity with capital market history, and expectations

2. Examine current and projected financial, economic, political, and social conditions
   Focus: Short-term and intermediate-term expected conditions to use in constructing a specific portfolio

3. Implement the plan by constructing the portfolio
   Focus: Meet the investor's needs at minimum risk levels

4. Feedback loop: Monitor and update investor needs, environmental conditions, portfolio performance

The third step is to construct the portfolio. With the investor's policy statement and financial market forecasts as inputs, the investor (or advisor) determines how to allocate available funds across different countries, asset classes, and securities. This involves constructing a portfolio that will minimize the investor's risks while meeting the needs specified in the policy statement. Knowledge of financial theory will assist portfolio construction, as we will discuss in Part 3. Some of the practical aspects of selecting specific investments are discussed in Parts 4 and 5.

The fourth step is the continual monitoring of the investor's needs, along with capital market conditions. When necessary, the investor (or advisor) will update the policy statement and modify the investment strategy accordingly. In addition, periodic rebalancing of the portfolio should occur if the asset allocation strays too much from its target level.[4] A major component of the monitoring process is to evaluate a portfolio's performance and compare results to the expectations and the requirements listed in the policy statement. We discuss the evaluation of portfolio performance in Chapter 21.

The Need for a Policy Statement

As we have noted, a policy statement is a road map that guides the investment process. This road map is an invaluable planning tool that will help the investor understand his or her own needs better as well as assist an advisor or portfolio manager in managing a client's

---

[4]This can happen, for example, if high returns in the stock market result in faster growth in the equity portion of the portfolio relative to bonds. If stocks represent a higher percentage allocation in the overall portfolio than originally desired, some stocks should be sold and the proceeds reinvested in other assets. The possible consequences of being over-exposed in an asset class must be balanced with the tax implications from realizing capital gains.

funds. While it does not guarantee investment success, a policy statement will provide discipline for the investment process and reduce the possibility of making hasty, inappropriate decisions. There are two important reasons for constructing a policy statement: First, it helps the investor decide on realistic investment goals. Second, it creates a standard by which to judge the performance of the portfolio manager.

REALISTIC INVESTOR GOALS

When asked what their investment goal is, people often say, "to make a lot of money." Such a goal has two drawbacks: First, it may not be achievable within the investor's risk preferences; and second, it is too open-ended to provide guidance for asset selection and time horizons. Thus, an important purpose of a policy statement is to help investors understand their own needs, objectives, and investment constraints. In the process of developing a policy statement, investors learn about financial markets, investment risks, and that a strong positive relationship exists between risk and return. For example, naïve investors will typically focus on a single statistic, such as a 12 percent average annual rate of return on stocks, and expect the market to match that statistic every year. Such thinking ignores the element of risk. The more educated investor will see that it is not unusual for asset prices to decline by 10 percent or even 20 percent or more (as the tech collapse and the Nasdaq returns of 2000–2002 proved) over several months.

As investors become educated about financial markets and risks, they are able to articulate realistic needs and goals that can be communicated in the policy statement. This information will help prevent future aggravation and dissatisfaction on the part of the investor.

STANDARD FOR EVALUATING PORTFOLIO PERFORMANCE

The policy statement also assists in judging the performance of the portfolio manager. For example, if an investor has stated a low tolerance for risky investments, the portfolio manager should not be fired when the portfolio of lower-risk investments does not perform as well as the risky S&P 500 stock index. Many times the policy statement will specify a *benchmark portfolio*, or comparison standard, aligned with the client's risk preferences and investment needs. The portfolio manager's investment performance is then compared to this benchmark portfolio.

Because it sets an objective performance standard, the policy statement acts as a starting point for periodic portfolio review and client communication with managers. Questions concerning portfolio performance or the manager's faithfulness to the policy can be addressed in the context of the written policy guidelines. It can and should be grounds for dismissal if a portfolio manager makes unilateral deviations from policy, even if those deviations result in higher portfolio returns.

The policy statement also protects the investor in case a current portfolio manager leaves and is replaced by someone else. A clearly written policy statement prevents costly delays during this transition and allows the new manager to "hit the ground running," creating a seamless transition from one money manager to another.[5]

Thus a clearly written policy statement acts as an objective performance measure, a guard against ethical lapses, and an aid in any transition between money managers.

---

[5]Investment policy statements are not only for individual financial plans; any investment fund, from a pension fund to endowment fund, should have a policy statement. Despite this "best practice" need, 36 percent of 401(k) plan sponsors do not have a policy statement. This was, however, an improvement over the 52 percent of the plans that lacked investment policy statements in 1998. Meg Glinska, "A Matter of Policy," *CFO* (August 2000): 99–106; Jill Elswick, *Employee Benefit News* (July 2003).

Input to the Policy Statement

Before an investor and advisor can construct a policy statement, they need to have an open and frank exchange of information, ideas, fears, and goals. To build a framework for this information-gathering process, the client and advisor need to discuss the client's investment objectives and constraints. We illustrate this framework by discussing the investment objectives and constraints that may confront "typical" twenty-five-year-old and sixty-five-year-old investors.

INVESTMENT OBJECTIVES

The investor's *objectives* are his or her investment goals expressed in terms of *both* risk and returns. Expressing goals only in terms of returns can lead to inappropriate and even unethical investment practices by the portfolio manager, such as the use of high-risk investment strategies or account "churning," which involves moving quickly in and out of commission-generating investments in an attempt to buy low and sell high.

A client must become informed of investment risks associated with a goal, including the possibility of loss. Since we know that risk drives expected returns, *a careful analysis of the client's risk tolerance should precede any discussion of return objectives.* Investment firms may survey clients directly to gauge their risk tolerance. Sometimes investment periodicals and Web sites contain tests such as Exhibit 5.4, which individuals can take to determine their own risk tolerance. An advisor will then use the results of such evaluations to categorize a client's risk tolerance and suggest, as a first step, asset allocations such as those in Exhibit 5.5.

Risk tolerance is more than a function of an individual's psychological makeup; it is also affected by factors such as an individual's family situation (for example, marital status and the number and ages of children), age, current net worth, and future income expectations. All else being equal, individuals with higher incomes have a greater propensity to take risk because their incomes can help cover any shortfall. Likewise, individuals with larger net worths can afford to place some assets in risky investments while the remaining assets provide a cushion against losses.

A person's return objective may be stated in terms of an absolute return (e.g., "seek an annual average return of 8 percent") or relative percentage return (e.g., "exceed the inflation rate by an average of 3 percent annually"). It may also be stated in terms of a general goal, such as capital preservation, current income, capital appreciation, or total return.

As we learned in Chapter 1, *capital preservation* means the investor wants to maintain the purchasing power of the investment and minimize the risk of loss. In other words, the desired return needs to be no less than the inflation rate. Generally, this is a strategy for strongly risk-averse investors or for funds that will soon be needed, say, for next year's tuition payment or a down payment on a house.

Capital appreciation is an appropriate objective for an investor who wants the portfolio to grow in real terms to meet future needs. Under this strategy, growth mainly occurs through capital gains, that is, buying assets at a low price and selling them later at a higher price. This is an aggressive strategy for investors willing to take on risk to meet their objective. Generally, longer-term investors seeking to build a retirement or college education fund may have this goal.

When *current income* is the return objective, an investor wants the portfolio to concentrate on generating income rather than capital gains. Retirees may favor this objective for part of their portfolio to help generate spendable funds.

The objective for the *total return* strategy is similar to that of capital appreciation; namely, the investor wants the portfolio to grow over time to meet a future need. Whereas

EXHIBIT 5.4	How Much Risk Is Right for You?

You've heard the expression "no pain, no gain"? In the investment world, the comparable phrase would be "no risk, no reward."

How you feel about risking your money will drive many of your investment decisions. The risk-comfort scale extends from very conservative (you don't want to risk losing a penny regardless of how little your money earns) to very aggressive (you're willing to risk much of your money for the possibility that it will grow tremendously). As you might guess, most investors' tolerance for risk falls somewhere in between.

If you're unsure of what your level of risk tolerance is, this quiz should help.

1. You win $300 in an office football pool. You:
   a) spend it on groceries b) purchase lottery tickets c) put it in a money market account d) buy some stock.

2. Two weeks after buying 100 shares of a $20 stock, the price jumps to over $30. You decide to: a) buy more stock; it's obviously a winner b) sell it and take your profits c) sell half to recoup some costs and hold the rest d) sit tight and wait for it to advance even more.

3. On days when the stock market jumps way up, you:
   a) wish you had invested more b) call your financial advisor and ask for recommendations c) feel glad you're not in the market because it fluctuates too much d) pay little attention.

4. You're planning a vacation trip and can either lock in a fixed room-and-meals rate of $150 per day or book stand-by and pay anywhere from $100 to $300 per day. You: a) take the fixed-rate deal b) talk to people who have been there about the availability of last-minute accommodations c) book stand-by and also arrange vacation insurance because you're leery of the tour operator d) take your chances with stand-by.

5. The owner of your apartment building is converting the units to condominiums. You can buy your unit for $75,000 or an option on it for $15,000. (Units have recently sold for close to $100,000, and prices seem to be going up.) For financing, you'll have to borrow the down payment and pay mortgage and condo fees higher than your present rent. You: a) buy your unit b) buy your unit and look for another to buy c) sell the option and arrange to rent the unit yourself d) sell the option and move out because you think the conversion will attract couples with small children.

6. You have been working three years for a rapidly growing company. As an executive, you are offered the option of buying up to 2% of company stock—2,000 shares at $10 a share. Although the company is privately owned (its stock does not trade on the open market), its majority owner has made handsome profits selling three other businesses and intends to sell this one eventually. You: a) purchase all the shares you can and tell the owner you would invest more if allowed b) purchase all the shares c) purchase half the shares d) purchase a small amount of shares.

7. You go to a casino for the first time. You choose to play: a) quarter slot machines b) $5 minimum-bet roulette c) dollar slot machines d) $25 minimum-bet blackjack.

8. You want to take someone out for a special dinner in a city that's new to you. How do you pick a place? a) read restaurant reviews in the local newspaper b) ask co-workers if they know of a suitable place c) call the only other person you know in this city, who eats out a lot but only recently moved there d) visit the city sometime before your dinner to check out the restaurants yourself.

9. The expression that best describes your lifestyle is: a) no guts, no glory b) just do it! c) look before you leap d) all good things come to those who wait.

10. Your attitude toward money is best described as: a) a dollar saved is a dollar earned b) you've got to spend money to make money c) cash and carry only d) whenever possible, use other people's money.

SCORING SYSTEM: Score your answers this way: 1) a-1, b-4, c-2, d-3 2) a-4, b-1, c-3, d-2 3) a-3, b-4, c-2, d-1 4) a-2, b-3 c-1, d-4 5) a-3, b-4, c-2, d-1 6) a-4, b-3, c-2, d-1 7) a-1, b-3, c-2, d-4 8) a-2, b-3, c-4, d-1 9) a-4, b-3, c-2, d-1 10) a-2, b-3, c-1, d-4.

What your total score indicates:

■ 10-17: You're not willing to take chances with your money, even though it means you can't make big gains.

■ 18-24: You're semi-conservative, willing to take a small chance with enough information.

■ 25-32: You're semi-aggressive, willing to take chances if you think the odds of earning more are in your favor.

■ 33-40: You're aggressive, looking for every opportunity to make your money grow, even though in some cases the odds may be quite long. You view money as a tool to make more money.

EXHIBIT 5.5	Initial Risk and Investment Goal Categories and Asset Allocations Suggested by Investment Firms

FIDELITY INVESTMENTS SUGGESTED ASSET ALLOCATIONS:

	Cash/Short-Term	Bonds	Domestic Equities	Foreign Equities
Short-term	100%	0%	0%	0%
Conservative	30	50	20	0
Balanced	10	40	45	5
Growth	5	25	60	10
Aggressive growth	0	15	70	15
Most aggressive	0	0	80	20

VANGUARD INVESTMENTS SUGGESTED ASSET ALLOCATIONS:

	Cash/Short-Term	Bonds	Stocks
Income-oriented	0%	100%	0%
	0	80%	20%
	0	70%	30%
Balanced	0%	60%	40%
	0	50%	50%
	0	40%	60%
Growth	0%	30%	70%
	0	20%	80%
	0	0%	100%

T. ROWE PRICE MATRIX

Nonretirement Goals Matrix

Your Time Horizon

Your Risk Tolerance	3–5 years	6–10 years	11+ years
Higher	**Strategy 2** 20% cash 40% bonds 40% stocks	**Strategy 3** 10% cash 30% bonds 60% stocks	**Strategy 5** 100% stocks
Moderate	**Strategy 1** 30% cash 50% bonds 20% stocks	**Strategy 2** 20% cash 40% bonds 40% stocks	**Strategy 4** 20% bonds 80% stocks
Lower	**All Cash** 100% cash	**Strategy 1** 30% cash 50% bonds 20% stocks	**Strategy 3** 10% cash 30% bonds 60% stocks

Source: Web sites accessed July 2004: http://personal.fidelity.com/planning/investment/?refhp=pr, http://flagship4 .vanguard.com/web/planret/AdvicePTCreatePlanStepIIIChooseYourAssetAlloc.html#, http://www.troweprice.com/ common/indexHtml3/0,0,htmlid=913,00.html?rfpgid=7934&rfpgid=7934.

the capital appreciation strategy seeks to do this primarily through capital gains, the total return strategy seeks to increase portfolio value by both capital gains and reinvesting current income. Because the total return strategy has both income and capital gains components, its risk exposure lies between that of the current income and capital appreciation strategies.

Investment Objective: Twenty-Five-Year-Old

What is an appropriate investment objective for a typical twenty-five-year-old investor? Let's assume he holds a steady job, is a valued employee, has adequate insurance coverage, and has enough money in the bank to provide a cash reserve. Let's also assume that his current long-term, high-priority investment goal is to build a retirement fund. Depending on his risk preferences, he can select a strategy carrying moderate to high amounts of risk because the income stream from his job will grow over time. For his retirement fund goal, a total return or capital appreciation objective would be most appropriate. Here's a possible objective statement:

> Invest funds in a variety of moderate- to high-risk investments. The average risk of the equity portfolio should exceed that of a broad stock market index such as the NYSE stock index. Equity exposure should range from 80 percent to 100 percent of the total portfolio with at least 10 percent of the funds in foreign investments. Remaining funds may be invested in intermediate- and long-term notes and bonds.

Investment Objective: Sixty-Five-Year-Old

Now let's consider a typical sixty-five-year-old investor who has adequate insurance coverage, a cash reserve, and is retiring this year. This individual will want less risk exposure than the twenty-five-year-old investor because her income stream from employment will soon be ending; she will not be able to recover any investment losses by saving more out of her paycheck. Depending on her income from Social Security and her pension, she may need some current income from her retirement portfolio to meet living expenses. Given that she can be expected to live about another fifteen to twenty years, she will need protection against inflation. A risk-averse investor will choose a combination of the current income and capital preservation strategies; a more risk-tolerant investor will choose a combination of current income and total return in an attempt to have principal growth outpace inflation. Here's an example of such an objective statement:

> Invest in stock and bond investments to meet income needs (from bond income and stock dividends) and to provide for real growth (from equities). Fixed-income securities should comprise 60–70 percent of the total portfolio; of this, 10–20 percent should be invested in short-term securities for extra liquidity and safety. The remaining 30–40 percent of the portfolio should be invested in high-quality stocks whose risk is approximate to those of the S&P 500 index.

More detailed analyses for our twenty-five- and our sixty-five-year-old investors would make more specific assumptions about the risk tolerance of each, as well as clearly enumerate their investment goals, return objectives, the funds they each have to invest at present, additional expected investment contributions, and expected cash flows each portfolio would need to generate to meet each investor's living expenses.

INVESTMENT CONSTRAINTS

In addition to the investment objective that sets limits on risk and return, certain other constraints affect the investment plan. These investment constraints include liquidity needs, an investment time horizon, tax factors, legal and regulatory constraints, and unique needs and preferences.

Liquidity Needs

An asset is *liquid* if it can be quickly converted to cash at a price close to fair market value. Generally, assets are more liquid if many traders are interested in a fairly standardized product. Treasury bills are a highly liquid security; real estate and venture capital are not.

Investors may have liquidity needs that the investment plan must take into consideration. Although an investor may have a primary long-term goal, several near-term goals may require available funds. For example, wealthy individuals with sizable tax obligations need adequate liquidity to pay their taxes without upsetting their investment plan. Families saving for retirement may need funds for shorter-term purposes such as buying a car or making college tuition payments.

Our typical twenty-five-year-old investor probably has little need for liquidity as he focuses on his long-term retirement fund goal. This constraint may change, however, should he face a period of unemployment or should near-term goals, such as honeymoon expenses or a house down payment, enter the picture. In contrast, our soon-to-be-retired sixty-five-year-old investor has a greater need for liquidity than the younger investor. She will want some of her portfolio in liquid securities to meet unexpected expenses or bills.

Time Horizon   Time horizon as an investment constraint briefly entered our earlier discussion of near-term and long-term goals. A close (but not perfect) relationship exists between an investor's time horizon, liquidity needs, and ability to handle risk. Investors with long investment horizons generally require less liquidity and can tolerate greater portfolio risk: less liquidity because the funds are not usually needed for many years; greater risk tolerance because any shortfalls or losses can be overcome by returns earned in subsequent years. Investors with shorter time horizons generally favor less risky investments because losses are harder to overcome during a short time frame.

Because of life expectancies, our twenty-five-year-old investor has a longer investment time horizon than our sixty-five-year-old investor. But, as discussed earlier, this does not mean the sixty-five-year-old should place all her money in short-term CDs; she needs the inflation protection that long-term investments such as common stock can provide. Still, because of the time horizon constraint, the twenty-five-year-old will probably have a greater proportion of his portfolio in equities—including stocks in small firms and international firms—than the sixty-five-year-old.

Tax Concerns   Investment planning is complicated by the tax code; taxes complicate the situation even more if international investments are part of the portfolio. Taxable income from interest, dividends, or rents is taxable at the investor's marginal tax rate. The marginal tax rate is the proportion of the next one dollar in income paid as taxes. Exhibit 5.6 shows the marginal tax rates for different levels of taxable income. As of 2003, the top federal marginal tax rate was 35 percent.

Capital gains or losses arise from asset price changes. They are taxed differently than income. Income is taxed when it is received; capital gains or losses are taxed only when an asset is sold and the gain or loss, relative to its initial cost or *basis,* is realized. *Unrealized capital gains* (or *losses*) reflect the price change in currently held assets that have *not* been sold; the tax liability on unrealized capital gains can be deferred indefinitely. If appreciated assets are passed on to an heir upon the investor's death, the basis of the assets is considered to be their value on the date of the holder's death. The heirs can then sell the assets and pay lower capital gains taxes if they wish. *Realized capital gains* occur when an appreciated asset has been sold; taxes are due on the realized capital gains only. As of 2003, the maximum tax rate on stock dividends and long-term capital gains is 15 percent.

Some find the difference between average and marginal income tax rates confusing. The *marginal tax rate* is the part of each additional dollar in income that is paid as tax. Thus, a married person, filing jointly, with an income of $50,000 will have a marginal tax rate of 15

EXHIBIT 5.6	Individual Marginal Tax Rates, 2003

For updates, go to the IRS Web site, *http://www.irs.gov.*

	IF TAXABLE INCOME		THE TAX IS		
			THEN		
	Is Over	But Not Over	This Amount	Plus This %	Of the Excess Over
Single	$0	$7,000	$0.00	10%	$0.00
	$7,000	$28,400	$700.00	15%	$7,000
	$28,400	$68,800	$3,910.00	25%	$28,400
	$68,800	$143,500	$14,010.00	28%	$68,800
	$143,500	$311,950	$34,926.00	33%	$143,500
	$311,950	—	$90,514.50	35%	$311,950
Married Filing Jointly	$0	$14,000	$0.00	10%	$0.00
	$14,000	$56,800	$1,400.00	15%	$14,000
	$56,800	$114,650	$7,820.00	25%	$56,800
	$114,650	$174,700	$22,282.50	28%	$114,650
	$174,700	$311,950	$39,096.50	33%	$174,700
	$311,950	—	$84,389.00	35%	$311,950

percent. The 15 percent marginal tax rate should be used to determine after-tax returns on investments.

The *average tax rate* is simply a person's total tax payment divided by their total income. It represents the average tax paid on each dollar the person earned. From Exhibit 5.6, a married person, filing jointly, will pay $6,800 in tax on a $50,000 income [$1,400 + 0.15($50,000 − $14,000)]. This average tax rate is $6,800/$50,000 or 13.6 percent. Note that the average tax rate is a weighted average of the person's marginal tax rates paid on each dollar of income. The first $14,000 of income has a 10 percent marginal tax rate; the next $36,000 has a 15 percent marginal tax rate:

$$\frac{\$14,000}{\$50,000} \times 0.10 + \frac{\$36,000}{\$50,000} \times 0.15 = 0.136, \text{ or the average tax rate of 13.6 percent}$$

Another tax factor is that some sources of investment income are exempt from federal and state taxes. For example, interest on federal securities, such as Treasury bills, notes, and bonds, is exempt from state taxes. Interest on municipal bonds (bonds issued by a state or other local governing body) is exempt from federal taxes. Further, if investors purchase municipal bonds issued by a local governing body of the state in which they live, the interest is exempt from both state and federal income tax. Thus, high-income individuals have an incentive to purchase municipal bonds to reduce their tax liabilities.

The after-tax return on taxable investment income is

After-Tax Income Return = Pre-Tax Income Return × (1 − Marginal Tax Rate)

Thus, the after-tax return on a taxable bond investment should be compared to that of municipals before deciding which a tax-paying investor should purchase.[6] Alternatively, we

---

[6]Realized capital gains on municipal securities are taxed, as are all other capital gains; similarly for capital losses. Only the income from municipals is exempt from federal income tax.

could compute a municipal's equivalent taxable yield, which is what a taxable bond investment would have to offer to produce the same after-tax return as the municipal. It is given by

$$\text{Equivalent Taxable Yield} = \frac{\text{Municipal Yield}}{(1 - \text{Marginal Tax Rate})}$$

To illustrate, if an investor is in the 28 percent marginal tax bracket, a taxable investment yield of 8 percent has an after-tax yield of 8 percent $\times$ (1 − 0.28) or 5.76 percent; an equivalent-risk municipal security offering a yield greater than 5.76 percent offers the investor greater after-tax returns. On the other hand, a municipal bond yielding 6 percent has an equivalent taxable yield of 6 percent/(1 − 0.28) = 8.33 percent; to earn more money after taxes, an equivalent-risk taxable investment has to offer a return greater than 8.33 percent.

There are other means of reducing investment tax liabilities. Contributions to an IRA (individual retirement account) may qualify as a tax deduction if certain income limits are met. Even without that deduction, taxes on any investment returns of an IRA, including any income, are deferred until the funds are withdrawn from the account. Any funds withdrawn from an IRA are taxable as current income, regardless of whether growth in the IRA occurs as a result of capital gains, income, or both. For this reason, to minimize taxes advisors recommend investing in stocks in taxable accounts and bonds in tax-deferred accounts such as IRAs. When funds are withdrawn from a tax-deferred account such as a regular IRA, assets are taxed (at most) at a 35 percent income tax rate (Exhibit 5.6)—even if the source of the stock return is primarily capital gains. In a taxable account, capital gains are taxed at the maximum 15 percent capital gains rate.[7]

The benefits of deferring taxes can dramatically compound over time, as we saw in Chapter 1. For example, $1000 invested in an IRA at a tax-deferred rate of 8 percent grows to $10,062.66 over thirty years; in a taxable account (assuming a 28 percent marginal (federal + state) tax rate), the funds would grow to only $5,365.91. After thirty years, the value of the tax-deferred investment has grown to nearly twice as large as the taxable investment.

With various stipulations, as of 2005 tax-deductible contributions of up to $4,000 (to be raised to $5,000 by 2008) can be made to a traditional IRA. A Roth IRA contribution is *not* tax deductible and contribution limits mirror those of the traditional IRA. The returns in a Roth IRA will grow on a tax-deferred basis and can be withdrawn, tax-free, if the funds are invested for at least five years and are withdrawn after the investor reaches age $59\frac{1}{2}$.[8]

For money you intend to invest in some type of IRA, the advantage of the Roth IRA's tax-free withdrawals will outweigh the tax-deduction benefit from the regular IRA—unless you expect your tax rate when the funds are withdrawn to be substantially less than when you initially invest the funds. Let's illustrate this with a hypothetical example.

Suppose you are considering investing $2,000 in either a regular or Roth IRA. Let's assume for simplicity that your combined federal and state marginal tax rate is 28 percent and that, over your twenty-year time horizon, your $2,000 investment will grow to $20,000, tax-deferred in either account; this represents an average annual return of 12.2 percent.

In a Roth IRA, no tax is deducted when the $2,000 is invested; in a regular IRA, the $2,000 investment is tax-deductible and will lower your tax bill by $560 (0.28 $\times$ $2,000).

---

[7]For a more complete analysis, see Terry Sylvester Charron, "Tax-Efficient Investing for Tax-Deferred and Taxable Accounts," *Journal of Private Portfolio Management* 2, no. 2 (Fall 1999): 31–37.

[8]Earlier tax-free withdrawals are possible if the funds are to be used for educational purposes or first-time home purchases.

EXHIBIT 5.7	Comparing the Regular versus Roth IRA Returns	
	Regular IRA	**Roth IRA**
Invested funds:	$2,000 + $560 tax savings on the tax-deductible IRA investment	$2,000 (no tax deduction)
Time horizon:	20 years	20 years
Rate of return assumption:	12.2 percent tax-deferred on the IRA investment; 8.8 percent on invested tax savings (represents the after-tax return on 12.2 percent)	12.2 percent tax-deferred on the IRA investment
Funds available after 20 years (taxes ignored)	$20,000 (pre-tax) from IRA investment; $3,025 (after-tax) from invested tax savings	$20,000 from IRA investment
Funds available after 20 years, 15 percent marginal tax rate at retirement	$20,000 less tax (0.15 × $20,000) plus $3,025 from invested tax savings equals **$20,025**	**$20,000**
Funds available after 20 years, 28 percent marginal tax rate at retirement	$20,000 less tax (0.28 × $20,000) plus $3,025 from invested tax savings equals **$17,425**	**$20,000**
Funds available after 20 years, 40 percent marginal tax rate at retirement	$20,000 less tax (0.40 × $20,000) plus $3,025 from invested tax savings equals **$15,025**	**$20,000**

Thus, in a Roth IRA, only $2,000 is assumed to be invested; for a regular IRA, both the $2,000 and the $560 tax savings are assumed to be invested. We will assume the $560 is invested at an after-tax rate of 12.2% × (1 − 0.28) = 8.8 percent. After twenty years, this amount will grow to $3,025. The calculations in Exhibit 5.7 show that at the end of the twenty-year time horizon the Roth IRA will give you more after-tax dollars unless you believe your tax bracket will be lower then *and you invest the regular IRA tax savings.*

Another tax-deferred investment is the cash value of life insurance contracts; these accumulate tax-free until the funds are withdrawn. Also, employers may offer 401(k) or 403(b) plans, which allow the employee to reduce taxable income by making tax-deferred investments. Many times employee contributions are matched by employer donations (up to a specified limit), thus allowing the employees to double their investment with little risk.

At times investors face a tradeoff between taxes and diversification needs. If entrepreneurs concentrate much of their wealth in equity holdings of their firm, or if employees purchase substantial amounts of their employer's stock through payroll deduction plans during their working life, their portfolios may contain a large amount of unrealized capital gains. In addition, the risk position of such a portfolio may be quite high because it is concentrated in a single company. The decision to sell some of the company stock in order to diversify the portfolio's risk by reinvesting the proceeds in other assets must be balanced against the resulting tax liability.

Our typical twenty-five-year-old investor probably is in a fairly low tax bracket, so detailed tax planning and tax-exempt income, such as that available from municipals, will not be major concerns. Nonetheless, he should still invest as much as possible into such tax-deferred plans as IRAs or 401(k)s for the retirement portion of his portfolio. If other funds are available for investment, they should be allocated based on his shorter- and longer-term investment goals.

Our sixty-five-year-old investor may face a different situation. If she had been in a high tax bracket prior to retiring—and therefore has sought tax-exempt income and tax-deferred investments—her situation may change shortly after retirement. After her retirement, without large regular paychecks, the need for tax-deferred investments or tax-exempt income becomes less. Taxable income may then offer higher after-tax yields than tax-exempt municipals if her tax bracket is lower. If her employer's stock is a large component of her retirement account, she must make careful decisions regarding the need to diversify versus the cost of realizing large capital gains (in her lower tax bracket).

Legal and Regulatory Factors   Both the investment process and the financial markets are highly regulated and subject to numerous laws. At times, these legal and regulatory factors constrain the investment strategies of individuals and institutions.

For example, funds removed from a regular IRA, Roth IRA, or 401(k) plan before age $59\frac{1}{2}$ are taxable and subject to an additional 10 percent withdrawal penalty. You may also be familiar with the tag line in many bank CD advertisements—"substantial interest penalty upon early withdrawal." Regulations and rules such as these may make such investments unattractive for investors with substantial liquidity needs in their portfolios.

Regulations can also constrain the investment choices available to someone in a fiduciary role. A *fiduciary*, or trustee, supervises an investment portfolio of a third party, such as a trust account or discretionary account.[9] The fiduciary must make investment decisions in accordance with the owner's wishes; a properly written policy statement assists this process. In addition, trustees of a trust account must meet the prudent-man standard, which means that they must invest and manage the funds as a prudent person would manage his or her own affairs. Notably, the prudent-man standard is based on the composition of the entire portfolio, not each individual asset.[10]

All investors must respect certain laws, such as insider trading prohibitions against the purchase and sale of securities on the basis of important information that is not publicly known. Typically, the people possessing such private, or insider, information are the firm's managers, who have a fiduciary duty to their shareholders. Security transactions based on access to insider information violates the fiduciary trust the shareholders have placed with management because the managers seek personal financial gain from their privileged position as agents for the shareholders.

For our typical twenty-five-year-old investor, legal and regulatory matters will be of little concern, with the possible exception of insider trading laws and the penalties associated with early withdrawal of funds from tax-deferred retirement accounts. Should he seek a financial advisor to assist him in constructing a financial plan, that advisor would have to obey the regulations pertinent to a client–advisor relationship. Similar concerns confront our sixty-five-year-old investor. In addition, as a retiree if she wants to do estate planning and set up trust accounts, she should seek legal and tax advice to ensure her plans are properly implemented.

Unique Needs and Preferences   This category covers the individual and sometimes idiosyncratic concerns of each investor. Some investors may want to exclude certain investments from their portfolio solely on the basis of personal preference or for social consciousness

---

[9]A discretionary account is one in which the fiduciary, many times a financial planner or stock broker, has the authority to purchase and sell assets in the owner's portfolio without first receiving the owner's approval.

[10]As we will discuss in Chapter 8, it is sometimes wise to hold assets that are individually risky in the context of a well-diversified portfolio, even if the investor is strongly risk averse.

reasons. For example, they may request that no firms that manufacture or sell tobacco, alcohol, pornography, or environmentally harmful products be included in their portfolio. Some mutual funds screen according to this type of social responsibility criterion.

Another example of a personal constraint is the time and expertise a person has for managing his or her portfolio. Busy executives may prefer to relax during nonworking hours and let a trusted advisor manage their investments. Retirees, on the other hand, may have the time but believe they lack the expertise to choose and monitor investments, so they also may seek professional advice.

In addition, a business owner with a large portion of her wealth—and emotion—tied up in her firm's stock may be reluctant to sell even when it may be financially prudent to do so and then reinvest the proceeds for diversification purposes. Further, if the stock holdings are in a private company, it may be difficult to find a buyer unless shares are sold at a discount from their fair market value. Because each investor is unique, the implications of this final constraint differ for each person; there is no "typical" twenty-five-year-old or sixty-five-year-old investor. Each individual will have to decide—and then communicate specific goals in a well-constructed policy statement.

Constructing the Policy Statement

As we have seen, the policy statement allows the investor to communicate his or her objectives (risk and return) and constraints (liquidity, time horizon, tax, legal and regulatory, and unique needs and preferences). This communication gives the advisor a better chance of implementing an investment strategy that will satisfy the investor. Even if an advisor is not used, each investor needs to take this first important step of the investment process and develop a financial plan to guide the investment strategy. To do without a plan or to plan poorly is to place the success of the financial plan in jeopardy.

GENERAL GUIDELINES

Constructing a policy statement is the investor's responsibility, but investment advisors often assist in the process. The following lists of recommendations for both the investor and the advisor provide guidelines for good policy statement construction.

In the process of constructing a policy statement, investors should think about the following set of questions and be able to explain their answers:

1. What are the real risks of an adverse financial outcome, especially in the short run?
2. What probable emotional reactions will I have to an adverse financial outcome?
3. How knowledgeable am I about investments and markets?
4. What other capital or income sources do I have? How important is this particular portfolio to my overall financial position?
5. What, if any, legal restrictions may affect my investment needs?
6. What, if any, unanticipated consequences of interim fluctuations in portfolio value might affect my investment policy?

Adapted from Charles D. Ellis, *Investment Policy: How to Win the Loser's Game,* Homewood IL: Dow Jones–Irwin, 1985, pp. 25–26. Reprinted by permission of The McGraw-Hill Companies.

In assisting an investor in the policy statement process, an advisor should ensure that the policy statement satisfactorily answers the following questions:

1. Is the policy carefully designed to meet the specific needs and objectives of this particular investor? (Cookie-cutter or one-size-fits-all policy statements are generally inappropriate.)
2. Is the policy written so clearly and explicitly that a competent stranger could manage the portfolio in conformance with the client's needs? In case of a manager transition, could the new manager use this policy to handle the portfolio in accordance with the client's needs?
3. Would the client have been able to remain committed to the policies during the capital market experiences of the past sixty to seventy years? That is, does the client fully understand investment risks and the need for a disciplined approach to the investment process?
4. Would the portfolio manager have been able to maintain fidelity to the policy over the same period? (Discipline is a two-way street; we do not want the portfolio manager to change strategies because of a disappointing market.)
5. Would the policy, if implemented, achieve the client's objectives? (Bottom line: would the policy have worked to meet the client's needs?)

Adapted from Charles D. Ellis, *Investment Policy: How to Win the Loser's Game,* Homewood, IL: Dow Jones–Irwin, 1985, p. 62. Reprinted by permission of The McGraw-Hill Companies.

FURTHER CONSIDERATIONS

When constructing their policy statements, participants in employer-sponsored retirement plans need to realize that through such plans 30–40 percent of their retirement funds may be invested in their employer's stock. Having so much money invested in one asset violates diversification principles and could be costly. To put this in context, most mutual funds are limited by law to having no more than 5 percent of their assets in any one company's stock; a firm's pension plan can invest no more than 10 percent of their funds in its own stock. Thus, individuals are unfortunately doing what government regulations prevent many institutional investors from doing.[11] In addition, some studies point out that the average stock allocation in retirement plans is lower than it should be to allow for growth of principal over time.

Another consideration is the issue of stock trading. A number of studies have shown that many individual investors trade stocks too often (driving up commissions), sell stocks with gains too early (prior to further price increases), and hold onto losers too long (as the price continues to fall).[12] These results are especially true for men and online traders.[13]

Investors, in general, seem to neglect that important first step to achieve financial success: they do not plan for the future. Studies of retirement plans show that Americans are not saving enough to finance their retirement years and they are not planning sufficiently

[11]Ellen R. Schultz, "Workers Put Too Much in Their Employer's Stock," *The Wall Street Journal,* September 13, 1996, pp. C1, C25.

[12]Brad Barber and Terrance Odean, "Trading Is Hazardous to Your Wealth: The Common Stock Investment Performance of Individual Investors," *Journal of Finance* 55, no. 2 (April 2000): 773–806; Terrance Odean, "Do Investors Trade Too Much?" *American Economic Review* 89 (December 1999): 1279–1298; Brad Barber and Terrance Odean, "The Courage of Misguided Convictions: The Trading Behavior of Individual Investors," *Financial Analyst Journal* 55, no. 6 (November/ December 1999): 41–55; Terrance Odean, "Are Investors Reluctant to Realize Their Losses?" *Journal of Finance* 53, no. 5 (October 1998): 1775–1798.

[13]Brad Barber and Terrance Odean, "Boys Will Be Boys: Gender, Overconfidence, and Common Stock Investment," *Quarterly Journal of Economics* 116, no. 1 (February 2001): 261–292; Brad Barber and Terrance Odean, "Online Investors: Do the Slow Die First?" University of California at Davis working paper.

for what will happen to their savings after they retire. Around 25 percent of workers have saved less than $50,000 for their retirement and 60 percent of workers surveyed confessed they were "behind schedule" in planning and saving for retirement.[14]

The Importance of Asset Allocation

A major reason for investors to develop policy statements is to determine an overall investment strategy. The policy statement should provide guidelines as to which asset classes to include and the relative proportions of funds to invest in each class. How the investor divides funds into different asset classes is the process of *asset allocation*. Asset allocation is usually expressed in ranges. This allows the investment manager some freedom, based on his or her reading of capital market trends, to invest toward the upper or lower end of the ranges. For example, suppose a policy statement requires that common stocks be 60 to 80 percent of the value of the portfolio and that bonds should be 20 to 40 percent. Should a manager be particularly bullish about stocks, he will increase the allocation of stocks toward the 80 percent upper end of the equity range and decrease bonds toward the 20 percent lower end of the bond range. Should he be more optimistic about bonds, that manager may shift the allocation closer to 40 percent of the funds invested in bonds with the remainder in stocks.

In general, four decisions are made when constructing an investment strategy:

1. What asset classes to consider for investment (e.g., stocks, bonds, and T-bills);
2. What normal or policy weights to assign to each eligible asset class, that is, what target asset allocation should be invested in each asset class (e.g., 60 percent stocks, 30 percent bonds, 10 percent T-bills);
3. The allowable allocation ranges based on policy weights (e.g., 50-70 percent stocks, 25-35 percent bonds, 5-15 percent T-bills);
4. What specific securities to purchase for the portfolio.

The asset allocation decision comprises the first two points. How important is this decision to an investor? In a word, *very*. Several studies have examined the effect of the normal policy weights on investment performance, using data from both pension funds and mutual funds, from periods of time extending from the early 1970s to the late 1990s.[15] The studies all found similar results: About 90 percent of a fund's returns over time can be explained by its target asset allocation policy. Exhibit 5.8 shows the relationship between returns on the target or policy portfolio allocation and actual returns on a sample mutual fund.

Rather than looking at just one fund and how the target asset allocation determines its returns, some studies have looked at how much the asset allocation policy affects returns on a variety of funds with different target weights. For example, Ibbotson and Kaplan found

---

[14]Glenn Ruffenach, "Fewer Americans Save for Their Retirement," *The Wall Street Journal,* May 10, 2001, p. A2; Jonathan Clements, "Curb Your Spending, Boost Your Saving and Watch Retirement Nest Egg Grow," *The Wall Street Journal,* September 2, 1997, p. C1; Jonathan Clements, "Squeezing the Right Amount from a Retirement Stash," *The Wall Street Journal,* February 25, 1997, p. C1; Jonathan Clements, "Retirement Honing: How Much Should You Have Saved for a Comfortable Life?" *The Wall Street Journal,* January 28, 1997, p. C1.

[15]Findings discussed in this section are based on Roger G. Ibbotson and Paul D. Kaplan, "Does Asset Allocation Policy Explain 40, 90, or 100 Percent of Performance?" *Financial Analysts Journal* 56, no. 1 (January/February 2000): 26–33; Gary P. Brinson, Brian D. Singer, and Gilbert L. Beebower, "Determinants of Portfolio Performance II: An Update," *Financial Analysts Journal* 47, no. 3 (May–June 1991): 40–48; Gary P. Brinson, L. Randolph Hood, and Gilbert L. Beebower, "Determinants of Portfolio Performance," *Financial Analysts Journal* 42, no. 4 (July–August 1986): 39–48.

EXHIBIT 5.8	Time-Series Regression of Monthly Fund Return versus Fund Policy Return: One Mutual Fund, April 1988–March 1998

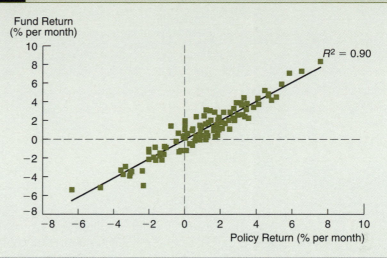

that across a sample of funds about 40 percent of the difference in fund returns is explained by their differences in asset allocation policy. And what does asset allocation tell us about the *level* of a particular fund's returns? The Brinson et. al and Ibbotson and Kaplan studies answered that question as well. They divided the policy return (what the fund return would have been had it been invested in indexes at the policy weights) by the actual fund return (which includes the effects of varying from the policy weights and security selection). A hypothetical fund passively invested at the target weights would have a ratio value of 1.0 or 100 percent. A hypothetical fund managed by someone with skill in market timing (for moving in and out of asset classes) and security selection would have a ratio less than 1.0 (or less than 100 percent); that is, the manager's skill would result in an actual fund return greater than the policy return. The studies showed the opposite: the policy-return–actual-return ratio averaged over 1.0, showing that asset allocation explains slightly more than 100 percent of the level of a fund's returns. Because of market efficiency, fund managers practicing market timing and security selection have, on average, difficulty surpassing passively invested index returns after taking into account the expenses and fees of investing.

Thus, asset allocation is a very important decision. Across all funds, the asset allocation decision explains an average of 40 percent of the variation in fund returns. For a single fund, asset allocation explains 90 percent of the fund's variation in returns over time and slightly more than 100 percent of the average fund's level of return. The desire to "get rich quick" by trading in the stock market may lead to a few success stories, but for most investors implementing a prudent asset allocation strategy and investing over time is a more likely means of investment success. A well-constructed policy statement can go a long way toward ensuring that an appropriate asset allocation decision is implemented.

RETURNS AND RISKS OF DIFFERENT ASSET CLASSES AND THE CASE FOR STOCKS

All investors with a long time horizon, even those who are very conservative and risk averse, should consider placing some of their portfolio in high-risk assets such as common

EXHIBIT 5.9	Higher Returns Offered by Equities Over Long Time Periods Time Frame: 1934–2003

Length of Holding Period (calendar years)	Percentage of Periods That Stock Returns Trailed T-Bill Returns*
1	35.7%
5	18.2
10	11.5
20	0.0
30	0.0

*Price change plus reinvested income

Source: Author calculations.

stocks. As we saw earlier, Exhibit 2.1 illustrated returns (unadjusted for costs and taxes) for several asset classes over time. The higher returns available from equities do come at the cost of higher risk. At times, Treasury bills will outperform equities. Because they are equities, common stocks sometimes lose significant value. These are times when undisciplined and uneducated investors sell their stocks at a loss and vow never to invest in equities again. In contrast, during such times disciplined investors stick to their investment plan and position their portfolio for the next bull market.[16] By holding on to their stocks and perhaps purchasing more at depressed prices, the equity portion of the portfolio will experience a substantial increase in the future. This is precisely why investors need a policy statement and why the investor and manager must understand the capital markets and have a disciplined approach to investing.

The asset allocation decision determines to a great extent both the returns and the volatility of the portfolio. Exhibit 2.1 indicated that stocks are riskier than bonds or T-bills. Exhibit 5.9, which examines the longer-term performance of a stock market index (the S&P 500) and T-bills, shows that stocks have sometimes earned returns lower than those of T-bills for extended periods of time. But over longer periods (twenty years or more) stocks have outperformed T-bills. Thus, sticking with an investment policy and riding out the difficult times can result in attractive long-term rates of return.[17]

One popular way to measure risk is to examine the variability of returns over time by computing a standard deviation or variance of annual rates of return for an asset class. This measure, as reported in Exhibit 2.1, indicates that stocks are risky and T-bills are not. Another intriguing measure of risk is the probability of *not* meeting a given investment return objective. From this perspective, if the investor has a long time horizon, the risk of equities is small and that of T-bills is large because their differences in expected returns leads to a greater possibility of stocks helping an investor meet an objective. T-bill income does not vary much since it depends on the overall level of interest rates. Income from common stock, on the other hand, may start out low but can rise as firms' earnings rise over time and they increase their dividends over time. And when we consider the growth

---

[16]Newton's law of gravity seems to work two ways in financial markets. What goes up may come down; it also appears that over time what goes down may come back up. Contrarian investors and some "value" investors use this concept to try to outperform the indexes over time.

[17]The added benefits of diversification may reduce overall portfolio risk without harming potential return.

in principal that stocks offer, we see that long-term "conservative," income-oriented T-bill investors are in fact exposed to substantial amounts of risk.

REAL INVESTMENT RETURNS AFTER TAXES AND COSTS

Depending on the measures used and the length of the time horizon, common stocks have been earning an average return between 11 percent and 13 percent over time in the United States. For the sake of illustration, let's call it a long-run average of 12 percent. But investors do not actually earn this return because of taxes on income and capital gains and because inflation erodes the real purchasing power of the invested funds.

For example, if the "typical" investor has, over time, an average tax rate of 25 percent, the annual average after-tax (nominal) return becomes 9 percent [12 percent $\times$ (1 $-$ 0.25)]. Inflation over time has averaged between 3 percent and 4 percent; using 3.5 percent, we calculate the real after-tax return on stocks to be

$$\textbf{Real Return} = \textbf{(1 + Nominal Return)/(1 + Inflation Rate)} - \textbf{1}$$

$$= \textbf{(1.09)/(1.035)} - \textbf{1} = \textbf{0.0531 or about 5.3 percent}$$

Any management fees and expenses for the investment account will lower this return even more.

The bond returns we saw in Exhibit 2.1 occurred over a time when interest rates were generally falling (thus leading to higher bond prices and bond returns). Over a longer period of time, an average return to bonds will be closer to 6 percent. With an average tax bracket of 25 percent, this pre-tax return becomes an after-tax return of 4.5 percent. Once inflation is considered, the real after-tax return on bonds becomes closer to 1.0 percent. Nominal rates on CDs and T-bills become close to zero—or even negative—once the effect of taxes and inflation is considered.

The income return on municipal bonds is tax-exempt, of course, and their yields are lower than taxable corporates and treasuries because of this. So the after-tax return on municipals should be approximately the same as the after-tax return on other bonds. After inflation is factored in, the real return on municipals will likely be in the 1–2 percent range.

As we learned in Chapter 3, TIPS (Treasury-Inflation Protected Securities) offer investors protection from inflation. But the income (including the added yield to compensate for the past year's inflation) is taxable at ordinary income tax rates. And taxes must be paid on all income, even the increased income to compensate for inflation. Thus a TIP paying 5 percent on a nominal basis has an after-tax return of 5 percent $\times$ (1 $-$ 0.25) = 3.75 percent; on a real basis, this return is less than 1 percent.

The results of this simple analysis imply that, for taxable investments, the only way to maintain purchasing power over time when investing in financial assets is to invest in common stocks. An asset allocation decision for a taxable portfolio that does not include a substantial commitment to common stocks may make it difficult for the portfolio to maintain real value over time.[18]

ASSET ALLOCATION SUMMARY

A carefully constructed policy statement determines the types of assets that should be included in a portfolio. The asset allocation decision, not the selection of specific stocks and

---

[18]Of course other equity-oriented investments, such as venture capital or real estate, may also provide inflation protection after adjusting for portfolio costs and taxes.

bonds, determines most of a portfolio's returns over time. Although seemingly risky, investors seeking capital appreciation, income, or even capital preservation over long time periods will do well to include an equity allocation in their portfolio. As reviewed in this section, a strategy's risk may depend on the investor's goals and time horizon. For long time horizons, investing in "safe" T-bills may be riskier than investing in common stocks due to reinvestment risks and the risk of not meeting long-term investment return goals.

Asset Allocation and Cultural Differences

Thus far our analysis has focused on U.S. investors. Non-U.S. investors approach their asset allocation decisions in much the same manner but the actual allocation decisions differ from those of U.S. investors because they face different social, economic, political, and tax environments. For example, Exhibit 5.10 shows the equity allocations of pension funds, a type of institutional investor, in several countries.

National differences can explain much of the divergent portfolio strategies. Of these four nations, the average age of the population is the highest in Germany and Japan and lowest in Ireland, Hong Kong, the United States, and the United Kingdom, which helps explain the greater use of equities in the latter countries. Government privatization programs during the 1980s in the United Kingdom encouraged equity ownership among individual and institutional investors. Since 1960, the cost of living in the United Kingdom has increased at a rate more than 4.5 times that of Germany; this inflationary bias in the U.K. economy favors equities in U.K. asset allocations. Exhibit 5.11 shows the positive relationship between the inflation level and pension fund equity allocation in various countries, indicating that the economic environment as well as demographics affect asset allocation in a country.

The need to invest in equities for portfolio growth is less in Germany, where workers receive generous state pensions. In addition, Germans tend to show a cultural aversion to the stock market; many are risk-averse and even consider stock investing a form of gambling.

Exhibit 5.10	Equity Allocations in Pension Fund Portfolios
Country	**Percentage in Equities**
Hong Kong	79
United Kingdom	78
Ireland	68
United States	58
Japan	37
Germany	8

Source: Copyright © 1998, Association for Investment Management and Research. "Client Expectations and the Demand to Minimize Downside Risk" by Mark Tapley in *Asset Allocation in a Changing World* edited by Terence E. Burns, pp. 85–91, with permission from CFA Institute. All Rights Reserved.

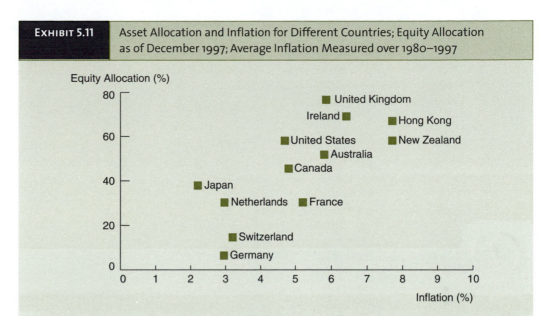

EXHIBIT 5.11 Asset Allocation and Inflation for Different Countries; Equity Allocation as of December 1997; Average Inflation Measured over 1980–1997

Although this attitude is showing signs of change, the German stock market is rather illiquid, with only a handful of stocks accounting for 50 percent of total stock trading volume.[19] Legislation in 2002 that encourages 401(k)-like plans in Germany may encourage citizens to invest more in equities, but in mid-2001, less than 10 percent of Germans over the age of fourteen owned stocks either directly or indirectly (e.g., in mutual funds).[20] As of May 2004, only 14 percent of households in all of western Europe owned stock and only 10 percent owned equity mutual funds.[21]

Legal and regulatory factors play a role in asset allocations across these countries. Until 2002, German regulations prevented pension firms from investing more than 30 percent of their assets in European Union equities. Since 2002, the regulated percentage has risen to 45 percent.[22] Other OECD (Organization for Economic Cooperation and Development) countries place regulatory restrictions on institutional investors as well. For example, pension funds in Austria must have at least 50 percent of their assets in bank deposits or schilling-denominated bonds. Belgium limits pension funds to a minimum 15 percent investment in government bonds. Finland places a 5 percent limit on investments outside its

---

[19]Peter Gumbel, "The Hard Sell: Getting Germans to Invest in Stocks," *The Wall Street Journal,* August 4, 1995, p. A2.

[20]Christopher Rhoads, "Germany Is Poised for a Pension Overhaul," *The Wall Street Journal,* May 10, 2001, p. A13.

[21]Sara Calian and Silvia Ascarelli, "Europeans Lose Love for Stocks," *The Wall Street Journal,* May 12, 2004, page C1, C2.

[22]Beatrix Payne, "Higher German Limits on Investment Seen as Boon for Equities," *Pension and Investments* (February 4, 2002): 14.

borders by pension funds, and French pension funds must invest a minimum of 34 percent in public debt instruments.[23]

Overall, asset allocation policy and strategy are determined mainly within the context of an individual investor's objectives and constraints. To explain differences in investor behavior across countries, however, we must look at each country's political and economic environment.

---

[23]Daniel Witschi, "European Pension Funds: Turning More Aggressive?" in *Asset Allocation in a Changing World,* edited by Terence E. Burns, (Charlottesville, VA: Association for Investment Management and Research, 1998): 72–84; Joel Chernoff, "OECD Eyes Pension Rules," *Pensions and Investments* (December 23, 1996): 2, 34.

Investments Online

Many inputs go into an investment policy statement as an investor maps out his or her objectives and constraints. Some inputs and helpful information are available in the following Web sites. Many of the sites mentioned in Chapter 1 also contain important information and insights about asset allocation decisions.

http://www.ssa.gov Information on a person's expected retirement funds from Social Security can be obtained by using the Social Security Administration's Web site.

http://www.ibbotson.com Ibbotson is the source of much data and analysis that is helpful in the investor-education and asset allocation process. Many professional financial planners make use of Ibbotson's data and education resources.

http://www.mfea.com/InvestmentStrategies/Calculators/default.asp This page contains links to calculators on Web sites of mutual fund families.

Sites with information and sample Monte Carlo simulations for spending plans in retirement include:

http://www.financialengines.com, http://www.troweprice.com (after getting to the individual investor page, click on investment planning and tools, investment planning, and select the investment strategy planner);
http://www3.troweprice.com/ric/RIC/ (for a retirement income calculator); and **http://www.decisioneering.com.**

Many professional organizations have Web sites for use by their members, those interested in seeking professional finance designations, and those interested in seeking advice from a professional financial advisor. These sites include:

http://www.cfainstitute.org CFA Institute awards the CFA (Chartered Financial Analyst) designation. This site provides information about the CFA designation, CFA Institute publications, investor education, and various Internet resources.

http://www.amercoll.edu This is the Web site for The American College, which is the training arm of the insurance industry. The American College offers the CLU and ChFC designations, which are typically earned by insurance professionals.

http://www.cfp.net The home page of Certified Financial Planner Board of Standards contains links to find a CFP™ mark holder and other information about the financial planning profession.

http://www.napfa.org This is the home page for the National Association of Personal Financial Advisors, the trade group for fee-only financial planners. Fee-only planners do not sell products on commission, or, should they recommend a commission-generating product, they pass the commission on to the investor. This site features press releases, finding a fee-only planner in your area, a list of financial resources on the Web, and position openings in the financial planning field.

http://www.fpanet.org The Financial Planning Association's Web site offers features and topics of interest to financial planners including information on earning the CFP designation and receiving the *Journal of Financial Planning*.

http://www.asec.org The home page of the American Saving Education Council.

Summary

- Investors need to prudently manage risk within the context of their investment goals and preferences. Income, spending, and investing behavior will change over a person's lifetime.

- Developing an investment policy statement is an important first step in implementing a serious investment plan. By forcing investors to examine their needs, risk tolerance, and familiarity with the capital markets, policy statements help investors correctly identify appropriate objectives and constraints. In addition, the policy statement serves as a standard by which to judge the performance of the portfolio and its manager.

- We reviewed the importance of the asset allocation decision in determining long-run portfolio investment returns and risks. Because the asset allocation decision follows the setting of objectives and constraints, it is clear that the success of the investment program depends on the first step, the construction of the policy statement.

- Asset allocation decisions will differ across countries because of different economic environments, demographics, and regulations.

Questions

1. What are some ways of managing risk in investments?
2. "Young people with little wealth should not invest money in risky assets such as the stock market because they can't afford to lose what little money they have." Do you agree or disagree with this statement? Why?
3. Your healthy sixty-three-year-old neighbor is about to retire and comes to you for advice. From talking with her, you find out she is planning to take all the money out of her company's retirement plan and invest it in bond mutual funds and money market funds. What advice would you give her?
4. Discuss how an individual's investment strategy may change as he or she goes through the accumulation, consolidation, spending, and gifting phases of life.
5. Why is a policy statement important?
6. Use the questionnaire in Exhibit 5.4 to evaluate your risk tolerance. Then use this information to write a policy statement for yourself.
7. Your forty-five-year-old uncle is twenty years away from retirement; your thirty-five-year-old older sister is thirty years away from retirement. How might their investment policy statements differ? What additional information do you need to know to put together a reasonable statement for each of them?
8. What information is necessary before a financial planner can assist a person in constructing an investment policy statement?
9. *CFA Examination Level III*

   Mr. Franklin is seventy years of age, in excellent health, pursues a simple but active lifestyle, and has no children.

He has interest in a private company for $90 million and has decided that a medical research foundation will receive half of the proceeds now; it will also be the primary beneficiary of his estate upon his death. Mr. Franklin is committed to the foundation's well-being because he believes strongly that, through it, a cure will be found for the disease that killed his wife. He now realizes that an appropriate investment policy and asset allocations are required if his goals are to be met through investment of his considerable assets. Currently, the following assets are available for use in building an appropriate portfolio:

$45.0 million cash (from sale of the private company interest, net of pending $45 million gift to the foundation)
10.0 million stocks and bonds ($5 million each)
9.0 million warehouse property (now fully leased)
1.0 million Franklin residence
$65.0 million total available assets

a. Formulate and justify an investment policy statement setting forth the appropriate guidelines within which future investment actions should take place. Your policy statement must encompass all relevant objective and constraint considerations. (10 minutes)
b. Recommend and justify a long-term asset allocation that is consistent with the investment policy statement you created in part (a) above. Briefly explain the key assumptions you made in generating your allocation. (15 minutes)

Problems

1. Suppose your first job pays you $28,000 annually. What percentage should your cash reserve contain? How much life insurance should you carry if you are unmarried? If you are married with two young children?
2. What is the marginal tax rate for a couple, filing jointly, if their taxable income is $20,000? $40,000? $60,000?

What is their tax bill for each of these income levels? What is the average tax rate for each of these income levels?

3. What is the marginal tax rate for a single individual if his taxable income is $20,000? $40,000? $60,000? What is his tax bill for each of these income levels? What is his average tax rate for each of these income levels?

4. a. Someone in the 36 percent tax bracket can earn 9 percent annually on her investments in a tax-exempt IRA account. What will be the value of a one-time $10,000 investment in five years? Ten years? Twenty years?

b. Suppose the 9 percent return in part (a) is taxable rather than tax-deferred and the taxes are paid annually. What will be the after-tax value of her $10,000 investment after five, ten, and twenty years?

5. a. Someone in the 15 percent tax bracket can earn 10 percent on his investments in a tax-exempt IRA account. What will be the value of a $10,000 investment in five years? Ten years? Twenty years?

b. Suppose the 10 percent return in part (a) is taxable rather than tax-deferred. What will be the after-tax value of his $10,000 investment after five, ten, and twenty years?

Web Exercises

1. Find at least three asset allocation strategies on the Internet (from mutual fund firms or brokerage houses) in addition to those in Exhibit 5.5. Compare and contrast their suggested allocations for different kinds of investors.

2. Use the Internet to find the home pages for some financial planning firms. What strategies do they emphasize? What do they say about their asset allocation strategy? What are their firms' emphases: value investing, international diversification, principal preservation, retirement and estate planning, and such?

3. Go to the Vanguard Web site (**http://www.vanguard.com**) and obtain information on the income return and capital return on their Vanguard 500 Index Fund. Assuming capital gains are realized every five years, develop a spreadsheet to compute before-tax and after-tax returns for an investor in the 28 percent income tax bracket. Assume all capital gains are taxed at 15 percent when they are realized. What is the average before-tax return during the fund's life? What is the average after-tax return?

4. The Web site of Ibbotson Associates (**http://www.ibbotson.com**) features research papers on a variety of investment topics. Read one of the papers and write a one or two page summary of its findings and suggestions for investors.

5. The use of an average annual return can be misleading. An average return of 10 percent annually can mask the variability in portfolio value that can arise because of year-to-year variation in returns. The use of Monte Carlo analysis is gaining popularity among investment professionals as a way of estimating future portfolio value. Find information about Monte Carlo analysis in the context of financial planning. What is it? How is it used? Describe some of the insights it provides investment professionals.

Spreadsheet Exercises

1. Use spreadsheet analysis to solve the following.
   a. How much money will you have at the end of the time horizon if you invest
      i. $2,000 over ten years at a return of 8 percent?
      ii. $5,000 over twenty years at a return of 7.5 percent?
      iii. $10,000 over twenty-five years at a return of 10 percent?
   b. How much money will you have at the end of the time horizon if you invest
      i. $1,000 a year over twenty years at a return of 10 percent?
      ii. $2,000 a year over fifteen years at a return of 6 percent?
      iii. $5,000 a year over twenty-five years at a return of 8.5 percent?
   c. How much money must you save every year if you want to meet the following investment goals?
      i. Having $100,000 for college tuition for your child in seventeen years if you can earn 7 percent on the funds
      ii. Having $1,000,000 for retirement in thirty-five years if you can earn 9 percent on the funds
      iii. Having $500,000 for retirement in twenty-five years if you can earn 11 percent on the funds

2. Replicate the analysis of Exhibit 5.7 for a Roth and a traditional IRA. Assume you are in the 25 percent tax bracket and you want to place $4,000 in one of the tax-deferred accounts. Which gives you the highest after-tax return if your time horizon is twenty-five years? Assume tax brackets of 10, 15, 25, 28 and 33 percent in your analysis.

3. Considering the effects of inflation, a person making $68,000 in 2004 had the equivalent income of a person

making $10,000 in 1955. Given the following tax rates from the 1950s, who was paying relatively more in taxes, the person in the 1950s or the person in the 2000s?

SINGLE		MARRIED, FILING JOINTLY	
Income	Marginal Tax Rate	Income	Marginal Tax Rate
$0-$2,000	20%	$0-$4,000	20%
$2,001-4,000	22	$4,001-8,000	22
$4,001-6,000	26	$8,001-12,000	26
$6,001-8,000	30		
$8,001-10,000	34		
$10,001-12,000	38		

4. Sam has just retired with $500,000 in savings. How long will it be before he runs out of money if the funds are invested to earn an average return of 6 percent and he withdraws (a) 4 percent annually, (b) 6 percent annually, (c) 8 percent annually? Assume the cash is withdrawn at the beginning of the year and the return on the remaining funds is credited at the end of the year.

5. How will the answers to Exercise 4 change if a bear market hits the investor shortly after retirement and the portfolio loses 15 percent of its value during the first year of retirement before it recovers to begin earning 6 percent annually? Assume the market fall occurs immediately after Sam removes funds from the account according to the three possible spending plans in Exercise 4.

6. You have $10,000 to invest this year; given your risk preferences and goals, you will invest 50 percent in common stocks and 50 percent in bonds. Your company retirement plan will allow you to invest $5,000 on a tax–deferred basis. Assume the stocks will average an annual price appreciation of 8 percent and distribute an additional 2 percent in dividends. The bonds will pay a coupon of 7 percent. Your income is taxed at a marginal rate of 25 percent and all your capital gains will be taxed at 18 percent. If your holding period is (a) ten years; (b) twenty years; (c) thirty years, is it better to place the stocks or the bonds in the tax-deferred account? Justify your answers.

REFERENCES

Bhatia, Sanjiv, ed. *Managing Assets for Individual Investors.* Charlottesville, VA: Association for Investment Management and Research, 1995.

Bronson, James W., Matthew H. Scanlan, and Jan R. Squires. "Managing Individual Investor Portfolios." In *2004 CFA Level III Candidate Readings: Portfolio Management.* Charlottesville, VA: CFA Institute, 2003.

Burns, Terence E., ed. *Asset Allocation in a Changing World.* Charlottesville, VA: Association for Investment Management and Research, 1998.

Ellis, Charles D. *Investment Policy: How to Win the Loser's Game.* Homewood, IL: Dow Jones–Irwin, 1985.

Maginn, John L., and Donald L. Tuttle. *Managing Investment Portfolios: A Dynamic Process*, 2nd ed. Charlottesville, VA: Association for Investment Management and Research, 1990.

Peavy, John. *Cases in Portfolio Management.* Charlottesville, VA: Association for Investment Management and Research, 1990.

Tschampion, R. Charles, Laurence B. Siegel, Dean J. Takahashi, and John L. Maginn. "Managing Institutional Investor Portfolios." In *2004 CFA Level III Candidate Readings: Portfolio Management.* Charlottesville, VA: CFA Institute, 2003.

GLOSSARY

Accumulation phase Phase in the investment life cycle during which individuals in the early-to-middle years of their working career attempt to accumulate assets to satisfy short-term needs and longer-term goals.

Actuarial rate of return The discount rate used to find the present value of a defined benefit pension plan's future obligations and thus determine the size of the firm's annual contribution to the plan.

Asset allocation The process of deciding how to distribute an investor's wealth among different asset classes for investment purposes.

Asset class A collection of securities that have similar characteristics, attributes, and risk–return relationships.

Average tax rate Average portion of income that is paid as taxes; equals the total tax payment divided by total income.

Basis (of an asset) For tax purposes, the cost of an asset.

Benchmark portfolio A comparison standard of risk and assets included in the policy statement and similar to the investor's risk preference and investment needs, which can be used to evaluate the investment performance of the portfolio manager.

Capital appreciation A return objective in which the investor seeks to increase the portfolio value, primarily through capital gains, over time to meet a future need; generally a goal of an investor willing to take on above-average risk to meet a goal.

Capital preservation A return objective in which the investor seeks to minimize the risk of loss; generally a goal of the risk-averse investor.

Consolidation phase Phase in the investment life cycle during which individuals who are typically past the midpoint of their career have earnings that exceed expenses and invest them for future retirement or estate-planning needs.

Current income A return objective in which the investor seeks to generate income rather than capital gains; generally a goal of an investor who wants to supplement earnings with income to meet living expenses.

Defined benefit pension plan A pension plan that promises to pay retirees a specific income stream that is based on years of service, salary, or both.

Defined contribution pension plan A pension plan in which the size of the employee's and employer's contribution is known but the benefits upon retirement depend on both the contributions and the returns earned on them.

Fiduciary A person who supervises or oversees the investment portfolio of a third party, such as in a trust account, and makes investment decisions in accordance with the owner's wishes.

Gifting phase Phase in the investment life cycle during which individuals use excess assets to financially assist relatives or friends, establish charitable trusts, or construct trusts to minimize estate taxes.

Liquid Term used to describe an asset that can be quickly converted to cash at a price close to fair market value.

Marginal tax rate The portion of each additional dollar in income that is paid as tax.

Objectives The investor's goals, expressed in terms of risk and return, included in the policy statement.

Overfunded plan A defined benefit pension plan in which the present value of the pension liabilities is less than the plan's assets.

Policy statement A statement in which the investor specifies investment goals, constraints, and risk preferences.

Realized capital gains Capital gains that result when an appreciated asset has been sold; realized capital gains are taxable.

Spending phase Phase in the investment life cycle during which individuals' earning years end as they retire. They pay for expenses with income from Social Security and prior investments and invest to protect against inflation.

Total return A return objective in which the investor wants to increase the portfolio value to meet a future need by both capital gains and current income reinvestment.

Underfunded plan A defined benefit pension plan in which the present value of the fund's liabilities to employees exceeds the value of the fund's assets.

Unrealized capital gains Capital gains that reflect the price appreciation of currently held assets; taxes on unrealized capital gains can be deferred indefinitely.

APPENDIX 5

Objectives and Constraints of Institutional Investors

Institutional investors manage large amounts of funds in the course of their business. They include pension funds, endowments, and insurance firms. In this section we review the characteristics of various institutional investors and discuss their typical investment objectives and constraints.

PENSION FUNDS

Pension funds are a major component of retirement planning for individuals. At the end of 2002, U.S. pension assets totaled nearly $10.0 trillion. A firm's pension fund receives contributions from the firm, its employees, or both. The funds are invested with the purpose of giving workers either a lump-sum payment or the promise of an income stream after their retirement. *Defined benefit pension plans* promise to pay retirees a specific income stream, usually based on the worker's salary, time of service, or both. The company contributes a certain amount each year to the pension plan; the size of the contribution depends on assumptions concerning future salary increases and the rate of return to be earned on the plan's assets. Under a defined benefit plan, the company carries the risk of paying the future pension benefit to retirees; should investment performance be poor, or should the company be unable to make adequate contributions to the plan, the shortfall must be made up in future years. "Poor" investment performance means the actual return on the plan's assets fell below the assumed *actuarial rate of return*. The actuarial rate is the discount rate used to find the present value of the plan's future obligations and thus determines the size of the firm's annual contribution to the pension plan.

Defined contribution pension plans do not promise set benefits; rather, employees' benefits depend on the size of the contributions made to the pension fund and the returns earned on the fund's investments. Thus, the plan's risk is borne by the employees. Unlike a defined benefit plan, employees' retirement income is not an obligation of the firm.

A pension plan's objectives and constraints depend on whether the plan is a defined benefit plan or a defined contribution plan. We review each separately below.

Defined Benefit Plan   The plan's risk tolerance depends on the plan's funding status and its actuarial rate. For *underfunded plans* (where the present value of the fund's liabilities to employees exceeds the value of the funds' assets), a more conservative approach toward risk is taken to ensure that the funding gap is closed over time. This may entail a strategy whereby the firm makes larger plan contributions and assumes a lower actuarial rate. *Overfunded plans* (where the present value of the pension liabilities is less than the plan's assets) allow a more aggressive investment strategy in which the firm reduces its contributions and increases the risk exposure of the plan. The return objective is to meet the plan's actuarial rate of return, which is set by actuaries who estimate future pension obligations based on assumptions about future salary increases, current salaries, retirement patterns, worker life expectancies, and the firm's benefit formula. The actuarial rate also helps determine the size of the firm's plan contributions over time.

The liquidity constraint on defined benefit funds is mainly a function of the average age of employees. A younger employee base means less liquidity is needed; an older employee base generally means more liquidity is needed to pay current and imminent pension obligations. The time horizon constraint is also affected by the average age of employees, although some experts recommend using a five- to ten-year horizon for planning purposes. Taxes are not a major concern to the plan, because pension plans are exempt from paying tax on investment returns. The major legal constraint is that the plan must be run in accordance with ERISA, the Employee Retirement and Income Security Act, and investments must satisfy the prudent-man standard when evaluated in the context of the overall pension plan's portfolio.

Defined Contribution Plan Since the individual worker decides how his contributions to the plan are to be invested, the objectives and constraints for defined contribution plans depend on the individual. Because the worker carries the risk of inadequate retirement funding rather than the firm, defined contribution plans are generally more conservatively invested (some suggest that employees tend to invest too conservatively). If, however, the plan is considered more of an estate-planning tool for a wealthy founder or officer of the firm, a higher risk tolerance and return objective is appropriate because most of the plan's assets will ultimately be owned by the individual's heirs.

The liquidity and time horizon needs for the plan differ depending on the average age of the employees and the degree of employee turnover within the firm. Similar to defined benefit plans, defined contribution plans are tax-exempt and are governed by the provisions of ERISA.

ENDOWMENT FUNDS

Endowment funds arise from contributions made to charitable or educational institutions. Rather than immediately spending the contributions, the organization invests the money for the purpose of providing a future stream of income to the organization. The investment policy of an endowment fund is the result of a tension between the organization's need for current income and the desire to plan for a growing stream of income in the future to protect against inflation.

To meet the institution's operating budget needs, the fund's return objective is often set by adding the spending rate (the amount taken out of the funds each year) and the expected inflation rate. Funds that have more risk-tolerant trustees may have a higher spending rate than those overseen by more risk-averse trustees. Because a total return approach usually serves to meet the return objective over time, the organization is generally withdrawing both income and capital gains returns to meet budgeted needs. The risk tolerance of an endowment fund is largely affected by the collective risk tolerance of the organization's trustees.

Due to the fund's long-term time horizon, liquidity requirements are minor except for the need to spend part of the endowment each year and maintain a cash reserve for emergencies. Many endowments are tax-exempt, although income from some private foundations can be taxed at either a 1 or 2 percent rate. Short-term capital gains are taxable, but long-term capital gains are not. Regulatory and legal constraints arise on the state level, where most endowments are regulated. Unique needs and preferences may affect investment strategies, especially among college or religious endowments, which sometimes have strong preferences about social investing issues.

INSURANCE COMPANIES

The investment objectives and constraints for an insurance company depend on whether it is a life insurance company or a nonlife (such as a property and casualty) insurance firm.

Cash outflows are somewhat predictable for life insurance firms, based on their mortality tables. In contrast, the cash flow required by major accidents, disasters, and lawsuit settlements are not as predictable for nonlife insurance firms.

Due to their fiduciary responsibility to claimants, risk exposures are low to moderate. Depending on the specific company and competitive pressures, premiums may be affected both by the probability of a claim and the investment returns earned by the firm. Typically, casualty insurance firms invest their insurance reserves in bonds for safety purposes and to provide needed income to pay claims; capital and surplus funds are invested in equities for their growth potential. As with life insurers, property and casualty firms have a stronger competitive position when their surplus accounts are larger than those of their competitors. Many insurers now focus on a total return objective as a means to increase their surplus accounts over time.

Because of uncertain claim patterns, liquidity is a concern for property and casualty insurers who also want liquidity so they can switch between taxable and tax-exempt investments as their underwriting activities generate losses and profits. The time horizon for investments is typically shorter than that of life insurers, although many invest in long-term bonds to earn the higher yields available on these instruments. Investing strategy for the firm's surplus account focuses on long-term growth.

Regulation of property and casualty firms is more permissive than for life insurers. Similar to life insurance companies, states regulate classes and quality of investments for a certain percentage of the firm's assets. But beyond this restriction, insurers can invest in many different types and qualities of instruments, except that some states limit the proportion of real estate assets.

INSTITUTIONAL INVESTOR SUMMARY

Among the great variety of institutions, each institution has its "typical" investment objectives and constraints. This appendix has given us a flavor of the differences that exist between types of institutions and some of the major issues confronting them. Notably, just as with individual investors, cookie-cutter policy statements are inappropriate for institutional investors. The specific objectives, constraints, and investment strategies must be determined on a case-by-case basis.

CHAPTER 6

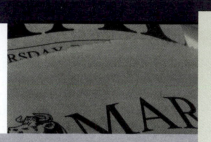

Organization and Functioning of Securities Markets*

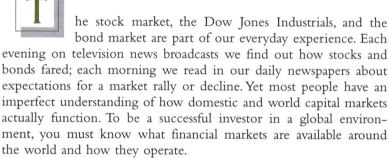

T he stock market, the Dow Jones Industrials, and the bond market are part of our everyday experience. Each evening on television news broadcasts we find out how stocks and bonds fared; each morning we read in our daily newspapers about expectations for a market rally or decline. Yet most people have an imperfect understanding of how domestic and world capital markets actually function. To be a successful investor in a global environment, you must know what financial markets are available around the world and how they operate.

In this chapter we take a broad view of securities markets and provide a detailed discussion of how major stock markets function. We conclude with a consideration of how global securities markets have changed during recent years and probably will change in the near future.

We begin with a discussion of securities markets and the characteristics of a good market. We describe two components of the capital markets: primary and secondary. Our main emphasis is on the secondary stock market. We consider the national stock exchanges around the world and how these markets, separated by geography and by time zones, are becoming linked into a twenty-four-hour market. We also consider regional stock markets and the Nasdaq market and provide a detailed analysis of how alternative exchange markets operate, including the Electronic Communication Networks (ECNs). In the final section we consider numerous historical changes in financial markets, additional current changes, and significant future changes expected. These numerous changes in our securities markets will have a profound effect on what investments are available from around the world and how we buy and sell them.

*The authors acknowledge the insights and help on this chapter provided by Robert Battalio from the University of Notre Dame. Any mistakes or oversights are the responsibility of the authors.

What Is a Market?

A *market* is the means through which buyers and sellers are brought together to aid in the transfer of goods and/or services. Several aspects of this general definition seem worthy of emphasis. First, a market need not have a physical location. It is only necessary that the buyers and sellers can communicate regarding the relevant aspects of the transaction.

Second, the market does not necessarily own the goods or services involved. For a good market, ownership is not involved; the important criterion is the smooth, cheap transfer of goods and services. In most financial markets, those who establish and administer the market do not own the assets but simply provide a physical location or an electronic system that allows potential buyers and sellers to interact. They help the market function by providing information and facilities to aid in the transfer of ownership.

Finally, a market can deal in any variety of goods and services. For any commodity or service with a diverse clientele, a market should evolve to aid in the transfer of that commodity or service. Both buyers and sellers benefit from the existence of a market.

CHARACTERISTICS OF A GOOD MARKET

Throughout this book, we will discuss markets for different investments such as stocks, bonds, options, and futures in the United States and throughout the world. We will refer to these markets using various terms of quality such as strong, active, liquid, or illiquid. There are many financial markets, but they are not all equal—some are active and liquid, others are relatively illiquid and inefficient in their operations. To appreciate these discussions, you should be aware of the following characteristics that investors look for when evaluating the quality of a market.

One enters a market to buy or sell a good or service quickly at a price justified by the prevailing supply and demand. To determine the appropriate price, participants must have timely and accurate information on the volume and prices of past transactions and all currently outstanding bids and offers. Therefore, one attribute of a good market is *timely and accurate information*.

Another prime requirement is *liquidity*, the ability to buy or sell an asset quickly and at a known price—that is, a price not substantially different from the prices for prior transactions, assuming no new information is available. An asset's likelihood of being sold quickly, sometimes referred to as its *marketability*, is a necessary, but not a sufficient, condition for liquidity. The expected price should also be fairly certain, based on the recent history of transaction prices and current bid–ask quotes.[1]

A component of liquidity is *price continuity*, which means that prices do not change much from one transaction to the next unless substantial new information becomes available. Suppose no new information is forthcoming, and the last transaction was at a price of $20; if the next trade were at $20.10, the market would be considered reasonably continuous.[2] A continuous market without large price changes between trades is a characteristic of a liquid market.

---

[1] For a more formal discussion of liquidity, see Puneet Handa and Robert A. Schwartz, "How Best to Supply Liquidity to a Securities Market," *Journal of Portfolio Management* 22, no. 2 (Winter 1996): 44–51. For a set of articles that consider liquidity and all components of trade execution, see *Best Execution and Portfolio Performance* (Charlottesville, VA: Association for Investment Management and Research, December 2000). For an outstanding book, see Larry Harris, *Trading and Exchanges* (New York: Oxford University Press, 2003).

[2] Common stocks are currently sold in decimals (dollars and cents), which is a significant change from the pre-2000 period when they were priced in eighths or sixteenths. We discuss the change to decimals in the next subsection.

A market with price continuity requires *depth,* which means that there are numerous potential buyers and sellers willing to trade at prices above and below the current market price. These buyers and sellers enter the market in response to changes in supply, demand, or both and thereby prevent drastic price changes. In summary, liquidity requires marketability and price continuity, which, in turn, requires depth.

Another factor contributing to a good market is the *transaction cost.* Lower costs (as a percent of the value of the trade) make for a more efficient market. An individual comparing the cost of a transaction between markets would choose a market that charges 2 percent of the value of the trade compared with one that charges 5 percent. Most microeconomic textbooks define an efficient market as one in which the cost of the transaction is minimal. This attribute is referred to as *internal efficiency.*

Finally, a buyer or seller wants the prevailing market price to adequately reflect all the information available regarding supply and demand factors in the market. If such conditions change as a result of new information, the price should change accordingly. Therefore, participants want prices to adjust quickly to new information regarding supply or demand, which means that prevailing market prices reflect all available information about the asset. This attribute is referred to as *external, or informational, efficiency.* We discuss this attribute extensively in Chapter 10.

In summary, a good market for goods and services has the following characteristics:

1. Timely and accurate information on the price and volume of past transactions.
2. Liquidity, meaning an asset can be bought or sold quickly at a price close to the prices for previous transactions (has price continuity), assuming no new information has been received. In turn, price continuity requires depth.
3. Low transactions costs, including the cost of reaching the market, the actual brokerage costs, and the cost of transferring the asset.
4. Prices that rapidly adjust to new information, so the prevailing price is fair since it reflects all available information regarding the asset.

DECIMAL PRICING

Prior to the initiation of changes in late 2000 that were completed in early 2001, common stocks in the United States were always quoted in fractions. Specifically, prior to 1997 they were quoted in eighths (e.g., $\frac{1}{8}, \frac{2}{8}, \ldots, \frac{7}{8}$), with each eighth equal to $0.125. This was modified in 1997 when the fractions for most stocks went to sixteenths (e.g., $\frac{1}{16}, \frac{2}{16}, \ldots, \frac{15}{16}$), equal to $0.0625. Now U.S. equities are priced in decimals (cents), so the minimum spread can be in cents (e.g., $30.10–$30.12).

The espoused reasons for the change to decimal pricing are threefold. First is the ease with which investors can understand the prices and compare them. Second, decimal pricing should save investors money since it reduces the size of the bid–ask spread from a minimum of 6.25 cents (when prices are quoted in sixteenths) to 1 cent (when prices are in decimals). (Of course, this is also why many brokers and investment firms were against the change—the spread is the price of liquidity for the investor and the compensation to the dealer.) Third, the change should make U.S. markets more competitive on a global basis since other countries price on a comparable basis. Thus, transactions costs should be lower.

The effect of decimalization has been substantial. Because it reduced spread size, there has been a decline in transaction costs. This has led to a decline in transaction size and a corresponding increase in the number of transactions—for example, the number of transactions on the NYSE doubled over the three years 2000–2003.

ORGANIZATION OF THE SECURITIES MARKET

Before we discuss the specific operation of the securities market, we need to understand its overall organization. The principal distinction is between *primary markets,* where new securities are sold, and *secondary markets,* where outstanding securities are bought and sold. Each of these markets is further divided based on the economic unit that issued the security. We will consider each of these major segments of the securities market, with an emphasis on the individuals involved and the functions they perform.

Primary Capital Markets

The primary market is where new issues of bonds, preferred stock, or common stock are sold by government units, municipalities, or companies to acquire new capital.

GOVERNMENT BOND ISSUES

All U.S. government bond issues are subdivided into three segments based on their original maturities. *Treasury bills* are negotiable, non-interest-bearing securities with original maturities of one year or less. *Treasury notes* have original maturities of two to ten years. Finally, *Treasury bonds* have original maturities of more than ten years.

To sell bills, notes, and bonds, the Treasury relies on Federal Reserve System auctions. (The bidding process and pricing are discussed in Chapters 3 and 12.)

MUNICIPAL BOND ISSUES

New municipal bond issues are sold by one of three methods: competitive bid, negotiation, or private placement. *Competitive bid* sales typically involve sealed bids. The bond issue is sold to the bidding syndicate of underwriters that submits the bid with the lowest interest cost in accordance with the stipulations set forth by the issuer. *Negotiated sales* involve contractual arrangements between underwriters and issuers wherein the underwriter helps the issuer prepare the bond issue and set the price and has the exclusive right to sell the issue. *Private placements* involve the sale of a bond issue by the issuer directly to an investor or a small group of investors (usually institutions).

Note that two of the three methods require an *underwriting* function. Specifically, in a competitive bid or a negotiated transaction, the investment banker typically underwrites the issue, which means the investment firm purchases the entire issue at a specified price, relieving the issuer from the risk and responsibility of selling and distributing the bonds. Subsequently, the underwriter sells the issue to the investing public. For municipal bonds, this underwriting function is performed by both investment banking firms and commercial banks.

The underwriting function can involve three services: origination, risk-bearing, and distribution. Origination involves the design of the bond issue and initial planning. To fulfill the risk-bearing function, the underwriter acquires the total issue at a price dictated by the competitive bid or through negotiation and accepts the responsibility and risk of reselling it for more than the purchase price. Distribution means selling it to investors, typically with the help of a selling syndicate that includes other investment banking firms and/or commercial banks.

In a negotiated bid, the underwriter will carry out all three services. In a competitive bid, the issuer specifies the amount, maturities, coupons, and call features of the issue and the competing syndicates submit a bid for the entire issue that reflects the yields they estimate for the bonds. The issuer may have received advice from an investment firm on the desirable characteristics for a forthcoming issue, but this advice would have been on a fee basis and would not necessarily involve the ultimate underwriter who is responsible for risk-bearing and distribution. Finally, a private placement involves no risk-bearing, but an investment banker would typically assist in locating potential buyers and negotiating the characteristics of the issue.

CORPORATE BOND ISSUES

Corporate bond issues are almost always sold through a negotiated arrangement with an investment banking firm that maintains a relationship with the issuing firm. In a global capital market that involves an explosion of new instruments, the origination function, which involves the design of the security in terms of characteristics and currency, is becoming more important because the corporate chief financial officer (CFO) will probably not be completely familiar with the availability and issuing requirements of many new instruments and the alternative capital markets around the world. Investment banking firms compete for underwriting business by creating new instruments that appeal to existing investors and by advising issuers regarding desirable countries and currencies. As a result, the expertise of the investment banker can help reduce the issuer's cost of new capital.

Once a stock or bond issue is specified, the underwriter will put together an underwriting syndicate of other major underwriters and a selling group of smaller firms for its distribution, as shown in Exhibit 6.1.

CORPORATE STOCK ISSUES

In addition to the ability to issue fixed-income securities to get new capital, corporations can also issue equity securities—generally common stock. For corporations, new stock

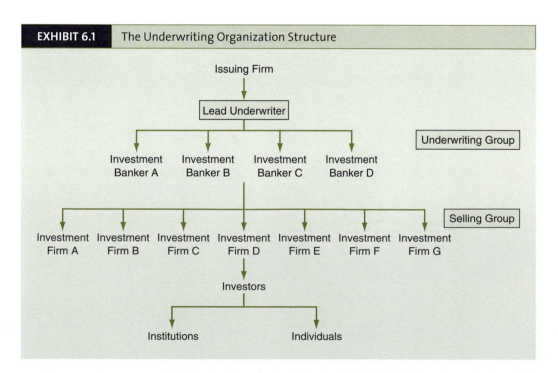

EXHIBIT 6.1   The Underwriting Organization Structure

issues are typically divided into two groups: (1) seasoned equity issues and (2) initial public offerings (IPOs).

Seasoned equity issues are new shares offered by firms that already have stock outstanding. An example would be General Electric, which is a large, well-regarded firm that has had public stock trading on the NYSE for over fifty years. If General Electric needed additional capital, it could sell additional shares of its common stock to the public at a price very close to the current price of the firm's stock.

Initial public offerings (IPOs) involve a firm selling its common stock to the public for the first time. At the time of an IPO offering, there is no existing public market for the stock; that is, the company has been closely held. An example was an IPO by Polo Ralph Lauren at $26 per share. At the time, the company was a leading manufacturer and distributor of men's clothing. The purpose of the offering was to get additional capital to expand its operations.

New issues (seasoned or IPOs) are typically underwritten by investment bankers, who acquire the total issue from the company and sell the securities to interested investors. The underwriter gives advice to the corporation on the general characteristics of the issue, its pricing, and the timing of the offering. The underwriter also accepts the risk of selling the new issue after acquiring it from the corporation.[3]

Relationships with Investment Bankers

The underwriting of corporate issues typically takes one of three forms: negotiated, competitive bids, or best-efforts arrangements. As noted, negotiated underwritings are the most common, and the procedure is the same as for municipal issues.

A corporation may also specify the type of securities to be offered (common stock, preferred stock, or bonds) and then solicit competitive bids from investment banking firms. This is rare for industrial firms but is typical for utilities, which may be required by law to sell the issue via a competitive bid. Although a competitive bid typically reduces the cost of an issue, it also means that the investment banker gives less advice but still accepts the risk-bearing function by underwriting the issue and fulfills the distribution function.

Alternatively, an investment banker can agree to sell an issue on a *best-efforts basis*. This is usually done with speculative new issues. In this arrangement, the investment banker does not underwrite the issue because it does not buy any securities. The stock is owned by the company, and the investment banker acts as a *broker* to sell whatever it can at a stipulated price. Because it bears no risk, the investment banker earns a lower commission on such an issue than on an underwritten issue.

Introduction of Rule 415

The typical practice of negotiated arrangements involving numerous investment banking firms in syndicates and selling groups has changed with the introduction of Rule 415, which allows large firms to register security issues and sell them piecemeal during the following two years. These issues are referred to as *shelf registrations* because, after they are registered, the issues lie on the shelf and can be taken down and sold on short notice whenever it suits the issuing firm. As an example, General Electric could register an issue of 5 million shares of common stock during 2006 and sell a million shares in early 2006, another million shares late in 2006, 2 million shares in early 2007, and the rest in late 2007.

Each offering can be made with little notice or paperwork by one underwriter or several. In fact, because relatively few shares may be involved, the lead underwriter often handles the

---

[3]For an extended discussion of the underwriting process, see Richard A. Brealey and Stewart C. Myers, *Principles of Corporate Finance,* 8th ed. (New York: McGraw-Hill, 2004), Chapter 15.

whole deal without a syndicate or uses only one or two other firms. This arrangement has benefited large corporations because it provides great flexibility, reduces registration fees and expenses, and allows firms issuing securities to request competitive bids from several investment banking firms.

On the other hand, some observers fear that shelf registrations do not allow investors enough time to examine the current status of the firm issuing the securities. Also, the follow-up offerings reduce the participation of small underwriters because the underwriting syndicates are smaller and selling groups are almost nonexistent. Shelf registrations have typically been used for the sale of straight debentures rather than common stock or convertible issues.[4]

PRIVATE PLACEMENTS AND RULE 144A

Rather than a public sale using one of these arrangements, primary offerings can be sold privately. In such an arrangement, referred to as a *private placement,* the firm designs an issue with the assistance of an investment banker and sells it to a small group of institutions. The firm enjoys lower issuing costs because it does not need to prepare the extensive registration statement required for a public offering. The institution that buys the issue typically benefits because the issuing firm passes some of these cost savings on to the investor as a higher return. In fact, the institution should require a higher return because of the absence of any secondary market for these securities, which implies higher liquidity risk.

The private placement market changed dramatically when Rule 144A was introduced by the SEC. This rule allows corporations—including non-U.S. firms—to place securities privately with large, sophisticated institutional investors without extensive registration documents. It also allows these securities to be subsequently traded among these large sophisticated investors (those with assets in excess of $100 million). The SEC intends to provide more financing alternatives for U.S. and non-U.S. firms and possibly increase the number, size, and liquidity of private placements.[5] Presently, over 80 percent of high-yield bonds are issued as 144A issues.

Secondary Financial Markets

In this section we first consider the purpose and importance of secondary markets and provide an overview of the secondary markets for bonds, financial futures, and stocks. Next, we consider national stock markets around the world. Finally, we discuss other primary listing markets, regional exchanges, third markets, and the rapidly growing electronic communication networks (ECNs) and provide a detailed presentation on the functioning of stock exchanges.

Secondary markets permit trading in outstanding issues; that is, stocks or bonds already sold to the public are traded between current and potential owners. The proceeds from a sale in the secondary market do not go to the issuing unit (the government, municipality, or company), but rather to the current owner of the security.

---

[4]For further discussion of Rule 415, see Robert J. Rogowski and Eric H. Sorensen, "Deregulation in Investment Banking: Shelf Registration, Structure and Performance," *Financial Management* 14, no. 1 (Spring 1985): 5–15.

[5]For a discussion of some reactions to Rule 144A, see John W. Milligan, "Two Cheers for 144A," *Institutional Investor* 24, no. 9 (July 1990): 117–119; and Sara Hanks, "SEC Ruling Creates a New Market," *The Wall Street Journal,* May 16, 1990, p. A12.

WHY SECONDARY MARKETS ARE IMPORTANT

Before discussing the various segments of the secondary market, we must consider its overall importance. Because the secondary market involves the trading of securities initially sold in the primary market, *it provides liquidity to the individuals who acquired these securities.* After acquiring securities in the primary market, investors may want to sell them again to acquire other securities, buy a house, or go on a vacation. The primary market benefits greatly from the liquidity provided by the secondary market because investors would hesitate to acquire securities in the primary market if they thought they could not subsequently sell them in the secondary market. That is, without an active secondary market, potential issuers of stocks or bonds in the primary market would have to provide a much higher rate of return to compensate investors for the substantial liquidity risk.

Secondary markets are also important to those selling seasoned securities because the prevailing market price of the securities (*price discovery*) is determined by transactions in the secondary market. New issues of outstanding stocks or bonds to be sold in the primary market are based on prices and yields in the secondary market.[6] Even forthcoming IPOs are priced based on the prices and values of comparable stocks or bonds in the public secondary market.

SECONDARY BOND MARKETS

The secondary market for bonds distinguishes among those issued by the federal government, municipalities, or corporations.

Secondary Markets for U.S. Government and Municipal Bonds

U.S. government bonds are traded by bond dealers that specialize in either Treasury bonds or agency bonds. Treasury issues are bought or sold through a set of thirty-five primary dealers, including large banks in New York and Chicago and some of the large investment banking firms (for example, Merrill Lynch, Goldman Sachs, Morgan Stanley). These institutions and other firms also make markets for government agency issues, but there is no formal set of dealers for agency securities.

The major market makers in the secondary municipal bond market are banks and investment firms. Banks are active in municipal bond trading and underwriting of general obligation issues since they invest heavily in these securities. Also, many large investment firms have municipal bond departments that underwrite and trade these issues.

Secondary Corporate Bond Markets

Currently, all corporate bonds are traded over the counter by dealers who buy and sell for their own accounts. The major bond dealers are the large investment banking firms that underwrite the issues: firms such as Merrill Lynch, Goldman Sachs, Salomon Brothers, Lehman Brothers, and Morgan Stanley. Because of the limited trading in corporate bonds compared to the fairly active trading in government bonds, corporate bond dealers do not carry extensive inventories of specific issues. Instead, they hold a limited number of bonds desired by their clients, and when someone wants to do a trade, they work more like brokers than dealers.

Notably, there is a movement toward a widespread transaction-reporting service as with stocks, especially for some large, actively traded bond issues. For example, *The Wall Street*

---

[6]In the literature on market microstructure, it is noted that the secondary markets also have an effect on market efficiency, the volatility of security prices, and the serial correlation in security returns. In this regard, see F. D. Foster and S. Viswanathan, "The Effects of Public Information and Competition on Trading Volume and Price Volatility," *Review of Financial Studies* 6, no. 1 (Spring 1993): 23–56; and C. N. Jones, G. Kaul, and M. L. Lipson, "Information, Trading and Volatility," *Journal of Financial Economics* 36, no. 1 (August 1994): 127–154.

Journal publishes a table entitled "Corporate Bonds" that contains daily trading information on forty active bonds. Also, as of September 2004, dealers were required to report trades on 17,000 bonds registered under the Securities Act of 1933.

FINANCIAL FUTURES

In addition to the market for the bonds, a market has developed for futures contracts related to these bonds. These contracts allow the holder to buy or sell a specified amount of a given bond issue at a stipulated price. The two major futures exchanges are the Chicago Board of Trade (CBOT) and the Chicago Mercantile Exchange (CME). We discuss these futures contracts and the futures market in Chapter 17.

SECONDARY EQUITY MARKETS

Before 2000, the secondary equity markets in the United States and around the world were divided into three segments: national stock exchanges, regional stock exchanges, and over-the-counter (OTC) markets for stocks not on an exchange. Because of numerous changes over the past decade, a better classification has been suggested by Harris, as presented later in Exhibit 6.2[7] Following our background discussions on alternative trading systems and call versus continuous markets, we will describe the market types listed in Exhibit 6.2 and discuss how they complement and compete against each other to provide price discovery and liquidity to individual and institutional investors.

Basic Trading Systems   Although stock exchanges are similar in that only qualified stocks can be traded by individuals who are members of the exchange, they can differ in their *trading systems.* There are two major trading systems, and an exchange can use one or a combination of them. One is a *pure auction market* (also referred to as an *order-driven market*), in which interested buyers and sellers submit bid-and-ask prices for a given stock to a central location where the orders are matched by a broker who does not own the stock but acts as a facilitating agent. Participants also refer to this system as *price-driven* because shares of stock are sold to the investor with the highest bid price and bought from the seller with the lowest offering price. Advocates of the auction system argue for a very centralized market that ideally will include all the buyers and sellers of the stock.

The other major trading system is a *dealer market* (also referred to as a *quote-driven* market) where individual dealers provide liquidity for investors by buying and selling the shares of stock for themselves. Ideally, with this system there will be numerous dealers who will compete against each other to provide the highest bid prices when you are selling and the lowest asking price when you are buying stock. Clearly, this is a very decentralized system that derives its benefit from the competition among the dealers to provide the best price for the buyer and seller. When we discuss the various equity markets, we will indicate the trading system used.

Call versus Continuous Markets   Beyond the different trading systems for equities, the operation of exchanges can differ in terms of when and how the stocks are traded.

In *call markets,* the intent is to gather all the bids and asks for the stock at a point in time and attempt to arrive at a single price where the quantity demanded is as close as possible to the quantity supplied. Call markets are generally used during the early stages of development of an exchange when there are few stocks listed or a small number of active investors–traders. For an exchange that is strictly a call market with a few listed stocks and

---

[7]Larry Harris, *Trading and Exchanges* (New York: Oxford University Press, 2003).

EXHIBIT 6.2	U.S. Secondary Equity Markets: Classification and Examples
Market Type	**Examples**
Primary listing markets	New York Stock Exchange
	American Stock Exchange
	Nasdaq National Market System (NMS)
	Nasdaq Small-Cap Market (SCM)
	Nasdaq OTC Electronic Bulletin Board
	National Quotation Bureau (NQB)
	Pink Sheets
Regional markets	Boston Stock Exchange
	Chicago Stock Exchange
	Cincinnati Stock Exchange
	Pacific Exchange
	Philadelphia Stock Exchange
Third-market dealers/brokers	Madoff Investment Securities
	Knight Trading Group
	Jefferies Group
	ITG
	Nasdaq InterMarket
Alternative Trading Systems (ATSs)	
Electronic Communications Networks (ECNs)	Archipelago
	BRUT
	Instinet
	Island
	REDIBook
Electronic Crossing Systems (ECSs)	POSIT
	Global Instinet Crossing
	Arizona Stock Exchange

Source: Adapted from Larry Harris, *Trading and Exchanges* (Oxford University Press, 2003), p. 49. Copyright © 2000 by Oxford University Press, Inc. Used by permission of Oxford University Press, Inc.

traders, a designated market maker would call the roll of stocks and ask for interest in one stock at a time. After determining the available buy and sell orders, exchange officials specify a single price that will satisfy *most* of the orders, and all orders are transacted at this price.

Notably, call markets also are used at the opening for stocks on a large exchange if there is an overnight buildup of buy and sell orders, in which case the opening price can differ from the prior day's closing price. Also, this concept is used if trading is suspended during the day because of some significant new information. In either case, the specialist or market maker would attempt to derive a new equilibrium price using a call-market approach that would reflect the imbalance and take care of most of the orders. For example, assume a stock had been trading at about $42 per share and some significant, new, positive information was released overnight or during the day. If it happened overnight it would affect the opening price; if it happened during the day, trading would be temporarily suspended and a call-market process would be used to determine a new equilibrium price that reflects the supply and demand due to the new information. If the buy orders were three or four times as numerous as the sell orders, the price based on the call market might be $44. Several studies have shown that using the call-market mechanism contributes to a more orderly market and less volatility in such instances.

In a *continuous market,* trades occur at any time the market is open wherein stocks are priced either by auction or by dealers. In a dealer market, dealers make a market in the stock, which means that they are willing to buy or sell for their own account at a specified bid-and-ask price. In an auction market, enough buyers and sellers are trading to allow the market to be continuous; that is, when one investor comes to buy stock, there is another investor available and willing to sell stock. A compromise between a pure dealer market and a pure auction market is a combination structure wherein the market is basically an auction market, but there exists an intermediary who is willing to act as a dealer if the pure auction market does not have enough activity. These intermediaries who act as both brokers and dealers provide temporary liquidity to ensure the market will be liquid and continuous.

The two tables in the chapter appendix list the characteristics of stock exchanges around the world and indicate whether the exchange provides a continuous market, a call-market mechanism, or a mixture of the two. Notably, many continuous market exchanges employ a call-market mechanism on specific occasions at the open and during trading suspensions. The NYSE is such a market.

Classification of U.S. Secondary Equity Markets

Now let's delve into the different secondary equity markets that currently exist in the United States as listed in Exhibit 6.2.

PRIMARY LISTING MARKETS

Primary listing markets are formal exchanges or markets where a corporate stock is primarily or formally listed. This category includes the two traditional national exchanges (New York Stock Exchange and American Stock Exchange) and the Nasdaq markets that previously were considered over-the-counter markets but are now recognized as equity markets that simply differ in how they trade securities (as will be discussed).

New York Stock Exchange (NYSE)   The New York Stock Exchange (NYSE), the largest organized securities market in the United States, was established in 1817 as the New York Stock and Exchange Board. The Exchange dates its founding to when the famous Buttonwood Agreement was signed in May 1792 by twenty-four brokers.[8] The name was changed to the New York Stock Exchange in 1863.

At the end of 2003, approximately 2,750 companies had stock issues listed on the NYSE, for a total of about 3,000 stock issues (common and preferred) with a total market value of more than $12 trillion. The specific listing requirements for the NYSE appear in Exhibit 6.3.

The average number of shares traded daily on the NYSE has increased steadily and substantially, as shown in Exhibit 6.4. Prior to the 1960s, the daily volume averaged less than 3 million shares, compared with the 2003 average daily volume of about 1.4 billion shares.

The NYSE has dominated the other exchanges in the United States in trading volume. Given its stringent listing requirements and its prestige, most of the largest and best known

---

[8]The NYSE considers the signing of this agreement the birth of the Exchange and celebrated its 200th birthday during 1992. For a pictorial history, see *Life,* collectors' edition, Spring 1992.

EXHIBIT 6.3	Listing Requirements for Stocks on the NYSE
Pretax income last year	$2,500,000
Pretax income last two years	2,000,000
Shares publicly held	1,100,000
Market value of publicly held shares[a]	100,000,000
Minimum number of holders of round lots (100 shares or more)	2,000

[a]This minimum required market value is $60 million for spin-offs, carve-outs, or IPOs and it varies over time, depending on the value of the NYSE Common Stock Index. For specifics, see the *2004 NYSE Fact Book*, 37.

Source: *NYSE Fact Book* (New York: NYSE, 2004): 37. Reprinted by permission of NYSE.

EXHIBIT 6.4	Average Daily Reported Share Volume Traded on Selected Stock Markets (×1,000)	
Year	**NYSE**	**Nasdaq**
1955	2,578	N.A.
1960	3,042	N.A.
1965	6,176	N.A.
1970	11,564	N.A.
1975	18,551	5,500
1980	44,871	26,500
1985	109,169	82,100
1990	156,777	131,900
1995	346,101	401,400
1996	411,953	543,700
1997	526,925	650,324
1998	673,590	801,747
1999	809,183	1,077,500
2000	1,041,578	1,759,900
2001	1,239,957	1,900,068
2002	1,441,015	1,752,643
2003	1,398,400	1,686,744

N.A. = not available.

Sources: *NYSE Fact Book* (New York: NYSE, various issues).

U.S. companies are listed on the NYSE. In addition, about 80 percent of the trading volume for these stocks takes place on the NYSE.

The volume of trading and relative stature of the NYSE is reflected in the price of a membership on the exchange (referred to as a *seat*). As shown in Exhibit 6.5, the price of membership has fluctuated in line with trading volume and other factors that influence the profitability of membership.[9]

---

[9]For a discussion of trading volume and membership prices, see Greg Ip, "Prices Soften for Exchange Seats," *The Wall Street Journal,* May 27, 1998, pp. C1, C17.

EXHIBIT 6.5	Membership Prices on the NYSE ($000)				
	High	Low		High	Low
1925	$150	$ 99	1995	$1,050	$ 785
1935	140	65	1996	1,450	1,225
1945	95	49	1997	1,750	1,175
1955	90	49	1998	2,000	1,225
1960	162	135	1999	2,650	2,000
1965	250	190	2000	2,000	1,650
1970	320	130	2001	2,300	2,000
1975	138	55	2002	2,550	2,000
1980	275	175	2003	2,000	1,300
1985	480	310			
1990	430	250			

Source: *NYSE Fact Book* (New York: NYSE, 2004): 110. Reprinted by permission of the NYSE.

American Stock Exchange (AMEX) The American Stock Exchange (AMEX) was begun by a group who traded unlisted shares at the corner of Wall and Hanover Streets in New York. It was originally called the Outdoor Curb Market. In 1910, it established formal trading rules and changed its name to the New York Curb Market Association. The members moved inside a building in 1921 and continued to trade mainly in unlisted stocks (stocks not listed on one of the registered exchanges) until 1946, when its volume in listed stocks finally outnumbered that in unlisted stocks. The current name was adopted in 1953.

The AMEX is a national exchange, distinct from the NYSE because, except for a short period in the late 1970s, no stocks have been listed on both the NYSE and AMEX at the same time. The AMEX has emphasized foreign securities and warrants.

The AMEX became a major stock options exchange in January 1975 and subsequently has added options on interest rates and stock indexes. In addition, exchange-traded funds (ETFs) that have grown in number and popularity (as discussed in Chapter 4) are almost all listed on the AMEX.

The AMEX and the Nasdaq merged in 1998, although they continued to operate as separate markets. In 2003 Nasdaq made overtures to sell the AMEX.

An aside on global stock exchanges. The equity-market environment outside the United States is similar in that each country typically will have one relatively large exchange that dominates the market. Examples would include the Tokyo Stock Exchange, the London Stock Exchange, the Frankfort Stock Exchange, and the Paris Bourse. Exhibit 6.A in the chapter appendix lists the exchanges in developed economies along with some descriptive characteristics of these exchanges.

In a few instances there may also be regional exchanges, but these are rare. Notably, even in small or emerging economies there are stock exchanges because of the liquidity that secondary equity markets provide. Exhibit 6.B in the chapter appendix lists and describes many of the emerging-market exchanges.

Three points about these international exchanges. First, there has been a trend toward consolidations or affiliations that will provide more liquidity and greater economies of scale to support the technology required by investors. Second, many of the larger companies in these countries that can qualify for listing on a U.S. exchange become dual-listed. As a result, about 20 percent of the stocks listed on the NYSE are non-U.S. firms. Third, the existence of these strong international exchanges has made possible a global equity market wherein stocks that have a global constituency can be traded around the world continuously, as discussed in the following section.

The global twenty-four-hour market. Our discussion of the global securities market will tend to emphasize the three markets in New York, London, and Tokyo because of their relative size and importance, and because they represent the major segments of a worldwide twenty-four-hour stock market. You will often hear about a continuous market where investment firms "pass the book" around the world. This means the major active market in securities moves around the globe as trading hours for these three markets begin and end.

Consider the individual trading hours for each of the three exchanges, translated into a twenty-four-hour eastern standard time (EST) clock:

	Local Time (24-hr. notations)	24-Hour EST
New York Stock Exchange (NYSE)	0930-1600	0930-1600
Tokyo Stock Exchange (TSE)	0900-1100	2300-0100
	1300-1500	0300-0500
London Stock Exchange (LSE)	0815-1615	0215-1015

Imagine trading starting in New York at 0930 and going until 1600 in the afternoon, being picked up by Tokyo late in the evening and going until 0500 in the morning, and continuing in London (with some overlap) until it begins in New York again (with some overlap) at 0930. Alternatively, it is possible to envision trading as beginning in Tokyo at 2300 hours and continuing until 0500, when it moves to London, then ends the day in New York. This latter model seems the most relevant because the first question a London trader asks in the morning is "What happened in Tokyo?" and the U.S. trader asks "What happened in Tokyo and what *is* happening in London?" The point is, the markets operate almost continuously and are related in their response to economic events. Therefore, investors are not dealing with three separate and distinct exchanges, but with one interrelated world market.[10] Clearly, this interrelationship is growing daily because of numerous multiple listings where stocks are listed on several exchanges around the world (such as the NYSE and TSE) and the availability of sophisticated telecommunications. Examples of stocks that are part of this global market are General Electric, Pfizer, Johnson and Johnson, and McDonald's.

Nasdaq National Market System (NMS)[11] This system has historically been known as the over-the-counter (OTC) market, which included stocks not formally listed on the two major exchanges (NYSE and AMEX). This description has changed since it has been recognized that this is an equity market similar to the major exchanges with several differences that are not relevant to the purpose of this market. The first difference is that it is a *dealer market,* in contrast to a broker/dealer (specialists) market as is the NYSE. Second, exchange trading takes place electronically rather than on a trading floor as in the other exchanges. What Nasdaq has in common with the other exchanges is a set of requirements for a stock

---

[10]In response to this trend toward global trading, the International Organization of Securities Commissions (IOSCO) has been established. For a discussion of it, see David Lascelles, "Calls to Bring Watchdogs into Line," *Financial Times,* August 14, 1989, p. 10.

[11]Nasdaq is an acronym for National Association of Securities Dealers Automated Quotations. (It is commonly spelled Nasdaq rather than NASDAQ.) We discuss the system in detail shortly.

to be traded on the Nasdaq NMS.[12] Also, while Nasdaq dealers do not have to pay for a seat (membership) on the exchange, they do have to be members of the National Association of Security Dealers (NASD) and abide by its rules.

Size of the Nasdaq NMS.   The Nasdaq NMS market is the largest segment of the U.S. secondary market in terms of the number of issues traded. As noted earlier, there are about 3,000 issues traded on the NYSE and about 600 issues on the AMEX. In contrast, more than 2,800 issues are actively traded on the Nasdaq NMS and almost 700 on the Nasdaq Small-Cap Market (SCM). The Nasdaq market is also the most diverse secondary market component in terms of quality because it has multiple minimum requirements. Stocks that trade on the total Nasdaq market (NMS and SCM) range from those of small, unprofitable companies to large, extremely profitable firms such as Microsoft and Intel.

Nasdaq's growth in average daily trading was shown in Exhibit 6.4 relative to the NYSE. As of the end of 2003 almost 600 issues of Nasdaq were either foreign stocks or American Depository Receipts (ADRs), representing over 8 percent of total Nasdaq share volume. About 300 of these issues trade on both Nasdaq and a foreign exchange such as Toronto. Nasdaq has developed a link with the Singapore Stock Exchange that allows twenty-four-hour trading from Nasdaq in New York to Singapore to a Nasdaq/London link and back to New York.

Although the Nasdaq market has the greatest number of issues, the NYSE has a larger total value of trading. In 2003 the approximate value of equity trading on the NYSE was about $13 billion and on Nasdaq was about $9 billion.

Operation of the Nasdaq market.   As noted, stocks can be traded on the Nasdaq market as long as there are dealers who indicate a willingness to make a market by buying or selling for their own account.[13]

The Nasdaq System   The *National Association of Securities Dealers Automated Quotation (Nasdaq) system* is an automated, electronic quotation system. Any number of dealers can elect to make markets in a Nasdaq stock. The actual number depends on the activity in the stock. In 2003, the average number of market makers for all stocks on the Nasdaq NMS was about eight.

Nasdaq makes all dealer quotes available immediately. The broker can check the quotation machine and call the dealer with the best market, verify that the quote has not changed, and make the sale or purchase. The Nasdaq quotation system has three levels to serve firms with different needs and interests.

Level 1 provides a single median representative quote for the stocks on Nasdaq. This quotation system is for firms that want current quotes on Nasdaq stocks but do not consistently buy or sell these stocks for their customers and are not market makers. This representative quote changes constantly to adjust for any changes by individual market makers.

Level 2 provides instantaneous current quotations on Nasdaq stocks by all market makers in a stock. This quotation system is for firms that consistently trade Nasdaq stocks. Given an order to buy or sell, brokers check the quotation machine, call the market maker with the best market for their purposes (highest bid if they are selling, lowest offer if buying), and consummate the deal.

---

[12]To be traded on the NMS, a firm must have a certain size and trading activity and at least four market makers. Requirements for trading on various components of the Nasdaq system are shown later, in Exhibit 6.6.

[13]The terms *dealer* and *market maker* are synonymous.

EXHIBIT 6.6	Nasdaq National Market Listing Requirements

A company must meet all of the requirements under at least one of three listing standards for initial listing on The Nasdaq National Market®. A company must continue to meet at least one continued listing standard to maintain its listing.

	Initial Listing			Continued Listing	
Requirements	**Standard 1 Marketplace Rule 4420(a)**	**Standard 2 Marketplace Rule 4420(b)**	**Standard 3 Marketplace Rule 4420(c)**	**Standard 1 Marketplace Rule 4450(a)**	**Standard 2 Marketplace Rule 4450(b)**
Stockholders' equity	$15 million	$30 million	N/A	$10 million	N/A
Market value of listed securities	N/A	N/A	$75 million[1,2]	N/A	$50 million
or			or		or
Total assets			$75 million		$50 million
and			and		and
Total revenue			$75 million		$50 million
Income from continuing operations before income taxes (in latest fiscal year or 2 of last 3 fiscal years)	$1 million	N/A	N/A	N/A	N/A
Publicly held shares[3]	1.1 million	1.1 million	1.1 million	750,000	1.1 million
Market value of publicly held shares	$8 million	$18 million	$20 million	$5 million	$15 million
Minimum bid price	$5	$5	$5[2]	$1	$1
Shareholders (round lot holders)[4]	400	400	400	400	400
Market makers[5]	3	3	4	2	4
Operating history	N/A	2 years	N/A	N/A	N/A
Corporate governance[6]	Yes	Yes	Yes	Yes	Yes

[1]For initial listing under Standard 3, a company must satisfy one of the following: the market value of listed securities requirement or the total assets and the total revenue requirement. Under Marketplace Rule 4200(a)(20), listed securities is defined as "securities quoted on Nasdaq or listed on a national securities exchange."

[2]Seasoned companies (those companies already listed or quoted on another marketplace) qualifying only under the market value of listed securities requirement of Standard 3 must meet the market value of listed securities and the bid price requirements for 90 consecutive trading days prior to applying for listing.

[3]Publicly held shares is defined as total shares outstanding less any shares held by officers, directors, or beneficial owners of 10 percent or more.

[4]Round lot holders are shareholders of 100 shares or more.

[5]An Electronic Communications Network (ECN) is not considered a market maker for the purpose of these rules.

[6]Marketplace Rules 4350 and 4351.

Source: The Nasdaq Listing Standards. Copyright © 2005, The Nasdaq Stock Market, Inc. Reprinted with permission.

Level 3 is for Nasdaq market makers. Such firms want Level 2, but they also need the capability to change their own quotations, which Level 3 provides.

Listing requirements for Nasdaq. Quotes and trading volume for the Nasdaq market are reported in two lists: a National Market System (NMS) list and a regular Nasdaq list. Exhibit 6.6 contains the alternative standards for initial listing and continued listing on the Nasdaq NMS as of 2004. A company must meet all of the requirements under at least one of the three listing standards for initial listing and then meet at least one continued listing standard to maintain its listing on the NMS. For stocks on this system, reports include up-to-the-minute volume and last-sale information for the competing market makers as well as end-of-the-day information on total volume and high, low, and closing prices.

A sample trade. Assume you are considering the purchase of 100 shares of Intel. Although Intel is large enough and profitable enough to be listed on the NYSE, the company has never applied for listing because it enjoys an active market on Nasdaq. (It is one of the volume leaders with daily volume typically above 25 million shares and often in excess of 50 million shares.) When you contact your broker, she will consult the Nasdaq electronic quotation machine to determine the current dealer quotations for INTC, the trading symbol for Intel.[14] The quote machine will show that about thirty-five dealers are making a market in INTC. An example of differing quotations might be as follows:[15]

Dealer	Bid	Ask
1	30.60	30.75
2	30.55	30.65
3	30.50	30.65
4	30.55	30.70

Assuming these are the best markets available from the total group, your broker would call either dealer 2 or dealer 3 because they have the lowest offering prices. After verifying the quote, your broker would give one of these dealers an order to buy 100 shares of INTC at $30.65 a share. Because your firm was not a market maker in the stock, the firm would act as a broker and charge you $3,065 plus a commission for the trade. If your firm had been a market maker in INTC, with an asking price of $30.65 the firm would have sold the stock to you at $30.65 net (without commission). If you had been interested in selling 100 shares of Intel instead of buying, the broker would have contacted dealer 1, who made the highest bid ($30.60).

Changing dealer inventory. Let's consider the price quotations by a Nasdaq dealer who wants to change his inventory on a given stock. For example, assume dealer 4, with a current quote of 30.55 bid–30.70 ask, decides to increase his holdings of INTC. The Nasdaq quotes indicate that the highest bid is currently 30.60. Increasing the bid to 30.60 would bring some of the business currently going to dealer 1. Taking a more aggressive action, dealer 4 might raise the bid to 30.63 and buy all the stock offered, because he has the highest bid. In this example, the dealer raises the bid price but does not change the ask price, which was above those of dealers 2 and 3. This dealer will buy stock but probably will not sell any. A dealer who had excess stock would keep the bid below the market (lower than 30.60) and reduce the ask price to 30.65 or less. Dealers constantly change their bid-and-ask prices, depending on their current inventories or changes in the outlook based on new information for the stock.

Other Nasdaq Market Segments Now that we are familiar with the Nasdaq system and its operation, we can easily describe the other segments of this market since the major differences relate to the size and liquidity of the stocks involved.[16]

[14]Trading symbols are one- to four-letter codes used to designate stocks. Whenever a trade is reported on a stock ticker, the trading symbol appears with the figures. Many symbols are obvious, such as GM (General Motors), F (Ford Motors), GE (General Electric), and T (American Telephone & Telegraph).

[15]While these quotes are interspersed for discussion purposes, the actual quotes would have two separate columns—one for the bids listed in order from highest to lowest and the second for ask prices listed in order from the lowest to highest.

[16]All issue numbers provided in this section are based on personal correspondence with the Nasdaq Economic Research Department.

- **The Nasdaq Small-Cap Market (SCM)** has initial listing requirements that consider the same factors as the NMS but are generally about one-half to one-third of the values required for the NMS. As of May 31, 2004, there were 683 stocks listed in the Nasdaq small-cap segment. This compares to about 600 stocks listed in the section entitled "Nasdaq NM Issues Under $100 million Market Cap" and about 2,200 in the section entitled "Nasdaq National Market Issues." In total, the Nasdaq NMS contained 2,819 issues as of May 31, 2004. Therefore, the total Nasdaq market includes 3,502 issues (2,819 NMS and 683 issues on the SCM).
- **The Nasdaq** *OTC Electronic Bulletin Board (OTCBB)* reports indications for smaller stocks sponsored by NASD dealers. As of May 31, 2004, there were 3,305 stocks included on the OTCBB.
- **The National Quotation Bureau (NQB) Pink Sheets** report order indications for the smallest publicly traded stocks in the United States. Pre-1970, these pink sheets (actually printed on pink sheets of paper) were the primary daily source of OTC stock quotes. With the creation of the Nasdaq electronic quotation system, the sheets were superseded. Currently, the NQB publishes a weekly edition on paper and distributes a daily edition electronically with these small-stock quotes.

REGIONAL STOCK EXCHANGES

The second category in Harris's classfication of U.S. secondary markets (Exhibit 6.2) is the regional market. Regional exchanges typically have the same operating procedures as national exchanges in the same countries, but they differ in their listing requirements and the geographic distributions of the listed firms. Regional stock exchanges exist for two main reasons: First, they provide trading facilities for local companies not large enough to qualify for listing on one of the national exchanges. Their listing requirements are typically less stringent than those of the national exchanges.

Second, regional exchanges in some countries list firms that also list on one of the national exchanges to give local brokers who are not members of a national exchange access to these securities. As an example, American Telephone & Telegraph and General Motors are listed on both the NYSE and several regional exchanges. This dual listing allows a local brokerage firm that is not large enough to purchase a membership on the NYSE to buy and sell shares of the dual-listed stock without going through the NYSE and giving up part of the commission. In addition, regional exchanges can trade some stocks on the Nasdaq market under *unlisted trading privileges* (UTP) granted by the SEC. The majority of trading on regional exchanges is due to dual-listed and UTP stocks.

The regional exchanges in the United States are shown in Exhibit 6.2. The Chicago, Pacific, and PBW exchanges account for about 90 percent of all regional exchange volume. In turn, total regional exchange volume is 9 to 10 percent of total exchange volume in the United States.

THE THIRD MARKET

Harris's third category is called the third market. The term *third market* involves dealers and brokers who trade shares that are listed on an exchange away from the exchange. Although most transactions in listed stocks do take place on an exchange, an investment firm that is not a member of an exchange can make a market in a listed stock away from the exchange. Most of the trading on the third market is in well-known stocks such as General Electric, IBM, and Ford. The success or failure of the third market depends on whether the non–exchange market in these stocks is as good as the exchange market and whether the relative cost of the transaction compares favorably with the cost on the exchange. This market is critical during the relatively few periods when trading is not available on the NYSE either because trading is suspended or the exchange is closed.[17] This market has also grown because of the quality and cost factors mentioned. These dealers typically display their quotes on the *Nasdaq InterMarket* system.

ALTERNATIVE TRADING SYSTEMS (ATSs)

The final category in Exhibit 6.2 is alternative trading systems. This is the facet of the equity market where the biggest changes have occurred during the last decade. *Alternative trading systems (ATSs)* are nontraditional, computerized trading systems that compete with or supplement dealer markets and traditional exchanges. These trading systems facilitate the exchange of millions of shares every day through electronic means. Notably, they do not provide listing services. The most well-known ATSs are the Electronic Communication Networks (ECNs) and the Electronic Crossing Systems (ECSs).

- *Electronic Communication Networks (ECNs)* are electronic facilities that match buy and sell orders directly via computer, mainly for retail and small institutional trading. ECNs do *not* buy or sell from their own account but act as very cheap, efficient electronic brokers. As shown in Exhibit 6.2, the major ECNs are Archipelago, BRUT, Instinet, Island, and REDIBook.
- *Electronic Crossing Systems (ECSs)* are electronic facilities that act as brokers to match *large* buy and sell orders. The most well-known ECSs are POSIT, Global Instinet Crossing, and Arizona Stock Exchange.

The trading of exchange-listed stocks using one of these ATSs has become the *fourth market*.

Detailed Analysis of Exchange Markets

The importance of listed exchange markets requires that we discuss them at some length. In this section, we discuss alternative members on the exchanges, the major types of orders, and exchange market makers—a critical component of a good exchange market.

EXCHANGE MEMBERSHIP

Stock exchanges typically have four major categories of membership: (1) specialist, (2) commission broker, (3) floor broker, and (4) registered trader. We will discuss specialists (or exchange market makers), who constitute about 25 percent of the total membership on exchanges, after our description of types of orders.

Commission brokers are employees of a member firm who buy or sell for the customers of the firm. When an investment firm receives an order to buy or sell a stock, it transmits it to a commission broker, who takes it to the appropriate trading post on the floor and completes the transaction.

---

[17]Three articles examine the impact of regional exchanges and the practice of purchasing order flow that would normally go to the NYSE; see Robert H. Battalio, "Third Market Broker-Dealers: Cost Competitors or Cream Skimmers?" *Journal of Finance* 52, no. 1 (March 1997): 341–352; Robert Battalio, Jason Greene, and Robert Jennings, "Do Competing Specialists and Preferencing Dealers Affect Market Quality?" *Review of Financial Studies*, 10 (1997): 969–993; and David Easley, Nicholas Kiefer, and Maureen O'Hara, "Cream-Skimming or Profit Sharing? The Curious Role of Purchased Order Flow," *Journal of Finance* 51, no. 3 (July 1996): 811–833.

Floor brokers are independent members of an exchange who act as brokers for other members. As an example, when commission brokers for Merrill Lynch become too busy to handle all of their orders, they will ask one of the floor brokers to help them.[18]

Registered traders use their memberships to buy and sell for their own accounts. While they save commissions on their trading, observers believe they provide the market with added liquidity, even though regulations limit how they trade and how many registered traders can be in a trading crowd around a specialist's booth at any time. Today they often are called *registered competitive market makers (RCMMs)* and have specific trading obligations set by the exchange. Their activity is reported as part of the specialist group.[19]

TYPES OF ORDERS

It is important to understand the different types of orders available to investors and the specialist as a dealer.

Market Orders The most frequent type of order is a *market order,* an order to buy or sell a stock at the best current price. An investor who enters a market sell order indicates a willingness to sell immediately at the highest bid available at the time the order reaches a specialist on an exchange, a Nasdaq dealer, or an ECN. A market buy order indicates the investor is willing to pay the lowest offering price available at the time on the exchange, Nasdaq, or an ECN. Market orders provide immediate liquidity for an investor willing to accept the prevailing market price.

Assume you are interested in General Electric (GE) and you call your broker to find out the current "market" on the stock. The quotation machine indicates that the prevailing market is 35 bid–35.10 ask. This means that the highest current bid on the books of the specialist is 35; that is, $35 is the most that anyone has offered to pay for GE. The lowest offer is 35.10; that is, this is the lowest price anyone is willing to accept to sell the stock. If you placed a market buy order for 100 shares, you would buy 100 shares at $35.10 a share (the lowest ask price) for a total cost of $3,510 plus commission. If you submitted a market sell order for 100 shares, you would sell the shares at $35 each and receive $3,500 less commission.

Limit Orders The individual placing a *limit order* specifies the buy or sell price. You might submit a limit-order bid to purchase 100 shares of Coca-Cola (KO) stock at $50 a share when the current market is 60 bid–60.10 ask, with the expectation that the stock will decline to $50 in the near future.

You must also indicate how long the limit order will be outstanding. Alternative time specifications are basically boundless. A limit order can be instantaneous ("fill or kill," meaning fill the order instantly or cancel it). It can also be good for part of a day, a full day, several days, a week, or a month. It can also be open-ended, or good until canceled (GTC).

Rather than wait for a given price on a stock, because KO is listed on the NYSE your broker will give the limit order to the specialist, who will put it in a limit-order book and act as the broker's representative. When and if the market price for KO reaches the limit-order price, the specialist will execute the order and inform your broker. The specialist receives a small part of the commission for rendering this service.

---

[18]These brokers received some unwanted notoriety in 1998: Dean Starkman and Patrick McGeehan, "Floor Brokers on Big Board Charged in Scheme," *The Wall Street Journal,* February 26, 1998, pp. C1, C21; and Suzanna McGee, "'$2 Brokers' Worried About Notoriety from Charges of Illegal Trading Scheme," *The Wall Street Journal,* March 5, 1998, pp. C1, C22.

[19]Prior to the 1980s, there also were odd-lot dealers who bought and sold to individuals with orders for less than round lots (usually 100 shares). Currently, this function is handled by either the specialist or some large brokerage firm.

Short Sales   Most investors purchase stock ("go long") expecting to derive their return from an increase in value. If you believe that a stock is overpriced, however, and want to take advantage of an expected decline in the price, you can sell the stock short. A *short sale* is the sale of stock that you do not own with the intent of purchasing it back later at a lower price. Specifically, you would *borrow* the stock from another investor through your broker, sell it in the market, and subsequently replace it at (you hope) a price lower than the price at which you sold it. The investor who lent the stock has the proceeds of the sale as collateral and can invest these funds in short-term, risk-free securities. Although a short sale has no time limit, the lender of the shares can decide to sell the shares, in which case your broker must find another investor willing to lend the shares.[20]

Three technical points affect short sales. First, a short sale can be made only on an *uptick trade,* meaning the price of the short sale must be higher than the last trade price. This is because the exchanges do not want traders to force a profit on a short sale by pushing the price down through continually selling short. Therefore, the transaction price for a short sale must be an uptick or, without any change in price, the previous price must have been higher than its previous price (a zero uptick). For an example of a zero uptick, consider the following set of transaction prices: 42, 42.25, 42.25. You could sell short at 42.25 even though it is no change from the previous trade at 42.25 because that previous trade was an uptick trade.

The second technical point concerns dividends. The short seller must pay any dividends due to the investor who lent the stock. The purchaser of the short-sale stock receives the dividend from the corporation, so the short seller must pay a similar dividend to the lender.

Finally, short sellers must post the same margin as an investor who had acquired stock. This margin can be in any unrestricted securities owned by the short seller.

Special Orders   In addition to these general orders, there are several special types of orders. A *stop loss order* is a conditional market order whereby the investor directs the sale of a stock if it drops to a given price. Assume you buy a stock at 50 and expect it to go up. If you are wrong, you want to limit your losses. To protect yourself, you could put in a stop loss order at 45. In this case, if the stock dropped to 45, your stop loss order would become a market sell order, and the stock would be sold at the prevailing market price. The stop loss order does not guarantee that you will get the $45; you can get a little bit more or a little bit less. Because of the possibility of market disruption caused by a large number of stop loss orders, exchanges have, on occasion, canceled all such orders on certain stocks and not allowed brokers to accept further stop loss orders on those issues.

A related stop loss tactic for an investor who has entered into a short sale is a *stop buy order.* Such an investor who wants to minimize loss if the stock begins to increase in value would enter this conditional buy order at a price above the short-sale price. Assume you sold a stock short at 50, expecting it to decline to 40. To protect yourself from an increase, you could put in a stop buy order to purchase the stock using a market buy order if it reached a price of 55. This conditional buy order would hopefully limit any loss on the short sale to approximately $5 a share.

Margin Transactions   When investors buy stock, they can pay for the stock with cash or borrow part of the cost, leveraging the transaction. Leverage is accomplished by buying on

Interactive e-lectures

For more explanation and an animated example of margins, go to: http://reillyxtra .swlearning.com.

---

[20]For a discussion of the negative short-selling result, see William Power, "Short Sellers Set to Catch Tumbling Overvalued Stocks," *The Wall Street Journal,* December 28, 1993, pp. C1, C2. For a discussion of short-selling events, see Carol J. Loomis, "Short Sellers and the Seamy Side of Wall Street," *Fortune* (July 22, 1996): 66–72; and Gary Weiss, "The Secret World of Short Sellers," *Business Week* (August 5, 1996): 62–68. For a discussion of short-selling during 2000–2001, see Allison Beard, "Short Selling Goes from Strength to Strength," *Financial Times,* March 16, 2001, p. 29.

EXHIBIT 6.7 NYSE Member Firm Customers' Margin Debt in Dollars and as a Percentage of U.S. Market Capitalization: 1993–2004

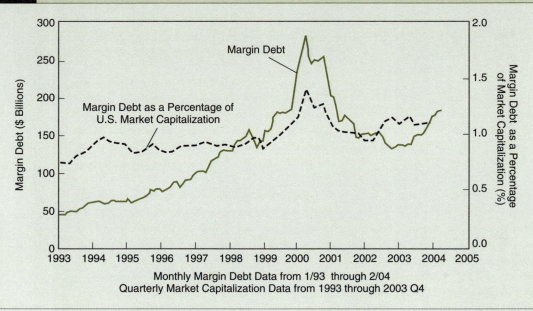

Monthly Margin Debt Data from 1/93 through 2/04
Quarterly Market Capitalization Data from 1993 through 2003 Q4

Sources: Federal Reserve Board; New York Stock Exchange; Goldman Sachs Portfolio Strategy.

margin, which means the investor pays for the stock with some cash and borrows the rest through the broker, putting up the stock for collateral.

As shown in Exhibit 6.7, the dollar amount of margin credit extended by NYSE members increased consistently since 1993, hitting a peak in early 2000 followed by a decline into 2003 and a subsequent increase in dollar terms but not as a percent of market capitalization. The interest rate charged on these loans by the investment firms is typically 1.50 percent above the rate charged by the bank making the loan. The bank rate, referred to as the *call money rate,* is generally about 1 percent below the prime rate. For example, in June 2004, the prime rate was 4.00 percent, and the call money rate was 2.75 percent.

Federal Reserve Board Regulations T and U determine the maximum proportion of any transaction that can be borrowed. This *margin requirement* (the proportion of total transaction value that must be paid in cash) has varied over time from 40 percent (allowing loans of 60 percent of the value) to 100 percent (allowing no borrowing). As of June 2004, the initial margin requirement specified by the Federal Reserve was 50 percent, although individual investment firms can require higher percents.

After the initial purchase, changes in the market price of the stock will cause changes in the *investor's equity,* which is equal to the market value of the collateral stock minus the amount borrowed. Obviously, if the stock price increases, the investor's equity as a proportion of the total market value of the stock increases, that is, the investor's margin will exceed the initial margin requirement.

Assume you acquired 200 shares of a $50 stock for a total cost of $10,000. A 50 percent initial margin requirement allowed you to borrow $5,000, making your initial equity $5,000. If the stock price increases by 20 percent to $60 a share, the total market value of your position is $12,000, and your equity is now $7,000, or 58 percent ($7,000/$12,000). In contrast, if the stock price declines by 20 percent to $40 a share, the total market value would be $8,000, and your investor's equity would be $3,000, or 37.5 percent ($3,000/$8,000).

This example demonstrates that buying on margin provides all the advantages and the disadvantages of leverage. Lower margin requirements allow you to borrow more, increasing the percentage of gain or loss on your investment when the stock price increases or decreases. The leverage factor equals 1/percent margin. Thus, as in the example, if the margin is 50 percent, the leverage factor is 2, that is, 1/0.50. Therefore, when the rate of return on the stock is plus or minus 10 percent, the return on your equity is plus or minus 20 percent. If the margin requirement declines to 33 percent, you can borrow more (67 percent), and the leverage factor is 3(1/0.33). When you acquire stock or other investments on margin, you are increasing the financial risk of the investment beyond the risk inherent in the security itself. You should increase your required rate of return accordingly.[21]

The following example shows how borrowing by using margin affects the distribution of your returns before commissions and interest on the loan. If the stock increased by 20 percent, your return on the investment would be as follows:

1. The market value of the stock is $12,000, which leaves you with $7,000 after you pay off the loan.
2. The return on your $5,000 investment is

$$\frac{7,000}{5,000} - 1 = 1.40 - 1$$

$$= 0.40 = 40\%$$

In contrast, if the stock declined by 20 percent to $40 a share, your return would be as follows:

1. The market value of the stock is $8,000, which leaves you with $3,000 after you pay off the loan.
2. The negative return on your $5,000 investment is

$$\frac{3,000}{5,000} - 1 = 0.60 - 1$$

$$= -0.40 = -40\%$$

Notably, this symmetrical increase in gains and losses is only true prior to commissions and interest. Obviously, if we assume a 6 percent interest on the borrowed funds (which would be $5,000 \times 0.06 = $300) and a $100 commission on the transaction, the results would indicate a lower increase and a larger negative return as follows:

$$\textbf{20\% increase: } \frac{\$12,000 - \$5,000 - \$300 - \$100}{5,000} - 1 = \frac{6,600}{5,000} - 1 = 0.32 = 32\%$$

$$\textbf{20\% decline: } \frac{\$8,000 - \$5,000 - \$300 - \$100}{5,000} - 1 = \frac{2,600}{5,000} - 1 = -0.48 = -48\%$$

---

[21]For a discussion of the investment environment in early 2000, see Greg Ip, "Margin Debt Set a Record in January, Sparking Fresh Fears Over Speculation," *The Wall Street Journal,* February 15, 2000, pp. C1, C2.

In addition to the initial margin requirement, another important concept is the *maintenance margin,* which is the required proportion of your equity to the total value of the stock; the maintenance margin protects the broker if the stock price declines. At present, the minimum maintenance margin specified by the Federal Reserve is 25 percent, but, again, individual brokerage firms can dictate higher margins for their customers. If the stock price declines to the point where your investor's equity drops below 25 percent of the total value of the position, the account is considered undermargined, and you will receive a *margin call* to provide more equity. If you do not respond with the required funds in time, the stock will be sold to pay off the loan. The time allowed to meet a margin call varies between investment firms and is affected by market conditions. Under volatile conditions, the time allowed to respond to a margin call can be shortened drastically.

Given a maintenance margin of 25 percent, when you buy on margin you must consider how far the stock price can fall before you receive a margin call. The computation for our example is as follows: If the price of the stock is P and you own 200 shares, the value of the position is 200P and the equity in the account is 200P − $5,000. The percentage margin is (200P − 5,000)/200P. To determine the price, P, that is equal to 25 percent (0.25), we use the following equation:

$$\frac{200P - \$5,000}{200P} = 0.25$$

$$200P - \$5,000 = 50P$$

$$150P = \$5,000$$

$$P = \$33.33$$

Therefore, when the stock is at $33.33, the equity value is exactly 25 percent; so if the stock declines from $50 to below $33.33, you will receive a margin call.

To continue the previous example, if the stock declines to $30 a share, its total market value would be $6,000 and your equity would be $1,000, which is only about 17 percent of the total value ($1,000/$6,000). You would receive a margin call for approximately $667, which would give you equity of $1,667, or 25 percent of the total value of the account ($1,667/$6,667). If the stock declined further, you would receive additional margin calls.

EXCHANGE MARKET MAKERS

Now that we have discussed the overall structure of the exchange markets and the orders that are used to buy and sell stocks, we can discuss the role and function of the market makers on the exchange. These people and the role they play differ among exchanges. For example, on U.S. exchanges these people are called *specialists*. Most exchanges do not have a single market maker but have competing dealers. On exchanges that have central market makers, these individuals are critical to the smooth and efficient functioning of these markets.

As noted, a major requirement for a good market is liquidity, which depends on how the market makers do their job. Our initial discussion centers on the specialist's role in U.S. markets, followed by a consideration of comparable roles on exchanges in other countries.

U.S. Markets The specialist is a member of the exchange who applies to the exchange to be assigned stocks to handle.[22] The typical specialist will handle ten to fifteen stocks. The

---

[22]Each stock is assigned to one specialist. Most specialists are part of a firm that can be a formal organization of specialists (a specialist firm) or a set of independent specialists who join together to spread the work load and the risk of the stocks assigned to the firm. As of July, 2004, a total of 467 individual specialists were affiliated with seven specialist firms (about sixty-seven specialists per firm).

minimum capital requirement for specialists is currently $1 million or the value of 15,000 shares of each stock assigned, whichever is greater.

Functions of the specialist.   Specialists have two major functions. First, they serve as *brokers* to match buy and sell orders and to handle special limit orders placed with member brokers. As noted earlier, an individual broker who receives a limit order (or stop loss or stop buy order) leaves it with the specialist, who executes it when the specified price occurs.

The second major function of a specialist is to act as a *dealer* to maintain a fair and orderly market by providing liquidity when the normal flow of orders is not adequate. As a dealer, the specialist must buy and sell for his or her own account (like a Nasdaq dealer) when public supply or demand is insufficient to provide a continuous, liquid market.

Consider the following example. If a stock is currently selling for about $40 per share, assume that the current bid and ask in an auction market (without the intervention of the specialist) was 40 bid–41 ask. Under such conditions, random market buy and sell orders might cause the stock price to fluctuate between 40 and 41 constantly—a movement of 2.5 percent between trades. Most investors would probably consider such a price pattern too volatile; the market would not be considered liquid. Under such conditions, the specialist is expected to provide "bridge liquidity" by entering alternative bids and asks or both to narrow the spread and improve the stock's price continuity. In this example, the specialist could enter a bid of 40.25 or 40.50 or an ask of 40.50 or 40.75 to narrow the spread to one-half or one-quarter point.

Specialists can enter either side of the market, depending on several factors, including the trend of the market. Notably, they are expected to buy or sell against the market when prices are clearly moving in one direction. Specifically, they are required to buy stock for their own inventories when there is a clear excess of sell orders and the market is definitely declining. Alternatively, they must sell stock from their inventories or sell it short (i.e., borrow shares) to accommodate an excess of buy orders when the market is rising. Specialists are not expected to prevent prices from rising or declining, but only to ensure that *prices change in an orderly fashion* (that is, to maintain price continuity). Evidence that they have fulfilled this requirement is that during recent years NYSE stocks traded unchanged from, or within ten cents of, the price of the previous trade about 95 percent of the time.

Assuming that there is not a clear trend in the market, several factors will affect how specialists close the bid–ask spread. One factor is their current inventory position in the stock. For example, if they have large inventories of a given stock, all other factors being equal, they would probably enter on the ask (sell) side to reduce these heavy inventories. In contrast, specialists who have little or no inventory of shares because they had been selling from their inventories, or selling short, would tend toward the bid (buy) side of the market to rebuild their inventories or close out their short positions.

Second, the position of the limit-order book will influence how they narrow the spread. Numerous limit buy orders (bids) close to the current market and few limit sell orders (asks) might indicate a tendency toward higher prices because demand is apparently heavy and supply is limited. Under such conditions, a specialist who is not bound by one of the other factors would probably opt to accumulate stock in anticipation of a price increase. The specialists on the NYSE have historically participated as dealers in about 15 percent of the trades, but this percent has been increasing in recent years—from about 18 percent in 1996 to about 27 percent in 2000.[23]

---

[23]For discussion of this trend and its effect on specialists' income, see Greg Ip, "Big Board Specialists: A Profitable Anachronism," *The Wall Street Journal,* March 12, 2001, p. A10.

Specialist income. The specialist derives income from the broker and dealer functions. The actual breakdown between the two sources depends on the specific stock. In an actively traded stock such as IBM or GE, a specialist has little need to act as a dealer because the substantial public interest in the stock creates a tight market (that is, a narrow bid–ask spread). In such a case, the main source of income would come from maintaining the limit orders for the stock. The broker income derived from a high-volume stock such as IBM is substantial and without risk.

In contrast, a stock with low trading volume and substantial price volatility would probably have a fairly wide bid–ask spread, and the specialist would have to be an active dealer. The specialist's income from such a stock would depend on his or her ability to trade it profitably. Specialists have a major advantage when trading because of their limit-order books. Officially, only specialists are supposed to see the limit-order book, which means that they would have a monopoly on very important information regarding the current supply and demand for a stock. The fact is, most specialists routinely share the limit-order book with other brokers, so it is not a competitive advantage.[24]

Most specialists attempt to balance their portfolios between strong broker stocks that provide steady, riskless income and stocks that require active dealer roles. It has been noted (see footnote 23) that the increase in dealer activity has been matched with an increase in return on capital for specialists.[25]

NEW TRADING SYSTEMS

As daily trading volume has gone from about 5 million shares to more than a billion shares on both the NYSE and Nasdaq, it has become necessary to introduce new technology into the trading process. Following are some technological innovations that assist in the trading process.

On the NYSE:

- **Super Dot.** Super Dot is an electronic order-routing system through which member firms transmit market and limit orders in NYSE-listed securities directly to the posts where securities are traded or to the member firm's booth. After the order has been executed, a report of execution is returned directly to the member firm office over the same electronic circuit, and the execution is submitted directly to the comparison systems. Member firms can enter market orders up to 2,099 shares and limit orders in round or odd lots up to 30,099 shares. An estimated 85 percent of all market orders enter the NYSE through the Super Dot system.
- **The Display Book.** The Display Book is an electronic workstation that keeps track of all limit orders and incoming market orders. This includes incoming Super Dot limit orders.
- **Opening Automated Report Service (OARS).** OARS, the opening feature of the Super Dot system, accepts member firms' preopening market orders up to 30,099 shares. OARS automatically and continuously pairs buy and sell orders and presents the

---

[24]If a major imbalance in trading arises due to new information, the specialist can request a temporary suspension of trading. For an analysis of what occurs during these trading suspensions, see Michael H. Hopewell and Arthur L. Schwartz Jr., "Temporary Trading Suspensions in Individual NYSE Securities," *Journal of Finance* 33, no. 5 (December 1978): 1355–1373; and Frank J. Fabozzi and Christopher K. Ma, "The Over-the-Counter Market and New York Stock Exchange Trading Halts," *The Financial Review* 23, no. 4 (November 1988): 427–437.

[25]For a rigorous analysis of specialist trading, see Ananth Madhaven and George Sofianos, "An Empirical Analysis of NYSE Specialist Trading," *Journal of Financial Economics* 48, no. 2 (May 1998): 189–210.

imbalance to the specialist prior to the opening of a stock. This system helps the specialist determine the opening price and the potential need for a preopening call market.

- **Market-Order Processing.** Super Dot's postopening market-order system is designed to accept member firms' postopening market orders up to 30,099 shares. The system provides rapid execution and reporting of market orders. During 2003, 94.5 percent of market orders were executed and reported in less than thirty seconds.

- **Limit-Order Processing.** The limit-order processing system electronically files orders to be executed when and if a specific price is reached. The system accepts limit orders up to 99,999 shares and electronically updates the Specialists' Display Book. Good-until-canceled orders that are not executed on the day of submission are automatically stored until executed or canceled.

On Nasdaq:

- *Small-Order Execution System (SOES).* SOES was introduced in 1984. Market makers receiving SOES orders must honor their bids for automatic executions up to 1,000 shares. SOES became compulsory following the October 1987 crash when many small investors could not trade and suffered significant losses.

- *SelectNet.* Introduced in 1990, **SelectNet** is an order-routing and execution service for institutional investors that allows brokers and dealers to communicate through Nasdaq terminals instead of the phone. Once two parties agree to a trade on SelectNet, the execution is automatic.

INNOVATIONS FOR COMPETITION

By this time you should realize that the U.S. secondary equity market is being served by two competing models. As mentioned early in this chapter, the first is the *order-driven* stock exchange market where buy and sell orders interact directly with the specialist market maker acting as both a broker and a dealer when necessary. This model is ideal for a secondary market when there is a concentration of participants and all orders come to one central location (either physically or electronically).

The second model is a *quote-driven* market, also referred to as a dealer market, where numerous dealers compete against each other by providing bid–ask quotations and commit to buy and sell given securities at these quoted prices. Generally, in this model buy and sell orders never interact directly, but the best prices are derived due to the competition among dealers who are independent and separated—it is a fragmented market.

Given these two models, the Securities and Exchange Commission has encouraged competition between the two market models by encouraging three innovations: the CQS, the ITS, and the CAES.

The *Consolidated Quotation System (CQS)* is an electronic service that provides quotations on issues listed on the NYSE, the AMEX, and regional exchanges, and issues traded by market makers in the Nasdaq InterMarket (the third market). Provided to subscribers by the Composite Quotation Service, the CQS makes it possible for subscribers to see all competing dealer and exchange quotes for a stock listed on any exchange. The volume of trading for stocks on the consolidated tape has grown dramatically and is now over 400 billion shares annually.

The *Intermarket Trading System (ITS)* is a centralized quotation and routing system developed by the American, Boston, Chicago, New York, Pacific, and Philadelphia Stock

EXHIBIT 6.8	Intermarket Trading System (ITS) Activity			
		DAILY AVERAGE		
Year	Issues Eligible	Share Volume	Executed Trades	Average Size of Trade
1980	884	1,565,900	2,868	546
1985	1,288	5,669,400	5,867	966
1990	2,126	9,387,114	8,744	1,075
1995	3,542	12,185,064	10,911	1,117
1996	4,001	12,721,968	11,426	1,113
1997	4,535	15,429,377	14,057	1,098
1998	4,844	18,136,472	17,056	1,063
1999	5,056	21,617,723	19,315	1,119
2000	4,664	28,176,178	23,972	1,175
2001	4,575	34,029,513	29,728	1,145
2002	4,718	50,036,437	37,694	1,327
2003	4,808	64,077,468	46,582	1,376

Source: *NYSE Fact Book* (New York: NYSE, 2004): 28. Reprinted by permission of NYSE.

Exchanges and the NASD. ITS consists of a central computer facility with interconnected terminals in the participating market centers. As shown in Exhibit 6.8, the number of issues included, the volume of trading, and the size of trades have all grown substantially. There were over 4,800 issues included on the system in 2003.

With ITS, brokers and market makers in each market center indicate specific buying and selling commitments through a composite quotation display that shows the current quotes for each stock in every market center. A broker is expected to go to the best market to execute a customer's order by sending a message committing to a buy or sell at the price quoted. When this commitment is accepted, a message reports the transaction. The following example illustrates how ITS works.

A broker on the NYSE has a market order to sell 100 shares of GE stock. Assuming the quotation display at the NYSE shows that the best current bid for GE is on the Pacific Stock Exchange (PSE), the broker will enter an order to sell 100 shares at the bid on the PSE. Within seconds, the commitment flashes on the computer screen and is printed out at the PSE specialist's post, where it is executed against the PSE bid. The transaction is reported back to New York and on the consolidated tape. Both brokers receive immediate confirmation and the results are transmitted at the end of each day. Thereafter, each broker completes his or her own clearance and settlement procedure.

The ITS system currently provides centralized quotations for stocks listed on the NYSE and specifies whether a bid or ask *away* from the NYSE market is superior to that *on* the NYSE. Note, however, that the system lacks several characteristics. It does not automatically execute at the best market. Instead, an investor must contact the market maker and indicate that he wants to buy or sell, at which time the bid or ask may be withdrawn. Also, it is not mandatory that a broker go to the best market. Although the best price may be at another market center, a broker might consider it inconvenient to trade on that exchange if the price difference is not substantial. Still, even with these shortcomings, substantial technical and operational progress has occurred through this central quotation and routing system.

The *Computer-Assisted Execution System (CAES)* is a service created by Nasdaq that automates order routing and transaction execution for securities listed on domestic exchanges that are part of the ITS. This system makes it possible for market makers who are involved with ITS to execute trades with specialists on the exchanges using CAES.

WHERE DO WE GO FROM HERE?

One cannot help but be struck by the significant changes that have taken place in both the U.S. and global equity markets during the new millennium. The technological advances and the decimalization of prices have contributed to significant reductions in trading costs for institutional and retail investors. Although we have two different trading models (order-driven and quote-driven), it appears that they can survive together. But both are challenged by the ECNs that can match orders electronically and provide faster, cheaper transactions. Based on the percent of Nasdaq transactions completed on the ECNs (about 25 to 30 percent), it appears that the ECNs are very good at finding, matching, and executing trades for dealer stocks (as brokers) and when they cannot broker the trade they send the orders to the Nasdaq market. The unknown factor with ECNs is "best price."

In response to challenge from the ECNs, the order-driven exchanges (mainly the NYSE) have attempted regulations to protect the exchange from competition. The first was Rule 390, which was motivated by the concept that the best auction market is one where *all* participants are *centralized* in one location so that the market benefits from having all bids and offers available to interact and provide the very best prices. To help create and protect this centralized auction market, the NYSE introduced Rule 390, which required members to obtain the exchange's permission to carry out a transaction in a listed stock off the exchange. The NYSE argued that without such a rule, the market would become fragmented and many orders would be internalized (members would match orders between customers) rather than exposed to the public. After several years of debate, in late 1999 the SEC ruled that this regulation was clearly anticompetitive and Rule 390 was rescinded (the final order was dated May 5, 2000).

The second regulation that constrains the ECNs from competing with the NYSE is the *trade-through rule*. Specifically, this rule dictates that markets *not* ignore superior prices that are available in competing markets. Put another way, traders are not allowed to "trade through" superior prices—e.g., if the best bid is at $30, a dealer cannot fill the order at $29.95. Notably, this rule almost always works to the advantage of the NYSE for stocks listed on the exchange because the bulk of trading in these listed stocks (about 70 to 80 percent) is done on the exchange, so one would expect it to have the best price. The problem is that the search for the best price and the ensuing order transfer can slow the trade by about thirty seconds, which is a long time on the exchange, and prices can change in the interim. Thus the debate is over *speed of execution* versus *best price*.[26] The speed-of-execution contingent (ECNs and other ATSs) wants some flexibility on the price: either allow the customer to specify a price range of one to three cents a share from the best price or have a general band whereby the order can be consummated if the electronic price is within one or two cents of the best price. The NYSE is considering such price bands but contend that block traders need to have the benefit of specialists who can ensure the best price for the

---

[26]The discussion was ongoing in 1999 and has continued into 2004—see Greg Ip and Randal Smith, "Big Board Member Face Off on the Issue of Automated Trading," *The Wall Street Journal*, November 15, 1999, p. 1; Deborah Soloman and Kate Kelly, "Wide SEC Review May Revamp Structure of U.S. Stock Markets," *The Wall Street Journal*, September 19, 2003, pp. A1, A2; Kate Kelly, "A Little Scary: NYSE's Chief Seeks to Sell Electronic Trading to the Floor," *The Wall Street Journal*, February 2, 2004, pp. C1, C6; Susanne Craig and Kate Kelly, "NYSE Chief has Balancing Act," *The Wall Street Journal*, February 3, 2004, pp. C1, C4; and Kate Kelly, "NYSE's Automatic Transition" *The Wall Street Journal*, June 22, 2004, pp. C1, C5.

total block. There is also a greater need for specialists for very small illiquid shares. The point is, relatively small transactions (e.g., under 5,000 shares) for large, liquid stocks (e.g., GE, IBM, 3M, and Johnson and Johnson) can be handled quickly and at very low cost via electronic trading and will typically be at the best price. But very large block trades for liquid stocks and most trades for very small illiquid stocks usually need human intervention.

So, where *do* we go from here? Most likely, further technological advances and the Internet will greatly influence the answer. But it is also likely that human financial experts will always be needed to exercise judgment in the investment process.

Summary

- The securities market is divided into primary and secondary markets. While primary markets are important sources of new capital for the issuers of securities, the secondary markets provide the liquidity that is critical to the primary markets.

- The composition of the secondary bond market has not changed very much over the past twenty years. In sharp contrast, the secondary equity market has experienced significant change and is continuing to evolve due to new technology and consolidation. In addition to several primary listing markets that include exchanges and several Nasdaq components, the secondary market includes several robust regional exchanges, a viable third market, and most recently, the creation, growth, and consolidation of numerous alternative trading systems that provide automatic electronic transactions for stocks on both exchanges and dealer markets.

Investments Online

Many Internet sites deal with different aspects of investing. Earlier site suggestions led you to information and prices of securities traded both in the U.S. and around the globe. Here are some additional sites of interest:

http://finance.yahoo.com One of the best sites for a variety of investments information including market quotes, commentary, and research, both domestic and international.

http://finance.lycos.com This site offers substantial market information, including price quotes on stocks, selected bonds, and options. Price charts are available.

http://www.sec.gov The Web site of the Securities and Exchange Commission (SEC) offers news and information, investor assistance and complaint handling, SEC rules, enforcement, and data.

http://www.nyse.com, http://www.amex.com, http://www.nasdaq.com The Web sites of the New York Stock Exchange (NYSE), the American Stock Exchange (AMEX), and the National Association of Securities Dealers Automated Quotation (Nasdaq) system offer information about the rele-

vant market, price quotes, listings of firms, and investor services. The AMEX site includes price quotes for SPDRs (S&P Depository Receipts, which represent ownership in the S&P 500 index or the S&P Midcap 400 index) and iShares MSCI Index Funds, which track the Morgan Stanley Capital International (MSCI) indexes of over twenty countries and regions.

https://www.etrade.com/global.html, http://www.schwab.com, http://www.ml.com Many brokerage houses have Web pages. These are three examples of such sites. E*Trade Securities is an example of an online brokerage firm that allows investors to trade securities over the Internet. Schwab is a discount broker, whereas Merrill Lynch is a full-service broker with a reputation for good research.

Links to country stock and other financial markets are available at:

http://www.internationalist.com/business/stocks/, http://biz.yahoo.com/ifc/, and **http://www.wall-street .com/foreign.html.**

- The components of a good exchange market include several types of membership as well as various types of orders. In addition, market makers play a critical role in maintaining the liquidity of the market.

- It appears that changes, especially those due to these technological innovations, have only just begun. Therefore, it is important for investors who will be involved in this market to understand how this market has evolved, what is its current structure, and how it can develop in the future. As an investor, you will need to understand how to analyze securities to find the best securities for your portfolio, but also you need to know the best way to buy/sell the security, that is, how and where to complete the transaction. Our discussion in this chapter should provide the background you need to make that trading decision.

QUESTIONS

1. Define *market* and briefly discuss the characteristics of a good market.
2. You own 100 shares of General Electric stock and you want to sell it because you need the money to make a down payment on a car. Assume there is absolutely no secondary market system in common stocks. How would you go about selling the stock? Discuss what you would have to do to find a buyer, how long it might take, and the price you might receive.
3. Define *liquidity* and discuss the factors that contribute to it. Give examples of a liquid asset and an illiquid asset, and discuss why they are considered liquid and illiquid.
4. Define a primary and secondary market for securities and discuss how they differ. Discuss how the primary market is dependent on the secondary market.
5. Give an example of an initial public offering (IPO) in the primary market. Give an example of a seasoned equity issue in the primary market. Discuss which would involve greater risk to the buyer.
6. Find an advertisement for a recent primary offering in *The Wall Street Journal*. Based on the information in the ad, indicate the characteristics of the security sold and the major underwriters. How much new capital did the firm derive from the offering before paying commissions?

7. Briefly explain the difference between a competitive-bid underwriting and a negotiated underwriting.
8. The figures in Exhibit 6.5 reveal a major change over time in the price paid for a membership (seat) on the NYSE. What has caused this change over time?
9. What are the major reasons for the existence of regional stock exchanges? Discuss how they differ from the national exchanges.
10. Which segment of the secondary stock market (listed exchanges or Nasdaq) is larger in terms of the number of issues? Which is larger in terms of the value of the issues traded?
11. Discuss the three levels of Nasdaq in terms of what each provides and who would subscribe to each.
12. a. Define the third market. Give an example of a third-market stock.
    b. Define the fourth market. Discuss why a financial institution would use the fourth market.
13. Briefly define each of the following terms and give an example.
    a. Market order
    b. Limit order
    c. Short sale
    d. Stop loss order
14. Briefly discuss the two major functions and sources of income for the NYSE specialist.

PROBLEMS

1. You have $40,000 to invest in a stock selling for $80 a share. The initial margin requirement is 60 percent. Ignoring taxes and commissions, show in detail the impact on your rate of return if the stock rises to $100 a share and if it declines to $40 a share assuming: (a) you pay cash for the stock, and (b) you buy it using maximum leverage.
2. Lauren has a margin account and deposits $50,000. Assuming the prevailing margin requirement is 40 percent, commissions are ignored, and The Gentry Shoe Corporation is selling at $35 per share.
    a. How many shares can Lauren purchase using the maximum allowable margin?
    b. What is Lauren's profit (loss) if the price of Gentry's stock

    i. rises to $45?
    ii. falls to $25?
    c. If the maintenance margin is 30 percent, to what price can Gentry Shoe fall before Lauren will receive a margin call?
3. Suppose you buy a round lot of Maginn Industries stock on 55 percent margin when the stock is selling at $20 a share. The broker charges a 10 percent annual interest rate, and commissions are 3 percent of the total stock value on both the purchase and sale. A year later you receive a $0.50 per share dividend and sell the stock for 27. What is your rate of return on the investment?
4. You decide to sell short 100 shares of Charlotte Horse Farms when it is selling at its yearly high of 56. Your broker tells you that your margin requirement is 45 percent and that the commission on the purchase is $155. While you are short the stock, Charlotte pays a $2.50

per share dividend. At the end of one year, you buy 100 shares of Charlotte at 45 to close out your position and are charged a commission of $145 and 8 percent interest on the money borrowed. What is your rate of return on the investment?

5. You own 200 shares of Shamrock Enterprises that you bought at $25 a share. The stock is now selling for $45 a share.
   a. You put in a stop loss order at $40. Discuss your reasoning for this action.
   b. If the stock eventually declines in price to $30 a share, what would be your rate of return with and without the stop loss order?

6. Two years ago, you bought 300 shares of Kayleigh Milk Co. for $30 a share with a margin of 60 percent. Cur-

rently, the Kayleigh stock is selling for $45 a share. Assuming no dividends and ignoring commissions,
(a) compute the annualized rate of return on this investment if you had paid cash, and (b) your rate of return with the margin purchase.

7. The stock of the Madison Travel Co. is selling for $28 a share. You put in a limit buy order at $24 for one month. During the month, the stock price declines to $20, then jumps to $36. Ignoring commissions, what would have been your rate of return on this investment? What would be your rate of return if you had put in a market order? If your limit order was at $18?

WEB EXERCISES

1. Explore the Web sites of five different stock exchanges including at least three non-U.S. markets (there are several Web sites, including *http://finance.wat.ch/*, that provide links to a myriad of exchanges in different countries). How do their listing requirements and trading mechanisms differ?

2. To practice making a market in a stock, go to *http://www.nasdaqtrader.com/HeadTrader*. How well can you do compared to others in your class?

3. Visit the Web sites of at least five different stock brokerages houses, including some online brokers. Gather and report information about their commission schedules. For example, do they advertise information on round lot trades? Is the commission based on the stock price? Number of shares? Value of the total trade (price multiplied by number of shares)? What information can you find about bond trading?

SPREADSHEET EXERCISES

1. Construct a spreadsheet to compute the percentage return on margin investments. Information input to the spreadsheet should include: initial stock price and shares purchased, initial equity in dollars, initial margin percentage, and maintenance margin percentage. The output should include in one column a series of ending stock prices and the percentage return in an adjoining column. The potential ending stock prices should range from 40 percent of the initial purchase price to 200 percent of the initial purchase price. The spreadsheet should compute the stock price at which a margin call will occur. Use the following scenario with the spread-

sheet: 1,000 shares of stock purchases at $50 a share; initial equity is $25,000; initial margin percentage is 50 percent; and the maintenance margin is 25 percent.

2. To make your spreadsheet from Exercise 1 more realistic, add the following features: dividends expected to be paid over the holding period and the interest paid on the margin loan. Assume a six-month holding period, that dividends are paid at the rate of $0.25 per share each quarter, and that the margin loan annual percentage rate is 8 percent. How does this affect the percentage returns on the investment over the range of stock prices?

3. How will the spreadsheets need to be adjusted for analyzing the use of margin on short sales?

REFERENCES

Barclay, Michael, Terrence Hendershott, and D. Timothy McCormick. "Competition among Trading Venues: Information and Trading on Electronic Communications Networks." *Journal of Finance* 58, no. 6 (December 2003).

Barclay, Michael J., William G. Christie, Jeffrey H. Harris, Eugene Kandel, and Paul Schultz. "The Effects of Market Reform on the Trading Costs and Depth of NASDAQ Stocks." *Journal of Finance* 54, no. 1 (March, 1999).

Blume, Marshall E., and Jeremy J. Siegel. "The Theory of Security Pricing and Market Structure." *Financial Markets, Institutions and Instruments* 1, no. 3 (1992). New York University Salomon Center.

Christie, William, and Paul Schultz. "Why Do NASDAQ Market-Makers Avoid Odd-Eighth Quotes?" *Journal of Finance* 49, no. 5 (December 1994).

Dutts, Prajit, and Ananth Madhaven. "Competition and Collusion in Dealer Markets." *Journal of Finance* 52, no. 1 (March 1997).

Economides, Nicholas, and Robert A. Schwartz. "Electronic Call Market Trading." *Journal of Portfolio Management* 21, no. 3 (Spring 1995).

Grossman, S. J., and Merton H. Miller. "Liquidity and Market Structure." *Journal of Finance* 43, no. 2 (June 1988).

Harris, Jeffrey, and Paul Schultz. "The Trading Profits of SOES Bandits." *Journal of Financial Economics* 50, no. 1 (October 1998).

Hasbrouck, Joel. "One Security, Many Markets: Determining the Contribution to Price Discovery." *Journal of Finance* 50, no. 4 (September, 1995).

Hendershott, Terrence, and Haim Mendelson. "Crossing Networks and Dealer Markets: Competition and Performance." *Journal of Finance* 55, no. 5 (October 2000).

Huang, Roger. "The Quality of ECN and Nasdaq Market-Maker Quotes." *Journal of Finance* 57, no. 3 (June, 2002).

Huang, Roger, and Hans Stoll. "Dealer versus Auction Markets: A Paired Comparison of Execution Costs on NASDAQ and the NYSE." *Journal of Financial Economics* 41, no. 3 (July 1996).

Madhaven, Ananth. "Consolidation, Fragmentation, and the Disclosure of Trading Information." *Review of Financial Studies* 8, no. 2 (June, 1995).

Neal, Robert. "A Comparison of Transaction Cost Between Competitive Market Maker and Specialist Market Structures." *Journal of Business* 65, no. 3 (July 1992).

NYSE Fact Book. New York: NYSE, published annually.

Pagano, M. "Trading Volume and Asset Liquidity." *Quarterly Journal of Economics* 104, no. 2 (1989).

Sherrerd, Katrina F., ed. *Execution Techniques, True Trading Costs, and the Microstructure of Markets.* Charlottesville, VA: Association for Investment Management and Research, 1993.

Stoll, Hans. *The Stock Exchange Specialist System: An Economic Analysis.* Monograph Series in Financial Economics. New York University, 1985.

Stoll, Hans, and Robert Whaley. "Stock Market Structure and Volatility." *Review of Financial Studies* 3, no. 1 (1990).

THOMSON ONE
Business School Edition

1. On which stock markets are the following firms traded: Abbott Labs, Apple Computer, ExxonMobil, Intel, Johnson and Johnson, Microsoft?
2. Suppose you purchased Microsoft stock on October 1, 2004 and sold it two months later on December 1, 2004. What would your percentage price return be? What would the percentage price change be if you had used 75 percent margin? 50 percent margin?
3. Redo exercise 2 but this time assume you purchased Microsoft on March 15, 2001 and sold it three months later on June 15, 2001. What would the annualized returns be if you bought the stock with cash? If you used 75 percent margin? 50 percent margin?

GLOSSARY

Alternative trading system (ATS) A nontraditional, computerized trading system that competes with or supplements dealer markets and traditional stock exchanges. While they facilitate trading in shares, they do not provide listing services.

Call market A market in which trading for individual stocks only takes place at specified times. All the bids and asks available at the time are combined and the market administrators specify a single price that will possibly clear the market at that time.

Commission broker An employee of a member firm who buys or sells for the customers of the firm.

Computer-Assisted Execution System (CAES) A service created by Nasdaq that automates order routing and execution for securities listed on domestic stock exchanges and involved in the Intermarket Trading System (ITS).

Consolidated Quotation System (CQS) An electronic quotation service for issues listed on the NYSE, the AMEX, or regional exchanges and traded on the Nasdaq InterMarket.

Continuous market A market where stocks are priced and traded continuously either by an auction process or by dealers during the time the market is open.

Electronic Communication Network (ECN) A computerized trading system that matches buy and sell orders, usually for retail and small institutional trading. ECNs act for customers as a broker—they do not buy or sell from their own account.

Electronic Crossing System (ECS) An electronic trading system that matches large buy and sell orders.

External (or informational) efficiency A market where prices adjust rapidly to the infusion of new information. As a result current security prices fully reflect all available information.

Floor broker An independent member of an exchange who acts as a broker for other members.

Fourth market Direct trading of exchange securities between owners (usually institutions) without any broker intermediation, often via an ATS.

Initial public offering (IPO) A new issue by a firm that has no existing public market.

Intermarket Trading System (ITS) A computerized system that connects competing exchanges and dealers who trade stocks listed on an exchange. Its purpose is to help customers find the best market for these stocks at a point in time.

Limit order An order that lasts for a specified time to buy or sell a security when and if it trades at a specified price.

Liquidity The ability to buy or sell an asset quickly and at a price that is not substantially different from the prices of prior transactions.

Maintenance margin The subsequent downside margin required after the purchase if the stock price declines.

Margin The percent of cash a buyer pays for a security, borrowing the balance from the broker. This introduces leverage, which increases the risk of the transaction.

Margin call If the value of your equity falls below the maintenance margin (currently 25 percent), you will receive a margin call that requires you to provide more equity to bring the equity up to the 25 percent requirement.

Market The means through which buyers and sellers are brought together to aid in the transfer of goods and/or services.

Market order An order to buy or sell a security immediately at the best price available.

Nasdaq InterMarket A trading system that includes Nasdaq market makers and ECNs that quote and trade stocks listed on the NYSE and the AMEX. It involves dealers from the Nasdaq market and the Intermarket Trading System (ITS). In many ways, this has become what had been labeled the third market.

National Association of Securities Dealers Automated Quotation (Nasdaq) system An electronic system for providing bid–ask quotes for securities traded on Nasdaq.

OTC Electronic Bulletin Board (OTCBB) A regulated quotation service that displays real-time quotes, last-sale prices, and volume information for a specified set of over-the-counter (OTC) securities that are not traded on the formal Nasdaq market.

Price continuity A feature of a liquid market in which prices change little from one transaction to the next due to the depth of the market.

Primary market The market in which newly issued securities are sold by their issuers, who receive the proceeds.

Private placement A new issue sold directly to a small group of investors, usually institutions.

Registered competitive market makers (RCMM) Members of an exchange who are allowed to use their memberships to buy or sell for their own account within the specific trading obligations set down by the exchange. Because they are on the floor, they have a better feel for the market and low commissions, but they provide liquidity to the market.

Seasoned equity issues New shares offered by firms that already have stock outstanding.

Secondary market The market in which outstanding securities are bought and sold by owners other than the issuers.

SelectNet An order-routing and trade-execution system for institutional investors (brokers and dealers) that allows communication through the Nasdaq system rather than by phone.

Short sale The sale of borrowed stock with the intention of repurchasing it later at a lower price and earning the difference.

Small-Order Execution System (SOES) A quotation and execution system for retail (nonprofessional) investors who place orders with brokers who must honor their prevailing bid–ask for automatic execution up to 1,000 shares.

Third market Trading of listed securities on Nasdaq.

Transaction cost The cost of executing a trade. Low costs characterize an internally efficient market.

Treasury bill A negotiable U.S. government security with a maturity of less than one year that pays no periodic interest but yields the difference between its par value and its discounted purchase price.

Treasury bond A U.S. government security with a maturity of more than ten years that pays interest periodically.

Treasury note A U.S. government security with maturities of one to ten years that pays interest periodically.

APPENDIX 6

Characteristics of Developed and Developing Markets around the World

EXHIBIT 6.A Developed Markets around the World

Country	Principal Exchange	Other Exchanges	Total Market Capitalization ($ billions)	Available Market Capitalization ($ billions)	Trading Volume ($ billions)	Domestic Issues Listed	Total Issues Listed	Auction Mechanism	Official Specialists	Options/Futures Trading	Price Limits	Principal Market Indexes
Australia	Sydney	5	82.3	53.5	39.3	N.A.	1,496	Continuous	No	Yes	None	All Ordinaries—324 issues
Austria	Vienna	—	18.7	8.3	37.2	125	176	Call	Yes	No	5%	GZ Aktienindex—25 issues
Belgium	Brussels	3	48.5	26.2	6.8	186	337	Mixed	No	Few	10%	Brussels Stock Exchange Index—186 issues
Canada	Toronto	4	186.8	124.5	71.3	N.A.	1,208	Continuous	Yes	Yes	None	TSE 300 Composite Index
Denmark	Copenhagen	—	29.7	22.2	11.1	N.A.	284	Mixed	No	No	None	Copenhagen Stock Exchange Index—38 issues
Finland	Helsinki	—	9.9	1.7	5.2	N.A.	125	Mixed	N.A.	N.A.	N.A.	KOP (Kansallis-Osake-Pannki) Price Index
France	Paris	6	256.5	137.2	129.0	463	663	Mixed	Yes	Yes	4%	CAC General Index—240 issues
Germany	Frankfurt	7	297.7	197.9	1,003.7	N.A.	355	Continuous	Yes	Options	None	DAX; FAZ (Frankfurter Allgemeine Zeitung)
Hong Kong	Hong Kong	—	67.7	37.1	34.6	N.A.	479	Continuous	No	Futures	None	Hang Seng Index—33 issues
Ireland	Dublin	—	8.4	6.4	5.5	N.A.	N.A.	Continuous	No	No	None	J&E Davy Total Market Index
Italy	Milan	9	137.0	73.2	42.6	N.A.	317	Mixed	No	No	10-20%	Banca Commerziale—209 issues
Japan	Tokyo	7	2,754.6	1,483.5	1,602.4	N.A.	1,576	Continuous	Yes	No	10% down	TOPIX—1,097 issues; TSE II—423 issues; Nikkei 225
Luxembourg	Luxembourg	—	1.5	0.9	0.1	61	247	Continuous	N.A.	N.A.	N.A.	Domestic Share Price Index—9 issues
Malaysia	Kuala Lumpur	—	199.3	95.0	126.4	430	478	Continuous	No	No	None	Kuala Lumpur Composite Index—83 issues
The Netherlands	Amsterdam	—	112.1	92.4	80.4	279	569	Continuous	Yes	Options	Variable	ANP—CBS General Index—51 issues

(continued)

EXHIBIT 6.A   Developed Markets around the World (concluded)

Country	Principal Exchange	Other Exchanges	Total Market Capitalization ($ billions)	Available Market Capitalization ($ billions)	Trading Volume ($ billions)	Domestic Issues Listed	Total Issues Listed	Auction Mechanism	Official Specialists	Options/ Futures Trading	Price Limits	Principal Market Indexes
New Zealand	Wellington	—	6.7	5.3	2.0	295	451	Continuous	No	Futures	None	Barclay's International Price Index—40 issues
Norway	Oslo	9	18.4	7.9	14.1	N.A.	128	Call	No	No	None	Oslo Bors Stock Index—50 issues
Singapore	Singapore	—	28.6	15.6	8.2	N.A.	324	Continuous	No	No	None	Straits Times Index—30 issues; SES—32 issues
South Africa	Johannesburg	—	72.7	N.A.	8.2	N.A.	N.A.	Continuous	No	Options	None	JSE Actuaries Index—141 issues
Spain	Madrid	3	86.6	46.8	41.0	N.A.	368	Mixed	No	No	10%	Madrid Stock Exchange Index—72 issues
Sweden	Stockholm	—	59.0	24.6	15.8	N.A.	151	Mixed	No	Yes	None	Jacobson & Ponsbach—30 issues
Switzerland	Zurich	6	128.5	75.4	376.6	161	380	Mixed	No	Yes	5%	Société de Banque Suisse—90 issues
United Kingdom	London	5	756.2	671.1	280.7	1,911	2,577	Continuous	No	Yes	None	Financial Times (FT)Ordinaries—750 issues; FTSE 100; FT 33
United States	New York	6	9,431.1	8,950.3	5,778.7	N.A.	3,358	Continuous	Yes	Yes	None	S&P 500; Dow Jones Industrial Average; Wilshire 5000; Russell 3000

Notes: Market capitalizations (both total and available) are as of December 31, 1990, except for South African market capitalization, which is from 1988. Available differs from total market capitalization by subtracting cross holdings, closely held and government-owned shares, and takes into account restrictions on foreign ownership. Number of issues listed are from 1988 except for Malaysia, which is from 1994. Trading volume data are from 1990 except for Switzerland, which are from 1988. Trading institutions data are from 1987. Market capitalizations (both total and available) for all countries except the United States and South Africa are from the Salomon-Russell Global Equity Indices. U.S. market capitalization (both total and available) is from the Frank Russell Company. All trading volume information (except for Switzerland) and Malaysian total issues listed are from the *Emerging Stock Markets Factbook: 1991,* International Finance Corp., 1991. Trading institutions information is from Richard Roll, "The International Crash of 1987," *Financial Analysts Journal,* September/October 1988. South African market capitalization, number of issues listed for all countries (except Malaysia), and Swiss trading volume are reproduced courtesy of Euromoney Books, extracted from *The G.T. Guide to World Equity Markets: 1989, 1988.*

Source: From *Global Investing: The Professional Guide to the World Capital Markets* by Roger G. Ibbotson and Gary P. Brinson, pp. 109–111. Copyright © 1993. Reprinted by permission of The McGraw-Hill Companies, Inc.

Exhibit 6.B	Emerging Markets around the World

Country	Principal Exchange	Other Exchanges	Market Capitalization ($ billions)	Trading Volume ($ billions)	Total Issues Listed	Auction Mechanism	Principal Market Indexes
Argentina	Buenos Aires	4	36.9	11.4	156	N.A.	Buenos Aires Stock Exchange Index
Brazil	São Paulo	9	189.2	109.5	544	Continuous	BOVESPA Share Price Index—83 issues
Chile	Santiago	—	68.2	5.3	279	Mixed	IGPA Index—180 issues
China	Shanghai	1	43.5	97.5	291	Continuous	Shanghai Composite Index
Colombia	Bogotá	1	14.0	2.2	90	N.A.	Bogotá General Composite Index
Greece	Athens	—	14.9	5.1	216	Continuous	Athens Stock Exchange Industrial Price Index
India	Bombay	14	127.5	27.3	4,413	Continuous	Economic Times Index—72 issues
Indonesia	Jakarta	—	47.2	11.8	216	Mixed	Jakarta Stock Exchange Index
Israel	Tel Aviv	—	10.6	5.5	267	Call	General Share Index—all listed issues
Jordan	Amman	—	4.6	0.6	95	N.A.	Amman Financial Market Index
Mexico	Mexico City	—	130.2	83.0	206	Continuous	Bolsa de Valores Index—49 issues
Nigeria	Lagos	—	2.7	N.A.	177	Call	Nigerian Stock Exchange General Index
Pakistan	Karachi	—	12.2	3.2	724	Continuous	State Bank of Pakistan Index
Philippines	Makati	1	55.5	13.9	189	N.A.	Manila Commercial & Industrial Index—25 issues
Portugal	Lisbon	1	16.2	5.2	195	Call	Banco Totta e Acores Share Index—50 issues
South Korea	Seoul	—	191.8	286.0	699	Continuous	Korea Composite Stock Price Index
Taiwan	Taipei	—	247.3	711.0	313	Continuous	Taiwan Stock Exchange Index
Thailand	Bangkok	—	131.4	80.2	389	Continuous	Securities Exchange of Thailand Price Index
Turkey	Istanbul	—	21.6	21.7	176	Continuous	Istanbul Stock Exchange Index—50 issues
Venezuela	Caracas	1	4.1	0.9	90	Continuous	Indice de Capitalization de la BVC
Zimbabwe	N.A.	—	1.8	0.2	64	N.A.	Zimbabwe S.E. Industrial Index

Notes: Market capitalizations, trading volume, and total issues listed are as of 1994. Market capitalization, trading volume, and total issues listed for India is Bombay only. Trading volume for the Philippines is for both Manila and Makati. Total issues listed for India is Bombay only. Trading institutions information is from 1987 and 1988. Market capitalizations, trading volume, and total issues listed are from the *Emerging Stock Markets Factbook: 1995*, International Finance Corp., 1995. Trading institutions information is from Richard Roll, "The International Crash of 1987," *Financial Analysts Journal*, September/October 1988.

Source: From *Global Investing: The Professional Guide to the World Capital Markets* by Roger G. Ibbotson and Gary P. Brinson, pp. 125–126. Copyright © 1993. Reprinted by permission of The McGraw-Hill Companies, Inc.

Security-Market Indexes

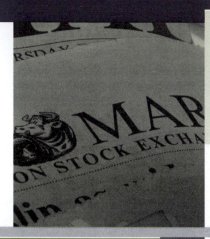

A fair statement regarding *security-market indexes*—especially those outside the United States—is that everybody talks about them but few people understand them. Even those investors familiar with widely publicized stock-market series, such as the Dow Jones Industrial Average (DJIA), usually know little about indexes for the U.S. bond market or for non-U.S. stock markets such as Tokyo or London.

Although portfolios are obviously composed of many different individual stocks, investors typically ask, "What happened to the market today?" The reason for this question is that if an investor owns more than a few stocks or bonds, it is cumbersome to follow each stock or bond individually to determine the composite performance of the portfolio. Also, there is an intuitive notion that most individual stocks or bonds move with the aggregate market. Therefore, if the overall market rose, an individual's portfolio probably also increased in value. To supply investors with a composite report on market performance, some financial publications or investment firms have developed stock-market and bond-market indexes.

In the initial section of this chapter we discuss several ways that investors use market indexes. An awareness of these significant functions should provide an incentive for becoming familiar with these series and indicates why we present a full chapter on this topic. In the second section we consider what characteristics cause various indexes to differ. Investors need to understand these differences and why one index is preferable for a given task because of its characteristics. In the third section we present the most well-known U.S. and global stock-market indexes, separated into groups based on the weighting scheme used. Then, in the fourth section, we consider bond-market indexes—a relatively new topic because the creation and maintenance of total return bond indexes are new. Again, we consider international bond indexes following the domestic indexes. In the fifth section we consider composite stock market–bond market series. In our final section we examine how alternative indexes relate to each other over monthly intervals. This comparison demonstrates the important factors that cause high or low correlation among series. With this background, you should be able to make an intelligent choice of the index that is best for you based on how you want to use it.

Uses of Security-Market Indexes

Security-market indexes have at least five specific uses. A primary application is to use the index values to compute total returns and risk for an aggregate market or some component of a market over a specified time period and use the computed return as a *benchmark* to judge the performance of individual portfolios. A basic assumption when evaluating portfolio performance is that any investor should be able to experience a risk-adjusted rate of return comparable to the market by randomly selecting a large number of stocks or bonds from the total market; hence, a superior portfolio manager should consistently do better than the market. Therefore, *an aggregate stock- or bond-market index can be used as a benchmark to judge the performance of professional money managers.*

An obvious use of indexes is to develop an index portfolio. As we have discussed, it is difficult for most money managers to consistently outperform specified market indexes on a risk-adjusted basis over time.[1] If this is true, an obvious alternative is to invest in a portfolio that will emulate this market portfolio. This notion led to the creation of *index funds* and *exchange-traded funds* (ETFs), whose purpose is to track the performance of the specified market series (index) over time.[2] The original index funds were common-stock funds. The development of comprehensive, well-specified bond-market indexes and bond-portfolio managers' inability to outperform these indexes has led to a similar phenomenon in the fixed-income area (bond-index funds).[3]

Securities analysts, portfolio managers, and academicians doing research use security-market indexes to examine the factors that influence aggregate security price movements (that is, the indexes are used to measure aggregate market movements) and to compare the risk-adjusted performance of alternative asset classes (e.g., stocks versus bonds versus real estate).

Another group interested in an aggregate market index is "technicians," who believe past price changes can be used to predict future price movements. For example, to project future stock price movements, technicians would plot and analyze price and volume changes for a stock-market series like the Dow Jones Industrial Average.

Finally, work in portfolio and capital market theory has implied that the relevant risk for an individual risky asset is its *systematic risk,* which is the relationship between the rates of return for a risky asset and the rates of return for a market portfolio of risky assets.[4] Therefore, in this case an aggregate market index is used as a proxy for the market portfolio of risky assets.

---

[1]We discuss specific evidence for this statement in Chapter 10, Efficient Markets.

[2]For a discussion of indexing, see Burton G. Malkiel, *A Random Walk Down Wall Street*, 7th ed., New York: W. W. Norton & Co., 2000, Chapter 14.

[3]See Fran Hawthorne, "The Battle of the Bond Indexes," *Institutional Investor* 20, no. 4 (April 1986).

[4]This concept and its justification are discussed in Chapters 8 and 9. Subsequently, we will consider the difficulty of finding an index that is an appropriate proxy for the market portfolio of risky assets.

Differentiating Factors in Constructing Market Indexes

Because the indexes are intended to reflect the overall movements of a group of securities, we need to consider three factors that are important when constructing an index intended to represent a total population.

THE SAMPLE

The first factor is the sample used to construct an index. The size, the breadth, and the source of the sample are all important.

A small percentage of the total population will provide valid indications of the behavior of the total population *if* the sample is properly selected. In fact, at some point the costs of taking a larger sample will almost certainly outweigh any benefits of increased size. The sample should be *representative* of the total population; otherwise, its size will be meaningless. A large biased sample is no better than a small biased sample. The sample can be generated by completely random selection or by a nonrandom selection technique designed to incorporate the important characteristics of the desired population. Finally, the *source* of the sample is important if there are any differences between segments of the population, in which case samples from each segment are required.

WEIGHTING SAMPLE MEMBERS

The second factor is the weight given to each member in the sample. Three principal weighting schemes are used for security-market indexes: (1) a price-weighted index, (2) a market-value-weighted index, and (3) an unweighted index, or what would be described as an equal-weighted index. We will discuss each of these in detail shortly.

COMPUTATIONAL PROCEDURE

The final consideration is the computational procedure used. One alternative is to take a simple arithmetic mean of the various members in the index. Another is to compute an index and have all changes, whether in price or value, reported in terms of the basic index. Finally, some prefer using a geometric mean of the components rather than an arithmetic mean.

Stock-Market Indexes

As mentioned previously, we hear a lot about what happens to the Dow Jones Industrial Average (DJIA) each day. You might also hear about other stock indexes, such as the S&P 500 index, the Nasdaq composite, or even the Nikkei Average. If you listen carefully, you will realize that these indexes change by differing amounts. Reasons for some differences are obvious, such as the DJIA versus the Nikkei Average, but others are not. In this section we briefly review how the major series differ in terms of the characteristics discussed in the prior section, which will help you understand why the movements over time for alternative indexes *should* differ.

We have organized the discussion of the indexes by the weighting of the sample of stocks. We begin with the price-weighted index because some of the most popular indexes are in this category. The next group is the value-weighted index, which is the technique currently used for most indexes. Finally, we will examine the unweighted indexes.

EXHIBIT 7.1	Example of Change in DJIA Divisor When a Sample Stock Splits	
Stock	**Before Split**	**After Three-for-One Split by Stock A**
	Prices	Prices
A	30	10
B	20	20
C	10	10
	60 ÷ 3 = 20	40 ÷ X = 20 X = 2 (New Divisor)

PRICE-WEIGHTED INDEX

A *price-weighted index* is an arithmetic mean of current prices, which means that index movements are influenced by the differential prices of the components.

Dow Jones Industrial Average   The best-known price-weighted index is also the oldest and certainly the most popular stock-market index, the Dow Jones Industrial Average (DJIA). The DJIA is a price-weighted average of thirty large, well-known industrial stocks that are generally the leaders in their industry (blue chips). The DJIA is computed by totaling the current prices of the thirty stocks and dividing the sum by a divisor that has been adjusted to take account of stock splits and changes in the sample over time.[5] The divisor is adjusted so the index value will be the same before and after the split. An adjustment of the divisor is demonstrated in Exhibit 7.1. The equation is

$$\text{DJIA}_t = \sum_{i=1}^{30} \frac{p_{it}}{D_{adj}}$$

where:

DJIA_t = the value of the DJIA on day t

p_{it} = the closing price of stock i on day t

D_{adj} = the adjusted divisor on day t

In Exhibit 7.1, we employ three stocks to demonstrate the procedure used to derive a new divisor for the DJIA when a stock splits. When stocks split, the divisor becomes smaller, as shown. The cumulative effect of splits can be derived from the fact that the divisor was originally 30.0, but as of October 2004 it was 0.13561241.

The adjusted divisor ensures that the new value for the index is the same as it would have been without the split. In this case, the presplit index value was 20. Therefore, after the split, given the new sum of prices, the divisor is adjusted downward to maintain this value of 20. The divisor is also changed when there is a change in the sample makeup of the index.

Because the index is price weighted, a high-priced stock carries more weight than a low-priced stock. As shown in Exhibit 7.2, a 10 percent change in a $100 stock ($10) will cause a larger change in the index than a 10 percent change in a $30 stock ($3). In case A,

[5]A complete list of all events that have caused a change in the divisor since the DJIA went to thirty stocks on October 1, 1928, is contained in Phyllis S. Pierce, ed., *The Business One Irwin Investor's Handbook*, Burr Ridge, IL: Dow Jones Books, annual. In May 1996, the DJIA celebrated its 100th birthday, which was acknowledged with two special sections entitled "A Century of Investing" and "100 Years of the DJIA," in *The Wall Street Journal*, May 28, 1996.

EXHIBIT 7.2	Demonstration of the Impact of Differently Priced Shares on a Price-Weighted Index		

| | | PERIOD T + 1 | |
Stock	Period T	Case A	Case B
A	100	110	100
B	50	50	50
C	30	30	33
Sum	180	190	183
Divisor	3	3	3
Average	60	63.3	61
Percentage change		5.5	1.7

when the $100 stock increases by 10 percent, the average rises by 5.5 percent; in case B, when the $30 stock increases by 10 percent, the average rises by only 1.7 percent.

The DJIA has been criticized on several counts. First, the sample used for the index is limited to thirty nonrandomly selected blue-chip stocks that cannot be representative of the thousands of U.S. stocks. Further, the stocks included are large, mature, blue-chip firms rather than typical companies. Several studies have shown that the DJIA has not been as volatile as other market indexes and its long-run returns are not comparable to other NYSE stock indexes.

In addition, because the DJIA is price weighted, when companies have a stock split, their prices decline and therefore their weight in the DJIA is reduced—even though they may be large and important. Therefore, the weighting scheme causes a downward bias in the DJIA; because high-growth stocks will have higher prices and because such stocks tend to split, they will consistently lose weight within the index.[6] Dow Jones also publishes a price-weighted index of twenty stocks in the transportation industry and fifteen utility stocks. Detailed reports of the averages are contained daily in *The Wall Street Journal* and weekly in *Barron's,* including hourly figures.

Nikkei–Dow Jones Average Also referred to as the Nikkei Stock Average Index, the Nikkei–Dow Jones Average is an arithmetic mean of prices for 225 stocks on the First Section of the Tokyo Stock Exchange (TSE). This best-known series in Japan shows stock price trends since the reopening of the TSE. Notably, it was formulated by Dow Jones and Company, and, similar to the DJIA, it is a price-weighted index. It is also criticized because the 225 stocks only comprise about 15 percent of all stocks on the First Section. It is reported daily in *The Wall Street Journal* and the *Financial Times* and weekly in *Barron's.*

VALUE-WEIGHTED INDEX

A *value-weighted index* is generated by deriving the initial total market value of all stocks used in the index (Market Value = Number of Shares Outstanding (or freely floating shares) × Current Market Price). Prior to 2004, the tradition was to consider all outstand-

---

[6]For several articles that consider the origin and performance of the DJIA during its 100 years, see "100 Years of the DJIA," *The Wall Street Journal,* May 28, 1996, pp. R29–R56. For discussion of differing results, see Greg Ip, "What's Behind the Trailing Performance of the Dow Industrials versus the S&P 500?" *The Wall Street Journal,* August 20, 1998, pp. C1, C17.

ing shares. In mid-2004, Standard & Poor's began only considering "freely floating shares" that excludes shares held by insiders. This initial figure is typically established as the base and assigned an index value (the most popular beginning index value is 100, but it can vary—say, 10, 50). Subsequently, a new market value is computed for all securities in the index, and the current market value is compared to the initial "base" market value to determine the percentage of change, which in turn is applied to the beginning index value.

$$\text{Index}_t = \frac{\sum P_t Q_t}{\sum P_b Q_b} \times \textbf{Beginning Index Value}$$

where:

Index_t = index value on day t
P_t = ending prices for stocks on day t
Q_t = number of outstanding or freely floating shares on day t
P_b = ending price for stocks on base day
Q_b = number of outstanding or freely floating shares on base day

A simple example for a three-stock index in Exhibit 7.3 indicates that there is an *automatic adjustment* for stock splits and other capital changes with a value-weighted index because the decrease in the stock price is offset by an increase in the number of shares outstanding.

In a value-weighted index, the importance of individual stocks in the sample depends on the market value of the stocks. Therefore, a specified percentage change in the value of a

EXHIBIT 7.3	Example of a Computation of a Value-Weighted Index		
Stock	**Share Price**	**Number of Shares**	**Market Value**
DECEMBER 31, 2004			
A	$10.00	1,000,000	$ 10,000,000
B	15.00	6,000,000	90,000,000
C	20.00	5,000,000	100,000,000
Total			$200,000,000
			Base Value Equal to an Index of 100
DECEMBER 31, 2005			
A	$12.00	1,000,000	$ 12,000,000
B	10.00	12,000,000[a]	120,000,000
C	20.00	5,500,000[b]	110,000,000
Total			$242,000,000

$$\text{New Index Value} = \frac{\text{Current Market Value}}{\text{Base Value}} \times \text{Beginning Index Value}$$

$$= \frac{\$242,000,000}{\$200,000,000} \times 100$$

$$= 1.21 \times 100$$

$$= 121$$

[a]Stock split two-for-one during the year.
[b]Company paid a 10 percent stock dividend during the year.

EXHIBIT 7.4	Demonstration of the Impact of Different Values on a Market-Value-Weighted Stock Index

	DECEMBER 31, 2004			DECEMBER 31, 2005				
					CASE A		CASE B	
Stock	Number of Shares	Price	Value	Price	Value	Price	Value	
A	1,000,000	$10.00	$ 10,000,000	$12.00	$ 12,000,000	$10.00	$ 10,000,000	
B	6,000,000	15.00	90,000,000	15.00	90,000,000	15.00	90,000,000	
C	5,000,000	20.00	100,000,000	20.00	100,000,000	24.00	120,000,000	
			$200,000,000		$202,000,000		$220,000,000	
Index Value			100.00		101.00		110.00	

large company has a greater impact than a comparable percentage change for a small company. As shown in Exhibit 7.4, if we assume that the only change is a 20 percent increase in the value of stock A, which has a beginning value of $10 million, the ending index value would be $202 million, or an index of 101. In contrast, if only stock C increases by 20 percent from $100 million, the ending value will be $220 million or an index value of 110. The point is, price changes for the large market value stocks in a value-weighted index will dominate changes in the index value over time.

UNWEIGHTED INDEX

In an *unweighted index,* all stocks carry equal weight regardless of their price or market value. A $20 stock is as important as a $40 stock, and the total market value of the company is unimportant. Such an index can be used by individuals who randomly select stock for their portfolio and invest the same dollar amount in each stock. One way to visualize an unweighted index is to assume that equal dollar amounts are invested in each stock in the portfolio (for example, an equal $1,000 investment in each stock would work out to 50 shares of a $20 stock, 100 shares of a $10 stock, and 10 shares of a $100 stock). In fact, the actual movements in the index are typically based on *the arithmetic mean of the percent changes in price or value for the stocks in the index.* The use of percentage price changes means that the price level or the market value of the stock does not make a difference—each percentage change has equal weight. This arithmetic mean of percent changes procedure is used in academic studies when the authors specify equal weighting.

In contrast to computing an arithmetic mean of percentage changes, both Value Line and the *Financial Times* Ordinary Share Index compute a *geometric* mean of the holding period returns *and* derive the holding period yield from this calculation. Exhibit 7.5, which contains an example of an arithmetic and a geometric mean, demonstrates the downward bias of the geometric calculation. Specifically, the geometric mean of holding period yields (HPY) shows an average change of only 5.3 percent versus the actual change in wealth of 6 percent.

STYLE INDEXES

Financial service firms such as Dow Jones, Moody's, Standard & Poor's, Russell, and Wilshire Associates are generally very fast in responding to changes in investment practices. One example is the growth in popularity of small-cap stocks following academic research in the 1980s that suggested that over long-term periods, small-cap stocks outperformed

EXHIBIT 7.5	Example of an Arithmetic and Geometric Mean of Percentage Changes

	SHARE PRICE			
Stock	T	T + 1	HPR	HPY
X	10	12	1.20	0.20
Y	22	20	.91	−0.09
Z	44	47	1.07	0.07

$$\prod = 1.20 \times .91 \times 1.07 \qquad \Sigma = 0.18$$

$$= 1.168 \qquad 0.18/3 = 0.06$$

$$1.168^{1/3} = 1.0531 \qquad = 6\%$$

$$\text{Index Value (T)} \times 1.0531 = \text{Index Value (T + 1)}$$

$$\text{Index Value (T)} \times 1.06 = \text{Index Value (T + 1)}$$

large-cap stocks on a risk-adjusted basis. In response to this, Ibbotson Associates created the first small-cap stock index, and this was followed by small-cap indexes by Frank Russell Associates (the Russell 2000 index), the Standard & Poor's 600, the Wilshire 1750, and the Dow Jones Small-Cap Index. This led to sets of size indexes, including large-cap, midcap, small-cap, and micro-cap. These new size indexes were used to evaluate the performance of money managers who concentrated in those size sectors.

The next innovation was for money managers to concentrate in *types* of stocks—that is, *growth* stocks or *value* stocks. We included a designation of these stocks in Chapter 2 in terms of what they are and how they are identified. As this innovation evolved, the financial services firms again responded by creating indexes of growth stocks and value stocks based on relative P/E, price–book value, price–cash flow ratios, and other metrics such as return on equity (ROE) and revenue growth rates.

Eventually, these two styles (size and type) were combined into six categories:

Small-cap growth	Small-cap value
Midcap growth	Midcap value
Large-cap growth	Large-cap value

Currently, most money managers identify their investment style as one of these, and consultants generally use these categories to identify money managers.

The most recent addition to style indexes are those created to track ethical funds referred to as *socially responsible investment* (sri) funds. These sri indexes are further broken down by country and include a global ethical stock index.

The best source for style stock indexes (both size and type of stock) is *Barron's*.

Exhibit 7.6 shows the "Stock-Market Data Bank" from *The Wall Street Journal* of October 5, 2004, which contains values for many of the U.S. stock indexes we have discussed. Exhibit 7.7 shows a table for numerous international stock indexes contained in *The Wall Street Journal*.

GLOBAL EQUITY INDEXES

As shown in Exhibit 7.7 and Exhibit 7.B in the appendix to this chapter, there are stock-market indexes available for most individual foreign markets. While these local indexes are

EXHIBIT 7.6	Stock-Market Data Bank

Major Stock Indexes

	DAILY					52-WEEK			YTD
Dow Jones Averages	HIGH	LOW	CLOSE	NET CHG	% CHG	HIGH	LOW	% CHG	% CHG
30 Industrials	10270.37	10191.40	10216.54	+23.89	+0.23	10737.70	9582.46	+ 6.48	− 2.27
20 Transportations	3329.46	3299.25	3318.62	+19.82	+0.60	3318.62	2750.80	+18.66	+10.36
15 Utilities	299.60	298.33	299.18	+ 0.86	+0.29	299.18	243.47	+17.86	+12.09
65 Composite	3119.17	3096.93	3107.93	+10.80	+0.35	3107.93	2781.59	+11.73	+ 3.57
Dow Jones Indexes									
Wilshire 5000	11149.23	11058.70	11099.85	+41.15	+0.37	11314.42	9983.50	+10.55	+ 2.78
US Total Market	270.34	268.15	269.12	+ 0.97	+0.36	274.54	242.66	+10.26	+ 2.45
US Large-Cap	245.23	243.43	244.20	+ 0.79	+0.32	250.84	223.78	+ 8.45	+ 1.16
US Mid-Cap	335.33	332.10	333.47	+ 1.38	+0.42	334.64	287.16	+15.90	+ 6.57
US Small-Cap	378.20	373.84	376.12	+ 2.26	+0.60	386.09	325.17	+14.39	+ 5.16
US Growth	1020.87	1010.93	1014.34	+ 3.42	+0.34	1069.37	944.85	+ 5.60	− 0.71
US Value	1427.74	1418.80	1423.73	+ 5.09	+0.36	1423.73	1230.42	+14.43	+ 5.50
Global Titans 50	185.03	184.06	184.44	+ 0.29	+0.16	191.85	169.35	+ 7.36	− 0.19
Asian Titans 50	108.72	106.07	108.21	+ 1.88	+1.77	118.74	96.87	+ 5.74	+ 2.48
DJ STOXX 50	2751.45	2723.84	2744.82	+23.77	+0.87	2804.06	2457.19	+10.58	+ 3.17
Nasdaq Stock Market									
Nasdaq Comp	1965.76	1950.17	1952.40	+10.20	+0.53	2153.83	1752.49	+ 3.11	− 2.54
Nasdaq 100	1472.21	1458.08	1459.01	+ 6.07	+0.42	1553.66	1304.43	+ 5.60	− 0.61
Biotech	735.82	729.37	733.18	+ 6.57	+0.90	845.11	622.19	− 2.41	+ 1.25
Computer	868.16	857.60	858.88	+ 4.05	+0.47	1012.13	768.60	− 3.97	− 8.13
Standard & Poor's Indexes									
500 Index	1140.19	1131.50	1135.17	+ 3.67	+0.32	1157.76	1028.91	+ 9.75	+ 2.09
MidCap 400	607.67	601.79	603.62	+ 1.83	+0.30	616.70	532.17	+13.27	+ 4.79
SmallCap 600	301.54	297.53	299.38	+ 1.85	+0.62	299.38	246.43	+19.94	+10.71
SuperComp 1500	255.03	252.98	253.83	+ 0.85	+0.34	258.20	228.69	+10.41	+ 2.64
New York Stock Exchange and Others									
NYSE Comp	6696.72	6662.73	6677.75	+14.57	+0.22	6780.03	5851.14	+13.99	+ 3.69
NYSE Financial	6874.99	6843.16	6855.65	+12.36	+0.18	7109.18	6102.46	+12.34	+ 2.68
Russell 2000	592.02	585.03	589.09	+ 4.06	+0.69	606.39	506.43	+14.01	+ 5.78
Value Line	369.73	365.71	368.00	+ 2.29	+0.63	386.84	330.12	+10.13	+ 1.47
Amex Comp	1279.83	1274.60	1276.34	− 2.93	−0.23	1279.27	1012.48	+26.06	+ 8.76

Source: Reuters

Source: From *The Wall Street Journal,* October 5, 2004, p. C2. Copyright © 2004 Dow Jones. Reprinted by permission of Copyright Clearance Center.

closely followed within each country, a problem arises in comparing the results implied by these indexes to one another because of a lack of consistency among them in sample selection, weighting, or computational procedure. To solve these comparability problems, several groups have computed a set of consistent country stock indexes. As a result, these indexes can be directly compared and combined to create various regional indexes (for example, Pacific Basin). We will describe the three major sets of global equity indexes.

FT/S&P-Actuaries World Indexes The FT/S&P-Actuaries World Indexes are jointly compiled by The Financial Times Limited, Goldman Sachs & Company, and Standard & Poor's (the "compilers") in conjunction with the Institute of Actuaries and the Faculty of Actuaries. Approximately 2,461 equity securities in thirty countries are measured, covering at least 70 percent of the total value of all listed companies in each country. All securities included must allow direct holdings of shares by foreign nationals.

EXHIBIT 7.7	International Stock-Market Indexes

International Stock Market Indexes

COUNTRY	INDEX	10/4/04 CLOSE	NET CHG	% CHG	YTD NET CHG	YTD % CHG	P/E
World	DJ World Index	194.20	+0.79	+0.41	+7.25	+3.88	17
Argentina	Merval	1167.09	+6.97	+0.60	+95.14	+8.88	...
Australia	S&P/ASX 200	3693.60	+34.00	+0.93	+393.80	+11.93	15
Belgium	Bel-20	2760.03	+34.91	+1.28	+515.85	+22.99	11
Brazil	Sao Paulo Bovespa	24150.39	+373.37	+1.57	+1914.00	+8.61	11
Canada	S&P/TSX Composite	8812.91	+65.82	+0.75	+592.02	+7.20	17
Chile	Santiago IPSA	1743.01	+11.85	+0.68	+258.21	+17.39	18
China	Dow Jones CBN China 600	11270.59	Closed	...	-946.02	-7.74	24
China	Dow Jones China 88	123.22	Closed	...	-12.51	-9.22	18
Europe	DJ STOXX 600	244.18	+2.33	+0.96	+14.87	+6.48	21
Europe	DJ STOXX 50	2744.82	+23.77	+0.87	+84.45	+3.17	20
Euro Zone	DJ Euro STOXX	254.66	+2.53	+1.00	+11.45	+4.71	21
Euro Zone	DJ Euro STOXX 50	2823.46	+27.38	+0.98	+62.80	+2.27	17
France	Paris CAC 40	3767.06	+36.90	+0.99	+209.16	+5.88	15
Germany	Frankfurt Xetra DAX	4033.28	+38.32	+0.96	+68.12	+1.72	15
Hong Kong	Hang Seng	13359.25	+239.22	+1.82	+783.31	+6.23	15
India	Bombay Sensex	5766.30	+90.76	+1.60	-72.66	-1.24	16
Israel	Tel Aviv 25	542.29	+2.67	+0.49	+38.14	+7.57	...
Italy	Milan MIBtel	21501.00	+114.00	+0.53	+1579.00	+7.93	14
Japan	Tokyo Nikkei 225	11279.63	+294.46	+2.68	+602.99	+5.65	...
Japan	Tokyo Nikkei 300	219.54	+4.46	+2.07	+16.00	+7.86	...
Japan	Tokyo Topix Index	1139.45	+22.16	+1.98	+95.76	+9.18	115
Mexico	I.P.C. All-Share	11181.63	+103.37	+0.93	+2386.35	+27.13	15
Netherlands	Amsterdam AEX	335.19	+4.32	+1.31	-2.46	-0.73	11
Russia	DJ Russia Titans 10	2552.70	+76.89	+3.11	+377.57	+17.36	37
Singapore	Straits Times	2013.89	+32.75	+1.65	+249.37	+14.13	12
South Africa	Johannesburg All Share	11795.02	-76.80	-0.65	+1407.80	+13.55	14
South Korea	KOSPI	880.84	+34.83	+4.12	+70.13	+8.65	15
Spain	IBEX 35	8304.90	+84.30	+1.03	+567.70	+7.34	16
Sweden	SX All Share	220.13	+2.70	+1.24	+25.96	+13.37	21
Switzerland	Zurich Swiss Market	5600.90	+72.00	+1.30	+113.10	+2.06	15
Taiwan	Weighted	6077.96	+132.61	+2.23	+187.27	+3.18	12
Turkey	Istanbul National 100	21987.74	+265.24	+1.22	+3362.72	+18.05	20
U.K.	London FTSE 100-share	4681.80	+22.20	+0.48	+204.90	+4.58	13
U.K.	London FTSE 250-share	6401.00	+68.00	+1.07	+598.70	+10.32	16

Source: From *The Wall Street Journal*, October 4, 2004, p. C17. Copyright © 2004 Dow Jones. Reprinted by permission of Copyright Clearance Center.

The indexes are market value weighted and have a base date of December 31, 1986 = 100. The index results are reported in U.S. dollars, U.K. pound sterling, Japanese yen, euros, and the local currency of the country. In addition to the individual countries and the world index, there are several geographic subgroups, as shown in Exhibit 7.8.

Morgan Stanley Capital International (MSCI) Indexes The Morgan Stanley Capital International Indexes consist of three international, nineteen national, and thirty-eight international industry indexes. The indexes consider some 1,673 companies listed on stock exchanges in nineteen countries with a combined market capitalization that represents approximately 60 percent of the aggregate market value of the stock exchanges of these countries. All the indexes are market value weighted. Exhibit 7.9 contains the countries included, the number of stocks, and market values for stocks in the various countries and groups.

In addition to reporting the indexes in U.S. dollars and the country's local currency, the following valuation information is available: (1) price-to-book value (P/BV) ratio, (2) price-to-cash earnings (earnings plus depreciation) (P/CE) ratio, (3) price-to-earnings (P/E) ratio,

EXHIBIT 7.8	Financial Times Global Equity Index Series

FTSE GLOBAL EQUITY INDEX SERIES

Sep 24

Countries & regions	No of stocks	US$ index	Day %	Mth %	YTD %	Total retn	YTD %	Gross Div Yield	FTSE All-World Industry Sectors	No of stocks	US$ index	Day %	Mth %	YTD %	Total retn	YTD %	Gross Div Yield
FTSE Global All-Cap	7352	270.57	-0.1	2.5	1.5	280.97	3.1	2.0	**Resources**	145	256.01	0.6	8.9	14.3	287.45	16.9	2.4
FTSE Global Large Cap	1038	258.52	-0.1	1.9	0.1	269.05	1.8	2.2	Mining	46	418.41	-0.2	4.9	0.0	469.45	1.9	2.0
FTSE Global Mid Cap	1844	300.11	0.1	3.8	4.8	310.33	6.3	1.7	Oil & Gas	99	241.63	0.7	9.6	16.9	271.41	19.6	2.5
FTSE Global Small Cap	4470	308.31	0.0	3.6	4.8	317.86	6.1	1.7	**Basic Industries**	330	265.22	0.0	3.1	3.1	294.56	5.2	2.3
FTSE All-World (Large/Mid Cap)	2882	162.67	-0.1	2.3	1.1	176.55	2.7	2.1	Chemicals	113	240.31	0.2	3.0	0.1	266.84	1.9	2.3
FTSE World (Large/Mid Cap)	2456	290.02	-0.1	2.2	1.0	422.29	2.7	2.1	Construction & Building Materials	117	272.38	-0.1	3.4	9.4	302.19	11.5	2.1
FTSE Global All-Cap ex UK	6847	270.88	-0.1	2.3	1.2	280.49	2.7	1.9	Forestry & Paper	31	265.80	0.1	-0.8	-2.5	300.32	-0.1	2.9
FTSE Global All-Cap ex USA	5130	286.09	-0.3	3.3	2.8	300.22	4.9	2.4	Steel & Other Metals	69	325.64	-0.2	5.7	4.8	356.65	7.0	2.1
FTSE Global All-Cap ex Japan	6009	269.86	0.1	2.9	1.4	280.74	3.1	2.1	**General Industrials**	285	166.76	-0.3	1.6	3.4	180.03	4.8	1.8
FTSE Global All-Cap ex Eurobloc	6599	268.77	-0.1	2.2	1.8	278.37	3.2	1.9	Aerospace & Defence	24	195.54	0.5	2.4	10.4	212.20	12.0	1.9
FTSE All-World Developed	1998	263.93	-0.1	2.1	0.8	274.15	2.4	2.0	Diversified Industrials	62	160.45	-0.3	1.7	7.4	175.27	9.2	2.1
FTSE Developed All-Cap	5832	268.56	-0.1	2.2	1.3	278.70	2.9	2.0	Electronic & Electrical Equipment	105	150.25	-1.2	0.6	-4.3	159.18	-3.3	1.3
FTSE Developed Large Cap	726	255.96	-0.1	1.7	-0.2	266.22	1.5	2.1	Engineering & Machinery	94	252.94	0.2	2.3	1.3	274.84	2.7	1.7
									Cyclical Consumer Goods	171	189.09	-0.3	1.2	1.4	204.90	2.8	1.8
FTSE Developed Europe Large Cap	190	266.99	0.0	4.2	0.1	282.85	2.8	2.8	Automobiles & Parts	79	200.01	-0.4	0.3	0.8	218.15	2.4	1.9
FTSE Developed Europe Mid Cap	324	295.64	0.1	4.3	5.4	311.96	7.9	2.6	Household Goods & Textiles	92	167.88	-0.2	3.0	2.6	179.44	3.7	1.6
FTSE Developed Europe Small Cap	1038	328.74	0.0	4.4	8.2	346.06	10.5	2.4	**Non-Cyclical Consumer Goods**	344	187.99	-0.1	-0.2	-1.5	203.00	0.0	2.0
FTSE All-World Developed Europe	514	169.25	0.1	4.2	1.1	189.96	3.7	2.8	Beverages	50	198.34	-0.1	-2.9	-5.2	215.50	-3.5	2.4
									Food Producers & Processors	91	236.04	-0.4	-1.6	-2.3	260.02	-0.5	2.5
FTSE North America Large Cap	236	247.09	0.1	0.9	-0.9	255.02	0.4	1.9	Health	71	226.42	1.0	4.5	3.9	234.52	4.4	0.5
FTSE North America Mid Cap	471	291.59	0.4	3.9	4.6	298.90	5.6	1.4	Personal Care & Household Products	27	238.53	-0.3	-2.7	4.9	256.96	6.4	1.9
FTSE North America Small Cap	1713	296.99	0.1	3.7	2.8	303.73	3.7	1.3	Pharmaceuticals	90	155.00	-0.2	0.4	-3.0	166.17	-1.6	1.9
FTSE All-World North America	707	157.34	0.2	1.6	0.3	168.18	1.6	1.8	Tobacco	15	293.79	-1.1	-3.6	-5.8	359.40	-2.0	5.3
FTSE All-World Dev ex North Am	1291	165.67	-0.4	2.7	1.4	183.29	3.7	2.4	**Cyclical Services**	467	178.46	0.3	2.4	1.1	187.61	2.0	1.2
									General Retailers	105	240.55	0.3	2.6	5.0	251.41	6.0	1.1
FTSE Japan Large Cap	177	263.22	-1.5	-2.4	0.0	267.59	0.6	1.0	Leisure & Hotels	60	168.59	0.7	4.5	11.8	177.00	13.0	1.5
FTSE Japan Mid Cap	304	312.08	-1.2	-1.8	4.0	317.64	4.7	0.9	Media & Entertainment	122	133.84	0.3	1.8	-7.0	140.66	-6.4	1.0
FTSE Japan Small Cap	862	342.27	-1.1	-1.7	14.1	350.11	15.0	1.1	Support Services	64	155.50	0.2	1.5	-0.7	164.59	0.5	1.4
FTSE Japan (Large/Mid Cap)	481	104.17	-1.5	-2.3	0.8	119.82	1.4	1.0	Transport	116	236.21	0.3	2.4	5.6	253.74	7.1	1.7
FTSE Asia Pacific Large Cap ex Japan	301	292.81	-0.8	4.5	3.3	310.46	6.0	3.0	**Non-Cyclical Services**	145	113.42	-0.3	2.3	0.4	123.30	2.3	2.4
FTSE Asia Pacific Mid Cap ex Japan	567	312.86	-0.5	5.9	2.6	329.37	5.2	2.7	Food & Drug Retailers	38	154.27	-0.1	1.6	-1.6	164.74	-0.3	1.6
FTSE Asia Pacific Small Cap ex Japan	734	293.42	-0.4	6.5	-0.8	308.59	1.6	2.8	Telecommunication Services	107	107.26	-0.3	2.5	0.9	117.05	2.9	2.5
FTSE All-World Asia Pacific ex Japan	868	222.66	-0.8	4.8	3.2	252.05	5.9	3.0	**Utilities**	142	181.62	0.0	2.8	8.2	212.36	11.4	3.6
									Electricity	92	200.34	0.0	2.4	7.1	235.59	10.3	3.7
FTSE All Emerging All-Cap	1520	313.97	-0.2	6.9	4.9	330.23	7.3	2.7	Utilities Other	50	187.99	-0.1	3.7	10.3	219.60	13.6	3.5
FTSE All Emerging Large Cap	312	308.92	-0.1	6.6	6.1	324.80	8.6	2.8	**Financials**	612	197.19	0.0	2.1	1.6	219.19	3.9	2.8
FTSE All Emerging Mid Cap	572	318.95	-0.3	7.4	2.8	334.04	5.2	2.6	Banks	258	223.52	0.3	2.3	1.1	254.23	3.9	3.3
FTSE All Emerging Small Cap	636	297.77	-0.1	8.1	-0.4	312.24	1.9	2.5	Insurance	62	155.89	-0.5	1.3	0.0	166.04	1.3	1.6
FTSE All-World All Emerging Europe	56	286.57	-0.1	10.0	16.0	312.50	18.2	2.6	Life Assurance	33	153.80	0.0	4.5	7.7	171.56	10.0	2.6
FTSE Latin Americas All-Cap	177	379.87	0.2	6.5	13.3	402.75	15.9	3.2	Investment Companies	21	189.44	0.0	6.4	6.1	209.67	8.8	2.8
FTSE Middle East Africa All-Cap	174	329.17	0.3	8.9	11.9	348.81	14.5	2.8	Real Estate	96	235.93	-0.6	1.7	13.2	272.69	16.2	3.5
									Speciality & Other Finance	142	174.39	-0.2	1.2	-0.6	185.60	0.6	1.6
FTSE UK All-Cap	505	267.96	0.4	4.2	3.7	285.61	6.6	3.2	**Information Technology**	241	76.30	-1.0	1.6	-10.8	78.10	-10.4	0.7
FTSE USA All-Cap	2222	257.98	0.2	1.7	0.3	265.58	1.5	1.7	Information Technology Hardware	159	66.31	-1.4	1.4	-14.5	68.01	-14.0	0.7
FTSE Europe All-Cap	1636	279.49	0.0	4.3	2.0	295.71	4.6	2.7	Software & Computer Services	82	106.98	-0.3	1.9	-4.1	109.07	-3.7	0.6
FTSE Eurobloc All-Cap	753	283.19	-0.1	4.4	-0.3	299.30	2.3	2.7									

www.ftse.com: On September 22 2003, FTSE launched the FTSE Global Equity Index Series. The family contains the new FTSE Global Small Cap Indices and broader FTSE Global All Cap Indices (large/mid/small cap) as well as the enhanced FTSE All-World Index Series (large/mid cap). This table has been updated to reflect the additional indices. The FTSE Industry Sectors table relates to the FTSE All-World Index Series Sectors (large/mid cap). To learn more about the enhancement and new indices, please visit www.ftse.com/geis. © FTSE International Limited 2004. All rights reserved. 'FTSE', 'FT-SE' and 'Footsie' are trade marks of the London Stock Exchange and The Financial Times and are used by FTSE International under license. **For constituent changes please see FTSE website.** Markets closed 24/9/04: Egypt, Israel and South Africa.

Source: "FTSE Global Equity Index Series" from *Financial Times,* September 27, 2004, p. 24. Reprinted by permission of The Financial Times Limited.

and (4) dividend yield (YLD). These ratios help in analyzing different valuation levels among countries and over time for specific countries.

Notably, the Morgan Stanley group index for Europe, Australia, and the Far East (EAFE) is the basis for futures and options contracts on the Chicago Mercantile Exchange and the Chicago Board Options Exchange. Several of the MSCI country indexes, the EAFE index, and a world index are reported daily in *The Wall Street Journal,* as shown in Exhibit 7.10.

Dow Jones World Stock Index   In January 1993, Dow Jones introduced its World Stock Index. Composed of more than 2,200 companies worldwide and organized into 120 industry groups, the index includes twenty-eight countries representing more than 80 percent of

| EXHIBIT 7.9 | Market Coverage of Morgan Stanley Capital International Indexes as of November 30, 2004 |

	GDP WEIGHTS[a]			WEIGHT AS PERCENT OF INDEX	
	Percent EAFE	Companies in Index	Market Cap. U.S. $ Billion	Free EAFE[b]	World
Austria	1.8	13	69.6	0.3	0.1
Belgium	2.3	20	239.5	1.3	0.5
Denmark	3.4	20	137.8	0.8	0.3
Finland	2.0	19	198.2	1.8	0.6
France	10.7	57	1,412.7	9.4	3.9
Germany	14.8	47	1,056.1	6.8	2.8
Greece	1.1	20	109.9	0.5	0.2
Ireland	1.0	15	93.9	0.8	0.3
Italy	9.6	41	606.7	4.0	1.6
The Netherlands	3.2	26	508.9	4.8	1.9
Norway	1.6	14	133.0	0.6	0.2
Portugal	0.9	10	67.2	0.4	0.1
Spain	5.3	31	774.7	3.8	1.5
Sweden	1.9	44	353.6	2.5	1.0
Switzerland	1.8	35	707.0	6.9	2.8
United Kingdom	10.8	121	2,560.0	25.2	10.3
Europe	69.1	563	9,118.0	69.5	28.5
Australia	3.5	72	675.0	5.4	2.2
Hong Kong	1.0	37	402.5	1.7	0.7
Japan	25.4	344	3,492.2	22.3	9.1
New Zealand	0.5	16	25.8	0.2	0.1
Singapore	0.6	35	169.0	0.6	0.3
Pacific	30.9	504	4,764.4	30.5	12.5
Pacific ex Japan	5.6	160	1,272.2	6.2	3.4
EAFE	100.0	1067	13,002.4	100.0	40.9
Canada	—	90	1,083.7	—	2.9
United States	—	51.6	14,816.4	—	51.3
The World Index	—	1,673	29,782.5	—	100.0
EMU	51.5	299	5,217.8	—	13.6
Europe ex UK	58.2	412	6,549.2	—	18.1
Far East	27.0	416	4,062.7	24.8	10.2
North America	—	606	15,900.1	—	54.1
Kokusai Index (World ex Japan)	—	1,329	29,453.7	—	90.9

[a]GDP weight figures represent the initial weights applicable for the first month. They are used exclusively in the MSCI "GDP weighted" indexes.

[b]Free indicates that only stocks that can be acquired by foreign investors are included in the index. If the number of companies is the same and the value is different, it indicates that the stocks available to foreigners are priced differently from domestic shares.

Source: Morgan Stanley Capital International (New York: Morgan Stanley & Co., 2004).

EXHIBIT 7.10   Listing of Morgan Stanley Capital International Stock Index Values

MSCI Indexes

	SEP 23	SEP 22	% CHG FROM 12/03
U.S.	1039.0	1044.1	−0.6
Britain	1375.8	1384.1	+2.0
Canada	1063.0	1064.2	+4.2
Japan	671.5	671.5	+5.4
France	1204.1	1216.4	+3.3
Germany	480.2	484.6	−2.4
Hong Kong	7065.8	7109.9	+11.4
Switzerland	722.3	730.4	+1.1
Australia	718.5	720.4	+9.6
World Index	1042.2	1045.3	+0.6
MSCI EAFE	1311.8	1313.0	+1.8

As calculated by Morgan Stanley Capital International Perspective, Geneva. Each index, calculated in local currencies, is based on the close of 1969 equaling 100.

Source: From *The Wall Street Journal,* September 27, 2004, p. C13. Copyright © 2004 Dow Jones. Reprinted by permission of Copyright Clearance Center.

EXHIBIT 7.11   Dow Jones Country Indexes

Dow Jones Country Indexes   Oct. 18, 2004 5:15 p.m. ET

In U.S. dollar terms

COUNTRY	INDEX	CHG	% CHG	YTD % CHG	COUNTRY	INDEX	CHG	% CHG	YTD % CHG
Australia	238.24	−2.32	−0.96	+9.24	Mexico	212.75	−0.35	−0.16	+21.18
Austria	221.95	+1.53	+0.69	+34.36	Netherlands	244.12	−0.11	−0.05	−2.29
Belgium	264.55	+1.89	+0.72	+21.76	New Zealand	208.79	−1.05	−0.50	+15.49
Brazil	413.93	+0.65	+0.16	+10.95	Norway	198.20	+2.23	+1.14	+27.23
Canada	264.39	−0.23	−0.09	+10.76	Philippines	82.18	+0.32	+0.39	+26.99
Chile	238.52	+2.41	+1.02	+10.28	Portugal	176.86	+0.09	+0.05	+8.93
Denmark	277.09	−0.75	−0.27	+15.91	Singapore	146.69	−0.90	−0.61	+10.13
Finland	748.47	−3.05	−0.41	−5.01	South Africa	172.56	+1.21	+0.71	+20.05
France	220.81	+0.03	+0.01	+3.21	South Korea	114.20	+1.04	+0.92	+7.29
Germany	175.93	+0.14	+0.08	−2.75	Spain	234.35	+0.88	+0.38	+5.63
Greece	153.76	−0.14	−0.09	+10.90	Sweden	303.97	+0.89	+0.29	+16.31
Hong Kong	229.22	−0.85	−0.37	+5.73	Switzerland	342.98	+1.05	+0.31	−0.56
Indonesia	63.73	−0.31	−0.48	+15.89	Taiwan	109.52	−1.00	−0.90	−3.35
Ireland	387.37	+1.61	+0.42	+13.46	Thailand	66.30	−0.08	−0.12	−17.09
Italy	182.96	+0.14	+0.08	+7.02	U.K.	185.43	−0.43	−0.23	+4.60
Japan	81.05	−0.42	−0.52	+4.33	U.S.	263.94	+1.37	+0.52	+0.48
Malaysia	112.42	−0.12	−0.11	+3.50	Venezuela	46.39	−0.70	−1.49	−14.81

Source: From *The Wall Street Journal,* October 19, 2004, p. C17. Copyright © 2004 Dow Jones. Reprinted by permission of Copyright Clearance Center.

the combined capitalization of these countries.[7] In addition to the thirty-four individual countries shown in Exhibit 7.11, the countries are grouped into three regions: Asia/Pacific, Europe/Africa, and the Americas. Finally, each country's index is calculated in its own currency as well as in U.S. dollars, British pounds, euros, and Japanese yen. The index for the individual countries is reported daily in *The Wall Street Journal* (domestic), in *The Wall Street Journal Europe,* and in *The Asian Wall Street Journal.* It is published weekly in *Barron's.*

[7]"Journal Launches Index Tracking World Stocks," *The Wall Street Journal,* January 5, 1993, p. C1.

EXHIBIT 7.12	Correlations of Percentage Price Changes of Alternative World Stock Indexes 12/31/91–12/31/03

	U.S. Dollars
FT–MS:	.997
FT–DJ:	.996
MS–DJ:	.994

Comparison of World Stock Indexes   As shown in Exhibit 7.12, the correlations between the three series since December 31, 1991, when the DJ series became available, indicate that the results with the various world stock indexes are quite comparable.

A summary of the characteristics of the major price-weighted, market-value-weighted, and equal-weighted stock price indexes for the United States and major foreign countries is contained in Exhibit 7.A in the chapter appendix. As shown, the major differences are the number of stocks in the index, but more important, the *source* of the sample (stocks from the NYSE, Nasdaq, all U.S. stocks, or from a foreign country such as the United Kingdom or Japan).

Bond-Market Indexes[8]

Investors know little about the several bond-market indexes because these indexes are relatively new and not widely published. Knowledge regarding these indexes is becoming more important because of the growth of fixed-income mutual funds and the consequent need to have a reliable set of benchmarks to use in evaluating their performance. Also, because the performance of many fixed-income money managers has been unable to match that of the aggregate bond market, interest has been growing in bond-index funds, which requires the development of an index to emulate.

Notably, it is more difficult to create and compute a bond-market index than a stock-market index for several reasons. First, the universe of bonds is much broader than that of stocks, ranging from U.S. Treasury securities to bonds in default. Second, the universe of bonds is changing constantly because of new issues, bond maturities, calls, and bond sinking funds. Third, the volatility of prices for individual bonds and bond portfolios changes because bond price volatility is affected by duration, which is likewise changing constantly because of changes in maturity, coupon, and market yield (see Chapter 12). Finally, significant problems can arise in correctly pricing the individual bond issues in an index (especially corporate and mortgage bonds) compared to the current and continuous transactions prices available for most stocks used in stock indexes.

Our subsequent discussion will be divided into the following three subsections: (1) U.S. investment-grade bond indexes, including Treasuries; (2) U.S. high-yield bond indexes; and (3) global government bond indexes. All of these indexes indicate total rates of return for the portfolio of bonds and the indexes are market value weighted. Exhibit 7.13 is a summary of the characteristics for the indexes available for these three segments of the bond market.

---

[8]The discussion in this section draws heavily from Frank K. Reilly and David J. Wright, "Bond Market Indexes," *Handbook of Fixed Income Securities,* 7th ed., edited by Frank J. Fabozzi (Chicago: Irwin Professional Publishing, 2005).

EXHIBIT 7.13 Summary of Bond-Market Indexes

Name of Index	Number of Issues	Maturity	Size of Issues	Weighting	Pricing	Reinvestment Assumption	Subindexes Available
U.S. Investment-Grade Bond Indexes							
Lehman Brothers	5,000+	Over 1 year	Over $100 million	Market value	Trader priced and model priced	No	Government, gov./corp., corporate mortgage-backed, asset-backed
Merrill Lynch	5,000+	Over 1 year	Over $50 million	Market value	Trader priced and model priced	In specific bonds	Government, gov./corp., corporate, mortgage
Ryan Treasury	300+	Over 1 year	All Treasury	Market value and equal	Market priced	In specific bonds	Treasury
Smith Barney	5,000+	Over 1 year	Over $50 million	Market value	Trader priced	In one-month T-bill	Broad inv. grade, Treas.-agency, corporate, mortgage
U.S. High-Yield Bond Indexes							
C. S. First Boston	423	All maturities	Over $75 million	Market value	Trader priced	Yes	Composite and by rating
Lehman Brothers	624	Over 1 year	Over $100 million	Market value	Trader priced	No	Composite and by rating
Merrill Lynch	735	Over 1 year	Over $25 million	Market value	Trader priced	Yes	Composite and by rating
Smith Barney	299	Over 7 years	Over $50 million	Market value	Trader priced	Yes	Composite and by rating
Global Government Bond Indexes							
Lehman Brothers	800	Over 1 year	Over $200 million	Market value	Trader priced	Yes	Composite and 13 countries, local and U.S. dollars
Merrill Lynch	9,736	Over 1 year	Over $50 million	Market value	Trader priced	Yes	Composite and 9 countries, local and U.S. dollars
J. P. Morgan	445	Over 1 year	Over $100 million	Market value	Trader priced	Yes in index	Composite and 11 countries, local and U.S. dollars
Smith Barney	400	Over 1 year	Over $250 million	Market value	Trader priced	Yes at local short-term rate	Composite and 14 countries, local and U.S. dollars

Source: Frank K. Reilly, Wenchi Kao, and David J. Wright, "Alternative Bond Market Indexes," *Financial Analysts Journal* 48, no. 3 (May–June, 1992): 14–58; Frank K. Reilly and David J. Wright, "An Analysis of High-Yield Bond Benchmarks," *Journal of Fixed Income* 3, no. 4 (March 1994): 6–24; and Frank K. Reilly and David J. Wright, "Global Bond Markets: Alternative Benchmarks and Risk–Return Performance," mimeo (May 2000).

U.S. Investment-Grade Bond Indexes

As shown in Exhibit 7.13, four investment firms have created and maintain indexes for Treasury bonds and other bonds considered investment grade, that is, the bonds are rated BBB or higher. As demonstrated in a subsequent section, the relationship among the returns for these investment-grade bonds is strong (that is, correlations average about 0.95), regardless of the segment of the market.

High-Yield Bond Indexes

One of the fastest-growing segments of the U.S. bond market during the past twenty years has been the high-yield bond market, which includes bonds that are not investment grade—that is, they are rated BB, B, CCC, CC, and C. Because of this growth, four investment firms created indexes related to this market. A summary of the characteristics for these indexes is included in Exhibit 7.13.

Global Government Bond Indexes

The global bond market has experienced significant growth in size and importance during the past fifteen years. Unlike the high-yield bond market, the global segment is completely dominated by government bonds because few non-U.S. countries have a corporate bond market. Once again, several major investment firms have created indexes that reflect the performance for the global bond market. As shown in Exhibit 7.13, the various indexes have similar characteristics. At the same time, the total sample sizes and the numbers of countries included differ.

Composite Stock-Bond Indexes

Beyond separate stock indexes and bond indexes for individual countries, a natural step is the development of a composite index that measures the performance of all securities in a given country. With a composite index investors can examine the benefits of diversifying with a combination of asset classes such as stocks and bonds in addition to diversifying within the asset classes of stocks or bonds. There are two such indexes available.

First, a market-value-weighted index called Merrill Lynch–Wilshire Capital Markets Index (ML–WCMI) measures the total return performance of the combined U.S. taxable fixed-income and equity markets. It is basically a combination of the Merrill Lynch fixed-income indexes and the Wilshire 5000 common-stock index. As such, it tracks more than 10,000 stocks and bonds and, as of March 2004, lists about 33 percent bonds and 67 percent stocks.

The second composite index is the Brinson Partner Global Security Market Index (GSMI), which contains U.S. stocks and bonds as well as non-U.S. equities and nondollar bonds along with an allocation to cash. The specific breakdown as of March 2004 was U.S. equities, 40 percent; non-U.S. equities, 25 percent; U.S. bonds, 24 percent; and non-U.S. bonds, 11 percent.

Although related to the relative market values of these asset classes, the weights specified were derived using optimization techniques to identify the portfolio mix of available global asset classes that matches the risk level of a typical U.S. pension plan. The index is balanced to the policy weights monthly.

Because the GSMI contains both U.S. and international stocks and bonds, it is clearly the most diversified benchmark available with a weighting scheme that approaches market values. As such, it is closest to the theoretically specified "market portfolio of risky assets" referred to in the CAPM literature.[9]

Comparison of Indexes over Time

We now look at price movements in the different indexes for monthly intervals.

CORRELATIONS AMONG MONTHLY EQUITY PRICE CHANGES

Exhibit 7.14 contains a listing of the correlation coefficients of the monthly percentage of price changes for a set of U.S. and non-U.S. equity-market indexes with the S&P 500 index during the twenty-two-year period from 1980 to 2001. Most of the correlation differences are attributable to the different sample of firms listed on the different stock exchanges. Most of the major indexes—except the Nikkei Stock Average—are market-value-weighted indexes that include a large number of stocks. Therefore, the computational procedure is generally similar and the sample sizes are large or all-encompassing. Thus, the major difference between the indexes is that the stocks are from different segments of the U.S. stock market or from different countries.

There is a high positive correlation (0.98–0.99) between the S&P 500 and the several comprehensive U.S. equity indexes, Wilshire, NYSE, and Russell. In contrast, there are lower correlations between these comprehensive indexes and various style indexes such as the Russell Large-Cap 1000 (0.886) or the Russell 2000 Small-Cap index (0.783).

The correlations among the S&P 500 and indexes from Canada, the United Kingdom, Germany, and Japan support the case for global investing. Specifically, the U.S.–Toronto correlation was about 0.75, the U.S.–*Financial Times* correlation was about 0.67, and the U.S.–Japan correlations (the Nikkei and the Tokyo S.E) averaged about 0.38. These diversification results were confirmed with the composite international series—with MSCI EAFE and the IFC Emerging Market the correlations were about 0.54 and 0.39, respectively. These results confirm the benefits of global diversification because such low correlations would reduce the variance of a pure U.S. stock portfolio.

CORRELATIONS AMONG MONTHLY BOND INDEXES

The correlations with the monthly Lehman Bros. Govt. bond return index in Exhibit 7.14 consider a variety of bond indexes. The correlations among the longer-term U.S. investment-grade bond indexes ranged from about 0.94 to 0.98, confirming that although the *level* of interest rates differs due to the risk premium, the overriding factors that determine the rates of return for investment-grade bonds over time are *systematic* interest rate variables.

The correlations among investment-grade bonds and high-yield bonds indicate significantly lower correlations (about 0.49) caused by definite equity characteristics of high-yield bonds.[10] Finally, the low and diverse relationships among U.S. investment-grade bonds and world government bonds without the United States (about 0.35) reflect different interest rate movements and exchange rate effects (these non-U.S. government results are U.S. dollar returns). Again, these results support global diversification.

---

[9]This GSMI series is used in a study that examines the effect of various benchmarks on the estimate of the security market line and individual stock betas. See Frank K. Reilly and Rashid A. Akhtar, "The Benchmark Error Problem with Global Capital Markets," *Journal of Portfolio Management* 22, no. 1 (Fall 1995).

[10]For a detailed analysis of this point, see Frank K. Reilly and David J. Wright, "The Unique Risk–Return Characteristics of High-Yield Bonds," *The Journal of Fixed Income* 10, no. 1 (Fall 2001).

EXHIBIT 7.14	Correlation Coefficients among Monthly Percentage Price Changes in Various Stock and Bond Indexes, 1980–2001

Stock Indexes	S&P 500	Bond Indexes	Lehman Brothers Govt. Bonds
Wilshire 5000	0.983	LB Aggregate Bonds	0.981
NYSE Composite	0.993	LB Corporate Bonds	0.945
Russell 3000	0.992	LB High-Yield Bonds	0.489
Russell 1000	0.886	ML World Govt Bonds[a]	0.596
Russell 2000	0.783	ML World Govt Bonds w/o U.S.[a]	0.345
MSCI EAFE	0.538	Treasury Bill—30-day	0.186
Toronto S.E. 300	0.753	Treasury Bill—6-month[b]	0.561
Financial Times All-Share	0.667	Treasury Bill—2-year[b]	0.917
Frankfurt (FAZ) Index	0.536		
Nikkei Index	0.418		
Tokyo S.E. Index	0.328		
IFC Emerging Mkt.	0.392		
M.S. World Index	0.604		
Brinson GSMI	0.915		

Notes: [a]Based on 1986–2001 data only

[b]Based on 1981–2001 data only

Source: Adapted from Frank K. Reilly and David J. Wright, "An Analysis of Risk-Adjusted Performance for Global Market Assets," *Journal of Portfolio Management* 30, no. 3 (Spring, 2004), pp. 63-77. Reprinted by permission of Institutional Investor.

MEAN ANNUAL SECURITY RETURNS AND RISK

The use of security indexes to measure returns and risk was demonstrated in Exhibit 3.14, which showed the average annual price change, or rate of return, and risk measure for a large set of asset indexes. As one would expect, there were clear differences among the indexes due to the different asset classes (e.g., stocks versus bonds) and the different samples within asset classes (e.g., the results for NYSE stocks versus Nasdaq stocks). Equally important, the results were generally consistent with what one should expect in a risk-averse world—that is, there was a positive relationship between the average rate of return for an asset and its measure of risk (e.g., the return-risk results for T-Bills versus the results for the S&P 500 stocks).

Summary

- Given the several uses of security-market indexes, it is important to know how they are constructed and the differences among them. To use one of the many indexes to learn how the "market" is doing, you need to be aware of what market you are dealing with so you can select the appropriate index. As an example, are you only interested in the NYSE or do you also want to consider Nasdaq? Beyond the U.S. market, are you interested in Japanese or U.K. stocks, or do you want to examine the total world market?[11]

---

[11]For a readable discussion on this topic, see Anne Merjos, "How's the Market Doing?" *Barron's,* August 20, 1990, pp. 18–20, 27, 28.

• Indexes are also used as benchmarks to evaluate portfolio performance.[12] In this case, you must be sure the index (benchmark) is consistent with your investing universe. If you are investing worldwide, you should not judge your performance relative to the DJIA, which is limited to thirty U.S. blue-chip stocks. For a

---

[12]Chapter 21 includes an extensive discussion of the purpose and construction of benchmarks and considers the use of benchmarks in the evaluation of portfolio performance.

bond portfolio, the index should match your investment philosophy. Finally, if your portfolio contains both stocks and bonds, you must evaluate your performance against an appropriate combination of indexes.

Investors need to examine numerous market indexes to evaluate the performance of their investments. The selection of the appropriate indexes for information or evaluation will depend on how knowledgeable you are regarding the various indexes. The background from this chapter should help you understand what to look for and how to make the right decision in this area.

QUESTIONS

1. Discuss briefly several uses of security-market indexes.
2. What major factors must be considered when constructing a market index? Put another way, what characteristics differentiate indexes?
3. Explain how a market index is price weighted. In such a case, would you expect a $100 stock to be more important than a $25 stock? Give an example.
4. Explain how to compute a value-weighted index.
5. Explain how a price-weighted index and a value-weighted index adjust for stock splits.

6. Describe an unweighted price index and describe how you would construct such an index. Assume a 20 percent price change in GM ($40/share; 50 million shares outstanding) and Coors Brewing ($25/share and 15 million shares outstanding). Explain which stock's change will have the greater impact on this index.
7. If you correlated percentage changes in the Wilshire 5000 equity index with percentage changes in the NYSE composite and the Nasdaq composite index, would you expect a difference in the correlations? Why or why not?

Investments Online

We have previously suggested several Web sites that offer online users a look at current market conditions in the form of a time-delayed market index (some sites offer real-time stock and index prices, but only at a cost to their customers). Here are a few others:

http://www.bloomberg.com This site is somewhat of an Internet version of the "Bloomberg machine" that is prevalent in many brokerage house offices. It offers both news and current data on a wide variety of global market securities and indexes, including historical charts. The site contains information on interest rates, commodities, and currencies.

http://www.barra.com Barra offers downloadable historical data on several S&P/Barra equity indexes, including S&P 500, midcap, and small-cap indexes as well as Canadian equity indexes. Also included is information about the characteristics of the indexes.

http://www.msci.com Morgan Stanley Capital International contains links to sites that offer downloadable data on several of its international equity indexes. Information and graphics on several fixed-income indexes are available, too.

http://www.barcap.com/euroidx/data/Summary.shtml and the home page of Barclays Capital, **http://www.barcap.com,** offer information on European bond-market indexes.

http://www.datastream.com/product/investor/index.htm Additional global bond index performance information can be found on this page of the Thomson Financial Web site.

http://www.dir.co.jp/InfoManage/dbi/menu.html. Information on Japanese bond indexes are available at a Daiwa Institute of Research site.

8. There are high correlations among the monthly percentage price changes for the alternative NYSE indexes. Discuss the reason for this similarity: Is it size of sample, source of sample, or method of computation?
9. Discuss the correlation of 0.82 between the two stock price indexes for the Tokyo Stock Exchange (TSE). Examine the correlations among the TSE and S&P 500 indexes. Explain why these relationships differ.
10. You learn that the Wilshire 5000 market-value-weighted index increased by 16 percent during a specified period, whereas a Wilshire 5000 equal-weighted index increased by 23 percent during the same period. Discuss what this difference in results implies.
11. Why is it contended that bond-market indexes are more difficult to construct and maintain than stock-market indexes?
12. Suppose the Wilshire 5000 market-value-weighted index increased by 5 percent, whereas the Merrill Lynch–Wilshire Capital Markets Index increased by 15

percent during the same period. What does this difference in results imply?
13. Suppose the Russell 1000 increased by 8 percent during the past year, whereas the Russell 2000 increased by 15 percent. Discuss the implication of these results.
14. Based on what you know about the *Financial Times* (FT) World Index, the Morgan Stanley Capital International World Index, and the Dow Jones World Stock Index, what level of correlation would you expect among monthly rates of return? Discuss the reasons for your answer based on the factors that affect indexes.
15. How would you explain that the ML High-Yield Bond Index was more highly correlated with the NYSE composite stock index than the ML Aggregate Bond Index?
16. Assuming that the mandate to a portfolio manager was to invest in a broadly diversified portfolio of U.S. stocks, which two or three indexes should be considered as an appropriate benchmark? Why?

PROBLEMS

1. You are given the following information regarding prices for a sample of stocks.

Stock	Number of Shares	PRICE	
		T	T + 1
A	1,000,000	60	80
B	10,000,000	20	35
C	30,000,000	18	25

a. Construct a *price-weighted* index for these three stocks, and compute the percentage change in the index for the period from T to T + 1.
b. Construct a *value-weighted* index for these three stocks, and compute the percentage change in the index for the period from T to T + 1.
c. Briefly discuss the difference in the results for the two indexes.
2. a. Given the data in Problem 1, construct an equal-weighted index by assuming $1,000 is invested in each stock. What is the percentage change in wealth for this portfolio?
b. Compute the percentage of price change for each of the stocks in Problem 1. Compute the arithmetic mean of these percentage changes. Discuss how this answer compares to the answer in part (a).
c. Compute the geometric mean of the percentage changes in part (b). Discuss how this result compares to the answer in part (b).
3. For the past five trading days, on the basis of figures in *The Wall Street Journal,* compute the daily percentage price changes for the following stock indexes.

a. DJIA
b. S&P 500
c. Nasdaq Composite Index
d. FT-100 Share Index
e. Nikkei 225 Stock Price Average

Discuss the difference in results for parts (a) and (b), (a) and (c), (a) and (d), (a) and (e), and (d) and (e). What do these differences imply regarding diversifying within the United States versus diversifying among countries?

4.

Company	PRICE			SHARES		
	A	B	C	A	B	C
Day 1	12	23	52	500	350	250
Day 2	10	22	55	500	350	250
Day 3	14	46	52	500	175[a]	250
Day 4	13	47	25	500	175	500[b]
Day 5	12	45	26	500	175	500

[a]Split at close of Day 2.
[b]Split at close of Day 3.

a. Calculate a Dow Jones Industrial Average for days 1 through 5.
b. What effects have the splits had in determining the next day's index? (*Hint:* Think of the relative weighting of each stock.)
c. From a copy of *The Wall Street Journal,* find the divisor that is currently being used in calculating the DJIA. (Normally this value can be found on pages C2 and C3.)
5. Utilizing the price and volume data in Problem 4,
a. Calculate a Standard & Poor's Index for days 1 through 5 using a beginning index value of 10.

b. Identify what effects the splits had in determining the next day's index. (*Hint:* Think of the relative weighting of each stock.)

6. Based on the following stock price and shares outstanding information, compute the beginning and ending values for a price-weighted index and a market-value-weighted index.

	December 31, 2004		**December 31, 2005**	
	Price	Shares Outstanding	Price	Shares Outstanding
Stock K	20	100,000,000	32	100,000,000
Stock M	80	2,000,000	45	4,000,000[a]
Stock R	40	25,000,000	42	25,000,000

[a]Stock split two-for-one during the year.

a. Compute the percentage change in the value of each index.
b. Explain the difference in results between the two indexes.
c. Compute the percentage change for an unweighted index and discuss why these results differ from those of the other indexes.

COMBINED WEB AND SPREADSHEET EXERCISES

1. Performance data on a variety of indexes are available at *http://www.msci.com* under "index tools." Download the performance data of any ten indexes. Compute and compare their five-year average returns and standard deviations. Graph the risk–return pairs. Does the resulting graph appear to be upward-sloping? Compute the correlations between the indexes. Which indexes are most highly correlated? Which are the least correlated?

2. a. Over a period of two weeks, record the closing prices of ten of the DJIA stocks from the newspaper or from an online source such as Yahoo! Finance. Compute and graph a price-weighted index for the stocks. What was the total percentage change in the value of the index over the two-week period?

   b. Find the number of shares outstanding from the Web sites of these ten companies and construct a market-value-weighted index and graph it. What was the total percentage change on this index over the two-week period?

   c. Construct an equal-weighted (sometimes called an unweighted) index for these ten stocks. Graph it and compute the percentage change over the two-week period.

   d. Compare and contrast the percentage changes and the behavior of the graphs over the two-week time frame.

REFERENCES

Fisher, Lawrence, and James H. Lorie. *A Half Century of Returns on Stocks and Bonds.* Chicago: University of Chicago Graduate School of Business, 1997.

Ibbotson Associates. *Stocks, Bonds, Bills and Inflation.* Chicago: Ibbotson Associates, annual.

Lorie, James H., Peter Dodd, and Mary Hamilton Kimpton. *The Stock Market: Theories and Evidence,* 2d ed. Homewood, IL: Richard D. Irwin, 1985.

Reilly, Frank K., and David J. Wright. "Bond Market Indexes." In *Handbook of Fixed Income Securities,* 7th ed., edited by Frank J. Fabozzi. New York: McGraw-Hill, 2005.

THOMSON ONE
Business School Edition

1. Collect price and number of outstanding share data from the past thirty days on the following firms: Amazon (AMZN), Family Dollar (FDO), J.C. Penney (JCP), Target (TGT), and Wal-mart (WMT). Using this data, create a "retail sales stock index" by computing a value-weighted index. What is the return on the index?

2. Using the data from the above problem, compute a price-weighted and unweighted stock index. What is the return on each index? How do the behaviors of the value-weighted, price-weighted, and unweighted indexes compare over the thirty days?

3. Compare the performance during the thirty-day time frame of a) the price-weighted retail sales stock index with the Dow Jones Industrial Average and b) the value-weighted retail sales stock index with the S&P 500.

4. Suppose Wal-Mart did a two-for-one stock split on day ten of the thirty-day set of data in problem 1. Compute the revised returns for the value-weighted, price-weighted, and unweighted stock indexes.

GLOSSARY

Price-weighted index An index calculated as an arithmetic mean of the current prices of the sampled securities.

Security-market index An index created as a statistical measure of the performance of an entire market or segment of a market based on a sample of securities from the market or segment of a market.

Unweighted index An index affected equally by the performance of each security in the sample regardless of price or market value. Also referred to as an equal-weighted index.

Value-weighted index An index calculated as the total market value of the securities in the sample. Market value is equal to the number of shares or bonds outstanding times the market price of the security.

APPENDIX 7

EXHIBIT 7.A	Summary of Stock-Market Indexes		
Name of Index	**Weighting**	**Number of Stocks**	**Source of Stocks**
Dow Jones Industrial Average	Price	30	NYSE, OTC
Nikkei–Dow Jones Average	Price	225	TSE
S&P 400 Industrial	Market value	400	NYSE, OTC
S&P Transportation	Market value	20	NYSE, OTC
S&P Utilities	Market value	40	NYSE, OTC
S&P Financials	Market value	40	NYSE, OTC
S&P 500 Composite	Market value	500	NYSE, OTC
NYSE			
Industrial	Market value	1,601	NYSE
Utility	Market value	253	NYSE
Transportation	Market value	55	NYSE
Financial	Market value	909	NYSE
Composite	Market value	2,818	NYSE
Nasdaq			
Composite	Market value	5,575	OTC
Industrial	Market value	3,394	OTC
Banks	Market value	375	OTC
Insurance	Market value	103	OTC
Other finance	Market value	610	OTC
Transportation	Market value	104	OTC
Telecommunications	Market value	183	OTC
Computer	Market value	685	OTC
Biotech	Market value	121	OTC
AMEX Market Value	Market value	900	AMEX
Dow Jones Equity Market Index	Market value	2,300	NYSE, AMEX, OTC
Wilshire 5000 Equity Value	Market value	5,000	NYSE, AMEX, OTC
Russell Indexes			
3000	Market value	3,000	NYSE, AMEX, OTC
1000	Market value	1,000 largest	NYSE, AMEX, OTC
2000	Market value	2,000 smallest	NYSE, AMEX, OTC
Financial Times Actuaries Index			
All Share	Market value	700	LSE
FT100	Market value	100 largest	LSE
Small-Cap	Market value	250	LSE
Midcap	Market value	250	LSE
Combined	Market value	350	LSE
Tokyo Stock Exchange Price Index (TOPIX)	Market value	1,800	TSE
Value Line Averages			
Industrials	Equal (geometric mean)	1,499	NYSE, AMEX, OTC
Utilities	Equal	177	NYSE, AMEX, OTC
Rails	Equal	19	NYSE, AMEX, OTC
Composite	Equal	1,695	NYSE, AMEX, OTC
Financial Times Ordinary Share Index	Equal (geometric mean)	30	LSE
FT-Actuaries World Indexes	Market value	2,275	24 countries, 3 regions (returns in $, £, ¥, DM, and local currency)
Morgan Stanley Capital International (MSCI) Indexes	Market value	1,375	19 countries, 3 international, 38 international industries (returns in $ and local currency)
Dow Jones World Stock Index	Market value	2,200	13 countries, 3 regions, 120 industry groups (returns in $, £, ¥, DM, and local currency)
Euromoney—First Boston Global Stock Index	Market value	—	17 countries (returns in $ and local currency)
Salomon-Russell World Equity Index	Market value	Russell 1000 and S-R PMI of 600 non-U.S. stocks	22 countries (returns in $ and local currency)

Source: Compiled by authors.

EXHIBIT 7.B	Foreign Stock-Market Indexes		
Name of Index	**Weighting**	**Number of Stocks**	**History of Index**
ATX-index (Vienna)	Market value	All listed stocks	Base year 1967, 1991 began including all stocks (Value = 100)
Swiss Market Index	Market value	18	Base year 1988, stocks selected from the Basle, Geneva, and Zurich Exchanges (Value = 1500)
Stockholm General Index	Market value	All listed stocks	Base year 1979, continuously updated (Value = 100)
Copenhagen Stock Exchange Share Price Index	Market value	All traded stocks	Share price is based on average price of the day
Oslo SE Composite Index (Sweden)	Market value	25	Base year 1972 (Value = 100)
Johannesburg Stock Exchange Actuaries Index	Market value	146	Base year 1959 (Value = 100)
Mexican Market Index	Market value	Variable number, based on capitalization and liquidity	Base year 1978, high dollar returns in recent years
Milan Stock Exchange MIB	Market value	Variable number, based on capitalization and liquidity	Change base at beginning of each year (Value = 1000)
Belgium BEL-20 Stock Index	Market value	20	Base year 1991 (Value = 1000)
Madrid General Stock Index	Market value	92	Change base at beginning of each year
Hang Seng Index (Hong Kong)	Market value	33	Started in 1969, accounts for 75 percent of total market
FT-Actuaries World Indexes	Market value	2,212	Base year 1986
FT-SE 100 Index (London)	Market value	100	Base year 1983 (Value = 1000)
CAC General Share Index (French)	Market value	212	Base year 1981 (Value = 100)
Morgan Stanley World Index	Market value	1,482	Base year 1970 (Value = 100)
Singapore Straits Times Industrial Index	Unweighted	30	
German Stock Market Index (DAX)	Market value	30	Base year 1987 (Value = 1000)
Frankfurter Allgemeine Zeitung Index (FAZ) (German)	Market value	100	Base year 1958 (Value = 100)
Australian Stock Exchange Share Price Indexes	Market value	250	Introduced in 1979
Dublin ISEQ Index	Market value	All stocks traded	Base year 1988 (Value = 1000)
HEX Index (Helsinki)	Market value	Varies with different indexes	Base changes every day
Jakarta Stock Exchange	Market value	All listed shares	Base year 1982 (Value = 100)
Taiwan Stock Exchange Index	Market value	All listed stocks	Base year 1966 (Value = 100)
TSE 300 Composite Index (Toronto)	Market value	300	Base year 1975 (Value = 1000)
KOSPI (Korean Composite Stock Price Index)	Market value (adjusted for cross-holdings)	All listed stocks	Base year 1980 (Value = 100)

Source: Compiled by authors.

Measurement and Management of Risk

At this point we are ready to discuss how to analyze and value various investments, which requires estimating expected returns (cash flow) and the risk involved in the securities. Therefore, before we can begin the valuation process, we need to understand several major developments in investment theory that have influenced the specification and measurement of risk. The three chapters in this part provide the necessary background on risk and asset valuation.

In Chapter 8 we provide an introduction to the portfolio theory developed by Harry Markowitz, which provided the first rigorous measure of risk for investors and showed how one selects alternative assets in order to diversify and reduce the risk of a portfolio. Markowitz also derived a risk measure for individual securities within the context of an efficient portfolio.

Subsequent to these developments, William Sharpe and several other academicians extended the Markowitz portfolio theory model into a general equilibrium asset pricing model that included an alternative risk measure for all risky assets. In Chapter 9 we give a detailed discussion of these developments and an explanation of the relevant risk measure implied by this valuation model, referred to as the *capital asset pricing model* (CAPM). We introduce the CAPM at this early point because the risk measure implied by this model has been used extensively in various valuation models.

We also discuss alternative asset pricing models in Chapter 9.

In Chapter 10 we describe the concept of *efficient capital markets* (ECM), which hypothesizes that security prices reflect the effect of all information. We consider why markets should be efficient, discuss how one goes about testing this hypothesis, describe the results of numerous tests, and consider the implications of the diverse results for those engaged in technical and fundamental analysis, as well as portfolio management.

An Introduction to Portfolio Management

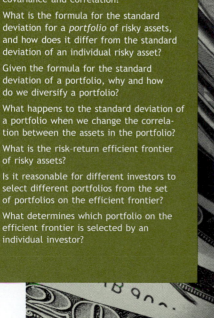

One of the major advances in the investment field during the past few decades has been the recognition that the creation of an optimum investment portfolio is not simply a matter of combining numerous unique individual securities that have desirable risk–return characteristics. Specifically, it has been shown that an investor must consider the relationship *among* the investments to build an optimum portfolio that will meet investment objectives. The recognition of what is important in creating a portfolio was demonstrated in the derivation of portfolio theory.

In this chapter we explain portfolio theory step by step. We introduce the basic portfolio risk formula for combining different assets. Once you understand this formula and its implications, you will understand not only *why* you should diversify your portfolio but also *how* you should diversify.

Some Background Assumptions

Before presenting portfolio theory, we need to clarify some general assumptions of the theory. This includes not only what we mean by an *optimum portfolio* but also what we mean by the terms *risk aversion* and *risk*.

One basic assumption of portfolio theory is that as an investor you want to maximize the returns from your total set of investments for a given level of risk. To adequately deal with such an assumption, certain ground rules must be laid. First, your portfolio should *include all of your assets and liabilities,* not only your stocks or even your marketable securities but also such items as your car, house, and less marketable investments such as coins, stamps, art, antiques, and furniture. The full spectrum of investments must be considered because the returns from all these investments interact and *this relationship among the returns for assets in the portfolio is important.* Hence, a good portfolio is not simply a collection of individually good investments.

RISK AVERSION

Portfolio theory also assumes that investors are basically *risk averse,* meaning that, given a choice between two assets with equal rates of return, they will select the asset with the lower level of risk. Evidence that most investors are risk averse is that they purchase various types of insurance, including life insurance, car insurance, and health insurance. Buying insurance basically involves an outlay of a given known amount to guard against an uncertain, possibly larger outlay in the future. Further evidence of risk aversion is the difference in promised yield (the required rate of return) for different grades of bonds that supposedly have different degrees of credit risk. Specifically, the promised yield on corporate bonds increases from AAA (the lowest risk class) to AA to A, and so on, indicating that investors require a higher rate of return to accept higher risk.

This does not imply that everybody is risk averse, or that investors are completely risk averse regarding all financial commitments. The fact is, not everybody buys insurance for everything. Some people have no insurance against anything, either by choice or because they cannot afford it. In addition, some individuals buy insurance related to some risks such as auto accidents or illness, but they also buy lottery tickets and gamble at race tracks or in casinos, where it is known that the expected returns are negative (which means that participants are willing to pay for the excitement of the risk involved). This combination of risk preference and risk aversion can be explained by an attitude toward risk that depends on the amount of money involved. Researchers speculate that this is the case for people who like to gamble for small amounts (in lotteries or slot machines) but buy insurance to protect themselves against large losses such as fire or accidents.[1]

While recognizing such attitudes, our basic assumption is that most investors committing large sums of money to developing an investment portfolio are risk averse. Therefore, we expect a positive relationship between expected return and expected risk. Notably, this is also what we generally find in terms of historical results—that is, most studies find a positive relationship between the rates of return on various assets and their measures of risk (as shown in Chapter 3).

DEFINITION OF RISK

Although there is a difference in the specific definitions of *risk* and *uncertainty,* for our purposes and in most financial literature the two terms are used interchangeably. For most investors, risk means *the uncertainty of future outcomes.* An alternative definition might be *the probability of an adverse outcome.* In our subsequent discussion of portfolio theory, we will consider several measures of risk that are used when developing and applying the theory.

Markowitz Portfolio Theory

In the early 1960s, the investment community talked about risk, but there was no specific measure for the term. To build a portfolio model, however, investors had to quantify their risk variable. The basic portfolio model was developed by Harry Markowitz, who derived the expected rate of return for a portfolio of assets and an expected risk measure.[2] Markowitz showed that the variance of the rate of return was a meaningful measure of

---

[1]Milton Friedman and Leonard J. Savage, "The Utility Analysis of Choices Involving Risk," *Journal of Political Economy* 56, no. 3 (August 1948): 279–304.

[2]Harry Markowitz, "Portfolio Selection," *Journal of Finance* 7, no. 1 (March 1952): 77–91; and Harry Markowitz, *Portfolio Selection—Efficient Diversification of Investments* (New York: John Wiley & Sons, 1959).

portfolio risk under a reasonable set of assumptions, and he derived the formula for computing the variance of a portfolio. This portfolio variance formula not only indicated the importance of diversifying investments to reduce the total risk of a portfolio but also showed *how* to effectively diversify. The Markowitz model is based on several assumptions regarding investor behavior:

1. Investors consider each investment alternative as being represented by a probability distribution of expected returns over some holding period.
2. Investors maximize one-period expected utility, and their utility curves demonstrate diminishing marginal utility of wealth.
3. Investors estimate the risk of the portfolio on the basis of the variability of expected returns.
4. Investors base decisions solely on expected return and risk, so their utility curves are a function of expected return and the expected variance (or standard deviation) of returns only.
5. For a given risk level, investors prefer higher returns to lower returns. Similarly, for a given level of expected return, investors prefer less risk to more risk.

Under these assumptions, *a single asset or portfolio of assets is considered to be efficient if no other asset or portfolio of assets offers higher expected return with the same (or lower) risk or lower risk with the same (or higher) expected return.*

ALTERNATIVE MEASURES OF RISK

One of the best-known measures of risk is the *variance,* or *standard deviation of expected returns.*[3] It is a statistical measure of the dispersion of returns around the expected value whereby a larger variance or standard deviation indicates greater dispersion. The idea is that the more disperse the expected returns, the greater the uncertainty of future returns.

Another measure of risk is the *range of returns.* It is assumed that a larger range of expected returns, from the lowest to the highest expected return, means greater uncertainty and risk regarding future expected returns.

Instead of using measures that analyze all deviations from expectations, some observers believe that investors should be concerned only with returns below expectations, which means only deviations below the mean value. A measure that only considers deviations below the mean is the *semivariance.* An extension of the semivariance measure only computes expected returns *below zero* (that is, negative returns), or returns below the returns of some specific asset such as T-bills, the rate of inflation, or a benchmark. These measures of risk implicitly assume that investors want to *minimize the damage* from returns less than some target rate. Assuming that investors would welcome returns above some target rate, the returns above a target rate are not considered when measuring risk.

Although there are numerous potential measures of risk, we will use the variance or standard deviation of returns because (1) this measure is somewhat intuitive, (2) it is a correct and widely recognized risk measure, and (3) it has been used in most of the theoretical asset pricing models.

EXPECTED RATES OF RETURN

We compute the expected rate of return for an *individual investment* as shown in Exhibit 8.1. The expected return for an individual risky asset with the set of potential returns and an assumption of the different probabilities used in the example would be 10.3 percent.

---

[3]We consider the variance and standard deviation as one measure of risk because the standard deviation is the square root of the variance.

EXHIBIT 8.1	Computation of the Expected Return for an Individual Asset	
Probability	**Possible Rate of Return (percent)**	**Expected Return (percent)**
0.35	0.08	0.0280
0.30	0.10	0.0300
0.20	0.12	0.0240
0.15	0.14	0.0210
		E(R) = 0.1030

EXHIBIT 8.2	Computation of the Expected Return for a Portfolio of Risky Assets	
Weight (w_i) (percent of portfolio)	**Expected Security Return (R_i)**	**Expected Portfolio Return ($w_i \times R_i$)**
0.20	0.10	0.0200
0.30	0.11	0.0330
0.30	0.12	0.0360
0.20	0.13	0.0260
		E(R$_{port}$) = 0.1150

The expected rate of return for a *portfolio* of investments is simply the weighted average of the expected rates of return for the individual investments in the portfolio. The weights are the proportion of total value for the individual investment.

The expected rate of return for a hypothetical portfolio with four risky assets is shown in Exhibit 8.2. The expected return for this portfolio of investments would be 11.5 percent. The effect of adding or dropping any investment from the portfolio would be easy to determine; we would use the new weights based on value and the expected returns for each of the investments. We can generalize this computation of the expected return for the portfolio $E(R_{port})$ as follows:

8.1
$$E(R_{port}) = \sum_{i=1}^{n} w_i R_i$$

where:

w_i = the weight of an individual asset in the portfolio, or the percent of the portfolio in asset i

R_i = the expected rate of return for asset i

VARIANCE (STANDARD DEVIATION) OF RETURNS FOR AN INDIVIDUAL INVESTMENT

As noted, we will be using the variance or the standard deviation of returns as the measure of risk. Therefore, at this point we demonstrate how to compute the standard deviation of returns for an individual investment. Subsequently, after discussing some other statistical concepts, we will consider the determination of the standard deviation for a *portfolio* of investments.

EXHIBIT 8.3	Computation of the Variance for an Individual Risky Asset				
Possible Rate of Return (R_i)	Expected Return $E(R_i)$	$R_i - E(R_i)$	$[R_i - E(R_i)]^2$	P_i	$[R_i - E(R_i)]^2 P_i$
0.08	0.103	−0.023	0.0005	0.35	0.000185
0.10	0.103	−0.003	0.0000	0.30	0.000003
0.12	0.103	0.017	0.0003	0.20	0.000058
0.14	0.103	0.037	0.0014	0.15	0.000205
					0.000451

Variance = σ^2 = 0.000451
Standard Deviation = σ = 0.021237

The variance, or standard deviation, is a measure of the variation of possible rates of return R_i from the expected rate of return $E(R_i)$ as follows:

8.2

$$\textbf{Variance} = \boldsymbol{\sigma^2} = \sum_{i=1}^{n} [\mathbf{R_i - E(R_i)}]^2 \mathbf{P_i}$$

where:
P_i = probability of the possible rate of return R_i

8.3

$$\textbf{Standard Deviation} = \boldsymbol{\sigma} = \sqrt{\sum_{i=1}^{n} [\mathbf{R_i - E(R_i)}]^2 \mathbf{P_i}}$$

The computation of the variance and standard deviation of returns for the individual risky asset in Exhibit 8.1 is set forth in Exhibit 8.3.

VARIANCE (STANDARD DEVIATION) OF RETURNS FOR A PORTFOLIO

Two basic concepts in statistics, covariance and correlation, must be understood before we discuss the formula for the variance of the rate of return for a portfolio.

Covariance of Returns In this subsection we discuss what the covariance of returns is intended to measure, give the formula for computing it, and present an example of its computation. *Covariance* is a measure of the degree to which two variables "move together" relative to their individual mean values over time. In portfolio analysis, we usually are concerned with the covariance of *rates of return* rather than prices or some other variable.[4] A positive covariance means that the rates of return for two investments tend to move in the same direction relative to their individual means during the same time period. In contrast, a negative covariance indicates that the rates of return for two investments tend to move in different directions relative to their means during specified time intervals over time. The *magnitude* of the covariance depends on the variances of the individual return series, as well as on the relationship between the series.

---

[4]Returns, of course, can be measured in a variety of ways, depending on the type of asset. For example, we could define returns R_i as

$$\mathbf{R_i} = \frac{\mathbf{EV - BV + CF}}{\mathbf{BV}}$$

where EV is ending value, BV is beginning value, and CF is the cash flow during the period.

EXHIBIT 8.4	Computation of Monthly Rates of Return for U.S. Stocks and Bonds	

	S&P 500 STOCK INDEX	LEHMAN BROTHERS TREASURY BONDS
Date	**Monthly Rate of Return (%)[a]**	**Monthly Rate of Return (%)[b]**
Jan-03	−2.66	−0.30
Feb-03	−1.52	1.72
Mar-03	1.03	−0.42
Apr-03	8.28	0.47
May-03	5.33	2.88
Jun-03	1.28	−0.61
Jul-03	1.79	−4.39
Aug-03	1.96	0.59
Sep-03	−1.07	3.02
Oct-03	5.56	−1.53
Nov-03	0.93	0.13
Dec-03	5.18	0.89
$\bar{R}_{S\&P\,500}$	2.17	$\bar{R}_{LBTB}$ 0.20

[a]Return includes dividends paid on stocks in the index.

[b]Return includes accrued interest on bonds in the index.

Source: Center for Research in Security Prices and Lehman Brothers.

Exhibit 8.4 contains the monthly closing index values for U.S. stocks (measured by the S&P 500 index) and bonds (measured by the Lehman Brothers Treasury Bond Index). Both indexes are total return indexes—that is, the stock index includes dividends paid and the bond index includes accrued interest, as discussed in Chapter 7. We can use these data to compute monthly rates of return for these two assets during 2003. Exhibits 8.5 and 8.6 contain a time-series plot of the monthly rates of return for the two assets during 2003. Although the rates of return for the two assets moved together during some months, in other months they moved in opposite directions. The covariance statistic provides an *absolute* measure of how they moved together over time.

For two assets, *i* and *j,* we define the covariance of rates of return as

8.4
$$\mathbf{Cov}_{ij} = \mathbf{E}\{[\mathbf{R}_i - \mathbf{E}(\mathbf{R}_i)][\mathbf{R}_j - \mathbf{E}(\mathbf{R}_j)]\}$$

When we apply this formula to the monthly rates of return for the S&P 500 and the Treasury bond indexes during 2003, it becomes

$$\frac{1}{11}\sum_{i=1}^{12}[\mathbf{R}_i - \overline{\mathbf{R}}_i][\mathbf{R}_j - \overline{\mathbf{R}}_j]$$

Note that when we apply formula 8.4 to actual sample data, we use the sample mean ($\bar{R}$) as an estimate of the expected return and divide the values by ($n - 1$) rather than by n to avoid statistical bias.

As can be seen, if the rates of return for one asset are above (below) its mean rate of return ($\bar{R}$) during a given period and the returns for the other asset are likewise above (below) its mean rate of return during this same period, then the *product* of these deviations

EXHIBIT 8.5   Time-Series Plot of Monthly Returns for S&P 500 Index, 2003

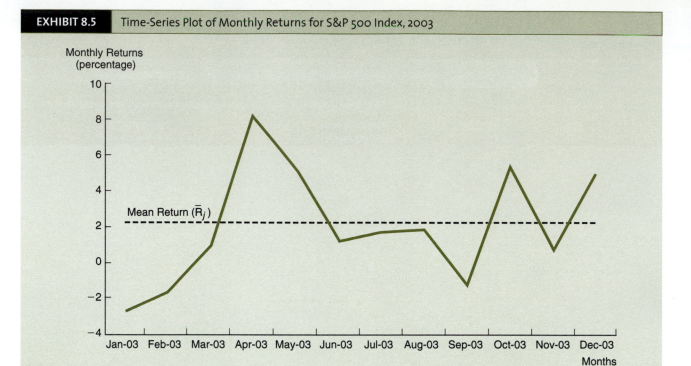

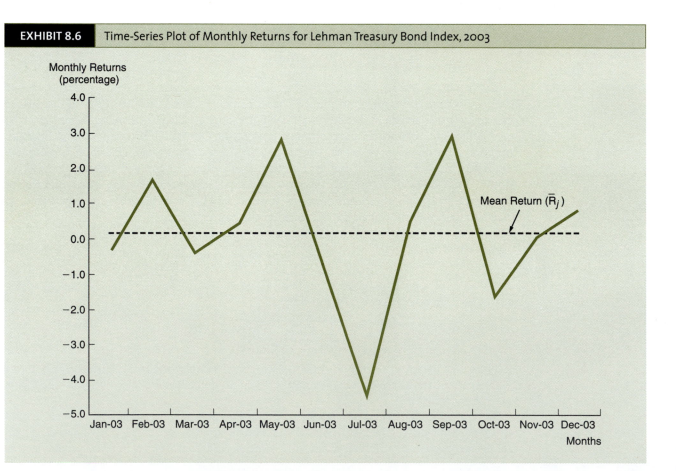

EXHIBIT 8.7	Computation of Covariance of Returns for S&P 500 Index and Lehman Brothers Treasury Bond Index, 2003

MONTHLY RETURN (%)

Date	S&P 500 (R_i)	Lehman Treasury Bond Index (R_j)	S&P 500 $R_i - \bar{R}_i$	Lehman Treasury Bond Index $R_j - \bar{R}_j$	S&P 500 $R_i - \bar{R}_i$ $\times$ Lehman Treasury Bond Index $R_j - \bar{R}_j$
Jan-03	−2.66	−0.30	−4.83	−0.50	2.44
Feb-03	−1.52	1.72	−3.70	1.52	−5.61
Mar-03	1.03	−0.42	−1.14	−0.62	0.71
Apr-03	8.28	−0.47	6.11	0.27	1.62
May-03	5.33	2.88	3.15	2.68	8.43
Jun-03	1.28	−0.61	−0.89	−0.81	0.73
Jul-03	1.79	−4.39	−0.38	−4.59	1.74
Aug-03	1.96	0.59	−0.21	0.39	−0.08
Sep-03	−1.07	3.02	−3.25	2.82	−9.15
Oct−03	5.56	−1.53	3.38	−1.73	−5.87
Nov-03	0.93	0.13	−1.25	−0.07	0.09
Dec-03	5.18	0.89	3.01	0.69	2.07
	$\bar{R}_i = 2.17$	$\bar{R}_j = 0.20$			Sum = −2.87

$$\text{Cov}_{ij} = -2.87/11 = -0.258$$

from the mean is positive. If this happens consistently, the covariance of returns between these two assets will be some large positive value. If, however, the rate of return for one of the securities is above its mean return while the return on the other security is below its mean return, the product will be negative. If this contrary movement happens consistently, the covariance between the rates of return for the two assets will be a large negative value.

Exhibit 8.7 contains the monthly rates of return during 2003 for the S&P 500 index and the Lehman Brothers Treasury Bond Index as computed in Exhibit 8.4. One might expect the returns for the two asset indexes to have reasonably low covariance because of the differences in the nature of these assets. The arithmetic mean of the monthly returns were

$$(\bar{R}_i) = \frac{1}{11} \sum_{i=1}^{12} R_{it}$$

and

$$(\bar{R}_j) = \frac{1}{11} \sum_{j=1}^{12} R_{jt}$$

We rounded all figures to the nearest hundredth of 1 percent, so there may be small rounding errors. The average monthly return was 2.17 percent for the S&P 500 and 0.20 percent for the Treasury bonds. The results in Exhibit 8.7 show that the covariance between the rates of return for these two assets was

$$\text{Cov}_{ij} = \frac{1}{11} \times -2.87$$

$$= -0.258$$

EXHIBIT 8.8	Scatterplot of Monthly Returns for S&P 500 and Lehman Brothers Treasury Bond Index, 2003

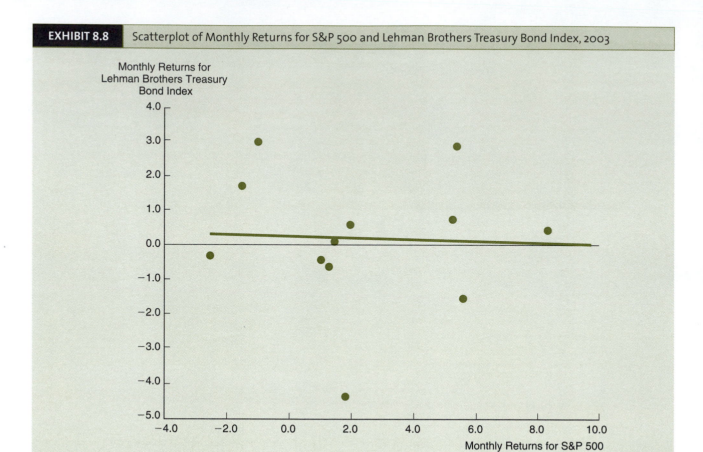

Interpretation of a number such as -0.258 is difficult; is it high or low for covariance? We know the relationship between the two assets is generally negative, but it is not possible to be more specific. Exhibit 8.8 contains a scatterplot with paired values of R_{it} and R_{jt} plotted against each other. This plot demonstrates the linear nature and strength of the relationship. It is not surprising that the relationship during 2003 is not very strong since during four months the two assets moved counter to each other and in three of those four months the size of the difference was so large that the overall covariance was a small negative value.

Covariance and Correlation   Covariance is affected by the variability of the two individual return indexes. Therefore, a number such as the -0.258 in our example might indicate a weak negative relationship if the two individual indexes were volatile, but would reflect a strong negative relationship if the two indexes were stable. Obviously, we want to "standardize" this covariance measure. We do so by taking into consideration the variability of the two individual return indexes, as follows:

Interactive e-lectures

For more explanation and an animated example of correlation, go to: http://reillyxtra .swlearning.com.

8.5

$$\mathbf{r}_{ij} = \frac{\mathbf{Cov}_{ij}}{\sigma_i \sigma_j}$$

where:

r_{ij} = the correlation coefficient of returns
σ_i = the standard deviation of R_{it}
σ_j = the standard deviation of R_{jt}

Standardizing the covariance by the product of the individual standard deviations yields the *correlation coefficient* r_{ij}, which can vary only in the range -1 to $+1$. A value of $+1$ would indicate a perfect positive linear relationship between R_i and R_j, meaning the returns for the two assets move together in a completely linear manner. A value of -1 indicates a perfect negative relationship between the two return indexes such that when one asset's rate of return is above its mean, the other asset's rate of return will be below its mean by the comparable amount.

To calculate this standardized measure of the relationship, we need to compute the standard deviation for the two individual return indexes. We already have the values for $R_{it} - (\bar{R}_i)$ and $R_{jt} - (\bar{R}_j)$ in Exhibit 8.7. We can square each of these values and sum them as shown in Exhibit 8.9 to calculate the variance of each return series (again we divide by $(n - 1)$ to avoid statistical bias).

$$\sigma_i^2 = \frac{1}{11}(119.15) = 10.83$$

and

$$\sigma_j^2 = \frac{1}{11}(43.5) = 3.95$$

EXHIBIT 8.9	Computation of Standard Deviation of Returns for S&P 500 Index and Lehman Brothers Treasury Bond Index, 2003

	S&P 500		LEHMAN TREASURY BOND INDEX	
Date	$R_i - \bar{R}_i$	$(R_i - \bar{R}_i)^2$	$R_j - \bar{R}_j$	$(R_j - \bar{R}_j)^2$
Jan-03	−4.83	23.34	−0.50	0.25
Feb-03	−3.70	13.68	1.52	2.30
Mar-03	−1.14	1.30	−0.62	0.39
Apr-03	6.11	37.29	0.27	0.07
May-03	3.15	9.93	2.68	7.16
Jun-03	−0.89	0.79	−0.81	0.66
Jul-03	−0.38	0.14	−4.59	21.11
Aug-03	−0.21	0.05	0.39	0.15
Sep-03	−3.25	10.55	2.82	7.93
Oct-03	3.38	11.45	−1.73	3.01
Nov-03	−1.25	1.56	−0.07	0.01
Dec-03	3.01	9.07	0.69	0.47
		Sum = 119.15		Sum = 43.50

$\text{Variance}_i = 119.15/11 = 10.83$ \qquad $\text{Variance}_j = 43.5/11 = 3.95$

$\text{Standard Deviation}_i = (10.83)^{1/2} = 3.29$ \qquad $\text{Standard Deviation}_j = (3.95)^{1/2} = 1.99$

The standard deviation for each index is the square root of the variance for each, as follows:

$$\sigma_i = \sqrt{10.83} = 3.29$$

$$\sigma_j = \sqrt{3.95} = 1.99$$

Thus, based on the covariance between the two indexes and the individual standard deviations, we can calculate the correlation coefficient between returns for common stocks and Treasury bonds during 2003:

$$r_{ij} = \frac{\text{Cov}_{ij}}{\sigma_i \sigma_j} = \frac{-0.258}{(3.29)(1.99)} = \frac{-0.258}{6.55} = -0.04$$

Obviously, this formula also implies that

$$\text{Cov}_{ij} = r_{ij}\sigma_i\sigma_j = (-0.04)(3.29)(1.99) = -0.26 \text{ (rounding difference)}$$

STANDARD DEVIATION OF A PORTFOLIO

As noted, a correlation of +1.0 indicates perfect positive correlation, and a value of −1.0 means that the returns moved in completely opposite directions. A value of zero means that the returns had no linear relationship, that is, they were uncorrelated statistically. That does *not* mean that they are independent. The value of $r_{ij} = -0.04$ is not significantly different from zero. This insignificant negative correlation is not unusual for stocks versus bonds during short time intervals such as one year.

Portfolio Standard Deviation Formula Now that we have discussed the concepts of covariance and correlation, we can consider the formula for computing the standard deviation of returns for a *portfolio* of assets, our measure of risk for a portfolio. In Exhibit 8.2, we showed that the expected rate of return of the portfolio was the weighted average of the expected returns for the individual assets in the portfolio; the weights were the percentage of value of the portfolio. One might assume it is possible to derive the standard deviation of the portfolio in the same manner, that is, by computing the weighted average of the standard deviations for the individual assets. This would be a mistake. Markowitz derived the general formula for the standard deviation of a portfolio as follows:[5]

8.6

$$\sigma_{\text{port}} = \sqrt{\sum_{i=1}^{n} w_i^2 \sigma_i^2 + \sum_{i=1}^{n} \sum_{\substack{j=1 \\ i \neq j}}^{n} w_i w_j \text{Cov}_{ij}}$$

where:

σ_{port} = the standard deviation of the portfolio
w_i = the weights of an individual asset in the portfolio, where weights are determined by the proportion of value in the portfolio
σ_i^2 = the variance of rates of return for asset i
Cov_{ij} = the covariance between the rates of return for assets i and j, where $\text{Cov}_{ij} = r_{ij}\sigma_i\sigma_j$

This formula indicates that the standard deviation for a portfolio of assets is a function of the weighted average of the individual variances (where the weights are squared), *plus* the weighted covariances between all the assets in the portfolio. The very important point is

---

[5]For the detailed derivation of this formula, see Markowitz, *Portfolio Selection*.

that the standard deviation for a portfolio of assets encompasses not only the variances of the individual assets but *also* includes the covariances between all the pairs of individual assets in the portfolio. Further, it can be shown that, in a portfolio with a large number of securities, this formula reduces to the sum of the weighted covariances.

Impact of a new security in a portfolio. Although in most of the following discussion we will consider portfolios with only two assets (because it is possible to show the effect in two dimensions), we will also demonstrate the computations for a three-asset portfolio. Still, it is important at this point to consider what happens in a large portfolio with many assets. Specifically, what happens to the portfolio's standard deviation when we add a new security to such a portfolio? As shown by the formula, we see two effects. The first is the asset's own variance of returns, and the second is the covariance between the returns of this new asset and the returns of *every other asset that is already in the portfolio.* The relative weight of these numerous covariances is substantially greater than the asset's unique variance; the more assets in the portfolio, the more this is true. This means that the important factor to consider when adding an investment to a portfolio that contains a number of other investments is *not* the new security's own variance but *its average covariance with all the other investments in the portfolio.*

Portfolio Standard Deviation Calculation Because of the assumptions used in developing the Markowitz portfolio model, any asset or portfolio of assets can be described by two characteristics: the expected rate of return and the expected standard deviation of returns. Therefore, the following demonstrations can be applied to two *individual* assets, two *portfolios* of assets, or two *asset classes* with the indicated return–standard deviation characteristics and correlation coefficients.

Equal risk and return—changing correlations. Consider first the case in which both assets have the same expected return and expected standard deviation of return. As an example, let's assume

$$E(R_1) = 0.20, \quad E(\sigma_1) = 0.10$$

$$E(R_2) = 0.20, \quad E(\sigma_2) = 0.10$$

To show the effect of different covariances, we assume different levels of correlation between the two assets. We also assume that the two assets have equal weights in the portfolio ($w_1 = 0.50$; $w_2 = 0.50$). Therefore, the only value that changes in each example is the correlation between the returns for the two assets.

Now consider the following five correlation coefficients and the covariances they yield. Since $Cov_{ij} = r_{ij}\sigma_i\sigma_j$, the covariance will be equal to $r_{1,2}(0.10)(0.10)$ because the standard deviation of both assets is 0.10.

a. For $r_{1,2} = 1.00$, $Cov_{1,2} = (1.00)(0.10)(0.10) = 0.01$
b. For $r_{1,2} = 0.50$, $Cov_{1,2} = (0.50)(0.10)(0.10) = 0.005$
c. For $r_{1,2} = 0.00$, $Cov_{1,2} = (0.00)(0.10)(0.10) = 0.000$
d. For $r_{1,2} = -0.50$, $Cov_{1,2} = (-0.50)(0.10)(0.10) = -0.005$
e. For $r_{1,2} = -1.00$, $Cov_{1,2} = (-1.00)(0.10)(0.10) = -0.01$

Now let's see what happens to the standard deviation of the portfolio under these five conditions.

When we apply the general portfolio formula from equation 8.6 to a two-asset portfolio, it is

8.7
$$\sigma_{port} = \sqrt{w_1^2\sigma_1^2 + w_2^2\sigma_2^2 + 2w_1w_2r_{1,2}\sigma_1\sigma_2}$$

or

$$\sigma_{port} = \sqrt{w_1^2\sigma_1^2 + w_2^2\sigma_2^2 + 2w_1w_2Cov_{1,2}}$$

Thus, in case (a).

$$\sigma_{port\,(a)} = \sqrt{(0.5)^2(0.10)^2 + (0.5)^2(0.10)^2 + 2(0.5)(0.5)(0.01)}$$

$$= \sqrt{(0.25)(0.01) + (0.25)(0.01) + 2(0.25)(0.01)}$$

$$= \sqrt{0.01}$$

$$= 0.10$$

In this case, where the returns for the two assets are perfectly positively correlated, the standard deviation for the portfolio is, in fact, the weighted average of the individual standard deviations. The important point is that we get no real benefit from combining two assets that are perfectly correlated; they are like one asset already because their returns move together.

Now consider case (b), where $r_{1,2}$ equals 0.50.

$$\sigma_{port\,(b)} = \sqrt{(0.5)^2(0.10)^2 + (0.5)^2(0.10)^2 + 2(0.5)(0.5)(0.005)}$$

$$= \sqrt{(0.0025) + (0.0025) + 2(0.25)(0.005)}$$

$$= \sqrt{0.0075}$$

$$= 0.0866$$

The only term that changed from case (a) is the last term, $Cov_{1,2}$, which changed from 0.01 to 0.005. As a result, the standard deviation of the portfolio declined by about 13 percent, from 0.10 to 0.0866. Note that *the expected return of the portfolio did not change* because it is simply the weighted average of the individual expected returns; it is equal to 0.20 in both cases.

You should be able to confirm through your own calculations that the standard deviations for portfolios (c) and (d) are as follows:

c. 0.0707
d. 0.05

The final case, where the correlation between the two assets is -1.00, indicates the ultimate benefits of diversification.

$$\sigma_{port\,(e)} = \sqrt{(0.5)^2(0.10)^2 + (0.5)^2(0.10)^2 + 2(0.5)(0.5)(-0.01)}$$

$$= \sqrt{(0.0050) + (-0.0050)}$$

$$= \sqrt{0}$$

$$= 0$$

Here, the negative covariance term exactly offsets the individual variance terms, leaving an overall standard deviation of the portfolio of zero. *This would be a risk-free portfolio.*

Exhibit 8.10 illustrates a graph of such a pattern. Perfect negative correlation gives a mean combined return for the two securities over time equal to the mean for each of them, so the returns for the portfolio show no variability. Any returns above and below the mean for each of the assets are *completely offset* by the return for the other asset, so there is

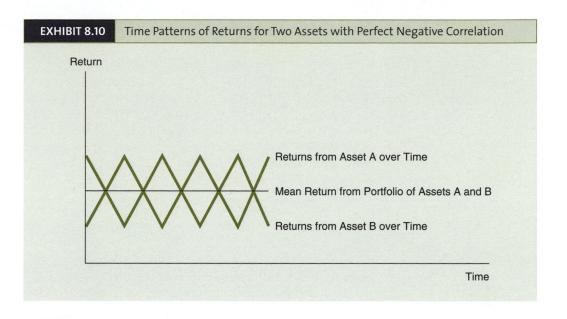

EXHIBIT 8.10 Time Patterns of Returns for Two Assets with Perfect Negative Correlation

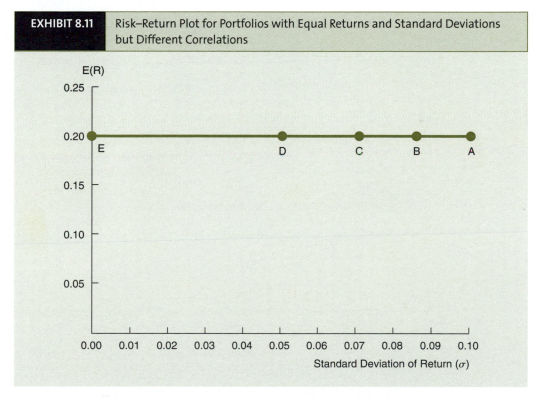

EXHIBIT 8.11 Risk–Return Plot for Portfolios with Equal Returns and Standard Deviations but Different Correlations

no variability in total returns—that is, *no risk*—for the portfolio. Thus, a pair of completely negatively correlated assets provides the maximum benefits of diversification by completely eliminating risk.

The graph in Exhibit 8.11 shows the difference in the risk–return posture for our five cases. As noted, the only effect of the change in correlation is the change in the standard deviation of this two-asset portfolio. Combining assets that are not perfectly correlated does *not* affect the expected return of the portfolio, but it *does* reduce the risk of the portfolio (as measured by its standard deviation). When we eventually reach the ultimate combination of perfect negative correlation, risk is eliminated.

Combining stocks with different returns and risk.   We have seen what happens when only the correlation coefficient (covariance) differs between the assets. We now consider two assets (or portfolios) with different expected rates of return and individual standard deviations.[6] We will show what happens when we vary the correlations between them. We will assume two assets with the following characteristics.

Asset	$E(R_i)$	w_i	σ_i^2	σ_i
1	0.10	0.50	0.0049	0.07
2	0.20	0.50	0.0100	0.10

We will use the previous set of correlation coefficients, but we must recalculate the covariances because this time the standard deviations of the assets are different. The results are shown in the following table.

Case	Correlation Coefficient ($r_{1,2}$)	Covariance ($r_{1,2}\sigma_1\sigma_2$)
a	+1.00	0.0070
b	+0.50	0.0035
c	0.00	0.0000
d	−0.50	−0.0035
e	−1.00	−0.0070

Because we are assuming the same weights in all cases ($0.50 - 0.50$), the expected return in every instance will be

$$E(R_{port}) = 0.50(0.10) + 0.50(0.20)$$

$$= 0.15$$

The portfolio standard deviation for case (a) will be

$$\sigma_{port\ (a)} = \sqrt{(0.5)^2(0.07)^2 + (0.5)^2(0.10)^2 + 2(0.5)(0.5)(0.0070)}$$

$$= \sqrt{0.007225}$$

$$= 0.085$$

Again, with perfect positive correlation, the portfolio standard deviation is the weighted average of the standard deviations of the individual assets:

$$(0.5)(0.07) + (0.5)(0.10) = 0.085$$

As you might envision, changing the weights with perfect positive correlation causes the portfolio standard deviation to change in a linear fashion. This will be an important point to remember when we discuss the capital asset pricing model (CAPM) in the next chapter.

---

[6]As noted, these could be two asset classes. For example, asset 1 could be low risk–return bonds and asset 2 could be higher risk–return stocks.

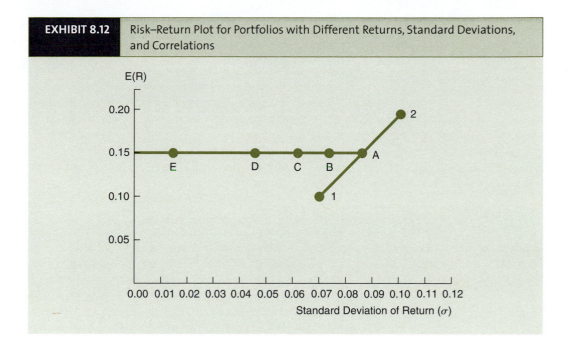

EXHIBIT 8.12 Risk–Return Plot for Portfolios with Different Returns, Standard Deviations, and Correlations

For cases (b), (c), (d), and (e), the portfolio standard deviations are as follows:[7]

$$\sigma_{\text{port (b)}} = \sqrt{(0.001225) + (0.0025) + (0.5)(0.0035)}$$

$$= \sqrt{0.005475}$$

$$= 0.07399$$

$$\sigma_{\text{port (c)}} = \sqrt{(0.001225) + (0.0025) + (0.5)(0.00)}$$

$$= 0.0610$$

$$\sigma_{\text{port (d)}} = \sqrt{(0.001225) + (0.0025) + (0.5)(-0.0035)}$$

$$= 0.0444$$

$$\sigma_{\text{port (e)}} = \sqrt{(0.003725) + (0.5)(-0.0070)}$$

$$= 0.015$$

Note that, in this example, with perfect negative correlation the portfolio standard deviation is not zero. This is because the different examples have equal weights, but the asset standard deviations are not equal.[8]

Exhibit 8.12 shows the results for the two individual assets and the portfolio of the two assets assuming the correlation coefficients vary as set forth in cases (a) through (e). As

---

[7]In all the following examples we will skip some steps because you are now aware that only the last term changes. You are encouraged to work out the individual steps to ensure that you understand the computational procedure.

[8]To see proofs for equal weights with equal variances and to solve for the appropriate weights to get zero standard deviation when standard deviations are not equal, see the appendixes to Chapter 7 in Frank K. Reilly and Keith C. Brown, *Investment Analysis and Portfolio Management*, 7th ed. (Mason: South-Western, © 2003), pp. 235–236.

before, the expected return does not change because the proportions are always set at 0.50–0.50, so all the portfolios lie along the horizontal line at the return, R = 0.15.

Constant correlation with changing weights.   If we changed the weights of the two assets while holding the correlation coefficient constant, we would derive a set of combinations that trace an ellipse starting at asset 2, going through the 0.50–0.50 point, and ending at asset 1. We can demonstrate this with case (c), in which the correlation coefficient of zero eases the computations. We begin with 100 percent in asset 2 [case (f)] and change the weights as follows, ending with 100 percent in asset 1 [case (l)]:

Case	w_1	w_2	$E(R_i)$
f	0.00	1.00	0.20
g	0.20	0.80	0.18
h	0.40	0.60	0.16
i	0.50	0.50	0.15
j	0.60	0.40	0.14
k	0.80	0.20	0.12
l	1.00	0.00	0.10

We already know the standard deviation (σ) for portfolio (i). In cases (f), (g), (h), (j), (k), and (l), the standard deviations are[9]

$$\sigma_{\text{port (g)}} = \sqrt{(0.20)^2 (0.07)^2 + (0.80)^2 (0.10)^2 + 2 (0.20) (0.80) (0.00)}$$

$$= \sqrt{(0.04) (0.0049) + (0.64) (0.01) + (0)}$$

$$= \sqrt{0.006596}$$

$$= 0.0812$$

$$\sigma_{\text{port (h)}} = \sqrt{(0.40)^2 (0.07)^2 + (0.60)^2 (0.10)^2 + 2 (0.40) (0.60) (0.00)}$$

$$= \sqrt{0.004384}$$

$$= 0.0662$$

$$\sigma_{\text{port (j)}} = \sqrt{(0.60)^2 (0.07)^2 + (0.40)^2 (0.10)^2 + 2 (0.60) (0.40) (0.00)}$$

$$= \sqrt{0.003364}$$

$$= 0.0580$$

$$\sigma_{\text{port (k)}} = \sqrt{(0.80)^2 (0.07)^2 + (0.20)^2 (0.10)^2 + 2 (0.80) (0.20) (0.00)}$$

$$= \sqrt{0.003536}$$

$$= 0.0595$$

---

[9]Again, you are encouraged to fill in the steps we skipped in the computations.

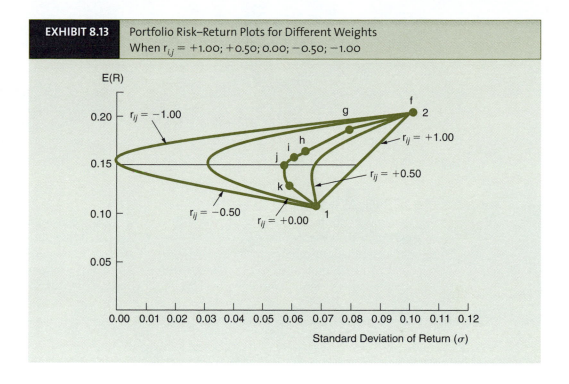

EXHIBIT 8.13	Portfolio Risk–Return Plots for Different Weights When $r_{i,j}$ = +1.00; +0.50; 0.00; −0.50; −1.00

The various weights with a constant correlation yield the following risk–return combinations.

Case	w_1	w_2	$E(R_i)$	$E(\sigma_{port})$
f	0.00	1.00	0.20	0.1000
g	0.20	0.80	0.18	0.0812
h	0.40	0.60	0.16	0.0662
i	0.50	0.50	0.15	0.0610
j	0.60	0.40	0.14	0.0580
k	0.80	0.20	0.12	0.0595
l	1.00	0.00	0.10	0.0700

A graph of these combinations appears in Exhibit 8.13. We could derive a complete curve by simply varying the weighting by smaller increments.

A notable result is that with low, zero, or negative correlations, it is possible to derive portfolios that have *lower risk than either single asset*. In our set of examples where r_{ij} = 0.00, this occurs in cases (h), (i), (j), and (k). This ability to reduce risk is the essence of diversification.

As shown in Exhibit 8.13, assuming the normal risk–return relationship where assets with higher risk (larger standard deviation of returns) provide high rates of return, it is possible for a conservative investor to experience *both* lower risk *and* higher return by diversifying into a higher-risk–higher-return asset, assuming that the correlation between the two assets is fairly low. Exhibit 8.13 shows that, in the case where we used the correlation of zero (0.00), the low-risk investor at point 1—who would receive a return of 10 percent and risk of 7 percent—could *increase* the return to 14 percent *and* experience a *decline* in risk to 5.8 percent by investing (diversifying) 40 percent of the portfolio in riskier asset 2.

As noted, the benefits of diversification are critically dependent on the correlation between assets. The exhibit shows that there is even some benefit when the correlation is 0.50 rather than zero.

Exhibit 8.13 also shows that the curvature in the graph depends on the correlation between the two assets or portfolios. With $r_{ij} = +1.00$, the combinations lie along a straight line between the two assets. When $r_{ij} = 0.50$, the curve is to the right of the $r_{ij} = 0.00$ curve; when $r_{ij} = -0.50$, it is to the left. Finally, when $r_{ij} = -1.00$, the graph would be two straight lines that would touch at the vertical line (zero risk) with some combination. It is possible to solve for the specified set of weights that would give a portfolio with zero risk. In this case, it is $w_1 = 0.412$ and $w_2 = 0.588$.

A THREE-ASSET PORTFOLIO

A demonstration of what occurs with a three-asset portfolio is useful because it shows the dynamics of the portfolio process when assets are added. It also shows the rapid growth in the computations required, which is why we will stop at three!

In this example, we will combine three asset classes we have been discussing: stocks, bonds, and cash equivalents.[10] We will assume the following characteristics:

Asset Classes	$E(R_i)$	$E(\sigma_i)$	w_i
Stocks (S)	0.12	0.20	0.60
Bonds (B)	0.08	0.10	0.30
Cash equivalent (C)	0.04	0.03	0.10

The correlations are

$$r_{S,B} = 0.25; \quad r_{S,C} = -0.08; \quad r_{B,C} = 0.15$$

Given the weights specified, the $E(R_{port})$ is

$$E(R_{port}) = (0.60)(0.12) + (0.30)(0.08) + (0.10)(0.04)$$
$$= (0.072 + 0.024 + 0.004) = 0.100 = 10.00\%$$

When we apply the generalized formula from equation 8.6 to the expected standard deviation of a three-asset portfolio, it is

8.8 $$\sigma_{port}^2 = (w_S^2 \sigma_S^2 + w_B^2 \sigma_B^2 + w_C^2 \sigma_C^2)$$
$$+ (2 w_S w_B \sigma_S \sigma_B r_{S,B} + 2 w_S w_C \sigma_S \sigma_C r_{S,C} + 2 w_B w_C \sigma_B \sigma_C r_{B,C})$$

From the characteristics specified, the standard deviation of this three-asset-class portfolio (σ_{port}) would be

$$\sigma_{port}^2 = [(0.6)^2(0.20)^2 + (0.3)^2(0.10)^2 + (0.1)^2(0.03)^2]$$
$$+ \{[2(0.6)(0.3)(0.20)(0.10)(0.25)] + [2(0.6)(0.1)(0.20)(0.03)(-0.08)]$$
$$+ [2(0.3)(0.1)(0.10)(0.03)(0.15)]\}$$
$$= [0.015309 + (0.0018) + (-0.0000576) + (0.000027)]$$
$$= 0.0170784$$
$$\sigma_{port} = (0.0170784)^{1/2} = 0.1306 = 13.06\%$$

---

[10]The asset allocation articles regularly contained in *The Wall Street Journal* generally refer to these three asset classes.

ESTIMATION ISSUES

It is important to keep in mind that the results of this portfolio asset allocation depend on the accuracy of the statistical inputs. In the current instance, this means that for every asset (or asset class) being considered for inclusion in the portfolio, we must estimate its expected returns and standard deviation. We must also estimate the correlation coefficient among the entire set of assets. The number of correlation estimates can be significant—for example, for a portfolio of 100 securities, the number is 4,950 (that is, $99 + 98 + 97 + \cdots$). The potential source of error that arises from these approximations is referred to as *estimation risk*.

We can reduce the number of correlation coefficients that must be estimated by assuming that stock returns can be described by a single index market model as follows:

8.9

$$R_i = a_i + b_i R_m + \varepsilon_i$$

where:

b_i = the slope coefficient that relates the returns for security i to the returns for the aggregate stock market

R_m = the returns for the aggregate stock market

If all the securities are similarly related to the market and a slope coefficient b_i is derived for each one, it can be shown that the correlation coefficient between two securities i and j is

8.10

$$r_{ij} = b_i b_j \frac{\sigma_m^2}{\sigma_i \sigma_j}$$

where:

σ_m^2 = the variance of returns for the aggregate stock market

This reduces the number of estimates from 4,950 to 100—that is, once we have derived a slope estimate b_i for each security, we can compute the correlation estimates. Keep in mind that this assumes that the single index market model provides a good estimate of security returns.

THE EFFICIENT FRONTIER

If we examined different two-asset combinations and derived the curves assuming all the possible weights, we would have a graph like that in Exhibit 8.14. The envelope curve that contains the best of all these possible combinations is referred to as the *efficient frontier*. Specifically, the efficient frontier represents that set of portfolios that has the maximum rate of return for every given level of risk or the minimum risk for every level of return. An example of such a frontier is shown in Exhibit 8.15. Every portfolio that lies on the efficient frontier has either a higher rate of return for equal risk or lower risk for an equal rate of return than some portfolio beneath the frontier. Thus, we would say that portfolio A in Exhibit 8.15 *dominates* portfolio C because it has an equal rate of return but substantially less risk. Similarly, portfolio B dominates portfolio C because it has equal risk but a higher expected rate of return. Because of the benefits of diversification among imperfectly correlated assets, we would expect the efficient frontier to be made up of *portfolios* of investments rather than individual securities. Two possible exceptions arise at the end points, which represent the asset with the highest return and the asset with the lowest risk.

As an investor, you will target a point along the efficient frontier based on your *utility function,* which reflects your attitude toward risk. No portfolio on the efficient frontier can

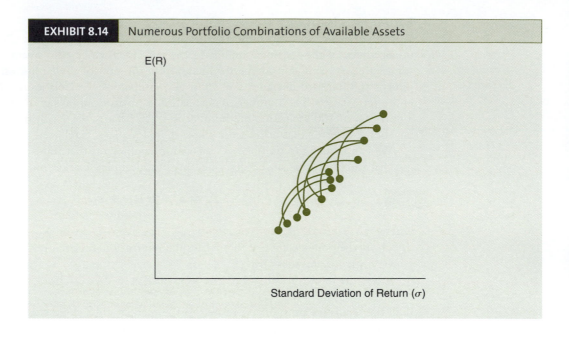

EXHIBIT 8.14 Numerous Portfolio Combinations of Available Assets

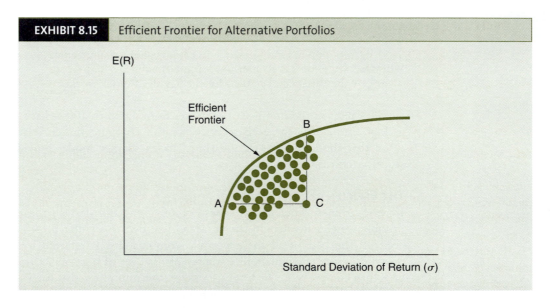

EXHIBIT 8.15 Efficient Frontier for Alternative Portfolios

dominate any other portfolio on the efficient frontier. All of these portfolios have different return and risk measures, with expected rates of return that increase with higher risk.

THE EFFICIENT FRONTIER AND INVESTOR UTILITY

The curve in Exhibit 8.15 shows that the slope of the efficient frontier curve decreases steadily as we move upward. This implies that adding equal increments of risk as we move

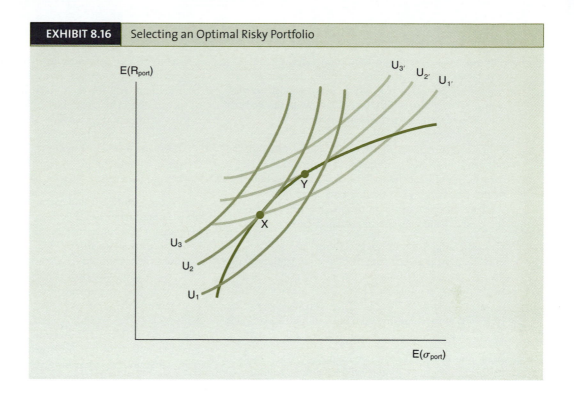

EXHIBIT 8.16   Selecting an Optimal Risky Portfolio

up the efficient frontier gives diminishing increments of expected return. To evaluate this situation, we calculate the slope of the efficient frontier as follows:

8.11

$$\frac{\Delta E\,(R_{port})}{\Delta E\,(\sigma_{port})}$$

An individual investor's utility curves specify the tradeoffs he or she is willing to make between expected return and risk. In conjunction with the efficient frontier, these utility curves determine which *particular* portfolio on the efficient frontier best suits an individual investor. Two investors will choose the same portfolio from the efficient set only if their utility curves are identical.

Exhibit 8.16 shows two sets of utility curves along with an efficient frontier of investments. The curves labeled U_1, U_2, and U_3 are for a strongly risk-averse investor. These utility curves are quite steep, indicating that the investor will not tolerate much additional risk to obtain additional returns. The investor is equally disposed toward any $E(R)$, $E(\sigma)$ combinations along the specific utility curve U_1.

The curves labeled $(U_{3'}\ U_{2'}\ U_{1'})$ characterize a less risk-averse investor. Such an investor is willing to tolerate a bit more risk to get a higher expected return.

The *optimal portfolio* is the efficient portfolio that has the highest utility for a given investor. It lies at the point of tangency between the efficient frontier and the U_1 curve with the highest possible utility. A conservative investor's highest utility is at point X in Exhibit 8.16, where the curve U_2 just touches the efficient frontier. A less risk-averse investor's highest utility occurs at point Y, which represents a portfolio on the efficient frontier with higher expected returns and higher risk than the portfolio at X.

Summary

- The basic Markowitz portfolio model derives the expected rate of return for a portfolio of assets and a measure of expected risk, which is the standard deviation of expected rate of return. Markowitz showed that the expected rate of return of a portfolio is the weighted average of the expected return for the individual investments in the portfolio. The standard deviation of a portfolio is a function not only of the standard deviations for the individual investments but *also* of the covariance between the rates of return for all the pairs of assets in the portfolio. In a large portfolio, these covariances are the important factors.

- Different weights or amounts of a portfolio held in various assets yield a curve of potential combinations. Correlation coefficients among assets are the critical factor to consider when selecting investments. Investors can maintain their rate of return while reducing the risk level of their portfolio by combining assets or portfolios that have low-positive or negative correlation.

- Assuming numerous assets and a multitude of combination curves, the efficient frontier is the envelope curve that encompasses all of the best combinations. It defines the set of portfolios that has the highest expected return for each given level of risk or the minimum risk for each given level of return. From this set of dominant portfolios, investors select the one that lies at the point of tangency between the efficient frontier and their highest utility curve. Because risk–return utility functions differ, the point of tangency and, therefore, the portfolio choice will differ among investors.

At this point, you understand that an optimum portfolio is a combination of investments, each having desirable individual risk–return characteristics that also fit together based on their correlations. This deeper understanding of portfolio theory should lead you to reflect back on our earlier discussion of global investing. Because many foreign stock and bond investments provide superior rates of return compared with U.S. securities *and* have low correlations with portfolios of U.S. stocks and bonds (as shown in Chapter 7), including these foreign securities in your portfolio will help you to reduce the overall risk of your portfolio while possibly increasing your rate of return.

Investments Online

By seeking to operate on the efficient frontier, portfolio managers try to minimize risk for a certain level of return, or maximize return for a given level of risk. Software programs called optimizers are used by portfolio managers to determine the shape of the efficient frontier as well as to determine some of the portfolios that lie on it. In addition to optimizers, financial planners use information on past returns and manager performance to make recommendations to their clients. Some interesting Web sites for money managers include:

http://www.pionline.com This is the home page for *Pensions & Investments,* a newspaper for money managers. Items on the home page include links to news of interest to managers, ePIPER performance data on a number of equity, fixed-income, real estate, and global portfolios from money manager and pension funds. The site also contains many links to organizations such as central banks, consultants, and sellers of investment-related products.

http://www.investmentnews.com *Investment News* is a sister publication to *Pensions & Investments,* with a focus toward the financial advisor. This site includes information on financial planning, the mutual fund industry, regulation, equity performance, and industry trends.

Software for creating efficient frontiers is available from firms such as Ibbotson Associates (**http://www.ibbotson.com**), Zephyr Associates (**http://www.styleadvisor.com**), Wagner Associates (**http://www.wagner.com**), and Efficient Solutions, Inc. (**http://www.effisols.com**).

QUESTIONS

1. Why do most investors hold diversified portfolios?
2. What is covariance, and why is it important in portfolio theory?
3. Why do most assets of the same type show positive covariances of returns with each other? Would you expect positive covariances of returns between *different* types of assets such as returns on Treasury bills, General Electric common stock, and commercial real estate? Why or why not?
4. What is the relationship between covariance and the correlation coefficient?
5. Explain the shape of the efficient frontier.
6. Draw a properly labeled graph of the Markowitz efficient frontier. Describe the efficient frontier in exact terms. Discuss the concept of dominant portfolios, and show an example of one on your graph.
7. Assume you want to run a computer program to derive the efficient frontier for your feasible set of stocks. What information must you input to the program?
8. Why are investors' utility curves important in portfolio theory?
9. Explain how a given investor chooses an optimal portfolio. Will this choice always be a diversified portfolio, or could it be a single asset? Explain your answer.
10. Assume that you and a business associate develop an efficient frontier for a set of investments. Why might the two of you select different portfolios on the frontier?
11. Draw a hypothetical graph of an efficient frontier of U.S. common stocks. On the same graph, draw an efficient frontier assuming the inclusion of U.S. bonds as well. Finally, on the same graph, draw an efficient frontier that includes U.S. common stocks, U.S. bonds, and stocks and bonds from around the world. Discuss the differences in these frontiers.

12. Stocks L, M, and N each have the same expected return and standard deviation. The correlation coefficients between each pair of these stocks are:

L and M correlation coefficient = +0.8

L and N correlation coefficient = +0.2

M and N correlation coefficient = −0.4

Given these correlations, a portfolio constructed of which pair of stocks will have the lowest standard deviation? Explain.

13. *CFA Examination Level II* **CFA**
A three-asset portfolio has the following characteristics.

Asset	Expected Return	Expected Standard Deviation	Weight
X	0.15	0.22	0.50
Y	0.10	0.08	0.40
Z	0.06	0.03	0.10

The expected return on this three-asset portfolio is
a. 10.3%.
b. 11.0%.
c. 12.1%.
d. 14.8%. (2 minutes)

14. *CFA Examination Level II* **CFA**
An investor is considering adding another investment to a portfolio. To achieve the maximum diversification benefits, the investor should add, if possible, an investment that has which of the following correlation coefficients with the other investments in the portfolio?
a. −1.0
b. −0.5
c. 0.0
d. +1.0 (1 minute)

PROBLEMS

1. Considering the world economic outlook for the coming year and estimates of sales and earning for the pharmaceutical industry, you expect the rate of return for Lauren Labs common stock to range between −20 percent and +40 percent with the following probabilities.

Probability	Possible Returns
0.10	−0.20
0.15	−0.05
0.20	0.10
0.25	0.15
0.20	0.20
0.10	0.40

Compute the expected rate of return $E(R_i)$ for Lauren Labs.

2. Given the following market values of stocks in your portfolio and their expected rates of return, what is the expected rate of return for your common stock portfolio?

Stock	Market Value ($ mil.)	E(R_i)
Phillips Petroleum	$15,000	0.14
Starbucks	17,000	−0.04
International Paper	32,000	0.18
Intel	23,000	0.16
Walgreens	7,000	0.12

3. The following are the monthly rates of return for Madison Corp. and for General Electric during a six-month period.

Month	Madison Corp.	General Electric
1	−0.04	0.07
2	0.06	−0.02
3	−0.07	−0.10
4	0.12	0.15
5	−0.02	−0.06
6	0.05	0.02

Compute the following.
   a. Average monthly rate of return $\overline{R_i}$ for each stock
   b. Standard deviation of returns for each stock
   c. Covariance between the rates of return
   d. The correlation coefficient between the rates of return

   What level of correlation did you expect? How did your expectations compare with the computed correlation? Would these two stocks offer a good chance for diversification? Why or why not?

4. You are considering two assets with the following characteristics.

   $E(R_1) = 0.15$ $E(\sigma_1) = 0.10$ $w_1 = 0.5$
   $E(R_2) = 0.20$ $E(\sigma_2) = 0.20$ $w_2 = 0.5$

   Compute the mean and standard deviation of two portfolios if $r_{1,2} = 0.40$ and -0.60, respectively. Plot the two portfolios on a risk–return graph and briefly explain the results.

5. Given: $E(R_1) = 0.10$
   $E(R_2) = 0.15$
   $E(\sigma_1) = 0.03$
   $E(\sigma_2) = 0.05$

   Calculate the expected returns and expected standard deviations of a two-stock portfolio in which stock 1 has a weight of 60 percent under the following conditions.
   a. $r_{1,2} = 1.00$
   b. $r_{1,2} = 0.75$
   c. $r_{1,2} = 0.25$
   d. $r_{1,2} = 0.00$
   e. $r_{1,2} = -0.25$
   f. $r_{1,2} = -0.75$
   g. $r_{1,2} = -1.00$

6. Given: $E(R_1) = 0.12$
   $E(R_2) = 0.16$

   $E(\sigma_1) = 0.04$
   $E(\sigma_2) = 0.06$

   Calculate the expected returns and expected standard deviations of a two-stock portfolio having a correlation coefficient of 0.70 under the following conditions.
   a. $w_1 = 1.00$
   b. $w_1 = 0.75$
   c. $w_1 = 0.50$
   d. $w_1 = 0.25$
   e. $w_1 = 0.05$

   Plot the results on a return–risk graph. Without calculations, draw in what the curve would look like first if the correlation coefficient had been 0.00 and then if it had been −0.70.

7. The following are monthly percentage price changes for four market indexes.

Month	DJIA	S&P 500	Russell 2000	Nikkei
1	0.03	0.02	0.04	0.04
2	0.07	0.06	0.10	−0.02
3	−0.02	−0.01	−0.04	0.07
4	0.01	0.03	0.03	0.02
5	0.05	0.04	0.11	0.02
6	−0.06	−0.04	−0.08	0.06

   Compute the following.
   a. Average monthly rate of return for each index
   b. Standard deviation for each index
   c. Covariance between the rates of return for the following indexes:
      DJIA–S&P 500
      S&P 500–Russell 2000
      S&P 500–Nikkei
      Russell 2000–Nikkei
   d. The correlation coefficients for the same four combinations
   e. Using the answers from parts (a), (b), and (d), calculate the expected return and standard deviation of a portfolio consisting of equal parts of (1) the S&P and the Russell 2000 and (2) the S&P and the Nikkei. Discuss the two portfolios.

8. The standard deviation of Shamrock Corp. stock is 19 percent. The standard deviation of Duke Co. stock is 14 percent. The covariance between these two stocks is 100. What is the correlation between Shamrock and Duke stock?

WEB EXERCISE

1. Read and summarize the lead articles from the past two issues of *Efficient Frontier* found at *http://www.efficientfrontier.com*.

SPREADSHEET EXERCISES

1. Using the indexes available from *http://www.barra.com,* compute correlations between the S&P 500, S&P Mid-Cap 400, and S&P Small-Cap 600 for the past five years. For the pair with the highest correlation, construct an equal-weighted portfolio (that is, each of the two indexes are weighted by 0.50). Construct the portfolio average return and standard deviation over the most recent five-year time frame. Do the same for the pair with the lowest correlation. Compute a weighted-average standard deviation for each portfolio, that is, 0.50 × standard deviation of the first index + 0.50 × standard deviation of second index. What is the difference between the portfolio standard deviations and the weighted-average standard deviations? What explains the difference?

2. For a pair of indexes from *http://www.msci.com,* compute the portfolio return and standard deviation for different weighting schemes: 10 percent/90 percent, 20 percent/80 percent, 30 percent/70 percent, and so on. Graph the risk–return combinations.

3. Repeat Exercise 2, only now change the correlation coefficient between the two indexes. Use the formula to compute the portfolio standard deviation using the different weights in Exercise 2 and a correlation coefficient of
   a. −0.80.
   b. −0.25.
   c. 0.00.
   d. How do the graphs of Exercise 2 and 3 differ?

4. Excel can assist the construction of efficient frontiers. Research how to use the Solver function of Excel (it should appear under Tools of the Excel bar. If not, click on Tools and click on Add-Ins. Scroll down and click the box next to "Solver Add-in." This should add Solver to the list of options on the Tools menu).

REFERENCES

Elton, Edwin J., Martin J. Gruber, Stephen J. Brown, and William N. Goetzmann. *Modern Portfolio Theory and Investment Analysis,* 6th ed. New York: John Wiley & Sons, 2003.

Farrell, James L. Jr. *Portfolio Management: Theory and Application,* 2d ed. New York: McGraw-Hill, 1997.

Maginn, John L., and Donald L. Tuttle, Eds. *Managing Investment Portfolios: A Dynamic Process,* 2nd ed. Sponsored by The Institute of Chartered Financial Analysts. Boston: Warren, Gorham and Lamont, 1990.

Markowitz, Harry. "Portfolio Selection." *Journal of Finance* 7, no. 1 (March 1952).

Markowitz, Harry. *Portfolio Selection: Efficient Diversification of Investments.* New York: John Wiley & Sons, 1959.

THOMSON ONE
Business School Edition

1. Compare and contrast the performance over the past six months of large-capitalization U.S. stocks (S&P 500) and small-capitalization U.S. stocks (S&P 600 small-cap). Compute daily returns for each series. What is the average daily return and variance for each series? What is the covariance and correlation between the two series?

2. If we assume the behavior of the stock markets in the near future will be similar to their behavior in the recent past, what is the expected return and standard deviation of a portfolio comprised of:
   a. 50 percent large-cap and 50 percent small-cap stocks?
   b. 75 percent large-cap and 25 percent small-cap stocks?
   c. 25 percent small-cap and 75 percent large-cap stocks?

3. Collect daily data for the past six months for the MSCI index for Germany. Compute average daily return, variance, and correlation with the S&P 500 and S&P 600. What is the expected return and standard deviation of a portfolio comprised of one-third S&P 500, one-third S&P 600, and one-third of the MSCI Germany index?

Glossary

Correlation coefficient A standarized measure of the relationship between two series that ranges from −1.00 to +1.00.

Covariance A measure of the degree to which two variables, such as rates of return for investment assets, move together over time relative to their individual mean returns.

Efficient frontier The curve that defines the set of portfolios with the maximum rate of return for every given level of risk or the minimum risk for a given rate of return.

Optimal portfolio The efficient portfolio with the highest utility for a given investor, found by the point of tangency between the efficient frontier and the investor's highest utility curve.

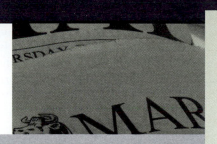

An Introduction to Asset Pricing Models

B uilding on the Markowitz portfolio theory, two major theories have been put forth to derive models for the valuation of risky assets—that is, asset pricing models. In this chapter we introduce these two models. We first provide background on asset pricing models because the risk measures implied by these models are a necessary input for our subsequent discussion on risky asset valuation. The bulk of the presentation concerns capital market theory and the capital asset pricing model (CAPM) that was developed almost concurrently by three individuals. Subsequent asset valuation models consider several variables that affect an asset's required rate of return. We will discuss this theory and the implied multifactor pricing models.

Capital Market Theory: An Overview

Because capital market theory builds on portfolio theory, we begin where our discussion of the Markowitz efficient frontier ended in Chapter 8. We assume that you have examined the set of risky assets and derived the aggregate efficient frontier. Further, we assume that you (and all other investors) want to maximize your utility in terms of risk and return, so you will choose portfolios of risky assets on the efficient frontier at points where your utility maps are tangent to this aggregate efficient frontier, as was shown in Exhibit 8.16. When you make your investment decision in this manner, you are called a *Markowitz efficient investor*.

Capital market theory extends portfolio theory by adding the very important assumption that a risk-free asset exists and then considering the implication of this for asset valuation. This leads to a model for pricing all risky assets. The final product, the *capital asset pricing model (CAPM),* allows us to determine the required rate of return for any risky asset. The CAPM is a single-factor model—that is, it assumes that the risk of an asset is determined by a single variable, its beta.

Notably, assuming the existence of a risk-free asset has significant implications for alternative risk–return combinations. In our discussion we assume a central portfolio of risky assets on the efficient frontier, which we call the *market portfolio*. We will discuss the market portfolio and what it implies regarding different types of risk.

We will also consider which types of risk are relevant to an investor who believes in capital market theory. Having defined a measure of risk that considers the implications of both portfolio theory and capital market theory, we consider how to determine the required rate of return on an investment. We can then compare this required rate of return to our estimate of the asset's expected rate of return during the investment horizon to determine whether the asset is undervalued or overvalued. In this discussion we will demonstrate how to calculate the risk measure implied by capital market theory.

Finally, we will discuss a set of alternative asset pricing models that contend that the required rate of return for a risky asset is a function of *multiple* factors. We will briefly demonstrate how to evaluate the risk of an asset and determine its required rate of return using multifactor models.

BACKGROUND FOR CAPITAL MARKET THEORY

When dealing with any theory in science, economics, or finance, it is necessary to articulate a set of assumptions that specify how the theory expects the world to act. This allows the theoretician to concentrate on developing a theory that explains how some facet of the world will respond to changes in the environment. Following are the main assumptions that underlie the development of capital market theory.

Assumptions of Capital Market Theory

Because capital market theory builds on the Markowitz portfolio model, it requires the same assumptions, along with some additional ones:

1. All investors are Markowitz efficient investors who want to target points on the efficient frontier. The exact location on the efficient frontier and, therefore, the specific portfolio selected, will depend on the individual investor's risk–return utility function.
2. Investors can borrow or lend any amount of money at the risk-free rate of return (RFR). Clearly, it is always possible to lend money at the nominal risk-free rate by buying risk-free securities such as government T-bills. It is not always possible to borrow at this risk-free rate, but we will see that assuming a higher borrowing rate does not change the general results.
3. All investors have homogeneous expectations; that is, they estimate identical probability distributions for future rates of return. Again, this assumption can be relaxed. As long as the differences in expectations are not vast, their effects are minor.
4. All investors have the same one-period time horizon such as one month, six months, or one year. The model will be developed for a single hypothetical period, and its results could be affected by a different assumption. A difference in the time horizon would require investors to derive risk measures and risk-free assets that are consistent with their investment horizons.
5. All investments are infinitely divisible, which means that it is possible to buy or sell fractional shares of any asset or portfolio. This assumption allows us to discuss investment alternatives as continuous curves. Changing it would have little impact on the theory.
6. There are no taxes or transaction costs involved in buying or selling assets. This is a reasonable assumption in many instances. Neither pension funds nor religious groups have to pay taxes, and the transaction costs for most financial institutions are less than 1 percent on

most financial instruments. Again, relaxing this assumption modifies the results, but it does not change the basic theory.

7. Either there is no inflation or any change in interest rates, or inflation is fully anticipated. This is a reasonable initial assumption, and it can be modified.

8. Capital markets are in equilibrium. This means that we begin with all investments properly priced in line with their risk levels.

You may consider some of these assumptions unrealistic and wonder how useful a theory we can derive with these assumptions. In this regard, two points are important. First, as mentioned, relaxing many of these assumptions would have only a minor effect on the model and would not change its main implications or conclusions. Second, a theory should never be judged on the basis of its assumptions, but rather on how well it explains and helps predict behavior in the real world. If this theory and the model it implies help explain the rates of return on a wide variety of risky assets, it is useful, even if some of its assumptions are unrealistic. Success in explaining real-world relationships implies that the questionable assumptions must be unimportant to the ultimate objective of the model, which is to explain the pricing and rates of return on assets.

Development of Capital Market Theory Following the development of the Markowitz portfolio model, several authors considered the implications of assuming the existence of a *risk-free asset,* that is, an asset with *zero variance.* This concept is the major factor that allowed portfolio theory to develop into capital market theory. As we will show, such an asset would have zero correlation with all other risky assets and would provide the *risk-free rate of return (RFR).* It would lie on the vertical axis of a portfolio graph.

This assumption allows us to derive a generalized theory of capital asset pricing under conditions of uncertainty from the Markowitz portfolio theory. This achievement is generally attributed to William Sharpe, for which he received the Nobel prize, but Lintner and Mossin derived similar theories independently.[1] Consequently, the literature also has references to the Sharpe–Lintner–Mossin (SLM) capital asset pricing model.

RISK-FREE ASSET

As noted, the assumption of a risk-free asset in the economy is critical to asset pricing theory. Therefore, we need to explain the meaning of a risk-free asset and show the effect on the risk and return measures when this risk-free asset is combined with a portfolio on the Markowitz efficient frontier.

A *risky asset* is one from which future returns are uncertain. In previous chapters we measured this uncertainty by the variance, or standard deviation of returns. Because the expected return on a risk-free asset is entirely certain, the standard deviation of its return is zero ($\sigma_{RF} = 0$). The rate of return earned on such an asset should be the risk-free rate of return (RFR), which, as we discussed in Chapter 2, should equal the expected long-run growth rate of the economy with an adjustment for short-run liquidity. We will now see what happens when we introduce this risk-free asset into the risky world of the Markowitz portfolio model.

---

[1] William F. Sharpe, "Capital Asset Prices: A Theory of Market Equilibrium Under Conditions of Risk," *Journal of Finance* 19, no. 3 (September 1964): 425–442; John Lintner, "Security Prices, Risk and Maximal Gains from Diversification," *Journal of Finance* 20, no. 4 (December 1965): 587–615; and J. Mossin, "Equilibrium in a Capital Asset Market," *Econometrica* 34, no. 4 (October 1966): 768–783.

Covariance with a Risk-Free Asset Recall that the covariance between two sets of returns is

$$\text{9.1} \quad \text{Cov}_{ij} = \frac{\sum_{i=1}^{n} [R_i - E(R_i)][R_j - E(R_j)]}{n - 1}$$

Because the returns for the risk-free asset are certain, $\sigma_{\text{RF}} = 0$, which means $R_i = E(R_i)$ during all periods. Thus, $[R_i - E(R_i)]$ will also equal zero, and the product of this expression and any other expression will equal zero. Consequently, the covariance of the risk-free asset with any risky asset or portfolio of assets will always equal zero. Similarly, the correlation between any risky asset j and the risk-free asset RF would be zero because it is equal to

$$\text{9.2} \quad r_{\text{RF},j} = \frac{\text{COV}_{\text{RF},j}}{\sigma_{\text{RF}}\sigma_j}$$

Combining a Risk-Free Asset with a Risky Portfolio What happens to the average rate of return and the standard deviation of returns when we combine a risk-free asset with a portfolio of risky assets such as those that exist on the Markowitz efficient frontier?

Expected return. Like the expected return for a portfolio of two risky assets, the expected rate of return for a portfolio that includes a risk-free asset is the weighted average of the two returns:

$$\text{9.3} \quad E(R_{\text{port}}) = w_{\text{RF}}(\text{RFR}) + (1 - w_{\text{RF}})E(R_j)$$

where:

    w_{RF} = the weight of the risk-free asset, or the proportion of the portfolio invested in the risk-free asset

    $E(R_j)$ = the expected rate of return on risky portfolio j

Standard deviation. Recall from Chapter 8 that the expected variance for a two-asset portfolio is

$$\text{9.4} \quad E(\sigma_{\text{port}}^2) = w_1^2\sigma_1^2 + w_2^2\sigma_2^2 + 2w_1w_2r_{1,2}\sigma_1\sigma_2$$

If we substitute the risk-free asset for security 1 and the risky-asset portfolio for security 2, this formula would become

$$\text{9.5} \quad E(\sigma_{\text{port}}^2) = w_{\text{RF}}^2\sigma_{\text{RF}}^2 + (1 - w_{\text{RF}})^2\sigma_j^2 + 2w_{\text{RF}}(1 - w_{\text{RF}})r_{\text{RF},j}\sigma_{\text{RF}}\sigma_j$$

We know that the variance of the risk-free asset is zero, that is, $\sigma_{\text{RF}}^2 = 0$. Because the correlation between the risk-free asset and any risky asset j is also zero, the factor $r_{\text{RF},j}$ in equation 9.5 also equals zero. Therefore, any component of the variance formula that has either of these terms will equal zero. When we make these adjustments, the formula becomes

$$\text{9.6} \quad E(\sigma_{\text{port}}^2) = (1 - w_{\text{RF}})^2\sigma_j^2$$

The standard deviation of the portfolio is

$$\text{9.7} \quad E(\sigma_{\text{port}}) = \sqrt{(1 - w_{\text{RF}})^2\sigma_j^2}$$
$$= (1 - w_{\text{RF}})\sigma_j$$

Therefore, the standard deviation of a portfolio that combines the risk-free asset with risky assets is *the linear proportion of the standard deviation of a portfolio of risky assets.*

EXHIBIT 9.1	Portfolio Possibilities Combining the Risk-Free Asset and Risky-Asset Portfolios on the Efficient Frontier

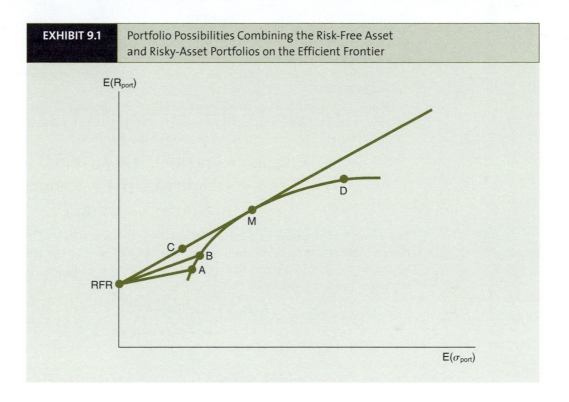

The risk–return combination. Because both the expected return *and* the standard deviation of return for such a portfolio are linear combinations, a graph of possible portfolio returns and risks looks like a straight line between the two assets. Exhibit 9.1 shows a graph depicting portfolio possibilities when a risk-free asset is combined with various portfolios of risky assets on the Markowitz efficient frontier.

We can attain any point along the straight line RFR-A by investing some portion of the portfolio in the risk-free asset w_{RF} and the remainder $(1 - w_{RF})$ in the risky-asset portfolio at point A on the efficient frontier. This set of portfolio possibilities dominates all the risky-asset portfolios on the efficient frontier below point A because some portfolio along line RFR–A has equal variance but a higher rate of return than the portfolio on the original efficient frontier. Likewise, we can attain any point along the line RFR–B by investing in some combination of the risk-free asset and the portfolio of risky assets at point B. Again, these potential combinations dominate all portfolio possibilities on the original efficient frontier below point B (including line RFR–A).

We can draw further lines from the RFR to the efficient frontier at higher and higher points until we reach the point where the line is tangent to the frontier, which occurs in Exhibit 9.1 at point M. The set of portfolio possibilities along line RFR–M dominates *all* portfolios below point M. For example, we could attain a risk and return combination between the RFR and point M (point C) by investing one-half of the portfolio in the risk-free asset (that is, lending money at the RFR) and the other half in the risky-asset portfolio at point M. This portfolio C would dominate the portfolios below it on lines RFR–A and RFR–B.

Risk–return possibilities with leverage. An investor may want to attain a higher expected return than is available at point M in exchange for accepting higher risk. One alternative would be to invest in one of the risky-asset portfolios on the efficient frontier beyond point M, such as the portfolio at point D. A second alternative is to add *leverage* to the portfolio by *borrowing* money at the risk-free rate and investing the proceeds of the loan in the risky-asset portfolio at point M. What effect would this leverage have on the return and risk for the portfolio?

If the investor borrows an amount equal to 50 percent of the original wealth at the risk-free rate, w_{RF} will not be a positive fraction, but rather a negative 50 percent ($w_{RF} = -0.50$). The effect on the expected return for the portfolio is

$$E(R_{port}) = w_{RF}(RFR) + (1 - w_{RF})E(R_M)$$
$$= -0.50(RFR) + [1 - (-0.50)]E(R_M)$$
$$= -0.50(RFR) + 1.50E(R_M)$$

The return will increase in a *linear* fashion along the line RFR–M because the gross return increases by 50 percent, but the investor must pay interest at the RFR on the money borrowed. For example, assume that $E(RFR) = 0.06$ and $E(R_M) = 0.12$. The return on the leveraged portfolio would be

$$E(R_{port}) = -0.50(0.06) + 1.5(0.12)$$
$$= -0.03 + 0.18$$
$$= 0.15$$

The effect on the standard deviation of the leveraged portfolio is similar.

$$E(\sigma_{port}) = (1 - w_{RF})\sigma_M$$
$$= [1 - (-0.50)]\sigma_M = 1.50\sigma_M$$

where:

σ_M = the standard deviation of portfolio M

Therefore, *both return and risk increase in a linear fashion along the original line RFR–M,* and this extension dominates everything below the line on the original efficient frontier. Thus, we have a new efficient frontier: the straight line from the RFR tangent to point M. This line is the *capital market line (CML)* and is shown in Exhibit 9.2.

Interactive e-lectures

For more explanation and an animated example of the capital market line, go to: http://reillyxtra.swlearning.com.

In our discussion of portfolio theory (Chapter 8), we stated that when two assets are perfectly correlated the set of portfolio possibilities falls along a straight line. Therefore, because the CML is a straight line, we infer that all the portfolios on the CML are perfectly positively correlated. This positive correlation appeals to our intuition because all these portfolios on the CML combine the risky-asset portfolio M and the risk-free asset. You either invest part of your portfolio in the risk-free asset (i.e., you *lend* at the RFR) and the rest in the risky-asset portfolio M, or you *borrow* at the risk-free rate and invest these funds in the risky-asset portfolio M. In either case, all the variability comes from the risky-asset portfolio M. The only difference between the portfolios on the CML is the proportion of the risky-asset portfolio in the total portfolio—i.e., the optimal risky-asset portfolio remains the same regardless of the investor's target risk and return.

THE MARKET PORTFOLIO

Because portfolio M lies at the point of tangency, it has the highest portfolio possibility line, and everyone will want to invest in portfolio M and borrow or lend to be somewhere on the CML (where depends on the investor's risk–return preference). This portfolio must,

EXHIBIT 9.2	Derivation of Capital Market Line Assuming Lending or Borrowing at the Risk-Free Rate

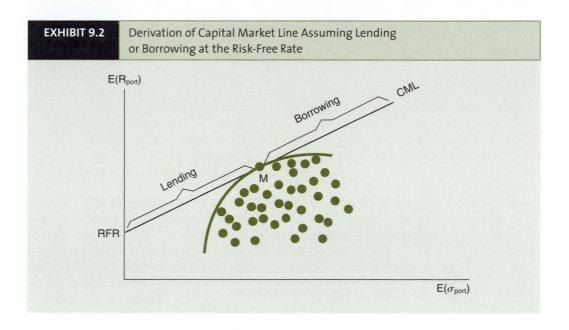

therefore, include *all risky assets.* If a risky asset were not in this portfolio in which everyone wants to invest, there would be no demand for it and therefore it would have no value.

Because the market is in equilibrium, it is also necessary to include all assets in this portfolio in *proportion to their market value.* If, for example, an asset accounts for a higher proportion of portfolio M than its market value justifies, excess demand for this asset will increase its price until its relative market value becomes consistent with its proportion in portfolio M.

This portfolio that includes all risky assets is referred to as the *market portfolio.* It includes not only common stocks, but *all* risky assets, such as non-U.S. stocks, U.S. and non-U.S. bonds, options, real estate, coins, stamps, art, or antiques. Because the market portfolio contains all risky assets, it is a *completely diversified portfolio,* which means that all the risk unique to individual assets in the portfolio is diversified away. Specifically, the unique risk (caused by microeconomic factors) of any single asset is offset by the unique variability of all the other assets in the portfolio.

This unique (diversifiable) risk is also referred to as *unsystematic risk.* This implies that only *systematic risk,* which is defined as the variability in all risky assets caused by macroeconomic variables, remains in the market portfolio. This systematic risk, measured by the standard deviation of returns of the market portfolio, can change over time if and when there are changes in the macroeconomic variables that affect the valuation of all risky assets.[2] Examples would be variability of growth in the money supply, interest rate volatility, and variability in such factors as industrial production, corporate earnings, and corporate

[2]For an analysis of changes in stock-market and bond-market return volatility, see G. William Schwert, "Why Does Stock Market Volatility Change over Time?" *Journal of Finance* 44, no. 5 (December 1989): 1115–1153; Peter S. Spiro, "The Impact of Interest Rate Changes on Stock Price Volatility," *Journal of Portfolio Management* 16, no. 2 (Winter 1990): 63–68; R. R. Officer, "The Variability of the Market Factor of the New York Stock Exchange," *Journal of Business* 46, no. 3 (July 1973): 434–453; and Frank K. Reilly, David J. Wright, and Kam C. Chan, "Bond Market Volatility Compared to Stock Market Volatility," *Journal of Portfolio Management* 27, no. 1 (Fall 2000): 82–92.

cash flow. We will discuss models that take micro- and macroeconomic factors into account later in the chapter.

How to Measure Diversification All portfolios on the CML are perfectly positively correlated, which means that all portfolios on the CML are perfectly correlated with the completely diversified market portfolio M. This implies a measure of complete diversification.[3] Specifically, a completely diversified portfolio would have a correlation with the market portfolio of +1.00. This is logical because complete diversification means the elimination of all the unsystematic or unique risk. Once we have eliminated all unsystematic risk, only systematic risk is left, which cannot be diversified away. Therefore, completely diversified portfolios would correlate perfectly with the market portfolio because it has only systematic risk.

Diversification and the Elimination of Unsystematic Risk As discussed in Chapter 8, the purpose of diversification is to reduce the standard deviation of the total portfolio. This assumes imperfect correlations among securities.[4] Ideally, as we add securities, the average covariance for the portfolio declines. An important question is, about how many securities must be included to arrive at a completely diversified portfolio? To discover the answer, we must observe what happens as we increase the sample size of the portfolio by adding securities that have some positive correlation. The typical correlation among U.S. securities is about 0.5 to 0.6.

One study examined the average standard deviation for numerous portfolios of randomly selected stocks of different sample sizes.[5] Specifically, the authors computed the standard deviation for portfolios of increasing numbers up to twenty stocks. The results indicated a large initial impact wherein the major benefits of diversification were achieved rather quickly. Specifically, about 90 percent of the maximum benefit of diversification was derived from portfolios of twelve to eighteen stocks. Exhibit 9.3 shows a graph of the effect. A subsequent study compared the benefits of lower risk from diversification to the added transaction costs with more securities.[6] It concluded that a well-diversified stock portfolio must include at least thirty stocks for a borrowing investor and forty stocks for a lending investor.

An important point to remember is that by adding stocks that are not perfectly correlated with stocks in the portfolio, we can reduce the overall standard deviation of the portfolio, but we *cannot eliminate variability*. The standard deviation of our portfolio will eventually reach the level of the market portfolio, where we will have diversified away all unsystematic risk, but we still have market or systematic risk. We cannot eliminate the variability and uncertainty of macroeconomic factors that affect all risky assets. At the same time (as discussed in Chapter 3), we can attain a lower level of systematic risk by diversifying globally because some of the systematic risk factors in the U.S. market (such as U.S. monetary policy) are not correlated with systematic risk variables in other countries such as Germany and Japan. As a result, if we diversify globally we eventually get down to a world systematic risk level, which will be at a lower level than only U.S. stock systematic risk.

---

[3]James Lorie, "Diversification: Old and New," *Journal of Portfolio Management* 1, no. 2 (Winter 1975): 25–28.

[4]The discussion in Chapter 8 leads one to conclude that securities with negative correlation would be ideal. Although this is true in theory, it is difficult to find such assets in the real world.

[5]John L. Evans and Stephen H. Archer, "Diversification and the Reduction of Dispersion: An Empirical Analysis," *Journal of Finance* 23, no. 5 (December, 1968); 761–767.

[6]Meir Statman, "How Many Stocks Make a Diversified Portfolio?" *Journal of Financial and Quantitative Analysis* 22, no. 3 (September, 1987): 353–363.

EXHIBIT 9.3	Number of Stocks in a Portfolio and the Standard Deviation of Portfolio Return

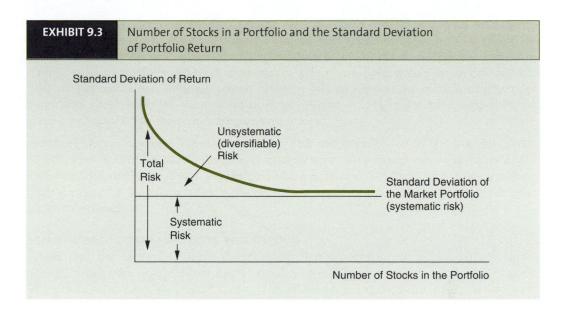

The CML and the Separation Theorem
We have seen that the CML leads all investors to invest in the same risky-asset portfolio M. Individual investors should only differ regarding their position on the CML, which depends on their risk preferences.

In turn, how they get to a point on the CML is based on their *financing decisions.* If you are relatively risk averse, you will lend some part of your portfolio at the RFR by buying some risk-free securities and investing the remainder in the risky-asset market portfolio. For example, you might invest in the portfolio combination at point A in Exhibit 9.4. In contrast, if you are willing to accept more risk, you might borrow funds at the RFR and invest everything (all of your capital plus what you borrowed) in the risky-asset market portfolio, building the portfolio at point B. This financing decision increases your risk but also provides greater returns than the market portfolio. As discussed earlier, because portfolios on the CML dominate other portfolio possibilities, the CML becomes the efficient frontier of portfolios, and investors decide where they want to be along this efficient frontier. This division of the investment decision from the financing decision has been called the *separation theorem*.[7] Specifically, to be somewhere on the CML efficient frontier, you initially decide to invest in the optimum risky-asset market portfolio M. This is your *investment* decision. Subsequently, based on your risk preferences, you make a separate *financing* decision either to borrow or to lend to attain your preferred risk position on the CML.

A Risk Measure for the CML
We now show that the relevant risk measure for risky assets is *their covariance with market portfolio M,* which is referred to as their systematic risk. The importance of this covariance is apparent from two points of view.

First, in discussing the Markowitz portfolio model, we noted that the relevant risk to consider when adding a security to a portfolio is *its average covariance with all other assets in the portfolio.* In this chapter, we have shown that *the only relevant portfolio is portfolio M.* Together, these two findings mean that the only important consideration for any individual

---

[7]James Tobin, "Liquidity Preference as Behavior Towards Risk," *Review of Economic Studies* 25, no. 2 (February 1958): 65–85.

| **EXHIBIT 9.4** | Choice of Optimal Portfolio Combinations on the CML |

risky asset is its average covariance with all the risky assets in portfolio M, or simply, *the asset's covariance with the market portfolio.* This covariance, then, is the relevant risk measure for an individual risky asset.

Second, because all individual risky assets are a part of portfolio M, we can describe their rates of return in relation to the returns for portfolio M using the following linear model:

9.8
$$R_{jt} = a_j + b_j R_{Mt} + \varepsilon$$

where:

R_{jt} = return for asset j during period t
a_j = constant term for asset j
b_j = slope coefficient for asset j
R_{Mt} = return for portfolio M during period t
ε = random error term

The variance of returns for a risky asset could be described as

$$\mathbf{Var}\,(R_{jt}) = \mathbf{Var}\,(a_j + b_j R_{Mt} + \varepsilon)$$

$$= \mathbf{Var}\,(a_j) + \mathbf{Var}\,(b_j R_{Mt}) + \mathbf{Var}\,(\varepsilon)$$

$$= 0 + \mathbf{Var}\,(b_j R_{Mt}) + \mathbf{Var}\,(\varepsilon)$$

Note that $\mathrm{Var}(b_j R_{Mt})$ is the variance of return for an asset related to the variance of the market portfolio return, or the *systematic variance or risk.* Also, $\mathrm{Var}(\varepsilon)$ is the residual variance of return for the individual asset that is not related to the market portfolio. This residual variance is the variability that we have referred to as the unsystematic or *unique risk or variance* because it arises from the unique features of the asset. Therefore,

9.9 $$\text{Var}\,(R_{jt}) = \text{Systematic Variance} + \text{Unsystematic Variance}$$

We know that a completely diversified portfolio such as the market portfolio has had all the unsystematic variance eliminated. Therefore, the unsystematic (unique) variance of an asset is not relevant to investors, because they can and do eliminate it when making an asset part of the market portfolio. Therefore, investors should not expect to receive added returns for assuming this unique risk. Only the systematic variance is relevant because it *cannot* be diversified away since, as we have said, it is caused by macroeconomic factors that affect all risky assets.

The Capital Asset Pricing Model: Expected Return and Risk

Interactive e-lectures

For more explanation and an animated example of the capital asset pricing model, go to: http://reillyxtra .swlearning.com.

Up to this point, we have considered how investors make their portfolio decisions, including the significant effects of a risk-free asset. The existence of this risk-free asset resulted in the derivation of a capital market line (CML) that became the relevant efficient frontier. Because all investors want to be on the CML, an asset's covariance with the market portfolio of risky assets emerged as the relevant risk measure.

Now that we understand this relevant measure of risk, we can use it to determine an appropriate expected rate of return on a risky asset. This step takes us into the *capital asset pricing model (CAPM)*, which is a model that indicates what should be the expected or required rates of return on risky assets. This transition is important because it helps us evaluate an asset by providing an appropriate discount rate to use in any valuation model. Alternatively, if we have already estimated the rate of return, we can compare this *estimated* rate of return to the *required* rate of return implied by the CAPM and determine whether the asset is undervalued, overvalued, or properly valued.

To accomplish the foregoing, we demonstrate the creation of a security market line (SML), which visually represents the relationship between risk and the expected or required rate of return on an asset. The equation of this SML, together with estimates for the return on a risk-free asset and on the market portfolio, can generate expected or required rates of return for any asset based on its systematic risk. After demonstrating this procedure, we will also demonstrate how to calculate the systematic risk variable for a risky asset.

THE SECURITY MARKET LINE (SML)

We know that the relevant risk measure for an individual risky asset is its covariance with the market portfolio (Cov_{jM}). Therefore, we draw the risk–return relationship as shown in Exhibit 9.5 with the systematic covariance variable (Cov_{jM}) as the risk measure.

The return for the market portfolio (R_M) should be consistent with its own risk, which is the covariance of the market with itself. If you recall the formula for covariance, you will see that the covariance of any asset with itself is its variance, $\text{Cov}_{jj} = \sigma_j^2$. In turn, the covariance of the market with itself is the variance of the market rate of return, $\text{Cov}_{MM} = \sigma_M^2$. Therefore, the equation for the risk–return line in Exhibit 9.5 is

9.10 $$E\,(R_j) = \text{RFR} + \frac{R_M - \text{RFR}}{\sigma_M^2}\,(\text{Cov}_{jM})$$

$$= \text{RFR} + \frac{\text{Cov}_{jM}}{\sigma_M^2}\,(R_M - \text{RFR})$$

Defining $\text{Cov}_{jM}/\sigma_M^2$ as beta (β_j), this equation can be stated

9.11 $$E\,(R_j) = \text{RFR} + \beta_j\,(R_M - \text{RFR})$$

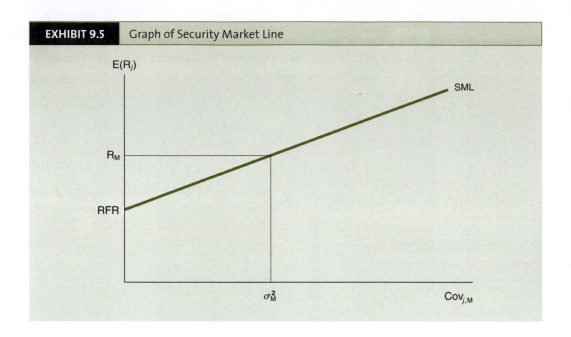

EXHIBIT 9.5 Graph of Security Market Line

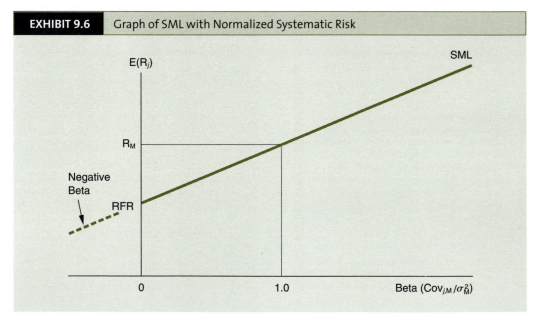

EXHIBIT 9.6 Graph of SML with Normalized Systematic Risk

Beta can be viewed as a *standardized* measure of systematic risk. Specifically, we already know that the covariance of any asset j with the market portfolio (Cov_{jM}) is the relevant risk measure. Beta is a standardized measure of risk because it relates this individual asset covariance to the variance of the market portfolio. As a result, the market portfolio has a beta of 1. Therefore, if the β_j for an asset is above 1.0, the asset has higher normalized systematic risk than the market, which means that it is more volatile (i.e., has more systematic risk) than the overall market portfolio.

Given this standardized measure of systematic risk, the SML graph can be expressed as shown in Exhibit 9.6. This is the same graph as in Exhibit 9.5, except there is a different measure of risk. Specifically, the graph in Exhibit 9.6 replaces the covariance of an asset's returns with the market portfolio as the risk measure with the standardized measure of systematic risk (beta) (the covariance of an asset with the market portfolio divided by the variance of the market portfolio).

Determining the Expected Rate of Return for a Risky Asset   Equation 9.11 and the graph in Exhibit 9.6 tell us that the expected (required) rate of return for a risky asset is determined by the RFR plus a risk premium for the individual asset. In turn, the risk premium is determined by the systematic risk of the asset (β_j) and the prevailing *market risk premium* (R_M − RFR). To demonstrate how to compute expected or required rates of return, let's consider the following example stocks, assuming we have already computed the betas for these stocks as follows:

Stock	Beta
A	0.70
B	1.00
C	1.15
D	1.40
E	−0.30

Assume that we expect the economy's RFR to be 6 percent (0.06) and the return on the market portfolio (R_M) to be 12 percent (0.12). This implies a market risk premium of 6 percent (0.06). With these inputs, the SML equation would yield the following expected (required) rates of return for these five stocks.

$$E(R_j) = RFR + \beta_j(R_M - RFR)$$

$$E(R_A) = 0.06 + 0.70(0.12 - 0.06)$$

$$= 0.102 = 10.2\%$$

$$E(R_B) = 0.06 + 1.00(0.12 - 0.06)$$

$$= 0.12 = 12\%$$

$$E(R_C) = 0.06 + 1.15(0.12 - 0.06)$$

$$= 0.129 = 12.9\%$$

$$E(R_D) = 0.06 + 1.40(0.12 - 0.06)$$

$$= 0.144 = 14.4\%$$

$$E(R_E) = 0.06 + (-0.30)(0.12 - 0.06)$$

$$= 0.06 - 0.018$$

$$= 0.042 = 4.2\%$$

As stated, these are the expected (required) rates of return that these stocks should provide based on their systematic risks and the prevailing SML.

Stock A has lower risk than the aggregate market, so we should not expect (require) its return to be as high as the return on the market portfolio of risky assets. We should expect (require) stock A to return 10.2 percent. Stock B has systematic risk equal to the market's (beta = 1.00), so its required rate of return should likewise be equal to the expected market return (12 percent). Stocks C and D have systematic risk greater than the market's so they should provide above-market returns consistent with their risk. Finally, stock E has a *negative* beta (which is quite rare in practice), so its required rate of return, if such a stock could be found, would be below the RFR.

In equilibrium, *all* assets and *all* portfolios of assets should plot on the SML. That is, all assets should be priced so that their *estimated rates of return,* which are the actual holding period rates of return that we anticipate, are consistent with their levels of systematic risk. Any security with an estimated rate of return that plots above the SML would be considered underpriced because it implies that we *estimated* we would receive a rate of return on the security that is above its *required* rate of return based on its systematic risk. In contrast, assets with estimated rates of return that plot below the SML would be considered overpriced. This position relative to the SML implies that the estimated rate of return is below what should be required based on the asset's systematic risk.

In an efficient market in equilibrium, we would not expect any assets to plot off the SML because, in equilibrium, all stocks should provide holding period returns equal to their required rates of return. Alternatively, a market that is "fairly efficient" but not completely efficient may misprice certain assets because not everyone will be aware of all the relevant information for an asset.

As we will discuss in Chapter 10, a superior investor has the ability to derive value estimates for assets that are consistently superior to the consensus market evaluation. As a result, such an investor will earn better rates of return than the average investor on a risk-adjusted basis.

Identifying Undervalued and Overvalued Assets Now that we understand how to compute the expected (required) rate of return for a specific risky asset using the SML, we can compare this *required* rate of return to the asset's *estimated* rate of return over a specific investment horizon to determine whether it would be an appropriate investment. To make this comparison, we need an independent estimate of the return outlook for the security based on either fundamental or technical analysis techniques that will be discussed in subsequent chapters. Let's continue the example for the five assets discussed in the previous section.

Assume that analysts in a major trust department have been following these five stocks. Based on extensive fundamental analysis, the analysts provide the expected price and dividend estimates contained in Exhibit 9.7. Given these projections, we can compute the estimated rates of return anticipated during this holding period.

Exhibit 9.8 summarizes the relationship between the *required* rate of return for each stock based on its systematic risk as computed earlier and its *estimated* rate of return (from Exhibit 9.7).

Plotting these estimated rates of return and stock betas on the SML we specified earlier gives the graph shown in Exhibit 9.9. Stock A is almost exactly on the line, so it is consid-

EXHIBIT 9.7	Price, Dividend, and Rate of Return Estimates			
Stock	Current Price (P_j)	Expected Price (P_{t+1})	Expected Dividend (D_{t+1})	Estimated Future Rate of Return
A	25	27	0.50	10.0%
B	40	42	0.50	6.2
C	33	39	1.00	21.2
D	64	65	1.10	3.3
E	50	54	—	8.0

EXHIBIT 9.8	Comparison of Required Rate of Return to Estimated Rate of Return				

Stock	Beta	Required Return $E(R_j)$	Estimated Return	Estimated Return Minus $E(R_j)$	Evaluation
A	0.70	10.2	10.0	−0.2	Properly valued
B	1.00	12.0	6.2	−5.8	Overvalued
C	1.15	12.9	21.2	8.3	Undervalued
D	1.40	14.4	3.3	−11.1	Overvalued
E	−0.30	4.2	8.0	3.8	Undervalued

EXHIBIT 9.9	Plot of Estimated Returns on SML Graph

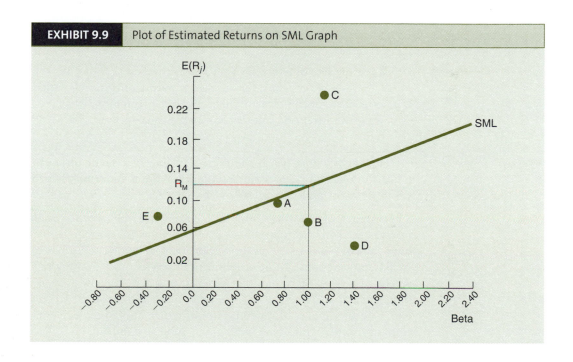

ered properly valued because its estimated rate of return is almost equal to its required rate of return. Stocks B and D are considered overvalued because their estimated rates of return during the coming period are below what an investor should expect (require) for the risk involved. As a result, they plot below the SML. In contrast, stocks C and E are expected to provide rates of return greater than we would require based on their systematic risk. Therefore, both stocks plot above the SML, indicating that they are undervalued stocks.

Assuming that you trusted your analyst to forecast estimated returns, you would take no action regarding stock A, but you would buy stocks C and E and sell stocks B and D if you owned them. You might even sell stocks B and D short if you favored such aggressive tactics.

Calculating Systematic Risk: The Characteristic Line The systematic risk input for an individual asset is derived from a regression model, referred to as the asset's characteristic line with the market portfolio:

9.12

$$R_{jt} = \alpha_j + \beta_j R_{Mt} + \varepsilon$$

EXHIBIT 9.10	Scatterplot of Rates of Return

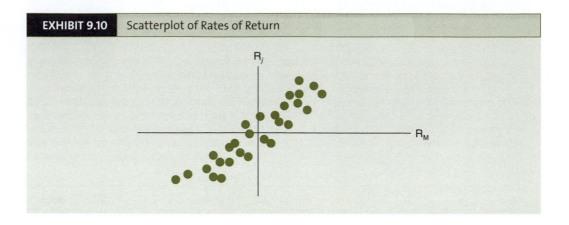

where:

R_{jt} = the rate of return for asset j during period t

R_{Mt} = the rate of return for the market portfolio M during period t

α_j = the constant term, or intercept, of the regression, which equals $R_j - \beta_j R_M$

β_j = the systematic risk (beta) of asset j equal to $\text{Cov}_{jM}/\sigma_M^2$

ε = the random error term

The *characteristic line* is the regression line of best fit through a scatterplot of rates of return for the individual risky asset and for the market portfolio of risky assets over some designated past period, as shown in Exhibit 9.10.

The impact of the time interval. In practice, the number of observations and the time interval used in the regression vary. Value Line Investment Services derives characteristic lines for common stocks using weekly rates of return for the most recent five years (260 weekly observations). Most other financial services use monthly rates of return for the most recent five years (sixty monthly observations). The fact is, there is no theoretically correct time interval for analysis, and we must make a tradeoff between enough observations to eliminate the impact of random rates of return and an excessive length of time such as fifteen or twenty years over which the subject company may have changed dramatically. Remember that what we really want is the *expected* systematic risk for the potential investment over our investment horizon. In this analysis, we are analyzing historical data to derive a reasonable estimate of the asset's expected systematic risk.

A couple of studies have considered the effect of the time interval used to compute betas (weekly versus monthly). Statman examined the relationship between Value Line (VL) weekly betas and Merrill Lynch (ML) monthly betas and found a relatively weak relationship.[8] Reilly and Wright analyzed the differential effects of return computation, market index, and the time interval and likewise found a weak relationship between VL and ML betas.[9] They showed that the major cause of the significant differences in beta was the use of monthly versus weekly intervals. They also found that the interval effect depended on the sizes of the firms. The shorter weekly interval caused a larger beta for large firms and a

---

[8]Meir Statman, "Betas Compared: Merrill Lynch vs. Value Line," *Journal of Portfolio Management* 7, no. 2 (Winter 1981): 41–44.

[9]Frank K. Reilly and David J. Wright, "A Comparison of Published Betas," *Journal of Portfolio Management* 14, no. 3 (Spring 1988): 64–69.

smaller beta for small firms. The authors concluded that the impact of the time interval increases as the size of the firm declines.

The effect of the market proxy.   Another significant decision when computing an asset's characteristic line is which index to use as a proxy for the market portfolio of all risky assets. Most investigators use the S&P 500 Composite Index because the stocks in this index encompass a large proportion of the total market value of U.S. stocks. Also, it is a value-weighted index, which is consistent with the theoretical market index. Still, this index only contains U.S. stocks, most of them listed on the NYSE. Recall that the theoretically correct market portfolio *of all risky assets* should include U.S. stocks and bonds, non-U.S. stocks and bonds, real estate, coins, stamps, art, antiques, and any other marketable risky asset from around the world.[10]

Example Computations of a Characteristic Line   The following examples show how to compute characteristic lines for Microsoft based on the monthly rates of return during 2003.[11] Twelve is not enough observations for statistical purposes, but it should provide a good example. We demonstrate the computations using two different proxies for the market portfolio. The first is the typical analysis in which the S&P 500 is used as the market proxy. The second analysis uses the Morgan Stanley Capital International (MSCI) World Equity Index as the market proxy, which allows us to demonstrate the effect of a more complete proxy of stocks.

The monthly price changes are computed using the closing prices for the last day of each month. These data for Microsoft, the S&P 500, and the MSCI World Index are contained in Exhibit 9.11. Exhibit 9.12 contains the scatterplot of the percentage price changes for Microsoft and the S&P 500. As shown in Exhibit 9.11, during this twelve-month period Microsoft had a beta of 0.32 relative to the S&P 500, which indicates that during this limited time period Microsoft was less risky than the aggregate market proxied by the S&P 500. The characteristic line on Exhibit 9.12 shows that the scatterplots are fairly dispersed from the characteristic line, which is consistent with the relatively low correlation coefficient of 0.22.

The computation of the characteristic line for Microsoft using the MSCI World Index as the market proxy is contained in Exhibit 9.11, and the scatterplots are in Exhibit 9.13. At this point, it is important to consider what one might expect to be the relationship between the S&P 500 beta and the MSCI World Index beta. This requires a consideration of the two components of beta: (1) the covariance between the stock and the market index and (2) the variance of returns for the market index. Notably, there are no obvious answers regarding what will happen for either series because we would typically expect both components to change. Specifically, the covariance of Microsoft with the S&P 500 will typically be higher than with the MSCI because we are matching a U.S. stock with a U.S. market index rather than a world stock index. At the same time, the variance of returns for the world stock index should be smaller than for the S&P 500 because the World Index is a more diversified stock portfolio.

---

[10]Substantial discussion surrounds the market index used and its impact on the empirical results and usefulness of the CAPM. This concern is discussed further and demonstrated in the section on computing an asset's characteristic line. The effect of the market proxy is also considered in Chapter 21 when we discuss the evaluation of portfolio performance.

[11]These betas are computed using only monthly price changes for Microsoft, the S&P 500, and the MSCI World Index (dividends are not included). This is done for simplicity but is also based on a study indicating that betas derived with and without dividends are correlated 0.99: William Sharpe and Guy M. Cooper, "Risk–Return Classes of New York Stock Exchange Common Stocks," *Financial Analysts Journal* 28, no. 2 (March–April 1972): 35–43.

EXHIBIT 9.11 Computation of Beta for Microsoft with Alternative Proxy Indexes

| | INDEX | | | RETURN (%) | | | S&P 500 $R_{S\&P} - (\bar{R}_{S\&P})$ | MSCI World $R_{MSCI} - (\bar{R}_{MSCI})$ | Microsoft $R_{MSFT} - (\bar{R}_{MSFT})$ | | |
| | | | | | | | (1) | (2) | (3) | (4)[a] | (5)[b] |
Date	S&P 500	MSCI World	Microsoft	S&P 500	MSCI World	Microsoft					
Dec-02	879.82	792.22	25.62								
Jan-03	855.70	767.48	23.52	−2.74	−3.12	−8.20	−4.76	−5.44	−8.85	42.12	48.15
Feb-03	841.15	752.86	23.57	−1.70	−1.90	0.21	−3.72	−4.22	−0.44	1.63	1.86
Mar-03	848.18	748.63	24.07	0.84	−0.56	2.12	−1.18	−2.88	1.47	−1.74	−4.24
Apr-03	916.92	813.30	25.43	8.10	8.64	5.65	6.09	6.32	5.00	30.42	31.59
May-03	963.59	857.65	24.47	5.09	5.45	−3.78	3.07	3.13	−4.43	−13.60	−13.87
Jun-03	974.51	871.07	25.50	1.13	1.56	4.21	−0.89	−0.76	3.56	−3.15	−2.69
Jul-03	990.31	887.78	26.26	1.62	1.92	2.98	−0.40	−0.40	2.33	−0.92	−0.93
Aug-03	1008.01	905.32	26.37	1.79	1.98	0.42	−0.23	−0.34	−0.23	0.05	0.08
Sep-03	995.97	909.64	27.64	−1.19	0.48	4.82	−3.21	−1.84	4.16	−13.38	−7.67
Oct-03	1050.71	962.71	26.14	5.50	5.83	−5.43	3.48	3.51	−6.08	−21.14	−21.36
Nov-03	1058.20	976.02	25.71	0.71	1.38	−1.64	−1.31	−0.94	−2.30	3.00	2.15
Dec-03	1111.92	1036.32	27.37	5.08	6.18	6.46	3.06	3.86	5.80	17.75	22.40
Average ($\bar{R}$)				2.02	2.32	0.65				41.05	55.47
Standard Deviation				3.29	3.54	4.64			Total =		

$Cov_{MSFT,S\&P} = 41.05/12 = 3.42$ $Var_{S\&P} = St.Dev._{S\&P}^2 = 3.29^2 = 10.82$ $Beta_{MSFT,S\&P} = 3.42/10.82 = 0.32$ $Alpha_{MSFT,S\&P} = 0.65 - (0.32 \times 2.02) = 0$

$Cov_{MSFT,MSCI} = 55.47/12 = 4.62$ $Var_{MSCI} = St.Dev._{MSCI}^2 = 3.54^2 = 12.53$ $Beta_{MSFT,MSCI} = 4.62/12.53 = 0.37$ $Alpha_{MSFT,S\&P} = 0.65 - (0.37 \times 2.32) = -0.21$

$Correlation\ Coef_{MSFT,S\&P} = 3.42/(3.29 \times 4.64) = 0.224$ $Correlation\ Coef_{MSFT,MSCI} = 4.62/(3.54 \times 4.64) = 0.281$

[a] Column (4) is equal to column (1) multiplied by column (3).

[b] Column (5) is equal to column (2) multiplied by column (3).

EXHIBIT 9.12   Scatterplot of Microsoft and the S&P 500 with Characteristic Line for Microsoft, 2003

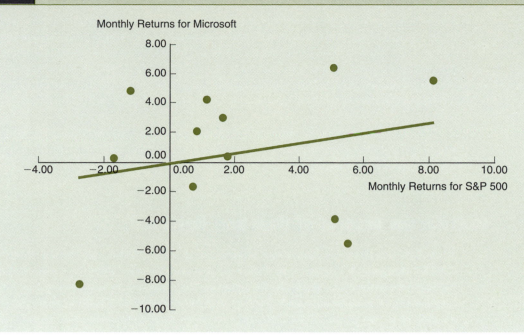

EXHIBIT 9.13   Scatterplot of Microsoft and the MSCI World Index with Characteristic Line for Microsoft, 2003

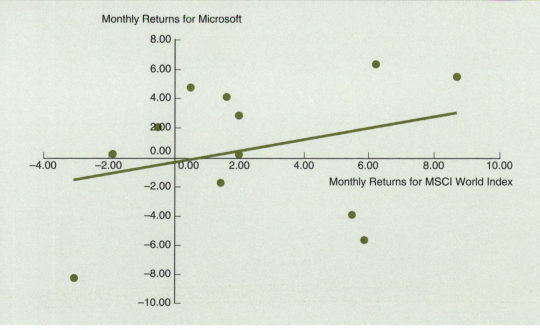

Regardless of our expectations, the direction of the actual change for the beta will depend on the relative change in the two components. The empirical results for this example indicate a larger beta for Microsoft using the world stock index as the market proxy (0.37 versus 0.32). The reason for the difference was counter to normal expectations. Specifically, the covariance of Microsoft with the MSCI was marginally higher than with the S&P 500 (4.62 versus 3.42) whereas the variance of the MSCI series was larger (12.53) than the variance for the S&P 500 (10.82). As a result, the beta of Microsoft relative to the MSCI was 0.37 (4.62/12.53) compared to a beta of 0.32 (3.42/10.82) relative to the S&P 500.

The fact that the betas differ is significant and reflects the potential problem that can occur in a global environment where it becomes difficult to select the appropriate proxy for the market portfolio.[12]

Multifactor Models of Risk and Return[13]

Now let's consider an important extension of the CAPM risk–return framework. The CAPM designated a single risk factor to account for the volatility (risk) inherent in an individual security or a portfolio of securities. In this section we develop the intuition and application of *multifactor models* used to explain risk and return. The wide variety of these models that are in use differ primarily in how they define the risk factors and can be broadly grouped into those that use *macroeconomic* factor definitions and those that specify *microeconomic* factors. We will look at several examples of the different multifactor approaches to illustrate the numerous forms these models can assume.

ESTIMATING RISK WITH MULTIFACTOR MODELS

When it comes to putting theory into practice, one advantage of the CAPM framework is that the single risk factor (i.e., the excess return to the market portfolio) is well specified. The empirical challenge in implementing the CAPM successfully is to accurately estimate the market portfolio, a process that requires identifying the relevant investment universe. As noted, however, this is not a trivial problem as an improperly chosen proxy for the market portfolio (e.g., using the S&P 500 index to represent the market when evaluating a global stock or portfolio) can lead to erroneous judgments. However, we also saw that, assuming an acceptable surrogate for the market portfolio is identified (i.e., R_M), the process for estimating the parameters of the CAPM is straightforward and can be accomplished using the following regression equation:

$$\mathbf{R}_{jt} = \alpha_j + \beta_j \mathbf{R}_{Mt} + \varepsilon_t$$

The first multifactor model to be developed was the *arbitrage pricing theory (APT)*. A practical problem with implementing the APT is that neither the identity nor the exact number of underlying risk factors are developed as part of the theory and, therefore, the risk factors must be specified in an ad hoc manner. A different approach to developing an empirical model that captures the essence of the APT relies on the direct specification of the form of

[12]For a demonstration of this effect for a large sample, see Frank K. Reilly and Rashid A. Akhtar, "The Benchmark Error Problem with Global Capital Markets," *Journal of Portfolio Management* 22, no. 1 (Fall 1995): 33–52.

[13]The authors acknowledge the collaboration of Professor Keith Brown of the University of Texas on this section.

the relationship to be estimated. That is, in a multifactor model, the investor chooses the exact number and identity of risk factors in the following equation:

9.13
$$R_{jt} = \alpha_j + [\beta_{j1}F_{1t} + \beta_{j2}F_{2t} + \cdots + \beta_{jk}F_{\kappa t}] + \varepsilon_{jt}$$

where F_{gt} is the period t return to the gth designated risk factor and R_{jt} is the nominal return to security j. The advantage of this approach, of course, is that the investor knows precisely how many and what things need to be estimated to fit the regression equation. On the other hand, the major disadvantage of a multifactor model is that it is developed with little theoretical guidance as to the true nature of the risk–return relationship. In this sense, developing a useful factor model is as much an art form as it is a theoretical exercise.

MULTIFACTOR MODELS IN PRACTICE

A wide variety of empirical factor specifications have been employed in practice. A hallmark of each alternative model that has been developed is that it attempts to identify a set of economic influences that is simultaneously broad enough to capture the major nuances of investment risk but small enough to provide a workable solution to the analyst or investor. Two general approaches have been employed in this factor identification process. First, risk factors can be *macroeconomic* in nature; that is, they can attempt to capture variations in the underlying reasons an asset's cash flows and investment returns might change over time (e.g., changes in inflation or real GDP growth). On the other hand, risk factors can also be identified at a *microeconomic* level by focusing on relevant characteristics of the securities themselves, such as the size of the firm in question or some of its financial ratios. A few examples representative of both of these approaches to the problem are discussed in the following sections.

Macroeconomic-Based Risk Factor Models   One particularly influential model was developed by Chen, Roll, and Ross, who hypothesized that security returns are governed by a set of broad economic influences in the following fashion:[14]

9.14
$$R_{jt} = \alpha_i + (\beta_{j1}R_{Mt} + \beta_{j2}MP_t + \beta_{j3}DEI_t + \beta_{j4}UI_t + \beta_{j5}UPR_t + \beta_{j6}UTS_t) + \varepsilon_{jt}$$

where:

R_M = the return on a value-weighted index of NYSE-listed stocks
MP = the monthly growth rate in U.S. industrial production
DEI = the change in inflation, measured by the U.S. consumer price index
UI = the difference between actual and expected levels of inflation
UPR = the unanticipated change in the bond credit spread (Baa yield − RFR)
UTS = the unanticipated term structure shift (long-term less short-term RFR)

In estimating this model, the authors used a series of monthly returns for a large collection of securities from the Center for Research in Security Prices (CRSP) database over the period 1958–1984. Exhibit 9.14 shows the factor sensitivities (along with the associated t-statistics in parentheses) that they established.[15] Notice two things about these findings. First, the economic significance of the designated risk factors changed dramatically over time. For instance, the inflation factors (DEI and UI) appear to only be relevant during the

---

[14]Nai-fu Chen, Richard Roll, and Stephen A. Ross, "Economic Forces and the Stock Market," *Journal of Business* 59, no. 3 (April 1986): 383–404.

[15]In regression analysis, it is customary to determine if a constant or a coefficient is statistically significant using a t-test that generates a t-statistic. If this t-statistic is approximately 2.00 or greater, the constant or coefficient is considered "significant."

EXHIBIT 9.14	Estimating a Multifactor Model with Macroeconomic Risk Factors						
Period	Constant	R_m	MP	DEI	UI	UPR	UTS
1958-84	10.71	−2.40	11.76	−0.12	−0.80	8.27	−5.91
	(2.76)	(−0.63)	(3.05)	(−1.60)	(−2.38)	(2.97)	(−1.88)
1958-67	9.53	1.36	12.39	0.01	−0.21	5.20	−0.09
	(1.98)	(0.28)	(1.79)	(0.06)	(−0.42)	(1.82)	(−0.04)
1968-77	8.58	−5.27	13.47	−0.26	−1.42	12.90	−11.71
	(1.17)	(−0.72)	(2.04)	(−3.24)	(−3.11)	(2.96)	(−2.30)
1978-84	15.45	−3.68	8.40	−0.12	−0.74	6.06	−5.93
	(1.87)	(−0.49)	(1.43)	(−0.46)	(−0.87)	(0.78)	(−0.64)

Source: Nai-fu Chen, Richard Roll, and Stephen A. Ross, "Economic Forces and the Stock Market," *Journal of Business* 59, no. 3 (April 1986). Reprinted by permission of The University of Chicago Press.

1968–1977 period. Second the parameter on the stock market proxy is never significant, suggesting that it contributes little to the explanation beyond the information contained in the other macroeconomic risk factors.

Burmeister, Roll, and Ross analyzed the predictive ability of a model based on a different set of macroeconomic factors.[16] Specifically, they define the following five risk exposures: (1) *confidence risk,* based on unanticipated changes in the willingness of investors to take on investment risk; (2) *time horizon risk,* which is the unanticipated changes in investors' desired time to receive payouts; (3) *inflation risk,* based on a combination of the unexpected components of short-term and long-term inflation rates; (4) *business cycle risk,* which represents unanticipated changes in the level of overall business activity; and (5) *market timing risk,* defined as the part of the S&P 500 total return that is not explained by the other four macroeconomic factors. Using monthly data through the first quarter of 1992, the authors estimated risk premiums (i.e., the market "price" of risk) for these factors:

Risk Factor	Risk Premium
Confidence	2.59%
Time horizon	−0.66
Inflation	−4.32
Business cycle	1.49
Market timing	3.61

They also compared the factor sensitivities for several different individual stocks and stock portfolios. Exhibit 9.15 shows these factor beta estimates for (A) a particular stock (Reebok International Ltd.) versus the S&P 500 index and (B) for a portfolio of large-cap firms versus a portfolio of small-cap firms. Also included in these graphs is the security's or portfolio's exposure to the BIRR composite risk index, which is designed to indicate which position has the most overall systematic risk. These comparisons highlight how a multifactor model can help investors distinguish the nature of the risk they are assuming when they

[16]Edwin Burmeister, Richard Roll, and Stephen A. Ross, "A Practitioner's Guide to Arbitrage Pricing Theory," in John Peavy, ed., *A Practitioner's Guide to Factor Models* (Charlottesville, VA: Research Foundation of the Institute of Chartered Financial Analysts), 1994.

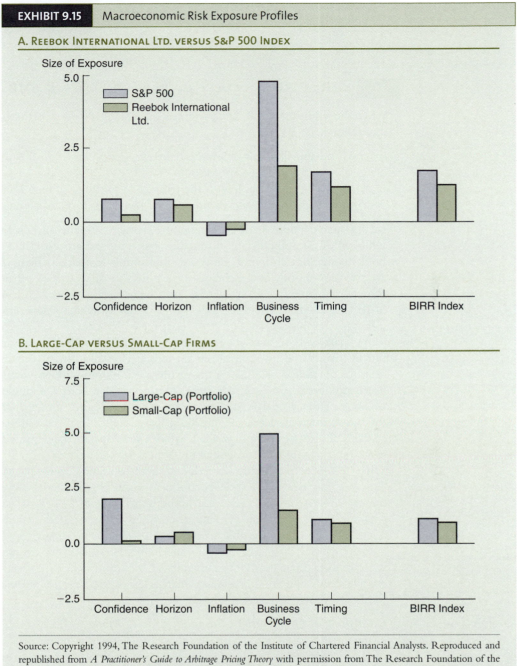

EXHIBIT 9.15 Macroeconomic Risk Exposure Profiles

A. Reebok International Ltd. versus S&P 500 Index

B. Large-Cap versus Small-Cap Firms

hold a particular position. For instance, notice that Reebok has greater exposures to all sources of risk than the S&P 500, with the incremental difference in the business cycle exposure being particularly dramatic. Additionally, smaller firms are more exposed to business cycle and confidence risk than larger firms but less exposed to horizon risk.

Microeconomic-Based Risk Factor Models   It is also possible to specify risk in microeconomic terms using certain characteristics of the underlying sample of securities. Typical of this *characteristic-based approach* to forming a multifactor model is the work of Fama and French, who use the following functional form:[17]

> **9.15** $$(R_{jt} - RFR_t) = \alpha_j + \beta_{j1}(R_{Mt} - RFR_t) + \beta_{j2}SMB_t + \beta_{j3}HML_t + \varepsilon_{jt}$$

where, in addition to the excess return on a stock market portfolio, two other risk factors are defined:[18]

> SMB (i.e., small minus big) is the return to a portfolio of small-cap stocks less the return to a portfolio of large-cap stocks
>
> HML (i.e., high minus low) is the return to a portfolio of high book-to-market value stocks less the return to a portfolio of low book-to-market value stocks

In this specification, SMB is designed to capture elements of risk associated with firm size while HML is intended to distinguish risk differentials associated with growth (i.e., low book-to-market ratio) and value (i.e., high book-to-market) firms. As we saw earlier, these are two dimensions of a security—or a portfolio of securities—that have consistently been shown to matter when evaluating investment performance. Also, notice that without the SMB and HML factors this model simply reduces to the excess returns form of the single-index market model.

As part of their analysis of the role that SMB and HML play in the return-generating process, Fama and French examined the behavior of a broad sample of stocks grouped into quintile portfolios by their price–earnings (P/E) ratios on a yearly basis over the period from July 1963 to December 1991. The results for both the single-index and multifactor versions of the model for the two extreme quintiles are shown in Exhibit 9.16 (*t*-statistics for the estimated coefficients are listed parenthetically). There are several important things to note about these findings. First, while the estimated beta from the single-factor model indicates that there are substantial differences between low and high P/E stocks (0.94 versus 1.10), this gap is dramatically reduced in the multifactor specification (1.03 versus 0.99). This suggests that the market portfolio in a one-factor model serves as a proxy for some, but not all, of the additional risk dimensions provided by SMB and HML. Second, it is apparent that low P/E stocks tend to be positively correlated with the small-firm premium, but the reverse is not reliably true for high P/E stocks. Finally, low P/E stocks also tend to have high book-to-market ratios while high P/E stocks tend to have low book-to-market ratios (i.e., estimated HML parameters of 0.67 and −0.50, respectively). Not surprisingly, relative levels of P/E and book-to-market ratios are both commonly employed in practice to classify growth and value stocks.

Extensions of Characteristic-Based Risk Factor Models   There have been other interesting characteristic-based approaches to estimating a multifactor model of risk and return. Three of those approaches are described here. First, Carhart directly extends the Fama–French three-factor model by including a fourth common risk factor that accounts for the tendency for firms with positive (negative) past returns to produce positive (negative) future

---

[17]Eugene F. Fama and Kenneth R. French, "Common Risk Factors in the Returns on Stocks and Bonds," *Journal of Financial Economics* 33, no. 1 (January 1993): 3–56.

[18]We will discuss the small capitalization phenomenon, the book-to-market ratio, and price–earning (P/E) ratios in the following section and in Chapter 10.

EXHIBIT 9.16	Estimating a Multifactor Model with Characteristic-Based Risk Factors				
Portfolio	Constant	Market	SMB	HML	R²
A. SINGLE-INDEX MODEL					
Lowest P/E	0.46	0.94	—	—	0.78
	(3.69)	(34.73)			
Highest P/E	−0.20	1.10	—	—	0.91
	(−2.35)	(57.42)			
B. MULTIFACTOR MODEL					
Lowest P/E	0.08	1.03	0.24	0.67	0.91
	(1.01)	(51.56)	(8.34)	(19.62)	
Highest P/E	0.04	0.99	−0.01	−0.50	0.96
	(0.70)	(66.78)	(−0.55)	(−19.73)	

Source: Reprinted from Eugene F. Fama and Kenneth R. French, "Common Risk Factors in the Returns on Stocks and Bonds." *Journal of Financial Economics* 33, no. 1 (January 1993), with permission from Elsevier Science.

returns.[19] He calls this additional risk dimension a *momentum factor* and estimates it by taking the average return to a set of stocks with the best performance over the prior year minus the average return to stocks with the worst returns. In this fashion, Carhart defines the momentum factor—which he labels PR1YR—in a fashion similar to SMB and HML. Formally, the model he proposes is

9.16

$$(R_{jt} - RFR_t) = \alpha_j + \beta_{j1}(R_{Mt} - RFR_t) + \beta_{j2}SMB_t + \beta_{j3}HML_t + \beta_{j4}PR1YR_t + \varepsilon_{jt}$$

He demonstrates that the typical factor sensitivity (i.e., factor beta) for the momentum variable is positive and its inclusion into the Fama–French model increases explanatory power by as much as 15 percent.

A second type of security characteristic-based method for defining systematic risk exposures involves the use of index portfolios (e.g., S&P 500, Wilshire 5000) as common factors. The intuition behind this approach is that, if the indexes themselves are designed to emphasize certain investment characteristics, they can act as proxies for the underlying exposure that determines returns to that characteristic. Examples of this include the Russell 1000 Growth index, which emphasizes large-cap stocks with low book-to-market ratios, or the EAFE (Europe, Australia, and the Far East) index that selects a variety of companies that are domiciled outside the United States. Typical of these index-based factor models is the work of Elton, Gruber, and Blake, who rely on four indexes: the S&P 500, the Lehman Brothers aggregate bond index, the Prudential Bache index of the difference between large- and small-cap stocks, and the Prudential Bache index of the difference between value and growth stocks.[20] Ferson and Schadt have developed an interesting variation on this approach, which, in addition to using stock and bond indexes as risk factors, also includes

[19]Mark M. Carhart, "On Persistence in Mutual Fund Performance." *Journal of Finance* 52, no. 1 (March 1997): 57–82.

[20]Edwin J. Elton, Martin J. Gruber, and Christopher R. Blake, "The Persistence of Risk-Adjusted Mutual Fund Performance," *Journal of Business* 69, no. 2 (April 1996): 133–157.

EXHIBIT 9.17	Description of Barra Characteristic-Based Risk Factors

- **Volatility (VOL)**   Captures both long-term and short-term dimensions of relative return variability
- **Momentum (MOM)**   Differentiates between stocks with positive and negative excess returns in the recent past
- **Size (SIZ)**   Based on a firm's relative market capitalization
- **Size Nonlinearity (SNL)**   Captures deviations from linearity in the relationship between returns and firm size
- **Trading Activity (TRA)**   Measures the relative trading in a stock, based on the premise that more actively traded stocks are more likely to be those with greater interest from institutional investors
- **Growth (GRO)**   Uses historical growth and profitability measures to predict future earnings growth
- **Earnings Yield (EYL)**   Combines current and historical earnings-to-price ratios with analyst forecasts under the assumption that stocks with similar earnings yields produce similar returns
- **Value (VAL)**   Based on relative book-to-market ratios
- **Earnings Variability (EVR)**   Measures the variability in earnings and cash flows using both historical values and analyst forecasts
- **Leverage (LEV)**   Measures the relative financial leverage of a company
- **Currency Sensitivity (CUR)**   Based on the relative sensitivity of a company's stock return to movements in a basket of foreign currencies
- **Dividend Yield (YLD)**   Computes a measure of the predicted dividend yield using a firm's past dividend and stock price history
- **Nonestimation Indicator (NEU)**   Uses returns to firms outside the equity universe to account for risk dimensions not captured by the other risk factors

Source: Barra.

other "public information" variables, such as the shape of the yield curve and dividend pay-outs.[21]

Barra, a leading risk forecasting and investment consulting firm, provides a final example of the microeconomic approach to building a multifactor model. In its most expansive form, the Barra model for analyzing U.S. equities includes as risk factors thirteen characteristic-based variables and more than fifty industry indexes.[22] Exhibit 9.17 provides a brief description of the thirteen characteristics based factors that form the heart of the Barra approach. One useful application for this model is to understand where the investment "bets" in an actively managed portfolio are being placed relative to a performance benchmark. Exhibit 9.18 illustrates this sort of comparison for a small-cap mutual fund (POOL2) versus the S&P 500 index (SAP500). As we would expect, there are dramatic differences between the fund and the benchmark in terms of the firm-size risk factors (i.e., size, SIZ, and size nonlinearity, SNL). However, it also appears that POOL2 contains more highly leveraged companies (LEV) with more emphasis on earnings momentum (MOM).

---

[21]Wayne R. Ferson and Rudi W. Schadt, "Measuring Fund Strategy and Performance in Changing Economic Conditions, *Journal of Finance* 51, no. 2 (June 1996): 425–462.

[22]A more complete description of the Barra approach to analyzing investment risk can be found in Richard Grinwold and Ronald N. Kahn, "Multiple-Factor Models for Portfolio Risk," in John Peavy, ed., *A Practitioner's Guide to Factor Models* (Charlottesville, VA: Research Foundation of the Institute of Chartered Financial Analysts), 1994.

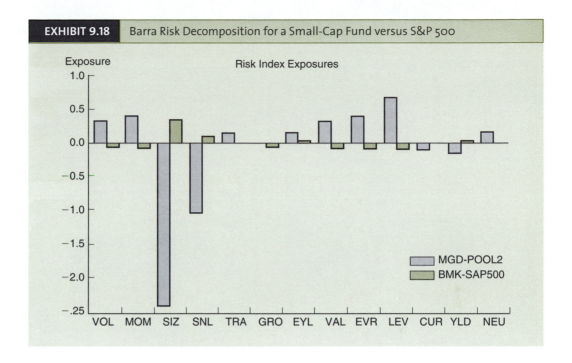

EXHIBIT 9.18 Barra Risk Decomposition for a Small-Cap Fund versus S&P 500

Conner analyzed the ability of the Barra model to explain the returns generated by a sample of U.S. stocks over the period from 1985 to 1993.[23] Interestingly, he found that the industry indexes, taken collectively, provided about four times the explanatory power as any single characteristic-based factor, followed in importance by volatility, growth, dividend yield, and momentum. Overall, the Barra model explained slightly more return variability than the other models to which it was compared, in part because of its large number of factors.

ESTIMATING RISK IN A MULTIFACTOR SETTING: EXAMPLES

Estimating Expected Returns for Individual Stocks

One direct way in which to employ a multifactor risk model is to use it to estimate the expected return for an individual stock position. To accomplish this task, we must take the following steps: (1) identify a specific set of G common risk factors, (2) estimate the risk premiums (F_j) for the factors, (3) estimate the sensitivities (β_{ij}) of the ith stock to each of those G factors, and (4) calculate the expected returns by combining the results of the previous steps in the appropriate way.

As an example of this process, we will use the Fama–French model discussed earlier. This immediately solves the first step by designating the following three common risk factors: the excess return on the market portfolio (R_M), the return differential between small- and large-cap stocks (SMB), and the return differential between high and low book-to-market stocks (HML). The second step is often addressed in practice by using historical return data to calculate the average values for each of the risk factors. However, it is important to recognize that these averages can vary tremendously depending on the time period the investor selects. For example, for the three-factor model, panel A of Exhibit 9.19 lists

[23]Gregory Connor, "The Three Types of Factor Models: A Comparison of Their Explanatory Power," *Financial Analysts Journal* 51, no. 3 (May–June 1995): 42–46.

| EXHIBIT 9.19 | Estimates for Risk Factor Premiums and Factor Sensitivities |

A. RISK FACTOR PREMIUM ESTIMATES USING HISTORICAL DATA

Risk Factor	Risk Premium Estimate		
	1996-2000	1981-2000	1928-2000
Market	11.50%	9.09%	7.02%
SMB	−1.44	−1.10	3.09
HML	−5.40	4.48	4.39

B. REGRESSION ESTIMATES OF RISK FACTOR SENSITIVITIES (JULY 1995–JUNE 2000)

Stock	Market	SMB	HML
INTC	0.615	−0.640	−1.476
	(1.63)	(−1.74)	(−2.55)
JPM	1.366	−0.387	0.577
	(7.15)	(−2.07)	(1.96)
WFMI	1.928	0.817	1.684
	(4.33)	(1.88)	(2.46)

the average annual risk premiums over three different time frames: a five-year period ending in June 2000, a twenty-year period ending in December 2000, and a seventy-three-year period ending in December 2000.[24] Notice that, while data for the longest time frame confirm that small stocks earn higher returns than large stocks and value stocks outperform growth stocks (i.e., positive risk premiums for the SMB and HML factors), this is not true over shorter periods. In particular, during the most recent five years, the opposite occurred in both cases.

To illustrate steps 3 and 4, we estimated risk factor sensitivities by regression analysis for three different stocks using monthly return data over the period from July 1995 to June 2000. The three stocks were Intel (INTC), a large semiconductor manufacturer; JP Morgan Chase (JPM), a large global banking firm; and Whole Foods Market (WFMI), a small specialty food retailer. The estimated factor betas are listed in panel B with the t-statistics associated with the various sensitivity estimates reported in parentheses. These factor betas provide some interesting comparisons between the three stocks. First, the positive coefficients on the market factor indicate that all of these stocks are positively correlated with general movement in the stock market. The coefficients on the SMB factor confirm that JPM and INTC produce returns consistent with large-cap stocks (i.e, negative SMB exposures), while WFMI acts like a small-cap stock. Finally, JPM and WFMI are more likely to be considered value stocks (i.e., positive HML exposures) while the technology company INTC can be considered a growth-oriented stock.

Whichever specific factor risk estimates are used, the expected return for any stock in excess of the risk-free rate (i.e., the expected risk premium) can be calculated with the formula

9.17

$$[E(R_j) - RFR] = \beta_{jM}\lambda_M + \beta_{jSMB}\lambda_{SMB} + \beta_{jHML}\lambda_{HML}$$

---

[24]The data used in these calculations are available from Professor Kenneth French's Web site at *http://mbatuck.dartmouth.edu/pages/faculty/ken.french/*.

where

λ_M = the market risk premium during a specified period

λ_{SMB} = the small cap stock premium during a specified period

λ_{HML} = the high to low book-to-market premium during a specified period

Using the data for the 1996–2000 period in Exhibit 9.19 the expected excess returns for the three stocks are as follows:

$$\text{INTC: } [E(R) - RFR] = (0.615)(11.50) + (-0.640)(-1.44) + (-1.476)(-5.40)$$
$$= 15.96\%$$

$$\text{JPM: } [E(R) - RFR] = (1.366)(11.50) + (-0.387)(-1.44) + (-0.577)(-5.40)$$
$$= 13.15\%$$

$$\text{WFMI: } [E(R) - RFR] = (1.928)(11.50) + (0.817)(-1.44) + (-1.684)(-5.40)$$
$$= 11.90\%$$

Notice that while these values are high relative to longer-term historical norms—especially the market factor premium—they reflect the conditions that prevailed in the capital markets at the time.

Investments Online

Asset pricing models show how risk measures or underlying return-generating factors will affect asset returns. Estimates from such models are usually proprietary and are available from providers only by buying their research. Of course, users can always purchase their raw data elsewhere (see some of our earlier Internet discussions) and develop their own estimates of beta and factor sensitivities.

http://www.valueline.com The Value Line Investment Survey has been a long-time favorite of investors and many local and college/university libraries subscribe to it. It is a popular source for finding stock's betas. Value Line Publishing, Inc.'s Web site contains useful information for the online researcher and student of investments. Its site features investment-related articles, sample pages from the Value Line Investment Survey, and a product directory that lists the venerable investment survey as well as Value Line's mutual fund, options, and convertibles survey, and others.

http://www.barra.com For subscribers, Barra's Web site offers a gold mine of data and analytical analysis. Links offer information on portfolio management, investment data, market indexes, and research. Barra offers its clients data, software, and consulting, as well as money management services

for equity, fixed-income, currency, and other global financial instruments. Barra estimates multiple factor models and their global and single-country equity models provide risk analyses on over 25,000 globally traded securities, including predicted and historical beta values. Explore this site to discover its data resources, charts, and graphs.

http://www.stanford.edu/~wfsharpe/ William F. Sharpe, the 1990 winner of the Nobel prize in Economics for his development of the capital asset pricing model, has a home page on the Internet. Among other items, Web surfers can read drafts of a sophisticated textbook in progress, some of his published papers, and case studies he has written. Sharpe's site offers monthly returns data on a number of mutual funds, stock indexes, and bond indexes, and links to other finance sites.

gsb.uchicago.edu/fac/eugene.fama/ The home page of Eugene Fama, whose empirical work first found support—and then lack of support—for beta as a risk measure.

http://www.moneychimp.com This is an informative educational site on investments that includes CAPM calculators for estimating a stock's return and a "market simulator" to show the effect of randomness on a portfolio's return over time.

Summary

- The assumptions of capital market theory expand on those of the Markowitz portfolio model and include consideration of the risk-free rate of return. The correlation and covariance of any asset with a risk-free asset are zero, so that any combination of an asset or portfolio with the risk-free asset generates a linear return and risk function. Therefore, when we combine the risk-free asset with any risky asset on the Markowitz efficient frontier, we derive a set of straight-line portfolio possibilities.

- The dominant portfolio possibility line is the one that is tangent to the efficient frontier. This dominant line is referred to as the capital market line (CML), and all investors should target points along this line that match their risk preferences.

- Because all investors want to invest in the risky portfolio at the point of tangency, this portfolio—referred to as the market portfolio or portfolio M—must contain all risky assets in proportion to their relative market values. Moreover, the investment decision and the financing decision can be separated because, although everyone will want to invest in the market portfolio, investors will make different financing decisions about whether to lend or borrow based on their individual risk preferences.

- The capital asset pricing model (CAPM) relates risk to a single factor (beta). Given the CML and the dominance of the market portfolio, the relevant risk measure for an individual risky asset is its covariance with the market portfolio, that is, its systematic risk. When this covariance is standardized by the covariance for the market portfolio, we derive the well-known beta measure of systematic risk and a security market line (SML) that relates the expected or required rate of return for an asset to its beta. Because all individual securities and portfolios should plot on this SML, we can determine the expected (required) return on a security based on its systematic risk (its beta).

- Alternatively, assuming security markets are not always completely efficient, we can identify undervalued and overvalued securities by comparing our estimate of the rate of return to be earned on an investment to its expected (required) rate of return. We compute the systematic risk variable (beta) for an individual risky asset using a regression model that generates an equation referred to as the asset's characteristic line.

- Multifactor models for determining the expected or (required) rates of return for a risky portfolio consider multiple sources of risk. These models can be grouped into those that use macroeconomic factors to measure risk (e.g., industrial production, changes in inflation, changes in credit spreads) and those that consider microeconomic factors (e.g., firm size, sales and earnings growth, financial leverage, earnings variability). One popular multifactor model considers a market factor (similar to CAPM) but also considers risk related to firm size and growth.

QUESTIONS

1. Explain why the set of points between the risk-free asset and a portfolio on the Markowitz efficient frontier is a straight line.
2. Draw a graph that shows what happens to the Markowitz efficient frontier when you combine a risk-free asset with alternative risky-asset portfolios on the Markowitz efficient frontier. Explain this graph.
3. Draw and explain why the line from the RFR tangent to the efficient frontier defines the dominant set of portfolio possibilities.
4. Discuss what risky assets are in portfolio M and why they are in it.
5. Discuss leverage and its effect on the CML.
6. Discuss and justify a measure of diversification for a portfolio in terms of capital market theory.
7. What changes would you expect in the standard deviation for a portfolio of randomly selected stocks between 4 and 10 stocks, between 10 and 20 stocks, and between 50 and 100 stocks?
8. Discuss why the investment and financing decisions are separate when you have a CML.
9. Given the CML, discuss and justify the relevant measure of risk for an individual security.
10. Capital market theory divides the variance of returns for a security into systematic variance and unsystematic or unique variance. Describe each of these terms.
11. The capital asset pricing model (CAPM) contends that there is systematic and unsystematic risk for an individual security. Which is the relevant risk variable and why is it relevant? Why is the other risk variable not relevant?
12. How does the SML differ from the CML?

13. *CFA Examination Level I*

Identify and briefly discuss *three* criticisms of beta as used in the capital asset pricing model (CAPM). (6 minutes)

14. *CFA Examination Level I*

Briefly explain whether investors should expect a higher return from holding portfolio A versus portfolio B under capital asset pricing theory (CAPM). Assume that both portfolios are fully diversified. (6 minutes)

	Portfolio A	Portfolio B
Systematic risk (beta)	1.0	1.0
Specific risk for each individual security	High	Low

15. *CFA Examination Level II*

You have recently been appointed chief investment officer of a major charitable foundation. Its large endowment fund is currently invested in a broadly diversified portfolio of stocks (60 percent) and bonds (40 percent). The foundation's board of trustees is a group of prominent individuals whose knowledge of modern investment theory and practice is superficial. You decide a discussion of basic investment principles would be helpful.

a. Explain the concepts of *specific risk, systematic risk, variance, covariance, standard deviation,* and *beta* as they relate to investment management. (12 minutes)

You believe that the addition of other asset classes to the endowment portfolio would improve the portfolio by reducing risk and enhancing return. You are aware that depressed conditions in U.S. real estate markets are providing opportunities for property acquisition at levels of expected return that are unusually high by historical standards. You believe that an investment in U.S. real estate would be both appropriate and timely, and have decided to recommend a 20 percent position be established with funds taken equally from stocks and bonds.

Preliminary discussions revealed that several trustees believe real estate is too risky to include in the portfolio. The board chairman, however, has scheduled a special meeting for further discussion of the matter and has asked you to provide background information that will clarify the risk issue.

To assist you, the following expectational data have been developed:

b. Explain the effect on *both* portfolio risk *and* return that would result from the addition of U.S. real estate. Include in your answer two reasons for any change you expect in portfolio risk. (*Note:* It is *not* necessary to compute expected risk and return.) (8 minutes)

c. Your understanding of capital market theory causes you to doubt the validity of the expected return and risk for U.S. real estate. Justify your skepticism. (5 minutes)

16. *CFA Examination Level I*

Which of the following statements about the security market line (SML) are *true*?

a. The SML provides a benchmark for evaluating expected investment performance.

b. The SML leads all investors to invest in the same portfolio of risky assets.

c. The SML is a graphic representation of the relationship between expected return and beta.

d. Properly valued assets plot exactly on the SML.

   i. I and III only

   ii. II and IV only

   iii. I, II, and IV only

   iv. I, III, and IV only (2 minutes)

17. *CFA Examination Level I*

Consistent with capital market theory, systematic risk:

a. refers to the variability in all risky assets caused by macroeconomic and other aggregate market-related variables.

b. is measured by the coefficient of variation of returns on the market portfolio.

c. refers to nondiversifiable risk.

   i. I only

   ii. II only

   iii. I and III only

   iv. II and III only (2 minutes)

CORRELATION MATRIX

Asset Class	Return	Standard Deviation	U.S. Stocks	U.S. Bonds	U.S. Real Estate	U.S. T-Bills
U.S. stocks	12.0%	21.0%	1.00			
U.S. bonds	8.0	10.5	0.14	1.00		
U.S. real estate	12.0	9.0	−0.04	−0.03	1.00	
U.S. Treasury bills	4.0	0.0	−0.05	−0.03	0.25	1.00

PROBLEMS

1. Assume that you expect the economy's rate of inflation to be 3 percent, giving an RFR of 6 percent and a market return (R_M) of 12 percent.
   a. Draw the SML under these assumptions.
   b. Subsequently, you expect the rate of inflation to increase from 3 percent to 6 percent. What effect would this have on the RFR and the R_M? Draw another SML on the graph from part (a).
   c. Draw an SML on the same graph to reflect an RFR of 9 percent and an R_M of 17 percent. How does this SML differ from that derived in part (b)? Explain what has transpired.

2. You expect an RFR of 10 percent and the market return (R_M) of 14 percent. Compute the expected (required) return for the following stocks, and plot them on an SML graph.

Stock	Beta	$E(R_j)$
U	0.85	
N	1.25	
D	−0.20	

3. You ask a stockbroker what her firm's research department expects for these three stocks over the next year. The broker responds with the following information:

Stock	Current Price	Expected Price	Expected Dividend
U	22	24	0.75
N	48	51	2.00
D	37	40	1.25

   Plot your estimated returns on the SML graph from Problem 2 and indicate what actions you would take with regard to these stocks. Discuss your decisions.

4. Select a stock from the NYSE and collect its month-end prices for the latest thirteen months to compute twelve monthly percentage price changes ignoring dividends. Do the same for the S&P 500 series. Prepare a scatterplot of these series on a graph and draw a visual characteristic line of best fit (the line that minimizes the deviations from the line). Compute the slope of this line from the graph.

5. Given the returns derived in Problem 4, compute the beta coefficient using the formula and techniques employed in Exhibit 9.11. How many negative products did you have for the covariance? How does this computed beta compare to the visual beta derived in Problem 4?

6. Look up the index values and compute the monthly percentage of price changes for either the FT World Index or the MSCI World Index.

   a. Compute the beta for your NYSE stock from Problem 4 using one of these world stock indexes as the proxy for the market portfolio.
   b. How does this world beta compare to your S&P beta? Discuss the difference.

7. Look up this stock in Value Line and record the beta derived by VL. How does this VL beta compare to the beta you computed using the S&P 500? Discuss reasons why the betas might differ.

8. Select a stock listed on the Nasdaq National market and plot the returns during the past twelve months relative to the S&P 500. Compute the beta coefficient. Did you expect this stock to have a higher or lower beta than the NYSE stock? Explain your answer based on the two components of beta.

9. Given the returns for the Nasdaq National market stock in Problem 8, plot the stock returns relative to monthly rates of return for the Nasdaq Composite Index and compute the beta coefficient. Does this beta differ from that derived in Problem 8? If so, how do you explain this? (*Hint:* Analyze the specific components of the formula for the beta coefficient. How did the components differ between Problems 8 and 9?)

10. Using the data from the prior questions, compute the beta coefficient for the Nasdaq Composite Index relative to the S&P 500 index. A priori, would you expect a beta less than or greater than 1.00? Discuss your expectations and the actual results.

11. Based on five years of monthly data, you derive the following information for the companies listed.

Company	a_j (Intercept)	σ_j	$r_{j,M}$
Intel	0.22	12.10%	0.72
General Motors	0.10	14.60	0.33
Anheuser Busch	0.17	7.60	0.55
Merck	0.05	10.20	0.60
S&P 500	0.00	5.50	1.00

   a. Compute the beta coefficient for each stock.
   b. Assuming a risk-free rate of 8 percent and an expected return for the market portfolio of 15 percent, compute the expected (required) return for all the stocks and plot them on the SML.
   c. Plot the following estimated returns for the next year on the SML and indicate which stocks are undervalued or overvalued.
   • Intel: 20%
   • General Motors: 15%
   • Anheuser Busch: 19%
   • Merck: 10%

12. Calculate the expected (required) return for each of the following stocks when the risk-free rate is 0.08 and you expect the market return to be 0.15.

Stock	Beta
A	1.72
B	1.14
C	0.76
D	0.44
E	0.03
F	−0.79

13. The following are the historic returns for the Denise Computer Company.

Year	Denise Computer	Market Index
1	37	15
2	9	13
3	−11	14
4	8	−9
5	11	12
6	4	9

Based on this information, compute the following.
a. The correlation coefficient between Denise Computer and the Market Index
b. The standard deviation for the company and the index
c. The beta for the Denise Computer Company

CFA 14. *CFA Examination Level II*
The following information describes the expected return and risk relationship for the stocks of two of WAH's competitors.

	Expected Return	Standard Deviation	Beta
Stock X	12.0%	20%	1.3
Stock Y	9.0	15	0.7
Market index	10.0	12	1.0
Risk-free rate	5.0		

Using only the data shown above:
a. Draw and label a graph showing the Security Market Line, and position stocks X and Y relative to it. (5 minutes)
b. Compute the alphas *both* for stock X *and* for stock Y. Show your work. (4 minutes)
c. Assume that the risk-free rate increases to 7 percent with the other data in the matrix above remaining unchanged. Select the stock providing the higher expected risk-adjusted return and justify your selection. Show your calculations. (6 minutes)

15. *CFA Examination Level II* **CFA**
An analyst expects a risk-free return of 4.5 percent, a market return of 14.5 percent, and the returns for stocks A and B that are shown in the following table.

STOCK INFORMATION

Stock	Beta	Analyst's Estimated Return
A	1.2	16%
B	0.8	14%

a. Show on a graph:
   i. where stock A and B would plot on the Security Market Line (SML) if they were fairly valued using the capital asset pricing model (CAPM).
   ii. where stock A and B actually plot on the same graph according to the returns estimated by the analyst and shown in the table. (6 minutes)
b. State whether stock A and B are undervalued or overvalued if the analyst uses the SML for strategic investment decisions. (4 minutes)

WEB EXERCISES

1. Obtain beta estimates for the following stocks from the NYSE, Nasdaq, Bloomberg, and Moneycentral Web sites for Microsoft (MSFT), ExxonMobil (XOM), McDonald's (MCD), and Apple (AAPL). How do the beta estimates compare across these sites? What reasons might exist for these differences?
   http://www.nyse.com: enter ticker symbol and click on "Quick Quote." Beta is among the information presented.
   http://www.nasdaq.com: enter ticker symbol and click on "info quotes."
   http://www.bloomberg.com: enter stock quote and click the arrow. Beta is included on the quote information page that appears.

   http://moneycentral.msn.com: go to "Investing"; enter the stock's ticker symbol, click on "Go," then choose "Company Report" under Research. Among the data in the report is the firm's beta (Volatility).

2. Examine Ken French's Web site and list of downloadable materials: (*http://mba.tuck.dartmouth.edu/pages/faculty/ken.french/* and *http://mba.tuck.dartmouth.edu/pages/faculty/ken.french/data_library.html#Research,* respectively). What information do you find that would be of interest to researchers and practitioners studying asset pricing models?

3. Go to *http://www.morningstar.com* and find the Fidelity Magellan report (type in FMAGX for the ticker symbol).

SPREADSHEET EXERCISES

1. Download S&P 500 monthly returns from *http://www.barra.com*. Using this as the market return, find the beta estimate of:
   a. the Small-Cap 600 from the Barra site.
   b. the MidCap 400 from the Barra site.
   c. the S&P 500 value index from the Barra site.
   d. the S&P 500 growth index from the Barra site.

2. Several mutual fund sites—such as *http://www.vanguard.com, https://www.fidelity.com,* and *http://www.troweprice.com*—list historic annual or quarterly returns for their mutual funds. Using the S&P 500 index from Barra as the market return, estimate beta, alpha, and R-squared for three mutual funds.

REFERENCES

Brinson, Gary P., Jeffrey J. Diermeier, and Gary Schlarbaum. "A Composite Portfolio Benchmark for Pension Plans." *Financial Analysts Journal* 42, no. 2 (March–April 1986).

Chen, F. N., Richard Roll, and Steve Ross. "Economic Forces and the Stock Market." *Journal of Business* (July 1986).

Handa, Puneet, S. P. Kothari, and Charles Wasley. "The Relation between the Return Interval and Betas: Implications of the Size Effect." *Journal of Financial Economics* 23, no. 1 (June 1989).

Reilly, Frank K., and Rashid A. Akhtar. "The Benchmark Error Problem with Global Capital Markets." *Journal of Portfolio Management* 22, no. 1 (Fall 1995).

THOMSON ONE
Business School Edition

1. Collect daily price data for the past year for the following four firms and find the daily price returns for each: Caterpillar, Intel, Bank of America, and Coca-Cola.
   a. Compute the standard deviation of each of these four firms. What is the "average" standard deviation? (Do this by summing the four standard deviations and dividing the sum by four.)
   b. Using all possible two-stock portfolios (50 percent invested in each stock), compute the standard deviation of each. What is the "average" standard deviation of all the possible two-stock portfolios? (There are six possible two-stock portfolios.)
   c. Repeat this process using all possible three-stock portfolios (there are four), and for a four-stock portfolio, assuming the stocks are equally-weighted in each.
   d. How does the average risk of the portfolio change as more firms enter the portfolio?

2. Collect daily price information for a year for Walgreens, ExxonMobil, and the S&P 500 index and compute daily returns for each.
   a. For each of the twelve months, compute the beta for Walgreens and ExxonMobil using the S&P 500 as the market index. (Excel's "slope" function will be helpful.) You will have twelve monthly estimates for beta for each stock. Are the monthly betas consistent over time?
   b. Using all the daily returns for the past year, compute beta for each stock. How do the monthly beta estimates compare to the annual beta calculation?
   c. For each of the twelve months, compute a monthly return for each stock and the S&P 500 index. Compute an annual beta estimate for Walgreens and for ExxonMobil using the twelve monthly returns. How does the beta computed using monthly data differ from the estimates using daily data?

GLOSSARY

Arbitrage pricing theory (APT) A theory concerned with deriving the expected (required) rates of return on risky assets based on the asset's systematic relationship to several risk factors. This multifactor model is in contrast to the single-factor CAPM.

Beta A standardized measure of systematic risk based on an asset's covariance with the market portfolio.

Capital asset pricing model (CAPM) A theory concerned with deriving the expected (required) rates of return on risky assets based on the assets' systematic risk levels.

Capital market line (CML) The line from the intercept point that represents the risk-free rate tangent to the original efficient frontier; it becomes the new efficient frontier.

Characteristic line The regression line of best fit through a scatterplot of rates of return for the individual risky asset and for the market portfolio of risky assets over some time period.

Completely diversified portfolio A portfolio in which all unsystematic risk has been eliminated by diversification.

Estimated rate of return The rate of return an investor anticipates earning from a specific investment over a particular future holding period.

Market portfolio The portfolio that includes all risky assets with relative weights equal to their proportional market values.

Market risk premium The amount of return above the risk-free rate that investors expect from the market in general as compensation for systematic risk.

Multifactor model A risk–return framework that considers multiple sources of both macroeconomic and microeconomic risk in deriving the expected (required) rates of return for a risky-asset portfolio.

Risk-free asset An asset with returns that exhibit zero variance.

Risky asset An asset with uncertain future returns.

Separation theorem The proposition that the investment decision, which involves investing in the market portfolio on the capital market line, is separate from the financing decision, which targets a specific point on the CML based on the investor's risk preference.

Systematic risk The variability of returns that is due to macroeconomic factors that affect all risky assets. Because it affects all risky assets, it cannot be eliminated by diversification.

Unsystematic risk Risk that is unique to an asset, derived from its particular characteristics (i.e., from microeconomic factors). It can be eliminated in a diversified portfolio.

Efficient Capital Markets

A n *efficient capital market* is one in which security prices adjust rapidly to the arrival of new information and, therefore, the current prices of securities reflect all information about the security. Some of the most interesting and important academic research during the past twenty years has analyzed whether our capital markets are efficient. This extensive research is important because its results have significant real-world implications for investors and portfolio managers. In addition, the question of whether capital markets are efficient is one of the most controversial areas in investment research. Recently, a new dimension has been added to the controversy: The rapidly expanding research in behavioral finance likewise has major implications regarding the concept of efficient capital markets.

Because of its importance and the controversy, investors need to understand the meaning of the terms *efficient capital markets* and *efficient market hypothesis (EMH)*. Our prior discussions have indicated how the capital markets function, so now it seems natural to consider the topic of efficient capital markets in terms of how prices react to new information. Investors should understand the analysis performed to test the EMH and the results of studies that either support or contradict the hypothesis. Finally, since the overall evidence on capital market efficiency is best described as mixed, investors need to be aware of the implications of these results when analyzing alternative investments to construct portfolios.

We first consider why we would expect capital markets to be efficient and the factors that contribute to an efficient market where the prices of securities reflect available information. We then describe the three subhypotheses of the EMH and the implications of each. In our subsequent review of the results of numerous studies on these hypotheses, we see diverse results: A large body of research supports the EMH, but a growing number of studies do not. Next we discuss the concept of behavioral finance and review the studies that relate to efficient markets and the implications for the EMH.

Finally, we discuss what these results imply for an investor who uses either technical or fundamental analysis, or for a portfolio manager who has access to superior or inferior analysts. We conclude with a brief discussion of the evidence for efficient markets in foreign countries.

Why Should Capital Markets Be Efficient?

As noted earlier, in an efficient capital market, security prices adjust rapidly to the infusion of new information, and, therefore, current security prices fully reflect all available information. To be absolutely correct, this is referred to as an *informationally efficient market*. Although the idea of an efficient capital market is relatively straightforward, we often fail to consider *why* capital markets *should* be efficient.

There is a set of three assumptions that imply an efficient capital market. The first is that an efficient market requires *a large number of profit-maximizing participants who analyze and value securities,* each independently of the others. Second, *new information regarding securities comes to the market in a random fashion,* and the timing of one announcement is generally independent of others.[1] The third assumption is especially crucial: *profit-maximizing investors adjust security prices rapidly to reflect the effect of new information.* Although the price adjustment may be imperfect, it is unbiased. Specifically, sometimes the market will overadjust and other times it will underadjust, but we cannot predict which will occur at any given time. Security prices adjust rapidly because of the many profit-maximizing investors competing against one another.

The combined effect of (1) information coming in a random, independent, unpredictable fashion and (2) numerous competing investors adjusting stock prices rapidly to reflect this new information means that price changes should be independent and random. Thus, the adjustment process requires a large number of investors analyzing the impact of new information on the value of a security and buying or selling the security until its price adjusts to reflect the new information. This scenario implies that informationally efficient markets require analysis and trading by numerous competing investors that cause a faster price adjustment, making the market more efficient. We will return to this need for trading and investor attention when we discuss some anomalies of the EMH.

Finally, because security prices adjust to all new information, these security prices should reflect all publicly available information. Therefore, the prevailing security prices should reflect all currently available information, including the risk of the security. Therefore, in an efficient market *the expected returns implicit in the current price of the security should reflect its risk.* This means that investors who buy at these informationally efficient prices should receive a rate of return that is consistent with the perceived risk of the stock. Put another way, in terms of the CAPM, all stocks should lie on the SML such that their expected rates of return are consistent with their perceived risk.

Efficient Market Subhypotheses

Most of the early work related to efficient capital markets was based on the *random walk hypothesis,* which contended that changes in stock prices occurred randomly. This early academic work contained extensive empirical analysis without much theory behind it. An article

---

[1]New information, by definition, must be information that was not known before, and it is not predictable. If it was predictable, it would have been impounded in the security price.

by Fama attempted to formalize the theory and organize the growing empirical evidence.[2] Fama presented the efficient market theory in terms of a *fair game model,* contending that investors can be confident that a current market price fully reflects all available information about a security and the expected return based on this price is consistent with its risk.

In his original article, Fama divided the overall efficient market hypothesis (EMH) and the empirical tests of the hypothesis into three subhypotheses, depending on the information set involved: (1) weak-form EMH, (2) semistrong-form EMH, and (3) strong-form EMH.

In a subsequent review article, Fama again divided the empirical results into three groups, but shifted empirical results among the prior categories.[3] Therefore, in the following discussion we use the original categories but organize the presentation of results using the new categories.

WEAK-FORM EFFICIENT MARKET HYPOTHESIS

The *weak-form EMH* assumes that current stock prices fully reflect *all security-market information,* including the historical sequence of prices, rates of return, trading volume data, and other market-generated information such as odd-lot transactions, block trades, and transactions by exchange specialists. Because it assumes that current market prices already reflect all past returns and any other security-market information, this hypothesis implies that past rates of return and other market data should have no relationship with future rates of return (that is, rates of return should be independent). Therefore, this hypothesis contends that an investor should gain little from buying or selling a security based on past rates of return or any other past market data.

SEMISTRONG-FORM EFFICIENT MARKET HYPOTHESIS

The *semistrong-form EMH* asserts that security prices adjust rapidly to the release of *all public information;* that is, current security prices fully reflect all public information. The semistrong hypothesis encompasses the weak-form hypothesis because all the market information considered by the weak-form hypothesis—such as stock prices, rates of return, and trading volume—is public. Public information also includes all nonmarket information, such as earnings and dividend announcements, price–earnings (P/E) ratios, dividend-yield (D/P) ratios, book value–market value (BV/MV) ratios, stock splits, news about the economy, and political news. This hypothesis implies that investors who base their decisions on important new *public* information should not derive above-average risk-adjusted profits after trading costs, because the security prices already reflect all new public information.

STRONG-FORM EFFICIENT MARKET HYPOTHESIS

The *strong-form EMH* contends that stock prices fully reflect *all information from public and private sources.* This means that no group of investors has monopolistic access to information relevant to the formation of prices. Therefore, this hypothesis contends that no group of investors should be able to consistently derive above-average risk-adjusted rates of return. The strong-form EMH encompasses both the weak-form and the semistrong-form EMH and extends the assumption of efficient markets—that prices adjust rapidly to the release of new public information—to assume perfect markets, in which all information is cost-free and available to everyone at the same time.

---

[2]Eugene F. Fama, "Efficient Capital Markets: A Review of Theory and Empirical Work," *Journal of Finance* 25, no. 2 (May 1970): 383–417.

[3]Eugene F. Fama, "Efficient Capital Markets: II," *Journal of Finance* 46, no. 5 (December 1991): 1575–1617.

Tests and Results of Efficient Market Hypotheses

With this background on the three components of the EMH and what each of them implies regarding the effect on security prices of different sets of information, we can consider the tests used to see whether the data support the hypotheses. Like most hypotheses in finance and economics, the evidence on the EMH is mixed. Some studies have supported the hypotheses and indicate that capital markets are efficient. Others have revealed some *anomalies* related to these hypotheses, raising questions about their validity.

WEAK-FORM EMH: TESTS AND RESULTS

Researchers have formulated two groups of tests of the weak-form EMH. The first category involves statistical tests of independence between rates of return. The second set of studies compare the risk–return results for *trading rules* that make investment decisions based on past market information relative to the results from a single buy-and-hold policy (which assumes that an investor buys stock at the beginning of a test period and holds it to the end).

Statistical Tests of Independence   As discussed earlier, the EMH contends that security returns over time should be independent of one another because new information comes to the market in a random, unpredictable, independent fashion, and security prices adjust rapidly to this new information. Two major statistical tests have been employed to verify this independence.

First, *autocorrelation tests* of independence measure the significance of positive or negative correlation in returns over time. Does the rate of return on day t correlate with the rate of return on day $t - 1$, $t - 2$, or $t - 3$?[4] Those who believe that capital markets are efficient would expect insignificant correlations for all such combinations.

Studies that examined the serial correlations among stock returns for short time horizons (one to sixteen days) typically indicated insignificant correlation in stock returns over time. Some recent studies that considered portfolios of stocks of different market size have indicated that the autocorrelation is stronger for portfolios of small-market-size stocks. Therefore, although the older results tend to support the hypothesis, the more recent studies cast doubt on it for portfolios of small firms, although these results could be affected by transaction costs of small-cap stocks and nonsynchronous trading for small-firm stocks.

The second statistical test of independence is the *runs test*.[5] Given a series of price changes, each price change is either designated a plus (+) if it is an increase or minus (−) if it is a decrease. The result is a set of pluses and minuses as follows: + + + − + − − + + − − + +. A run occurs when two consecutive changes are the same; that is, two or more consecutive positive or negative price changes constitute one run. When the price changes in a different direction, such as when a negative price change is followed by a positive price change, the run ends and a new run may begin. To test for independence, one would compare the number of runs for a given series to the number in a table of expected values for the number of runs that should occur in a random series.

Studies that have examined stock price runs have confirmed the independence of stock price changes over time. Because the actual number of runs for stock price series consistently fell into the range expected for a random series, these statistical tests confirmed the

---

[4]For a discussion of tests of independence, see S. Christian Albright, *Statistics for Business and Economics*, New York: MacMillan Publishing, 1987, 515–517.

[5]For the details of a runs test, see Albright, *Statistics for Business and Economics*, 695–699.

independence of stock price changes over time. Finally, several studies that examined price changes for individual *transactions* on the NYSE found significant serial correlations but this dependence of transaction price movements could not be used to earn above-average risk-adjusted returns after considering the substantial transaction costs.

Tests of Trading Rules

The second group of tests of the weak-form EMH were developed in response to the assertion that the prior statistical tests of independence were too rigid to identify the intricate price patterns examined by technical analysts. In response to this objection, investigators attempted to examine alternative technical trading rules through simulation. Advocates of the EMH contend that investors could not derive abnormal profits above a buy-and-hold policy using any trading rule that depended solely on past market information.

The trading-rule studies compared the risk–return results from trading-rule simulations (including transactions costs) to the results from a simple buy-and-hold policy. Three major pitfalls can negate the results of a trading-rule study:

1. The investigator should *use only publicly available data* when implementing the trading rule. As an example, the trading activities of specialists as of December 31 may not be publicly available until February 1, so one should not factor in information about specialist trading activity until then.
2. When computing the returns from a trading rule, the investigator should *include all transactions costs* involved in implementing the trading strategy because most trading rules involve many more transactions than a simple buy-and-hold policy.
3. The investigator must *adjust the results for risk* because a trading rule might simply select a portfolio of high-risk securities that should experience higher returns.

Researchers have encountered two operational problems in carrying out these tests of specific trading rules. First, some trading rules require too much subjective interpretation of data to simulate mechanically. Second, the almost infinite number of potential trading rules makes it impossible to test all of them. As a result, only the better-known technical trading rules have been examined.

In addition, the studies have typically examined relatively simple trading rules (which many technicians contend are rather naive) and employed readily available data for well-known, heavily traded stocks that certainly should trade in efficient markets. Recall the contention that *more trading in a security should promote market efficiency.* Alternatively, for securities with relatively few stockholders and little trading activity, the market could be inefficient simply because too few investors would be analyzing the effect of new information and trading the stock to move the price of the security quickly to a new equilibrium value. Therefore, using only active, heavily traded stocks could bias the results toward finding efficiency.

Results of Simulations of Specific Trading Rules

In the most popular trading technique, *filter rules,* an investor trades a stock when the price change exceeds a filter value set for it. As an example, an investor using a 5 percent filter would envision a positive (or negative) breakout if the stock were to rise (or fall) 5 percent from some base, suggesting that the stock price would continue to rise (or fall). A technician would buy (or sell) the stock to take advantage of the expected continued rise (or decline).

Studies that used a range of filters from 0.5 percent to 50 percent found that small filters yield above-average profits *before* taking account of trading commissions. However, because small filters generate numerous trades and substantial trading costs, when trading commissions were considered, the trading profits turned to losses. Alternatively, trading using larger filters did not yield returns above those of a simple buy-and-hold policy.

Researchers have simulated other trading rules that used other past market data such as advanced-decline ratios, short sales, short positions, and specialist activities.[6] These simulation tests have generated mixed results wherein most of the studies suggested that these trading rules generally would not outperform a buy–and–hold policy on a risk-adjusted basis after commissions, although several studies indicated support for specific trading rules. Therefore, most evidence from simulations of specific trading rules have supported the weak-form EMH, but the results are not unanimous.

Conclusions Regarding the Weak-Form EMH

The results generated by the two sets of tests of the weak-form hypothesis were fairly consistent in supporting the weak-form EMH. However, the results were not unanimous. There is always the caveat that there are some trading rules that are too subjective to test and there are obviously some trading rules that are not disclosed.

SEMISTRONG-FORM EMH: TESTS AND RESULTS

Recall that the semistrong-form EMH asserts that security prices adjust rapidly to the release of all public information; that is, security prices fully reflect all public information. These studies attempt to predict future rates of return using available public information beyond the pure market information (such as prices and trading volume) considered in the weak-form tests. Studies that have tested the semistrong-form EMH can be divided into the following three sets:

1. *Time-series analysis* of returns or *return prediction studies*. Advocates of the EMH contend that it would not be possible to predict future returns using the past time series of returns.
2. *Prediction of cross-sectional* returns for individual stocks based on some public information like size, P/E ratios, or P/BV ratios.
3. *Event studies.* These examine how fast stock prices adjust to specific significant economic events. A corollary approach would be to test whether it is possible to invest in a security after the public announcement of a significant event and experience significant abnormal rates of return. If markets are efficient, this should not be possible after transactions costs.

Adjustment for Market Effects

For any of these tests, we need to adjust the security's rates of return for the rates of return of the overall market during the period considered. A 5 percent return in a stock during the period surrounding an announcement is meaningless until we know what the aggregate stock market did during the same period and how this stock normally acts under such conditions. If the market had experienced a 10 percent return during this period, the 5 percent return for the stock may be lower than expected.

Authors of studies prior to 1970 typically assumed that the individual stocks should experience returns equal to the aggregate stock market. Therefore, the market adjustment process simply entailed subtracting the market return from the return for the individual security to derive its *abnormal rate of return,* as follows:

10.1
$$AR_{it} = R_{it} - R_{mt}$$

where:

AR_{it} = abnormal rate of return on security i during period t
R_{it} = rate of return on security i during period t
R_{mt} = rate of return on a market index during period t

If the stock experienced a 5 percent increase while the market increased 10 percent, the stock's abnormal return would be minus 5 percent.

---

[6]We discuss many of these trading rules in Chapter 16.

Since the 1970s, many authors have adjusted the rates of return for securities by an amount different from the market rate of return because the CAPM indicated that all stocks do not change by the same amount as the market—that is, some stocks are more volatile than the market and some are less. Therefore, we must determine an *expected rate of return* for the stock based on the market rate of return *and* the stock's relationship with the market (its beta). As an example, suppose stock A is generally 20 percent more volatile than the market (that is, it has a beta of 1.20). If the market experiences a 10 percent rate of return, we would expect this stock to experience a 12 percent rate of return. Therefore, a stock's abnormal return is the difference between the stock's actual rate of return and its *expected rate of return* as follows:

10.2

$$AR_{it} = R_{it} - E(R_{it})$$

where:

$E(R_{it})$ = the expected rate of return for stock i during period t based on the market rate of return and the stock's normal relationship with the market (its beta)

Thus if stock A had only a 5 percent return, its abnormal rate of return during the period would be minus 7 percent. Over the normal long-run period, we would expect the abnormal returns for a stock to sum to zero. Specifically, during one period the returns may exceed expectations, and during the next period they may fall short of expectations.

Let's summarize the three sets of tests of the semistrong-form EMH listed on the preceding page. First, in *return prediction studies* investigators attempt to predict the time series of future rates of return for individual stocks or the aggregate market using public information. For example, is it possible to predict abnormal market returns based on public information such as changes in the aggregate dividend yield or the risk premium spread for bonds?

In the second set of studies researchers attempt to *predict cross-sectional returns* using public information to predict the cross-sectional distribution of future risk-adjusted rates of return. For example, they use variables such as the price–earnings (P/E) ratio, the price–earnings/growth-rate (PEG) ratio, market value size, the price–book value ratio (P/BV), or the dividend yield (D/P) to predict which stocks will experience positive or negative abnormal rates of return in the future. Finally, in *event studies*, researchers examine abnormal rates of return for a period immediately after an announcement of a significant economic event—such as a stock split, proposed merger, or stock/bond issue—to determine whether an investor can derive abnormal rates of return by investing after the release of significant public information.

In all three sets of tests, the emphasis is on the analysis of abnormal rates of return that deviate from long-term expectations.

Results of Return Prediction Studies   The *time-series tests* assume that in an efficient market the best estimate of *future* rates of return will be the long-run *historical* rates of return. The point of the tests is to determine whether any public information will provide superior estimates of returns for a short horizon (one to six months) or a long horizon (one to five years).

The results of these studies have indicated limited success in predicting short-horizon returns, but the analysis of long-horizon returns has been quite successful. A prime example is dividend-yield studies. After postulating that the aggregate dividend yield (D/P) was a proxy for the risk premium on stocks, researchers found a significant positive relationship between the D/P and long-run stock-market returns.

In addition, several studies have considered two variables related to the term structure of interest rates: (1) a *default spread,* which is the difference between the yields on lower-grade and Aaa-rated long-term corporate bonds, and (2) the *term structure spread,* which is the difference between the long-term Aaa yield and the yield on one-month Treasury bills. These variables have been used to predict stock and bond returns.

The reasoning for these empirical results is as follows: When the two most significant variables—the dividend yield (D/P) and the default spread—are high, it implies that investors are expecting or requiring a high return on stocks and bonds. Notably, this occurs during poor economic environments, when investors perceive higher risk for investments and require a high rate of return. It is suggested that if you invest during this risk-averse period, your subsequent returns will be above normal. In contrast, when these values are small, it implies that investors have reduced their required rates of return, and future returns will be below normal.

Quarterly earnings reports.   Studies that address quarterly reports are considered part of the times-series analysis. Specifically, these studies question whether it is possible to predict future returns for a stock based on publicly available quarterly earnings reports. The typical test examined firms that experienced changes in quarterly earnings that differed from expectations. The results generally indicated abnormal returns during the thirteen or twenty-six weeks *following* the announcement of a large unanticipated earnings change (referred to as an *earnings surprise*). These results suggest that the earnings surprise is not instantaneously reflected in security prices.

An extensive analysis by Rendleman, Jones, and Latané (RJL) using a large sample and daily data from twenty days before a quarterly earnings announcement to ninety days after the announcement indicated that 31 percent of the total response in stock returns came before the announcement, 18 percent on the day of the announcement, and 51 percent afterward.[7]

Several authors contend that the reason for the stock price drift was the *earnings revisions* that followed the earnings surprises and contributed to the positive correlations of prices.

In summary, these results indicate that the market has not adjusted stock prices to reflect the release of quarterly earnings surprises as fast as expected by the semistrong EMH. This implies that earnings surprises and earnings revisions can be used to predict returns for individual stocks. These results using public information are evidence against the EMH.[8]

A set of calendar studies questioned whether some regularities in the rates of return during the calendar year would allow investors to predict returns on stocks. These studies include numerous studies on the January anomaly and studies that consider a variety of other daily and weekly regularities.

The January anomaly.   Several years ago Branch proposed a unique trading rule for those interested in taking advantage of tax selling.[9] Investors (including institutions) tend to sell stocks that have declined toward the end of the year to establish tax losses. After the new year, the tendency is to reacquire these stocks or to buy other stocks that look attractive. This scenario would produce downward pressure on stock prices in late November and

---

[7]Richard J. Rendleman Jr., Charles P. Jones, and Henry A. Latané, "Empirical Anomalies Based on Unexpected Earnings and the Importance of Risk Adjustments," *Journal of Financial Economics* 10, no. 3 (November 1982): 269–287; and C. P. Jones, R. J. Rendleman Jr., and H. A. Latané, "Earnings Announcements: Pre- and Post-Responses," *Journal of Portfolio Management* 11, no. 3 (Spring 1985): 28–32.

[8]Academic studies such as these that have indicated the importance of earnings surprises have led *The Wall Street Journal* to publish a section on "earnings surprises" in connection with regular quarterly earnings reports.

[9]Ben Branch, "A Tax Loss Trading Rule," *Journal of Business* 50, no. 2 (April 1977): 198–207. These results were generally confirmed in Ben Branch and Kyun Chun Chang, "Tax-Loss Trading—Is the Game Over or Have the Rules Changed?" *Financial Review* 20, no. 1 (February 1985): 55–69.

December and positive pressure in early January. Such a seasonal pattern is inconsistent with the EMH since it should be eliminated by arbitrageurs who would buy in December and sell in early January.

A study that did not support the EMH found December trading volume abnormally high for stocks that declined during the previous year and significant abnormal returns during January for these loss stocks. It was concluded that because of transaction costs, arbitrageurs must not be eliminating the January tax-selling anomaly. Subsequent analysis showed that most of the January effect was concentrated in the first week of trading, particularly on the first day of the year.

Several studies provided support for a January effect inconsistent with the tax-selling hypothesis by examining what happened in foreign countries that did not have U.S. tax laws or a December year-end. They found abnormal returns in January, but the results could not be explained by tax laws.

In summary, despite numerous studies, the January anomaly poses as many questions as it answers.[10]

Other calendar effects. Several other calendar effects have been examined, including a monthly effect, a weekend/day-of-the-week effect, and an intraday effect. One study found a significant monthly effect wherein all the market's cumulative advance occurred during the first half of trading months.

An analysis of the weekend effect found that the mean return for Monday was significantly negative during five-year subperiods and a total period. In contrast, the average return for the other four days was positive.

One study decomposed the Monday effect (typically measured from Friday close to Monday close) into a *weekend effect* (from Friday close to Monday open), and a *Monday trading effect* (from Monday open to the Monday close). It was shown that the negative Monday effect found in prior studies actually occurs from the Friday close to the Monday open, so it is really a weekend effect. After adjusting for the weekend effect, the Monday trading effect was positive. Subsequently it was shown that the Monday effect was on average positive in January and negative for all other months.

Finally, for *large firms,* the negative Monday effect occurred before the market opened (it was a weekend effect), whereas for *smaller firms* most of the negative Monday effect occurred during the day on Monday (it was a Monday trading effect).

Predicting Cross-Sectional Returns

Assuming an efficient market, *all securities should have equal risk-adjusted returns* because security prices should reflect all public information that would influence the security's risk. These studies test if an investor can use public information to predict what stocks will have above or below average risk-adjusted returns.

These studies examine alternative measures of size or quality to rank stocks in terms of risk-adjusted returns. Notably, all of these tests involve a *joint hypothesis* because they not only consider the efficiency of the market, but also depend on the asset pricing model that provides the measure of risk. Specifically, if a test indicates it is possible to predict risk-adjusted returns, these results could occur either because the market is not efficient *or* because the risk measure is faulty and, therefore, the risk-adjusted returns are wrong.

Price–earnings (P/E) ratios. Several studies have examined the relationship between the historical price–earnings (P/E) ratios for stocks and the returns on the stocks. It has been

---

[10]An article that reviews these studies and others is Donald B. Keim, "The CAPM and Equity Return Regularities," *Financial Analysts Journal* 42, no. 3 (May–June 1986): 19–34.

suggested that low P/E stocks will outperform high P/E stocks because the market tends to overestimate the growth potential and the value of high-growth companies while undervaluing low-growth firms with low P/E ratios. A consistent relationship between P/E ratios and subsequent abnormal risk-adjusted performance is evidence against the semistrong EMH, because it implies that investors could use publicly available P/E ratios to predict future abnormal returns.

Performance measures indicated that low P/E stocks experienced superior abnormal risk-adjusted results relative to the market, whereas high P/E ratio stocks had significantly inferior risk-adjusted results.[11] These results imply that publicly available P/E ratios possess valuable information regarding future returns, which is inconsistent with semistrong market efficiency.

Another study examined P/E ratios with adjustments for firm size, industry effects, and infrequent trading and likewise found that the risk-adjusted returns for stocks in the lowest P/E ratio quintile were superior to those in the highest P/E ratio quintile.

Price–earnings/growth-rate (PEG) ratios.   During the past decade there has been a significant increase in the use of the ratio of a stock's price–earnings ratio divided by the firm's expected growth rate of earnings (referred to as the PEG ratio) as a relative valuation tool, especially for stocks of growth companies that have P/E ratios substantially above average. Advocates of the PEG ratio hypothesize an inverse relationship between the PEG ratio and subsequent rates of return—that is, they expect that stocks with relatively low PEG ratios (i.e., less than 1) will experience above-average rates of return while stocks with relatively high PEG ratios (i.e., in excess of 3 or 4) will have below-average rates of return. A study by Peters using quarterly rebalancing supported the hypothesis of an inverse relationship.[12] These results would constitute an anomaly and would not support the EMH. A subsequent study by Reilly and Marshall assumed annual rebalancing and divided the sample on the basis of a risk measure (beta), market value size, and by expected growth rate.[13] Except for stocks with low betas and very low expected growth rates, the results were not consistent with the hypothesis of an inverse relationship between the PEG ratio and subsequent rates of return.

In summary, the results related to using the PEG ratio to select stocks are mixed—several studies that assume either monthly or quarterly rebalancing indicate an anomaly because the authors use public information and derive above-average rates of return. In contrast, a study with annual rebalancing indicated that no consistent relationship exists between the PEG ratio and subsequent rates of return.

The size effect.   Several authors have examined the impact of size (measured by total market value) on the risk-adjusted rates of return. The risk-adjusted returns for extended periods (twenty to thirty-five years) indicated that the small firms consistently experienced significantly larger risk-adjusted returns than the larger firms. It was contended that it was the size, not the P/E ratio, that caused the results discussed in the prior subsection, but this contention was disputed.

Recall that abnormal returns may occur either because the markets are inefficient or because the market model provides incorrect estimates of risk and expected returns.

---

[11]We discuss composite performance measures in Chapter 20.

[12]Donald J. Peters, "Valuing a Growth Stock," *Journal of Portfolio Management* 17, no. 3 (Spring 1991): 49–51.

[13]Frank K. Reilly and Dominic R. Marshall, "Using P/E/Growth Ratios to Select Stocks," Financial Management Association Meeting (October 1999).

It was suggested that the riskiness of the small firms was improperly measured because small firms are traded less frequently. An alternative risk measure technique confirmed that small firms had much higher risk, but even assuming an increase in the beta did not account for the large difference in rates of return for small-cap firms.

A study that examined the impact of transaction costs confirmed the size effect, but also found that firms with small market value have low stock prices. Because transaction costs vary inversely with price per share, these costs must be considered in size-effect studies. Studies found a significant difference in the percentage total transaction cost for large firms (2.71 percent) versus small firms (6.77 percent). Such a differential, with frequent trading, can have a significant impact on the results. Assuming daily transactions, the original small-firm effects are reversed. The point is that size-effect studies must consider realistic transaction costs and specify holding period assumptions. Studies that have considered both factors over long periods have demonstrated that infrequent rebalancing (about once a year) is almost ideal. The investment results are better than long-run buy-and-hold and this trading rule avoids frequent rebalancing that results in high trading costs.

In summary, the small firms outperformed the large firms after considering risk and transaction costs, assuming annual rebalancing.

Most studies on the size effect employed large databases and long time periods (over fifty years) to show that this phenomenon has existed for many years. In contrast, a study that examined the performance over various intervals of time concluded that *the small-firm effect is not stable.* During most periods they found the negative relationship between size and return, but during others (such as, 1967 to 1975) they found that large firms outperformed the small firms. Notably, this positive relationship held during the following recent periods: 1984–87; 1989–90; and 1995–99. A study by Reinganum acknowledges this instability but contends that the small-firm effect is still a long-run phenomenon.[14]

In summary, firm size is a major efficient market anomaly. Numerous attempts to explain the size anomaly indicate that the two strongest explanations are the risk measurements and the higher transaction costs. Depending on the frequency of trading, these two factors may account for much of the differential. These results indicate that the size effect must be considered in any event study that uses long intervals and contains a sample of firms with significantly different market values.

Neglected firms and trading activity. Arbel and Strebel considered an additional influence beyond size—attention or neglect.[15] They measured attention in terms of the number of analysts who regularly follow a stock and divided the stocks into three groups: (1) highly followed, (2) moderately followed, and (3) neglected. They confirmed the small-firm effect but also found a neglected-firm effect caused by the lack of information and limited institutional interest. The neglected-firm concept applied across size classes. Contrary results are reported by Beard and Sias, who found no evidence of a neglected-firm premium after controlling for capitalization.[16]

Another study examined the impact of trading volume by considering the relationship between returns, market value, and trading activity. The results confirmed the relationship

[14]Marc R. Reinganum, "A Revival of the Small Firm Effect," *Journal of Portfolio Management* 18, no. 3 (Spring 1992): 55–62.

[15]Avner Arbel and Paul Strebel, "Pay Attention to Neglected Firms!" *Journal of Portfolio Management* 9, no. 2 (Winter 1983): 37–42.

[16]Craig Beard and Richard Sias, "Is There a Neglected-Firm Effect?" *Financial Analysts Journal* 53, no. 5 (September–October 1997): 19–23.

between size and rates of return but the results indicated no significant difference between the mean returns of the highest and lowest trading activity portfolios. A subsequent study hypothesized that firms with less information require higher returns. Using the period of listing as a proxy for information, they found a negative relationship between returns and the period of listing after adjusting for firm size and the January effect.

Book value–market value (BV/MV) ratio. This ratio relates the book value (BV) of a firm's equity to the market value (MV) of its equity. Rosenberg, Reid, and Lanstein found a significant positive relationship between current values for this ratio and future stock returns and contended that such a relationship between available public information on the BV/MV ratio and future returns was evidence against the EMH.[17]

Strong support for this ratio was provided by Fama and French, who evaluated the joint effects of market beta, size, P/E ratio, leverage, and the BV/MV ratio (referred to as BE/ME) on a cross section of average returns.[18] They analyzed the hypothesized positive relationship between beta and expected returns and found that this positive relationship held before 1969 but disappeared during the period 1963 to 1990. In contrast, the negative relationship between size and average return was significant by itself and significant after inclusion of other variables.

In addition, they found a significant positive relationship between the BV/MV ratio and average return that persisted even when other variables are included. Most important, *both* size and the BV/MV ratio are significant when included together and they dominate other ratios. Specifically, although leverage and the P/E ratio were significant by themselves or when included with size, these variables become insignificant when *both* size and the BV/MV ratio are considered.

The results in Exhibit 10.1 show the separate and combined effect of the two variables. As shown, going across the Small-ME (small size) row, BV/MV (BE/ME in the table) captures strong variation in average returns (0.70 to 1.92 percent). Alternatively, controlling for the BV/MV ratio leaves a size effect in average returns (the high BV/MV results decline from 1.92 to 1.18 percent when going from small to large). These positive results for the BV/MV ratio were replicated for returns on Japanese stocks.

In summary, studies that have used publicly available ratios to predict the cross section of expected returns for stocks have provided substantial evidence in conflict with the semistrong-form EMH. Significant results were found for P/E ratios, market value size, neglected firms, and BV/MV ratios. Although the Fama–French work indicated that the optimal combination appears to be size and the BV/MV ratio, a study by Jensen, Johnson, and Mercer indicates that this combination only works during periods of expansive monetary policy.[19]

Results of Event Studies Recall that the intent of event studies is to examine abnormal rates of return surrounding significant economic information. Those who advocate the EMH would expect returns to adjust quickly to announcements of new information. As a

[17]Barr Rosenberg, Kenneth Reid, and Ronald Lanstein, "Persuasive Evidence of Market Inefficiency," *Journal of Portfolio Management* 11, no. 3 (Spring 1985): 9–17. Many studies define this ratio as "book-to-market value" (BV/MV) because it implies a positive relationship, but most practitioners refer to it as the "price-to-book value" (P/B) ratio. Obviously the concept is the same, but the sign changes.

[18]Eugene F. Fama and Kenneth R. French, "The Cross-Section of Expected Stock Returns," *Journal of Finance* 47, no. 2 (June 1992): 427–465.

[19]Gerald R. Jensen, Robert R. Johnson, and Jeffrey M. Mercer, "New Evidence on Size and Price-to-Book Effects in Stock Returns," *Financial Analysts Journal* 53, no. 6 (November–December 1997): 34–42.

EXHIBIT 10.1	Average Monthly Returns on Portfolios Formed on Size and Book-to-Market Equity; Stocks Sorted by ME (Down) and then BE/ME (Across); July 1963 to December 1990

In June of each year t, the NYSE, AMEX, and NASDAQ stocks that meet the CRSP-COMPUSTAT data requirements are allocated to ten size portfolios using the NYSE size (ME) breakpoints. The NYSE, AMEX, and Nasdaq stocks in each size decile are then sorted into ten BE/ME portfolios using the book-to-market ratios for year $t - 1$. BE/ME is the book value of common equity plus balance-sheet deferred taxes for fiscal year $t - 1$, over market equity for December of year $t - 1$. The equal-weighted monthly portfolio returns are then calculated for July of year t to June of year $t + 1$.

Average monthly return is the time-series average of the monthly equal-weighted portfolio returns (in percent).

The All column shows average returns for equal-weighted size decile portfolios. The All row shows average returns for equal-weighted portfolios of the stocks in each BE/ME group.

					BOOK-TO-MARKET PORTFOLIOS						
	All	Low	2	3	4	5	6	7	8	9	High
All	1.23	0.64	0.98	1.06	1.17	1.24	1.26	1.39	1.40	1.50	1.63
Small-ME	1.47	0.70	1.14	1.20	1.43	1.56	1.51	1.70	1.71	1.82	1.92
ME-2	1.22	0.43	1.05	0.96	1.19	1.33	1.19	1.58	1.28	1.43	1.79
ME-3	1.22	0.56	0.88	1.23	0.95	1.36	1.30	1.30	1.40	1.54	1.60
ME-4	1.19	0.39	0.72	1.06	1.36	1.13	1.21	1.34	1.59	1.51	1.47
ME-5	1.24	0.88	0.65	1.08	1.47	1.13	1.43	1.44	1.26	1.52	1.49
ME-6	1.15	0.70	0.98	1.14	1.23	0.94	1.27	1.19	1.19	1.24	1.50
ME-7	1.07	0.95	1.00	0.99	0.83	0.99	1.13	0.99	1.16	1.10	1.47
ME-8	1.08	0.66	1.13	0.91	0.95	0.99	1.01	1.15	1.05	1.29	1.55
ME-9	0.95	0.44	0.89	0.92	1.00	1.05	0.93	0.82	1.11	1.04	1.22
Large-ME	0.89	0.93	0.88	0.84	0.71	0.79	0.83	0.81	0.96	0.97	1.18

Source: From Eugene F. Fama and Kenneth French, "The Cross-Section of Expected Stock Returns," *Journal of Finance* 47, no. 2 (June 1992): 446. Reprinted by permission of Blackwell Publishing Ltd.

result, investors should not experience positive abnormal rates of return by acting after the announcement. Because of space constraints, we can only summarize the results for some of the more popular events considered.

The discussion of results is organized by event or item of public information. Specifically, we will examine the price movements and profit potential surrounding stock splits, the sale of initial public offerings, exchange listings, unexpected world or economic events, the announcements of significant accounting changes, and corporate events. Notably, the results for most of these studies have supported the semistrong-form EMH.

Stock split studies. Many investors believe that the prices of stocks that split will increase in value because the shares are priced lower, which increases demand for them. In contrast, those who believe in efficient markets would not expect a change in value because the firm has simply issued additional stock and nothing fundamentally affecting the value of the firm has occurred.

The classic FFJR study hypothesized no significant price change following a split because any relevant information (such as, earnings growth) that caused the split would have already been discounted.[20] The FFJR study analyzed abnormal price movements surrounding the time of the split and divided the stock split sample into those stocks that did or did not raise their dividends. Both groups experienced positive abnormal price changes

---

[20]E. F. Fama, L. Fisher, M. Jensen, and R. Roll, "The Adjustment of Stock Prices to New Information," *International Economic Review* 10, no. 1 (February 1969): 1–21.

prior to the split. Stocks that split but did *not* increase their dividend experienced abnormal price *declines* following the split and within twelve months lost all their accumulated abnormal gains. In contrast, stocks that split and also increased their dividend experienced no abnormal returns after the split.

These results support the semistrong-form EMH because they indicate that investors cannot gain from the information on a split after the public announcement. These results were confirmed by most (but not all) subsequent studies.

In summary, most studies found no short-run or long-run positive impact on security returns because of a stock split, although the results are not unanimous.

Initial public offerings (IPOs).   During the past twenty years a number of closely held companies have gone public by selling some of their common stock. Because of uncertainty about the appropriate offering price and the risk involved in underwriting such issues, it has been hypothesized that the underwriters would tend to underprice these new issues.

Given this general expectation of underpricing, the studies in this area have generally considered three sets of questions: (1) How great is the underpricing on average, does the underpricing vary over time, and if so, why? (2) What factors cause different amounts of underpricing for different issues? (3) How fast does the market adjust the price for the underpricing?

The answer to the first question is an average underpricing of almost 18 percent, but it varies over time as shown by the results in Exhibit 10.2. The major variables that cause differential underpricing for various issues seem to be: various risk measures, the size of the firm, the prestige of the underwriter, and the status of the firm's accounting firms. Finally, on the question of direct interest to the EMH, results indicate that the price adjustment to the underpricing takes place within one day after the offering.[21] Therefore, it appears that some underpricing occurs based on the original offering price, but the only ones who benefit from this underpricing are investors who receive allocations of the original issue. Further, a more recent study showed that institutional investors captured most (70 percent) of the short-term profits. This rapid adjustment of the initial underpricing would support the semistrong EMH. Finally, there have been several studies that examined the long-run returns on IPOs and the results indicate that investors who acquire the stock after the initial adjustment do *not* experience abnormal returns.[22]

Exchange listings.   A significant economic event for a firm's stock is being listed on a national exchange, especially the NYSE. Such a listing is expected to increase the market liquidity of the stock and add to its prestige. An important question is, can an investor derive abnormal returns from investing in the stock when a new listing is announced or around the time of the actual listing? The results about abnormal returns from such investing were mixed. All the studies agreed that: (1) the stocks' prices increased before any listing announcements, and (2) stock prices consistently declined after the actual listing. The crucial question is, what happens between the announcement of the application for listing and the actual listing (a period of four to six weeks)? Recent studies point toward profit opportunities immediately after the announcement that a firm is applying for listing and there is the

---

[21]In this regard, see Robert E. Miller and Frank K. Reilly, "An Examination of Mispricing, Returns, and Uncertainty for Initial Public Offerings," *Financial Management* 16, no. 2 (January 1987): 33–38. For an excellent review of the research on this topic, see Roger G. Ibbotson, Jody L. Sindelar, and Jay R. Ritter, "The Market Problems with the Pricing of Initial Public Offerings," *Journal of Applied Corporate Finance* 7, no. 1 (Spring 1994): 66–74.

[22]This is documented in Jay R. Ritter, "The Long-Run Performance of Initial Public Offerings," *Journal of Finance* 46, no. 1 (March 1991): 3–27; Richard B. Carter, Frederick Dark, and Asah Singh, "Underwriter Reputation, Initial Returns, and the Long-Run Performance of IPO Stocks," *Journal of Finance* 53, no. 1 (February 1998): 285–311; and Timothy Loughran and Jay Ritter, "The New Issues Puzzle," *Journal of Finance* 50, no. 1 (March, 1995).

EXHIBIT 10.2	Number of Offerings, Average First-Day Returns, and Gross Proceeds of Initial Public Offerings in 1975–2000		
Year	Number of Offerings[a]	Average First-Day Return, %[b]	Gross Proceeds, $ Millions[c]
1975	12	−1.5	262
1976	26	1.9	214
1977	15	3.6	127
1978	20	11.2	209
1979	39	8.5	312
1980	78	15.2	962
1981	202	6.4	2,386
1982	83	10.6	1,081
1983	523	8.8	12,047
1984	227	2.6	3,012
1985	215	6.2	5,488
1986	464	6.0	16,195
1987	322	5.5	12,160
1988	121	5.6	4,053
1989	113	7.8	5,212
1990	111	10.5	4,453
1991	287	11.7	15,765
1992	396	10.0	22,198
1993	503	12.6	29,232
1994	412	9.7	18,103
1995	464	21.1	28,866
1996	664	16.7	41,916
1997	483	13.7	33,216
1998	318	20.1	34,856
1999	491	69.0	65,471
2000	385	55.5	66,100
1975-79	112	5.7	1,124
1980-89	2,348	6.8	62,596
1990-99	4,129	20.9	294,076
2000	385	55.5	66,100
TOTAL	6,974	17.8	423,896

[a]The number of offerings excludes IPOs with an offer price of less than $5.00, ADRs, best efforts offers, unit offers, Regulation A offerings (small issues, raising less than $1.5 million during the 1980s), real estate investment trusts (REITs), partnerships, and closed-end funds.

[b]First-day returns are computed as the percentage return from the offering price to the first closing market price.

[c]Gross proceeds data are from Securities Data Co., and exclude overallotment options but include the international tranche, if any. No adjustments for inflation have been made.

Source: Reprinted by permission of Jay R. Ritter, University of Florida.

possibility of excess returns from price declines after the actual listing.[23] Finally, studies that have examined the impact of listing on the risk of the securities found no significant change in systematic risk or the firm's cost of equity.

---

[23]See John J. McConnell and Gary Sanger, "A Trading Strategy for New Listings on the NYSE," *Financial Analysts Journal* 40, no. 1 (January–February 1989): 38–39.

In summary, these studies that provide some evidence of short-run profit opportunities for investors using public information do not support the semistrong-form EMH.

Unexpected world events and economic news. The results of several studies that examined the response of security prices to world or economic news have supported the semistrong-form EMH. An analysis of the reaction of stock prices to unexpected world events—such as the Eisenhower heart attack, the Kennedy assassination, and military events—found that prices adjusted to the news before the market opened or before it reopened after the announcement (generally, as with the World Trade Center attack, the exchanges are closed immediately for various time periods—e.g., one to four days). A study that examined the response to announcements about money supply, inflation, real economic activity, and the discount rate found either no impact or an impact that did not persist beyond the announcement day. Finally, an analysis of hourly stock returns and trading volume response to *surprise* announcements about money supply, prices, industrial production, and the unemployment rate found that unexpected information about money supply and prices had an impact on stock prices that was reflected in about one hour.

Announcements of accounting changes. Numerous studies have analyzed the impact of announcements of accounting changes on stock prices. In efficient markets, security prices should react quickly and predictably to announcements of accounting changes. An announcement of an accounting change that affects the economic value of the firm should cause a rapid change in stock prices. An accounting change that affects reported earnings, but has no economic significance, should not affect stock prices. For example, when a firm changes its depreciation accounting method for reporting purposes from accelerated to straight-line, the firm should experience an increase in reported earnings but there is no economic consequence. An analysis of stock price movements surrounding this accounting change supported the EMH because (1) there were no positive price changes following the change, and (2) there were some negative price changes because firms making such a change are typically performing poorly.

During periods of high inflation, many firms will change their inventory method from first-in, first-out (FIFO) to last-in, first-out (LIFO), which causes a decline in reported earnings but benefits the firm because it reduces its taxable earnings and, therefore, its tax expenses. Advocates of efficient markets would expect positive price changes because of the tax savings; study results confirmed this expectation.

Therefore, these studies provide support for the EMH because they indicate that the securities markets react quite rapidly to accounting changes and adjust security prices as expected on the basis of the true value (that is, analysts are able to pierce the accounting veil and value securities on the basis of relevant economic events).[24]

Corporate events. Corporate financial events such as mergers and acquisitions, reorganization, and various security offerings (common stock, straight bonds, convertible bonds) have been examined relative to two general questions: (1) What is the market impact of these events? (2) How fast does the market adjust the security prices?

Regarding the reaction to corporate events, the stock price reactions were consistent with the underlying economic impact of the action. For example, the reaction to mergers is that the stock of the firm being acquired increases in line with the premium offered by the acquiring firm, whereas the stock of the acquiring firm typically declines because of the concern that they overpaid for the firm. Also, the evidence indicates fairly rapid adjustment.

---

[24]For a review of studies on this contention, see V. Bernard and J. Thomas, "Evidence That Stock Prices Do Not Fully Reflect the Implications of Current Earnings for Future Earnings," *Journal of Accounting and Economics* (December 1990): 305–341.

Studies related to financing decisions are reviewed by Smith.[25] Studies that consider mergers and reorganizations are reviewed by Jensen and Warner.[26]

Conclusions Regarding the Semistrong-Form EMH   Clearly, the evidence from tests of the semistrong EMH is mixed. The hypothesis receives almost unanimous support from the numerous event studies on a range of events including stock splits, initial public offerings, world events and economic news, accounting changes, and a variety of corporate financial events. About the only mixed results come from exchange-listing studies.

In sharp contrast, the numerous studies on predicting rates of return over time or returns for a cross section of stocks presented evidence counter to semistrong efficiency. This included time-series studies on risk premiums, calendar patterns, and quarterly earnings surprises. Similarly, the results for cross-sectional predictors such as size, the BV/MV ratio (when there is expansive monetary policy), P/E ratios, and neglected firms indicated nonefficiencies.

STRONG-FORM EMH: TESTS AND RESULTS

The strong-form EMH contends that stock prices fully reflect *all information,* public and private. This implies that no group of investors has access to *private information* that will allow them to consistently experience above-average profits. This extremely rigid hypothesis requires not only that stock prices adjust rapidly to new public information but also that no group has access to private information.

Tests of the strong-form EMH have analyzed returns over time for different identifiable investment groups to determine whether any group consistently received above-average risk-adjusted returns. Such a group must have access to important private information or an ability to act on public information before other investors, which would indicate that security prices were not adjusting rapidly to *all* new information.

Investigators have tested this form of the EMH by analyzing the performance of the following four major groups of investors: (1) *corporate insiders,* (2) *stock exchange specialists,* (3) *security analysts* at Value Line and elsewhere, and (4) *professional money managers.*

Corporate Insiders   Corporate insiders are required to report monthly to the SEC on their transactions (purchases or sales) in the stock of the firm for which they are insiders. Insiders include major corporate officers, members of the board of directors, and owners of 10 percent or more of any equity class of securities. About six weeks after the reporting period, this insider trading information is made public by the SEC. These insider trading data have been used to identify how corporate insiders have traded and determine whether they bought on balance before abnormally good price movements and sold on balance before poor market periods for their stock.[27] These studies have generally indicated that corporate insiders consistently enjoyed above-average profits especially on purchase transactions. This implies that many insiders had private information from which they derived above-average returns on their company stock.

---

[25]Clifford W. Smith Jr., "Investment Banking and the Capital Acquisition Process," *Journal of Financial Economics* 15, no. 1–2 (January–February 1986): 3–29.

[26]Michael C. Jensen and Jerald B. Warner, "The Distribution of Power Among Corporate Managers, Shareholders, and Directors," *Journal of Financial Economics* 20, no. 1–2 (January–March 1988): 3–24.

[27]Studies on this topic include M. Chowdhury, J. S. Howe, and J. C. Lin, "The Relation Between Aggregate Insider Transactions and Stock Market Returns," *Journal of Financial and Quantitative Analysis* 28, no. 3 (September 1993); 431–437; and R. R. Pettit and P. C. Venkatesh, "Insider Trading and Long-Run Return Performance," *Financial Management* 24, no. 2 (Summer 1995): 88–103.

In addition, an early study found that *public* investors who consistently traded with the insiders based on announced insider transactions would have enjoyed excess risk-adjusted returns (after commissions). However, a subsequent study concluded that the market had eliminated this inefficiency after considering total transaction costs.

Overall, these results provide mixed support for the EMH because several studies indicate that insiders experience abnormal profits, while subsequent studies indicate it is no longer possible for noninsiders to use this information to generate excess returns. Notably, because of investor interest in these data as a result of academic research, *The Wall Street Journal* currently publishes a monthly column entitled "Inside Track" that discusses the largest insider transactions.

Stock Exchange Specialists Several studies have determined that specialists have monopolistic access to certain important information about unfilled limit orders and should be able to derive above-average returns from this information. This expectation is generally supported by the data. First, specialists generally make money because they typically sell shares at higher prices than their purchase price. Also, they apparently make money when they buy or sell after unexpected announcements and when they trade in large blocks of stock. An article in *The Wall Street Journal* supported this belief; it contended that specialists are doing more trading as dealers, and they had experienced a return on their capital during 2000 of 26 percent.[28]

Security Analysts Several tests have considered whether it is possible to identify a set of analysts who have the ability to select undervalued stocks. The analysis involves determining whether, after a stock selection by an analyst is made known, a significant abnormal return is available to those who follow these recommendations. These studies and those that discuss performance by money managers are more realistic and relevant than those that considered corporate insiders and stock exchange specialists because these analysts and money managers are full-time investment professionals with no obvious advantage except emphasis and training. If anyone should be able to select undervalued stocks, it should be these "pros." In our discussion of these tests, we initially examine Value Line rankings and then analyze what returns investors experience when they follow the recommendations by individual analysts.

The Value Line enigma. Value Line (VL) is a large well-known advisory service that publishes financial information on approximately 1,700 stocks. Included in its report is a timing rank, which indicates Value Line's expectation regarding a firm's common stock performance over the coming twelve months. A rank of 1 indicates an expectation of the most favorable performance and 5 the worst. This ranking system, initiated in April 1965, assigns numbers based on four factors:

1. An earnings and price rank of each security relative to all others
2. A price momentum factor
3. Year-to-year relative changes in quarterly earnings
4. A quarterly earnings "surprise" factor (actual quarterly earnings compared with VL estimated earnings)

The firms are ranked based on a composite score for each firm. The top and bottom 100 are ranked 1 and 5, respectively, the next 300 from the top and bottom are ranked 2 and 4,

---

[28]Greg Ip, "If Big Board Specialists Are an Anachronism, They're a Profitable One," *The Wall Street Journal,* March 12, 2001, pp. A1, A10.

and the rest (approximately 900) are ranked 3. Rankings are assigned every week based on the latest data. Notably, all the data used to derive the four factors are public information.

Several years after the ranking was started, Value Line contended that the stocks rated 1 substantially outperformed the market and that the stocks rated 5 seriously underperformed the market (the performance figures did not include dividend income but also did not charge commissions). Several early studies on the Value Line enigma indicate that there is information in the VL rankings (especially either rank 1 or 5) and in changes in the rankings (especially going from 2 to 1). Further, most of the recent evidence indicates that the market is fairly efficient, because the abnormal adjustments appear to be complete by Day + 2. An analysis of study results over time indicates a faster adjustment to the rankings during recent years. Also, despite statistically significant price changes, mounting evidence indicates that it is not possible to derive abnormal returns from these announcements after considering realistic transaction costs. Some of the strongest evidence in this regard is the fact that Value Line's Centurion Fund, which concentrates on investing in rank-1 stocks, has consistently underperformed the market over the past decade.

Analysts' recommendations.   There is evidence in favor of the existence of superior analysts who apparently possess private information. This evidence is provided in two studies where the authors found that the prices of stocks mentioned in *The Wall Street Journal* column "Heard on the Street" experience a significant change on the day that the column appears. A study by Womach found that analysts appear to have both market timing and stock-picking ability, especially in connection with relatively rare sell recommendations.[29]

Professional Money Managers   The studies of professional money managers are more realistic and widely applicable than the analysis of insiders and specialists because money managers typically do not have monopolistic access to important new information but are highly trained professionals who work full-time at investment management. Therefore, if any "normal" set of investors should be able to derive above-average profits, it should be this group. Also, if any noninsider should be able to derive inside information, professional money managers should because they conduct extensive management interviews.

Most studies on the performance of money managers have examined mutual funds because performance data is readily available for them. Recently, data have become available for bank trust departments, insurance companies, and investment advisors. The original mutual fund studies indicated that most funds did not match the performance of a buy-and-hold policy.[30] When risk-adjusted returns were examined *without* considering commission costs, slightly more than half of the money managers did better than the overall market. When commission costs, load fees, and management costs were considered, approximately two-thirds of the mutual funds did *not* match aggregate market performance. It was also found that individual funds were inconsistent in their performance.

Now that it is possible to get performance data for pension plans and endowment funds, several studies have documented that the performances of pension plans and endowments likewise did not match that of the aggregate market.

The figures in Exhibit 10.3 provide a rough demonstration of these results for recent periods. These data are collected by Russell/Mellon Analytical Services as part of its performance evaluation service. Exhibit 10.3 contains the median rates of return for several investment groups compared to a set of Russell indexes, including the very broad Russell

---

[29]Kent L. Womach, "Do Brokerage Analysts' Recommendations Have Investment Value?" *Journal of Finance* 51, no. 1 (March 1996): 137–167.

[30]We review these studies and others on this topic in Chapter 19.

EXHIBIT 10.3	Annualized Rates of Return for Russell/Mellon U.S. Equity Universes and for Benchmark Indexes during Alternative Periods Ending December 31, 2003

	1 YEAR	2 YEARS	3 YEARS	4 YEARS	5 YEARS	8 YEARS	10 YEARS
U.S. Equity Universe-Medians							
Equity accounts	30.0	1.0	−2.3	−2.2	2.2	10.6	11.8
Equity oriented accounts	30.3	1.0	−2.4	−2.5	2.7	10.7	11.8
Equity pooled	29.6	0.9	−2.3	−2.2	1.2	10.1	11.5
Special equity pooled	47.0	11.3	13.0	14.0	13.6	13.5	14.1
Value equity accounts	31.1	5.0	3.7	6.0	5.8	11.3	12.6
Market oriented accounts	29.3	0.7	−2.7	−3.0	1.2	10.5	11.7
Midcap equity accounts	38.6	6.5	4.6	7.4	9.4	13.1	13.8
Growth equity accounts	29.1	−2.8	−9.0	−9.9	−1.6	9.9	10.6
Small cap accounts	45.7	10.4	10.8	11.6	13.3	13.4	13.9
Mutual Fund Universe-Medians							
Balanced mutual funds	18.6	2.6	0.3	0.6	2.6	7.3	7.8
Equity mutual funds	−1.7	−8.4	−6.6	−3.3	−0.3	8.4	8.9
Benchmark Indexes							
Russell 1000 Growth Index	29.75	−3.27	−9.36	−12.82	−5.11	6.97	9.21
Russell 1000 Index	29.89	0.88	−3.78	−4.79	−0.13	9.41	11.00
Russell 1000 Value Index	30.03	4.81	1.22	2.64	3.56	10.76	11.88
Russell 2000 Growth Index	48.54	1.78	−2.03	−7.59	0.86	3.61	5.43
Russell 2000 Index	47.25	8.21	6.27	3.86	7.13	8.78	9.47
Russell 2000 Value Index	46.03	13.73	13.83	16.01	12.28	13.06	12.70
Russell 2500 Index	45.51	9.37	6.58	6.00	9.40	11.15	11.74
Russell 3000 Index	31.06	1.40	−3.08	−4.19	0.37	9.25	10.77
Russell Midcap Index	40.06	8.35	3.47	4.65	7.23	11.54	12.18

Source: "Annualized Rates of Return for Russell/Mellon U.S. Equity Universes during Alternate Periods Ending December 31, 2003" from Russell/Mellon. Reprinted by permission of Russell/Mellon. "Benchmark Indexes during Alternative Periods Ending December 31, 2003" from Frank Russell Company. Reprinted by permission of Russell Investment Group, Tacoma, WA.

3000 index.[31] These results show that all but one equity universe always beat the Russell 3000 index in all periods. In contrast, the Russell 3000 beat the mutual fund universes for periods of five years and longer, but not for periods of three years and less. Therefore, for these periods, the money manager results are clearly mixed related to the strong-form EMH.

Conclusions Regarding the Strong-Form EMH The tests of the strong-form EMH have generated mixed results. The results for two unique groups of investors (corporate insiders and stock exchange specialists) did not support the hypothesis because both groups apparently have monopolistic access to important information and use it to derive above-average returns.

Tests to determine whether there are any analysts with private information concentrated on the Value Line rankings and publications of analysts' recommendations. The results for Value Line rankings have changed over time and currently tend toward support for the

[31]The results for these individual accounts have an upward bias because they consider only accounts retained (for example, if a firm or bank does a poor job on an account and the client leaves, those results would not be included).

EMH. Specifically, the adjustment to rankings and ranking changes is fairly rapid, and it appears that trading is not profitable after transactions costs. Alternatively, individual analysts' recommendations seem to contain significant information.

Finally, the recent performance by professional money managers provided mixed support for the strong-form EMH. Most money manager performance studies done pre-2000 have indicated that these highly trained, full-time investors could not consistently outperform a simple buy-and-hold policy on a risk-adjusted basis. In contrast, the recent results in Exhibit 10.3 show that about half the non–mutual fund universes beat the broad Russell 3000 index, while the equity mutual fund results supported the EMH for long term periods. Because money managers are similar to most investors who do not have access to inside information, these latter results are considered more relevant to the hypothesis. Therefore, there is mixed support for the strong-form EMH as applied to most investors.

Behavioral Finance

Our discussion up to this point has dealt with standard finance theory, how this theory assumes that capital markets function, and how to test within this theoretical context whether capital markets are informationally efficient. However in the 1990's a new branch of financial economics has been added to the mix. *Behavioral finance* considers how various psychological traits affect how individuals or groups act as investors, analysts, and portfolio managers. As noted by Olsen, behavioral finance advocates recognize that the standard finance model of rational behavior and profit maximization can be true within specific boundaries but assert that it is an *incomplete* model since it does not consider individual behavior.[32] Specifically, behavioral finance

> Seeks to understand and predict systematic financial market implications of psychological decisions processes . . . behavioral finance is focused on the implication of psychological and economic principles for the improvement of financial decision-making.[33]

While it is acknowledged that currently there is no unified theory of behavioral finance, the emphasis has been on identifying portfolio anomalies that can be explained by various psychological traits in individuals or groups or pinpointing instances where it is possible to experience above-normal rates of return by exploiting the biases of analysts or portfolio managers.

EXPLAINING BIASES

Over time it has been noted that investors have a number of biases that negatively affect their investment performance. Advocates of behavioral finance have been able to explain a number of these biases based on psychological characteristics. One major documented bias is the propensity of investors to hold on to "losers" too long and sell "winners" too soon.[34] Apparently, investors fear losses much more than they value gains. This is explained by *prospect theory,* which contends that utility depends on deviations from moving reference points rather than absolute wealth.

---

[32]Robert A. Olsen, "Behavioral Finance and Its Implications for Stock-Price Volatility," *Financial Analysts Journal* 54, no. 2 (March–April 1998): 10–18.

[33]Ibid., p. 11.

[34]This is discussed in J. Scott, M. Stumpp, and P. Xu, "Behavioral Bias Valuation, and Active Management," *Financial Analysts Journal* 55, no. 4 (July–August 1999): 49–57.

Another bias is overconfidence in forecasts, which causes analysts to overestimate growth rates for growth companies and overemphasize good news and ignore negative news for these firms. They generally believe that the stocks of growth companies will be "good" stocks. This bias is also referred to as *confirmation bias,* where investors look for information that supports their prior opinion and decision. As a result, they will misvalue the stocks of these generally popular companies.

A study by Brown examined the effect of *noise traders* (nonprofessionals with no special information) on the volatility of closed-end mutual funds. When there is a shift in sentiment, these traders move heavily, which increases the prices and the volatility of these securities during trading hours.[35] Also, Clark and Statman find that noise traders tend to follow newsletter writers, who in turn tend to "follow the herd." These writers and "the herd" are almost always wrong, which contributes to excess volatility.[36]

There is also *escalation bias,* which causes investors to put more money into a failure that they feel responsible for rather than into a success.[37] This leads to the relatively popular investor practice of "averaging down" on an investment that has declined in value since the initial purchase rather than consider selling the stock if it was a mistake. The thinking is that if it was a "buy" at $40, it is a screaming bargain at $30. Obviously, the investor's solution is to reevaluate the stock to see if some important bad news was missed in the initial valuation (therefore, sell it and accept the loss), or to confirm the initial valuation and acquire more of the "bargain." The difficult psychological factor is to seriously look for the bad news and consider the effects of that on the valuation.[38]

FUSION INVESTING

According to Charles M. C. Lee, *fusion investing* is the integration of two elements of investment valuation—fundamental value and investor sentiment.[39] In Robert Shiller's formal model, the market price of securities is the expected dividends discounted to infinity (its fundamental value) plus a term that indicates the demand from noise traders who reflect investor sentiment.[40] It is contended that when noise traders are bullish, stock prices will be higher than normal or higher than what is justified by fundamentals. Under this combination pricing model of fusion investing, investors will engage in fundamental analysis but also will consider investor sentiment in terms of "fads" and "fashions." During some periods, investor sentiment is rather muted and noise traders are inactive such that fundamental valuation dominates market returns. In other periods when investor sentiment is strong, noise traders are very active and market returns are more heavily impacted by investor sentiments. Both investors and analysts should be cognizant of these dual effects on the aggregate market, various economic sectors, and individual stocks.

Beyond advocating awareness of the dual components of fusion investing, results from other studies documented that fundamental valuation may be the dominant factor but takes

[35]Gregory Brown, "Volatility, Sentiment, and Noise Traders," *Financial Analysts Journal* 55, no. 2 (March–April 1999): 82–90.

[36]R. G. Clark and M. Statman, "Bullish or Bearish," *Financial Analysts Journal* 54, no. 3 (May–June 1998): 63–72.

[37]Hersh Shefrin, "Behavioral Corporate Finance," *Journal of Applied Corporate Finance* 14, no. 3 (Fall 2001): 113–124.

[38]For an extended presentation on this topic, see Hersh Shefrin, *Beyond Greed and Fear: Understanding Behavioral Finance and the Psychology of Investing,* Boston: Harvard Business School Press, 1999.

[39]Charles M. C. Lee, "Fusion Investing," in *Equity Valuation in a Global Context,* a conference sponsored by AIMR, 2003.

[40]Robert J. Shiller, "Stock Prices and Social Dynamics," *Brookings Papers on Economic Activity,* vol. 2 (1984): 457–510.

much longer to assert itself—about three years. To derive some estimate of changing investor sentiment, Lee proposes several measures of investor sentiment, most notably analysts recommendations, price momentum, and high trading turnover. Significant changes in these variables for a stock will indicate a movement from a glamour stock to a neglected stock or vice versa.

Implications of Efficient Capital Markets

Having reviewed the results of numerous studies related to different facets of the EMH, we can now look at what this means to individual investors, financial analysts, portfolio managers, and institutions. Overall, the results of many studies indicate that the capital markets are efficient as related to numerous sets of information. At the same time, research has uncovered a substantial number of instances where the market fails to adjust rapidly to public information. Given these mixed results regarding the existence of efficient capital markets, it is important to consider the implications.

The following discussion considers the implications of both sets of evidence. Specifically, given results that support the EMH, we consider what techniques will not work and what we do if we cannot beat the market. In contrast, because of the evidence that fails to support the EMH, we discuss what information and psychological biases should be considered when attempting to derive superior investment results through active security valuation and portfolio management.

EFFICIENT MARKETS AND TECHNICAL ANALYSIS

The assumptions of technical analysis directly oppose the notion of efficient markets. A basic premise of technical analysis is that stock prices move in trends that persist.[41] Technicians believe that when new information comes to the market, it is not immediately available to everyone but is typically disseminated from the informed professional to the aggressive investing public and then to the great bulk of investors. Also, technicians contend that investors do not analyze information and act immediately. This process takes time. Therefore, they hypothesize that stock prices move to a new equilibrium after the release of new information in a gradual manner, which causes trends in stock price movements that persist.

Technical analysts believe that nimble traders can develop systems to detect the beginning of a movement to a new equilibrium (called a *breakout*). Hence, they hope to buy or sell the stock immediately after its breakout to take advantage of the subsequent gradual price adjustment.

The belief in this pattern of price adjustment directly contradicts advocates of the EMH, who believe that security prices adjust to new information very rapidly. These EMH advocates do not contend, however, that prices adjust perfectly, which implies a chance of overadjustment or underadjustment. Still, because it is uncertain whether the market will over- or underadjust at any time, an investor cannot derive abnormal profits from adjustment errors.

If the capital market is weak-form efficient as indicated by most of the results, then prices fully reflect all relevant market information. So technical trading systems that depend only on past trading data cannot have any value. By the time the information is public, the price adjustment has taken place. Therefore, a purchase or sale using a technical trading rule should not generate abnormal returns after taking account of risk and transaction costs.

---

[41]Chapter 16 contains an extensive discussion of technical analysis.

Efficient Markets and Fundamental Analysis

As we have previously noted, fundamental analysts believe that, at any time, there is a basic intrinsic value for the aggregate stock market, various industries, or individual securities and that these values depend on underlying economic factors. Therefore, investors should determine the intrinsic value of an investment asset at a point in time by examining the variables that determine value—such as current and future earnings or cash flows, interest rates, and risk variables. If the prevailing market price differs from the estimated intrinsic value by enough to cover transaction costs, the investor should take appropriate action: buy if the market price is substantially below intrinsic value and sell if it is above. Investors who engage in fundamental analysis believe that occasionally market price and intrinsic value differ, but eventually investors recognize the discrepancy and correct it.

An investor who can do a superior job of *estimating* intrinsic value can consistently make superior market timing (asset allocation) decisions or acquire undervalued securities and generate above-average returns. Fundamental analysis involves aggregate market analysis, industry analysis, company analysis, and portfolio management. The divergent results from the EMH research has important implications for all of these components.

Aggregate Market Analysis with Efficient Capital Markets In Chapter 13 we make a strong case that intrinsic value analysis should begin with aggregate market analysis. Still, the EMH implies that an investor who examines only *past* economic events is unlikely to outperform a buy-and-hold policy because the market rapidly adjusts to known economic events. Evidence suggests that the market experiences long-run price movements, but to take advantage of these movements in an efficient market, an investor must do a superior job of *estimating* the relevant variables that cause these long-run movements. Put another way, an investor who uses only *historical* data to estimate future values and invests on the basis of these estimates will *not* experience superior risk-adjusted returns.

Industry and Company Analysis with Efficient Capital Markets As we will discuss in Chapter 13, the wide distribution of returns from different industries and companies clearly justifies industry and company analysis. Again, the EMH does not contradict the potential value of such analysis but implies that an investor must (1) understand the relevant variables that affect rates of return and (2) do a superior job of *estimating future* values for these relevant valuation variables. To demonstrate this, Malkiel and Cragg developed a model that did an excellent job of explaining past stock price movements using historical data. When this valuation model was employed to project *future* stock price changes using *past* company data, however, the results were consistently inferior to a buy-and-hold policy.[42] This implies that, even with a good valuation model, one cannot select stocks that will provide superior returns using only past data as inputs. The point is, most analysts are aware of the several well-specified valuation models, so the factor that differentiates superior from inferior analysts is the ability to *estimate* the inputs to the models.

Another study showed that the crucial difference between the stocks that enjoyed the best and worst price performance during a given year was the relationship between expected earnings of professional analysts and actual earnings (that is, it was *earnings surprises*). Specifically, stock prices increased if actual earnings substantially exceeded expected earnings, and stock prices fell if actual earnings did not reach expected levels. Thus, if an investor can do a superior job of projecting earnings and her expectations *differ from the consensus,* she will have

---

[42]Burton G. Malkiel and John G. Cragg, "Expectations and the Structure of Share Prices," *American Economic Review* 60, no. 4 (September 1970): 601–617.

a superior stock selection record.[43] Put another way, there are two factors that are required to be a superior analyst: you must be *correct* in your estimates, and you must be *different* from the consensus. If you are only correct and not different, you were predicting the consensus and the consensus was correct, which implies no surprise and no abnormal price movement.

The quest to be a superior analyst holds some good news and some suggestions. The good news is related to the strong-form tests that indicated the likely existence of superior analysts. It was shown that the rankings by Value Line contained information value, even though it might not be possible to profit from the work of these analysts after transaction costs. Also, the price adjustments to the publication of analyst recommendations also points to the existence of superior analysts. The point is, there are some superior analysts, but a limited number, and it is *not* an easy task to be among this select group. Most notably, a superior analyst must do a superior job of *estimating* the relevant valuation variables and *predicting earning surprises.*

The suggestions for those involved in fundamental analysis are based on the studies that considered the cross section of future returns. As noted, these studies indicated that P/E ratios, size, and the BV/MV ratios were able to differentiate future return patterns with size and the BV/MV ratio appearing to be the optimal combination. Therefore, these factors should be considered when selecting a universe or analyzing firms. In addition, the evidence suggests that neglected firms should be given extra consideration. Although these ratios and characteristics have been shown to be useful in isolating superior stocks from a large sample, it is our suggestion that they are best used to derive a viable sample to analyze from the total universe (e.g., select 200 stocks to analyze from a universe of 3,000). Then the 200 stocks should be rigorously valued using the techniques discussed in this text.

How to Evaluate Analysts or Investors To determine whether an individual is a superior analyst or investor, one should examine the performance of numerous securities that this analyst or investor recommends over time in relation to the performance of a set of randomly selected stocks of the same risk class. The stock selections of a superior analyst or investor should *consistently* outperform the randomly selected stocks. The consistency requirement is crucial because a portfolio developed by random selection will outperform the market about half the time.

Conclusions about Fundamental Analysis A text on investments can indicate the relevant variables that should be analyzed and describe the important analysis techniques, but actually estimating the relevant variables is as much an art and a product of hard work as it is a science. If the estimates could be done on the basis of some mechanical formula, we could program a computer to do it, and there would be no need for analysts. Therefore, the superior analyst or successful investor must understand what variables are relevant to the valuation process and have the ability to do a superior job of *estimating* these variables. Alternatively, one could be superior if one has the ability to interpret the impact or estimate the effect of some public information better than others.

EFFICIENT MARKETS AND PORTFOLIO MANAGEMENT

As noted, studies have indicated that the majority of professional money managers cannot beat a buy-and-hold policy on a risk-adjusted basis. One explanation for this generally inferior performance is that there are no superior analysts and the cost of research and trading forces the results of merely adequate analysis into the inferior category. Another explana-

---

[43]This is a major point made in H. Russell Fogler, "A Modern Theory of Security Analysis," *Journal of Portfolio Management* 19, no. 3 (Spring 1993): 6–14.

tion, which we favor and which has some empirical support from the Value Line and analyst recommendation results, is that money management firms employ both superior and inferior analysts and the gains from the recommendations by the few superior analysts are offset by the costs and the poor results derived from the recommendations of the inferior analysts.

This raises the question, should a portfolio be managed actively or passively? The point of the following discussion is that the decision of how to manage the portfolio (actively or passively) should depend on whether the manager has access to superior analysts. A portfolio manager with superior analysts or an investor who believes that he or she has the time and expertise to be a superior investor can manage a portfolio actively by attempting to time major market trends or looking for undervalued securities and trading accordingly. In contrast, without access to superior analysts or the time and ability to be a superior investor, one should manage passively and assume that all securities are properly priced based on their levels of risk.

Portfolio Management with Superior Analysts

A portfolio manager with access to superior analysts who have unique insights and analytical ability should follow their recommendations. The superior analysts should make investment recommendations for a certain proportion of the portfolio, and the portfolio manager should ensure that the risk preferences of the client are maintained.

Also, the superior analysts should be encouraged to concentrate their efforts in mid-cap stocks that possess the liquidity required by institutional portfolio managers. But because they do not receive the attention given the top-tier stocks, the markets for these neglected stocks may be less efficient than the market for large well-known stocks.

Recall that capital markets are expected to be efficient because many investors receive new information and analyze its effect on security values. If the number of analysts following a stock differ, one could conceive of differences in the efficiency of the markets. New information on top-tier stocks is well publicized and rigorously analyzed, so the price of these securities should adjust rapidly to reflect the new information. In contrast, middle-tier firms receive less publicity and fewer analysts follow these firms, so prices might be expected to adjust less rapidly to new information. Therefore, the possibility of finding temporarily undervalued securities among these neglected stocks is greater. Again, in line with the cross-sectional study results, these superior analysts should pay particular attention to the BV/MV ratio, to the size of stocks being analyzed, and to the monetary policy environment.

Portfolio Management without Superior Analysts

A portfolio manager who does not have access to superior analysts should proceed as follows. First, he should *measure the risk preferences* of his client. Then he should build a portfolio to match this risk level by investing a certain proportion of the portfolio in risky assets and the rest in a risk-free asset as discussed in Chapter 9.

The risky asset portfolio must be *completely diversified* on a global basis so it moves consistently with the world market. In this context, proper diversification means eliminating all unsystematic (unique) variability. In our prior discussion, it was estimated that about twenty securities are required to gain most of the benefits (more than 90 percent) of a completely diversified portfolio. More than one hundred stocks are required for complete diversification. To decide how many securities to actually include in a global portfolio, the portfolio manager must balance the added benefits of complete worldwide diversification against the costs of research for the additional stocks.

Finally, the portfolio manager should *minimize transaction costs.* Assuming that the portfolio is completely diversified and is structured for the desired risk level, excessive transaction costs that do not generate added returns will detract from the expected rate of return. Three factors are involved in minimizing total transaction costs.

1. *Minimize taxes.* Methods of accomplishing this objective vary, but it should receive prime consideration.
2. *Reduce trading turnover.* Trade only to liquidate part of the portfolio or to maintain a given risk level.
3. When trading, *minimize liquidity costs* by trading relatively liquid stocks. To accomplish this, submit limit orders to buy or sell several stocks at prices that approximate the specialist's quote. That is, put in limit orders to buy stock at the bid price or sell at the ask price. The stock bought or sold first is the most liquid one; all other orders should be withdrawn.

In summary, a manager who lacks access to superior analysts should do the following:

1. Determine and quantify risk preferences.
2. Construct the appropriate risk portfolio by dividing the total portfolio between risk-free and risky assets.
3. Diversify completely on a global basis to eliminate all unsystematic risk.
4. Maintain the specified risk level by rebalancing when necessary.
5. Minimize total transaction costs.

The Rationale and Use of Index Funds and Exchange-Traded Funds

As the preceding discussion indicates, efficient capital markets and a lack of superior analysts imply that many portfolios should be managed *passively* so that their performance matches that of the aggregate market, minimizing the costs of research and trading. In response to this demand, several institutions have introduced *market funds,* also referred to as *index funds,* which are security portfolios designed to duplicate the composition, and therefore the performance, of a selected market index series.

Notably, this concept of stock-market index funds has been extended to other areas of investments and has been enhanced by the introduction of exchange-traded funds (ETFs).[44] Index bond funds attempt to emulate the bond-market indexes discussed in Chapter 4. Also, some index funds focus on specific segments of the market such as international bond-index funds, international stock-index funds that target specific countries, and index funds that target small-cap stocks in the United States and Japan. When portfolio managers decide that they want a given asset class in their portfolio, they often look for index funds or to ETFs to fulfill this need. The use of index funds or ETFs are less costly in terms of research and commissions, and during almost all time periods they can provide the same or better performance than what is available from the majority of active portfolio managers.

Insights from Behavioral Finance

As noted earlier, the major contributions of behavioral finance researchers are explanations for some of the anomalies discovered by prior academic research and opportunities to derive abnormal rates of return by acting on some of the deeply ingrained biases of investors. Clearly, their findings support the notion that the stocks of growth companies typically will not actually be growth stocks because analysts become overconfident in their ability to predict future growth rates and eventually derive valuations that either fully value or overvalue future growth. Behavioral finance research also supports the notion of contrary investing, confirming the notion of the "herd mental-

---

[44]Leonard Kostovetsky, "Index Mutual Funds and Exchange-Traded Funds," *Journal of Portfolio Management* 29, no. 4 (Summer 2003): 80–92; and G.L. Gastineau, "Exchange-Traded Funds: An Introduction," *Journal of Portfolio Management* 27, no. 3 (Spring 2001): 88–96.

ity" of analysts in stock recommendations or quarterly earning estimates and the recommendations by newsletter writers. Also, it is important to recall the loss aversion and escalation bias that causes investors to ignore bad news and hold losers too long and in some cases acquire additional shares of losers to average down the cost. Finally, recognize that valuation is a combination of fundamental value and investor sentiment.

Summary

- The efficiency of capital markets has implications for the investment analysis and management of a portfolio. Capital markets should be efficient because numerous rational, profit-maximizing investors react quickly to the release of new information. Assuming prices reflect new information, they are unbiased estimates of the securities' true, intrinsic value, and there should be a consistent relationship between the return on an investment and its risk.

- The weak-form EMH states that stock prices fully reflect all market information, so any trading rule that uses past market data to predict future returns should have no value. Most studies consistently supported this hypothesis.

- The semistrong-form EMH asserts that security prices adjust rapidly to the release of all public information. The tests of this hypothesis either examine the opportunities to predict future rates of return, or they involve event studies that analyze whether investors could profit from trading on the basis of public information. The test results for this hypothesis were clearly mixed. The results for almost all the event studies consistently supported the semistrong hypothesis while several studies that examined the ability to predict rates of return generally did not support the hypothesis.

- The strong-form EMH states that security prices reflect all information. This implies that nobody has private information, so no group should be able to derive above-average returns consistently. Studies of corporate insiders and stock exchange specialists do not support the strong-form hypothesis. An analysis of the recommendations by analysts indicated the

Investments Online

Capital market prices reflect current news items fairly quickly. On the other hand, a portfolio manager should not ignore news just because prices adjust quickly. News provides information a manager can use to structure portfolios and to update potential future scenarios.

A number of news sources are available on the Internet. Some of them, such as **http://www.bloomberg.com, http://news.ft.com,** and **http://online.wsj.com,** were listed in previous chapters. Other sites include:

http://finance.yahoo.com This site contains links to a number of news, information, commentary, and finance-related sites.

http://money.cnn.com This is the financial network site for the Cable News Network and Money magazine. The CNN Web site is **http://www.cnn.com.**

http://moneycentral.msn.com The Web site of the CNBC cable TV station has moved to this site.

http://www.foxnews.com, http://www.abcnews.go.com, http://www.cbsnews.com, and **http://www.msnbc.msn.com/** are the URLs for news from Fox, ABC, CBS, and NBC, respectively. Meir Statman (**http://lsb.scu.edu/finance/faculty/ Statman/**) and Richard Thaler (**http://gsbwww.uchicago.edu/ fac/richard.thaler/research/**) are two leading researchers in the area of behavioral finance. These pages contain links to their research.

existence of private information. In contrast, the performance by professional money managers supported the strong-form EMH because their risk-adjusted investment performance was typically inferior to results achieved with buy-and-hold-policies.

- During the past decade research in behavioral finance has contended that the standard finance theory model is incomplete since it does not consider implications of psychological traits of individuals that explain many anomalies and the existence of several biases. These biases can lead to inferior performance by analysts and portfolio managers and can be exploited for excess returns.

- Given the mixed results, it is important to consider the implications of all of this for technical or fundamental analysts, and for portfolio managers. All forms of fundamental analysis are useful, but they are difficult to implement because they require the ability *to estimate future economic values.* Superior analysis is possible but it requires superior projections. Portfolio managers should constantly evaluate investment advice to determine whether it is superior.

- Without access to superior analytical advice, investors should run their portfolios like an index fund or ETF. In contrast, superior analysts should concentrate their efforts on mid-cap firms and neglected firms where there is a higher probability of discovering misvalued stocks. The analysis should concentrate on a firm's P/E ratio, BV/MV ratio, its size, and the monetary environment.

This chapter contains some good news and some bad news. The good news is that the practice of investment analysis and portfolio management is not an art that has been lost to the great computer in the sky. Viable professions still await those willing to extend the effort and able to accept the pressures. The bad news is that many bright, hardworking people with extensive resources make the game tough. In fact, those competitors have created a fairly efficient capital market in which it is extremely difficult for most analysts and portfolio managers to achieve superior results.

QUESTIONS

1. Discuss the rationale for expecting an efficient capital market. What factor would you look for to differentiate the market efficiency for two stocks?
2. Define and discuss the weak-form EMH. Describe the two sets of tests used to examine the weak-form EMH.
3. Define and discuss the semistrong-form EMH. Describe the two sets of tests used to examine the semistrong-form EMH.
4. What is meant by the term *abnormal rate of return*?
5. Describe how to compute the abnormal rate of return for a stock for a period surrounding an economic event. Give a brief example for a stock with a beta of 1.40.
6. Assume you want to test the EMH by comparing alternative trading rules to a buy-and-hold policy. Discuss the three common mistakes that can bias the results against the EMH.
7. Describe the results of a study that supported the semistrong-form EMH. Discuss the nature of the test and specifically why the results support the hypothesis.
8. Describe the results of a study that did *not* support the semistrong-form EMH. Discuss the nature of the test and specifically why the results did not support the hypothesis.
9. For many of the EMH tests, it is really a test of a "joint hypothesis." Discuss what is meant by this concept and what joint hypotheses are being tested.

10. Define and discuss the strong-form EMH. Why do some observers contend that the strong-form hypothesis really requires a perfect market in addition to an efficient market? Be specific.
11. Discuss how you would test the strong-form EMH. Why are these tests relevant? Give a brief example.
12. Describe the results of a study that did *not* support the strong-form EMH. Discuss the test involved and specifically why the results reported did not support the hypothesis.
13. Describe the results of a study that supported the strong-form EMH. Discuss the test involved and specifically why these results support the hypothesis.
14. Describe the general goal of behavioral finance.
15. Why do the advocates of behavioral finance contend that the standard finance theory is incomplete?
16. What does the EMH imply for the use of technical analysis?
17. What does the EMH imply for fundamental analysis? Discuss specifically what it does *not* imply.
18. In a world of efficient capital markets, what do you have to do to be a superior analyst? How would you test whether an analyst was superior?
19. Discuss what advice you would give to your superior analysts in terms of the set of firms to analyze and variables that should be considered in the analysis.
20. How should a portfolio manager without any superior analysts run his or her portfolio?

21. Describe the goals of an index fund. Discuss the contention that index funds are the ultimate answer in a world with efficient capital markets.
22. At a social gathering you meet the portfolio manager for the trust department of a local bank. He confides to you that he has been following the recommendations of the department's six analysts for an extended period and has found that two are superior, two are average, and two are clearly inferior. What would you recommend that he do to run his portfolio?

CFA 23. *CFA Examination Level I*
   a. List and briefly define the *three* forms of the efficient market hypothesis. (6 minutes)
   b. Discuss the role of a portfolio manager in a perfectly efficient market. (9 minutes)

CFA 24. *CFA Examination Level II*
   Tom Max, TMP's quantitative analyst, has developed a portfolio construction model about which he is excited. To create the model, Max made a list of the stocks currently in the S&P 500 stock index and obtained annual operating cash flow, price, and total return data for each issue for the past five years. As of each year-end, this universe was divided into five equal-weighted portfolios of 100 issues each, with selection based solely on the price–cash flow rankings of the individual stocks. Each portfolio's average annual return was then calculated.

   During this five-year period, the linked returns from the portfolios with the lowest price–cash flow ratio generated an annualized total return of 19.0 percent, or 3.1 percentage points better than the 15.9 percent return on the S&P 500 stock index. Max also noted that the lowest price–cash flow portfolio had a below-market beta of 0.91 over this same time span.
   a. Briefly comment on Max's use of the beta measure as an indicator of portfolio risk in light of recent academic tests of its explanatory power with respect to stock returns. (5 minutes)
   b. You are familiar with the literature on market anomalies and inefficiencies. Against this background, discuss Max's use of a single-factor model (price–cash flow) in his research. (8 minutes)
   c. Identify and briefly describe *four* specific concerns about Max's test procedures and model design. (The issues already discussed in your answers to parts (a) and (b) may *not* be used in answering part (c). (12 minutes)

CFA 25. *CFA Examination Level III*
   a. Briefly explain the concept of the *efficient market hypothesis* (EMH) and each of its three forms—*weak, semistrong, and strong*—and briefly discuss the degree to which existing empirical evidence supports each of the three forms of the EMH. (8 minutes)
   b. Briefly discuss the implications of the efficient market hypothesis for investment policy as it applies to:
      i. technical analysis in the form of charting, and
      ii. fundamental analysis. (4 minutes)
   c. Briefly explain *two* major roles or responsibilities of portfolio managers in an efficient market environment. (4 minutes)
   d. Briefly discuss whether active asset allocation among countries could consistently outperform a world market index. Include a discussion of the implications of *integration versus segmentation* of international financial markets as it pertains to portfolio diversification, but ignore the issue of stock selection. (6 minutes)

PROBLEMS

1. Compute the abnormal rates of return for the following stocks during period t (ignore differential systematic risk).

Stock	R_{it}	R_{mt}
B	11.5%	4.0%
F	10.0	8.5
T	14.0	9.6
C	12.0	15.3
E	15.9	12.4

R_{it} = return for stock i during period t
R_{mt} = return for the aggregate market during period t

2. Compute the abnormal rates of return for the five stocks in Problem 1 assuming the following systematic risk measures (betas).

Stock	β_i
B	0.95
F	1.25
T	1.45
C	0.70
E	−0.30

3. Compare the abnormal returns in Problems 1 and 2 and discuss the reason for the difference in each case.

4. Look up the daily trading volume for the following stocks during a recent five-day period.
   - Merck
   - Anheuser Busch
   - Intel
   - McDonald's
   - General Electric

Randomly select five stocks from the NYSE and examine their daily trading volume for the same five days.
   a. What are the average daily volumes for the two samples?
   b. Would you expect this difference to have an impact on the efficiency of the markets for the two samples? Why or why not?

WEB EXERCISES

1. Undiscovered Managers (*http://www.undiscoveredmanagers.com*) is a mutual fund group that uses the concepts of behavioral finance in managing its portfolios.
   a. Comment on the performance of their funds against their benchmarks. Do the performance figures, when compared to the benchmarks, indicate that the insights from behavioral finance provide a superior way to invest? Why or why not?
   b. Are the benchmarks noted in the "performance" section appropriate for the funds? Why or why not?
   c. The Web site contains research papers on behavioral finance. Read one of the papers and summarize the research in one or two pages. What implications do the findings have for the efficient market hypothesis?

2. The Web site *http://finance.yahoo.com* provides information on recent earnings announcements and earnings surprises. (Click on "Today's Markets," then click on "Earnings" under "Today's Events.") Select the three stocks with the largest earnings surprises (positive or negative). On the main page, enter the ticker symbols for each of the stocks and get a price chart. Does the chart reflect market anticipation of the earnings surprise? Or did the market react after the news?

3. What is a "whisper number?" What is the relationship between whisper numbers, earnings announcements, and stock price reaction? See Internet sites such as *http://www.earningswhispers.com* and *http://www.whispernumber.com*.

REFERENCES

Ball, Ray. "The Theory of Stock Market Efficiency: Accomplishments and Limitations." *Journal of Applied Corporate Finance* 8, no. 1 (Spring 1995).

Barry, Christopher B., and Stephen J. Brown. "Differential Information and the Small Firm Effect." *Journal of Financial Economics* 13, no. 2 (June 1984).

Basu, Senjoy. "Investment Performance of Common Stocks in Relation to Their Price-Earnings Ratios: A Test of the Efficient Market Hypothesis." *Journal of Finance* 32, no. 3 (June 1977).

Berkowitz, Stephen A., Louis D. Finney, and Dennis Logue. *The Investment Performance of Corporate Pension Plans.* New York: Quorum Books, 1988.

Bernard, Victor. "Capital Markets Research in Accounting During the 1980's: A Critical Review." In *The State of Accounting Research as We Enter the 1990's,* edited by Thomas J. Frecka. Urbana: University of Illinois Press, 1989.

Bernard, Victor L., and Jacob K. Thomas. "Post–Earnings–Announcements Drift: Delayed Price Response or Risk Premium?" *Journal of Accounting Research* 27, (Supplement, 1989).

Fama, Eugene F. "Efficient Capital Market: II." *Journal of Finance* 46, no. 5 (December 1991).

Fisher, Kenneth and Meir Statman, "A Behavioral Framework for Time Diversification," *Financial Analysts Journal* 55, no. 3 (May–June, 1999).

Huberman, Gur, and Shmuel Kandel. "Market Efficiency and Value Line's Record." *Journal of Business* 63, no. 2 (April 1990).

Ibbotson, Roger G., Jody Sindelar, and Jay R. Ritter. "Initial Public Offerings." *Journal of Applied Corporate Finance* 1, no. 3 (Summer 1988).

Jain, Prem C. "Response of Hourly Stock Prices and Trading Volume to Economic News." *Journal of Business* 61, no. 2 (April 1988).

Keim, Donald B. "Size-Related Anomalies and Stock Return Seasonality." *Journal of Financial Economics* 12, no. 1 (June 1983).

Keim, Donald B., and Robert F. Stambaugh. "Predicting Returns in Stock and Bond Markets." *Journal of Financial Economics* 17, no. 2 (December 1986).

Lev, Baruch. "On the Usefulness of Earnings and Earning Research: Lessons and Directions from Two Decades of Empirical Research," *Journal of Accounting Research* (Supplement, 1989).

Loughran, Timothy, and Jay Ritter. "The New Issues Puzzle." *Journal of Finance* 50, no. 1 (March 1995).

Malkiel, Burton G. *A Random Walk Down Wall Street.* New York: Norton, 2000.

Miller, Robert E., and Frank K. Reilly. "Examination of Mispricing, Returns, and Uncertainty for Initial Public Offerings." *Financial Management* 16, no. 2 (January 1987).

Nofsinger, John R. *The Psychology of Investing,* 2nd ed., New Jersey: Pearson Prentice Hall, 2005.

Ou, J., and S. Penman. "Financial Statement Analysis and the Prediction of Stock Returns." *Journal of Accounting and Economics* (November 1989).

Shefrin, Hersh. *Beyond Greed and Fear: Understanding Behavioral Finance and the Psychology of Investing.* Boston: Harvard Business School Press, 1999.

Shefrin, Hersh, and Meir Statman. "Behavioral Capital Asset Pricing Theory." *Journal of Financial and Quantitative Analysis,* no. 3 (September 1995).

Wood, Arnold S., ed. *Behavioral Finance and Decision Theory in Investment Management.* Charlottesville, VA: Association for Investment Management and Research, 1995.

THOMSON ONE
Business School Edition

1. Find a firm which has had an earnings surprise at the end of a recent quarter (select a firm, click the "estimate" tab, then click on "consensus estimate" and "Thomson Surprise Report"). How did the stock price react to the earnings surprise relative to the overall market?

2. For a firm of your choice, review news listings by clicking the "news" tab. Find a significant firm or industry event. How did the stock price react that day compared to the overall market?

GLOSSARY

Abnormal rate of return The amount by which a security's return differs from the market's expected rate of return based on the market's rate of return and the security's relationship with the market.

Anomalies Security price relationships that appear to contradict a well-regarded hypothesis; in this case, the efficient market hypothesis.

Autocorrelation test A test of the weak-form efficient market hypothesis that compares security price changes over time to check for predictable correlation patterns.

Behavioral finance A branch of financial economics that considers how psychological traits affect how individuals or groups act as investors.

Earnings surprise A company announcement of earnings that differ from analysts' prevailing expectations.

Efficient capital market A market in which security prices rapidly reflect all information about securities.

Expected rate of return The return that analysts' calculations suggest a security should provide, based on the market's rate of return during the period and the security's relationship to the market.

Filter rule A trading rule that recommends security transactions when price changes exceed a previously determined percentage.

Fusion investing Investing with awareness of the dual effects of fundamental value and investor sentiment.

Informationally efficient market A more technical term for an efficient capital market that emphasizes the role of information.

Runs test A test of the weak-form efficient market hypothesis that checks for trends that persist longer in terms of positive or negative price changes than one would expect for a random series.

Semistrong-form efficient market hypothesis The belief that security prices fully reflect all publicly available information, including information from security transactions and company, economic, and political news.

Strong-form efficient market hypothesis The belief that security prices fully reflect all information from both public and private sources.

Trading rule A formula for deciding on current transactions based on historical data.

Weak-form efficient market hypothesis The belief that security prices fully reflect all security market information.

Valuation: Review and Fixed-Income Applications

In the realm of investor excitement, bonds are near the bottom of the list; it's stocks that draw attention from both the print and broadcast media. The perception that bonds are boring and not a very important component of the capital market is pervasive—ask any investor under sixty years old or a college finance student. This is surprising when one considers that in the United States and most other countries, the total market value of the bond market is very similar to that of the stock market. For example, in the United States as of year-end 2003, the market value of all publicly issued bonds was more than $21 trillion while the market value of all stocks was about $23 trillion. On a global basis the market value of bonds was almost $45 trillion.[1]

Bonds also have a reputation for offering low, unexciting rates of return. While this may have been true fifty or sixty years ago, it has certainly not been true during the past twenty years. Specifically, from 1980 to 2001, the average compound rate of return for an aggregate bond portfolio was about 10 percent a year (including 32.64 percent in

1982, six other years where the returns exceeded 14 percent, and only two years of small negative returns). This compares to an annual average return for the Wilshire 5000 index of about 14 percent.[2] The point is, there are substantial investment opportunities in fixed-income securities for individual and institutional investors.

In Chapter 3 we provided a basic discussion of fixed-income securities and an overview of the global markets for bonds. We also discussed several new corporate bond instruments developed in the United States, such as asset-backed securities, zero coupon bonds, and high-yield bonds. All of these instruments are being or will eventually be used around the world. In this section we build on this background, starting in Chapter 11 where we introduce the general topic of the valuation of assets, including the valuation of option-free bonds as a precursor to Chapter 12 (and the valuation of common stocks as a precursor to Chapter 15 in Part 3). We discuss the two major inputs in the valuation process, as well as various approaches and models used to estimate these

inputs and derive the intrinsic value of an asset in order to make sound investment decisions.

In Chapter 12 we cover the analysis of fixed-income securities in more detail. We discuss the various rate of return measures for bonds, factors that affect yields on bonds, and influences on the volatility of bond returns including bond duration and the convexity of alternative bonds.

The fact that we have devoted several chapters to the study of bonds attests to the importance of the topic and the extensive research being done in this area. During the past fifteen years, there have probably been more developments related to the valuation and portfolio management of bonds than of stocks. This growth in bond theory and practice does not detract from the importance of equities but certainly enhances the significance of fixed-income securities. In addition, this growth in size and sophistication of the bond market means there are numerous career opportunities in the fixed-income field including the trading of these securities, credit analysis, and portfolio management both domestically and globally.

---

[1]Merrill Lynch, "Size and Structures of the World Bond Market," New York: Merrill Lynch, May 2004.

[2]Frank K. Reilly and David J. Wright, "Analysis of Risk-Adjusted Performance of Global Market Assets," *Journal of Portfolio Management* 30, no. 3 (Spring 2004): 63–77.

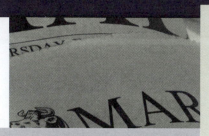

An Introduction to Valuation

T he purpose of this chapter is to provide a background in the general topic of valuation as a prelude to both bond valuation (Chapter 12) and to common-stock valuation (Chapter 15). Therefore, we begin with some very general topics: What determines the value of an asset? What is the best investment process? How do we make the investment decision? Then we apply these valuation concepts to bonds, preferred stocks, and common stocks. In the final section, we emphasize the estimation of the variables that determine value—the required rate of return and the expected future cash flows from the asset.

What Determines the Value of an Asset?

By now you should be familiar with the concept that *the value of an earning or financial asset is the present value of expected future cash flows received from the asset.* Within this concept, there are two necessary inputs when deriving a specific value for an asset: (1) a discount rate used to calculate the present value of the cash flows and (2) an estimate of the future stream of cash flows.

- **Discount rate.** We noted at the start of this book that an investment is a commitment of funds for a period of time in order to derive a rate of return that compensates the investor for (1) the time for which the funds are invested, (2) the expected rate of inflation during that time, and (3) the uncertainty of the future cash flows. This rate of return is the investor's *required rate of return* and, therefore, is the appropriate *discount rate* to use when estimating the value of an asset. The first two components of this rate of return would be the same for any investment and thus are the components of the *nominal risk-free rate.* Therefore, the third component, which requires the estimation of the *required risk premium,* most heavily affects the discount rate.

- **Estimate of the future stream of cash flows.** The difficulty of estimating future cash flows can vary dramatically since assets range from noncallable government bonds, where the cash flows are contractual and virtually guaranteed (i.e., they are free of credit risk) to high-risk common stocks of oil exploration firms with very uncertain cash flows.

The calculation of a value for an asset is the same for a government bond, a piece of real estate, a blue-chip common stock, or a very high-risk common stock. However, while the valuation process always entails calculating the present value of future cash flows, the discount rates will differ because the uncertainly of cash flows differ. Likewise, the future cash flows will differ, not only because of the nature of the asset (e.g., bond versus common stock) but also because analysts differ in their methods of estimation. Because of these differences in discount rates and estimates of future cash flows, two analysts can derive two very different estimates of the value for the same asset.

Once a value for an asset has been estimated, the *investment decision process* is quite straightforward—we simply compare the estimated *intrinsic value* of the asset to its prevailing *market price,* and

If Estimated Intrinsic Value > Market Price → BUY

If Estimated Intrinsic Value < Market Price → DO NOT BUY
(or sell it if you own it)

In other words, if you believe the asset is worth more than the price you must pay for it, you will buy it. If its estimated value is less than its current price, you will consider it overpriced and not buy it or, if you owned it, you will sell it.

The Valuation Process

We start our investigation of security valuation by discussing the *valuation process,* that is, the part of the investment decision process in which we estimate the value of an asset. There are two general approaches to the valuation process: (1) the top-down, three-step approach and (2) the bottom-up, stock valuation, stock-picking approach. Both can be implemented by either fundamentalists or technicians. The difference between the two is the perceived importance of the economy and a firm's industry in the valuation of a firm and its stock.

Advocates of the *top-down, three-step approach* believe that both the economy/market and the industry effect have a significant impact on the total returns for individual stocks. In contrast, those who employ the *bottom-up, stock-picking approach* contend that it is possible to find stocks that are undervalued relative to their market price, and these stocks will provide superior returns *regardless* of the market and industry outlook.

Both approaches have numerous supporters, and advocates of both approaches have been quite successful.[1] In this book, we advocate and present the top-down, three-step approach because of its logic and empirical support. Although we believe that a portfolio manager or an investor can be successful using the bottom-up approach, we believe that it is more difficult because this approach ignores substantial information from the market and

---

[1]For the history and selection process of a legendary stock picker, see Robert G. Hagstrom Jr., *The Essential Buffett,* New York: John Wiley & Sons, 2001; or Roger Lowenstein, *Buffett: The Making of an American Capitalist,* New York: Random House, 1995.

the firm's industry. Notably, both approaches employ the same valuation models and techniques during the stock valuation phase of the process.

AN OVERVIEW OF THE TOP-DOWN VALUATION PROCESS

Although we know that the value of a security is essentially determined by its quality and profit potential, we also believe that the economic environment and the performance of a firm's industry influence the value of a security and its rate of return. Because of the importance of these economic and industry factors, we first present an overview of the valuation process that describes these influences and explains how they can be incorporated into the analysis of security value. Subsequently, we describe the theory of value and emphasize the factors that affect the value of securities.

Psychologists suggest that the success or failure of an individual can be caused as much by his or her social, economic, and family environment as by genetic gifts. Extending this idea to the valuation of securities means we should consider a firm's economic and industry environment during the valuation process. Regardless of the qualities or capabilities of a firm and its management, the economic and industry environment will have a major influence on the success of a firm and the realized rate of return on its stock.

As an example, assume you own shares of the strongest and most successful firm producing home furnishings. If you own the shares during a strong economic expansion, the sales and earnings of the firm will increase and your rate of return on the stock should be quite high. In contrast, if you own the same stock during a major economic recession, the sales and earnings of this firm (and probably most or all of the firms in the industry) would likely experience a decline and the price of its stock would be stable or decline. Therefore, when assessing the future value of a security, it is necessary to analyze the outlook for the aggregate economy and the firm's specific industry.

The valuation process is like the chicken-and-egg dilemma. Do we start by analyzing the macroeconomy and various industries before individual stocks, or do we begin with individual securities and gradually combine these firms into industries and the industries into the entire economy? For reasons discussed in the next section, we contend that the discussion should begin with an analysis of aggregate economies and overall securities markets and progress to different industries with a global perspective. Only after a thorough analysis of a global industry are we in a position to properly evaluate the securities issued by individual firms within the better industries. Thus, we recommend a top-down three-step valuation process in which we first examine the influence of the general economy on all firms and the security markets, then analyze the prospects for various global industries with the best outlooks in this economic environment, and finally turn to the analysis of individual firms in the preferred industries and to the common stock of these firms. Exhibit 11.1 indicates the procedure recommended.

Why a Three-Step Valuation Process?

GENERAL ECONOMIC INFLUENCES

Monetary and fiscal policy measures enacted by various agencies of national governments influence the aggregate economies of those countries. The resulting economic conditions influence all industries and companies within the economies.

Fiscal policy initiatives such as tax credits or tax cuts can encourage spending, whereas additional taxes on income, gasoline, cigarettes, and liquor can discourage spending. Increases

EXHIBIT 11.1	Overview of the Investment Process

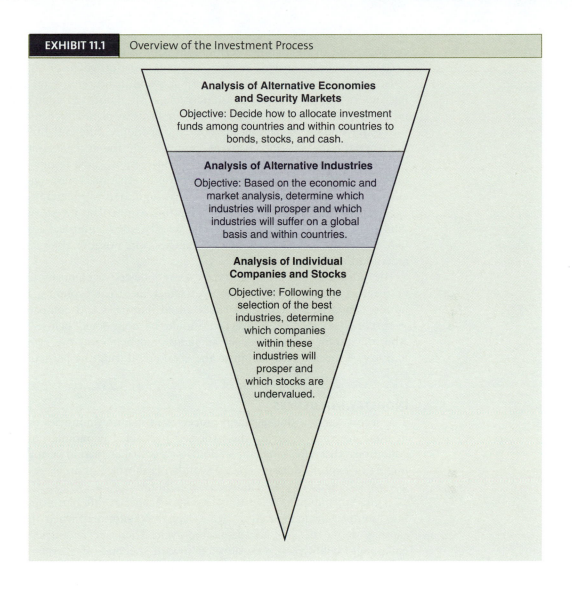

Analysis of Alternative Economies and Security Markets

Objective: Decide how to allocate investment funds among countries and within countries to bonds, stocks, and cash.

Analysis of Alternative Industries

Objective: Based on the economic and market analysis, determine which industries will prosper and which industries will suffer on a global basis and within countries.

Analysis of Individual Companies and Stocks

Objective: Following the selection of the best industries, determine which companies within these industries will prosper and which stocks are undervalued.

or decreases in government spending on defense, on unemployment insurance or retraining programs, or on highways also influence the general economy. All such policies influence the business environment for firms that rely directly on such expenditures. In addition, we know that government spending has a strong *multiplier effect*. For example, increases in road building increase the demand for earthmoving equipment and concrete materials. As a result, in addition to construction workers, the employees in those industries that supply the equipment and materials have more to spend on consumer goods, which raises the demand for consumer goods, which affects another set of suppliers.

Monetary policy produces similar economic changes. A restrictive monetary policy that reduces the growth rate of the money supply reduces the supply of funds for working capital and expansion for all businesses. Alternatively, a restrictive monetary policy that targets interest rates would raise market interest rates and therefore firms' costs and make it more expensive for individuals to finance home mortgages and the purchase of other durable goods such as autos and appliances. Monetary policy therefore affects all segments of an economy and that economy's relationship with other economies.

Any economic analysis requires the consideration of inflation. As we have discussed, inflation causes differences between real and nominal interest rates and changes the spending and savings behavior of consumers and corporations. In addition, unexpected changes in the rate of inflation make it difficult for firms to plan, which inhibits growth and innovation. Beyond the impact on the domestic economy, differential inflation and interest rates influence the trade balance between countries and the exchange rate for currencies.

In addition to monetary and fiscal policy actions, such events as war, terrorist attacks, political upheavals in foreign countries, or international monetary devaluations produce changes in the business environment that add to the uncertainty of sales and earnings expectations and therefore the risk premium required by investors. For example, the September 11, 2001, terrorist attack on the World Trade Center had a significant impact on the U.S. economy that affected other countries and possibly slowed the recovery from the recession during that period.

In short, it is difficult to conceive of any industry or company that can avoid the impact of macroeconomic developments that affect the total economy. Because aggregate economic events have a profound effect on all industries and companies within these industries, these macroeconomic factors should be considered before industries are analyzed. Also, the future performance of an industry depends on the economic outlook *and* the industry's expected relationship to the economy during the particular phase of the business cycle.

Industry Influences

The second step in the valuation process is to identify industries that will prosper or suffer in the long run or during the expected near-term economic environment. Examples of conditions that affect specific industries are strikes within a major producing country, import or export quotas or taxes, a worldwide shortage or an excess supply of a resource, or government-imposed regulations on an industry.

Different industries react to economic changes at different points in the business cycle. For example, firms typically increase capital expenditures when they are operating at full capacity at the peak of the economic cycle. Therefore, industries that provide plant and equipment will typically be affected toward the end of a cycle. In addition, alternative industries have different responses to the business cycle. Cyclical industries such as steel or autos typically do much better than the aggregate economy during expansions, but they suffer more during contractions. In contrast, noncyclical industries such as retail food would not experience a significant decline during a recession but also would not experience a strong increase during an economic expansion.

Another factor that will have a differential effect on industries is demographics. For example, it is widely recognized that the U.S. population is aging; baby boomers are entering their late fifties and there is a large group of citizens over sixty-five. These two groups have heavy demand for second homes and medical care and the industries related to these segments (e.g., home furnishings and pharmaceuticals).

Firms that sell in international markets can benefit or suffer as foreign economies shift. An industry with a substantial worldwide market might experience low demand in its domestic market but benefit from growing demand in its international market. As an example, much of the growth for Coca-Cola and Pepsi as well as fast-food chains such as McDonald's and Burger King has come from international expansion in Europe and the Far East.

In general, an industry's prospects will determine how well or poorly an individual firm will fare. Few companies perform well in a poor industry, so even the best company in a poor industry is a bad prospect for investment. For example, poor sales and earnings in the farm equipment industry during 2001–2002 had a negative impact on Deere and Co., a well-managed firm and probably the best firm in its industry. Even though Deere performed better than other firms in the industry (some went bankrupt), its earnings and stock performance still fell far short of its past performance and the company did poorly compared to firms in most other industries.

Notably, even money managers who are essentially stock pickers consider industry analysis important because it determines a firm's business risk due to sales volatility and operating leverage, and a firm's profitability is impacted by the competitive environment in its industry.

COMPANY ANALYSIS

After determining that an industry's outlook is good, an investor can analyze and compare individual firms' performance within the entire industry using financial ratios and cash flow values. As we will discuss in Chapter 14, many financial ratios for firms are valid only when they are compared to the performance of their industries.

Company analysis tries to identify the best company in a promising industry. This involves examining a firm's past performance but, more important, its future prospects. After we understand the firm and its outlook, we can determine its value and then compare this estimated intrinsic value to the price of the firm's stock to decide whether its stock or bonds are good investments.

The final goal is to select undervalued stocks within a desirable industry and include them in a portfolio based on their relationship (correlation) with all other assets in the portfolio. As we discuss in more detail in Chapter 15, the best stock for investment purposes may not necessarily be issued by the best company because the stock of the finest company in an industry may be overpriced, which would cause it to be a poor investment. You cannot know whether a security is undervalued or overvalued until you have analyzed the company, estimated its intrinsic value, and compared your estimated intrinsic value to the market price of the firm's stock.

DOES THE THREE-STEP PROCESS WORK?

While the logic of the three-step investment process is compelling, you might wonder how well this process works in practice. Several academic studies have indicated that most changes in an individual firm's *earnings* could be attributed to changes in aggregate corporate earnings and changes in the firm's industry, with the aggregate earnings changes being more important. The results consistently demonstrated that the economic environment had a significant effect on firm earnings.

Studies have also found a relationship between aggregate stock prices and various economic series, which supported the view that a relationship exists between stock prices and economic expansions and contractions.[2] In addition, an analysis of the relationship between *rates of return* for the aggregate stock market, alternative industries, and individual stocks showed that most of the changes in individual stock returns could be explained by changes in the rates of return for the aggregate stock market and the stock's industry. Although the importance of the market effect tended to decline over time and the significance of the

---

[2]See Geoffrey Moore and John P. Cullity, "Security Markets and Business Cycles," in *The Financial Analysts Handbook,* 2nd ed., edited by Sumner N. Levine (Homewood, IL: Dow Jones–Irwin, 1988).

industry effect varied among industries, the combined market–industry effect on an individual stock's rate of return was still important.[3]

These results that support the three-step valuation process are consistent with our contention in Chapter 2 that the most important decision is the asset allocation decision.[4] The asset allocation specifies: (1) what proportion of your portfolio will be invested in various nations' economies; (2) within each country, how you will divide your assets among stocks, bonds, or other assets; and (3) your industry selections, based on expected industry performance in the projected economic environment.

Given the three-step process, we need to consider the theory of valuation, which allows us to compute estimated values for the market, for alternative industries, and for individual stocks.

Review of the Components of Valuation

The valuation theory states that the value of an asset is the present value of future expected cash flows. In turn, the two components required to calculate value are (1) the required rate of return (discount rate) of the investment and (2) the stream of expected cash flows.

REQUIRED RATE OF RETURN

Uncertainty of Cash Flows   As mentioned earlier, the required rate of return on an investment is determined by (1) the economy's real risk-free rate of return, plus (2) the expected rate of inflation during the holding period, plus (3) a risk premium that is determined by the uncertainty of returns (cash flows). The factor that causes a difference in required rates of return is the risk premium for the investment, which depends on the uncertainty of returns or cash flows from the investment. We can identify the sources of the uncertainty of returns by the internal characteristics of an asset or by market-determined factors. In Chapters 2 and 3 we subdivided the internal characteristics for a firm into business risk (BR), financial risk (FR), liquidity risk (LR), exchange rate risk (ERR), and country risk (CR). The market-determined factors are the systematic risk of the asset, its beta, or its systematic risk as specified by multiple factors as discussed in Chapter 9.

STREAM OF CASH FLOWS

An estimate of the expected cash flows from an investment encompasses not only the size but also the form, time pattern, and the uncertainty of the cash flows, which affect the required rate of return.

Form of Returns   The cash flows from an investment can take many forms, including earnings cash flows, dividends, interest payments, or return of principal during a period. We will consider several valuation techniques that use different forms of returns. As an example, one common-stock valuation model computes the present value of a firm's operating cash

---

[3]For a study that documents the impact of the economy and industry but indicates the growing importance of the global industry effect, see S. Cavaglia, C. Brightman, and M. Aked, "The Increasing Importance of Industry Factors," *Financial Analysts Journal* 56, no. 5 (September–October 2000): 41–54.

[4]An application of these concepts is contained in Abby J. Cohen, "Economic Forecasts and the Asset Allocation Decision," in *Economic Analysis for Investment Professionals* (Charlottesville, VA: AIMR, November, 1996).

flows, and another model estimates the present value of dividend payments. Since cash flows can come in many forms, we must consider all of them to evaluate an investment accurately.

Interactive e-lectures
For more explanation and an animated example of time value of money, go to: **http://reillyxtra**.swlearning.com.

Time Pattern and Growth Rate of Cash Flows   An accurate value for a security must include an estimate of the timing and amount of future cash flows. Because money has a time value, we must know the time pattern and estimate the growth rate of cash flows from an investment.

INVESTMENT DECISION PROCESS: AN EXAMPLE

As noted earlier, to ensure the required return on an investment, we must estimate the intrinsic value of the investment at the required rate of return and then compare this estimated intrinsic value to the prevailing market price. We will illustrate with an example.

Suppose you read about an athletic shoe manufacturer whose stock is listed on the NYSE. Using one of the valuation models we will discuss and making estimates of future cash flow, you estimate that the intrinsic value of the company's stock using your required rate of return is $20 a share. After estimating this value, you look in the paper and see that the stock is currently being traded at $15 a share. You would want to buy this stock because you think it is worth $20 a share and you can buy it for $15 a share. In contrast, if the current market price were $25 a share, you would not want to buy the stock because, based on your valuation, it is overvalued. Not only do you not want to buy the stock, but you should sell it if it is in your portfolio because going forward from this point and based on this price, you will not earn your required rate of return. You would do better selling this stock and reinvesting the funds into another asset that will provide at least your required rate of return.

Valuation Overview

VALUATION OF BONDS

Calculating the value of bonds is relatively easy because the size and time pattern of cash flows from the bond over its life are known. A bond typically promises

Interactive e-lectures
For more explanation and an animated example of bond valuation, go to: **http://reillyxtra**.swlearning.com.

1. Interest payments every six months equal to one-half the coupon rate times the face value of the bond
2. The payment of the principal on the bond's maturity date

As an example, in 2006, a $10,000 bond due in 2021 with a 10 percent coupon will pay $500 every six months for its fifteen-year life. In addition, the bond issuer promises to pay the $10,000 principal at maturity in 2021. Therefore, assuming the bond issuer does not default, the investor knows what payments (cash flows) will be made and when they will be made.

Based on valuation theory, the value of the bond is the present value of the interest payments, which we can think of as an annuity of $500 every six months for fifteen years, and the present value of the principal payment, which in this case is the present value of $10,000 in fifteen years. The only unknown for this asset (assuming the borrower does not default) is the required rate of return that should be used to discount the expected stream of returns (cash flows). If the prevailing nominal risk-free rate is 9 percent and the investor requires a 1 percent risk premium on this bond because there is some probability of default, the required rate of return would be 10 percent.

Interactive e-lectures

For more explanation and an animated example of annuity, go to: http://reillyxtra .swlearning.com.

The present value of the interest payments is an annuity for thirty periods (fifteen years every six months) at one-half the required return (5 percent):[5]

$$\$500 \times 15.3725 = \$7,686$$

(Present Value of Interest Payments at 10 Percent)

The present value of the principal is likewise discounted at 5 percent for thirty periods:[6]

$$\$10,000 \times 0.2314 = \$2,314$$

(Present Value of the Principal Payment at 10 Percent)

We can summarize as follows:

Present Value of Interest Payments $500 × 15.3725 = $ 7,686
Present Value of Principal Payment $10,000 × 0.2314 = 2,314
Total Value of Bond at 10 Percent = $10,000

This is the amount that an investor should be willing to pay for this bond, assuming that the required rate of return on a bond of this risk class is 10 percent. If the market price of the bond is above this value, the investor should not buy it because the promised yield to maturity at this higher price will be less than the investor's required rate of return. Notice that the value of the bond is equal to its par value, which will always be true if the required rate of return (the discount rate) is equal to the coupon rate. What the calculations demonstrate is that this relationship is due to the mathematics of the calculations to compute the value of the asset.

Alternatively, suppose another investor requires a 3 percent risk premium in addition to the 9 percent nominal risk-free rate. This implies a 12 percent required return on the bond. Therefore, the expected cash flows are the same but they would be discounted at 12 percent. The recalculated value would be

$$\$500 \times 13.7648 = \$6,882$$
$$\$10,000 \times 0.1741 = 1,741$$
Total Value of Bond at 12 Percent = $8,623

This example shows that an investor who wants a higher rate of return will not pay as much for an asset; that is, the same stream of cash flows has a lower value to this investor. As before, this computed value is compared to the market price of the bond to determine whether to invest in it.

Finally, suppose a third investor expects a lower rate of inflation, so his nominal risk-free rate is only 6 percent. This investor wants a risk premium of 2 percent, which implies a required rate of return on this bond of 8 percent. To test your understanding of bond valuation, you should calculate the value of this bond using an 8 percent discount rate (the computed value should be $11,729). This example shows that the investor who has a lower required rate of return will pay more for this asset; this same cash flow stream is worth more to this investor.

In considering the preceding calculations, notice two important points. First, the *value* of a bond moves in the opposite direction of the *discount rate*. Second, for a given change in

---

[5]The annuity factors and present value factors are contained in Appendix C at the end of the book.

[6]If we used annual compounding, this would be 0.239 rather than 0.2314. We use semiannual compounding because it is consistent with the interest payments and is used in practice.

the discount rate (e.g., one percent), the change in value will differ depending on the characteristics of the bond. We will discuss this important point in Chapter 12.

VALUATION OF PREFERRED STOCK

Interactive e-lectures

For more explanation and an animated example of perpetuity, go to:
http://reillyxtra
.swlearning.com.

The owner of a preferred stock receives a promise to pay a stated dividend, usually each quarter, for an infinite period. Preferred stock is a **perpetuity** because it has no maturity. As was true with a bond, stated payments are made on specified dates although the issuer of this stock does not have the same legal obligation to pay investors as do issuers of bonds. Payments are made only after the firm meets its bond interest payments. Because this reduced legal obligation increases the uncertainty of returns, investors should require a higher rate of return on a firm's preferred stock than on its bonds. Although this differential in required return should exist in theory, it generally does not exist in practice because of the tax treatment accorded dividends paid to corporations. As described in Chapter 3, 80 percent of intercompany preferred dividends are tax-exempt, making the effective tax rate on them about 6.8 percent, assuming a corporate tax rate of 34 percent. This tax advantage stimulates the demand for preferred stocks by corporations. Because of this demand, the yield on them has generally been below that on the highest-grade corporate bonds.

Because preferred stock is a perpetuity, its value is simply the stated annual dividend divided by the required rate of return on preferred stock (k_p) as follows:

11.1
$$V = \frac{\text{Dividend}}{k_p}$$

Assume a preferred stock has a $100 par value and a dividend of $8 a year. Because of the expected rate of inflation, the uncertainty of the dividend payment, and the tax advantage to a corporate investor, the required rate of return on this stock is 9 percent. Therefore, the value of this preferred stock is

$$V = \frac{\$8}{0.09}$$

$$= \$88.89$$

Given this estimated value, if the current market price is $95, the investor would decide against a purchase because the stock is overpriced relative to this estimated intrinsic value. In contrast, if it is $80, the investor would buy the stock. Also, given the market price of preferred stock, we can derive its promised yield. Assuming a current market price of $85, the promised yield would be

$$k_p = \frac{\text{Dividend}}{\text{Price}} = \frac{\$8}{\$85.00} = 0.0941$$

VALUATION OF COMMON STOCK: TWO APPROACHES

Because of the complexity and importance of valuing common stock, various techniques for accomplishing this task have been devised over time. These techniques fall into one of two general approaches: (1) the discounted cash flow valuation techniques, where the value of the stock is estimated based on the present value of some measure of cash flow, including dividends, operating cash flow, and free cash flow; and (2) the relative valuation techniques, where the value of a stock is estimated based on its current price relative to variables considered to

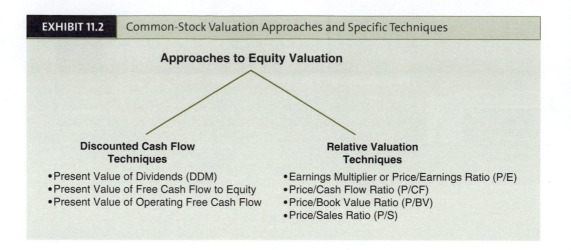

EXHIBIT 11.2 Common-Stock Valuation Approaches and Specific Techniques

Approaches to Equity Valuation

Discounted Cash Flow Techniques
- Present Value of Dividends (DDM)
- Present Value of Free Cash Flow to Equity
- Present Value of Operating Free Cash Flow

Relative Valuation Techniques
- Earnings Multiplier or Price/Earnings Ratio (P/E)
- Price/Cash Flow Ratio (P/CF)
- Price/Book Value Ratio (P/BV)
- Price/Sales Ratio (P/S)

be significant to valuation such as earnings, cash flow, book value, or sales. Exhibit 11.2 provides a visual presentation of the alternative approaches and specific techniques.

An important point is that *both of these approaches and all of these valuation techniques have several common factors*. First, all of them are significantly affected by the investor's *required rate of return* on the stock because this rate either becomes the discount rate or is a major component of the discount rate. Second, all valuation approaches are affected by the *estimated growth rate of the variable* used in the valuation technique—for example, dividends, earnings, cash flow, or sales. As noted in the efficient market discussion, both of these critical variables must be *estimated*. As a result, different analysts using the same valuation techniques will derive different estimates of value for a stock because they have different estimates for these critical variable inputs.

The following discussion of equity valuation techniques considers the specific models and the theoretical and practical strengths and weaknesses of each of them. Notably, our intent is to present these two approaches as complementary, *not* competitive, approaches. That is, you should learn and use both of them.

Why and When to Use Discounted Cash Flow Valuation

Discounted cash flow valuation techniques are obvious choices for valuation because they are the epitome of how we describe value—that is, the present value of expected cash flows. The major difference between the alternative techniques is how one specifies cash flow—that is, the measure of cash flow used.

The cleanest and most straightforward measure of cash flow is *dividends* because these are clearly cash flows that go directly to the investor, which implies that we should use the *cost of equity* as the discount rate. However, this dividend technique is difficult to apply to firms that do not pay dividends during periods of high growth or that currently pay very limited dividends because they have high rate of return investment alternatives available. On the other hand, an advantage is that the reduced form of the dividend discount model (DDM) is very useful when discussing valuation for a stable, mature entity where the assumption of relatively constant growth for the long term is appropriate.

The second cash flow measure is *free cash flow to equity*, which is a measure of cash flows available to the equityholder after payments to debt holders and after allowing for expenditures to maintain the firm's asset base. Because these are cash flows available to equity owners, the appropriate discount rate is the firm's *cost of equity*.

The third specification of cash flow is the *operating free cash flow,* which is generally described as cash flows after direct costs (cost of goods and S, G, & A expenses) and before any payments to capital suppliers. Because we are dealing with the cash flows available for all capital suppliers, the discount rate employed is the firm's *weighted average cost of capital* (WACC). This is a very useful model when comparing firms with diverse capital structures because we determine the value of the total firm and then subtract the value of the firm's debt obligations to arrive at a value for the firm's equity.

Beyond being theoretically correct, these models allow substantial flexibility in terms of changes in sales and expenses that implies changing growth rates over time. Once you understand how to compute each measure of cash flow, you can estimate the specific cash flow for each year by constructing a pro forma statement for each year or you can estimate overall growth rates for the alternative cash flow values (as we will demonstrate with the DDM).

A potential difficulty with these cash flow techniques is that they are very dependent on the two significant inputs—(1) the growth rates of cash flows (both the *rate* of growth and the *duration* of growth) and (2) the estimate of the discount rate. As we will show in several instances, a small change in either of these values can have a significant impact on the estimated value. This is a critical realization when using any theoretical model: Virtually everyone knows and uses the same valuation models, so the *inputs* are critical—GIGO: garbage in, garbage out!

Why and When to Use Relative Valuation   As noted, a potential benefit and a problem with the discounted cash flow valuation models is that it is possible to derive intrinsic values that are substantially above or below prevailing prices depending on how you adjust your estimated inputs to the prevailing environment. An advantage of the relative valuation techniques is that they provide information about how the market is *currently* valuing stock at several levels—that is, relative to the aggregate market, various industries, and individual stocks within industries. Following this chapter, which provides the background for these two approaches, we will demonstrate the relative valuation ratios for the aggregate market, for an industry relative to the market, and for an individual company relative to the aggregate market, to its industry, and to other stocks in its industry.

The good news is that this relative valuation approach provides information on how the market is currently valuing securities. The bad news is that it is providing information on current valuation. The point is, the relative valuation approach provides information on current valuation, but it does *not* provide guidance on whether these current valuations are appropriate; *all* valuations at a point in time could be too high or too low. For example, assume that the market becomes significantly overvalued (as in 1999–early 2000). Given such a market environment, if we compare the value for an industry to the very overvalued market, we might contend that an industry is undervalued relative to the market. Unfortunately, our judgment may be wrong because of the benchmark used—that is, we might be comparing a fully valued industry to a *very* overvalued market. Obviously, we could do the same faulty comparison for a stock to an overvalued industry.

Put another way, the relative valuation techniques are appropriate to consider under two conditions:

1. You have a good set of comparable entities—that is, comparable companies that are similar in terms of industry, size, and, hopefully risk.
2. The aggregate market and the company's industry are not at a valuation extreme—that is, they are not either seriously undervalued or overvalued.

Which Approach Is Preferable? Now that we have presented the two approaches, a natural question is, which should we use? The bottom-line answer is *both*! While this answer may not be very satisfying, it is based on our view that equity valuation is extremely difficult and, therefore, you should use *all* the tools available when attempting to make a sound decision. The good news related to this decision is that *the major inputs* (i.e., the required rate of return [discount rate] and the estimated future stream of cash flows) *that determine the final valuation are basically the same for either approach.* Clearly, the analyst who is best at making these estimates will generate the best valuations and will be a superior analyst.

In the following sections we describe each of the equity valuation techniques shown in Exhibit 11.2. In the following chapters there will be demonstrations of these techniques, where the emphasis will be on estimating the critical inputs described above.

Discounted Cash Flow Valuation Techniques

All of these valuation techniques are based on the basic valuation model, which asserts that the value of an asset is the present value of its expected future cash flows as follows:

11.2

$$V_j = \sum_{t=1}^{n} \frac{CF_t}{(1 + k)^t}$$

where:

V_j = value of stock j
n = life of the asset
CF_t = cash flow in period t
k = the discount rate, which is the investors' required rate of return for asset j determined by the uncertainty (risk) of the stock's cash flows

As noted, the specific cash flows used will differ between techniques. They range from dividends (the best-known model) to free cash flow to equity and operating free cash flow. We begin with a presentation of the present value of dividend model, referred to as the dividend discount model (DDM), because it is intuitively appealing and the best-known model. Also, its general approach is similar to the other discounted cash flow models.

THE DIVIDEND DISCOUNT MODEL (DDM)

The *dividend discount model (DDM)* assumes that the value of a share of common stock is the present value of all future dividends:[7]

11.3

$$V_j = \frac{D_1}{(1 + k)} + \frac{D_2}{(1 + k)^2} + \frac{D_3}{(1 + k)^3} + \cdots + \frac{D_\infty}{(1 + k)^\infty}$$

$$= \sum_{t=1}^{n} \frac{D_t}{(1 + k)^t}$$

Interactive e-lectures
For more explanation and an animated example of the dividend discount model, go to: **http://reillyxtra .swlearning.com.**

[7]This model was initially set forth in J. B. Williams, *The Theory of Investment Value,* Cambridge, MA: Harvard, 1938. It was subsequently reintroduced and expanded by Myron J. Gordon, *The Investment, Financing, and Valuation of the Corporation,* Homewood, IL: Irwin, 1962.

where:

V_j = value of common stock j
D_t = dividend during period t
k = discount rate, or required rate of return on stock j

An obvious question is: What happens when the stock is not held for an infinite period? A sale of the stock at the end of year 2 would imply the following formula:

$$V_j = \frac{D_1}{(1 + k)} + \frac{D_2}{(1 + k)^2} + \frac{SP_{j2}}{(1 + k)^2}$$

In other words, the value is equal to the two dividend payments during years 1 and 2 plus the sale price (SP) for stock j at the end of year 2. The expected selling price of stock j at the end of year 2 (SP_{j2}) is simply the value of all remaining dividend payments.

$$SP_{j2} = \frac{D_3}{(1 + k)} + \frac{D_4}{(1 + k)^2} + \cdots + \frac{D_\infty}{(1 + k)^\infty}$$

If SP_{j2} is discounted back to the present by $1/(1 + k)^2$, this equation becomes

$$PV(SP_{j2}) = \frac{\dfrac{D_3}{(1 + k)} + \dfrac{D_4}{(1 + k)^2} + \cdots + \dfrac{D_\infty}{(1 + k)^\infty}}{(1 + k)^2}$$

$$= \frac{D_3}{(1 + k)^3} + \frac{D_4}{(1 + k)^4} + \cdots + \frac{D_\infty}{(1 + k)^\infty}$$

which is simply an extension of the original equation. Whenever the stock is sold, its value (that is, the sale price at that time) will be the present value of all future dividends. When this ending value is discounted back to the present, we are back to the original dividend discount model.

What about stocks that pay no dividends? Again, the concept is the same, except that some of the early dividend payments are zero. Notably, there are expectations that *at some point* the firm will start paying dividends. If investors lacked such an expectation, nobody would be willing to buy the security. It would have zero value. A firm with a non-dividend-paying stock is reinvesting its capital in very profitable projects rather than paying current dividends so that its earnings and dividend stream will be larger and grow faster in the future. In this case, we would apply the DDM as

$$V_j = \frac{D_1}{(1 + k)} + \frac{D_2}{(1 + k)^2} + \frac{D_3}{(1 + k)^3} + \cdots + \frac{D}{(1 + k)^\infty}$$

where:

$D_1 = 0; D_2 = 0$

The investor here expects that when the firm starts paying dividends in period 3, it will be a large initial amount and dividends will grow faster than those of a comparable stock that had paid out dividends all along. The stock has value because of these *future* dividends. Because it can be very difficult to estimate when a firm will initiate a dividend, most analysts do not apply this model if a company is not paying a dividend.

For short holding periods such as one or two years, the DDM would show that the value is the present value of several dividend payments plus the present value of a closing price that would reflect all future dividend payments. For longer holding periods we use the infinite period model, which is used extensively in corporate finance and can indicate what factors affect the price–earnings ratio.

Infinite Period DDM The infinite period dividend discount model assumes investors estimate future dividend payments for an infinite number of periods. Needless to say, this is a formidable task! We must make some simplifying assumptions about this future stream of dividends to make the model viable. The easiest assumption is that *the future dividend stream will grow at a constant rate for an infinite period.* This is a rather heroic assumption in many instances, but where it does hold we can use the model to value individual stocks as well as the aggregate market and alternative industries. This model is generalized as follows:

11.4
$$V_j = \frac{D_0(1 + g)}{(1 + k)} + \frac{D_0(1 + g)^2}{(1 + k)^2} + \cdots + \frac{D_0(1 + g)^n}{(1 + k)^n}$$

where:

V_j = the value of stock j
D_0 = the dividend payment in the current period
g = the constant growth rate of dividends
k = the required rate of return on stock j (discount rate)
n = the number of periods, which we assume to be infinite

In the appendix to this chapter, we show that with certain assumptions this infinite period constant growth rate model can be simplified to the following expression:

11.5
$$V_j = \frac{D_1}{k - g}$$

You will probably recognize this formula as one that is widely used in corporate finance to estimate the cost of equity capital for the firm—that is, $k = D/V + g$.

To use this model for valuation, we must estimate (1) the required rate of return k and (2) the expected constant growth rate of dividends g. After estimating g, it is a simple matter to estimate D_1 because it is the current dividend D_0 times $(1 + g)$.

Consider the example of a stock with a current dividend of $1 a share. You believe that, over the long run, this company's earnings and dividends will grow at 6 percent; therefore, your estimate of g is 0.06, which implies an expectation of D_1 equal to $1.06 ($1.00 × 1.06). For the long run, given your risk expectations for this stock, you set your required rate of return on this stock at 10 percent; your estimate of k is 0.10. Let's summarize the relevant estimates:

$$g = 0.06$$
$$k = 0.10$$
$$D_1 = \$1.06 \ (\$1.00 \times 1.06)$$
$$V = \frac{\$1.06}{0.10 - 0.06}$$
$$= \frac{\$1.06}{0.04}$$
$$= \$26.50$$

A small change in any of the original estimates will have a large impact on V, as shown by the following examples:

1. For an increase in k: $g = 0.06$; $k = 0.11$; $D_1 = \$1.06$

$$V = \frac{\$1.06}{0.11 - 0.06}$$

$$= \frac{\$1.06}{0.05}$$

$$= \$21.20$$

2. For an increase in g: $g = 0.07$; $k = 0.10$; $D_1 = \$1.07$

$$V = \frac{\$1.07}{0.10 - 0.07}$$

$$= \frac{\$1.07}{0.03}$$

$$= \$35.67$$

These examples show that as small a change as 1 percent in either g or k produces a large difference in the estimated value of the stock. The crucial relationship that determines the value of the stock is the *spread between the required rate of return (k) and the expected growth rate of dividends* (g). Anything that causes a decline in the spread will cause an increase in the computed value, whereas any increase in the spread will decrease the computed value of the stock.

Infinite Period DDM and Growth Companies As noted in the appendix, the infinite period DDM has the following assumptions:

1. Dividends grow at a constant rate.
2. The constant growth rate will continue for an infinite period.
3. The required rate of return (k) *is greater than the infinite growth rate* (g). If it is not, the model gives meaningless results because the denominator becomes negative.

What is the effect of these assumptions if we want to use this model to value the stock of growth companies such as Dell, Intel, Microsoft, Pfizer, and Wal-Mart? **Growth companies** are firms that have the opportunities and abilities to earn rates of return on investments that are consistently above their required rates of return.[8] Recall that the required rate of return for a corporation is its weighted average cost of capital (WACC). An example might be Intel, which has a WACC of about 10 percent, but is currently earning about 20 percent on its invested capital. Therefore, we would consider Intel a growth company. To exploit these outstanding investment opportunities, these growth firms generally retain a high percentage of earnings for reinvestment, and their earnings will grow faster than those

---

[8]Growth companies are discussed in Ezra Salomon, *The Theory of Financial Management,* New York: Columbia University Press, 1963; and Merton Miller and Franco Modigliani, "Dividend Policy, Growth, and the Valuation of Shares," *Journal of Business* 34, no. 4 (October 1961): 411–433. We will also discuss growth companies in Chapter 15.

of the typical firm. As will be discussed in Chapter 14 a firm's substainable growth is a function of its retention rate and its return on equity (ROE).

The earnings growth pattern for these growth companies is inconsistent with the assumptions of the infinite period DDM. First, the infinite period DDM assumes dividends will grow at a constant rate for an infinite period. This assumption seldom holds for companies currently growing at above-average rates. As an example, both Intel and Wal-Mart have grown at rates in excess of 15 percent a year for several years. It is unlikely that they can maintain such high rates of growth because of the inability to continue earning the ROEs implied by this growth for an infinite period in an economy where other firms will compete with them for these high rates of return.

Second, during the periods when these firms experience abnormally high rates of growth, their rates of growth probably exceed their required rates of return. There is *no* automatic relationship between growth and risk; a high-growth company is not necessarily a high-risk company. In fact, a firm growing at a high *constant rate* would have lower risk (less uncertainty) than a low-growth firm with an unstable earnings pattern.

Valuation with Temporary Supernormal Growth   Some firms experience periods of abnormally high rates of growth for some finite periods of time. The infinite period DDM cannot be used to value these true growth firms because these high-growth conditions are temporary and therefore inconsistent with the constant growth assumptions of the DDM. However, we can supplement the DDM to value a firm with temporary supernormal growth.

A company cannot permanently maintain a growth rate higher than its required rate of return because competition will eventually enter this apparently lucrative business, which will reduce the firm's profit margins and therefore its ROE and growth rate. Therefore, after a few years of exceptional growth—that is, a period of temporary supernormal growth—a firm's growth rate is expected to decline. Eventually its growth rate is expected to stabilize at a constant level, which is consistent with the assumptions of the infinite period DDM.

To determine the value of a temporary supernormal growth company, we must combine the previous models. During the initial years of exceptional growth, we examine each year individually. If the company is expected to have two or three stages of supernormal growth (each stage above normal but at declining rates) we must examine each year during these stages of growth. When the firm's growth rate eventually stabilizes at a rate below the required rate of return, we can compute the remaining value of the firm using the DDM since it assumes constant growth. Finally, we discount this lump-sum constant growth value back to the present. The technique should become clear as you work through the following example.

Suppose the Bourke Company has a current dividend D_0 of $2 a share. The following are the expected annual growth rates for dividends.

Year	Dividend Growth Rate
1-3	25%
4-6	20
7-9	15
10 on	9

The required rate of return for the stock (the company's cost of equity) is 14 percent. Therefore, the value equation becomes

$$
\begin{aligned}
V_i =\ & \frac{2.00\,(1.25)}{1.14} + \frac{2.00\,(1.25)^2}{(1.14)^2} + \frac{2.00\,(1.25)^3}{(1.14)^3} \\[2mm]
& + \frac{2.00\,(1.25)^3(1.20)}{(1.14)^4} + \frac{2.00\,(1.25)^3(1.20)^2}{(1.14)^5} \\[2mm]
& + \frac{2.00\,(1.25)^3(1.20)^3}{(1.14)^6} + \frac{2.00\,(1.25)^3(1.20)^3(1.15)}{(1.14)^7} \\[2mm]
& + \frac{2.00\,(1.25)^3(1.20)^3(1.15)^2}{(1.14)^8} + \frac{2.00\,(1.25)^3(1.20)^3(1.15)^3}{(1.14)^9} \\[2mm]
& + \frac{\dfrac{2.00\,(1.25)^3(1.20)^3(1.15)^3(1.09)}{(0.14 - 0.09)}}{(1.14)^9}
\end{aligned}
$$

We can take this very scary equation and put it into a table that lists the estimated dividend for each year based on the growth rates specified and the discount factor for each year assuming the 14 percent rate, as shown in Exhibit 11.3. The computations indicate a total value for this stock of $94.36. Note that the bulk of the stock's estimated value is due to the continuing value of the dividend starting in year 10, when it is assumed the dividend will experience constant growth at 9 percent. As before, we would compare this estimate of intrinsic value to the market price of the stock when deciding whether to purchase the stock. The difficult part of the valution is estimating the supernormal growth rates and determining *how long* each of the growth rates will last.

EXHIBIT 11.3	Computation of Value for the Stock of a Company with Temporary Supernormal Growth		

Year	Dividend	Discount Factor (14 percent)	Present Value
1	$ 2.50	0.8772	$ 2.193
2	3.12	0.7695	2.401
3	3.91	0.6750	2.639
4	4.69	0.5921	2.777
5	5.63	0.5194	2.924
6	6.76	0.4556	3.080
7	7.77	0.3996	3.105
8	8.94	0.3506	3.134
9	10.28	0.3075[b]	3.161
10	11.21		
	$224.20[a]	0.3075[b]	68.941
		Total value =	$94.355

[a]Value of dividend stream for year 10 and all future dividends (that is, $11.21/(0.14 − 0.09) = $224.20).

[b]The discount factor is the ninth-year factor because the valuation of the remaining stream is made at the end of year 9 to reflect the dividend in year 10 and all future dividends.

PRESENT VALUE OF OPERATING FREE CASH FLOWS

In this model, we derive the value of the total firm because we discount the operating free cash flows prior to the payment of interest to the debt holders but after deducting funds needed to maintain the firm's asset base (capital expenditures). Because we discount the total firm's operating free cash flow, we use the firm's weighted average cost of capital (WACC) as the discount rate. Therefore, to estimate the value of the firm's equity, once we estimate the value of the total firm we subtract the value of debt. The total value of the firm is then

11.6
$$V_j = \sum_{i=1}^{n} \frac{OFCE_t}{(1 + WACC_j)^t}$$

where:

V_j = value of the total firm j

n = number of periods assumed to be infinite

$OFCF_t$ = the firm's operating free cash flow in period t. The specification of operating free cash flow will be discussed in Chapter 15.

$WACC_j$ = firm j's weighted average cost of capital. The computation of the firm's WACC will be discussed in Chapter 15.

Similar to the process with the DDM, it is possible to envision this as a model that requires estimates for an infinite period. Alternatively, if we are dealing with a mature firm whereby its operating cash flows have reached a stage of stable growth, we can employ the reduced form used in the infinite period constant growth DDM as follows:

11.7
$$V_j = \frac{OFCF_1}{WACC_j - g_{OFCF}}$$

where:

$OFCF_1$ = operating free cash flow in period 1 equal to $OFCF_0(1 + g_{OFCF})$

g_{OFCF} = long-term constant growth rate of operating free cash flow

Alternatively, assuming that the firm is in a true growth period and is expected to experience several different rates of growth for OFCF, these estimates can be divided into three or four stages, as demonstrated with the temporary supernormal dividend growth model. Similar to the dividend model, we must estimate the *rate* of growth and the *duration* of growth for each of these periods of supernormal growth as follows:

Year	OFCF Growth Rate
1-4	20%
5-7	16
8-10	12
11 on	7

Therefore, the calculations would estimate the specific OFCFs for each year through year 10 based on the expected growth rates. We would subsequently use the infinite growth model estimate when the growth rate reached stability after Year 10. As noted, after determining the value of the total firm V_j, we must subtract the value of all nonequity items, including accounts payable, total interest-bearing debt, deferred taxes, and preferred stock, to arrive at the estimated total value of the firm's equity. This calculation will be demonstrated in Chapter 15.

PRESENT VALUE OF FREE CASH FLOWS TO EQUITY

The third discounted cash flow technique deals with "free" cash flows to equity, which would be derived *after* operating free cash flows have been adjusted for debt payments (interest and principle). Also, these cash flows precede dividend payments to the common stockholder. Such cash flows are referred to as "free" because they are what is left after meeting all obligations to other capital suppliers (debt and preferred stock) and after providing the funds needed to maintain the firm's asset base (similar to operating free cash flow).

Notably, because these are cash flows available to equity owners, the discount rate used is the firm's cost of equity (k) rather than the firm's WACC.

11.8

$$V_j = \sum_{t=1}^{n} \frac{FCFE_t}{(1 + k_j)^t}$$

where:

V_j = value of the stock of firm j
n = number of periods assumed to be infinite
$FCFE_t$ = the firm's free cash flow to equity in period t. The specification of free cash flow to equity will be discussed in Chapter 15.

Again, how an analyst would implement this general model depends on the firm's position in its life cycle. That is, if the firm is expected to experience stable growth, analysts can use an adaptation of the infinite growth model. In contrast, if the firm is expected to experience a period of temporary supernormal growth, analysts should use the multistage growth model similar to the process used with dividends and for operating free cash flow.

Relative Valuation Techniques

In contrast to the various discounted cash flow techniques that attempt to estimate a specific value for a stock based on its estimated growth rates and its discount rate, the relative valuation techniques implicitly contend that it is possible to determine the value of an economic entity (i.e., the market, an industry, or a company) by comparing it to similar entities on the basis of several relative ratios that compare its stock price to relevant variables that affect a stock's value, such as earnings, cash flow, book value, and sales. Therefore, in this section, we discuss the following relative valuation ratios: (1) price–earnings (P/E), (2) price–cash flow (P/CF), (3) price–book value (P/BV), price–sales (P/S), and entity value/EBITDA (EV/EBITDA). We begin with the P/E ratio, also referred to as the earnings multiplier, because it is the most popular relative valuation ratio. In addition, we will show that the P/E ratio can be directly related to the DDM in a manner that indicates the variables that affect the P/E ratio.

EARNINGS MULTIPLIER MODEL

As noted, many investors prefer to estimate the value of common stock using an **earnings multiplier model.** The reasoning for this approach recalls the basic concept that the value of any investment is the present value of future returns. In the case of common stocks, the returns that investors are entitled to receive are the net earnings of the firm. Therefore, one way investors can estimate value is by determining how many dollars they are willing to pay for a dollar of expected earnings (typically represented by the estimated per share earnings during the following twelve-month period). For example, if investors are willing to pay ten times expected earnings, they would value a stock they expect to earn $2 a share during the following year at $20. We compute the prevailing earnings multiplier, also referred to as the *price–earnings (P/E) ratio,* as follows:

11.9

$$\text{Earnings Multiplier} = \text{Price–Earnings Ratio}$$

$$= \frac{\textbf{Current Market Price}}{\textbf{Expected 12-Month Earnings}}$$

Interactive e-lectures

For more explanation and an animated example of the price–earnings ratio, go to: **http://reillyxtra .swlearning.com.**

This computation indicates the prevailing attitude of investors toward a stock's value. Investors must decide if they agree with the prevailing P/E ratio (that is, is the earnings multiplier too high or too low?) based on how it compares to the P/E ratio for the aggregate market, for the firm's industry, and for similar firms and stocks.

To decide whether a given P/E ratio is too high or low, we must consider what influences the P/E ratio over time. For example, over time the aggregate stock market P/E ratio, as represented by the S&P Industrials Index, has varied from about 6 times earnings to about 30 times earnings.[9] The infinite period DDM can be used to indicate the variables that should determine the value of the P/E ratio as follows:[10]

11.10

$$P_i = \frac{D_1}{k - g}$$

If we divide both sides of the equation by E_1 (expected earnings during the next twelve months), the result is

11.11

$$\frac{P_i}{E_1} = \frac{D_1/E_1}{k - g}$$

Thus, the future P/E ratio is determined by

1. The *expected* dividend payout ratio (dividends divided by earnings)
2. The *estimated* required rate of return on the stock (k)
3. The *expected* growth rate of dividends for the stock (g)

As an example, if we assume a stock has an expected dividend payout of 50 percent, a required rate of return of 12 percent, and an expected growth rate for dividends of 8 percent, we would have the following regarding the stock's future P/E ratio:

$$D/E = 0.50; \; k = 0.12; \; g = 0.08$$

$$P/E = \frac{0.50}{0.12 - 0.08} = \frac{0.50}{0.04} = 12.5$$

---

[9]When computing historical P/E ratios, the practice is to use earnings for the past twelve months rather than expected earnings. Although this will influence the level, it demonstrates the changes in the P/E ratio over time. Although it is acceptable to use historical P/E ratios that use past earnings for historical comparison, we strongly believe that investment decisions should emphasize future P/E ratios that use *expected* earnings.

[10]In this formulation of the model we use P rather than V (that is, the value is stated as the estimated price of the stock). Although the factors that determine the P/E are the same for growth companies, this formula cannot be used to estimate a specific value because many of these firms do not pay dividends and the $(k - g)$ assumptions don't apply.

Again, a small difference in either k or g or both will have a large impact on the earnings multiplier, as shown in the following three examples.

1. For a higher k: $D/E = 0.50$; $k = 0.13$; $g = 0.08$.

$$P/E = \frac{0.50}{0.13 - 0.08} = \frac{0.50}{0.05} = 10$$

2. For a higher g and the original k: $D/E = 0.50$; $k = 0.12$; $g = 0.09$.

$$P/E = \frac{0.50}{0.12 - 0.09} = \frac{0.50}{0.03} = 16.7$$

3. For a lower k and a higher g: $D/E = 0.50$; $k = 0.11$; $g = 0.09$.

$$P/E = \frac{0.50}{0.11 - 0.09} = \frac{0.50}{0.02} = 25$$

As before, *the spread between* k *and g is the main determinant of the size of the P/E ratio.* Although the dividend payout ratio has an impact, we are generally referring to a firm's long-run target payout, which is typically rather stable with little effect on year-to-year changes in the P/E ratio (earnings multiplier).

After estimating the earnings multiple, we apply it to our estimate of earnings for the next year (E_1) to arrive at an estimated value. In turn, E_1 is based on the earnings for the current year (E_0) and the expected growth rate of earnings. Using these two estimates, we compute an estimated value of the stock and compare this estimated value to its market price.

Consider the following estimates for an example firm:

$$D/E = 0.50; \; k = 0.12; \; g = 0.09; \; E_0 = \$2.00;$$

Using these estimates, we compute a future earnings multiple of

$$P/E = \frac{0.50}{0.12 - 0.09} = \frac{0.50}{0.03} = 16.7$$

Given current earnings (E_0) of $2.00 and a g of 9 percent, we would expect E_1 to be $2.18. Therefore, we estimate the intrinsic value of the stock as

$$V = 16.7 \times \$2.18$$

$$= \$36.41$$

As always we would compare this estimated intrinsic value of the stock to its current market price to decide whether to invest in it. This estimate of value requires you to estimate future earnings (E_1) and a P/E ratio based on expectations of k and g. We will further discuss these two estimates in Chapter 15.

PRICE–CASH FLOW RATIO MODEL

The growth in the popularity of this relative valuation ratio can be traced to concern over the propensity of some firms to manipulate earnings per share, whereas cash flow values are generally less prone to manipulation. Also, as noted, cash flow values are important in fundamental valuation (when computing the present value of cash flow), and they are critical when doing credit analysis where "cash is king." The price to cash flow ratio is computed as follows:

11.12

$$P/CF_j = \frac{P_t}{CF_{t+1}}$$

where:

$$P/CF_j = \text{the price–cash flow ratio for firm } j$$
$$P_t = \text{the price of the stock in period } t$$
$$CF_{t+1} = \text{the expected cash flow per share for firm } j$$

The variables that affect this valuation ratio are similar to the P/E ratio. Specifically, the main variables should be: (1) the expected growth rate of the cash flow variable used, and (2) the risk of the stock as indicated by the uncertainty or variability of the cash flow series over time. The specific cash flow measure used will vary depending on the nature of the company and industry and which cash flow specification (for example, operating cash flow or free cash flow) is the best measure of performance for this industry. An appropriate ratio can also be affected by the firm's capital structure.

PRICE–BOOK VALUE RATIO MODEL

The price–book value (P/BV) ratio has been widely used for many years by analysts in the banking industry as a measure of relative value. The book value of a bank is typically considered a good indicator of intrinsic value because most bank assets, such as bonds and commercial loans, have a value equal to book value. This ratio gained in popularity and credibility as a relative valuation technique for all types of firms based on a study by Fama and French that indicated a significant inverse relationship between P/BV ratios and excess rates of return for a cross section of stocks.[11] The P/BV ratio is specified as follows:

| 11.13 |

$$P/BV_j = \frac{P_t}{BV_{t+1}}$$

where:

$$P/BV_j = \text{the price–book value ratio for firm } j$$
$$P_t = \text{the price of the stock in period } t$$
$$BV_{t+1} = \text{the estimated end-of-year book value per share for firm } j$$

As with other relative valuation ratios, it is important to match the current price with the book value that is expected to prevail at the end of the year. The difficulty is that this future book value is not generally available. We can estimate the end-of-year book value based on the historical growth rate for the series or use the growth rate implied by the sustainable growth formula: g = (ROE)(Retention Rate).

The factors that determine the size of the P/BV ratio are a function of ROE relative to the firm's cost of equity since the ratio would be 1 if they were equal—that is, if the firm earned its required return on equity. In contrast, if the ROE is much larger, it would be considered a growth company and investors would be willing to pay a premium for the stock over its book value.

PRICE–SALES RATIO MODEL

The price–sales (P/S) ratio has a volatile history. It was a favorite of Phillip Fisher, a well-know money manager in the late 1950s, his son, and others.[12] Recently, the P/S ratio has

---

[11]Eugene Fama and Kenneth French, "The Cross Section of Expected Returns," *Journal of Finance* 47, no. 2 (June 1992). We discussed this study in Chapter 10.

[12]Phillip A. Fisher, *Common Stock and Uncommon Profits,* rev. ed., Woodside, CA: PSR Publications, 1984; Kenneth L. Fisher, *Super Stocks,* Homewood, IL: Dow Jones–Irwin, 1984, and A. J. Senchak Jr. and John D. Martin, "The Relative Performance of the PSR and PER Investment Strategies," *Financial Analysts Journal* 43, no. 2 (March–April, 1987): 46–56.

been recommended by Martin Leibowitz, a widely admired stock and bond portfolio manager.[13] These advocates consider this ratio meaningful for two reasons. First, they believe that strong and consistent sales growth is a requirement for a growth company. Although they note the importance of an above-average profit margin, they contend that *the growth process must begin with sales*. Second, given the numerous data items in the balance sheet and income statement, sales information is subject to less manipulation than most other data items. The specific P/S ratio is

11.14

$$P/S_j = \frac{P_t}{S_{t+1}}$$

where:

P/S_j = the price to sales ratio for firm j
P_t = the price of the stock in period t
S_{t+1} = the expected sales per share for firm j

Again, it is important to match the current stock price with the firm's *expected* sales per share, which may be difficult to derive for a large cross section of stocks. Two caveats are relevant to the price to sales ratio. First, this relative valuation ratio varies dramatically by industry. For example, the sales per share for retail firms, such as Kroger or Wal-Mart, are typically much higher than sales per share for computer or microchip firms. The second consideration is the profit margin on sales. The point is, retail food stores have high sales per share, which will cause a low P/S ratio, which is considered good until one realizes that these firms have low net profit margins. Therefore, it is recommended that relative valuation analysis using the P/S ratio should be between firms in the same or similar industries.

IMPLEMENTING THE RELATIVE VALUATION TECHNIQUE

As noted, the relative valuation technique considers several valuation ratios—such as P/E and P/BV—to derive a value for a stock. To properly implement this technique, it is essential to compare the various ratios but also to recognize that the analysis needs to go beyond simply comparing the ratios to understanding what factors affect each of the valuation ratios and, therefore, knowing why they should differ. The first step is to compare the valuation ratio (e.g., the P/E ratio) for a company to the comparable ratio for the market, for the stock's industry, and to other stocks in the industry to determine how it compares—that is, is it similar to these other P/Es, or is it consistently at a premium or discount? Beyond knowing the overall relationship to the market, industry, and competitors, the real analysis involves understanding *why* the ratio has this relationship or why it should *not* have this relationship and the implications of this mismatch. Specifically, the second step is to explain the relationship. To do this, we need to understand what factors determine the specific valuation ratio and then compare these factors for the stock versus the same factors for the market, industry, and other stocks.

To illustrate this process, suppose you want to value the stock of a pharmaceutical company and decide to employ the P/E as a relative valuation technique. You compare the P/E ratios for this firm over time (e.g., the last fifteen years) to similar ratios for the S&P Industrials, the pharmaceutical industry, and competitors. Let us assume that the results of this comparison indicate that the company P/E ratios are consistently above all the other sets. The obvious question (why?) leads you into the second part of the analysis—whether the

---

[13]Martin L. Leibowitz, *Sales Driven Franchise Value,* Charlottesville, VA: The Research Foundation of the Institute of Chartered Financial Analysts, 1997.

fundamental factors that affect the P/E ratio (i.e., the firm's growth rate and required rate of return) justify the higher P/E. A positive scenario would be that the firm had a historical and expected growth rate that was substantially above all the comparables and a lower required rate of return due to a lower beta. This analysis would indicate that the higher P/E ratio is justified; the only question that needs to be considered is, how much higher should the P/E ratio be? Alternatively, a negative scenario would be if the company that had a high P/E ratio had an expected growth rate that was equal to or lower than the industry and competitors and its required k was higher than for the industry and competitors. This would signal a stock that should have a lower P/E, which implies that it is overpriced based on the fundamental factors that determine a stock's P/E ratio.

Estimating the Inputs: The Required Rate of Return and the Expected Growth Rate of Valuation Variables

This section deals with estimating two critical inputs to the valuation process (irrespective of which approach or technique is being used): the required rate of return (k) and the expected growth (g) rate of earnings and other valuation variables—that is, book value, cash flow, sales, and dividends.

REQUIRED RATE OF RETURN

The nominal required rate of return on an investment will be the discount rate for most cash flow models and affects all the relative valuation techniques. The only difference in the discount rate is between the present value of dividends and the present value of free cash flow to equity techniques, which use the required rate of return on equity (k), and the present value of operating free cash flow technique, which uses the weighted average cost of capital WACC, wherein the cost of equity is a critical input to estimating the firm's WACC.

Recall that three factors influence an investor's required rate of return:

1. The economy's real risk-free rate (RRFR)
2. The expected rate of inflation (I)
3. A risk premium (RP)

The Economy's Real Risk-Free Rate   As discussed in Chapter 1, this is the absolute minimum rate that an investor should require. It depends on two factors: first, the real growth rate of the investor's home economy because capital invested should grow at least as fast as the economy, and second, this rate can be affected for short periods by temporary tightness or ease in the capital markets.

The Expected Rate of Inflation   Investors are interested in real rates of return that will allow them to increase their rate of consumption. Therefore, if investors expect a given rate of inflation, they should increase their required nominal risk-free rate of return (NRFR) to reflect any expected inflation as follows:

11.15
$$NRFR = [1 + RRFR][1 + E(I)] - 1$$

where:

$E(I)$ = expected rate of inflation

Consider the following example. Suppose the long-run growth rate of real GDP in the United States has been about 2.5 percent (0.025) and you expect this to continue into the future. In addition, you have read numerous reports that indicate that the consensus expected rate of inflation over the next five years (your investment horizon) is 3.0 percent (0.030). Thus your NRFR should be

$$\text{NRFR} = \left[(1 + 0.025)(1 + 0.030) \right] - 1$$

$$= 1.05575 - 1$$

$$= 0.05575 = 5.575\%$$

Because it is an estimate, you would probably round it off to 5.6%. Alternatively, some would simply add the two values and use 5.5% (0.025 + 0.030). At this point, the exact mathematics is not as important as the understanding of the two components and the fact that this NRFR is the base rate for all investments. Of the two components, the expected inflation rate is the tougher estimate due to its volatility.

The Risk Premium   The risk premium (RP) causes differences in the required rates of return among alternative investments that range from government bonds to corporate bonds to common stocks. The RP also explains the difference in the expected return among securities of the same type. For example, this is the reason corporate bonds with different ratings of Aaa, Aa, or A have different yields, and why different common stocks have widely varying earnings multipliers despite similar growth expectations.

Recall that investors demand a risk premium because of the uncertainty of returns expected from an investment. A measure of this uncertainty of returns is the dispersion of expected returns. Several internal factors influence a firm's variability of returns, such as its business risk, financial risk, and liquidity risk. Securities of foreign firms or of domestic companies with significant foreign sales and earnings (e.g., Coca-Cola and McDonald's) bring additional risk factors, including exchange rate risk and country (political) risk.

Changes in the risk premium.   Because different securities have different patterns of returns and different guarantees to investors, we expect their risk premiums to differ. In addition, the risk premiums for the same securities can *change over time*. For example, Exhibit 11.4 shows the spread between the yields to maturity for Aaa-rated corporate bonds and Baa-rated corporate bonds from 1974 through 2004. This yield spread, or difference in yield, is a measure of the risk premium for investing in higher-risk bonds (Baa) compared to low-risk bonds (Aaa). As shown, the yield spread varied from about 0.40 percent to 2.69 percent (from less than one-half of 1 percent to almost 3 percent). This change in risk premium over time occurs because either investors perceive change in the level of risk of Baa bonds compared to Aaa bonds or there is a change in the amount of return that investors require to accept the same risk differential. In either case, this change in the risk premium for a set of assets implies a change in the slope of the security market line (SML) (see Chapter 9).

EXPECTED GROWTH RATES

After arriving at a required rate of return, we must estimate the growth rate of cash flows, earnings, and dividends because valuation models for common stock depend heavily on good estimates of growth (g) for these variables in order to estimate future cash flows, earnings, or dividends. The initial procedure we describe here is similar to the presentation forthcoming in Chapter 14, where we will use financial ratios to measure a firm's growth potential. Subsequently, we discuss the use of historical growth rates as an input to the estimate.

EXHIBIT 11.4 | Time-Series Plot of Moody's Corporate Bond Yield Spreads (Baa–Aaa): Monthly 1974–2004

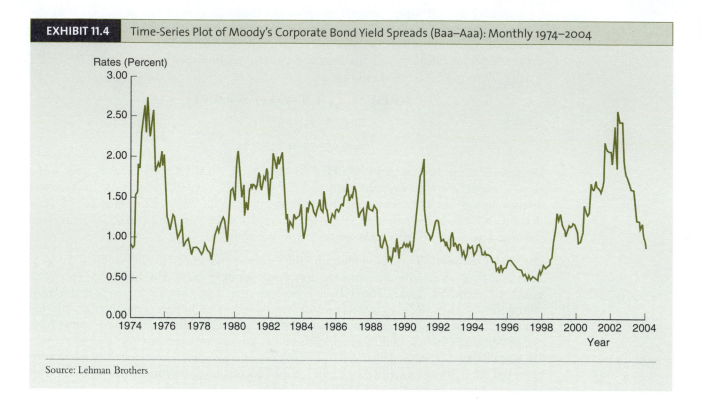

Source: Lehman Brothers

Estimating Growth from Fundamentals   The growth rate of dividends is determined by the growth rate of earnings and the proportion of earnings paid out in dividends (the payout ratio). Over the short run, dividends can grow faster or slower than earnings if the firm changes its payout ratio. Specifically, if a firm's earnings grow at 6 percent a year and it consistently pays out exactly 50 percent of earnings in dividends, then the firm's dividends will likewise grow at 6 percent a year. Alternatively, if a firm's earnings grow at 6 percent a year and the firm increases its payout, then during the period when the payout ratio increases, dividends will grow faster than earnings. In contrast, if the firm reduces its payout ratio, dividends will grow slower than earnings for a period of time. Because there is a limit to how long this difference in growth rates can continue, most investors assume that the long-run dividend payout ratio is fairly stable. Therefore, analysis of the growth rate of dividends typically concentrates on an analysis of the growth rate of equity earnings. Also, as we will show in Chapter 15, these earnings are the major factor driving the operating cash flows or the free cash flows for the firm.

When a firm retains earnings and acquires additional assets, if it earns some positive rate of return on these additional assets the total earnings of the firm will increase because its asset base is larger. How rapidly a firm's earnings increase depends on (1) the proportion of earnings it retains and reinvests in new assets and (2) the rate of return it earns on these new assets. Specifically, the growth rate (g) of equity earnings (that is, earnings per share) without any external financing is equal to the percentage of net earnings retained (the retention rate, which equals 1 − the payout ratio) times the rate of return on equity capital.

11.16

$$g = (\text{Retention Rate}) \times (\text{Return on Equity})$$

$$= RR \times ROE$$

Therefore, a firm can increase its growth rate by increasing its retention rate (reducing its payout ratio) and investing these added funds at its ROE. Alternatively, the firm can maintain its retention rate but increase its ROE. For example, if a firm retains 50 percent of net earnings and consistently has an ROE of 10 percent, its net earnings will grow at the rate of 5 percent a year:

$$g = RR \times ROE$$
$$= 0.50 \times 0.10$$
$$= 0.05$$

If, however, the firm increases its retention rate to 75 percent and invests these additional funds in internal projects that earn 10 percent, its growth rate will increase to 7.5 percent:

$$g = 0.75 \times 0.10$$
$$= 0.075$$

If, instead, the firm continues to reinvest 50 percent of its earnings but derives a higher rate of return on these investments, say 15 percent, it can likewise increase its growth rate, as follows:

$$g = 0.50 \times 0.15$$
$$= 0.075$$

Breakdown of ROE   Although the retention rate is a management decision, changes in the firm's ROE result from changes in its operating performance or its financial leverage. As will be discussed in Chapter 14, we can divide the ROE ratio into three components.

11.17

$$ROE = \frac{Net\ Income}{Sales} \times \frac{Sales}{Total\ Assets} \times \frac{Total\ Assets}{Equity}$$
$$= Net\ Profit\ Margin \times Total\ Asset\ Turnover \times Financial\ Leverage$$

This breakdown allows us to consider the three factors that determine a firm's ROE. Because it is a multiplicative relationship, an increase in any of the three ratios will cause an increase in ROE. The first two of the three ratios reflect operating performance, and the third one indicates a firm's financing decision.

The first operating ratio, net profit margin, indicates the firm's profitability on sales. This ratio changes over time for some companies and is highly sensitive to the business cycle. For growth companies, this is one of the first ratios to decline because the increased competition increases the supply of the goods or services and forces price cutting, which leads to lower profit margins. Also, during recessions, profit margins decline because of price cutting or because of higher percentages of fixed costs due to lower sales.

The second component, total asset turnover, is the ultimate indicator of operating efficiency and reflects the asset and capital requirements of the business. Although this ratio varies dramatically by industry, within an industry it is an excellent indicator of management's operating efficiency.

The product of these first two components (profit margin and total asset turnover) equals the firm's return on assets (ROA), which reflects the firm's operating performance before the financing impact.[14]

---

[14]In Chapter 13 we will discuss a study that analyzes why and how alternative industries differ regarding the return on assets and the two components.

The final component, total assets/equity, does not measure operating performance but, rather, financial leverage. Specifically, it indicates how management has decided to finance the firm. In turn, this management decision regarding the financing of assets can contribute to a higher ROE, but it also has financial risk implications for the stockholder.

Knowing this breakdown of ROE, analysts must examine past results and expectations for a firm and develop *estimates* of the three components and therefore an estimate of a firm's ROE. This estimate of ROE combined with the firm's expected retention rate will indicate its future growth potential. Finally, it is important to note that when estimating growth, it is necessary to estimate not only the *rate* of growth but also the *duration* of growth (i.e., how long can the firm sustain this rate of growth?). Clearly, the higher the rate of growth the more significant the estimate of the duration of growth to the ultimate value of the stock.

Estimating Growth Based on History   Although we have a strong bias in favor of using the fundamentals to estimate future growth, which involves estimating the components of ROE, we also believe in using all the information available to make this critical estimate. Therefore, we suggest that analysts also consider the historical growth rate of sales, earnings, cash flow, and dividends in this process.

Although we will demonstrate these computations for the market, for an industry, and for a company in subsequent chapters, the following discussion considers some suggestions on alternative calculations. In terms of the relevant period to consider, "more is better" as long as you recognize that "recent is relevant." Specifically, about twenty years of annual observations would be ideal, but it is important to consider subperiods as well as the total period—that is, twenty years, two ten-year periods, and four five-year periods would indicate the overall growth rate as well as whether there were any *changes* in the growth rate in recent periods.

The specific measurement can be done using one or more of three techniques: (1) arithmetic or geometric mean of annual percentage changes, (2) linear regression models, and (3) log-linear regression models. Irrespective of the measurement techniques used, we strongly encourage a time-series plot of the annual percentage changes.

The arithmetic or geometric mean technique involves computing the annual percentage change and then computing either the simple arithmetic mean or the geometric mean of these values for the different periods. As you will recall from the discussion in Chapter 2, the arithmetic mean will always be a higher value than the geometric mean (except when the annual values are constant) and the difference between the means will increase with volatility. As noted previously, we generally prefer the geometric mean because it provides the average annual compound growth rate.

The linear regression model goes well with the suggested time-series plot and is as follows:

11.18
$$\text{EPS}_t = a + bt$$

where:

EPS_t = earnings per period in period t

t = year t where t goes from 1 to n

b = the coefficient that indicates the average absolute change in the series during the period

This regression line superimposed on the time-series plot would provide insights on changes in absolute growth.

The log-linear model considers that the series might be better described in terms of a constant *growth rate*. This model is

11.19

$$\ln(EPS_t) = a + bt$$

where:

$\ln(EPS_t)$ = the natural logarithm of earnings per share in period t
b = the coefficient that indicates the average percentage change in the series during the period

The analysis of these historical growth rates both visually with a time-series graph and through calculations provides significant insights into the trend of the growth rates as well as the *variability* of the growth rates over time.

Summary

- Investors want to select investments that will provide a rate of return that compensates for their time, the expected rate of inflation, and the risk involved. The theory of valuation by which the value of an investment is derived using the required rate of return can greatly aid in this selection. Both the top-down, three-step approach and the bottom-up, stock-picking approach to the investment decision processes can provide abnormal positive returns if the analyst is superior. However, the top-down approach—in which we initially consider the aggregate economy and market, then examine global industries, and finally analyze individual firms and determine the value of their stocks—is preferable.

- The valuation theory can be applied to a range of investments including bonds, preferred stock, and common stock. Because the valuation of common stock is more complex and difficult, we suggest two approaches (the present value of cash flows and the relative valuation approach) and several techniques for each of these approaches. Notably, we do *not* believe that these are competitive approaches but suggest that *both* approaches be used. Although we suggest using several different valuation models, the investment decision rule is always the same: If the estimated intrinsic value of the investment is greater than the market price, you should buy the investment; if the estimated intrinsic value of an investment is less than its market price, you should not invest in it and you should sell it if you own it.

- The necessary factors when estimating the value of stock with either approach are the required rate of return on an investment and the growth rate of earnings, cash flow, and dividends.

Investments Online

Several sites that we discussed in earlier chapters contained financial calculators. By inputting the required data, users can determine if it is better to buy or lease a car, calculate returns, and determine how much money they will have if funds are invested at a certain rate of return over time. The sites listed here all contain financial calculators that may be of use to investors and financial planners.

http://www.financenter.com

http://www.jamesko.com/FinCalc

http://www.numeraire.com

http://www.moneychimp.com

QUESTIONS

1. Discuss the difference between the top-down and bottom-up approaches. What major assumption causes the difference in these two approaches?
2. What is the benefit of analyzing the market and the industry before an individual security?
3. Discuss why you would not expect all industries to have a similar relationship to the economy. Give an example of two industries that have different relationships to the economy.
4. Discuss why estimating the value for a bond is easier than estimating the value for common stock.
5. Would you expect the required rate of return for a U.S. investor in U.S. common stocks to be the same as the required rate of return on Japanese common stocks? What factors would determine the required rate of return for stocks in these countries?
6. Given the factors that determine the value of an asset, why is there an emphasis on estimating the growth rate of earnings, cash flows, or dividends?
7. What are the two facets of growth that must be considered when estimating growth? Use an example to clarify your answer.
8. What are the three components of the required rate of return for an investment? Which of the three components differentiates investments? Why is this true?

9. With regard to the investment decision process, it is specified that if the intrinsic value of an asset is less than its market price, you should not buy the asset and if you own it, you should sell it. Discuss the rationale for this sell decision.
10. Give an example of a stock where it would be appropriate to use the reduced form DDM for valuation and discuss why you feel that it is appropriate. Similarly, give an example of and discuss a stock where it would not be appropriate to use the reduced form DDM.
11. Give an example of and discuss a stock that has temporary supernormal growth where it would be appropriate (necessary) to use the modified DDM.
12. When we use the term *supernormal growth,* why do we refer to it as "temporary"?
13. Under what conditions will it be ideal to use one or several of the relative valuation ratios to evaluate a stock?
14. Discuss a scenario where it would be appropriate to use one of the present value of cash flow techniques for the valuation.
15. Discuss why the two valuation approaches (present value of cash flows and the relative valuation ratios) are competitive or complementary.

PROBLEMS

1. What is the value to you of a 9 percent coupon bond with a par value of $10,000 that matures in ten years if you want a 7 percent return? Use semiannual compounding.
2. What would be the value of the bond in Problem 1 if you wanted an 11 percent rate of return?
3. An AA-rated corporate bond has a par value of $1,000, an 8 percent coupon rate, and a twenty-year maturity. If your required rate of return for this bond is 10 percent, what is its value to you? If the bond is currently priced at $950 (95 percent of par), would you buy it?
4. If you owned the bond in Problem 3, what would you do? If this bond was downgraded by a rating agency to A, what would happen to the market price of the bond (no calculations required)? Discuss the reason for the price change.
5. The preferred stock of the Clarence Radiology Company has a par value of $100 and a $9 dividend rate. You require an 11 percent rate of return on this stock. What is the maximum price you would pay for it? Would you buy it at a market price of $96?

6. The Baron Basketball Company (BBC) earned $10 a share last year and paid a dividend of $6 a share. Next year, you expect BBC to earn $11 and continue its payout ratio. Assume that you expect to sell the stock for $132 a year from now. If you require a 12 percent return on this stock, how much would you be willing to pay for it?
7. Given the expected earnings and dividend payments in Problem 6, if you expected a selling price of $110 and required an 8 percent return on this investment, how much would you pay for the stock?
8. Over the long run, you expect dividends for BBC in Problem 6 to grow at 8 percent and you require an 11 percent return on the stock. Using the infinite period DDM, how much would you pay for this stock?
9. Based on new information regarding the popularity of basketball, you revise your growth estimate for BBC in Problem 6 to 9 percent. What is the maximum P/E ratio you will apply to BBC, and what is the maximum price you will pay for the stock?
10. The Shamrock Dogfood Company (SDC) has consistently paid out 40 percent of its earnings in dividends.

The company's return on equity is 16 percent. What would you estimate as its dividend growth rate?

11. Given the low risk in dog food, your required rate of return on SDC (Problem 10) is 13 percent. What P/E ratio would you apply to the firm's earnings?

12. What P/E ratio would you apply if you learned that SDC (Problem 10) had decided to increase its payout to 50 percent? (*Hint:* This change in payout has multiple effects.)

13. Discuss three ways a firm can increase its ROE. Make up an example to illustrate your discussion.

14. The Sophie Silk Company (SSC) has a profit margin of 4 percent, an asset turnover of 2.5 times, a retention rate of 90 percent, and total assets to equity of 2.2. The company earned $1.75 per share this year.
    a. How much do you expect SSC to earn next year?
    b. What would you estimate as the firm's dividend next year?
    c. Assume a required cost of equity (*k*) of 12 percent and use the DDM to determine the stock's P/E and its value.
    d. What other valuation models should be used to value Sophie's stock (no calculations required)? Why?

15. It is widely known that grocery chains have low profit margins; on average they earn about 1 percent on sales. How would you explain the fact that their ROE is about 12 percent? Does this seem logical?

16. Compute a recent five-year average of the following ratios for three companies of your choice (attempt to select diverse firms):
    a. Retention rate
    b. Net profit margin
    c. Equity turnover
    d. Total asset turnover
    e. Total assets/equity
    Based on these ratios, explain which firm should have the highest growth rate of earnings.

17. You have been reading about the Madison Computer Company (MCC), which currently retains 90 percent of its earnings ($5 a share this year). It earns an ROE of almost 30 percent. Assuming a required rate of return of 14 percent, how much would you pay for MCC on the basis of the earnings multiplier model? Discuss your answer. What would you pay for Madison Computer if its retention rate was 60 percent and its ROE was 19 percent? Show your work.

18. Gentry Can Company's (GCC) latest annual dividend of $1.25 a share was paid yesterday and maintained its historic 7 percent annual rate of growth. You plan to purchase the stock today because you believe that the dividend growth rate will increase to 8 percent for the next three years and the selling price of the stock will be $40 per share at the end of that time.
    a. How much should you be willing to pay for the GCC stock if you require a 12 percent return?
    b. What is the maximum price you should be willing to pay for the GCC stock if you believe that the 8 percent growth rate can be maintained indefinitely and you require a 12 percent return?
    c. If the 8 percent rate of growth is achieved, what will the price be at the end of year 3, assuming the conditions in part (b)?

19. In the *Federal Reserve Bulletin,* find the average yield of AAA and BBB bonds for a recent month. Compute the risk premium (in basis points) on BBB bonds relative to AAA bonds. Discuss how these values compare to those shown in Exhibit 11.4.

REFERENCES

Arzac, Enrique R. *Valuation for Mergers, Buyouts, and Restructuring.* New York: Wiley, 2005.

Bhatia, Sanjiv, ed. *Global Equity Investing.* Proceedings of a seminar by the Association of Investment Management and Research. Charlottesville, VA: AIMR, 1995.

Billingsley, Randall, ed. *Corporate Financial Decision Making and Equity Analysis.* Proceedings of a seminar by the Association of Investment Management and Research. Charlottesville, VA: AIMR, 1995.

Copeland, T. E., Tim Koller, and Jack Murrin. *Valuation: Measuring and Managing the Value of Companies,* 3d ed. New York: John Wiley & Sons, 2001.

Cornell, Bradford. *Corporate Valuation.* Burr Ridge, IL: Irwin Professional Publishing, 1993.

Damodaran, Aswath. *Damodaran on Valuation.* New York: John Wiley & Sons, 1994.

Damodaran, Aswath. *Investment Valuation.* New York: John Wiley & Sons, 1996.

Farrell, James L. "The Dividend Discount Model: A Primer." *Financial Analysts Journal* 41, no. 6 (November–December 1985).

Greenwald, B. C. N., J. Kahn, P. D. Sonkin, and M. van Biema. *Value Investing.* New York: John Wiley & Sons, 2001.

Helfert, Erich A. *Techniques of Financial Analysis,* 10th ed. Burr Ridge, IL: Irwin McGraw-Hill, 2000.

Higgins, Robert C. *Analysis for Financial Management,* 5th ed. Chicago: Richard D. Irwin, 2000.

Levine, Sumner N., ed. *The Financial Analysts Handbook,* 2nd ed. Homewood, IL: Dow Jones–Irwin, 1988.

Palepu, Krishna, Victor Bernard, and Paul Healy. *Business Analysis and Valuation*. Cincinnati, OH: South-Western Publishing, 1996.

Sharpe, William, and Katrina Sherrerd, eds. *Quantifying the Market Risk Premium Phenomenon for Investment Decision Making*. Proceedings of a seminar by the Association of Investment Management and Research. Charlottesville, VA: AIMR, 1989.

Squires, Jan, ed. *Equity Research and Valuation Techniques*. Proceedings of a seminar by the Association of Investment Management and Research. Charlottesville, VA: AIMR, 1997.

Squires, Jan, ed. *Practical Issues in Equity Analysis*. Conference proceedings by the Association of Investment Management and Research. Charlottesville, VA: AIMR, 2000.

Stowe, J. D., T. R. Robinson, J. E. Pinto, and D. W. McLeavey. *Analysis of Equity Investments: Valuation*. Charlottesville, VA: AIMR, 2002.

Sullivan, Rodney N., ed. *Equity Analysis Issues, Lessons, and Techniques*. Proceedings of a seminar by the Association of Investment Management and Research. Charlottesville, VA: AIMR, 2003.

Whitman, Martin J. *Value Investing*. New York: John Wiley & Sons, 1999.

THOMSON ONE
Business School Edition

1. Using Ford, General Electric, McDonald's, Nike, and Walgreens, find the five-year estimate for net income growth, dividend yield, P/E, Price/Cash Flow, and Price/Book Value ratios. Do any positive or negative relationships or correlations exist between these data items?
2. Assume that the five-year estimates for net income growth for General Electric, McDonald's, and Walgreens are the same as their dividend growth rates.

a. For each of these three firms, estimate the dollar amount of dividends per share over each of the next five years.
b. Find the present value of each dividend stream from part a. Use a discount rate of 10 percent for each firm. (This is a simplification; in reality we would need to estimate the required rate of return for each firm.)
c. For each firm, compare its current stock price with the estimated present value of its dividends over the next five years. Given our assumptions, what proportion of the stock price arises from cash flows *beyond* the next five years?

GLOSSARY

Bottom-up, stock-picking approach A forward-looking approach to evaluating securities in which trends are forecast based on an analysis of microeconomic, or firm-specific, factors.

Dividend discount model (DDM) A technique for estimating the value of a stock issue as the present value of all future dividends.

Earnings multiplier model A technique for estimating the value of a stock issue as a multiple of its expected earnings per share.

Growth company A firm that has opportunities and the ability to earn rates of return on investments that are consistently above its required rate of return.

Investment decision process The comparison of the estimated intrinsic value of an asset to its market price to determine whether or not to invest.

Perpetuity An annuity payable forever; a preferred stock with no maturity.

Price–earnings (P/E) ratio The number by which expected earnings per share is multiplied to estimate a stock's value; also called the *earnings multiplier.*

Top-down, three-step approach A forward-looking approach to evaluating securities in which trends are forecast based on a three-step analysis of macroeconomic factors; industry outlook and company analysis and valuation.

Valuation process Part of the investment decision process in which the intrinsic value of an asset is derived using estimates of the required rate of return (the discount rate) and the stream of expected cash flows, earnings, and dividends.

Derivation of Constant Growth Dividend Discount Model (DDM)

The basic dividend discount model is

$$P_0 = \frac{D_1}{(1 + k)^1} + \frac{D_2}{(1 + k)^2} + \frac{D_3}{(1 + k)^3} + \cdots + \frac{D_n}{(1 + k)^n}$$

where:

P_0 = current price
D_i = expected dividend in period i
k = required rate of return on asset j

The model assumes

• A constant growth rate
• An infinite time period
• That the required return on the investment (k) is greater than the expected growth rate (g)

If growth rate (g) is constant,

$$P_0 = \frac{D_0(1 + g)^1}{(1 + k)^1} + \frac{D_0(1 + g)^2}{(1 + k)^2} + \cdots + \frac{D_0(1 + g)^n}{(1 + k)^n}$$

This can be written

$$P_0 = D_0\left[\frac{(1 + g)}{(1 + k)} + \frac{(1 + g)^2}{(1 + k)^2} + \frac{(1 + g)^3}{(1 + k)^3} + \cdots + \frac{(1 + g)^n}{(1 + k)^n}\right]$$

Multiplying both sides of the equation by $\dfrac{1 + k}{1 + g}$ gives

$$\left[\frac{(1 + g)}{(1 + k)}\right]P_0 = D_0\left[1 + \frac{(1 + g)}{(1 + k)} + \frac{(1 + g)^2}{(1 + k)^2} + \cdots + \frac{(1 + g)^{n-1}}{(1 + k)^{n-1}}\right]$$

Subtracting the previous equation from this equation gives

$$\left[\frac{(1 + k)}{(1 + g)} - 1\right]P_0 = D_0\left[1 - \frac{(1 + g)^n}{(1 + k)^n}\right]$$

$$\left[\frac{(1 + k) - (1 + g)}{(1 + g)}\right]P_0 = D_0\left[1 - \frac{(1 + g)^n}{(1 + k)^n}\right]$$

Assuming $k > g$ as $n \rightarrow \infty$, the term in brackets on the right side of the equation goes to 1, leaving

$$\left[\frac{(1 + k) - (1 + g)}{(1 + g)}\right]P_0 = D_0$$

This simplifies to

$$\left[\frac{(1 + k - 1 - g)}{(1 + g)}\right] P_0 = D_0$$

which equals

$$\left[\frac{k - g}{(1 + g)}\right] P_0 = D_0$$

This equals

$$(k - g) P_0 = D_0 (1 + g)$$

$$D_0 (1 + g) = D_1$$

so

$$(k - g) P_0 = D_1$$

$$P_0 = \frac{D_1}{k - g}$$

Analysis of Fixed-Income Securities

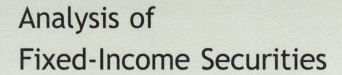

We begin this chapter with several measures of yields for bonds. Then, to understand why bond values and yields change over time, we review the value estimation for bonds that allows us to understand and compute the expected rates of return on bonds, which are their yields. We then consider what factors influence the level of bond yields and the economic forces that cause changes in yields over time. We discuss various characteristics and indenture provisions that affect the required returns and value of specific bond issues such as time to maturity, coupon, callability, and sinking funds.

With this background we return to the consideration of bond value and examine the characteristics that cause different changes in a bond's price. We will see that when yields change, the prices of different bonds do not change in the same way.

An understanding of the factors that affect the price changes for bonds has become more important during the past several decades because the price volatility of bonds has increased substantially. Before 1950, bond yields were fairly low, both yields and prices were stable, bonds were considered a safe investment, and most bond investors intended to hold them to maturity. During the past several decades, the level of interest rates has increased substantially because of inflation. In addition, interest rates have become more volatile because of frequent changes in the rate of inflation and monetary policy. As a result, rates of return on bonds have increased and become much more volatile.

The Fundamentals of Bond Valuation

The value of bonds can be described in terms of either dollar values or the rates of return that the bonds promise under some set of assumptions. In this section, we briefly recall the present value model, which computes a specific value for the bond, and describe

EXHIBIT 12.1	Price–Yield Relationship for a Twenty-Year, 8 Percent Coupon Bond ($1,000 Par Value)

Required Yield	Price of Bond
2	$1,985.09
4	1,547.12
6	1,231.19
8	1,000.00
10	828.36
12	699.05
14	600.07
16	522.98

the yield model, which computes the promised rate of return based on the bond's current price.

THE PRESENT VALUE MODEL

Previously we saw that the value of a bond (or any asset) equals the present value of its expected cash flow. Therefore, the value of a bond is the present value of the semiannual interest payments plus the present value of the principal payment, typically found by using a single interest rate discount factor, which is the required rate of return on the bond. We can express this in the following present value formula, which assumes semiannual compounding.[1]

12.1

$$P = \sum_{t=1}^{2n} \frac{C_i/2}{(1 + Y_m/2)^t} + \frac{P_p}{(1 + Y_m/2)^{2n}}$$

where:

- P = the current market price of the bond
- n = the number of years to maturity
- C_i = the annual coupon payment for bond i
- Y_m = the prevailing yield to maturity for this bond issue
- P_p = the par value of the bond

The Price–Yield Curve When we know the basic characteristics of a bond in terms of its coupon, maturity, and par value, the only factor that determines its value (price) is the market discount rate—its required rate of return. As shown in Chapter 11, as we increase the required rate, the price declines. We can demonstrate the specific relationship between the price of a bond and its yield by computing the bond's price at a range of yields, as shown in Exhibit 12.1.

---

[1]Almost all U.S. bonds pay interest semiannually, so it is appropriate to use semiannual compounding wherein we cut the annual coupon rate in half and double the number of periods. To be consistent, we should also use semiannual compounding when discounting the principal payment of a coupon bond or even a zero coupon bond. All our present value calculations assume semiannual compounding.

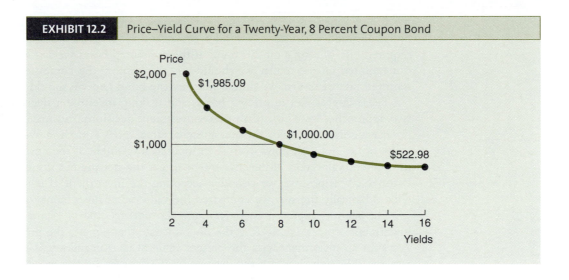

EXHIBIT 12.2   Price–Yield Curve for a Twenty-Year, 8 Percent Coupon Bond

A graph of this relationship between the required return (yield) on the bond and its price is referred to as the *price–yield curve,* as shown in Exhibit 12.2. Besides demonstrating that price moves inverse to yields, it shows three other important points:

1. When the yield is below the coupon rate, the bond will be priced at a *premium* to its par value.
2. When the yield is above the coupon rate, the bond will be priced at a *discount* to its par value.
3. The price–yield relationship is not a straight line; rather, it is *convex*. As the yield declines, the price increases at an increasing rate; as the yield increases, the price declines at a declining rate. This concept of a convex price–yield curve is referred to as *convexity* and will be discussed further in a later section.

THE YIELD MODEL

Instead of determining the value of a bond in dollar terms, investors often price bonds in terms of *yields,* which are the promised rates of return on bonds under certain assumptions. Thus far we have used cash flows and the required rate of return to compute an estimated value for the bond, which we then compared to its market price P. To compute an expected yield, we use the current market price P with the expected cash flows and *compute the expected yield on the bond.* We can express this approach using the present value model as follows:

12.2

$$P = \sum_{t=i}^{n} C_t \frac{1}{(1 + Y)^t}$$

where:

P = the current market price of the bond
C_t = the cash flow received in period t
Y = the discount rate that will discount the cash flows to equal the current market price of the bond

This Y value gives the yield of the bond. We will discuss several different bond yields that arise from alternative assumptions of the valuation model.

When approaching the investment decision using the bond's yield figure rather than a dollar amount, we need to consider the relationship of the computed bond yield to our required rate of return on this bond. If the computed bond yield is equal to or greater than our required rate of return, we should buy the bond; if the computed yield is less than our required rate of return, we should not buy the bond and we should sell it if we own it.

These approaches to pricing bonds and making investment decisions are similar to the two approaches by which firms make investment decisions. You may recall from a corporate finance course that with the net present value (NPV) method we compute the present value of the net cash flows from the proposed investment at the cost of capital and subtract the present value cost of the investment to get the net present value (NPV) of the project. If this NPV is positive, we consider accepting the investment; if it is negative, we reject it. This is basically the way we compared the value of an investment to its market price.

The second approach is to compute the *internal rate of return (IRR)* on a proposed investment project. The IRR is the discount rate that equates the present value of cash outflows for an investment with the present value of its cash inflows. We compare this discount rate, or IRR (which is also the expected rate of return on the project), to our cost of capital and accept any investment proposal with an IRR equal to or greater than that cost of capital. We do the same thing when we price bonds on the basis of yield. If the expected yield on the bond is equal to or exceeds our required rate of return on the bond, we should invest in it; if the expected yield is less than our required rate of return on the bond, we should not invest in it and we should sell it if we own it.

Computing Bond Yields

Bond investors use five measures of yield for the following purposes:

Yield Measure	Purpose
Coupon rate	Measures the coupon rate or the percentage of par paid out annually as interest.
Current yield	Measures current income rate.
Promised yield to maturity	Measures expected rate of return for bond held to maturity.
Promised yield to call	Measures expected rate of return for bond held to first call date.
Realized (horizon) yield	Measures expected rate of return for a bond likely to be sold prior to maturity. It considers specific reinvestment assumptions and an estimated sales price. It can also measure the actual rate of return on a bond during some past period of time.

Coupon rate and current yields are mainly descriptive. The last three yields are all derived from the present value model as described in equations 12.1 and 12.2. We advocate using these last three yields to get accurate values. A financial calculator or spreadsheet software can be used to determine exact returns from a series of cash flows.

To measure an expected realized yield (also referred to as the *horizon yield*), we must estimate a bond's future selling price. Following our presentation of bond yields, we will present the procedure for finding these prices.

COUPON RATE

The *coupon rate* merely measures the annual income that a bond investor receives expressed as a percent of the bond's par value. It is of little use in determining a bond's actual return, as the bond's price may differ from par when purchased or when sold if the bond is sold before maturity.

CURRENT YIELD

Current yield (CY) is to bonds what dividend yield is to stocks. It is computed as

12.3

$$CY = \frac{C}{P}$$

where:

CY = the current yield on a bond
C = the annual coupon payment of the bond
P = the current market price of the bond

Because this yield measures the current income from the bond as a percentage of its price, it is important to income-oriented investors who want current cash flow from their investment portfolios, such as a retired person who lives on this investment income. Current yield has little use for investors who are interested in total return because it excludes the important capital gain or loss component.

PROMISED YIELD TO MATURITY (Y_M)

Promised yield to maturity (Y_m) is the most widely used bond yield figure because it indicates the fully compounded rate of return *promised* to an investor who buys the bond at prevailing prices, *if two assumptions hold true.* The first assumption is that the investor holds the bond to maturity. This assumption gives this yield its shortened name, *yield to maturity.* The second assumption is implicit in the present value method of computation, namely that all the bond's cash flows are reinvested at the computed yield to maturity.

To see this, recall that equation 12.2 related the current market price of the bond to the present value of all cash flows as follows:

$$P = \sum_{t=i}^{n} C_t \frac{1}{(1 + Y)^t}$$

To compute the Y_m for a bond, we solve for the rate Y that will equate the current price P to all cash flows from the bond to maturity. As noted, this resembles the computation of the internal rate of return (IRR) on an investment project, which implies a reinvestment rate assumption because it discounts the cash flows. That is, the equation assumes that *all interim cash flows (interest payments) are reinvested at the computed* Y_m. That is why this is referred to as a *promised* Y_m; the bond will provide this computed Y_m only *if* we meet its conditions:

1. Hold the bond to maturity.
2. Reinvest all the interim cash flows at the computed Y_m rate.

For example, if a bond promises an 8 percent nominal Y_m, we must reinvest coupon income at 8 percent to realize that promised return. If we spend (do not reinvest) the coupon payments or cannot find opportunities to reinvest these coupon payments at rates as high as its promised Y_m, then the actual *realized* yield we earn will be less than the promised

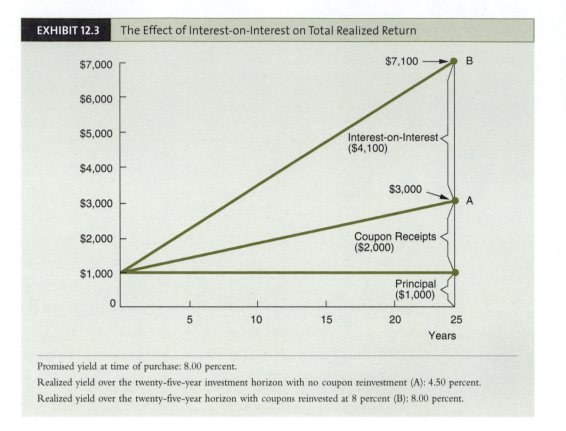

EXHIBIT 12.3 The Effect of Interest-on-Interest on Total Realized Return

Promised yield at time of purchase: 8.00 percent.

Realized yield over the twenty-five-year investment horizon with no coupon reinvestment (A): 4.50 percent.

Realized yield over the twenty-five-year horizon with coupons reinvested at 8 percent (B): 8.00 percent.

yield to maturity. The income earned on the reinvestment of the interim interest payments is referred to as *interest-on-interest.*[2]

The impact of the reinvestment assumption (the interest-on-interest earnings) on the realized return from a bond varies directly with the bond's coupon and maturity. Higher coupons and longer terms to maturity increase the loss in value from failure to reinvest at the Y_m. These conditions make the reinvestment assumption more important.

Exhibit 12.3 illustrates the impact of interest-on-interest for an 8 percent, twenty-five-year bond bought at par to yield 8 percent. If we invested $1,000 today at 8 percent for twenty-five years and reinvested all the coupon payments at 8 percent, we would have approximately $7,100 at the end of twenty-five years. We will refer to the money that we have at the end of our investment horizon as our ending-wealth value. To prove that we would have an ending-wealth value of $7,100, look up the compound interest factor for 8 percent for twenty-five years (which is 6.8493) or 4 percent for fifty periods (which assumes semiannual compounding and is 7.1073).

Exhibit 12.3 shows that this $7,100 is made up of $1,000 principal return, $2,000 of coupon payments over the twenty-five years ($80 a year for twenty-five years), and $4,100 in interest earned on the coupon payments reinvested at 8 percent. If we had saved but never reinvested any of the coupon payments, we would have an ending-wealth value of only $3,000. This ending-wealth value of $3,000 derived from the beginning investment of

---

[2]This concept is developed in Sidney Homer and Martin L. Leibowitz, *Inside the Yield Book,* Englewood Cliffs, NJ: Prentice-Hall, 1972, Chapter 1.

$1,000 gives an actual (realized) yield to maturity of only 4.5 percent. That is, the rate that will discount $3,000 back to $1,000 in twenty-five years is 4.5 percent. Reinvesting the coupon payments at some rate between 0 and 8 percent would cause the ending-wealth position to be above $3,000 and below $7,100; therefore, the actual rate of return would be somewhere between 4.5 percent and 8 percent. Obviously if we managed to reinvest the coupon payments at rates consistently above 8 percent, the ending-wealth position would be above $7,100 and the actual realized rate of return would be above 8 percent.

Interestingly, during periods of high interest rates, we often hear investors talk about "locking in" high yields. Many of these people are subject to yield illusion—they do not realize that attaining the high promised yield requires that they reinvest all the coupon payments at the same high yields. As an example, if we buy a twenty-year bond with a promised yield to maturity of 15 percent, we will actually realize the 15 percent yield only if we reinvest all the coupon payments at 15 percent over the next twenty years.

Computing the Promised Yield to Maturity   We can compute the promised yield to maturity using the present value model with semiannual compounding.[3] The present value model in equation 12.4 is the technique used by investment professionals.

12.4
$$P = \sum_{t=i}^{2n} \frac{C_t/2}{(1 + Y/2)^t} + \frac{P_p}{(1 + Y/2)^{2n}}$$

All variables are as described previously. This formula reflects the semiannual interest payments. We adjust for these semiannual payments by doubling the number of periods (two times the number of years to maturity) and dividing both the annual coupon value and interest rate in half.

This model is more complex because the solution requires iteration. The present value equation is a variation of the internal rate of return (IRR) calculation where we want to find the discount rate i that will equate the present value of the stream of coupon receipts (C_t) and principal value (par) with the current market price of the bond (P). For an 8 percent, twenty-year bond priced at $900, the equation gives us a semiannual promised yield to maturity of 4.545 percent, which implies a nominal Y_m of 9.09 percent:[4]

$$900 = 40 \sum_{t=1}^{40} \left[\frac{1}{(1.04545)^t} \right] + 1,000 \left[\frac{1}{(1.04545)^{40}} \right]$$
$$= 40(18.2574) + 1,000(0.1702)$$
$$= 900$$

A WORD ON YIELD CALCULATIONS

We quote yield to maturity for bonds paying semiannual coupons in two ways: as nominal rates or effective rates. The yield to maturity, quoted on a nominal basis, is equal to the bond's semiannual rate of return multiplied by two:

Nominal Y_m = Semiannual Return × 2

[3]We can compute promised Y_m assuming annual compounding, but practitioners use semiannual compounding because the interest cash flows are semiannual. Even when the cash flows are not semiannual, bond analysts use this assumption for calculating the yield. Therefore, all our calculations employ this assumption.

[4]Recall from your corporate finance course that you would start with one rate (for example, 9 percent or 4.5 percent semiannual) and compute the value of the stream. In this example, the value would exceed $900, so you would select a higher rate until you had a present value for the stream of cash flows of less than $900. Given the discount rates above and below the true rate, you would do further calculations or interpolate between the two rates to arrive at the correct discount rate that would give you a value of $900.

A bond with a semiannual return of 4.545 percent has a nominal Y_m of 4.545×2 or 9.09 percent. The more formal term used in practice for this yield is the *bond-equivalent yield (BEY)*. Put another way, when one uses the convention of doubling the semiannual yield, it is said that they are computing the measure on a *bond-equivalent basis*.

The second method, the *effective yield to maturity*, considers the effect of semiannual period-by-period compounding on the annual return: interest earned in one six-month period earns interest when reinvested in subsequent periods. That is, a bond with a 4.545 percent semiannual return has an effective Y_m of

$$(1 + 0.04545)^2 - 1 = 0.0930 \text{ or } 9.30 \text{ percent}$$

Alternatively, a bond with an effective yield to maturity of 9.30 percent has a semiannual return of

$$\sqrt{1 + 0.0930} - 1 = 0.04545 \text{ or } 4.545 \text{ percent}$$

As bond returns may be quoted using either bond-equivalent yields or effective yields, it is important to know how the reported rate was calculated.

Y_m for a Zero Coupon Bond In several instances we have discussed the existence of zero coupon bonds that only have the one cash inflow at maturity. This single cash flow means that the calculation of Y_m is substantially easier, as shown by the following example.

Assume a zero coupon bond, maturing in ten years with a maturity value of $1,000, selling for $311.80. Because we are dealing with a zero coupon bond, there is only the one cash flow from the principal payment at maturity. Therefore, we simply need to determine the discount rate that will discount $1,000 to equal the current market price of $311.80 in twenty periods (ten years of semiannual payment). The equation is as follows:

$$\$311.80 = \frac{\$1,000}{(1 + Y/2)^{20}}$$

Thus, the semiannual discount rate is 6 percent, which implies a bond-equivalent yield to maturity rate of 12 percent.

PROMISED YIELD TO CALL (Y_c)

Although investors use promised Y_m to value most bonds, they must estimate the return on certain callable bonds with a different measure—the *promised yield to call (Y_c)*. Whenever a bond with a call feature is selling for a price equal to or greater than its par value plus one year's interest, a bond investor should value the bond in terms of Y_c rather than Y_m. The reason is that the market uses the lowest, most conservative yield measure in pricing a bond. When bonds are trading at or above a specified *crossover point*, which approximates the bond's par value plus one year's interest, the yield to call will normally provide the lowest yield measure.[5] The price at the crossover point is important because when the bond rises to this price above par, the computed Y_m becomes low enough that it would be profitable for the issuer to call the bond and finance the call by selling a new bond at the prevailing market interest rate.[6] Therefore, the Y_c measures the promised rate of return the

---

[5] For a discussion of the crossover point, see Homer and Leibowitz, *Inside the Yield Book*, Chapter 4.

[6] Extensive literature treats the refunding of bond issues, including A. J. Kalotay, "On the Structure and Valuation of Debt Refundings," *Financial Management* 11, no. 1 (Spring 1982): 41–42; and John D. Finnerty, "Evaluating the Economics of Refunding High-Coupon Sinking-Fund Debt," *Financial Management* 12, no. 1 (Spring 1983): 5–10.

investor will receive from holding this bond until it is retired at the first available call date, that is, at the end of the deferred call period. Investors should consider computing the Y_c for their bonds after a period when numerous high-yielding, high-coupon bonds have been issued. Following such a period, interest rates will decline, bond prices will rise, and the high-coupon bonds will subsequently have a high probability of being called.

Computing the Promised Yield to Call   To compute the Y_c by the present value method, we adjust the semiannual present value equation (equation 12.4) to give

12.5
$$P = \sum_{t=1}^{2nc} \frac{C_t/2}{(1 + Y_c/2)^t} + \frac{P_c}{(1 + Y_c/2)^{2nc}}$$

where:

P = market price of the bond
C_t = annual coupon payment
nc = number of years to first call
P_c = call price of the bond

Assume a 12 percent, twenty-year bond trading at 115 ($1,150) with five years to first call and a call price of 112 ($1,120). Following the present value method, we solve for the semiannual yield to obtain an answer of 5.01 percent. The bond-equivalent (nominal) yield to call will be 5.01 × 2 or 10.02 percent. The yield to call Y_c, quoted as an effective yield, will be $(1 + 0.0501)^2 - 1$ or 10.27 percent.

As with the Y_m, the Y_c calculation depends on two assumptions: first, the number of years until first call; second, that all cash flows will be reinvested at the Y_c. This means the example bond's coupon cash flows of $60 will be reinvested at a semiannual rate of 5.01 percent.

REALIZED YIELD (Y_R)

The final measure of bond yield, *realized yield (Y_R)* (or *horizon yield*), measures the expected rate of return of a bond that an investor expects to sell prior to its maturity. In terms of the equation, the investor has a holding period (hp) less than n. Realized (horizon) yield can be used to estimate rates of return attainable from various trading strategies. It is a useful measure that requires several additional estimates not required by the other yield measures. Specifically, the investor must estimate (1) the expected future selling price of the bond at the end of the holding period, and (2) an explicit estimate of the reinvestment rate for the coupon flows prior to selling the bond. This technique can also be used to measure an investor's actual yields after selling bonds.

Computing Realized (Horizon) Yield   The realized yields are variations on the promised yield equations (equations 12.4 and 12.5). The substitution of P_f and hp into the present value model provides the following realized yield model:

12.6
$$P = \sum_{t=1}^{2hp} \frac{C_t/2}{(1 + Y_R/2)^t} + \frac{P_f}{(1 + Y_R/2)^{2hp}}$$

where:

C_t = annual coupon payment
P_f = estimated future selling price of the bond
hp = holding period of the bond in years

Note that the coupon flows are implicitly discounted at the computed realized (horizon) yield. In many cases, this is an inappropriate assumption because available market rates might be very different from the computed realized (horizon) yield. Therefore, to derive a realistic estimate of the expected realized yield, we also need to estimate the expected reinvestment rate during the investment horizon, as we will demonstrate.

Calculating Future Bond Prices

Interactive e-lectures

For more explanation and an animated example of bond valuation, go to: http://reillyxtra .swlearning.com.

Dollar bond prices need to be calculated in two instances: (1) when computing realized (horizon) yield, we must determine the future selling price P_f of a bond if it is to be sold before maturity or first call, and (2) when issues are quoted on a promised yield basis, as with municipals. We can easily convert a yield-based quote to a dollar price by using equation 12.1, which does not require iteration. (We need only solve for P.) The coupon C_i is given, as is par value P_p and the promised Y_m that is used as the discount rate.

Consider a 10 percent, twenty-five-year bond with a promised Y_m of 12 percent. We would compute the price of this issue as

$$P = \frac{100}{2} \sum_{t=1}^{50} \frac{1}{(1 + 0.120/2)^t} + 1000 \frac{1}{(1 + 0.120/2)^{50}}$$

$$= 50(15.7619) + 1000(0.0543)$$

$$= \$842.40$$

In this instance, we are determining the prevailing market price of the bond based on the current market Y_m. These market figures indicate the consensus of all investors regarding the value of this bond. An investor with a required rate of return on this bond that differs from the market Y_m would estimate a different value for the bond.

In contrast to the current market price, we need to compute a future price P_f when estimating the expected realized (horizon) yield performance of bonds. Investors or portfolio managers who consistently trade bonds for capital gains need to compute expected realized (horizon) yield rather than promised yield. They would compute P_f through the following variation of the bond value equation:

12.7
$$P_f = \sum_{t=1}^{2n-2hp} \frac{C_i/2}{(1 + Y_m/2)^t} + \frac{P_p}{(1 + Y_m/2)^{2n-2hp}}$$

where:

P_f = the future selling price of the bond
P_p = the par value of the bond
n = the number of years to maturity
hp = the holding period of the bond (in years)
C_i = the annual coupon payment of bond i
Y_m = the expected market Y_m at the end of the holding period

Equation 12.7 is the version of the present value model used to calculate the expected price of the bond at the end of the holding period (hp). The term $2n - 2hp$ equals the bond's remaining term to maturity at the end of the investor's holding period, that is, the number of six-month periods remaining after the bond is sold. Therefore, the determination of P_f is based on four variables, two that are known and two that must be estimated by the investor.

Specifically, the coupon C_i and the par value P_p are given. We must forecast the length of the holding period and therefore the number of years remaining to maturity at the time the bond is sold ($n - hp$). We also must forecast the expected market Y_m at the time of sale (i). With this information, we can calculate the future price of the bond. The real difficulty (and the potential source of error) in estimating P_f lies in predicting hp and the Y_m at i.

Suppose you bought the 10 percent, twenty-five-year bond just discussed at $842, giving it a promised Y_m of 12 percent. Based on an analysis of the economy and the capital market, you expect this bond's market Y_m to decline to 8 percent in five years. Therefore, you want to compute its future price P_f at the end of year 5 to estimate your expected rate of return, assuming you are correct in your assessment of the decline in overall market interest rates. As noted, you estimate the holding period (five years), which implies a remaining life of twenty years, and the market Y_m of 8 percent. A semiannual model would give you the following estimated future selling price (P_f):

$$P_f = 50 \sum_{t=1}^{40} \frac{1}{(1.04)^t} + 1000 \frac{1}{(1.04)^{40}}$$

$$= 50(19.7928) + 1000(0.2083)$$

$$= 989.64 + 208.30$$

$$= \$1,197.94$$

Using this estimate of the selling price, you would estimate the realized (horizon) yield on this investment.

REALIZED (HORIZON) YIELD WITH DIFFERENTIAL REINVESTMENT RATES

The realized yield equation 12.6 is the standard present value formula with the changes in holding period and ending price. As such, it includes the implicit reinvestment rate assumption that all cash flows are reinvested at the computed i rate. There may be instances where such an implicit assumption is not appropriate, given our expectations for future interest rates. Assume that current market interest rates are very high and we invest in a long-term bond (e.g., a twenty-year, 14 percent coupon) at par to take advantage of an expected decline in rates from 14 percent to 10 percent over a two-year period. Computing the future price of this bond (which will be an eighteen-year bond at a 10 percent Y_m, which implies a future price of $1,330.95) and using the realized yield equation to estimate the realized (horizon) yield Y_R, we will get the following fairly high realized rate of return:

$$P = \$1,000$$

$$hp = 2 \text{ years}$$

$$P_f = \sum_{t=1}^{36} \frac{70}{(1 + 0.05)^t} + \frac{\$1,000}{(1.05)^{36}}$$

$$= \$1,158.30 + \$172.65$$

$$= \$1,330.95$$

$$\$1,000 = \sum_{t=1}^{4} \frac{70}{(1 + Y_R/2)^t} + \frac{1330.95}{(1 + Y_R/2)^4}$$

$$Y_R = 27.5\%$$

As noted, this calculation assumes that all cash flows are reinvested at the computed Y_R (27.5 percent). However, it is unlikely that during a period when market rates are going from 14 percent to 10 percent we could reinvest the coupon at 27.5 percent. It is more appropriate and realistic to explicitly estimate the reinvestment rates and calculate the realized yields based on the *ending-wealth position*. This procedure is more precise and realistic, and it is easier because it does not require iteration.

The basic technique calculates the value of all cash flows at the end of the holding period, which is the investor's ending-wealth value. We compare this ending-wealth value to our *beginning-wealth value* to determine the *compound rate of return that equalizes these two values*. Adding to our prior example, assume we have the following cash flows:

$$P = \$1,000$$

$$i = \text{interest payments of } \$70 \text{ in } 6, 12, 18, \text{ and } 24 \text{ months}$$

$$P_f = \$1,330.95 \text{ (the ending market value of the bond)}$$

The ending value of the four interest payments is determined by our assumptions regarding specific reinvestment rates. Assume each payment is reinvested at a different declining rate that holds for its time period (that is, the first three interest payments are reinvested at progressively lower rates and the fourth interest payment is received at the end of the holding period).

$$i_1 \text{ at } 13\% \text{ for } 18 \text{ months} = \$70 \times (1 + 0.065)^3 = \$\,84.55$$

$$i_2 \text{ at } 12\% \text{ for } 12 \text{ months} = \$70 \times (1 + 0.06)^2 = 78.65$$

$$i_3 \text{ at } 11\% \text{ for } 6 \text{ months} = \$70 \times (1 + 0.055) = 73.85$$

$$i_4 \text{ not reinvested} = \$70 \times (1.0) = \underline{70.00}$$

$$\text{Future Value of Interest Payments} = \$307.05$$

Therefore, our total ending-wealth value is

$$\$1,330.95 + \$307.05 = \$1,638.00$$

The compound realized (horizon) rate of return is calculated by comparing our ending-wealth value ($1,638) to our beginning-wealth value ($1,000) and determining what interest rate would equalize these two values over a two-year holding period. To find this, we compute the ratio of ending wealth to beginning wealth (1.638). We find this ratio in a compound value table for four periods (assuming semiannual compounding). Table C.3 at the end of the book indicates that the Y_R is somewhere between 12 percent (1.5735) and 14 percent (1.6890). Interpolation gives an estimated semiannual rate of 13.16 percent, which indicates a bond–equivalent annual rate of 26.32 percent. Using a calculator or computer, we compute $(1.638)^{1/4} - 1$. This compares to an estimate of 27.5 percent when we assume an implicit reinvestment rate of 27.5 percent.

This realized (horizon) yield computation specifically states the expected reinvestment rates as contrasted to assuming the reinvestment rate is equal to the computed realized yield. The actual assumption regarding the reinvestment rate can be very important.

Thus the steps to calculate an expected realized (horizon) yield Y_R are as follows:

1. Calculate the future value at the horizon date of all coupon payments reinvested as estimated rates.
2. Calculate the expected sales price of the bond at your expected horizon date based on your estimate of the required yield to maturity at that time.

3. Sum the values in steps 1 and 2 to arrive at the total ending-wealth value.
4. Calculate the ratio of the ending-wealth value to the beginning-wealth value (the purchase price of the bond). Given this ratio and the time horizon, compute the compound rate of interest that will grow to this ratio over this time horizon.

$$\left(\frac{\textbf{Ending-Wealth Value}}{\textbf{Beginning-Wealth Value}} \right)^{1/2n} - 1$$

5. If all calculations assume semiannual compounding, double the interest rate derived from step 4 to get the bond-equivalent Y_R.

YIELD ADJUSTMENTS FOR TAX-EXEMPT BONDS

Municipal bonds, Treasury issues, and many agency obligations possess one common characteristic: their interest income is partially or fully tax-exempt. This tax-exempt status affects the valuation of taxable versus nontaxable bonds. Although we could adjust each present value equation for the tax effects, it is not necessary for our purposes. We can approximate the effect of such an adjustment, however, by computing the equivalent taxable yield, which is one of the most often cited measures of performance for municipal bonds.

Fully taxable equivalent yield (FTEY) adjusts the promised yield computation for the bond's tax-exempt status. To compute the FTEY, we determine the promised yield on a tax-exempt bond using one of the yield formulas and adjust the computed yield to reflect the rate of return that must be earned on a fully taxable issue. It is measured as

12.8

$$\textbf{FTEY} = \frac{\textbf{Tax-Free Annual Return}}{1 - \textbf{T}}$$

where:

T = amount and type of tax exemption (i.e., the investor's marginal tax rate)

For example, if the promised yield on a tax-exempt bond is 6 percent and the investor's marginal tax rate is 30 percent, the FTEY would be

$$\textbf{FTEY} = \frac{0.06}{1 - 0.30} = \frac{0.06}{0.70}$$

$$= 0.0857 = 8.57\%$$

The FTEY equation has some limitations. It is applicable only to par bonds or current coupon obligations, such as new issues, because the measure considers only interest income and ignores capital gains. Therefore, we cannot use it for issues trading at a significant variation from par value (premium or discount).

What Determines Interest Rates?

Now that we have learned to calculate various yields on bonds, the question arises as to what causes differences and changes in yields over time. Market interest rates cause these effects because the interest rates reported in the media are simply the prevailing Y_m's for the bonds being discussed. For example, when you hear on television that the interest rate on long-term government bonds declined from 6.40 percent to 6.30 percent, this means that the price of this particular bond increased such that the computed Y_m at the former price was 6.40 percent but the computed Y_m at the new, higher price is 6.30 percent. Yields and interest rates are the same; they are different terms for the same concept.

We have discussed the inverse relationship between bond prices and interest rates. When interest rates decline, bond prices increase; when interest rates rise, bond prices decline. It is natural to ask which of these is the driving force, bond prices or bond interest rates. It is a simultaneous change, and you can envision *either* factor causing it. Most practitioners probably envision the changes in interest rates as causes because they constantly use interest rates to describe changes. They use interest rates because these rates are comparable across bonds, whereas the price of a bond depends not only on the interest rate but also on its specific characteristics, including its coupon and maturity. The point is, when you change the interest rate (yield) on a bond, you simultaneously change its price in the opposite direction. Later in the chapter we will discuss the specific price–yield relationship for individual bonds and demonstrate that this relationship differs among bonds based on their particular coupon and maturity.

Understanding interest rates and what makes them change is necessary for an investor who hopes to maximize returns from investing in bonds. Therefore, in this section we will review our prior discussion of the following topics: what causes overall market interest rates to rise and fall, why do alternative bonds have different interest rates, and why the difference in rates (the yield spread) between various bonds changes over time. To accomplish this, we begin with a general discussion of the influences on interest rates, and then consider the *term structure of interest rates* (shown by yield curves), which relates the interest rates on a set of comparable bonds to their terms to maturity. The term structure is important because it reflects what investors expect to happen to interest rates in the future and also dictates their current risk attitude. Finally, we turn to the concept of *yield spreads,* which measures the differences in yields between alternative bonds.

FORECASTING INTEREST RATES

As discussed, the ability to forecast interest rates and changes in these rates is critical to successful bond investing. Subsequent presentations consider the major determinants of interest rates, but for now keep in mind that interest rates *are the price for loanable funds.* Like any price, they are determined by the supply and demand for these funds. On the one side, investors are willing to provide the funds (the supply) at prices based on their required rates of return for a particular borrower. On the other side, borrowers need the funds (the demand) to support budget deficits (government), to invest in capital projects (corporations), or to acquire durable goods (cars, appliances) or homes (individuals).

Although the lenders and borrowers have some fundamental factors that determine the supply and demand curves, the prices for these funds (interest rates) are also affected for short time periods by events that shift the curves. Examples include major government bond issues that affect the demand for funds, or significant changes in Federal Reserve monetary policy that affect the supply of money.

Our treatment of interest rate forecasting recognizes the need to be aware of the basic determinants of interest rates and monitor these factors. We also recognize that detailed forecasting of interest rates is a complex task that is best left to professional economists. Therefore, our goal as bond investors and bond-portfolio managers is to monitor current and expected interest rate behavior. We should attempt to continuously assess the major factors that affect interest rate behavior but also rely on others, such as economic consulting firms, banks, or investment banking firms, for detailed insights on such topics as the real

EXHIBIT 12.4 International Long-Term Government Bond Yields

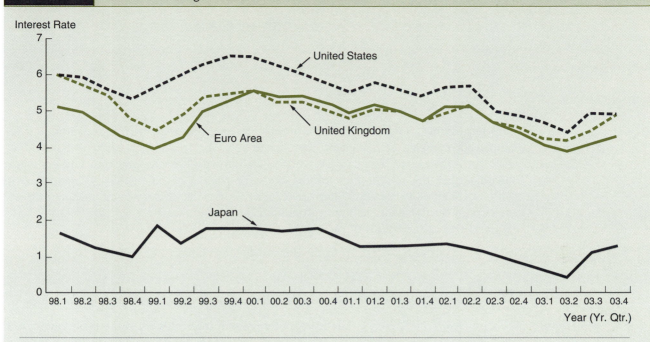

Source: Federal Reserve Bank of St. Louis, *International Economic Trends.*

RFR and the expected rate of inflation.[7] This is precisely the way most bond-portfolio managers operate.

FUNDAMENTAL DETERMINANTS OF INTEREST RATES

As shown in Exhibit 12.4, average interest rates for long-term (ten-year) U.S. government bonds during the period 1998–2003 fluctuated between 4.50 and 6.55 percent. The level of U.S. interest rates was always above Euro Area rates and almost always above United Kingdom rates. As a result of Japan's slow economy and troubled financial sector, Japan's bond rates were consistently under 2 percent during this six-year period as they attempted to use lower rates to overcome their recession.

Bond investors need to understand *why* these differences occur and *why* interest rates change this way. Tracking both domestic and international influences over time can provide information regarding interest rate behavior and expectations for future interest rate changes. Some of these factors will be reviewed in the rest of this section.

As we know, bond prices can increase dramatically during periods when market interest rates drop, and some bond investors experience attractive returns. In contrast, some investors have experienced substantial losses during several periods when interest rates increased. A casual analysis of Exhibit 12.4, which covers six years, indicates the need for monitoring

---

[7]Examples of publications on the bond market and interest rate forecasts would include Merrill Lynch's *Fixed Income Weekly* and *World Bond Market Monitor,* Goldman, Sach's *Financial Market Perspectives,* and Morgan Stanley's *U.S. and the Americas Investment Perspectives.*

interest rates. Essentially, the factors causing interest rates (Y) to rise or fall are described by the following model:

12.9
$$Y = RFR + I + RP$$

where:

$$RFR = \text{real risk-free rate of interest}$$
$$I = \text{expected rate of inflation}$$
$$RP = \text{risk premium}$$

This relationship should be familiar from our presentation in Chapter 2. Equation 12.9 is a simple but complete statement of interest rate behavior. It is a more difficult task to estimate the *future* behavior of variables such as real growth, expected inflation, and economic uncertainty. In this regard, interest rates, like stock prices, are extremely difficult to forecast with any degree of accuracy.[8] Alternatively, we can visualize the source of changes in interest rates in terms of the economic conditions and issue characteristics that determine the required rate of return (yield) on a bond:

$$Y = f(\textbf{Economic Forces} + \textbf{Issue Characteristics})$$
$$= (\textbf{RFR} + \textbf{I}) + \textbf{RP}$$

This rearranged version of equation 12.9 helps to isolate the determinants of interest rates.[9]

Effect of Economic Factors The real risk-free rate of interest RFR is the economic cost of money, that is, the opportunity cost necessary to compensate individuals for forgoing consumption. As discussed previously, it is basically determined by the real growth rate of the economy with short-run effects due to ease or tightness in the capital market.

The expected rate of inflation is the other economic influence on interest rates. We add the expected level of inflation I to the real RFR to specify the nominal RFR, which is a market rate like the current rate on government T-bills. Given the stability of the real RFR, it is clear that most changes in government interest rates during the six years covered by Exhibit 12.4 occurred because of changes in the expected inflation. Besides the unique country and exchange rate risk (which we discuss shortly), differences in the rates of inflation between countries have a major impact on their level of interest rates.

To sum up, one way to estimate the nominal RFR is to begin with the real growth rate of the economy, adjust for short-run ease or tightness in the capital market, and then adjust this real rate of interest for the expected rate of inflation.

Another approach to estimating the nominal rate or changes in the rate is the macroeconomic view, where the supply and demand for loanable funds are the fundamental economic determinants of Y. As the supply of loanable funds increases, the level of interest rates declines, other things being equal. Several factors influence the supply of funds. Government monetary policies imposed by the Federal Reserve have a significant impact on the supply of money. The savings pattern of U.S. and non-U.S. investors also affects the supply of funds. Non-U.S. investors have become a stronger influence on the U.S. supply of loanable funds during recent years, as shown by the significant purchases of U.S. securities by non-U.S. investors. It is widely acknowledged that this increase in foreign purchases has

---

[8]For an overview of interest rate forecasting, see W. David Woolford, "Forecasting Interest Rates," in *Handbook of Fixed-Income Securities,* 7th ed., edited by Frank J. Fabozzi, New York: McGraw-Hill, 2005.

[9]For an extensive exploration of interest rates and interest rate behavior, see James C. Van Horne, *Financial Market Rates and Flows,* 6th ed., Upper Saddle River, NJ: Prentice-Hall, 2001.

added to the supply of funds invested in U.S. bonds and benefited the United States in terms of reducing interest rates and the cost of capital.

Interest rates increase when the demand for loanable funds increases. The demand for loanable funds is affected by the capital and operating needs of the U.S. government, federal agencies, state and local governments, corporations, institutions, and individuals. Federal budget deficits or surpluses change the Treasury's demand for loanable funds.[10] Likewise, the level of consumer demand for funds to buy houses, autos, and appliances affects rates, as does corporate demand for funds to pursue investment opportunities. The total of all groups determines the aggregate demand and supply of loanable funds and the level of the nominal RFR.

Impact of Bond Characteristics

The interest rate of a specific bond issue is influenced not only by all these factors that affect the nominal RFR, but also by its unique issue characteristics. These issue characteristics influence the bond's risk premium RP. The economic forces that determine the nominal RFR affect all securities (that is, these are systematic factors), whereas issue characteristics are unique to individual securities, market sectors, or countries. Thus, the differences in the yields of corporate and Treasury bonds are not caused by economic forces but rather by different issue characteristics that cause differences in the risk premiums.

Bond investors separate the risk premium into four components:

1. The credit quality of the issue as determined by its risk of default relative to other bonds
2. The term to maturity of the issue, which can affect yield and price volatility
3. Indenture provisions, including collateral, call features, and sinking-fund provisions
4. Foreign bond risk, including exchange rate risk and country risk

Of the four factors, credit quality and maturity have the greatest impact on the risk premium for domestic bonds, while exchange rate risk and country risk are important components of risk for non-U.S. bonds.

The credit quality of a bond reflects the ability of the issuer to service outstanding debt obligations. This information is largely captured in the ratings issued by the bond-rating firms. As a result, bonds with different ratings have different yields. For example, AAA-rated obligations possess lower risk of default than BBB obligations, so they can provide lower yield.

Notably, the risk premium differences between bonds of different quality levels have changed dramatically over time, depending on prevailing economic conditions. When the economy experiences a recession or a period of economic uncertainty, the desire for quality increases, and investors bid up prices of higher-rated bonds, which reduces their yields. This is referred to as the *credit quality spread*. It has also been suggested that this spread is influenced by the volatility of interest rates.[11] This variability in the risk premium over time was demonstrated and discussed in Chapters 2 and 11.

Term to maturity also influences the risk premium because it affects an investor's level of uncertainty as well as the price volatility of the bond. In the next section, we will discuss

[10]Historically, the U.S. budget had deficits that added to the stock of Treasury debt. During the four-year period of 1998–2001, the budget experienced a surplus and Treasury debt was repurchased. It then swung back to deficits in 2002 and the current long-term outlook is not encouraging, as outlined in William C. Dudley and Edward F. McKelvey, "The U.S. Budget Outlook: A Surplus of Deficits," *Goldman Sachs Global Economics* (March 31, 2004).

[11]Chris P. Dialynas and David H. Edington, "Bond Yield Spreads: A Postmodern View," *Journal of Portfolio Management* 19, no. 1 (Fall 1992): 68–75.

the typical positive relationship between the term to maturity of an issue and its interest rate.

Indenture provisions indicate the collateral pledged for a bond, its callability, and its sinking-fund provisions. Collateral gives protection to the investor if the issuer defaults on the bond, because the investor has a specific claim on some set of assets in case of liquidation.

Call features indicate when an issuer can buy back the bond prior to its maturity. A bond is called by an issuer when interest rates have declined, so it is typically not to the advantage of the investor who must reinvest the proceeds at a lower interest rate. Therefore, more protection against having the bond called reduces the risk premium. The significance of call protection to an investor increases during periods of high interest rates. When an investor buys a bond with a high coupon, he or she wants protection from having the bond called away when rates decline.[12]

A sinking fund reduces the investor's risk and causes a lower yield for several reasons. First, a sinking fund reduces default risk because it requires the issuer to reduce the outstanding issue systematically. Second, purchases of the bond by the issuer to satisfy sinking-fund requirements provide price support for the bond because of the added demand. These purchases by the issuer also contribute to a more liquid secondary market for the bond because of the increased trading. Finally, sinking-fund provisions require that the issuer retire a bond before its stated maturity, which causes a reduction in the issue's average maturity. The decline in average maturity tends to reduce the risk premium of the bond much as a shorter maturity would reduce yield.[13]

We know that foreign currency exchange rates change over time and that this increases the risk of global investing. Differences in the variability of exchange rates among countries arise because the trade balances and rates of inflation differ among countries. More volatile trade balances and inflation rates in a country make its exchange rates more volatile, which increase the uncertainty of future exchange rates. These factors increase the exchange rate risk premium.

In addition to the ongoing changes in exchange rates, investors are always concerned with the political and economic stability of a country. If investors are unsure about the political environment or the economic system in a country, they will increase the risk premium they require to reflect this country risk.

TERM STRUCTURE OF INTEREST RATES

The *term structure of interest rates* (or the *yield curve,* as it is more popularly known) is a static function that relates the term to maturity to the yield to maturity for a sample of bonds at *a given point in time.* Thus, it represents a cross section of yields for a category of bonds that are comparable in all respects but maturity. Specifically, the quality of the issues should be constant, and ideally an investor should have issues with similar coupons and call features. We can construct different yield curves for Treasuries, government agencies, prime-grade municipals, AAA utilities, and so on. The accuracy of the yield curve will depend on the comparability of the bonds in the sample.

As an example, Exhibit 12.5 shows yield curves for a sample of U.S. Treasury obligations. It is based on the yield-to-maturity information for a set of comparable Treasury

---

[12]William Marshall and Jess B. Yawitz, "Optimal Terms of the Call Provision on a Corporate Bond," *Journal of Financial Research* 3, no. 3 (Fall 1980): 203–211.

[13]For a further discussion of sinking funds, see Edward A. Dyl and Michael D. Joehnk, "Sinking Funds and the Cost of Corporate Debt," *Journal of Finance* 34, no. 4 (September 1979): 887–893; and A. J. Kalotay, "Sinking Funds and the Realized Cost of Debt," *Financial Management* 11, no. 1 (Spring 1982): 43–54.

EXHIBIT 12.5	Treasury Yield Curve

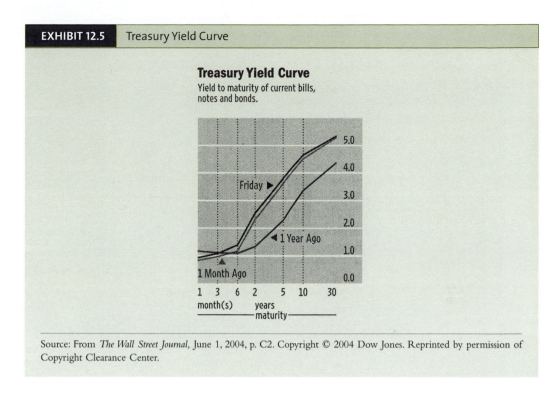

Treasury Yield Curve
Yield to maturity of current bills, notes and bonds.

Source: From *The Wall Street Journal,* June 1, 2004, p. C2. Copyright © 2004 Dow Jones. Reprinted by permission of Copyright Clearance Center.

issues from a publication such as the *Federal Reserve Bulletin* or *The Wall Street Journal.* These promised yields were plotted on the graph, and the yield curve drawn represents the general configuration of rates.

Not all yield curves, of course, have the same shape as those in Exhibit 12.5. The point of the example is that although individual yield curves are static, their behavior over time is quite fluid. For instance, in Exhibit 12.5, during the four-week period from April 28 to May 28, 2004, there was a very small increase in rates along the yield curve. In contrast, there was a substantial increase in rates from a year ago—about 150 basis points at five years and 100 basis points at ten- and thirty-year maturities.

Also, the shape of the yield curve can undergo dramatic alterations, following one of the four patterns shown in Exhibit 12.6. The rising yield curve is the most common and tends to prevail when interest rates are at low or modest levels. The declining yield curve tends to occur when rates are relatively high. The flat yield curve rarely exists for any period of time. The humped yield curve prevails when extremely high rates are expected to decline to more normal levels. The slope of the curve tends to level off after fifteen years.

Three major theories attempt to explain why the term structure assumes different shapes: the expectations hypothesis, the liquidity preference hypothesis, and the segmented-market hypothesis.

Interactive e-lectures

For more explanation and an animated example of the expectations hypothesis, go to: **http://reillyxtra .swlearning.com.**

Expectations Hypothesis   According to the expectations hypothesis, the shape of the yield curve results from the interest rate expectations of market participants. More specifically, it holds that *any long-term interest rate simply represents the geometric mean of current and future one-year interest rates expected to prevail over the maturity of the issue.* In essence, the term structure involves a series of intermediate and long-term interest rates, each of which is a reflection of the geometric mean of current and expected one-year interest rates. Under such conditions, the equilibrium long-term rate is the rate the long-term bond investor would expect

EXHIBIT 12.6	Types of Yield Curves

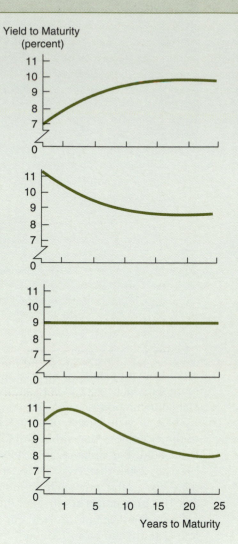

A rising yield curve is formed when the yields on short-term issues are low and rise consistently with longer maturities and flatten out at the extremes.

A declining yield curve is formed when the yields on short-term issues are high and yields on subsequently longer maturities decline consistently.

A flat yield curve has approximately equal yields on short-term and long-term issues.

A humped yield curve is formed when yields on intermediate-term issues are above those on short-term issues and the rates on long-term issues decline to levels below those for the short-term and then level out.

to earn through successive investments in short-term bonds over the term to maturity of the long-term bond.

The expectations theory can explain any shape of yield curve. Expectations for rising short-term rates in the future will cause a rising yield curve; expectations for falling short-term rates in the future will cause long-term rates to lie below current short-term rates, and the yield curve will decline. Similar explanations account for flat and humped yield curves. Consider the following example using arithmetic means.

$_tR_1 = 5\frac{1}{2}\%$ **the one-year rate of interest prevailing now (period _t_)**

$_{t+1}R_1 = 6\%$ **the one-year rate of interest expected to prevail next year (period _t_ + 1)**

$_{t+2}\mathbf{R}_1 = 7\frac{1}{2}\%$ **the one-year rate of interest expected to prevail two years from now (period $t + 2$)**

$_{t+3}\mathbf{R}_1 = 8\frac{1}{2}\%$ **the one-year rate of interest expected to prevail three years from now (period $t + 3$)**

Using these values and the known rate on a one-year bond, we compute rates on two-, three-, or four-year bonds (designated R_2, R_3, and R_4) as follows:

$$_t\mathbf{R}_1 = 5\frac{1}{2}\%$$

$$_t\mathbf{R}_2 = (0.055 + 0.06)/2 = 5.75\%$$

$$_t\mathbf{R}_3 = (0.055 + 0.06 + 0.075)/3 = 6.33\%$$

$$_t\mathbf{R}_4 = (0.055 + 0.06 + 0.075 + 0.085)/4 = 6.88\%$$

In this illustration (which uses the arithmetic mean as an approximation of the geometric mean), the yield curve is upward-sloping because, at present, investors expect future short-term rates to be above current short-term rates. This is not the formal method for constructing the yield curve. Rather, it is constructed as demonstrated in Exhibit 12.5 on the basis of the prevailing promised yields for bonds with different maturities.

The expectations hypothesis attempts to explain *why* the yield curve is upward-sloping, downward-sloping, humped, or flat by explaining the expectations implicit in yield curves with different shapes. The evidence is fairly substantial and convincing that the expectations hypothesis is a workable explanation of the term structure. Because of the supporting evidence, its relative simplicity, and the intuitive appeal of the theory, the expectations hypothesis of the term structure of interest rates is rather widely accepted.

Besides the theory and empirical support, it is also possible to present a scenario wherein *investor actions will cause the yield curve postulated by the theory*. The expectations hypothesis predicts a declining yield curve when interest rates are expected to fall in the future rather than rise. One might expect such a scenario toward the end of an economic expansion when rates are generally high due to strong demand, and short-term rates are high due to Federal Reserve actions to slow down inflationary pressures (wherein the Fed concentrates its tightening at the short end of the yield curve). In such a case, long-term bonds would be considered attractive investments to buy for two reasons. First, investors would want to lock in prevailing higher yields (which are not expected to be as high in the future). Second, they would want to capture the increase in bond prices (as capital gains) that will accompany a decline in rates, and long-term bonds, which are more volatile (as will be explained shortly), will provide a larger capital gain. By the same reasoning, investors will avoid short-term bonds or sell them and reinvest the funds in the more desirable long-term bonds. The point is, investor actions based on their expectations will reinforce the declining shape of the yield curve as they bid up the prices of long-maturity bonds (forcing yields to decline) at the same time that they avoid or sell short-term bond issues (so prices decline and yields rise). At the same time, there is confirming action by suppliers of bonds. Specifically, government or corporate issuers will avoid selling long-term bonds at the current high rates, wanting to wait until the rates decline. In the meantime, they will issue short-term bonds if they need funds while waiting for lower long-term rates. Therefore, in the long-term market we observe an increase in demand and a decline in the supply, which will cause an increase in price and a decline in yields for long-term bonds. The opposite will occur in the short-term market. There will be lower demand for short-term bonds and an increase in the supply of these securities. As a result, the price of short-term bonds will decline and yields on these bonds will increase. These shifts between long- and short-term maturities will continue until equilibrium occurs or expectations change.

Liquidity Preference Hypothesis   The theory of liquidity preference holds that long-term securities should provide higher returns than short-term obligations because investors are willing to accept lower yields to invest in short-maturity obligations to avoid the higher price volatility of long-maturity bonds. Another way to interpret the liquidity preference hypothesis is to say that lenders prefer short-term loans, and to induce them to lend long term, higher yields must be offered.

The liquidity preference theory contends that uncertainty causes investors to favor short-term issues over bonds with longer maturities because short-term bonds can easily be converted into predictable amounts of cash should unforeseen events occur. This theory argues that the yield curve should slope upward and that any other shape should be viewed as a temporary aberration.

This theory is generally considered an extension of the expectations hypothesis because the formal liquidity preference position contends that the liquidity premium inherent in the yields for longer-maturity bonds should be added to the expected future rate implied by the expectations hypothesis in arriving at long-term yields. Specifically, the liquidity premium compensates the investor in long-term bonds for the added uncertainty caused by the greater volatility of long-maturity bonds.

Combining this risk premium perspective with the expectations hypothesis explains term structure behavior better than the expectations hypothesis alone. The term structure should slope upward, presumably because of the liquidity-preference–risk-premium effect as seen in panel (a) in Exhibit 12.7. The term structure may become downward-sloping, however, if substantial declines in future rates are expected, as shown in panel (b).

As a matter of historical fact, the yield curve shows a definite upward bias, which implies that some combination of the expectations theory and the liquidity preference theory will more accurately explain the shape of the yield curve than either of them alone. Specifically, actual long-term rates consistently tend to be above what is envisioned from the pure price expectations hypothesis. This consistent bias implies the existence of a liquidity premium.

Segmented-Market Hypothesis   A third theory that attempts to explain the shape of the yield curve is the segmented-market hypothesis, which enjoys wide acceptance among market practitioners. Also known as the *preferred habitat,* the *institutional theory,* or the *hedging pressure theory,* this hypothesis asserts that financial institutions tend to structure their investment policies in line with factors such as their tax obligations and the types and maturity structure of their liabilities. As an example, because commercial banks are subject to normal corporate tax rates and their liabilities are generally short- to intermediate-term time-and-demand deposits, they have a propensity to invest in short- to intermediate-term municipal bonds. This theory contends that the shape of the yield curve is ultimately a function of these investment policies of major financial institutions.

In its strongest form, the segmented-market theory holds that the maturity preferences of investors and borrowers are so strong that investors never purchase securities outside their preferred maturity range to take advantage of yield differentials. As a result, the short- and long-maturity portions of the bond market are effectively segmented, and yields for a particular maturity segment depend on the supply and demand *within* that maturity segment.

Trading Implications of the Term Structure   Information on maturities can help investors formulate yield expectations by simply observing the shape of the yield curve. If the yield

| EXHIBIT 12.7 | The Combined Effects of the Expectations and Liquidity Preference Hypotheses |

Panel (a). Upward-sloping term structure, showing the combined effects of the liquidity premium and expectations for higher future interest rates.

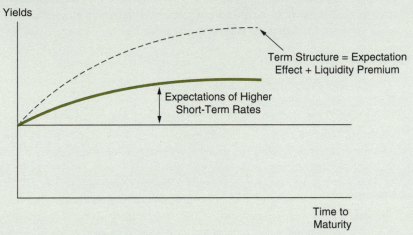

Panel (b). Downward-sloping term structure, showing the combined effects of the liquidity premium and expectations of lower future interest rates.

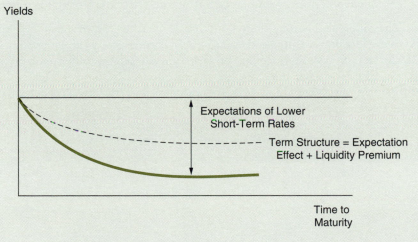

curve is declining sharply, historical evidence suggests that interest rates will probably decline in the future. Expectations theorists would suggest that one needs to examine only the prevailing yield curve to predict the direction of interest rates in the future.

Based on these theories, bond investors use the prevailing yield curve to predict the shapes of future yield curves. Using this prediction and knowledge of current interest rates, investors can determine expected yield volatility by maturity sector. In turn, the maturity segments that experience the greatest yield changes give the investor the largest potential price appreciation.[14]

---

[14]Gikas A. Hourdouvelis, "The Predictive Power of the Term Structure During Recent Monetary Regimes," *Journal of Finance* 43, no. 2 (June 1988): 339–356.

YIELD SPREADS

Another technique that can be used to help make good bond investments or profitable trades is the analysis of *yield spreads,* which are the differences in promised yields between bond issues or segments of the market at any point in time. Such differences in yield are specific to the particular issues or segments of the bond market.

There are four major yield spreads:

1. Different *segments* of the bond market may have different yields. For example, pure government bonds will have lower yields than government agency bonds; and government bonds will have much lower yields than corporate bonds.
2. Bonds in different *sectors* of the same market segment may have different yields. For example, yield differences between AAA corporates versus BBB corporates is a very popular spread to consider, and yields for various high-yield bond ratings (BB, B, CCC) versus ten-year Treasuries are closely followed, as are spreads between AAA industrial bonds and AAA public utility bonds.
3. Different *coupons* or *seasoning* within a given market segment or sector may cause yield spreads. Examples would include current coupon government bonds versus deep-discount government bonds, or recently issued AA industrials versus seasoned AA industrials.
4. Different *maturities* within a given market segment or sector also cause differences in yields. You will see maturity spreads or term yield spreads between short-term agency issues and long-term agency issues, between three-year prime municipals and twenty-five-year prime municipals, or between one-year Treasuries versus thirty-year Treasuries.

The differences among these bonds cause yield spreads that may be either positive or negative. More important, *the magnitude or the direction of a yield spread can change over time.* These changes in size or direction of yield spreads offer profit opportunities. We say that the spread narrows whenever the differences in yield become smaller, and it widens as the differences increase. Exhibit 12.8 contains data on a variety of past yield spreads that demonstrate the size of these spreads and show some large changes over time. The two most interesting changes during this six-year period were the long- versus short-term spread (#1), and the CCC rated bonds versus BB corporate credit spread (#7).

Bond investors evaluate yield-spread changes because these changes influence bond price behavior and comparative return performance. Those with an interest in this technique need to identify (1) any normal yield spread that is expected to become abnormally

EXHIBIT 12.8	Selected Mean Yield Spreads (Reported in Basis Points)					
Comparisons	1998	1999	2000	2001	2002	2003
1. Long governments–short governments	67	111	12	215	343	371
2. Long Aaa corporates–long governments	65	69	125	116	111	95
3. Long Aaa corporates–long Aaa municipals	146	152	180	177	178	164
4. Long Baa municipals–long Aaa municipals	17	24	54	62	51	71
5. Utilities–industrials	−10	−16	−12	19	106	18
6. Industrials–financials	31	39	44	85	44	60
7. Long CCC corporates–long BB corporates	601	871	1205	1587	1445	859

Note: Yield spreads are equal to the yield on the first bond minus the yield on the second bond—for example, the yield on long governments minus the yield on short governments.

Sources: Federal Reserve Bank of St. Louis, Merrill Lynch Fixed Income Research.

wide or narrow in response to an anticipated swing in market interest rates, or (2) an abnormally wide or narrow yield spread that is expected to become normal. A correct estimate of a change in either direction will provide profit opportunities.

Economic and market analyses would help in developing these expectations of potential for a yield spread to change. Taking advantage of these changes requires a knowledge of historical spreads and an ability to *predict* not only future changes in the overall market, but also why and when specific spreads will change.[15]

What Determines the Price Volatility for Bonds?

Thus far we have learned about alternative bond yields, how to calculate them, what determines bond yields (interest rates), and what causes them to change. Now that we understand why yields change, we can logically ask, what is the effect of these yield changes on the prices and rates of return for different bonds? We have discussed the inverse relationship between changes in yields and the price of bonds, so we can now discuss *the specific factors that affect the amount of price change for a yield change* in different bonds.

The fact is, a given change in interest rates can cause vastly different percentage price changes for different bonds. Understanding what causes these differences among percentage price changes will help in the bond selection decision. To maximize the rate of return received from a correct forecast of a decline in interest rates, for example, we need to know which bonds will benefit the most from the yield change.

Throughout this section we will talk about bond price changes or bond price volatility interchangeably. A bond price change is measured as the percentage change in the price of the bond, computed as follows:

12.10
$$\text{Percent Change in Bond Price} = \frac{\text{EPB}}{\text{BPB}} - 1$$

where:

EPB = the ending price of the bond
BPB = the beginning price of the bond

Bond price volatility is also measured in terms of percentage changes in bond prices. A bond with high price volatility is one that experiences large percentage price changes for a given change in yields.

Bond price volatility is influenced by more than yield behavior alone. Malkiel used the bond valuation model to demonstrate that the market price of a bond is a function of four factors: (1) its par value, (2) its coupon, (3) the number of years to its maturity, and (4) the prevailing market interest rate.[16] Malkiel's mathematical proofs showed the following relationships between yield (interest rate) changes and bond price behavior:

1. Bond prices move inversely to bond yields (interest rates).
2. For a given change in yields (interest rates), longer-maturity bonds post larger price changes; thus, bond price volatility is *directly* related to term to maturity.

---

[15]For an article that identifies four determinants of relative market spreads and suggests scenarios when they will change, see Chris P. Dialynas and David H. Edington, "Bond Yield Spreads: A Postmodern View," *Journal of Portfolio Management* 19, no. 1 (Fall 1992): 68–75.

[16]Burton G. Malkiel, "Expectations, Bond Prices, and the Term Structure of Interest Rates," *Quarterly Journal of Economics* 76, no. 2 (May 1962): 197–218.

3. Price volatility (percentage of price change) increases at a diminishing rate as term to maturity increases.
4. Price movements resulting from equal absolute increases or decreases in yield are *not* symmetrical. A decrease in yield raises bond prices by more than an increase in yield of the same amount lowers prices.
5. Higher coupon issues show smaller percentage price fluctuation for a given change in yield; thus, bond price volatility is *inversely* related to coupon.

Homer and Leibowitz showed that the absolute level of market yields also affects bond price volatility.[17] As the level of prevailing yields rises, the price volatility of bonds increases, *assuming a constant percentage change in market yields.* It is important to note that if we assume a constant percentage change in yield, the basis-point change will be greater when rates are high. For example, a 25 percent change in interest rates when rates are at 4 percent will be a 100 basis-point change; the same 25 percent change when rates are at 8 percent will be a 200 basis-point change. In the discussion of bond duration, we will see that this difference in basis-point change is important.

THE MATURITY EFFECT

Exhibit 12.9 demonstrates the effect of maturity on price volatility. In all four maturity classes, we assume a bond with an 8 percent coupon and assume the discount rate (nominal Y_m) changes from 7 to 10 percent. The only difference among the four cases is the maturities of the bonds. The demonstration involves computing the value of each bond at a 7 percent yield and at a 10 percent yield and noting the percentage change in price. As shown, this change in yield caused the price of the one-year bond to decline by only 2.9 percent, whereas the thirty-year bond declined by almost 29 percent. Clearly, the longer-maturity bond experienced the greater price volatility.

Also, price volatility increased at a decreasing rate with maturity. When maturity doubled from ten years to twenty years, the percent change in price increased by less than 50 percent (from 18.5 percent to 25.7 percent). A similar change occurred when going from twenty years to thirty years. Therefore, this table demonstrates the first three of our price–yield relationships: Bond price is inversely related to yields, bond price volatility is positively related to term to maturity, and bond price volatility increases at a decreasing rate with maturity.

EXHIBIT 12.9	Effect of Maturity on Bond Price Volatility							
	PRESENT VALUE OF AN 8 PERCENT BOND ($1,000 PAR VALUE)							
Term to Maturity	**1 Year**		**10 Years**		**20 Years**		**30 Years**	
Discount rate (nominal YTM)	7%	10%	7%	10%	7%	10%	7%	10%
Present value of interest	$ 75	$ 73	$ 569	$498	$ 858	$686	$1,005	$757
Present value of principal	934	907	505	377	257	142	132	54
Total value of bond	$1,009	$980	$1,074	$875	$1,115	$828	$1,137	$811
Percentage change in total value	−2.9		−18.5		−25.7		−28.7	

[17]Sidney Homer and Martin L. Leibowitz, *Inside the Yield Book,* Englewood Cliffs, NJ: Prentice-Hall, 1972.

It is also possible to demonstrate the fourth relationship with this table. Using the twenty-year bond, if we computed the percentage change in price related to an increase in rates (for example, from 7 to 10 percent), we would get the answer reported—a 25.7 percent decrease. In contrast, if we computed the effect on price of a *decrease* in yields from 10 percent to 7 percent, we would get a 34.7 percent increase in price ($1,115 versus $828). This demonstrates that prices change more in response to a decrease in rates (from 10 percent to 7 percent) than to a comparable increase in rates (from 7 percent to 10 percent).

THE COUPON EFFECT

Exhibit 12.10 demonstrates the coupon effect. In this set of examples, all the bonds have equal maturity (twenty years) and experience the same change in nominal Y_m (from 7 percent to 10 percent). The table shows the inverse relationship between a bond's coupon rate and its price volatility: The smallest coupon bond (the zero) experienced the largest percentage price change, almost 45 percent versus a 24 percent change for the 12 percent coupon bond.

THE YIELD LEVEL EFFECT

Exhibit 12.11 demonstrates the yield level effect. In these examples, all the bonds have the same twenty-year maturity and the same 4 percent coupon. In the first three cases the

EXHIBIT 12.10 Effect of Coupon on Bond Price Volatility

	PRESENT VALUE OF A 20-YEAR BOND ($1,000 PAR VALUE)							
	0 Percent Coupon		3 Percent Coupon		8 Percent Coupon		12 Percent Coupon	
Discount rate (nominal YTM)	7%	10%	7%	10%	7%	10%	7%	10%
Present value of interest	$ 0	$ 0	$322	$257	$ 858	$686	$1,287	$1,030
Present value of principal	257	142	257	142	257	142	257	142
Total value of bond	$257	$142	$579	$399	$1,115	$828	$1,544	$1,172
Percentage change in total value	−44.7		−31.1		−25.7		−24.1	

EXHIBIT 12.11 Effect of Yield Level on Bond Price Volatility

	PRESENT VALUE OF A 20-YEAR, 4 PERCENT BOND ($1,000 PAR VALUE)							
	(1) Low Yield		(2) Intermediate Yields		(3) High Yields		(4) 100 Basis-Point Change at High Yields	
Discount rate (nominal YTM)	3%	4%	6%	8%	9%	12%	9%	10%
Present value of interest	$ 602	$ 547	$462	$396	$370	$301	$370	$343
Present value of principal	562	453	307	208	175	97	175	142
Total value of bond	$1,164	$1,000	$769	$604	$545	$398	$545	$485
Percentage change in total value	−14.1		−21.5		−27.0		−11.0	

nominal Y_m changed by a constant 33.3 percent (from 3 percent to 4 percent, from 6 percent to 8 percent, and from 9 percent to 12 percent). Note that the first change is 100 basis points, the second is 200 basis points, and the third is 300 basis points. The results in the first three columns confirm the statement that when higher yields change by a *constant percentage,* the change in the bond price is larger.

The fourth column shows that if we assume a *constant basis-point change in yields,* we get the opposite results. Specifically, a 100 basis-point change in yields from 3 percent to 4 percent provides a price change of 14.1 percent, while the same 100 basis-point change from 9 percent to 10 percent results in a price change of only 11 percent. Therefore, in this case of a constant basis-point change in rates, there is an inverse relationship, with a larger price change at lower yields. Therefore, the yield level effect can differ depending on whether the yield change is specified as a constant percentage change or a constant basis-point change.

In summary, the price volatility of a bond for a given change in yield is affected by the bond's term to maturity, its coupon, the level of yields (depending on what kind of change in yield), and the direction of the yield change. However, although both the level and direction of change in yields affect price volatility, they cannot be used for trading strategies. When yields change, the two variables the investor or portfolio manager can control that have a dramatic effect on bond price volatility are coupon and maturity.

SOME TRADING STRATEGIES

Knowing that coupon and maturity are the major variables that influence bond price volatility, we can develop some strategies for maximizing rates of return when interest rates change. Specifically, if we expect a major *decline* in interest rates, we know that bond prices will increase, so we want a portfolio of bonds with the *maximum price volatility* to enjoy maximum price changes (capital gains) from the change in interest rates. In this situation, the previous discussion regarding the effect of maturity and coupon indicates that we should attempt to build a portfolio of long-maturity bonds with low coupons (ideally a zero coupon bond). A portfolio of such bonds (long-term, zeros) should experience the maximum price appreciation for a given decline in market interest rates.

In contrast, if we expect an *increase* in market interest rates, we know that bond prices will decline and we want a portfolio with *minimum price volatility* to minimize the capital losses caused by the increase in rates. Therefore, given these expectations we would want to change our portfolio to short-maturity bonds with high coupons. This combination should provide the minimum price volatility for an increase in market interest rates.

THE DURATION MEASURE

Interactive e-lectures

For more explanation and an animated example of duration, go to: http://reillyxtra .swlearning.com.

Because the price volatility of a bond varies inversely with its coupon and directly with its term to maturity, it is necessary to determine the best combination of these two variables to achieve our objective. This effort would benefit from a composite measure that considers both coupon and maturity. Fortunately, such a measure, the *duration* of a security, was developed almost 70 years ago by Macaulay.[18] Macaulay showed that the duration of a bond was a more appropriate measure of the time characteristics of bond cash flows than the term to maturity of the bond because duration considers both the repayment of capital at maturity and the size and timing of coupon payments prior to final maturity. Duration is defined as

---

[18]Frederick R. Macaulay, *Some Theoretical Problems Suggested by the Movements of Interest Rates, Bond Yields, and Stock Prices in the United States Since 1856,* New York: National Bureau of Economic Research, 1938.

the weighted average time to full recovery of principal and interest payments in present value terms. Using annual compounding, duration D is

12.11

$$D = \frac{\displaystyle\sum_{t=1}^{n} \frac{C_t(t)}{(1 + Y_m)^t}}{\displaystyle\sum_{t=1}^{n} \frac{C_t}{(1 + Y_m)^t}} = \frac{\displaystyle\sum_{t=1}^{n} [t \times PV(C_t)]}{P}$$

where:

t = time period in which the coupon or principal payment occurs
C_t = interest or principal payment that occurs in period t
Y_m = yield to maturity on the bond
PV = the present value of each of the annual cash flows
P = the current market price of the bond

The denominator in equation 12.11 is the price of a bond as determined by the present value model. The numerator is the present value of all cash flows *weighted according to the time to cash receipt.* The following example, which demonstrates the specific computations for two bonds, shows the procedure and highlights some of the properties of duration. Consider the following two sample bonds:

	Bond A	Bond B
Face value	$1,000	$1,000
Maturity	10 years	10 years
Coupon	4%	8%

Assuming annual interest payments and an 8 percent effective yield to maturity on the bonds, duration is computed as shown in Exhibit 12.12. Duration computed by discounting flows using the yield to maturity of the bond is called *Macaulay duration.*

Characteristics of Macaulay Duration   The example in Exhibit 12.12 illustrates several characteristics of Macaulay duration. First, the duration of a coupon bond will always be less than its term to maturity because duration gives weight to these interim payments.

Second, *an inverse relationship exists between coupon and duration.* A bond with a larger coupon will have a shorter duration because more of the total cash flows come earlier in the form of interest payments. As shown in Exhibit 12.12, the 8 percent coupon bond has a shorter duration than the 4 percent coupon bond.

A bond with no coupon payments (a zero coupon bond or a pure-discount bond such as a Treasury bill) will have Macaulay duration *equal* to its term to maturity. In Exhibit 12.12, if we assume a single payment at maturity, we will see that duration will equal term to maturity because the only cash flow comes in the final (maturity) year.

Third, *a positive relationship generally holds between term to maturity and duration,* but duration increases at a decreasing rate with maturity. Therefore, all else being the same, a bond with longer term to maturity will almost always have a higher duration. Note that the relationship is not direct, because as maturity increases, the present value of the principal declines in value.

As shown in Exhibit 12.13, the shape of the duration–maturity curve depends on the coupon and the yield to maturity. The curve for a zero coupon bond is a straight line, indicating that duration equals term to maturity. In contrast, the curve for a low-coupon bond selling at a deep discount (due to a high YTM) will turn downward at long maturities, which means that under these conditions the longer-maturity bond will have lower duration.

EXHIBIT 12.12	Computation of Duration (Assuming 8 Percent Market Yield)

BOND A

(1) Year	(2) Cash Flow	(3) PV at 8%	(4) PV of Flow	(5) PV as % of Price	(6) (1) × (5)
1	$ 40	0.9259	$ 37.04	0.0506	0.0506
2	40	0.8573	34.29	0.0469	0.0938
3	40	0.7938	31.75	0.0434	0.1302
4	40	0.7350	29.40	0.0402	0.1608
5	40	0.6806	27.22	0.0372	0.1860
6	40	0.6302	25.21	0.0345	0.2070
7	40	0.5835	23.34	0.0319	0.2233
8	40	0.5403	21.61	0.0295	0.2360
9	40	0.5002	20.01	0.0274	0.2466
10	1,040	0.4632	481.73	0.6585	6.5850
Sum			$731.58	1.0000	8.1193

Duration = 8.12 Years

BOND B

(1) Year	(2) Cash Flow	(3) PV at 8%	(4) PV of Flow	(5) PV as % of Price	(6) (1) × (5)
1	$ 80	0.9259	$ 74.07	0.0741	0.0741
2	80	0.8573	68.59	0.0686	0.1372
3	80	0.7938	63.50	0.0635	0.1906
4	80	0.7350	58.80	0.0588	0.1906
5	80	0.6806	54.44	0.0544	0.2720
6	80	0.6302	50.42	0.0504	0.3024
7	80	0.5835	46.68	0.0467	0.3269
8	80	0.5403	43.22	0.0432	0.3456
9	80	0.5002	40.02	0.0400	0.3600
10	1,080	0.4632	500.26	0.5003	5.0030
Sum			$1,000.00	1.0000	7.2470

Duration = 7.25 Years

Fourth, all else the same, there is an *inverse relationship between YTM and duration*. A higher yield to maturity of a bond reduces its duration. As an example, in Exhibit 12.12, if the yield to maturity had been 12 percent rather than 8 percent, the durations would have been about 7.75 and 6.80 rather than 8.12 and 7.25.[19]

Finally, sinking funds and call provisions can have a dramatic effect on a bond's duration. They can accelerate the total cash flows for a bond and, therefore, significantly reduce

---

[19]These properties are discussed and demonstrated in Frank K. Reilly and Rupinder Sidhu, "The Many Uses of Bond Duration," *Financial Analysts Journal* 36, no. 4 (July–August 1980): 58–72.

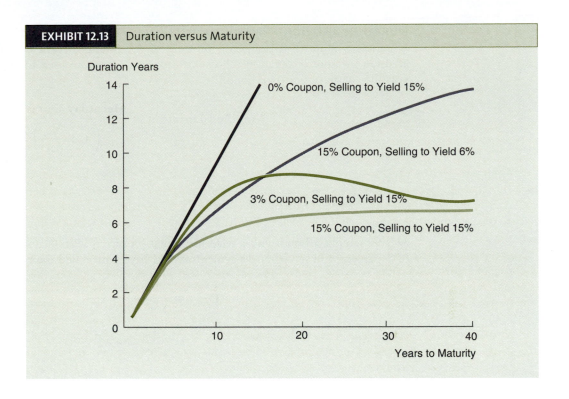

EXHIBIT 12.13 Duration versus Maturity

its duration.[20] Between these two factors, the factor that causes the greatest uncertainty is the call feature because it is difficult to estimate when it will be exercised. We will consider this further in a later section.

A summary of the characteristics of Macaulay duration is as follows:

- The duration of a zero coupon bond will *equal* its term to maturity.
- The duration of a coupon bond will always be less than its term to maturity.
- An *inverse* relationship exists between coupon and duration.
- There is generally a *positive* relationship between term to maturity and duration. Note that duration increases at a decreasing rate with maturity. Also, the duration of a deep-discount bond will decline at long maturities (over twenty years).
- An *inverse* relationship exists between yield to maturity and duration.
- Sinking funds and call provisions can cause a dramatic decline in the duration of a bond because of an early payoff (maturity).

The Macaulay duration measure can be useful to bond investors because it combines the properties of maturity and coupon to measure the time flow of cash from the bond. This measure of the timing of cash flows from a bond is superior to the term-to-maturity measure, which only considers when the principal will be repaid at maturity.

---

[20]An example of the computation of duration with a sinking fund is contained in Reilly and Sidhu, "The Many Uses of Bond Duration."

DURATION AND BOND PRICE VOLATILITY

Duration is more than a superior measure of the timing of cash flow from the bond. An adjusted measure of duration called *modified duration* can be used to approximate the price volatility of an option-free bond:[21]

12.12

$$\text{Modified Duration} = \frac{\textbf{Macaulay Duration}}{\left(1 + \dfrac{Y_m}{m}\right)}$$

where:

m = number of payments a year
Y_m = nominal yield to maturity

As an example, a bond with a Macaulay duration of ten years, a nominal yield to maturity of 8 percent, and semiannual payments would have a modified duration of

$$D_{mod} = \frac{10}{1 + (0.08/2)}$$

$$= \frac{10}{1.04} = 9.62$$

It has been shown, both theoretically and empirically, that bond price movements *will vary proportionally* with modified duration *for small changes in yields*.[22] Specifically, as shown in equation 12.13, an estimate of the percentage change in bond price equals the change in yield times modified duration. It is also the expected percentage change in price for a 100 basis-point change in yield.

12.13

$$\frac{\Delta P}{P} \times 100 = -D_{mod} \times \Delta Y_m$$

where:

ΔP = change in price for the bond
P = beginning price for the bond
D_{mod} = modified duration of the bond
ΔY_m = yield change in basis points divided by 100 (For example, if interest rates go from 8.00 to 8.50 percent, $\Delta Y_m = 50/100 = 0.50$.)

The negative sign indicates that the price change is in the opposite direction of the interest rate change (i.e., when interest rates fall, prices rise, and vice versa).

Consider a bond with $D = 8$ years and $Y_m = 0.08$. Assume we expect the bond's Y_m to decline by 75 basis points (for example, from 8 percent to 7.25 percent). The first step is to compute the bond's modified duration as follows:

---

[21]Notably, at this point, with modified duration we are measuring the interest rate sensitivity of the bond's price, so the modified duration value is an estimate of the percentage change in price for a 100 basis-point change in yield.

[22]A generalized proof of this is contained in Michael H. Hopewell and George Kaufman, "Bond Price Volatility and Term to Maturity: A Generalized Respecification," *American Economic Review* 63, no. 4 (September 1973): 749–753. The importance of the specification "for small changes in yields" will become clear when we discuss convexity.

$$D_{mod} = \frac{8}{1 + (0.08/2)}$$

$$= \frac{8}{1.04} = 7.69$$

The estimated percentage change in the price of the bond using equation 12.13 is

$$\% \Delta P = -(7.69) \times \frac{-75}{100}$$

$$= (-7.69) \times (-.75)$$

$$= 5.77$$

This indicates that the price of the bond should increase by approximately 5.77 percent in response to the 75 basis-point decline in Y_m. If the price of the bond before the decline in interest rates was $900, the price after the decline in interest rates should be approximately $900 \times 1.0577 = $951.93.

The modified duration will always have a negative sign for a noncallable bond because of the inverse relationship between yield changes and bond price changes. Also, remember that this formulation provides an *estimate* or *approximation* of the percentage change in the price of the bond. In the following section on convexity, we will show that the formula that only includes modified duration provides an exact estimate of the percentage price change only for small changes in yields.

Trading Strategies Using Duration   We know from the prior discussion on the relationship between modified duration and bond price volatility that the longest-duration security provides the maximum price variation. Exhibit 12.14 demonstrates the numerous ways to achieve a given level of duration. The duration measure has become increasingly popular because it conveniently specifies the time flow of cash from a security considering both coupon and term to maturity. The following discussion indicates that an active bond investor can also use this measure to structure a portfolio to take advantage of changes in market yields.

EXHIBIT 12.14	**Bond Duration in Years for Bond Yielding 6 Percent under Different Terms**			
		COUPON RATES		
Years to Maturity	**0.02**	**0.04**	**0.06**	**0.08**
1	0.995	0.990	0.985	0.981
5	4.756	4.558	4.393	4.254
10	8.891	8.169	7.662	7.286
20	14.981	12.980	11.904	11.232
50	19.452	17.129	16.273	15.829
100	17.567	17.232	17.120	17.064
∞	17.167	17.167	17.167	17.167

Source: From "Coping with the Risk of Interest Rate Fluctuations: Returns to Bondholders from Naive and Optimal Strategies" by L. Fisher and R. L. Weil, *Journal of Business* 44, no. 4 (October 1971): 418. Copyright © 1971. Reprinted by permission of The University of Chicago Press.

If we expect a *decline* in interest rates, we should *increase* the average duration of our bond portfolio to experience maximum price volatility. Alternatively, if we expect an *increase* in interest rates, we should *reduce* the average duration of our portfolio to minimize our price decline. Notably, most bond-portfolio managers specify their duration targets relative to their benchmark portfolios. For example, a portfolio manager who expects lower interest rates would set a duration target of 1.10 of the benchmark duration. A manager who expects an increase in rates would reduce the duration of the portfolio to 0.90 of the duration for the benchmark portfolio so the portfolio would be less volatile than the benchmark. Note that the duration of the portfolio is the market-value-weighted average of the durations of the individual bonds in the portfolio.

BOND CONVEXITY

Modified duration allows us to estimate bond price changes for a change in interest rates. Equation 12.13 is, however, accurate only for *small changes* in market yields. We will see that the accuracy of the estimate of the price change deteriorates with larger changes in yields because the modified duration calculation specified in equation 12.13 is a *linear* approximation of a bond price change, which, in fact, follows a *curvilinear* (convex) function. To understand the effect of this convexity, we must consider the price–yield relationship for alternative bonds.[23]

Price–Yield Relationship for Bonds   Because the price of a bond is the present value of its cash flows at a particular discount rate, if we are given the coupon, maturity, and a yield for a bond, we can calculate its price at a point in time. The *price–yield curve* provides a set of prices for a specific maturity and coupon bond at a point in time using a range of yields to maturity (discount rates). As an example, Exhibit 12.15 lists the computed prices for a 12

| EXHIBIT 12.15 | Price–Yield Relationships for Alternative Bonds |

A. 12 PERCENT, 20-YEAR BOND		B. 12 PERCENT, 3-YEAR BOND		C. ZERO COUPON, 30-YEAR BOND	
Yield	Price	Yield	Price	Yield	Price
1.0%	$2,989.47	1.0%	$1,324.30	1.0%	$741.37
2.0	2,641.73	2.0	1,289.77	2.0	550.45
3.0	2,346.21	3.0	1,256.37	3.0	409.30
4.0	2,094.22	4.0	1,224.06	4.0	304.78
5.0	1,878.60	5.0	1,192.78	5.0	227.28
6.0	1,693.44	6.0	1,162.52	6.0	169.73
7.0	1,533.88	7.0	1,133.21	7.0	126.93
8.0	1,395.86	8.0	1,104.84	8.0	95.06
9.0	1,276.02	9.0	1,077.37	9.0	71.29
10.0	1,171.59	10.0	1,050.76	10.0	53.54
11.0	1,080.23	11.0	1,024.98	11.0	40.26
12.0	1,000.00	12.0	1,000.00	12.0	30.31

[23]For a further discussion of this topic, see Mark L. Dunetz and James M. Mahoney, "Using Duration and Convexity in the Analysis of Callable Bonds," *Financial Analysts Journal* 44, no. 3 (May–June 1988): 53–73.

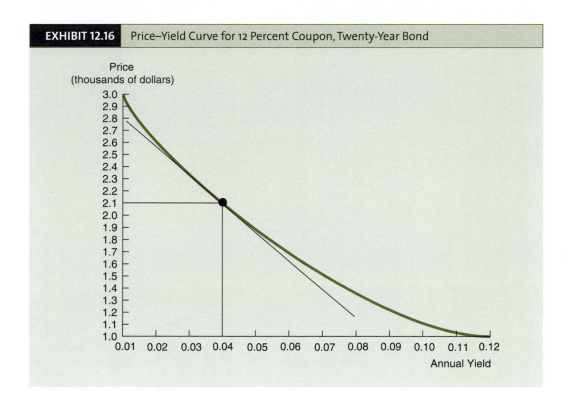

| **EXHIBIT 12.16** | Price–Yield Curve for 12 Percent Coupon, Twenty-Year Bond |

percent, twenty-year bond assuming nominal yields from 1 percent to 12 percent. For example, the table shows that discounting the flows from this 12 percent, twenty-year bond at a yield of 1 percent gives a price of $2,989.47; discounting these same flows at 10 percent gives a price of $1,171.59. The graph of these prices relative to the yields that produced them in Exhibit 12.16 indicates that the price–yield relationship for this bond is not a straight line but a curvilinear relationship. That is, it is convex.

Three points are important about the price–yield relationship:

1. This relationship can be applied to a single bond, a portfolio of bonds, or any stream of future cash flows.
2. The convex price–yield relationship will differ among bonds or other cash flow streams, depending on the nature of the cash flow stream, that is, its coupon and maturity. As an example, the price–yield relationship for a high-coupon, short-term security will be almost a straight line (i.e., it is not very convex) because the price does not change as much for a change in yields (for example, the 12 percent, three-year bond in Exhibit 12.15). In contrast, the price–yield relationship for a low-coupon, long-term bond will curve radically (that is, be strongly convex), as shown by the zero coupon, thirty-year bond in Exhibit 12.15. These differences in convexity are shown graphically in Exhibit 12.17. The curved nature of the price–yield relationship is referred to as the bond's *convexity.*
3. As shown by the graph in Exhibit 12.16, because of the convexity of the price–yield relationship, as yield increases, the rate at which the price of the bond declines becomes slower. Similarly, when yields decline, the rate at which the price of the bond increases becomes faster. Convexity is therefore a desirable trait.

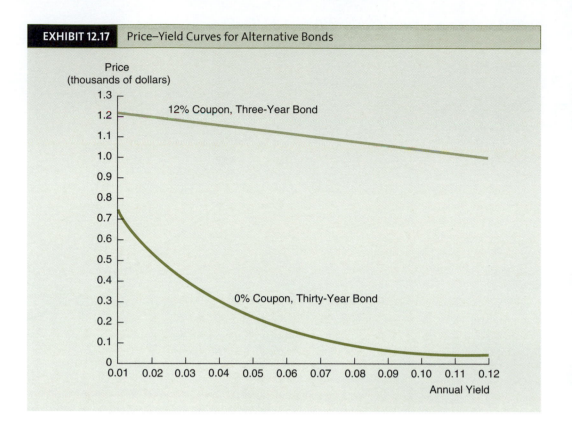

EXHIBIT 12.17 Price–Yield Curves for Alternative Bonds

Given this price–yield curve, modified duration is the percentage change in price for a 100 basis-point change in yield as follows:[24]

12.14

$$D_{mod} = \frac{dP/dY}{P}$$

Notice that the dP/dY line is tangent to the price–yield curve *at a given yield*, as shown in Exhibit 12.18. The slope of this line at the point of tangency is the modified duration of the bond at this yield. For *small* changes in yields (i.e., from $y^\star$ to either y_1 or y_2), this tangent straight line gives a good estimate of the actual price changes. In contrast, for larger changes in yields (from $y^\star$ to either y_3 or y_4), the straight line will estimate the new price of the bond at less than the actual price shown by the price–yield curve. This misestimate arises because the modified duration line is a linear estimate of a curvilinear relationship. Specifically, the estimate using only modified duration will *underestimate* the actual price *increase* caused by a yield decline and *overestimate* the actual price *decline* caused by an increase in yields. This graph, which demonstrates the convexity effect, also shows that price changes are *not* symmetric when yields increase or decrease. As shown, when rates decline, a larger price error occurs than when rates increase because when yields decline prices rise at an *increasing* rate, while when yields rise prices decline at a *decreasing* rate.

---

[24]In mathematical terms, modified duration is the first derivative of this price–yield relationship with respect to yield.

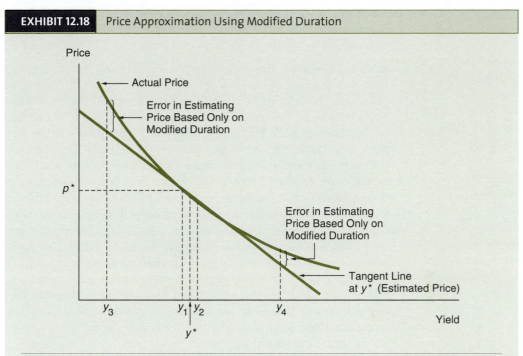

EXHIBIT 12.18 Price Approximation Using Modified Duration

Source: "Measuring Interest Rate Risk," Table 5.11, page 104 of *The Handbook of Fixed Income Securities,* 6th Edition by Frank Fabozzi. Copyright © 2001, 1997, 1995, 1991, 1987, 1983 by The McGraw-Hill Companies. Reprinted by permission.

Determinants of Convexity   Convexity is a measure of the curvature of the price–yield relationship. Mathematically, convexity is the second derivative of price with respect to yield (d^2P/dY^2) divided by price. Specifically, convexity is the percentage change in dP/dY for a given change in yield:

12.15
$$\text{Convexity} = \frac{d^2P/dY^2}{P}$$

Convexity is a measure of how much a bond's price–yield curve deviates from the linear approximation of that curve. As indicated by Exhibits 12.16 and 12.18 for *noncallable* bonds, convexity is always a positive number, implying that the price–yield curve lies above the modified duration (tangent) line. Exhibit 12.17 illustrates the price–yield relationship for two bonds with widely different coupons and maturities. (The yields and prices are contained in Exhibit 12.15.)

These graphs demonstrate the following relationship between these factors and the convexity of a bond.

- An *inverse* relationship exists between coupon and convexity (yield and maturity constant).
- A *direct* relationship exists between maturity and convexity (yield and coupon constant).
- An *inverse* relationship exists between yield and convexity (coupon and maturity constant). This means that the price–yield curve is more convex at its lower-yield (upper-left) segment.

Therefore, a short-term, high-coupon bond, such as the 12 percent coupon, three-year bond in Exhibit 12.17, has low convexity—it is almost a straight line. In contrast, the zero coupon, thirty-year bond has high convexity.

Modified Duration–Convexity Effects In summary, the change in a bond's price resulting from a change in yield can be attributed to two sources: the bond's modified duration and its convexity. The relative effect of these two factors on the price change will depend on the characteristics of the bond (its convexity) and the size of the yield change. For example, if we are estimating the price change for a 300 basis-point change in yield for a zero coupon, thirty-year bond, the convexity effect would be fairly large because this bond would have high convexity and a 300 basis-point change in yield is relatively large. In contrast, if we are dealing with only a 10 basis-point change in yields, the convexity effect would be minimal because it is a small change in yield. Similarly, the convexity effect would be relatively small for a larger yield change if we are concerned with a bond with small convexity (high coupon, short maturity) because its price–yield relationship is almost a straight line.

In conclusion, modified duration can be used to derive an *approximate* percentage bond price change for a given change in interest rates, but it is only a good estimate for small yield changes. We must also consider the convexity effect when we are dealing with large yield changes or when the security has high convexity. Investors see convexity as something desirable. Given two bonds with identical durations, they prefer the one with the greater convexity. The higher-convexity bond will give greater price appreciation if rates fall and a smaller price loss should rates rise.

DURATION AND CONVEXITY FOR BONDS WITH EMBEDDED OPTIONS

The discussion and presentation thus far regarding Macaulay and modified durations and convexity have been concerned with option-free bonds. A callable bond is different because it provides the issuer with an option to call the bond under certain conditions and pay it off with funds from a new issue sold at a lower yield. Observers refer to this as a bond with an

Investments Online

Bond valuation focuses on bond mathematics, the term structure, and bond features that add to the yield (such as callability) or lead to lower yields (such as putability). Bonds are normally easier to evaluate than stocks, given their stated life, cash flows, and discount rates which can be read from the term structure. Nonetheless, bond pricing can become quite complicated if the bond has complex options or attributes. It is not surprising that bond market commentary typically focuses on interest rate trends and factors that can favorably or unfavorably affect credit quality.

http://www.bonds-online.com Perhaps the best source for bond market information on the Internet. It includes prices, yields, and market commentary for Treasuries, corporates, munis, and U.S. savings bonds. It contains several links to sites of interest to bond investors.

http://www.bondmarkets.com The Bond Market Association web page contains market information, products of interest to bond traders, links, and research.

http://www.bondcalc.com This site discusses a software pricing system for fixed income securities. It includes a description of basic and sophisticated bond analyses.

http://www.bondtrac.com This site offers much bond data to subscribers. It has links to various bond market pages, including municipals, corporate, and agency sites. It also includes a fixed income glossary of terms and description of various bonds, including treasuries, corporates, strips, inflation-indexed, mortgaged-backed, and others.

embedded option. We noted earlier that the duration of a bond can be seriously affected by an embedded call option if interest rates decline substantially below a bond's coupon rate. In such a case, the issuer will likely call the bond, which will dramatically change the maturity and the duration of the bond. A full discussion of what happens to the duration and convexity of bonds with embedded call or put options is beyond the scope of this text.[25]

Summary

- The value of a bond equals the present value of all future cash flows accruing to the investor. Cash flows for the conservative bond investor include periodic interest payments and principal return; cash flows for the aggressive investor include periodic interest payments and the capital gain or loss when the bond is sold prior to its maturity. Bond investors can maximize their rates of return by accurately estimating the level of interest rates and, more important, changes in interest rates and yield spreads.

- The five bond yield measures are coupon rate, current yield, promised yield to maturity, promised yield to call, and realized (horizon) yield. The promised Y_m and promised Y_c equations include an implied interest-on-interest, or coupon reinvestment, assumption. For the realized (horizon) yield computation, the investor estimates the reinvestment rate and may need to also estimate the future selling price for the bond. The fundamental determinants of interest rates are a real risk-free rate, the expected rate of inflation, and a risk premium.

- The yield curve (or the term structure of interest rates) shows the relationship between the yields on a set of comparable bonds and the term to maturity. Yield curves exhibit four basic patterns. Three theories attempt to explain the shape of the yield curve: the expectations hypothesis, the liquidity preference hypothesis, and the segmented-market hypothesis.

- It is important to understand what causes changes in interest rates and also how these changes in rates affect the prices of bonds. Differences in bond price volatility are mainly a function of differences in yield, coupon, and term to maturity. The duration measure incorporates coupon, maturity, and yield in one measure that provides an estimate of the response of bond prices to changes in interest rates. Because modified duration provides a straight-line estimate of the curvilinear price–yield function, investors must consider modified duration together with the convexity of a bond when estimating price changes for large changes in yields and/or when dealing with securities that have high convexity. The presentation in this chapter is related to option-free bonds. There are significant differences when dealing with bonds that have embedded put and call options.

Questions

1. Why does the present value equation appear to be more useful for the bond investor than for the common stock investor?

2. What important assumptions are made when calculating the promised yield to maturity? What are the assumptions when calculating promised yield to call?

3. a. Define the variables included in the following model:
   $$Y = RFR + I + RP$$
   b. Assume the firm whose bonds you are considering is not expected to break even this year. Discuss which factor will be affected by this information.

4. We discussed three hypotheses to explain the term structure of interest rates. Which one do you think best explains the various shapes of a yield curve? Defend your choice.

5. *CFA Examination Level I*
   a. Explain *term structure of interest rates.* Explain the theoretical basis of an upward-sloping yield curve. (8 minutes)
   b. Explain the economic circumstances under which you would expect to see the inverted yield curve prevail. (7 minutes)
   c. Define "real" rate of interest. (2 minutes)

---

[25]For discussion on these topics, see Frank K. Reilly and Keith Brown, *Investment Analysis and Portfolio Management,* 7th ed., Mason, OH: South-Western, 2003, Chapter 16; Frank J. Fabozzi, *Fixed Income Analysis,* New Hope, PA: Frank J. Fabozzi Associates, 2000; and Frank J. Fabozzi, Gerald W. Buetow Jr., and Robert R. Johnson, "Measuring Interest Rate Risk," in *Handbook of Fixed Income Securities,* 6th ed., edited by Frank J. Fabozzi, New York: McGraw-Hill, 2001.

d. Discuss the characteristics of the market for U.S. Treasury securities. Compare it to the market for AAA corporate bonds. Discuss the opportunities that may exist in bond markets that are less than efficient. (8 minutes)

e. Over the past several years, fairly wide yield spreads between AAA corporates and Treasuries have occasionally prevailed. Discuss the possible reasons for this. (5 minutes)

CFA 6. *CFA Examination Level III*

As the portfolio manager for a large pension fund, you are offered the following bonds:

	Coupon	Maturity	Price	Call Price	Yield to Maturity
Edgar Corp. (new issue)	14.00%	2012	$101¾	$114	13.75%
Edgar Corp. (new issue)	6.00	2012	48⅛	103	13.60
Edgar Corp. (1982 issue)	6.00	2012	48⅞	103	13.40

Assuming you expect a decline in interest rates over the next three years, identify and justify which of these bonds you would select. (10 minutes)

7. You expect interest rates to decline over the next six months.

a. Given your interest rate outlook, state what kind of bonds you want in your portfolio in terms of duration. Explain your reasoning for this choice.

b. You must make a choice between the following three sets of noncallable bonds. In each case, select the bond that would be best for your portfolio given your interest rate outlook and the strategy suggested in part (a). In each case, briefly discuss why you selected the bond.

		Maturity	Coupon	Yield to Maturity
Case 1:	Bond A	15 years	10%	10%
	Bond B	15 years	6%	8%
Case 2:	Bond C	15 years	6%	10%
	Bond D	10 years	8%	10%
Case 3:	Bond E	12 years	12%	12%
	Bond F	15 years	12%	8%

8. At the present time you expect a decline in interest rates and must choose between two portfolios of bonds with the following characteristics.

	Portfolio A	Portfolio B
Average maturity	10.5 years	10.0 years
Average Y_m	7%	10%
Modified duration	5.7 years	4.9 years
Modified convexity	125.18	40.30
Call features	Noncallable	Deferred call features that range from 1 to 3 years

Select one of the portfolios and discuss three factors that would *justify* your selection.

9. *CFA Examination Level 1* **CFA**

Bill Peters is the investment officer of a $60 million pension fund. He has become concerned about the big price swings that have occurred lately in the fund's fixed-income securities. Peters has been told that such price behavior is only natural given the recent behavior of market yields. To deal with the problem, the pension fund's fixed-income money manager keeps track of exposure to price volatility by closely monitoring bond duration. The money manager believes that price volatility can be kept to a reasonable level as long as portfolio duration is maintained at approximately seven to eight years.

Discuss the concepts of duration and convexity and explain how each fits into the price–yield relationship. In the situation described above, explain why the money manager should have used both duration and convexity to monitor the bond portfolio's exposure to price volatility. (15 minutes)

10. *CFA Examination Level I* **CFA**

A bond analyst is looking at a twenty-year, AA-rated corporate bond. The bond is noncallable and carries a coupon of 7.50 percent. The analyst computes both the standard yield to maturity and horizon return for this bond, which are as follows:

Yield to maturity	8.00%
Horizon return	8.96%

Assuming the bond is held to maturity, explain why these *two* measures of return differ. (5 minutes)

11. *CFA Examination Level I* **CFA**

Which of the following statements is correct? The yield to maturity on a bond is:

a. below the coupon rate when the bond sells at a discount and above the coupon rate when the bond sells at a premium.

b. the interest rate that makes the present value of the payments equal to the bond price.

c. based on the assumption that all future payments received are reinvested at the coupon rate.

d. based on the assumption that all future payments received are reinvested at future market rates.

CFA 12. *CFA Examination Level I*
Which *one* of the following statements about the term structure of interest rates is *true*?
a. The expectations hypothesis indicates a flat yield curve if anticipated future short-term rates exceed current short-term rates.
b. The expectations hypothesis contends that the long-term rate is equal to the anticipated short-term rate.
c. The liquidity premium theory indicates that, all else being equal, longer maturities will have lower yields.
d. The market-segmentation theory contends that borrowers and lenders prefer particular segments of the yield curve.

13. Bond price volatility is normally highest for bonds with what coupon, duration, and maturity characteristics?
14. Under what circumstances will the yield to maturity and current yield be equal?
15. Which of the following bonds has the longest duration?
a. Nine-year maturity, 8% coupon
b. Nine-year maturity, 12% coupon
c. Sixteen-year maturity, 8% coupon
d. Sixteen-year maturity, 12% coupon
16. What is the relationship between the Macaulay duration and time to maturity of a zero coupon bond?

PROBLEMS

1. Four years ago your firm issued $1,000 par, twenty-five-year bonds, with a 7 percent coupon rate and a 10 percent call premium.
a. If these bonds are now called, what is the *approximate* yield to call for the investors who originally purchased them at par?
b. If these bonds are now called, what is the *actual* yield to call for the investors who originally purchased them at par? Quote it both on a nominal and an effective annual yield.
c. If the current interest rate is 5 percent and the bonds were not callable, at what price would each bond sell?

2. Assume you purchased an 8 percent, twenty-year, $1,000 par, semiannual payment bond priced at $1,012.50 when it has twelve years remaining until maturity. Compute:
a. Its yield to maturity (nominal *and* effective)
b. Its yield to call if the bond is callable in three years with an 8 percent premium

3. Calculate the duration of an 8 percent, $1,000 par bond that matures in three years if the bond's Y_m is 10 percent and interest is paid semiannually.
a. Calculate this bond's modified duration.
b. Assuming the bond's Y_m goes from 10 percent to 9.5 percent, calculate an estimate of the price change.

4. Two years ago you acquired a ten-year, zero coupon, $1,000 par value bond at a 12 percent nominal Y_m. Recently you sold this bond at an 8 percent nominal Y_m. Using semiannual compounding, compute the annualized horizon return for this investment.

5. A bond for the Edgar Corporation has the following characteristics:

Maturity—12 years
Coupon—10 percent
Yield to maturity—9.50 percent
Macaulay duration—5.7 years
Convexity—48
Noncallable

Calculate the approximate price change for this bond using only its duration assuming its yield to maturity increased by 150 basis points. Discuss (without calculations) the impact of including the convexity effect in the calculation.

6. *CFA Examination Level I* **CFA**
Philip Morris has issued bonds that pay semiannually with the following characteristics:

Coupon—8 percent
Yield to maturity—8 percent
Maturity—15 years
Macaulay duration—10 years

a. Calculate modified duration using the information above. (5 minutes)
b. Explain why modified duration is a better measure than maturity when calculating the bond's sensitivity to changes in interest rates. (5 minutes)
c. Identify the direction of change in modified duration if:
   i. the coupon of the bond were 4 percent, not 8 percent.
   ii. the maturity of the bond were seven years, not fifteen years. (5 minutes)
d. Define convexity and explain how modified duration *and* convexity are used to approximate the bond's percentage change in price, given a change in interest rates. (5 minutes)

CFA 7. *CFA Examination Level I*

Bonds of Zello Corporation with a par value of $1,000 sell for $960, mature in five years, and have a 7 percent annual coupon rate paid semiannually.

a. Calculate the:
   i. current yield;
   ii. yield to maturity (to the nearest whole percent, i.e., 3 percent, 4 percent, 5 percent, etc.); *and*
   iii. horizon yield (also called total return) for an investor with a three-year holding period and a reinvestment rate of 6 percent over the period. At the end of three years the 7 percent coupon bonds with two years remaining will sell to yield 7 percent.

   Show your work. (9 minutes)

b. Cite *one* major shortcoming for *each* of the following fixed-income yield measures:
   i. current yield;
   ii. yield to maturity; *and*
   iii. horizon yield (also called realized yield or total return). (6 minutes)

8. A bond with ten years to maturity has a yield to maturity of 12 percent and a Macaulay duration of seven years. If the market yield falls by 100 basis points, what will be the bond's expected price change?

WEB EXERCISES

1. Go to *http://www.bloomberg.com/markets;* the site contains information on yields on government bonds for a number of countries. Compare the horizontal (or time) spread of the bonds in the different countries. Which has the steepest yield curve? The flattest? What do the spreads tell us about the condition of the bond market in these countries?

2. Go to the Web site of the St. Louis Federal Reserve Bank (*http://www.stlouisfed.org*). Click on the link that will take you to FRED, the Federal Reserve Economic Database, which contains a variety of downloadable interest rate data. How has the yield spread between Treasuries and corporate bonds behaved over time? When was there a flight to quality? What was happening to the slope of the yield curve during these times?

3. The Web site of *SmartMoney* magazine (*http://www.smartmoney.com*) has innovative features in its bond section. Under "Economy," click on the "Living Yield Curve" link and view the changing yield curve over time. Were periods of steep yield curves followed by rising interest rates and periods of inverted yield curves followed by falling interest rates? What does this imply for the expectations hypothesis of the term structure of interest rates?

SPREADSHEET EXERCISES

1. Given the coupon rate, yield to maturity, time to maturity, and par value, compute the price of the following bonds:
   a. Coupon rate 8%, yield to maturity 10%, time to maturity ten years, par value $1,000
   b. Coupon rate 6%, yield to maturity 6.5%, time to maturity five years, par value $5,000
   c. Coupon rate 4%, yield to maturity 3.3%, time to maturity fifteen years, par value $1,000

2. Use the computed prices in Exercise 1 and the IRR function to estimate the yields to maturity for the three bonds.

3. Set up a table that lists the cash flows of a bond. Use it to compute the bond price and duration for the bonds in Exercise 1. Estimate the change in price of the bonds if their yields to maturity change by +1 percent and −1 percent.

4. Construct a spreadsheet showing the effect of interest-on-interest to a bond investor. Assume a $1,000 par value bond and a coupon rate of 8 percent paid annually. All interest is reinvested at 8 percent. After ten years,
   a. What is the total value of the invested funds?
   b. How much interest would have been received under simple interest?
   c. How much interest has been received and reinvested over time?
   d. What proportion of the total dollar return is due to interest-on-interest?

REFERENCES

Fabozzi, Frank J. *Fixed Income Analysis for the Chartered Financial Analyst Program.* 2nd ed. New Hope, PA: Frank J. Fabozzi Associates, 2004.

Fabozzi, Frank J. *Bond Markets, Analysis and Strategies*, 5th ed. Upper Saddle River, NJ: Pearson Prentice-Hall, 2004.

Kritzman, Mark. "What Practitioners Need to Know about Duration and Convexity." *Financial Analysts Journal* 48, no. 6 (November–December 1992).

Sundaresan, Suresh. *Fixed Income Markets and Their Derivatives.* 2nd ed. Mason, OH: South-Western Publishing, 2002.

Tuckman, Bruce. *Fixed Income Securities.* New York: John Wiley & Sons, 1995.

Van Horne, James C. *Financial Market Rates and Flows.* 6th ed. Upper Saddle River, NJ: Prentice-Hall, 2001.

GLOSSARY

Bond-equivalent yield (BEY) One of the conventions for quoting yield to maturity for bonds that pay semiannual coupons. If you provide BEY, it is equal to the bond's semiannual rate of return multiplied by two.

Bond price volatility The percentage changes in bond prices over time.

Convexity A measure of the degree to which a bond's price–yield curve departs from a straight line. This characteristic affects estimates of a bond's price volatility.

Coupon rate Measures the annual income that a bond investor receives expressed as a percent of the bond's par value.

Crossover point The price at which it becomes profitable for an issuer to call a bond. Above this price, yield to call is the appropriate yield measure.

Current yield (CY) A bond's yield as measured by its current income (coupon) as a percentage of its market price.

Discount A bond selling at a price below par value because its Y_m is above its coupon rate.

Duration A composite measure of the timing of a bond's cash flow characteristics taking into consideration its coupon and term to maturity.

Effective yield to maturity One of the conventions for quoting yield to maturity for bonds that pay semi-annual coupons. If you provide effective yield to maturity, you compound the bond's semiannual rate of return.

Ending-wealth value The total amount of money derived from investment in a bond until maturity, including principal, coupon payments, and income from reinvestment of coupon payments.

Fully taxable equivalent yield (FTEY) A yield on a tax-exempt bond that adjusts for its tax benefits to allow comparisons with taxable bonds.

Interest-on-interest Bond income from reinvestment of coupon payments.

Internal rate of return (IRR) The discount rate at which cash outflows of an investment equal cash inflows.

Modified duration A measure of Macaulay duration adjusted to help estimate a bond's price volatility.

Premium A bond selling at a price above par value because its Y_m is below its coupon rate.

Price–yield curve The relationship between the required return (yield) on a bond and its price. Provides a set of prices for a specific maturity and coupon bond at a point in time using a range of yields to maturity (discount rates).

Promised yield to call (Y_c) A bond's yield if held until the first available call date, with reinvestment of all coupon payments at the Y_c rate.

Promised yield to maturity (Y_m) The most widely used measure of a bond's yield that states the fully compounded rate of return on a bond bought at market price and held to maturity with reinvestment of all coupon payments at the Y_m rate.

Realized (horizon) yield The expected compounded yield on a bond that is sold before it matures assuming a sales price and the reinvestment of all cash flows at an explicit rate.

Term structure of interest rates The relationship between term to maturity and yield to maturity for a sample of comparable bonds at a given time. Popularly known as the *yield curve.*

Yield The promised rate of return on an investment under certain assumptions.

Yield illusion The erroneous expectation that a bond will provide its stated yield to maturity without recognizing the implicit coupon reinvestment assumption related to the Y_m calculation.

Yield spread The difference between the promised yields of various bond issues or market segments at a given time.

Equity Securities: Valuation and Management

Thus far we have examined the purpose of investing, the importance of an appropriate asset allocation decision, and the numerous investment instruments available on a global basis. We have also given an overview of the institutional characteristics of capital markets and of the major developments in investment theory as they relate to portfolio theory, capital asset pricing, and efficient capital markets. In addition, we have considered the theory and practice of valuing fixed-income securities and are now ready to extend those principles to equity securities. Valuation is the heart of investing and leads to the construction of a portfolio that is consistent with our risk–return objectives.

We begin in Chapter 13 with a discussion of generic approaches to estimating a security's intrinsic value, which starts with developing a perspective on global markets and which economies and industries will be more favorable for investing over the investment horizon. We examine factors that affect the long-term economic growth rate and those that will lead to short-term deviations from this growth rate. We review several economic forecasting tools, including anticipated relationships between economic and industry forecasts, and factors that affect the attractiveness of an industry for investment purposes, including structural changes in the economy, the industry's competitive structure, and its stage in the industry life cycle.

The major source of information regarding a stock or bond is the particular corporation's financial statements. In Chapter 14 we consider the financial statements available and the information they provide, followed by an extended discussion of the financial ratios used to answer important questions about a firm's liquidity, its operating performance, its risk profile, and its growth potential.

In Chapter 15 we apply the basic principles of valuation to common stock. Prior to the demonstration of the valuation models, we discuss the important difference between a company and its stock—i.e., in many instances the common stock of a very fine company may *not* be a good investment. We then use the two general approaches to valuing common stock—discounted cash flow valuation techniques and several relative valuation techniques—to value the stock of an example company.

In Chapter 16 we deal with technical analysis, an alternative to the fundamental approach discussed in the previous chapters. Rather than attempting to estimate value based on numerous external variables, the technical analyst contends that the market is its own best estimator. Therefore, he or she believes that it is possible to project future stock price movement based on past stock price changes or other stock-market data. We discuss and demonstrate various techniques used by technical analysts for U.S. and world markets.

Economic and Industry Analysis

Analysis of the economy—where we are and where we are headed—should be the first component of security analysis. By studying the big picture of the national and international economy, we can better identify factors and trends that will affect industries and firms in the future and make security buy-and-sell decisions accordingly.

Economic analysis may appear difficult because leading economists disagree on some points of economic theory and policy prescriptions. Still, there is enough agreement to aid those who wish to buy and sell securities and manage portfolios. In this chapter we avoid discussion of theory and focus instead on the practice of economic forecasting and its role in portfolio management and security selection.

Recall that the concept of present value states that the value of an asset today is the sum of the expected cash flows from the asset discounted to the present at a discount rate k. For a simple one-period cash flow, we have

13.1
$$\text{Price} = \text{Present Value of Expected Cash Flows}$$
$$= \frac{\text{E}(\text{CF}_1)}{1 + k}$$

This equation shows us what the focus of economic and industry analysis should be: helping the analyst determine expected future cash flows and discount rates for these cash flows. We need to develop insight into the level of future cash flows, their growth, and the duration of that growth over time. As far as discount rates are concerned, monetary conditions and the role of monetary policy will be important to the analysis, as will investor expectations about future risk.

Therefore, useful economic analysis should provide insights regarding cash flow trends, interest rate trends, and risk premium analysis. This may involve analysis of the economy's expected growth, inflation, demographic shifts, the political environment, and industry competition.

The global economy affects the domestic economy; for large economies such as the United States, the opposite may be true as well. Fluctuating exchange rates affect prices of imports and exports. Growing consumer demand for goods can lead to increases in imports. Attractive financial conditions overseas may cause investment dollars to be funneled to other countries. Thus, the sales and profitability of firms and industries are not necessarily tied into their home markets.

Relating Economic Analysis to Efficient Markets

Our discussion of efficient capital markets in Chapter 10 may have led some to believe that attempts to outperform the market indexes on a risk-adjusted basis is an exercise in futility. But perhaps we can produce superior risk-adjusted performance by focusing our analysis on some of the apparent anomalies discovered through research on efficient markets. Smaller firms, firms with low P/E ratios, firms with low BV/MV ratios, firms with earnings surprises, and neglected firms not heavily scrutinized by Wall Street analysts may give amateur investors or analysts a chance to concentrate their research efforts and outperform the market indexes.

Another implication of the efficient market hypothesis is that the market consensus for expectations about the economy, firms, and interest rate trends is incorporated into asset prices. *Therefore, for an analyst to experience above-average risk-adjusted returns, he or she must have well-reasoned, usually correct expectations that differ from the market consensus.* Perhaps a disciplined approach to analyzing information—an approach that removes the emotions that sometimes blind proper decision making—can foster such expectations. We discuss this method—expectational analysis—later in the chapter.

Our prior study on efficient capital markets provided a dose of reality: Identifying undervalued securities is not easy. However, in this and the next few chapters we will give the basic tools analysts use in attempting to identify mispriced securities. Use of these tools to analyze equities (and fixed-income securities) may lead to superior returns.

Generic Approaches to Security Analysis

EMPHASIZING HISTORY

Two basic approaches are useful in evaluating securities. One is generally backward-looking. Specifically, investors select securities for purchase or sale by examining past data, trends, and relationships and by assuming the future will be an extension of the past. Advocates of this approach may attempt to exploit market anomalies by using quantitative screens to construct portfolios (for example, buy only low P/E stocks or only stocks with small market capitalizations), or they may use technical analysis, which we will discuss in some detail in Chapter 16.

FOCUSING ON THE FUTURE

The second approach is forward-looking. In this approach, although proponents might use some historical information, they focus mainly on determining likely future trends and invest accordingly. As we learned in Chapter 11, investors may take either a top-down or a bottom-up approach to investing.

In this text we focus on the top-down approach that was shown in Exhibit 11.1. In the *top-down approach,* we first review a country's macroeconomy and forecast likely trends.

From this analysis arise implications for different industries and economic sectors. By combining both the economic and industry analysis, we identify buy candidates that are best positioned to take advantage of the expected trends; those firms that will suffer in the expected economic/industry environment are sell candidates. Industries that are expected to do better than other industries under the expected economic conditions should be *overweighted* in a portfolio; that is, the proportion of the industry's holdings should be larger than its market-value weight in the benchmark portfolio (such as the S&P 500). Industries that are expected to do poorly under the economic forecast should be *underweighted*.[1]

From a global portfolio perspective, the asset allocation for a country within a global portfolio will be affected by its economic outlook. If a recession were imminent in a country, we would expect a negative impact on its security prices except possibly for those securities with a global presence. Such a country should be underweighted in a portfolio. Further, given these pessimistic expectations, any funds invested in the country would be directed to low-risk sectors of the economy. (For example, many portfolio managers underweighted the Japanese stock market relative to its weight in the EAFE index based on the continuing economic troubles of that country in the late 1990s and early 2000s.) In contrast, a country with an optimistic economic and stock-market outlook should be overweighted in a global portfolio.

MARKET ANALYSIS

Much data is available on the performance of U.S. stocks in different economic scenarios. For example, Exhibit 13.1 shows the average price–earnings ratios for the S&P 500 index under different categories of inflation. The table shows that stocks have higher P/E ratios at lower rates of inflation; conversely, higher inflation results in lower P/E ratios. One reason for the high P/E ratio is the expectation of higher earnings growth.[2] Yet studies have found

EXHIBIT 13.1	Price–Earning Ratios under Various Inflation Conditions
Inflation	**Average S&P 500 P/E**
Less than 3.5%	16.2
Less than 4.5%	15.3
4.5-5.5%	15.6
5.5-6.5%	12.1
6.5-7.5%	10.0
Greater than 7.5%	8.6

Source: Copyright © 1997, Association for Investment Management and Research. Reproduced and republished from "Economic Forecasts and the Asset Allocation Decision" by Abby Joseph Cohen from *Economic Analysis for Investment Professionals*, pp. 24–34, with permission from CFA Institute. All Rights Reserved.

---

[1]A good question is: if some industries are expected to perform poorly, why invest in them at all? We still want to maintain an investment presence for two reasons. First is the concept of diversification. No economic forecast will be 100 percent correct. Even in scenario analysis we know there is a most likely, or expected, scenario and others with a lower probability. In case our forecast is incorrect, we want some exposure to a diversified set of industries. Second, transactions costs and portfolio reallocation costs will increase the expense of making wholesale changes in the portfolio. The costs, coupled with the benefits of diversification, will lead us to maintain an underweighted allocation to the industry.

[2]Recall the basic dividend growth model, $P_0 = D_0(1 + g)/(k - g)$. Dividing each side by earnings, E, we have an estimate for the P/E ratio: $P/E = \text{Dividend Payout}/(k - g)$. Higher expected growth rates will result in higher P/E ratios.

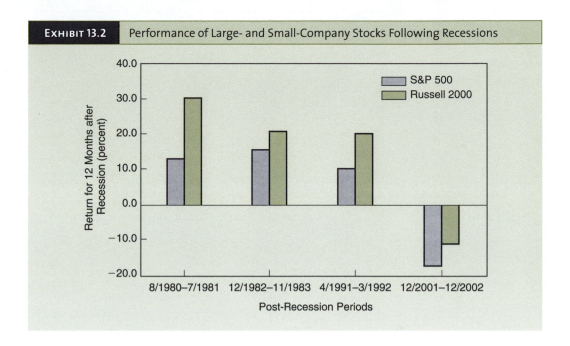

EXHIBIT 13.2	Performance of Large- and Small-Company Stocks Following Recessions

that these expectations are not met. In the years following high P/E ratios, high earnings growth has not occurred and stock prices on average have declined.[3]

The inverse of the P/E ratio is the E/P ratio, which represents the average earnings per dollar invested in stocks. This measure, called the *earnings yield,* is frequently used in financial research as it allows comparisons to an interest rate, which represents the interest received per dollar invested in bonds. When the earnings yield is low, risky stocks are poor alternatives to fixed-income securities. Since 1959, when the difference between the earnings yield and the three-month T-bill rate has been less than zero (i.e., the T-bill rate exceeds the earnings yield), the average annual return on S&P 500 has been a dismal −2.13 percent.

The state of the economy has implications for other asset categories, too. Exhibit 13.2 shows the return performance of large- and small-company stocks in the twelve months after a recession has ended. Small-cap stocks generally outperform large-cap stocks following recessions for two reasons. First, they are less diversified than large firms and therefore have large relative earnings gains when the economy turns around. Second, smaller firms are likely to be more leveraged, so when sales gains arise the effect is magnified on earnings. Therefore, when analysts predict that a recession is ending, history implies that smaller firms are relatively attractive investments.

Bond returns behave differently during and after recessions. High-quality bonds such as government bonds generally perform well during a recession and less well in the twelve months following a recession. During the last ten recessions (1948 to the present), the average annual return on long-term government bonds was 11.0 percent; for the twelve months following each of these recessions these bonds averaged only 3.0 percent annual returns. High-yield (junk) corporate bonds, on the other hand, perform stellarly in the

---

[3]John Y. Campbell and Robert J. Shiller, "Valuation Ratios and the Long-Run Stock Market Outlook," *Journal of Portfolio Management* 24, no. 2 (1998): 11–26; Pu Shen, "The P/E Ratio and Stock Market Performance," *Federal Reserve Bank of Kansas City Economic Review* (fourth quarter 2000): 23–36.

twelve months following recession (average annual return of 12.5 percent) and less so during recession. The reason for these differences has to do with the quality of the investment and the cash flow supporting the bonds. With government bonds, their good returns during a recession arises from the falling interest rates that occur during such times. High-yield bonds, on the other hand, are like small-cap stocks in that when the economy starts to recover their issuers experience relatively larger gains in sales, earnings, and cash flow and the prices of high yield bonds rise because of lower default risk perceptions.

A Quick Review of Economic Concepts

A discussion of the macroeconomy usually has at least two components: (1) the national economy and (2) how the international economy affects the national economy.

DOMESTIC ECONOMIC ACTIVITY

Economic forecasters attempt to determine trends in major economic variables such as gross domestic product (GDP), inflation, and interest rates. *Gross domestic product (GDP)* is the sum total of the goods and services produced within a nation's borders in a year. To be useful to investment analysts, GDP estimates need to be broken down into their components, so analysts can derive sector and industry growth forecasts. Economic variables such as income, interest rates, and exchange rates have differential effects on the components of GDP.

GDP has five major components: consumption spending, investment spending, government expenditures, goods and services produced domestically for export, and the production of goods and services consumed in the process of distributing imports to the domestic consumer. *Consumption spending* represents purchases by households and consumers and comprises about two-thirds of GDP. Changes in consumption spending are affected by changes in income, consumer sentiment, and taxes. *Investment spending* is mainly investments by businesses in their assets. It is affected by factors such as expectations of future sales and interest rates. *Government spending* includes government budget plans. *Export and import activity* encompasses spending relevant to the shipment of goods into or out of the domestic economy and is affected by exchange rates and the strength or weakness of the economies of both the United States and other countries.

These components of GDP can be broken down further to provide additional detail on sector and industry growth prospects. For example, consumption spending has three main components: spending on consumer durable goods (such as refrigerators, autos, and televisions), consumer nondurables (such as food and pharmaceuticals), and services. Spending on consumer durables is sensitive to the stage of the business cycle, expectations, and income. Consumer nondurables, by their nature, are less sensitive to these influences. Consumption spending is reported by spending category, too; this provides a finer breakdown of spending by various categories for analysis. For example, Exhibit 13.3 shows that the three largest categories for consumption spending in 2003 were medical care, housing, and food.

Investment spending also has several elements. It includes nonresidential investment spending on buildings and equipment used in the course of business as well as residential investing such as home purchases, which are sensitive to demographic influences as well as income and interest rate levels. Another component of investment spending is business inventory investment. Unlike the first two elements, this one can be positive or negative, depending on whether businesses are adding to their inventories or facing inventory reductions.

Exhibit 13.3	Breakdown of Personal Consumption Expenditures, 2003		
	2003	**2000**	**Percentage Change**
Personal consumption expenditures	$7,919.1	$6,728.4	17.7
Durable goods	$967.0	$819.6	18.0
Motor vehicles and parts	432.2	346.8	24.6
Furniture and household equipment	345.1	307.3	12.3
Other	189.7	165.5	14.6
Nondurable goods	$2,262.2	$1,989.6	13.7
Food	1,094.2	957.5	14.3
Clothing and shoes	317.3	319.1	−0.6
Gasoline, fuel oil, and other energy goods	212.7	183.3	16.0
Other	637.9	529.8	20.4
Services	$4,689.9	$3,919.2	19.7
Housing	1,216.4	958.8	26.9
Household operation	428.3	385.7	11.0
Transportation	294.1	272.8	7.8
Medical care	1,342.3	996.5	34.7
Recreation	325.7	256.2	27.1
Other	1,083.1	1,049.3	3.2

Source: *http://www.bea.doc.gov.*

Government spending also has several components: federal, state, and local. Federal spending can also be divided into various elements, including defense and nondefense spending.

From this we see that a forecast of, say, 5 percent GDP growth next year is important information, but for investment purposes it would be more valuable to know the main impetus for that growth. For example, will the growth be due to consumer spending in the durable goods market, residential construction, or businesses building their inventories? Knowing the source of the growth will identify industries or sectors deserving of closer scrutiny for possible investment. Of course, if the market has already anticipated this growth, stock P/E ratios and prices may reflect this optimism.

DOMESTIC ECONOMIC POLICIES

The federal government and Federal Reserve Board use fiscal and monetary policy tools in their attempts to guide the economy. By their effects on the interest rate and economic growth, monetary and fiscal policy can affect financial market behavior and price levels.

Monetary policy involves the use of the power of the Fed to affect the money supply and aggregate economic activity. Many economists believe that the growth rate of the money supply has broad implications for future economic growth and future levels of inflation. As a consequence, most investment managers are interested in changes in the growth rate of the money supply and the current status of monetary policy. Many analysts are "Fed watchers," who seek to glean information from Fed pronouncements and data that may indicate potential future changes in money supply growth, interest rates, and the inflation rate.

The Federal Reserve Board has three basic instruments with which it can administer its monetary policy:

1. Open market operations, in which it purchases or sells government securities
2. Determination of the discount rate (the interest rate banks pay when they borrow from the Fed)
3. The setting of reserve requirements for banks

Open market operations are the most frequently used tool of monetary policy. The term *open market* simply means the Fed will buy or sell securities (usually Treasury bills) from any market participant, rather than, for example, dealing only with the U.S. Treasury. You may recall from a macroeconomics course that *reserve requirements* determine the proportion of deposited funds that must be kept on reserve in a bank. When the Fed purchases or sells government securities in the open market, a bank's loanable reserves will change. Subsequently, through a multiplier process, deposits (and the money supply) in the U.S. banking system will change. Financial and market analysts eagerly watch money-supply figures, reported weekly in the financial press, for insight into the Fed's policy and its desire to either slow down or speed up the economy. The effect of open market operations may also be evaluated through changes in the *federal funds rate,* the interest rate that banks charge each other for short-term interbank loans. Many Fed watchers predict monetary policy and future interest rate trends by observing the federal funds rate; it is considered to be a better indicator of Fed policy than watching for *discount rate* announcements.

Fiscal policy involves the use of government spending and taxing powers to influence the economy. Both tax laws and government expenditures affect the disposable incomes of consumers and corporations as well as the level of aggregate demand in the economy. Many analysts believe that efforts to reduce the federal budget deficit in the 1990s helped contribute to lower interest rates and a rising stock market. Some believe that capital gains tax cuts help stimulate investment in equities due to higher expected after-tax returns.

THE GLOBAL ECONOMY

With the development of global trade and finance, analysts developing forecasts must consider the effects of international factors on domestic economies. Because many firms are affected by worldwide competition, top-down analysis in many instances must begin with an examination of *global* economic growth rather than domestic growth alone.

Global influences can have numerous effects on domestic economies. The health of foreign economies affects domestic industries and U.S. exports. If foreign economies are enjoying growth, U.S. exports will likely rise and export-based firms will prosper. These same industries will face a slowdown if foreign economies go into recession.

Movements toward freer trade, with the elimination of tariffs, quotas, and other trade restraints between countries, is generally a positive sign for economic growth. Although some domestic industries may do better than others in the short run, in general free trade helps expand markets and contributes to economic growth.

Trade is affected by changes in exchange rates. Thus, an analysis of global industries needs to review national growth forecasts as well as exchange rate trends. An *exchange rate* is the price of one currency in terms of another currency, such as ¥110/$ (110 yen to the dollar) or €1.10/$ (1.10 euros to the dollar). Should the U.S. dollar strengthen against a foreign currency (meaning one U.S. dollar can purchase more foreign currency units), imports from that nation may rise because the goods from that country become cheaper in U.S.-dollar terms. For example, if we assume an exchange rate of 105 yen to the dollar, a car that costs ¥2,100,000 in Japan will cost $20,000 in the United States. Should the dollar strengthen to 110 yen to the dollar, this same car can sell for about $19,091 and provide the same amount of yen revenue as before. A strengthening dollar helps make imports less expensive in U.S.-dollar terms; insomuch as this increases demand for imported goods, competing domestic sectors may suffer. Also, because it can reduce import prices, a strengthening U.S. dollar may ease U.S. inflation rates.

There is a mirror effect: as one currency gets stronger, the other currency necessarily becomes weaker. For example, a stronger dollar means it takes more yen to purchase one U.S. dollar; therefore, U.S.-manufactured goods will become more expensive for the Japanese consumer unless U.S. producers reduce their prices. In turn, Japan will import less and the United States will export less and the profitability of industries with large Japanese exports will decline.

Global events also affect interest rates in an investor's home country. Recall from Chapter 3 (equation 3.1) that the relation between a U.S. investor's dollar returns and foreign returns was given by

13.2

$$1 + \text{U.S. Dollar Return} = (1 + \text{Foreign Return})\left(\frac{\text{Current Exchange Rate}}{\text{Initial Exchange Rate}}\right)$$

or

$$1 + \text{U.S. Dollar Return} = (1 + \text{Foreign Return})$$
$$(1 + \text{Change in the Exchange Rate})$$

where the exchange rate is defined as the home currency per unit of foreign currency, such as U.S. dollar per peso or U.S. dollar per euro for a U.S. investor. For a foreign investor, the return on a U.S. investment is

13.3 $$(1 + \text{Foreign Return}) = \frac{1 + \text{U.S. Dollar Return}}{1 + \text{Change in the Exchange Rate}}$$

Just as a U.S. investor will demand higher nominal interest rates when faced with higher inflationary expectations (the Fisher effect), foreign investors will want higher returns on their U.S. investments when faced with a falling dollar. Suppose current interest rates in Europe are 6 percent and European investors expect the dollar to weaken from \$0.90/euro to \$0.945/euro (a decline of 5 percent). To determine what U.S. interest rate will give European investors the same 6 percent return they can receive in their home economy, we use equation 13.3 to solve for the U.S. dollar return:

$$(1 + 0.06) = \frac{1 + \text{U.S. Dollar Return}}{1 + 0.05}$$

or

$$1 + \text{U.S. Dollar Return} = (1 + 0.06)(1 + 0.05) = 1.113 \text{ or } 11.3\%$$

If the U.S. dollar is expected to fall 5 percent, the Euro-based investor will require a U.S. interest rate of 11.3 percent to entice an investment in U.S. securities. Thus a falling dollar puts upward pressure on U.S. interest rates and makes borrowing more expensive for the U.S. government, corporations, and individuals. The effect of exchange rate fluctuations on U.S. interest rates are virtually all-encompassing, from rates paid on Treasury bills to rates on home mortgages.

According to this perspective, called *interest rate parity,* countries with weakening currencies will have higher domestic interest rates. Exhibit 13.4 shows that this hypothesized relationship has been seen in many different countries.

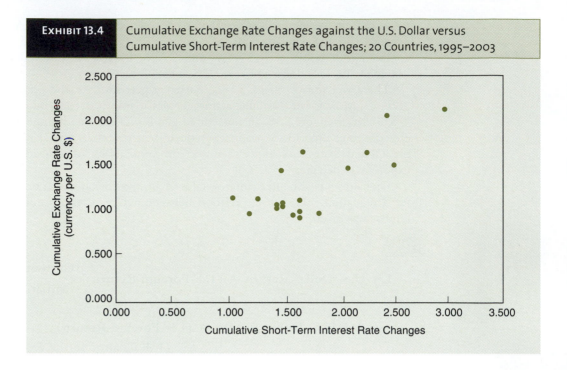

EXHIBIT 13.4   Cumulative Exchange Rate Changes against the U.S. Dollar versus Cumulative Short-Term Interest Rate Changes; 20 Countries, 1995–2003

Influences on the Economy and Security Markets

Several factors affect future real economic growth, that is, the growth in output that occurs after the effects of inflation are removed. In this section we discuss factors that influence long-term and short-term growth expectations.

INFLUENCES ON LONG-TERM EXPECTATIONS

The long-term growth path of the economy is determined by supply factors. Growth will be constrained in the long run by limits in technology, the size and training of the labor force, and the availability of adequate resources and incentives to expand. Exhibit 13.5 illustrates these factors. Positive or negative changes in these factors may lead to changes in future economic growth.

Another, perhaps simpler, way of viewing growth prospects is to focus on specific components of real output, as follows:

13.4   **Real Output = Population × Labor Force Participation Rate × Average Number of Hours Worked per Week × Labor Productivity**

Population multiplied by the proportion of the population that is in the labor force equals the number of workers in the economy; multiplying this by the average number of hours worked per week gives the total number of labor-hours over a week's time. Labor productivity is defined as output per labor-hour; thus, total labor-hours multiplied by output per labor-hour results in economic output.

When focusing on long-term economic growth, we are not interested in the *levels* of the variables on the right-hand side of equation 13.4 but rather in their *changes* over time. It is the changes, or growth, of the population, labor force participation, the workweek, and

EXHIBIT 13.5	Foundations of Long-Term Growth Expectations

LABOR EFFECT

Population
Labor participation rate
          Labor force
          Percentage employed
                    Workforce
                    Hours worked per employee
                              Total hours worked
                              Business training
                              Education

CAPITAL EFFECT

Capital stock (net)
          Capital employed
          Technology/R&D
          Capacity utilization

CONTRIBUTING FACTORS

          Economic mix (manufacturing versus service)
          Peace expectations
          Energy availability
          Economic stability
          Foreign competition
          Incentives
                    Regulation
                    Tax mix
                    Government share of output

Source: First Chicago Investment Advisors, as reported in Jeffrey J. Diermeier, "Capital Market Expectations: The Macro Factors," in *Managing Investment Portfolios: A Dynamic Process,* 2nd ed., edited by John L. Maginn and Donald L. Tuttle (Boston: Warren, Gorham, and Lamont, 1990), pp. 5–32. Reprinted by permission of Jeffrey J. Diermeier.

labor productivity that will lead to *growth* in real output over time. Thus we see that demographic changes and technological improvements have a major effect on an economy's growth trends. Sectors serving higher-growth global industries and higher-growth economies should benefit in the years ahead. Free trade will spur economic growth by allowing developed nations to meet the economic needs of developing nations.

Deviations from the economy's long-term trend will cause business cycles. Short-term growth above the trend gives the appearance of an economic "boom" and is manifested by higher production, higher spending, and maybe signs of inflation. Slower or negative short-term growth causes recessions, identified by slower or negative growth in output and higher unemployment.

INFLUENCES ON SHORT-TERM EXPECTATIONS

Fluctuations in demand relative to long-term supply constraints create fluctuations in real GDP, known as *business cycles.* When demand exceeds supply, inflation results; when demand is less than supply, rising unemployment and recession may occur. Therefore, short-term economic forecasting should focus on sources of demand or variations in short-term supply to predict future trends in economic variables.

Liquidity and Monetary Policy   Businesses need access to funds in order to borrow, raise capital, and invest in their assets. If monetary policy is too tight, sources of capital become scarce and economic activity will slow or decline. Lack of liquidity can also occur if banks tighten their lending practices.

In this sense, liquidity is the availability of funds to invest. Liquidity comes into the stock market as investors sell other assets, or take cash reserves, to invest them in stocks. Such liquidity can come from either home-country or foreign investors if the economy and stock market are relatively attractive for investment purposes.

Some popular measures of liquidity include the difference between the growth in money supply (using a measure such as M2 or MZM[4]) and GDP growth; a narrowing in the difference between the commercial paper and T-bill rate;[5] and changes in the federal funds rate.[6] Some analysts use public announcements of discount rate changes as a proxy for "expansionary" or "restrictive" monetary policy. Studies have shown that stock returns are higher and exhibit less volatility in expansionary stages than in restrictive stages of monetary policy. Treasury bond returns are, on average, higher in expansive periods while Treasury bill returns are generally higher when the Fed is being restrictive.[7]

Fiscal Policy   Fiscal policy affects short-term demand. Government spending can directly affect economic sectors and geographic regions. All else constant, some economists believe larger-than-expected increases in government spending will increase short-term demand and slower-than-expected increases may harm short-term demand. Tax changes influence incentives to save, work, and invest, and may therefore affect both short-term expectations as well as long-term supply.

Real Effects   Real effects differ from monetary effects in that they influence the operations and manufacture of goods and services. Some economic theorists argue that economic fluctuations can be traced to random real shocks in the economy. Examples of real shocks include major political occurrences such as embargoes, declarations of war and peace, technological advances, tax code changes, and extended labor strikes. Although the effect of these shocks can concentrate in one industry or sector, multiplier effects can spread their expansionary or recessionary effects throughout the economy.

Inflation   Although inflation is mainly a monetary phenomenon, at times outside shocks to the system (such as raw material shortages) can cause increases, albeit temporary, in the inflation rate. Inflation usually occurs when short-term economic demand exceeds the long-term supply constraint. As such, inflation is typically seen as a sign that the end of an economic expansion is near. An increase in the expected rate of inflation will cause nomi-

---

[4]M2 is equal to M1 (generally, currency, traveler's checks, and other checkable deposits) plus savings deposits (including money market deposit accounts), small-denomination (less than $100,000) time deposits, and shares of retail money market mutual funds (funds with initial investments of less than $50,000). MZM (Money, Zero Maturity) equals M2 minus small-denomination time deposits plus institutional money market funds (funds with initial investments of more than $50,000).

[5]Robert F. Whitelaw, "Time Variations and Covariations in the Expectation and Volatility of Stock Market Returns," *Journal of Finance* 49 (1994): 515–541; Ben S. Bernanke and Alan S. Blinder, "The Federal Funds Rate and the Channels of Monetary Transmission," *American Economic Review* 82 (1992): 901–921; Benjamin M. Friedman and Kenneth N. Kuttner, "Money, Income, Prices, and Interest Rates," *American Economic Review* 82 (1992): 472–492.

[6]Willem Thorbecke, "On Stock Market Returns and Monetary Policy," *Journal of Finance* 52 (1997): 635–654.

[7]Gerald R. Jensen, Robert R. Johnson, and Jeffrey M. Mercer, *The Role of Monetary Policy in Investment Management*, Charlottesville, VA: Research Foundation of AIMR, 2000. A good review of different influences is contained in David A. Becher, Gerald R. Jensen, and Jeffrey M. Mercer, "Monetary Policy Indicators as Predictors of Stock and Bond Returns," unpublished working paper, 2004.

nal interest rates to rise, as predicted by the Fisher effect. Inflation in the United States may raise the price of our exports, thus reducing foreign sales while making imports appear more price competitive. Inflation adds a layer of uncertainty to future business and investment decisions, which in turn increases risk premiums. It is not surprising that many studies find negative correlations between a country's inflation rate and its short-term stock market returns.[8]

Interest Rates   In general, increases in interest rates—whether caused by inflation, Fed policy, rising risk premiums, or other factors—will lead to reduced borrowing and an economic slowdown. Rising interest rates typically lead to falling stock prices for several other reasons, too. First, when interest rates rise, investors' required rate of return on stocks will rise as well, causing prices to fall. Second, rising interest rates also make bond yields look more attractive relative to stock dividend yields.

Reductions in real short-term rates mean cheaper financing costs. This will be favorable to companies with relatively more variable-rate debt and to small-cap firms who have few financing alternatives. Larger credit spreads between AAA and BB rated bonds (or AAA and Treasuries) indicate investor concerns about larger firms' creditworthiness. A steep yield curve (short-term rates much lower than long-term rates) will favor firms with relatively more short-term debt; generally, this will be smaller firms.

International Influences   Rapid real growth in other countries can create surges in demand for U.S. exports, leading to growth in export-sensitive industries and overall GDP. In contrast, the imposition of trade barriers, quotas, nationalistic fervor, and currency restrictions can hinder the free flow of currency, goods, and services and harm the export sector of the U.S. economy. Therefore, a strong U.S. economy can at times assist economies experiencing a recession by importing their products, and vice versa.

Summary of Short-Term Influences   A variety of influences affect short-run demand. Changes in demand, relative to long-term supply growth, result in business cycles and concomitant fluctuations in cash flows, interest rates, and risk premiums. As part of the top-down investment approach, analysts should examine short-term demand trends and influences. These influences can then be evaluated to estimate their influence on different economic sectors, industries, and investments.

Some Forecasting Tools

Despite some of the practical difficulties in preparing consistently accurate forecasts, some general economic signals provide us with insights regarding future economic trends without requiring us to be experts in economics.

INFLATION INDICATORS

Investors want to predict inflation trends for two reasons. First, inflation generally rises before the onset of an economic downturn. Second, inflation is a great destroyer of wealth: Principal and fixed-income streams lose purchasing power and value as the price level rises.

One indicator of future inflation trends is actions by the Federal Reserve Board. Rapid growth in the money supply *relative* to the real growth rate of the economy is often a precursor to inflation; slow money-supply growth typically means inflation should not be a

---

[8]See, for example, Claude B. Erb, Campbell R. Harvey, and Tadas E. Viskanta, "Inflation and World Equity Selection," *Financial Analysts Journal* (November–December 1995): 28–42, and the references therein.

concern. Thus analysts will keep an eye on the rate of money-supply growth measures such as M2 and changes in free reserves as indicators of current and future money-supply growth.

Another indicator is commodity prices; adherents of cost-push or demand-pull inflation view commodity prices as the first indicator of inflation trends. Commodities used in these indexes include agricultural products such as wheat, beans, livestock, and sugar as well as minerals such as aluminum and copper. Several raw materials price indexes have gained popularity as inflation indicators. The *Journal of Commerce* publishes a price index of eighteen industrial-use raw materials (e.g., aluminum and lead). The Commodity Research Bureau compiles indexes of commodity spot and futures market prices for foretelling price trends in commodities, although they are biased toward the grain markets. The Goldman Sachs Commodity Index also can be used to gauge future price trends; its drawback is that nearly 50 percent of the index is affected by oil prices.[9]

If interest rates follow the Fisher effect, increases in short-term T-bill rates may be a precursor of inflation. Differences between interest rates on Treasury securities and the relatively new inflation-indexed notes issued by the Treasury can also provide an indication of the market's expectations about future inflation.

Professional economists may also be a source of expertise on inflation trends. The Philadelphia Federal Reserve Bank publishes the Livingston surveys wherein economists are asked to forecast future inflation. Twice a year, in January and July, *The Wall Street Journal* publishes its own survey of economists who likewise forecast future price levels.

DIFFERENCES BETWEEN LONG-TERM AND SHORT-TERM INTEREST RATES

Studies have found that tracking the difference between long-term and short-term interest rates on government securities (referred to as a *maturity spread*) is a useful predictor of the trend of economic activity. Usually, long-term interest rates exceed short-term rates, giving an upward-sloping yield curve. It is contended that no difference or a negative difference between the ten-year and three-month interest rate foretells an economic recession. Between 1955 and 2004, the United States went through nine recessions; all nine followed an interest rate differential between long-term and short-term bonds that was zero or negative. When this maturity spread became positive again, economic growth followed.

CYCLICAL ECONOMIC INDICATORS

Leading indicators are a set of economic variables whose values reach peaks and troughs before aggregate economic activity (as measured by real GDP) does. For example, the housing industry serves as such a leading indicator. Generally, if the housing market picks up, it is expected that after a short lag the general economy will follow because the increase in demand for housing will stimulate increased demand for construction materials, workers, and durables to furnish the home. The lag arises because of the time lapse between the first evidence of increased housing demand (that is, an increase in housing starts) and a noticeable effect on overall economic activity.

The Conference Board publishes an index of economic data on ten leading economic indicators (LEI) in the business cycle (listed in Exhibit 13.6) and a composite *index of leading economic indicators.* The Economic Cycle Research Institute, another private organiza-

---

[9]Some evidence exists that over time individual indicators may not perform well as inflation predictors but combinations of indicators produce fairly accurate forecasts. See Stephen G. Cecchetti, Rita S. Chu, and Charles Steindel, "The Unreliability of Inflation Indicators," *Current Issues in Economics and Finance,* 6, no. 4 (April 2000): Federal Reserve Bank of New York; James H. Stock and Mark W. Watson, "Forecasting Inflation," *Journal of Monetary Economics* 44, no. 2 (October 1999): 293–335.

EXHIBIT 13.6	Economic Series Included in the Conference Board Indicators

LEADING INDEX

1. Average weekly hours of manufacturing workers
2. Average weekly initial claims for unemployment insurance
3. Real value of manufacturers' new orders for consumer goods and materials
4. Index of consumer expectations
5. Index of 500 common stock prices
6. Manufacturers' new orders, nondefense capital goods in 1992 dollars
7. Index of new private housing starts authorized by local building permits
8. Vendor performance (the percentage of companies receiving delivery later than the industry average)
9. Real money supply, M2
10. Interest rate spread, ten-year Treasury bonds less federal funds rate

COINCIDENT INDEX

1. Number of employees on nonagricultural payrolls
2. Personal income less transfer payments, expressed in 1992 dollars
3. Index of industrial production
4. Manufacturing and trade sales, expressed in 1992 dollars

LAGGING INDEX

1. Average duration of unemployment
2. Ratio of manufacturing and trade inventories to sales
3. Percentage change in the labor cost per unit of output in manufacturing
4. Average prime rate charged by banks
5. Commercial and industrial loans outstanding
6. Ratio of consumer installment credit outstanding to personal income
7. Change in the consumer price index (inflation rate) for services

tion, has developed an 11-item index of leading economic indicators as well as a "Long Leading Index" and a "Short Leading Index." Exhibit 13.7 shows the performance of the Conference Board's and ECRI's leading economic indicators over time.

The leading-indicator approach to forecasting requires no assumptions about what causes economic behavior. Instead, it is an empirical process that relies on statistically detected patterns among economic variables, which are then used to forecast turning points in overall economic activity. Because it relies on historical relationships to determine the index included, it sometimes gives incorrect signals. Also, no relationship exists between changes in the leading economic indicator index and the strength and duration of business expansions or recessions.

Just as the leading index helps us to see where we are going, the Conference Board's *coincident index of economic indicators* shows where we are. Similar to the LEI, the coincident index is composed of economic indexes whose trends have been found to change direction at about the same time the business cycle hits a peak or trough. The Board's *lagging index of economic indicators* discloses where the economy has been. It is composed of a variety of economic indexes, such as the unemployment rate, whose values follow the pattern of general economic activity but with a lag of several months. The economic variables comprising the coincident and lagging indicators are listed in Exhibit 13.6.

| **EXHIBIT 13.7** | Conference Board and Economic Cycle Research Institute Leading Indicators |

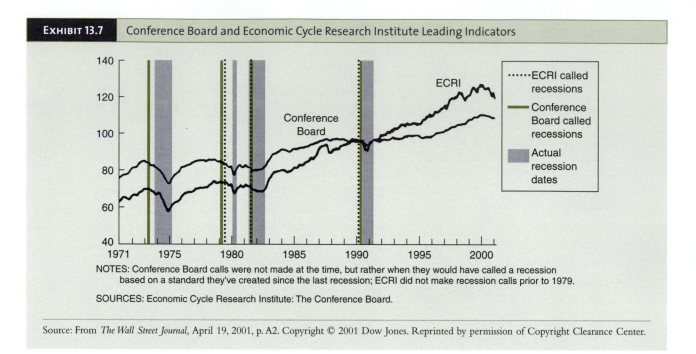

NOTES: Conference Board calls were not made at the time, but rather when they would have called a recession based on a standard they've created since the last recession; ECRI did not make recession calls prior to 1979.

SOURCES: Economic Cycle Research Institute: The Conference Board.

Source: From *The Wall Street Journal*, April 19, 2001, p. A2. Copyright © 2001 Dow Jones. Reprinted by permission of Copyright Clearance Center.

Economic statistics released by the government provide another source of helpful information about current economic trends, particularly concerning various economic sectors. These statistics are regularly published in *The Wall Street Journal* and other business periodicals.

ECONOMETRIC MODELS

Econometric models are the most sophisticated of the forecasting tools. Based on economic theory and mathematics, an *econometric model* specifies the statistical relationships between economic variables. The number of equations in econometric models ranges from a few to several hundred.

The more complex models allow computers to simulate the behavior of economic and industry variables for years into the future. They can be used to estimate the impact of virtually any important economic occurrence, including oil price changes, the effects of removing trade barriers, and currency devaluations. Econometric models also are useful in generating country market and asset class forecasts, which in turn can be used to allocate assets in a global portfolio.

Risks in Economic Forecasting[10]

Economic forecasting is not an easy task. Even professional economists and market strategists can and do disagree at times on the economy's direction. There are several reasons for this situation. The first we can label "group think." Recall that in our initial discussion of the secret of successful investing we mentioned that in order to consistently earn above-

---

[10]Our discussion in this section is based on D. Bostian, "The Nature of Effective Forecasts," in *Improving the Investment Decision Process—Better Use of Economic Inputs in Securities Analysis and Portfolio Management*, edited by H. Kent Baker (Charlottesville, VA: AIMR, 1992).

average risk-adjusted returns, our expectations (forecast) *must differ* from the market consensus, and our forecast *must be correct* more often than it is incorrect. Unfortunately, human psychology being what it is, it is difficult to stray from the consensus opinion of other professionals. Also, by keeping economic forecasts close to that of other economists, analysts can more easily deflect criticism if their estimates are incorrect.

Another reason is that too many analysts are shortsighted. They assume the future will be like the recent past—which is a great way to miss turning points and profit opportunities in the economy and financial markets. For example, too many analysts in the 1970s were stuck in the 1960s' growth mindset; too many analysts in the 1980s were still concerned about 1970s inflation. Too many analysts in the late 1980s had forgotten about risk and were spoiled by declining interest rates and rising stock prices; the crash of October 1987 and the minicrash of October 1989 helped to refresh their memories about risk. The bull markets of the 1990s climbed a wall of fear as investors looked at higher and higher valuations and feared another 1987-like crash. Finally, people assumed we had a "new economy" and could value start-up technology firms at stratospheric P/E multiples while ignoring profit-generating "old economy" firms. Reality hit in March 2000 when technology stocks fell precipitously and investors realized a slowing economy meant sales forecasts would not be met. The lesson? What happens in the future will be based on *future* events, not on simple extrapolations of the past.

A third reason may be that economists and other forecasters are overwhelmed by the quantity of statistical data available. Poor forecasting may be a problem of not seeing the forest because of the trees. Also, problems can arise with government-issued data, which is often preliminary in nature and later updated or revised.

Finally, economic forecasts are based on the forecaster's assumptions regarding what the Fed, Congress, and other countries' leaders will do. However, monetary policy, fiscal policy, real shocks, and political factors are difficult to predict.

Expectational Analysis

To help increase the usefulness of economic forecasts, we suggest a mix of quantitative and qualitative approaches to develop a *disciplined* approach to economic forecasting. The underlying concept is that the forecasting and analytical process should take into account (1) the current environment, (2) the analyst's assumptions behind his or her estimates, and (3) a procedure for monitoring data and events to identify changes in the environment or violations of the analyst's assumptions. This process is called *expectational analysis*. The key thought is to *identify and monitor key assumptions and variables* throughout the top-down approach.

For example, the first step in the top-down analysis is to forecast broad economic, political, and demographic trends. During this process, the analyst will have to make certain assumptions about monetary and fiscal policy, important political initiatives, and relationships with trading partners, among other items. At the end of this process, the analyst should have estimated important economic variables and identified the key assumptions made and what important variables or events must be monitored over time due to their importance to the forecast.

The second step of the top-down analysis is to relate the macroeconomic forecast to sectors of the economy. That is, how will the components of GDP (consumption, investment, government spending, and net exports) and their subcomponents change? What is different (or similar) about this time period from previous periods during this stage of the business cycle, or during this period of rising (or falling) inflation (or interest rates, or consumer expectations, etc.)? The analyst should identify key assumptions driving the analysis and monitor the important variables over time.

The third step is to relate the macro and sector forecast to specific industries. Microeconomics and industry competition factors (price elasticities, competitive positioning, technological trends, etc.) must be examined in the context of the assumed macroenvironment. The industry analyst must identify both macro and micro trends and influences that are especially relevant to his or her industry specialization and monitor them over time.

Finally, economic and industry analyses are applied to the individual firm, as we will examine in Chapter 15. As in the prior stages, the analyst needs to identify key assumptions in the top-down approach that are most important to support his or her recommendations concerning individual firms. These important economic–industry–firm assumptions must be monitored for changes that may affect the recommendation.[11]

ILLUSTRATIONS OF EXPECTATIONAL ANALYSIS

Occasionally *The Wall Street Journal* and other business periodicals and Web sites review the state of the economy and expectations for future stock-market performance. Many times they present two or more perspectives on the current state of the economy and stock market. Reading these different perspectives provides examples that allow us to identify the forecaster's key assumptions and insights. So doing gives insight into possible investment sectors to consider. Also, it gives information concerning what news events investors should monitor to determine if the forecaster's assumptions are holding true or are being violated. Exhibit 13.8 features some examples of market strategists' perceptions of the stock market in recent years.

EXHIBIT 13.8	Economic Assumptions to Monitor
Bearish	**Bullish**
EARLY 2001	
ECONOMIC OUTLOOK[a]	**ECONOMIC OUTLOOK**[b]
Corporate earnings will decline; the bottom of the economic slowdown has not yet been reached. The Fed's rate cuts are too late. Overall weakness in the U.S. economy due to technology and telecom overcapacity and excessive consumer debt.	Fed is cutting interest rates to stimulate the economy; recovery is ahead. Excesses of the tech stock bubble have been removed. We are going through an awkward transitional period with no dramatic downside risk in stock prices. Corporate earnings should rise.
INVESTMENT SUGGESTION	**INVESTMENT SUGGESTION**
Expect further declines in tech stocks as more air is let out of the bubble. Bonds are favored due to the poor outlook for stocks and the possibility for declining interest rates.	Technology stocks; overweight stocks as an asset class. *(continued)*

---

[11]Viewers of "Louis Rukeyser's Wall Street" (on MSNBC) will be familiar with expectational analysis, although it is not mentioned by name during the broadcast. Frequently, after guests discuss securities that they recommend for purchase, one of the panelists asks what would change their mind about their selections. This is expectational analysis—knowing why an asset is recommended for purchase and knowing what may change your opinion about its attractiveness.

Exhibit 13.8	Economic Assumptions to Monitor (*continued*)

Bearish	Bullish
EARLY 2002[c]	
ECONOMIC OUTLOOK	**ECONOMIC OUTLOOK**
Fed's policy may not create a turnaround; P/E ratios are still above historical averages despite market losses in recent years. Consumers are overspent and in too much debt to lead an economic recovery.	Hopes for economic recovery and growth in corporate profits to boost the stock market. Recovery is expected to begin in the first quarter of the year. Inflation will likely be low, helped by falling oil prices.
INVESTMENT SUGGESTION	**INVESTMENT SUGGESTION**
Overweight Treasury bonds and bonds selling at high yields relative to Treasuries. They will perform relatively well in a slow or declining economy.	Consider cyclical and small-cap stocks, which will likely lead a market recovery. Bonds, which will benefit from further drops in inflation, are good possibilities, too.
EARLY 2003[d]	
ECONOMIC OUTLOOK	**ECONOMIC OUTLOOK**
Pessimism about corporate profit growth, negative effects of geopolitical concerns on the economy.	Faster-than-expected earnings growth, no/little change in interest rates. Stimulative fiscal and monetary policy environment. Pessimism about Iraq, corporate accounting scandals, and earnings will diminish.
INVESTMENT SUGGESTION	**INVESTMENT SUGGESTION**
Reduce stock, increase bond allocation. Focus on buying stocks of high-quality companies with large dividends.	Increase allocation to stocks. Favor large-cap stocks over small caps for now. Focus on defensive stocks; avoid tech stocks, which are still recovering from the sector crash that started in Spring 2000.
EARLY 2004	
ECONOMIC OUTLOOK[e]	**ECONOMIC OUTLOOK**[f]
Slowdown in profit growth will slow or stop growth in capital spending and job creation.	Interest rates will not change much from 2003 levels; profit growth and capital spending growth will continue.
INVESTMENT SUGGESTION	**INVESTMENT SUGGESTION**
Buy stocks of firms producing consumer staples.	Consider stocks of technology firms and "rust belt" manufacturers as the economic growth cycle continues. For bond investors, consider buying bonds that offer better protection from inflation: high-yield bonds, emerging-market bonds, TIPS.

[a]Ken Brown, "Points of View: Economists See Darker Future Than Strategists," *The Wall Street Journal*, March 13, 2001, pp. C1, C2; Cassell Bryan-Low, "Bulls Remain Uncowed Amid Market's Slide," *The Wall Street Journal*, January 16, 2001, p. C12; E. S. Browning, "Is This Really a Bear Market or Some Other Animal?" *The Wall Street Journal*, January, 16, 2001, p. C1.

[b]Ibid.

[c]Both perspectives are based on comments in E. S. Browning, "Floating on the Winds of Uncertainty," *The Wall Street Journal*, January 2, 2002, pp. R1, R6; Gregory Zuckerman, "Bonds Outperformed Stocks Again in Banner Year for Debt Markets," *The Wall Street Journal*, January 2, 2002, p. R6.

[d]Quoted from *http://www.usatoday.com/money/markets/2002-01-02-stratpack.htm*.

[e]Richard Bernstein, Merrill Lynch; quoted from *http://www.usatoday.com/money/markets/us/2004-01-02-bear_x.htm*.

[f]Quotes from *http://www.usatoday.com/money/markets/us/2003-12-19-intro-story_x.htm*.

Although expectational analysis can involve quantitative models,[12] the analyst's expertise is involved in identifying the important driving variables behind the analysis and in knowing what questions to ask and what numbers and events to watch closely. A disciplined approach such as expectational analysis can help mitigate some of the practical problems, such as group think and simple extrapolation, that arise in forecasting. In addition, it forces discipline on the investment analysis process by removing some of the emotion from buy-and-sell decisions; if an assumption is violated, the recommendation needs to be reexamined, regardless of what the analyst may believe about the stock's attractiveness.

Industry Analysis

Now let's examine the second step of the top-down valuation process: industry analysis.[13] The economic setting is more than just the macroeconomy (the national and global factors such as exchange rates, inflation, interest rates, fiscal policy, and monetary policy). Economic analysis can and should also delve into the competitive structure—the microeconomics—of industries.

An *industry* is a set of businesses that produce similar products used by customers for similar purposes. We can define an industry broadly or narrowly, depending on the purposes of the analysis. For example, the "computer industry" includes a variety of specialty areas: software, hardware, and peripheral devices, as well as personal computers, servers, and mainframe computers. The federal government's North American Industry Classification System (NAICS) code system[14] assigns numbers to industries, ranging from a single digit for broad classifications (agriculture, for example) to seven digits for specific products. For practical purposes, most industry analysis is done at the two-, three-, or four-digit level. For example, the NAICS code "44" represents retail trade; "446" is for health and personal care stores; "4461" is a subcategory for health and personal care stores, and "44611" represents pharmacies and drug stores.

Links between the Economy and Industry Sectors

Economic trends can and do affect industry performance. To track the relationships between an analyst's economic expectations and expected industry performance, we can use expectational analysis to gauge the implications of new information on our original economic outlook and industry analysis.

---

[12]For a more quantitative review of links between the economy, stock market, and industries, see Frank K. Reilly and Keith C. Brown, *Investment Analysis and Portfolio Management,* 8th ed. (Mason, OH: South-Western, 2006).

[13]As it focuses on expectations, expectational analysis is relevant both to top-down and bottom-up analysts. Bottom-up analysts focus mainly on microeconomic, firm-specific factors that make a security an attractive purchase candidate (that is, it has a good story behind it). Bottom-up analysts would emphasize assumptions and key microeconomic variables; top-downers would examine both macro and micro factors. Nonetheless, both sets of analysts need to identify and monitor key assumptions and variables important to the investment decision.

[14]At the current time the government is phasing out the SIC (Standard Industrial Classification) system and phasing in NAICS; the transition should be complete soon. NAICS is an update of the SIC, which was developed in the 1930s and was oriented toward manufacturing and outputs. NAICS includes many new industries not present in SIC (such as convenience stores, bed-and-breakfasts, and many new electronic, software, and telecommunications industries) and is more process-oriented, not output-oriented, in its industry classifications. The number of broad industry categories in NAICS doubles those available in SIC, from ten to twenty. Most of the change is in service industries. For more information, see *http://www.census.gov/epcd/www/pdf/naicsdat.pdf.*

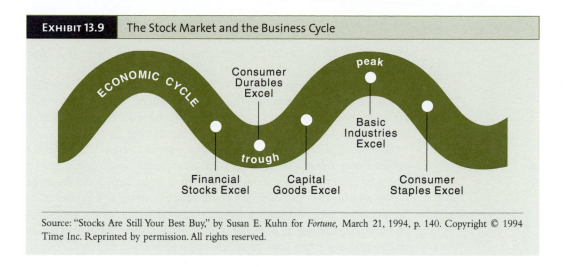

| **EXHIBIT 13.9** | The Stock Market and the Business Cycle |

Economic trends can take two basic forms: *cyclical changes* in the economy that arise from the ups and downs of the business cycle and *structural changes* that lack a cyclical pattern. Structural changes occur when the economy is undergoing a major change in organization (e.g., from a manufacturing to a service economy) or in how it functions (e.g., technological change).

Industry performance is related to the stage of the business cycle. What makes industry analysis challenging is that every business cycle is different and those who look only at history are in danger of missing the current and evolving trends that will determine future market performance. Switching from one industry group to another over the course of a business cycle is known as a *rotation strategy*. When trying to determine which industry groups will benefit from the next stage of the cycle, investors can apply expectational analysis.

Exhibit 13.9 presents a stylized graphic of which industry groups typically perform well in the different stages of the business cycle. Toward the end of a recession, financial stocks begin to rise in value as investors begin to anticipate a recovery. They anticipate that banks' earnings will rise as both the economy and loan demand recover. Brokerage houses may also be attractive investments; their sales and earnings will rise as investors trade securities and as businesses sell debt and equity during the economic recovery. These industry selections assume that the recession will end shortly, followed by positive economic news including increases in loan demand, housing construction, and security offerings.

After the economy has hit bottom and begins its recovery, consumer durable stocks typically make attractive investments. Such stocks include industries that produce expensive consumer items, such as cars, personal computers, refrigerators, lawn tractors, and snow blowers. These industries are attractive investments because a reviving economy will increase consumer confidence and personal income. Pent-up demand for expensive consumer purchases, delayed during the recession, may be fulfilled during the coming recovery.

Once businesses finally recognize the economy is recovering and current levels of consumer spending are sustainable, they begin to think about modernizing, renovating, or purchasing new equipment to satisfy rising demand, lower costs, expand markets, or provide better service to customers. Thus, capital goods industries become attractive investments. Examples of capital goods industries include heavy equipment manufacturers, machine and tool die makers, and airplane manufacturers.

Traditionally, toward the business cycle peak, the rate of inflation increases as demand starts to outstrip supply. Basic materials industries, which transform raw materials into finished products, become investor favorites. These industries include the oil, gold, aluminum, and timber industries. Because inflation has little influence on the cost of extracting or finishing these products, the higher prices allow these industries to experience higher profit margins.

During a recession, some industry sectors typically do better than others. Consumer staples, such as pharmaceuticals, food, and beverages, tend to perform better than other sectors because people still spend money on these necessities. As a result, these "defensive" industries generally maintain their values during market declines.

If a weak domestic economy means a weak currency, industries with large export components may benefit because their goods become more cost competitive in foreign markets. The most attractive industries will be those with large markets in growing economies.

In addition to industry or sector rotation strategies, *capitalization rotation* strategies may be attractive to some, that is, rotating among large-, mid-, and small-cap stocks. For example, a strengthening U.S. dollar will typically harm large-cap stocks more than small-cap stocks as larger firms have greater foreign presence and larger foreign sales volume. Low real interest rates will favor small caps over large caps as smaller firms generally use more debt financing and more variable-rate debt financing than larger firms.

Generally, investors should not invest with the current economic situation in mind because the efficient market has already incorporated current economic news into security prices. Rather, investors must forecast important economic variables three to six months into the future and invest accordingly while monitoring their key assumptions and variables.

Structural Influences on the Economy and Industries

Influences other than the economy are part of the business environment. Social trends and changes in technology as well as political and regulatory environments all play a role in affecting the cash flow and risk prospects of different industries.

SOCIAL INFLUENCES

Societal changes affect the economy and relevant industries in various ways. Changes in the composition of the population, lifestyle choices, and social values can lead to the rise and fall of industries, products, and corporate strategies irrespective of overall economic growth.

Between the 1990 and 2000 U.S. census, the U.S. population grew about 14 percent. The fastest-growing age group over this decade was those between the ages of thirty-four and fifty-four, which grew over 30 percent, while the number of twenty to thirty-four year olds shrank by about 5 percent.[15] Almost 13 percent of Americans are currently sixty-five or older, and this number is expected to reach 70 million by 2030. This changing age mix has implications for financial services, health care—even the retail sector since older people have different preferences and shopping habits than younger people. The changing age profile of Americans also has implications for resource availability, namely, a possible shortage of entry-level workers, leading to an increase in labor costs.

In terms of family lifestyle, in the 2000 census only 24 percent of homes were the "traditional" American family with a husband, a wife, and children under 18. The segment of households with children headed by single mothers had risen 25 percent since 1990. The increase in divorce rates, dual-career families, population shifts away from cities, and computer-

---

[15]Anonymous, "Census 2000: The New Demographics," *The Wall Street Journal,* May 15, 2001, p. B1.

based education and entertainment will continue to influence numerous industries, including housing, child care, automobiles, convenience and catalog shopping, services, and home entertainment.

Similarly, changes in society's values and outlook on issues can lead to changes in labor force participation, education, and consumption patterns. These, in turn, may have a positive or negative effect on different industries and sectors of the economy.

For example, changes in retail sales over time and across regions in the United States are mainly due to changes in population and per capita income. Still, this provides little guidance to an analyst studying the retail apparel sector or the drugstore industry. More helpful are studies that have found that different social factors influence the sales of the various subsectors of the aggregate retail industry.[16] For example, unmarried young singles were found to spend more money in furniture stores and restaurants and less at drugstores. "Full-nesters"—households with children—spend more money in virtually all store categories except for restaurants when compared to other households. Studies also found that the degree of mobility within a region, measured by relative automobile ownership, was statistically related to higher levels of spending in apparel, department, general merchandise, and variety stores; it had no impact on furniture store and drugstore sales. Another factor is the rise of Internet purchasing, which requires retailers to have "bricks and clicks"—both a physical ("bricks") and an Internet ("clicks") presence.

Such variables deal with the demand side of retailing. Studies have also found supply-side influences on retail spending per household. Factors such as assortment, service quality, and service quantity have been found to lead to higher retailing expenditures, although the size of the effect differs depending on the type of retailing establishment.

TECHNOLOGY

Trends in technology can affect both the competitiveness of an industry's product and its manufacturing and delivery processes. Changes in technology have spurred capital spending in technological equipment as firms try to use microprocessors and software as a means to gain competitive advantages.

For example, in the retail industry major retailers already use a great deal of technology. Bar code scanning and radio frequency identification (RFID) speed the checkout process and allow the firm to track inventory. Use of customer credit cards allows firms to track customer purchases and send custom-made sales announcements. Electronic data interchange (EDI) allows the retailer to electronically communicate with suppliers to order new inventory and pay accounts payable. Electronic funds transfer allows retailers to move funds quickly and easily between local banks and headquarters. Some forecasters envision "relationship merchandising," in which customer databases will allow closer links between retail stores and customer needs.[17]

POLITICS AND REGULATIONS

Because political change reflects social values, today's social trend may be tomorrow's law, regulation, or tax. The industry analyst needs to project and assess political changes relevant

---

[16]Charles A. Ingene, "Using Economic Data in Retail Industry Analysis," in *The Retail Industry—General Merchandisers and Discounters, Specialty Merchandisers, Apparel Specialty, and Food/Drug Retailers,* edited by Charles A. Ingene (Charlottesville, VA: AIMR, 1993), pp. 18–25.

[17]Carl E. Steidtmann, "General Trends in Retailing," in *The Retail Industry—General Merchandisers and Discounters, Specialty Merchandisers, Apparel Specialty, and Food/Drug Retailers,* edited by Charles A. Ingene (Charlottesville, VA: AIMR, 1993), pp. 6–9.

to the industry under study. In addition, the analyst must consider the effect of laws and regulations on the industry's future.

For example, patents give a legal monopoly to drug manufacturers to help them recover R&D costs and to give firms incentives to innovate. As drug patents expire, generic copies may legally be sold. Consumers and drug chains will soon experience substantial savings as generics are expected to account for over 55 percent of all prescriptions by 2004, up from 47 percent in 1999 and 35 percent in 1992.

Some regulations and laws are based on economic reasoning. Due to utilities' positions as natural monopolies, their rates must be reviewed and approved by a regulatory body.[18] The Food and Drug Administration protects consumers by reviewing new drugs. Public and worker safety concerns spurred the creation of the Consumer Product Safety Commission, Environmental Protection Agency, and laws such as OSHA.

Regulatory changes sometimes remove competitive obstacles. Changing markets and technology helped to spur the passage of the Gramm-Leach-Bliley Act, which reversed prior regulations that had separated aspects of the financial services industry—banking, insurance, investment banking, and investment services.

The retail industry is affected by several political and regulatory factors. One is the minimum-wage law, which specifies the minimum wage that can be paid to workers. A second factor is health-care costs. Employer-paid health insurance dramatically affects the labor costs (and thus the incentive to use part-time workers) of labor-intensive service industries such as retailing. Third, because goods must first be delivered to the stores, regulations that affect the cost of shipping by airplane, ship, or truck will affect retailers' costs. Finally, trends toward open international markets can assist retailers, because the elimination or reduction of tariffs and quotas will allow retailers to offer imported goods at lower prices and expand their international marketing.

Competitive Structure of an Industry

Porter's concept of *competitive strategy* is the search by a firm for a favorable competitive position in an industry.[19] The potential profitability of a firm is heavily influenced by the inherent profitability of its industry. Hence, industry analysts need to determine the competitive structure of their industry and examine the factors that determine the relative competitive position of firms within the industry.

Porter believes that the *competitive environment* of an industry—the intensity of competition among the firms in that industry—determines the ability of the firms to sustain above-average rates of return on invested capital. As seen in Exhibit 13.10, he suggests that five competitive forces determine the intensity of competition:

---

[18]Technology can change natural monopolies. We mentioned earlier how some firms are generating their own electrical power. Advancing technology resulted in AT&T losing its monopoly in the early 1980s. An antitrust suit filed against IBM in the 1960s was subsequently thrown out because changing computer technology and growing competition made such a suit moot. By the mid- and late-1990s, several states were allowing electric utilities, once considered a natural monopoly, to compete for customers in test markets. The U.S. government's antitrust case against Microsoft moved away from a demand to break up the firm, in part because of continuing hardware and software technological advances.

[19]Michael E. Porter, *Competitive Strategy: Techniques for Analyzing Industries and Competitors*, New York: Free Press, 1980; Michael Porter, "Industry Structure and Competitive Strategy; Keys to Profitability," *Financial Analysts Journal* 36, no. 4 (July–August 1980); and Michael Porter, *Competitive Advantage: Creating and Sustaining Superior Performance*, New York: Free Press, 1985.

| **Exhibit 13.10** | Forces Driving Industry Competition |

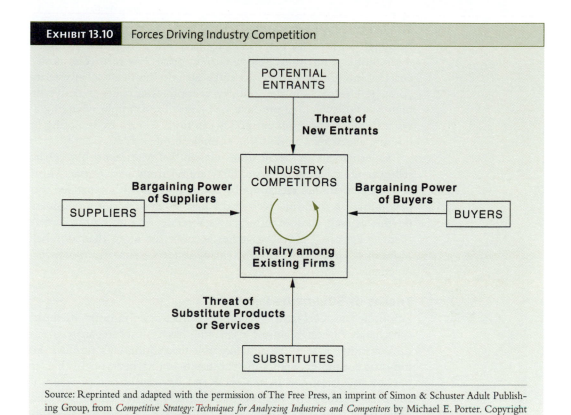

Source: Reprinted and adapted with the permission of The Free Press, an imprint of Simon & Schuster Adult Publishing Group, from *Competitive Strategy: Techniques for Analyzing Industries and Competitors* by Michael E. Porter. Copyright © 1980, 1998 by The Free Press.

1. Rivalry among existing competitors
2. Threat of new entrants
3. Threat of substitute products
4. Bargaining power of buyers
5. Bargaining power of suppliers

RIVALRY AMONG EXISTING COMPETITORS

The industry analyst must examine in each industry the levels of price-based and non-price-based (e.g., ads, quality claims, warranties, service, convenience) competition among domestic and international firms over time. Rivalry increases when many firms of relatively equal size compete in an industry. Slow growth causes competitors to fight for market share and increases competition. High fixed costs stimulate the desire to operate at full capacity, which can lead to price cutting and greater competition. Finally, exit barriers, such as specialized facilities or labor agreements, will keep firms in an industry despite below-average or negative rates of return.

For example, the retail drugstore (RDS) industry has enjoyed sales gains but with fewer competitors and lower profit margins. Managed health-care plans have been a driving force behind this trend. Stores are using segmentation strategies, enhanced customer service, and broadened product offerings (such as food, seasonal goods, and alternative (non-drug) therapies and "nutraceuticals") in an attempt to diversify from the low-margin prescription market.

THREAT OF NEW ENTRANTS

Although an industry may currently have few competitors within it, new firms may enter the industry at any time. Setting current prices low relative to costs keeps the threat of new entrants low. Other barriers to entry include the need to invest large financial resources to compete effectively in the industry, economies of scale, extensive distribution channels, and high costs of switching products or brands (for example, changing a computer or telephone system). Finally, government policy can restrict entry by imposing licensing requirements or limiting access to materials (for example, lumber, coal).

Supermarkets and retail stores such as Wal-Mart, who have pharmacies in their stores or sell over-the-counter drug products, are relatively new entrants in the RDS industry. Some drugstore chains are retaliating by opening stores with expanded food departments. Another new entrant is firms involved in the mail-order prescription business. Although many chains do this as well, newcomers such as Veterans Administration and American Association of Retired Persons (AARP) together account for more than one-half of all mail-order prescriptions. There now are also many Internet sites from which RDS products can be obtained.

THREAT OF SUBSTITUTE PRODUCTS

Substitute products limit the profit potential of an industry by limiting the prices that firms can charge. Although almost everything has a substitute, analysts must determine how close the substitute is in price and function to an industry's product. For example, in the food industry, consumers constantly substitute among beef, pork, chicken, and fish, or they may opt for vegetarianism. In the RDS industry, the threat of a substitute product is rather a threat of a substitute delivery system that improves consumer convenience. Supermarkets, other retail stores, mail order, and the Internet have grown as substitute delivery systems to offer consumers many ways to purchase the items they need. Most drugstore chains have responded with expanded delivery options, from mail to Internet ordering.

BUYER BARGAINING POWER

When they bid down prices or demand higher quality or more services, buyers influence industry profitability by bargaining among competitors. When they purchase a large volume relative to the sales of a supplier, buyers become powerful. Buyers will be more conscious of the costs of items that represent a significant percentage of the firm's total costs. In addition, buyers can affect an industry's competitive structure if they decide to vertically integrate and start supplying the product in-house rather than purchase it from an existing vendor.

In the RDS industry, managed-care providers wield the buyer bargaining power. As third-party payers, their prescription-drug reimbursement rate policies have cut into RDS prescription sales profits. The industry is reacting to this by seeking to diversify their product base to lessen the impact of large managed-care providers on overall industry sales.

SUPPLIER BARGAINING POWER

Suppliers can alter future industry returns if they increase prices or reduce the quality or services they provide. Suppliers (which can include raw material and other input providers, such as labor unions) are more powerful if they are few and more concentrated than the industry to which they sell and if they supply critical input for which few if any substitutes exist to several industries. Similar to buyer bargaining power, a supplier can change the competitive structure of an industry by deciding to vertically integrate forward in order to produce the final product.

The suppliers of the RDS industry's mainstay products are pharmaceutical firms. RDS firms have historically been price-takers; they have tried to cut costs and increase efficiencies to maintain profitability as pharmaceutical prices rose while managed-care reimbursements fell. Some drugstores have sought legal remedy by filing lawsuits against several pharmaceutical firms, alleging illegal discriminatory pricing.

To summarize, an investor can analyze these competitive forces to determine the intensity of the competition in an industry and assess its long-run profit potential. Analysts should examine each of these factors for every industry and develop a relative competitive-force profile. It is important to periodically update this analysis because an industry's competitive structure can and will change over time.

Industry Life-Cycle Analysis

Another way to predict industry sales is to view the industry over time and divide its development into stages. The number of stages in this *industry life-cycle analysis* can vary; a five-stage model would include the following:

1. Pioneering development
2. Rapidly accelerating industry growth
3. Mature industry growth
4. Stabilization and market maturity
5. Deceleration of growth and decline

Exhibit 13.11 shows the growth path of sales during each stage. The vertical scale reflects sales levels; the horizontal scale represents different time periods. To estimate industry sales, an analyst must predict the length of time for each stage.

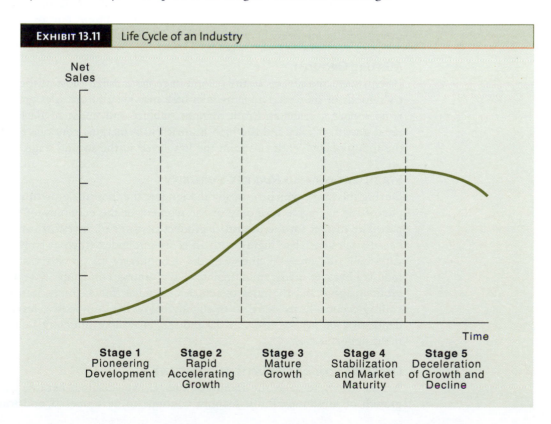

EXHIBIT 13.11　Life Cycle of an Industry

Net Sales

Time

Stage 1	Stage 2	Stage 3	Stage 4	Stage 5
Pioneering Development	Rapid Accelerating Growth	Mature Growth	Stabilization and Market Maturity	Deceleration of Growth and Decline

Besides sales estimates, this analysis of an industry's life cycle can also provide some insights into risk, profit margins, and earnings growth. The profit margin series typically peaks early in the total cycle and then levels off and declines as competition is attracted by the early success of the industry.

To illustrate the contribution of life-cycle stages to sales estimates, we will briefly describe these stages and their identifiable characteristics. The current growth stage of an industry can be determined by comparing its characteristics to the following factors.

PIONEERING DEVELOPMENT

This stage begins following some type of marketing or technological breakthrough. The market for the industry's product or service during this time is small, and firms incur major development costs. Cash flow is usually negative as cash is reinvested to finance growth, and outside financing sources usually are tapped to finance growth. Because of an uncertain industry future and the competition to come, it is difficult to identify "winners" at this stage.

RAPID ACCELERATING GROWTH

During this stage, a market develops for the product or service and demand becomes substantial. The limited number of firms in the industry face little competition, and individual firms can experience substantial backlogs. The profit margins are high. The high profit levels attract new entrants; in the ensuing competitive battle some firms will ultimately be forced to exit the industry. Over time, the industry builds its productive capacity as existing firms and new entrants attempt to meet excess demand. High sales growth and high profit margins that increase as firms become more efficient cause industry and firm profits to explode. Some firms emerge as industry leaders, both in terms of product offerings and market share. These firms may be attractive for investment purposes—if their shares are not overpriced. Some firms may begin to pay small cash dividends.

MATURE GROWTH

By this stage, the success in the second stage has satisfied most of the demand for the industry's goods or services. The large sales base may keep future sales growth above normal, but it no longer accelerates. Profit margins stabilize and begin to decline to normal levels as rapid growth of sales and the high historic profit margins continue to attract competitors to the industry. Dividends rise from the low levels in the second stage.

STABILIZATION AND MARKET MATURITY

During this stage, which is usually the longest, the industry growth rate matches the growth rate of the aggregate economy or the segment of the economy of which the industry is a part. The market for the industry's product is saturated. Investors can estimate growth easily because sales correlate highly with an economic index (such as consumption expenditures). Although sales grow in line with the economy, profit growth varies by firms within the industry because management ability differs among companies. Competition produces tight profit margins, and the rates of return on capital (for example, return on assets, return on equity) eventually are equal to or slightly below the competitive level. More generous dividends may be paid as firms in the industry may have difficulty finding attractive reinvestment opportunities.

DECELERATION OF GROWTH AND DECLINE

At this life-cycle stage, the industry's sales growth declines because of shifts in demand or growth of substitutes. Profit margins continue to be squeezed, and some firms experience low profits or even losses. Firms that remain profitable may show low rates of return on capital. A current example of an industry in this stage is the U.S. cigarette industry because of a changing social and political climate, i.e., a shift in demand.

The industry life cycle can be invigorated in any stage by product innovations that attract new consumers to use the product or that convince existing consumers to buy the new product. Traditional roller skates have been replaced by in-line skates and have led to growing popularity of street hockey in some communities. Bicycles have been redesigned to be lighter and more durable. The game industry has been invigorated by the advent of computerized, high-quality graphic entertainment systems. Once found only in athletic clubs, smaller, durable exercise equipment is now found in many homes.

Sources of Industry Information

Careful research is required to properly conduct an industry analysis. We discuss several major sources of industry information in this section and provide additional source listings in the Investments Online feature.

Standard & Poor's Industry Survey covers over fifty major domestic industries. Coverage in each area is divided into a basic analysis and a current analysis. The basic analysis examines the long-term prospects for a particular industry based on an analysis of historical trends and problems. Major segments of the industry are spotlighted, and a comparative analysis of the principal companies in the industry is included. The current analysis discusses recent developments and provides statistics for an industry and specific companies along with appraisals of the industry's investment outlook.

Standard & Poor's Analysts Handbook contains selected income account and balance sheet items along with related financial ratios for S&P's industry groups. These fundamental income and balance-sheet indexes allow comparisons of the major factors bearing on group stock price movements.

Value Line Industry Survey is an integral part of the *Value Line Investment Survey*. The reports for the 1,700 companies included are divided into ninety-one industries and updated by industry. In the binder containing these reports, the industry evaluation precedes the individual company reports. The industry report contains summary statistics for the industry on assets, earnings, and important ratios, similar to what is included for companies. An industry stock price index is included, as well as a table that provides comparative data for all the individual companies in the industry ranked on timeliness, safety, and financial strength. The discussion considers the major factors affecting the industry and concludes with an investment recommendation for the industry.

Other valuable sources of industry information include trade associations, trade magazines, the business press, corporate SEC filings, and industry-average data, available from Dun and Bradstreet, the *IRS Corporation Source Book of Statistics of Income*, and publications from the U.S. Census Bureau (such as the *Census of Manufactures* or the *Census of Retail Trade*) and the Bureau of Labor Statistics (such as the *Wholesale Price Index*). Web browsers and Internet-based research from reliable sources offer additional opportunities to research industry and competitor characteristics. Exhibit 13.12 lists several industry references for the retailing industry.

Among the most valuable information sources are field interviews with industry management, members of sales forces, customers, suppliers, union leaders, technical consultants, and trade association officials. Since these may offer contradictory perspectives, the analyst must cross-check references and sources to construct a consistent evaluation.

Exhibit 13.12	Industry References for the Retail Industry	

Publication	Frequency of Publication	Content
Chain Store Age http://www.chainstoreage.com	Monthly	Merchandising information, operating techniques, training material, and industry news for headquarters executives and store managers
Drug Store News http://www.drugstorenews.com	Bimonthly	National news and features of the drugstore industry
Drug Topics http://www.drugtopics.com	Semimonthly	National news and features of the drugstore industry
MMR (Mass Market Retailers) http://www.massmarketretailers.com	Biweekly	Features stories on mass merchandisers, drug chains, and supermarkets
Progressive Grocer http://www.progressivegrocer.com	Monthly	Includes articles about trends in the industry, companies, and statistics
Supermarket News http://www.supermarketnews.com	Weekly	Covers industry in general, with financial highlights and weekly chronology of major companies

Investments Online

The Internet contains a great many sources for economic and financial market information. Many banks, research firms, investment banks, stock brokerages, and government agencies feature data, analysis, or commentaries on their Web sites.

U.S. Government Sources

It should come as no surprise that the main source of information on the U.S. economy is the federal government, which issues a variety of publications on the topic.

Federal Reserve Bulletin (http://www.federalreserve.gov/pubs/bulletin) is a monthly publication issued by the Board of Governors of the Federal Reserve System. It is the primary source for almost all monetary data. In addition, it contains figures on financial markets, including interest rates and some stock-market statistics; data for corporate finance, including profits, assets, and liabilities of corporations; extensive nonfinancial statistics on output, the labor force, and the GNP; and a major section on international finance.

Survey of Current Business (http://www.bea.doc.gov/bea/pubs.htm) is a monthly publication issued by the U.S. Department of Commerce that gives details on national income and production figures. It is probably the best source for current, detailed information on all segments of the gross domestic product (GDP) and national income. It also contains industrial production data for numerous segments of the economy.

Economic Indicators (http://www.gpoaccess.gov/indicators/browse.html) is a monthly publication prepared for the Joint Economic Committee by the Council of Economic Advisers. It contains monthly and annual data on output, income, spending, employment, production, prices, money and credit, federal finance, and international economies.

The *Quarterly Financial Report (QFR) (http://www.census.gov/csd/qfr)* is prepared by the Federal Trade Commission and contains aggregate statistics on the financial position of U.S. corporations. Based on an extensive quarterly sample survey, the QFR presents estimated statements of income and retained earnings, balance sheets, and related financial and operating ratios for all manufacturing corporations. The publication also includes data on mining and trade corporations. The statistical data are classified by industry and, within the manufacturing group, by size.

Each January, the president of the United States prepares the *Economic Report of the President (http://www.gpoaccess.gov/*

eop), which he transmits to the Congress. The report indicates what has transpired during the past year and discusses the current environment and what the president considers the major economic problems to face the country during the coming year. An appendix contains statistical tables relating to income, employment, and production. The tables typically provide annual data from the 1940s and in some instances from 1929.

Statistical Abstract of the United States (*http://www .census.gov/statab/www/*), published annually since 1878, is the standard summary of statistics on the social, political, and economic organization of the United States. Prepared by the U.S. Bureau of the Census, it is designed to serve as a convenient statistical reference and as a guide to other statistical publications and sources.

PUBLICATIONS OF FEDERAL RESERVE BANKS

The Federal Reserve System (*http://www.federalreservebanks .org*) is divided into twelve Federal Reserve districts; each of the Federal Reserve district banks has a research department that issues periodic reports. A notable source of analysis and data is the St. Louis Federal Reserve Bank (*http://www.stlouisfed .org*), which publishes statistical releases that contain extensive national and international data (*http://research.stlouisfed .org/fred2*). The Philadelphia Fed's site includes access to the Livingston Surveys and Surveys of Professional Forecasters (*http://www.phil.frb.org/econ/index.html*); both provide professional economists' judgments about future economic trends.

NON-U.S. ECONOMIC DATA

In addition to data on the U.S. economy, data on other countries in which you might consider investing are also important to acquire. Some of the available sources follow.

The *Economic Intelligence Unit* (*http://www.eiu.com*) publishes 83 separate quarterly reviews and an annual supplement covering the economic and business conditions and outlook for 160 countries. For each country the reviews consider the economy, trade and finance, trends in investment and consumer spending, along with comments on its political environment. Tables contain data on economic activity and foreign trade.

The Organization for Economic Cooperation and Development, or OECD (*http://www.oecd.org*), publishes semiannual surveys showing recent trends and policies and assessing short-term prospects for each country. An annual volume, *His-*

torical Statistics, contains annual percentage change data for the most recent twenty years.

The *Economist* (*http://www.economist.com*) prepares country reports that contain extensive economic and demographic statistics on more than 100 countries around the world. Of greater importance is a detailed discussion that critically analyzes the current economic and political environment in the country and considers the future outlook. You may subscribe to reports for a selected list of countries or for all of them. The reports are updated twice yearly.

United Nations Statistical Yearbook (*http://unstats.un.org/ unsd*) is a basic reference book that contains extensive economic statistics on all UN countries (population, construction, industrial production, and so on). *United Nations Yearbook of International Trade Statistics* is an annual report on import statistics over a four-year period for each of 166 countries. The commodity figures for each country are given by commodity code. *United Nations Yearbook of National Accounts Statistics* is a comprehensive source of national account data that contains detailed statistics for 155 countries on domestic product and consumption expenditures, national income, and disposable income for a twelve-year period.

Eurostatistics, a monthly publication of the *Statistical Office of the European Communities (Luxembourg)* (*http://europa.eu .int*), contains statistics for short-term economic analysis in ten European community countries and the United States. It generally includes data for six years on industrial production, employment and unemployment, external trade, prices, wages, and finance.

International Financial Statistics, a monthly publication (with a yearbook issue) of the International Monetary Fund (*http:// www.imf.org*), is an essential source of current financial statistics such as exchange rates, fund position, international liquidity, money and banking statistics, interest rates (including LIBOR), prices, and production.

International Monetary Fund Balance of Payments Yearbook (*http://www.imf.org*) is a two-part publication. The first part contains detailed balance-of-payments figures for more than 110 countries, and the second part contains world totals for balance-of-payments components and aggregates.

http://www.morganstanley.com The Web site of Morgan Stanley includes the Global Economic Forum. The Forum is a compilation of reports filed by economists located around the world. The Forum is updated daily, and prior reports are available in an archive. This site features daily updates of the MSCI indexes of international markets.

http://www.globalinsight.com The Web site of Global Insight features information and links to global economic and industry news.

http://www.whitehouse.gov/fsbr/esbr.html This is the Economics Statistics Briefing Room of the White House Web site. It includes links to data produced by certain federal agencies.

http://www.worldbank.org World Bank's site features useful global data and articles on a variety of economic policy and foreign investment topics.

INDUSTRY

The Web can help researchers find information about an industry, but many industry analyses and studies are available online only to registered and paying clients of research firms, investment banks, and brokerage houses. You probably will not find up-to-date Porter analyses free on the Internet, at least not for a wide variety of industries. Instead, in Web searches for industry information you can focus on exploring Web sites of competitors in the industry. You also may find trade group Web sites through key word searches using terms and phrases relevant to the industry you wish to study.

Because we used the retail drugstore industry as our example industry in this chapter, we include in the following list several sites relevant to the RDS industry.

http://www.lf.com This is the home page for Lebhar-Friedman, Inc., a publisher and provider of information about retailers.

http://www.nacds.org Sponsored by the National Association of Chain Drug Stores, this page contains much data relevant to chain drugstores, from sales in different product categories to projected numbers of prescriptions. It also offers news and links to related sites.

http://www.healthcaredistribution.org The Web site of the Healthcare Distribution Management Association features links to managed-care issues, public policy issues, information for pharmacies, consumers, the press, manufacturers, analysts, and investors. It also contains links to a number of related sites.

http://retailindustry.about.com A part of the about.com Web site, this site contains a number of links to other Web sites that deal with the retail industry and the analysis of the retail industry.

http://www.valuationresources.com This site contains links to industry information sources and economic information sources. Industry report information is segmented by SIC code.

Summary

- Economic analysis should give the analyst insight into the determinants of asset value, namely, the level of interest rates, asset risk premiums, and asset cash flow. In efficient markets, it will be difficult to find assets with intrinsic values different from their current market prices. A successful analyst must have insights that differ from the market consensus and must be right often enough to outperform the market on a risk-adjusted basis over time.

- Analysts use many concepts and forecasting tools to identify long- and short-term trends in the economy, which they then relate to industry and firm conditions in top-down analysis. These tools will work best when combined with human judgment and experience in a disciplined process that identifies and monitors the analyst's key assumptions and variables over time. This

will help the analyst determine when to sell currently owned securities and when securities previously shunned should be considered for purchase.

- Industries are affected by economic events and trends. The rise and fall of the business cycle will make some industries look alternately attractive and unattractive for investment purposes. Fluctuations in such economic variables as inflation, interest rates, or exchange rates may affect the investment potential of an industry irrespective of the stage of the business cycle.

- Other structural influences affect industries. Changing social factors, such as demographics, lifestyles, and values, may affect industries over and above the effect of the business cycle. Similarly, changing technology and political and regulatory environments can also affect industry prospects. Throughout the process of industry analysis, the analyst needs to identify and monitor the key assumptions and variables that drive the forecast.

- An important part of industry analysis is the examination of five factors that determine the competitive environment in an industry, which in turn affects its

long-run profitability. In addition, an industry's life cycle stage may affect investors' desires to invest at the current time.

- Analysts can access a wealth of industry information from a variety of sources. Thorough research will provide the details needed for competent analysis.

QUESTIONS

1. How can what you have learned about efficient markets and valuation analysis assist the process of analyzing stocks using the top-down approach?
2. Why is it important to develop sectoral forecasts of GDP?
3. Describe how exchange rate changes affect U.S. exports, imports, and interest rates.
4. What factors affect exchange rates over time?
5. What is the expected effect on U.S. dollar exchange rates of each of the following events?
   a. The U.S. inflation rate increases relative to the rates of other economies.
   b. German interest rates rise.
   c. The Fed moves to increase interest rates.
   d. The United States goes into a recession.
   e. The Fed purchases U.S. dollars in the currency market.
6. Describe how monetary policy and fiscal policy affect the economy.
7. What factors influence long-term expectations of economic growth? Explain their effect on the economy.
8. What factors influence short-term expectations of economic growth? Explain their effect on the economy.
9. Describe the various indicators of inflation trends. How do they differ from one another?
10. Define leading, coincident, and lagging economic indicators. Give an example of an economic index in each category and discuss why you think the index belongs in that particular category.
11. It is fairly easy to determine the effect of a change in interest rates on the price of a bond. In contrast, some observers contend that it is harder to estimate the effect of such a change on common stocks. Discuss this contention.
12. What are the risks of forecasting the economy?
13. What is expectational analysis?
14. *CFA Examination Level II*
    The Board of Directors of Evergreen Pension Fund asked consultant Whitney Hannah to review two approaches to forecasting economic trends: econometric and consensus.
    a. Discuss whether econometric approaches and consensus approaches to forecasting economic trends are different or similar with respect to:

    i. Role of historical data
    ii. Number of analysts reflected in the forecast
    iii. Nature of assumptions about future economic relationships (6 minutes)
  b. State and discuss whether econometric approaches or consensus approaches to forecasting economic trends are more likely to be distorted by:
    i. Group think
    ii. Inability to test sensitivity
    iii. Simultaneity
    iv. Data mining (8 minutes)
  c. State and discuss whether econometric approaches or consensus approaches to forecasting economic trends are more likely to reflect the following strengths:
    i. Ability to identify turning points in trends
    ii. Ease of construction
    iii. Ability to capture multiple market influences (6 minutes)

15. Some observers have contended that differences in the performance of various firms within an industry limit the usefulness of industry analysis. Discuss this contention.
16. How do cyclical changes in the economy differ from structural changes? How do each affect industry analysis?
17. Discuss some examples of structural changes that may affect an industry.
18. You believe the current recession is about to end. How would you adjust an equity portfolio to take advantage of your forecast?
19. As a stock-portfolio manager, you believe the current growth phase of the business cycle will persist for the next year. A friend of yours who manages a portfolio at a rival firm believes the economic cycle has peaked and a recession will soon begin. How might the composition of your portfolios differ from each other?
20. Identify an industry that is likely to do well and one that is likely to do poorly in each of the following situations:
    a. Rising inflation
    b. Health-care reform places price controls on the pharmaceutical industry
    c. Interest rates decline
    d. The dollar strengthens against other currencies

e. Oil prices rise

f. The average age of the U.S. population is rising

21. How do demographics, lifestyles, and social values affect industry analysis?

22. Assume that you are analyzing an industry in the fourth stage of the industrial life cycle. How would you react if your industry–economic analysis predicted that sales per share for this industry would increase by 20 percent? Discuss your reasoning.

23. Discuss at what stage in the industrial life cycle you would like to discover a firm. Justify your choice.

24. Discuss an example of the impact of one of the five competitive forces on an industry's profitability.

CFA 25. *CFA Sample Examination Level I*

Which of the following are characteristics of the maturity stage of the industry life cycle:

a. Slowly growing sales

b. A highly competitive environment

c. Many new competitors enter the market

d. Price tends to be a major competitive weapon

e. Technological advances occur

CFA 26. *CFA Examination Level II*

Katherine Cooper is preparing a report on the optical network component business. She begins her research by analyzing the competitive conditions of the industry.

One of the dominant firms in the industry is Rubylight Inc. Below is an excerpt from the President's Letter in the annual report.

> **Rubylight Inc.**
> **2000 Annual Report**
> **Excerpt from President's Letter**
> **The reference number preceding each sentence is for your use in answering the question.**
>
> [1]Rubylight Inc. had an exceptional year in 2000. [2]The results in almost every corner of the business exceeded our expectations. [3]Sales at Rubylight climbed 73 percent over fiscal 1999 to $135 million, representing the strongest year-on-year sales growth in the company's history. [4]Our gross margin remained constant, compared to the prior year, at a respectable 67 percent. [5]We managed to maintain our margins, despite an increase in direct materials cost, through an improvement in product mix and price increases. [6]The capital markets have rewarded us for this superior financial performance; the company's stock price closed the year at an all time high. [7]We have an outstanding team here at Rubylight, deserving high praise for performance.
>
> [8]The backlog (unfulfilled orders) expanded by 39 percent. [9]This was principally due to an inabil-

ity of our supplier to ship two application-specific integrated circuits ("ASIC") that are critical to the superior performance of the Rubylight product. [10]Although the ASIC designs are owned by Rubylight, the integrated circuits must be fabricated in highly specialized facilities, of which there are only two worldwide. [11]The extremely capital intensive nature of these facilities prevents us from manufacturing the integrated circuits ourselves. [12]Shortages of electronic component supplies and fabrication time are worldwide phenomena that have also plagued our major competitor.

[13]One of the strategic imperatives in the optical components industry is to get your components incorporated into the designs of your customers' products, known as "design wins," which makes it very expensive for the customer to make a component substitution. [14]Early in the year we announced the appointment of Dr. Brian Richards as the Chief Technology Officer. [15]Dr. Richards is one of the pioneers of the optical switching industry and has numerous patents to his credit. [16]He and his very fine team in our Research and Development department continue to work closely with our customers to ensure design wins for the next generation of products.

[17]On the competitive landscape, we have seen some interesting developments over the last year. [18]Our major competitor has focused on building distribution in the European market. [19]That competitor appears to be exiting North America and the Far East, which are our strongholds. [20]However, we have seen several start-ups enter the North American market. [21]They have been able to attract significant venture capital financing, which gives them greater ability to build brand recognition than start-ups have enjoyed in the past.

[22]On the technology front, recent developments in micro-electronic mechanical technology have created the promise of a dramatic improvement in product performance. [23]Typically the start-ups have been focused on this technology.

Name each of the competitive forces faced by Rubylight, using Porter's five-force model. Determine whether each competitive force is favorable or unfavorable for Rubylight. Select, for each competitive force, only two sentences from the President's Letter that support whether the competitive force is favorable or unfavorable for Rubylight.

Note: No sentence may be selected more than once; only the sentence reference numbers are needed for your selection. (16 minutes)

PROBLEMS

1. What is the expected level of U.S. interest rates based on the following conditions?
   a. Expected change in exchange rate is 4 percent; foreign interest rate is 9 percent.
   b. Expected change in exchange rate is −4 percent; foreign interest rate is 9 percent.
   c. Expected change in exchange rate is 2.5 percent; foreign interest rate is 18 percent.
   d. Expected change in exchange rate is −1.3 percent; foreign interest rate is 5 percent.

2. The current rate of inflation is 3 percent and long-term bonds are yielding 8 percent. You estimate that the rate of inflation will increase to 6 percent. What do you expect to happen to long-term bond yields? Compute the effect of this change in inflation on the price of a fifteen-year, 8 percent coupon bond.

3. You are told an investment firm projects a 10 percent return next year for U.S. stocks while European stocks are expected to give investors a 13 percent return.
   a. Assuming that all risks except exchange rate risk are equal and that you expect the euro/U.S. dollar exchange rate to go from 1.20 to 1.10 during the year, discuss where you would invest and why.
   b. Discuss where and why you would invest if you expected the exchange rate to go from 1.20 to 1.30.

4. Prepare a table showing the percentage change for each of the past ten years in (a) the Consumer Price Index (all items), (b) nominal GDP, (c) real GDP (in constant dollars), and (d) the GDP deflator. Discuss how much of nominal growth was caused by *real* growth and how much was caused by inflation. Is the outlook for next year any different from last year? Discuss.

5. *CFA Examination Level I*
   Assume you are a fundamental research analyst following the automobile industry for a large brokerage firm. Identify and briefly explain the relevance of *three* major economic time series, economic indicators, or economic data items that would be significant to automotive industry and company research. (12 minutes)

6. World Stock Market Indexes are published weekly in *Barron's* in the section labeled "Market Laboratory/ Stocks." Consult the latest available issue of this publication and the issue one year earlier to find the following information.
   a. Show the closing value of each index on each date relative to the yearly high for each year.
   b. Name the countries with markets in downtrends. Name those in uptrends.
   c. For the two time periods, calculate the year's change relative to the beginning price. Based on this and the range of annual values, which markets seem the most volatile?

7. Using a source of financial data such as *Barron's* or *The Wall Street Journal,* do the following.
   a. Plot the weekly percentage changes in the S&P 400 index (*y*-axis) versus comparable weekly percentage changes in the M2 money supply figures (*x*-axis) for the past ten weeks. Do you see a positive, negative, or zero correlation? (Monetary aggregates will lag the stock-market aggregates.)
   b. Examine the relationship between the weekly percentage changes in the S&P 400 index and the DJIA for the past ten weeks. Plot the weekly percentage changes in each index using S&P as the *x*-axis and DJIA as the *y*-axis. Discuss your results as they relate to diversification. Do a similar comparison for the S&P 400 and the Nikkei indexes and discuss these results.

8. Select three industries from the *S&P Analysts Handbook* with different demand factors. For each industry, indicate what economic series you would use to help you predict the growth for the industry. Discuss why the economic series selected is relevant for this industry.

9. Prepare a scatterplot for one of the industries in Problem 8 of industry sales per share and observations from the economic series you suggested for this industry. Do this for the most recent ten years using information available in the *S&P Analysts Handbook.* Based on the results of the scatterplot, discuss whether the economic series was closely related to this industry's sales.

10. Using the *S&P Analysts Handbook,* calculate the means for the following variables of the S&P 400 and the industry of your choice during the past ten years.
    a. Price–earnings multiplier
    b. Retention rate
    c. Return on equity
    d. Equity turnover
    e. Net profit margin
    (*Note:* Each of these entries is a ratio, so take care when averaging.) Briefly comment on how your industry and the S&P 400 differ for each of the variables.

11. Where is your industry in its industrial life cycle? Justify your answer.

12. Evaluate your industry in terms of the five factors that determine an industry's competitive structure. Discuss your expectations for this industry's long-run profitability.

13. Industry information can be found in Barron's *Market Laboratory/Economic Indicators.* Using issues over the past six months, plot the trend for the following.
    a. Auto production
    b. Auto inventories (domestic and imports)
    c. Newsprint production

d. Newsprint inventories

e. Business inventories

What tentative conclusions do these data support regarding the current economic environment?

14. *CFA Examination Level II*

Universal Auto is a large multinational corporation headquartered in the United States. For segment reporting purposes, the company is engaged in two businesses: production of motor vehicles and information processing services.

The motor vehicle business is by far the larger of Universal's two segments. It consists mainly of domestic U.S. passenger car production, but also includes small truck manufacturing operations in the U.S. and passenger car production in other countries. This segment of Universal has had weak operating results for the past several years, including a large loss in 1992. While the company does not break out the operating results of its domestic passenger car business, that part of Universal's business is generally believed to be primarily responsible for the weak performance of its motor vehicle segment.

Idata, the information processing services segment of Universal, was started by Universal about fifteen years ago. This business has shown strong, steady growth that has been entirely internal; no acquisitions have been made.

A research report on Universal Auto was recently written by Paul Adam, a CFA candidate. In an excerpt from the research report, Adam states:

> Based on our assumption that Universal will be able to increase prices significantly on U.S. passenger cars in 1993, we project a multibillion dollar profit improvement . . .

a. Discuss the concept of an industrial life cycle by describing *each* of its *five* phases. (8 minutes)

b. Identify where *each* of Universal's two primary businesses, passenger cars and information processing, is in such a cycle. (2 minutes)

c. Discuss how product pricing should differ between Universal's two businesses, based on the location of each in the industrial life cycle. (4 minutes)

Adam's research report continued as follows:

> With a business recovery already under way, the expected profit surge should lead to a much higher price for Universal Auto stock. We strongly recommend purchase.

d. Discuss the business cycle approach to investment timing. (Your answer should describe actions to be taken on *both* stocks *and* bonds at different points over a typical business cycle.) (6 minutes)

e. Assuming Adam's assertion is correct—that a business recovery is already under way, evaluate the timeliness of his recommendation to purchase Universal Auto, a cyclical stock, based on the business cycle approach to investment timing. (6 minutes)

15. *CFA Examination Level II*

Pat Johnson, CFA, is a stock analyst who follows the toy industry. Johnson has concluded that the two major macroeconomic factors influencing the toy industry's U.S. domestic nominal sales (in $ millions, $SALES_t$) are

- the population (in millions) of children 3–14 years old ($CHILD_t$), and
- nominal per capita GDP in U.S. dollars (GDP_t).

Using monthly data, Johnson obtains the following regression results (*t*-values shown in parentheses):

$$SALES_t = 62.10 + 87.50\ CHILD_t + 0.1974\ GDP_t$$
$$\quad\ \ (2.49)\quad\ (2.02)\qquad\qquad (3.03)$$

Number of observations:	30
Unadjusted R^2:	0.9699
F-statistic:	112.64
Multiple standard error:	13.31
Correlation between CHILD and GDP:	0.25 (*t*-value = 0.75)

a. Evaluate the goodness of fit of the regression equation. (4 minutes)

b. Calculate, based on the regression equation,

i. the forecasted "industry nominal sales volume" if nominal per capita GDP (GDP_t) is expected to be $500 and the population of children 3–14 years old ($CHILD_t$) is expected to be 100 million;

ii. the approximate 95 percent confidence interval for the predicted nominal sales. Show your calculations. (6 minutes)

Johnson's results are evaluated by the firm's chief economist, Susan Yost, CFA. Yost suggests that the results can be improved by removing the effects of inflation on $SALES_t$ and GDP_t.

c. Justify Yost's suggestion. (4 minutes)

WEB EXERCISES

1. A popular measure of liquidity is the difference between the growth in money supply (using a measure such as M2 or MZM) and GDP growth. Obtain data on these measures from the Internet and discuss how the relationship between these growth measures has affected the behavior of the stock market in recent months.

2. Examine the trend in money rates (for example, federal funds, ninety-day T-bills, etc.) over the past ten weeks. Is there a correlation between these money rates? Estimate the correlation between the individual money rates and

percentage changes in M1 money supply. Run a regression with percentage changes in M1 as the independent variable and money rates as the dependent variable. What does your analysis show?

3. Obtain a copy of Table B 95 from the Internet version of the latest *Economic Report of the President*. Find the average return on the S&P 500 since 1959 in years when the difference between the earnings yield and the three-month T-bill rate is (a) less than zero (meaning the T-bill rate exceeds the earnings yield); (b) less than 1 percent.

4. Use the Internet to locate data on inflation indicators. Evaluate how well they have indicated inflation trends.

5. By searching the Internet, locate two contrasting positions about the near-term economic and market environment. Explain the differing positions and their investment recommendations. What different assumptions or expectations do their proponents hold?

SPREADSHEET EXERCISES

1. Obtain data, from print or Internet sources, on GDP and its components since 1985. Graph the main components of GDP spending (consumption, investment, government, and net exports) as a percentage of total GDP each year. Discuss what the graph indicates about the behavior of spending over time. What is the correlation coefficient between GDP and consumption spending?

2. Let's take a closer look at the behavior of consumption spending. Collect data on consumption spending components since 1985. Graph the components as a percentage of GDP and of consumption. Describe the behavior of the components over time. Assuming 2003 proportions, by how many dollars would durable goods spending rise if GDP increased by one percentage point?

3. Describe the changes in the components of investment spending since 1985.

REFERENCES

Baker, H. Kent, Ed. *Improving the Investment Decision Process—Better Use of Economic Inputs in Securities Analysis and Portfolio Management.* Charlottesville, VA: AIMR, 1992.

Balog, James. *The Health Care Industry.* Charlottesville, VA: AIMR, 1993.

Bhatia, Sanjiv, Ed. *The Media Industry.* Charlottesville, VA: AIMR, 1996.

Billingsley, Randall S., Ed. *The Telecommunications Industry.* Charlottesville, VA: AIMR, 1994.

Hyman, Leonard. S., Ed. *Deregulation of the Electric Utility Industry.* Charlottesville, VA: AIMR, 1997.

Ingene, Charles A., Ed. *The Retail Industry—General Merchandisers and Discounters, Specialty Merchandisers, Apparel Specialty, and Food/Drug Retailers.* Charlottesville, VA: AIMR, 1993.

Jensen, Gerald R., Robert R. Johnson, and Jeffrey M. Mercer. *The Role of Monetary Policy in Investment Management.* Charlottesville, VA: The Research Foundation of AIMR, 2000.

Morley, Alfred C., Ed. *The Financial Services Industry—Banks, Thrifts, Insurance Companies, and Securities Firms.* Charlottesville, VA: AIMR, 1992.

Petrie, Thomas A., Ed. *The Oil and Gas Industries.* Charlottesville, VA: AIMR, 1993.

Porter, Michael E. *Competitive Strategy: Techniques for Analyzing Industries and Competitors.* New York: Free Press, 1980.

Porter, Michael E. *Competitive Advantage: Creating and Sustaining Superior Performance.* New York: Free Press, 1985.

Sherrerd, Katrina F., Ed. *Economic Analysis for Investment Professionals.* Charlottesville, VA: AIMR, 1997.

THOMSON ONE
Business School Edition

1. Compare the behavior of the following U.S. industry indexes (use either MSCI or DJ) over the past five or ten years in the U.S. market: auto, biotech, chemicals, electric utility, financials, and machinery. Which industries appear to be most sensitive to business cycle movements? Which are least sensitive? Given your knowledge of recent business cycle history, do any of these industries appear to perform better during the growth stage of the business cycle? Which do relatively better in the recession phase?

2. Obtain data on the following two MSCI USA industry indexes: "biotec" and "beverages." What is the price-to-book ratio and the price-earnings ratio of each? Do you expect there to be differences in these market ratios in light of their industry life cycle stages?

GLOSSARY

Coincident index of economic indicators An index that consists of a set of economic variables whose values reach peaks and troughs at about the same time as the aggregate economy.

Competitive environment The level of intensity of competition among firms in an industry, determined by an examination of five competitive forces.

Competitive strategy The search by a firm for a favorable competitive position within an industry, which affects evaluation of the industry's prospects.

Cyclical change A type of economic trend resulting from the ups and downs of the business cycle.

Discount rate The interest rate at which banks can borrow from the Federal Reserve Board.

Earnings yield Ratio of earnings per share divided by price; the inverse of the P/E ratio.

Econometric model A statistical estimation of mathematical relationships between economic variables as posited by economic theory.

Exchange rate The price of one nation's currency in terms of another nation's currency.

Expectational analysis A forecasting approach that includes an analysis of the current environment, the analyst's assumptions, and a procedure for monitoring data and events to identify changes in the environment or violations of the analyst's assumptions.

Federal funds rate The interest rate banks charge each other for short-term loans.

Fiscal policy The use of government spending and taxing powers.

Gross domestic product (GDP) The sum total of the goods and services produced within a nation's borders. The five major components of GDP are consumption spending, investment spending, government expenditures, export production, and import production.

Index of leading economic indicators An index consisting of a set of economic variables whose values reach peaks and troughs in advance of the aggregate economy.

Industry A set of businesses producing similar products used by customers for similar purposes.

Industry life-cycle analysis An analysis that focuses on the industry's stage of development.

Lagging index of economic indicators An index consisting of a set of economic variables whose values reach peaks and troughs after the aggregate economy.

Monetary policy The use of the Federal Reserve Board's power to affect the money supply and aggregate economic activity.

Open market operations The most frequently used tool of monetary policy in which the Federal Reserve Board buys or sells securities from any market participant.

Overweighted A condition in which a portfolio, for whatever reason, includes more of a class of securities than the relative market value alone would justify.

Reserve requirement The ratio of required reserves to total deposits at a bank.

Structural change A type of economic trend resulting from a major organizational change in the economy or in how it functions.

Underweighted A condition in which a portfolio, for whatever reason, includes less of a class of securities than the relative market value alone would justify.

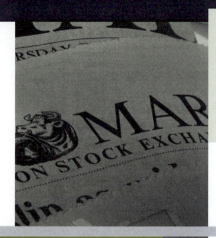

CHAPTER 14

Analysis of Financial Statements

In this chapter we answer the following questions:

What are the major financial statements provided by firms and what specific information does each of them contain?

Why do we use financial ratios to examine the performance of a firm, and why is it important to examine performance relative to the economy and to a firm's industry?

What are the major categories for financial ratios and what questions are answered by the ratios in these categories?

What specific ratios help determine a firm's internal liquidity, operating performance, risk profile, and growth potential?

How can DuPont analysis help evaluate a firm's past and future return on equity?

What is a quality balance sheet or income statement?

Why is financial statement analysis done if markets are efficient and forward-looking?

What major financial ratios are used by analysts in the following areas: stock valuation, estimating and evaluating systematic risk, predicting the credit ratings on bonds, and predicting bankruptcy?

Purpose of This Chapter

You have probably already noted that this is a fairly long chapter with several financial statements and numerous financial ratios. The reason for this extensive discussion of how to analyze financial statements is that our ultimate goal (as noted earlier) is to construct a portfolio of investments that will provide rates of return that are consistent with the risk of the portfolio. In turn, to determine the expected rates of return on different assets we must *estimate the future value* of each asset since a major component of the rate of return is the change in value for the asset over time. Therefore, the crux of investments is *valuation*. Although we will consider various valuation models for common stocks in the next chapter, you are already aware that the value of any earning asset is the present value of the expected cash flows generated by the asset. Therefore, as noted in previous chapters, to estimate the value of an asset we must derive an estimate of the discount rate for the asset (the required rate of return) and its expected cash flows. The main source of the information needed to make these two estimates is the financial statements. To derive an estimate of the required rate of return, we need to understand the business and financial risk of the firm. To estimate future cash flows, we must understand the composition of cash flows and what will contribute to the short-run and long-run growth of these cash flows. Financial statements, business and financial risk, and analysis of the composition and growth of cash flow are all topics of this chapter. In other words, a primary purpose of this chapter is to help you understand how to estimate the variables in valuation models.

Financial statements are also the main source of information when deciding whether to lend money to a firm (invest in its bonds) or to buy warrants or options on a firm's stock. In this chapter, we first introduce a corporation's major financial statements and discuss why and how financial ratios are useful. We also provide example computations of ratios that reflect internal liquidity, operating performance, risk analysis, and growth analysis. In addition, we address four major areas in investments where financial ratios have been effectively employed.

Our example company in this chapter is Walgreens Co., the largest retail drugstore chain in the United States. It operates 4,227 drugstores in 44 states and Puerto Rico. General merchandise accounts for 26 percent and pharmacy generates over 62 percent of total sales. The firm leads its industry (retail drugstores) in sales, profit, and store growth. The firm's goal is to be America's most convenient and technologically advanced health-care retailer. It takes great pride in its steady sales and earnings growth that have been reflected in outstanding stock performance—e.g., dividends have increased in each of the past 28 years and since 1980 the stock has been split two-for-one seven times.

Major Financial Statements

Financial statements are intended to provide information on the resources available to management, how these resources were financed, and what the firm accomplished with them. Corporate shareholder annual and quarterly reports include three required financial statements: the balance sheet, the income statement, and the statement of cash flows. In addition, reports that must be filed with the Securities and Exchange Commission (SEC) (for example, the 10-K and 10-Q reports) carry detailed information about the firm, such as information on loan agreements and data on product line and subsidiary performance. Information from the basic financial statements can be used to calculate financial ratios and to analyze the operations of the firm to determine what factors influence a firm's earnings, cash flows, and risk characteristics.

GENERALLY ACCEPTED ACCOUNTING PRINCIPLES

Among the input used to construct the financial statements are *generally accepted accounting principles (GAAP),* which are formulated by the Financial Accounting Standards Board (FASB). The FASB recognizes that it would be improper for all companies to use identical and restrictive accounting principles. Some flexibility and choice are needed because industries and firms within industries differ in their operating environments. Therefore, the FASB allows companies some flexibility to choose among appropriate GAAP. This flexibility allows the firm's managers to choose accounting standards that best reflect company practice. On the negative side, this flexibility can allow firms to appear healthier than they really are.[1] Given this possibility, the financial analyst must rigorously analyze the available financial information to separate those firms that *appear* attractive from those that actually are in good financial shape.

Fortunately, the FASB requires that financial statements include footnotes that indicate which accounting principles were used by the firm. Because accounting principles frequently differ among firms, the footnote information assists the financial analyst in adjusting the financial statements of companies so the analyst can better compare "apples with apples."

BALANCE SHEET

The *balance sheet* shows what resources (assets) the firm controls and how it has financed these assets. Specifically, it indicates the current and fixed assets available to the firm *at a*

---

[1]The recent Enron fiasco clearly makes this point. For a general discussion on this topic, see Nanette Byrnes and David Henry, "Confused About Earnings?" *Business Week* (November 26, 2001): 77–84; David Henry, "The Numbers Game," *Business Week* (May 14, 2001): 100–110; and Mike McNamee et al., "Accounting in Crises," *Business Week* (January 28, 2002): 44–48.

point in time (the end of the fiscal year or the end of a quarter). In most cases, the firm owns these assets, but some firms lease assets on a long-term basis. How the firm has financed the acquisition of these assets is indicated by its mixture of current liabilities (accounts payable or short-term borrowing), long-term liabilities (fixed debt and leases), and owners' equity (preferred stock, common stock, and retained earnings).

The balance sheet for Walgreens in Exhibit 14.1 represents the *stock* of assets and its financing mix as of the end of Walgreens' fiscal year, August 31, 2001, 2002, and 2003.

EXHIBIT 14.1	Walgreen Co. and Subsidiaries Consolidated Balance Sheet ($ Millions), Years Ended August 31, 2001, 2002, and 2003		
	2003	**2002**	**2001**
Assets			
Current Assets			
Cash and cash equivalents	$ 1,017	$ 450	$ 17
Accounts receivable, net of allowances	1,018	955	798
Inventories	4,203	3,645	3,482
Other Current Assets	121	117	96
Total Current Assets	6,358	5,167	4,394
Property, Plant, and Equipment, Gross	6,362	5,918	5,503
Less accumulated depreciation and amortization	1,422	1,327	1,158
Property, Plant, and Equipment, Net	4,940	4,591	4,345
Other Noncurrent Assets	108	121	95
Total Assets	$11,406	$9,879	$8,834
Liabilities and Shareholders' Equity			
Current Liabilities			
Short-term borrowings	$ 0	$ 0	$ 441
Current maturities of long-term debt	0	0	0
Trade accounts payable	2,077	1,836	1,547
Total accrued expenses and other liabilities	1,238	1,018	938
Accrued expenses and other liabilities	0	0	0
Income taxes payable	106	101	87
Total Current Liabilities	3,421	2,955	3,012
Deferred Income Taxes	228	177	137
Long-Term Debt, Net of Current Maturities	0	0	0
Other Noncurrent Liabilities	562	517	478
Preferred Stock, $0.0625 par value; authorized 32 million shares; none issued			
Common Shareholders' Equity			
Common stock, $0.078125 par value; authorized 3.2 billion shares; issued and outstanding 1,024,908,276 in 2003, 2002	80	80	80
Paid-in capital	698	748	597
Retained earnings	6,418	5,402	4,531
Total Shareholders' Equity	7,196	6,230	5,207
Total Liabilities and Common Shareholders' Equity	$11,406	$9,879	$8,834

Source: Reprinted with permission of Walgreen Co.

EXHIBIT 14.2	Walgreen Co. and Subsidiaries Consolidated Statement of Income ($ Millions, Except Per Share Data) Years Ended August 31, 2001, 2002, and 2003

	2003	2002	2001
Net Sales	$32,505	$28,681	$24,623
Cost of sales	23,706	21,076	18,049
Gross Profit	8,799	7,605	6,574
Selling, occupancy and administrative expense	6,951	5,981	5,176
Operating Profit (EBIT)	1,848	1,624	1,398
Interest income	11	7	5
Interest expense	0	0	3
Other income	30	6	22
Operating Income before Income Taxes	1,889	1,637	1,423
Provision for income taxes	713	618	537
Reported Net Income	1,176	1,019	886
Reported Net Income Available for Common	1,176	1,019	886
Net Earnings (Loss) Per Share	$ 1.14	$ 0.99	$ 0.86
Dividends Per Common Share	$ 0.16	$ 0.15	$ 0.14
Average Number of Common Shares Outstanding (millions)	1,032	1,032	1,029

Source: Reprinted with permission of Walgreen Co.

INCOME STATEMENT

The *income statement* contains information on the operating performance of the firm during some *period of time* (a quarter or a year). In contrast to the balance sheet, which is at a fixed point in time, the income statement indicates the *flow* of sales, expenses, and earnings during a period of time. The income statement for Walgreens for the years 2001, 2002, and 2003 appears in Exhibit 14.2. We concentrate on earnings from operations after tax as the relevant net earnings figure. For Walgreens, this is typically the same as net income because the firm generally has no nonrecurring or unusual income or expense items.

STATEMENT OF CASH FLOWS

Our earlier discussion on valuation indicates that cash flows are a critical input. Therefore accountants now require firms to provide such information. The *statement of cash flows* integrates the information on the balance sheet and income statement to show the effects on the firm's cash flow of income flows (based on the most recent year's income statement) and changes on the balance sheet (based on the two most recent annual balance sheets) that imply an effect on cash flows. Analysts can use these cash flow values to estimate the value of a firm and to evaluate the risk and return of the firm's bonds and stock.

The statement of cash flows has three sections: cash flows from operating activities, cash flows from investing activities, and cash flows from financing activities. The total cash flows from the three sections is the net change in the cash position of the firm that should equal the difference in the cash balance between the ending and beginning balance sheets. The statements of cash flow for Walgreens for 2001, 2002, and 2003 appear in Exhibit 14.3.

Cash Flows from Operating Activities This section of the statement lists the sources and uses of cash that arise from the normal operations of a firm. In general, the net cash flow from operations is computed as the net income reported on the income statement includ-

EXHIBIT 14.3	Walgreen Co. and Subsidiaries Consolidated Statement of Cash Flows ($ Millions), Years Ended August 31, 2001, 2002, and 2003

	2003	2002	2001
Cash Flow from Operating Activities:			
Net Income	$1,176	$1,019	$ 886
Adjustments to Reconcile Net Income to Net Cash Provided by Operating Activities:			
Cumulative effect of accounting changes	0	0	0
Depreciation and amortization	346	307	269
Deferred income taxes	59	23	47
Income tax savings from employee stock plans	24	57	67
Other net income adjustments	29	(9)	2
Changes in Operating Assets and Liabilities (used in) Provided from Continuing Operations:			
(Increase) decrease in inventories	(558)	(163)	(652)
(Increase) decrease in accounts receivable	(57)	(171)	(177)
(Increase) decrease in other current assets	0	0	0
Increase (decrease) in trade accounts payable	241	290	183
Increase (decrease) in accrued expenses and other liabilities	178	75	82
Income taxes	5	14	(5)
Other operating assets and liabilities	48	31	17
Net Cash Flows from Operating Activities	$1,492	$1,474	$ 719
Cash Flows from Investing Activities:			
Additions to property and equipment	(795)	(934)	(1237)
Disposition of property and equipment	85	368	44
Net proceeds from corporate-owned life insurance	8	14	59
Net (purchases) sales of marketable security	0	0	0
Net Cash Flows from Investing Activities	$ (702)	$ (552)	$(1,135)
Cash Flows from Financing Activities:			
(Payments of) proceeds from short-term borrowing	0	(441)	441
Cash dividends paid	(152)	(147)	(141)
(Costs) proceeds from employee stock plans	(67)	111	126
Other	(3)	(12)	(7)
Net Cash Flows from Financing Activities	$ (222)	$ (489)	$ 419
Net Increase (decrease) in cash and cash equivalents	567	433	4
Cash and cash equivalents at beginning of year	450	17	13
Cash and cash equivalents at end of year	$1,017	$ 450	$ 17

Source: Reprinted with permission of Walgreen Co.

ing changes in net working capital items (i.e., receivables, inventories, and so on) plus adjustments for noncash revenues and expenses (such as depreciation), or:

14.1

Cash Flow from Operating Activities

= Net Income + Noncash Revenue and Expenses

+ Changes in Net Working Capital Items

Consistent with our previous discussion, the cash account is not included in the calculations of cash flow from operations. Notably, Walgreens has been able to generate consistently large and growing cash flows from operations even after accounting for consistent increases in receivables and inventory required by the firm's growth.

Cash Flows from Investing Activities   A firm makes investments in both its own noncurrent and fixed assets and the equity of other firms (which may be subsidiaries or joint ventures of the parent firm. They are listed in the "investment" account of the balance sheet). Increases and decreases in these noncurrent accounts are considered investment activities. The cash flow from investing activities is the change in gross plant and equipment plus the change in the investment account. The changes are positive if they represent a source of funds (e.g., sale of some plant and/or equipment); otherwise they are negative. The dollar changes in these accounts are computed using the firm's two most recent balance sheets. Most firms (including Walgreens) experience negative cash flows from investments due to significant capital expenditures.

Cash Flows from Financing Activities   Cash inflows are created by increasing notes payable and long-term liability and equity accounts, such as bond and stock issues. Financing uses (outflows) include decreases in such accounts (that is, the pay down of liability accounts or the repurchase of common shares). Dividend payments are a significant financing cash outflow.

The total cash flows from operating, investing, and financing activities are the net increase or decrease in the firm's cash. The statement of cash flows provides cash flow detail that is lacking in the balance sheet and income statement.

MEASURES OF CASH FLOW

There are several cash flow measures an analyst can use to determine the underlying health of the corporation.

Traditional Cash Flow   The traditional measure of cash flow equals net income plus depreciation expense and deferred taxes. But as we have just seen, it is also necessary to adjust for changes in operating (current) assets and liabilities that either use or provide cash. These changes can add to or subtract from the cash flow estimated from the traditional measure of cash flow: net income plus noncash expenses.

The table below compares the cash flow from operations figures (Exhibit 14.3) to the traditional cash flow figures for Walgreens from 2001 to 2003.

	Traditional Cash Flow Equals Net Income + Depreciation + Change in Def. Taxes	Cash Flow from Operations from Statement of Cash Flows
2003	1,581	1,492
2002	1,349	1,474
2001	1,202	719

In two of the three years the cash flow from operations was less than the traditional cash flow estimate because of the several adjustments needed to arrive at cash flow from operations. Therefore, using this more exact measure of cash flow for these two years, the Walgreens ratios would not have been as strong. For many firms, this is fairly typical because the effect of working capital changes is often a large negative cash flow due to necessary increases in receivables or inventory to support sales growth (especially for high-growth companies).

Free Cash Flow   *Free cash flow* modifies cash flow from operations to recognize that some investing and financing activities are critical to the firm. It is assumed that these expenditures must be made before a firm can use its cash flow for other purposes such as reducing debt outstanding or repurchasing common stock. Two additional items are considered: (1) capital expenditures (an investing expenditure) and (2) the disposition of property and equipment (a divestment source of cash). These two items are used to modify Walgreens' cash flow from operations as follows (some analysts only subtract capital expenditures but conservative analysts also subtract dividends).

	Cash Flow from Operations	−	Capital Expenditures	+	Disposition of Property and Equipment	=	Free Cash Flow
2003	1,492	−	795	+	85	=	781
2002	1,474	−	934	+	368	=	908
2001	719	−	1,237	+	44	=	(474)

For firms involved in leveraged buyouts, this free cash flow number is critical because the new owners typically want to use the firm's free cash flow as funds available for retiring outstanding debt. It is not unusual for a firm's free cash flow to be a negative value. The free cash flow for Walgreens was negative in 2001 even though the firm had large cash flow from operations because of heavy capital expenditures in connection with opening new stores. Notably, this free cash flow value or a variation of it will be used in the subsequent cash flow valuation models.[2]

EBITDA   The EBITDA (earnings before interest, taxes, depreciation, and amortization) measure of cash flow is extremely liberal. This very generous measure of operating earnings does not consider any of the adjustments noted previously. Specifically, it adds back depreciation and amortization (as in the traditional measure) along with both interest expense and taxes, but does not consider the effect of changes in working capital items (such as additions to receivables and inventory) or the significant impact of capital expenditures. The following table, which compares this measure to the other three measures of cash flow for Walgreens, demonstrates the large differences among these measures.

Year	EBITDA	Traditional Cash Flow	Cash Flow from Operations	Free Cash Flow
2003	2,235	1,581	1,492	781
2002	1,944	1,349	1,474	908
2001	1,695	1,202	719	(474)

Some analysts have used EBITDA as a proxy for cash flow and a metric for valuation similar to earnings—i.e., they refer to EBITDA multiples as other analysts would refer to price-earnings (P/E) multiples. Yet given what this measure does not consider, this is a very questionable practice and is not recommended by the authors.[3]

---

[2]As we will show in the next chapter, small modifications of this free cash flow—entitled free cash flow to equity (FCFE), free cash flow to the firm (FCFF), and NOPLAT—are used in valuation models and also the Economic Value Added (EVA) model.

[3]For a detailed discussion of the problems with using EBITDA, see Pamela M. Stumpp, "Putting EBITDA in Perspective," *Moody's Investors Service* (June 2000).

PURPOSE OF FINANCIAL STATEMENT ANALYSIS

Financial statement analysis seeks to evaluate management performance in several important areas, including profitability, efficiency, and risk. Although we will necessarily analyze historical data, the ultimate goal of this analysis is to provide insights that will help us to project *future* management performance, including pro forma balance sheets, income statements, cash flows, and risk. It is the firm's *expected future* performance that determines whether we should lend money to a firm or invest in it.

Analysis of Financial Ratios

Analysts use financial ratios because numbers in isolation typically convey little meaning. For example, knowing that a firm earned a net income of $100,000 is not very informative unless we also know the sales figure that generated this income ($1 million or $10 million) and the assets or capital committed to the enterprise. Thus, ratios are intended to provide meaningful *relationships* between individual values in the financial statements.

Because the major financial statements report numerous individual items, it is possible to produce a vast number of potential ratios, many of which will have little value. Therefore, we limit our examination to the most relevant ratios and group them into categories that will provide information on important economic characteristics of the firm.

IMPORTANCE OF RELATIVE FINANCIAL RATIOS

Just as a single number from a financial statement is of little use, an individual financial ratio has little value except in relation to comparable ratios for other entities. That is, *only relative financial ratios are relevant*. Therefore, it is important to compare a firm's performance relative to

- The aggregate economy
- Its industry or industries
- Its major competitors within the industry
- Its past performance (time-series analysis)

The comparison to the aggregate economy is important because almost all firms are influenced by economic fluctuations. For example, it is unreasonable to expect an increase in the profit margin for a firm during a recession; a stable margin might be encouraging under such conditions. In contrast, a small increase in a firm's profit margin during a major business expansion may be a sign of weakness. Thus, this comparison helps investors understand how a firm reacts to the business cycle and *estimate* the future performance of the firm during subsequent business cycles.

Probably the most significant comparison relates a firm's performance to that of its industry. Different industries affect the firms within them differently, but this relationship is always significant. The industry effect is strongest for industries with homogeneous products such as steel, rubber, glass, and wood products, because all firms within these industries experience coincidental shifts in demand. In addition, these firms employ fairly similar technology and production processes. For example, even the best-managed steel firm experiences a decline in sales and profit margins during a recession. In such a case, the relevant question is not whether sales and margins declined, but how bad was the decline relative to other steel firms? In addition, investors should examine an industry's performance relative to the economy to understand how the industry responds to the business cycle.

When comparing a firm's financial ratios to industry ratios, investors may not want to use the average (mean) industry value when there is wide variation among firms in the industry. Alternatively, if we believe that a firm has a "unique" component, a *cross-sectional analysis* in which we compare the firm to a subset of industry firms comparable in size or characteristics, may be appropriate. As an example, we would compare the performance of Kroger to that of other national food chains rather than regional food chains or specialty food chains.

Another practical problem with comparing a firm to its industry is that many large firms are multi-industry. Inappropriate comparisons can arise when a multi-industry firm is evaluated against the ratios from a single industry. To mitigate this problem, we can use a cross-sectional analysis that compares the firm against a rival that operates in many of the same industries. Alternatively, we can construct composite industry average ratios for the firm. To do this, we use the firm's annual report or 10-K filing to identify each industry in which the firm operates and the proportion of total firm sales derived from each industry. The composite industry ratios would be the weighted-average ratios based on the proportion of firm sales derived from each industry.

Finally, *time-series analysis,* in which we examine a firm's relative performance over time to determine whether it is progressing or declining, is helpful when estimating future performance. Calculating the five or ten year average of a ratio without considering the time-series trend can result in misleading conclusions. For example, an average rate of return of 10 percent can be the result of rates of return that have increased from 5 percent to 15 percent over time or the result of a series that declined from 15 percent to 5 percent. Obviously, the difference in the trend for these series would have a major impact on our estimate for the future. Ideally, we would examine a firm's time series of *relative* financial ratios compared to its industry and the economy.

Computation of Financial Ratios

In the ensuing discussion we divide the financial ratios into five major categories that underscore the important economic characteristics of a firm. The five categories are

1. Common size statements
2. Internal liquidity (solvency)
3. Operating performance
    a. Operating efficiency
    b. Operating profitability
4. Risk analysis
    a. Business risk
    b. Financial risk
    c. External liquidity risk
5. Growth analysis

COMMON SIZE STATEMENTS

Common size statements "normalize" balance sheet and income statement items to allow easier comparison of different sized firms. A common size *balance sheet* expresses all balance sheet accounts as a *percentage of total assets.* A common size *income statement* expresses all income statement items as a *percentage of sales.* Exhibit 14.4 is the common size balance sheet for Walgreens, and Exhibit 14.5 contains the common size income statement. Common size ratios are useful to quickly compare two different sized firms and to examine trends over time within a single firm. Common size statements also give insight into a firm's financial condition, for example, the proportion of liquid assets or the proportion of short-term liabilities, and the percentage of sales consumed by production costs or interest

EXHIBIT 14.4	Walgreen Co. and Subsidiaries Common Size Balance Sheet ($ Millions). Years Ended August 31, 1999, 2000, 2001, 2002, and 2003				
	2003	**2002**	**2001**	**2000**	**1999**
Assets					
Current Assets					
Cash and cash equivalents	8.92%	4.55%	0.19%	0.18%	2.40%
Accounts receivable, net of allowances	8.92	9.67	9.04	8.65	8.24
Inventories	36.85	36.90	39.42	39.85	41.69
Other current assets	1.06	1.18	1.09	1.30	2.21
Total Current Assets	55.74	52.30	49.74	49.98	54.54
Property, Plant and Equipment, gross	55.78	59.91	62.30	62.22	58.79
Less accumulated depreciation and amortization	12.47	13.43	13.11	13.96	14.88
Property, plant, and equipment, net	43.31	46.48	49.19	48.26	43.91
Other Noncurrent Assets	0.95	1.22	1.07	1.77	1.54
Total Assets	100.00%	100.00%	100.00%	100.00%	100.00%
Liabilities and Shareholders' Equity					
Current Liabilities					
Short-term borrowings	0%	0%	4.99%	0%	0%
Current maturities of long-term debt	0	0	0	0	0
Trade accounts payable	18.21	18.59	17.51	19.20	19.14
Total accrued expenses and other liabilities	10.85	10.30	10.61	11.93	12.36
Accrued expenses and other liabilities	—	—	—	—	—
Income taxes payable	0.93	1.02	0.98	1.30	1.07
Total Current Liabilities	29.99	29.91	34.09	32.43	32.57
Deferred income taxes	2.00	1.79	1.55	1.43	1.27
Long-term debt, net of current maturities	0	0	0	0	0
Other noncurrent liabilities	4.92	5.23	5.41	6.54	7.17
Preferred stock, $0.0625 par value; authorized 32 million shares; none issued	0	0	0	0	0
Common Shareholders' Equity					
Common stock, $0.078125 par value; authorized 3.2 billion shares; issued and outstanding 1,024,908,276 in 2003, 2002	0.70	0.81	0.90	1.11	1.33
Paid-in capital	6.12	7.58	6.75	5.17	4.38
Retained earnings	56.27	54.68	51.29	53.32	53.28
Total Shareholders' Equity	63.09	63.07	58.95	59.60	58.99
Total Liabilities and Common Shareholders' Equity	100.00%	100.00%	100.00%	100.00%	100.00%

expense. In the case of Walgreens, the common size balance sheet shows a small decline and then an increase in the percent of current assets (due to a cash increase), and an increase followed by a decline in the proportion of net property. Alternatively, the common size income statement shows that Walgreens' cost of goods sold and its selling and administrative expenses were quite stable from 1999 to 2003 in proportion to sales. As a result of this stability, the firm has experienced virtually a constant operating profit margin before and after

EXHIBIT 14.5 Walgreen Co. and Subsidiaries Common Size Income Statement, Years Ended August 31, 1999, 2000, 2001, 2002, and 2003

	2003	%	2002	%	2001	%	2000	%	1999	%
Net Sales	$32,505	100.00	$28,681	100.00	$24,623	100.00	$21,207	100.00	$17,839	100.00
Cost of sales	23,706	72.93	21,076	73.48	18,049	73.30	15,466	72.93	12,979	72.75
Gross Profit	8,799	27.07	7,605	26.52	6,574	26.70	5,741	27.07	4,860	27.25
Selling, occupancy, and administrative expense	6,951	21.38	5,981	20.85	5,176	21.02	4,517	21.30	3,845	21.55
Operating Profit (EBIT)	1,848	5.69	1,624	5.66	1,398	5.68	1,224	5.77	1,015	5.69
Interest income	11	0.03	7	0.02	5	0.02	6	0.03	12	0.07
Interest expense	0	0.00	0	0.00	3	0.01	0	0.00	0	0.00
Other income	30	0.09	6	0.02	22	0.09	34	0.16	0	0.00
Operating Income before Income Taxes	1,889	5.81	1,637	5.71	1,423	5.78	1,263	5.96	1,027	5.76
Provision for income taxes	713	2.19	618	2.16	537	2.18	486	2.29	403	2.26
Reported Net Income	1,176	3.62	1,019	3.55	886	3.60	777	3.66	624	3.50
Reported Net Income Available for Common	$ 1,176	3.62	$ 1,019	3.55	$ 886	3.60	$ 777	3.66	$ 624	3.50

Note: Percentages may not add to 100% due to rounding.

Source: Reprinted with permission from Walgreen Co.

taxes. The ability of Walgreens to experience strong growth in sales (over 14 percent a year) *and* a constant profit margin during a period that included a recession is very impressive.

Evaluating Internal Liquidity

Interactive e-lectures
For more explanation and an animated example of liquidity, go to:
http://reillyxtra.swlearning.com.

Internal liquidity (solvency) ratios are intended to indicate the ability of the firm to meet future short-term financial obligations. They compare near-term financial obligations, such as accounts payable or notes payable, to current assets or cash flows that will be available to meet these obligations.

INTERNAL LIQUIDITY RATIOS

Current Ratio   Clearly the best-known liquidity measure is the current ratio, which examines the relationship between current assets and current liabilities as follows:

14.2
$$\text{Current Ratio} = \frac{\text{Current Assets}}{\text{Current Liabilities}}$$

For Walgreens, the current ratios were (all ratios are computed using dollars in 000s)

$$2003: \quad \frac{6,358}{3,421} = 1.86$$

$$2002: \quad \frac{5,167}{2,955} = 1.75$$

$$2001: \quad \frac{4,394}{3,012} = 1.46$$

These current ratios experienced a consistent increase during the three years and are consistent with the "typical" current ratio. As always, it is important to compare these values with similar figures for the firm's industry and the aggregate market. If the ratios differ from the industry results, we need to determine what might explain it. (We will discuss comparative analysis in a later section.)

Quick Ratio   Some observers question using total current assets to gauge the ability of a firm to meet its current obligations because inventories and some other current assets might not be very liquid. They prefer the quick ratio, which relates current liabilities to only relatively liquid current assets (cash items and accounts receivable) as follows:

14.3
$$\text{Quick Ratio} = \frac{\text{Cash} + \text{Marketable Securities} + \text{Receivables}}{\text{Current Liabilities}}$$

Walgreens' quick ratios were

$$2003: \quad \frac{2,035}{3,421} = 0.59$$

$$2002: \quad \frac{1,405}{2,955} = 0.48$$

$$2001: \quad \frac{815}{3,012} = 0.27$$

These quick ratios were below the norm but increased over the three years. As before, we should compare these values relative to other firms in the industry and to the aggregate economy.

Cash Ratio   The most conservative liquidity ratio is the cash ratio, which relates the firm's cash and short-term marketable securities to its current liabilities as follows:

14.4
$$\text{Cash Ratio} = \frac{\textbf{Cash and Marketable Securities}}{\textbf{Current Liabilities}}$$

Walgreens' cash ratios were

$$2003: \quad \frac{1{,}017}{3{,}421} = 0.30$$

$$2002: \quad \frac{450}{2{,}955} = 0.15$$

$$2001: \quad \frac{17}{3{,}012} = 0.01$$

The cash ratios were quite low in 2001 but grew substantially during 2002 and 2003 to a point that they were almost excessive for a fast-growing retailer with inventories being financed by accounts payable to its suppliers. In addition, the firm has strong lines of credit at various banks.

Receivables Turnover   In addition to examining total liquid assets, it is useful to analyze the quality (liquidity) of the accounts receivable by calculating how often the firm's receivables turn over, which implies an average collection period. The faster these accounts are paid, the sooner the firm gets the funds to pay off its own current liabilities. Receivables turnover is computed as

14.5
$$\text{Receivable Turnover} = \frac{\textbf{Net Annual Sales}}{\textbf{Average Receivables}}$$

The average receivables figure is typically equal to the beginning receivables figure plus the ending value divided by two. Walgreens receivables turnover ratios were

$$2003: \quad \frac{32{,}505}{(1018 + 955)/2} = 32.95 \text{ times}$$

$$2002: \quad \frac{28{,}681}{(955 + 798)/2} = 32.72 \text{ times}$$

We cannot compute a turnover value for 2001 because the tables used do not include a beginning receivables figure for 2001 (that is, we lack the ending receivables figure for 2000).

Given these annual receivables turnover figures, the average collection period is

14.6 $$\text{Average Receivable Collection Period} = \frac{\textbf{365 Days}}{\textbf{Annual Receivables Turnover}}$$

For Walgreens,

$$2003: \quad \frac{365}{32.95} = 11.1 \text{ days}$$

$$2002: \quad \frac{365}{32.72} = 11.2 \text{ days}$$

These results indicate that Walgreens currently collects its accounts receivable in about eleven days on average. To determine whether these account collection numbers are good or bad, it is essential that they be related to the firm's credit policy and to comparable numbers for other firms in the industry. The point is, the receivables collection period value varies dramatically for different firms (e.g., from ten to over sixty) and it is mainly due to the product and the industry. An industry comparison would indicate similar rapid collection periods for other drugstore chains since most sales are for cash. The reason for the small increase in the collection period over several years is that a significant change has occurred in pharmacy sales: About 90 percent of pharmacy sales are now to a third party (i.e., they are reimbursed by a managed-care company), which has caused the increase in receivables.

The receivables turnover is one of the ratios where a firm *does not want to deviate too much from the norm*. In an industry where the norm is forty days, a collection period of eighty days would indicate slow-paying customers, which increases the capital tied up in receivables and the possibility of bad debts. Therefore, the firm wants to be somewhat below the norm (for example, thirty-five days versus forty days), but a figure *substantially below* the norm (e.g., 20 days) might indicate overly stringent credit terms relative to the competition, which could be detrimental to sales.

INVENTORY TURNOVER

We should also examine the liquidity of inventory based on the firm's inventory turnover and the implied processing time. Inventory turnover can be calculated relative to sales or cost of goods sold. The preferred turnover ratio is relative to cost of goods sold (CGS), which does not include the profit implied in sales.

14.7
$$\text{Investory Turnover} = \frac{\text{CGS}}{\text{Average Inventory}}$$

For Walgreens the inventory turnover ratios were

$$2003: \quad \frac{23,706}{(4,203 + 3,645)/2} = 6.04 \text{ times}$$

$$2002: \quad \frac{21,076}{(3,645 + 3,482)/2} = 5.91 \text{ times}$$

Given these turnover values, we can compute the average inventory processing time as follows:

14.8
$$\text{Average Investory Processing Period} = \frac{365}{\text{Annual Inventory Turnover}}$$

For Walgreens,

$$2003: \quad \frac{365}{6.04} = 60.4 \text{ days}$$

$$2002: \quad \frac{365}{5.91} = 61.7 \text{ days}$$

Although this seems like a low turnover figure, it is encouraging that the inventory processing period is very stable and has declined over the longer run. Still, it is essential to examine this turnover ratio relative to an industry norm and/or the firm's prime competition. Notably, this ratio will also be affected by the products carried by the chain—for instance, if a drugstore chain adds high profit margin items, such as cosmetics and liquor, these products may have a lower turnover.

As with receivables, a firm does not want an extremely low inventory turnover value and long processing time because this implies that capital is being tied up in inventory and could signal obsolete inventory (especially for firms in the technology sector). Alternatively, an abnormally high inventory turnover and a short processing time could mean inadequate inventory that could lead to outages, backorders, and slow delivery to customers, which would eventually have an adverse effect on sales.

Cash Conversion Cycle   A very useful measure of overall internal liquidity is the cash conversion cycle, which combines information from the receivables turnover, the inventory turnover, and the accounts payable turnover. Cash is tied up in assets for a certain number of days. Specifically, cash is committed to receivables for the collection period and in inventory for a number of days—the inventory processing period. At the same time, the firm receives an offset to this capital commitment from its own suppliers who provide interest-free loans to the firm by carrying the firm's payables. Specifically, the payables' payment period is equal to 365 divided by the payables' turnover ratio. In turn, the payables turnover ratio is

14.9
$$\text{Payables Turnover Ratio} = \frac{\text{Cost of Goods Sold}}{\text{Average Trade Payables}}$$

For Walgreens the payables turnover ratios were

$$2003: \quad \frac{23,706}{(2,077 + 1,836)/2} = 12.1 \text{ times}$$

$$2002: \quad \frac{21,076}{(1,836 + 1,547)/2} = 12.5 \text{ times}$$

14.10
$$\text{Payables Payment Period} = \frac{365 \text{ days}}{\text{Payable Turnover}}$$

$$2003: \quad \frac{365}{12.1} = 30.1 \text{ days}$$

$$2002: \quad \frac{365}{12.5} = 29.2 \text{ days}$$

Therefore, the cash conversion cycle for Walgreens (with components rounded) equals:

Year	Receivables Collection Days	+	Inventory Processing Days	−	Payables Payment Period	=	Cash Conversion Cycle
2003	11	+	60	−	30	=	41 days
2002	11	+	62	−	29	=	44 days

Walgreens has experienced stability in its receivables days, has had a small increase in its inventory processing days, and is paying its bills at about the same speed. The overall result is a small decline in its cash conversion cycle. Although the overall cash conversion cycle appears to be quite good (about forty-one days), as always we should examine the firm's long-term trend and compare it to other drugstore chains.

Evaluating Operating Performance

The operating performance ratios can be divided into two subcategories: (1) *operating efficiency ratios* and (2) *operating profitability ratios*. Efficiency ratios examine how the management uses its assets and capital, measured by dollars of sales generated by various asset or capital categories. Profitability ratios analyze the profits as a percentage of sales and as a percentage of the assets and capital employed.

OPERATING EFFICIENCY RATIOS

Total Asset Turnover   The total asset turnover ratio indicates the effectiveness of the firm's use of its total asset base (net assets equals gross assets minus depreciation on fixed assets). It is computed as

14.11
$$\text{Total Asset Turnover} = \frac{\text{Net Sales}}{\text{Average Total Net Assets}}$$

Walgreens' total asset turnover values were

$$2003: \quad \frac{32,505}{(11,406 + 9,879)/2} = 3.05 \text{ times}$$

$$2002: \quad \frac{28,681}{(9,879 + 8,834)/2} = 3.07 \text{ times}$$

This ratio must be compared to that of other firms *within* an industry because it varies substantially between industries. For example, total asset turnover ratios range from less than one for large, capital-intensive industries (steel, autos, and heavy manufacturing companies) to over ten for some retailing or service operations. It also can be affected by the use of leased facilities.

Again, we must consider a *range* of turnover values consistent with the industry. It is poor management to have an exceedingly high asset turnover relative to the industry because this might imply too few assets for the potential business (sales), or it could be due to the use of outdated, fully depreciated assets. It is equally poor management to have an extremely low asset turnover because this implies that the firm is tying up capital in excess assets relative to the needs of the firm and its competitors.

Beyond the analysis of the firm's total asset base, it is insightful to examine the utilization of some specific assets, such as receivables, inventories, and fixed assets. This is especially important if the firm has experienced a major decline in its total asset turnover because we want to know the cause of the decline, that is, which of the component turnovers (receivables, inventory, fixed assets) contributed to the decline. We have already examined the receivables and inventory turnover as part of our liquidity analysis; we now examine the fixed asset turnover ratio.

Net Fixed Asset Turnover   The net fixed asset turnover ratio reflects the firm's utilization of fixed assets. It is computed as

14.12
$$\text{Fixed Asset Turnover} = \frac{\text{Net Sales}}{\text{Average Net Fixed Assets}}$$

Walgreens' fixed asset turnover ratios were

$$2003: \quad \frac{32,505}{(4,940 + 4,591)/2} = 6.82 \text{ times}$$

$$2002: \quad \frac{28,681}{(4,591 + 4,345)/2} = 6.42 \text{ times}$$

These turnover ratios, which indicate a small increase for Walgreens during the last few years, must be compared with industry competitors and should consider the impact of leased assets (this is especially significant for retail firms). Again, an abnormally low turnover implies capital tied up in excessive fixed assets. An abnormally high asset turnover ratio can indicate a lack of productive capacity to meet sales demand, or it might imply the use of old, fully depreciated plant and equipment that may be obsolete.[4]

Equity Turnover   In addition to specific asset turnover ratios, it is useful to examine the turnover for capital components. An important one, equity turnover, is computed as

14.13

$$\textbf{Equity Turnover} = \frac{\textbf{Net Sales}}{\textbf{Average Equity}}$$

Equity includes preferred and common stock, paid-in capital, and total retained earnings.[5] This ratio differs from total asset turnover in that it excludes current liabilities and long-term debt. Therefore, when examining this series, we must consider the firm's capital structure ratios because the firm can increase its equity turnover ratio by increasing its proportion of debt capital.

Walgreens' equity turnover ratios were

$$2003: \quad \frac{32,505}{(7,196 + 6,230)/2} = 4.84 \text{ times}$$

$$2002: \quad \frac{28,681}{(6,230 + 5,207)/2} = 5.02 \text{ times}$$

Walgreens experienced a small decline in this ratio during the past several years. In our later analysis of sustainable growth, we examine the variables that affect the equity turnover ratio to understand what caused any changes.

Following an analysis of the firm's operating efficiency, the next step is to examine its profitability in relation to its sales and capital.

OPERATING PROFITABILITY RATIOS

There are two facets of profitability: (1) the rate of profit on sales (profit margin) and (2) the percentage return on capital employed. The analysis of profitability of sales actually entails several component profit margins that consider various expense categories. These component margins provide important information relative to the final net profit margin. Thus, if we determine that a firm has experienced a significant increase or decrease in its net profit margin, the analysis of the component profit margins will help us to determine the specific causes of the change. Therefore, we will briefly discuss each of the margins but

---

[4]There will be a longer-term analysis of this total asset turnover ratio in the "DuPont System" section of this chapter.

[5]Some investors prefer to consider only *owner's* equity, which would not include preferred stock.

will defer calculation's and comments on the trends until we discuss the common size income statement.

Gross Profit Margin Gross profit equals net sales minus the cost of goods sold. The gross profit margin is computed as

14.14

$$\text{Gross Profit Margin} = \frac{\text{Gross Profit}}{\text{Net Sales}}$$

This ratio indicates the basic cost structure of the firm. An analysis of this ratio over time relative to a comparable industry figure shows the firm's relative cost–price position. As always, we must compare these margins to the industry and major competitors. Notably, this margin can also be impacted by a change in the firm's product mix toward higher or lower profit margin items.

Operating Profit Margin Operating profit is gross profit minus sales, general, and administrative (SG&A) expenses. It is also referred to as EBIT—earnings before interest and taxes.

14.15

$$\text{Operating Profit Margin} = \frac{\text{Operating Profit}}{\text{Net Sales}}$$

The variability of the operating profit margin over time is a prime indicator of the business risk for a firm.

There are two additional deductions from operating profit—interest expense and net foreign exchange loss. After these deductions, we have income before income taxes.

Some investors add back to the operating income value (EBIT) the firm's depreciation expense and compute a profit margin that consists of earnings before interest, taxes, depreciation, and amortization (EBITDA). This alternative operating profit margin has been used by some analysts as a proxy for pre-tax cash flow.[6]

Net Profit Margin This margin relates after-tax net income to sales. In the case of Walgreens, this is the same as operating income after taxes because the firm does not have any significant nonoperating adjustments. This margin is equal to

14.16

$$\text{Net Profit Margin} = \frac{\text{Net Income}}{\text{Net Sales}}$$

This ratio should be computed using sales and earnings from *continuing* operations because our analysis seeks to derive insights about *future* expectations. Therefore, we do not consider earnings from discontinued operations, the gain or loss from the sale of these operations, or any nonrecurring income or expenses.

Common Size Income Statement As noted earlier, these ratios are basically included in a common size income statement, which lists all expense and income items as a percentage of sales. This statement provides useful insights regarding the trends in cost figures and profit margins.

Exhibit 14.5 showed a common size statement for Walgreens for 1999–2003. As noted earlier in the chapter when Exhibit 14.5 was presented, the most striking characteristic of

---

[6]While this measure of "cash flow" has grown in popularity, there are a growing number of concerned observers who point out that this measure does *not* consider the necessary cash outflows for working capital items (which are considered in "Cash Flow from Operations") or capital expenditures (which are considered in "Free Cash Flow"). For a brief discussion, see Herb Greenberg, "Alphabet Dupe: Why EBITDA Falls Short," *Fortune* (July 10, 2000): 240–241.

the various profit margins for Walgreens (gross, operating, and net) is the *significant stability* in those margins over time. This stability is notable for two reasons: First, the firm experienced significant sales growth during this period (about 14 percent a year) and it is generally a challenge to control costs when growing rapidly. Second, this time interval included the economic recession of 2001–2002 (the official recession was during 2001, but it carried over for most corporations into 2002) and the sales and profit margins of most corporations were negatively impacted by this environment. Therefore, the stability of profit margins for Walgreens is an impressive accomplishment by management.

Beyond the analysis of earnings on sales, the ultimate measure of management performance is the profits earned on the assets or the capital committed to the enterprise. Several ratios help us evaluate this important relationship.

Return on Total Capital   The return on total capital ratio relates the firm's earnings to all the capital involved in the enterprise (debt, preferred stock, and common stock). Therefore, the earnings figure used is the net income from continuing operations (before any dividends) *plus* the interest paid on debt.

14.17

$$\text{Return on Total Capital} = \frac{\text{Net Income} + \text{Interest Expense}}{\text{Average Total Capital}}$$

Walgreens incurred interest expense for long- and short-term debt. The gross interest expense value used in this ratio differs from the "net" interest expense item in the income statement, which is measured as gross interest expense minus interest income.

Walgreens' rates of return on total capital were

$$2003: \quad \frac{1,176 + 0.2}{(11,406 + 9,879)/2} = 11.05\%$$

$$2002: \quad \frac{1,019 + 0.3}{(9,879 + 8,834)/2} = 10.89\%$$

This ratio indicates the firm's return on all the capital it employed. It should be compared with the ratio for other firms in the industry and the economy. For Walgreens, the results are stable with an increase during the last several years.

Consideration of Lease Obligations   Many firms lease facilities (buildings) and equipment rather than borrow the funds and purchase the assets—it is basically a lease or borrow decision since the lease contract is like a bond obligation. The accounting for the lease obligation depends on the type of lease. If it is a *capital* lease, the value of the asset and the lease obligation is included on the balance sheet as an asset and liability. If it is an *operating* lease, it is noted in the footnotes but not specifically included on the balance sheet.[7] Because operating leases are a form of financing used extensively by retailers (like Walgreens, Sears, and McDonalds') and airlines, it is necessary to recognize this obligation, capitalize estimated future lease payments, and include this value on the balance sheet as both an asset and a long-term liability. In this section we will discuss how to do this and demonstrate the significant impact this adjustment can have on several financial ratios.

Capitalizing Operating Leases   Capitalizing leases basically involves an estimate of the present value of a firm's future required lease payments. Therefore, an analyst must estimate:

---

[7]A discussion of the technical factors that will cause a lease to be capital versus operating is beyond the scope of this book, but it is covered in most intermediate accounting texts.

(1) an appropriate discount rate (typically the firm's long-term debt rate) and (2) the firm's future lease payment obligations as specified in a footnote.

An estimate of the discounted value of the future lease payments can be done one of two ways: (1) a multiple of the forthcoming minimum lease payments or (2) the discounted value of the future lease payments provided in the annual report at the firm's cost of long-term debt. The traditional multiple technique multiplies the minimum lease payment in year $t + 1$ by 8. In the case of Walgreens, the future minimum lease payments in the annual report for the year 2003 are as follows:

Years Relating to Year-End	1	2	3	4	5	Later
Minimum Payments ($ millions)	1,188	1,219	1,188	1,149	1,082	13,490

Given these data, the estimate using the first technique would produce an estimate of 8 × $1,188 million = $9.50 billion. To derive an estimate using the second technique, we need to estimate the firm's cost of long-term debt and consider how to handle the lump-sum "later" payments. Our debt rate estimate is 5.60 percent, which is consistent with the prevailing rate on 20 year, AA rated corporate bonds. For the later lump-sum payment, we need to derive a reasonable estimate regarding how many years to assume for this payout. A liberal assumption is that the lump-sum payment is spread evenly over fifteen years, based on a typical building lease of twenty years ($13,490/15 = $899.3 million per year). An alternative estimate of the spread period is derived by dividing the lump-sum payment in period $t + 6$ by the $t + 5$ payment, which implies a time estimate ($13,490/1,082 = 12.5$). If we round this up to thirteen years, we have an annual payment of $1,037.7 million per year for thirteen years.

If we discount at 5.60 percent all the annual flows and the later flows over fifteen years, we derive an estimate of the lease debt of $11.80 *billion*. A similar computation using the thirteen-year spread indicates an estimate of lease debt of $12.14 *billion*. Therefore, we have the following three estimates:[8]

Eight times the $t + 1$ lease payment	$9.50 billion
Discounting the lease payments assuming a 15-year spread	$11.80 billion
Discounting the lease payments assuming a 13-year spread	$12.14 billion

We will use the $9.50 billion traditional estimate since this estimate is reasonably close to the discounted value estimates. Also, it is clearly easier to estimate not only this year's lease debt but also prior years' implied debt obligations as well as the implied interest component. If we add this amount (or that estimated by discounting the future payments) to both fixed assets and long-term debt we will have a better measure of the assets utilized by the firm and the complete funding of the assets (recognition of more debt).

Implied interest for leased assets.   When computing the return on total capital (ROTC) that considers these leased assets, we must also add the implied interest expense for the leases. The interest expense component of a lease is typically estimated by bond-rating agencies and many other analysts as equal to one-third of the lease payment in year $t + 1$ (in our example, $1,188 million/3 = $396 million).

An alternative to this rule of thumb would be to derive a specific estimate based on an estimate of the firm's cost of debt capital (5.60 percent) and the estimate of the present value (PV) of the lease obligation, as follows:

---

[8]Notably, the "8 times" estimate almost always provides the lowest estimate of debt value, which means that this rule of thumb will tend to underestimate the financial leverage for these firms and the resulting implied interest expense. Still, this underestimate is minor compared to not capitalizing these lease obligations.

Estimating Technique	PV of Lease Obligation ($ Billion)	Interest Expense at 5.60 Percent ($ Million)
Eight times estimate of rent	9.50	532
PV with 15-year spread	11.80	661
PV with 13-year spread	12.14	680

Notably, all of these estimates of the implied interest expense are substantially higher than the one-third rule-of-thumb estimate of $396 million. Again, the rule of thumb underestimates the financial leverage related to these lease obligations.

To calculate the ROTC for 2002 and 2003, we need to compute the value of the lease obligations and the implied interest expense for the three years (2001, 2002, and 2003) as follows:

Year	Lease Payments for Period $t + 1$ ($ Million)	Multiple	Estimate of PV of Lease Obligation ($ Billion)	Estimate of Interest Component of Lease* ($ Million)
2003	$1,188	8	$9.50	$396
2002	898	8	7.18	299
2001	783	8	6.26	261

*Equal to one-third of lease payment for year.

Adding these values to the prior ratios results in the following lease-adjusted return on total capital values:

$$2003: \frac{1,176 + 0.2 + 396}{(20,910 + 17,062)/2} = \frac{1,572.2}{18,986} = 8.28\%$$

$$2002: \frac{1,019 + 0.3 + 299}{(17,062 + 15,096)/2} = \frac{1,318.3}{16,079} = 8.20\%$$

As shown, the ROTCs that include the leased assets and lease debt are lower (over 8 percent versus 12 percent), but they are still quite reasonable and the firm experienced an increase over the two years.

Implied depreciation on leased assets. Another factor is the implied depreciation expense that would be taken if these were not leased assets. One way to calculate this value is to simply use the typical term of the lease or weighted-average term. In the case of Walgreens, this is reasonably clear since almost all leases are twenty-year leases on buildings. However, if the value were not clear, a second alternative would be the average percent of depreciation as a percent of beginning-of-year net fixed assets. In the case of Walgreens, for 2002 this would be

Depreciation: $346 million;   **Net Fixed Assets at End of 2002: $4,591**

This implies a percent of 0.075 (346/4,591), which is clearly higher than the 5 percent on buildings. Obviously, Walgreens has many assets being depreciated over shorter lives. For these calculations we assume the twenty-year life as follows:

Year	Estimate of PV of Lease Obligation ($ Billion)	Estimate of Implied Depreciation Expense of Lease* ($ Million)
2003	9.50	475
2002	7.18	359
2001	6.26	313

*Assumes straight-line depreciation over a twenty-year life.

These implied depreciation charges should be included in ratios that include depreciation expenses.

Return on Owner's Equity   The return on owner's equity (ROE) ratio is extremely important to the owner of the enterprise (the common stockholder) because it indicates the rate of return that management has earned on the capital provided by stockholders after accounting for payments to all other capital suppliers. If we consider all equity (including preferred stock), this return would equal

14.18
$$\text{Return on Total Equity} = \frac{\text{Net Income}}{\text{Average Total Equity}}$$

If we are concerned only with owner's equity (the common stockholder's equity), the ratio would be

14.19
$$\text{Return on Owner's Equity} = \frac{\text{Net Income} - \text{Preferred Dividend}}{\text{Average Common Equity}}$$

Walgreens generated return on owner's equity of

$$2003: \frac{1,176 - 0}{(7,196 + 6,230)/2} = 17.52\%$$

$$2002: \frac{1,019 - 0}{(6,230 + 5,207)/2} = 17.82\%$$

This ratio reflects the rate of return on the stockholder's capital. It should be consistent with the firm's overall business risk, but it also should reflect the financial risk assumed by the common stockholder because of the prior claims of the firm's bondholders.

The DuPont System   The importance of ROE as an indicator of performance makes it desirable to divide the ratio into several component ratios that provide insights into the causes of a firm's ROE or any changes in it. This breakdown is generally referred to as the *DuPont System*. First, the return on equity (ROE) ratio can be broken down into two ratios that we have discussed—net profit margin and equity turnover.

14.20
$$\text{ROE} = \frac{\text{Net Income}}{\text{Common Equity}} = \frac{\text{Net Income}}{\text{Net Sales}} \times \frac{\text{Net Sales}}{\text{Common Equity}}$$

This breakdown is an identity because we have both multiplied and divided by net sales. To maintain the identity, the common equity value used is the year-end figure rather than the average of the beginning and ending value. This identity reveals that ROE equals the net profit margin times the equity turnover, which implies that a firm can improve its return on equity by *either* using its equity more efficiently (increasing its equity turnover) *or* by becoming more profitable (increasing its net profit margin).

As noted previously, a firm's equity turnover is affected by its capital structure. Specifically, a firm can increase its equity turnover by employing a higher proportion of debt capital. We can see this effect by considering the following relationship:

14.21
$$\frac{\text{Net Sales}}{\text{Common Equity}} = \frac{\text{Net Sales}}{\text{Total Assets}} \times \frac{\text{Total Assets}}{\text{Common Equity}}$$

Similar to the prior breakdown, this is an identity because we have both multiplied and divided the equity turnover ratio by total assets. This equation indicates that the equity turnover ratio equals the firm's *total asset turnover* (a measure of efficiency) times the ratio of *total assets to equity* (a measure of financial leverage). Specifically, this leverage ratio indicates the proportion of total assets financed with debt. *All assets have to be financed by either equity or some form of debt* (either current liabilities or long-term debt). Therefore, the higher the ratio of assets to equity, the higher the proportion of debt to equity. A total asset–equity ratio of 2, for example, indicates that for every two dollars of assets there is a dollar of equity, which means the firm financed one-half of its assets with equity and the other half with debt. Likewise, a total asset–equity ratio of 3 indicates that only one-third of total assets was financed with equity and two-thirds must have been financed with debt. Thus a firm can increase its equity turnover either by increasing its total asset turnover (becoming more efficient) or by increasing its financial leverage ratio (financing assets with a higher proportion of debt capital). This financial leverage ratio is also referred to as the financial leverage multiplier because the first two ratios (profit margin times total asset turnover) equal return on total assets (ROTA) and ROTA times the financial leverage multiplier equals ROE.

Combining these two breakdowns, we see that a firm's ROE is composed of three ratios, as follows:

14.22
$$\frac{\text{Net Income}}{\text{Common Equity}} = \frac{\text{Net Income}}{\text{Net Sales}} \times \frac{\text{Net Sales}}{\text{Total Assets}} \times \frac{\text{Total Assets}}{\text{Common Equity}}$$

$$= \frac{\text{Profit}}{\text{Margin}} \times \frac{\text{Total Asset}}{\text{Turnover}} \times \frac{\text{Financial}}{\text{Leverage}}$$

As an example of this important set of relationships, the figures in Exhibit 14.6 indicate what has happened to the ROE for Walgreens and the components of its ROE during the twenty-two-year period from 1982 to 2003. As noted, these ratio values employ year-end balance sheet figures (assets and equity) rather than the average of beginning and ending data, so they will differ from our individual ratio computations.

The DuPont results in Exhibit 14.6 indicate several significant trends:

1. The total asset turnover ratio was relatively stable: a total range of 2.79 to 3.31, with a small decline in the ratio to its level in 2003 of 2.85.
2. The profit margin series experienced a stable increase from 2.75 to almost a peak value of 3.62 in 2003.
3. The product of the total asset turnover and the net profit margin is equal to return on total assets (ROTA), which experienced an overall increase from 9.09 percent to a peak of 10.94 percent in 2000 followed by a small decline to 10.31 percent in 2003.
4. The financial leverage multiplier (total assets/equity) experienced a steady decline from 2.06 to 1.59. Notably, most of this debt is trade credit, which is non-interest-bearing. The fact is, the firm has almost no interest-bearing debt, except for the long-term leases on drugstores that are not on the formal balance sheet but were discussed and analyzed in the prior subsection and will be considered in the financial risk section.
5. Finally, as a result of the overall increasing ROTA and a clear decline in financial leverage, the firm's ROE has experienced a small decline overall, beginning at 18.73 and ending at 16.34.

Extended DuPont System.   Some analysts employ an *extended DuPont System,* which provides additional insights into the effect of financial leverage on the firm and also pinpoints the effect of income taxes on the firm's ROE. The concept and use of this model is the same as the basic DuPont system except for a further breakdown of components.[9]

---

[9]A full-blown discussion of this model is beyond our scope. For a detailed presentation and demonstration see Frank K. Reilly and Keith Brown, *Investment Analysis and Portfolio Management,* 8th ed., Mason, OH: South-Western, 2006.

EXHIBIT 14.6		Components of Return on Total Equity for Walgreen Co.[a]			
Year	(1) Sales–Total Assets	(2) Net Profit Margin (%)	(3)[b] Return on Total Assets	(4) Total Assets–Equity	(5)[c] Return on Equity (%)
1982	3.31	2.75	9.09	2.06	18.73
1983	3.29	2.96	9.72	2.04	19.84
1984	3.26	3.11	10.16	2.03	20.60
1985	3.29	2.98	9.79	2.00	19.58
1986	3.06	2.82	8.62	2.16	18.64
1987	3.14	2.42	7.60	2.19	16.63
1988	3.23	2.64	8.54	2.12	18.12
1989	3.20	2.87	9.18	2.04	18.74
1990	3.16	2.89	9.12	2.02	18.42
1991	3.21	2.90	9.31	1.94	18.04
1992	3.15	2.95	9.30	1.92	17.90
1993	3.27	2.67	8.74	1.84	16.07
1994	3.17	3.05	9.69	1.85	17.91
1995	3.20	3.09	9.86	1.81	17.85
1996	3.24	3.16	10.23	1.78	18.19
1997	3.18	3.26	10.37	1.77	18.35
1998	3.12	3.34	10.42	1.72	17.93
1999	3.02	3.50	10.57	1.70	17.91
2000	2.99	3.66	10.94	1.68	18.35
2001	2.79	3.60	10.03	1.70	17.01
2002	2.90	3.55	10.32	1.59	16.36
2003	2.85	3.62	10.31	1.59	16.34

[a]Ratios use year-end data for total assets and common equity rather than averages of the year.

[b]Column (3) is equal to column (1) times column (2).

[c]Column (5) is equal to column (3) times column (4).

Risk Analysis

Risk analysis examines the uncertainty of income flows for the total firm and for the individual sources of capital (that is, debt, preferred stock, and common stock). The typical approach examines the major factors that cause a firm's income flows to vary. More volatile income flows mean greater risk (uncertainty) facing the investor.

The total risk of the firm has two internal components: business risk and financial risk. We first discuss the concept of business risk: how to measure it, what causes it, and how to measure its individual causes. Then we consider financial risk and the several ratios by which we measure it. Following this analysis of a firm's internal risk factors, we discuss an important external risk factor, external liquidity risk—i.e., the ability to buy or sell the firm's stock in the secondary equity market.

BUSINESS RISK

Recall that *business risk* is the uncertainty of operating income, which is heavily impacted by the firm's industry. In turn, this uncertainty of operating earnings (EBIT) is a function of two components: (1) the volatility of sales and (2) the firm's cost structure in terms of fixed and variable costs (its operating leverage). We will discuss these in the following subsections. For now, consider the earnings for a steel firm, which will probably vary more than those of, say, a grocery chain because (1) over the business cycle, steel sales are more volatile than grocery sales and (2) the steel firm's large fixed production costs (operating leverage) make its operating earnings vary more than its sales.

Business risk is generally measured by the variability of the firm's operating income over time. In turn, the earnings variability is measured by the normalized standard deviation of the historical operating earnings series. These volatility measures are adjusted for size and for sales and earnings growth.[10]

Besides measuring overall business risk, it is very helpful to examine the two factors that contribute to the variability of operating earnings: sales variability and operating leverage.

Sales Variability   Sales variability is the prime determinant of earnings variability. Operating earnings must be as volatile as sales. Notably, the variability of sales is mainly caused by a firm's industry and is largely outside the control of management. For example, sales for a firm in a cyclical industry, such as automobiles or steel, will be quite volatile over the business cycle compared to sales of a firm in a noncyclical industry, such as retail food or hospital supplies. Like operating earnings, the variability of a firm's sales is typically measured by the normalized standard deviation of sales during the most recent five to ten years.

Operating Leverage   The variability of a firm's operating earnings also depends on its mixture of production costs. Total production costs of a firm with no *fixed* production costs would vary directly with sales, and operating profits would be a constant proportion of sales. In such an idealized example, the firm's operating profit margin would be constant and its operating profits would have the same relative volatility as its sales. Realistically, firms always have some fixed production costs such as buildings, machinery, or relatively permanent personnel.

Fixed production costs cause operating profits to vary more than sales over the business cycle. Specifically, during slow periods, profits decline by a larger percentage than sales, and during an economic expansion, profits will increase by a larger percentage than sales.

The employment of fixed production costs is referred to as *operating leverage*. Clearly, greater operating leverage makes the operating earnings series more volatile relative to the sales series.[11]

FINANCIAL RISK

Financial risk, you will recall, is the *additional* uncertainty of returns to equityholders due to a firm's use of fixed obligation debt securities. This financial uncertainty is in addition to the firm's business risk. When a firm sells bonds to raise capital, the required interest payments on this capital precede the computation of common stock earnings, and these interest payments are fixed obligations. As with operating leverage, during good times the net

Interactive e-lectures

For more explanation and an animated example of solvency, go to: http://reillyxtra .swlearning.com.

---

[10]It is beyond the scope of this text to discuss the computation details. For a further discussion on this general topic, see Eugene Brigham and Louis C. Gapenski, *Financial Management: Theory and Practice,* 10th ed., Fort Worth, TX: Dryden, 2003, Chapters 6 and 10. For a detailed discussion and demonstration of the computations that adjust for size and growth, see Frank K. Reilly and Keith Brown, *Investment Analysis and Portfolio Management,* 8th ed., Mason, OH: South-Western, 2006.

[11]See C. F. Lee, Joseph Finnerty, and Edgar Norton, *Foundations of Financial Management,* Mason, OH: South-Western, 1997, Chapter 5 for further discussion. For detailed computations, see Frank K. Reilly and Keith Brown, *Investment Analysis and Portfolio Management,* 8th ed., Mason, OH: South-Western, 2006.

earnings available for common stock after interest payments will experience a larger percentage increase than operating earnings, whereas during a business decline the earnings available to stockholders will decline by a larger percentage than operating earnings because of these fixed financial costs. Obviously, as a firm increases the proportion of financing using fixed contractual obligations (bonds), it increases its financial risk and the possibility of default and bankruptcy.

A very important point to remember is that *the acceptable level of financial risk for a firm depends on its business risk.* If the firm has low business risk (i.e., stable operating earnings), investors are willing to accept higher financial risk. For example, retail food companies typically have stable operating earnings over time, which implies *low* business risk, and means that investors and bond-rating firms will allow the firms to have *higher* financial risk.[12]

In our analysis, we employ three sets of financial ratios to measure financial risk, and *all three* sets should be considered. First, there are balance sheet ratios that indicate the proportion of capital derived from debt securities compared to equity capital. Second are ratios that consider the earnings or cash flows available to pay fixed financial charges. Third are ratios that consider the cash flows available and relate these cash flows to the book value of the outstanding debt.

PROPORTION OF DEBT (BALANCE SHEET) RATIOS

The proportion of debt ratios indicate what proportion of the firm's capital is derived from debt compared to other sources of capital, such as preferred stock, common stock, and retained earnings. A higher proportion of debt capital compared to equity capital makes earnings more volatile (i.e., more financial leverage) and increases the probability that a firm could default on the debt. Therefore, higher proportion of debt ratios indicate greater financial risk. The following are the major proportion of debt ratios used to measure financial risk.

Debt–Equity Ratio   The debt–equity ratio is

14.23
$$\text{Debt–Equity Ratio} = \frac{\text{Total Long-Term Debt}}{\text{Total Equity}}$$

The debt figure includes all long-term fixed obligations, including subordinated convertible bonds. The equity typically is the book value of equity and includes preferred stock, common stock, and retained earnings. Some analysts prefer to exclude preferred stock and consider only common equity. Total equity is preferable if some of the firms being analyzed have preferred stock.

Notably, debt ratios can be computed *with and without deferred taxes.* Most balance sheets include an accumulated deferred tax figure. There is some controversy regarding whether these deferred taxes should be treated as a liability or as part of permanent capital. Some argue that if the deferred tax has accumulated because of the difference in accelerated and straight-line depreciation, this liability may never be paid. That is, as long as the firm continues to grow and add new assets, this total deferred tax account continues to grow. Alternatively, if the deferred tax account is caused by differences in the recognition of income on long-term contracts, there will be a reversal and this liability must eventually be paid. To resolve this question, the analyst must determine the reason for the deferred tax account

---

[12]Support for this specific relationship is a set of tables published by Standard & Poor's Credit Rating division that suggests specific required ratios needed to be considered for a specific rating. In these tables, the required financial risk ratios differ based on the specification of the business risk of the firm.

and examine its long-term trend.[13] Walgreens' deferred tax account is because of a depreciation difference and it has typically grown over time.

A second consideration when computing debt ratios is the existence of operating leases, as mentioned in a prior section. As noted, given a firm like Walgreens with extensive leased facilities, it is necessary to include an estimate of the present value of the lease payments as long-term debt.

To show the effect of these two significant items on the financial risk of Walgreens, we define the ratios to include both of these factors, but they will be broken out to identify the effect of each of the components of total debt. Thus, the debt–equity ratio is

14.24 $$\text{Debt–Equity Ratio} = \frac{\text{Total Long-Term Debt}}{\text{Total Equity}}$$

$$= \frac{\text{Noncurrent Liabilities} + \text{Deferred Taxes} + \text{PV of Lease Obligations}}{\text{Total Equity}}$$

For Walgreens, the debt–equity ratios were

$$2003: \frac{562 + 228 + 9,504}{7,196} = \frac{10,294}{7,196} = 143.1\%$$

$$2002: \frac{517 + 177 + 7,183}{6,230} = \frac{7,877}{6,230} = 126.4\%$$

$$2001: \frac{478 + 137 + 6,262}{5,207} = \frac{6,877}{5,207} = 132.1\%$$

These ratios demonstrate the significant impact of including the present value of the lease payments as part of long-term debt—for example, the debt–equity percent for 2003 went from less than 11 percent without lease obligations to over 143 percent when capitalized leases are included.

Long-Term Debt–Total Capital Ratio   The long-term debt–total capital ratio indicates the proportion of long-term capital derived from long-term debt capital. It is computed as

14.25 $$\text{Long-Term Debt} - \text{Total Capital Ratio} = \frac{\text{Total Long-Term Debt}}{\text{Total Long-Term Capital}}$$

The total long-term debt values are the same as above. The total long-term capital would include all long-term debt, any preferred stock, and total equity. The long-term debt–total capital ratios for Walgreens were

Including Deferred Taxes and Lease Obligations as Long-Term Debt

$$2003: \frac{10,294}{10,294 + 7,196} = \frac{10,294}{17,490} = 58.9\%$$

$$2002: \frac{7,877}{7,877 + 6,230} = \frac{7,877}{14,107} = 55.8\%$$

$$2001: \frac{6,877}{6,877 + 5,207} = \frac{6,877}{12,084} = 56.9\%$$

[13]For a further discussion of this, see Gerald I. White, Ashwinpaul C. Sondhi, and Dov Fried, *The Analysis and Use of Financial Statements,* 3rd ed., New York: John Wiley & Sons, 2001, pp. 1017–1018.

Again, this ratio, which includes the present value of lease obligations, shows that a significant percent of long-term capital is debt obligations, which differs substantially from a ratio without the lease obligations.

Total Debt–Total Capital Ratios In many cases, it is useful to compare *total* debt to *total* capital, computed as

14.26
$$\frac{\text{Total Debt}}{\text{Total Capital}} = \frac{\text{Current Liabilities} + \text{Total Long-Term Debt}}{\text{Total Debt} + \text{Total Equity}}$$

This ratio is especially revealing for a firm that derives substantial capital from short-term borrowing. The total debt–total capital ratios for Walgreens were

Including Deferred Taxes and Lease Obligations as Long-Term Debt

$$2003: \frac{3,421 + 10,294}{13,715 + 7,196} = \frac{13,715}{20,911} = 65.6\%$$

$$2002: \frac{2,955 + 7,877}{10,832 + 6,230} = \frac{10,832}{17,062} = 63.5\%$$

$$2001: \frac{3,102 + 6,877}{9,979 + 5,207} = \frac{9,979}{15,186} = 65.7\%$$

These ratios, which indicate that about 66 percent of Walgreens' assets are financed with debt, should be compared with those of industry competitors to evaluate their consistency with the business risk of this industry. This comparison would also indicate how much higher this ratio can go (i.e., the firm's unused debt capacity).

Some observers would consider this ratio too conservative because it includes accounts payable and accrued expenses, which are *non-interest-bearing debt*. If this non-interest-bearing debt along with deferred taxes is excluded from debt and from total capital, the ratio declines as follows:

14.27
$$\frac{\text{Total Interest-Bearing Debt}}{\text{Total Capital}} = \frac{\text{Total Interest-Bearing Debt}}{\text{Total Capital} - \text{Non-Interest Liabilities}}$$

For Walgreens,

$$2003: \frac{562 + 9,504}{20,911 - 3,421} = \frac{10,066}{17,490} = 57.6\%$$

$$2002: \frac{517 + 7183}{17,062 - 2,955} = \frac{7,700}{14,107} = 54.6\%$$

$$2001: \frac{478 + 6,262}{15,186 - 3,012} = \frac{6,740}{12,174} = 55.4\%$$

While these debt percents are lower, they are still quite high, which confirms the importance of considering the impact of lease obligations on the financial risk of firms like Walgreens who employ this form of financing.

EARNINGS AND CASH FLOW COVERAGE RATIOS

In addition to ratios that indicate the proportion of debt on the balance sheet, investors are very conscious of ratios that relate the *flow* of earnings or cash flows available to meet the required interest and lease payments. A higher ratio of available earnings or cash flow relative to fixed financial charges indicates lower financial risk.

Interest Coverage Ratio   The standard interest coverage ratio is computed as

14.28

$$\text{Interest Coverage} = \frac{\text{Income before Interest and Taxes (EBIT)}}{\text{Debt Interest Charges}}$$

$$= \frac{\text{Net Income + Income Taxes + Interest Expense}}{\text{Interest Expense}}$$

This ratio indicates how many times the fixed interest charges are earned, based on the earnings available to pay these expenses.[14] Alternatively, one minus the reciprocal of the interest coverage ratio indicates how far earnings could decline before it would be impossible to pay the interest charges from current earnings. For example, a coverage ratio of five means that earnings could decline by 80 percent (1 minus $\frac{1}{5}$), and the firm could still pay its fixed financial charges. Again, it is necessary to consider the impact of the lease obligations on this ratio because if we only consider the firm's public interest-bearing debt, the interest cost is about one-half million dollars and the coverage ratio exceeds 3,000 times. In contrast, if we recognize the lease obligations as debt and use the assumption by the rating agencies that one-third of the lease payment in year $t + 1$ is interest (as computed earlier), the coverage ratio would be restated as follows:

14.29

$$\frac{\text{Fixed Financial}}{\text{Cost Coverage}} = \frac{\text{Earnings before Interest and Taxes} + (1/3)\text{Lease Payment}_{t+1}}{\text{Gross Interest Expense} + (1/3)\text{Lease Payment}_{t+1}}$$

Hence, the fixed financial cost coverage ratios for Walgreens were

$$2003: \frac{1{,}175 + 713 + 396}{396} = \frac{2{,}284}{396} = 5.8 \text{ times}$$

$$2002: \frac{1{,}019 + 618 + 299}{299} = \frac{1{,}936}{299} = 6.5 \text{ times}$$

$$2001: \frac{886 + 537 + 261}{261} = \frac{1{,}684}{261} = 6.5 \text{ times}$$

These fixed financial cost coverage ratios show a substantially different picture than the coverage ratios that do not consider the impact of the lease obligations. Even so, these coverage ratios show reasonable financial risk for a firm with very low business risk.

The trend of Walgreens' coverage ratios has been consistent with the overall trend in the proportion of debt ratios. The point is, the proportion of debt ratios and the earnings flow ratios do not always give consistent results because the proportion of debt ratios are not sensitive to changes in earnings or to changes in the interest rates on the debt. For example, if interest rates increase or if the firm replaces old debt with new debt that has a higher interest rate, no change would occur in the proportion of debt ratios but the interest coverage

---

[14]The net income figure used in the analysis is the operating income after taxes because, once again, it is important to exclude earnings and cash flows that are considered nonrecurring. The idea is to consider only those earnings that should be available in the future (that is, earnings from ongoing operations).

ratio would decline. Also, the interest coverage ratio is sensitive to an increase or decrease in earnings. Therefore, the results using balance sheet ratios and coverage ratios can differ. Given a difference between the two sets of ratios, we have a strong preference for the coverage ratios that reflect the ability of the firm to meet its financial obligations.

Alternatives to these earnings coverage ratios are several ratios that relate the cash flow available from operations to either interest expense or total fixed charges.

Cash Flow Coverage Ratio   The motivation for this ratio is that a firm's earnings and cash flow typically will differ substantially (these differences have been noted and will be considered in a subsequent section). The cash flow value used is the cash flow from operating activities figure contained in the cash flow statement. As such, it includes depreciation expense, deferred taxes, and the impact of all working capital changes. Again, it is appropriate to specify the ratio in terms of total fixed financial costs including leases, as follows:

14.30   **Cash Flow Coverage of Fixed Financial Cost**

$$= \frac{\text{Net Cash Flow from Operating Activities} + \text{Interest Expense} + (1/3)\,\text{Lease Obligations}}{\text{Interest Expense} + (1/3)\,\text{Lease Obligations}}$$

We use the values given in the cash flow statement since we are specifically interested in the cash flow effect.

The cash flow coverage ratios for Walgreens were

$$2003: \frac{1{,}492 + 0.2 + 396}{0.02 + 396} = \frac{1{,}888}{396} = 4.77 \text{ times}$$

$$2002: \frac{1{,}474 + 0.3 + 299}{0.03 + 299} = \frac{1{,}773}{299} = 5.93 \text{ times}$$

$$2001: \frac{719 + 3.4 + 261}{3.4 + 261} = \frac{983}{264} = 3.72 \text{ times}$$

These coverage ratios are not overpowering but are respectable for a firm with low business risk.

Cash Flow–Long-Term Debt Ratio   Several studies have used a ratio that relates cash flow to a firm's outstanding debt. The cash flow–outstanding debt ratios are unique because they relate the *flow* of earnings plus noncash expenses to the *stock* of outstanding debt. These ratios have been significant variables in numerous studies concerned with predicting bankruptcies and bond ratings. (These studies are listed in the reference section.) The cash flow figure we use is the cash flow from operating activities. Obviously, the higher the percent of cash flow to long-term debt, the stronger the company—i.e., the lower its financial risk. This ratio would be computed as

14.31 $\dfrac{\textbf{Cash Flow}}{\textbf{Long-Term Debt}}$

$$= \frac{\text{Cash Flow from Operating Activities}}{\text{Book Value of Long-Term Debt} + \text{Present Value of Lease Obligations}}$$

For Walgreens, the ratios were as follows. Again, these ratios assume that deferred taxes and lease obligations are included as long-term debt.

$$2003: \quad \frac{1{,}492}{228 + 9{,}504} = \frac{1{,}492}{9{,}732} = 15.3\%$$

$$2002: \quad \frac{1{,}474}{177 + 7{,}183} = \frac{1{,}474}{7{,}360} = 20.0\%$$

$$2001: \quad \frac{719}{137 + 6{,}262} = \frac{719}{6{,}399} = 11.2\%$$

The large increase in percent during 2002 was caused by the increase in cash flow due to a smaller increase in inventory during the year (see Exhibit 14.3).

Cash Flow–Total Debt Ratio   Investors also should consider the relationship of cash flow to *total* debt to check that a firm has not had a significant increase in its short-term borrowing.

14.32

$$\frac{\text{Cash Flow}}{\text{Total Debt}} = \frac{\text{Cash Flow from Operating Activities}}{\text{Total Long-Term Debt} + \text{Interest-Bearing Current Liabilities}}$$

For Walgreens, these ratios were

$$2003: \quad \frac{1{,}492}{9{,}732 + 3{,}421} = \frac{1{,}492}{13{,}153} = 11.3\%$$

$$2002: \quad \frac{1{,}474}{7{,}360 + 2{,}955} = \frac{1{,}474}{10{,}315} = 14.3\%$$

$$2001: \quad \frac{719}{6{,}399 + 3{,}012} = \frac{719}{9{,}411} = 7.6\%$$

When we compare these ratios to those with only long-term debt, they reflect the firm's proportion of short-term debt due to short-term borrowing. We excluded accounts payable because they are non-interest-bearing. In the case of Walgreens, this eliminated almost all current liabilities. As before, it is important to compare these flow ratios with similar ratios for other companies in the industry and with the overall economy to gauge the firm's relative performance.

Alternative Measures of Cash Flow[15]   As noted, many past studies that included a cash flow variable used the traditional measure of cash flow. The requirement that companies must prepare and report the statement of cash flows to stockholders has raised interest in other exact measures of cash flow. The first alternative measure is the *cash flow from operations,* which is taken directly from the statement of cash flows and is the one we have used. A second alternative measure is *free cash flow,* which is a modification of the cash flow from operations—that is, capital expenditures (minus the cash flow from the sale of assets) are

---

[15]A list of studies in which financial ratios or cash flow variables are used to predict bankruptcies or bond ratings is included in the reference section.

also deducted and some analysts also subtract dividends. The following table summarizes the values derived earlier in the chapter (page 431) for Walgreens.

Year	Traditional Cash Flow	Cash Flow from Operations	Net Cap Exp	FREE CASH FLOW		
				Before Div.	Div.	After Div.
2003	1581	1492	711	781	152	629
2002	1349	1474	566	908	147	761
2001	1202	719	1,193	(474)	141	(615)

As shown, Walgreens has strong and growing cash flow from operations even after considering significant working capital requirements, but the firm experiences small or negative free cash flow because of substantial net capital expenditures necessitated by the firm's growth.

EXTERNAL MARKET LIQUIDITY RISK

External Market Liquidity Defined   In Chapter 4 we discussed external market liquidity as the ability to buy or sell an asset quickly with little price change from a prior transaction assuming no new information. GE and Pfizer are examples of liquid common stocks because investors can sell them quickly with little price change from the prior trade. Investors might be able to sell an illiquid stock quickly, but the price would be significantly different from the prior price. Alternatively, the broker might be able to get a specified price, but could take several days doing so.

Determinants of External Market Liquidity   Investors should know the liquidity characteristics of the securities they currently own or may buy because liquidity can be important if they want to change the composition of their portfolios. Although the major determinants of market liquidity are reflected in market trading data, several internal corporate variables are good proxies for these market variables. The most important determinant of external market liquidity is the number of shares or the dollar value of shares traded (the dollar value adjusts for different price levels). More trading activity indicates a greater probability that one can find someone to take the other side of a desired transaction. A very good measure that is usually available is *trading turnover* (the percentage of outstanding shares traded during a period of time), which indicates relative trading activity. During calendar year 2003 about 835 million shares of Walgreens were traded, which indicates annual trading turnover of approximately 81 percent (835 million/1,032 million). This compares with the average turnover for the NYSE of about 95 percent. Another measure of market liquidity is the bid–ask spread, where a smaller spread indicates greater liquidity. In addition, certain corporate variables are correlated with these trading variables:

1. Total market value of outstanding securities (number of common shares outstanding times the market price per share)
2. Number of security owners

Numerous studies have shown that the main determinant of the bid–ask spread (besides price) is the dollar value of trading.[16] In turn, the value of trading correlates highly with the market value of the outstanding securities and the number of security holders because with more shares outstanding, there will be more stockholders to buy or sell at any time for a variety of purposes. Numerous buyers and sellers provide liquidity.

---

[16]Studies on this topic were discussed in Chapter 4.

We can estimate the market value of Walgreens' outstanding stock as the average number of shares outstanding during the year (adjusted for stock splits) times the average market price for the year (equal to the high price plus the low price divided by two) as follows:[17]

$$2003: 1{,}032 \times \frac{36 + 27}{2} = \$32.51 \text{ billion}$$

$$2002: 1{,}032 \times \frac{40 + 31}{2} = \$36.65 \text{ billion}$$

$$2001: 1{,}029 \times \frac{45 + 31}{2} = \$39.10 \text{ billion}$$

These market values would place Walgreens in the large-cap category, which usually begins at about \$5 billion. Walgreens' stockholders number 600,000, including more than 650 institutions that own approximately 56 percent of the outstanding stock. These large values for market value, the number of stockholders, institutional holders, and the high trading turnover indicate a highly liquid market in Walgreens stock, which implies extremely low external liquidity risk.

Analysis of Growth Potential

IMPORTANCE OF GROWTH ANALYSIS

The analysis of *sustainable growth potential* examines ratios that indicate how fast a firm should grow. Analysis of a firm's growth potential is important for both lenders and owners. Owners know that the value of the firm depends on its future growth in earnings, cash flow, and dividends. In the following chapter, we discuss various valuation models that are based on alternative cash flows, the investor's required rate of return for the stock, and the firm's expected growth rate of cash flows.

Creditors also are interested in a firm's growth potential because the firm's future success is the major determinant of its ability to pay obligations, and the firm's future success is influenced by its growth. Some credit analysis ratios measure the book value of a firm's assets relative to its financial obligations, assuming that the firm can sell these assets to pay off the loan in case of default. Selling assets in a forced liquidation will typically yield only about ten to fifteen cents on the dollar. Currently, it is widely recognized that the more relevant analysis is the ability of the firm to pay off its obligations as an ongoing enterprise, which is impacted by its growth potential. This analysis is also relevant to changes of bond ratings.

DETERMINANTS OF GROWTH

The growth of business, like the growth on any economic entity, including the aggregate economy, depends on

1. The amount of resources retained and reinvested in the entity
2. The rate of return earned on the reinvested funds

The more a firm reinvests, the greater its potential for growth. Alternatively, for a given level of reinvestment, a firm will grow faster if it earns a higher rate of return on the funds

---

[17]These stock prices (which are for the calendar year) are rounded to the nearest whole dollar.

reinvested. Therefore, the growth rate of equity earnings is a function of two variables: (1) the percentage of net earnings retained (the firm's retention rate) and (2) the rate of return earned on the firm's equity capital (the firm's ROE) because when earnings are retained they become part of the firm's equity.

14.33   **g = Percentage of Earnings Retained × Return on Equity**

$$= \text{RR} \times \text{ROE}$$

where:

$$
\begin{aligned}
g &= \text{potential (i.e., sustainable) growth rate} \\
\text{RR} &= \text{the retention rate of earnings} \\
\text{ROE} &= \text{the firm's return on equity}
\end{aligned}
$$

The retention rate is a decision by the board of directors based on the investment opportunities available to the firm. Theory suggests that the firm should retain earnings and reinvest them as long as the expected rate of return on the investment exceeds the firm's cost of capital.

As discussed earlier regarding the DuPont System, a the firm's ROE is a function of three components:

- Net profit margin
- Total asset turnover
- Financial leverage (total assets/equity)

Therefore, a firm can increase its ROE by increasing its profit margin, by becoming more efficient (increasing its total asset turnover), or by increasing its financial leverage (and its financial risk). As discussed, investors should examine and estimate each of the components when estimating the ROE for a firm.

The sustainable growth potential analysis for Walgreens begins with the retention rate (RR):

14.34 $$\text{Retention Rate} = 1 - \frac{\text{Dividends Declared}}{\text{Operating Income after Taxes}}$$

Walgreens' RR figures were

$$
\begin{aligned}
2003: &\quad 1 - \frac{0.16}{1.14} = 0.86 \\[6pt]
2002: &\quad 1 - \frac{0.15}{0.99} = 0.85 \\[6pt]
2001: &\quad 1 - \frac{0.14}{0.86} = 0.84
\end{aligned}
$$

The historical results in Exhibit 14.7 indicate that the retention rate for Walgreens has been relatively stable during the twenty-two-year period in excess of 70 percent including recent increases to over 80 percent.

Exhibit 14.6 contains the three components of ROE for the period 1982–2003. Exhibit 14.7 contains the two factors that determine a firm's growth potential and the implied growth rate during the past twenty-two-years. Overall, Walgreens experienced a slight decline in its growth potential during the early 1990s, but since 1995 the firm has experienced a potential growth rate in excess of 14 percent, which is very consistent with its actual performance.

EXHIBIT 14.7	Walgreen Co. Components of Growth and the Implied Sustainable Growth Rate		
Year	(1) Retention Rate	(2) Return on Equity[a]	(3)[b] Sustainable Growth Rate
1982	0.72	18.73	13.49
1983	0.74	19.84	14.68
1984	0.74	20.60	15.24
1985	0.71	19.58	13.90
1986	0.70	18.64	13.05
1987	0.68	16.63	11.31
1988	0.71	18.12	12.87
1989	0.73	18.74	13.68
1990	0.72	18.42	13.26
1991	0.71	18.04	12.81
1992	0.71	17.90	12.71
1993	0.67	16.07	10.77
1994	0.70	17.91	12.54
1995	0.69	17.85	12.32
1996	0.71	18.19	12.91
1997	0.73	18.35	13.40
1998	0.75	17.93	13.44
1999	0.79	17.91	14.15
2000	0.82	18.35	15.05
2001	0.84	17.01	14.29
2002	0.85	16.36	13.91
2003	0.86	16.34	14.05

[a]From Exhibit 14.6.

[b]Column (3) is equal to column (1) times column (2).

Exhibit 14.7 reinforces our understanding of the importance of the firm's ROE. Walgreens' retention rate was quite stable throughout the period with an increase during the last five years. Even with this, it has been the firm's ROE that has mainly determined its sustainable growth rate. This analysis indicates that the important consideration is *the long-run outlook for the components of sustainable growth.* Investors need to *project* changes in each of the components of ROE and employ these projections to estimate an ROE to use in the growth model along with an estimate of the firm's long-run retention rate. We will come back to these concepts on numerous occasions when discussing stock valuation. This detailed analysis of ROE is extremely important for growth companies where the ROEs are notably above average for the economy and, therefore, vulnerable to competition.

Comparative Analysis of Ratios

We have discussed the importance of comparative analysis, but so far we have concentrated on the selection and computation of specific ratios. Exhibit 14.8 contains most of the ratios discussed for Walgreens, the retail drug store industry (as derived from the *S&P Analysts Handbook*), and the S&P Industrials Index. The three-year comparison should provide some

EXHIBIT 14.8 Summary of Financial Ratios for Walgreens, S&P Retail Drugstores, S&P Industrials Index, 2000–2002

	2002			2001			2000		
	Walgreens	Drugstores	S&P Industrials	Walgreens	Drugstores	S&P Industrials	Walgreens	Drugstores	S&P Industrials
Internal Liquidity									
Current ratio	1.75	1.81	1.36	1.46	1.58	1.29	1.54	1.53	1.19
Quick ratio	0.48	0.47	0.98	0.27	0.32	0.92	0.27	0.32	0.84
Cash ratio	0.15	0.16	0.32	0.01	0.04	0.26	0.01	0.06	0.21
Receivables turnover	32.72	27.54	4.24	34.86	27.03	4.30	27.8	25.50	4.55
Average collection period	11.2	13.3	86.1	10.5	13.5	84.9	13.1	14.3	80.2
Working capital sales	0.06	0.09	0.11	0.05	0.08	0.09	0.06	0.08	0.08
Operating Performance									
Total asset turnover	3.07	2.80	0.76	3.09	2.69	0.79	3.3	2.14	0.86
Inventory turnover (sales)[a]	8.05	6.68	10.89	7.80	6.29	10.94	8.01	5.48	11.29
Working capital turnover	15.96	11.74	8.88	18.73	13.07	11.34	16.67	12.12	12.72
Net fixed asset turnover	6.42	8.11	2.77	6.34	7.71	2.80	7.04	6.22	2.97
Equity turnover	5.02	5.05	2.38	5.22	4.99	2.32	5.50	5.14	2.63
Profitability									
Gross profit margin	26.52	—	—	26.7	—	—	27.1	—	—
Operating profit margin	5.71	5.41	12.81	5.78	5.38	10.53	5.8	5.82	14.34
Net profit margin	3.62	3.29	7.07	3.55	2.81	4.89	3.7	2.87	8.17
Return on total capital[b]	10.89	9.54	6.85	11.15	9.01	5.41	11.9	7.74	8.72
Return on owner's equity	17.82	16.64	16.80	18.76	15.86	11.33	20.1	17.49	21.51
Financial Risk									
Debt–equity ratio[c]	126.43	17.82	139.93	132.07	16.91	113.60	140.67	15.79	106.58
Long-term debt–long-term capital[b]	55.84	15.12	58.32	56.91	14.46	53.18	58.45	13.64	51.59
Total debt–total capital[b]	63.49	42.17	69.81	65.71	45.70	66.09	66.11	45.33	65.98
Interest coverage	6.45	49.18	6.68	6.47	30.77	5.24	6.6	26.20	7.30
Cash flow–long-term debt[b]	24.09	194.24	36.78	15.37	231.48	37.78	16.32	266.13	58.03
Cash flow–total debt[b]	17.19	28.12	17.11	10.45	25.49	16.92	11.77	27.76	23.25
Growth Analysis[c]									
Retention rate	0.85	0.86	0.72	0.84	0.81	0.58	0.82	0.84	0.76
Return on equity	16.36	15.37	17.84	17.01	13.14	11.02	18.35	13.38	20.60
Total asset turnover	2.90	2.69	0.76	2.99	2.59	0.76	2.99	2.66	0.85
Total assets–equity	1.59	1.73	3.30	1.68	1.88	2.96	1.68	1.83	2.95
Net profit margin	3.55	3.29	3.12	3.66	2.81	2.26	3.66	2.87	6.52
Sustainable growth rate	13.96	13.18	12.77	14.24	10.67	6.38	15.05	11.18	15.60

[a]Computed using sales since cost of sales not available for industry and S&P Industrials.

[b]Ratios for Walgreens include deferred taxes and leased obligations as long-term debt, which is not available for Industry and Industrials.

[c]Calculated using year-end data.

insights, although we typically would want to examine data for a five- to ten-year period. It was necessary to do the comparison for the period 2000–2002 because industry and market data from Standard and Poor's were not available for 2003 at the time of this writing.

INTERNAL LIQUIDITY

The three basic ratios (current ratio, quick ratio, and cash ratio) provided mixed results regarding liquidity for Walgreens relative to the industry and market. The current ratio is about equal to the industry and above the market. The firm's receivables collection period is substantially less than the S&P Industrials and below the retail drugstore industry. Because the collection period has been fairly steady, the difference is due to the firm's basic credit policy.

Overall, the comparisons indicate reasonably strong internal liquidity. An additional positive liquidity factor is the firm's ability to sell high-grade commercial paper and several major bank credit lines.

OPERATING PERFORMANCE

This segment of the analysis considers efficiency ratios (turnovers) and profitability ratios. The major comparison is relative to the industry. Walgreens' turnover ratios were consistently substantially above those of the retail drugstore industry.

The comparison of profitability from sales was mixed. Operating profit margins were about equal to the industry, but net margins beat the industry performance. The strong operating profit margin was in spite of the higher growth rate of new stores relative to the competition, and the fact that new stores require eighteen to twenty-four months to reach the firm's "normal" profit rate.

The profit performance related to invested capital was historically strong. The return on total capital (including capitalized leases) for Walgreens was consistently above both the S&P Industrials and the retail drugstore industry. Walgreens likewise always attained higher ROEs than its industry and the market.

RISK ANALYSIS

Walgreens' financial risk ratios, measured in terms of proportion of debt, were consistently inferior to those of the industry and the market when both deferred taxes and capitalized leases were included as long-term debt for Walgreens, but it was not possible to do a comparable adjustment for the S&P Industrials or the industry. Such an adjustment would have a significant impact on the industry results. Similarly, the financial risk ratios that use cash flow for Walgreens were below the market and its industry. These comparisons indicate that Walgreens has a reasonable amount of financial risk, but it is not of major concern because the firm has very low business risk based on consistently high growth in sales and operating profit. Notably, there are no specific comparative ratios available for both business and external liquidity risk. Still, in both cases the analysis of the Walgreens ratios shows that Walgreens had very low business and external liquidity risk.

GROWTH ANALYSIS

Walgreens has generally maintained a sustainable growth rate above its industry and the aggregate market, based on both a higher ROE and a consistently higher retention rate.

In sum, Walgreens has adequate liquidity, a good operating record including a very consistent growth record that implies low business risk, relatively low financial risk even when we consider the leases on stores, and clearly above-average growth performance. Your success as an investor depends on how well you use these historical numbers to derive meaningful *estimates* of *future* performance for use in a valuation model. As noted previously, everybody is generally aware of the valuation models, so it is the individual who can provide the best *estimates* of relevant valuation variables who will experience superior risk-adjusted performance.

Analysis of Non-U.S. Financial Statements

As we have stressed several times, your portfolio should encompass other economies and markets, numerous global industries, and many foreign firms in these global industries. However, because accounting conventions differ among countries, non-U.S. financial statements will differ from those in this chapter and from what you will see in a typical accounting course. While it is beyond the scope of this text to discuss these alternative accounting conventions in detail, we encourage you to examine the section in the references entitled "Analysis of International Financial Statements." Also, there is a discussion of some of these differences in Reilly and Brown.[18]

The Quality of Financial Statements

Analysts sometimes speak of the quality of a firm's earnings or the quality of a firm's balance sheet. In general, *quality financial statements* are a good reflection of reality; accounting tricks and one-time changes are not used to make the firm appear stronger than it really is. Some factors that lead to lower-quality financial statements were mentioned previously when we discussed ratio analysis. Other quality influences are discussed here.[19]

BALANCE SHEET

A high-quality balance sheet typically has a conservative use of debt or leverage. Therefore, the potential of financial distress resulting from the need to service debt is quite low. Little use of debt also implies the firm has unused borrowing capacity, which implies that the firm can draw on that unused capacity to make profitable investments.

A quality balance sheet contains assets with market values greater than their book value. The capability of management and the existence of intangible assets—such as goodwill, trademarks, or patents—will make the market value of the firm's assets exceed their book values. In general, as a result of inflation and historical cost accounting, we might expect the market value of assets to exceed their book values. Overpriced assets on the books occur when a firm has outdated, technologically inferior assets; obsolete inventory; and nonperforming assets such as a bank that has not written off nonperforming loans.

The presence of off-balance-sheet liabilities also harms the quality of a balance sheet. Such liabilities may include joint ventures and loan commitments or guarantees to subsidiaries.[20]

---

[18]Frank K. Reilly and Keith Brown, *Investment Analysis and Portfolio Management,* 8th ed., Mason, OH: South-Western, 2006, Chapter 12.

[19]For additional discussion, see K. G. Palepu, P. M. Healy, and Victor L. Bernard, *Business Analysis and Valuation,* 3rd ed., Mason, OH: South-Western, 2004, Chapter 3.

[20]For detailed analysis of these items, see Clyde P. Stickney, Paul Brown, and James Wahlen, *Financial Reporting and Statement Analysis,* 5th ed., Mason, OH: South-Western, 2004, Chapter 6.

INCOME STATEMENT

High-quality earnings are *repeatable* earnings. For example, they arise from sales among customers who are expected to do repeat business with the firm and from costs that are not artificially low as a result of unusual and short-lived input price reductions. One-time and nonrecurring items—such as accounting changes, mergers, and asset sales—should be ignored when examining earnings. Unexpected exchange rate fluctuations that work in the firm's favor to raise revenues or reduce costs should also be viewed as nonrecurring.

High-quality earnings result from the use of conservative accounting principles that do not result in overstated revenues and understated costs. The closer the earnings are to cash, the higher the quality of the income statement. Suppose a firm sells furniture "on time" by allowing customers to make monthly payments. A higher-quality income statement will recognize revenue using the "installment" principle; that is, as the cash is collected each month, in turn, annual sales will reflect only the cash collected from sales during the year. A lower-quality income statement will recognize 100 percent of the revenue at the time of sale, even though payments may stretch well into next year.[21]

FOOTNOTES

A word to the wise: **read the footnotes!** The purpose of the footnotes (that have come to include three or more pages in most annual reports) is to provide information on how the firm handles balance sheet and income items. While the footnotes may not reveal everything you should know (e.g., Enron), if you do not read them you cannot hope to be informed.

The Value of Financial Statement Analysis

Financial statements, by their nature, are backward-looking. They report the firm's assets, liabilities, and equity as of a certain (past) date; they report a firm's revenues, expenses, or cash flows over some (past) time period. An efficient capital market will have already incorporated this past information into security prices; so it may seem, at first glance, that analysis of a firm's financial statements and ratios is a waste of the analyst's time.

The fact is, the opposite is true. Analysis of financial statements allows the analyst to gain knowledge of a firm's operating and financial strategy and structure. This, in turn, assists the analyst in determining the effects of *future* events on the firm's cash flows. Combining knowledge of the firm's strategy, operating and financial leverage, and possible macro- and microeconomic scenarios is necessary to determine an appropriate market value for the firm's stock. Combining the analysis of historical data with potential future scenarios allows analysts to evaluate the risks facing the firm and then to develop an expected return forecast based on these risks. The final outcome of the process, as future chapters will detail, is the determination of the firm's current value based on expected cash flows, which is compared to its security price. The point is, the detailed analysis of the historical results ensures a better estimation of the expected cash flows and thus a superior valuation of the firm.

---

[21]For detailed analysis of income items, see Clyde P. Stickney, Paul Brown, and James Wahlen, *Financial Reporting and Statement Analysis,* 5th ed., Mason, OH: South-Western, 2004, Chapter 5.

Specific Uses of Financial Ratios

In addition to measuring firm performance and risk, financial ratios have been used in four major areas in investments: (1) stock valuation, (2) the identification of internal corporate variables that affect a stock's systematic risk (beta), (3) assigning credit quality ratings on bonds, and (4) predicting insolvency (bankruptcy) of firms.

STOCK VALUATION MODELS

As we will discuss in the following chapter, most valuation models attempt to derive a value based on one of several present value of cash flow models or appropriate relative valuation ratios for a stock. As will be noted, all the valuation models require an estimate of the expected growth rate of earnings, cash flows, or dividends and the required rate of return on the stock. Clearly, financial ratios can help in estimating these critical inputs. The growth rate estimate for earnings, cash flow, or dividends employs the ratios discussed in the potential growth rate section.

When estimating the required rate of return on an investment (i.e., either the cost of equity, k, or the weighted average cost of capital, WACC), recall that these estimates depend on the risk premium for the security, which is a function of business risk, financial risk, and liquidity risk. Business risk typically is measured in terms of earnings variability; financial risk is identified by either the debt proportion ratios or the earnings or cash flow ratios. Insights regarding a stock's liquidity risk can be obtained from the external liquidity measures we discussed.

The typical empirical valuation model has examined a cross section of companies and used a multiple regression model that relates one of the relative valuations ratios for the sample firms to some of the following corporate variables (the averages generally consider the past five or ten years):[22]

Financial Ratios

1. Average debt–equity
2. Average interest coverage
3. Average dividend payout
4. Average return on equity
5. Average retention rate
6. Average market price to book value
7. Average market price to cash flow
8. Average market price to sales

Variability Measures

1. Coefficient of variation of operating earnings
2. Coefficient of variation of sales
3. Coefficient of variation of net income
4. Systematic risk (beta)

Nonratio Variables

1. Average growth rate of earnings

---

[22]A list of studies in this area appears in the reference section at the end of the chapter.

ESTIMATING SYSTEMATIC RISK

As discussed in Chapter 9, the capital asset pricing model (CAPM) asserts that the relevant risk variable for an asset should be its systematic risk, which is its beta coefficient related to the market portfolio of all risky assets. In efficient markets, a relationship should exist between internal corporate risk variables and market-determined risk variables such as beta. Numerous studies have tested the relationship between a stock's systematic risk (beta) and the firm's internal corporate variables intended to reflect business risk and financial risk.[23] The significant variables (usually five-year averages) included were as follows.

Financial Ratios

1. Dividend payout
2. Total debt–total assets
3. Cash flow–total debt
4. Interest coverage
5. Working capital–total assets
6. Current ratio

Variability Measures

1. Coefficient of variation of net earnings
2. Coefficient of variation of operating earnings
3. Coefficient of variation of operating profit margins
4. Operating earnings beta (company earnings related to aggregate earnings)

Nonratio Variables

1. Asset size
2. Market value of stock outstanding

ESTIMATING THE RATINGS ON BONDS

As discussed in Chapter 3, three financial services assign credit ratings to bonds on the basis of the issuing company's ability to meet all its obligations related to the bond. An AAA or Aaa rating indicates high quality and almost no chance of default, whereas a C rating indicates the bond is already in default. Numerous studies have used financial ratios to predict the rating to be assigned to a bond.[24] The major financial variables considered in these studies were

Financial Ratios

1. Long-term debt–total assets
2. Total debt–total capital
3. Net income plus depreciation (cash flow)–long-term senior debt
4. Cash flow–total debt
5. Earnings before interest and taxes (EBIT)–interest expense (fixed charge coverage)
6. Cash flow from operations plus interest–interest expense
7. Market value of stock–par value of bonds

---

[23]A list of studies in this area appears in the reference section at the end of the chapter.

[24]A list of studies in this area appears in the reference section at the end of the chapter.

8. Net operating profit–sales
9. Net income–owners' equity (ROE)
10. Net income–total assets (ROA)
11. Working capital–sales
12. Sales–net worth (equity turnover)

Variability Measures

1. Coefficient of variation of sales
2. Coefficient of variation of net earnings
3. Coefficient of variation of return on assets

Nonratio Variables

1. Subordination of the issue
2. Size of the firm (total assets)
3. Issue size
4. Par value of all publicly traded bonds of the firm

PREDICTING INSOLVENCY (BANKRUPTCY)

Analysts have always been interested in using financial ratios to identify firms that might default on a loan or declare bankruptcy.[25] The typical study examines a sample of firms that have declared bankruptcy against a matched sample of firms in the same industry and of comparable size that have not failed. The analysis involves examining a number of financial ratios expected to reflect declining liquidity for several years prior to the declaration of bankruptcy. The goal is to determine which set of ratios correctly predict that a firm will be in the bankrupt or nonbankrupt group. The better models have typically correctly classified more than 80 percent of the firms one year prior to failure. Some of the financial ratios included in successful models were[26]

Financial Ratios

1. Cash flow–total debt
2. Cash flow–long-term debt
3. Sales–total assets★
4. Net income–total assets
5. EBIT/total assets★
6. Total debt/total assets
7. Market value of stock–book value of debt★
8. Working capital–total assets★
9. Retained earnings–total assets★
10. Current ratio
11. Working capital–sales

---

[25]A list of studies on this topic appears in the reference section at the end of the chapter.

[26]In addition to the several studies that have used financial ratios to predict bond ratings and failures, other studies have also used cash flow variables or a combination of financial ratios and cash flow variables for these predictions, and the results have been quite successful. These studies are listed in the reference section at the end of the chapter. The five ratios designated by an asterisk (★) are the ratios used in the well-known Altman Z-score model following Edward I. Altman, "Financial Ratios, Discriminant Analysis and the Prediction of Corporate Bankruptcy," *Journal of Finance* 23, no. 4 (September 1968): 589–609.

LIMITATIONS OF FINANCIAL RATIOS

We must reinforce an earlier point: you should always consider *relative* financial ratios. In addition, you should be aware of other questions and limitations of financial ratios:

1. Are alternative firms' accounting treatments comparable? As you know from prior accounting courses, there are several generally accepted methods for treating various accounting items, and the alternatives can cause a difference in results for the same event. Therefore, you should check on the accounting treatment of significant items and adjust the values for major differences. Comparability becomes a critical consideration when dealing with non–U.S. firms.

2. How homogeneous is the firm? Many companies have divisions that operate in different industries, which can make it difficult to derive comparable industry ratios.

3. Are the implied results consistent? It is important to develop a total profile of the firm and not depend on only one set of ratios (for example, internal liquidity ratios). As an example, a firm may be having short-term liquidity problems but be very profitable—the profitability will eventually alleviate the short-run liquidity problems.

4. Is the ratio within a reasonable range for the industry? As noted on several occasions, you typically want to consider a *range* of appropriate values for the ratio because a value that is either too high or too low for the industry can be a problem.

Investments Online

Many publicly traded companies have Web sites that contain financial information. Sometimes complete copies of the firm's annual report and SEC filings are on their home page. Since the focus of this chapter has been Walgreens' financial statements, here are some relevant sites:

http://www.walgreens.com Walgreens' home page. Financial information is available through links from this page. At least four of Walgreens' competitors have Web sites featuring financial information. These include:

http://www.cvs.com The home page for CVS Pharmacy.

http://www.riteaid.com Rite Aid Corporation's home page.

http://www.longs.com The Web site for Longs Drug Stores.

http://www.duanereade.com The home page of Duane Reade, a New York drug store.

The following commercially oriented and government-sponsored databases are available on the Web:

http://www.sec.gov The home page for the Securities and Exchange Commission allows entrance into the SEC's EDGAR (electronic data gathering, analysis, and retrieval) database. Most firms' SEC filings are accessible through EDGAR, including filings for executive compensation, 10-K, and 10-Q forms.

http://www.hoovers.com Hoovers Online is a commercial source of company-specific information, including financial statements and stock performance. Some data are available for free, including a company profile, news, stock price, and a chart of recent stock price performance. It contains links to a number of sources, including the firm's annual report, SEC filings, and earnings per share estimates by First Call.

http://www.dnb.com Dun & Bradstreet is a well-known gatherer of financial information. Corporations use its business credit reporting services. In addition, D&B publishes industry financial ratios that are useful in equity and fixed-income analysis.

Summary

- The overall purpose of financial statement analysis is to help investors make decisions on investing in a firm's bonds or stock. Financial ratios should be examined relative to the economy, the firm's industry, the firm's main competitors, and the firm's past relative ratios.

- The specific ratios can be divided into four categories, depending on the purpose of the analysis: internal liquidity, operating performance, risk analysis, and growth analysis.

- When analyzing the financial statements for non-U.S. firms, analysts must consider differences in format and in accounting principles that cause different values for specific ratios.

- Four major uses of financial ratios are (1) stock valuation, (2) analysis of variables affecting a stock's systematic risk (beta), (3) assigning credit ratings on bonds, and (4) predicting insolvency (bankruptcy).

A final caveat: you can envision numerous financial ratios to examine almost every possible relationship. The goal is not more ratios, but to limit and group the ratios so you can examine them in a meaningful way. This entails analyzing the ratios over time relative to the economy, the industry, or the past. You should concentrate on deriving better comparisons for a limited number of ratios that provide insights into the questions of interest to you.

QUESTIONS

1. Discuss briefly two decisions that require the analysis of financial statements.
2. Why do analysts use financial ratios rather than the absolute numbers? Give an example.
3. Besides comparing a company's performance to its total industry, discuss what other comparisons should be considered *within* the industry.
4. How might a jewelry store and a grocery store differ in terms of asset turnover and profit margin? Would you expect their return on total assets to differ assuming equal business risk? Discuss.
5. Describe the components of business risk, and discuss how the components affect the variability of operating earnings (EBIT).
6. Would you expect a steel company or a retail food chain to have greater business risk? Discuss this expectation in terms of the components of business risk.
7. When examining a firm's financial structure, would you be concerned with the firm's business risk? Why or why not?
8. Give an example of how a cash flow ratio might differ from a proportion of debt ratio. Assuming these ratios

differ for a firm (for example, the cash flow ratios indicate high financial risk, while the proportion of debt ratio indicates low risk), which ratios would you follow? Justify your choice.
9. Why is the analysis of growth potential important to the common stockholder? Why is it important to the debt investor?
10. Discuss the general factors that determine the rate of growth of *any* economic unit.
11. A firm is earning 24 percent on equity and has low business and financial risk. Discuss why you would expect it to have a high or low retention rate.
12. The Orange Company earned 18 percent on equity, whereas the Blue Company earned only 14 percent on equity. Does this mean that Orange will grow faster than Blue? Explain.
13. In terms of the factors that determine market liquidity, why do investors consider real estate to be a relatively illiquid asset?
14. Discuss some internal company factors that would indicate a firm's market liquidity.
15. Select one of the limitations of ratio analysis and indicate why you believe it is a major limitation.

PROBLEMS

1. The Shamrock Vegetable Company has the following results.

Net sales	$6,000,000
Net total assets	4,000,000
Depreciation	160,000
Net income	400,000
Long-term debt	2,000,000
Equity	1,160,000
Dividends	160,000

a. Compute Shamrock's ROE directly. Confirm this using the three components.
b. Using the ROE computed in part (a), what is the expected sustainable growth rate for Shamrock?

c. Assuming the firm's net profit margin went to 0.04, what would happen to Shamrock's ROE?

d. Using the ROE in part (c), what is the expected sustainable growth rate? What if dividends were only $40,000?

2. Three companies have the following results during the recent period.

	K	L	M
Net profit margin	0.04	0.06	0.10
Total assets turnover	2.20	2.00	1.40
Total assets/equity	2.40	2.20	1.50

a. Derive for each its return on equity based on the three DuPont components.

b. Given the following earnings and dividends, compute the estimated sustainable growth rate for each firm.

	K	L	M
Earnings/share	2.75	3.00	4.50
Dividends/share	1.25	1.00	1.00

3. Given the following balance sheet, fill in the ratio values for 2006 and discuss how these results compare with both the industry average and past performance of Sophie Enterprises.

SOPHIE ENTERPRISES
CONSOLIDATED BALANCE SHEET,
YEARS ENDED DECEMBER 31, 2005 AND 2006

ASSETS ($ THOUSANDS)

	2006	2005
Cash	$ 100	$ 90
Receivables	220	170
Inventories	330	230
Total current assets	650	490
Property, plant, and equipment	1,850	1,650
Depreciation	350	225
Net properties	1,500	1,425
Intangibles	150	150
Total assets	2,300	2,065

LIABILITIES AND SHAREHOLDERS' EQUITY

	2006	2005
Accounts payable	$ 85	$ 105
Short-term bank notes	125	110
Current portion of long-term debt	75	—
Accruals	65	85
Total current liabilities	350	300
Long-term debt	625	540

	2006	2005
Deferred taxes	100	80
Preferred stock (10%, $100 par)	150	150
Common stock ($2 par, 100,000 issued)	200	200
Additional paid-in capital	325	325
Retained earnings	550	470
Common shareholders' equity	1,075	995
Total liabilities and shareholders' equity	2,300	2,065

SOPHIE ENTERPRISES
CONSOLIDATED STATEMENT OF INCOME,
YEARS ENDED DECEMBER 31, 2005 AND 2006
($ THOUSANDS)

	2006	2005
Net sales	$3,500	$2,990
Cost of goods sold	2,135	1,823
Selling, general, and administrative expenses	1,107	974
Operating profit	258	193
Net interest expense	62	54
Income from operations	195	139
Income taxes	66	47
Net income	129	91
Preferred dividends	15	15
Net income available for common shares	114	76
Dividends declared	40	30

	Sophie (2006)	Sophie's Average	Industry Average
Current ratio	_____	2.000	2.200
Quick ratio	_____	1.000	1.100
Receivables turnover	_____	18.000	18.000
Average collection period	_____	20.000	21.000
Total asset turnover	_____	1.500	1.400
Inventory turnover	_____	11.000	12.500
Fixed-asset turnover	_____	2.500	2.400
Equity turnover	_____	3.200	3.000
Gross profit margin	_____	0.400	0.350
Operating profit margin	_____	8.000	7.500
Return on capital	_____	0.107	0.120
Return on equity	_____	0.118	0.126
Return on common equity	_____	0.128	0.135
Debt–equity ratio	_____	0.600	0.500
Debt–total capital ratio	_____	0.400	0.370
Interest coverage	_____	4.000	4.500
Fixed charge coverage	_____	3.000	4.000
Cash flow–long-term debt	_____	0.400	0.450
Cash flow–total debt	_____	0.250	0.300
Retention rate	_____	0.350	0.400

4. *CFA Examination Level I (Adapted)*
(Question 4 is composed of two parts, for a total of 20 minutes.)

The DuPont formula defines the net return on shareholders' equity as a function of the following components:

- Operating margin
- Asset turnover
- Interest burden
- Financial leverage
- Income tax rate

Using *only* the data in the table shown below:

a. Calculate *each* of the *five* components listed above for 2002 *and* 2006, and calculate the return on equity (ROE) for 2002 *and* 2006, using all of the *five* components. Show calculations. (15 minutes)

b. Briefly discuss the impact of the changes in asset turnover *and* financial leverage on the change in ROE from 2002 to 2006. (5 minutes)

	2002	2006
INCOME STATEMENT DATA		
Revenues	$542	$979
Operating income	38	76
Depreciation and amortization	3	9
Interest expense	3	0
Pretax income	32	67
Income taxes	13	37
Net income after tax	19	30
BALANCE SHEET DATA		
Fixed assets	$ 41	$ 70
Total assets	245	291
Working capital	123	157
Total debt	16	0
Total shareholders' equity	159	220

5. *CFA Examination Level II*
Mike Smith, CFA, an analyst with Blue River Investments, is considering buying a Montrose Cable Company corporate bond. He has collected the following balance sheet and income statement information for Montrose as shown in Exhibit 5-1. He has also calculated the three ratios shown in Exhibit 5-2, which indicate that the bond is currently rated "A" according to the firm's internal bond-rating criteria shown in Exhibit 5-4.

EXHIBIT 5-1
MONTROSE CABLE COMPANY
YEAR ENDED MARCH 31, 1999
(US$ THOUSANDS)
Balance Sheet

Current assets	$ 4,735
Fixed assets	43,225
Total assets	$47,960
Current liabilities	$ 4,500
Long-term debt	10,000
Total liabilities	$14,500
Shareholders' equity	33,460
Total liabilities and shareholder's equity	$47,960

Income Statement

Revenue	$18,500
Operating and administrative expenses	14,050
Operating income	$ 4,450
Depreciation and amortization	1,675
Interest expense	942
Income before income taxes	$ 1,833
Taxes	641
Net income	$ 1,192

EXHIBIT 5-2
SELECTED RATIOS AND CREDIT YIELD PREMIUM DATA FOR MONTROSE

EBITDA/interest expense	4.72
Long-term debt/equity	0.30
Current assets/current liabilities	1.05
Credit yield premium over U.S. Treasuries	55 basis points

EXHIBIT 5-3
MONTROSE OFF-BALANCE-SHEET ITEMS

- Montrose has guaranteed the long-term debt (principal only) of an unconsolidated affiliate. This obligation has a present value of $995,000.
- Montrose has sold $500,000 of accounts receivable with recourse at a yield of 8 percent.
- Montrose is a lessee in a new noncancelable operating leasing agreement to finance transmission equipment. The discounted present value of the lease payments is $6,144,000 using an interest rate of 10 percent. The annual payment will be $1,000,000.

EXHIBIT 5-4
BLUE RIVER INVESTMENTS: INTERNAL
BOND-RATING CRITERIA AND CREDIT
YIELD PREMIUM DATA

Bond Rating	Interest Coverage (EBITDA/interest expense)	Leverage (Long-term debt/equity)	Current Ratio (Current assets/ current liabilities)	Credit Yield Premium over U.S. Treasuries (in basis points)
AA	5.00 to 6.00	0.25 to 0.30	1.15 to 1.25	30 bps
A	4.00 to 5.00	0.30 to 0.40	1.00 to 1.15	50 bps
BBB	3.00 to 4.00	0.40 to 0.50	0.90 to 1.00	100 bps
BB	2.00 to 3.00	0.50 to 0.60	0.75 to 0.90	125 bps

Smith has decided to consider some off-balance-sheet items in his credit analysis, as shown in Exhibit 5-3. Specifically, Smith wishes to evaluate the impact of each of the off-balance-sheet items on each of the ratios found in Exhibit 5-2.

a. Calculate the combined effect of the *three* off-balance-sheet items in Exhibit 5-3 on *each* of the following *three* financial ratios shown in Exhibit 5-2.
 i. EBITDA/interest expense
 ii. Long-term debt/equity
 iii. Current assets/current liabilities (9 minutes)

The bond is currently trading at a credit premium of 55 basis points. Using the internal bond-rating criteria in Exhibit 5-4, Smith wants to evaluate whether or not the credit yield premium incorporates the effect of the off-balance-sheet items.

b. State and justify whether or not the current credit yield premium compensates Smith for the credit risk of the bond based on the internal bond-rating criteria found in Exhibit 5-4. (6 minutes)

6. *CFA Examination Level II*
 Patricia Bouvier, CFA, is an analyst following Telluride. In reviewing Telluride's 1999 annual report, Bouvier discovers the following footnotes:

 Footnote (1) During the fourth quarter of 1999, Telluride changed its accounting policy from expensing to capitalizing software expenditures. The amount capitalized in 1999 was $15 million, including $12 million that had been expensed during the first three quarters of the year.

 Footnote (2) On December 31, 1999, Telluride established a restructuring charge of $20 million of which $8 million was for severance pay for workers who will be terminated in the year 2000 and $12 million was for the write down of assets on December 31, 1999.

 Footnote (3) Telluride leases assets under an operating lease that expired on December 31, 1999. The lease renewal terms required Telluride to capitalize the lease, which has a present value of $50 million. The amount of the monthly lease payment does not change.

Indicate, for *each* of the *three* footnotes, the effect of the adjustments on the financial ratios shown in the following template for:
 i. the year 1999
 ii. the year 2000 compared to adjusted 1999
Note: Assume all financial information remains unchanged from 1999 through 2000, except that referenced in the footnotes above.

Answer Question 6 using the following template. (18 minutes)

TEMPLATE FOR QUESTION 6

Ratio	Effect on 1999 Ratio (circle one)	Effect on 2000 Ratio Compared to Adjusted 1999 Ratio (circle one)
FOOTNOTE (1)		
Operating Cash Flow/Sales	Increase / Decrease / No Effect	Increase / Decrease / No Effect
Net Income/Sales	Increase / Decrease / No Effect	Increase / Decrease / No Effect
Sales/Net Fixed Assets	Increase / Decrease / No Effect	Increase / Decrease / No Effect
FOOTNOTE (2)		
Operating Cash Flow/Sales	Increase / Decrease / No Effect	Increase / Decrease / No Effect
Net Income/Sales	Increase / Decrease / No Effect	Increase / Decrease / No Effect
Sales/Net Fixed Assets	Increase / Decrease / No Effect	Increase / Decrease / No Effect

(continued)

Ratio	Effect on 1999 Ratio (circle one)	Effect on 2000 Ratio Compared to Adjusted 1999 Ratio (circle one)
FOOTNOTE (3)		
Operating Cash Flow/Sales	Increase Decrease No Effect	Increase Decrease No Effect
Net Income/Sales	Increase Decrease No Effect	Increase Decrease No Effect
Sales/Net Fixed Assets	Increase Decrease No Effect	Increase Decrease No Effect

CFA

7. *CFA Examination Level II*

Candidates should use Exhibits 7-1, 7-2, and 7-3 to answer Question 7.

One of the companies that Jones is researching is Mackinac Inc., a U.S.–based manufacturing company. Mackinac has released its June 2001 financial statements, which are shown in Exhibits 7-1, 7-2, and 7-3.

EXHIBIT 7-1
MACKINAC INC.
ANNUAL INCOME STATEMENT FOR THE YEAR ENDED JUNE 30, 2001
(IN THOUSANDS, EXCEPT PER-SHARE DATA)

Sales	$250,000
Cost of Goods Sold	125,000
Gross Operating Profit	$125,000
Selling, General, and Administrative Expenses	50,000
Earnings Before Interest, Taxes, Depreciation, and Amortization (EBITDA)	$ 75,000
Depreciation and Amortization	10,500
Earnings Before Interest and Taxes (EBIT)	$ 64,500
Interest Expense	11,000
Pretax Income	$ 53,500
Income Taxes	16,050
Net Income	$ 37,450
Shares Outstanding	13,000
Earnings Per Share (EPS)	$ 2.88

EXHIBIT 7-2
MACKINAC INC.
BALANCE SHEET AS OF JUNE 30, 2001
(IN THOUSANDS)

Current Assets:		
Cash and Equivalents	$ 20,000	
Receivables	40,000	
Inventories	29,000	
Other Current Assets	23,000	
Total Current Assets		$112,000
Noncurrent Assets:		
Property, Plant, and Equipment	$145,000	
Less: Accumulated Depreciation	(43,000)	
Net Property, Plant, and Equipment	$102,000	
Investments	70,000	
Other Noncurrent Assets	36,000	
Total Noncurrent Assets		$208,000
Total Assets		$320,000
Current Liabilities:		
Accounts Payable	$ 41,000	
Short-Term Debt	12,000	
Other Current Liabilities	17,000	
Total Current Liabilities		$ 70,000

(continued)

Noncurrent Liabilities:		
Long-Term Debt	$100,000	
Total Noncurrent Liabilities		$100,000
Total Liabilities		$170,000
Shareholders' Equity:		
Common Equity	$ 40,000	
Retained Earnings	110,000	
Total Equity		$150,000
Total Liabilities and Equity		$320,000

EXHIBIT 7-3
MACKINAC INC.
CASH FLOW STATEMENT FOR THE YEAR
ENDED JUNE 30, 2001 (IN THOUSANDS)

Cash Flow from Operating Activities:		
Net Income		$37,450
Depreciation and Amortization		10,500
Change in Working Capital:		
(Increase) Decrease in Receivables	($ 5,000)	
(Increase) Decrease in Inventories	(8,000)	
Increase (Decrease) in Payables	6,000	
Increase (Decrease) in Other Current Liabilities	1,500	
Net Change in Working Capital		($ 5,500)
Net Cash from Operating Activities		$42,450
Cash Flow from Investing Activities:		
Purchase of Property, Plant, and Equipment	($15,000)	
Net Cash from Investing Activities		($15,000)
Cash Flow from Financing Activities:		
Change in Debt Outstanding	$ 4,000	
Payment of Cash Dividends	(22,470)	
Net Cash from Financing Activities		($18,470)
Net Change in Cash and Cash Equivalents		$8,980
Cash at Beginning of Period		11,020
Cash at End of Period		$20,000

Jones is particularly interested in Mackinac's sustainable growth and sources of return.

a. Calculate Mackinac's sustainable growth rate. Show your calculations.
   Note: Use June 30, 2001, year-end balance sheet data rather than averages in ratio calculations. (4 minutes)

b. Name *each* of the *five* components in the extended DuPont System and calculate a value for *each* component for Mackinac.
   Note: Use June 30, 2001, year-end balance sheet data rather than averages in ratio calculations. (10 minutes)

WEB EXERCISES

1. Visit the SEC's EDGAR (accessible from *http://www.sec.gov*) Web site. What information is available to assist with the analysis of financial statements? What information is available on a 10-K form? A 10-Q form?

2. Visit *http://www.fasb.org*. What issues and changes to financial statements is the Financial Accounting Standards Board considering?

SPREADSHEET EXERCISES

1. With common size financial statements and many ratios, spreadsheets are helpful tools to manipulate raw financial data into a form that can be used by analysts. Construct a spreadsheet to compute the common size statements and financial ratios discussed in this chapter.

2. Assume the retail drugstore industry is composed of only five firms: Walgreens, CVS, Duane Reed, Long's Drug Stores, and Rite-Aid. Visit each firm's Web site, obtain financial statement data for the most recent three years, and enter the data into a spreadsheet. For each year, sum the accounts across the five firms to generate a sample "industry" set of financial statements. Use the spreadsheet from Exercise 1 to compute ratios for Walgreens and the "industry" for each of the past three years. Use your program's graphing abilities to create graphs showing the behavior of the firm and industry ratios. How does Walgreens compare to the industry ratios for internal liquidity, operating performance, risk analysis, and growth analysis?

REFERENCES

General

Beaver, William H. *Financial Reporting: An Accounting Revolution.* Englewood Cliffs, NJ: Prentice-Hall, 1989.

Bernstein, Leopold A., and John J. Wild. *Financial Statement Analysis: Theory, Application, and Interpretation,* 6th ed. Homewood, IL: Irwin/McGraw-Hill, 1998.

Frecka, Thomas J., and Cheng F. Lee. "Generalized Financial Ratio Adjustment Processes and Their Implications." *Journal of Accounting Research 27,* no. 1 (Spring 1983).

Fridson, Martin, and Fernando Alvarez. *Financial Statement Analysis*, 3rd ed. New York: John Wiley & Sons, 2002.

Heckel, Kenneth S., and Joshua Livnat. *Cash Flow and Security Analysis,* 2nd ed. Burr Ridge, IL: Business One Irwin, 1996.

Helfert, Erich A. *Techniques of Financial Analysis,* 10th ed. New York: McGraw-Hill, 2000.

Higgins, Robert C. *Analysis for Financial Management,* 5th ed. Chicago: Irwin, 1998.

Lev, Baruch, and S. Ramu Thiagarajan. "Fundamental Information Analysis." *Journal of Accounting Research* 37, no. 2 (Fall 1993).

Peterson, Pamela P., and Frank J. Fabozzi. *Analysis of Financial Statements.* New Hope, PA: Frank J. Fabozzi Associates, 1999.

Stickney, Clyde P., Paul R. Brown, and James Wahlen. *Financial Reporting and Statement Analysis*, 5th ed. Mason, OH: South-Western, 2004.

White, Gerald I., Ashwinpaul Sondhi, and Dov Fried. *The Analysis and Use of Financial Statements,* 2nd ed. New York: John Wiley & Sons, 1998.

Analysis of International Financial Statements

Choi, Frederick D. S., Carol Ann Frost, and Gary Meek. *International Accounting.* Englewood Cliffs, NJ: Prentice-Hall, 2000.

Evans, Thomas G., Martin E. Taylor, and Oscar Holzmann. *International Accounting and Reporting.* New York: MacMillan, 1985.

Iqbal, M. Zafar. *International Accounting: A Global Approach.* Cincinnati: South-Western, 2002.

Rueschhoff, Norlin, and David Strupeck. "Equity Returns: Local GAAP versus US GAAP for Foreign Issuers from Developing Countries." *Journal of International Accounting* 33, no. 3 (Spring 2000).

Saudagaran, Shakrokh. *International Accounting: A User Perspective.* Cincinnati: South-Western, 2001.

Financial Ratios and Stock Valuation Models

Babcock, Guilford. "The Concept of Sustainable Growth." *Financial Analysts Journal* 26, no. 3 (May–June 1970).

Beaver, William, and Dale Morse. "What Determines Price-Earnings Ratios?" *Financial Analysts Journal* 34, no. 4 (July–August 1978).

Copeland, Tom, Tim Koller, and Jack Murrin. *Valuation: Measuring and Managing the Value of Companies,* 3rd ed. New York: John Wiley & Sons, 2000.

Damodaran, Aswath. *Damodaran on Valuation.* New York: John Wiley & Sons, 1994.

Danielson, M. G. "A Simple Valuation Model and Growth Expectations." *Financial Analysts Journal* 54, no. 3 (May–June 1998).

Fairfield, Patricia M. "P/E, P/B and the Present Value of Future Dividends." *Financial Analysts Journal* 50, no. 4 (July–August 1994).

Farrell, James L. "The Dividend Discount Model: A Primer." *Financial Analysts Journal* 41, no. 6 (November–December 1985).

Hickman, Kent, and Glenn Petry. "A Comparison of Stock Price Predictions Using Court Accepted Formulas, Dividend Discount, and P/E Models." *Financial Management* (Summer 1990).

Kaplan, S. N., and R. S. Ruback. "The Valuation of Cash Flow Forecasts: An Empirical Analysis." *Journal of Finance* 50, no. 4 (September 1995).

Leibowitz, M. L., and S. Kogelman. "Inside the P/E Ratio: The Franchise Factor." *Financial Analysts Journal* 46, no. 6 (November–December 1990).

Palepu, Krishna G., Paul M. Healy, and Victor L. Bernard. *Business Analysis and Valuation,* 3rd ed. Mason, OH: South-Western, 2004.

Penman, S. H. "The Articulation of Price-Earnings Ratios and Market-to-Book Ratios and the Evaluation of Growth." *Journal of Accounting Research* 34, no. 2 (Spring 1996).

Wilcox, Jarrod W. "The P/B-ROE Valuation Model." *Financial Analysts Journal* 40, no. 1 (January–February 1984).

Financial Ratios and Systematic Risk (Beta)

Beaver, William H., Paul Kettler, and Myron Scholes. "The Association Between Market-Determined and Accounting-Determined Risk Measures." *Accounting Review* 45, no. 4 (October 1970).

Gahlon, James M., and James A. Gentry. "On the Relationship Between Systematic Risk and the Degrees of Operating and Financial Leverage." *Financial Management* 11, no. 2 (Summer 1982).

Mandelker, Gershon M., and S. Ghon Rhee. "The Impact of the Degrees of Operating and Financial Leverage on the Systematic Risk of Common Stock." *Journal of Financial and Quantitative Analysis* 19, no. 1 (March 1984).

Rosenberg, Barr. "Prediction of Common Stock Investment Risk." *Journal of Portfolio Management* 11, no. 1 (Fall 1984).

Rosenberg, Barr. "Prediction of Common Stock Betas." *Journal of Portfolio Management* 11, no. 2 (Winter 1985).

Financial Ratios and Bond Ratings

Cantor, R., and F. Packer. "The Credit Rating Industry." *The Journal of Fixed Income* 5, no. 3 (December 1995).

Fisher, Lawrence. "Determinants of Risk Premiums on Corporate Bonds." *Journal of Political Economy* 67, no. 3 (June 1959).

Fons, Jerome S. "An Approach to Forecasting Default Rates." New York: Moody's Investors Services (August 1991).

Gentry, James A., David T. Whitford, and Paul Newbold. "Predicting Industrial Bond Ratings with a Probit Model and Funds Flow Components." *Financial Review* 23, no. 3 (August 1988).

Kaplan, Robert S., and Gabriel Urwitz. "Statistical Models of Bond Ratings: A Methodological Inquiry." *Journal of Business* 52, no. 2 (April 1979).

Standard and Poor's Corporation. "Corporate Ratings Criteria," 2000.

Zhou, Chunsheng. "Credit Rating and Corporate Defaults." *Journal of Fixed Income* 11, no. 3 (December 2001).

Financial Ratios and Corporate Bankruptcy

Altman, Edward I. "Financial Ratios, Discriminant Analysis, and the Prediction of Corporate Bankruptcy." *Journal of Finance* 23, no. 4 (September 1968).

Altman, Edward I. *Corporate Financial Distress and Bankruptcy.* 2nd ed. New York: John Wiley & Sons, 1993.

Altman, Edward I., Robert G. Haldeman, and P. Narayanan. "Zeta Analysis: A New Model to Identify Bankruptcy Risk of Corporations." *Journal of Banking and Finance* 1, no. 2 (June 1977).

Aziz, A., and G. H. Lawson. "Cash Flow Reporting and Financial Distress Models: Testing of Hypothesis." *Financial Management* 18, no. 1 (Spring 1989).

Beaver, William H. "Financial Ratios as Predictors of Failure." *Empirical Research in Accounting: Selected Studies*, 1966, supplement to vol. 4, *Journal of Accounting Research*.

Beaver, William H. "Market Prices, Financial Ratios, and the Prediction of Failure." *Journal of Accounting Research* 6, no. 2 (Autumn 1968).

Casey, Cornelius, and Norman Bartczak. "Using Operating Cash Flow Data to Predict Financial Distress: Some Extensions." *Journal of Accounting Research* 23, no. 1 (Spring 1985).

Dumbolena, I. G., and J. M. Shulman. "A Primary Rule for Detecting Bankruptcy: Watch the Cash." *Financial Analysts Journal* 44, no. 5 (September–October 1988).

Gentry, James A., Paul Newbold, and David T. Whitford. "Classifying Bankrupt Firms with Funds Flow Components." *Journal of Accounting Research* 23, no. 1 (Spring 1985).

Gentry, James A., Paul Newbold, and David T. Whitford. "Predicting Bankruptcy: If Cash Flow's Not the Bottom Line, What Is?" *Financial Analysts Journal* 41, no. 5 (September–October 1985).

Gombola, M. F., M. E. Haskins, J. E. Katz, and D. D. Williams. "Cash Flow in Bankruptcy Prediction." *Financial Management* 16, no. 4 (Winter 1987).

Helwege, J., and P. Kleiman. "Understanding High Yield Bond Default Rates." *Journal of Fixed Income* 7, no. 1 (June 1997).

Jonsson, J. G., and M. S. Fridson. "Forecasting Default Rates on High Yield Bonds." *Journal of Fixed Income* 6, no. 1 (June 1996).

Largay, J. A., and C. P. Stickney. "Cash Flows Ratio Analysis and the W. T. Grant Company Bankruptcy." *Financial Analysts Journal* 36, no. 4 (July–August 1980).

Ohlson, J. A. "Financial Ratios and the Probabalistic Prediction of Bankruptcy." *Journal of Accounting Research* 18, no. 2 (Spring 1980).

Reilly, Frank K. "Using Cash Flows and Financial Ratios to Predict Bankruptcies." In *Analyzing Investment Opportunities in Distressed and Bankrupt Companies*, edited by Thomas A. Bowman. Charlottesville, VA: The Institute of Chartered Financial Analysts, 1991.

THOMSON ONE
Business School Edition

1. Update the ratio analysis for Walgreens presented in this chapter.
2. In Chapter 7 you made a "retail sales stock index" using price and share data from Amazon (AMZN), Family Dollar (FDO), J.C. Penney (JCP), Target (TGT), and Wal-mart (WMT). Now download balance sheet and income statement data into a spreadsheet and sum similar accounting categories to create an "industry" balance sheet and an "industry" income statement. Compute the following ratios and compare the performance of Wal-mart's ratios against the "industry" ratios:

   a. Current Ratio
   b. Inventory Turnover
   c. Total Asset Turnover
   d. Net Profit Margin
   e. Debt-Equity

3. Using common-size financial statements, compare the operating characteristics of a retail firm (Walgreens), a technology firm (Microsoft) and one involved in oil production and distribution (ExxonMobil).
4. Using the firms in problem 3, compare their returns on equity using DuPont analysis.
5. Find Walgreens' "peers" using Thomson One: Business School Edition. Click on "financials" and review the financial ratios of Walgreens and its peers. Comment on the strengths and weaknesses of Walgreens compared to these firms.

GLOSSARY

Balance sheet A financial statement that shows what assets the firm controls at a fixed point in time and how it has financed these assets.

Business risk The variability of operating income arising from the characteristics of the firm's industry. Two sources of business risk are sales variability and operating leverage.

Common size statements The normalization of balance sheet and income statement items to allow for easier comparison of different-sized firms.

Cross-sectional analysis An examination of a firm's performance in comparison to other firms in the industry with similar characteristics to the firm being studied.

DuPont System A method of examining ROE by breaking it down into three component parts.

Extended DuPont System A method of examining ROE by breaking it down into five component parts.

Financial risk The variability of future income arising from the firm's fixed financing costs, for example, interest payments. The effect of fixed financial costs is to magnify the effect of changes in operating profit on net income or earnings per share.

Free cash flow A cash flow measure that equals cash flow from operations minus capital expenditures and dividends (by some analysts).

Generally accepted accounting principles (GAAP) Accounting principles formulated by the Financial Accounting Standards Board and used to construct financial statements.

Income statement A financial statement that shows the flow of the firm's sales, expenses, and earnings over a period of time.

Internal liquidity (solvency) ratios Relationships between items of financial data that indicate the firm's ability to meet short-term financial obligations.

Operating efficiency ratios Ratios that measure a firm's utilization of its assets and capital.

Operating leverage The use of fixed-production costs in the firm's operating cost structure. The effect of fixed costs is to magnify the effect of a change in sales on operating profits.

Operating profitability ratios Ratios that measure the ability of the firm to earn returns on sales.

Quality financial statements A term analysts use to describe financial statements that are conservative and a good reflection of reality.

Statement of cash flows A financial statement that shows the effects on the firm's cash flow of income flows and changes in its balance sheet.

Sustainable growth potential A measure of how fast a firm can grow based upon a firm's retention rate (RR) and its return on equity (ROE).

Time-series analysis An examination of a firm's performance data over a period of time.

Trading turnover The percentage of outstanding shares traded during a period of time.

Company Analysis and Stock Valuation

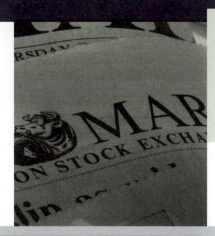

A t this point we have made two decisions about our investment in equity markets. First, after analyzing the economy and stock markets for several countries, we have decided our portfolio allocation to stocks. Second, we have identified those industries that appear to offer above-average risk-adjusted performance over our investment horizon. We must now answer the final question in the fundamental analysis procedure: Which stocks within these desirable industries are underpriced? Specifically, is the intrinsic value of the stock above its market price, or is the expected rate of return on the stock equal to or greater than its required rate of return?

We begin this chapter with a discussion of the difference between company analysis and stock selection. Company analysis should occur in the context of the prevailing economic and industry conditions. We discuss some competitive strategies that can help firms maximize returns in an industry's competitive environment. We also discuss a number of methods used by practicing analysts to estimate intrinsic values. Then we demonstrate several cash flow models and relative valuation ratios that can be used to estimate the intrinsic value of a stock and thereby identify undervalued stocks. We also review factors that an investor should consider when deciding to sell a stock. We conclude with a discussion of the pressures and influences that affect professional stock analysts.

Company Analysis versus the Valuation and Selection of Stock

This chapter is titled "Company Analysis and Stock Valuation" to convey the idea that the common stocks of good companies are not necessarily good investments. As a final step of the analysis, investors must compare the intrinsic value of a stock to its market price to determine if it should be purchased. The stock of a wonderful firm with superior management and strong performance measured by sales and earnings or cash flow growth can be priced so high that the intrinsic value of the stock is below its current market price—i.e., it is overpriced. In contrast, the stock of a company with less success based on its sales and earnings growth may have a stock market price that is below its intrinsic value. In this case, although the company is not as good, its stock could be the better investment.

The classic confusion in this regard concerns growth companies versus growth stocks. The stock of a growth company is not necessarily a growth stock. Recognition of this difference between the quality of the company and the desirability of the stock as an investment is crucial for successful investing.

GROWTH COMPANIES AND GROWTH STOCKS

Observers have historically defined growth companies as those that consistently experience above-average increases in sales and earnings. This definition has some limitations because many firms could qualify due to certain accounting procedures, mergers, or other external temporary events.

In contrast, financial theorists define a *growth company* as a firm with the management ability and the opportunities to make investments that yield rates of return greater than the firm's required rate of return.[1] This required rate of return is the firm's weighted average cost of capital (WACC). As an example, a growth company might be able to acquire capital at an average cost of 10 percent and yet have the management ability and the opportunity to invest those funds at rates of return of 15 to 20 percent. As a result of these investment opportunities, the firm's sales and earnings will grow faster than those of similar-risk firms and the overall economy. In addition, because a growth company has above-average investment opportunities it should, and typically does, retain a large portion of its earnings to fund these superior investment projects (i.e., they have low dividend payout ratios).

Growth stocks are *not* necessarily shares in growth companies. A *growth stock* is a stock expected to experience a higher rate of return than other stocks in the market with similar risk characteristics. The stock achieves this superior risk-adjusted rate of return because at some point in time the market undervalued it compared to other stocks. Although the stock market adjusts stock prices relatively quickly and accurately to reflect new information, available information is not always perfect or complete. Therefore, the use of imperfect or incomplete information by most analysts may cause a given stock to be undervalued or overvalued at a point in time.[2]

If the stock is undervalued, its price should eventually increase to reflect its true fundamental value when the correct information becomes available. During this period of price adjustment, the stock's realized return will exceed the required return for a stock with its risk, and during this period of adjustment it will be considered a growth stock. Growth stocks are not necessarily limited to growth companies. A future growth stock can be the stock of any type of company, the stock need only be undervalued by the market.

The fact is, if investors recognize a growth company and discount its future earnings or cash flow stream properly, the current market price of the growth company's stock will reflect its future earnings (cash flow) stream. Those who acquire the stock of a growth

---

[1]Ezra Solomon, *The Theory of Financial Management,* New York: Columbia University Press, 1963, 55–68; and Merton Miller and Franco Modigliani, "Dividend Policy, Growth and the Valuation of Shares," *Journal of Business* 34, no. 4 (October 1961): 411–433.

[2]An analyst is more likely to find such misvalued stocks outside the top tier of companies where information is rapidly and widely broadcast and is scrutinized by numerous analysts; in other words, look for "neglected" stocks.

company at this correct market price will receive a rate of return consistent with the risk of the stock, even when the superior earnings growth is attained. In many instances overeager investors tend to overestimate the expected growth rate of earnings or the period of growth for the growth company and therefore overestimate the intrinsic value of a growth company's stock. Investors who pay the inflated stock price for a growth company will earn a rate of return below the risk-adjusted required rate of return, despite the fact that the growth company experiences above-average growth of sales and earnings. Several studies that have examined the stock price performance for samples of growth companies have found that their stocks performed poorly—that is, the stocks of growth companies have generally *not* been growth stocks.[3]

COMPANY TYPES

In addition to growth companies, investors and analysts have developed other descriptive titles for firms including cyclical, defensive, and even speculative. These descriptions are based on the nature of the firm's sales, earnings, and cash flows over time.

Sales, earnings, and cash flows of a *cyclical company* will be heavily influenced by aggregate business activity. Examples would be firms in the steel, auto, or heavy machinery industries. Such companies will do quite well during economic expansions and poorly during economic contractions. This volatile earnings pattern is typically a function of the firm's high business risk (both substantial sales volatility over the business cycle and high operating leverage).

Defensive companies are those firms whose sales, earnings, and cash flows are likely to withstand changes caused by the economic environment. Specifically, they would have low business risk so they would not experience abnormal success during an economic expansion or suffer major declines in performance during recessions. Typical examples would be public utilities, grocery and drugstore chains, and food processing firms that supply basic consumer necessities.

Finally, *speculative companies* have extremely uncertain sales, earnings, and cash flows that are not necessarily related to the economy. Prime examples would be oil exploration firms that are dependent on "striking oil" or biotech firms that are attempting to discover and patent significant medical breakthroughs. Clearly the valuation of these firms is very difficult due to the extreme uncertainty of their cash flows.

STOCK TYPES—THERE ARE ONLY TWO!

As we discussed in Chapter 7, some analysts and most consultants advocate describing stocks as either "growth" or "value" stocks based on firms' price–earning ratios, price–book value ratios, or dividend policy. But it is difficult to determine in which category a stock belongs; often a stock can qualify for both, depending on the ratio used to classify the stock. There is also a question of how relevant these labels are in terms of valuation and asset allocation. In addition to the growth/value categories, some analysts also want to divide the universe by size—i.e., large-cap, mid-cap, and small-cap firms based on the aggregate market value of common stock. By combining size categories with growth/value divisions, it is possible to create a matrix of six styles from large-cap growth to small-cap value.

---

[3]Michael Solt and Meir Statman, "Good Companies, Bad Stocks," *Journal of Portfolio Management* 15, no. 4 (Summer 1989): 39–44; Hersh Shefrin and Meir Statman, "Making Sense of Beta, Size, and Book-to-Market," *Journal of Portfolio Management* 21, no. 2 (Winter 1995): 26–34; and Michelle Clayman, "In Search of Excellence: The Investor's Viewpoint," *Financial Analysts Journal* 43, no. 3 (May–June 1987): 54–63.

In contrast to this "mechanical" classification, the authors of this book (and some academicians and practitioners like Warren Buffett) contend that there are only two relevant stock types. First are stocks that are *undervalued* relative to the prevailing market price—i.e., the intrinsic value of the stock exceeds its market price. These are *growth stocks,* which are expected to provide an excess rate of return. Second are *overvalued* stocks with intrinsic values less than their market price; these are *non-growth stocks,* which are expected to provide a rate of return less than what is required based on their risk.

In other words, the type of company does *not* determine the type of stock. There are several types of company, and which type of company it is will impact the stream of cash flows that, in turn, will determine the intrinsic value of a stock. Once the intrinsic value is determined (by whatever valuation technique), the only relevant analysis is to compare this intrinsic value to the stock's market price. This comparison will indicate whether the stock is a growth (undervalued) or a non-growth (overvalued) stock. Any type of company—growth, cyclical, defensive, or speculative; large or small—can have a stock that is undervalued or overvalued at a point in time. It is important to recognize that *this stock type can change over time* depending on the stock's market price. For example, the stock of a growth company can be seriously overpriced and, therefore, it would be considered a non-growth stock. But if the stock's price declines substantially for any reason while its intrinsic value does not change, it can become a growth (undervalued) stock. Alternatively, the valuation of a growth company can indicate a growth (undervalued) stock, but if the market price increases substantially and its intrinsic value is stable, it eventually can become a non-growth (overvalued) stock.

Thus, we contend that the only relevant stock types are growth (undervalued) and non-growth (overvalued). We further contend that comparison of the intrinsic value of the stock with its market price is what determines the type of stock.

The Search for True Growth Stocks

Now that we have differentiated the alternative companies and stocks, we can return to the major goal—finding true growth stocks that will provide rates of return that exceed the required rates of return for them, that is, stocks that are undervalued. To find these true growth (undervalued) stocks, we use the theory of valuation, which we introduced in Chapter 11. Once we briefly review the basic theory of valuation, we can consider various approaches to applying this theory to the valuation of common stocks.

VALUATION BRIEFLY REVISITED

Recall that the value of an asset is the present value of its expected returns. Specifically, we expect an asset to provide a stream of returns during the period of time we own it. To convert this estimated stream of returns to a value for the security, we must discount this stream at the required rate of return. This *valuation process* requires estimates of (1) the stream of expected returns and (2) the required rate of return on the investment (i.e., the discount rate).

Stream of Expected Returns   An estimate of the expected returns from an investment encompasses not only the size but also the form, time pattern, and the uncertainty of returns, which affect the required rate of return.

Form of returns.   The returns from an investment can take many forms, including earnings, cash flows, dividends, interest payments, or capital gains (increases in value) during a period. We will consider several valuation techniques that use different forms of returns. As an example, one common-stock valuation model applies a multiplier to a firm's earnings, another model computes the present value of a firm's operating cash flows, and a third model estimates the present value of dividend payments. Returns or cash flows can come in many forms, and we must consider all of them to evaluate an investment accurately.

Time pattern and growth rate of returns. We cannot calculate an accurate value for a security unless we can estimate when we will receive the returns or cash flows. Because money has a time value, we must know the time pattern and growth rate of returns from an investment. This makes it possible to properly value the stream of returns relative to investments with a different time pattern and growth rate of returns.

Required Rate of Return

Uncertainty of returns. Recall from Chapter 2 that the required rate of return on an investment is determined by (1) the economy's real risk-free rate of return plus (2) the expected rate of inflation during the holding period plus (3) a risk premium that is determined by the uncertainty of returns. All investments are affected by the risk-free rate and the expected rate of inflation because these two variables determine the nominal risk-free rate. Therefore, the factor that causes a difference in required rates of return is the risk premium. In turn, this risk premium depends on the uncertainty of returns on the assets.

We can identify the sources of the uncertainty of returns by the internal characteristics of assets or by market-determined factors. Earlier, we subdivided the internal characteristics into business risk (BR), financial risk (FR), liquidity risk (LR), exchange rate risk (ERR), and country risk (CR). The market-determined risk measures are the systematic risk of the asset, its beta, or its multivariate risk factors.

Investment Decision Process As we discussed in Chapter 11, the investment decision process is relatively straightforward: estimate the intrinsic value of the investment using the estimated required rate of return and expected growth rate and then compare this estimated intrinsic value to the prevailing market price.

If Estimated Intrinsic Value > Market Price, Buy

If Estimated Intrinsic Value < Market Price, Do Not Buy or Sell It If You Own It

Application of Valuation Theory We covered the details of valuation theory along with techniques for estimating the inputs for valuation models in Chapter 11. In the remainder of this chapter we provide a detailed application of this theory in the valuation of our example company, Walgreens. We begin with an overview of the economic, industry, and structual links to company analysis, followed by a discussion of firm competitive strategies and the very insightful SWOT analysis of the firm.

Economic, Industry, and Structural Links to Company Analysis

We began our discussion of the top-down approach to investing in Chapter 11. The analysis of companies and their stocks is the final step in the top-down approach. Rather than selecting stocks on the basis of company-specific factors (as with bottom-up analysis), top-down analysts review the current state and future outlook for domestic and international sectors of the economy. On the basis of this macroeconomic analysis, they identify industries that are expected to offer attractive returns in the expected future environment. After we review these macro analyses, we turn our attention to the process of analyzing firms in the selected industries. Our analysis concentrates on the two major determinants of a stock's intrinsic value: (1) growth of the firm's expected cash flows (g), and (2) its risk, which is the factor that will impact its differential required rate of return, discount rate, (k).

ECONOMIC AND INDUSTRY INFLUENCES

If economic trends are favorable for an industry, the company analysis should focus on firms in that industry that are well positioned to benefit from the economic trends. For example, the expectation of lower interest rates and strong economic growth will be beneficial to such industries as housing, heavy equipment, durable goods, and automotive. But for investment purposes, the most attractive firms within those industries will be those that possess strong leadership positions in terms of innovation, quality, and/or lower costs. In contrast, a firm that has been losing market share and finds it difficult to control costs may not be as attractive a purchase candidate.

Firms with sales or earnings particularly sensitive to macroeconomic variables should also be considered. For example, although auto sales are related to the business cycle and consumer sentiment, sales of high-margin luxury and sports cars are even more sensitive to these factors. Thus, expectations of rapid economic growth may be beneficial to all auto manufacturers, but especially to those that sell to the high end of the market. If the U.S. dollar is strengthening against European currencies but declining against Pacific Rim currencies, it will benefit U.S. firms that export their goods to Asia rather than to Europe.

In addition, research analysts need to be familiar with the cash flow and risk attributes of their firms. In times of strong industry growth, the most attractive candidates for purchase may be the firms in the industry with high levels of operating leverage and financial leverage because a modest percentage increase in revenue can be magnified into a much larger percentage rise in earnings and cash flow for the highly leveraged firm. The point is that all firms in an industry are not identical. They will have varying sensitivities to economic variables such as economic growth, interest rates, input costs, and exchange rates, and they will have different competitive strategies. Because each firm is different, an investor must examine each firm to determine what will happen to its intrinsic value under current and expected economic conditions.

Although our discussion has implied that all firms in an industry will be affected by future economic trends, this is not necessarily the case. Sometimes, although poor economic news implies tough times for an industry, certain firms in that industry may have positioned themselves in anticipation of difficult economic times or have a well-diversified international revenue base. As a result, these firms may do well while their rivals suffer from an economic recession. The stock of such firms can become attractive when investors become overly pessimistic about an industry's prospects and heavy selling of *all* the stocks in the industry leads to inappropriate stock price declines for selected stocks in the industry.

STRUCTURAL INFLUENCES

In addition to economic variables, other trends such as social trends, technology, and political and regulatory influences can have a major effect on some firms in an industry. Some firms in the industry can try to take advantage of demographic changes or shifts in consumer tastes and lifestyles, or they may invest in technology as part of a strategy to lower costs and better serve their customers. Such firms may be able to grow and succeed despite unfavorable industry or economic conditions. For example, Wal-Mart has become the nation's leading retailer because of innovative management. The geographic location of many of its stores has allowed it to benefit from rising regional population and lower labor costs. Its strategy, which has emphasized everyday low prices, appeals to consumers. In addition, Wal-Mart's technologically advanced inventory and ordering systems and the logistics of its distribution system has given the retailer a competitive advantage over less technically progressive rivals.

During the initial stage of an industry's life cycle, the original firms in the industry can refine their technologies and move down the learning curve. Subsequent entrants into the industry may benefit from these initial actions and learn from the leaders' mistakes and take market share away from them. Investors need to be aware of such strategies when they evaluate companies and their stocks.

Political and regulatory events can create opportunities in an industry even when economic influences appear weak. Deregulation in trucking, airlines, and the financial services industries has led to the creation of new companies and innovative strategies. Sharp price declines following bad industry news may be a good buying opportunity for investors with good analytical skills and cool heads. The point is, some stocks may deserve lower prices following some political or regulatory events; but if the market also sends down the stock prices of good companies or companies with smaller exposures to the bad news, then an astute analyst can identify buying opportunities of undervalued stocks within such an industry.

The bottom line is that, although the economy plays a major role in determining overall market trends and industry groups display sensitivity to economic variables, other structural changes may counterbalance the economic effects or company management may be able to minimize the impact of economic events on a company. Analysts who are familiar with industry trends and unique company strategies can provide well-reasoned buy-and-sell recommendations irrespective of the economic forecast.

Company Analysis

In this section we discuss several analytical components. As we consider firms' competitive strategies, we continue our discussion (from Chapter 13) of Porter's analysis of an industry's competitive environment. Subsequently we consider the basic SWOT analysis, where the objective is to articulate a firm's strengths, weaknesses, opportunities, and threats. These two analyses should provide a complete understanding of a firm's overall *strategic* approach. Given this background, we are in a position to apply several fundamental valuation models.

FIRMS' COMPETITIVE STRATEGIES

In describing competition within industries in Chapter 13, we identified five competitive forces that could affect the competitive structure and profit potential of an industry: (1) current rivalry, (2) threat of new entrants, (3) potential substitutes, (4) bargaining power of suppliers, and (5) bargaining power of buyers. After we have determined the competitive structure of an industry, we need to identify the specific competitive strategy employed by each firm and evaluate these strategies in terms of the overall competitive structure of the industry.

A company's competitive strategy can either be *defensive* or *offensive*. A *defensive competitive strategy* involves positioning the firm so that its capabilities deflect the effect of the competitive forces in the industry. Examples may include investing in fixed assets and technology to lower production costs or creating a strong brand image with increased advertising expenditures.

An *offensive competitive strategy* is one in which the firm attempts to use its strengths to affect the competitive forces in the industry and improve its relative position in the industry. For example, Microsoft's domination in personal computer software has been due to its ability to preempt rivals and write operating system software for a large portion of the PC market. Similarly, Wal-Mart has used its buying power to obtain price concessions from its suppliers. This cost advantage, coupled with a superior delivery system to its stores, has allowed Wal-Mart to grow against larger competitors to become the leading U.S. retailer.

Analysts must understand what strategies exist, determine each firm's strategy, judge whether the firm's strategy is reasonable for its industry, and finally, evaluate how successful the firm is in implementing its strategy.

In the following sections, we discuss a firm's competitive position and strategy. Analysts must decide whether the firm's management is correctly positioning the firm to take advantage of industry and economic conditions. Their opinion about management's decisions will subsequently be reflected in their estimates of the firm's future cash flows, its inherent risk (which determines its required discount rate), and, therefore, its intrinsic value.

Porter suggests two major competitive strategies: low-cost leadership and differentiation.[4] These two competitive strategies indicate how a firm has decided to cope with the five competitive forces that define an industry's environment. The strategies available and the ways of implementing them differ within each industry.

LOW-COST (COST-LEADERSHIP) STRATEGY

The firm that pursues the low-cost strategy is determined to become *the* low-cost producer and, hence, the cost leader in its industry. Cost advantages vary by industry and might include economies of scale, proprietary technology, or preferential access to raw materials. To benefit from cost leadership, the firm must command prices near the industry average, which means that it must differentiate itself about as well as other firms. If the firm discounts price too much, it could erode the superior rates of return available because of its low cost. Wal-Mart has become a low-cost source due to volume purchasing of merchandise and lower-cost operations. As a result, the firm charges less but still enjoys higher profit margins and returns on capital than its competitors.

DIFFERENTIATION STRATEGY

With the differentiation strategy, a firm seeks to be unique in its industry in an area that is important to buyers. Again, the possibilities for differentiation vary widely by industry. For example, a company can differentiate itself based on its distribution system (selling in stores, by mail order, on the Internet, or door-to-door), or some unique marketing approach such as high price but exceptional quality and service (e.g., Neiman Marcus, Tiffany, Bloomingdales, and Burberry). A firm employing the differentiation strategy will enjoy above-average rates of return only if the price premium attributable to its differentiation exceeds the extra cost of being unique. Therefore, when analyzing a firm using this strategy, we must determine whether the differentiating factor is truly unique, whether it is sustainable, its cost, and if the price premium derived from the uniqueness is greater than its cost (i.e., whether the firm is experiencing above-average rates of return on its sales and/or capital).

FOCUSING A STRATEGY

Whichever strategy it selects, a firm must determine where it will focus this strategy by selecting segments in the industry and tailoring its strategy to serve these specific groups.

---

[4]Michael E. Porter, *Competitive Strategy: Techniques for Analyzing Industries and Companies*, New York: The Free Press, 1980; Michael E. Porter, *Competitive Advantage: Creating and Sustaining Superior Performance*, New York: The Free Press, 1985.

EXHIBIT 15.1	Skills, Resources, and Organizational Requirements Needed to Successfully Apply Cost-Leadership and Differentiation Strategies	
Generic Strategy	**Commonly Required Skills and Resources**	**Common Organizational Requirements**
Overall cost leadership	Sustained capital investment and access to capital Process engineering skills Intense supervision of labor Products designed for ease in manufacture Low-cost distribution system	Tight cost control Frequent, detailed control reports Structured organization and responsibilities Incentives based on meeting strict quantitative targets
Differentiation	Strong marketing abilities Product engineering Creative flair Strong capability in basic research Corporate reputation for quality or technological leadership Long tradition in the industry or unique combination of skills drawn from other businesses Strong cooperation from channels	Strong coordination among functions in R&D, product development, and marketing Subjective measurement and incentives instead of quantitative measures Amenities to attract highly skilled labor, scientists, or creative people

Source: Reprinted and adapted with the permission of The Free Press, an imprint of Simon & Schuster Adult Publishing Group, from *Competitive Strategy: Techniques for Analyzing Industries and Competitors* by Michael E. Porter, pp. 40–41. Copyright © 1980, 1998 by The Free Press.

For example, a cost-leadership strategy might focus on being the low-cost producer for an expensive segment of the market. Similarly, a differentiation focus would target specific segments. For example, athletic shoe companies that have developed shoes for unique sport segments such as tennis, basketball, aerobics, or walkers and hikers, rather than only running shoes. These companies thought that participants in these activities needed shoes with characteristics different from those desired by joggers. Equally important, they believed that participants in these athletic activities would pay a premium for these special shoes. In analyzing firms, we must ascertain if such special possibilities exist, if they are being served by another firm, and if they can be priced to generate abnormal returns to the firm. Exhibit 15.1 details some of Porter's ideas for the skills, resources, and company organizational requirements needed to successfully develop a cost-leadership or differentiation strategy.

In analyzing a specific firm, we must determine which strategy the firm is pursuing, its success in its strategy, and whether the strategy can be sustained. Further, we should evaluate a firm's competitive strategy *over time,* because strategies need to change as an industry evolves; different strategies work during different phases of an industry's life cycle. For example, a differentiation strategy may work for a firm during an industry's growth stages, but when the industry is in its mature stage, firms may try the low-cost strategy.

Throughout the analysis process, we identify what the company does well, what it does not do well, and where the firm is vulnerable to the five competitive forces. Some call this process developing a company's "story." This evaluation enables us to determine the outlook and risks facing the firm. In summary, the industry's competitive forces and the firm's strategy for dealing with them is the key to estimating the firm's long-run cash flows and risks.

SWOT ANALYSIS

Another framework for examining a firm's competitive position and its strategy is SWOT analysis. *SWOT analysis* involves examining a firm's Strengths, Weaknesses, Opportunities, and *Threats* to evaluate a firm's strategies to exploit its competitive advantages or defend against its weaknesses. Strengths and weaknesses involve identifying the firm's *internal* abilities, or lack thereof. Opportunities and threats include *external* factors such as competitive forces, discovery and development of new technologies, government regulations, and domestic and international economic trends.

The *strengths* of a company give the firm a comparative advantage in the marketplace. Perceived strengths can include good customer service, high-quality products, strong brand image, customer loyalty, innovative R&D, market leadership, or strong financial resources. To remain strengths, they must continue to be developed, maintained, and defended.

Weaknesses result when competitors have potentially exploitable advantages over the firm. Once weaknesses are identified, the firm can select strategies to mitigate or correct the weaknesses. For example, a firm that is only a domestic producer in a global market can make investments that will allow it to export or produce its product overseas. Alternatively, a firm with poor financial resources would enter into joint ventures with financially stronger firms.

Opportunities, or environmental factors that favor the firm, can include a growing market for the firm's products, shrinking competition, favorable exchange rate shifts, or identification of a new market or product segment.

Threats are environmental factors that can hinder the firm in achieving its goals. Examples would include impending negative legislation, an increase in industry competition, threats of entry, buyers or suppliers seeking to increase their bargaining power, or new technology that could preempt a firm's product. By recognizing and understanding opportunities and threats, an investor can make informed decisions about how the firm might exploit opportunities and mitigate threats.

FAVORABLE ATTRIBUTES OF FIRMS

Peter Lynch, the former portfolio manager of Fidelity Investments' highly successful Magellan Fund, looks for the following attributes when he analyzes firms.[5]

1. The firm's product is not faddish; it is one that consumers will continue to purchase over time.
2. The firm has some sustainable comparative competitive advantage over its rivals.
3. The firm's industry or product has the potential for market stability because it has little or no need to innovate, create product improvements, or fear that it may lose a technological advantage. Market stability means less potential for entry and limited need for costly investments or R&D.
4. The firm can benefit from cost reductions (for example, a computer manufacturer that uses supplier technology to deliver a faster and less-expensive machine).
5. The firm buys back its shares and/or has management (insiders) buying shares.

Estimating Intrinsic Values for Walgreens

Now that we know how to analyze the economy, structural forces, the industry, a company, and its competitors, it is time to apply the valuation techniques discussed in Chapter 11 to Walgreens to estimate the intrinsic value of the firm's common stock. If our intrinsic value estimate exceeds the stock's current market price, we should purchase the stock. If the current market price exceeds our intrinsic value estimate, we should avoid or sell the stock.

---

[5]See his two books: Peter Lynch, *One Up on Wall Street*, New York: Simon & Schuster, 1989; and Peter Lynch, *Beating the Street*, New York: Simon & Schuster, 1993.

We first consider the *present value of cash flow (PVCF) models*. Exhibit 15.2 contains historical data for Walgreens related to variables required for the PVCF models.

PRESENT VALUE OF DIVIDENDS

As noted in Chapter 11, determining the present value of future dividends is a difficult task. Therefore, analysts apply one or more simplifying assumptions to dividend discount models (DDMs). The typical assumption is that the stock's dividends will grow at a constant rate over time. Although unrealistic for fast-growing or cyclical firms, the constant growth assumption may be appropriate for some mature slow-growing firms. More complex DDMs exist for more complicated growth forecasts. These include two-stage growth models (a period of fast growth followed by a period of constant growth) and three-stage growth models (a period of fast growth followed by a period of diminishing growth rates followed by a period of constant growth).

For simplicity, we will initially discuss the constant growth dividend model. As shown in Chapter 11, when dividends grow at a constant rate, a stock's price should equal next year's dividend, D_1, divided by the difference between investors' required rate of return on the stock (k) and the dividend growth rate (g):

15.1
$$\text{Intrinsic Value} = \frac{D_1}{(k - g)}$$

With constant dividend growth, next year's dividend should equal the current dividend, D_0, increased by the constant dividend growth rate: $D_1 = D_0(1 + g)$. Because the current dividend is known, to estimate intrinsic value we need only estimate two parameters: the dividend growth rate and investors' required rate of return.

Growth Rate Estimates   If the stock has had fairly constant dividend growth over the past five to ten years, one estimate of the constant growth rate is to use the actual percentage growth rate of dividends over this time period. The average compound annual growth rate (CAGR) is found by computing

15.2
$$\text{CAGR of Dividends} = \sqrt[n]{\frac{D_n}{D_0}} - 1$$

In the case of Walgreens, the 1983 dividend (D_0) was $0.02 a share and the 2003 dividend (D_{10}) was $0.16 a share. The average dividend growth rate was

$$\sqrt[20]{\frac{\$0.16}{\$0.02}} - 1 = 0.1096$$

or 10.96 percent. Clearly, it is inappropriate to blindly plug historical growth rates into our formulas because if we do, we have wasted our time analyzing economic, structural, industry, and company influences. Our analysis may have indicated that growth is expected to increase or decrease due to factors such as changes in government programs, demographic shifts, or changes in product mix. The historical growth rate may need to be raised or lowered to incorporate our prior analysis.

In Chapter 14, we learned other ways to compute growth. The sustainable growth rate

15.3
$$g = RR \times ROE$$

assumes the firm will maintain a constant debt–equity ratio as it finances asset growth. We know that ROA can be expressed as the product of the firm's net profit margin and total asset turnover; ROE is the product of the net profit margin, total asset turnover, and the

EXHIBIT 15.2   Walgreens Input Data for Alternative Present Value of Cash Flow Models (Dollars in Millions, Except per Share Data)

Year	Dividend per Share	Net Income	Depreciation Expense	Capital Spending	Change in Working Capital	Principal Repayment	New Debt Issues	FCFE	EBIT	Tax Rate	FCFF	1-Tax Rate	Time
1983	0.02	70	25	-71	-15	-3	0	6	147	45%	19.9	55%	1
1984	0.03	85	29	-68	-56	-3	0	-13	181	45%	4.6	55%	2
1985	0.03	94	34	-97	-61	-3	20	-13	209	46%	-11.1	54%	3
1986	0.03	103	44	-156	-72	-5	92	6	229	45%	-58.1	55%	4
1987	0.04	104	54	-122	-118	-4	5	-81	243	46%	-54.8	54%	5
1988	0.04	129	59	-114	49	-4	31	150	263	38%	157.1	62%	6
1989	0.05	154	64	-121	-97	-4	0	-4	301	37%	35.6	63%	7
1990	0.05	175	70	-192	-69	-4	0	-20	344	38%	22.3	62%	8
1991	0.06	195	84	-202	-129	-24	0	-76	381	38%	-10.8	62%	9
1992	0.07	221	92	-145	-32	-6	0	130	429	37%	185.3	63%	10
1993	0.08	245	105	-185	-28	-112	0	25	483	39%	186.6	61%	11
1994	0.09	282	118	-290	-58	-6	0	46	550	38%	111.0	62%	12
1995	0.10	321	132	-310	-104	-7	0	32	629	39%	101.7	61%	13
1996	0.11	372	147	-364	-116	0	2	41	725	39%	109.3	61%	14
1997	0.12	436	164	-485	34	-1	0	148	842	39%	226.6	61%	15
1998	0.13	511	189	-641	-143	0	0	-84	878	39%	-59.4	61%	16
1999	0.13	624	210	-696	-206	0	0	-68	1028	39%	-64.9	61%	17
2000	0.14	777	230	-1119	-140	0	0	-252	1264	39%	-258.0	61%	18
2001	0.14	886	269	-1237	-569	0	0	-651	1426	38%	-652.9	62%	19
2002	0.15	1,019	307	-934	46	0	0	438	1,624	38%	429.4	62%	20
2003	0.16	1,176	346	-795	-191	0	0	536	1,848	38%	510.5	62%	21
Annual compound growth rate 1983-2003	10.96%	15.15%	14.04%	12.84%					13.49%		~17%		
Annual compound growth rate 1993-2003	7.18%	16.98%	12.67%	15.70%					14.36%		~11%		
Compound sales per share growth rate 1993-2003	14.25%												
Compound BV/PS growth rate 1993-2003	17.50%												
ROE	16.34												

financial leverage multiplier. Thus, a firm's future growth rate and its components can be compared to its competitors, its industry, and the market. Although there is not necessarily a close relationship between the year-to-year growth in a firm's assets and its dividend cash flows, these calculations provide insight that, along with the rest of the top-down analysis, can assist the analyst in determining whether dividend growth may rise or fall in the future.

For Walgreens, the sustainable growth rate calculation using 2003 data is[6]

$$g = RR \times ROE = 0.86 \times 0.1634$$

$$= 0.1405 = 14.05\%$$

The dividend growth rate will be influenced by the stage of the industry life cycle, structural changes, and economic trends. Economic–industry–firm analysis provides valuable information regarding future trends in dividend growth. Analysts who ask questions during interviews about management's plans to expand the firm, diversify into new areas, or change dividend policy can gather useful information about the firm's dividend policy. Averaging the historical growth rate of dividends (10.96 percent) and the implied sustainable growth estimate above (14.05 percent) indicates a value of 12.51 percent. For simplicity, we will use 13 percent for the estimated g because it is consistent with the fundamentals and with the growth of earnings.

Required Rate of Return Estimate

We know an investor's required rate of return has two basic components: the nominal risk-free interest rate and a risk premium. If the market is efficient, over time the return earned by investors should compensate them for the risk of the investment.

Notably, we must estimate *future* risk premiums to determine the stock's current intrinsic value. Estimates of the nominal risk-free interest rate are available from the initial analysis of the economy during the top-down approach. The risk premium of the firm must rely on other information derived from the top-down company analysis, including evaluation of the financial statements and capital market relationships.

In Chapter 14 we examined ratios that measure several aspects of the risk of a firm and its stock. Business risk, financial risk, liquidity risk, exchange rate risk, and country risk are additional components of risk to be reviewed in the context of our economy–industry–firm analysis. These measures can be compared against the firm's major competitors, its industry, and the overall market. This comparison will indicate whether the firm should have a higher or lower risk premium than other firms in the industry, the overall market, or the firm's historical risk premium. Accounting-based risk measures use historical data, whereas investment analysis requires an estimate of the future. Investors need to incorporate into the risk analysis any information uncovered during the top-down process that would lead to higher or lower risk estimates.

For a market-based risk estimate, the firm's characteristic line is estimated by regressing market returns on the stock's returns. We know the slope of this regression line is the stock's beta, or measure of systematic risk. Estimates of next year's risk-free rate and the long-run market return and an estimate of the stock's beta indicate the required rate of return:

15.4 $$E(R_{stock}) = E(RFR) + \beta_{stock}[E(R_{market}) - E(RFR)]$$

Again, this estimate of beta begins with historical market information. Because beta is affected by changes in a firm's business and financial risks, as well as other influences, an

---

[6]This sustainable growth rate value differs from the one in Chapter 14 because this calculation uses year-end values for ROE, while in Chapter 14 the equity value is an average of the beginning and ending values.

investor should increase or lower the historical beta estimate based on an analysis of the firm's future.

To demonstrate the estimate of the required rate of return equation for Walgreens, we make several assumptions regarding components of the security market line (SML) discussed in Chapter 9. First is the prevailing nominal risk-free rate (RFR), which is estimated at about 5.0 percent—the current yield to maturity for the intermediate-term government bond. The expected equity-market rate of return (R_{Mkt}) depends on the expected market risk premium on stocks. There is substantial controversy on the appropriate estimate for the equity-market risk premium—that is, the estimates range from a high of about 8 percent (the arithmetic mean of the actual risk premium since 1926) to a low of about 3 percent, which is the risk premium suggested in several academic studies. We question both of these extreme values and suggest using a 4.5 percent risk premium (0.045). The final estimate is the firm's systematic risk value (beta), which is typically derived from the following regression model (the characteristic line) noted in Chapter 9.

15.5
$$R_{WAG} = \alpha + \beta_{WAG}R_{Mkt}$$

where:

R_{WAG} = monthly rate of return for Walgreens
α = constant term
β_{WAG} = beta coefficient for Walgreens equal to $\dfrac{Cov_{WM}}{\sigma_m^2}$
R_{Mkt} = monthly rate of returns for a market proxy—typically the S&P 500 index

When we ran this regression using monthly rates of return during the five-year period 1999–2003 (sixty observations), the beta coefficient was estimated at 0.90.

Putting together the RFR of 0.05 and the market risk premium of 0.045 implies an expected market return (R_{Mkt}) of 0.095. This, combined with the Walgreens beta of 0.90, indicates the following expected rate of return for Walgreens:

15.6
$$E(R) = RFR + \beta_i(R_{Mkt} - RFR)$$
$$= 0.05 + 0.90(0.095 - 0.05)$$
$$= 0.05 + 0.90(0.045)$$
$$= 0.05 + 0.040$$
$$= 0.09 = 9.0\%$$

Present Value of Dividends Model At this point, we face a problem: The intent was to use the basic DDM that assumed a constant growth rate for an infinite period. Recall that the model also required that $k > g$ (the required rate of return is larger than the expected growth rate), which is not true in this case because k = 9 percent and g = 13 percent (see Exhibit 15.2). Therefore, we must employ a two- or three-stage growth model. Because of the fairly large difference in the current growth rate of 13 percent and the long-run constant growth rate of 8 percent, it seems reasonable to use a three-stage model that includes a gradual transition period.

We assume that the growth periods are as follows:

g_1 = **seven years (growing at 13 percent a year)**
g_2 = **five years (during this period it is assumed that the growth rate declines 1 percent per year for five years)**
g_3 = **constant growth at 8 percent into the future**

Therefore, beginning with 2004, when dividends were expected to be $0.17, the future dividend payments will be as follows (the growth rate is in parenthesis):

Year	HIGH-GROWTH PERIOD	Div.	PV @ 9%	Year	DECLINING-GROWTH PERIOD	Div.	PV @ 9%
2005	(13%)	0.19	0.17	2012	(12%)	0.45	0.23
2006	(13%)	0.22	0.18	2013	(11%)	0.50	0.23
2007	(13%)	0.25	0.19	2014	(10%)	0.55	0.23
2008	(13%)	0.28	0.20	2015	(9%)	0.60	0.23
2009	(13%)	0.31	0.20	2016	(8%)	0.64	0.23
2010	(13%)	0.35	0.21			Total	$1.15
2011	(13%)	0.40	0.22				
		Total	$1.37				

$$\text{Constant Growth Period: } P_{2016} = \frac{0.64\,(1.08)}{0.09 - 0.08} = \frac{0.69}{0.09 - 0.08} = \frac{0.69}{0.01} = \$69.00$$

The total value of the stock is the sum of the three present value streams discounted at 9 percent:

1. Present value of high-growth period dividends — $ 1.37
2. Present value of declining-growth period dividends — 1.15
3. Present value of constant-growth period dividends — 24.53
   Total present value of dividends — $27.05

The estimated value based on the DDM is lower than the market price in mid-2004 of about $36.00. This estimated value also implies a low P/E ratio based on expected earnings in 2004 of about $1.30 per share (that is, about 21 times earnings) compared to the prevailing market P/E of about 18 times 2004 earnings. In a subsequent section on relative valuation techniques, we compare the Walgreens P/E ratio to that of its industry and the market. As we will discuss, Walgreens should definitely sell at a premium P/E compared to the market.

Present Value of Free Cash Flow to Equity   This technique resembles a present value of earnings concept except that it considers the capital expenditures required to maintain and grow the firm and the change in working capital required for a growing firm (that is, an increase in accounts receivable and inventory). The specific definition of free cash flow to equity (FCFE) is

Net Income + Depreciation Expense − Capital Expenditures
− Change in Working Capital − Principal Debt Repayments
+ New Debt Issues

This technique attempts to determine the free cash flow available to the stockholders after payments to all other capital suppliers and after providing for the continued growth of the firm. Because we are dealing with the cash flow available to stockholders, the discount rate used is the firm's cost of equity (k), which we estimated to be 9 percent.

Given the current FCFE values, the alternative forms of the model are similar to those available for the DDM, which in turn depends on the firm's growth prospects. Specifically, if the firm is in its mature constant growth phase, it is possible to use a model similar to the reduced-form DDM:

15.7

$$\text{Value} = \frac{FCFE_1}{k - g_{FCFE}}$$

where:

$FCFE$ = the expected free cash flow to equity in period 1

k = the required rate of return on equity for the firm

g_{FCFE} = the expected constant growth rate of free cash flow to equity for the firm

We can see from Exhibit 15.2 that during the period 1983–2003 Walgreens' net income grew between 15 percent and 17 percent, and its EBIT grew at about 14 percent. These rates of growth exceed the firm's k rate of 9 percent. In the case of FCFE, we need to consider the effect of capital expenditures relative to depreciation and changes in working capital as well as debt repayments and new-debt issues. The historical data in Exhibit 15.2 shows that the FCFE series has had a volatile history with a growth rate that exceeded 20 percent during some periods since 1983, in contrast to the negative values in 1999–2002. The reason for the dramatic change is evident—it is the very heavy capital expenditures that have grown at almost a 13 percent rate for the total period and the significant negative working capital items (including a special problem with inventories). The firm returned to positive cash flows in 2003 because of a reduction in the growth rate of stores—from a net increase (new stores minus closings) of about 475 stores per year to about 360 a year. Based on discussions with management, this slowdown in growth was due to the prevailing shortage of pharmacists. While Walgreens continued to add stores, the slower *rate* of growth and the elimination of the inventory buildup problem allowed the firm to return to positive cash flows in 2002. Going forward, it is conservatively estimated that in 2004, the FCFE will be about 500 million and the FCFF (free cash flow to the firm) will be about $550 million. Such volatility makes it appropriate to use a conservative 12 percent growth rate going forward after 2004 and assume it declines to a 7 percent constant rate. Therefore, the following example again uses a three-stage growth model with the following characteristics.

g_1 = **12 percent for the six years after 2004**

g_2 = **a constantly declining growth rate to 7 percent over five years**

g_3 = **a long-run constant rate of growth of 7 percent**

k = **9 percent cost of equity**

The specific estimate of annual FCFE beginning with the actual estimated value of $500 million in 2004 are as follows:

	HIGH-GROWTH PERIOD				DECLINING-GROWTH PERIOD		
Year	Growth Rate	$ Million	PV at 9%	Year	Growth Rate	$ Million	PV at 9%
2004	—	500	—	2011	11%	1,096	$ 600
2005	12%	560	$ 514	2012	10	1,205	605
2006	12	627	528	2013	9	1,314	605
2007	12	702	542	2014	8	1,419	599
2008	12	787	558	2015	7	1,518	588
2009	12	881	573			Total	$2,997
2010	12	987	589				
		Total	$3,304				

$$\text{Constant Growth Period Value} = \frac{\$1,625}{0.09 - 0.07} = \$81,250$$

$$\text{PV at 9\%} = \$31,484$$

The total value of the stock is the sum of the three present value streams discounted at 9 percent:

	$ Million
1. Present value of high-growth cash flows	3,304
2. Present value of declining-growth cash flows	2,997
3. Present value of constant-growth cash flows	31,484
Total present value of FCFE	$37,785

The outstanding shares estimated for the end of 2004 were 1,050 million. Therefore, the per share value of the present value of FCFE is $35.99 ($36 for simplicity), which is almost exactly the market price as of mid-2004 ($35.65 close, twelve-month range $29–37). This implies a P/E for Walgreens relative to 2004 earnings ($1.30) of about 28 times and relative to 2005 earnings ($1.45) of almost 25 times. These multiples compare to a current forward multiple for the S&P 500 of about 18 times. This differential is reasonable based on a much higher growth rate for Walgreens and a below-market risk measure (beta = 0.90).

Present Value of Operating Free Cash Flow   This is also referred to as *free cash flow to the firm* by Damodaran and *the entity DCF model* by Copeland, Koller, and Murrin.[7] The object is to determine a value for the total firm and subtract the value of the firm's debt obligations to arrive at a value for the firm's equity. Notably, in this valuation technique, because we are dealing with the cash flows available to all capital suppliers (both equity and debt), we discount the firm's operating free cash flow (OFCF) or the free cash flow to the firm (FCFF) at the firm's weighted-average cost of capital (WACC) rather than its cost of equity.

Operating free cash flow or free cash flow to the firm is equal to

EBIT(1 − Tax Rate) + Depreciation Expense − Capital Spending − Change in Working Capital − Change in Other Assets

This is the cash flow generated by a company's operations and available to both equity and debt. As noted, because it is the cash flow from *all capital suppliers,* it is discounted at the firm's WACC.

Again, the specifications of this operating FCF model are similar to the DDM—that is, the specification depends on the firm's growth prospects. Assuming an expectation of constant growth, we can use the reduced-form model

15.8

$$\text{Firm Value} = \frac{\text{FCFF}_1}{\text{WACC} - \text{g}_{\text{FCFF}}} \quad \text{or} \quad \frac{\text{OFCF}_1}{\text{WACC} - \text{g}_{\text{OFCF}}}$$

where:

FCFF_1 = the free cash flow for the firm in period 1
OFCF_1 = the firm's operating free cash flow in period 1
WACC = the firm's weighted-average cost of capital
g_{FCFF} = the constant infinite growth rate of free cash flow for the firm
g_{OFCF} = the constant infinite growth rate of operating free cash flow

As noted in Exhibit 15.2, the compound annual growth rate for operating free cash flow (also referred to as free cash flow to the firm) during the twenty-year period was quite

---

[7]Aswath Damodaran, *Damodaran on Valuation*, New York: John Wiley & Sons, 1994, Chapter 8; and Tom Copeland, Tim Koller, and Jack Murrin, *Valuation: Measuring and Managing the Value of Companies,* 3rd ed., New York: John Wiley & Sons, 2000, Chapter 5.

volatile but it has been a positive value during the past two years with a slowdown in the growth of new drugstores and lower working capital needs. An alternative measure of long-run growth is the growth implied by the equation

$$g = (RR)(ROIC)$$

where:

$$RR = \text{the average retention rate}$$
$$ROIC = EBIT(1 - \text{Tax Rate})/\text{Total Capital}$$

For Walgreens, the recent retention rate is about 80 percent and the ROIC for 2003 (assuming a tax rate of 38 percent) is equal to

15.9

$$ROIC = \frac{\textbf{EBIT}(1 - \textbf{Tax Rate})}{\textbf{Average Total Capital}} = \frac{(1,848)(0.62)}{(6,924 + 7,986)/2}$$

$$= \frac{1146}{7455}$$

$$= 0.1537 = 15.37\%$$

(*Note:* Total capital is equal to shareholders equity plus noncurrent liabilities. The average is equal to the beginning and ending values divided by two. The specific values used are from Exhibits 14.1 and 15.2.)

Therefore,

$$g = (0.80)(0.1537)$$

$$= 0.1230 = 12.30\%$$

Therefore, in the subsequent valuation calculation we will begin with a conservative growth estimate for FCFF of 12 percent.

Calculation of WACC We calculate the discount rate (i.e., the firm's WACC) using the following formula:

15.10

$$\textbf{WACC} = \textbf{W}_E k + \textbf{W}_D i$$

where:

$$W_E = \text{the proportion of equity in total capital}$$
$$k = \text{the after-tax cost of equity (from the SML)}$$
$$W_D = \text{the proportion of debt in total capital}[8]$$
$$i = \text{the after-tax cost of debt}[9]$$

For Walgreens,

$$\textbf{W}_E = \textbf{0.70}; \quad k = \textbf{0.09}; \quad \textbf{W}_D = \textbf{0.30}; \quad i = (\textbf{0.07})(\textbf{1} - \textbf{0.38})$$

$$= \textbf{0.043}$$

---

[8]The proportion of debt capital used in the WACC estimate is based on the book value of the debt and includes the value of capitalized lease payments as debt as computed in Chapter 14.

[9]For this estimate we use the prevailing interest rate on corporate A rated bonds (7 percent), and Walgreens' recent tax rate of 38 percent.

so

$$\mathbf{WACC} = (0.70)(0.09) + (0.30)(0.043)$$

$$= 0.063 + 0.013 = 0.076 = 7.6\%$$

Again, to be conservative we will round off the WACC estimate and use 8 percent in the calculations.

Again, because the expected growth rate of operating free cash flow is greater than the firm's WACC, we cannot use the reduced-form model that assumes constant growth at this relatively high rate for an infinite period. Therefore, we will employ the three-stage growth model with growth duration assumptions similar to the prior examples.

Given these inputs for recent growth and the firm's WACC, the growth estimates for a three-stage growth model are

g_1 = 12 percent for six years

g_2 = a constantly declining rate to 6 percent over six years[10]

g_3 = a constant long-run growth rate

The specific estimates for future operating FCF (or FCFF) are as follows, beginning from the estimated 2004 value of $550 million.

HIGH-GROWTH PERIOD				DECLINING-GROWTH PERIOD			
Year	Growth Rate	FCFF	PV at 8%	Year	Growth Rate	FCFF	PV at 8%
2004	—	550	—	2011	(11%)	1,205	703
2005	(12%)	616	570	2012	(10%)	1,326	716
2006	(12%)	690	592	2013	(9%)	1,445	723
2007	(12%)	773	614	2014	(8%)	1,561	723
2008	(12%)	865	636	2015	(7%)	1,670	716
2009	(12%)	969	660	2016	(6%)	1,770	703
2010	(12%)	1,086	684			Total	4,284
		Total	$3,756				

$$\textbf{Constant Growth Period Value} = \frac{1,770 \times (1.06)}{0.08 - 0.06} = \$93,800$$

$$\textbf{PV at 8\%} = \$37,248$$

Thus the total value of the firm is equal to

	$ Million
1. Present value of high-growth cash flows	$3,756
2. Present value of declining-growth cash flows	4,284
3. Present value of constant-growth cash flows	37,248
Total present value of operating FCF (FCFF)	$45,288

---

[10]This 6 percent long-run growth rate assumption implies that we do not believe that FCFF can grow as fast as FCFE. Given a beginning growth rate of 12 percent and a long-run rate of 6 percent means that the growth rate will decline by 0.01 per year.

Recall that the value of equity is the total value of the firm (PV of operating FCF) minus the current market value of debt, which is the present value of debt payments at the firm's cost of debt (0.07). The values are as follows:

Total present value of operating FCF	$45,288
Minus value of debt	10,500
Value of equity	34,788
Number of common shares	1,050 million
Value of equity per share	$33.13

(*Note:* Value of debt includes an estimate of the present value of minimum lease payments for the firm at the and of 2004.)

Again, this estimated value compares to the recent market value of almost $36. The $33.13 value implies a P/E of about 25.5 times estimated 2004 earnings of $1.30 per share.

To summarize, the valuations derived from the present value of cash flow techniques are as follows:

Present value of dividends	$23.11
Present value of FCFE	36.00
Present value of operating FCF	33.13
(or, the PV of FCFF)	

All of these prices must be compared to the prevailing market price of $35.65 to determine the investment decision.

RELATIVE VALUATION TECHNIQUES

In this section we present the data required to compute the several relative valuation ratios and demonstrate the use of these relative valuation techniques for Walgreens compared to the retail drugstore industry and the S&P Industrials index.

Exhibit 15.3 contains the basic data required to compute the relative valuation ratios, and Exhibit 15.4 contains the four sets of relative valuation ratios for Walgreens, its industry, and the aggregate market. This table also contains a comparison of the company ratios to similar ratios for the company's industry and the market. Such a comparison highlights the changes in the relative valuation ratio over time and helps in the determination of whether the current valuation ratio for the company (Walgreens) is reasonable based on the financial characteristics of the firm versus its industry and the market. To aid in the analysis, four graphs contain the time series of the relative valuation ratios for the company, its industry, and the market. Four additional graphs show the relationship between the relative valuation ratios: for the company compared to its industry, and for the company compared to the stock market.

Price–Earnings Ratio This is the most widely used and well-documented relative valuation ratio. We saw in Chapter 11 that the P/E ratio can be derived from the DDM as follows:

15.11

$$P/E_1 = \frac{D_1/E_1}{k - g}$$

This equation indicates that the P/E ratio is affected by two major variables:

1. The firm's required rate of return on its equity (*k*)
2. The firm's expected growth rate of dividends (*g*)

Therefore, the object of the analysis is to relate the firm's risk and expected growth to that of its industry and the market and determine if the firm's earnings multiplier should be less than or greater than its industry and the market multiplier.

EXHIBIT 15.3 Inputs for Relative Valuation Ratios: Walgreens, Retail Drugstore Industry, S&P Industrials Index, 1992–2002

Year	WALGREENS					RETAIL DRUG INDUSTRY					S&P INDUSTRIAL INDEX				
	Mean Price	EPS	CF per Share	BV per Share	Sales per Share	Mean Price	EPS	CF per Share	BV per Share	Sales per Share	Mean Price	EPS	CF per Share	BV per Share	Sales per Share
1992	4.69	0.22	0.39	1.25	7.54	89.56	4.52	5.80	33.59	162.55	490.34	20.82	51.11	201.12	617.41
1993	4.96	0.23	0.44	1.40	8.37	91.00	5.29	6.97	36.84	189.10	519.39	22.62	55.59	192.86	639.77
1994	5.06	0.29	0.50	1.60	9.32	91.27	4.73	6.08	38.69	202.91	535.90	35.17	69.56	211.51	672.04
1995	6.64	0.33	0.57	1.82	10.49	120.77	6.65	8.59	42.76	233.78	638.89	38.12	75.45	226.64	715.38
1996	9.10	0.38	0.65	2.08	11.85	158.78	8.73	11.01	44.28	265.94	796.69	41.74	80.76	240.07	736.65
1997	13.22	0.44	0.61	2.40	13.57	231.01	6.24	10.15	60.88	308.30	1,002.28	41.67	81.94	249.57	741.52
1998	22.50	0.54	0.73	2.86	15.43	368.63	8.96	13.25	68.07	343.36	1,278.87	40.79	83.16	265.27	738.82
1999	28.31	0.62	0.83	3.47	17.83	403.33	9.01	12.11	61.88	397.78	1,650.56	50.25	93.26	304.45	801.29
2000	33.91	0.76	1.00	4.19	21.05	385.22	11.69	14.36	69.34	337.40	1,702.23	53.85	98.54	332.81	838.78
2001	38.98	0.86	0.71	5.11	24.15	416.50	9.80	12.18	72.69	354.38	1,357.55	19.82	64.33	352.26	794.48
2002	35.71	0.99	1.44	6.08	27.98	348.15	13.26	15.57	85.75	400.24	1,136.17	22.57	61.43	313.56	790.86

EXHIBIT 15.4	Relative Valuation Ratios: Walgreens, Retail Drugstore Industry, S&P Industrials Index, 1992–2002

PRICE/EARNINGS RATIO

Year	Walgreens	Retail Drug	Ratio Co./Ind.	S&P Ind.	Ratio Co./Mkt.
1992	21.32	19.81	1.08	23.55	0.91
1993	21.57	17.20	1.25	22.96	0.94
1994	17.45	19.29	0.90	15.24	1.15
1995	20.12	18.16	1.11	16.76	1.20
1996	23.95	18.19	1.32	19.09	1.25
1997	30.05	37.02	0.81	24.05	1.25
1998	41.67	41.14	1.01	31.35	1.33
1999	45.66	44.76	1.02	32.85	1.39
2000	44.62	32.95	1.35	31.61	1.41
2001	45.33	42.50	1.07	68.49	0.66
2002	36.07	26.26	1.37	50.34	0.72
Mean	31.62	28.84	1.12	30.57	1.11

PRICE/CASH FLOW RATIO

Walgreens	Retail Drug	Ratio Co./Ind.	S&P Ind.	Ratio Co./Mkt.
12.03	15.44	0.78	9.59	1.25
11.27	13.06	0.86	9.34	1.21
10.12	15.01	0.67	7.70	1.31
11.65	14.06	0.83	8.47	1.38
14.00	14.42	0.97	9.86	1.42
21.67	22.76	0.95	12.23	1.77
30.82	27.82	1.11	15.38	2.00
34.11	33.31	1.02	17.70	1.93
33.91	26.83	1.26	17.27	1.96
55.25	34.20	1.62	21.10	2.62
24.83	22.36	1.11	18.50	1.34
23.61	21.75	1.02	13.38	1.65

PRICE/BOOK VALUE

Year	Walgreens	Retail Drug	Ratio Co./Ind.	S&P Ind.	Ratio Co./Mkt.
1992	3.75	2.67	1.41	2.44	1.54
1993	3.54	2.47	1.43	2.69	1.32
1994	3.16	2.36	1.34	2.53	1.25
1995	3.65	2.82	1.29	2.82	1.29
1996	4.38	3.59	1.22	3.32	1.32
1997	5.51	3.79	1.45	4.02	1.37
1998	7.87	5.42	1.45	4.82	1.63
1999	8.16	6.52	1.25	5.42	1.50
2000	8.09	5.56	1.46	5.11	1.58
2001	7.63	5.73	1.33	3.85	1.98
2002	5.87	4.06	1.45	3.62	1.62
Mean	5.60	4.09	1.37	3.70	1.49

PRICE/SALES RATIO

Walgreens	Retail Drug	Ratio Co./Ind.	S&P Ind.	Ratio Co./Mkt.
0.62	0.55	1.13	0.79	0.78
0.59	0.48	1.23	0.81	0.73
0.54	0.45	1.21	0.80	0.68
0.63	0.52	1.23	0.89	0.71
0.77	0.60	1.29	1.08	0.71
0.97	0.75	1.30	1.35	0.72
1.46	1.07	1.36	1.73	0.84
1.59	1.01	1.57	2.06	0.77
1.61	1.14	1.41	2.03	0.79
1.61	1.18	1.37	1.71	0.94
1.28	0.87	1.47	1.44	0.89
1.06	0.78	1.32	1.34	0.78

Exhibit 15.5 contains the three time series of P/E multipliers for 1992–2002. The P/E ratio used is equal to the mean price during year t (the mean price equals the average of the high and low price during the year) divided by the earnings per share during year t. This is referred to as the *historical* P/E ratio. All three series show an overall rising trend beginning at about 20 times earnings and ending at between 30 and 50 times earnings. Notably, Walgreens' P/E ratio was initially between its industry and the market, and was also between both series at the end of 2002. Specifically, as shown in Exhibit 15.6, the Co/Ind ratio of P/E ratios went from about 1.08 (that is, Walgreens' P/E was about 108 percent of the value of the industry P/E) to about 1.37 (Walgreens' P/E ratio was about 37 percent greater than the industry P/E ratio). In contrast, the Co/Mkt ratio of P/Es declined from about 0.91 to 0.72. The question an analyst must ask is whether Walgreens'

EXHIBIT 15.5	Time-Series Plot of Mean Historical Price–Earnings Ratios: Walgreens, RDS Industry, and S&P Industrials, 1992–2000

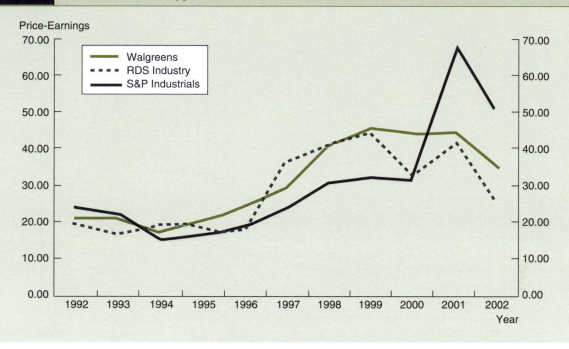

EXHIBIT 15.6	Time-Series Plot of Relative Price–Earnings Ratios: Walgreens/Industry and Walgreens/Market, 1992–2002

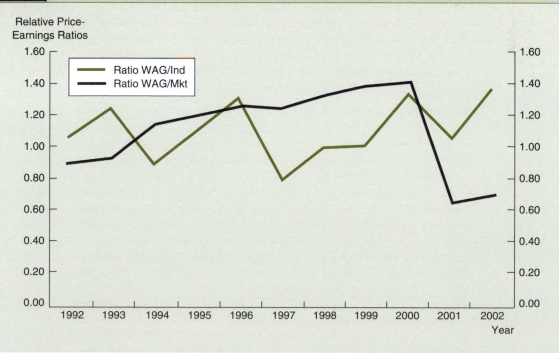

EXHIBIT 15.7	Time-Series Plot of Mean Historical Price–Cash Flow Ratios: Walgreens, RDS Industry, and S&P Industrials, 1992–2002

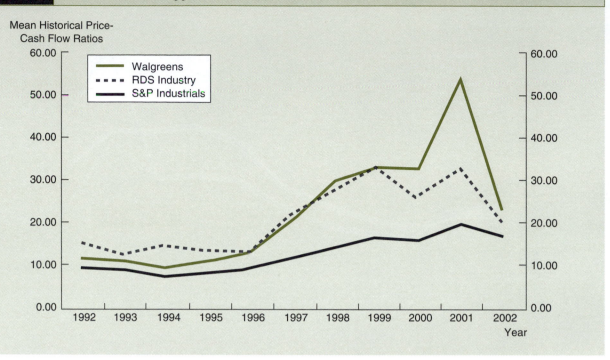

relative risk and its expected growth rate justify this premium P/E ratio relative to its industry and the discounted P/E relative to the market. The quick answers are that Walgreens *does* deserve a premium relative to its industry because it has a higher growth rate than any of its competitors and is less risky in terms of fundamentals or market risk. Alternatively, Walgreens does *not* deserve to sell at a discount to the market because it is growing much faster and has a lower risk measure than the market. Note that this discount is because the market P/E was abnormally high (50–68 times) during 2001 and 2002.

Price–Cash Flow Ratio The price–cash flow (P/CF) ratio has grown in prominence and use because many observers contend that a firm's cash flow is less subject to manipulation than its earnings per share and because cash flows are widely used in the present value of cash flow models discussed earlier. An important question is, which of the several cash flow specifications should we employ? In this analysis, we use the "traditional" cash flow measure, equal to net income plus the major noncash expense (depreciation), because this cash flow measure can be derived for both the retail drugstore industry and the market. Although it is certainly possible to employ any of the other cash flow measures discussed, a demonstration using this measure should provide a valid comparison for learning purposes.[11]

The time-series graph of the P/CF ratios in Exhibit 15.7 show a general increase for Walgreens and its industry from about 10 times in 1992 to 22–24 times in 2002, while the

---

[11]In an ideal world where all cash flow measures are available, the authors would prefer either "cash flow from operations" or a free cash flow series, but both of these are difficult to compute for the industry and market and are not generally available.

| EXHIBIT 15.8 | Time-Series Plot of Relative Price–Cash Flow Ratios: Walgreens/Industry and Walgreens/Market, 1992–2002 |

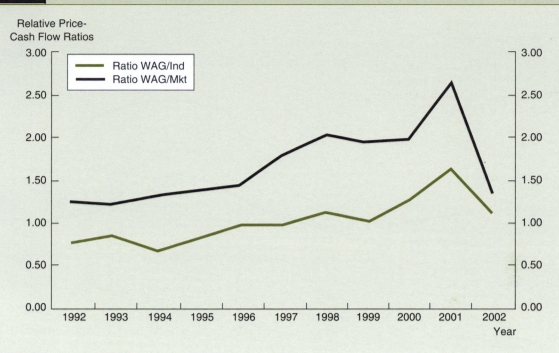

markct P/CF ratio went from 10 times to 19 times. Notably, although the absolute values of the ratios increased, the graphs in Exhibit 15.8 show that Walgreens P/CF ratios relative to its industry experienced an overall increase from 0.78 to 1.11. Similarly, the Co/Mkt comparison started at 1.25, reached a high of 2.62, and ended at 1.34. This indicates an overall increase in the P/CF ratio, and an increase in the firm's P/CF ratio relative to its industry and the overall market. The question to the investor therefore becomes, what has happened to the firm's growth rate of cash flow and the risk of its cash flows that would justify these increases in the relative P/CF ratio?

Price–Book Value Ratio The price–book value (P/BV) ratio has gained prominence because of the studies by Fama and French and several subsequent authors.[12] The rationale is that if individual firms have consistent accounting practice (for example, firms in the same industry), they can be meaningfully compared using this ratio. Notably, this measure of relative value can be used for firms with negative earnings or even negative cash flows. Investors should not attempt to use this ratio for firms with different levels of hard assets— that is, do not compare a heavy industrial firm to a service firm using this ratio.

The annual P/BV ratios for Walgreens, its industry, and the market are shown in Exhibit 15.9. Exhibit 15.10 contains the ratio of the company P/BV ratio relative to its industry

[12]Eugene F. Fama and Kenneth R. French, "The Cross Section of Expected Stock Returns," *Journal of Finance* 47, no. 2 (June 1992): 427–450; Barr Rosenberg, Kenneth Raid, and Ronald Lanstein, "Persuasive Evidence of Market Ineffi- ciency," *Journal of Portfolio Management* 11, no. 3 (Spring 1985): 9–17; and Patricia Fairfield, "P/E, P/B and the Present Value of Future Dividends," *Financial Analysts Journal* 50, no. 4 (July–August 1994): 23–31.

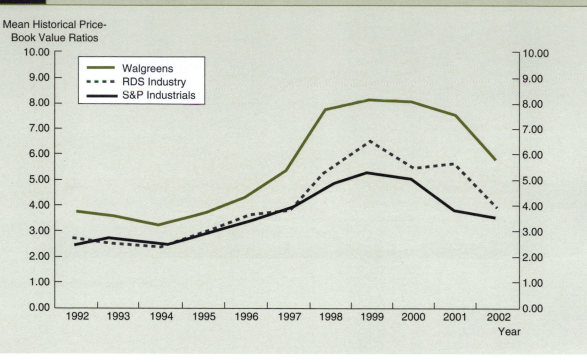

EXHIBIT 15.9 Time-Series Plot of Mean Historical Price–Book Value Ratios: Walgreens, RDS Industry, and S&P Industrials, 1992–2002

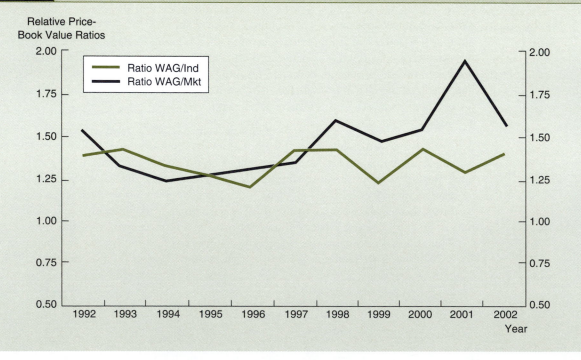

EXHIBIT 15.10 Time-Series Plot of Relative Price–Book Value Ratios: Walgreens/Industry and Walgreens/Market, 1992–2002

and the market. The major variable that should cause a difference in the P/BV ratio is the firm's ROA relative to its cost of capital (its WACC). Assuming that most firms in an industry have comparable WACCs, the major differential should be the firm's ROA because the larger the ROA–WACC difference, the greater the justified P/BV ratio. (This indicates that a firm is earning more on all its assets than is required in terms of its WACC.)

As shown in Exhibit 15.9, the P/BV ratios for the three components have increased from about 2.5–3.50 to about 4.0–6.0 (down from a peak in 1999). As shown in Exhibit 15.10, Walgreens has experienced a similar increase in its P/BV ratio to that of its industry— its Co/Ind ratio has gone from 1.41 to 1.45. The Co/Mkt ratio for Walgreens experienced a similar small increase from 1.54 to 1.62. These small increases in the relative ratios are justified by the larger ROAs for Walgreens compared to both its industry and the market.

Price–Sales Ratio The price–sales (P/S) ratio has had a long but generally neglected existence followed by a recent reawakening. In the late 1950s, Phillip Fisher in his classic book suggested this ratio as a valuable tool when considering investments, including growth stocks.[13] Subsequently, his son, Kenneth Fisher, used the ratio as a major stock selection variable in his widely read book.[14] Recently, P/S has been suggested as a valuable tool in a monograph by award-winning author Martin Leibowitz, and the ratio was espoused by O'Shaughnessy in his book that compared several stock selection techniques.[15] Leibowitz makes the point that sales growth drives all subsequent earnings and cash flow. Additionally, those who are concerned with accounting manipulation point out that sales is one of the purest numbers available. This ratio is equal to the P/E ratio times the net profit margin (Earnings/Sales), which implies that it is heavily influenced by the profit margin of the entity being analyzed. Its makeup also means that it is best used for comparing companies in the same industry. Put another way, it should definitely *not* be used to compare firms in very different industries such as heavy industrial versus service firms.

As shown in Exhibit 15.4 and Exhibit 15.11, the P/S ratio for Walgreens has experienced an increase from 0.62 to 1.28 compared to a moderate increase by its industry from 0.55 to 0.87, and an increase by the market from 0.79 to 1.44. This relative performance by Walgreens is reflected in Exhibit 15.12, which shows the plot of relative ratios wherein the Co/Ind ratio increased from 1.13 to 1.47, while the Co/Mkt ratio experienced a small increase from 0.78 to 0.89. Similar to prior comparisons, the relevant question the analyst must ask is whether the growth rate of sales, the risk related to the sales growth, and the profit margin of Walgreens can justify a much higher P/S ratio than its industry.

Summary of Relative Valuation Ratios Notably, all four relative valuation ratios increased during the eleven-year period for Walgreens, its industry, and the aggregate stock market. The widespread increases suggest that the changes are caused by changes in some aggregate economic variables such as economic growth and economic risk factors. Interestingly, Dudley and McKelvey from Goldman Sachs & Co. argued in 1997 that the U.S. economy had experienced several significant changes during the past two decades that have caused an important change in the nature and length of our economic expansions and contractions.[16]

---

[13] Phillip A. Fisher, *Common Stocks and Uncommon Profits,* Woodside, CA: PSR Publications, 1958, 1960 rev. ed., 1984.

[14] Kenneth L. Fisher, *Super Stocks,* Woodside, CA: Business Classics, 1984.

[15] Martin L. Leibowitz, *Sales-Driven Franchise Value,* Charlottesville, VA: The Research Foundation of the Institute of Chartered Financial Analysis, 1997; and James P. O'Shaughnessy, *What Works on Wall Street,* New York: McGraw-Hill, 1997.

[16] William C. Dudley and Edward F. McKelvey, *The Brave New Business Cycle,* New York: Goldman Sachs & Co., October 1997.

EXHIBIT 15.11 Time-Series Plot of Mean Historical Price–Sales Ratios: Walgreens, RDS Industry, and S&P Industrials, 1992–2002

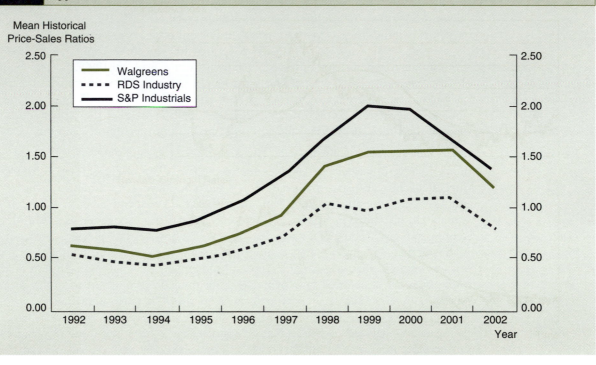

EXHIBIT 15.12 Time-Series Plot of Relative Price–Sales Ratios: Walgreens/Industry and Walgreens/Market, 1992–2002

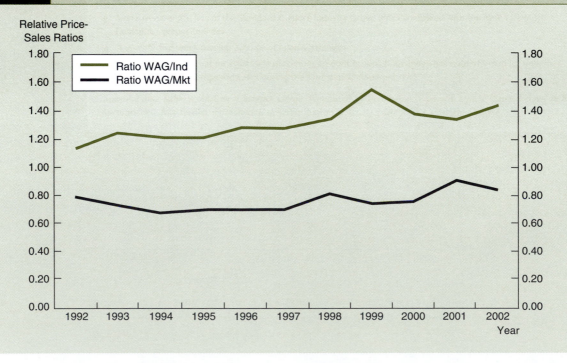

In addition to these overall increases for all three segments (firm, industry, and market), Walgreens has experienced a larger increase than its industry in terms of all of its ratios. Compared to the market, the firm's P/CF, P/BV, and P/S ratios increased by more than the market, while it lagged the market in terms of the P/E ratio because the market P/E ratio exploded in 2001 and 2002. Assuming that we want to use these ratios to determine relative value or to make an investment decision, we must examine the basic valuation factors to explain the differentials.

Specific Valuation with the P/E Ratio

In addition to judging the relative valuation for a firm by comparing several ratios, analysts also use the P/E ratio to determine a specific value for a firm. Such a valuation is relatively common and requires the analyst to estimate next year's earnings per share (EPS) and the firm's expected earnings multiplier (P/E ratio). Because we have already discussed P/E ratio analysis, we consider several methods for estimating EPS in this section.

EARNINGS PER SHARE ESTIMATES

Earnings estimates can be derived using statistical or judgmental analyses. Studies have found that earnings usually have time-series properties, meaning that future earnings levels have a statistical relationship with prior earnings.

Using *statistical analysis* to estimate earnings is as much an art as a science. The analyst must determine the independent variables that appear in the model, the estimation technique to use, and the historical time period over which the relationship is to be estimated.

Judgmental forecasts depend on subjective evaluation of many factors rather than a mathematical formula. Most analysts' forecasts are judgmental in nature, although many are the result of both statistical and judgmental analysis. A statistical relationship may give the analyst a base estimate, which is then adjusted up or down based on knowledge of quantitative and qualitative influences affecting the firm. Use of the judgmental approach has an advantage over the statistical method because the human mind can implicitly consider the data developed from the economy–industry–firm analysis and adjust the estimate accordingly. It is almost impossible to develop statistical models that include the effects of industry life-cycle changes, competitive forces, and alternative strategies. A judgmental model requires the analyst to be knowledgeable about key assumptions and the significant variables driving the estimate.

Earnings estimates can have a top-down orientation, a bottom-up orientation, or a mixture of both. A top-down forecast relates (statistically or judgmentally) the sensitivity of company earnings to macroeconomic and industry variables. By forecasting these economic and industry variables and knowing the sensitivity of company earnings to them, the analyst can forecast an earnings estimate.

A bottom-up forecast focuses on earnings' sensitivity to firm-specific variables, such as sales growth and changes in the operating profit margin or tax rate. Estimates of future values for these firm variables, coupled with knowledge of profits' sensitivity to them, result in an earnings forecast. Should firm sales be related to economic and industry events, it is easy to combine the top-down and bottom-up approaches to arrive at an estimate of earnings.

TIME SERIES APPROACH

Typically, the time-series approach relates earnings per share in time period t to earnings in earlier time periods. The model states that current earnings are statistically related to prior period's earnings. Once this time-series model is estimated, earnings for time period $t + 1$

are forecast by inserting the current and prior period's earnings. The analyst will typically adjust the resulting estimate to reflect the forecast of economic, industry, and firm-specific factors.

SALES–PROFIT MARGIN APPROACH

This method is a direct approach to estimating net income and EPS. Under this technique, a sales forecast is multiplied by a net profit margin (NI/Sales) estimate, resulting in a net income forecast. Thus, earnings per share is equal to:

15.12

$$\text{EPS} = \frac{\text{Sales Forecast} \times \text{Net Profit Margin}}{\text{Estimated Number of Shares Outstanding}}$$

$$= \frac{\text{Net Income}}{\text{Estimated Number of Shares Outstanding}}$$

The sales forecast can be developed using a number of statistical and judgmental tools. Past sales trends or growth rates can be extrapolated into the future; sales can be estimated from a regression relationship relating firm sales to industry or economic variables; market share forecasts can be combined with industry sales forecasts to develop the firm's sales forecast. If the firm is in the retail industry, sales can be estimated by multiplying the forecasted number of stores next year by the expected average sales volume per store. The analyst can use insights from the economic–industry–firm analysis to judgmentally adjust these estimates.

Net profit margins can be affected by various factors. The firm's internal performance should be reviewed, including general company trends and consideration of any problems that might affect future performance. The firm's operating and financial leverage should be estimated to show the relationship between sales changes and profit variability. The firm's profit margins should be reviewed historically against the industry's margins to determine if past firm performance is attributable to its industry or is unique to the firm. As always, this history-oriented analysis must be supplemented with the analyst's forecasts of future economic, industry, and firm developments.

PURELY JUDGMENTAL APPROACHES TO ESTIMATING EARNINGS

The above methods could use statistical, judgmental, or both methods to estimate earnings. Here we present two purely judgmental analyses of earnings estimation.

Last Year's Income Statement Plus Judgmental Evaluations Starting with last year's income statement and a brief review of historical changes and expected future developments leads to an earnings forecast. As always, analysts need to identify and monitor the key assumptions and variables that are driving expected firm sales and profitability.

For example, the analyst may start with the sales revenue of the most recent year. A historical review will inform the analyst of the average sales growth rate during some recent period—say, the past ten years. He can then determine the maximum and minimum sales growth rates along with a review of economic, industry, and firm factors that explain the reason for good and poor sales growth rates. Reasons may include economic expansion or recession or new product introductions by the firm or its competitors. Based on these bounds of sales growth, the analyst would evaluate favorable and unfavorable influences expected to affect the firm, its industry, and the economy in the coming year to produce a sales growth forecast.

The operating profit margin can likewise be evaluated beginning with the historical average and its upper and lower range. The analyst would subjectively evaluate alternative pricing strategies that may affect the operating profit margin. The operating profit margin times the sales forecast generates an estimate of the firm's operating income.

The difference between the firm's operating income and net income is affected by the firm's other income, its interest expense, and taxes. Based on reading the footnotes and talking with management, the analyst can estimate changes in other income sources (such as income from subsidiaries or marketable securities). Interest expense will be affected by the firm's debt outstanding and expected interest rates. Expectations about future firm financing can be estimated by forecasting the firm's free cash flow in the coming year; negative cash flow means the firm may have to raise capital, depending on the firm's capital spending plans. The firm's tax obligation can be estimated by analyzing the firm's past tax rates along with any expected changes in tax rates. Operating income, plus other income, less interest expense and taxes equals the analyst's estimate of net income.

An estimate of the number of shares outstanding over the coming year is based on the firm's plans to issue equity, to force conversion of convertible bonds or preferred stock, or to repurchase stock. The earnings per share estimate will equal the analyst's judgmental estimate of net income divided by the estimate of shares outstanding.

The analyst may also want to use a scenario analysis to estimate expected earnings per share. Various sales growth rates can be combined with a range of operating profit margins in pessimistic, neutral, and optimistic scenarios. By assigning probabilities to each scenario, the analyst can calculate an expected earnings per share estimate.

Using the Consensus of Analysts' Earnings Estimates   Zacks and IBES are two Wall Street research firms that systematically collect analysts' earnings estimates. Although specific analysts are not identified, Zacks and IBES report the average of the earnings per share estimates from analysts that cover the firm as well as the variance of the estimates from the consensus. Because these earnings estimates are widely distributed and followed by investors, we would expect them to be reflected in the stock's current price.

Some analysts use the consensus estimate and work their way up a firm's income statement to check its reasonableness. If they believe the consensus estimate reflects overly optimistic (or pessimistic) expectations, they will flag the stock for further analysis.

For example, multiplying a firm's IBES consensus earnings estimate by the number of shares outstanding indicates a net income forecast.[17] Combining this with an estimate of the firm's average tax rate allows the analyst to forecast the firm's earnings before tax. Interest expense can be approximated using the prior year's numbers and expected financing changes based on news releases by the firm or the previous year's free cash flow analysis. Adding interest expense to pre-tax earnings gives the IBES consensus estimate of operating income.

This is compared to the previous year's actual operating income. If the percentage difference cannot be explained by reasonable sales growth or operating profit margin changes, the IBES earnings consensus may be in error, reflecting extreme optimism or pessimism by analysts. The analyst may then decide the firm is a candidate for sale (if the IBES consensus is too optimistic) or for purchase (if the IBES consensus is too pessimistic). The reason is, if the IBES consensus is incorrect, the resulting positive or negative earnings surprise will lead to a large change in the stock's price, as discussed in Chapter 10.

IMPORTANCE OF QUARTERLY ESTIMATES

Once the analyst has derived an estimate of next year's sales and net earnings, it is essential to also derive an estimate of each of the quarterly results for two important reasons. First,

---

[17]A discussion of this method is found in Lawrence J. Haverty Jr., "Interpreting the Retail Numbers," in *The Retail Industry: General Merchandisers and Discounters, Specialty Merchandisers, Apparel Specialty, and Food/Drug Retailers,* edited by Charles A. Ingene (Charlottesville, VA: AIMR, 1993), 75–80.

this is a way to confirm the annual estimate—that is, do the quarterly estimates required to arrive at the annual estimate seem reasonable? If not, the analyst needs to reevaluate the annual forecast. Second, unless quarterly forecasts confirm the annual forecast, the analyst will not be in a position to determine whether the subsequent *actual* results are a positive surprise, negative surprise, or no surprise. Further, if the actual results are a surprise relative to her estimate, the analyst will want to understand the reason for the surprise—for example did she under- or overestimate sales growth and/or was it due to differences in the profit margin from her estimates? This understanding is needed for an estimated *earnings revision* that reflects the new information from the company. With this new information, the analyst would probably revise each of our future quarterly estimates to arrive at a new annual estimate.

SITE VISITS, CORPORATE INTERVIEWS, AND FAIR DISCLOSURE REQUIREMENTS

Historically, brokerage house analysts and portfolio managers have had access to persons that were not available to the typical small investor. In addition, analysts would frequently contact corporate personnel by telephone, at formal presentations, or during plant site visits. Although insider trading laws restricted the analyst's ability to obtain material nonpublic information, these visits facilitated dialog between the corporation and the investor community. The function of the analyst was to gather information about the firm's plans and strategies to create a mosaic that would help the analyst understand the firm's prospects as an investment—that is, to estimate the firm's intrinsic value.

The idea was always that analysts were able to create this mosaic from numerous sources (including the company, its customers, its suppliers, and its competitors) and transmit this information to the market by sending research reports to brokerage clients and portfolio managers of pensions and mutual funds. This traditional way of doing research was changed by the SEC in 2000 when they issued the Fair Disclosure (FD) guidelines that required all disclosure of "material information" to be made public to all interested parties at the same time. The intent was to level the playing field by ensuring that professional analysts did not have a competitive advantage over nonprofessional investors. The result of this law is that many firms will not agree to interviews with analysts and will only provide information during large public presentations over the Internet.

The long-run impact of this FD requirement is not clear in terms of how firms will relate to the professional analyst community. One benefit is that analysts will spend even more time with information sources beyond the firm such as trade shows, customers, suppliers, and competitors to build the mosaic.

Now the analyst must talk to people other than top managers. Visiting stores and talking with customers provides insights beyond those of management. The firm's major customers can provide information regarding product quality and customer satisfaction. The firm's suppliers can furnish information about rising or falling supply orders and the timeliness of payments.

Making the Investment Decision

Once again, the investment decision rule (noted in Chapter 11 and earlier in this chapter) is

If Estimated Intrinsic Value > Market Price → Buy

If Estimated Intrinsic Value < Market Price → Do Not Buy or Sell
If You Own It

Let's look at the rationale for this decision rule. First, if the estimated intrinsic value *equals* the market price and you buy the stock at this price and hold it over time, *you will receive your required rate of return k.* That was your discount rate, so the value of the stock should increase at this rate over time. In turn, if the estimated intrinsic value is *above* the market price and you buy the stock at this price, you will receive a rate of return *that exceeds your required rate of return.* That is, during the future period you will not only receive the normal required return implied by the discount rate but also an additional capital gain. The above-market intrinsic value means that you expect the stock to be repriced to correct for the fact that it is underpriced. Finally if the estimated intrinsic value is *less* than the market price and you buy the stock at this price above its intrinsic value, you will receive a rate of return *that is less than your required rate of return.* In this case, the market will eventually reprice the stock to reflect that it is overpriced. The investment decision rule specifies you should not buy such a stock and if you own it, you should sell it and reinvest the proceeds into an underpriced stock.

Although we can determine the intrinsic value using any of the valuation models we have discussed, the objective is always the same: Derive an estimate that reflects the intrinsic value of the stock. The approaches are different and we suggest that you consider several of them, but the results should generally agree. Substantially different intrinsic values from different valuation models should be rare, assuming that our risk and growth inputs to the models are similar. That is why we emphasize the two critical value estimates (risk and growth)—they are the factors that drive intrinsic value irrespective of the models.

RANKING UNDERVALUED STOCKS

Suppose we identify several enticing undervalued stocks using the basic decision rule. The question now becomes, how do we rank our set of stocks if we have a budget constraint and can't buy all the stocks we want? The process is fairly straightforward: We rank on the basis of the excess return ratio, intrinsic value–market price. The larger this ratio, the larger the percent underpricing and, therefore, the larger the excess return potential. For example, if a stock has a market price of $40 and an estimated intrinsic value of $50, it has an excess return ratio of 50/40 = 1.25 and should experience an excess return of 25 percent during the future period when the price is adjusted to its intrinsic value. Also, this ratio determines the "margin of safety" employed by some analysts, that is, the difference they want between their estimated intrinsic value and the market price. For example, a 20 percent margin of safety means the analyst wants the intrinsic value to be at least 20 percent above the market price (in our example, they would want an intrinsic value of at least $48) before buying the stock with a market value of $40.

WHEN TO SELL

Our analysis has focused on determining if a stock should be purchased. In fact, when we make a purchase, a subsequent question gains prominence: When should the stock be sold? Many times holding onto a stock too long leads to a return below expectations or less than what was available earlier. Alternatively, when stocks decline in value immediately following a purchase, is this a further buying opportunity, or does the decline indicate that the stock analysis was incorrect?

The answer to when to sell a stock is contained in the research that convinced the analyst to initially purchase the stock. The analyst should have identified the key assumptions and variables driving the expectations for the stock. Analysis of the stock does not end when the intrinsic value is computed and the research report is written. Once the key value drivers are identified, the analyst must continually monitor and update his or her knowledge base about the firm. If and when the key assumptions and variables change (i.e., weaken), it is necessary to re-estimate the firm's intrinsic value and possibly sell the stock holding.

The stock should also be closely evaluated when the market price approaches the intrinsic value estimate. When the stock becomes fairly priced, it may be time to sell it and reinvest the funds in other underpriced stocks. In short, if the "story" for buying the stock still appears to be true such that its intrinsic value exceeds its market price, continue to hold it. If the "story" changes, it may be time to sell the stock.

In short, if you know why you bought the stock, you will be able to recognize when to sell it. The key to success is to maintain your discipline and be willing to sell a stock that has become fully priced even though the company is still doing well. It still may be a growth company, but it is not a growth stock because its future rates of return (based on the current price) will not exceed its required rate of return.

Influences on Analysts

Stock analysts and portfolio managers are, for the most part, highly trained individuals who possess expertise in financial analysis and background in their industry. A computer hardware analyst knows as much about industry trends and new product offerings as any industry insider. A pharmaceutical analyst is able to independently determine the market potential of drugs undergoing testing and the FDA approval process. So, in theory, all brokerage house customers and portfolio managers who receive the analysts' expert advice should achieve investment success. In reality, however, there are several factors that make it difficult to consistently outperform the aggregate market.

EFFICIENT MARKETS

As noted in Chapter 10, an efficient market is difficult to outsmart, especially for actively traded and frequently analyzed companies. Information about the economy, a firm's industry, and the firm itself are reviewed by numerous bright analysts, investors, and portfolio managers. Because of the market's ability to review and absorb information, stock prices generally approximate fair market value. Investors look for situations where stocks may not be fairly valued. However, with many market players, it is difficult to successfully, frequently, and consistently find undervalued shares. The analyst's best place to seek attractive stocks is not among well-known companies and actively traded stocks that are analyzed by dozens of Wall Street researchers. Stocks with smaller market capitalizations, those not covered by many analysts, or those whose shares are mainly held by individual investors may be the best places to search for inefficiencies. Smaller capitalization stocks sometimes are too small for time-constrained analysts or too small for purchase by institutional investors.[18] The price of stocks not researched by many analysts ("neglected stocks") may not reflect all relevant information.[19]

PARALYSIS OF ANALYSIS

Most analysts spend most of their time in a relentless search for one more contact or one more piece of information. This preoccupation with more information can keep the ana-

---

[18]According to SEC regulations, mutual funds cannot own more than 10 percent of a firm's shares. For some large funds, this constraint will make the resulting investment too small to have any significant impact on fund returns, so they do not bother to consider such stocks for purchase.

[19]Information on the number of analysts covering a stock is available from research firms such as IBES and Zacks.

lyst's mind off the final output—that is, their stock recommendation. Analysts need to develop a systematic approach for gathering, monitoring, and reviewing relevant information about economic trends, industry competitive forces, and company strategy. Otherwise they become too busy collecting data, searching for *all* the answers. The analyst must evaluate the information as a whole to discern patterns that indicate the intrinsic value of the stock rather than searching for that one more piece of information.

Because markets are generally efficient, the consensus view about the firm is typically reflected in its stock price. As we have said before, to earn above-average returns the analyst must have expectations that differ from the consensus *and* the analyst must be correct. Thus, analysts need to concentrate on identifying what is wrong with the market consensus, or what events or factors would contribute to changes in the market consensus—that is, they should attempt to *estimate earnings surprises.*

FORCES PULLING ON THE SELL-SIDE ANALYST

Although such linkages should not exist, at times communication occurs between a firm's investment banking and stock analysis division. If the investment bankers are assisting a firm in a stock or bond offering, it will be difficult for an analyst at the investment banking firm to issue a negative evaluation of the company. Advisory fees have been lost because of a negative stock recommendation. Despite attempts to ensure the independence of stock analysts, at times firm politics get in the way.

The analyst is in frequent contact with the top officers of the company he or she analyzes. Although there are guidelines about receiving gifts and favors, it is sometimes difficult to separate personal friendship and impersonal corporate relationships. Corporate officials

Investments Online

Many helpful sites have been reviewed in prior chapters, for example, individual firm sites and the SEC's EDGAR database for firm-specific information. Investment bank and brokerage house sites may also prove valuable, though they may expect payment for access to their published research on different firms. Still, many sites allow users to examine free information and investing tips.

http://www.better-investing.com The home page for the National Association of Investment Clubs offers company information and investing ideas in addition to resources for those interested in setting up their own investment club.

http://www.fool.com This is the home page for the Motley Fool; despite its name, it is a well-known and popular site for investors. It is chock-full of data, articles, educational resources, news, and investing ideas.

http://www.cfonews.com Corporate Financials Online provides links to news about selected publicly traded firms.

http://www.zacks.com At the Web site for Zacks Investment Research, when the user types in a ticker symbol, Zacks provides links to a company profile, financials, analysts' current stock ratings, consensus earnings estimates, and the number of analysts recommending strong buy, moderate buy, hold, moderate sell, and strong sell. Links allow the user to order brokerage reports. The site provides aggregate earnings growth estimates for the S&P 500, the market, and various economic sectors.

http://moneycentral.msn.com/investor/home.asp This site offers stock screens, price charts, and links to earnings estimates and analyst reports.

http://www.nyssa.org The home page of the New York Society of Security Analysts includes many financial Web links and sources of market and company information.

may try to convince the analyst that a pessimistic report is in error or does not fully consider some recent positive developments. To mitigate these problems, an analyst should call the company's investor relations department immediately *after* changing a recommendation to explain the new perspective. In short, the analyst needs to maintain *independence* and have confidence in his or her analysis.

Summary

- The fundamental analysis process involves analyzing a company and deciding whether or not to buy its stock. This requires a separate analysis of a company and its stock. A wonderful firm can have an overpriced stock, or a mediocre firm can have an underpriced stock.

- The valuation theory applies to a range of investments, as discussed in detail in Chapter 11. Although analysts may use several different valuation models, the investment decision rule is always the same: if the estimated intrinsic value of the investment is greater than the market price, buy the investment; if the estimated intrinsic value of an investment is less than the market price, do not buy it or sell it if you own it.

- Company analysis logically follows from our earlier research on economic, structural, and industry influences. In this analysis, it is important to determine what competitive strategy—low-cost leadership or differentiation—the firm has adopted in response to different competitive pressures in its industry. Also important is SWOT analysis, which helps an analyst assess a firm's internal strengths and weaknesses and its external opportunities and threats. In addition, a careful review of the firm's financial statements gives insight into the firm's future potential. Interviews of top and middle managers, suppliers, and customers can also provide valuable information.

- There are two major approaches—present value of cash flow and relative valuation ratios—for estimating a stock's intrinsic value. Several techniques are available for these approaches. We reviewed and demonstrated how to estimate the major inputs to these techniques and evaluated the results as applied to Walgreens.

- After the analyses are completed, the investment decision process is the same as noted above irrespective of the approach used to estimate the stock's intrinsic value. Then, after a buy decision, the analyst must still continually monitor assumptions and variables used—the firm's "story" may change and the stock may need to be sold.

- Analysts have a difficult job because of several factors. The efficient market makes it difficult to find truly underpriced securities due to the efforts of numerous bright, hardworking analysts. In addition, the quantity of information available for an analyst to review can be overwhelming. Finally, there are inherent conflicts of interest for analysts from investment banking firms.

QUESTIONS

1. Define a growth company and a speculative stock.
2. Give an example of a growth company and discuss why you identify it as such.
3. Give an example of a cyclical stock and discuss why you have designated it as such. Is it issued by a cyclical company?
4. A biotechnology firm is growing at a compound rate of more than 21 percent a year. (Its ROE is over 30 percent, and it retains about 70 percent of its earnings.) The stock of this company is priced at about 65 times next year's earnings. Discuss whether you consider this a growth company and a growth stock.
5. Select a company and, based on reading its annual report and other public information, discuss its competitive strategy (low-cost producer or differentiation). Is the firm successful in implementing this strategy?
6. Discuss a company known to be a low-cost producer in its industry and consider what makes it possible for the firm to be a cost leader. Do the same for a firm known for differentiation.
7. You are told that a growth company has a P/E ratio of 12 times and a growth rate of 15 percent compared to the aggregate market, which has a growth rate of 8 percent and a P/E ratio of 15 times. What does this comparison imply regarding the growth company? What else do you need to know to properly compare the growth company to the aggregate market?
8. Select a company and discuss the economic and structural influences that are affecting it.
9. Choose a firm and discuss its strengths and opportunities. How might the firm best address its weaknesses and threats?
10. How might an analyst determine the value for a firm that pays no dividends and is expected to operate at a loss next year?
11. How can an investor determine when it might be time to sell an investment?
12. Is being an accurate estimator of earnings a guarantee for success in stock investing? Why or why not?

PROBLEMS

1. The Lauren Kilt Company has been experiencing a growth rate of almost 14 percent a year in its free cash flow to equity (FCFE), which as of the end of 2006 is $150 million. The management projects (and you agree) that the firm should experience the following annual growth rates going forward:

2007–2010	12 percent
2011–2012	10 percent
2013–2014	8 percent
2015 forward	6 percent

   The Lauren Kilt Company has 50 million shares outstanding and its stock has a Beta of 0.80. The current 10-year Treasury note has a yield of 5.00 percent, and the consensus is that the equity risk premium (ERP) for the market is 4 percent.

   Using a multi-stage cash flow valuation model, determine the intrinsic value of Lauren's stock and compare its value to the current per share market price of $25.00. Would you buy the stock?

2. Compute the value of Lauren Kilt if all the assumptions from Problem 1 were the same except the company stock Beta was equal to 1.20. Would you buy the stock?

3. Compute the value of Lauren Kilt with all the assumptions from Problem 1 except that the estimated growth rates are as follows:

2007–2010	10 percent
2011–2012	8 percent
2013 forward	6 percent

   Would you buy the stock?

4. To confirm your valuation of Lauren Kilt, you decide to value the stock using the firm's operating free cash flow (equal to $200 million in 2006) that is expected to grow at the same rate as specified in Problem 1 for FCFE.

   To compute the firm's WACC, you will use the same Beta (0.80) and market expectations. In addition, you estimate a cost of debt for the firm of 7 percent, an equity-debt mix (using market values) of 75 percent equity, 25 percent debt ($1 billion) and a tax rate of 35 percent.

   Using a multi-stage cash flow valuation model, determine an intrinsic value for Lauren's stock. Would you buy the stock at $25 per share?

5. Compute the value of Lauren Kilt with all the assumptions in Problem 4 except that the Beta is 1.10, the firm's cost of debt is 8 percent, and the growth rates are

2007–2012	10 percent
2013–forward	6 percent

   Would you buy the stock?

WEB EXERCISES

1. Go to a Web site in the "Investments Online" box (or one of your own choosing) that offers "best" or "top" stock picks. Select any five such stocks. Into which of Lynch's six categories does each of the firms fall? What reasons are given in the Web site for their appearance on such a list? Do you agree or disagree with their "story"? Why?

2. Select two companies in the same industry that pay dividends. Using Web resources, find and report the following information: recent price history; current dividend; analyst report and outlook; earnings estimate; earnings growth rate; price forecast. Using this data, what prices do you estimate for each of the firms using the constant dividend growth model? How does your calculation differ from the price estimates offered on the Web? What growth and discount rate assumptions are needed so the price forecast from the dividend discount model agrees with those on the Web? How reasonable is the price forecast from the Web source?

3. Using an Internet search function, try to find earnings or price forecast models. Download and experiment with any that are available in spreadsheet form. For earnings and price forecast models that are proprietary, that is, for sale, what information does the Web site provide about how the model estimates stock prices or earnings?

SPREADSHEET EXERCISES

1. In this chapter we develop a number of models for estimating a stock's intrinsic value. Develop a spreadsheet and the inputs to it so that price estimates can be computed using the different techniques.
2. Develop a spreadsheet for the two-stage growth model. What inputs do you need? Construct it so it will develop price estimates assuming one, two, . . . , ten years of above-normal growth. Using the following information, show how the price estimate changes as the assumptions vary:

Current dividend: $2.00
Supernormal growth rate: 18%
Duration of supernormal growth: 5 years
Normal growth rate: 5%
Discount rate: 12%

REFERENCES

Billingsley, Randall, ed. *Corporate Financial Decision Making and Equity Analysis.* Proceedings of a seminar by the Association of Investment Management and Research. Charlottesville, VA: AIMR, 1995.

Copeland, T. E., Tim Koller, and Jack Murrin. *Valuation: Measuring and Managing the Value of Companies,* 3rd ed. New York: John Wiley & Sons, 2000.

Damodaran, Aswath. *Damodaran on Valuation.* New York: John Wiley & Sons, 1994.

Farrell, James L. "The Dividend Discount Model: A Primer." *Financial Analysts Journal* 41, no. 6 (November–December 1985).

Fogler, H. Russell, ed. *Developments in Quantitative Investment Models.* Proceedings of a seminar by the Association of Investment Management and Research. Charlottesville, VA: AIMR, 2001.

Jost, Kathryn. *Equity Valuation in a Global Context.* Proceedings of a seminar by the Association of Investment Management and Research. Charlottesville, VA: AIMR, 2003.

Palepu, Krishna, Paul Healy, and Victor Bernard. *Business Analysis and Valuation,* 3rd ed. Mason, OH: South-Western, 2004.

Sharpe, William, and Katrina Sherrerd, eds. *Quantifying the Market Risk Premium Phenomenon for Investment Decision Making.* Proceedings of a seminar by the Association of Investment Management and Research. Charlottesville, VA: AIMR, 1990.

Sherrerd, Katrina, ed. *Equity Research and Valuation Techniques.* Proceedings of a conference by the Association of Investment Management and Research, Charlottesville, VA: AIMR, 2002.

Squires, Jan, ed. *Equity Research and Valuation Techniques.* Proceedings of a seminar by the Association of Investment Management and Research. Charlottesville, VA: AIMR, 1998.

Squires, Jan R., ed. *Practical Issues in Equity Analysis.* Proceedings of seminars by the Association of Investment Management and Research. Charlottesville, VA: AIMR, 2000.

Sullivan, Rodney N., ed. *Equity Analysis Issues, Lessons, and Techniques.* Proceedings of a seminar by the Association of Investment Management and Research. Charlottesville, VA: AIMR, 2003.

THOMSON ONE
Business School Edition

1. Identify two firms in an industry, one of which seems to follow a "cost leadership" strategy and one of which tries to be a "differentiator." How do their common-size financial statements differ? Examine their trends in ROE using DuPont analysis. Comment on the differences and/or similarities you find.
2. Update the analysis of Walgreens in this chapter by computing the following:
   a. average compound dividend growth rate from 1983 until the most recent year
   b. sustainable growth rate
   c. expected return, based on Thomson One: Business School Edition's beta estimate and estimates you obtain of the current risk-free rate and market risk premium
   d. present value of dividends, using the growth assumptions in the chapter.
3. Estimate Walgreens' free cash flow to equity and its operating free cash flow for the most recent year.
4. Using peer analysis, compare Walgreens' relative valuation ratios with those of its peers (click on the "peers" tab, then click on "overviews" and "valuation comparison").

GLOSSARY

Cyclical company A firm whose earnings rise and fall with general economic activity.

Defensive company Firms whose future earnings are likely to withstand an economic downturn.

Defensive competitive strategy A competitive strategy in which the firm positions itself so its capabilities provide the best means to deflect the effect of industry competitive forces.

Growth company A company that consistently has the opportunities and ability to invest in projects that provide rates of return that exceed the firm's cost of capital. Because of these investment opportunities, it retains a high proportion of earnings, and its earnings grow faster than those of average firms.

Growth stock A stock with an intrinsic value greater than its market price, which implies that it should generate a higher rate of return than other stocks with similar risk characteristics; an *undervalued* stock.

Non-growth stock A stock with an intrinsic value less than its market price, which implies that it should generate a lower rate of return than other stocks with similar risk characteristics; an *overvalued* stock.

Offensive competitive strategy A competitive strategy in which the firm uses its strengths to affect the competitive forces in the industry.

Present value of cash flow (PVCF) models Valuation models used to determine intrinsic value by discounting alternative cash flows at the firm's cost of equity or weighted-average cost of capital (WACC). Cash flows used are either free cash flow to equity (FCFE) or free cash flow to the firm (FCFF).

Speculative company A firm with a great degree of business or financial risk, or both.

SWOT analysis An examination of a firm's internal strengths and weaknesses and its external opportunities and threats.

Information Sources for Company Analysis

Extensive material is available on individual firms' stocks and bonds. Sources of these publications include individual companies; commercial publishing firms, which produce a vast array of material; reports provided by investment firms; and several investment magazines that discuss the overall financial markets and provide opinions on individual companies and their stocks or bonds. We will discuss each of these sources and specific publications. Keep in mind that many of the sources described in the economy and industry analysis chapters also include discussions of individual stocks or bonds.

Company-Generated Information

An obvious source of information about a company is the company itself. Indeed, some small firms may have no other source of information because trading activity in their stock is insufficient to justify inclusion in publications of commercial services or brokerage firms.

ANNUAL REPORTS

Every firm with publicly traded stock must prepare and distribute to its stockholders an annual report of financial operations and current financial position. In addition to basic information, most reports discuss what happened during the year and outline future prospects. Most firms also publish quarterly financial reports that include brief income statements for the interim period and, sometimes, a balance sheet. These reports can be obtained directly from the company. To find an address for a company, you can consult Volume 1 of *Standard & Poor's Register of Corporations, Directors, and Executives,* which contains an alphabetical listing, by business name, of approximately 37,000 corporations.

SECURITY PROSPECTUS

When a firm wants to sell securities (bonds, preferred stock, or common stock) in the primary market to raise new capital, the Securities and Exchange Commission (SEC) requires that it file a registration statement describing the securities being offered. It must provide extensive financial information beyond what is required in an annual report as well as nonfinancial information on its operations and personnel. A condensed version of the registration statement, referred to as a *prospectus,* is published by the underwriting firm and contains most of the relevant information. Copies of a prospectus for a current offering can be obtained from the underwriter or from the company. Investment banking firms will often advertise offerings in publications such as *The Wall Street Journal, Barron's,* or *Financial Times.*

REQUIRED SEC REPORTS

In addition to registration statements, the SEC requires three *periodic* statements from publicly held firms. First, the 8-K form is filed each month, reporting any action that affects the debt, equity, amount of capital assets, voting rights, or other changes that might have a significant impact on the stock.

Second, the 9-K form is an unaudited report filed every six months that contains revenues, expenses, gross sales, and special items. It typically contains more extensive information than the quarterly statement.

Finally, the 10-K form is an annual version of the 9-K but is even more comprehensive. The SEC requires that firms indicate in their annual reports that a copy of their 10-K is available from the company upon request without charge.

Commercial Publications

Numerous advisory services supply information on the aggregate market and individual stocks. A partial list follows.

STANDARD & POOR'S PUBLICATIONS

Standard & Poor's Corporation Records is a set of seven volumes. The first six contain basic information on all types of corporations (industrial, financial) arranged alphabetically. The volumes are in binders and are updated throughout the year. The seventh volume is a daily news volume that contains recent data on all companies listed in all the volumes.

Standard & Poor's Stock Reports are comprehensive two-page reports on numerous companies with stocks listed on the NYSE, AMEX, and Nasdaq. They include the near-term sales and earnings outlook, recent developments, key income statement and balance sheet items, and a chart of stock price movements. They are in bound volumes by exchange and are revised every three to four months.

Standard & Poor's Stock Guide is a monthly publication that contains, in compact form, pertinent financial data on more than 5,000 common and preferred stocks. A separate section covers more than 400 mutual fund issues. For each stock, the guide contains information on price ranges (historical and recent), dividends, earnings, financial position, institutional holdings, and a ranking for earning and dividend stability. It is a useful quick reference for almost all actively traded stocks.

Standard & Poor's Bond Guide is a monthly publication that contains the most pertinent comparative financial and statistical information on a broad list of bonds including domestic and foreign bonds (about 3,900 issues), 200 foreign government bonds, and about 650 convertible bonds.

The Outlook is a weekly publication of Standard & Poor's Corporation that advises investors about the general market environment and specific groups of stocks or industries (for example, high-dividend stocks, stocks with low price–earnings ratios, high-yielding bonds, stocks likely to increase their dividends). Weekly stock index figures for eighty-eight industry groups and other market statistics are included.

Daily Stock Price Records is published quarterly by Standard & Poor's, with individual volumes for the NYSE, the AMEX, and Nasdaq. Each quarterly book is divided into two parts. Part 1, "Major Technical Indicators of the Stock Market," is devoted to market indicators widely followed as technical guides to the stock market and includes price indicator series, volume series, and data on odd lots and short sales. Part 2, "Daily and Weekly Stock Action," gives daily high, low, close, and volume information as well as monthly data on short interest for individual stocks, insider trading information, a 200-day moving average of prices, and a weekly relative strength series. The books for the NYSE and AMEX are available from 1962 on; the Nasdaq books begin in 1968.

MOODY'S PUBLICATIONS

Moody's Industrial Manual resembles the Standard & Poor's records service except it is organized by type of corporation (industrial, utility, and so on). The two-volume service is published once a year and covers industrial companies listed on the NYSE, the AMEX, and regional exchanges. One section concentrates on international industrial firms. Like all Moody's manuals, a news report volume covers events that occurred after publication of the basic manual.

Moody's OTC Industrial Manual is similar to the *Moody's Industrial Manual* of listed firms but is limited to stocks traded on Nasdaq.

Moody's has manuals for various industries as well. *Moody's Public Utility Manual* provides information on public utilities, including electric and gas, gas transmission, telephone, and water companies. *Moody's Transportation Manual* covers the transportation industry, including railroads, airlines, steamship companies, electric railway, bus and truck lines, oil pipe lines, bridge companies, and automobile and truck leasing companies. *Moody's Bank and Finance Manual* covers the field of financial services represented by banks, credit agencies of the U.S. government, all facets of the insurance industry, investment companies, real estate firms, real estate investment trusts, and miscellaneous financial enterprises.

Moody's Municipal and Government Manual contains data on the U.S. government, all the states, state agencies, more than 13,500 municipalities, and some excellent information on foreign governments and international organizations.

Moody's International Manual provides financial information on about 3,000 major foreign corporations.

VALUE LINE PUBLICATIONS

The *Value Line Investment Survey* is published in two parts. Volume I contains basic historic information on about 1,700 companies including a number of analytical measures of earnings stability, growth rates, a common-stock safety factor, and a timing factor rating. Various studies have examined the usefulness of the timing factor ratings for investment purposes. These studies were discussed in Chapter 10.

The *Investment Survey* also includes extensive two-year *projections* for the given firms and three-year *estimates* of performance. As an example, in 2006 it included an earnings projection for 2006, 2007, and 2008–2010. The second volume includes a weekly service that provides general investment advice and recommends individual stocks for purchase or sale.

The *Value Line Special Situations Service* is published twenty-four times a year. It serves the experienced investor who is willing to accept high risk in the hope of realizing exceptional capital gains. Each issue discusses past recommendations and presents eight to ten new stocks for consideration.

Brokerage Firm Reports

Many brokerage firms prepare reports on individual companies and their securities. Some of these reports contain only basic information, but others make specific recommendations.

Computerized Data Sources

In addition to the numerous published sources of data, some financial service firms have developed computerized data sources. Space limitations restrict the discussion to major sources.

Compustat is a computerized bank of financial data developed by Standard & Poor's and currently handled by a subsidiary, Investors Management Services. The *Compustat* tapes contain twenty years of data for approximately 2,400 listed industrial companies, 1,000 Nasdaq companies, 175 utilities, 120 banks, and 500 Canadian firms. Quarterly tapes contain twenty years of quarterly financial data for more than 2,000 industrial firms and twelve years of quarterly data for banks and utilities. The financial data on the annual tapes include almost every possible item from each firm's balance sheet and income statement as well as stock-market data (stock prices and trading volume).

Value Line Data Base contains historical annual and quarterly financial and market data for 1,600 industrial and finance companies beginning in 1954. It also provides quarterly data from 1963. In addition to historical data, it gives estimates of dividends and earnings for the coming year and the Value Line opinion regarding stock price stability and investment timing.

University of Chicago Stock Price Tapes is a set of monthly and daily stock price tapes developed by the Center for Research in Security Prices (CRSP) at the University of Chicago Graduate School of Business. The monthly tapes contain month-end prices from January 1926 to the present (updated annually) for every stock listed on the NYSE. Stock prices are adjusted for all stock splits, dividends, and any other capital changes. CRSP added monthly AMEX data beginning from July 1962 to the NYSE monthly file to create the current NYSE/AMEX monthly file with information on approximately 6,100 securities.

The daily stock price tape contains the daily high, low, close, and volume figures since July 1962 for every stock listed on the NYSE and AMEX (approximately 5,600 securities). In 1988 the CRSP developed its Nasdaq historical data file with daily price quotes, volume, and information about capitalization and distributions to shareholders for more than 9,600 common stocks traded on Nasdaq since December 14, 1972. These tapes are updated annually.

The Media General Data Bank, compiled by Media General Financial Services, Inc., includes current price and volume data plus major corporate financial data on 2,000 major companies. In addition, it contains ten years of daily price and volume information on more than 8,000 issues. Finally, it includes price and volume data on major market indexes.

ISL Daily Stock Price Tapes are prepared by Interactive Data Corporation. They contain the same information as the *Daily Stock Price Records,* published by Standard & Poor's.

Technical Analysis*

In this chapter we will answer the following questions:

How does technical analysis differ from fundamental analysis?

What are the underlying assumptions of technical analysis?

What major assumption causes a difference between technical analysis and the efficient market hypothesis?

What are the major advantages of technical analysis?

What are the major challenges to technical analysis?

What is the logic for the major contrary-opinion rules used by technicians?

What rules are used by technicians who want to "follow the smart money"?

What is the breadth of market measures, and what are they intended to indicate?

What are the three types of price movements postulated in the Dow Theory, and how are they used?

Why is trading volume important and how do technicians use it?

What are support and resistance levels and how are they used?

How do technicians use moving-average lines to detect changes in trends?

What is the rationale behind relative-strength line?

How are bar charts different from point-and-figure charts?

What are some uses of technical analysis in foreign security markets?

How is technical analysis used when analyzing bonds?

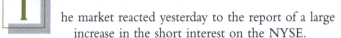

T he market reacted yesterday to the report of a large increase in the short interest on the NYSE.

Although the market declined today, it was not considered bearish because of the light volume.

The market declined today after three days of increases due to profit taking by investors.

These and similar statements appear daily in the financial news. All of them have as their rationale one of numerous technical trading rules. *Technical analysts,* or *technicians,* develop technical trading rules from observations of past price movements of the stock market and individual stocks. The philosophy behind technical analysis is in sharp contrast to the efficient market hypothesis that we studied, which contends that past performance has no influence on future performance or market values. It also differs from what we learned about fundamental analysis, which involves making investment decisions based on the examination of the economy, an industry, and company variables that lead to an estimate of intrinsic value for an investment, which is then compared to its prevailing market price. In contrast to the efficient market hypothesis or fundamental analysis, *technical analysis* involves the examination of past market data such as prices and the volume of trading, which leads to an estimate of future price trends and, therefore, an investment decision. Whereas fundamental analysts use economic data that are usually separate from the stock or bond market, the technical analyst uses data *from the market itself* because "the market is its own best predictor." Therefore, technical analysis is an alternative method of making the investment decision and answering the questions: What securities should an investor buy or sell? When should these investments be made?

---

*Richard T. McCabe, Chief Market Analyst at Merrill Lynch Capital Markets, provided helpful comments and material for this chapter.

Technical analysts see no need to study the multitude of economic, industry, and company variables to arrive at an estimate of future value because they believe that past price movements will signal future price movements. Technicians also believe that a change in the price trend may predict a forthcoming change in the fundamental variables such as earnings and risk before the change is perceived by most fundamental analysts. Are technicians correct? Many investors using these techniques claim to have experienced superior rates of return on many investments. In addition, many newsletter writers base their recommendations on technical analysis. Finally, even the major investment firms that employ many fundamental analysts also employ technical analysts to provide investment advice. Numerous investment professionals and individual investors believe in and use technical trading rules to make their investment decisions. Therefore, whether a fan of technical analysis or an advocate of the efficient market hypothesis, investors should still have an understanding of the basic philosophy and reasoning behind technical approaches. Thus, we begin this chapter with an examination of the basic philosophy underlying technical analysis. Subsequently, we consider the advantages and potential problems with the technical approach. Finally, we present alternative technical trading rules applicable to both the U.S. and foreign securities markets.

Underlying Assumptions of Technical Analysis

Technical analysts base trading decisions on examinations of prior price and volume data to determine past market trends from which they predict future behavior for the market as a whole and for individual securities. Several assumptions lead to this view of price movements. Certain aspects of these assumptions are controversial, leading fundamental analysts and advocates of efficient markets to question their validity. We have italicized those aspects in our list.

1. The market value of any good or service is determined solely by the interaction of supply and demand.
2. Supply and demand are governed by numerous rational and irrational factors. Included in these factors are those economic variables relied on by the fundamental analyst as well as opinions, moods, and guesses. The market weighs all these factors continually and automatically.
3. Disregarding minor fluctuations, *the prices for individual securities and the overall value of the market tend to move in trends, which persist for appreciable lengths of time.*
4. Prevailing trends change in reaction to shifts in supply and demand relationships. These shifts, no matter why they occur, *can be detected sooner or later in the action of the market itself.*[1]

The first two assumptions are almost universally accepted by technicians and nontechnicians alike. Almost anyone who has had a basic course in economics would agree that, at any point in time, the price of a security (or any good or service) is determined by the interaction of supply and demand. In addition, most observers would acknowledge that supply and demand are governed by many variables. The only difference in opinion might concern the influence of the irrational factors. Certainly, everyone would agree that the market continually weighs all these factors.

---

[1] These assumptions are summarized in Robert A. Levy, "Conceptual Foundations of Technical Analysis," *Financial Analysts Journal* 22, no. 4 (July–August 1966): 83.

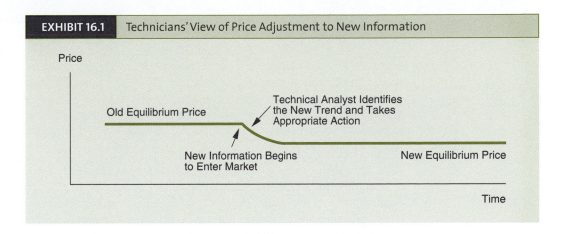

EXHIBIT 16.1 Technicians' View of Price Adjustment to New Information

In contrast, there is a difference of opinion regarding the assumption about the *speed of adjustment* of stock prices to changes in supply and demand. Technical analysts expect stock prices to move in trends that persist for long periods because they believe that new information does *not* come to the market at one point in time but rather enters the market *over a period of time.* This pattern of information access occurs because of different sources of information or because certain investors receive the information or perceive fundamental changes earlier than others. As various groups—ranging from insiders to well-informed professionals to the average investor—receive the information and buy or sell a security accordingly, its price moves gradually toward the new equilibrium. Therefore, technicians do not expect the price adjustment to be as abrupt as fundamental analysts and efficient market supporters do; rather, they expect a *gradual price adjustment* to reflect the gradual flow of information.

Exhibit 16.1 shows this process wherein new information causes a decrease in the equilibrium price for a security but the price adjustment is not rapid. It occurs as a trend that persists until the stock reaches its new equilibrium. Technical analysts look for the beginning of a movement from one equilibrium value to a new equilibrium value but do not attempt to predict the new equilibrium value. They look for the start of a change so that they can get on the bandwagon early and benefit from the move to the new equilibrium price by buying if the trend is up or selling if the trend is down. Obviously, if there is a rapid adjustment of prices to the new information (as expected by those who espouse an efficient market), the ride on the bandwagon would be so short that investors could not benefit.

Advantages of Technical Analysis

Although technicians understand the logic of fundamental analysis, they see several benefits in their approach. Most technical analysts admit that a fundamental analyst with good information, good analytical ability, and a keen sense of information's impact on the market should achieve above-average returns. However, this statement requires qualification. According to technical analysts, it is important to recognize that the fundamental analysts can experience superior returns *only* if they obtain new information before other investors and process it *correctly* and *quickly.* Technical analysts do not believe the majority of investors can consistently get new information before other investors and consistently process it correctly and quickly.

In addition, technical analysts claim that a major advantage of their method is that *it is not heavily dependent on financial accounting statements*—the major source of information about the past performance of a firm or industry. As we know from Chapters 14 and 15, the fundamental analyst evaluates such statements to help project future return and risk characteristics for industries and individual securities. The technician contends that there are several major problems with accounting statements:

1. They lack a great deal of information needed by security analysts, such as information related to sales, earnings, and capital utilized by product line and customers.
2. According to GAAP (Generally Accepted Accounting Principles), corporations may choose among several procedures for reporting expenses, assets, or liabilities. Notably, these alternative procedures can produce vastly different values for expenses, income, return on assets, and return on equity, depending on whether the firm is conservative or aggressive. As a result, an investor can have trouble comparing the statements of two firms within the same industry, much less firms across industries.
3. Many psychological factors and other nonquantifiable variables do not appear in financial statements. Examples include employee training and loyalty, customer goodwill, and general investor attitude toward an industry. Investor attitudes could be important when investors become concerned about the risk from restrictions or taxes on products such as tobacco or alcohol or when firms do business in countries that have significant political risk.

Therefore, because technicians are suspicious of financial statements, they consider it advantageous not to depend on them. As we will show, most of the data used by technicians, such as security prices, volume of trading, and other trading information, are derived from the stock market itself.

Also, a fundamental analyst must process new information correctly and *quickly* to derive a new intrinsic value for the stock or bond before the other investors can. Technicians, on the other hand, only need to quickly recognize a movement to a new equilibrium value *for whatever reason*—that is, they do not need to know about a specific event and determine the effect of the event on the value of the firm and its stock.

Finally, assume a fundamental analyst determines that a given security is under- or overvalued a long time before other investors. He or she still must determine when to make the purchase or sale. Ideally, the highest rate of return would come from making the transaction just before the change in market value occurs. For example, assume that based on your analysis in February, you expect a firm to report substantially higher earnings in June. Although you could buy the stock in February, you would be better off waiting until about May to buy the stock so your funds would not be tied up for an extra three months, but you may be reticent to wait that long. Because most technicians do not invest until the move to the new equilibrium is under way, they contend that they are more likely than a fundamental analyst to experience ideal timing.

Challenges to Technical Analysis

Those who doubt the value of technical analysis for investment decisions question the usefulness of this technique in two areas. First, they challenge some of its basic assumptions. Second, they challenge some specific technical trading rules and their long-run usefulness. In this section we consider these challenges.

CHALLENGES TO TECHNICAL ANALYSIS ASSUMPTIONS

The major challenge to technical analysis is based on the results of empirical tests of the efficient market hypothesis (EMH). As discussed in Chapter 10, for technical trading rules to generate superior risk-adjusted returns after taking account of transactions costs, the market would have to be slow to adjust prices to the arrival of new information; that is, it would have to be inefficient. This is referred to as the weak-form efficient market hypothesis. The two sets of tests of the weak-form EMH are: (1) the statistical analysis of prices to determine if prices moved in trends or were a random walk, and (2) the analysis of specific trading rules to determine if their use could beat a buy-and-hold policy after considering transactions costs and risk. Almost all the studies testing the weak-form EMH using statistical analysis have found that prices do not move in trends based on statistical tests of autocorrelation and runs. These results support the EMH.

Regarding the analysis of specific trading rules, as discussed in Chapter 10, numerous technical trading rules exist that have not been or cannot be tested. Still, the vast majority of the results for the trading rules that have been tested support the EMH.

CHALLENGES TO TECHNICAL TRADING RULES

An obvious challenge to technical analysis is that the past price patterns or relationships between specific market variables and stock prices may not be repeated. As a result, a technique that previously worked might miss subsequent market turns. This possibility leads most technicians to follow several trading rules and to seek a consensus of all of them to predict the future market pattern.

Other critics contend that many price patterns become self-fulfilling prophecies. For example, assume that many analysts expect a stock selling at $40 a share to go to $50 or more if it should rise above its current pattern and "break through" its channel at $45. As soon as it reaches $45, enough technicians will buy to cause the price to rise to $50, exactly as predicted. In fact, some technicians may place a limit order to buy the stock at such a breakout point. Under such conditions, the increase will probably be only temporary and the price will return to its true equilibrium.

Another problem with technical analysis is that the success of a particular trading rule will encourage many investors to adopt it. It is contended that this popularity and the resulting competition will eventually neutralize the technique. If numerous investors focus on a specific technical trading rule, some of them will attempt to anticipate the price pattern and either ruin the expected historical price pattern or eliminate profits for most traders by causing the price to change faster than expected. For example, suppose it becomes known that technicians who employ short-selling data have been enjoying high rates of return. Based on this knowledge, other technicians will likely start using these data and thus accelerate the stock price pattern following changes in short selling. As a result, this profitable trading rule may no longer be profitable after the first few investors react.

Further, as we will see when we examine specific trading rules, *they all require a great deal of subjective judgment.* Two technical analysts looking at the same price pattern may arrive at widely different interpretations of what has happened and, therefore, will come to different investment decisions. This implies that the use of various techniques is neither completely mechanical nor obvious. Finally, as we will discuss in connection with several trading rules, *the standard values that signal investment decisions can change over time.* Therefore, in some instances technical analysts adjust the specified values that trigger investment decisions to conform to the new environment. In other cases, trading rules have been abandoned because they no longer work.

Technical Trading Rules and Indicators

To illustrate the specific technical trading rules, Exhibit 16.2 shows a typical stock price cycle that could be an example for the overall stock market or for an individual stock. The graph shows a peak and trough, along with a rising trend channel, a flat trend channel, a declining trend channel, and indications of when a technical analyst would ideally want to trade.

The graph begins with the end of a declining (bear) market that finishes in a *trough,* followed by an upward trend that breaks through the *declining trend channel.* Confirmation that the declining trend has reversed would be a buy signal. The technical analyst would buy stocks that showed this pattern.

The analyst would then expect the development of a *rising trend channel.* As long as the stock price stayed in this rising channel, the technician would hold the stock(s). Ideally, they want to sell at the *peak* of the cycle, but they cannot identify a peak until after the trend changes.

If the stock (or the market) begins trading in a flat pattern, it will necessarily break out of its rising trend channel. At this point, some technical analysts would sell, but most would hold to see if the stock experiences a period of consolidation and then breaks out of the *flat trend channel* on the upside and begins rising again. Alternatively, if the stock were to break out of the channel on the downside, the technician would take this as a sell signal and would expect a declining trend channel. The next buy signal would come after the trough when the price breaks out of the declining channel and establishes a rising trend. We will consider strategies to detect these changes in trend and the importance of volume in this analysis shortly.

There are numerous technical trading rules and a range of interpretations for each of them. Almost all technical analysts watch many alternative rules and decide on a buy or sell decision based on a *consensus* of the signals because complete agreement of all the rules is rare. In the following discussion of several well-known techniques, we have divided the rules into four groups based on the attitudes of technical analysts. The first group includes trading rules used by analysts who like to trade against the crowd using contrary-opinion signals. The second group attempts to emulate astute investors, that is, the smart money. The third

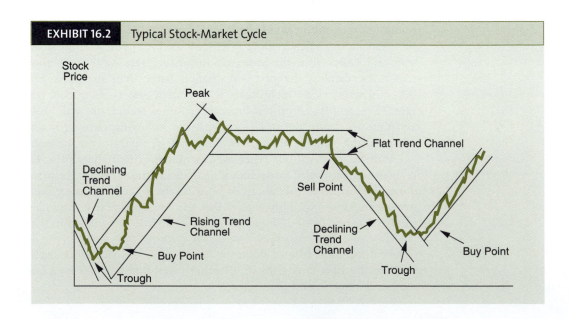

| EXHIBIT 16.2 | Typical Stock-Market Cycle |

group includes popular technical indicators that are not easily classified. Finally, the fourth group includes pure price and volume techniques, including the famous Dow Theory.

CONTRARY-OPINION RULES

Many technical analysts rely on technical trading rules that assume that the majority of investors are wrong as the market approaches peaks and troughs. Therefore, these technicians try to determine when the majority of investors is either strongly bullish or bearish and then trade in the opposite direction.

Mutual Fund Cash Positions   Mutual funds hold some part of their portfolio in cash for one of several reasons. One is that they need cash to liquidate shares submitted by fundholders. Another is that new investments in the mutual fund may not have been invested. Third, the portfolio manager might be bearish on the market and want to increase the fund's defensive cash position.

Mutual funds' ratios of cash as a percentage of the total assets in their portfolios (the *cash ratio* or *liquid asset ratio*) are reported in the press, including monthly figures in *Barron's*.[2] This percentage of cash has varied in recent years from a low point of about 4 percent to a high point near 11 percent, although there appears to be a declining trend to the series.

Contrary-opinion technicians believe that mutual funds usually are wrong at peaks and troughs. Thus, they expect mutual funds to have a high percentage of cash near a market trough—the time when they should be fully invested to take advantage of the impending market rise. At the market peak, these technicians expect mutual funds to be almost fully invested with a low percentage of cash when they should be selling stocks and realizing gains. Therefore, contrary-opinion technicians watch for the mutual fund cash position to approach one of the extremes and act contrary to the mutual funds. Specifically, they would tend to buy when the cash ratio approaches 11 percent and to sell when the cash ratio approaches 4 percent.

An alternative rationale is that a high cash position is a bullish indicator because of potential buying power. Irrespective of the reason for a large cash balance, these technicians believe the cash funds will eventually be invested and will cause stock prices to increase. Alternatively, a low cash ratio would mean that the institutions have bought heavily and are left with little potential buying power.

Credit Balances in Brokerage Accounts   Credit balances result when investors sell stocks and leave the proceeds with their brokers, expecting to reinvest them shortly. The amounts are reported by the SEC and the NYSE in *Barron's*. Because technical analysts view these credit balances as potential purchasing power, a decline in these balances is considered bearish because it indicates lower purchasing power as the market approaches a peak. Alternatively, a buildup of credit balances indicates an increase in buying power and is a bullish signal.

Investment Advisory Opinions   Many technicians believe that if a large proportion of investment advisory services are bearish, this signals the approach of a market trough and the onset of a bull market. Because most advisory services tend to be trend followers, the number of bears usually is greatest when market bottoms are approaching. This trading rule is specified in terms of the percent of advisory services that are bearish/bullish given the number of services expressing an opinion.[3] A 60 percent bearish and/or 20 percent bullish reading indicates a major market bottom (a bullish indicator), while a 60 percent bullish

---

[2]*Barron's* is a prime source for numerous technical indicators. For a readable discussion of relevant data and their use, see Martin E. Zweig, *Understanding Technical Forecasting*, New York: Dow Jones & Co., 1987.

[3]This ratio is compiled by Investors Intelligence, Larchmont, NY 10538. Richard McCabe at Merrill Lynch uses this series as one of his "Investor Sentiment Indicators."

EXHIBIT 16.3 Time-Series Plot of Dow Jones Industrial Average and the Bullish and Bearish Advisory Services

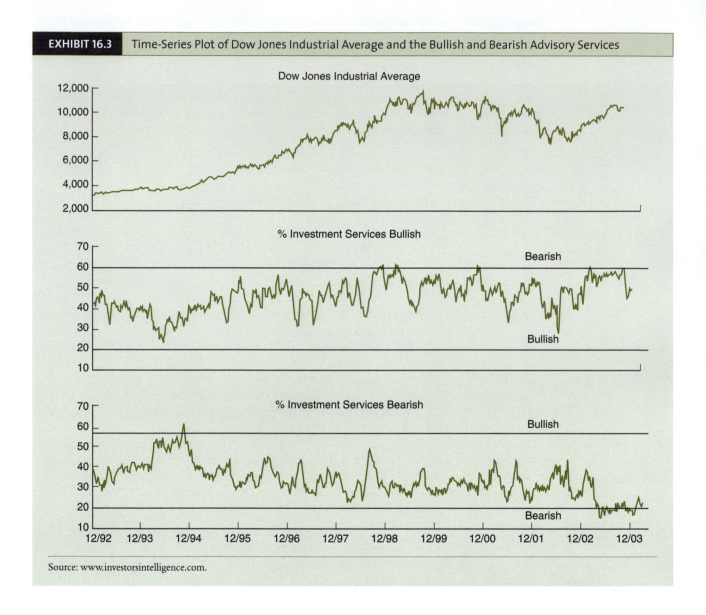

Source: www.investorsintelligence.com.

and/or 20 percent bearish reading suggests a major market top (a bearish signal). Exhibit 16.3 shows a time-series plot of the DJIA and both the bearish sentiment index and the bullish sentiment index. As of mid-2004, both indexes are either at or near the bearish boundary values.

OTC versus NYSE Volume This ratio of trading volume is considered a measure of speculative activity. Speculative trading typically peaks at market peaks. Notably, the interpretation of the ratio has changed—that is, the decision rules have changed. Specifically, during the mid-1990s, the decision rule was in terms of specific percentages—112 percent was considered heavy speculative trading and an overbought market while 87 percent was considered low speculative trading and an oversold market. The problem was that the percentages kept increasing because of faster growth in OTC trading volume and dominance of the OTC market by a few large-cap stocks. It was subsequently decided to detect excess speculative activity by using the *direction* of the volume ratio as a guide. For example, if this ratio is increasing, it would indicate a bearish speculative environment.

Chicago Board Options Exchange (CBOE) Put–Call Ratio   Contrary-opinion technicians use put options, which give the holder the right to sell stock at a specified price for a given time period, as signals of a bearish attitude. A higher put–call ratio indicates a pervasive bearish attitude for investors, which technicians consider a bullish indicator.

This ratio fluctuates between 0.60 and 0.40 and has typically been substantially less than 1 because investors tend to be bullish and avoid selling short or buying puts. The current decision rule states that a put–call ratio above 0.60—that is, sixty puts are traded for every one hundred calls—indicates that investors are generally bearish, so it is considered bullish, while a relatively low put–call ratio of 0.40 or less is considered bearish.

Futures Traders Bullish on Stock-Index Futures   Another relatively new contrary-opinion measure is the percentage of speculators in stock-index futures who are bullish regarding stocks based on a survey of individual futures traders. These technicians would consider it a bearish sign when more than 70 percent of the speculators are bullish, and a bullish sign when this ratio declines to 30 percent or lower. The plot in Exhibit 16.4 shows that as of mid-2004 this indicator was at the upper bound, which is bearish.

EXHIBIT 16.4	Time-Series Plot of Dow Jones Industrial Average and the Market Percentage of Futures Traders Bullish on Stock-Index Futures

Source: Market Vane.

As we have shown, contrary-opinion technicians have several measures of how the majority of investors are investing that prompt them to take the opposite action. They generally employ several of these series to provide a consensus regarding investors' attitudes.

FOLLOW THE SMART MONEY

Some technical analysts have created a set of indicators and corresponding rules that they believe indicate the behavior of smart, sophisticated investors. We discuss three such indicators in this section.

Confidence Index   Published by *Barron's*, the Confidence Index is the ratio of *Barron's* average yield on ten top-grade corporate bonds to the yield on the Dow Jones average of forty bonds.[4] This index measures the difference in yield spread between high-grade bonds and a large cross section of bonds. Because the yields on high-grade bonds always should be lower than those on a large cross section of bonds, this ratio should approach 100 as the spread between the two sets of bonds gets smaller.

Technicians believe the ratio is a bullish indicator because, during periods of high confidence, investors are willing to invest in lower-quality bonds for the added yield, which causes a decrease in the average yield for the large cross section of bonds relative to the yield on high-grade bonds. Therefore, this ratio of yields—the Confidence Index—will increase. In contrast, when investors are pessimistic, they avoid investing in low-quality bonds, which increases the yield spread between high-grade and average bonds, which in turn causes the Confidence Index to decline.

Unfortunately, this interpretation assumes that changes in the yield spread are caused almost exclusively by changes in investor demand for different quality bonds. In fact, the yield differences have frequently changed because of changes in the supply of bonds. For example, a large issue of high-grade AT&T bonds could cause a temporary increase in yields on all high-grade bonds, reduce the yield spread, and increase the Confidence Index without any change in investors' attitudes. Such a change can generate a false signal of a change in confidence.

T-Bill–Eurodollar Yield Spread   A popular measure of investor attitude or confidence on a global basis is the spread between T-bill yields and Eurodollar rates. It is reasoned that, at times of international crisis, this spread widens as the smart money flows to safe-haven U.S. T-bills, which causes a decline in this ratio to a trough. The stock market typically experiences a trough shortly thereafter.

Debit Balances in Brokerage Accounts (Margin Debt)   Debit balances in brokerage accounts represent borrowing (margin debt) by knowledgeable investors from their brokers. Hence, these balances indicate the attitude of sophisticated investors who engage in margin transactions. Therefore, an increase in debit balances implies buying by these sophisticated investors and is considered a bullish sign, while a decline in debit balances would indicate selling and would be a bearish indicator.

Monthly data on margin debt is reported in *Barron's*. Unfortunately, this index does not include borrowing by investors from other sources such as banks. Also, because it is an absolute value, technicians would look for changes in the trend of borrowing.

MOMENTUM INDICATORS

In addition to contrary-opinion and smart money signals, there are several indicators of overall market momentum that are used to make aggregate market decisions.

---

[4]Historical data for this index are contained in the *Dow Jones Investor's Handbook*, Princeton, NJ: Dow Jones Books, annual. Current figures appear in *Barron's*.

EXHIBIT 16.5	Daily Advances and Declines on the New York Stock Exchange				
Day	**1**	**2**	**3**	**4**	**5**
Issues traded	3,608	3,641	3,659	3,651	3,612
Advances	2,310	2,350	1,558	2,261	2,325
Declines	909	912	1,649	933	894
Unchanged	389	379	452	457	393
Net advances (advances minus declines)	+1,401	+1,438	−91	+1,328	+1,431
Cumulative net advances	+1,401	+2,839	+2,748	+4,076	+5,507
Changes in DJIA	+40.47	+95.75	−15.25	+108.42	+140.63

Sources: New York Stock Exchange and *Barron's*.

Breadth of Market   Breadth of market measures the number of issues that have increased each day and the number of issues that have declined. It helps explain the cause of a change of direction in a composite market index such as the DJIA. As we discussed in Chapter 7, most stock-market indexes are heavily influenced by the stocks of large firms because they are value weighted. Therefore, a stock-market index can experience an increase while the majority of the individual issues do not, which means that most stocks are not participating in the rising market. Such a divergence can be detected by examining the advance–decline figures for all stocks on the exchange, along with the overall market index.

The advance–decline index is typically a cumulative index of net advances or net declines. Specifically, each day major newspapers publish figures on the number of issues on the NYSE that advanced, declined, or were unchanged. The figures for a five-day sample, as would be reported in *Barron's,* are shown in Exhibit 16.5. These figures, along with changes in the DJIA at the bottom of the table, indicate a strong market advance because the DJIA was increasing and the net advance figure was strong, indicating that the market increase was broadly based. Even the results on day 3, when the market declined 15 points, were encouraging since it was a small decline and the individual stock issues were split just about 50–50, which points toward a fairly even environment.

Stocks above Their 200-Day Moving Average   Technicians often compute moving averages of an index to determine its general trend. To examine individual stocks, the 200-day *moving average* of prices has been fairly popular. From these moving-average indexes for numerous stocks, Media General Financial Services calculates how many stocks currently are trading above their 200-day moving-average index, and this is used as an indicator of general investor sentiment. The market is considered to be *overbought* and subject to a negative correction when more than 80 percent of the stocks are trading above their 200-day moving average. In contrast, if less than 20 percent of the stocks are selling above their 200-day moving average, the market is considered to be *oversold,* which means investors should expect a positive correction. As shown in Exhibit 16.6, as of mid-2004 the percent of stocks selling above their 200-day moving average was correcting its previous overbought position and was considered neutral.

STOCK PRICE AND VOLUME TECHNIQUES

In the introduction to this chapter, we examined a hypothetical stock price chart that demonstrated market peaks and troughs along with rising and declining trend channels and breakouts from channels that signal new price trends or reversals of the price trends. While

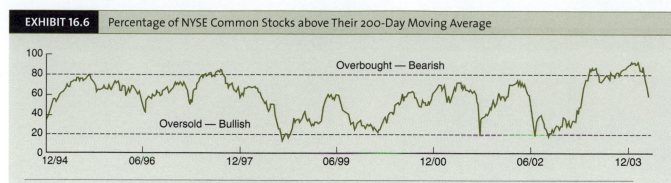

EXHIBIT 16.6 Percentage of NYSE Common Stocks above Their 200-Day Moving Average

Source: From *Where the Indicators Stand,* May 2004. Reprinted and adapted by permission of Merrill Lynch, Pierce, Fenner & Smith Incorporated. Any further reproduction or redistribution is strictly prohibited. Copyright © 2004.

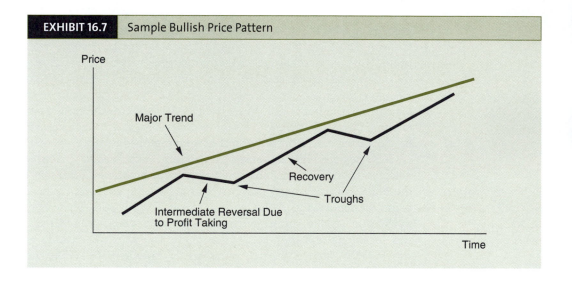

EXHIBIT 16.7 Sample Bullish Price Pattern

price patterns alone are important, most technical trading rules consider both stock price and corresponding volume movements.

Dow Theory Any discussion of technical analysis using price and volume data should begin with a consideration of the Dow Theory because it was among the earliest work on this topic and remains the basis for many technical indicators.[5] Dow described stock prices as moving in trends analogous to the movement of water. He postulated three types of price movements over time: (1) major trends that are like tides in the ocean, (2) intermediate trends that resemble waves, and (3) short-run movements that are like ripples. Followers of the Dow Theory attempt to detect the direction of the major price trend (tide), recognizing that intermediate movements (waves) may occasionally move in the opposite direction. They recognize that a major market advance does not go straight up, but rather includes small price declines as some investors decide to take profits.

Exhibit 16.7 shows the typical bullish pattern. The technician would look for every recovery to reach a new peak above the prior peak, and this price rise should be accompanied by heavy trading volume. Alternatively, each profit-taking reversal that follows an

[5]A study that discusses and provides support for the Dow Theory is David A. Glickstein and Rolf E. Wubbels, "Dow Theory Is Alive and Well," *Journal of Portfolio Management* 9, no. 3 (Spring 1983): 28–32.

increase to a new peak should have a trough above the prior trough, with relatively light trading volume during the profit-taking reversals. When this pattern of price and volume movements changes, the major trend may be entering a period of consolidation (a flat trend) or a major reversal.

Importance of Volume As noted, technicians watch volume changes along with price movements as an indicator of changes in supply and demand. A price movement in one direction means that the net effect on price is in that direction, but the price change alone does not indicate the breadth of the excess demand or supply. Therefore, the technician looks for a price increase on heavy volume relative to the stock's normal trading volume as an indication of bullish activity. Conversely, a price decline with heavy volume is bearish. A generally bullish pattern would be when price increases are accompanied by heavy volume and small price reversals occur with light trading volume.

Technicians also use a ratio of upside–downside volume as an indicator of short-term momentum for the aggregate stock market. Each day the stock exchanges announce the volume of trading in stocks that experienced an increase divided by the volume of trading in stocks that declined. These data are reported daily in *The Wall Street Journal* and weekly in *Barron's*. This ratio is used as an indicator of market momentum. Specifically, technicians believe that a value of 1.75 or more indicates an overbought position that is bearish. Alternatively, a value of 0.75 and lower supposedly reflects an oversold position and is considered bullish.

Support and Resistance Levels A *support level* is the price range at which the technician would expect a substantial increase in the demand for a stock. Generally, a support level will develop after a stock has enjoyed a meaningful price increase and the stock experiences profit taking. Technicians reason that at some price below the recent peak other investors who did not buy during the first price increase (waiting for a small reversal) will get into the stock. When the price reaches this support price, demand surges and price and volume begin to increase again.

A *resistance level* is the price range at which the technician would expect an increase in the supply of stock and a price reversal. A resistance level develops after steady decline from a higher price level—that is, the decline in price leads some investors who acquired the stock at a higher price to look for an opportunity to sell it near their breakeven points. Therefore, the supply of stock owned by these investors is *overhanging* the market. When the price rebounds to the target price set by these investors, this overhanging supply of stock comes to the market and there is a price decline on heavy volume. It is also possible to envision a rising trend of support and resistance levels for a stock. For example, the rising support prices would be a set of higher prices where investors over time would see the price increase and would take the opportunity to buy when there is profit taking. In this latter case, there would be a succession of higher support levels over time.

Exhibit 16.8 contains the daily stock prices for Gillette (G) with support and resistance lines. The graphs show a rising pattern since Gillette has experienced strong price increases during this period. At present, the resistance level is at about 44 and is rising, while the support level is about $40 and is also rising. The bullish technician would look for future prices to rise in line with this channel. If prices fell below the support line, it would be considered a bearish signal, while an increase above the $44.00 resistance price would be bullish.

Moving-Average Lines Earlier, we discussed how technicians use a moving average of past stock prices as an indicator of the long-run trend and how they examine current prices relative to this trend for signals of a change. We also noted that a 200-day moving average is a relatively popular measure for individual stocks and the aggregate market. In this discussion, we add a fifty-day moving-average price line and consider large volume.

EXHIBIT 16.8   Daily Stock Prices and Volume for Gillette with Indications of Support and Resistance Levels

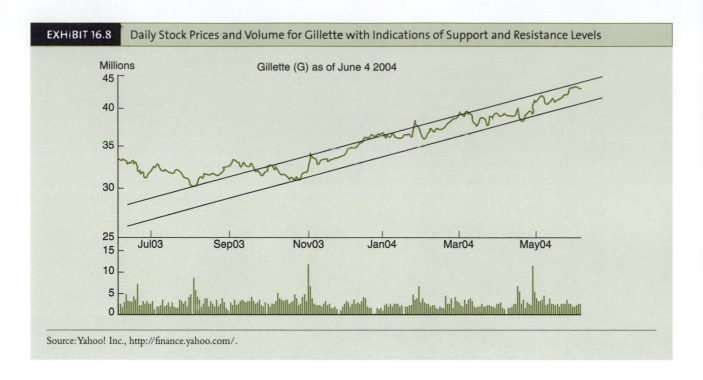

Source: Yahoo! Inc., http://finance.yahoo.com/.

Exhibit 16.9 is a daily stock price chart from Yahoo! Inc. for Pfizer, Inc. (PFE) for the year ending June 4, 2004. It also contains 50-day and 200-day moving-average (MA) lines. As noted, MA lines are meant to reflect the overall trend for the price index, with the shorter MA index (the 50-day versus 200-day) reflecting shorter trends. Two comparisons involving the MA index are considered important. The first comparison is the specific prices to the shorter-run 50-day MA index. If the overall price trend of a stock or the market has been down, the moving-average price line generally would lie above current prices. If prices reverse and break through the moving-average line *from below* accompanied by heavy trading volume, most technicians would consider this a *positive* change and speculate that this breakthrough could signal a reversal of the declining trend. In contrast, if the price of a stock had been rising, the moving-average line would also be rising, but it would be below current prices. If current prices broke through the moving-average line *from above* accompanied by heavy trading volume, this would be considered a bearish pattern that would possibly signal a reversal of the long-run rising trend.

The second comparison is between the 50- and 200-day MA lines. Specifically, when these two lines cross, it signals a change in the overall trend. Specifically, if the 50-day MA line crosses the 200-day MA line from below on good volume, this would be a bullish indicator (buy signal) because it signals a reversal in trend from negative to positive. In contrast, when the 50-day line crosses the 200-day line from above, it signals a change to a negative trend and would be a sell signal. As shown in Exhibit 16.9, in the case of Pfizer (PFE) there was a bearish crossing in late September 2003, but it was reversed in December 2003 when there was a bullish crossing. Following this bullish crossing, the 50-day line has been consistently above the 200-day line as prices reached a peak of about $38 and were at about $36 at the end of the period.

Overall, for a *bullish* trend the 50-day MA line should be above the 200-day MA line, as it has been for Pfizer since December 2003. Notably, if this positive gap gets too large (which happens with a fast run up in price), a technician might consider this an indication

EXHIBIT 16.9	Daily Stock Prices for Pfizer, Inc. with 50-Day and 200-Day Moving-Average Lines

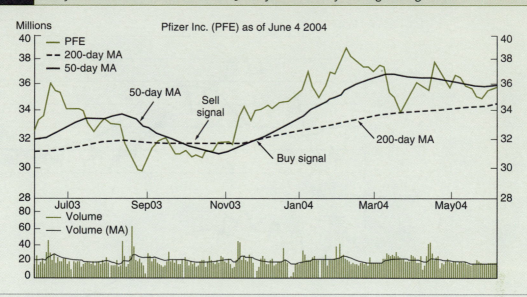

Source: Yahoo! Inc., http://finance.yahoo.com/.

that the stock is temporarily overbought, which is bearish in the short run. A *bearish* trend is when the 50-day MA line is always below the 200-day MA line. If the gap gets large on the downside, it might be considered a signal of an oversold stock, which is bullish for the short-run.

Relative Strength   Technicians believe that once a trend begins, it will continue until some major event causes a change in direction. They believe this is also true of *relative* performance. If an individual stock or an industry group is outperforming the market, technicians believe it will continue to do so.

Therefore, technicians compute weekly or monthly *relative-strength (RS) ratios* for individual stocks and industry groups. The RS ratio is equal to the price of a stock or an industry index divided by the value for some stock-market index such as the S&P 500. If this ratio increases over time, it shows that the stock or industry is outperforming the overall stock market, and a technician would expect this superior performance to continue. Relative-strength ratios work during declining as well as rising markets. In a declining market, if a stock's price declines less than the market does, the stock's relative-strength ratio will continue to rise. Technicians believe that if this ratio is stable or increases during a bear market, the stock should do well during the subsequent bull market.

Merrill Lynch publishes relative-strength charts for industry groups. Exhibit 16.10 describes how to read the charts. Further, some technicians construct graphs of stocks relative to their industry in addition to the comparison relative to the market.

Bar Charting   Technicians use charts that show daily, weekly, or monthly time series of stock prices. For a given interval, the technical analyst plots the high and low prices and connects the two points vertically to form a bar. Typically, he or she will also draw a small horizontal line across this vertical bar to indicate the closing price. Finally, almost all bar charts include the volume of trading at the bottom of the chart so that the technical analyst

EXHIBIT 16.10 How to Read Industry Group Charts

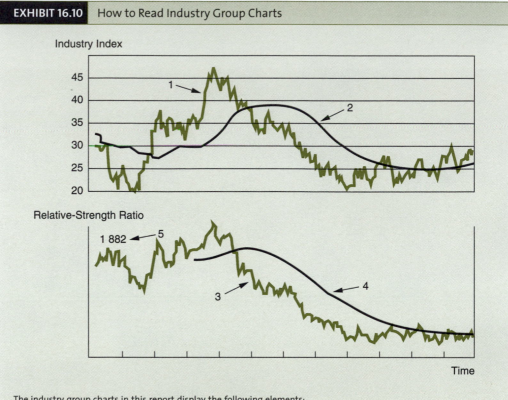

The industry group charts in this report display the following elements:

1. A line chart of the weekly close of the Standard & Poor's Industry Group Index for the past nine and one-half years, with the index range indicated to the left.

2. A line of the seventy-five-week moving average of the Standard & Poor's Industry Group Index.

3. A relative-strength line of the Standard & Poor's Industry Group Index compared with the New York Stock Exchange Composite Index.

4. A seventy-five-week moving average of relative strength.

5. A volatility reading that measures the maximum amount by which the index has outperformed (or underperformed) the NYSE Composite Index during the time period displayed.

Source: From *Technical Analysis of Industry Groups.* Reprinted by permission of Merrill Lynch, Pierce, Fenner & Smith Incorporated. Any further reproduction or redistribution is strictly prohibited. Copyright © 2002.

can relate the price and volume movements. A typical bar chart in Exhibit 16.11 shows data for the DJIA from *The Wall Street Journal* along with volume figures for the NYSE.

Multiple-Indicator Charts Thus far we have presented charts that deal with only one trading technique such as moving-average lines or relative-strength rules. In the real world, it is fairly typical for technical charts to contain several indicators that can be used together like the two MA lines (50- and 200-day) and the RS line, because they can provide added support to the analysis. Technicians include as many price and volume indicators as are reasonable on one chart and then, based on the performance of *several* technical indicators, try to arrive at a consensus about the future movement for the stock.

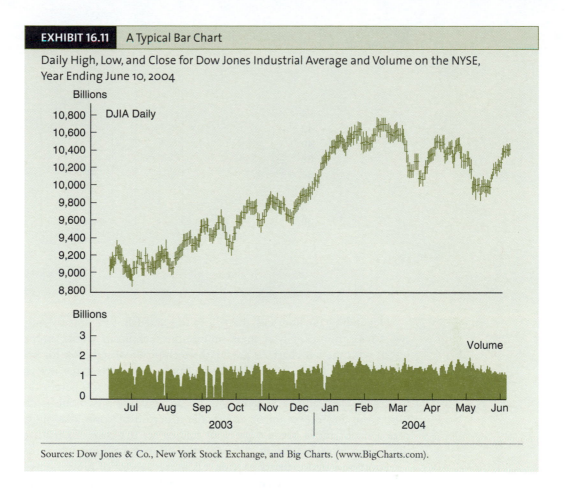

EXHIBIT 16.11 A Typical Bar Chart

Daily High, Low, and Close for Dow Jones Industrial Average and Volume on the NYSE, Year Ending June 10, 2004

Sources: Dow Jones & Co., New York Stock Exchange, and Big Charts. (www.BigCharts.com).

Point-and-Figure Charts Another graph that is popular with technicians is the point-and-figure chart. Unlike the bar chart, which typically includes all ending prices and volumes to show a trend, the point-and-figure chart includes only significant price changes, regardless of their timing. The technician determines what price interval to record as significant (one point, two points, and so on) and when to note price reversals.

To demonstrate how a technical analyst would use such a chart, suppose we want to chart a volatile stock that is currently selling for $40 a share. Because of its volatility, we believe that anything less than a two-point price change is not significant. Also, we consider anything less than a four-point reversal, meaning a movement in the opposite direction, quite minor. Therefore, we would set up a chart similar to the one in Exhibit 16.12, which starts at 40 and progresses in two-point increments. If the stock moves to 42, we would place an X in the box above 40 and do nothing else until the stock rose to 44 or dropped to 38 (a four-point reversal from its high of 42). If it dropped to 38, we would move a column to the right, which indicates a reversal in direction, and begin again at 38 (fill in boxes at 42 and 40). If the stock price dropped to 34, we would enter an X at 36 and another at 34. If the stock then rose to 38 (another four-point reversal), we would move to the next column and begin at 38, going up (fill in 34 and 36). If the stock then went to 46, we would fill in more Xs as shown and wait for further increases or a reversal.

EXHIBIT 16.12	Sample Point-and-Figure Chart

50									
48									
46			X						
44			X						
42	X	X	X						
40	X	X	X						
38		X	X						
36		X	X						
34		X	X						
32									
30									

Depending on how fast the prices rise and fall, this process might take anywhere from two to six months. Given these figures, the technician would attempt to determine trends just as with the bar chart. As always, the technician would look for breakouts to either higher or lower price levels. A long horizontal movement with many reversals but no major trends up or down would be considered a *period of consolidation* wherein the stock is moving from buyers to sellers and back again with no strong consensus about its direction. Once the stock breaks out and moves up or down after a period of consolidation, technical analysts anticipate a major move because previous trading set the stage for it. In other words, the longer the period of consolidation, the larger the subsequent move when there is finally a breakout.

Point-and-figure charts provide a compact record of movements because they only consider significant price changes for the stock being analyzed. Therefore, some technicians contend they are easier to work with and give more vivid pictures of price movements.

Technical Analysis of Foreign Markets

Our discussion thus far has concentrated on U.S. markets, but analysts have discovered that these techniques apply to foreign markets as well. Merrill Lynch, for instance, prepares separate technical analysis publications for individual countries such as Japan, Germany, and the United Kingdom as well as a summary of all world markets. The examples that follow show that when analyzing non-U.S. markets, many techniques are limited to price and volume data rather than the more detailed U.S. market information. The reason is that the detailed information available on the U.S. market through the SEC, the stock exchanges, the Nasdaq system, and various investment services is not always available for other countries.

FOREIGN STOCK-MARKET INDEXES
Exhibit 16.13 contains the daily time-series plot for the Japanese Nikkei Index. This chart shows the generally declining trend by the Japanese stock market during the period May 1999–April 2003 followed by a strong reversal and rising stock prices through May 2004. In the written analysis, the market analyst at Merrill Lynch estimated support and resistance

EXHIBIT 16.13 Graph and Summary Comments on the Japanese Stock Market

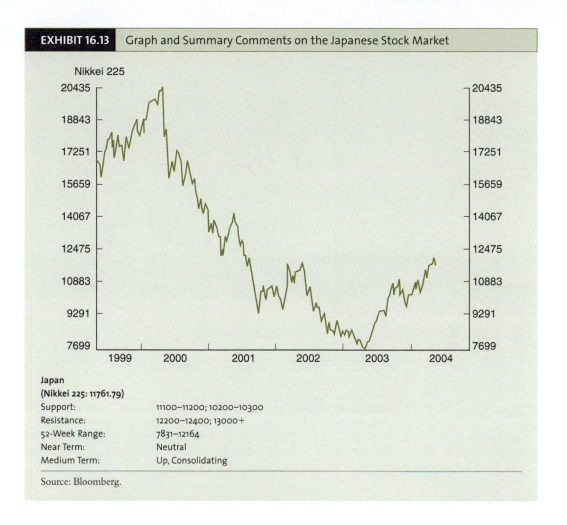

Japan
(Nikkei 225: 11761.79)

Support:	11100–11200; 10200–10300
Resistance:	12200–12400; 13000+
52-Week Range:	7831–12164
Near Term:	Neutral
Medium Term:	Up, Consolidating

Source: Bloomberg.

levels for the Japanese Stock Exchange index and commented on the medium-term outlook for this market.

Merrill Lynch publishes similar charts for ten other countries and compares the countries and ranks them by stock and currency performance.

TECHNICAL ANALYSIS OF FOREIGN EXCHANGE RATES

On numerous occasions, we have discussed the importance of changes in foreign exchange rates on the rates of return on foreign securities. Because of the importance of these relationships, bond-and-stock traders in world markets examine the time-series data of various currencies such as the British pound. They also analyze the spread between currencies, such as the difference between the Japanese yen and the British pound. Finally, they would typically examine the time series for the U.S. dollar trade-weighted exchange rate that experienced significant weakness during 2003–2004.

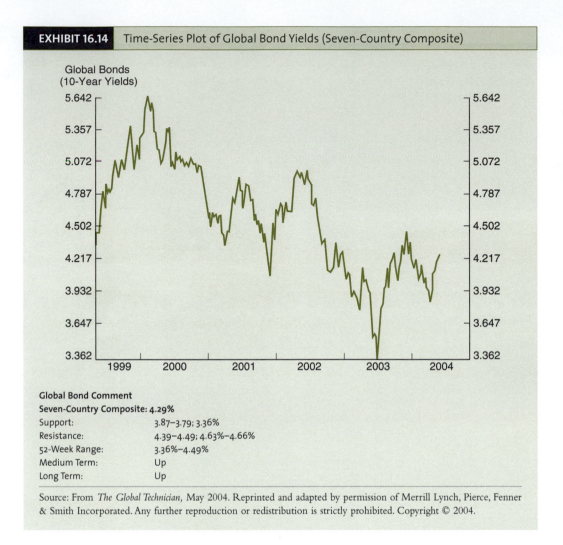

| **EXHIBIT 16.14** | Time-Series Plot of Global Bond Yields (Seven-Country Composite) |

Global Bonds
(10-Year Yields)

Global Bond Comment

Seven-Country Composite: 4.29%

Support:	3.87–3.79; 3.36%
Resistance:	4.39–4.49; 4.63%–4.66%
52-Week Range:	3.36%–4.49%
Medium Term:	Up
Long Term:	Up

Source: From *The Global Technician,* May 2004. Reprinted and adapted by permission of Merrill Lynch, Pierce, Fenner & Smith Incorporated. Any further reproduction or redistribution is strictly prohibited. Copyright © 2004.

Technical Analysis of Bond Markets

Thus far, we have emphasized the use of technical analysis in stock markets. These techniques can also be applied to the bond market. The theory and rationale for technical analysis of bonds is the same as for stocks, and many of the same trading rules are used. A major difference is that it was generally not possible to consider the volume of trading of bonds because most bonds are traded OTC, where volume was not reported.

Exhibit 16.14 demonstrates the use of technical analysis techniques applied to bond-yield series. Specifically, the graph contains a time-series plot of yields for world bond yields based on a seven-country composite. As shown, yields declined steadily until a trough in June 2003, followed by a sharp recovery. Such a technical graph provides important insights to a global bond-portfolio manager interested in adjusting his or her portfolio.

Summary

- Numerous investors believe in and use the principles of technical analysis. The fact is, the large investment houses provide extensive support for technical analysis, and a large proportion of the discussion related to securities markets in the media is based on a technical view of the market.

- Their answers to two main questions separate technical analysts and efficient market advocates. First, in the information dissemination process does everybody get the information at about the same time? Second, how quickly do investors adjust security prices to reflect new information? Technical analysts believe that news takes time to travel from the insider and expert to the individual investor. They also believe that price adjustments are not instantaneous. As a result, they contend that security prices move in trends that persist and, therefore, they can use past price trends and volume information along with other market indicators to determine future price trends.

- Technical trading rules fall into four general categories: contrary-opinion rules, follow-the-smart-money tactics, momentum indicators, and stock price and volume techniques. These techniques and trading rules can be applied to both domestic and foreign markets. They can also be used to analyze currency exchange rates and determine the prevailing sentiment in the bond market.

- Most technicians employ several indicators and attempt to derive a consensus to guide their decision to buy, sell, or do nothing.[6]

---

[6]An analysis using numerous indicators is Jerome Baesel, George Shows, and Edward Thorp, "Can Joe Granville Time the Market?" *Journal of Portfolio Management* 8, no. 3 (Spring 1982): 5–9.

Investments Online

By its nature, technical analysis uses charts and graphs. Many Web sites offer such tools; some are free, but some of the sites for more sophisticated users require payment for access. Here are several interesting sites:

http://www.mta-usa.org Market Technicians Association is a professional group of chartists whose goal is to enhance technical analysis and educate investors about its role. The group sponsors the Chartered Market Technician (CMT) designation. This site features news groups, investment links, training and education sources, a journal, and a variety of technical analysis charts.

http://www.bigcharts.marketwatch.com This site offers free intraday and historical charts and price quotes. Its database includes stocks, mutual funds, and indexes. Users can learn which stocks have the largest percentage gain (loss) in price and volume and which stocks are hitting new 52-week highs (lows). Other features include charts showing momentum, stocks with the largest short interest, and a variety of other data of interest to technicians.

http://www.equis.com/ A Reuters company, Equis sells software used by market technicians. Their Web site contains links to free downloads, education, and information about technical analysis.

http://www.investools.com The INVESTools home page offers news, reports, data, links to a variety of charts, investment newsletter links, and insights from featured advisors.

http://www.stockmaster.com This site offers basic stock charts, including price and volume charts.

QUESTIONS

1. Technical analysts believe that one can use past price changes to predict future price changes. How do they justify this belief?
2. Technicians contend that stock prices move in trends that persist for long periods of time. What do technicians believe happens in the real world to cause these trends?
3. Briefly discuss the problems related to fundamental analysis that are considered advantages for technical analysis.
4. Discuss some disadvantages of technical analysis.
5. If the mutual fund cash position were to increase close to 10 percent, would a technician consider this cash position bullish or bearish? Give two reasons why the technical analyst would think this way.
6. Assume a significant decline in credit balances at brokerage firms. Discuss why a technician would consider this bearish.
7. If the bearish sentiment index of advisory service opinions were to increase to 61 percent, discuss why a technician would consider this bullish or bearish.
8. Why is an increase in debit balances considered bullish?
9. Describe the Dow Theory and its three components. Which component is most important? What is the reason for an intermediate reversal?
10. Describe a bearish price and volume pattern, and discuss why it is considered bearish.
11. Discuss the logic behind the breadth of market index. How is it used to identify a peak in stock prices?
12. During a ten-day trading period, the cumulative net advance index goes from 1,572 to 1,053. During this same period of time, the DJIA goes from 11,200 to 12,100. As a technician, discuss what this set of events would mean to you.
13. Explain the reasoning behind a support level and a resistance level.
14. What is the purpose of computing a moving-average line for a stock? Describe a bullish pattern using a fifty-day moving-average line and the stock volume of trading. Discuss why this pattern is considered bullish.
15. Assuming a stock price and volume chart that also contains a 50-day and a 200-day MA line, describe a bearish pattern with the two MA lines and discuss why it is bearish.
16. Explain how you would construct a relative-strength ratio for an individual stock or an industry group. What would it mean to say a stock experienced good relative strength during a bear market?
17. Discuss why most technicians follow several technical rules and attempt to derive a consensus.

PROBLEMS

1. Select a stock on the NYSE and construct a daily high, low, and close bar chart for it that includes its volume of trading for ten trading days.
2. Compute the relative-strength ratio for the stock in Problem 1 relative to the S&P 500 index. Prepare a table that includes all the data and indicates the computations as follows:

Closing Price		Relative-Strength Ratio
Day	Stock	S&P 500	Stock Price/S&P 500

3. Plot the relative-strength ratio computed in Problem 2 on your bar chart. Discuss whether the stock's relative strength is bullish or bearish.
4. Currently Charlotte Art Importers is selling at $23 per share. Although you are somewhat dubious about technical analysis, you want to know how technicians who use point-and-figure charts would view this stock. You decide to note one-point movements and three-point reversals. You gather the following historical price information:

Date	Price	Date	Price	Date	Price
4/1	$23\frac{1}{2}$	4/18	33	5/3	27
4/4	$28\frac{1}{2}$	4/19	$35\frac{3}{8}$	5/4	$26\frac{1}{2}$
4/5	28	4/20	37	5/5	28
4/6	28	4/21	$38\frac{1}{2}$	5/6	$28\frac{1}{4}$
4/7	$29\frac{3}{4}$	4/22	36	5/9	$28\frac{1}{8}$
4/8	$30\frac{1}{2}$	4/25	35	5/10	$28\frac{1}{4}$
4/11	$30\frac{1}{2}$	4/26	$34\frac{1}{4}$	5/11	$29\frac{1}{8}$
4/12	$32\frac{1}{8}$	4/27	$33\frac{1}{8}$	5/12	$30\frac{1}{4}$
4/13	32	4/28	$32\frac{7}{8}$	5/13	$29\frac{7}{8}$

Plot the point-and-figure chart using Xs for uptrends and Os for downtrends. How would a technician evaluate these movements? Discuss why you would expect a technician to buy, sell, or hold the stock based on this chart.

5. Assume the following daily closings for the Dow Jones Industrial Average:

Day	DJIA	Day	DJIA
1	12,010	7	12,220
2	12,100	8	12,130
3	12,165	9	12,250
4	12,080	10	12,315
5	12,070	11	12,240
6	12,150	12	12,310

a. Calculate a four-day moving average for days 4 through 12.
b. Assume that the index on day 13 closes at 12,300. Would this signal a buy or sell decision?

6. The cumulative advance–decline line reported in *Barron's* at the end of the month is 21,240. During the first week of the following month, the daily report for the *Exchange* is as follows:

Day	1	2	3	4	5
Issues traded	3,544	3,533	3,540	3,531	3,521
Advances	1,737	1,579	1,759	1,217	1,326
Declines	1,289	1,484	1,240	1,716	1,519
Unchanged	518	470	541	598	596

a. Compute the daily net advance–decline line for each of the five days.
b. Compute the cumulative advance–decline line for each day and the final value at the end of the week.

WEB EXERCISES

1. Visit the Web site of the Market Technicians Association (*http://www.mta-usa.org*). What qualifications must someone have before they are awarded the Chartered Market Technician (CMT) designation?
2. Throughout this book, we have mentioned many Web sites with stock, currency, and index price charts. Using your knowledge of indicators, what do they forecast for the overall stock market (proxied by the S&P 500)? For stocks such as Intel, Microsoft, Wendy's, Walgreens, and K-Mart?
3. There are many technical indicators we could not discuss in this single chapter. Search the Web for information, explanations, and charts for tools such as "candlestick graphs" and "Bollinger bands."

REFERENCES

Benning, Carl J. "Prediction Skills of Real-World Market Timers." *The Journal of Portfolio Management* 23, no. 2 (Winter, 1997).

Blume, Lawrence, David Easley, and Maureen O'Hara. "Market Statistics and Technical Analysis: The Role of Volume." *Journal of Finance* 49, no. 1 (March, 1994).

Brown, David P., and Robert H. Jennings. "On Technical Analysis." *The Review of Financial Studies* 2, no. 4 (October 1989).

Colby, Robert W., and Thomas A. Mayers. *The Encyclopedia of Technical Market Indicators.* Homewood, IL: Dow Jones–Irwin, 1988.

DeMark, Thomas R. *The New Science of Technical Analysis.* New York: John Wiley & Sons, 1994.

Edwards, R. D., and John Magee, Jr. *Technical Analysis of Stock Trends,* 6th ed. Boston: New York Institute of Finance, 1992.

Farinella, Joseph A., Edward Graham, and Cynthia McDonald. "Does High Short Interest Lead Underperformance?" *Journal of Investing* 10, no. 2 (Summer 2001).

Jagadeesh, Narasimhan. "Evidence of Predictable Behavior of Security Returns." *Journal of Finance* 45, no. 3 (July 1990).

Lo, Andrew W., and A. Craig MacKinley. *A Non-Random Walk Down Wall Street.* Princeton, NJ: Princeton University Press, 1999.

Lo, Andrew W., Harry Mamasky, and Jiang Wang. "Foundations of Technical Analysis: Computational Algorithms, Statistical Inference, and Empirical Implementation." *Journal of Finance* 55, no. 4 (August 2000).

Meyers, Thomas A. *The Technical Analysis Course.* Chicago: Probus, 1989.

Pring, Martin J. *Technical Analysis Explained,* 3rd ed. New York: McGraw-Hill, 1991.

Pruitt, Stephen, and Robert White. "The CRISMA Trading System: Who Says Technical Analysis Can't Beat the Market?" *Journal of Portfolio Management* 14, no. 3 (Spring 1988).

Shaw, Alan R. "Market Timing and Technical Analysis." In *The Financial Analysts Handbook,* 2nd ed., edited by Sumner N. Levine. Homewood, IL: Dow Jones–Irwin, 1988.

Sweeney, Richard J. "Some New Filter Rule Tests: Methods and Results." *Journal of Financial and Quantitative Analysis* 23, no. 3 (September 1988).

Zweig, Martin E. *Winning on Wall Street.* New York: Warner Books, 1986.

THOMSON ONE
Business School Edition

1. Examine the recent (past six months) price charts for Walgreens, Intel, and Merck (or any three firms of your choosing). What channels, buy/sell points, and patterns do you see in them?
2. What does the price and volume chart of the Dow Jones Industrial and S&P 500 imply for future price trends in the overall market?
3. For a stock of your choice, obtain daily price data for the past three years and download it into a spreadsheet. Compute and graph five-day and ten-day moving averages of the price data along with the daily price data. How successful were the signals generated by the moving average lines?
4. What does the relative strength measure indicate for trends in Walgreens' stock?
5. Using data for the most recent two months, construct a point-and-figure chart for Walgreens.

GLOSSARY

Declining trend channel The range defined by security prices as they move progressively lower.

Flat trend channel The range defined by security prices as they maintain a relatively steady level.

Moving average The continually recalculated average of security prices for a period, often 200 days, to serve as an indication of the general trend of prices and also as a benchmark price.

Peak The culmination of a bull market when prices stop rising and begin declining.

Relative-strength (RS) ratio The ratio of a stock price or an industry index value to a market index, indicating performance relative to the overall market.

Resistance level A price at which a technician would expect a substantial increase in the supply of a stock to reverse a rising trend.

Rising trend channel The range defined by security prices as they move progressively higher.

Support level A price at which a technician would expect a substantial increase in price and volume for a stock to reverse a declining trend that was due to profit taking.

Technical analysis Estimation of future security price movements based on past price and volume movements.

Trough The culmination of a bear market at which prices stop declining and begin rising.

P A R T

6

Derivative Securities

Thus far we have examined stocks and bonds that have value because the underlying assets they represent have value. If these real assets cannot generate future cash flows, a company's stocks and bonds would have no value today.

A major development in the past thirty years has been the creation and growth of new markets and instruments beyond stocks and bonds. This growth has occurred in *derivatives*, so named because they *derive* their value from an underlying financial security such as a firm's common stock. These instruments create a wider range of risk–return opportunities for investors. In Chapter 17 we provide a description of these instruments and markets, including the fundamental principles that determine their prices.

In Chapter 18 we delve deeper into the analysis and valuation of derivatives, particularly futures and option contracts. We discuss how futures and options prices should be determined in markets. We examine option pricing in some detail, including the sensitivity of option prices to different influences such as time to expiration and price volatility. We review two models used to price options, the binomial option pricing model and the Black–Scholes option pricing model. In addition, we look at sophisticated investment strategies and arbitrage possibilities with derivatives. Since convertible and callable bonds have option-like characteristics, we also review how these embedded options can affect bond pricing.

An Introduction to Derivative Instruments

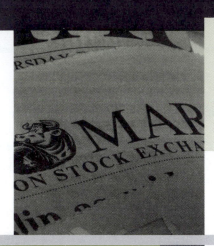

A *derivative instrument* has its value determined by, or derived from, the value of another investment vehicle, called the underlying asset or security. In Chapter 3 we briefly described options and futures, which form the basis for much derivative trading. The incredible growth in the use of derivatives and the occasional controversy they engender make it all the more important that we develop an understanding of derivatives and their role in our financial markets. In this chapter we introduce the basic derivative instruments—forwards, futures, and options—and describe their characteristics, pricing, and some selected investment strategies.

Forward contracts are agreements between two parties, the buyer and seller, for the former to purchase an asset from the latter at a specific future date at a price agreed on up front. No money changes hands between the buyer and seller when the forward contract is initiated, thus, a forward contract itself is not an asset but merely an agreement. Forward contracts are created in the over-the-counter market. *Futures contracts* are somewhat like forward contracts as they represent an agreement between a buyer and a seller to exchange a specified amount of cash for an asset at a specified future date. Unlike forward contracts, futures contracts trade on an exchange and are subject to a daily settling-up process, which will be described in more detail later. *Options* are instruments that grant to their owners the right, but not the obligation, to buy or sell something at a fixed price, either on a specific date or any time up to a specific date. Unlike a forward or futures contract, the owner of an option contract is not obliged to follow through on it if the transaction is not in his or her best interest; thus the name "option" contract.[1]

---

[1]Another type of derivative, called a *swap,* is an agreement between two investors to exchange a series of cash flows over time. For example, a borrower paying a fixed rate of interest who believes interest rates will fall can enter a swap agreement in which he will pay a floating interest rate to a counterparty while the counterparty will pay a fixed interest rate to him. The actual amount of cash that changes hands is based on the *notional*

In derivatives parlance, the buyer and seller of a contract are sometimes referred to as *counterparties* in the derivatives transaction. The buyer of a contract is said to be *long* in the contract. The seller, or writer of the contract, is *short* in the contract.

Although their names are different, forwards, futures, and options have similar general characteristics. First, they all specify the asset underlying the contract and the quantity of the asset to be traded. Second, they all specify a length of time over which the contract is in force. The transaction is to be completed, or the option exercised, on or before the contract's expiration date. Third, they allow the buyer of the contract to lock in a transaction price; we call this the *exercise* or *strike price*. If the purchaser exercises the option, or when the forward or futures contract is fulfilled, the trade occurs at the exercise price specified in the contract. Fourth, the profit or loss on the contract depends on the relationship between the asset's *market price* (or *spot price*) and the exercise price at the time the contract is executed or when it expires.

Why Do Derivatives Exist?

Most assets—such as stocks, bonds, gold, or real estate—are traded in the cash or *spot market*. The primary and secondary markets we examined earlier in the text are examples of spot markets. In these markets trades occur, and cash, along with ownership of the asset, is transferred between buyer and seller.

At times, it may be advantageous to enter into a transaction immediately with the promise that the exchange of the asset and money will take place at a future time. As an illustration, a portfolio manager may anticipate month-end cash flows from investors but wishes to purchase attractively priced securities now, fearing their prices will rise. A corporate treasurer may want to lock in today's borrowing rates, fearing they will rise in the future. A farmer may want to lock in attractive July corn prices, although his crops will not be harvested for several months.

Over time, derivatives such as forwards, futures, and options have evolved to fulfill these desirable economic purposes. They help shift risk from those who do not want to carry it to those who are willing to bear it. They also assist in forming cash prices and provide additional information to the market. Finally, the trading mechanisms for derivatives have evolved so that in many cases it may be less costly, in terms of both commissions and required investment, to invest in derivatives than in the cash market. In the following sections, we discuss each of these benefits.

Risk Shifting

Investors who want to reduce their exposure to a fluctuating spot price can do so by using derivatives. Similarly, investors or speculators who are willing to increase (or "leverage") their exposure to risk can do so via appropriate derivatives trades. For example, the farmer who wants to reduce his risk can hedge by locking in a price for wheat to be delivered at harvest. He does this by entering into a forward or futures contract with someone who is

---

principal. The interest cash flows equal the party's interest rate times the notional amount. The notional principal is never paid to anyone; its purpose is to be a scaling factor to determine the size of the interest payments in the swap agreement. A party paying a fixed rate of 0.5 percent a month with a notional amount of $100 million will make monthly payments of $500,000; with a notational principal of $1 billion the monthly payments will be $5 million. Equity swaps exist, too. An example of an equity swap will have a portfolio manager paying the S&P 500 monthly return to a counterparty who in turn will pay a fixed percentage return to the portfolio manager. In a bearish market environment such a swap can protect a portfolio against a decline in value but at the cost of giving up some of the portfolio's upside potential.

willing to bear the risk of fluctuating spot prices. The buyer of the contract may be a spec-ulator or grain processor who believes that wheat will sell at a higher spot price in the future and so agrees to buy the wheat in the future at the preset price.

Option contracts allow the option owner to decide not to exercise it if the transaction becomes disadvantageous. Thus, options can be used to control risk by limiting losses while protecting profit opportunities.

PRICE FORMATION

Speculators trade in the derivatives markets because they believe the asset is incorrectly priced based on their analysis and information. Because speculators bring additional infor-mation into the market, the prices of the underlying assets and their corresponding futures and option contracts should more accurately reflect the intrinsic values of the assets.

Derivative prices also provide information that can be analyzed to assist decision mak-ing. For example, some investors use futures prices as the market's best estimate for future spot prices. The price formation function enhances market efficiency as participants in both the spot and derivatives markets trade based on their information and analysis.

INVESTMENT COST REDUCTION

As the derivatives markets have evolved, commissions are generally lower than in the corre-sponding cash market. Liquidity in this market is also enhanced as many hedgers and spec-ulators trade derivatives. Investors can easily bet on the direction of the stock market by purchasing a single futures contract that represents an entire index. Portfolio managers can quickly adjust their portfolio's risk exposures to commodities, currencies, stocks, or interest rates at lower cost by using futures instead of spot-market trades. Unlike a spot-market transaction, commodity derivative contracts do not require the purchaser to pay for storing the commodity. Additionally, margin requirements are less in futures transactions than they are on the spot market.

Although they may seem esoteric and daunting at first, derivatives play an important economic role in allocating risk, forming prices, and facilitating transactions. Similar to other investment vehicles, careless or improper use of derivatives can lead to large losses. When taking a large position in one market, even risk-loving speculators will often hedge their risk to limit their loss by taking an offsetting position in another market.

Forward Contracts

Interactive e-lectures

For more expla-nation and an animated example of for-ward contracts, go to: http://reillyxtra .swlearning.com.

A *forward contract* is an agreement between two parties to exchange an asset at a specified price at a specified date. Because it is a contract, the buyer is obligated to purchase the asset and the seller is obligated to sell at the predetermined price (the exercise price) on the specified date (the expiration date). The buyer of the contract is said to be *long forward;* the seller is said to be *short forward.*

Forward contracts are traded over the counter and are generally not standardized, mean-ing that as long as the buyer and seller negotiate agreeable terms, they can create their own forward contract on virtually any commodity. But this flexibility has a major drawback: *for-ward contracts are not liquid.* Should a buyer (or seller) wish to get out of a forward agree-ment, she needs to find another party to purchase it. Another potential problem with forwards is credit risk or default risk. The contract may not be executed as planned if the buyer can-not raise the cash needed to purchase the asset, or if the seller commits fraud by not deliv-ering the asset to be sold.

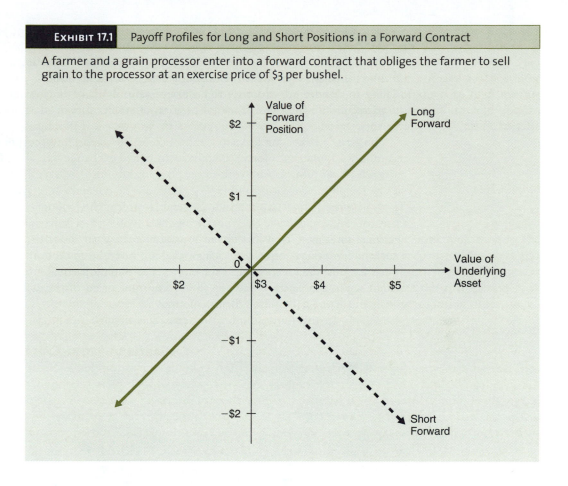

EXHIBIT 17.1 Payoff Profiles for Long and Short Positions in a Forward Contract

A farmer and a grain processor enter into a forward contract that obliges the farmer to sell grain to the processor at an exercise price of $3 per bushel.

The profit or loss on a forward contract relates directly to the relationship between the actual market price of the underlying asset and the exercise price contained in the contract. The value of a forward contract is realized only at the expiration date; no payments are made at the initiation of the contract and no cash transfers are made prior to expiration.

As shown in Exhibit 17.1, if the market price rises above the exercise price, the buyer gains (and the seller loses, because the asset will be sold at a price below current value); should the price fall below the exercise price, the buyer loses (and the seller gains, because the asset is sold for a price greater than its current value). Suppose a grain processor buys a forward contract from a farmer for October delivery of grain at a price of $3 a bushel. Exhibit 17.1 shows the grain processor's payoff profile for her long forward position (heavy arrow). Should the October spot-market price be $3 a bushel, the processor breaks even as the spot price equals the previously set forward price. If the October spot price is $4 a bushel, the processor gains $1 a bushel by purchasing grain that has a $4 market value at the $3 forward price. The processor's profits rise dollar for dollar as the spot price rises above the $3 forward price. Conversely, the processor's losses increase dollar for dollar if the spot price falls below the $3 forward price. For instance, if the October spot price is only $2, the processor loses $1 per bushel; she is obligated to buy grain that has a $2 market value for the $3 forward price.

The situation is reversed for the farmer, who is short forward (dotted arrow). As the October spot-market price rises above $3 a bushel, the farmer suffers an *opportunity loss* since he is obligated to sell his grain for $3 a bushel. For example, if the market price is $4, he has a $1–per–bushel opportunity loss. Conversely, for October spot prices under $3, the farmer gains a dollar-for-dollar *opportunity profit*.

The diagram in Exhibit 17.1 is called a *payoff profile*; it illustrates the profits and losses on an investment. The payoff profile for a long forward position is similar to that from owning the underlying asset outright; price increases make the owner wealthier. Similarly, the payoff profile for a short forward position resembles that from a short sale of the underlying asset.

The large market for forward contracts in currencies allows corporations and financial institutions to enter into forward contracts to hedge exchange rate risks. The spot market for currencies is an informal network of financial institutions that trade large volumes of currencies by telephone or wire. Exhibit 17.2 illustrates the currency spot quotations that appear in *The Wall Street Journal*. Most major currencies of capitalist countries are included, although many of these currencies do not freely float with other currencies. In these cases, the exchange rates are established either by government order or by the country's central bank, which intervenes to keep the exchange rate at a given level. Note that quotes for a spot and several forward rates are included for most major trading partners of the United States.

For the example day—July 28, 2004—the spot price of the U.K. pound was $1.8229, which means that 1 million British pounds are equivalent to £1,000,000($1.8229/£) = $1,822,900. In the third column the same quote is inverted, that is, expressed as units of

---

EXHIBIT 17.2 Spot and Forward Exchange Rates

Exchange Rates

July 28, 2004

The foreign exchange mid-range rates below apply to trading among banks in amounts of $1 million and more, as quoted at 4 p.m. Eastern time by Reuters and other sources. Retail transactions provide fewer units of foreign currency per dollar.

Country	U.S. $ EQUIVALENT Wed	U.S. $ EQUIVALENT Tue	CURRENCY PER U.S. $ Wed	CURRENCY PER U.S. $ Tue
Argentina (Peso)-y	.3362	.3366	2.9744	2.9709
Australia (Dollar)	.6991	.6993	1.4304	1.4300
Bahrain (Dinar)	2.6526	2.6525	.3770	.3770
Brazil (Real)	.3275	.3265	3.0534	3.0628
Canada (Dollar)	.7522	.7506	1.3294	1.3323
1-month forward	.7518	.7502	1.3301	1.3330
3-months forward	.7512	.7496	1.3312	1.3340
6-months forward	.7504	.7488	1.3326	1.3355
Chile (Peso)	.001562	.001552	640.20	644.33
China (Renminbi)	.1208	.1208	8.2781	8.2781
Colombia (Peso)	.0003810	.0003779	2624.67	2646.20
Czech. Rep. (Koruna)				
Commercial rate	.03803	.03794	26.295	26.357
Denmark (Krone)	.1620	.1620	6.1728	6.1728
Ecuador (US Dollar)	1.0000	1.0000	1.0000	1.0000
Egypt (Pound)-y	.1612	.1610	6.2023	6.2100
Hong Kong (Dollar)	.1282	.1282	7.8003	7.8003
Hungary (Forint)	.004878	.004861	205.00	205.72
India (Rupee)	.02163	.02165	46.232	46.189
Indonesia (Rupiah)	.0001098	.0001100	9107	9091
Israel (Shekel)	.2209	.2213	4.5269	4.5188
Japan (Yen)	.008953	.009012	111.69	110.96
1-month forward	.008965	.009024	111.54	110.82
3-months forward	.008991	.009051	111.22	110.49
6-months forward	.009043	.009104	110.58	109.84
Jordan (Dinar)	1.4104	1.4104	.7090	.7090
Kuwait (Dinar)	3.3929	3.3921	.2947	.2948
Lebanon (Pound)	.0006606	.0006606	1513.78	1513.78
Malaysia (Ringgit)-b	.2632	.2632	3.7994	3.7994
Malta (Lira)	2.8367	2.8366	.3525	.3525
Mexico (Peso)				
Floating rate	.0874	.0871	11.4377	11.4877

Country	U.S. $ EQUIVALENT Wed	U.S. $ EQUIVALENT Tue	CURRENCY PER U.S. $ Wed	CURRENCY PER U.S. $ Tue
New Zealand (Dollar)	.6282	.6283	1.5918	1.5916
Norway (Krone)	.1427	.1418	7.0077	7.0522
Pakistan (Rupee)	.01718	.01714	58.207	58.343
Peru (new Sol)	.2922	.2923	3.4223	3.4211
Philippines (Peso)	.01787	.01781	55.960	56.148
Poland (Zloty)	.2732	.2725	3.6603	3.6697
Russia (Ruble)-a	.03438	.03437	29.087	29.095
Saudi Arabia (Riyal)	.2667	.2666	3.7495	3.7509
Singapore (Dollar)	.5786	.5797	1.7283	1.7250
Slovak Rep. (Koruna)	.03003	.03014	33.300	33.179
South Africa (Rand)	.1596	.1582	6.2657	6.3211
South Korea (Won)	.0008565	.0008587	1167.54	1164.55
Sweden (Krona)	.1306	.1308	7.6570	7.6453
Switzerland (Franc)	.7832	.7831	1.2768	1.2770
1-month forward	.7840	.7838	1.2755	1.2758
3-months forward	.7855	.7854	1.2731	1.2732
6-months forward	.7881	.7880	1.2689	1.2690
Taiwan (Dollar)	.02941	.02934	34.002	34.083
Thailand (Baht)	.02412	.02420	41.459	41.322
Turkey (Lira)	.00000067	.00000067	1492537	1492537
U.K. (Pound)	1.8229	1.8217	.5486	.5489
1-month forward	1.8178	1.8164	.5501	.5505
3-months forward	1.8085	1.8071	.5529	.5534
6-months forward	1.7952	1.7937	.5570	.5575
United Arab (Dirham)	.2723	.2723	3.6724	3.6724
Uruguay (Peso)				
Financial	.03400	.03410	29.412	29.326
Venezuela (Bolivar)	.000521	.000521	1919.39	1919.39
SDR	1.4565	1.4682	.6866	.6811
Euro	1.2046	1.2049	.8302	.8299

Special Drawing Rights (SDR) are based on exchange rates for the U.S., British, and Japanese currencies. Source: International Monetary Fund.

a-Russian Central Bank rate. b-Government rate. y-Floating rate.

Source: From *The Wall Street Journal*, July 29, 2004, p. C12. Copyright © 2004 Dow Jones. Reprinted by permission of Copyright Clearance Center.

U.K. currency per U.S. dollar; $1 million is equivalent to $1,000,000(£0.5486/$) = £548,600. On that same day, the one-month forward rate for pounds was $1.8178, which means that one could have entered into an agreement to buy £1,000,000 in one month at a price of $1,817,800. Of course, these quotes should not be interpreted as precise because they are based on a sampling of banks and represent large transactions. Moreover, the bid–ask spread does not appear in these quotes.

Futures Contracts

A *futures contract* is much like a forward contract in some ways. As with a forward, a futures contract obliges the owner to purchase the underlying asset at a specified price (the exercise price or futures price) on a specified day. The long (short) futures payoff profile is identical to the long (short) forward payoff profile shown in Exhibit 17.1. Futures, however, have two major distinctions that differentiate them from forwards.

First, futures have *less liquidity risk* because they are traded on major futures exchanges. Futures contracts have standardized terms and conditions, such as quality and quantity of the underlying asset and expiration dates. This standardization allows futures to be bought and sold in secondary markets, just like common stocks. Someone purchasing (or selling) a futures contract can offset his obligation by selling (or purchasing) the identical type of contract.

Second, futures have *less credit risk* or default risk than forwards. Purchasers and sellers of futures are required to deposit funds, the *initial margin,* in a margin account with the exchange's clearing corporation or clearinghouse. The initial margin requirement is usually 3 percent to 6 percent of the value of the contract. Funds are added to or subtracted from the margin account daily, reflecting that day's price changes in the futures contract (at the end of each trading day, a special exchange committee determines the approximate closing price, called the *settlement price,* for each futures contract). Thus, futures are cash-settled every day through this process known as *marking to the market.* Similar to common stocks, if an investor's margin account becomes too low, the maintenance margin limit is reached and the investor must place additional funds in the margin account or have his position closed.

Thus, rather than buying or selling futures from a specific investor, the futures exchange becomes the counterparty to all transactions. Should an investor default, the exchange, rather than a specific investor, covers any losses. But the daily settling of accounts through marking to the market and the maintenance margin requirements helps to prevent an investor's deficit from growing unchecked until contract maturity.

Futures markets are regulated by the Commodity Futures Trading Commission (CTFC), which oversees the exchanges and approves new contracts for trading. At contract expiration, cash or assets may be exchanged between the counterparties. Agricultural futures settle "in kind" (with assets) while financial contracts—futures on stock indexes or interest rates—settle in cash. Non-farmers can participate in agricultural futures; they just need to close out their contracts before expiration to prevent having to make or take delivery.

Exhibit 17.3 lists global futures exchanges and provides a few details about them. The Chicago Board of Trade (CBOT) remains the largest futures exchange, but it is rivaled by the Chicago Mercantile Exchange (CME). Although the CBOT specializes in grains, its biggest contract is its highly successful U.S. Treasury bond futures, which was launched in 1977 and has traditionally experienced the largest volume of any futures contract. The CME originally specialized in livestock futures, but most of its current volume comes from numerous successful futures on foreign currencies, stock indexes, and the Eurodollar. The third largest exchange is the New York Mercantile Exchange (NYMEX), which specializes

Exhibit 17.3	Global Futures Exchanges

Chicago Board of Trade (CBOT) Referred to as "The Board of Trade." The world's oldest and largest futures exchange. The primary exchange for futures on agricultural commodities and a major market for trading in financial futures, particularly on intermediate and long-term Treasury securities.

Chicago Mercantile Exchange (CME) Referred to as "The Merc." The second largest futures exchange. Originally specialized in livestock futures, but now most trading is in stock-index, interest rate, and foreign currency futures through its subsidiaries the Index and Option Market and the International Monetary Market.

Commodity Exchange (COMEX) Referred to as "Comex." The primary market for metal futures.

Eurex US An electronic futures exchange with trading in Treasury bond futures. Part of a global exchange, Eurex, which facilitates trading in a number of euro-denominated derivative products.

Kansas City Board of Trade (KCBT) Specializes in grain and has a small volume in stock-index futures. It was the first exchange to offer trading in stock index futures.

London International Financial Futures Exchange (LIFFE) Offers trading in interest rate and equity futures, options, swaps, and selected commodities including cocoa, sugar, and wheat.

Marche a Terme International de France (MATIF) Offers trading in short-term, medium-term, and long-term Eurobond futures; selected stock-index futures; and commodities.

MidAmerica Commodity Exchange (MCE) Referred to as "The MidAm." Trades scaled-down versions of many of the contracts on the Chicago Board of Trade and Chicago Mercantile Exchange.

Minneapolis Grain Exchange (MGE) Small volume of trading in grain futures.

New York Board of Trade (NYBOT) Trades in cocoa, coffee, sugar, cotton, and other commodities.

New York Futures Exchange (NYFE) Referred to as "NYFE" (pronounced "Nife"). Created out of the New York Stock Exchange. Specializes in stock-index futures and has a small volume of trading in a commodity futures index and in Treasury bond futures.

New York Mercantile Exchange (NYMEX) Referred to as "NYMEX." The primary market for energy futures.

Philadelphia Board of Trade (PBT) Created out of the Philadelphia Stock Exchange. Has a small volume of trading in currency futures. Features industry-based index options for gold and silver mining, oil service, bank, and utility industry sectors.

Twin Cities Board of Trade (TCBT) Created out of the Minneapolis Grain Exchange. Has a small volume of trading in currency futures.

in futures on energy products such as crude oil, gasoline, and heating oil. Trading on NYMEX has exploded in recent years because NYMEX's contracts enable firms to hedge the extremely volatile energy market.

As part of their marketing function, the futures exchanges develop futures contracts for outstanding assets that they believe will meet the needs of various traders and investors. In recent years futures trading began on two new contracts that may be of interest to individual and institutional investors. One, called the "mini" S&P 500 futures, allows futures trading on a contract that is one-tenth the value of the regular S&P 500 futures contract. The second allows futures trading on the value of the Dow Jones Industrial Average, one of the world's best-known stock-market indexes.

Exhibit 17.4 presents a sample of the futures quotation page from *The Wall Street Journal*. For example, a corn futures contract trades at the Chicago Board of Trade (CBT in *The Wall Street Journal*) and trades in units of 5,000 bushels. The price quoted is in cents per bushel. The September 2005 contract (on the sixth line of the left-hand column) opened at 251 cents per bushel, had a high of 251 cents per bushel, and a low of 248 cents per bushel. The settlement price, which is roughly the closing price and the price at which contracts are marked to market, was 248 cents per bushel. The settlement price was down by 3 cents per bushel from the previous day. During the lifetime of the September 2005 contract, its high was 299 and its low was 248. The open interest—the number of contracts currently outstanding—was 4,329. At the bottom of each commodity listing is summary information

EXHIBIT 17.4 Selected Futures Prices

Wednesday, July 28, 2004

Grain and Oilseed Futures

Corn (CBT)-5,000 bu.; cents per bu.

	OPEN	HIGH	LOW	SETTLE	CHG	LIFETIME HIGH	LIFETIME LOW	OPEN INT
Sept	222.00	223.25	217.50	218.50	-3.75	341.00	217.50	148,945
Dec	230.25	231.75	225.50	226.75	-4.00	341.50	225.50	310,364
Mr05	239.00	240.00	234.25	235.50	-3.75	342.00	234.25	59,766
May	245.00	245.25	240.50	241.50	-3.75	344.00	240.50	22,039
July	250.00	250.25	245.00	246.25	-3.75	342.00	245.00	18,805
Sept	251.00	251.00	248.00	248.00	-3.00	299.00	248.00	4,329
Dec	254.00	254.00	251.50	252.25	-2.25	288.50	235.00	11,703

Est vol 61,555; vol Tue 64,700; open int 576,695, +2,308.

Oats (CBT)-5,000 bu.; cents per bu.

	OPEN	HIGH	LOW	SETTLE	CHG	LIFETIME HIGH	LIFETIME LOW	OPEN INT
Sept	127.25	127.50	125.25	125.75	-2.00	190.00	123.25	2,633
Dec	135.00	135.25	133.25	133.25	-2.50	193.00	131.00	6,483
Mr05	140.00	140.25	139.75	140.25	-2.75	191.00	138.25	697

Est vol 624; vol Tue 759; open int 9,915, -265.

Soybeans (CBT)-5,000 bu.; cents per bu.

	OPEN	HIGH	LOW	SETTLE	CHG	LIFETIME HIGH	LIFETIME LOW	OPEN INT
Aug	662.00	666.00	625.00	627.00	-38.50	1026.00	521.00	18,325
Sept	604.00	608.75	580.50	582.50	-26.50	904.50	528.00	14,248
Nov	594.25	597.75	575.00	575.75	-21.25	802.00	483.00	108,095
Ja05	600.00	601.00	583.00	583.50	-19.50	800.00	573.00	10,530
Mar	607.00	607.00	590.00	590.75	-20.25	787.00	570.00	6,066
May	609.00	609.00	594.50	595.25	-18.25	775.00	594.50	5,450
July	609.00	611.00	598.00	598.00	-16.00	773.00	598.00	2,075
Aug	600.00	600.00	596.00	596.00	-9.00	712.00	596.00	25

Est vol 65,605; vol Tue 73,583; open int 166,302, +578.

Soybean Meal (CBT)-100 tons; $ per ton.

	OPEN	HIGH	LOW	SETTLE	CHG	LIFETIME HIGH	LIFETIME LOW	OPEN INT
Aug	212.70	212.70	197.50	198.80	-13.90	326.00	154.00	14,606
Sept	200.00	200.00	188.00	188.80	-11.20	299.50	154.00	21,656
Oct	182.10	184.00	178.00	178.80	-7.40	257.00	150.50	19,269
Dec	184.50	184.80	177.00	177.90	-6.90	252.00	150.00	46,336
Ja05	183.00	184.00	177.50	178.50	-6.80	249.50	161.50	8,139
Mar	186.00	186.10	180.00	181.80	-6.70	245.50	168.50	6,889
May	186.50	188.50	182.50	182.80	-6.00	242.00	182.50	6,439
July	191.30	191.50	186.00	188.00	-4.50	239.00	172.00	5,080
Aug	189.00	189.50	187.00	188.00	-4.00	231.00	185.00	1,802

Est vol 37,657; vol Tue 39,725; open int 133,006, +801.

Soybean Oil (CBT)-60,000 lbs.; cents per lb.

	OPEN	HIGH	LOW	SETTLE	CHG	LIFETIME HIGH	LIFETIME LOW	OPEN INT
Aug	24.24	24.24	23.23	23.25	-.99	34.52	19.05	12,275
Sept	23.42	23.47	22.60	22.64	-.94	33.45	19.01	17,592
Oct	22.71	22.76	22.00	22.03	-.86	30.85	19.00	15,727
Dec	22.20	22.20	21.40	21.49	-.68	29.55	18.98	60,429
Ja05	22.00	22.05	21.48	21.50	-.61	29.20	21.48	9,814
Mar	21.95	22.05	21.50	21.58	-.52	28.66	21.50	8,057
May	22.03	22.03	21.55	21.80	-.30	27.50	21.55	5,897
July	22.04	22.04	21.60	21.73	-.30	27.42	21.60	4,233
Aug	22.00	22.00	21.55	21.70	-.15	26.65	21.55	1,127

Est vol 32,647; vol Tue 34,945; open int 138,162, -239.

Rough Rice (CBT)-2,000 cwt.; cents per cwt.

	OPEN	HIGH	LOW	SETTLE	CHG	LIFETIME HIGH	LIFETIME LOW	OPEN INT
Sept	720.00	740.00	713.00	713.00	-5.50	955.00	688.00	1,099
Nov	725.00	738.00	708.00	708.00	-9.00	944.00	690.00	1,816
Ja05	728.00	728.00	728.00	728.00	-12.00	959.00	720.00	556

Est vol 392; vol Tue 221; open int 3,847, +41.

Wheat (CBT)-5,000 bu.; cents per bu.

	OPEN	HIGH	LOW	SETTLE	CHG	LIFETIME HIGH	LIFETIME LOW	OPEN INT
Sept	321.00	322.00	314.00	314.75	-6.50	432.50	314.00	87,664
Dec	335.00	336.00	327.00	327.50	-7.50	440.00	327.00	51,445
Mr05	345.00	347.50	339.00	339.25	-7.25	441.50	339.00	11,840
May	351.00	351.00	344.50	345.25	-5.75	430.00	344.50	724
July	353.00	353.00	350.00	350.00	-3.00	400.00	342.00	2,552

Est vol 23,311; vol Tue 16,312; open int 154,277, -401.

Wheat (KC)-5,000 bu.; cents per bu.

	OPEN	HIGH	LOW	SETTLE	CHG	LIFETIME HIGH	LIFETIME LOW	OPEN INT
Sept	349.50	350.50	342.50	343.00	-7.25	437.50	330.50	35,749
Dec	361.00	361.50	354.00	354.50	-6.50	444.00	341.00	28,384
Mr05	371.00	371.00	363.50	364.00	-6.75	443.00	363.50	6,991
May	373.00	373.00	368.50	368.50	-4.50	428.00	368.50	1,010
July	370.00	370.00	367.50	368.50	-3.50	405.00	365.00	554

Est vol 13,510; vol Tue 6,917; open int 72,704, +664.

Wheat (MPLS)-5,000 bu.; cents per bu.

	OPEN	HIGH	LOW	SETTLE	CHG	LIFETIME HIGH	LIFETIME LOW	OPEN INT
Sept	370.00	370.25	361.00	361.00	-9.00	453.50	346.00	13,794
Dec	376.50	377.25	370.00	370.00	-7.00	457.00	355.00	14,122
Mr05	383.75	383.75	378.00	378.00	-6.25	453.00	378.00	3,312
May	384.00	385.50	382.75	384.50	-3.50	440.00	382.75	634
July	386.00	386.00	384.50	384.50	-3.50	419.00	384.50	63

Est vol 9,285; vol Tue 4,508; open int 31,940, +820.

Index Futures

DJ Industrial Average (CBT)-$10 x index

	OPEN	HIGH	LOW	SETTLE	CHG	YIELD	CHG	OPEN INT
Sept	10062	10133	9975	10110	48	10557	9835	40,437
Dec	10030	10120	9980	10107	48	10575	8440	371

Est vol 11,349; vol Tue 8,164; open int 40,808, -161.
Idx prl: Hi 10146.86; Lo 9994.22; Close 10117.07, +31.93.

Mini DJ Industrial Average (CBT)-$5 x index

	OPEN	HIGH	LOW	SETTLE	CHG	YIELD	CHG	OPEN INT
Sept	10061	10134	9975	10110	48	10629	9840	48,861

Vol Wed 105,733; open int 48,945, +156.

DJ-AIG Commodity Index (CBT)-$100 x index

	OPEN	HIGH	LOW	SETTLE	CHG	YIELD	CHG	OPEN INT
Aug	...	...	...	460.2	4.3	485.0	449.4	2,886

Est vol 0; vol Tue 0; open int 2,886, unch.
Idx prl: Hi 147.050; Lo 144.121; Close 145.746, +1.405.

S&P 500 Index (CME)-$250 x index

	OPEN	HIGH	LOW	SETTLE	CHG	YIELD	CHG	OPEN INT
Sept	109580	109840	108100	109520	270	116080	78100	576,363
Dec	108600	109850	108240	109590	300	116010	78100	13,757

Est vol 41,751; vol Tue 40,253; open int 590,945, +1,457.
Idx prl: Hi 1098.84; Lo 1082.17; Close 1095.42, +.59.

Mini S&P 500 (CME)-$50 x index

	OPEN	HIGH	LOW	SETTLE	CHG	YIELD	CHG	OPEN INT
Sept	109575	109575	109525	109520	270	114850	107500	584,465

Vol Wed 803,233; open int 632,008, -10,108.

S&P Midcap 400 (CME)-$500 x index

	OPEN	HIGH	LOW	SETTLE	CHG	YIELD	CHG	OPEN INT
Sept	572.50	573.50	564.75	571.25	-2.15	616.50	508.70	13,543

Est vol 424; vol Tue 407; open int 13,543, -97.
Idx prl: Hi 574.02; Lo 565.22; Close 571.02, -3.00.

Nasdaq 100 (CME)-$100 x index

	OPEN	HIGH	LOW	SETTLE	CHG	YIELD	CHG	OPEN INT
Sept	138450	139500	136150	138500	-550	156500	136000	70,777

Est vol 14,056; vol Tue 12,979; open int 73,072, +753.
Idx prl: Hi 1387.62; Lo 1360.27; Close 1374.84, -16.66.

Mini Nasdaq 100 (CME)-$20 x index

	OPEN	HIGH	LOW	SETTLE	CHG	YIELD	CHG	OPEN INT
Sept	1384.5	1386.0	1384.5	1385.0	-5.5	1528.5	1360.0	228,151

Vol Wed 428,512; open int 233,013, +3,001.

GSCI (CME)-$250 x nearby index

	OPEN	HIGH	LOW	SETTLE	CHG	YIELD	CHG	OPEN INT
Aug	...	...	...	304.40	4.00	308.50	279.45	16,480

Est vol 322; vol Tue 47; open int 16,480, +6.
Idx prl: Hi 305.28; Lo 300.32; Close 304.95, +5.08.

Interest Rate Futures

Treasury Bonds (CBT)-$100,000; pts 32nds of 100%

	OPEN	HIGH	LOW	SETTLE	CHG	YIELD	CHG	OPEN INT
Sept	106-16	106-28	106-05	106-26	3	114-30	101-24	517,124
Dec	105-13	105-20	105-00	105-20	3	113-07	100-24	18,169

Est vol 292,509; vol Tue 357,491; open int 535,533, +10,056.

Treasury Notes (CBT)-$100,000; pts 32nds of 100%

	OPEN	HIGH	LOW	SETTLE	CHG	YIELD	CHG	OPEN INT
Sept	109-17	09-275	09-115	09-265	5.5	15-095	106-13	1,392,182
Dec	08-115	08-195	108-07	08-195	5.5	13-045	105-14	50,328

Est vol 899,198; vol Tue 870,279; open int 1,442,701, +64,902.

5 Yr. Treasury Notes (CBT)-$100,000; pts 32nds of 100%

	OPEN	HIGH	LOW	SETTLE	CHG	YIELD	CHG	OPEN INT
Sept	08-235	109-00	108-20	08-305	4.5	112-15	106-29	1,186,864

Est vol 520,849; vol Tue 399,990; open int 1,287,718, +34,675.

2 Yr. Treasury Notes (CBT)-$200,000; pts 32nds of 100%

	OPEN	HIGH	LOW	SETTLE	CHG	YIELD	CHG	OPEN INT
Sept	105-08	05-117	105-07	05-115	2.5	106-01	04-187	191,177

Est vol 29,485; vol Tue 23,643; open int 191,577, -251.

30 Day Federal Funds (CBT)-$5,000,000; 100 - daily avg.

	OPEN	HIGH	LOW	SETTLE	CHG	YIELD	CHG	OPEN INT
July	...	...	...	98.740	...	98.970	97.750	124,453
Aug	98.57	98.58	98.57	98.58	...	98.94	98.37	211,048
Sept	98.42	98.43	98.41	98.43	.01	98.90	98.14	74,132
Oct	98.25	98.26	98.24	98.26	.01	98.85	98.24	79,329
Nov	98.04	98.06	98.03	98.05	.01	98.96	97.74	68,218
Dec	97.87	97.88	97.83	97.86	...	98.93	97.55	38,638
Ja05	97.77	97.78	97.77	97.78	.01	98.30	97.47	12,121

Est vol 38,473; vol Tue 42,111; open int 609,719, +5,461.

10 Yr. Interest Rate Swaps (CBT)-$100,000; pts 32nds of 100%

	OPEN	HIGH	LOW	SETTLE	CHG	YIELD	CHG	OPEN INT
Sept	106-05	106-18	106-03	106-17	3	108-16	103-19	51,838

Est vol 1,202; vol Tue 687; open int 51,838, -52.

10 Yr. Muni Note Index (CBT)-$1,000 x index

	OPEN	HIGH	LOW	SETTLE	CHG	YIELD	CHG	OPEN INT
Sept	100-14	100-28	100-14	100-25	2	102-00	97-25	2,483

Est vol 74; vol Tue 536; open int 2,483, -69.
Index: Close 101-15; Yield 4.815.

1 Month Libor (CME)-$3,000,000; pts of 100%

	OPEN	HIGH	LOW	SETTLE	CHG	YIELD	CHG	OPEN INT
Aug	98.39	98.40	98.39	98.39	...	1.61	...	183,713
Sept	98.20	98.20	98.20	98.20	...	1.80	...	29,899
Oct	98.06	98.07	98.06	98.07	.01	1.93	-.01	252,910
Nov	97.83	97.83	97.82	97.83	.01	2.17	-.01	98,653

Est vol 11,746; vol Tue 6,669; open int 571,014, +174.

on the overall volume, the volume on the previous day, and the overall open interest for the commodity.

The upper right-hand column of the exhibit contains the stock-index futures contracts. For instance, S&P 500 futures trades at the Chicago Mercantile Exchange (CME) and its price is 250 times the index. The December contract opened at 1086.00, which means the value of the contract was actually 250×1086.00 or $271,500. The high during the day was 1098.50, the low was 1082.40, and the settlement price was 1095.90, up 3.00 from the previous day. At the bottom of the S&P 500 listing is information on futures volume, open interest, and the value of the S&P 500 index, which closed at 1095.42 the previous day.

The lower right-hand column of the exhibit contains information on interest rate futures. For example, the Treasury bond contract on the Chicago Board of Trade is for $100,000 face value of Treasury bonds and the price quote is in $\frac{1}{32}$ of 100 percent of face value. The settlement price of the December contract is $105\frac{20}{32}$, up $\frac{3}{32}$ from the previous day. This is an actual price of $(105\frac{20}{32}) \times \$100,000 = \$105,625$. The rightmost column of the exhibit contains the open interest, and the bottom line below the Treasury bond futures listing contains volume and open interest information on all contracts.

The Chicago Mercantile Exchange trades futures based on the currencies of the leading trading partners of the United States. The currency futures market is quite active, although it is smaller than the over-the-counter currency forward market. Current trading is in the Japanese yen, Canadian dollar, British pound, Swiss franc, Australian dollar, Mexican peso, and the euro. The most active trading is in the yen and euro contracts.

Exhibit 17.5 presents a sample of the quotations from *The Wall Street Journal* for currency futures. For example, a yen contract is for 12.5 million yen, with the settlement price

EXHIBIT 17.5	Currency Futures Prices

	OPEN	HIGH	LOW	SETTLE	CHG	LIFETIME HIGH	LIFETIME LOW·	OPEN INT
Japanese Yen (CME)-¥12,500,000; $ per ¥								
Sept	.9038	.9042	.8952	.8968	−.0055	.9705	.8575	96,721
Dec	.9035	.9073	.9004	.9013	−.0055	.9740	.8800	10,441
Mr05	.9060	.9060	.9060	.9067	−.0055	.9762	.8873	5
Est vol 12,902; vol Tue 28,442; open int 107,170, −117.								
Canadian Dollar (CME)-CAD 100,000; $ per CAD								
Sept	.7500	.7536	.7466	.7522	.0028	.7815	.6505	69,921
Dec	.7471	.7530	.7462	.7515	.0028	.7800	.6940	4,585
Mr05	.7500	.7505	.7472	.7510	.0028	.7775	.7150	785
June	.7515	.7515	.7515	.7505	.0028	.7760	.7150	562
Est vol 8,649; vol Tue 16,068; open int 75,905, −308.								
British Pound (CME)-£62,500; $ per £								
Sept	1.8135	1.8182	1.8076	1.8153	.0016	1.8712	1.6330	66,824
Dec	1.7940	1.8040	1.7940	1.8009	.0016	1.8648	1.6850	428
Est vol 9,914; vol Tue 21,625; open int 67,259, −2,860.								
Swiss Franc (CME)-CHF 125,000; $ per CHF								
Sept	.7846	.7874	.7822	.7847	.0002	.8209	.7110	39,908
Dec	.7888	.7888	.7859	.7872	.0002	.8260	.7264	138
Est vol 10,253; vol Tue 21,291; open int 40,111, +430.								
Australian Dollar (CME)-AUD 100,000; $ per AUD								
Sept	.6964	.6987	.6915	.6960	.0009	.7780	.5756	28,008
Dec	.6865	.6906	.6865	.6899	.0009	.7705	.6150	278
Est vol 4,830; vol Tue 14,268; open int 28,377, −4,755.								
Mexican Peso (CME)-MXN 500,000; $ per MXN								
Aug	...	...	...	.08732	00050	.08760	.08730	400
Sept	.08650	.08720	.08630	.08682	00050	.08935	.08370	38,161
Dec	.08505	.08530	.08505	.08552	00050	.08855	.08270	1,350
Est vol 5,126; vol Tue 17,647; open int 40,408, −3,562.								

Source: From *The Wall Street Journal*, July 29, 2004, p. C12. Copyright © 2004 Dow Jones. Reprinted by permission of Copyright Clearance Center.

of the March 2005 yen contract equal to 0.9067. However, because there are so many yen in a dollar, it is understood that two decimal places precede the price. Thus, the actual price is $.009067 per yen. For a full contract, the price is ¥12,500,000 × $.009067/¥ = $113,337.5.

The use of futures contracts in investment portfolios is widespread among professional managers. Cash inflows to an equity portfolio can be used to purchase S&P 500 futures to prevent the cash from diluting the portfolio's equity exposure. Because of the use of margin, only a fraction of the cash inflows need to be invested to maintain the appropriate equity exposure for the portfolio. After suitable stocks for investment are selected, the futures positions are sold and the excess cash is invested in the selected securities. Futures can be used to assist an indexing strategy and to adjust portfolio asset allocation quickly. Equity and bond futures can be traded to immediately tilt a portfolio toward the preferred asset class. Then, over time, asset positions can be liquidated and new securities purchased while the futures positions are unwound.

Options

As described earlier, an *option* grants an investor the right to buy or sell an asset at a fixed price on or before a specific point in time. An option to buy an asset is referred to as a *call option,* whereas an option to sell an asset is called a *put option.* Buyers of options (either calls or puts) are said to be *long* and sellers (or option writers) are said to be *short.*

The price paid for the option itself is called the **option premium**. The price at which the asset can be acquired or sold is the *exercise price* or *strike price.* For example, if a stock call option has an exercise price of $45, it means that this call option permits the owner of the option to buy the stock for $45 a share. If the underlying stock's current market price is $50, the call option has an intrinsic value of $5, as it allows the holder to pay $45 for something that has a market value of $50. If the underlying stock's price is $40, the call option's intrinsic value is $0; it is worthless, and the holder will choose not to exercise the option as it makes little sense to pay $45 (the exercise price) for something that has a spot-market value of $40. In general, if V is the underlying stock's price and X is the option's exercise price, the call option's intrinsic value is

17.1 **Call Option Intrinsic Value = Max $\left[0, V - X\right]$**

or the maximum of $0 and the value of the underlying stock price minus the exercise price.

Suppose a put option permits its owner to sell the stock for $45 a share. If the underlying stock's current market price is $40, the put option has an intrinsic value of $5 as it allows the holder to sell for $45 an asset that has a market value of only $40. If the underlying stock's price is $50, the put option's intrinsic value is $0; it is worthless, and the holder will choose not to exercise the option as it makes little sense to sell an asset for $45 (the exercise price) when he can go to the spot market and sell it for $50. In general, a put option's intrinsic value is

17.2 **Put Option Intrinsic Value = Max $\left[0, X - V\right]$**

or the maximum of $0 and the value of the exercise price minus the underlying stock price.

For both puts and calls, an *at-the-money option* has an exercise price approximately equal to the stock price. An *in-the-money option* has an intrinsic value. An *out-of-the-money option* has no intrinsic value and will not be exercised because the holder can buy the stock for less in the market (out-of-the-money call) or sell it for more (out-of-the-money put). However, an out-of-the-money option can subsequently become in-the-money and vice

EXHIBIT 17.6	Important Option Terminology
Term	**Definition**
Call option	Right to purchase an asset at a specific price on or before a specific date
Put option	Right to sell an asset at a specific price on or before a specific date
Option premium	Price paid by the investor to purchase the option contract
Exercise or strike price	Price at which the underlying asset can be bought or sold
Expiration date	Date on which the option to exercise the contract expires
Write an option	Sell an option contract
At-the-money	Exercise price is the same as the underlying asset spot price
In-the-money	The option has some positive intrinsic value; trading at the exercise price is more attractive to the option holder than trading at the market price for the underlying asset. For calls, asset spot price exceeds exercise price; it is cheaper to buy the asset at the exercise price. For puts, asset spot price is less than exercise price; more is gained by selling the asset at the exercise price.
Out-of-the-money	The option has no intrinsic value; trading at the spot price is more attractive to the option holder rather than trading at the exercise price. For calls, asset spot price is less than exercise price; it is cheaper to buy the asset at the spot price. For puts, asset spot price exceeds exercise price; more is gained by selling the asset at the spot price.

versa prior to expiration. In reality, few options are exercised; in-the-money options are usually closed out before the expiration date, giving the holder a profit on the difference between the premium paid for the option and the premium received when it is sold.

The date on which the option expires, or the last date on which it can be exercised, is the *expiration date*. For options trading on exchanges, expiration dates are typically specified in terms of a given month, and the time within the month is likewise specified as the Saturday following the third Friday. Thus, a July option would expire the Saturday following the third Friday in July. However, off the exchanges, options can be created by any two parties and can have any expiration date desired. Options that trade on exchanges are generally fairly liquid so that they can be sold before expiration.

Some options permit the holder to exercise them only on the expiration day. These are called *European options*. Those that permit the holder to exercise any time up to and including the expiration day are called *American options*. These names have no relationship to geography; both European and American options trade extensively on exchanges and in OTC markets throughout the world.

Exhibit 17.6 summarizes some option-contract terminology. Exhibit 17.7 summarizes some of the major distinctions between forwards, futures, and option contracts.

OPTION EXCHANGES

In 1973 the Chicago Board of Trade (CBOT), then the largest futures exchange, created a separate exchange called the Chicago Board Options Exchange (CBOE). Since then, other options exchanges have appeared, including the American, Philadelphia, Boston, Pacific, and International Security Exchange. Exchange-traded options offer traders a number of features that did not exist in the OTC options markets. On the exchanges, options are traded in a central marketplace with regulatory, surveillance, disclosure, and price discovery capabilities. The Clearing Corporation is the guarantor of every CBOE option; similar arrangements exist for other exchanges. Standing as the opposite party to every trade, the Clearing Corporation all but eliminates counterparty risk and enables buyers and sellers of options to terminate their positions in the market at any time by making an offsetting transaction.

Exhibit 17.7	Differences between Forwards, Futures, and Options	
Forward Contract	**Futures Contract**	**Option Contract**
Obligation to trade at time T at a specified price	Obligation to trade at time T at a specified price	Option to trade at time T at a specified price
Traded OTC	Exchange traded	Exchange traded
Terms are not standardized	Standardized terms	Standardized terms
Poor secondary market (not liquid)	Liquid (varies among contracts)	Liquid (varies among contracts)
Settlement occurs at expiration	Daily settlement (marking to the market)	Daily settlement
Close long position by selling identical contract to another party or to the original seller	Close long position by selling the contract on the exchange	Close long position by selling the contract on the exchange
Exposed to credit/default risk by the counterparty	No credit/default risk	No credit/default risk
Can earn a profit or loss on the position	Can earn a profit or loss on the position	Can limit losses by choosing not to exercise the option

Exhibit 17.8	Examples of Exchange-Traded Options
Stocks	**Market Sectors**
Indexes:	Gold index
Dow Jones Industrial Average	Internet index
NYSE	Oil index
Russell 2000	Technology index
Nasdaq 100	Interest rates:
S&P 500	13-week Treasury bills
Japan	5-year Treasury notes
Mexico	10-year Treasury notes
	Commodities:
	Corn
	Wheat

In addition, exchange-traded options have standardized expiration dates and standardized exercise prices. Options are available with exercise prices that bracket the current stock price. Exercise prices are generally set in five-dollar intervals. As a stock price moves, additional options with new exercise prices are added. Contracts are standardized, too, at 100 shares per contract. Adjustments are made for stock splits and stock dividends, which can create odd-lot option contracts.

Before option exchanges were established, the buyers and sellers of over-the-counter options were essentially committed to their positions until the expiration date. The Clearing Corporation and the standardization of contract features make feasible a secondary market for options.

Exhibit 17.8 lists index options that trade on various exchanges. Index options have special appeal because they involve taking a position on a market or sector as a whole, rather than on individual stocks.

Exhibit 17.9 presents a sample of the option quotation page from *The Wall Street Journal*. Let's consider buying a call option on Microsoft. Under Microsoft's name is the prior day's closing price on Microsoft stock: $28.48. Next to Microsoft's name, in the second and third columns, are the exercise (or strike) prices and expiration dates on Microsoft option contracts. The fourth and fifth columns give the day's trading volume and the last price (or premium) for a call option contract trade; the sixth and seventh columns present the trad-

EXHIBIT 17.9	Stock Option Quotations					
			CALL		PUT	
	OPTION/STRIKE	EXP	VOL	LAST	VOL	LAST
MerrLyn	50	Aug	3,812	1.40	371	1.05
50.36	55	Sep	1,032	0.35	1	5.10
50.36	55	Oct	892	0.85	12	5.20
MetLife	35	Aug	1,480	0.70	. . .	. . .
MicrochpT	30	Aug	2,097	0.60	42	2
MicronT	12	Aug	2,881	1.55	1	0.10
13.52	13	Aug	1,618	0.85	121	0.35
13.52	14	Aug	716	0.35	149	0.85
13.52	14	Sep	1,266	0.65	75	1.15
13.52	17.50	Jan	3,092	0.45	40	4.30
Microsft	25	Oct	425	3.50	65	0.20
28.48	27.50	Aug	7,543	1	2,080	0.20
28.48	27.50	Sep	221	1.40	655	0.50
28.48	27.50	Jan	893	2.15	1,042	1.20
28.48	30	Aug	2,026	0.10	878	1.75
28.48	30	Sep	1,011	0.25	1,462	1.90
28.48	30	Oct	957	0.45	176	2
28.48	**30**	**Jan**	**1,802**	**0.95**	**10,048**	**2.50**
28.48	32.50	Jan	7,292	0.35	115	4.30
MidwyGm	10	Aug	94	1.55	617	0.10
Mohawk	65	Aug	. . .	. . .	1,000	0.15
MorgStan	50	Aug	3,656	1.10	247	1.15
49.90	50	Jan	122	3.60	1,592	3.80
49.90	55	Oct	502	0.65	. . .	. . .
49.90	60	Oct	505	0.15	. . .	. . .
Motorola	16	Aug	678	0.60	431	0.55
MultimGm	20	Aug	. . .	. . .	1,831	0.35
24.54	22.50	Aug	20	2.85	475	0.85
Mylan	15	Aug	7,974	0.60	1,259	0.75
14.83	15	Sep	1,591	0.80	63	0.95
NCR	50	Sep	407	0.55	. . .	. . .
NTL Inc	50	Sep	670	4.60	. . .	. . .
Nabors	45	Aug	2,948	1.80	65	0.70

Source: From *The Wall Street Journal*, July 30, 2004. Copyright © 2004 Dow Jones. Reprinted by permission of Copyright Clearance Center.

ing volume and last price (or premium) for a put option trade. If ". . ." appears under the call or put columns, it indicates that the option contract did not trade that day. Look at the last trade on the Microsoft January 30 call: The option premium is $0.95 per share. Because each contract is for 100 calls, the total option premium cost is $95.00.

The fact that option premiums are small, in comparison to the stock's market price, can lead to rather large percentage gains (or losses) on the option buyer's invested capital. This is called *leverage* by option investors. Let's look at what happens when the price of the underlying stock rises before the option expires. Suppose we purchase the above-mentioned January 30 call option for $0.95 per share and Microsoft's stock rises to $31.33 by the option expiration date, an increase of 10 percent. The stockholder's return would be the same as this increase, 10 percent. But the call option's intrinsic value on the expiration date will be $1.33—namely, $31.33 less the exercise price of $30. The investment of $0.95 per share grew to a value of $1.33 per share, a percentage return of ($1.33 − $0.95)/$0.95 = 40 percent, far above the stockholder's percentage return.

What if Microsoft's stock price fell 10 percent, so by the expiration date the call option is out of the money? The stockholder faces a 10 percent loss on her investment. But the option holder faces a 100 percent loss; his option expires out of the money, worthless.[2] The option's leverage is clear: Because a relatively small premium controls much value, small percentage changes in the value of the stock can result in large percentage changes for an option position.

OPTION TRADING STRATEGIES

Investors quickly learned that option trading greatly increases the number and complexity of investment strategies. We will not attempt to cover all the strategies, but will limit our discussion to the major alternatives. We explicitly take option premiums into consideration as we consider profits and losses from various option positions.

For the option trading strategies we shall examine, let's assume that the following options are available for trading.

Exercise Price (per share)	Call Premium (per share)	Put Premium
70	6.13	2.25
75	3.50	4.75

We will assume the stock price is $73.25, and, for simplicity, we will ignore taxes and commissions and treat the options as European options. In addition, we will assume all strategies are held to expiration. Although this is not required and usually is not done, we cannot understand how to evaluate trading strategies closed out before expiration without a better grasp of option-pricing theory.

Buying Call Options   Investors buy call options because they expect the price of the underlying stock to increase during the period prior to the expiration of the option. If this occurs, the purchase of an option may yield a large return on a small dollar investment.

Consider the purchase of the call option with a $70 exercise price (we will refer to this as the 70 call). We would pay 100 × $6.13 or $613.00 for this call. The overall profit from the long call option transaction can be stated as

17.3 $$\text{Long Call Option Profit} = \text{Max}\,[\,0,\,V - X\,] - \text{Call Premium}$$

---

[2]We ignore commissions and taxes for simplicity in this example.

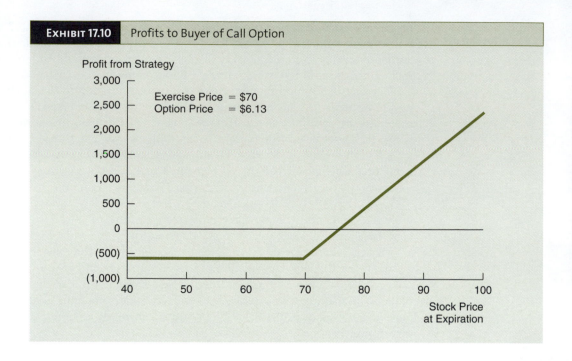

EXHIBIT 17.10 Profits to Buyer of Call Option

If the stock price ends up at $68, the profit is Max $[0, 68 - 70] - 6.13 = -6.13$, or a loss of $6.13 per option. If the stock price ends up at $75, the profit is Max $[0, 75 - 70] - 6.13 = -1.13$, or a loss of $1.13 per option. We would break even if the stock price at expiration is $70 (the exercise price) + $6.13 (the call premium), or $76.13.

Exhibit 17.10 illustrates these results in the form of a payoff diagram that reflects the initial cost of the option premium. Losses for the call-buying strategy are limited to the option premium, $613.00 per contract. No limit exists on the upside because the stock price can rise without limit. Investors need to be careful about interpreting potential option profits and losses. The lure of potentially large profits with limited dollar losses must be tempered with the fact that the large profits occur quite rarely, whereas small losses occur quite frequently.

Suppose we had chosen the out-of-the-money option with the $75 exercise price and paid a call premium of only $3.50. This option would have limited our overall loss to $350. However, the stock price will have to rise to $78.50 ($75 exercise price + $3.50 call premium) at expiration before we will make a profit.

Buying call options can be part of a prudent tax strategy for some investors. For example, suppose a portfolio manager owns stock that has fallen in value but the manager still likes the stock's longer-term prospects. Here's the strategy: Toward the end of the calendar year (usually toward the end of November), the portfolio manager can buy a call option that expires sometime in the next year, say January. Thirty-one days[3] after buying the call but before the end of the tax year the manager can sell the stock, thereby generating a cap-

---

[3]Any buying and selling of similar securities is called a *wash sale,* and the U.S. tax code disallows any tax advantage—such as capital losses offsetting other capital gains—from a wash sale. This is why the investor cannot sell the shares at a depressed price and immediately repurchase them. But the use of the call option helps to preserve the currently depressed price of the stock until the option expires, allowing the investor to avoid the wash sale problem.

| EXHIBIT 17.11 | Profits to Seller of Uncovered Call Option |

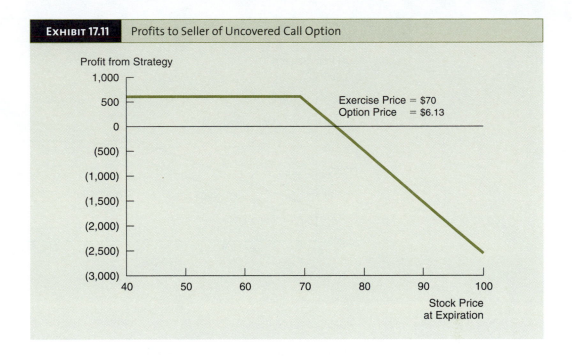

ital loss that can be used to offset any capital gains and reduce taxes. Before the option expires in January, the manager can exercise it and reestablish a position in the stock at the low exercise price.

Selling Call Options   Now let's look at the profits for the individual who sold, or wrote, the 70 call. When a call is sold, the writer receives the premium, which in this case is $6.13 (or, more properly, $6.13 × 100 shares or $613.00). If we assume the seller does not own the stock, this transaction is referred to as an *uncovered* or *naked call option,* for reasons that will become apparent.

The seller of the call will *owe* the value Max [0, V − X] at expiration because the seller may have to buy the stock at its market price, V, and sell it at X. If the stock price is substantially greater than the exercise price, the seller of the option can incur a large loss.

Exhibit 17.11 is a graph of the seller's profits, which you should recognize as simply Exhibit 17.10 inverted. The seller of the option can earn a maximum amount equal to the premium of $613.00, which is retained if the option ends up out of the money. The seller's loss is potentially unlimited.[4]

The risk of unlimited losses explains why we refer to this option writing strategy as uncovered or naked. If, however, the writer owns the stock, this is a *covered call option.* In this case, if the call option is exercised, the covered call writer need not buy the stock in the market. He or she simply delivers the stock held, effectively selling it for the exercise price. Thus out-of-pocket losses are minimal, aside from an opportunity cost if the option expires in the money (that is, the writer of the call option sells the stock at a price below current market value).

---

[4]Clearly, the seller can be "wiped out." For that reason, the seller's broker will generally require the seller to post margin money. Another way to reduce the risk of disaster is for the seller to own the stock, a strategy we shall examine next.

EXHIBIT 17.12 Profits to Seller of Covered Call Option

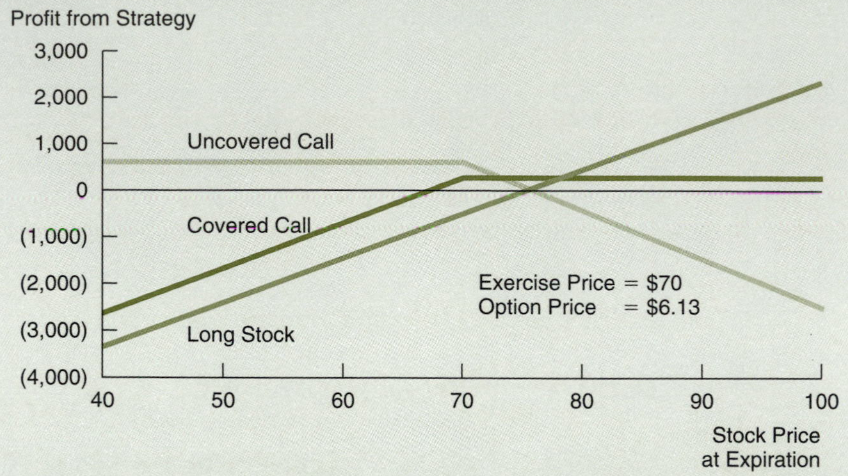

Profit from Strategy

Uncovered Call

Covered Call

Long Stock

Exercise Price = $70
Option Price = $6.13

Stock Price
at Expiration

The profit to the call writer from a covered call can be broken down into two components: the profit from writing the call and the profit on the stock held. The profit from writing the call is

17.4   **Short Call Option Profit = $-$Max $[0, V - X]$ + Call Premium**

The profit on the stock is either the current value V minus the original price the investor paid for the stock if the call expires out of the money, or the exercise price minus the original stock purchase price if the call expires in the money.

Exhibit 17.12 shows the profits of the writer of the covered call; graphically as well as arithmetically it equals the combined profits of its component strategies, the long position in the stock plus an uncovered call. If the stock falls, the covered call writer keeps the premium and the stock, while the premium received cushions against the loss in value of the stock. On the upside, however, the covered call writer's gains are limited because the stock must be sold for the exercise price regardless of how much it is worth in the market.

Covered call writers are considered to be smart option traders because they capitalize on the public's excessive optimism about potential stock price moves. If the public is indeed overly optimistic, a covered call writer can collect the premiums, knowing that the stock is unlikely to move high enough to justify the premium. Many covered call writers view this as an opportunity to generate income from a slow-moving stock.

Buying Put Options   Several major reasons exist for acquiring a put option on a stock. The most obvious is that an investor expects a particular stock to decline in price and wants to profit from this decline. Buying put options offers two advantages over selling the stock short: (1) the losses are limited to the put premium and (2) costly short-sale margin requirements are avoided. In addition, put options can serve as a hedge if you own a stock and do not want to sell it at the present time although you believe it might decline in the near term. In this case, you can buy a put option on the stock you own as a hedge against the decline; if the stock does decline, you will offset the decline with an increase in the value of the put option.

Exhibit 17.13	Profits to Buyer of Put Option

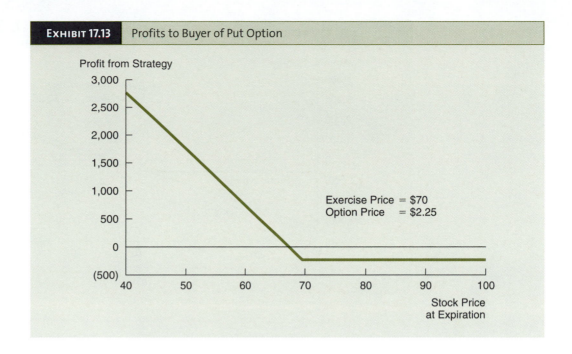

Consider the strategy of purchasing the 70 put for $2.25. The put will be worth Max [0, X − V] at expiration. Thus, the profit from buying the put can be expressed as

17.5   **Long Put Option Profit = Max [0, X − V] − Put Option Premium**

Suppose the stock price ends up at $60. The $60 stock can be sold for $70, netting a profit of $10 − $2.25 = $7.75 per share, or $775 per contract. If the stock price ends up at $80, the option expires worthless and the put holder loses the $225 premium. Exhibit 17.13 shows the profits for the put buyer and that the put buyer's loss is limited to the premium of $225. The gains are limited because the stock price can never fall below zero. If the company went bankrupt, the stock could theoretically fall to zero and the put buyer would make $70 − $2.25 = $67.75 per option or $6,775 overall. Of course, this extreme case is quite unlikely.

One of the more attractive strategies employing puts is called the *protective put*. This involves the purchase of a put accompanied by a long position in the stock. Should the price of the stock decline below the exercise price, the rising value of the put option will offset the decline in the stock price. Similar to the covered call, the profit from this strategy can be broken down into the profit from the stock plus the profit from the put option.

Exhibit 17.14 graphically illustrates the returns on a protective put by combining the payoff diagrams for a stock purchase with those of a long put position. Notice that the protective put payoff diagram resembles that of the long call in Exhibit 17.10. In fact, it is sometimes referred to as a *synthetic call* because the holder of the protective put has limited losses and unlimited gains. Thus, two different option trading strategies result in similar payoffs regardless of the stock's price at expiration. We will return to this interesting point in our discussion of put/call parity later in this chapter.

The protective put is also a classic example of how to insure (hedge) a stock position. The holder of the stock can be viewed as someone holding an asset at risk of losing value. Some investors might be interested in purchasing insurance that would limit the losses on

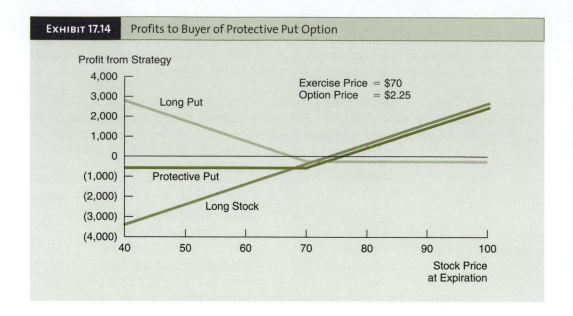

EXHIBIT 17.14 Profits to Buyer of Protective Put Option

the asset. The put serves as this insurance. By paying the premium up front, the insurer (the put writer) promises to absorb all stock price decreases below the exercise price. If the stock price rises, the put expires worthless, which is equivalent to an insurance policy expiring without having had a claim.

Selling Put Options The seller or writer of the put option, like the seller of the call option, has a profit that can be expressed as simply −1 times the put option buyer's profit. The seller of the put is accepting the premium up front for his willingness to purchase the stock at expiration at the exercise price. The put seller's gains are limited. His losses (like the put buyer's gains), although limited, can be quite large if the stock price experiences a dramatic decline.

Exhibit 17.15 illustrates the profits to the seller of the put option. Comparing this with Exhibit 17.13, we can see that these two exhibits are mirror images of each other.

Option Spreads Rather than simply buying or selling a call option, an investor can do both by entering into a spread. There are two basic types of spreads. First, a *price spread* (also called a *vertical spread*) involves buying the call option for a given stock, expiration date, and strike price, and selling the call option for the same stock and expiration date but at a different strike price (for example, buying a Ford October 20 and selling a Ford October 30). The second type, a *time spread* (also called a *horizontal* or *calendar spread*), involves both buying and selling options for the same stock and strike price but with different expiration dates (for example, buying a Ford October 30 and selling a Ford January 30). Option spreads can serve a variety of investment goals.

Bullish Spreads. You might consider a *bullish spread* strategy if you were generally bullish (optimistic) on the underlying stock but you wanted to be conservative. Assume you are optimistic on the outlook for Ford stock, which is currently selling for, say, $22, and want to enter into a price spread. Assume also that a Ford October 20 option is currently priced at 7, whereas a Ford October 30 option is priced at 2.

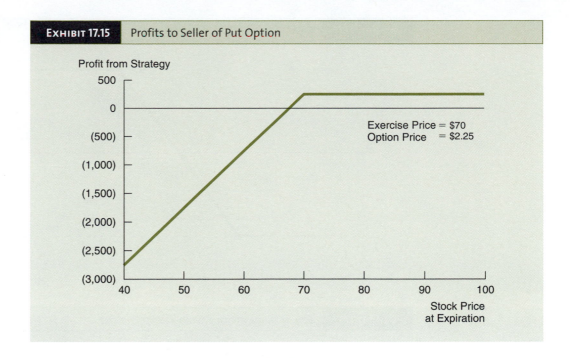

EXHIBIT 17.15	Profits to Seller of Put Option

Profit from Strategy

Exercise Price = $70
Option Price = $2.25

Stock Price
at Expiration

Because you are bullish you would buy the higher-priced Ford October 20 option and sell the lower-priced Ford October 30 option. The net cost of 5 ($500) is your maximum loss. If your expectations are correct and the stock rises from $22 to $35, the October 20 option will be worth about 15, its intrinsic value, whereas the October 30 will sell for about 5. Closing out both positions would give you a $500 gain, as follows:

October 20: Bought at 7, Sold at 15 = Gain 8
October 30: Sold at 2, Bought at 5 = Loss 3
Overall   = Gain 5

If the stock were to decline dramatically, your maximum loss would be $500 (your initial cost), even though both options would expire worthless. Your maximum gain would also be $500. At some high stock price, the value of the options will differ by 10, which would give you a gross profit of $1,000 less the $500 initial cost. The payoff diagram for this option trading strategy is shown in Exhibit 17.16.

Bearish spreads.   Assume, on the other hand, that you are generally bearish (pessimistic) on a stock or the market and want to act using a conservative strategy. You could enter into a *bearish spread,* selling the higher-priced option and buying the lower-priced option. You would sell the Ford October 20 at 7, and buy the Ford October 30 at 2, generating an immediate gain of $500.

If you are correct and Ford stock declines below 20, both options will expire worthless and you will have the $500 profit. In contrast, if the stock rises to 35, the results would be as follows:

October 20: Sold at 7, Bought at 15 = Loss 8
October 30: Bought at 2, Sold at 5 = Gain 3
Overall   = Loss 5

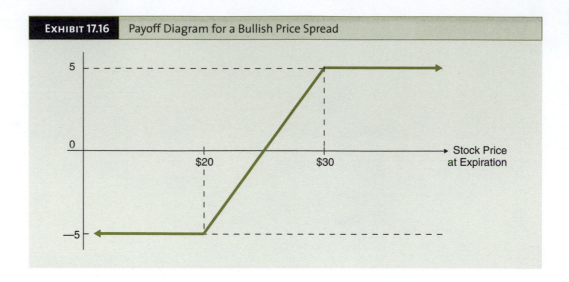

EXHIBIT 17.16   Payoff Diagram for a Bullish Price Spread

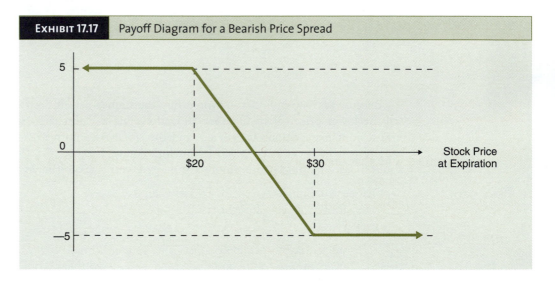

EXHIBIT 17.17   Payoff Diagram for a Bearish Price Spread

The loss of $500 compares favorably with the potential loss of $800 or more if the spread had not partially offset the adverse movement. At a high stock price, the two options will differ in price by 10, so your maximum loss is $500, or a gross loss of $1,000 less a $500 gain on the original transaction. This payoff diagram is shown in Exhibit 17.17.

Option spreads allow numerous other potential transactions to meet almost any possible set of risk–return conditions. Ever inventive, option traders have labeled certain strategies as *straddles, strangles,* and *butterfly spreads.*

Straddle   A *straddle* is a combination of a call and a put with the same expiration date and the same exercise price, which will be close to the underlying security's current value. Buying a straddle (buying the call and the put) is used when an investor expects a large price move in the underlying security but is not sure whether the price will rise or fall. A short

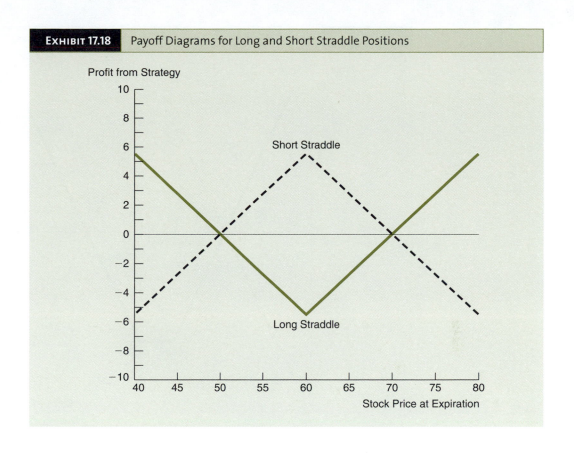

EXHIBIT 17.18 Payoff Diagrams for Long and Short Straddle Positions

straddle position (writing a call and writing a put) is entered when an investor believes the underlying security's price will not be very volatile. Exhibit 17.18 shows the straddle payoff diagrams.

Strangle A *strangle* is similar to a straddle. A strangle is a combination of a call and put with the same expiration date but with *different* exercise prices. The investor will purchase out-of-the-money calls and puts—that is, a call with an exercise price above that of the underlying security's current price and a put with an exercise price below the underlying security's current price. The motivation for entering a strangle position is similar to that of a straddle, although the range over which the underlying security's price can vary before the position gains a profit (long strangle) or loss (short strangle) is larger than that of the straddle. Exhibit 17.19 presents the strangle payoff diagrams.

Butterfly Spread The risk of a straddle or strangle position is the loss if the underlying security's price stays within a narrow range (long straddle or strangle) or varies widely (short straddle or strangle). A *butterfly spread* reduces the risk exposure, as well as the potential profitability, of these trading strategies. A long butterfly spread would entail buying a call with a low exercise price, buying a call with a high exercise price, and selling two calls with an exercise price in between the two. A short butterfly spread involves the opposite positions, namely selling or writing call options with a low and a high exercise price and buying two calls with a moderate exercise price. Exhibit 17.20 illustrates the butterfly spread payoff diagrams.

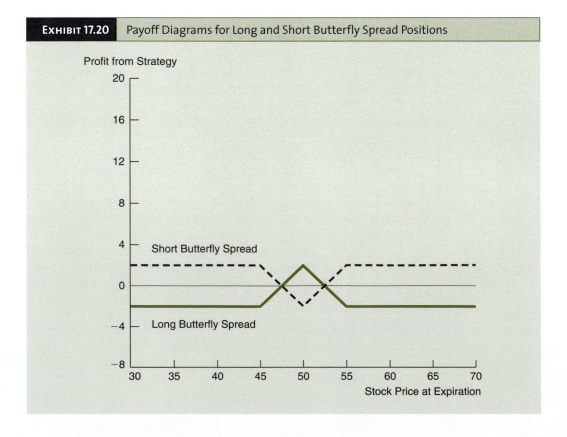

EXHIBIT 17.19 Payoff Diagrams for Long and Short Strangle Positions

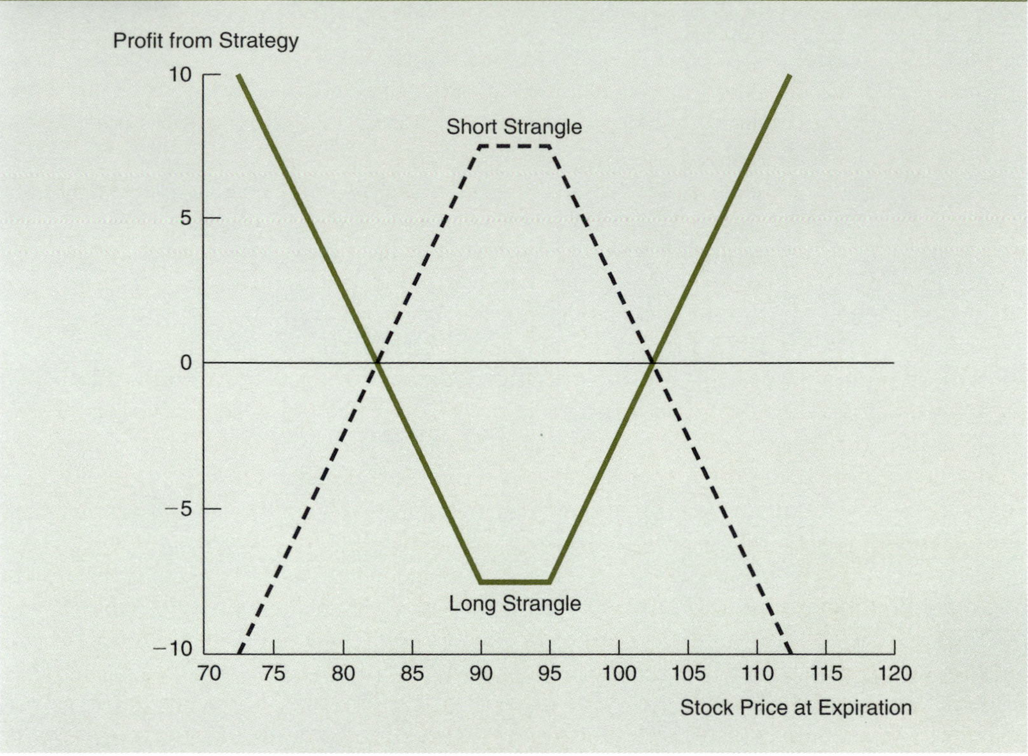

EXHIBIT 17.20 Payoff Diagrams for Long and Short Butterfly Spread Positions

Expected Return and Risk   A review of the payoff diagrams will show differing levels of possible returns and risks with different option trading strategies. Least risky (in terms of potential variability in return) are the butterfly spreads, bullish price spreads, and bearish price spreads. Strategies that provide downside protection with potential for participating in favorable underlying security price moves include buying a call, buying a put, a long straddle, and a long strangle. Income-generating strategies include writing calls, writing puts, and covered call strategies, but each of these has the potential for large losses if the underlying security price moves against the position. The riskiest strategies, in terms of loss potential, are the short straddle, short strangle, and writing uncovered calls and puts. Which strategy should be used depends on the purpose of the position (for example, to hedge, generate extra income, or take advantage of an expected price move in the underlying security), the investor's expectations about future price direction and volatility, and the investor's preferences, including, of course, risk preferences.

Put/Call Parity

Interactive e-lectures

For more explanation and an animated example of put/call parity, go to: **http://reillyxtra .swlearning.com.**

As it turns out, the prices of calls and puts are not completely independent of one another. They are related to each other through a concept known as *put/call parity*. The basic intuition behind this concept is that if two portfolios will have the same value at some future time T, the prices of the two portfolios should be the same today. Arbitrage will result if this is not true because investors will buy the underpriced portfolio and sell the overpriced one until their prices are equivalent.

Consider four securities: one call and one put option (each with an exercise price of $50, on one share of the same stock), one share of the stock, and one risk-free zero-coupon bond with par value of $50. The two options and the bond mature or expire on the same day, T. Suppose we construct portfolio A consisting of the share of stock and the put option. Suppose we also construct portfolio B consisting of the call option and the risk-free discount bond with a par value of $50.

We know the values of the options depend on the stock's value, V, at expiration and the option's exercise price, X. Let's examine these two portfolios under two situations: first with the stock's price V less than the exercise price X ($50) at expiration; and then with V exceeding X ($50) at expiration. These results are shown in Exhibit 17.21.

In the first case, V (say, $40) is less than or equal to X ($50). In portfolio A, the put option expires in the money and will have a value equal to X − V; the stock itself has a price of V. The value of portfolio A at option expiration is $50 − $40 (value of the put option) + V ($40 value of the stock); this sums to $50. In portfolio B, the call option is out of the money and expires worthless. The value of portfolio B will be 0 (value of call option) + $50 (par value of the matured bond), which sums to $50. Thus, if the stock's price is less than $50 when the options expire, the values of portfolios A and B are both $50.

In the second case, V (say, $60) is greater than X ($50). The put option expires out of the money and has a value of 0. The stock itself has a price of V. The value of portfolio A at option expiration is 0 (value of the put option) + V ($60 value of the stock), which sums to $60. In portfolio B, the call option expires in the money, with a value of $60 − $50 = $10. The value of portfolio B will then be $60 − $50 (value of call option) + $50 (par value of matured bond), which sums to $60. Thus, if the stock's price is greater than $50 when the options expire, the values of portfolios A and B are both V ($60 in this example).

So we see that portfolios A and B will have the same value when the options expire under each possibility. Because they both have the same value at time T, both portfolios

EXHIBIT 17.21	Values of Portfolios A and B on the Option Expiration Date, Time T				
	VALUE AT EXPIRATION, TIME T				
	Stock Price $<$	Exercise Price		Stock Price $>$	Exercise Price
Portfolio					
A					
One share of stock	V			V	
One put option	X – V			0	
	X			V	
B					
One call option	0			V – X	
Risk-free discount bond	X			X	
	X			V	

must have the same price today. Thus, the value of portfolio A must equal the value of portfolio B:

17.6   **Stock Price + Put Premium**

= Call Premium + Risk-Free Discount Bond Price

This result is not really all that surprising. Recall that earlier we saw that the payoff diagrams of Exhibit 17.14 (protective put) and Exhibit 17.10 (call option) are identical. That is what the relationship in equation 17.6 expresses algebraically. The left-hand side of the equation is the protective put strategy: long on the stock and long on a put option. The right-hand side represents a long call position, with the extra cash invested in a risk-free security (the extra cash represents the difference between the stock's price and the call premium). Arbitrage will ensure that the value of a protective put strategy will be in parity with that of a long call position.

By rearranging equation 17.6, we can determine the appropriate price of a put option as a function of the call price, stock price, and the price of risk-free discount bonds.

17.7   **Put Premium = Call Premium + Risk-Free Discount Bond − Stock Price**

Sketching a payoff diagram of a combination of a long call and a short stock position shows a payoff resembling that of a long put position; buying a call and shorting the stock is a *synthetic put*. Similarly, we can determine the call's price from the values of the other three assets. We can also estimate the stock's price using information about the prices of call and put options and risk-free discount bonds:

17.8   **Stock Price = Call Premium − Put Premium + Risk-Free Discount Bond**

This shows that the payoff diagram for a long stock position results from combining the payoffs of a long call and short put position.

Futures prices are also related to call and put option prices. To see this intuitively, recall that the payoff diagram for a long futures position is identical to that of a long position in the underlying asset. The same applies to a short futures position and its underlying asset. We will examine futures valuation in Chapter 18.

Investments Online

A good way to learn more about the basics of futures and options is to visit some derivative-related Web sites. Interesting futures and options exchange sites include:

http://www.cboe.com The Web site of the Chicago Board Options Exchange presents an overview of the exchange and options on equities, indexes, and LEAPS and FLEX options. Market data, including quotes, are available. The site offers educational materials for beginners and discussions of investment strategies. By inputting some data, users can compute the theoretical value of an option using the site's options calculator.

http://www.cbot.com The home page of the Chicago Board of Trade, the world's largest futures exchange, includes an overview of the board, a dictionary of trading jargon, and price quotes and charts. The site offers government agriculture reports (many commodities are traded on the CBOT) and weather reports (weather affects commodity yields).

http://www.cme.com The Chicago Mercantile Exchange's Web site features information similar to that of the other exchanges: news, price quotes, information on products, and educational resources. The Merc's site offers Web-based lessons on derivative strategies and even offers an "Introduction to Hand Signals" used by floor traders.

http://www.eurexus.com The home page of the U.S. branch of Europe-based Eurex, an electronic derivatives trading market that offers 21-hour-a-day global trading of Treasury futures.

http://www.iseoptions.com The International Securities Exchange is an all-electronic options exchange. It facilitates trading in equity options and equity index options. The site offers pricing information, option calculators, education, and a description of its primary market maker and competitive market maker structure.

http://www.liffe.com LIFFE stands for the London International Financial Futures and Options Exchange. It is Europe's premier derivatives exchange. The site includes information on money market, bond, equity, index, and commodity trading.

http://www.schaeffersresearch.com The Web site of the Investment Research Institute serves the investing public. It advertises option trading resources, but it also has several valuable (and free) educational resources. The site reviews option basics and option trading strategies (from simple to complex). It offers users a daily option market commentary, a market forecast, and free option quotes. This site is useful for those who want to get a flavor for how traders and investors use options.

Summary

- Derivative securities are rising in importance and popularity. Forwards, futures, and options are used in a variety of ways, both by investors and corporations. They can be used to control risk through hedging, to generate income through writing puts and calls, or to earn capital gains.

- Forward contracts are the oldest derivative; a forward contract represents an obligation by the owner to buy the underlying asset on or before a specified date (the expiration date) at a specified price (the exercise or strike price). The gain or loss on a forward contract is transmitted on the contract's expiration date. The value of a forward contract rises and falls with increases and decreases in the value of the underlying asset. Curren-

cies are the underlying asset for many forward contracts.

- Futures contracts also represent an obligation by the owner to purchase the underlying asset on a specified day and at a specified price. Notably, the futures' liquidity is enhanced by standardized contracts. Credit risk is also reduced because buyers and sellers of futures must post a margin account. Through the process of marking to the market, the daily change in the value of an investor's position is added to or subtracted from the margin accounts. If the balance in the margin account becomes too low, a margin call will be issued.

- A major distinction between option and futures contracts is that the option contract provides the owner with the *right,* rather than an obligation, to buy an asset (call options) or sell an asset (put options). This feature allows options buyers to limit their losses if the price of the underlying asset moves adversely to their position. Various trading strategies are available to options investors, including buying and selling calls and puts, writing covered calls, and using protective puts.

- Investors can use option trading strategies as an uncovered position or to hedge existing investment positions. Many expected return-risk possibilities exist among the different option trading strategies.

- Puts, calls, and the same underlying asset will have prices that are related to each other; this is called put/call parity. Arbitrage among the spot market, futures market, and options market will ensure that put/call parity holds rather closely over time.

QUESTIONS

1. How are options like forward contracts? How are they different?
2. How do forward contracts differ from futures contracts? How are they similar?
3. Identify the maximum and minimum prices of puts and calls and explain why they are the maximum and minimum.
4. If the price of a stock and a put option exceeded the price of a call option and a risk-free bond with a face value equal to the exercise price, what kind of transaction should you make? Explain.
5. What is a derivative security? Why would an investor want to own or sell a derivative instead of the underlying asset?
6. Why do futures contracts have less credit or default risk than forward contracts?
7. Discuss the ways a portfolio manager can use futures contracts.
8. Why are futures and option contracts available on only a limited set of assets?
9. For options written on the same stock and at the same exercise price, would the price of an American option be greater than, less than, or equal to the price of a European option? Explain.
10. Is it riskier to write covered or uncovered calls? Explain.
11. Compare and contrast the following options strategies: buy a call option, long straddle, long strangle, and long butterfly spread.
12. When might an investor use a bullish or bearish price spread rather than a butterfly spread?
13. How can buying call options help reduce the possible tax obligation from an investor's portfolio?
14. *CFA Examination Level II*
   Current equity call prices for Furniture City are contained in the table below. In reviewing these prices Jim Smith, CFA, notices discrepancies between several option prices and basic option-pricing relationships.

Closing Prices, Furniture City Equity Call Options

May 30, 1998					
Expiration Month					
Close	Strike	June	July	August	September
$119\frac{1}{2}$	110	$8\frac{7}{8}$	$12\frac{1}{2}$	$15\frac{1}{2}$	$18\frac{1}{2}$
$119\frac{1}{2}$	120	$1\frac{1}{2}$	$3\frac{3}{4}$	$3\frac{1}{2}$	$4\frac{1}{4}$
$119\frac{1}{2}$	130	1	$2\frac{1}{4}$	$2\frac{7}{8}$	$5\frac{1}{2}$

   Identify *three different* apparent pricing discrepancies in the table. Identify which of the basic option-pricing relationships *each* discrepancy violates.

   [*Note:* The fact that option contracts do not always trade at the same time as the underlying stock should *not* be identified as a discrepancy.] (12 minutes)

15. *CFA Examination Level I*
   Michelle Industries issued a Swiss franc–denominated five-year discount note for SFr200 million. The proceeds were converted to U.S. dollars to purchase capital equipment in the United States. The company wants to hedge this currency exposure and is considering the following alternatives:
   a. At-the-money Swiss franc call options
   b. Swiss franc forwards
   c. Swiss franc futures
   Contrast the essential characteristics of *each* of these *three* derivative instruments. Evaluate the suitability of *each* in relation to Michelle's hedging objective, including both advantages and disadvantages. (15 minutes)

16. *CFA Examination Level II*
   Linda Morgan is evaluating option strategies that will allow her to profit from large moves in a stock's price, either up or down. She believes that a combination of a long put and a long call option with the same expiration and exercise price (straddle) would meet her objective.

   Price information on APEX stock and options is presented below.

   APEX Stock and Option Current Market Prices
   APEX stock: $50

Call option with an exercise price of $50 expiring
   December: $4
Put option with an exercise price of $50 expiring
   December: $3
No transactions costs or taxes exist.

a. Draw a net-profit-and-loss diagram at expiration for
   the straddle, using the above information. Calculate
   and label the following on a graph:
   i. Maximum loss
   ii. The breakeven points of the position (10 minutes)
b. Morgan is considering a lower-cost strategy that
   would allow her to profit from large changes in the
   stock's price.

   APEX Stock and Option Current Market Prices
   APEX stock: $50

PROBLEMS

1. The current stock price is 56. Find the lower bound of
   the option prices assuming the following exercise prices.
   a. 55 call
   b. 60 call
   c. 55 put
   d. 60 put
2. Find the value at expiration of the following options if
   the stock price at expiration is 41.
   a. 40 call
   b. 45 call
   c. 40 put
   d. 45 put
3. Using the information in Exhibit 17.2, how much more
   or less expensive is it to buy Swiss francs with a one-
   month forward contract rather than purchase francs in
   the spot market? In the three-month forward market?
   In the six-month forward market? Redo these calculations, this time using the Japanese yen.
4. Answer the following using the futures price data in
   Exhibit 17.4.
   a. What is the dollar value of the July 2005 corn
      futures contract at the settlement price?
   b. Suppose the initial margin requirement is 5 percent
      of the contract value. How much must you deposit
      in a margin account on this contract if you pur-
      chase it at the settlement price?
   c. Suppose the contract expires at a price of 275 cents
      per bushel. What is your percentage return?
5. Answer the following using the futures price data in
   Exhibit 17.4.
   a. The notation by the future price quotation for the
      S&P Midcap 400 Index states the value of the con-
      tract is $500 times the index. Suppose the initial
      margin is 10 percent. How much must you deposit

Call option with an exercise price of $55 expiring
   December: $2.50
Put option with an exercise price of $45 expiring
   December: $2.00
No transactions costs or taxes exist.

c. Draw a net-profit-and-loss diagram at expiration for
   the alternative option strategy, using the above
   information. Calculate and label the following on a
   graph:
   i. Maximum loss
   ii. The breakeven points of the position (10 minutes)

in the margin account if you buy the September
contract at the settlement price?
   b. Compare the return on your futures investment to
      the return on a cash investment in the index if the
      September contract expires at 600. The cash market
      value of the index is listed in the last line of the
      Midcap Index quotes.
   c. Compare the return on your futures investment to
      the return on a cash investment in the index if the
      September contract expires at 530.
6. IBM's options listing appears in Exhibit 17.22.
   a. What was the closing price of IBM stock?
   b. Which options are in the money? Out of the
      money?
   c. What is the dollar return on the August 105 call
      option if you purchased it and the expiration date
      price of IBM stock is $100? $105? $110?
   d. What is the dollar return on the September 110 put
      option if you purchased it and the expiration date
      price of IBM stock is $105? $110? $115?
7. Answer the following using the data for Microsoft's
   options appearing in Exhibit 17.22.
   a. What is the value of the time premium between
      the September and January 60 call options? Put
      options?
   b. What is the intrinsic value of the October 65 call
      and put options? The January 70 call and put
      options?
   c. What arbitrage would investors do if the September
      55 call was priced at 7.25?
   d. What arbitrage would investors do if the September
      65 put was priced at 0.50?
8. Do the following using the data for Microsoft's options
   appearing in Exhibit 17.22.
   a. Draw the payoff diagram if an October 60 call is
      purchased.

EXHIBIT 17.22	Sample Option Data												

			CALL		**PUT**					**CALL**		**PUT**	
Option	Strike	Exp.	Vol.	Last	Vol.	Last	Option	Strike	Exp.	Vol.	Last	Vol.	Last
Intel	30	Aug	16058	0.35	16108	0.55	Microsoft	55	Sep	35	9.60	394	0.65
29.78	30	Sep	7741	1.65	12241	1.70	63.20	55	Oct	. . .	. . .	5205	1.40
29.78	30	Oct	370	2.35	193	2.30	63.20	60	Aug	329	3.70	2242	0.20
29.78	32.50	Aug	6987	0.05	3798	2.75	63.20	60	Sep	55	5.40	7018	1.75
29.78	32.50	Sep	1426	0.70	14521	3.50	63.20	60	Oct	25	6.70	3431	2.75
29.78	35	Oct	553	0.65	49	5.80	63.20	60	Jan	211	9.00	2404	4.70
29.78	35	Jan	492	1.70	49	6.30	63.20	65	Aug	8573	0.30	7730	2.00
29.78	50	Jan	400	0.15	2000	22.00	63.20	65	Sep	2968	2.30	949	3.80
							63.20	65	Oct	451	3.70	2450	4.70
IBM	95	Oct	. . .	. . .	403	2.00	63.20	65	Jan	1266	6.20	4762	6.70
105.01	100	Aug	10822	5.20	2010	0.15	63.20	70	Aug	579	0.05	3288	7.10
105.01	100	Sep	1042	7.20	1077	1.60	63.20	70	Sep	23523	0.75	152	7.30
105.01	100	Oct	10	9.80	690	3.40	63.20	70	Oct	1429	1.75	273	7.70
105.01	105	Aug	1200	1.00	1448	1.00	63.20	70	Jan	474	4.10	179	9.70
105.01	110	Aug	682	0.10	273	5.90	63.20	75	Sep	397	0.20	. . .	. . .
105.01	110	Sep	211	1.60	557	6.20	63.20	75	Oct	2901	0.80	36	12.00
105.01	115	Sep	4639	0.65	11	10.10	63.20	75	Jan	2091	2.55	13	13.30

b. Draw the payoff diagram for writing an uncovered call using the October 60 call option.

c. Draw the payoff diagram for writing a covered call using the October 60 call option.

9. Do the following using the data for Microsoft's options appearing in Exhibit 17.22.

a. Draw the payoff diagram if a January 65 put is purchased.

b. Draw the payoff diagram for a protective put strategy using the January 65 put option.

c. Draw the payoff diagram for writing the January 65 put option.

10. Using the data from Exhibit 17.22, compute the following:

a. The dollar return from a bullish spread of buying the IBM September 110 call and selling the September 115 call if the expiration price is $95; $105; $115; $125.

b. The dollar return from a bearish spread of buying the IBM September 115 call and selling the September 110 call if the expiration price is $95; $105; $115; $125.

11. Using the stock price, call premium, and put premium data for Intel's October 30 options (from Exhibit 17.22), use put/call parity to estimate the price of a risk-free discount bond.

12. Assume the appropriate risk-free discount bond has a par value of 34.24. Using the stock price and call premium for the Intel January 35 option (from Exhibit 17.22), what should be the premium for the January 35 put option?

13. A put option on a stock has an exercise price of $35 and is priced at $2 a share. A call option with the same exercise price is priced at $4. What is the maximum loss per share to a writer of an uncovered put and the maximum profit per share to a writer of an uncovered call?

14. An investor buys 200 shares of stock for $43 per share and sells call options for all this stock, with an exercise price of $45, for a premium of $3 per share. Ignoring dividends and transaction costs, what is the maximum profit the investor can earn if this position is held to expiration?

15. An investor buys an ExxonMobil August 80 call for $5.00 and an August 80 put for $1.25.

a. What is this option trading strategy called?

b. Determine the dollar payoff if the price of ExxonMobil at the expiration date is $65; $75; $85; $95.

16. An investor buys a McDonald's call option with a June expiration and an exercise price of $40 at a premium of $8; he also purchases a June 50 call option at a premium of $2.50. In addition, he writes two June 45 McDonald's call options and collects the premium of $3.75 for each.

a. What is the name of this option trading strategy?
b. What is the dollar payoff if, at June expiration, the price of McDonald's stock is $30? $35? $42.50? $45? $47.50? $50? $60?

17. An investor buys a Coca-Cola September 60 call for $6.00 and a September 50 put for $0.25.

a. What is this option trading strategy called?
b. Determine the dollar payoff if the price of Coca-Cola at the expiration date is $40; $45; $50; $55; $60; $70.

WEB EXERCISES

1. Your supervisor at Amijo Financial Institution wants you to investigate the possibility of using interest rate futures of bunds, bobls, and schatz to hedge some of Amijo's foreign risk. Since these futures are one of the variety of contracts traded on the CBOT, go to *http://www.cbot.com* and investigate them. Specifically, what item is "traded" when buying and selling bunds, bobls, and schatz futures? How is delivery made? What is the settlement price underlying these futures contracts and how is it calculated?

2. Explain the differences between the Chicago Board of Trade (*http://www.cbot.com*), Chicago Board Options Exchange (*http://www.cboe.com*), and the Chicago Mercantile Exchange (*http://www.cme.com*). What kinds of educational resources are offered through each organization for your further study?

3. Two types of options traded on the CBOE are FLEX and LEAPS options. From information found on the CBOE Web site, write a paragraph explaining what each of these are.

4. What new options and futures products have been recently introduced by the options and futures exchanges? How might the new contracts assist investors?

5. Locate, from doing a Web search, firms that offer forward contracts in currencies and agricultural products.

SPREADSHEET EXERCISES

1. Develop a spreadsheet using logical operators to determine the intrinsic value of (a) a call option and (b) a put option.

2. Develop a spreadsheet to determine, for different levels of stock prices, the intrinsic value of the following for both long and short option positions.
   a. Bullish and bearish spreads
   b. Straddle
   c. Strangle
   d. Butterfly spread

3. Develop a spreadsheet to estimate the returns (based on different final stock prices) of (a) owning stock; (b) owning call options; (c) owning stock plus put options (a protective put strategy). Using a stock purchase price of $45 and an exercise price of $50, estimate the returns on each of these three strategies if the final stock price falls within a price range of $35 to $65. (*Hint:* Compute the returns at $5 increments of the stock price.)

4. Extend the spreadsheet from Exercise 3 to estimate the average percent return and standard deviation; assume that all prices in the $35–$65 price range are equally likely to occur.

REFERENCES

Burns, Terence, Ed. *Derivatives in Portfolio Management.* Charlottesville, VA: AIMR, 1998.

Chance, Don M. *Analysis of Derivatives for the CFA® Program.* Charlottesville, VA: CFA Institute, 2003.

Clarke, Roger C. *Options and Futures: A Tutorial.* Charlottesville, VA: The Research Foundation of the Institute of Chartered Financial Analysts, 1992.

Dubosky, David A. *Options and Financial Futures: Valuation and Uses.* New York: McGraw-Hill, 1992.

Kolb, Robert W. *Futures, Options, and Swaps,* 3rd ed. Malden, MA: Blackwell Publishers, 2000.

Stoll, Hans R., and Robert E. Whaley. *Futures and Options: Theory and Applications.* Cincinnati: South-Western, 1993.

GLOSSARY

American option An option that allows the holder to exercise the option any time up to and including the expiration day.

At-the-money option An option with an exercise price approximately equal to the underlying stock's market price; its intrinsic value equals zero.

Counterparty The name used for investors in derivative security positions.

Covered call option Selling an option contract against stock that you own.

Derivative instrument An investment that has its value determined by, or derived from, the value of an underlying asset or security.

European option An option that allows the holder to exercise the option only on the expiration day.

Exercise price or **strike price** The transaction price specified in an option contract.

Forward contract An agreement between two traders for delivery of an asset at a fixed time in the future for a specified price.

Futures contract An agreement between a trader and an exchange clearinghouse for the exchange of an asset at a fixed, standardized time in the future for a specified price.

Initial margin The funds that buyers and sellers of futures are required to deposit in a margin account with an exchange's clearing corporation or clearinghouse.

In-the-money option An option with a favorable exercise price in relation to the underlying stock's market price; its intrinsic value is positive.

Option An investment instrument that grants to the owner the right to buy or sell something at a fixed price, either on a specific date or any time up to a specific date.

Option premium The price paid for an option.

Out-of-the-money option An option with an unfavorable exercise price in relation to the underlying stock's market price; its intrinsic value is negative.

Price spread Simultaneously buying and selling options that are identical except for their exercise prices.

Protective put A put option strategy that involves the purchase of a put accompanied by a long position in the stock.

Put/call parity The relationship between put and call options on the same underlying asset with the same exercise price.

Settlement price The approximate closing price of the futures contract determined by a special exchange committee at the end of each trading day.

Spot market The trading market in which cash and asset ownership are transferred between the buyer and the seller.

Synthetic call Another name for a protective put; so called because the payoff diagram for a protective put resembles that of a call option.

Synthetic put A put-like position that arises from having a short stock position together with a long call position in the same stock.

Time spread Simultaneously buying and selling options that are identical except for their expiration dates.

Uncovered (naked) call option Selling a call option contract on a stock that you do not own; you would have to acquire it if the option owner called for the stock.

Derivatives: Analysis and Valuation

I n this chapter we focus on advanced analysis of derivatives. We discuss futures valuation concepts, basis risk, and popular applications of futures strategies, such as index arbitrage and speculating on changing yield curve spreads. We also examine the use of options on futures, an example of a "derivative on a derivative" that is growing in popularity. As we then study option valuation, we look at factors that affect option prices and how to estimate option prices using the binomial and Black–Scholes option-pricing models. Finally, we examine several option-like securities such as callable bonds, warrants, and convertible bonds. Although they have been in existence for many years, the growth in knowledge and popularity of pure options has enhanced the use and valuation of these securities and has led to further innovations.

Futures Valuation Issues

When a commodity can be purchased both in the spot (or cash) market and a futures market, an investor has two ways to arrange a purchase of the commodity so he will own it in say, six months: buy it now in the spot market and hold it for six months or buy a futures contract for delivery in six months. Say the current spot price of gold is S_0 and the expected spot price in six months is S_6. What is an appropriate price for a gold futures contract today for delivery at that time? To answer this, we will compare the prices of a spot and futures position at time 0 and any future time T using a technique we used in Chapter 17 to examine put/call parity.

COST OF CARRY MODEL
The first strategy is to buy the gold today (time 0) at the spot price S_0. The funds needed equal S_0 and the position will be worth S_T at time T. The second strategy is to enter a long futures position for gold today, time 0, that requires the investor to purchase gold at a

futures price $F_{0,T}$ at time T. The investor needs to set aside sufficient funds at time 0 so he can pay the futures price $F_{0,T}$ when the contract ends. The investor need not set aside the entire amount of this price; rather he can invest a smaller sum in risk-free securities so that, with interest, he will have the needed amount at time T. If the one-period risk-free rate is r_f, the investor will need to invest an amount equal to $F_{0,T}/(1 + r_f)^T$ in order to have the needed funds. To summarize the cash flows of these two strategies:

Strategy	Cash Flow at Time 0	Value of Gold at Time T
Buy Gold	$-S_0$ (outflow equals current spot price of gold)	S_T (market price of gold at time T)
Buy Futures Contract Maturing at Time T	$-F_{0,T}/(1 + r_f)^T$ (outflow equals funds invested to purchase gold at time T at futures price)	S_T (regardless of futures price paid, the gold's value will equal its spot price at time T)

Since either strategy results in the same portfolio value S_T, their values at time 0 must also be the same; otherwise arbitrage by knowing investors will occur until the values are made equal. This means the cash outflow from the "buy gold" strategy must equal the cash outflow from "buy futures" strategy:

$$S_0 = \frac{F_{0,T}}{(1 + r_f)^T}$$

or, alternatively,

18.1
$$F_{0,T} = S_0(1 + r_f)^T$$

This is the *cost of carry model* for determining futures prices. In this case, the cost of carrying (or owning) gold is the forgone interest income from investing the funds in risk-free securities. For other commodities, the cost of carrying may include storage charges (as in the case of grains such as wheat and corn) as well as insurance costs.

Suppose the price of gold is $300 per ounce and the monthly risk-free interest rate is 0.25 percent. Using equation 18.1, we can determine what the price of a gold futures contract should be for delivery of gold in six months:

$$F_{0,T} = S_0(1 + r_f)^T = \$300(1 + 0.0025)^6 = \$304.53 \text{ per ounce}$$

Suppose the current futures price for gold is $310 per ounce for six-month contracts. Arbitrageurs can lock in a risk-free profit (ignoring commissions) by borrowing to buy gold at the $300 spot price and selling a six-month futures contract. The arbitrageurs would pay $304.53 after six months to repay the loan ($300 plus six month's interest at 0.25 percent per month) and collect $310 from selling gold on the futures contract, netting a risk-free profit of $5.47 per ounce. However, the heavy demand for gold in the spot market and the heavy selling pressure for gold futures contracts would result in the spot and futures prices adjusting quickly to eliminate the arbitrage opportunity. Such is an example of market efficiency, with the spot and futures markets working in tandem to eliminate anomalous prices.

Suppose a portfolio manager wants to increase her holdings of gold bullion over the next nine months. Suppose six- and nine-month futures contracts exist in addition to the spot market. That means the manager has several means of increasing her allocation to gold:

(a) buying in the spot market and holding the gold for nine months; (b) buying a six-month futures contract and then holding the purchased gold for three months; or (c) buying a nine-month futures contract and taking delivery of the gold after nine months.

What should be the pricing relationship between the six- and nine-month futures? We have seen that the difference between the spot price and six-month futures price is the cost of carry over the six months. By the same logic, the difference in the price of the six- and nine-month futures contracts will simply be the cost of carrying gold over the three-month period:

$$F_{0,9} = F_{0,6}(1 + r_f)^{9-6} = F_{0,6}(1 + r_f)^3$$

Thus, the relationship between the spot price, the six-month futures, and the nine-month futures is

$$F_{0,9} = S_0(1 + r_f)^9 = F_{0,6}(1 + r_f)^3$$

Market Imperfections

The real world contains market imperfections, and not all commodities and financial assets have the low storage costs and lack of income cash flows that gold does. However, we can adjust the cost of carry model to take such real-world implications into account.

Storage Costs   In the case of physical commodities, ownership of the commodity requires that it be stored and insured. The cost of carry will then include the costs of storage and insuring (SI) per period as well as the cost of the foregone interest that could have been earned on the funds. Equation 18.1 then becomes

18.2
$$F_{0,T} = S_0(1 + r_f + SI)^T$$

Cash Flows from Ownership   Some assets, when owned, provide cash flows to benefit the owner. For example, interest on bonds or dividends on stocks will make owning those assets more attractive than owning the futures contract. To include the lost periodic cash flow benefit from ownership (call it d) in the cost of carry model, we must reduce the cost of carry by d:

18.3
$$F_{0,T} = S_0(1 + r_f + SI - d)^T$$

Transactions Costs   Many markets have a bid-and-ask spread for asset prices. A dealer or market maker purchases items at a (lower) bid price and sells them at a (higher) ask price. In addition, trading commissions increase the net price to buyers and lower the net receipts to sellers. Thus, transactions costs have the effect of increasing the effective futures price for buyers of futures and lowering the effective futures price for sellers of futures. This leads to a range of possible prices for futures contracts as both futures buyers and sellers have to pay the commission and/or spread. If the market price of the futures contract falls within the range, profitable arbitrage is not possible. Should the price rise above or fall below the range, arbitrage can be profitable and will occur to restore an appropriate price to the futures contract. If we let TC denote transactions costs as a percentage of the spot price, the range of trading prices for a futures contract becomes

18.4
$$S_0(1 - TC)(1 + r_f + SI - d)^T \leq F_{0,T} \leq S_0(1 + TC)(1 + r_f + SI - d)^T$$

THE BASIS

The difference between a spot and futures price is called *basis.* More precisely, the basis at time *t* between the spot price S_t and a futures contract expiring at time T is

18.5

$$B_{t,T} = S_t - F_{t,T}$$

When the futures contract expires at time T the futures price $F_{t,T}$ must equal the spot price S_T. Futures market participants call this process *convergence.* This means that as we approach time T, the basis goes to zero. Between the time the futures contract is purchased and time T, the difference between spot and futures prices may vary; this is known as *basis risk.* This is of special interest to hedgers who expect to unwind their futures position before maturity (time T) since the basis may not approach the spot price in a smooth and predictable manner. Speculators sometimes bet on the direction of the basis, taking positions to profit if they expect the basis to widen or narrow.

The left graph of Exhibit 18.1 shows the behavior of gold spot and future prices. The behavior of the basis is graphed on the right-hand side of the exhibit. The spot and futures

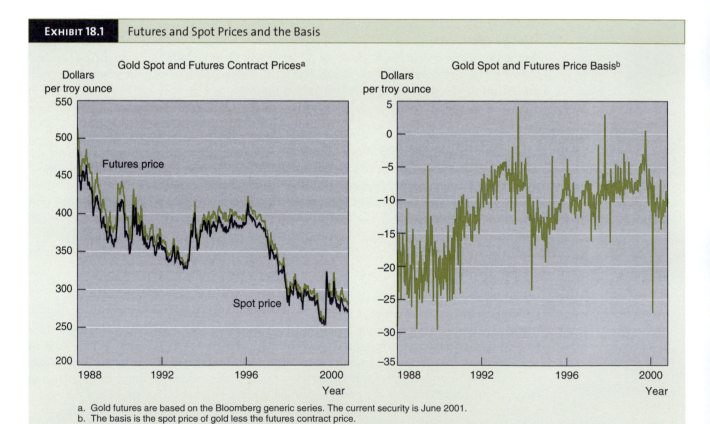

| **EXHIBIT 18.1** | Futures and Spot Prices and the Basis |

Gold Spot and Futures Contract Prices[a]

Gold Spot and Futures Price Basis[b]

a. Gold futures are based on the Bloomberg generic series. The current security is June 2001.
b. The basis is the spot price of gold less the futures contract price.
SOURCES: World Gold Council, *Gold Demand Trends;* and Bloomberg Financial Information Services.

Source: Federal Reserve Bank of Cleveland, *Economic Trends,* November 2000; available on the Internet at *http://www.clevelandfed.org/Research/ Et2000/1100/Html/gold.htm.*

prices closely follow each other, but the process is not a smooth one. The basis fluctuates over time depending on market conditions, interest rates, and cash flow expectations of other assets.

Some indirect evidence indicates that minimizing basis risk is the primary goal for most hedgers in the futures markets. For example, the growth of OTC products to help institutions manage interest rate risk, despite the existence of exchange-traded futures and options products, is a response to create customized risk management solutions to satisfy specific hedging needs.[1]

Advanced Applications of Financial Futures

Portfolio managers use futures to immediately "invest" cash inflows until such time as the futures are sold and the inflows are invested in specifically selected securities. Managers also use futures to shift an asset allocation. Buying and shorting the appropriate futures contracts can result in an immediate shift in exposure and can allow time for the manager to prudently sell positions in order to establish new ones. In this section we examine other strategies that use financial futures.

STOCK-INDEX ARBITRAGE

Stock-index futures are settled in cash; that is, at expiration an appropriate cash balance, not a bundle of stock certificates, is delivered. Hedging strategies can be applied against a full spectrum of equity positions, from diversified portfolios to individual stocks. Hedging an individual stock with an index futures contract is done in an attempt to isolate the unsystematic portion of that security's risk. Additionally, stock-index futures often are used to convert entire stock portfolios into synthetic riskless positions to exploit an apparent mispricing between stock in the cash (that is, the spot) and futures markets. This strategy is called *stock-index arbitrage* and is an example of a wider class of computer-assisted trading schemes known as *program trading*.

To illustrate, we will use equation 18.3 over one period (T = 1). As storage costs are nil for stocks and since buying and selling among arbitrageurs trading in both the stock and futures markets should ensure that profits are zero, the futures price set at date 0 will be

| 18.6 | $$F_{0,T} = S_0 + S_0(r_f - d)$$ |

As in the cost of carry model, the futures price could be set below the spot level of the index if $(r_f - d) < 0$. That is, the index futures contract will be priced lower than the current level of the stock price whenever the dividends received by holding stock exceed the borrowing cost.

To see how this parity relationship helps establish the appropriate level of the stock-index futures price, assume that one "share" of the S&P 500 index can be purchased for 1250.00 and that the dividend yield and risk-free rate over a six-month holding period are 1.5 percent and 2.5 percent, respectively. Under these conditions, the contract price on a six-month S&P 500 futures should be $F_{0,0.5} = 1250 + 1250(0.025 - 0.015) = 1262.50$. Now suppose that we construct a short hedge position by (1) purchasing the index at 1250.00 and (2) shorting the futures at 1262.50. If the position is held to expiration, the

---

[1]Keith C. Brown and Donald J. Smith, *Interest Rate and Currency Swaps: A Tutorial*, Charlottesville, VA: Research Foundation of the Institute of Chartered Financial Analysts, 1995.

profit at various expiration date levels of the S&P is shown in Exhibit 18.2. Notice that the net profit remains constant no matter the level of the index at the expiration date since spot and futures price parity holds in this example.

Implementing an Index Arbitrage Strategy What if the parity condition between the stock index and the stock–index futures price does not hold? Could we design a portfolio to take advantage of the situation? Specifically, suppose that in the preceding example the actual contract price on a six-month S&P 500 futures was 1265.50 (i.e., $F_{0,T} > S_0 + S_0(r_f - d)$. We could then implement the following arbitrage transaction: (1) short the stock-index future at a price of 1265.50; (2) borrow money at 2.5 percent to purchase the stock index at 1250.00; and (3) hold the position until maturity, collecting 18.75 in dividends and then selling the stock to repay the loan. The net profit at maturity would be $1265.50 - 1250.00 - 1250.00(0.025 - 0.015) = 3.00$ regardless of the value of the S&P 500 index at expiration. Exhibit 18.3 illustrates this. This strategy was riskless (i.e., the sales price of the stock and dividends were known in advance) and none of our own capital was used; it is an arbitrage profit.

This is *stock-index arbitrage,* which is possible whenever the index futures price is set at a level sufficiently different from the theoretical value for $F_{0,T}$ to account for trading costs. For example, if the actual level of $F_{0,T}$ were less than $S_0 + S_0(r_f - d)$, the previous strategy could be reversed: (1) buy the stock-index future at a price of $F_{0,T}$; (2) lend money at r_f and short the stock index at S_0; and (3) cover the position at the expiration date of the futures contract. Indeed, index arbitrage is a very popular form of trading. Exhibit 18.4 reports that for the week noted about 12 percent of all computer-assisted program trading used this

EXHIBIT 18.2	Stock-Index Arbitrage Example—No Profit				
	S&P at Expiration Is:				
	1220	**1240**	**1260**	**1280**	**1300**
Net futures profit	42.50	22.50	2.50	−17.50	−37.50
Net index profit	−30.00	−10.00	10.00	30.00	50.00
Borrowing cost (2.5%)	−31.25	−31.25	−31.25	−31.25	−31.25
Dividend (1.5%)	18.75	18.75	18.75	18.75	18.75
Net profit	0.00	0.00	0.00	0.00	0.00

EXHIBIT 18.3	Stock-Index Arbitrage Example—With Riskless Profit				
	S&P at Expiration Is:				
	1220	**1240**	**1260**	**1280**	**1300**
Net futures profit	45.50	25.50	5.50	−14.50	−34.50
Net index profit	−30.00	−10.00	10.00	30.00	50.00
Borrowing cost (2.5%)	−31.25	−31.25	−31.25	−31.25	−31.25
Dividend (1.5%)	18.75	18.75	18.75	18.75	18.75
Net profit	3.00	3.00	3.00	3.00	3.00

strategy. Further, program trading accounted for about one-half of trading volume on the New York Stock Exchange. Both of these totals can get much higher around contract expiration dates (i.e., the so-called triple witching days around the third Friday of the contract expiration month).

T-Bond/T-Note (NOB) Futures Spread

Frequently, speculators in the bond market will forecast a change in the overall shape of the yield curve but be less certain as to the actual direction in future rate movements. Suppose, for instance, a speculator thinks an upward-sloping yield curve will flatten. One way to invest in such a situation is to go both long and short in contracts representing different points on the yield curve. This is known as the Treasury *notes over bond (NOB) spread* strategy.

EXHIBIT 18.4	Program Trading Statistics

Program Trading

NEW YORK—Program trading in the week ended July 23 accounted for 51%, or an average of 770.5 million shares daily, of New York Stock Exchange volume. Brokerage firms executed an additional 552.5 million daily shares of program trading away from the NYSE, with 4.6% of the overall total on foreign markets. Program trading is the simultaneous purchase or sale of at least 15 different stocks with a total value of $1 million or more.

Of the program total on the NYSE, 12% involved stock-index arbitrage. In this strategy, traders dart between stocks and stock-index options and futures to capture fleeting price differences. Another 0.1% involved derivative product-related strategies. Index arbitrage can be executed only in a stabilizing manner when the Dow Jones Industrial Average moves 200 points or more from its previous day's close.

Some 52% of program trading was executed by firms for their clients, while 46% was done for their own accounts, or principal trading. An additional 2% was designated as customer facilitation, in which firms use principal positions to facilitate customer trades.

Of the five most-active firms overall for the week, **UBS** AG's UBS Securities and **Credit Suisse Group**'s Credit Suisse First Boston executed most of their program trading as principal for their own accounts. **Morgan Stanley** and **Deutsche Bank** AG's Deutsche Bank Securities executed most of their program trading activity for customers, as agent. **Lehman Brothers** split its activity between its own accounts and those of its customers.

NYSE PROGRAM TRADING
Volume in millions of shares for the week ended July 23, 2004

TOP 15 FIRMS	INDEX ARBITRAGE	DERIVATIVE-RELATED*	OTHER STRATEGIES	TOTAL
UBS Securities	.....	.....	603.4	603.4
Morgan Stanley	17.4	1.2	573.5	592.1
Deutsche Bank Securities	102.5	.....	335.4	437.9
Credit Suisse First Boston	13.2	.....	292.5	305.7
Lehman Brothers	.....	.....	291.0	291.0
Goldman Sachs Group	1.6	.....	241.6	243.2
Merrill Lynch	.....	.....	226.3	226.3
RBC Capital Markets	124.0	.....	43.7	167.7
CIBC World Markets	51.3	.....	91.3	142.6
Nomura Securities	78.9	.....	39.9	118.8
Salomon Smith Barney	.....	.....	102.7	102.7
Bear Stearns	13.7	.....	84.7	98.4
J.P. Morgan	.....	.....	90.8	90.8
Banc of America Sec.	.....	.....	83.5	83.5
Interactive Brokers	.....	.....	60.7	60.7
OVERALL TOTAL	**460.0**	**1.2**	**3391.2**	**3852.4**

*Other derivative-related strategies besides index arbitrage

Source: New York Stock Exchange

Source: From *The Wall Street Journal*, July 30, 2004, p. C6. Copyright © 2004 Dow Jones. Reprinted by permission of Copyright Clearance Center.

If the yield curve flattens, the price of long-term bonds will rise relative to those of intermediate-term notes. Speculators will want to be long in the long-term bond contract and short in the notes contract.

Suppose in mid–February you observe the price quotes shown in the table (along with their implied yields to maturity) for T-Bond and T-Note futures contracts maturing in June. (Remember, Treasuries are quoted in 32nds; 103-02 corresponds to $103\frac{2}{32}$ percent of par. Par value is $100,000.)

Contract	Settle Price	Price in Dollars	Implied Yield
20-yr, 6% T-bond	103–02	$103,062.5	5.70
10-yr, 6% T-note	104–02	$104,062.5	5.42

Notice that your expectation of a flattening yield curve is identical to the view that the twenty-eight basis-point gap $(0.0570 - 0.0542)$ between the longer- and shorter-term contracts will shrink. If you also feel this will occur by mid-June, the appropriate strategy would be (1) go long in one Treasury bond futures; and (2) go short in one Treasury note futures. The net profit from this joint position when you close out the two contracts is calculated as the sum of the profits on the long T-bond position and the short T-note position or,

Profit on Long T–Bond Position + Profit on Short T–Note Position

(June T–bond Price − $103,062.5) + ($104,062.5 − June T–Note Price)

To see how this combined position would pay off if your view is correct, suppose the yield curve flattens so that both securities offer 6% yields by the time you close your positions in June.

In this case, both futures contracts will sell at par, so your net profit will be

($100,000 − $103,062.5) + ($104,062.5 − $100,000)

= (−3,062.50) + ($4,062.50) = $1,000

This means you lost $3,062.50 on the long position in the T-bond contract but gained $4,062.50 on your short T-note position for a net gain of $1,000 on the NOB spread.

Other spread bets are possible with futures contracts. The TED (Treasury–Eurodollar) spread allows speculators to take positions when they believe credit spreads will widen or narrow. The Treasury bill futures has the risk-free Treasury bill as the underlying security. Eurodollar futures are based on three-month (ninety-day) LIBOR rates, which contain some credit risk. If traders expect a widening credit spread, such as in a "flight to quality" when investors are very risk-averse, traders will take a long TED spread position by buying T-bill futures and shorting Eurodollar futures. Conversely, when they expect a narrowing credit spread they will short a TED spread by shorting T-bill futures and going long on Eurodollar futures.

Options on Futures

Options on futures, which are called *futures options*, offer investors additional ways to hedge or speculate. Let's assume that a call option exists to buy an S&P 500 index futures with an exercise price of 1080. If the option is exercised, the owner of the call establishes a long position in the March futures contract at 1080, which is equivalent to buying the futures at a price of 1080. If we assume that when the option is exercised the futures price is 1085, the call holder receives a long position in the futures at 1080, and this futures contract is immediately marked to market at 1085, which gives the call holder a credit of 5. Margin on the futures must be deposited as usual. The writer of the call establishes a short futures position at 1080 that is marked to 1085 and the writer is charged 5. The exercise of a put establishes a short futures position for the owner and a long futures position for the writer.

Some of the contracts have the options expire at the same time the futures contract expires; others have the options expire as much as a month earlier than the futures. The options and the underlying futures contract trade side by side on a futures exchange in contrast to options on stocks, which do not trade side by side with the underlying stocks. This side-by-side trading makes it easy to execute arbitrage transactions between the options and the futures, which makes the market more efficient. In addition, because there are options on commodity futures but not options on the commodities themselves, these options allow investors to take option positions based on expected price movements in commodities.

Exhibit 18.5 contains a sample of the price quotations for options on futures taken from *The Wall Street Journal*. The quotes are grouped by type of instrument (agricultural, interest rate, and index). Below the name of the underlying asset is an indication of the size of the contract. For example, one S&P 500 contract is priced at $250 times the premium. The premium of the September 1100 call is shown as 22.30. Thus, the total price paid for this call option contract is: $22.30 × 250 = $5,575. This call option contract permits the purchase of the September S&P 500 futures at a price of 1100. The futures price is not indicated but can be found on the pages containing futures prices, which are usually located near the futures options quotes. In this example, the September S&P futures was selling for 1095.20, which meant that the call option on this futures contract was out of the money.

Treasury bond futures as traded by the Chicago Board of Trade are based on an "assumed" underlying twenty-year Treasury bond with a 6 percent coupon. Many Treasury bonds of varying maturities and coupons are actually deliverable, though, because Treasury bond futures provide an example of "basket delivery." A contract summary for U.S. Treasury bond futures is as follows:

Exchange	Chicago Board of Trade
Contract unit	U.S. Treasury bond, $100,000 par value, nominal 6 percent coupon
Good delivery	Any U.S. Treasury bond with a minimum of fifteen years remaining to call date or maturity date, whichever is shorter
Settlement	Upon delivery of $100,000 par amount of eligible Treasury bonds, the seller receives the contract settlement price times a delivery factor for the bonds delivered, plus any accrued interest
Daily price change limit	2 points ($2,000 per contract)
Delivery months	March, June, September, December

Treasury bond futures have a maximum price change or "limit move" of 2 points per day, which represents $2,000 per contract. Should the futures price increase or decrease by more than 2 points, trading is halted and no transactions beyond the limit can be completed. Futures transactions also require margin on both sides of the market (buy and sell), requiring initial deposits when each transaction is executed and maintenance margin should adverse market changes cause the margin to fall below a maintenance level.

To be eligible for delivery, a Treasury bond must have at least fifteen years remaining before it is callable or it matures, whichever is sooner. The Treasury bonds delivered must

EXHIBIT 18.5 Options on Futures Quotations

FUTURES OPTIONS PRICES

Wednesday, July 28, 2004

Final or settlement prices of selected contracts. Volume and open interest are totals in all contract months.

Grain and Oilseed

Corn (CBT)
5,000 bu.; cents per bu.

STRIKE	CALLS-SETTLE			PUTS-SETTLE		
Price	Sep	Oct	Dec	Sep	Oct	Dec
200	19.625	...	28.250	1.250	...	1.875
210	12.125	...	20.500	3.625	...	4.125
220	6.625	...	14.375	8.125	...	8.000
230	3.500	...	9.875	15.000	...	13.125
240	2.000	...	6.750	23.500	...	20.000
250	1.125	...	4.750	32.625	...	28.000

Est vol 22,680 Tu 20,263 calls 8,824 puts
Op int Tues 440,116 calls 251,542 puts

Soybeans (CBT)
5,000 bu.; cents per bu.

Price	Sep	Oct	Nov	Sep	Oct	Nov
540	...	...	54.750	10.500	15.000	19.000
560	39.500	39.000	43.625	17.000	...	28.000
580	28.750	29.500	34.000	26.250	34.000	38.000
600	20.250	21.500	27.000	37.750	46.000	51.000
620	14.000	...	21.000	51.500	...	65.000
640	10.000	11.500	16.500	67.250	...	80.250

Est vol 24,695 Tu 13,513 calls 8,338 puts
Op int Tues 134,246 calls 112,500 puts

Soybean Meal (CBT)
100 tons; $ per ton

Price	Sep	Oct	Dec	Sep	Oct	Dec
180	...	9.50	11.25	5.50	10.70	13.25
185	...	...	9.50	7.75	13.75	16.55
190	...	6.35	7.85	10.25	17.40	19.85
195	...	5.00	6.45	13.40	21.10	23.45
200	5.50	4.00	5.30	16.70	25.25	27.25
205	...	...	...	...	...	...

Est vol 4,531 Tu 1,870 calls 878 puts
Op int Tues 21,336 calls 30,455 puts

Soybean Oil (CBT)
60,000 lbs.; cents per lb.

Price	Sep	Oct	Dec	Sep	Oct	Dec
215	...	...	...	...	.650	...
220	...	...	...	.450	.900	1.530
225	...	...	.850	...	1.200	1.860
230	.560	...	...	.900	1.550	2.230
235	...	...	...	1.250	1.900	2.610
240	.300	.350	.510	1.650	2.300	3.010

Est vol 3,075 Tu 2,176 calls 1,109 puts
Op int Tues 33,031 calls 30,431 puts

Wheat (CBT)
5,000 bu.; cents per bu.

Price	Sep	Oct	Dec	Sep	Oct	Dec
290	...	...	...	1.000	...	...
300	17.625	...	...	2.875	...	5.000
310	11.250	...	...	6.500	...	8.500
320	6.750	...	20.375	11.875	...	13.000
330	4.000	...	15.875	19.250	...	18.375
340	2.250	8.000	12.375	27.500	...	24.875

Est vol 5,573 Tu 2,456 calls 494 puts
Op int Tues 71,069 calls 40,251 puts

Wheat (KC)
5,000 bu.; cents per bu.

Price	Sep	Oct	Dec	Sep	Oct	Dec
320	...	...	2.875	...	...	2.875
330	...	...	...	2.500	...	...
340	9.125	...	23.125	6.125	...	8.750
350	4.875	...	17.750	11.875	8.000	13.250
360	2.375	...	13.250	19.375	13.375	18.750
370	1.125	4.875	9.625	28.125	20.250	25.125

Est vol 1,561 Tu 279 calls 150 puts
Op int Tues 17,917 calls 14,886 puts

Interest Rate

STRIKE	CALLS-SETTLE	PUTS-SETTLE

T-Bonds (CBT)
$100,000; points and 64ths of 100%

Price	Sep	Oct	Dec	Sep	Oct	Dec
105	2-23	2-03	...	0-35	1-27	2-14
106	1-44	1-33	...	0-56	1-57	2-45
107	1-08	1-06	...	1-20	2-29	3-16
108	0-45	0-49	...	1-57	3-08	3-55
109	0-26	0-32	...	2-38	3-56	4-33
110	0-14	0-21	...	3-26	4-43	5-16

Est vol 55,302;
Tu vol 33,298 calls 39,663 puts
Op int Tues 354,443 calls 315,927 puts

T-Notes (CBT)
$100,000; points and 64ths of 100%

Price	Sep	Oct	Dec	Sep	Oct	Dec
108	2-07	1-38	...	0-18	0-63	1-15
109	1-24	1-04	...	0-35	1-29	1-45
110	0-52	0-42	...	0-62	2-03	...
111	0-27	0-25	...	1-37	2-50	...
112	0-12	0-14	...	2-23	...	...
113	0-05	0-08	0-13	3-16	...	...

Est vol 284,764 Tu 75,238 calls 122,232 puts
Op int Tues 1,068,420 calls 1,304,148 puts

5 Yr Treas Notes (CBT)
$100,000; points and 64ths of 100%

Price	Sep	Oct	Dec	Sep	Oct	Dec
10750	1-39	1-06	1-30	0-10	0-40	...
10800	1-13	0-53	1-13	0-16	0-55	...
10850	0-55	0-38	0-61	0-26	1-08	...
10900	0-37	0-26	0-48	0-40	1-28	...
10950	0-22	0-18	0-37	0-57	...	...
11000	0-13	0-11	0-28	1-16	...	...

Est vol 136,005 Tu 7,810 calls 98,461 puts
Op int Tues 300,707 calls 621,806 puts

Eurodollar (CME)
$ million; pts. of 100%

Price	Aug	Sep	Oct	Aug	Sep	Oct
9775	.270	.275	.042	.000	.005	.257
9800	.050	.070	.015	.030	.050	...
9825	.005	.012	.005	.235	.242	...
9850	.000	.002	...	.480	.482	...
9875	.000	.000	...	.730	.730	...
9900	...	...	...	.980	...	...

Est vol 764,552;
Tu vol 260,082 calls 278,523 puts
Op int Tues 6,042,161 calls 5,031,245 puts

Index

STRIKE	CALLS-SETTLE	PUTS-SETTLE

DJ Industrial Avg (CBOT)
$100 times premium

Price	Aug	Sep	Oct	Aug	Sep	Oct
99	27.25	35.25	...	6.00	14.25	...
100	19.75	28.50	...	8.75	17.60	24.75
101	13.50	22.50	...	12.50	21.50	...
102	8.50	17.00	23.80	17.25	26.00	...
103	4.75	12.50	...	23.75	31.40	...
104	2.75	8.50	...	37.40	...	...

Est vol 426 Tu 237 calls 37 puts
Op int Tues 3,366 calls 5,251 puts

S&P 500 Stock Index (CME)
$250 times premium

Price	Aug	Sep	Oct	Aug	Sep	Oct
1085	21.60	31.10	...	11.10	20.60	28.50
1090	18.30	28.00	...	12.80	22.50	...
1095	15.30	25.10	...	14.80	24.60	...
1100	12.60	22.30	30.70	17.10	26.80	34.80
1105	10.20	19.70	...	19.70	29.20	...
1110	8.10	17.30	...	22.60	31.80	...

Est vol 8,986 Tu 8,276 calls 9,022 puts
Op int Tues 101,403 calls 226,550 puts

EXHIBIT 18.6   Comparative Profit–Loss Graphs for Alternative Strategies
Alternative A: Investor buys June T-bond futures at 120
Alternative B: Investor buys June T-bond futures 120 call option at 2

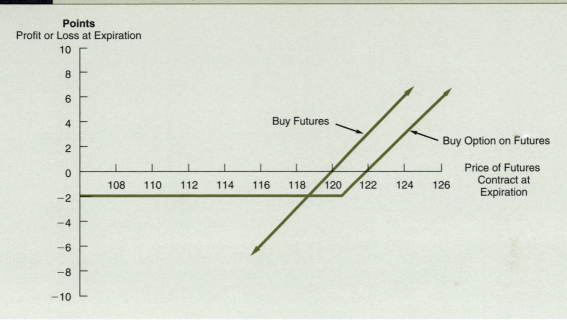

have a par value of $100,000. The bond chosen for delivery will be the one that is "cheap-est to deliver," that is, the bond with the lowest price that meets the above criteria.

Treasury bond futures rise and fall with the value of the underlying security. A call option on a Treasury bond futures contract, however, limits losses to the size of the call pre-mium. Exhibit 18.6 shows the behavior of the futures contract and the option on the futures. The option contract limits losses but profits will be less than those on the futures contract by the size of the option premium.

Another benefit of the call option as opposed to the actual financial futures contract is that no maintenance margin is required. Once the option premium is paid, no matter how far the price of the futures contract moves adversely, the option holder has the chance that the price will rebound and will potentially provide a profit. There is no need to provide additional capital under adverse circumstances. This is not the case with the holder of the futures contract; an additional margin is constantly required as the price moves adversely.

Valuation of Call and Put Options

Just as there are means for valuing futures contracts, sophisticated techniques exist to deter-mine option values. In this section we review the factors that affect the value of an option contract. In the following section we introduce the binomial option-pricing model as a means of estimating option prices. Then we expand our discussion to include the more complex Black–Scholes option-pricing formula for valuing options.

We use five factors to calculate the value of an American call or put option, assuming the stock does not pay a dividend: (1) the stock price, (2) the exercise price, (3) the time to maturity, (4) the interest rate, and (5) the volatility of the underlying stock. We can allow for dividends through an additional calculation. First we will briefly describe how each of these factors relate to the value of a call option. Then, we will note how they relate to the value of a put option.

Stock Price   The value of a call option is positively related to the price of the underlying stock. With a given exercise price, the price of the stock determines whether the option is in the money, and therefore has an intrinsic value, or out of the money, with only speculative or time value.

Exercise Price   The value of a call option is inversely related to its exercise price. For a given stock price, a lower exercise price raises the value of a call on the stock. As an example, consider a stock selling at $70 a share. A call option with an exercise price of $50 would certainly be worth more than a call option with an exercise price of $60. The first option is in the money by $20, the second by only $10.

Time to Expiration   The value of an option depends to a great extent on its time to expiration. All other factors being equal, a longer time to expiration increases the value of the option because it lengthens the span of time during which gains are possible. The longer option allows investors to reap all the benefits of a shorter option for a longer time.

Interest Rate   An investor can use funds to purchase 100 shares of stock or buy one call option and invest the difference in risk-free securities. A higher market interest rate increases the benefit from using call options. This creates a *positive* relationship between the market interest rate and the value of the call option.

Volatility of Underlying Stock Price   For call options on a stock, an option's value has a positive relationship with the volatility of the underlying stock. This is because greater volatility implies greater upside potential; the downside protection of the option, which limits the maximum loss, is also worth more.

VALUATION FACTORS AND PUT OPTIONS

As noted, the same five factors determine the value of put options, although several of the relationships differ. First, the value of put options relates *inversely* to the price of the underlying stock, all else remaining the same. This is because the intrinsic value of a put option is the difference between the exercise price and the stock price; the exercise price of an in-the-money put option exceeds the stock price. Following from this, the value of the put option relates *positively* to the exercise price.

The relationship of put option value to the time-to-expiration factor is positive, as for a call option. Again, the reasoning is that the longer maturity provides more time for the put option to increase in value. The interest rate effect on the value of a put option is *negative* because buying a put option is like deferring the *sale* of stock because the investor receives the proceeds of the sale in the future. Therefore, we are dealing with the present value of the future proceeds, and a higher interest rate reduces the present value of those proceeds. Finally, the effect of the volatility of the stock price on the value of the put option is the same as for the call option. Higher price volatility increases the value of the put option because it increases the probability of the put option being in the money. These relationships are summarized in Exhibit 18.7.

EXHIBIT 18.7	Option-Pricing Relationships		
		Call Option	**Put Option**
Stock price		+	−
Exercise price		−	+
Time to expiration		+	+
Interest rate		+	−
Volatility of underlying stock		+	+

The Binomial Option-Pricing Model

What is an appropriate price for an option contract? Complicated option-pricing models exist but we first examine option pricing in a simple context. We simplify the analysis by assuming an asset today (which we assume is a share of stock) can only have two possible prices one year from now. We want to create a perfectly hedged portfolio of stock call options. That is, the portfolio will have a known value regardless of which of the two stock prices exist a year from now. And if the portfolio has a known value, it is a riskless security; investors will discount the known value, using the risk-free rate of interest, to determine the current price of the portfolio.

The fundamental intuition behind the process is straightforward and can be illustrated quite simply. Suppose we have just purchased a share of stock in WYZ Corp. for $50. The stock is not expected to pay a dividend during the time we plan to hold it, and we have forecast that in one year the stock price will either rise 30 percent to $65 or fall 20 percent to $40. We can summarize this as follows:

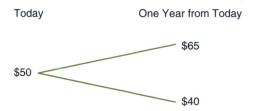

Suppose further that we can either buy or sell a call option on WYZ stock with an exercise price of $52.50. If this is a European-style contract that expires in exactly one year, it will have the following possible expiration values:

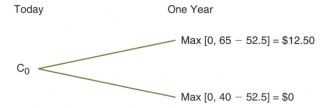

Although we do not know what the call option is worth today, we know what it is worth at expiration, given our forecast of future WYZ stock prices. The dilemma is establishing what the option should sell for today (i.e., C_0).

This dilemma can be solved in three steps. First, create a *hedge portfolio* consisting of one share of stock held long and some number of call options so that the combined position will be riskless, that is, so that the portfolio's value in the future is the same regardless of whether the stock rises or falls. Second, use the risk-free rate (probably the T-bill rate) to discount the hedge portfolio's future value to the present. Third, using the information obtained (stock price, present and future value to the portfolio, and the number of call options in the hedge portfolio), compute the price of a call option. Let's apply this process to find the value of the above call option.

Step 1: Estimate the number of call options needed. In one year we have two possibilities: the WYZ stock price rises to $65 and each call option has an intrinsic value of $12.50, or the stock price falls to $40 and the options have no intrinsic value, $0. Our portfolio of stock and call options will have the following values:

Value of portfolio if stock price rises: $65 + (n)($12.50)
Value of portfolio if stock price falls: $40 + (n)($0)

Estimating n, the number of call options to write, requires that the hedge portfolio have the same value regardless of whether the stock price rises or falls:

Portfolio Value if Stock Price Rises = Portfolio Value if Stock Price Falls

$$\$65 + (n)(\$12.50) = \$40 + (n)(\$0) = \$40$$

Solving for n, we have

$$n = \frac{\$40 - \$65}{\$12.50} = -2.0$$

Note that this number has both *direction* and *magnitude*. The negative sign indicates that call options must be *sold* to hedge a long stock position. Further, given that the range of possible call option values (i.e., 12.5 − 0 = 12.5) is only half as large as the range for WYZ stock (i.e., 65 − 40 = 25), twice as many options must be sold as there is stock in the hedge portfolio. Thus, we can create a risk-free hedge portfolio by purchasing one share of stock and selling two call options.

The value of $1/n$ is called the *hedge ratio*. In this example the hedge ratio is $\frac{1}{2}$ or 0.50, indicating that the portfolio should hold one share of stock for every two call options written (or one-half share of stock for every written call).

The cost of the hedge portfolio today is the price of a share of WYZ, $50, minus the premiums received from selling two call options:

Values of hedge portfolio today: $\$50 - (2.00)(C_0)$

Step 2: Determine the present value of the hedge portfolio. In the second step we assume that capital markets are free from arbitrage possibilities. This means all risk-free investments are priced to earn the risk-free rate over time. In the first step we learned the value of the hedge portfolio equals $40 in one year regardless of whether the stock price rises or falls; with a known value, it is riskless. To find the value of the portfolio and the call option, we discount the $40 value to the present using the risk-free rate:

Value of Portfolio Today = Present Value of $40

$$\$50 - (2.00)(C_0) = \frac{\$40}{(1 + \text{RFR})^T}$$

where:

RFR = the annualized risk-free rate

T = the time to expiration (i.e., one year)

Two unknown values exist in this formula: C_0 and RFR. Finding a suitable estimate for RFR seldom is a problem; we can use as a proxy the yield to maturity on a U.S. Treasury security of appropriate length. For example, if the one-year T-bill yield is 8 percent, the formula for C_0 can be solved as follows:

$$\$50 - 2(C_0) = \frac{\$40}{1.08} = \$37.04$$

Step 3: Compute the price of a call option. The final step is a continuation of step 2, namely, solving the equation for the value of C_0, the price of the call option:

$$C_0 = \frac{\$50 - \$37.04}{2} = \$6.48$$

This value, $6.48, represents the fundamental value of a one-year call option on WYZ stock, given the prevailing market price for WYZ stock, our forecast of future share values, and the risk-free rate. The single unknown is our forecast of future share values, namely, $65 and $40. The value of the call option will change as the spread between the forecasted prices widens or narrows (or, to think of it another way, as the stock prices become more or less volatile). Finally, recall that the current price of the stock is $50 and the option's exercise price is $52.50. Since the call option is currently out of the money, the call price represents a time premium as it has zero intrinsic value.

GENERALIZING THE PROCESS

It is unrealistic to assume only two possible outcomes for future WYZ share prices. To improve the accuracy of this process, we can expand the forecast of stock prices at the expiration date to allow for more possibilities. For example, what happens if in addition to $65 and $40 we include a forecast of $50.99?

The solution involves dividing the one-year time to expiration into two six-month subintervals, each allowing a subsequent price move up or down. Exhibit 18.8 shows how we apply this to WYZ stock. Before the current stock price can reach $65 in one year, it

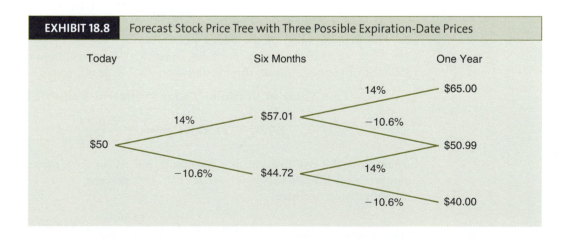

EXHIBIT 18.8 Forecast Stock Price Tree with Three Possible Expiration-Date Prices

Today	Six Months	One Year
$50	14% → $57.01	14% → $65.00
	−10.6% → $44.72	−10.6% → $50.99
		14% → $50.99
		−10.6% → $40.00

must first move up to $57.01 in the first six-month period before moving up a second time to its final value of $65. Here each price increase is forecast to be about 14 percent. Similarly, the lower extreme of $40 can only be reached by two consecutive downward price changes, each losing about 10.6 percent. On the other hand, there are two different paths to the $50.99 price in the middle: one upward movement followed by one downward, or one downward movement followed by an upward.

Once we fill in all the stock prices, we find the call option's value by working backward. If, for instance, starting at a six-month price of $57.01, the price changes over the remaining subperiod are

The change in the value of the call option from this uppermost part of the stock price tree is

We use the symbol C_u as the value of the call option after the stock price has already increased (moved up) in value once. Using this notation, C_{uu} (the value of the option after two consecutive price increases) would equal $12.50 and C_{ud} (the value after an upward followed by a downward price move) would equal $0.

Using the option's exercise price of $52.50, we can employ our three-step process:

1. **Number of call options needed:**

   Portfolio Value if Stock Price Rises = Portfolio Value if Stock Price Falls

   $$\$65 + (n)(\$12.50) = \$50.99 + (n)(\$0) = \$50.99$$

   Solving for n, we have

   $$n = \frac{\$50.99 - \$65}{\$12.50} = -1.12$$

2. **The present value of the hedge portfolio:**
   Since the value of the hedge portfolio equals $50.99 in six months, we need to discount $50.99 to the present using the risk-free rate:

   Value of Portfolio Today = Present Value of $50.99

   $$\$57.01 - (1.12)(C_u) = \frac{\$50.99}{(1 + \text{RFR})^T}$$

   where now the risk-free rate is a six-month rate. With an 8 percent annual rate, the six-month rate will be $\sqrt{1.08} - 1 = 0.0392$ or 3.92 percent.
   Simplifying, we have

   $$\$57.01 - 1.12(C_u) = \frac{\$50.99}{1.0392} = \$49.07$$

3. The price of a call option:

Solving the equation for the value of C_u, we obtain

$$C_u = \frac{\$57.01 - \$49.07}{1.12} = \$7.09$$

Now we can establish the value for the option corresponding to a share price of \$44.72 (i.e., C_d) using the same three-step procedure with the stock and option price trees truncated as follows:

The change in the value of the call option from this lowermost part of the stock price tree is

Notice that in this case the call option is certain to be out of the money at the expiration date, six months hence. That is, given this forecast of potential stock prices, if the WYZ stock falls in value to \$44.72 after one subperiod, even a subsequent recovery to \$50.99 (i.e., an upward move in the second subperiod) leaves the share price below the \$52.50 exercise price of the call option. Thus, it is clear that C_d must be \$0.00; any security that is certain to be worthless in the future is also worthless today.

These intermediate calculations are necessary; C_0 cannot be established before determining C_u and C_d. With these values in hand, the relevant part of the stock price tree is its initial two branches:

The call option values from this part of the stock price tree are

Once again applying our three-step process, we estimate today's value of the call option, C_0:

1. Number of call options needed:

Portfolio Value if Stock Price Rises = Portfolio Value if Stock Price Falls

$$\$57.01 + (n)(\$7.09) = \$44.72 + (n)(\$0) = \$44.72$$

Solving for *n*, we have

$$n = \frac{\$44.72 - \$57.01}{\$7.09} = -1.73$$

So the riskless hedge portfolio requires the holder to short 1.73 call options for every share held long, or, alternatively, to hold long 0.58 shares (1/1.73) for every call option written.

2. The present value of the hedge portfolio:
Since the value of the hedge portfolio equals $44.72 in six months, we need to discount $44.72 to the present using the risk-free rate. Recalling that the six-month risk-free rate in this example is 3.92 percent, we have

Value of Portfolio Today = Present Value of $44.72

$$\$50 - (1.73)(C_0) = \frac{\$44.72}{1.0392} = \$43.03$$

3. The price of a call option:

$$C_0 = \frac{\$50 - \$43.03}{1.73} = \$4.03$$

These initial, intermediate, and terminal option values are summarized in Exhibit 18.9.

Notice two interesting results from this expansion from two to three possible stock price outcomes. First, the addition of a third potential terminal stock price had the effect of reducing the Date 0 option value from $6.48 to $4.03. Although this reduction was a consequence of choosing a third stock price (i.e., $50.99) that caused the option to be out of the money (selecting a value closer to $65.00 would have increased C_0), it does underscore once again that the option valuation process critically depends on the investor's stock price forecast. Second, notice that the hedge ratio changes with stock price changes prior to the expiration date. That is, the composition of the riskless hedge portfolio must be rebalanced after each stock price movement. For example, from the initial position of being short 1.73 calls against one share held long, an upward movement in WYZ stock from $50.00 to $57.01

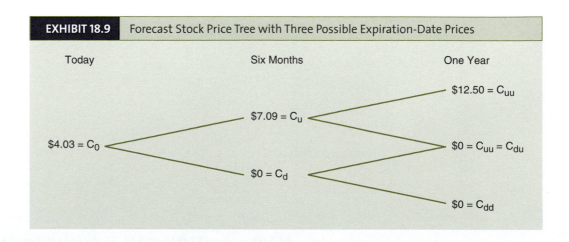

EXHIBIT 18.9   Forecast Stock Price Tree with Three Possible Expiration-Date Prices

Today

Six Months

One Year

$12.50 = C_{uu}

$7.09 = C_u

$4.03 = C_0

$0 = $C_{uu} = C_{du}$

$0 = C_d

$0 = C_{dd}

would require buying back 0.61 (1.73 − 1.12) options. Thus, replicating a risk-free position with stock and call options is a *dynamic* process requiring rebalancing and readjustments.

This valuation process can become even more precise as more terminal stock price outcomes are included in the forecast. Of course, as this happens, the number of pairwise calculations and the number of necessary subperiods will also increase. Consequently, although the three-step valuation method is quite flexible, there is a tradeoff between realism and the volume of required calculations.

We have applied the first step of our three-step process often enough that the astute student may have noticed a short-cut calculation. We can compute the hedge ratio in step 1 as

$$\textbf{Hedge Ratio} = \frac{C_u - C_d}{S_u - S_d}$$

or the difference in call option values (C) at the end of the subperiod divided by the difference in stock prices (S) at the end of the subperiod. In the preceding examples C_d was always zero, but that does not need to be the case. For example, had we used an intermediate price of \$54 rather than \$50.99 in Exhibit 18.8, the intrinsic value of either C_{ud} or C_{du} would have been \$54 − \$52.50 = \$1.50. The hedge ratio would then be

$$\textbf{Hedge Ratio} = \frac{C_u - C_d}{S_u - S_d} = \frac{\$12.50 - \$1.50}{\$65.00 - \$54.00} = \frac{\$11.00}{\$11.00} = 1.00$$

Thus the hedge portfolio would contain 1.00 shares of stock for every call option written, or conversely, 1/1.00 or 1.00 written calls for every share owned.

One difficulty with this process is the requirement that the investor specify future potential stock prices in all subperiods demanded by the forecast. This can be a rather daunting task as the number of possible expiration prices grows larger with the time to expiration of the contract.[2] To simplify, we can, as we did in our examples, assume that each subperiod price move contains one upward movement and one downward movement.[3] We can also focus our estimates on how stock prices change from one subperiod to the next, rather than on the dollar levels. That is, beginnning with today's known price for a stock, for the next subperiod we forecast: (1) one plus the percentage change associated with an upward (u) movement and (2) one plus the percentage change associated with a downward (d) movement. Further, to limit the number of required forecasts, we also assume that the same values for (u) and (d) apply to every upward and downward price movement in all subsequent subperiods. With these assumptions, we need only forecast three things: u, d, and the total number of subperiods. These simplifications represent the essence of the *binomial option-pricing model*. It is a discrete model, using distinct stock price forecasts and definite subperiod intervals (such as six months in our example) to examine option-pricing behavior over time. A more complex model—the Black–Scholes option-pricing model—allows for continuous stock price changes over any number of time periods to estimate the value of call options today.

---

[2] As we have seen in our examples, one interval (say, one year) requires forcasts of two terminal stock prices and two intervals (six months each) requires estimates of three. Using three four-month intervals requires four terminal stock price estimates; four three-month intervals requires five.

[3] For this reason, this analytical development is part of a more general valuation methodology known as the *two state option-pricing* model. See Richard J. Rendleman Jr. and Brit J. Bartter, "Two-State Option Pricing," *Journal of Finance* 34, no. 5 (December 1979): 1093–1110; and John C. Cox, Stephen A. Ross, and Mark Rubinstein, "Option Pricing: A Simplified Approach," *Journal of Financial Economics* 1, no. 3 (September 1979): 229–264.

Black-Scholes Option-Pricing Formula

Black and Scholes developed a formula for determining the value of American call options in a classic article published in 1973.[4] Merton later refined this formula under less restrictive assumptions.[5]

Although the formula appears rather forbidding, one can observe almost all the required inputs directly in the market. Further, although the calculations are rather difficult, numerous programs for computers and hand-held calculators can expedite the process.

The basic Black–Scholes and Merton valuation formula is[6]

18.7

$$P_c = P_s[N(d_1)] - X(e^{-rt})[N(d_2)]$$

where:

P_c = market value of call option

P_s = current market price of underlying common stock

$N(d_1)$ = the probability of a random draw in the standard normal distribution being less than d_1, as defined below

X = exercise price of call option

r = current annualized market interest rate for prime commercial paper

t = time remaining before expiration in years (90 days = 0.25)

$N(d_2)$ = the probability of a random draw in the standard normal distribution being less than d_2, as defined below

The values for d_1 and d_2 are defined as

$$d_1 = \frac{\ln(P_s/X) + (r + 0.5\sigma^2)t}{\sigma(t)^{1/2}}$$

$$d_2 = d_1 - [\sigma(t)^{1/2}]$$

where:

$$\ln\left(\frac{P_s}{X}\right) = \text{natural logarithm of } \left(\frac{P_s}{X}\right)$$

σ = standard deviation of annual rate of return on underlying stock

Note that if both $N(d_1)$ and $N(d_2)$ are close to one, the formula gives a call premium value of (stock price − exercise price), which is the intrinsic value of the option when it is in the money. Similarly, if both $N(d_1)$ and $N(d_2)$ are close to zero, the call option's value is zero, which is its intrinsic value when it is out of the money. $N(d_1)$ is of special significance; it measures the sensitivity of the call premium to a change in the underlying stock price (that is, the change in the call premium for a $1 change in stock price). If $N(d_1)$ equals 0.25, that means a $1 change in the underlying stock price will change the call option premium by

---

[4]Fischer Black and Myron Scholes, "The Pricing of Options and Corporate Liabilities," *Journal of Political Economy* 81, no. 2 (May–June 1973): 637–654. For a background discussion, see Fischer Black, "How We Came Up with the Option Formula," *Journal of Portfolio Management* 15, no. 2 (Winter 1989): 4–8.

[5]Robert C. Merton, "The Theory of Rational Option Pricing," *Bell Journal of Economics and Management Science* 4, no. 3 (August 1973): 141–183.

[6]Fischer Black and Myron Scholes, "The Pricing of Options and Corporate Liabilities," *Journal of Political Economy* 81, no. 2 (May–June 1973): 637–654; Robert C. Merton, "The Theory of Rational Option Pricing," *Bell Journal of Economics and Mangement Science* 4, no. 3 (August 1973): 141–183.

$0.25. Or, put another way, we will need four call options (each changing in value by 25 cents) to fully hedge one share of stock. Thus, the reciprocal of $N(d_1)$ is the *hedge ratio* showing how many call options are needed to hedge each share of stock.

IMPLEMENTING THE BLACK–SCHOLES FORMULA

Although the formula appears quite complicated almost all the required data are observable. The major inputs are current stock price (P_s), exercise price (X), market interest rate (r), time to expiration (t), and standard deviation of annual returns (σ). Once these are determined, a programmable calculator or computer spreadsheet can ease the calculations. For example, the following Excel functions will make the calculation process easier:

"exp" for the terms that are a power of *e*
"Normdist" for determining the probability of having a value less than d_1 and d_2
"ln" for taking natural logs
"sqrt" for taking square roots

With these functions, the value of the call option can be estimated in just a few lines of an Excel spreadsheet. The initial step would be to compute the value of d_1. The second is to calculate d_2. The third is to find the normal probabilities using the "Normdist" function; then it is straightforward to calculate the call option value. Spreadsheet exercises at the end of this chapter will give you practice in doing this.

Using put/call parity (see Chapter 17), we can use the calculated value for the call option to estimate the put option value:

Put Premium = Call Premium + Risk-Free Discount Bond − Stock Price

Or, using the mathematical symbols, we have

$$\text{Put Value } (P_p) = P_c + Xe^{-rt} - P_s$$

which can also be easily computed on a spreadsheet.

Of the five inputs to the Black–Scholes formula, the only variable that is not observable is the volatility of price changes as measured by the standard deviation of returns (σ); it must be estimated. There are several ways to estimate the appropriate level of standard deviation. First, knowledge of past price volatility should be helpful, but volatility of an individual stock changes over time. Second, we can (subjectively or via quantitative modeling) consider factors that change volatility such as industry factors or internal corporate variables (changes in business risk, financial risk, or liquidity risk). Third, by using the Black–Scholes model and the known values used in the model (stock price, exercise price, time to maturity, risk-free rate, and the option's market price), we can find the market's estimate of standard deviation. This estimate is called the *implied volatility* since it is the value for σ that equates the market option price to the pricing equation.[7,8]

---

[7]Implied volatility of several market indexes are estimated and reported minute by minute by the Chicago Board Options Exchange. The VIX (short for Volatility Index) is a weighted average of eight S&P 500 options. It represents the implied volatility for a hypothetical OEX (S&P 500) at-the-money option with thirty calendar days to expiration. Similarly, the VNX is identical to the VIX except that it represents the implied volatility of the Nasdaq 100 (NDX) index.

[8]From this perspective, the standard deviation parameter in the option-pricing model is similar to yield to maturity in bond-pricing models. By equating a bond's observable market price to the present value of its coupon and par value when solving for the interest rate, we are estimating the market-determined yield to maturity for a bond.

One other variable requires some attention: the interest rate. We must use a rate that corresponds to the term of the option. The interest rate on prime commercial paper is quoted daily in *The Wall Street Journal* for maturities of 30, 60, 90, and 240 days.

To demonstrate the application of the formula, let's consider an example with the following variables:

$$P_s = \$36$$

$$X = \$40$$

$$r = 0.10 \text{ (the rate on 90-day prime commercial paper)}$$

$$t = 90 \text{ days (0.25 year)}$$

$$\text{Historical } \sigma = 0.40$$

$$\text{Expected } \sigma = 0.50 \text{ (analysts expect an increase in the stock's volatility because of a new debt issue)}$$

Exhibit 18.10 details the calculations for this option using both the historical and expected volatility measures. These results indicate the importance of estimating stock price volatility. A 25 percent increase in volatility (0.50 versus 0.40) causes a 36 percent increase in the value of the option. Because everything else is observable, this variable will differentiate estimates.

EXHIBIT 18.10 Option Value Calculations

A. Calculation of option value ($\sigma = 0.40$)

$$d_1 = \frac{\ln(36/40) + [0.10 + 0.5(0.4)^2]0.25}{0.4(0.25)^{1/2}}$$

$$= \frac{-0.1054 + 0.045}{0.2}$$

$$= -0.302$$

$$d_2 = -0.302 - [0.4(0.25)^{1/2}]$$

$$= -0.302 - 0.2$$

$$= -0.502$$

$$N(d_1) = 0.3814$$

$$N(d_2) = 0.3079$$

$$P_0 = P_s[N(d_1)] - X(e^{-rt})[N(d_2)]$$

$$= (36)(0.3814) - (40)(e^{-0.025})(0.3079)$$

$$= 13.7304 - (40)(0.9753)(0.3079)$$

$$= 13.7304 - 12.0118$$

$$= 1.7186$$

B. Calculation of option value ($\sigma = 0.50$)

$$d_1 = \frac{\ln(36/40) + [0.10 + 0.5(0.5)^2]0.25}{0.5(0.25)^{1/2}}$$

$$= \frac{(-0.1054 + 0.05625)}{0.25}$$

$$= -0.1966$$

$$d_2 = -0.1966 - [0.5(0.25)^{1/2}]$$

$$= -0.1966 - 0.25$$

$$= -0.4466$$

$$N(d_1) = 0.4199$$

$$N(d_2) = 0.3275$$

$$P_0 = (36)(0.4199) - (40)(e^{-0.025})(0.3275)$$

$$= 15.1164 - (40)(0.9753)(0.3275)$$

$$= 15.1164 - 12.7764$$

$$= 2.34$$

Option-Like Securities

Option contracts can trade over exchanges such as the Chicago Board Options Exchange or over the counter. But several securities with option-like features are also traded in the market. Examples include callable and putable bonds (bonds with a call option and a put option, respectively, included as part of the bond offering), warrants (which, when they are issued, are usually attached to a stock or bond issue), and convertible securities such as bonds or preferred stock that can be converted into a stated number of shares of common stock.

CALLABLE AND PUTABLE BONDS

Callable bonds allow the issuer the option of redeeming the bonds at a call price (typically par value plus one year's coupon interest) rather than waiting until the bonds mature. The call option is unattractive to investors as the call will most likely be exercised after interest rates have fallen and the issuer wishes to replace the higher coupon debt with lower coupon debt. To make the issue more attractive to investors, the issuer will offer the bonds at a lower price or offer a higher coupon rate than straight debt. Over time, a callable bond will typically trade at a price no higher than its call price. This effectively places a ceiling on the bond's price. The difference between the price of the callable bond and a similar straight-debt issue will reflect the value of the call option. This is illustrated in Exhibit 18.11.

Although not as prevalent, putable bonds have been issued by corporations, too. Unlike callable bonds where the issuer owns the call option, investors own the put feature. Investors may put the bonds back to the issuer and receive a specified price for the bonds. Typically, there are two types of events that will trigger the ability of bondholders to put the bonds to the issuer, both of which are related to events that ordinarily would reduce the credit rating of the bond. One is the occurrence of a prospectus-specified "designated

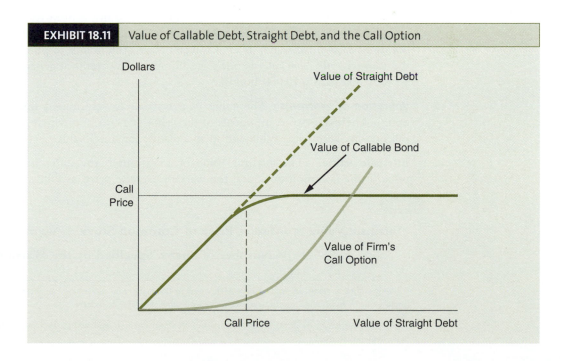

EXHIBIT 18.11 Value of Callable Debt, Straight Debt, and the Call Option

event" such as a leveraged merger or buyout. The second type of putable bond allows investors to put the bonds under any circumstances that result in a reduction in the bond rating below a specified rating. For example, the put option may become active should the bond's rating slip to "junk" levels with a rating of BB or lower. As in the case of a callable bond, the value of the put option to the investor equals the price difference between the putable bond and straight debt with a similar rating and time to maturity.

WARRANTS

A *warrant* is an option to buy a stated number of shares of common stock at a specified price at any time during the life of the warrant. Although this definition is quite similar to the description of a call option, it has several important differences. First, when originally issued, the life of a warrant is usually much longer than that of a call option. Although the listed option markets have introduced long-term options (LEAPS), the typical exchange-traded call option has a term to expiration that ranges from three to nine months. In contrast, a warrant generally has an original term to maturity of at least two years, and most are between five and ten years. Some are much longer, including a few perpetual warrants.

A second major difference is that warrants are usually issued by the company on whose stock the warrant is written. As a result, when the warrant is exercised, the investor buys the stock from the company, and the proceeds from the sale are new capital to the issuing firm.[9]

Consider the following hypothetical example. The Becking Corporation is going to issue $10 million in bonds but knows that within the next five years it will also need an additional $5 million in new external equity beyond the expected retained earnings. One way to make the bond issue more attractive, and also possibly sell the required stock, is to attach warrants to the bonds. To keep things simple, we shall assume the warrants are European-style, that is, they cannot be exercised before the expiration.[10] If Becking common stock is currently selling at $45 a share, the firm may decide to issue five-year warrants that will allow the holder to acquire the company's common stock at an exercise price of $50. Because the firm wants to raise $5 million in equity, it must issue warrants for 100,000 shares ($5 million/$50). To raise $10 million in debt, the firm will need to sell 10,000 bonds (at $1,000 par value). If each warrant allows the holder to purchase one share (that is, the *warrant conversion ratio* is one), the number of warrants attached to each bond will be 10 (100,000 shares/10,000 bonds).

Valuation of Warrants   The value of a warrant is determined much like that of a call option. There are two components of the value of a warrant, which are similar to those of a call option: its intrinsic value and its speculative (or time) value.

Intrinsic value.   The intrinsic value of a warrant is the difference between the market price of the common stock and the warrant exercise price, as follows:

18.8

$$\textbf{Intrinsic Value} = \textbf{(Market Price of Common Stock} - \textbf{Warrant Exercise Price)}$$
$$\times \textbf{ Number of Shares Specified by the Warrant}$$

---

[9]Although most warrants outstanding have been issued in this manner, in recent years an increasing number of warrants issued by firms and foreign governments are written on other securities or indexes.

[10]Most warrants issued by firms on their own shares are American-style and will be exercised early only if sufficiently high dividends are paid.

Consider a firm that has outstanding warrants that expire in 2008 and allow the holder of the warrant to buy two shares of stock at $17 a share. The common stock is currently selling for $21, and the warrant is priced at $10. The warrant has an intrinsic value of $8: ($21.00 − $17.00) × 2 = $8. Since the market price of the warrant ($10) is above its intrinsic value ($8), the warrant has a speculative value of $2.

Similar to a call option, a warrant's leverage is an important investment consideration. As an example, assume a stock is selling for $48, and a warrant for the stock with an exercise price of $50 is selling for $3. This warrant has no intrinsic value because its exercise price is above the market price. The $3 price represents speculative value. If the stock were to increase 15 percent to $55, the warrant would rise to at least $5, its new intrinsic value. Thus, a stock price increase of about 15 percent would cause the price of the warrant to increase by at least 67 percent, from $3 to $5. Any speculative value would boost the price of the warrant even higher.

CONVERTIBLE SECURITIES

A *convertible security* gives the holder the right to convert one type of security into a stipulated amount of another (usually common stock) at the investor's discretion. Convertibles exhibit some characteristics of a bond and other characteristics of the security they are convertible into. Convertible issues generally are subordinated to the firm's other debt. Like warrants, convertibles are usually offered to attract investors to a bond issue.

As an example of a typical convertible bond, consider an issue offered by Amoco that matures in the year 2013, carries a coupon of $7\frac{3}{8}$ percent, and pays interest semiannually on March 1 and September 1. It has a face value of $1,000 and can be converted into 19.048 shares of Amoco Corporation common stock. This value, 19.048, is the *conversion ratio*. Alternatively, when the face value of $1,000 is divided by the conversion ratio of 19.048, it gives $52.50, which is called the *conversion price*. A convertible can be thought of as an ordinary bond with a call option attached, which in this case allows the bondholder to buy 19.048 shares of stock by simply tendering the bond.

Issuing convertible bonds is considered attractive for a company for several reasons. By attaching the convertible feature, a firm can often get a *lower interest rate* on its debt. If the firm's common stock subsequently rises in value and the securities are converted to common stock, the firm reduces its financial leverage and gains equity financing.

Convertibles provide investors with the upside potential of common stock and the downside protection of a bond. If the stock price increases, the convertible bond gains in value due to the increased value of the stock into which it can be converted. The convertible bond has downside protection because, no matter what happens to the stock, the price of the bond will not decline below what it would be worth as a straight bond. In addition, the convertible usually has a higher current yield than the underlying common stock. Suppose Amoco pays a dividend of $2.20 per share. The Amoco bond is convertible into 19.048 shares of stock, which means that the total dividends on the stock would be 19.048 × $2.20 = $41.91. In contrast, the bond pays $7\frac{3}{8}$ percent interest, which gives $73.75.

Valuation of Convertibles[11]   The value of the convertible as a bond is called its *bond* or *investment value* (also called *floor value*). To determine the bond value, we must determine the bond's required yield as though it had no conversion feature attached. A simple (but not always feasible) way to do this is to identify a nonconvertible bond with similar characteristics

---

[11]We examine valuation issues in the context of convertible bonds; the concepts are applicable to analyzing convertible preferred stock, too.

issued by the company. Let's assume a comparable straight issue of Amoco is its $8\frac{5}{8}$s of 2016 and that these bonds are priced at 110 for a yield of 7.72 percent. Let us round this off and assume the convertible as a straight bond would yield 7.70 percent and have a maturity of twenty years. Using these assumptions, the bond value of the Amoco convertible bond with a $7\frac{3}{8}$ coupon would be about $950. Comparing this bond value to the current market price of the convertible (about $1,215) the *investment premium* is

$$\frac{1,215.00 - 950.00}{1,215.00} = 21.81\%$$

This is a measure of the downside risk assuming the bond's yield would not change if the firm's performance deteriorated. But if the stock price falls substantially because of a perceived bankruptcy threat, the bond's required yield would rise and its investment value would fall.

The bond's *conversion* or *equity value* (also caled *parity*) is the value of the common stock the investor will receive if she converts the bond. The conversion value equals the conversion ratio of 19.048 multiplied by the current stock price. If Amoco was trading at 57, the conversion value would be 19.048 × $57 = $1,085.74. Obviously, the conversion value is linearly related to the stock price.

The value of the convertible bond must at least equal the conversion value or the bond value, whichever is larger. Thus we can state:

18.9   **Minimum Price of Convertible = Max [Bond Value, Conversion Value]**

In this case, the minimum value is the conversion value of $1,085.74, which exceeds the bond value of $950.

Because of the speculative value of the option to convert, the market value of the convertible should be higher than its minimum value except at maturity. This amount over its minimum value is called the *conversion premium* and is calculated as

18.10 $$\text{Conversion Premium} = \frac{\text{Market Price} - \text{Minimum Value}}{\text{Minimum Value}}$$

If the Amoco convertible was selling at $1,215, the conversion premium would be

$$\frac{\$1,215.00 - \$1,085.74}{\$1,085.74} = 11.91\%$$

This indicates that the option value adds about 12 percent to the minimum value of the bond.

Another useful measure for a convertible bond is the *conversion parity price*. This is defined as

18.11 $$\text{Conversion Parity Price} = \frac{\text{Market Price of Convertible Bond}}{\text{Conversion Ratio}}$$

For Amoco, this is

$$\frac{\$1,215.00}{19.048} = \$63.79$$

The conversion parity price indicates that if the bond were purchased and immediately converted, the effective price paid for the common stock would be $63.79 compared to the current stock price of $57.

Exhibit 18.12 illustrates the factors involved in the value of a convertible bond. There is an upper bound for the value of a convertible; it cannot sell for more than the firm's assets.

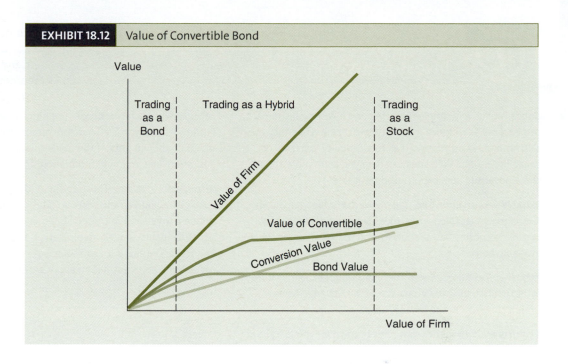

EXHIBIT 18.12   Value of Convertible Bond

Thus, the value of the convertible must be below the forty-five-degree line. Note that the line for the bond value is relatively flat for a wide range of firm values—higher firm values do not increase the value of the bond because the bondholders receive only their promised payments. In contrast, at fairly low firm values the value of the convertible drops off as bankruptcy becomes more likely. Conversion value rises directly with the value of the firm. This graph shows that for low firm values, the bond value will be the minimum value of the convertible; for high firm values, the conversion value will be the minimum value of the convertible. Finally, the line for the value of the convertible shows that when the firm value is low, the convertible will act more like a bond, trading for only a slight premium over the bond value. Alternatively, when firm values are high, the convertible will act more like a stock, selling for only a slight premium over the conversion value. In the fairly wide middle range, the convertible will trade as a hybrid security that acts somewhat like a bond and somewhat like a stock.

Convertible Arbitrage   One means for explicitly trading on the conversion option with the bond is to do convertible arbitrage. By owning the convertible bond and shorting the issuer's stock using an appropriate hedge ratio, investors can try to isolate the value of the conversion option. Increases in the stock price will result in offsetting changes as the convertible bond increases in value and the short stock position loses value; the opposite is true if the stock price falls. If an investor thinks the convertible bond is underpriced relative to the conversion option, conversion arbitrage may be a means of capturing some of the expected bond undervaluation while hedging the overall position with a short stock position. Another source of return from this strategy is income. The convertible bond will pay more coupon income than the dividend on the stock. In addition, short-sale proceeds on the stock can be invested in safe securities and earn interest.

Sources of Information on Convertibles   Information on many convertible bonds is available in reference books on ordinary bonds such as *Standard & Poor's Bond Guide* and *Mergent Bond Record*. *Value Line Convertibles* also has information on convertibles as well as warrants.

Investments Online

Bonds, a relatively simple financing and investing instrument, can become as complex as an equity to value when they contain embedded options such as convertibility, warrants, or callability. Several Web sites can help you learn more about these advanced applications of derivatives.

http://www.calamos.com Calamos Asset Management, Inc., specializes in research, investment, and management of convertible securities. News, analysis, and market updates are available here.

http://www.optionscentral.com The Options Clearing Corporation is the issuer and guarantor of all exchange-traded option contracts in the United States.

http://www.optionetics.com This home page offers free and purchased information to visitors, including price and volume analysis for stock option contracts.

http://www.nfa.futures.org/ The home page of the National Futures Association is an industry group whose purpose is to maintain the integrity of the marketplace. It features investor education links, training information, and regulatory issues.

http://www.cftc.gov The Web site of the Commodities Futures Trading Commission regulates commodity futures and option markets in the United States. The agency protects market participants against manipulation, abusive trade practices, and fraud. The site is a good source of information on laws, regulations, and information about exchanges.

Summary

- In futures valuation, the cost of carry model is used to determine futures prices. Market imperfections—such as storage costs, cash flows from ownership, and transactions costs—need to be included in the futures valuation relationship.

- The concept of arbitrage is used many ways in derivative security pricing. The cost of carry model uses arbitrage to derive an appropriate price for futures contracts. Advanced applications of futures contracts for hedging, speculating, or taking advantage of arbitrage opportunities include stock-index arbitrage and the NOB futures spread.

- Options on futures are useful for investors who want to participate in the futures market but want the downside protection of options. With options on futures, the loss is limited to the price (premium) for the option and the investor is not subject to marking to market every day.

- There are five factors essential to the valuation of call and put options. These are the stock price, exercise

price, time to maturity, interest rate, and volatility of the underlying stock.

- The binomial option-pricing model is a simplified way to estimate option prices. The model assumes that stock prices either rise or fall by a given percentage over consecutive time intervals.

- The Black–Scholes option-pricing model is a powerful tool for estimating call option prices (and, via put/call parity, put prices). Spreadsheets and specialized financial calculators can be used to estimate option prices or to use market prices of options to determine the market's value of implied volatility.

- Many securities—such as callable and putable bonds, warrants, and convertible securities—have the characteristics of options. Callable and putable bonds contain embedded options. Issuing firms may exercise the call option by redeeming a callable bond at a specified call (or exercise) price. The investor may exercise the put option by putting the bonds to the issuer at the exercise price if specific events occur. Warrants are options written by firms and are similar to ordinary calls, except that they tend to have longer original maturities and when they are exercised the number of firms' shares increases. Convertible securities give the holder the right to convert one type of security into a stipulated amount of another type. The two most popular types of convertibles are convertible bonds and convertible preferred stock.

- Convertibles can be priced using some principles derived from option theory.

- All derivative instruments provide additional investment opportunities. The analysis and valuation of these instruments are complex, but they add the potential for an improved risk–return profile and should not be ignored when constructing diversified global portfolios.

QUESTIONS

CFA

1. *CFA Examination Level II*
   Four factors affect the value of a futures contract on a stock index. Three of these factors are the current price of the stock index, the time remaining until the contract maturity (delivery) date, and the dividends on the stock index. Identify the fourth factor and explain how and why changes in this factor affect the value of the futures contract. (5 minutes)

2. Explain what is meant by *cost of carry*. How does it affect futures valuation?

3. Show how arbitrage can be used to determine the proper price for a futures contract.

4. How do storage costs, insurance, and cash flows (such as dividends or interest) affect the pricing of futures contracts? Can market prices still be affected by arbitrage in the face of these additional variables?

5. How do transactions costs, such as bid–ask spreads and commissions, affect futures valuation and the ability to arbitrage if the futures price deviates from its cost of carry value?

6. What is basis? What should happen to the basis as the expiration of a futures contract approaches?

CFA

7. *CFA Examination Level II*
   Mike Lane will have $5 million to invest in five-year U.S. Treasury bonds three months from now. Lane believes interest rates will fall during the next three months and wants to take advantage of prevailing interest rates by hedging against a decline in interest rates. Lane has sufficient funds to pay the costs of entering into and maintaining a futures position.
   a. Describe what action Lane should take using five-year U.S. Treasury note futures contracts to protect against declining interest rates. (5 minutes)
   Assume three months have gone by and despite Lane's expectations, five-year cash and forward market interest rates have increased by 100 basis points compared with the five-year forward market interest rates of three months ago.
   b. Discuss the effect of higher interest rates on the value of the futures position that Lane entered into in part (a). (4 minutes)

   c. Discuss how the return from Lane's hedged position differs from the return he could now earn if he had not hedged in part (a). (4 minutes)

8. It is often stated that a stock-index arbitrage trade is easier to implement when the stock-index futures contract price is above its theoretical level than when it is below that value. What institutional realities make this statement true? Describe the steps involved in forming the arbitrage transaction in both circumstances. To the extent that the statement is valid, what does it suggest about the ability of the stock-index futures market to remain efficient?

9. Briefly explain an option on a futures contract.

10. If there are futures contracts and option contracts, what economic purpose is served by having an option on a futures contract?

11. Assuming the underlying asset for a futures contract goes up in value by 15 percent, would you be better off owning a futures contract or an option on the futures? Which instrument would you want if the asset declined by 20 percent?

12. What factors affect the price of an option contract? Explain how each affects the option premium.

13. What purpose does the hedge portfolio serve in the binomial option-pricing model?

14. What is a hedge ratio? Interpret the meaning of a hedge of 1.5; of 0.60.

15. If a stock's standard deviation of returns rises, what happens to the value of its call and put options? If the stock's beta rises, what happens to the value of its call and put options?

16. How can implied volatility be estimated?

17. What adjustment should be made to the Black–Scholes option-pricing model if a stock pays dividends?

18. Who owns the call option in a callable bond? All else constant, how should a callable bond be priced relative to a noncallable bond? Who owns the put option in a putable bond? How should investors price putable bonds relative to nonputable bonds?

19. What are the major differences between a warrant and a call option?

20. Identify and discuss the factors that influence the value of a warrant.

21. What condition must exist at expiration for the holder of a warrant to decide to exercise it?

22. The Baron Corporation debentures are rated Aa by Moody's and are selling to yield 9.30 percent. The firm's subordinated convertible bonds are rated A by Moody's and are selling to yield 8.20 percent. Explain how this phenomenon could exist.

23. Describe what is meant by the upside potential of convertible bonds. How do convertible bonds also provide downside protection?

24. What is convertible arbitrage? Why is it done?

25. Assume a convertible bond's conversion value is substantially above par. Why would the bondholder continue holding the bond rather than converting?

PROBLEMS

1. The spot price of gold is $275 an ounce. The T-bill rate is 0.33 percent per month. What is the appropriate price for a three-month futures contract for gold?

2. Using the information in Problem 1, compute the futures prices for contracts requiring delivery of gold in three, six, nine, and twelve months.

3. Wheat futures are selling at 305 (cents per bushel) for six-month futures contracts. If storage and insurance for wheat is ½ percent per month and the six-month T-bill rate is 1.5 percent, what should be the current spot price for wheat?

4. What would be a nonarbitragable price range for wheat in Problem 3 if the commission for buying or selling wheat was 0.75 percent?

5. Suppose the market price for gold is $275. What is the value of the basis for each of the futures prices calculated in Problem 2? For the three-month futures contract, what will be the value of the basis after three months?

6. You are a cocoa dealer anticipating the purchase of seventy-five metric tons in three months. You are concerned that the price of cocoa will rise, so you take a long position in cocoa futures. Since cocoa futures do not expire every month, you purchase a four-month futures contract. Each contract covers ten metric tons; you decide to go long seven contracts. The futures price at the time you initiate your hedge is $1,028 per ton and the spot price is $1,005. Three months later the actual spot price of cocoa turns out to be $1,039 per ton and the futures price is $1,045.
   a. Determine the effective price at which you purchased your cocoa. How do you account for the difference in the amounts for the spot and hedge positions?
   b. How did the basis change during the time you held the contracts? Describe the nature of the basis risk in this long hedge.

7. *CFA Examination Level II*
   Donna Doni, CFA, wants to explore potential inefficiencies in the futures market. The TOBEC stock index has a spot value of 185.00 now. TOBEC futures contracts are settled in cash and underlying contract values

are determined by multiplying $100 times the index value. The current annual risk-free interest rate is 6.0 percent.
   a. Calculate the theoretical price of the futures contract expiring six months from now, using the cost of carry model. Show your calculations. (4 minutes)
   The total (round-trip) transaction cost for trading a futures contract is $15.00.
   b. Calculate the lower bound for the price of the futures contract expiring six months from now. Show your calculations. (6 minutes)

8. *CFA Examination Level II*
   Joan Tam, CFA, believes she has identified an arbitrage opportunity for a commodity as indicated by the information given below.

Commodity Price and Interest Rate Information

Spot price for commodity	$120
Futures price for commodity expiring in 1 year	$125
Interest rate for one year	8%

   a. Describe the transactions necessary to take advantage of this specific arbitrage opportunity. (6 minutes)
   b. Calculate the arbitrage profit. (3 minutes)
   c. Describe *two* market imperfections that could limit Tam's ability to implement this arbitrage strategy. (6 minutes)

9. An investment bank engages in stock-index arbitrage for its own and customer accounts. On a particular day, the S&P 500 index is 1060.23 when the futures contract for delivery in ninety days is 1083.56. If the annualized ninety-day interest rate is 8 percent and the annualized dividend yield is 3 percent, could program trading involving stock-index arbitrage possibly take place? If so, describe the transactions that should be undertaken and calculate the profit that would be made per each "share" of the S&P 500 index used in the trade.

10. Consider the following price quotes in mid-October for T-bond and T-note futures contracts maturing in December.

Contract	Settle Price
20-year 6% T-bond	103-25
20-year 6% T-note	104-15

You believe the yield curve will steepen in the next few months. Suppose the rate on the twenty-year bond rises to 8 percent while the yield on the ten-year bond moves to 7 percent.

a. How much money do you gain or lose on the NOB spread?

b. How much money do you gain or lose if the yield curve flattens and both securities yield 7 percent?

11. Assuming the probability of a stock price increase or decrease is equally likely, compute the probability of being on each branch of stock price trees with two, three, four, and five subintervals. (*Hint:* Exhibit 18.8 presents a tree with two subintervals.) It is said that the binomial option-pricing model approximates the Black–Scholes' model assumption of normally distributed stock price as the number of subintervals rises. Does this approximation seem reasonable?

12. Use the binomial option-pricing model to estimate the value of a call option with an exercise price of $24 if the stock currently sells for $20 and is equally likely to rise or fall by 21 percent in the next year. Use a one-year risk-free rate of 4 percent.

13. Compute the value of the call option in Problem 12 if (examine each of these changes separately from the others):

a. The exercise price is $22.

b. The time frame is 6 months.

c. The annual risk-free rate is 8 percent.

14. Use the binomial option-pricing model to estimate the value of a call option that expires in one year. It has an exercise price of $24. The stock currently sells for $20 and is equally likely to rise or fall by 10 percent in each six-month period. After one year, the stock's price will be $16.20, $19.80, or $24.20. Use a one-year risk-free rate of 4 percent.

15. Use the binomial option-pricing model to estimate the value of a call option that expires in one year. It has an exercise price of $24. The stock currently sells for $20 and is equally likely to rise or fall by 10 percent in the first six-month period. After one year, the stock's price will be $16.20, $21, or $24.20. Use a one-year risk-free of 4 percent.

16. Estimate the Black–Scholes price for a call option of a stock with a current price of $50 and an expected volatility of 60 percent (0.60). The option's exercise price is $55, and it expires in two months (sixty days). The risk-free rate is 2 percent (0.02) over this time frame.

17. What is the appropriate price of the corresponding put option in Problem 16?

18. What is the price of a call option for a stock with a current price of $24 and an historical volatility of 25 percent that is expected to rise to 40 percent? The option expires in three months (ninety days) and has an exercise price of $20. The risk-free rate is 1 percent (0.01).

19. What is the appropriate price of the corresponding put option in Problem 18?

20. A firm has 100,000 shares of stock outstanding priced at $40. It has no debt. The firm issues 10,000 warrants, each allowing the purchase of one share of stock at a price of $50. The warrants expire in five years and currently are priced at $2.

a. Estimate the intrinsic value of the warrants.

b. Determine the speculative value of the warrant and discuss the justification for this value.

c. Assume the stock price increases by 50 percent. What will be the minimum increase in the value of the warrant?

21. The Harley Corporation has an 8 percent subordinated convertible debenture outstanding that is due in ten years. The current yield to maturity on this A-rated bond is 5 percent. The current yield on nonconvertible A-rated bonds is 10 percent. This bond is convertible into twenty-one shares of common stock and is callable at 106 of par, which is $1,000. The company's $10 par value common stock is currently selling for $54.

a. What is the straight-debt value of this convertible bond, assuming semiannual interest payments?

b. What is the conversion value of this bond?

c. At present, what would be the minimum value of this bond?

d. At present, could the Harley Corporation get rid of this convertible debenture? If so, discuss specifically how it would do so.

22. *CFA Examination Level II*   **CFA**

Singh is also analyzing a convertible bond. The characteristics of the bond and the underlying common stock are given below.

Convertible Bond and Underlying Stock Characteristics

Convertible Bond Characteristics	
Par Value	$1,000
Annual Coupon Rate (annual pay)	6.5%
Conversion Ratio	22
Market Price	105% of par value
Straight Value	99% of par value

Underlying Stock Characteristics	
Current Market Price	$40 per share
Annual Cash Dividend	$1.20 per share

a. Compute the bond's:

i. Conversion value

ii. Market conversion price (6 minutes)

b. Determine whether the value of a callable convertible bond will increase, decrease, or remain unchanged in response to *each* of the following changes, and justify *each* of your responses with *one* reason:
   i. An increase in stock price volatility
   ii. An increase in interest rate volatility (6 minutes)
23. Extractive Industries has debentures outstanding (par value $1,000) that are convertible into the company's common stock at a price of $25. The convertibles have a coupon interest rate of 11 percent and mature ten years from today. Interest is payable semiannually, and the convertible debenture is callable with a one-year interest premium.
   a. Calculate the conversion value if the stock price is $20 per share.
   b. Calculate the conversion value if the stock price is $28 per share.
   c. Calculate the straight-bond value, assuming that nonconvertible bonds of equivalent risk and maturity are yielding 12 percent per year compounded semiannually.

d. Assume the stock price is $28. The convertible is selling for $1,225. Calculate the conversion parity price.
e. Using the information in part (d), calculate the conversion premium.
24. Sitting next to Dan at a business luncheon, Rachel explained, "I bought American Desk at $20 a share and it's gone to $40." Dan said, "You would have done better to buy American's warrants, as I did."
   a. Why did Dan say this?
   b. The exercise price of American Desk warrants is $18. Dan purchased the warrants for $4 each when American Desk's stock price was $20 a share. Each warrant entitles Dan to purchase one share of American stock. Assuming the original $2 time value of the warrant dropped to $1, what is the current price of the warrant?
   c. Calculate Rachel's percentage gain.
   d. Calculate Dan's percentage gain when the stock price is $40 and the time value of the warrant is $1.

WEB EXERCISES

1. The Web site *http://www.pmpublishing.com* contains a wealth of data about traded options. Click on the section of the home page dealing with volatility and then select the Chicago Merc's S&P 500 options. Interpret the information it contains on implied volatilities.
2. Visit the Web site *http://www.business.com/directory/financial_services/investment_banking_and_brokerage/sales_and_trading/calculators/options/* and evaluate at least three of the options calculators it offers. Do they all give the

same answers to the data you input? Compare the performance of binomial and Black–Scholes option-pricing model calculators. How do their estimates differ for small volatility and large volatility inputs?
3. Calamos Asset Management, Inc., is a leading firm in the research, investment, and management of convertible securities. Study their Web site, *http://www.calamos.com,* and summarize their perspectives on the current market environment for convertible securities.

SPREADSHEET EXERCISES

1. What inputs do you need to price call options? Create a spreadsheet that will allow you to input the necessary values in separate cells and allow you to estimate call prices using the Black–Scholes option-pricing model (BSOPM).
2. (a) Using the spreadsheet you created in Exercise 1, calculate the value of the following call option: $P_s = \$75$; $X = \$70$; r = 5% (or 0.05); $t = 90$ days (or 0.25 years); $\sigma = 0.30$. (b) Change the inputs, one at a time, and recalculate the call option price to verify the information in Exhibit 18.7. After each recalculation, revert to

the original input values and recalculate using the next variable change. Use these values as the new inputs: $P_s = \$85$; $X = \$73$; r = 0.07; $t = 0.33$ years; $\sigma = 0.50$.
3. Expand your spreadsheet from Exercise 1 to include a calculation of the put option price using put/call parity to compute the price of the corresponding put option. Repeat parts (a) and (b) of Exercise 2.
4. Create a spreadsheet to assist the trial-and-error process of finding the implied volatility of an option. This spreadsheet will require the basic BSOPM inputs but also needs to include the current market price of the option (from the newspaper or a market news Web site). By trial and error, input different values for the standard

deviation until the BSOPM price estimate is very close to that of the actual market price. The resulting standard deviation will be the implied volatility estimate.

5. Construct a spreadsheet for evaluating convertible bonds using the following input values in different cells: Par Value, Coupon Rate, Years to Maturity, Current Convertible Market Price, Yield to Maturity as a Straight Bond, Conversion Factor, Current Common Stock Price, Dividends Per Share of Common Stock. Use the spreadsheet to calculate the following information: Conversion Price, Annual Common Stock Dividends, Annual Coupon Income, Straight Bond Price Estimate, Conversion Value, Conversion Premium, Conversion Parity Price. Estimate these values for a convertible bond with a $1,000 par value, 8 percent coupon, and fifteen years until maturity. The convertible's current price is $1,050. If it were nonconvertible, its yield to maturity would be 8.30 percent. The conversion factor is 15, with a current common stock price of $65. The stock pays a quarterly dividend of 50 cents per share.

6. How would the spreadsheet in Exercise 5 need to be modified for analysis of convertible preferred stock?

REFERENCES

Benninga, Simon. *Financial Modelling,* 2nd ed. Cambridge, MA: MIT Press, 2000.

Bhattacharya, Mihir, and Yu Zhu. "Valuation and Analysis of Convertible Securities." In *The Handbook of Fixed Income Securities,* 4th ed., edited by Frank J. Fabozzi and T. Dessa Fabozzi. Chicago: Irwin, 1995.

Black, Fischer, and Myron Scholes. "The Pricing of Options and Corporate Liabilities." *Journal of Political Economy* 81, no. 2 (May–June 1973).

Burns, Terence E. *Derivatives in Portfolio Management.* Charlottesville, VA: AIMR, 1998.

Carow, Kenneth A., Gayle R. Erwin, and John J. McConnell. "A Survey of U.S. Corporate Financing Innovations: 1970–1997." *Journal of Applied Corporate Finance* 12, no. 1 (Spring 1999): 55–69.

Hull, John. *Fundamentals of Futures and Options Markets,* 4th ed. Englewood Cliffs, NJ: Prentice-Hall, 2001.

Ingersoll, Jonathan E. Jr. "A Contingent Claims Valuation of Convertible Securities." *Journal of Financial Economics* 4, no. 4 (May 1977).

Kolb, Robert W. *Futures, Options, and Swaps,* 3rd ed. Boston: Blackwell Publishers, 2000.

Glossary

Basis The difference between a spot and a futures price.

Basis risk Risk arising from variability in basis over time.

Binomial option-pricing model A discrete model that uses distinct price forecasts and definite subperiod intervals to examine option-pricing behavior over time.

Bond value *See* Investment value.

Convergence At futures contract expiration, the futures price must equal the spot price.

Conversion parity price The market value of a convertible bond divided by the number of shares into which it can be converted (its conversion ratio).

Conversion premium The excess of the market value of the convertible over its equity value if immediately converted into common stock. Typically expressed as a percentage of the equity value.

Conversion (or exercise) price The price at which common stock can be obtained by surrendering the convertible instrument at par value.

Conversion ratio The number of shares of common stock for which a convertible security may be exchanged.

Conversion value *See* Equity value.

Convertible security A security that gives the holder the right to convert one type of security into a stipulated amount of another security at the investor's discretion.

Equity value The value of the convertible security if converted into common stock at the stock's current market price. Also referred to as *parity* or *conversion value*.

Floor value *See* Investment value.

Hedge portfolio A portfolio created by combining securities and derivative securities so that its value at a future time is known and is not dependent on market moves.

Hedge ratio The number of securities held for each derivative security in a hedge portfolio.

Investment value The price at which a convertible would have to sell as a straight-debt instrument. Also referred to as *bond value* or *floor value*.

Notes over bond (NOB) spread Buying and selling Treasury note and Treasury bond futures to take advantage of anticipated changes in the slope of the yield curve.

Options on futures An option contract where the underlying security is a futures contract.

Parity (or conversion parity) *See* Equity value.

Stock-index arbitrage Buying and selling of stocks and stock futures contracts to take advantage of mispricing between the spot and futures markets.

Warrant An option to buy a stated number of shares of common stock from the company at a specified price at any time during the life of the warrant.

Warrant conversion ratio The number of shares of stock that can be purchased for each warrant.

Portfolio Management Applications

Pulling together what we have learned of stock analysis, bond analysis, portfolio theory, and derivative securities, we examine practical portfolio management in this section. In Chapter 19 we discuss active and passive equity portfolio management. We consider several investing styles such as value, growth, large-cap, and small-cap. We also illustrate the use of futures and options contracts in managing equity portfolios and the effect of taxes on portfolio management decisions.

In Chapter 20 we employ our background in bond fundamentals and analysis to examine bond-portfolio management. There are three major bond-portfolio strategies; we consider each of them in detail. The first set consists of passive strategies, which include either a simple buy-and-hold strategy or an indexing strategy. The second set consists of active management strategies, which involve one of six alternatives: interest rate anticipation, valuation analysis, credit analysis, yield-spread analysis, bond swaps, and core-plus management. The third set consists of matched-funding strategies, which include dedicated portfolios, classical immunization portfolios, and horizon matching techniques. We also review the use of derivatives in managing bond portfolios.

The final step in the money management process is to evaluate the performance of the portfolio manager relative to the client's goals and objectives. Therefore, we review and illustrate several methods of evaluating performance on a risk-adjusted basis. Since an appropriate benchmark that reflects the client's risk-return objectives is needed to properly evaluate portfolio performance, we discuss the characteristics of a good benchmark portfolio and issues surrounding benchmarks for tax-exempt and taxable portfolios. We illustrate how attribution analysis can be used in both equity and bond portfolios to determine the source of a portfolio's over- (or under-) performance versus its benchmark.

Equity-Portfolio Management

I n previous chapters we have reviewed how to analyze industries and companies, how to estimate a stock's intrinsic value, and how technical analysis can assist in stock picking. Some equity portfolios are constructed one stock at a time. Research staffs analyze the economy, industries, and companies; evaluate firms' strategies and competitive advantages; and recommend individual stocks for purchase or for sale. Other equity portfolios use quantitative methods. Computers analyze relationships between stocks and market sectors in an attempt to identify undervalued stocks. Numerical "screens" and factor models help construct portfolios of stocks with certain attributes, such as low P/E ratios, low price–book value ratios, or stocks whose returns are strongly correlated with economic variables such as interest rates. Computer programs detect trading patterns that allow portfolio managers to place buy and sell orders based on past price movements. Armed with computer-generated pricing relationships across markets, managers place orders to arbitrage small price differences between stocks, options, and futures.

Portfolio managers can modify equity-portfolio return profiles through futures and options. Futures contracts on major indexes as well as options on indexes, selected industry groups, and individual stocks help portfolio managers shift a portfolio's systematic and unsystematic risk exposure.

Introduction

Equity-portfolio management styles fall into one of two categories: passive or active.[1] In the following discussion we give the traditional definitions of these categories.

---

[1]Some argue that hybrid active/passive equity-portfolio management styles exist, but such styles actually reflect active management philosophies. An example of this is enhanced indexing, which seeks to provide returns above those of a specified index by investing in

Passive equity-portfolio management is a buy-and-hold strategy. Usually the manager purchases stocks so that the portfolio's returns track those of an index over time. Occasional rebalancing occurs as dividends are reinvested and because stocks merge or drop out of the target index and other stocks are added. Notably, the portfolio is designed not to "beat" the target index but to match its performance, and the manager is judged on how well it does so.

Active equity-portfolio management attempts to outperform, on a risk-adjusted basis, a passive benchmark portfolio.[2] A *benchmark portfolio* is a passive portfolio whose average characteristics (in terms of beta, dividend yield, industry weighting, firm size, and so on) match the risk–return objectives of the client and serves as a basis for evaluating the performance of an active manager.

In the next sections we will examine more closely the mechanics of passive and active equity-portfolio management.

Passive Management Strategies

The aim of passive equity-portfolio management is a portfolio that replicates the performance of an index. The key word here is *replicate*. A true passive manager earns his or her fee by constructing a portfolio that closely tracks the performance of a specified index that meets the client's needs and objectives. Any attempts by the manager to do better than the selected index violate the passive premise of the portfolio and should be cause for dismissal. In actuality, a passive index portfolio may slightly underperform the target index after fees and commissions are deducted from the gross returns.

In Chapter 10 we presented several reasons for investing in a passive equity portfolio in our discussion of market efficiency. In Chapter 7 we described many different market indexes. Domestic U.S. indexes include the S&P 500, 400, and 100; the Value Line index; and the Wilshire 5000. *The Wall Street Journal* publishes the daily values of indexes for the organized exchanges, Nasdaq, and various industry groups. Indexes exist for small-cap stocks (Russell 2000), for value- or growth-oriented stocks (Russell Growth Index and Russell Value Index), for numerous world regions (such as the EAFE index), as well as for smaller regions and individual countries. As passive investing has grown in popularity, money managers have created an index fund for virtually every broad market category.

Some passive portfolios are not based on a published index. "Customized" passive portfolios, called *completeness funds,* can be constructed to complement active portfolios that do not cover the entire market. For example, suppose a pension fund hires three active managers to invest part of the fund's money. One manager emphasizes small-cap U.S. stocks; the second invests only in Pacific Rim countries, and the third invests in U.S. stocks with low P/E ratios. To ensure adequate diversification, the pension fund may want to passively invest the remaining funds in a completeness fund. In this case, the completeness fund's specialized benchmark would include large-cap and midcap U.S. stocks, U.S. stocks with normal to high P/E ratios, and international stocks outside the Pacific Rim. The manager would compare

stocks whose overall characteristics (such as P/E, dividend yield, beta, sector weights, and so forth) are close to those of the index. Two basic strategies for enhanced indexing are (a) a tilt strategy, where the portfolio is overweighted in some stocks/sectors because of beliefs of superior return performance by the portfolio manager, and (b) derivatives-based strategies such as using futures exposure coupled with investments in one-year T-bills, shorter-term Treasuries, or commercial paper. See Mark W. Riepe, "Are Enhanced Index Mutual Funds Worthy of Their Name?" *Journal of Investing* 7, no. 2 (Summer 1998): 6–15; and Matthew R. Smith, Stephen K. Bosu, and Robert W. Harless, "Gone Fishing: Some Hard Facts and Straight Talk on Enhanced Indexing," *Derivatives Quarterly* 4, no. 1 (Fall 1997): 66–75.

[2]Evaluating the risk-adjusted performance of a portfolio is the subject of Chapter 21.

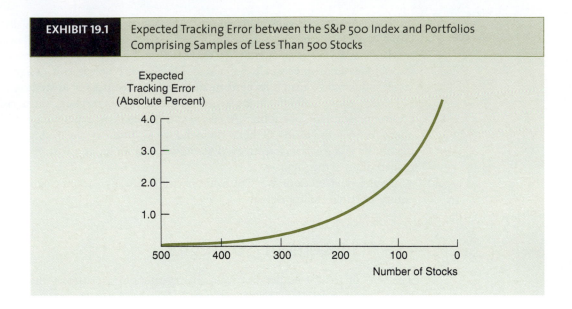

EXHIBIT 19.1 Expected Tracking Error between the S&P 500 Index and Portfolios Comprising Samples of Less Than 500 Stocks

the performance of the completeness fund to a specialized benchmark that incorporates the characteristics of the stocks not covered by the active managers.

The three basic techniques for constructing a passive index portfolio are full replication, sampling, and quadratic optimization or programming. The first, and most obvious, technique is *full replication*. With this technique, all the securities in the index are purchased in proportion to their weights in the index. This technique helps ensure close tracking, but it may backfire for two reasons. First, buying many securities increases transaction costs. Second, dividend reinvestment results in high commissions when many firms pay small dividends at different times in the year.

The second technique addresses these problems. With *sampling,* a portfolio manager attempts to buy a representative sample of stocks that comprise the benchmark index. Stocks with larger index weights are purchased according to their weight in the index; smaller issues are purchased so that their aggregate characteristics (industry distribution, dividend yield, and so on) approximate the rest of the underlying benchmark. With fewer stocks to purchase, the buyer can take larger positions in the issues acquired, which should incur proportionately lower commissions. Reinvestment of dividend cash flows becomes less problematic because fewer securities must be purchased to rebalance the portfolio. The disadvantage of sampling is that portfolio returns will not track the index as closely as with full replication; there will be some *tracking error*.[3]

Exhibit 19.1 estimates the tracking error that occurs from sampling. For example, full replication of the S&P 500 would (in theory) have no tracking error. As smaller samples are used to replicate the S&P's performance, the potential tracking error increases (tracking error can be positive or negative as the sample may overperform or underperform the index over any period of time). Therefore, managers who use this technique must weigh the costs (tracking error) and the benefits (easier management, lower trading commissions) of using smaller samples.

---

[3]For a period of time (a month or a quarter) the difference between an indexed portfolio's return and the index return is the tracking error. Over time we can compute the average tracking error (which is the sum of the periodic errors divided by the number of observations) and the standard deviation of the tracking error.

EXHIBIT 19.2	Dollar-Cost Averaging versus Lump-Sum Investing

DOLLAR-COST AVERAGING					LUMP SUM	
$1,000 INVESTED AT $t = 1, 2, 3$					$3,000 INVESTED AT $t = 1$ (PRICE = $10)	
	$t = 1$	$t = 2$	$t = 3$	Total Number of Shares	Market Value at $t = 3$	Number of Shares	Market Value at $t = 3$
Scenario 1: Rising stock price							
Stock price	$10	$15	$20				
Number of shares	100	66.67	50	216.67	216.67 × $20 = $4,333.40	300	300 × $20 = $6,000
Scenario 2: Falling stock price							
Stock price	$10	$7	$5				
Number of shares	100	142.86	200	442.86	442.86 × $5 = $2,214.30	300	300 × $5 = $1,500
Scenario 3: Rising, then falling, stock price							
Stock price	$10	$15	$10				
Number of shares	100	66.67	100	266.67	266.67 × $10 = $2,666.70	300	300 × $10 = $3,000
Scenario 4: Falling, then rising, stock price							
Stock price	$10	$5	$10				
Number of shares	100	200	100	400	400 × $10 = $4,000	300	300 × $10 = $3,000

With the third technique that managers use to construct a passive portfolio—*quadratic optimization or programming*—historical information on price changes and correlations between securities are input to a computer program that determines the composition of a portfolio that will minimize tracking error with the benchmark. The drawback of this technique is that it relies on historical correlations; if these change over time portfolio performance may fail to closely track the index.

Dollar-cost averaging is an investment method popular with many who passively invest. Rather than trying to predict the time of market highs and lows, managers using this strategy invest an equal amount of funds each period. With dollar-cost averaging, the manager purchases fewer shares with the fixed-dollar investment when stock prices are high and more shares when the stock prices fall. This disciplined approach to investing prevents investors from buying too many shares when they may be overly optimistic after prices have risen. On the other hand, buying more shares when prices are low will position the portfolio for attractive gains if prices rebound.

As a simple example, suppose we can invest $3,000 all at once in a stock or $1,000 per month over the next three months. If the price of the stock is $10, our $3,000 will purchase 300 shares. Exhibit 19.2 presents the effects of dollar-cost averaging in four scenarios. In the first scenario, prices rise; in the second, prices fall. In scenarios 3 and 4, prices rise or fall before returning to their original level. More shares are purchased over time in scenarios 2 and 4, and the dollar-cost-averaged portfolio outperforms the lump-sum investment.

In a market that initially rises (scenarios 1 and 3), dollar-cost averaging underperforms the lump-sum strategy.

Dollar-cost averaging is an attractive strategy to prevent attempts to time the market or to prevent investing a large sum at an inopportune time. It performs best when the market declines sometime after the initial investment. Because the market never continually rises, dollar-cost averaging is a favored investment strategy of many individual investors.[4]

Active Management Strategies

The goal of active equity-portfolio management is a portfolio that earns a return that exceeds the return of a passive benchmark portfolio, net of transaction costs, on a risk-adjusted basis. An important issue for active managers and their clients is the selection of an appropriate benchmark (sometimes called a "normal" portfolio).[5] The benchmark should incorporate the average qualities of the client's portfolio strategy. Thus, the performance of an actively managed portfolio with mainly small-cap stocks with low P/E ratios (because the client specified this strategy) should not be compared to a broad market index such as the S&P 500. A better strategy is to construct a *specialized* benchmark portfolio that reflects the average characteristics of the actively managed portfolio and the client's risk tolerance. For example, a first step in constructing a normal benchmark portfolio for this example may be to include, on an equally weighted basis, all stocks with market capitalizations under $1 billion and P/E ratios less than 80 percent of the S&P 500 P/E ratio. Computerized databases allow managers to construct such passive benchmarks and monitor returns over time.

The job of an active equity manager is not easy. If transaction costs total 1.5 percent of the portfolio's assets annually, the portfolio has to earn a return 1.5 percentage points above the passive benchmark just to keep pace with it. If the manager's strategy involves over-weighting market sectors in anticipation of price increases, the risk of the active portfolio will exceed that of the passive benchmark, so the active portfolio's return will have to exceed the benchmark by an even wider margin to compensate. Thus, active managers must overcome two difficulties relative to the benchmark: higher transaction costs and, in all likelihood, higher risk.

One key to success is for managers to be *consistent* in their area of expertise. Market gyrations occur and investment styles go in and out of favor. Successful long-term investing requires that managers maintain their investment philosophy and composure in the face of bear markets. Another key is to minimize the trading activity of the portfolio. Attempts to time price movements over short horizons may result in profits disappearing because of growing commissions (and taxes, if capital gains are realized in a taxable portfolio).

Managers of global portfolios can apply the economic analysis discussed in Chapter 13 to identify different countries whose equity markets are potentially undervalued or overvalued. The global portfolio can then overweight or underweight those countries relative to a global benchmark portfolio based on the active manager's forecast of their return potential. Or global managers can review the portfolio from an industry perspective rather than from a country perspective. More analysts are employing this strategy as companies and competi-

---

[4]Persons who have money deducted from their paycheck and invested in insurance products, variable annuities, and 401(k) and other retirement plans are automatic dollar-cost averagers; their fixed-amount funds are invested on a periodic basis, every pay period.

[5]We discuss in Chapter 21 the construction of benchmark portfolios.

tion become more global.[6] For example, Caterpillar and Komatsu compete globally in the heavy-equipment industry; Boeing and Airbus compete globally in the airline manufacturing industry. Evidence of the global automobile market is on every street.

Global portfolio managers focus on global economic trends, industry competitive forces, and company strengths and strategies. They apply their analyses of financial statements (Chapter 14), industries (Chapter 13), and companies (Chapter 15) in a global, rather than a national, setting in order to identify undervalued industrial sectors and firms.

Managers use three generic strategies in their attempts to add value to their equity portfolios in comparison to the benchmark:

- Sector rotation: shifting funds among different equity sectors and industries (financial stocks, consumer cyclicals, durable goods, and so on).
- Style investing: focusing on a particular investment style (large capitalization, small capitalization, value, growth, and so on) and seeking to add value compared to that style's benchmark.
- Stock picking: looking at individual stocks in an attempt to buy low and sell high regardless of industry, economic sector, or style. Many times stock pickers base their selections on broad economic or market-based themes such as aging demographics, growing global trade, or technology. In some respect, all active management strategies involve some aspect of stock picking.

In the following sections we more closely examine the strategies of sector rotation and style investing. To review the techniques and philosophy of stock picking, reread Chapters 13–16.

SECTOR ROTATION

A *sector rotation strategy*, used by managers who invest in domestic equities, involves positioning the portfolio to take advantage of the market's next move. Often this means emphasizing or overweighting (relative to the benchmark portfolio) certain economic sectors or industries in response to the next expected phase of the business cycle. Exhibit 13.9, on page 407, contains suggestions on how sector rotators may position their portfolios to take advantage of stock market trends during the economic cycle.

"Sector" can also include different stock attributes. Sector rotation can also involve overweighting stocks with certain characteristics, such as small- or large-cap stocks, high- or low-P/E stocks, or stocks classified as value or growth stocks.

The existence of computer databases has encouraged the use of computer screening and other quantitatively based methods of evaluating stocks. Using computers, some managers invest in stocks with certain characteristics rather than examining individual stocks to determine whether they are underpriced. Others narrow the list of thousands of stocks to a manageable few that can then be evaluated using more traditional analytical means. Stocks can be screened on many company and stock price characteristics. For example, programs can generate a list of value stocks that had at least a 20 percent return on equity and stable or growing dividends over the past ten years.

Some more complicated quantitative strategies are similar to sector rotation. Factor models, similar to those used in the APT, can identify stocks whose earnings or prices are

---

[6]Peter J. B. Hopkins and C. Hayes Miller, *Country, Sector, and Company Factors in Global Equity Portfolios,* Charlottesville, VA: Research Foundation of the Association for Investment Management and Research, 2001; Leila Heckman, Singanallur R. Narayanan, and Sandeep A. Patel, "Country and Industry Importance in European Returns," *Journal of Investing* 10, no. 1 (Spring 2001): 27–34.

sensitive to economic variables such as exchange rates, inflation, interest rates, or consumer sentiment. With this information, managers can tilt portfolios by trading those stocks most sensitive to the analyst's economic forecast. The manager can try to improve the portfolio's relative performance in a recession by purchasing stocks that are *least* sensitive to the analyst's pessimistic forecast.

Some quantitatively oriented portfolio managers use a "long–short" approach to investing. In this approach, stocks are passed through a number of screens and assigned a rank. Stocks at the top of the ranking are purchased; stocks at the bottom are sold short. Such a strategy can be neutral on the overall market because the value of the long position can approximate that of the short position. The performance of the top-ranked stocks is expected to exceed that of the lower-ranked stocks, regardless of whether the overall stock market rises, falls, or trades in a narrow range.

How do managers know that these and other quantitative models have the potential to offer above-average risk-adjusted returns? The answer is that they hope the future will resemble the past. These quantitative strategies have been *backtested,* which involves using computers to examine the composition and returns of portfolios based on historical data to determine if the strategy would have worked successfully in the past. The risk of this testing is that relationships that existed in the past are not guaranteed to hold in the future.

Active managers also use quadratic programming to solve the efficient frontier optimization problem of Markowitz. The optimizer uses the manager's expectations about returns, risk, and correlations to select portfolios that offer the optimal risk–return tradeoff. Linear programming techniques help construct portfolios that maximize an objective (such as expected return) while satisfying linear constraints dealing with items such as the portfolio's beta, dividend yield, and diversification.

STYLE INVESTING

Most equity-portfolio managers follow an investing style. *Style investing* involves constructing portfolios in such a way as to capture one or more of the characteristics of equity securities. Though it has been around in a variety of forms for many years, style investing has had its most recent endorsement in the efficient markets anomaly literature. Research studies purporting to show above-average risk-adjusted returns to small-cap stocks, low-P/E stocks, and the like lead some investment managers to focus on segments of the market, hoping to capture extra return.

A variety of investing styles exist. Some investment managers favor large-cap stocks, those on the higher tiers of market capitalization. These managers focus on the stocks that comprise the S&P 500 index and seek to outperform the index by overweighting the various industries and sectors they anticipate will do well and underweighting the expected poorer-performing sectors. Other managers favor small-cap stocks. They believe that, since small firms are less analyzed than larger firms, the market may not be as efficient for small firms. Or they may focus on small-cap firms to take advantage of the alleged "small-firm effect" anomaly, which finds that small firms' returns have been overcompensated for their systematic risk over time. Still others may focus on midcap stocks. These managers believe that both large- and small-cap styles are now well recognized, have attracted many investors in search of higher returns, and thus are both efficient. But they hope that inefficiencies exist in the neglected mid-range.

Still other managers place themselves in the value or growth camp. *Value stocks* are those that appear to be underpriced because either their price–book or price–earnings ratio is low or their dividend yield is high compared to the rest of the market. *Growth stocks,* according to popular terminology, are stocks of firms that are enjoying above-average earnings-per-

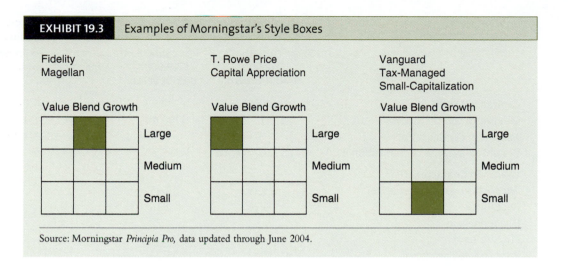

EXHIBIT 19.3 Examples of Morningstar's Style Boxes

Source: Morningstar *Principia Pro,* data updated through June 2004.

share increases and usually have above-average price–book and price–earnings ratios. Similar to this are the *earnings momentum* and *price momentum* strategies. The market at times seems to reward the stocks of companies whose earnings have steady, above-average growth or whose prices are rising because of market optimism.

Some managers combine styles along the large-cap–small-cap and value–growth continuums, creating many possible mixes: large-cap value, large-cap growth, small-cap value, small-cap growth, midcap value, and midcap growth. Morningstar's mutual fund analysis, which we saw in Chapter 4, has used a 3 × 3 style box to graphically show investors where a given mutual fund lies along the small-cap–large-cap and value–growth continuums. Exhibit 19.3 shows an example.

Not every manager falls into one of these categories; their portfolio's exposure to small- or large-cap, value or growth may change over time. Some managers may emphasize one style, while others may tilt or bias a portfolio only slightly toward one style. Many indexes exist that can form the basis for judging the performance of these varied investment styles.[7]

Exhibit 19.4 illustrates the characteristics of the four main investment styles. Value stocks generally have smaller capitalizations than growth stocks (columns 1 and 2), but their profile is much different from that of the typical small-stock fund (columns 2 and 4). Value stocks have P/E and P/B ratios significantly lower than those of growth stocks while their dividend yield is much higher. As expected, earnings growth is higher in growth stocks, and growth stocks favor industries such as technology and health care. Value stocks were more likely to involve firms in the energy sector and financial services.

Distinctions between large- and small-cap stocks are obvious in the size category. Small-cap stocks have some value stock characteristics in terms of P/E, P/B, and price–sales ratios, but with a few exceptions their sector weightings are not markedly different from larger-cap stocks. Small-cap stocks tend to favor technology, health care, consumer cyclicals, and financial services. Thus, a growth or value portfolio, or any style portfolio, is not as well diversified as the market portfolio. A style portfolio will contain some unsystematic risk that

---

[7]Melissa R. Brown and Claudia E. Mott, "Understanding the Differences and Similarities of Equity Style Indexes," in *The Handbook of Equity Style Management,* 2nd ed., edited by T. Daniel Coggin, Frank J. Fabozzi, and Robert D. Arnott, New Hope, PA: Frank J. Fabozzi Associates, 1997, pp. 21–53.

EXHIBIT 19.4	Comparison of Growth, Value, Large-Cap, and Small-Cap Portfolios			
	Growth S&P 500/ BARRA Growth	Value S&P 500/ BARRA Value	Market-Oriented S&P 500	Small-Cap S&P Small-Cap 600
Capitalization (millions)				
Maximum capitalization	$341,961	$290,443	$341,961	$3,136
Minimum capitalization	$887	$919	$887	$64
Weighted-average capitalization	$116,449	$67,277	$91,840	$1,077
Valuation Characteristics				
Price/earnings (excl negative)	25.39	16.25	19.89	20.76
Price/book	5.36	2.14	3.05	2.29
Dividend yield	1.52	2.20	1.86	0.93
Price/sales	2.35	1.18	1.57	1.03
Price to free cash flow	27.47	15.23	20.82	20.23
Growth Characteristics				
Implied growth rate (%, 5-yr average)	18.13	8.08	13.21	10.17
Economic Sectors (percent)				
Basic materials	3.70	4.43	4.06	6.96
Energy	0.94	11.52	6.24	5.28
Consumer noncyclicals	14.99	2.32	8.65	2.94
Consumer cyclicals	10.58	5.93	8.26	14.82
Consumer services	1.77	8.53	5.15	6.32
Industrials	3.36	3.10	3.23	6.54
Utilities	0.12	4.85	2.48	3.43
Transportation	1.47	1.63	1.55	3.13
Health care	22.63	4.34	13.48	11.39
Technology	27.67	8.50	18.08	16.96
Telecommunications	0.67	5.78	3.23	0.31
Commercial services	4.11	2.87	3.49	7.19
Financial services	7.99	36.19	22.11	14.74

Source: *www.barra.com*, data updated of 6/30/2004.

will not be diversified away. A style investor must be willing to take on this risk exposure, and the investment policy statement should reflect it.

Data show that large- and small-stock returns seem to move, at times, in cycles, as do value and growth stocks. Exhibit 19.5A shows the annual difference between a growth index and a value index; positive values show times when growth outperformed value. Exhibit 19.5B shows the annual differences between a large- and a small-cap index; positive values indicate when large stocks earned higher returns. Over time one style overperforms, then underperforms. Attempts to time styles rely on forecasting stages of the business cycle. Firms whose earnings growth mirrors the cycles of the economy may comprise many of the value stocks. The ideal time to purchase value stocks is when the economy is nearing a business cycle trough and preparing for the next expansion phase. Growth stocks, on the other hand, have earnings growth patterns that arise from these firms' ability to generate

EXHIBIT 19.5 Relative Performance of Styles over Time

A. Growth index return minus value index return (S&P/BARRA)

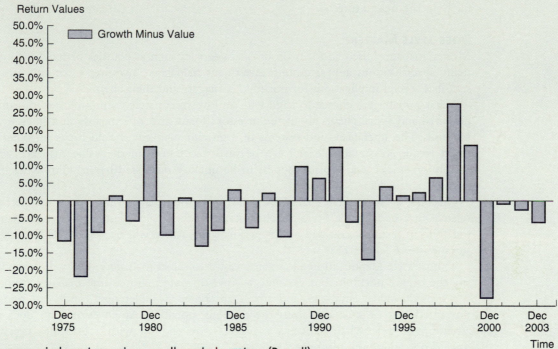

B. Large-cap index return minus small-cap index return (Russell)

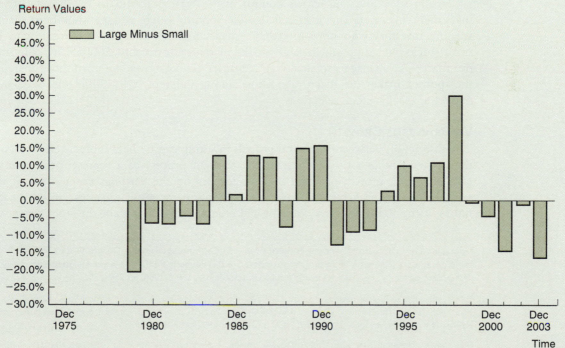

their own demand, irrespective of the overall state of the economy. With little sensitivity to the state of the business cycle, portfolio managers may consider selling value stocks and buying growth stocks as the economy nears the peak of an expansion and a downturn is likely in the near future.[8]

DOES STYLE MATTER?

Money managers used to focus on broad categories such as equities or fixed income. Now many specializations appear among investment managers. Investing according to a certain style has several implications for portfolio managers and their clients.[9]

First, a manager's choice to align with an investment style communicates information to potential and actual clients about the investor's focus, area of expertise, and stock evaluation methods. The operations and systems of a growth manager should focus on whether past profit trends are sustainable and can be surpassed. Those of the value manager will focus mainly on stocks whose prices appear to be unfairly depressed by an unknowing or overly pessimistic market.

Second, an investment manager's style can be used to measure his or her performance relative to a benchmark. Style benchmarks show the characteristics of an unmanaged style portfolio in terms of risk and return performance. More will be said on performance measurement in Chapter 21.

Third, style identification allows an investor to select managers who will properly diversify the overall portfolio. For example, an investor could choose one manager from each of the growth, value, large-cap, and small-cap styles. Completeness funds can remove any unwanted bias or style tilts from the resulting portfolio. An investor who does not pay attention to style when choosing managers may end up with a portfolio overweighted toward one style over another.

Finally, style investing allows control of the total portfolio to be shared between the investment managers and a knowledgeable sponsor (such as a pension fund manager or wealthy investor) who hires investment managers. For example, a sponsor who believes small stocks will outperform large stocks in the early to mid 2000s can reallocate funds from large-cap managers to small-cap managers. Control over the portfolio is shared in that the sponsor makes the macro allocation among different styles while the hired managers make the specific stock selections.

VALUE VERSUS GROWTH

The distinction between value and growth investing can be best appreciated by focusing on the price–earnings ratio to consider the thought process of a representative manager for each style.[10] A growth-oriented investor focuses on the earnings component of the P/E ratio. He looks for firms that have the expectation for rapid earnings growth in the near future. If the P/E ratio stays constant and earnings growth occurs, the stock price will rise,

---

[8]A business-cycle discussion of switching between value and growth stocks appears in Douglas W. Case and Steven Cusimano, "Historical Tendencies of Equity Style Returns and the Prospects for Tactical Style Allocation," in *Equity Style Management,* edited by Robert A. Klein and Jess Lederman, Chicago: Irwin, 1995, pp. 259–287.

[9]For a fuller discussion, see Charles Trzcinka, "Is Equity Style Management Worth the Effort? Some Critical Issues for Plan Sponsors," in *The Handbook of Equity Style Management,* 2nd ed., edited by T. Daniel Coggin, Frank J. Fabozzi, and Robert D. Arnott, New Hope, PA: Frank J. Fabozzi Associates, 1997, pp. 301–312.

[10]See Jon A. Christopherson and C. Nola Williams, "Equity Style: What It Is and Why It Matters," in *The Handbook of Equity Style Management,* edited by T. Daniel Coggin and Frank J. Fabozzi, New Hope, PA: Frank J. Fabozzi Associates, 1995.

and he will benefit. On the other hand, the value-oriented investor focuses on the price component of the P/E ratio. She looks for stock that is priced cheaply compared to its potential, with a P/E ratio that is too low. In this case, the market will realize the undervaluation, the stock price will rise, and she will benefit.

Over the long run studies indicate, on average, that value stocks offer somewhat higher returns than growth stocks.[11] In the United States, for example, the S&P/BARRA value index has had an average arithmetic return of 15.7 percent since 1975; the S&P/BARRA growth index's return has averaged 14.3 percent with a much higher standard deviation (19.2 percent for the growth returns, only 15.4 percent for the value index). Several reasons can be offered for this empirical finding. First, studies have focused on before-tax returns of value and growth stocks. If investors are concerned with after-tax returns, they will demand a return premium from value stocks, which typically have higher dividends and lower expected capital gains than growth stocks. Second, the typical value stock may have a low comfort level with investors. Bad news, disappointments, or an uncertain future lead investors to perceive them to be riskier and less desirable. This results in a higher-risk premium for value stocks. Investors' negative perceptions about a value stock can lead to pessimism about the firm's future sales and earnings, which itself can lead to positive earnings surprises and superior stock returns when better times arrive. The apparent superior risk–return tradeoff for value stocks compared to growth stocks is a subject of ongoing research and investigation.

Expectational Analysis and Value/Growth Investing

Analysts recommending stocks to a portfolio manager need to identify and monitor key assumptions and variables related to their suggested stocks. Value investors focus on one set of key assumptions and variables, whereas growth investors focus on another. To more closely examine growth and value, let's look at Exhibit 19.6, which represents the cycle of rising and falling expectations about a firm's earnings over time. This is a stylistic drawing; it tells nothing about the relative length of its various stages. Indeed, the length of the stages is firm-specific. It is the job of the analyst and portfolio manager to make decisions regarding where firms are in this cycle and how long they may stay in their current position or if they even will move to the next position.

Investors known as *contrarians* (1) invest in beaten-down stocks that usually have poor consensus earnings forecasts. These stocks are unattractive and are generally thought of as risky and poor investment selections. Some of these firms really are down and out; others eventually show signs of renewal and start to experience good news about their markets, sales, and earnings. After some initial good news, investors who used to ignore the firm start paying attention to it. Quantitative analysts who focus on positive earnings surprises begin to examine the firm as well (2). If earnings continue to rise, more and more investors pay attention to it and consider it for their portfolios. Soon, investors begin to feel optimistic about the firm. In time, analysts revise earnings estimates upward (3). Earnings surprises continue. The momentum of earnings increases attracts the attention of still more investors and analysts, who then proclaim the stock a growth stock (4).

But all good things come to an end; at some point the firm's stock will be "torpedoed" by an earnings disappointment. Earnings may still be up, but maybe not as high as analysts

[11]Carlo Capaul, Ian Rowley, and William F. Sharpe, "International Value and Growth Stock Returns," *Financial Analysts Journal* (January–February 1993): 27–36; David Umstead, "International Equity Style Management," in *Equity Style Management,* edited by Robert A. Klein and Jess Lederman, Chicago, IL: Irwin, 1995, pp. 118–140; and J. Lakonishok, A. Shleifer, and R. Vishny, "Contrarian Investment, Extrapolation, and Risk," *Journal of Finance* 49, no. 5 (December 1994): 1541–1578.

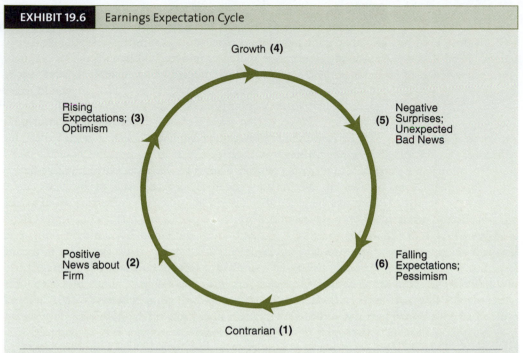

expected, or earnings may decline (5). Some investors will sell the stock. In the future, the earnings may recover and make such investors look foolish. Or the firm may continue in the cycle, but now on the downside. Negative surprises continue; the firm's upward trend in earnings starts to level off or become a downward trend. Problems develop within the firm, its strategy, or its markets. After a time, pessimism about the firm grows and the stock price continues to fall (6). Fewer and fewer investors hold the stock in high regard, and many direct their attention to other companies. Soon, the neglected stock once again becomes the kind that is owned by contrarians (1), who hope for a recovery that may or may not come.

The expectational perspective illustrated in Exhibit 19.7 has implications for the kinds of stocks that make those with a value or growth tilt successful over time. One skill that separates a successful value-oriented portfolio manager from a poor one is knowing when to buy a stock. Buying a stock too early results in poor stock performance as bad or disappointing news continues. But a value manager who picks the right time to buy enjoys benefits from a growing collection of good news about a firm and from a rising stock price as other investors jump on the bandwagon and buy into the stock.

One skill that separates a successful growth-oriented portfolio manager from a bad one is knowing when to sell. Less-successful growth managers remain optimistic about the firm or believe that *any* bad news will soon be replaced by good news. They characteristically hold onto their stocks so long that previously earned returns shrink or disappear. Portfolio managers who consider themselves growth or value investors need to have systems or processes in place to monitor the key variables about their holdings and potential investments so they can, on average, buy in and sell out at appropriate times.

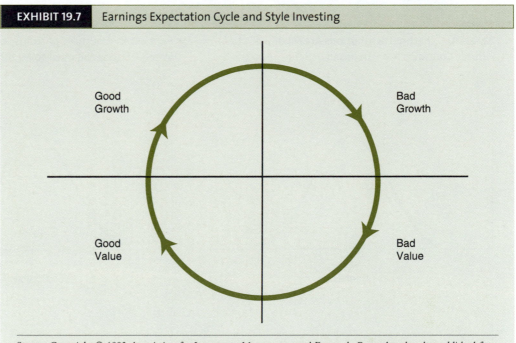

EXHIBIT 19.7 Earnings Expectation Cycle and Style Investing

Good
Growth

Bad
Growth

Good
Value

Bad
Value

Derivatives in Equity-Portfolio Management

The systematic and unsystematic risk of equity portfolios can be modified by using futures and options derivatives. The portfolio mix between equities and other assets can be adjusted by the use of equity derivatives. In addition, cash inflows and outflows can be hedged through appropriate derivative strategies. Selling futures contracts or purchasing puts are attractive alternatives to short selling for long–short managers.

MODIFYING PORTFOLIO RISK AND RETURN: A REVIEW

As discussed in Chapters 17 and 18, futures and options can affect the risk and return distribution for a portfolio. In general, a dollar-for-dollar relationship exists between changes in the price of the underlying security and the price of the corresponding futures contract. In effect, buying (selling) futures is identical to subtracting (adding) cash from or to the portfolio. Purchasing futures has the effect of increasing the exposure to the asset; selling futures decreases the portfolio's exposure. Suppose Exhibit 19.8A represents a portfolio's probability distribution of returns. Buying futures on the portfolio's underlying asset increases the portfolio's exposure (or sensitivity) to price changes of the asset. As shown in Exhibit 19.8B, the return distribution widens, indicating a larger return variance. Selling futures has the effect of decreasing the portfolio's sensitivity to the underlying asset. Exhibit 19.8C shows the effect on the portfolio if futures are sold; the variance of returns declines, causing a "narrower" return distribution.

As Exhibit 19.8A–C illustrates, futures have a symmetrical impact on portfolio returns; their impact on the portfolio's upside and downside return potential is the same. This will not be true if options are used.

EXHIBIT 19.8 Return Distributions

Panels A–C Return Distributions Are Modified When Futures Contracts Are Purchased or Sold

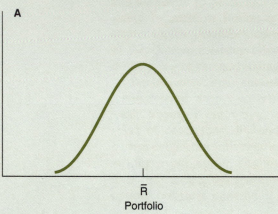

A

$\overline{R}$
Portfolio

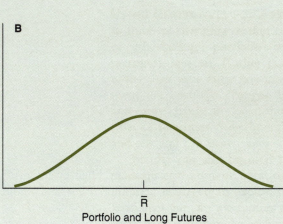

B

$\overline{R}$
Portfolio and Long Futures

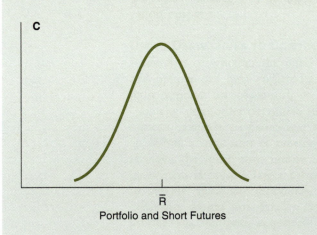

C

$\overline{R}$
Portfolio and Short Futures

Panels D–F Examples of Truncated Return Distributions When Options Are Used to Modify Portfolio Risk

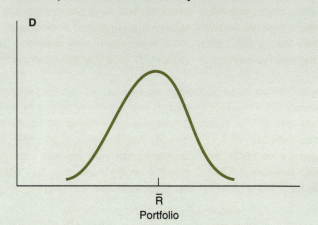

D

$\overline{R}$
Portfolio

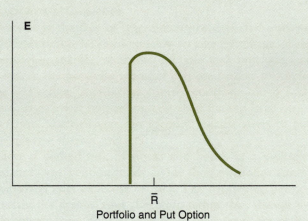

E

$\overline{R}$
Portfolio and Put Option

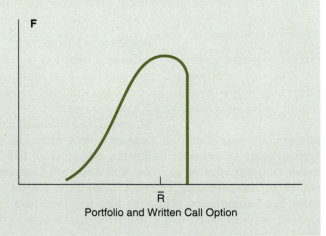

F

$\overline{R}$
Portfolio and Written Call Option

The choice of whether or not to exercise an option means that options do not have a symmetrical impact on returns. For example, as discussed in Chapter 17, buying a call option limits losses; buying a put when the investor owns the underlying security has the effect of controlling downside risk, as shown in Figure 19.8E. Writing a covered call, on the other hand, limits upside returns while not affecting loss potential, as seen in Figure 19.8F; writing a put option has the same effect.

USING DERIVATIVES TO CONTROL PORTFOLIO CASH FLOWS

Regardless of whether the equity portfolio is passively or actively managed, futures and options can help control cash inflows and outflows from the portfolio. In reality, most options used to modify portfolio risk are options whose underlying security is another derivative security—a futures contract. These options are called future options or options on futures, which we discussed in Chapter 18.

Hedging Portfolio Inflows A fund's asset composition changes when cash flows into a portfolio from investors. The accumulating cash inflows have the effect of reducing the portfolio's exposure to equities because a larger proportion of the portfolio's assets are in cash. The portfolio manager who makes hurried investments in the market runs a greater chance of purchasing inappropriate securities. Also, large purchases can lead to sizable commissions and a price-pressure influence on the stocks purchased.

A better strategy is to use part of the cash inflow to purchase stock-index futures contracts so that the total contract value approximates the size of the inflow. Alternatively, the manager could purchase call options. In doing so, the money is immediately invested with lower commissions and the price impact is less than if stocks had been purchased outright. Once the futures are purchased, the manager has time to decide what assets to buy, and the smaller purchases over time will reduce the price pressure. As these purchases are made, the futures contracts can be sold.

Hedging Portfolio Outflows A large planned withdrawal from a portfolio is usually accomplished by selling securities over time so that when the withdrawal date occurs, the needed funds are available for transfer. Similar to a cash deposit, the sale of securities causes an increase in cash holdings, thus reducing the portfolio's equity exposure. A possible strategy to counterbalance the effect of a larger cash position is to buy futures contracts or call options as securities are sold. The net effect is to maintain the portfolio's overall exposure to stocks while accumulating cash. On the cash withdrawal date, the futures contracts can be sold and the portfolio's operations have not been disrupted.

STANDARD & POOR'S 500 INDEX FUTURES CONTRACT

We focus on futures contracts in this overview because futures, and options on the futures, are the derivative tools that portfolio managers typically use.[12]

Exhibit 19.9 lists the various exchange-traded financial futures contracts. Although a complete review of the numerous futures contracts is beyond our current discussion, we will use the Chicago Mercantile Exchange's S&P 500 index futures contract as an illustration. As with any futures contract, purchasers of this contract must place funds in a margin account. Initial margin requirements are $6,000 for those buying for speculative purposes and $2,500 for those buying for hedging purposes. Hedgers must show current ownership of an equity portfolio whose market value approximates that of the futures traded.

The value of the S&P 500 futures contract is equal to $250 times the value of the index, so each one-point change in the index leads to a $250 change in the value of the

[12]In addition to futures, options, and options on futures, swaps are another derivative security useful in portfolio management.

EXHIBIT 19.9	Selected Financial Futures Contracts Available on U.S. Exchanges (as of June 2004)

Type of Contract	Exchange
Treasury bonds	CBOT
Six and one-half- to ten-year Treasury notes	CBOT
Five-year Treasury notes	CBOT
Two-year Treasury notes	CBOT
Thirty-day Federal funds rate	CBOT
Municipal Bond Index	CBOT
One-month Eurodollars	CME
One-month LIBOR	CME
Euroyen	CME
Dow Jones Industrial Average	CBOT
S&P 500 Index	CME
Mini-S&P 500 Index	CME
S&P 400 MidCap Index	CME
Nikkei 225 Stock Average	CME
Nasdaq 100	CME
Mini-Nasdaq 100	CME
Russell 2000	CME
Russell 1000	NYBOT
NYSE Composite Index	NYBOT

contract. When the S&P 500 futures contract expires, delivery or settlement of the contract is *not* made in the shares of 500 different stocks, but in cash. Every day the contract is marked to the market, which means its change in value is added to or subtracted from the investors' margin account. When investors close out their position, or when the futures contract expires, they receive the funds in their margin accounts. The difference between the funds in their account when it is closed and their initial margin deposit represents their profit or loss, which equals the change in value of the futures contract over the holding period.

There is one exception to this. Should the funds in the investors' margin account become too low because of adverse price movements, investors will receive a margin call. Maintenance margin requires that the account balance be increased to at least $2,500 for speculators and $1,500 for hedgers using the S&P 500 index futures contract.

Prior to discussing how portfolio managers use S&P 500 futures, we need to discuss how managers determine the appropriate number of S&P 500 futures to buy or sell—that is, the *hedge ratio*. We will examine two scenarios.

Determining How Many Contracts to Trade to Hedge a Deposit or Withdrawal

As discussed, futures can help maintain the desired exposure to stocks when the portfolio experiences a cash inflow or outflow. The number of futures contracts to be traded will equal

$$\frac{\textbf{Cash Flow}}{\textbf{Value of One Contract}} \times \textbf{Portfolio Beta}$$

In our example, the value of one contract is the price times $250. If the price of the S&P 500 futures contract is quoted as 1100.00, the value of the contract will be $275,000.

The beta of the underlying futures index is taken to be 1.0. To determine the portfolio's beta to be used in the hedge ratio formula, we regress the portfolio returns on those of the underlying index:

19.1
$$R_{portfolio} = \alpha + \beta(R_{index})$$

The resulting slope estimate is the relative volatility of the portfolio's returns compared to those of the underlying index. We multiply the number of contracts by beta so the value of the futures position will change in line with the value of the portfolio.

Given the existence of several stock-index futures contracts listed in Exhibit 19.9, one way to determine which contract is best for a particular portfolio is to examine the coefficient of determination (R^2) from estimating Equation 19.1 with different indexes. The index with the highest R^2 is the one that best follows the variations in the portfolio over time, which indicates it may be the most appropriate index. Generally, R^2 will be higher for well-diversified portfolios.

For example, assume an equity-portfolio manager will receive a $5 million cash inflow today. The beta of the portfolio, measured against the S&P 500, is 1.15. If the futures price is 1100, the value of the contract is $275,000. The number of S&P 500 futures contracts that should be purchased to hedge this cash inflow is

$$\frac{\$5 \text{ million}}{\$275,000} \times 1.15 = 20.91 \text{ contracts}$$

Because fractional contracts do not exist, managers typically round this number to the nearest integer; in this case, the manager would purchase twenty-one contracts to hedge the cash inflow. These twenty-one contracts will be sold over time as the $5 million in cash is invested in stocks.

Determining How Many Contracts to Trade to Adjust Portfolio Beta In Chapter 9, we learned that the beta of a stock portfolio equals the weighted average of its components' betas. This concept also serves to determine how many futures contracts to buy or sell to increase or decrease a portfolio's beta.

Suppose a $25 million equity portfolio has $22.5 million invested in stocks and $2.5 million is invested in Treasury bills. The equity component of the portfolio has a beta of 0.95. Assume that we expect rising stock prices, so we want to increase the overall portfolio's beta to 1.10. As above, we will assume the value of a futures contract is $275,000. The beta of the cash or T-bill component of a portfolio is usually assumed to be zero and thus is ignored in the analysis.

Currently, the weight of the equity component of the portfolio is $22.5 million/$25 million or 0.90; the beta of the equity component is 0.95. The beta of the futures contract is 1.0. The weight of the futures component of the portfolio will be (F × 275,000)/$25 million, where F represents the number of futures contracts to be traded. Because the target beta for the entire portfolio is 1.10, the weighted average of the portfolio's components must equal 1.10:

$$1.10 = \quad 0.90 \times 0.95 \quad + \quad F \times \frac{\$275,000}{\$25 \text{ million}} \times 1.0$$

| Target Beta | Contribution of Common-Stock Portfolio | Contribution of the Futures Component |

Solving for F, we find that 22.27 contracts must be purchased to attain the target beta. Rounding to the nearest integer, we will buy twenty-two contracts.

If we forecast a falling market and want to reduce the beta of the portfolio to 0.80, the number of futures contracts required is determined as follows:

$$0.80 = \underset{\textbf{Target Beta}}{0.90 \times 0.95} + \underset{\substack{\textbf{Contribution of the} \\ \textbf{Futures Component}}}{F \times \frac{\$275,000}{\$25 \text{ million}} \times 1.0}$$

$$\underset{\substack{\textbf{Contribution of} \\ \textbf{Common-Stock Portfolio}}}{}$$

Solving for F, we find the answer is −5.00. The negative sign indicates that futures contracts must be sold to reduce the portfolio beta to 0.80. We will sell five contracts to attain the desired portfolio. Note that options contracts *cannot* be easily used to adjust a portfolio's beta because they have an asymmetrical effect on a portfolio's return distribution.

USING DERIVATIVES IN PASSIVE EQUITY-PORTFOLIO MANAGEMENT

Because a passive investment strategy generally is a buy-and-hold strategy that seeks to replicate a stock-market index, passive managers will not try to change a portfolio's beta based on an economic forecast. However, a passive manager is expected to manage cash inflows and outflows without harming the ability of the portfolio to track its target index. The prior example on hedging a cash inflow or outflow is directly applicable to passive portfolio management. Instead of investing all cash inflows in the index or a subsample of the index, the manager can purchase an appropriate number of futures contracts to maintain the portfolio's structure and reduce the portfolio's tracking error relative to the index while determining where to invest the funds. Similarly, anticipated cash outflows can be hedged by liquidating part of the portfolio over time while maintaining the portfolio's exposure to the market through the use of futures contracts.

Options can only be used to a limited extent in passive management. When cash rebalancing is imperfect and an index fund becomes overweighted in a sector or in individual stocks relative to its index, it is possible to sell call options on firms or industry groups to correct the portfolio's weights.

USING DERIVATIVES IN ACTIVE EQUITY-PORTFOLIO MANAGEMENT

Active management often attempts to adjust the portfolio's systematic risk, unsystematic risk, or both. As we have discussed, systematic risk is a portfolio's exposure to price fluctuations caused by changes in the overall stock market. Unsystematic risk includes the portfolio's exposure to industries, sectors, or firms different from the benchmark.

Modifying Systematic Risk An equity portfolio's systematic risk is the sensitivity of the portfolio's value to changes in the benchmark index as measured by the portfolio's beta. If a rising market is expected, active portfolio managers want to increase their portfolio's beta; if a falling market is expected, they want to reduce their portfolio's beta.

Traditionally, when the market was expected to rise, active managers would sell low-beta stocks and buy high-beta stocks to raise the portfolio's weighted average beta. But the use of futures provides a quicker and cheaper way to increase or decrease a portfolio's beta with less disruption to the traits of the portfolio.[13]

---

[13]This is an important advantage. Should the active managers believe they have expertise in identifying mispriced or undervalued securities, they may want to continue holding them in spite of predictions of an adverse market move.

It is possible to sell futures so the value of the overall portfolio will be unaffected by market changes over the length of the futures contract. This is accomplished by selling a sufficient number of futures so the portfolio's beta becomes zero. To illustrate, assume a $25 million portfolio with $22.5 million invested in stocks and the rest in T-bills. The equity portfolio has a beta of 0.95 and T-bills have zero beta. The beta of the futures contract is 1.0, and the value of a futures contract is $275,000. To determine the required number of futures to sell to make the beta of the portfolio zero, we need to solve the following equation:

$$0.00 = \underset{\textbf{Target Beta}}{0.90 \times 0.95} + \underset{\substack{\textbf{Contribution of the} \\ \textbf{Futures Component}}}{F \times \frac{\$275{,}000}{\$25 \text{ million}} \times 1.0}$$

Target Beta   **Contribution of**   **Contribution of the**
Common-Stock Portfolio   **Futures Component**

We find that F equals −77.73, which means we must sell seventy-eight futures contracts to make the portfolio market-neutral. By setting the portfolio beta equal to zero, the return earned on the portfolio should approximate that of a risk-free asset such as short-term T-bills. An active manager who has the ability to identify mispriced or undervalued securities may generate an extra return component.

Modifying Unsystematic Risk   Opportunities also exist for controlling the unsystematic risk in an equity portfolio. Futures and options on futures exist for a limited number of sectors, whereas options exist for numerous components of the equity market. Option contracts are also available on market indexes such as the S&P 100 and 500; for stock groups such as consumer goods and cyclicals; and for selected industries such as technology, oil service, banks, utilities, pharmaceuticals, and semiconductors. Options can be traded on over 1,400 individual stocks. Thus, even when industry option contracts do not exist, portfolio managers can buy or sell individual stock options for the industry to modify their exposure.

A manager can buy call options when anticipating a rise in the market, in a sector or industry, or in a group of individual stocks. The lower call premiums can provide more leverage than buying futures, and options contracts can allow greater precision in targeting sectors of the market rather than an entire index. The maximum loss for such strategies is limited to the call premium.

Similarly, managers can buy put options on index futures, a sector, or group of stocks in anticipation of a decline in value. Calls can be written on the market and subsets of the market when declining or stable values are forecast. Writing put options on the market and its subsectors can generate income when the portfolio managers expect their values to be stable or to rise.

Modifying the Characteristics of a Global Equity Portfolio   As noted, global portfolios represent positions in both securities and currencies. Futures and options contracts on major currencies allow the portfolio manager to manage the risks of each of these separately. Currency futures and options on currency futures can help modify the currency exposure without affecting the actual holdings of the portfolios. For example, a portfolio manager who is bullish on European stocks but believes that the euro is currently overvalued relative to the U.S. dollar can purchase the European securities and then adjust the overall currency exposure of the portfolio through currency options and futures.

Consider the following example. A stock portfolio has the equivalent of $30 million invested: $12 million in the United States; $9 million in Japan; the remainder in the United Kingdom. Thus, the current allocation across countries and currencies is: 40 percent United States, 30 percent Japan, and 30 percent United Kingdom. The manager believes that the yen is overvalued and expects a strengthening pound. Given this outlook, the manager wishes to reduce exposure to the yen by $4.5 million (or -15 percent of the portfolio) while increasing exposure to the pound by $4.5 million (or $+15$ percentage points). In other words, the *desired currency allocation* is: 40 percent U.S. dollar, 15 percent Japanese yen, and 45 percent U.K. pound.

Traditional currency rebalancing required rebalancing the country allocation, but the manager would lose the chance to participate in security markets she thinks are undervalued. Also, such security rebalancing would be costly and time consuming. Such a rebalancing scenario would cause the manager to ignore what presumably she does best—identifying undervalued markets and securities. Instead, she would be forced to make decisions based on currency forecasts.

With derivatives, the manager can maintain the desired country exposure while modifying the currency exposure. Assume the futures dollar/pound exchange rate is £1 = $1.44. Because the pound futures contract calls for the delivery of £62,500, the value of one contract is 1.44 $/£ × £62,500 = $90,000. If the yen/dollar futures exchange rate is yen 1 = $0.00835 and the yen contract calls for the delivery of 12.5 million yen, the value of the yen futures contract is 0.00835 $/yen × yen 12.5 million = $104,375.

If the manager wants to reduce the yen exposure of the portfolio by $4.5 million, she will sell $4,500,000/$104,375 = 43.11 (rounded off to 43) futures contracts on the Japanese yen. She can increase the portfolio's exposure to the pound by $4.5 million, by purchasing $4,500,000/$90,000 = 50.00 British pound futures contracts.

Following these transactions, the security allocation across these countries remains as before: 40 percent United States, 30 percent Japan, 30 percent United Kingdom. But through the use of currency hedging, the portfolio's exposure to the (presumably overvalued) yen is only 15 percent, whereas exposure to the (presumably undervalued) pound is 45 percent. The use of derivatives has allowed the portfolio manager to shift currency exposures in a quicker, less costly manner than reallocating stocks across countries, while maintaining her desired exposure to undervalued securities.

Taxable Portfolios

Most investment discussions are done in the context of tax-exempt accounts such as IRAs and 401(k) plans. But for many individuals—and the financial planners and advisors who try to manage their investments—taxes are a fact of investing life. Among corporations the amount of funds invested in taxable accounts exceeds that in tax-exempt accounts.[14] For private (taxable) clients, taxes are the largest expense to be managed and minimized, far surpassing that of fees and transactions costs. The combined effect of state and federal taxes is over 20 percent for capital gains and may be more than double that for income receipts. Exhibit 19.10 shows the effect of taxes on the efficient frontier. When after-tax data is used, the efficient frontier is shifted down and to the left. The shift downward is obvious as investors have lower returns after paying taxes. The leftward shift occurs as the U.S. tax code allows capital losses to be netted against capital gains so the variation in returns over time is reduced.

Taxes bring many complications to the asset allocation and portfolio management process. First, plans to take a client's current portfolio and reallocate assets so it will lie on

---

[14]Robert D. Arnott, Andrew L. Berkin, and Jia Ye, "The Management and Mismanagement of Taxable Assets," *Journal of Investing* 10, no. 1 (Spring 2001): 15–21.

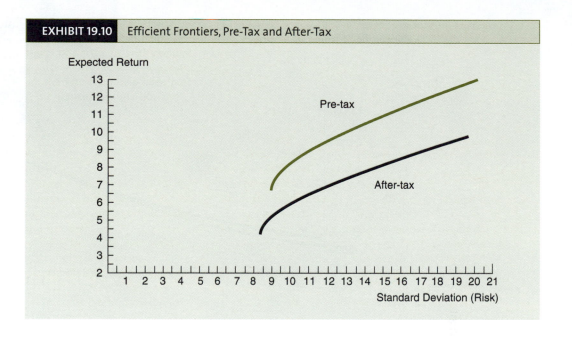

EXHIBIT 19.10   Efficient Frontiers, Pre-Tax and After-Tax

an efficient frontier will trigger capital gains taxes and reduce the client's wealth. Any portfolio reallocation process needs to consider unrealized capital gains and will likely result in a tradeoff between (a) selling assets and paying capital gains and (b) reinvesting assets for a more optimal risk–expected return tradeoff. Because of tax considerations, the resulting portfolio will likely be somewhere between the ideal efficient frontier and the current portfolio.

Second, the need to periodically rebalance the portfolio and bring the allocation back to the target will cause taxable events.

Third, Markowitz mean-variance optimization is a single-period model and is indifferent to the investor's time horizon. The optimal portfolio management decision, however, will depend on the investor's finite claim to his wealth. For example, whether the client should diversify out of a low-basis-cost stock depends on his life expectancy. If the expected life span is short, diversification and paying capital gains taxes may not be a good decision as the stock can be passed to heirs on a "stepped-up" basis, meaning the market value on the date of death becomes the cost basis to the heirs. For a longer life expectancy, the tradeoff between the tax consequences of selling and the return potential from reinvesting in diversified assets may be such that diversification is a proper solution.[15]

To see the implications of taxation on a portfolio, consider the following example. Suppose the founder of a company is invested 100 percent in a single stock with a zero cost basis that has been held for many years. Assume the expected future return on the stock is 8 percent a year and, to keep the numbers simple, assume the value of the stock is $1,000. If he were to sell the stock today, pay a 20 percent capital gains tax, and reinvest the proceeds ($800) in a diversified portfolio expected to return 10 percent annually, it will be

---

[15]Some would add a fourth consideration. The optimal portfolio suggested by mean-variance optimization may not be optimal for a taxable investor. It may include high-yield debt generating taxable income or may contain assets with deceptively low standard deviations, such as real estate and low-volatility income hedge funds. Special software, and special attention to the inputs, is required to consider such complicated situations.

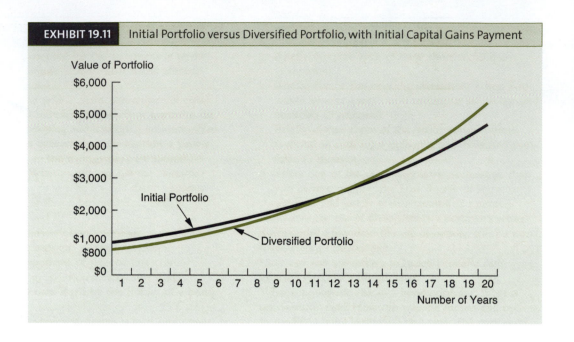

EXHIBIT 19.11 Initial Portfolio versus Diversified Portfolio, with Initial Capital Gains Payment

12.2 years before the future value of the diversified portfolio would equal the expected future value of the single stock portfolio.[16] Exhibit 19.11 shows the growth of both portfolios. Despite 25 percent higher returns (10 percent versus 8 percent) compounding over time, the initial loss of wealth because of capital gains taxes still takes a long time to recover.

Passive managers or those following an index strategy are not immune to tax problems. An index manager following a style index will have "drift" in the portfolio that will require rebalancing and the realization of capital gains and lower after-tax returns.

Active managers face the difficulty of the tax cost of trading even more so. They need to consider the following thought process:

1. If a security is sold at a profit, capital gains are paid, leaving less wealth in the portfolio to reinvest in another stock.
2. The new security to be purchased needs to have an expected return advantage (the difference between the expected return of the new security and the expected return of the old security) to recover the tax cost.
3. The size of the expected return advantage depends on the expected length of the holding period and the cost basis of the original security.

For example, suppose the expected return on a currently held security is 8 percent annually and the capital gains tax rate is 20 percent. The current value of the security is $100. The security has a cost basis of 50 percent, meaning the purchase price was 50 percent of its current market price. We are considering two options:

Option 1: Continue to hold the security for another year, earn an expected return of 8 percent, then sell the security and pay the capital gains tax rate.

---

[16]This can be modeled as a spreadsheet exercise with graphs showing the compounding growth of each alternative. It can be solved mathematically as well by finding the value of n, the number of years, such that the value of $1,000 compounded at 8 percent annually equals the value of $800 compounded at 10 percent annually: $1,000(1 + 0.08)^n = $800(1 + 0.10)^n$. Using logarithms, the solution for n is 12.16 years.

Option 2: Sell the security, pay capital gains tax, and reinvest the proceeds in another security for a year before selling it and paying capital gains on the profits from the second purchase.

What expected rate of return do we need under option 2 in order to have the same after-tax dollars as if we continued to hold the original security? Under option 1, with a cost basis of 50 percent, our original purchase price was $50. If we hold it, we expect its value of $100 to grow to $108 after one year. At that time we sell the security and, assuming all returns are capital gains, the after-tax proceeds are $108 − ($108 − $50) × 0.20 = $96.40.

Under option 2, we sell the security today for $100 and reinvest the proceeds. The after-tax proceeds from selling the security are $100 − ($100 − $50) × 0.20 = $90. We invest the $90 (which now becomes the cost basis for the new investment) in another security. The minimum expected return on the new investment must leave us no worse off than option 1's after-tax value of $96.40 after one year. That is, we want to find the value P such that the after-tax value from reinvesting the $90 sale proceeds equals $96.40:

$$\textbf{Price} - \textbf{Tax} \qquad = \textbf{\$96.40}$$

$$\textbf{P} - (\textbf{P} - \textbf{\$90}) \times \textbf{0.2} = \textbf{\$96.40}$$

where we assume only capital gains taxes are relevant and the amount of the tax is (P − $90) × 0.20. Solving for the price P, we see that the minimum price is $98; this represents a one-year return of $98/90 − 1 = 8.89 percent.

Thus, with a one-year holding period with all returns in the form of capital gains, we need to expect a return of 8.89 percent before we would consider selling a security with a 50 percent cost basis that is expected to return 8.00 percent. If a two-year holding period is used, the minimum expected annual return from reinvesting the sale proceeds is 8.85 percent.[17]

In general, the longer the expected holding period, the lower the expected return advantage needs to be. Also, the lower the original security's cost basis, the larger the capital gains tax paid if it is sold and the larger the expected return advantage will need to be to make the transaction profitable.

TAX-EFFICIENT INVESTMENT STRATEGIES

Even "average" investors will become more tax-aware because of SEC regulations that require mutual funds to disclose after-tax fund returns based on a set of assumptions. There are several well-recognized strategies for managing a portfolio to minimize capital gains taxes.[18] First, since unrealized capital gains are not taxed, a buy-and-hold strategy will defer capital gains. This works best for returns compounding over a number of years. Second, a loss harvesting or tax-loss offset strategy takes advantage of tax laws that allow the netting of capital gains and capital losses. The investment manager can sell securities with unrealized losses to offset realized capital gains.[19] Options can be used to maintain some exposure to

---

[17]Holding the current security for two additional years gives an expected value of $100(1.08)(1.08) = $116.64; selling the security and paying tax on the $50 cost basis leaves $103.31 after-tax dollars. Selling the security today and reinvesting the $90 after-tax proceeds requires the security have an expected price of $106.64 after two years [which is the solution to P − (P − $90) × 0.2 = $103.31]. This is equivalent to an annual average return of $\sqrt{(\$106.64/\$90)} − 1 = 8.85$ percent.

[18]This discussion is based on Joanne M. Hill, "Equity Derivative Strategies," in *Investment Counseling for Private Clients*, edited by Terence E. Burns (Charlottesville, VA: AIMR), 1999; and Robert Levitt, "Searching for an Answer," *Dow Jones Asset Management* (July–August 1999): 59–61.

[19]Over time this strategy will be difficult to implement. The portfolio will become increasingly concentrated and have larger unsystematic risk as winners increase or maintain their value while losing securities are sold.

the sold stock. For example, suppose a stock has declined to $60 a share for an investor who sells it to net out a capital gain from another security. The investor can sell a put on the stock with a strike price of $65 that expires in more than thirty days; let's say he receives a $6 premium.[20] If the stock price remains below $65, the put will be exercised and he will buy the stock back for an effective price of $59 ($65 strike price less the $6 premium received). The risks of this strategy are twofold: Should the price plummet, the investor's effective price of $59 may be higher than the current market price. If the price rises, he will have to pay a much higher price to reestablish the position.

Third, options can be used to help convert a short-term capital gain into a long-term gain for more favorable tax treatment. An investor can do so by writing an at-the-money or out-of-the-money call option. The strike price becomes a maximum selling price should the stock price continue to rise, but the option premium provides some downside protection in case of a price decline. As long as the price decline is not too severe, the combined stock and option position will allow the investor to maintain some profits for long-term capital gains treatment.

Fourth is a method called tax-lot accounting, wherein investors specify which shares to sell. To minimize taxes, the investor or fund manager will select those securities with the highest cost basis. The fifth strategy may not be suitable for all investors; it suggests buying growth stocks and focusing the portfolio on capital appreciation rather than income.

---

[20]The thirty-day delay is needed before repurchasing the shares to prevent a wash sale. Should that happen, the original sale is deemed not to have occurred for tax purposes and the capital loss is disallowed.

Investments Online

Equity-portfolio management is the "how-to"—it combines what we know of stock selection and portfolio theory with the practice of constructing, monitoring, and updating equity portfolios to meet the needs of individual or institutional clients. Several professional money managers describe their services on the Internet. Here's a sampling:

http://www.russell.com The home page of Frank Russell and Company contains descriptions of Russell's many services. Of special interest to us here are the links to Russell's indexes, including its various style indexes, for the United States and several other countries.

http://www.panagora.com The Web site of PanAgora Asset Management contains their investment philosophy, performance data and characteristics of their investment funds, and research papers on investment management topics authored by their staff.

http://www.firstquadrant.com First Quadrant is a leader in the application of quantitative investment techniques to equity portfolio management. The product section of this site features a description of its quantitative perspective of style management. Other sections allow users to order copies of research monographs and published articles by First Quadrant personnel.

http://www.wilshire.com Wilshire Associates, Inc., offers indexes, consulting, and other services to investors. This home page offers links to information about its indexes (the Wilshire 5000 is a widely used benchmark to represent the total equity market in the United States). The site offers a description of each Wilshire index, including such helpful information as the fundamental characteristics of each index and downloadable data.

Summary

- Passive equity portfolios attempt to track the returns of an established benchmark such as the S&P 500 or some other index that meets the investor's needs. Active portfolios attempt to add value relative to their benchmark by market timing and/or by seeking to buy undervalued stocks.

- Managers use several methods for constructing and managing a passive portfolio, including full replication, sampling, and quadratic optimization. Active management strategies include sector rotation, the use of factor models, quantitative screens, and linear programming methods.

- Investment styles include small-cap, large-cap, value, and growth. Style investing tries to take advantage of possible anomalies or strengths of the portfolio manager. Identifying with a certain style conveys information to potential clients and helps identify appropriate benchmark portfolios. Just as asset allocation models exist, some have tried to develop models to predict when one style will outperform another. A value manager focuses on the best time to buy undervalued securities; a growth manager focuses on determining appropriate times to sell securities before they are harmed by bad or disappointing news.

- Derivative securities are used by both passive and active managers for equity-portfolio management. Futures can be used to hedge against portfolio cash inflows and outflows, to keep a passive portfolio fully invested and help minimize tracking error, and to change an actively managed portfolio's beta. Options can be employed to modify a portfolio's unsystematic risk. Finally, derivatives can be used in managing currency exposures in global equity portfolios.

- Tax issues are an important consideration in many portfolios. Equity-portfolio managers use trading and derivative strategies to minimize the loss of wealth due to taxes and to get the portfolio closer to an efficient frontier offering higher returns and less risk.

QUESTIONS

1. Why have passive portfolio management strategies increased in use over time?
2. What do we mean by an indexing portfolio strategy, and what is the justification for this strategy? How might it differ from another passive portfolio?
3. Why might it be more difficult to construct a bond-market index than a stock-market index portfolio?
4. Describe several techniques for constructing a passive portfolio.
5. What tradeoffs are involved when constructing a portfolio using full replication? A sampling method?
6. Briefly describe three techniques that are considered active portfolio management strategies.
7. Discuss three strategies active managers can use to try to add value to their portfolios.
8. Because of inflation expectations, you expect natural-resource stocks such as mining companies and oil firms to perform well over the next three to six months. As an active portfolio manager, describe the various methods you might use to take advantage of this forecast.
9. How do trading costs and market efficiencies affect the active manager? How might an active manager try to overcome these obstacles to success?
10. *CFA Examination Level III*
   Global Advisors Company (GAC) is an SEC-registered investment counseling firm solely involved in managing international securities portfolios. After much research on the developing economy and capital markets of the country of Otunia, GAC has decided to include an investment in the Otunia stock market in its Emerging Market Commingled fund. However, GAC has not yet decided whether to invest actively or by indexing. Your opinion on the active versus indexing decision has been solicited. A summary of the research findings follows.

   > Otunia's economy is fairly well diversified across agricultural and natural resources, manufacturing (both consumer and durable goods), and a growing finance sector. Transaction costs in securities markets are relatively large in Otunia because of high commission and government "stamp taxes" on securities trades. Accounting standards and disclosure regulations are quite detailed, resulting in wide public availability of reliable information about companies' financial performance.
   >
   > Capital flows into and out of Otunia, and foreign ownership of Otunia securities is strictly regulated by an agency of the national government. The settlement procedures under these ownership rules often cause long delays in settling trades made by nonresidents. Senior finance officials in the government are working to deregulate capital flows and foreign ownership, but GAC's political consultant believes that isolationist sentiment may prevent much real progress in the short run.

   a. Briefly discuss four aspects of the Otunia environment that favor investing actively and four aspects that favor indexing.

b. Recommend whether GAC should invest in Otunia actively or by indexing and justify your recommendation based on the factors identified in part (a). (20 minutes)

11. What is meant by an investment style? How do value stocks differ from growth stocks?

12. Explain how style identification is an important component of the client–portfolio manager relationship.

CFA 13. *CFA Examination Level III*

Recent empirical research has suggested that holding portfolios of stocks classified as value (low price–book ratio) as opposed to growth (high price–book ratio) in both U.S. and international markets results in enhanced risk-adjusted returns. Critique the efficient market hypothesis in light of these findings.

14. Some studies suggest that value investors earn higher risk-adjusted returns than growth investors. Does this mean investors should always focus on value investing and never on other styles?

CFA 15. *CFA Examination Level III*

Betty Black's investment club wants to buy the stock of either NewSoft Inc. or Capital Corp. Black has prepared the table shown below. You have been asked to help her interpret the data, based on your forecast for a healthy economy and a strong market over the next twelve months.

	NewSoft Inc.	Capital Corp.	S&P 500 Index
Current price	$30	$32	n/a
Industry	Computer software	Capital goods	n/a
P/E ratio (current)	25 ×	14 ×	16 ×
P/E ratio (5-yr avg.)	27 ×	16 ×	16 ×
P/B ratio (current)	10 ×	3 ×	3 ×
P/B ratio (5-yr avg.)	12 ×	4 ×	2 ×
Beta	1.5	1.1	1.0
Dividend yield	0.3%	2.7%	2.8%

NewSoft's shares have higher price–earnings (P/E) and price–book (P/B) ratios than those of Capital Corp. Identify and briefly discuss three reasons why the disparity in ratios may not indicate that NewSoft's shares are overvalued relative to the shares of Capital Corp. Answer the question in terms of the two ratios, and assume that there have been no extraordinary events affecting either company. (6 minutes)

16. What are the characteristics of a good value stock portfolio manager? A good growth stock portfolio manager?

17. How are completeness funds used with style investing?

18. *CFA Examination Level III* **CFA**

Futures contracts and options on futures contracts can be used to modify risk.

a. Identify the fundamental distinction between a futures contract and an option on futures contract, and briefly explain the difference in the manner that futures and options modify portfolio risk.

b. The risk or volatility of an individual asset can be reduced either by writing a covered call option against the asset or by purchasing a put option on the asset. Explain the difference in the extent to which each of these two option strategies modifies an individual asset's risk. In your answer, describe the effect of each strategy on the potential upside and downside performance of the asset.

19. What is a hedge ratio? Why is it useful?

20. Is it possible to immunize an equity portfolio so its value is not affected by changes in the overall market? Why or why not?

21. Why might an after-tax portfolio lie below and to the left of a pretax efficient frontier?

22. Should a poorly diversified portfolio in a taxable account be rebalanced and reinvested so as to lie on an efficient frontier? Why or why not?

23. Would you expect a value manager or a growth manager to have higher after-tax returns over time? Explain.

24. Discuss three complications that taxes bring to the asset allocation and portfolio management process.

25. A manager of an actively managed portfolio is considering selling stock A and buying stock B. What factors must she consider before executing the trade?

26. Describe four different tax-efficient investing strategies.

27. How can options be used to convert a short-term capital gain situation into a long-term capital gain situation?

PROBLEMS

1. You have a portfolio with a market value of $50 million and a beta (measured against the S&P 500) of 1.2. If the market rises 10 percent, what value would you expect your portfolio to have?

2. Given the monthly returns below, how well did the passive portfolio track the S&P 500 benchmark? Find the R^2, alpha, and beta of the portfolio.

Month	Portfolio Return	S&P 500 Return
January	5.0%	5.2%
February	−2.3	−3.0
March	−1.8	−1.6
April	2.2	1.9
May	0.4	0.1

(*continued*)

Month	Portfolio Return	S&P 500 Return
June	−0.8	−0.5
July	0.0	0.2
August	1.5	1.6
September	−0.3	−0.1
October	−3.7	−4.0
November	2.4	2.0
December	0.3	0.2

3. Using the data on asset returns from Chapter 3 (Exhibit 3.13), what percentage of the equity risk premium is consumed by trading costs of 1.5 percent? Assuming a normal distribution of returns, what is the probability that an active manager can earn a return that will overcome these trading costs?

4. Solve the following algebraically:
   a. A portfolio's investment in a stock with a zero cost basis is $1,000,000. The expected after-tax return is 6 percent. An advisor has presented the owner an alternative: sell the shares, pay the 20 percent capital gains tax, and reinvest the proceeds in a set of securities with an 8 percent after-tax return. How long will it be before the compounded value of the new investment will equal the compounded value of the current investment if the shares are not sold?
   b. Assume now that part of the new portfolio's return is in the form of income; this will reduce the effective after-tax return to 7.5 percent. Assume all income and capital gains are reinvested. How long will it take for the compounded value of the new portfolio to equal that of the old investment?
   c. Now assume the income portion of the return is kept and spent by the investor. Thus, the annual compounded return on the new portfolio is only 6.5 percent. How long will it take the new portfolio to equal the value of the current portfolio?

5. You sell a stock at a loss to offset a capital gain on another security. You sell the shares at $50 per share. A put option with a strike price of $55 has a premium of $6. A call option with a strike price of $45 sells for $7. Explain what the investor should do to maintain his exposure to the sold stock. What effective price will be paid if the stock is repurchased thirty-one or more days later at a stock price of $43? $50? $57?

6. Assume you actively manage a $100 million portfolio, 95 percent invested in equities, with a portfolio beta of 1.05. Your passive benchmark is the S&P 500. The current S&P 500 index value is 1010.50.
   a. You anticipate a $3 million cash inflow from a pension fund next week. How many futures contracts should you buy or sell to mitigate the effect of this inflow on the portfolio's performance?

   b. Rather than a cash inflow, suppose you expected a cash outflow of $8 million. How many futures contracts should you buy or sell to mitigate the effect of this outflow on the portfolio's performance?

7. You manage the portfolio described in Problem 6. How many S&P 500 futures contracts must you buy or sell to
   a. increase the portfolio beta to 1.15?
   b. increase the portfolio beta to 1.30?
   c. reduce the portfolio beta to 0.95?
   d. reduce the portfolio beta to 0?

8. You own a stock portfolio worth $1.5 million with a beta of 1.3. The current value of the S&P 500 index is 985.37.
   a. What is the value of one S&P 500 futures contract traded on the Chicago Mercantile Exchange?
   b. How many futures contracts must you buy or sell to completely hedge the value of the portfolio against an expected market decline?
   c. Suppose the market, as measured by the S&P 500, drops 10 percent over the course of the next several months. Given the answer to part (b),
      i. What is the profit or loss on your futures position?
      ii. What is the expected profit or loss for your stock portfolio (unhedged)?
      iii. What is the overall impact of the market decline on your hedged portfolio?
   d. Suppose the market, as measured by the S&P 500, increases 10 percent over the course of the next several months. Given the answer to part (b),
      i. What is the profit or loss on your futures position?
      ii. What is the expected profit or loss for your stock portfolio (unhedged)?
      iii. What is the overall impact of the market rise on your hedged portfolio?

9. You own a stock portfolio worth $2.3 million with a beta of 1.1. The current value of the S&P 500 index is 1051.73.
   a. What is the value of one S&P 500 futures contract traded on the Chicago Mercantile Exchange?
   b. How many futures contracts must you buy or sell to hedge the portfolio against an expected market decline?
   c. Suppose the market, as measured by the S&P 500, drops 10 percent over the course of the next several months, but your portfolio, because of unsystematic risk, falls 13 percent in value. Given the answer to part (b),
      i. What is the profit or loss on your futures position?
      ii. What is the profit or loss for your stock portfolio (unhedged)?

iii. What is the overall impact of the market decline on your hedged portfolio? Why is this number not closer to zero?

d. Suppose the market, as measured by the S&P 500, increases 10 percent over the course of the next several months while your stock portfolio rises 15 percent. Given the answer to part (b),
  i. What is the profit or loss on your futures position?
  ii. What is the profit or loss for your stock portfolio (unhedged)?
  iii. What is the overall impact of the market rise on your hedged portfolio? Why is this number not closer to zero?

 10. *CFA Examination Level III*

Alex Andrew, who manages a $95 million large-capitalization U.S. equity portfolio, currently forecasts that equity markets will decline soon. Andrew prefers to avoid the transactions costs of making sales but wants to hedge $15 million of the portfolio's current value using S&P 500 futures.

Because Andrew realizes that his portfolio will not track the S&P 500 index exactly, he performs a regression analysis on his actual portfolio returns versus the S&P futures returns over the past year. This regression analysis indicates a risk-minimizing beta of 0.88 with an R^2 of 0.92.

FUTURES CONTRACT DATA

S&P 500 futures price	1,000
S&P 500 index	999
S&P 500 index multiplier	250

Calculate the number of futures contracts required to hedge $15 million of Andrew's portfolio, using the data above. State whether the hedge is long or short. Show all calculations. (6 minutes)

 11. *CFA Examination Level III*

Dinah Kees, the chief financial officer of Murphy Corporation, is reviewing a performance measurement report for Murphy's defined benefit pension plan. She notes that Arctic Asset Management (Arctic), a large capitalization U.S. equity value manager, has significantly underperformed the S&P 500 for the year to date and past one- and three-year periods.

The exhibit identifies factors that are included in the performance measurement report.

PERFORMANCE MEASUREMENT FACTORS

Arctic's portfolio return	P
S&P 500 index return	M
Salomon World ex-U.S. index return	E
Russell 1000 Value index return	B
Russell 2000 Growth index return	X
Risk-free rate of return	R

a. Construct a formula, using factors from the exhibit, that measures the contribution of *style* to Arctic's relative performance.

b. Construct a formula, using factors from the exhibit, that measures the contribution of *stock selection* to Arctic's relative performance. (6 minutes)

12. Sam owns 500 shares of FAB stock; its current price is $45 and he purchased the shares at $20. He expects the stock to average a 7 percent price increase into the foreseeable future with no dividends. He expects the capital gains tax rate to be 20 percent.

a. What return must he earn if he sells his FAB stock and reinvests the proceeds if he sells the new investment after one year?

b. What return must he earn if the holding period on the new investment is likely to be five years?

13. Sam's colleague, Marcia, purchased FAB stock before Sam did, when the stock's price was $12.

a. What return must she earn if she sells her FAB stock and reinvests the proceeds if she sells the new investment after one year?

b. What return must she earn if the holding period on the new investment is likely to be five years?

14. Using your answers from Problems 12 and 13, discuss the impact of length of holding period and cost basis on the return of a follow-on investment.

15. Using the data in Problem 12, suppose Sam's expected return on FAB stock is now 14 percent. Do the answers to parts (a) and (b) in Problem 12 double as well? Why or why not?

16. Redo parts (a) and (b) of Problem 12, assuming a capital gains tax rate of 10 percent. How sensitive are the answers to a change in the capital gains tax rate?

WEB EXERCISES

1. A variety of data is available from BARRA's Web site (*http://www.barra.com*). BARRA index data can be downloaded from *http://www.barra.com/Research/DownloadMonthlyReturns.aspx*. Data is available on returns on several growth and value indexes. Compute the mean and standard deviation of each growth and value index and compare them to the "straight" index (S&P 500, Midcap 400, Smallcap 600).

2. Find and visit the Web site of a growth manager and a value manager. What are their current market outlooks and investment strategies? Compare their performance with that of the BARRA indexes.

3. Professor Ken French (of Fama and French) has a personal Web site: *http://mba.tuck.dartmouth.edu/pages/faculty/ken.french/*. What information is available in his data library? Why might it be of interest to an equity-portfolio manager?

4. Dimensional Fund Advisors' Web site is *http://www.dfaus.com*. Explain its equity investing strategies and how it fits in with the EMH and an investing style. How does DFA construct its indexes? Report on the interviews with Eugene Fama and other well-known academic researchers that are available on the site.

5. Go to Vanguard's Web site (*http://www.vanguard.com*) and obtain annual (or quarterly) return data for its equity index funds. Compare their after-tax and before-tax returns. Is there a difference in the tax efficiency of their large-cap versus small-cap funds? Growth versus value? Explain why there might be a difference.

SPREADSHEET EXERCISES

1. Suppose the founder of a company is invested 100 percent in a single stock with a zero cost basis that has been held for many years. Assume the expected future return on the stock is 8 percent a year and, to keep the numbers simple, assume the value of the stock is $1,000. If he were to sell the stock today, pay a 20 percent capital gains tax, and reinvest the proceeds ($800) in a diversified portfolio expected to return 10 percent annually, how long will it be before the value of the diversified portfolio equals the expected value of the single-stock portfolio? Graph the dollar values of each portfolio over time on the same graph.

2. An entrepreneur owns $2 million of his company's stock. The expected return on the single-stock portfolio is 6 percent annually, after taxes. A well-diversified portfolio is expected to have an after-tax return of 8 percent. If capital gains taxes of 20 percent are to be paid when the entrepreneur sells his shares and reinvests in the diversified portfolio, how long will it be before the value of the diversified portfolio equals the expected value of the single-stock portfolio? Graph the dollar values of each portfolio over time on the same graph.

3. Suppose in Exercise 2 that 1.5 percent of the diversified portfolio's return is from income. Given the entrepreneur's income, this cash flow is taxed at a higher rate than the portfolio's capital returns. Suppose this will reduce the after-tax return on the portfolio to 7.5 percent annually. Under these conditions, how long will it be before the value of the diversified portfolio equals the expected value of the single-stock portfolio?

4. Suppose in Exercise 2 that part of the diversified portfolio's return is income of 1.5 percent annually. Rather than reinvesting, the entrepreneur spends this income. This will reduce the after-tax return that is reinvested in the portfolio to 6.5 percent. How long will it be before the value of the diversified portfolio equals the value of the single-stock portfolio?

5. A company has achieved great growth in recent years but its short-term outlook is cloudy. You have $800,000 in this stock with a cost basis of $100,000. The capital gains tax rate is 20 percent. You believe the after-tax return on the stock will be −5 percent in each of the next two years; after that the stock will enjoy an after-tax return of +5 percent. You are thinking of selling the position and investing in a portfolio with an expected after-tax return of 6 percent into the foreseeable future. Evaluate the wealth you will have in each of the positions over time. Does the trade make economic sense if your time horizon is two years? Five years? Ten years?

6. Your company's stock continues to have a rosy forecast. Analysts expect it to gain 10 percent per year, after-tax, for the next four years and then earn a more sustainable 6 percent after-tax annually. Wary of risk from your undiversified position, you are also considering selling the position and investing in a portfolio with an expected after-tax return of 8 percent annually. If your stock holding is worth $1.2 million with a cost basis of zero, compare the wealth position of each portfolio over time.

REFERENCES

Bhatia, Sanjiv, Ed. *Global Equity Investing*. Charlottesville, VA: AIMR, May 1996.

Burns, Terence E., Ed. *Derivatives in Portfolio Management*. Charlottesville, VA: AIMR, 1998.

Coggin, Daniel T., Frank J. Fabozzi, and Robert D. Arnott, Eds. *The Handbook of Equity Style Management*, 3rd ed. Hoboken, NJ: John Wiley & Sons, 2003.

Jost, Kathryn Dixon., Ed. *Investment Counseling for Private Clients III*. Charlottesville, VA: AIMR, 2001.

Jost, Kathryn Dixon, ed. *Investment Counseling for Private Clients IV*. Charlottesville, VA: AIMR, 2002.

Jost, Kathryn Dixon, Ed. *Equity Portfolio Management*. Charlottesville, VA: AIMR, 2002.

Klein, Robert A., and Jess Lederman, Eds. *Equity Style Management*. Chicago: Irwin Professional Publishing, 1995.

Maginn, John L., and Donald L. Tuttle, eds. *Managing Investment Portfolios*, 2nd ed. Boston, MA: Warren, Gorham, and Lamont, 1990.

Squires, Jan, Ed. *Value and Growth Styles in Equity Investing*. Charlottesville, VA: AIMR, 1995.

THOMSON ONE
Business School Edition

1. Examine the behavior of the following market capital-ization-weighted indexes: S&P 600 small-cap index, S&P 400 mid-cap index, the S&P 500 large-cap index, and the S&P 1500 composite. Which market capitaliza-tion style has performed best over the past year? The past five years? Estimate the return to each style for each of the past five years. What would your compound return be if you were able to forecast the best-perform-ing index in each of the past five years?

2. Examine the behavior of the S&P 500 Barra/Growth and S&P 500 Barra/Value indexes. Which style has per-formed best over the past year? The past five years? Esti-mate the return to each style for each of the past five years. What would your compound return be if you were able to forecast the best-performing style in each of the past five years?

GLOSSARY

Active equity-portfolio management An attempt by the manager to outperform, on a risk-adjusted basis, a pas-sive benchmark portfolio.

Backtest A method of testing a quantitative model in which computers are used to examine the composition and returns of portfolios based on historical data to determine if the selected strategy would have worked in the past.

Benchmark portfolio A passive portfolio whose average characteristics (in terms of beta, dividend yield, industry weighting, firm size, and so on) match the risk–return objectives of the client and serves as a basis for evaluating the performance of an active manager.

Completeness fund A specialized index used to form the basis of a passive portfolio whose purpose is to provide diversification to a client's total portfolio by excluding those segments in which the client's active managers invest.

Dollar-cost averaging A passive investment strategy where equal amounts of funds are invested each period.

Earnings momentum A strategy in which portfolios are constructed of stocks of firms with rising earnings.

Full replication A technique for constructing a passive index portfolio in which all securities in an index are pur-chased in proportion to their weights in the index.

Growth stocks Stocks of firms enjoying above-average earnings per share increases and that usually have above-average price–book and price–earnings ratios.

Passive equity-portfolio management A long-term buy-and-hold strategy so that returns will track those of an index over time.

Price momentum A portfolio strategy in which the investor acquires stocks that have enjoyed above-market stock price increases.

Quadratic optimization A technique in which historical correlations are used to construct a portfolio that seeks to minimize tracking error with an index.

Sampling A technique for constructing a passive index portfolio in which the portfolio manager buys a representa-tive sample of stocks that comprise the benchmark index.

Sector rotation strategy An active strategy that involves purchasing stocks in specific industries or stocks with spe-cific characteristics (low P/E, growth, value) that are antici-pated to rise in value more than the overall market.

Style investing An investment strategy that involves con-structing portfolios that capture one or more of the charac-teristics of equity securities.

Tracking error The difference between a passively man-aged portfolio's returns and that of the index it seeks to imi-tate.

Value stocks Stocks that appear to be underpriced because either their price–book or price–earnings ratio is low or their dividend yield is high compared to the rest of the market.

Bond-Portfolio Management

S uccessful bond-portfolio management involves far more than mastering vast amounts of technical information. Such information is useful only to the extent that it helps generate higher risk-adjusted returns. In this chapter, we shift attention from the technical dimensions of bond-portfolio management to the equally important strategic dimension. We first discuss several portfolio management strategies. Then we examine how the use of derivative securities can assist fixed-income portfolio managers.

In this chapter we will answer the following questions:

What are three major bond-portfolio management strategies?

What are the two specific strategies for passive portfolio management?

What are six strategies for active portfolio management?

What do we mean by matched-funding techniques, and what are the four specific strategies?

How are futures contracts used to hedge against cash deposits or withdrawals from a bond portfolio?

How are futures used to change the systematic risk (i.e., duration) of an actively managed portfolio?

What are some of the general advantages of using derivatives in bond-portfolio management?

Introduction

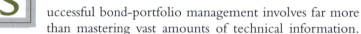

Bond-portfolio management strategies can be divided into three groups:

1. Passive strategies
   a. Buy and hold
   b. Indexing
2. Active strategies
   a. Interest rate anticipation
   b. Valuation analysis
   c. Credit analysis
   d. Yield-spread analysis
   e. Bond swaps
   f. Core-plus
3. Matched-funding techniques
   a. Classical ("pure") immunization
   b. Pure cash-matched dedicated portfolio
   c. Dedication with reinvestment
   d. Horizon matching

We will discuss each of these alternatives because they are all viable for certain portfolios with different needs and risk profiles. Prior to the 1960s, only the passive and active strategies were available, and most bond portfolios were managed on a buy-and-hold basis. The 1960s and early 1970s saw growing interest in alternative active strategies. The investment environment since the late 1970s has been characterized by periods of record-breaking inflation and interest rates, declining inflation and interest rates, extremely volatile rates of return in bond markets, the introduction of many new financial instruments in response to the increase in return volatility, and the development of several new funding techniques or contingent portfolio management techniques to meet the emerging needs of institutional clients. Several of these new management techniques have become possible because of the rediscovery of the concept of *duration* in the early 1970s.

Passive Management Strategies

Managers employ two specific passive management strategies. First is a *buy-and-hold strategy*, in which a manager selects a portfolio of bonds based on the objectives and constraints of the client with the intent of holding these bonds to maturity. In the second strategy, *indexing*, the objective is to construct a portfolio of bonds that will match the performance of a specified bond index, such as the Lehman Brothers Government Bond Index.

BUY-AND-HOLD STRATEGY

The simplest portfolio management strategy is to buy and hold the securities until maturity. Well-known to bond investors, buy and hold involves finding issues with desired quality, coupon levels, term to maturity, and important indenture provisions, such as a call feature. Tradeoffs include the fact that investors recognize that agency issues generally provide incremental returns relative to Treasuries with little sacrifice in quality, that utilities generally provide higher returns than comparably rated industrials, and that various embedded options affect the risk and realized yield of an issue. Thus, buy-and-hold managers use their knowledge of markets and issue characteristics to select the appropriate bonds for a portfolio.

Buy-and-hold managers do not consider active trading to achieve attractive returns, but rather look for vehicles whose maturities (or duration) approximate the stipulated investment horizon to reduce price and reinvestment risk. A modified buy-and-hold strategy involves investing in an issue with the intention of holding it until the end of the investment horizon, while actively looking for opportunities to trade into more desirable positions.[1]

INDEXING STRATEGY

As discussed in Chapter 10 on efficient capital markets, numerous empirical studies have demonstrated that the majority of money managers fail to match the risk–return performance of common-stock or bond indexes. As a result, many clients opt to have some part of their bond portfolios indexed to a selected bond-market index such as the Lehman Brothers, Merrill Lynch, or Salomon Brothers index. In such a case, the portfolio manager is not judged on the basis of risk and return compared to an index but by how closely the portfolio tracks the index. Specifically, the analysis of performance involves examining the *tracking error*, the difference between the rate of return for the portfolio and the rate of return for the index.

When the manager initiates an indexing strategy, selection of the appropriate market index is critical to meeting the need for consistency with the client's risk–return preferences and the investment policy statement. This requires the manager to be familiar with all

---

[1]If this strategy became too modified, it would become an active strategy.

the characteristics of the index,[2] which can change over time. For example, studies have shown that the market experienced significant changes in composition, maturity, and duration during the period 1975 to 2000.[3]

Active Management Strategies[4]

Managers can choose from six active management strategies that range from interest rate anticipation, which involves economic forecasting, to valuation analysis and credit analysis, which require detailed bond and company analysis. Yield-spread analysis and bond swaps require economic and market analysis. Core–plus bond management combines passive management of part of the portfolio with active management of the remainder in market segments in which the manager believes he can earn above-normal returns.

INTEREST RATE ANTICIPATION

Interest rate anticipation is perhaps the riskiest active management strategy because it involves making portfolio changes based on uncertain forecasts of future interest rates. As discussed in Chapter 12, the idea is to preserve capital by reducing portfolio duration when interest rates are expected to increase and achieve attractive capital gains by increasing portfolio duration when a decline in yields is anticipated.

When managers expect a rate decline, portfolio liquidity is important; managers must be able to close out the position quickly when the drop in rates is complete. Therefore, they would prefer high-grade securities such as Treasuries, agencies, or corporates rated AAA through Baa. Another reason for using these securities is that the higher the quality of an obligation, the more sensitive its value to interest rate changes.

Obviously, shifting portfolio duration in anticipation of rate changes incurs risk. When durations are shortened in the face of an expected rate increase, one risk is that the rate forecast turns out to be incorrect and the portfolio will be poorly positioned to earn capital gains should rates fall. In addition, income returns are generally lower for shorter-term bonds, so a strategy to lower duration also leads to lower portfolio coupon income.

Portfolio shifts prompted by the anticipation of declining rates are also very risky. By lengthening duration, the portfolio's value could sharply decline should rates rise rather than fall as anticipated. Also, if rates are forecast to fall at a time when the yield curve is inverted, the manager will sacrifice current income by shifting from high-coupon short bonds to longer-duration bonds that have a lower yield.

To avoid the risks of having an all-short or all-long duration portfolio built to take advantage of a specific rate forecast, some managers prefer to take a more neutral stance by

---

[2]An article that describes a couple of the indexes and discusses how their characteristics affect their performance in different interest rate environments is Chris P. Dialynas, "The Active Decisions in the Selection of Passive Management and Performance Bogeys," in *The Handbook of Fixed-Income Securities,* 6th ed., edited by Frank J. Fabozzi (New York: McGraw-Hill, 2001).

[3]An article that describes the major indexes, analyzes the relationship among them, and also examines how the aggregate bond market has changed is Frank K. Reilly and David J. Wright, "Bond Market Indexes," in *The Handbook of Fixed-Income Securities,* 6th ed., edited by Frank J. Fabozzi (New York: McGraw-Hill, 2001).

[4]For further discussion on this topic, see H. Gifford Fong, "Bond Management: Past, Current, and Future," in *The Handbook of Fixed-Income Securities,* 6th ed., edited by Frank J. Fabozzi (New York: McGraw-Hill, 2001). Another interesting source is Dwight D. Churchill, ed., *Fixed-Income Management: Techniques and Practices* (Charlottesville, VA: AIMR, 1994).

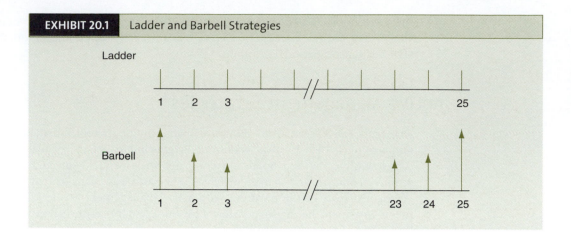

EXHIBIT 20.1 Ladder and Barbell Strategies

spreading the maturities of their holdings using *ladder* and *barbell* strategies, as illustrated in Exhibit 20.1.

The *ladder strategy* places an equal amount of the portfolio's holdings in a wide range of maturities. Maturing bonds are reinvested in the longest-term bonds. To reduce reinvestment risk, coupon income is reinvested across the maturity spectrum. With this strategy, the increases and declines in interest rates are averaged out over the business cycle, leading to less risky returns when compared to the all-short or all-long strategy.

In the *barbell strategy,* about one-half of the funds are invested in short-duration securities and the remainder are invested in long-duration securities. This combines the high-return, high-income potential of long-term bonds with the lower-risk, high-liquidity aspects of shorter-term securities. This strategy is especially appropriate for times when short-term rates are expected to rise and long-term rates are expected to be stable or decline (that is, when the term structure of interest rates is expected to flatten).

VALUATION ANALYSIS

With *valuation analysis,* the portfolio manager attempts to select bonds based on their intrinsic value. In turn, a bond's value is based on its coupon cash flows, market interest rates, and its characteristics such as callability, the existence of a sinking fund, and credit rating. The average value placed on these characteristics in the marketplace can be estimated by examining bond-market data or by running multiple regression models. As an example, a bond's rating will dictate a certain spread, or yield differential, relative to comparable Treasury bonds; long maturity might be worth additional basis points relative to short maturity (that is, the maturity spread); a given deferred call feature might require a lower yield compared to a bond that is currently callable. Given all the characteristics of the bond and their average impact on a bond's yield, we can determine the required yield, and therefore, the bond's implicit intrinsic value. After we have done this for a number of bonds, we would compare these derived bond values to the prevailing market prices to determine which bonds are undervalued or overvalued. The strategy would be to buy the undervalued issues and ignore or sell the overvalued issues. Success in valuation analysis arises from understanding the characteristics that are important in valuation and being able to accurately estimate the value of these characteristics over time.

A difficulty in implementing valuation analysis is that the price the market is willing to pay for certain characteristics varies across time. For example, the value of a call or put option will vary with interest rate volatility and the credit spread across bond ratings will change dramatically over time depending on the overall economic environment (e.g., the credit spread increases during periods of recession and economic uncertainty).

CREDIT ANALYSIS

A *credit analysis* strategy involves detailed analysis of the bond issuer to determine expected changes in its default risk. As such, it is similar in scope and detail to equity analysis. Credit analysis involves attempts to project changes in the quality ratings assigned to bonds by the three rating agencies.[5] These rating changes are affected by internal changes in the entity (for example, changes in important financial ratios) and also by changes in the external environment (changes in the firm's industry and the economy). During periods of strong economic expansion, even financially weak firms may be able to survive and perhaps prosper. In contrast, during severe economic contractions, normally strong firms may find it difficult or impossible to meet financial obligations. Therefore, rating changes have shown a strong cyclical pattern—typically, downgradings increase during economic contractions and decline during economic expansions.

To employ credit analysis as a management strategy, the manager must *project* rating changes prior to the announcement by the rating agencies. Studies have found that the bond market adjusts rather quickly to bond rating changes—especially downgradings. Therefore, the manager should acquire bond issues *expected* to experience upgradings and sell or avoid those *expected* to be downgraded.

YIELD-SPREAD ANALYSIS

As discussed in Chapter 12, spread analysis assumes normal relationships between the yields for bonds in alternative sectors (for example, the spread between high-grade versus low-grade industrial or between industrial versus utility bonds). Therefore, a bond-portfolio manager would monitor these relationships and, when an abnormal relationship occurs, would execute various sector swaps. The crucial factor is to develop the background to know the normal yield relationship and evaluate the liquidity necessary to buy or sell the required issues quickly enough to take advantage of the supposedly temporary abnormality. *Yield-spread analysis* differs from valuation analysis in that valuation analysis examines many issue-specific influences on yield whereas yield-spread analysis focuses only on the difference in yield between specific sectors.

Changes in yield spreads are related to the economic environment. For example, the credit spreads widen during periods of economic uncertainty and recession because investors require larger risk premiums (that is, larger spreads) on riskier issues. In contrast, spreads decline during periods of economic confidence and expansion.

BOND SWAPS

Bond swaps involve selling a bond (frequently called the *S bond,* as it may be sold) and simultaneously buying a different issue (called the *P bond,* as it may be purchased) with similar attributes but a chance for improved return.[6] Swaps can be executed to increase

---

[5]For a discussion of credit analysis that takes this approach, see Jane Tripp Howe, "Credit Analysis for Corporate Bonds," in *The Handbook of Fixed-Income Securities,* 6th ed., edited by Frank J. Fabozzi (New York: McGraw-Hill, 2001).

[6]The bond swaps we are discussing here should not be confused with interest rate swaps. Interest rate swaps involve an agreement in which two parties agree to exchange interest cash flows, typically one based on a fixed-interest rate and the other based on a variable or floating rate.

current yield, to increase yield to maturity, to take advantage of shifts in interest rates or the realignment of yield spreads, to improve the quality of a portfolio, or for tax purposes.

Inputs to the swap analysis include current interest rates and prices on the S and P bonds as well as predictions for future interest rates. The input to the analysis also includes a time horizon, called the *work-out time,* over which the forecasted interest rate change will occur. Typical work-out times are six months or one year. Swap analysis examines the three components of bond return (coupon income, interest earned on reinvested bond income, and the change in the bond's price) over the work-out time to determine whether the S or P bond offers better returns given the interest rate forecast. Of course, commissions and taxes paid from selling one bond and buying another should also figure in the analysis by using prices net of commissions.

The analysis must also examine the several different types of risk to which swaps are exposed. One obvious risk is that the market will move against you while the swap is outstanding. In other words, interest rates may behave differently than forecasted by moving up when they were expected to fall, or yield spreads may fail to respond as anticipated.

Another risk is that the P bond may not be a true substitute for the S bond; for example, the S bond may receive a credit-rating upgrade while the P bond's rating remains unchanged. In this case, even if the expectations and interest rate formulations are correct, the swap may be unsatisfactory because the wrong issue was selected.

Finally, a problem can occur if the work-out time is longer than anticipated, in which case the realized return from selling the S bond and buying the P bond might be less than expected. Such risks can be evaluated by using a variety of interest rate assumptions and work-out times to compare the sensitivity of the swap's incremental return to these risks.

In the following subsections we consider three of the more popular bond swaps.[7]

Pure Yield Pickup Swap   The pure yield pickup involves swapping out of a low-coupon bond into a comparable higher-coupon bond to realize an automatic and instantaneous increase in current yield and yield to maturity. One risk inherent in this type of swap is that the market may be pricing the issues differently because of an anticipated credit-rating change for one of the issues. Another risk is the higher probability that the higher-coupon bond will be called in the event of a future interest rate decline.

An example of a pure yield pickup swap would be an investor who currently holds a thirty-year, Aa-rated, 10 percent issue that is trading at an 11.50 percent yield. Assume that a comparable thirty-year, Aa-rated obligation bearing a 12 percent coupon priced to yield 12 percent becomes available. The investor would report (and realize) some book loss if the original issue was bought at par but is able to improve current yield and yield to maturity simultaneously if the new obligation is held to maturity, as shown in Exhibit 20.2.

The investor need not predict rate changes, and the swap is not based on any imbalance in yield spread. The object is simply to seek higher yields. Quality and maturity stay the same, as do all other factors except coupon.

As an example of the risk of this swap, consider the situation in which the 12 percent yield on the candidate bond is correct because the market anticipates the Aa candidate bond will be downgraded to an A rating. Suppose this occurs, and by the end of the one-year time frame the candidate bond has an A rating and is selling to yield 12.5 percent. In this case, the return calculations for the candidate bond are as follows:

[7]For additional information on these and other types of bond swaps, see Sidney Homer and Martin L. Leibowitz, *Inside the Yield Book* (Princeton Bloomberg Press, 2004).

	P Bond
Dollar investment	$1,000.00
Coupon income	120.00
Interest from reinvesting one coupon	3.60
Principal value at year-end (selling at a 12.5% yield)	961.15
Total accrued value at year-end	$1,084.65
Realized compound yield	8.47%

The 8.47 percent realized compound yield is far below that expected on the S bond shown in Exhibit 20.2. Thus, some credit analysis should be undertaken before swaps are completed to ensure the credit quality of the bonds is similar.

Substitution Swap   The substitution swap is done to exploit an apparent short-term mispricing between two bond issues that are identical with respect to coupon rate, credit rating, and time to maturity. It is subject to considerably more risk than the pure yield pickup swap, as the apparent mispricing may persist because of quality differences that the market perceived before the bond-rating agencies.

For example, an investor might hold a thirty-year, 12 percent issue that is yielding 12 percent (the S bond) and be offered a comparable thirty-year, 12 percent bond that is yielding 12.20 percent (the P bond). Because it has a higher yield but the same coupon and maturity, the P bond will sell for a lower price than the current value of the S bond.

Ideally, the yield spread imbalance would be corrected over a short period of time as the yield on the P bond declines to 12 percent and the P bond rises in value. But the yield difference may persist if, despite their credit ratings, the quality of the bonds is not really identical. The work-out time will have an important effect on the differential realized return. Even if the yield is not corrected until maturity, thirty years hence, the investor will

---

EXHIBIT 20.2   A Pure Yield Pickup Swap

Pure yield pickup swap: A bond swap that involves a switch from a low-coupon bond to a higher-coupon bond of similar quality and maturity to pick up higher current yield and a better yield to maturity.

Example:
Currently held: thirty-year. Aa, 10.0 percent coupon priced at 874.12 to yield 11.5 percent.
Swap candidate: thirty-year, Aa 12 percent coupon priced at $1,000 to yield 12.0 percent.
The analysis for a one-year time frame appears below. For simplicity, we assume the next semiannual coupon payment occurs in six months. Cash flows are reinvested at 12 percent.

	S Bond	P Bond
Dollar investment	$874.12	$1,000.00
Coupon income	100.00	120.00
Interest from reinvesting one coupon	3.00	3.60
Principal value at year-end	874.66	1,000.00
Total accrued value at year-end	977.66	1,123.60
Realized compound yield	11.85%	12.36%

Value of swap: 57.0 basis points in one year (using above interest rate assumptions)

EXHIBIT 20.3	A Substitution Swap

Substitution swap: A swap executed to take advantage of temporary market anomalies in yield spreads between issues that are equivalent with respect to coupon, quality, and maturity.

Example:

Currently held: thirty-year, Aa 12 percent coupon priced at $1,000 to yield 12 percent.

Swap candidate: thirty-year, Aa 12 percent coupon priced at $984.08 to yield 12.2 percent, which we believe will fall to equal the 12 percent yield of the currently held bond.

Assumed work-out period: one year; cash flows reinvested at 12 percent.

	S Bond	P Bond
Dollar investment	$1,000.00	$984.08
Coupon income	120.00	120.00
Interest from reinvesting one coupon	3.60	3.60
Principal value at year-end	1,000.00	1,000.00
Total accrued value at year-end	1,123.60	1,123.60
Realized compound yield (one year work-out period)	12.36%	14.18%

Value of swap: 182 basis points in one year

still experience a small increase in realized yield (about ten basis points). In contrast, if the correction takes place within one year, the differential realized return is much greater, as shown in Exhibit 20.3.

Another possibility is that the value of the P bond may remain constant while the 12 percent yield on the S bond *rises* to 12.2 percent. In this case, a loss in the value of the S bond is avoided if the swap is completed. Exhibit 20.3 shows a basic analysis, but a more complete analysis would consider different scenarios to gauge the risk and return potential of the transaction.

Tax Swap   The tax swap is popular with individual investors because it is a relatively simple procedure that involves no interest rate projections and few risks. Investors' reasons for entering into tax swaps often include tax law provisions and realized capital gains in their portfolios. Suppose an investor had acquired $100,000 worth of corporate bonds and after two years sold the securities for $150,000, giving a capital gain of $50,000. One way to eliminate the tax liability of that capital gain is to sell an issue that has a comparable long-term capital loss.[8] A long-term investment of $100,000 with a current market value of $50,000 could be swapped to establish the $50,000 capital loss. By offsetting this capital loss and the comparable capital gain, the investor's income taxes would be reduced.

Municipal bonds are considered particularly attractive tax swap candidates because tax-free income can be increased and the capital loss (which is subject to normal federal and state taxation) can be used to reduce capital gains tax liability. The money saved by avoiding the tax liability can then be used to increase the portfolio's yield, as shown in Exhibit 20.4.

An important caveat is that *you cannot swap identical issues,* such as selling the New York 4s in Exhibit 20.4 to establish a loss and then buying back the same New York 4s. If the

---

[8]Although this discussion deals with tax swaps that involve bonds, comparable strategies apply to other types of investments.

EXHIBIT 20.4	A Tax Swap

Tax swap: A swap you undertake when you wish to offset capital gains through the sale of a bond currently held and selling at a discount from the price paid at purchase. By swapping into a bond with as nearly identical features as possible, you can use the capital loss on the sale of the bond for tax purposes and still maintain your current position in the market.

Example: You currently hold two sets of bonds. One set is corporate bonds purchased for $100,000; their current market value is $150,000. The second set is municipal bonds (New York, twenty-year, 4 percent coupon) purchased for $100,000 with a current market value of $50,000. The swap candidate is $50,000 in New York twenty-year, 4.1 percent bonds.

A. Corporate bonds sold and long-term capital gains profit established	$50,000
Capital gains tax liability, assuming a 20 percent capital gains tax rate	($50,000 × .20) = $10,000
B. N.Y. 4s sold and long-term capital *loss* established	($50,000)
Reduction in capital gains tax liability	(loss of $50,000 × .20 = $10,000)
Net capital gains tax liability	$0
Tax savings realized	$10,000
C. Complete tax swap by buying New York 4.1s from proceeds of New York 4s sale	
(therefore, amount invested remains largely the same)[a]	
Annual tax-free interest income—New York 4s	$4,000
Annual tax-free interest income—New York 4.1s	$4,100
Net increase in annual tax-free interest income	$100

[a]New York 4.1s will show a substantial price rise when liquidated at maturity (because they were bought at deep discounts) and, therefore, will be subject to future tax liability. The swap is designed to use the capital loss resulting from the swap to offset capital gains from other investments. At the same time, your funds remain in a security almost identical to your previous holding while you receive a slight increase in both current income and YTM. Because the tax swap involves no projections in terms of work-out period, interest rate changes, and so on, it has minimal risk. Your major concern should be to avoid potential wash sales.

same issue is purchased within thirty days, the IRS considers the transaction a *wash sale* and does not allow the loss. It is easier to avoid wash sales in the bond market than it is in the stock market because every bond issue, even with identical coupons and maturities, is considered distinct. Likewise, it is easier to find comparable bond issues with only modest differences in coupon, maturity, and quality. Tax swaps are common at year-end as investors establish capital losses, because the capital loss must occur in the same taxable year as the capital gain. This procedure differs from other swap transactions in that it exists because of tax statutes rather than temporary market anomalies.

CORE-PLUS BOND MANAGEMENT

The sixth active portfolio management style is actually a combination approach. In *core-plus bond management,* a significant (core) part of the portfolio (e.g., 70 percent to 75 percent) is managed passively in a widely recognized sector such as the U.S. Aggregate Sector or the U.S. Government/Corporate sector (the difference between these two sectors is that the aggregate includes the rapidly growing mortgage-backed and asset-backed sectors). It is suggested that this core of the portfolio be managed passively because these segments of the bond market are so efficient that it is not worth the time and cost to attempt to derive excess returns within these sectors. The rest of the portfolio would be managed actively in one or several additional "plus" sectors, where it is felt that there is a higher probability of achieving positive abnormal rates of return because of potential inefficiencies. The major areas suggested for the plus of the portfolio include high-yield bonds (HY bonds), foreign bonds, and emerging-market debt. These are considered good candidates for active management since they generally experience above-average rates of return, but while they have *high total risk* as measured by their standard deviation of returns, they have relatively *low systematic risk* relative to a total bond-market portfolio because they have low correlations with other fixed-income sectors. An example would be HY bonds that have *very high* standard deviations but are correlated only about 0.30 with investment-grade bonds and/or other large bond benchmarks so they have *very low* systematic risk.[9]

A WORD ON STYLE

Just as managers employ various investment styles in the equity markets (as we saw in Chapter 19), managers have various investing styles in the fixed-income markets. Although valuation analysis, taking advantage of yield spreads, bond swaps, and core-plus can add incremental return to a bond portfolio, the two main determinants of a portfolio's return are duration and overall credit quality. The term structure of interest rates illustrates the effect of time to maturity and duration on overall yield to maturity; generally, longer-duration securities offer higher yields to maturity. Credit quality reflects a default risk premium on a bond; higher-quality bonds have lower default risk premiums and therefore have lower yields than lower-quality issues.

Comparing a bond manager's performance or selecting a bond manager requires sharing information regarding the portfolio style characteristics of duration and credit quality characteristics. It makes little sense to judge a small-cap stock portfolio on the basis of the S&P 500. Neither is it appropriate to compare the performance of a manager investing in high-yield bonds to an investment-grade corporate bond index, nor the performance of a manager who focuses on the short-end of the term structure with a long-duration benchmark.

Matched-Funding Techniques[10]

As discussed previously, an increase in interest rate volatility and the needs of many institutional investors has led to growth in the use of matched-funding techniques ranging from pure cash-matched dedicated portfolios to portfolios that employ immunization.

IMMUNIZATION STRATEGIES

Immunization attempts to earn a specified rate of return (generally quite close to the current market rate) over a given investment horizon regardless of what happens to market interest rates. Whether market rates rise or fall, the value of the portfolio at the end of the time horizon (that is, the ending-wealth value) should be close to its target value in an immunized portfolio. Portfolio immunization attempts to balance the two components of interest rate risk: price risk and reinvestment risk.

[9]Two conferences by the Association for Investment Management and Research (now known as CFA Institute) consider this concept and discuss potential areas for active management. See *Global Bond Management II: The Search for Alpha* (Charlottesville, VA: AIMR, August 2000); and *Core-Plus Bond Management* (Charlottesville, VA: AIMR, March 2001).

[10]An overview of these alternative strategies is contained in Martin L. Leibowitz, "The Dedicated Bond Portfolio in Pension Funds—Part I: Motivation and Basics," *Financial Analysts Journal* 42, no. 1 (January–February 1986): 68–75; and Martin L. Leibowitz, "The Dedicated Bond Portfolio in Pension Funds—Part II: Immunization, Horizon Matching, and Contingent Procedures," *Financial Analysts Journal* 42, no. 2 (March–April 1986): 47–57.

Components of Interest Rate Risk If the term structure of interest rates were flat and market rates never changed between the time of purchase and the date the bond is to be sold or redeemed, a bond-portfolio manager could acquire a bond with a term to maturity equal to the desired *investment horizon,* and the ending wealth from the bond would equal the promised wealth position implied by the promised yield to maturity. As an example, suppose an investor acquired at par a ten-year, $1 million bond with an 8 percent coupon. The wealth position at the end of the ten-year investment horizon (assuming semiannual compounding) would be $1,000,000 \times (1.04)^{20} = \$1,000,000 \times 2.1911 = \$2,191,100$. This is the same as taking each $40,000 interest payment received every six months and compounding it to the end of the period at a 4 percent nominal rate every six months and adding the $1,000,000 principal at maturity.

Unfortunately, in the real world, the term structure of interest rates typically is not flat and the level of interest rates is constantly changing. *Interest rate risk* is the uncertainty regarding the ending-wealth value of the portfolio due to changes in market interest rates between the time of purchase and the target date. It involves two component risks in turn: price risk and coupon-reinvestment risk.

Price risk occurs because varying interest rates may cause the market price for the bond to change over time. If rates were to increase after the time of purchase, the market price for the bond would fall, whereas if rates declined, the realized price would rise. The point is, because we do not know whether rates will increase or decrease, we are uncertain about the bond's future price prior to maturity.

The *reinvestment risk* arises because the yield-to-maturity computation implicitly assumes all coupon cash flows will be reinvested at the promised yield to maturity. If, after the purchase of the bond, interest rates decline, the coupon cash flows will be reinvested at rates below the promised YTM, and the ending wealth will be below expectations. In contrast, if interest rates increase, the coupon cash flows will be reinvested at rates above expectations, and the ending wealth will be above expectations. Again, because we are uncertain about future interest rates, we are uncertain about these reinvestment rates.

Classical Immunization and Interest Rate Risk Notably, the price risk and the reinvestment risk caused by a change in interest rates have opposite effects on the ending-wealth position. Clearly, a bond-portfolio manager with a specific target date (investment horizon) will attempt to balance these two interest rate risk effects. The process intended to eliminate interest rate risk is referred to as *immunization.*

Assuming a flat yield curve and parallel shifts in the yield curve as interest rates change, a portfolio of bonds is immunized from interest rate risk if the modified duration of the portfolio is always equal to the desired investment horizon. As an example, if the investment horizon of a bond portfolio is eight years, the *modified duration* (recall equation 12.12) of the bond portfolio should be eight years to immunize the portfolio. To attain a given modified duration, the weighted-average modified duration (with weights equal to the proportion of value) is set at the desired length and all subsequent cash flows are invested in securities to keep the modified duration of the portfolio equal to the remaining investment horizon.[11]

---

[11]Some researchers have pointed out several specifications of the duration measure. The Macaulay duration measure, which is used throughout this book, discounts all flows by the prevailing yield to maturity on the bond being measured. Alternatively, some have defined duration using future one-period interest rates (forward rates) to discount the future flows. Depending on the shape of the yield curve, the two definitions could give different answers. If the yield curve is flat, the two definitions will compute equal durations. It has been discovered that, except at high coupons and long maturities, the values of both definitions are similar, and the Macaulay definition is preferable because it is a function of the yield to maturity of the bond. This means we do not need a forecast of one-period forward rates over the maturity of the bond.

EXHIBIT 20.5	The Effect of a Change in Market Rates on a Bond (Portfolio): Maturity Strategy versus the Duration Strategy

	RESULTS WITH MATURITY STRATEGY			RESULTS WITH DURATION STRATEGY		
Year	Cash Flow	Reinvestment Rate	End Value	Cash Flow	Reinvestment Rate	End Value
1	80	0.08	$ 80.00	80	0.08	$ 80.00
2	80	0.08	166.40	80	0.08	166.40
3	80	0.08	259.71	80	0.08	259.71
4	80	0.08	360.49	80	0.08	360.49
5	80	0.06	462.12	80	0.06	462.12
6	80	0.06	596.85	80	0.06	596.85
7	80	0.06	684.04	80	0.06	684.04
8	$1,080	0.06	$1,805.08	$1,120.64[a]	0.06	$1,845.72

Expected-Wealth Ratio = 1.8509 or $1,850.90.

[a]The bond could be sold at its market value of $1,040.64, which is the value for an 8 percent bond with two years to maturity priced to yield 6 percent.

Example of classical immunization. Exhibit 20.5 shows the effect of attempting to immunize a portfolio by matching the investment horizon and the duration of a bond portfolio using a single bond. The portfolio manager's investment horizon is eight years, and the current yield to maturity for eight-year bonds is 8 percent. Therefore, if we assumed no change in yields, the ending-wealth ratio for an investor should be $(1.08)^8$ or 1.8509 with annual compounding.[12] As noted, this should also be the ending-wealth ratio for a completely immunized portfolio.

The example considers two portfolio strategies: (1) the *maturity strategy,* where the portfolio manager would acquire a bond with a term to maturity of eight years, and (2) the *duration strategy,* where the portfolio manager sets the duration of the portfolio at eight years. For the maturity strategy, the manager acquires an eight-year, 8 percent bond; for the duration strategy, the manager acquires a ten-year, 8 percent bond that has approximately an eight-year duration (8.12 years), assuming an 8 percent YTM. We assume a single shock to the interest rate structure at the end of year 4, when rates go from 8 percent to 6 percent and stay there through year 8.

Although the maturity strategy eliminates price risk (because the bond matures at the end of year 8), the ending-wealth ratio for the maturity strategy bond is below the expected-wealth ratio because of the shortfall in the reinvestment cash flow after year 4.

The duration strategy portfolio performs much better in terms of attaining the desired ending-wealth ratio. Although it suffers a shortfall in reinvestment cash flow because of the change in market rates (similar to the maturity strategy), this shortfall is partially offset by an increase in the ending value for the bond because of the decline in market rates. Under the duration strategy the original ten-year bond sells at the end of year 8 for $1,040.64, which is the price of an 8 percent coupon bond with two years to maturity selling to yield 6 percent. Because the price increase (i.e., the price risk was positive) helps to offset the reinvestment shortfall, the ending-wealth value ($1,845.72) of the duration strategy is much closer to the expected-wealth ($1,850.90) than that of the maturity strategy ($1,805.08).

---

[12]We use annual compounding to compute the ending-wealth ratio because the example uses annual observations.

Had market interest rates increased, the maturity strategy portfolio would have experienced an excess of reinvestment income compared to the expected cash flow, and the ending-wealth ratio for this strategy would have been above expectations. In contrast, in the duration portfolio, the excess cash flow from reinvestment under this assumption would have been partially offset by a decline in the ending price for the bond (that is, it would have sold at a small discount to par value because the price risk would have been negative). Although the ending-wealth ratio for the duration strategy would have been lower than that of the maturity strategy, it would have been closer to the expected-wealth ratio. The point is, the whole purpose of immunization is to *eliminate uncertainty* due to interest rate changes by having the ending-wealth position equal the expected-wealth position.

Application of classical immunization. Once you understand the reasoning behind immunization (that it is meant to offset the components of interest rate risk) and the general principle (that you need to match modified duration and the investment horizon), you might conclude that this strategy is fairly simple to apply. You might even consider it a passive strategy; simply match modified duration and the investment horizon, and you can ignore the portfolio until the end of the horizon period. The following discussion will show that immunization is neither a simple nor a passive strategy.

An immunized portfolio requires *frequent rebalancing;* bonds with various modified durations must be sold and bought to keep the portfolio's weighted-average duration approximately equal to the remaining time horizon.[13] Several characteristics of duration make this difficult.

First, assuming no change in market interest rates, *duration declines more slowly than term to maturity.* As an example, consider a security with a computed modified duration of five years at a 10 percent market yield. A year later, at a 10 percent market rate, its modified duration will be approximately 4.2 years; that is, although the term to maturity has declined by a year, the modified duration has declined by only 0.8 years. This means that, assuming no change in market rates, the portfolio manager must rebalance the portfolio to reduce its modified duration to four years. Typically, this is not too difficult because cash flows from the portfolio can be invested in short-term T-bills to shorten the modified duration.

Second, *modified duration changes with a change in market interest rates.* In Chapter 12 we discussed the inverse relationship between market rates and duration—higher market rates lead to lower duration and vice versa. Therefore, a portfolio's modified duration changes immediately if market rates change. If this occurs, a portfolio manager would have to rebalance the portfolio if the deviation from the required modified duration becomes too large.

Third, the assumption that when market rates change, they all will change by the same amount and in the same direction (a parallel shift of the yield curve) is frequently violated. As an example, assume you own a portfolio of long- and short-term bonds with a weighted-average six-year duration (say, one-half two-year duration bonds and one-half ten-year duration bonds). Suppose short-term rates decline and long-term rates rise (an increase in the slope of the yield curve). In such a case, you would experience a major price decline in the long-term bonds but would also be penalized on reinvestment, assuming you generally reinvest the cash flow in short-term securities. This potential problem suggests that you should bunch your portfolio selections close to the desired modified

---

[13]The zero coupon bond is unique because the duration of a zero coupon bond is always equal to its terms to maturity. It incurs *no reinvestment risk* because it has no intermediate cash flows and incurs *no price risk* if the zero's maturity equals our time horizon because we will receive the face value of the bond at maturity. Zero coupon bonds can be ideal instruments for immunization.

duration. For example, an eight-year duration portfolio should be made up of seven- to nine-year duration securities to avoid this term structure risk.

Finally, acquiring the bonds selected as optimum for a portfolio can be a problem. For instance, are long-duration bonds available? Is the price acceptable? Are bonds being offered at the desired interest rate? In other words, patience may be required to achieve the optimum bonds.

DEDICATED PORTFOLIOS

Dedication refers to bond-portfolio management techniques used to generate cash payments to service a prescribed set of liabilities such as monthly pension checks. Those responsible for administering these liabilities want a money manager to construct a portfolio of assets with cash flows that will match this liability stream. We discuss two ways a dedicated portfolio can be created.

A *pure cash-matched dedicated portfolio* is the most conservative strategy. Specifically, the objective of pure cash matching is to develop a portfolio of bonds that will provide a stream of payments from coupons, sinking funds, and maturing principal payments that will exactly match the specified liability schedules. The goal is to build a portfolio that will generate sufficient funds in advance of each scheduled payment to ensure that the payment will be met. One alternative is to find zero coupon Treasury securities that will exactly cash-match each liability. Such an exact cash match is referred to as a *total passive portfolio* because it is designed so that any prior receipts would not be reinvested (that is, it assumes a zero reinvestment rate).

Dedication with reinvestment is the same as the pure cash-matched technique except that the bonds and other cash flows do not have to exactly match the liability stream. Specifically, any inflows that precede liability claims can be reinvested at some reasonably conservative rate (say at 3 percent in an environment where market interest rates are currently ranging from 4 to 6 percent). This assumption allows the portfolio manager to consider a substantially wider set of bonds that may have higher return characteristics. In addition, it will generate a higher return for the asset portfolio. As a result, the net cost of the portfolio will be lower.

Potential problems exist with both of these dedicated portfolio strategies. For example, in selecting potential bonds for these dedicated portfolios, it is critical to be aware of call and prepayment possibilities (refundings, calls, sinking funds) with specific bonds or mortgage-backed securities.

Although quality is also a legitimate concern, it is probably not necessary to invest only in Treasury bonds if the portfolio manager diversifies across industries and sectors. A diversified portfolio of AA or A industrial bonds can provide a current and total annual return of 50 to 75 basis points above Treasuries. This differential over a thirty-year period can significantly affect the net cost of funding a liability stream.

HORIZON MATCHING

Horizon matching combines cash-matching dedication and immunization. As shown in Exhibit 20.6, the liability stream is divided into two segments. In the first segment, the portfolio is constructed to provide a cash match for the liabilities (say, the first five years). In the second segment, the liabilities are covered by a duration-matched strategy based on immunization principles. As a result, the client receives the certainty of cash matching during the early years and the cost savings and flexibility of duration-matched flows thereafter.

The combination technique also helps alleviate one of the problems with classical immunization—the potential for nonparallel shifts in the yield curve. Most of the problems related to nonparallel shifts are concentrated in the short end of the yield curve because

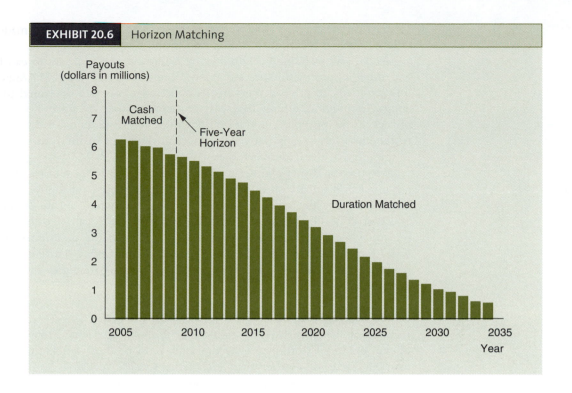

EXHIBIT 20.6 Horizon Matching

this is where the most severe curve reshaping occurs. In horizon matching, the short end is taken care of by the cash matching and these curve reshapings are not of concern.

An important decision when using horizon matching is the length of the horizon period. The tradeoff when making this decision is between the safety and certainty of cash matching and the cost and flexibility of duration-based immunization. The portfolio manager should provide the client with a set of horizon alternatives along with the costs and benefits of each of them, and allow the client to make the decision.

It is also possible to consider rolling out the cash-matched segment over time. Specifically, after the first year the portfolio manager would restructure the portfolio to provide a cash match during the original year 6, which would mean that there would still be a five-year horizon. The ability and cost of rolling out the cash-matched segment depends on movements in interest rates.

Derivative Securities in Bond-Portfolio Management

Derivative securities can play a major role in managing fixed-income portfolios. Their use can modify a portfolio's risk–return profile and change a portfolio's sensitivity to overall interest rate changes or to those of broad sectors. Portfolio managers use them in other ways as well—for example, to lower the cost of trading, to shift asset allocations, and to maintain a fund's investment exposure following a large cash inflow.

MODIFYING PORTFOLIO RISK AND RETURN: A REVIEW

As we first saw in Chapter 17, futures and options can affect the risk and return distribution for a portfolio. For the most part, a dollar-for-dollar relationship exists between changes in the price of the underlying security and the price of the corresponding futures contract. In effect, purchasing futures is identical to subtracting cash from the portfolio, and selling futures is identical to adding cash to the portfolio.

As we saw in Exhibit 19.8B, buying futures increases exposure to the underlying asset and amplifies portfolio return variability. Selling futures (Exhibit 19.8C) reduces the portfolio's sensitivity to price changes in the underlying asset and decreases portfolio return variability. In addition, futures have a symmetrical impact on portfolio returns, because their impact on the portfolio's upside and downside return potential is the same. This occurs due to the close relationship between changes in the price of the futures contract and changes in the price of the underlying asset.

Because the owner chooses to exercise or not to exercise an option, options do *not* have a symmetrical impact on returns. For example, buying a call option (Exhibit 17.10) limits losses; buying a put when you are long the underlying security (Exhibit 17.14) has the effect of controlling downside risk. Writing a covered call (Exhibit 17.12) limits upside returns while not affecting loss potential (except that the premium is an offset to a loss); writing a put option (Exhibit 17.15) has the same effect. Exhibit 19.8D–F showed the truncated return distributions that arise from various strategies that combine the use of options and their underlying asset.

USING DERIVATIVES FOR ASSET ALLOCATION CHANGES

In times of changing market conditions or in the face of large inflows or expected outflows of cash, shifting a portfolio's asset allocation must be done quickly to take advantage of the manager's forecast. Rather than identifying specific securities for sale and purchase, and rather than issue large buy-and-sell orders, the portfolio manager can use futures to implement the portfolio changes. Buying and selling appropriate futures contracts can quickly and easily change the portfolio's asset mix at lower transaction cost than trading large quantities of securities. Subsequently, over time, the manager can identify specific assets to buy and sell, and can time trades to avoid adverse market impacts.

Futures can also be used to achieve a desired mix of stocks and bonds in a multiple-manager environment. Most medium and large pension funds divide their portfolios among different managers to exploit the specialized asset expertise of each. The overseeing pension fund manager can use futures to maintain the desired asset allocation rather than disrupt the specialized managers by adding or removing large sums of cash from their funds for reallocation purposes.

USING DERIVATIVES TO CONTROL PORTFOLIO CASH FLOWS

Regardless of whether the fixed-income portfolio is passively or actively managed, futures and options can help control cash inflows and outflows from the portfolio. In reality, the most frequent use of options to modify portfolio risk is to use options whose underlying "security" is another derivative security—a futures contract. These options are called futures options or *options on futures* and were discussed in Chapter 18.

When a large sum of money is deposited with a manager, the fund's asset composition changes; the lump sum inflow of cash reduces the portfolio's exposure to fixed-income investment because a larger proportion of the portfolio's assets are in cash. Also, the desire to quickly invest the funds may cause the manager to purchase securities that he or she otherwise would not. Finally, large purchases can lead to sizable commissions and price pressure on the bonds acquired.

A better strategy would be to use part of the cash inflow to purchase appropriate bond futures contracts that have a value equal to the deposit; purchasing call options may be another possibility. The effect is that the money is immediately invested with lower commissions and less price impact than an outright purchase of bonds. Subsequently, the manager has time to decide on the specific assets to be purchased. Then, as bond purchases are made, the futures contracts can be sold.

A large, planned withdrawal from a portfolio is accomplished by selling securities to generate cash prior to the withdrawal date. Similar to a cash deposit, the sale of securities causes an increase in cash holdings, which reduces the portfolio's exposure to bonds. A strategy to counterbalance the temporary cash increase is to buy an appropriate number of futures contracts or call options as bonds are sold. The net effect will be to maintain the portfolio's overall exposure to bonds while accumulating cash. When the cash is paid out, the futures contracts can be sold and the portfolio's characteristics have not been disrupted.

TREASURY BOND FUTURES CONTRACT

To illustrate the use of derivative securities in bond-portfolio management, we will focus on futures. Futures, and options on futures, are the derivative tool bond-portfolio managers typically use. In Chapter 17 we listed the various financial futures contracts traded on an exchange. Here, to illustrate our examples, we will use the Treasury bond futures contract.

When the Treasury bond (T-bond) futures contract expires, *delivery* or settlement of the contract is made in the actual underlying security—a T-bond. Bonds with a par value of $100,000 must be delivered to settle the contract. With the variety of Treasury bonds available, the futures contract has to be written with a specific Treasury bond in mind. The contract specifies that the underlying security be a 6 percent coupon Treasury bond with at least fifteen years until maturity or first call. The fact is, only rarely does such a bond actually exist! How can delivery occur in a nonexistent bond? More important, why would anyone trade a futures contract based on a fictitious underlying security?

The answer is that a T-bond is delivered to settle the contract, but another T-bond can be substituted for the 6 percent coupon, fifteen-years-to-maturity bond. The contract allows for any bond with fifteen years until maturity or first call to be delivered. If a bond is delivered with a coupon rate above (or below) 6 percent, the person accepting delivery pays a higher (or lower) price. The bond delivered by the seller of the futures contract will be the *cheapest-to-deliver (CTD)* Treasury bond that satisfies the contract's specifications. In other words, the seller will deliver the lowest-price bond possible to satisfy the terms of the futures contract. At any point in time, the CTD bond will be known to both buyers and sellers of the futures contract, and the price of the contract will be set using the known CTD bond as the underlying asset. Over time, the effects of changing market interest rates on the duration and convexity of bonds will cause the CTD bond to change. For example, as interest rates rise, longer-duration bonds become CTD. Whenever a new bond becomes CTD, the futures price follows that bond until it is replaced by another bond as CTD.

Before we review the variety of ways that portfolio managers buy and sell T-bond futures, we will discuss how managers determine the appropriate number of T-bond futures to buy or sell—that is, the *hedge ratio.*

Determining How Many Contracts to Trade to Hedge a Cash Deposit or Withdrawal
As discussed previously, futures can be used to maintain the desired exposure to bonds while the portfolio receives or distributes a cash flow. The number of futures contracts to be traded will equal[14]

$$\boxed{20.1} \qquad \frac{\text{Cash Flow}}{\text{Value of 1 Contract}} \times \text{Conversion Factor} \times \text{Duration Adjustment Factor}$$

---

[14]This relationship is identical to the "basis-point value" (BPV) method that appears in Chicago Board of Trade materials on the use of bond futures.

The value of one contract is the price times $100,000. T-bond futures price quotes are always in terms of thirty-seconds. If the price of the T-bond futures contract is quoted as 114–26, the price is $114\frac{26}{32}$, or 114.8125. Therefore, the value of the contract will be $114,812.50.

The *conversion factor* is necessary because the deliverable bond will probably *not* have a 6 percent coupon. The conversion factor adjusts the current CTD bond to reflect the fact that $100,000 par value of the CTD bond will not cost the same to deliver as a 6 percent coupon, fifteen-year T-bond. Tables listing conversion factors for bonds of different coupons and maturities are available from the futures exchanges and many financial institutions.

The *duration adjustment factor* reflects the difference in interest rate sensitivity between the portfolio and the CTD bond. It equals the ratio of the portfolio duration divided by the duration of the CTD bond.[15]

An important caveat: because we are using durations to find the hedge ratio, our analysis is subject to the duration assumptions. Namely, we are assuming a flat yield curve and that all yield curve shifts are parallel.

Consider the following example of how to compute the number of futures contracts to hedge a cash inflow. Assume a bond-portfolio manager receives a $5 million cash inflow today when the current conversion factor is 0.90. The bond portfolio under management has a duration of 7.5; the duration of the CTD bond is 6.5. The value of the futures contract is $114,812.50. The number of T-bond futures contracts required to hedge this cash inflow is equal to

$$\frac{\$5 \text{ million}}{\$114,812.50} \times 0.90 \times \frac{7.5 \text{ years}}{6.5 \text{ years}} = 45.22 \text{ contracts}$$

Because fractional futures contracts do not exist, the bond-portfolio manager will round this number to the nearest integer and purchase forty-five contracts to hedge the cash inflow. These forty-five contracts will be sold over time as the $5 million in cash is invested in bonds.

As a simplifying assumption, in the rest of this chapter we will assume no adjustment for a conversion factor is needed.

USING FUTURES IN PASSIVE BOND-PORTFOLIO MANAGEMENT

As we have said, a passive investment strategy generally seeks to buy and hold a portfolio of fixed-income securities. Many times the portfolio manager attempts to replicate a bond-market index, such as those described in Chapter 7.

In a passive investment strategy, the manager attempts to manage deposits and withdrawals without harming the ability of the portfolio to achieve its stated goal. Sometimes, instead of investing all cash inflows immediately in the specified index, the manager can purchase an appropriate number of futures contracts. This will maintain the portfolio structure and reduce index tracking error while the manager determines how to invest the funds.[16]

---

[15]Those who manage corporate-bond portfolios have no corporate-bond futures contract with which to hedge; thus, they are forced to use the T-bond futures contract. In this case, the ratio of durations does not measure the different price sensitivities to interest rate changes between Treasury and corporate bonds. An alternative method is to use the slope from a regression that uses the portfolio's value as the dependent variable and the price of the CTD bond as the independent variable. Recall from the discussion in Chapter 12 that when we progress from Macaulay duration to modified duration, we are dealing with interest rate sensitivity and we do not refer to duration in years—it is simply the percent change in price for a 100 basis-point change in interest rates.

[16]When a portfolio's goal is to mimic an index, the portfolio's returns should closely follow, or track, those of the index. An index fund's quality is not measured by the magnitude of its returns but by its tracking error, or the degree to which the portfolio's returns deviate from those of the specified index.

Similarly, anticipated cash withdrawals can be hedged by liquidating part of the portfolio while maintaining the portfolio's exposure to the bond market using futures contracts.

USING FUTURES IN ACTIVE BOND-PORTFOLIO MANAGEMENT

Active management may focus on adjusting the portfolio's systematic risk, unsystematic risk, or both. Systematic risk in the fixed-income arena involves a portfolio's exposure to price fluctuations caused by changes in interest rates. Unsystematic risk includes the portfolio's exposure to changes in sector or maturity spreads. It is difficult to control a bond portfolio's unsystematic risk (except through diversification), but there are well-developed tools available to modify systematic risk.

Modifying Systematic Risk   In a fixed-income portfolio, market or systematic risk arises from the sensitivity of the portfolio's value to changes in interest rates. This sensitivity is the portfolio's duration. Thus, adjusting the portfolio's duration changes the portfolio's systematic (interest rate) risk. If we expect rising interest rates, we will want to reduce the portfolio's duration. If we expect falling interest rates, we will want to increase the duration of the portfolio.

In Chapter 12 we learned that the duration of a bond portfolio equals the weighted average of its component durations. This concept is used when computing how many futures contracts must be bought or sold to increase or decrease the duration of a portfolio. This is called the *weighted-average-duration approach*.[17]

Suppose a \$25 million bond portfolio has \$22.5 million invested in bonds and the remainder invested in T-bills. The duration of the bond component of the portfolio is 5.5. Because the manager expects falling interest rates, he wants to increase the portfolio's duration to 7.5. We will assume the value of a futures contract is \$114,812.50, the duration of the futures contract is seven, and the duration of the T-bill component is zero.

Currently the weight of the bond component of the portfolio is \$22.5 million/\$25 million or 0.90. The weight of the futures component of the portfolio will be (F × \$114,812.50)/\$25 million, where F represents the required number of futures contracts. Assuming a target portfolio duration of 7.5, the weighted average of the portfolio's components must equal 7.5:

$$\underset{\textbf{Target Duration}}{7.5} \quad = \quad \underset{\substack{\textbf{Contribution of Current} \\ \textbf{Bond Portfolio}}}{0.90 \times 5.5} \quad + \quad \underset{\substack{\textbf{Contribution of the} \\ \textbf{Futures Component}}}{\frac{F \times \$114{,}812.50}{\$25 \text{ million}} \times 7.0}$$

Solving for F, we find that 79.32 contracts must be purchased to increase the duration of this portfolio from 5.5 to 7.5. To the nearest integer, the manager will purchase seventy-nine contracts.

Suppose the manager forecasts a sharp increase in interest rates and wants to reduce the duration of the portfolio to 2.0. To find this required number of future contracts, we need to solve the following equation for F:

$$\underset{\textbf{Target Duration}}{2.0} \quad = \quad \underset{\substack{\textbf{Contribution of Current} \\ \textbf{Bond Portfolio}}}{0.90 \times 5.5} \quad + \quad \underset{\substack{\textbf{Contribution of the} \\ \textbf{Futures Component}}}{\frac{F \times \$114{,}812.50}{\$25 \text{ million}} \times 7.0}$$

---

[17]This is identical to the BPV method used in Chicago Board of Trade materials.

EXHIBIT 20.7	Hedging a Long Position in Treasury Bonds

Intent: Sell futures contracts against a long position in Treasury bonds to hedge an unexpected increase in interest rates.

	Spot	Futures
Nov. 1:	You own $1 million of 21-year, $8\frac{3}{8}$ percent Treasury bonds priced at 82–17, yielding 10.45 percent. Your portfolio value is $825,312.50.	Sell ten March Treasury bond futures at a price of 80–09. The basis is $2\frac{8}{32}$ ($82\frac{17}{32} - 80\frac{9}{32}$).
Mar. 3:	You sell the $8\frac{3}{8}$ percent bonds at 70–26 to yield 12.31 percent. Your portfolio value is $708,125. This is a loss of $11\frac{23}{32}$ per bond or $117,187.50 overall.	Buy ten March Treasury bond futures at 66–29. This is a gain of $13\frac{12}{32}$ per contract or $133,750. The basis is now $3\frac{29}{32}$ ($70\frac{26}{32} - 66\frac{29}{32}$).

Conclusion: The overall transaction resulted in a portfolio value gain. The loss of $117,187.50 was offset by a gain on the futures transaction of $133,750 for a net gain of $16,562.50. Another way of looking at the gain is the strengthening of the basis of $3\frac{29}{32}$ that resulted from the futures price decreasing more than the spot price. Because the position is long spot and short futures, the overall position benefits from the stronger basis. The basis went from $2\frac{8}{32}$ to $3\frac{21}{32}$ for an increase of $1\frac{21}{32}$, which is $16,562.50, the overall gain.

or −91.76. The negative sign indicates that it is necessary to sell futures contracts to shorten the duration to 2.0. To the nearest integer, the manager will sell ninety-two futures contracts to attain the desired portfolio position.

It is also possible to sell futures so the overall portfolio will be unaffected by interest rate changes over the length of the futures contract. This is accomplished by selling a specified number of futures so the portfolio's duration becomes zero.[18] To illustrate, we return to our prior assumptions. The goal is to sell an appropriate number of futures to bring the duration of the portfolio to zero.

$$0.0 = 0.90 \times 5.5 + \frac{F \times \$114,812.50}{\$25\text{ million}} \times 7.0$$

| **Target Duration** | **Contribution of Current Bond Portfolio** | **Contribution of the Futures Component** |

Solving this, we find that F equals −153.98, which means that to make the portfolio rate-neutral, 154 futures contracts would have to be sold. Because the portfolio duration is equal to zero, the return earned on the portfolio should approximate that of a risk-free asset such as short-term T-bills. An extra return component may be earned if the active manager can identify mispriced or undervalued securities.

Consider the hedge example in Exhibit 20.7. Assume that to hedge a $1 million portfolio of Treasury bonds against an interest rate increase you decide to sell ten Treasury bond futures contracts. Exhibit 20.7 shows that a potential loss of $117,187.50 in the portfolio is offset by a gain of $133,750 on the futures position. Fortuitously, your hedged portfolio had an overall gain of $16,562.50 following the rise in rates.

---

[18]Note: This is *not* the same as immunizing a portfolio. Immunization is a carefully planned asset allocation strategy wherein the portfolio is constructed to earn a target rate of return that will not be affected by changing interest rates over a known time horizon. Immunization by active managers would be frowned upon by their clients who hired them for their active investment expertise. Constructing an interest-rate-neutral active portfolio would be a *temporary* defensive measure during a period of interest rate uncertainty or volatility. Also, some managers may use it as part of a strategy to take advantage of mispricing between the futures and cash markets, or to create "synthetic" securities.

Modifying Unsystematic Risk   Unlike the situation with equities, few opportunities exist for controlling the unsystematic risk in a fixed-income portfolio. Futures and options exist only in a limited number of broad sectors and maturities. Sectors include Treasury bonds, mortgage-backed securities, and municipal bonds. Different maturity sectors include short-term (Treasury bills, Eurodollars), intermediate-term (Treasury notes), and long-term (Treasury bonds) maturities approximated by the noted futures contracts.

By buying or selling an appropriate number of futures or option contracts, active managers can increase or decrease their portfolios' exposure to these sectors or yield curve maturities to take advantage of expected sector yield shifts. Thus, changes in portfolio asset allocation among alternative sectors can be accomplished faster and at lower cost.

Changing the Duration of a Corporate Bond Portfolio   Because no corporate bond futures currently exist, strategies involving corporate bonds can be implemented using T-bond futures. We generally determine the number of T-bond futures to be traded as shown in our prior examples, but it is not always appropriate to use durations in the calculation. The problem arises because the prices of default-free Treasury securities only change in response to changes in interest rates, whereas the value of corporate bonds is affected by both interest rates and fluctuations in the yield spread between corporate and Treasury bonds. Rather than rely solely on durations, some managers will regress the price changes of their corporate bond portfolio to the price changes of the T-bond contract:

20.2
$$\text{Change in Price of Corporate Bond Portfolio} = \alpha + \beta\left(\text{Change in Price of Futures Contracts}\right)$$

The slope of this equation is used to determine the hedge ratio. Taking the number of futures as computed in previous examples and multiplying it by the slope estimate will tell the manager the appropriate number of T-bond futures required to cross-hedge the corporate bond portfolio.

For example, previously we showed that 91.76 (rounded to 92) futures contracts must be sold to reduce a portfolio's duration from 5.5 to 2.0 when (1) the value of a T-bond futures contract is $114,812.50, (2) the portfolio has a value of $25 million, and (3) $22.5 million of the portfolio is in bonds. For a *corporate* bond portfolio, historical regression analysis finds that a $1.00 change in the value of the futures contract is associated with an $0.88 change in the value of the corporate bond portfolio. Given this result, the appropriate number of T-bond futures that need to be sold to reduce the duration of this corporate bond portfolio is 91.76 × 0.88, or 80.75. With rounding, this implies that eighty-one T-bond contracts need to be sold.

Modifying the Characteristics of a Global Bond Portfolio   Futures and options also can be used to modify or hedge positions in global bond portfolios. For example, if a manager believes that German bonds are attractive investments, she can purchase them directly or be exposed to them through a German government bond-futures contract (traded on LIFFE). Similarly, positions in British gilts or long-term British government bonds can be established by purchasing the specific securities, by purchasing long gilt futures, or by buying an option where the long gilt futures contract is the underlying security.

The fact is, global bond portfolios represent positions in both securities and currencies. Fortunately, the existence of futures and option contracts on major currencies allows the portfolio manager to manage the risks of the security and the currency separately. Currency futures and options on currency futures serve to modify the currency exposure of a global bond portfolio without affecting the actual holdings of the portfolios. For example, a portfolio manager may be bullish on Japanese bonds because of expectations of falling Japanese interest rates, but may also believe that the yen is currently overvalued relative to the U.S. dollar. She can purchase the Japanese securities and then adjust the currency exposure of the portfolio through use of currency options and futures.

For illustrative purposes, consider a bond portfolio with the equivalent of $30 million invested: $9 million is invested in the United States; $12 million is invested in Japan; the remainder is invested in the United Kingdom. Thus, the allocation across countries and currencies is currently 30 percent United States, 40 percent Japan, and 30 percent United Kingdom. Because of fears that the yen is overvalued and a forecast of a strengthening pound, the manager wishes to reduce his exposure to the yen by $4.5 million (or −15 percentage points) while increasing his exposure to the pound by $4.5 million (or +15 percentage points). In other words, his *desired currency allocation* is 30 percent U.S. dollar, 25 percent Japanese yen, and 45 percent British pound.

Traditional currency rebalancing meant rebalancing the country allocation, too, thus preventing the manager from fully participating in security markets that were thought to be undervalued. Such security rebalancing would also be costly and time consuming. Rather than being able to do what they do best, which is identifying undervalued markets and securities, portfolio managers would have to make decisions based on currency forecasts.

The derivatives market helps the manager maintain the country exposure while modifying the currency exposure. If we assume that the futures dollar/pound exchange rate is £1 = $1.62 and the pound futures contract calls for the delivery of £62,500, the value of one contract is 1.62 $/£ × £62,500 = $101,250. If the yen/dollar futures exchange rate is ¥1 = $0.008185 (122.17 ¥/$1) and the yen contract calls for the delivery of ¥12.5 million, the value of the yen futures contract is 0.008185 $/¥ × ¥12.5 million = $102,312.50.

If our manager wants to reduce his yen exposure by $4.5 million, he accomplishes this by selling $4,500,000/$102,312.50 = 43.98 (rounded to 44) futures contracts on the yen. To increase the portfolio's exposure to the pound by $4.5 million, he must purchase $4,500,000/$101,250 = 44.44 (or 44) British pound futures contracts.

Once these transactions are completed, the allocation of the securities across these countries remains as before: 30 percent United States, 40 percent Japan, 30 percent United Kingdom. Through the use of currency hedging, the manager's portfolio's exposure to the (presumably overvalued) yen is only 25 percent while his exposure to the (presumably undervalued) pound is 45 percent. The use of derivatives allows the portfolio manager to shift currency exposures faster and at less cost than reallocating bonds across countries. These techniques allow the manager to maintain the desired exposure to securities he believes are undervalued.

Summary

- The past decade has seen a significant increase in the number and range of available bond-portfolio management strategies, including the relatively straightforward passive strategies of buy-and-hold and bond indexing; several active portfolio strategies; a core-plus strategy that combines passive and active management; and various matched-funding techniques including classical immunization, dedication, and horizon matching. It is important to understand the alternatives available and how to implement them. Equally important is that the choice of a specific strategy is based on the needs and desires of the client. In turn, the success of any strategy will depend on the background and talents of the portfolio manager.

- Derivative securities such as futures and options can help hedge against portfolio cash inflows and outflows in bond-portfolio management. They can help keep passive portfolios fully invested and help minimize tracking error. In active portfolios they can help change duration. Managers of portfolios with combinations of active and passive strategies, such as immunized portfolios, can use derivatives to help keep portfolio duration equal to the remaining time horizon.

- Derivatives can also be used in managing currency exposures in global bond portfolios.

Questions

1. Explain the difference between a pure buy-and-hold strategy and a modified buy-and-hold strategy.
2. What is an indexing portfolio strategy, and what is the justification for using this strategy?
3. Briefly define the following bond swaps: pure yield pickup swap, substitution swap, and tax swap.
4. Briefly describe three active bond-portfolio management strategies.
5. What are the advantages of a cash-matched dedicated portfolio? Discuss the difficulties of developing such a portfolio and the added costs.
6. Identify and describe the two components of interest rate risk.
7. What is bond-portfolio immunization?
8. If the yield curve were flat and did not change, how would you immunize your portfolio?
9. You begin with an investment horizon of four years and a portfolio with a duration of four years with a market interest rate of 10 percent. A year later, what is your investment horizon? Assuming no change in interest rates, what is the duration of your portfolio relative to your investment horizon? What does this imply about your ability to immunize your portfolio?

Investments Online

Fixed-income management analytics and software are typically proprietary. The sites listed below offer some additional information about the techniques discussed in the text and will give you insight into the use of various analytical and portfolio management techniques.

http://www.ryanlabs.com Ryan Labs Inc. is a leader in the construction and analysis of fixed-income indexes. Their site offers information on their research, data, indexing, consulting, and asset/liability management skills (this latter feature is of particular importance to portfolios that must meet a stream of cash outflows, such as a pension fund). The site discusses the quantitative nature of bond-portfolio management, fixed-income index construction, and the variety of risk and reward measures used for bond investment analysis.

http://www.cmsbondedge.com The home page of CMS BondEdge allows users to move to sites featuring CMS's various products. CMS sells fixed-income analytical software to

institutional investment managers. Research papers on fixed-income security analysis are offered free of charge to users who fill out an online form. BondEdge is a product offering "what-if" simulations, volatility appraisals, and other analytics to fixed-income portfolio managers.

Several brokerage houses offer fixed-income portfolio information and strategies with an orientation to the individual investor. Several such sites are

http://individual.ml.com/individual/pages/prodserv.asp?Rep TypeID=19

http://individual.ml.com/individual/CmaFiles/M221.pdf

http://www.bergencapital.com/research/files/ LadderedPortfolio.htm

http://www.smithbarney.com/products_services/fixed_inco me/taxable_fixed_income/research.html

10. It has been contended that a zero coupon bond is the ideal financial instrument to use for immunizing a portfolio. Discuss the reasoning for this statement in terms of the objective of immunization (that is, the elimination of interest rate risk).

11. During a conference with a client, the subject of classical immunization is introduced. The client questions the fee charged for developing and managing an immunized portfolio. The client believes that it is basically a passive investment strategy, so the management fee should be substantially lower. What would you tell the client to show that it is not a passive policy and that it requires more time and talent than a buy-and-hold policy?

CFA 12. *CFA Examination Level III*
The ability to immunize a bond portfolio is desirable for bond-portfolio managers in some instances.
   a. Discuss the components of interest rate risk— assuming a change in interest rates over time, explain the two risks faced by the holder of a bond. (4 minutes)
   b. Define immunization and discuss why a bond manager would immunize a portfolio. (4 minutes)
   c. Explain why a duration-matching strategy is a superior technique to a maturity-matching strategy for the minimization of interest rate risk. (3 minutes)
   d. Explain in specific terms how you would use a zero coupon bond to immunize a bond portfolio. Discuss why a zero coupon bond is an ideal instrument in this regard. (4 minutes)

CFA 13. *CFA Examination Level III*
After you have constructed a structured fixed-income portfolio (one that is dedicated, indexed, or immunized), it may be possible over time to improve on the initial optimal portfolio while continuing to meet the primary goal. Discuss three conditions that would be considered favorable for a restructuring, assuming no change in objectives for the investor, and cite an example of each condition. (10 minutes)

CFA 14. *CFA Examination Level III*
The use of bond-index funds has grown dramatically in recent years.
   a. Discuss the reasons you would expect it to be easier or more difficult to construct a bond-market index than a stock-market index. (3 minutes)
   b. It is contended that the operational process of managing a corporate-bond-index fund is more difficult than managing an equity-index fund. Discuss three examples that support this contention. (6 minutes)

CFA 15. *CFA Examination Level III (adapted)*
During the past several years substantial growth has occurred in the dollar amount of portfolios managed using immunization and dedication techniques. Assume a client wants to know the basic differences between

(1) classical immunization, (2) cash-matched dedication, and (3) duration-matched dedication.
   a. Briefly describe each of these three techniques. (3 minutes)
   b. Briefly discuss the ongoing investment action you would have to carry out if managing an immunized portfolio. (3 minutes)
   c. Briefly discuss three of the major considerations involved in creating a cash-matched dedicated portfolio. (2 minutes)
   d. Select one of the three alternative techniques that you believe requires the least degree of active management and justify your selection. (2 minutes)

16. How does the use of futures affect a portfolio's return distribution? How does the use of options affect a portfolio's return distribution?

17. How can you use futures to hedge portfolio cash inflows? Portfolio cash outflow?

18. What is systematic risk in a bond portfolio? What is unsystematic risk? How can you use futures and options to modify a bond portfolio's systematic risk exposure?

19. How is it possible to modify a bond portfolio's currency exposure without buying or selling the bonds of different countries?

20. *CFA Examination Level II*　　　　　　　　　**CFA**
The shape of the U.S. Treasury yield curve appears to reflect two expected Federal Reserve reductions in the Federal Funds rate. The first reduction of approximately fifty basis points (bp) is expected six months from now, and the second reduction of approximately fifty bp is expected one year from now. The current U.S. Treasury term premiums are ten bp per year for each of the next three years (throughout the three-year benchmark).

You agree that the two Federal Reserve reductions described above will occur. However, you believe that they will be reversed in a single 100 bp increase in the Federal Funds rate two and a half years from now. You expect term premiums to remain ten bp per year for each of the next three years (throughout the three-year benchmark).
   a. Describe or draw the shape of the Treasury yield curve out through the three-year benchmark. (1 minute)
   b. State which term structure theory supports the shape of the U.S. Treasury yield curve described in part (a). Justify your choice. (3 minutes)

Kent Lewis, an economist, also expects two Federal Reserve reductions in the Federal Funds rate, but believes that the market is too optimistic about how soon they will occur. Lewis believes that the first fifty bp reduction will be made one year from now and that the second fifty bp reduction will be made one and a half years from now. He expects these reductions to be reversed by a single 100 bp increase two and a half years from now. He believes that the market will adjust to reflect his beliefs when new economic data are released over the next two weeks.

Assume you are convinced by Lewis's argument and are authorized to purchase either the two-year benchmark U.S. Treasury or a cash/three-year benchmark U.S. Treasury barbell weighted to have the same duration as the U.S. Treasury.

c. Select an investment in *either* the two-year benchmark U.S. Treasury (bullet) or the cash/three-year benchmark U.S. Treasury barbell. Justify your choice. (3 minutes)

CFA 21. *CFA Examination Level II*

Mike Lane will have $5 million to invest in five-year U.S. Treasury bonds three months from now. Lane believes interest rates will fall during the next three months and wants to take advantage of prevailing interest rates by hedging against a decline in interest rates. Lane has sufficient funds to pay the costs of entering into and maintaining a futures position.

a. Describe what action Lane should take using five-year U.S. Treasury note futures contracts to protect against declining interest rates. (2 minutes)

Assume three months have gone by and, despite Lane's expectations, five-year cash and forward markets interest rates have increased by 100 basis points compared with the five-year forward market interest rates of three months ago.

b. Discuss the effect of higher interest rates on the value of the futures position that Lane entered into in part (a). (2 minutes)

c. Discuss how the return from Lane's hedged position differs from the return he could now earn if he had not hedged in part (a). (2 minutes)

22. *CFA Examination Level I*

What two sources of bond risk have offsetting effects?

a. Default risk and interest rate risk
b. Reinvestment risk and default risk
c. Interest rate risk and reinvestment risk
d. None of the above (1 minute)

PROBLEMS

1. You have a portfolio with a market value of $50 million and a Macaulay duration of seven years (assuming a market interest rate of 10 percent). If interest rates jump to 12 percent, what would be the estimated value of your portfolio using duration? Show all your computations.

2. Answer the following questions, assuming that at the initiation of an investment account, the market value of your portfolio is $200 million, and you immunize the portfolio at 12 percent for six years. During the first year, interest rates are constant at 12 percent.
   a. What is the market value of the portfolio at the end of year 1?
   b. Immediately after the end of the year, interest rates decline to 10 percent. Estimate the new value of the portfolio assuming you did the required rebalancing (use only modified duration).

3. Compute the Macaulay duration under the following conditions:
   a. A bond with a five-year term to maturity, a 12 percent coupon (annual payments), and a market yield of 10 percent.
   b. A bond with a four-year term to maturity, a 12 percent coupon (annual payments), and a market yield of 10 percent.
   c. Compare your answers to parts (a) and (b), and discuss the implications of this for classical immunization.

4. Compute the Macaulay duration under the following conditions:
   a. A bond with a four-year term to maturity, a 10 percent coupon (annual payments), and a market yield of 8 percent.
   b. A bond with a four-year term to maturity, a 10 percent coupon (annual payments), and a market yield of 12 percent.
   c. Compare your answers to parts (a) and (b). Assuming it was an immediate shift in yields, discuss the implications of this for classical immunization.

5. Answer the following questions about a zero coupon bond with a term to maturity at issue of ten years (assume semiannual compounding).
   a. What is the duration of the bond at issue assuming a market yield of 10 percent? What is its duration if the market yield is 14 percent? Discuss these two answers.
   b. Compute the initial issue price of this bond at a market yield of 14 percent.
   c. Compute the initial issue price of this bond at a market yield of 10 percent.
   d. A year after issue, the bond in part (c) is selling to yield 12 percent. What is its current market price? Assuming you owned this bond during this year, what is your rate of return?

6. Evaluate the following pure yield pickup swap: You currently hold a twenty-year, Aa-rated, 9 percent coupon bond priced to yield 11 percent. As a swap candidate,

you are considering a twenty-year, Aa-rated, 11 percent coupon bond priced to yield 11.5 percent. (Assume reinvestment at 11.5 percent.)

	Current Bond	Candidate Bond
Dollar investment		
Coupon		
i on one coupon		
Principal value at year-end		
Total accrued		
Realized compound yield		
Value of swap: basis points in one year		

7. Evaluate the following substitution swap: You currently hold a twenty-five-year, 9.0 percent coupon bond priced to yield 10.5 percent. As a swap candidate, you are considering a twenty-five-year, Aa-rated, 9.0 percent coupon bond priced to yield 10.75 percent. (Assume a one-year work-out period and reinvestment at 10.5 percent.)

	Current Bond	Candidate Bond
Dollar investment		
Coupon		
i on one coupon		
Principal value at year-end		
Total accrued		
Realized compound yield		
Value of swap: basis points in one year		

8. *CFA Examination Level III*

Reinvestment risk is a major factor for bond managers to consider when determining the most appropriate or optimal strategy for a fixed-income portfolio. Briefly describe each of the following bond-portfolio management strategies, and explain how each deals with reinvestment risk:
a. Active management
b. Classical immunization
c. Dedicated portfolio (10 minutes)

9. "The risks involved in implementing an interest rate anticipation strategy are not equal. Shortening durations when an interest rate rise is expected is much less risky than lengthening durations when a decline in rates is anticipated." Is this statement true? Why or why not?

10. Having attracted a large pension fund as a new client, you are expecting a rather large cash deposit of $25 million into your bond portfolio next month. If the conversion factor between the current CTD bond and the 6 percent coupon, fifteen-years-to-maturity bond specified in the Treasury bond futures contract is 1.05, the duration of the CTD bond is 6.0, and your portfolio has a duration of 8.5, how many T-bond futures contracts should you purchase or sell to hedge this cash flow? Assume the T-bond futures contract value is $121,156.25.

11. Assume all the information in Problem 10 still holds, except that you manage a corporate bond portfolio. Regression analysis gives you this additional information:

Δ Price of Corporate Bond Portfolio
= 980 + 0.92(Δ Price of the Futures Contract)

How many T-bond futures contracts should you buy or sell to hedge this expected cash inflow?

12. Your $50 million bond portfolio is currently 95 percent invested in bonds and has a 5 percent cash reserve. The bond component of the portfolio has a duration of 4.3. If the T-bond futures contract has a duration of 8.0, a value of $105,000 per contract, and the conversion factor is 0.95, how many futures contracts must you buy or sell to change your portfolio's duration
a. to 5?
b. to 8?
c. to 3?
d. to make the portfolio insensitive to changes in interest rates?

13. A $100 million international bond portfolio has 20 percent of its assets in U.S. bonds, 30 percent in European Union bonds, 15 percent in U.K. gilts, and 35 percent in Japanese bonds. Assume the current futures prices are $1 = €1.10, $1 = £0.75, $1 = ¥100. What must you do to change your currency exposure to those given below? Note: Look in the financial section of a newspaper such as *The Wall Street Journal* to determine the characteristics of the currency future contracts.

	U.S.	Europe	U.K.	Japan
a.	25%	25%	25%	25%
b.	20%	50%	25%	5%
c.	30%	10%	20%	40%

WEB EXERCISES

1. What examples of ladder and barbell strategies can you find on the Internet? Of bond swaps?
2. Visit the Chicago Board of Trade Web site (http://www.cbot.com). What information and ideas do they offer for fixed-income portfolio managers who want to hedge risk or who believe they have insight about future interest rate moves?

SPREADSHEET EXERCISES

1. Construct a spreadsheet to analyze a bond swap. Test it using the data of Exhibit 20.2 and Exhibit 20.3 (pure yield pickup and substitution swaps).
2. Using the duration spreadsheet from Chapter 12 Spreadsheet Exercise 3, use trial-and-error to find the coupon rate of a fifteen-year bond with a $1000 par value that has a duration of seven years and a yield to maturity of 6 percent. What is the price of the bond?

   a. What is the realized yield of the bond over a seven-year holding period should interest rates (and yield to maturity) suddenly rise by 1 percentage point? If rates suddenly fall by 1 percentage point?
   b. What is the realized yield over a seven-year holding period if interest rates suddenly rise by 2 percentage points? If rates suddenly fall by 2 percentage points?

REFERENCES

Barnhill, Theodore M., William F. Maxwell, and Mark R. Shenkman, Eds. *High Yield Bonds.* New York: McGraw-Hill, 1999.

Dattatreya, Ravi E., and Frank J. Fabozzi. *Active Total Return Management of Fixed Income Portfolios,* rev. ed. Burr Ridge, IL: Irwin, 1995.

Fabozzi, Frank J., Ed. *Fixed Income Readings for the Chartered Financial Analysts Program,* 2nd ed. New Hope, PA: Frank J. Fabozzi Associates, 2004.

Fabozzi, Frank J. *Bond Markets, Analysis and Strategies,* 5th ed. Upper Saddle River, NJ: Pearson, 2004.

Global Bond Management II: The Search for Alpha. Charlottesville, VA: AIMR, 2000.

Jost, K. D., Ed., *Fixed Income Management for the 21st Century.* Charlottesville, VA: CFA Institute, 2002.

Reilly, Frank K., and David J. Wright. "The Unique Risk–Return Characteristics of High-Yield Bonds." *Journal of Fixed Income* 11, no. 2 (September 2001).

Rosenberg, Michael R. *Currency Forecasting.* Burr Ridge, IL: Irwin, 1996.

Ryan, Ronald J., Ed. *Yield Curve Dynamics.* Chicago: Glen Lake Publishing, 1997.

Squires, Jan R., Ed. *Credit Analysis Around the World.* Charlottesville, VA: AIMR, 1998.

Squires, Jan R., Ed. *Global Bond Management.* Charlottesville, VA: AIMR, 1997.

GLOSSARY

Barbell strategy A bond-portfolio strategy in which about one-half of the funds are invested in short-duration securities and the remainder are invested in long-duration securities. This combines the high-return, high-income potential of long-term bonds with the lower-risk, high-liquidity aspects of shorter-term securities.

Bond swap An active bond-portfolio management strategy that exchanges one position for another to take advantage of some difference between them.

Buy-and-hold strategy A passive bond-portfolio management strategy in which bonds are bought and held to maturity.

Cheapest-to-deliver (CTD) bond The bond the seller of a Treasury bond futures contract will deliver to the buyer to settle the futures contract, because the bond specified in the futures contract (6 percent coupon, fifteen years to maturity or first call) rarely exists.

Conversion factor Used to adjust the value of the CTD bond to reflect the cost to deliver the 6 percent coupon, fifteen-years-to-maturity Treasury bond specified in the T-bond futures contract.

Core-plus bond management A combination portfolio management technique wherein a significant part of the portfolio (about 75 percent) is managed passively in an index, while the rest (the plus component) is managed actively in sectors such as high-yield bonds, foreign bonds, or emerging-market debt.

Credit analysis An active bond-portfolio management strategy designed to identify bonds expected to experience changes in rating. This strategy is critical when investing in high-yield bonds.

Dedication A portfolio management technique in which the portfolio's cash flows are used to retire a set of liabilities over time.

Dedication with reinvestment A dedication strategy in which portfolio cash flows may precede their corresponding liabilities. Such cash flows can be reinvested to earn a return until the date the liability is due to be paid.

Delivery The settlement of a Treasury-bond futures contract made in the actual underlying security, a T-bond.

Duration adjustment factor A factor that reflects the difference in interest rate sensitivity between the bond portfolio and the cheapest-to-deliver Treasury bond.

Duration strategy A bond-portfolio management strategy employed to reduce the interest rate risk of a bond portfolio by matching the modified duration of the portfolio with its investment horizon. Also referred to as *immunization of the portfolio.*

Immunization A bond-portfolio management technique of matching modified duration to the investment horizon of the portfolio to eliminate interest rate risk.

Indexing A passive bond-portfolio management strategy that seeks to match the composition, and therefore the performance, of a selected market index.

Interest rate anticipation An active bond-portfolio management strategy designed to preserve capital or take advantage of capital gains opportunities by predicting interest rate changes and their effects on bond prices.

Interest rate risk The uncertainty of returns on an investment due to possible changes in interest rates over time. Composed of price risk and reinvestment risk.

Investment horizon The time period used for planning and forecasting purposes or the future time at which the investor requires the invested funds.

Ladder strategy A portfolio strategy that places an equal amount of the portfolio's holdings in a wide range of maturities. Maturing bonds are reinvested in the longest-term bonds. To reduce reinvestment risk, coupon income is reinvested across the maturity spectrum.

Maturity strategy A portfolio management strategy employed to reduce the interest rate risk of a bond portfolio by matching the maturity of the portfolio with its investment horizon.

Price risk The component of interest rate risk due to the uncertainty of the market price of a bond caused by possible changes in market interest rates.

Pure cash-matched dedicated portfolio A conservative dedicated portfolio management technique aimed at developing a bond portfolio that will provide payments exactly matching the specified liability schedules.

Reinvestment risk The component of interest rate risk due to the uncertainty of the rate at which coupon payments will be reinvested.

Tracking error The difference between the return of a portfolio that is constructed to replicate an index and the return on the index itself.

Valuation analysis An active bond–portfolio management strategy designed to capitalize on expected price increases in temporarily undervalued issues.

Wash sale The term for selling an issue for a capital loss and repurchasing it within thirty days. In such cases the IRS does not allow the loss.

Weighted–average–duration approach An approach used to determine how many futures contracts should be bought or sold to quickly increase or decrease a portfolio's duration.

Yield spread analysis An active bond–portfolio management strategy that focuses only on the difference in yield between specific investment sectors.

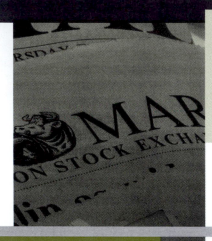

Evaluation of Portfolio Management

I nvestors are always interested in evaluating the performance of their portfolios. Active managers want to know if they beat their benchmark; passive managers want to know if their performance closely tracks that of their index. Performance evaluation is a very important step in the portfolio management process. Exhibit 5.3 on page 117 shows the four-step portfolio management process. The all-important fourth step is to monitor the investor's needs, economic and market performance, and the portfolio. In this last step, which is a feedback loop to all the other portfolio management processes, we determine whether the portfolio is meeting the investor's needs or if adjustments are needed.

In this chapter we outline the theory and practice of evaluating investment portfolio performance. In the initial sections, we discuss basic portfolio performance evaluation techniques and issues. Then we review performance measures that evaluate a portfolio's risk-adjusted return.

In our discussion of benchmark portfolios, we first consider what is required of portfolio managers. Because selection of an appropriate benchmark is paramount to performance evaluation, we review the required characteristics of benchmark portfolios as well as some of the difficulties that arise in using them, especially with taxable portfolios. We also discuss how to determine a manager's investment style and adherence to that style.

Then we examine performance attribution analysis, which seeks to discover why a particular portfolio strategy resulted in returns that were higher (or lower) than the benchmark portfolio. Finally, since the factors that determine the performance of a bond portfolio differ from those that affect common stocks, we consider several models specifically developed to evaluate the performance of bond portfolios.

In this chapter we will answer the following questions:

What are some methods used to evaluate portfolio performance?

What are the differences and similarities between the various portfolio performance measures?

What are clients' major requirements of their portfolio managers?

What important characteristics should any benchmark possess?

What is the benchmark error problem, and how does it affect portfolio performance measures?

What two methods can be used to determine a portfolio's style exposure over time?

What is portfolio performance attribution analysis? How does it assist the process of analyzing a manager's performance?

How do bond-portfolio performance measures differ from equity-portfolio performance measures?

What measure of risk is used in the Wagner and Tito bond-portfolio performance measure?

Composite Measures of Portfolio Performance

Many risk-adjusted portfolio performance measures are based on the theories reviewed in Chapters 8 and 9. In those chapters we learned about the capital market line, which shows that the expected return on a portfolio is a function of its total risk; the security market line, which is based on a model that assumes we can diversify some risk so that the market rewards systematic risk only; and the arbitrage pricing theory, which explains that factor sensitivities and the level of return-generating factors affect the level of expected returns.

All of these perspectives can be used to evaluate portfolio performance. Three general methods exist that are based on these models:

1. Excess return methods, which compare the return on the portfolio to that expected under the capital asset pricing model (CAPM) or other return-generating models;
2. Relative return ratio measures of return, which evaluate portfolio performance on the basis of return per unit of risk;
3. Scaled return methods, which adjust a portfolio's risk (and hence its return) in such a way that the portfolio and its benchmark are equally risky, thus allowing an easy comparison of returns.

We examine each of these methods in the following sections.

EXCESS RETURN METHODS

All the excess return methods compare the portfolio's return to an expected return, where the expected return is based on CAPM, an APT-based model, or the portfolio's benchmark.

Jensen Measure Based on the CAPM, the Jensen measure is the best known of the excess return methods. All other excess return methods are variations of this measure.[1] The CAPM calculates the expected one-period return on any security or portfolio by the following expression:

21.1
$$E(R_j) = RFR + \beta_j[E(R_M) - RFR]$$

where:

$$E(R_j) = \text{expected return on security or portfolio } j$$
$$RFR = \text{one-period risk-free interest rate}$$
$$\beta_j = \text{systematic risk (beta) for security or portfolio } j$$
$$E(R_M) = \text{expected return on the market portfolio of risky assets}$$

Assuming the CAPM is empirically valid, we can express the expectations formula in terms of *realized* rates of return over time period *t* as follows:

21.2
$$R_{jt} = RFR_t + \beta_j(R_{Mt} - RFR_t) + U_{jt}$$

That is, the realized rate of return on a security or portfolio during a given time period is a linear function of the risk-free rate of return during the period plus a risk premium that

---

[1]Michael C. Jensen, "The Performance of Mutual Funds in the Period 1945–1964," *Journal of Finance* 23, no. 2 (May 1968): 389–416.

depends on the systematic risk of the security or portfolio during the period plus a random error term (U_{jt}).

Subtracting the risk-free return from both sides, we have

21.3

$$R_{jt} - RFR_t = \beta_j(R_{Mt} - RFR_t) + U_{jt}$$

This indicates that, according to the security market line, the risk premium earned on the *j*th security or portfolio *j* is equal to β_j times a market risk premium plus a random error term.

Superior portfolio managers would have consistently positive random error terms because the actual returns for their portfolios would consistently exceed the expected returns implied by this model. Inferior managers would have negative terms because returns for their portfolios would fall below the implied expected returns.

To detect and measure for superior or inferior performance, we need to allow for an intercept (a nonzero constant) to measure consistent differences from the model. Equation 21.3 becomes

21.4

$$R_{jt} - RFR_t = \alpha_j + \beta_j(R_{Mt} - RFR_t) + U_{jt}$$

In this equation, the α_j value (or "alpha") represents how much of the rate of return on the portfolio is attributable to the manager's ability to derive above-average returns adjusted for risk. A superior manager's returns will have a significant positive alpha; an inferior manager's returns will have a significant negative alpha. A portfolio manager who basically matched the market on a risk-adjusted basis will have an alpha value that is not significantly different from zero. When investors and the financial press discuss a manager's alpha or seek information about positive-alpha managers, they are referring to this α_j intercept term.

Manager alphas can be computed two different ways. First, we can compute period-by-period alphas using equation 21.4, assuming a zero residual (U_{jt}) term. That is, we rearrange equation 21.4 to solve for alpha:

21.5

$$\alpha_j = (R_{jt} - RFR_t) - \beta_j(R_{Mt} - RFR_t)$$

Second, we can gather time-series data on a portfolio's returns, the risk-free rate, and the market return and then estimate equation 21.4 using simple linear regression. The constant or intercept term from the regression is the estimate of the manager's alpha. Most computer regression packages will also report the standard error of the alpha estimate, so a statistical *t*-test can be done to determine whether the alpha value is significantly positive (superior performance), significantly negative (inferior performance), or not different from zero (average performance).

As an example, let's use the first method to compute the alphas for portfolio managers W, X, and Y. Assume during the past year the actual market return was 11 percent and the risk-free rate was 5 percent. The results for the three portfolio managers were as follows:

Portfolio Manager	Rate of Return	Beta
W	9%	0.90
X	14%	1.05
Y	13%	1.20

Using equation 21.5, we can find each manager's alpha over the past year.

$$\alpha_W = (9 - 5) - 0.90(11 - 5) = -1.40$$

$$\alpha_X = (14 - 5) - 1.05(11 - 5) = 2.70$$

$$\alpha_Y = (13 - 5) - 1.20(11 - 5) = 0.80$$

Of the three managers, manager X had the best risk-adjusted performance according to the Jensen measure.

APT-Type Regressions   Jensen's alpha is a simplified form of more complex return-generating models. Examples of models used in research to evaluate the portfolio performance of mutual funds include three-factor and four-factor models in the form of

$$\alpha_{jt} = R_{jt} - [\Sigma (\beta_{jt} \times F_t)]$$

That is, the excess return on the portfolio is the actual portfolio return minus the sum of the return-generating factors (F_t) multiplied by the factor sensitivities (β_{jt}). Factors used in portfolio performance studies have included variables measuring size (market capitalization), book-to-market equity, price momentum, and the market return.[2]

RELATIVE RETURN RATIOS

Relative ratios are computed by dividing a measure of portfolio return by portfolio risk. As such, they provide data on which portfolio has the best return per unit of risk exposure. We determine a portfolio's relative performance by comparing a portfolio's relative ratio to that of its benchmark. If its ratio exceeds that of its benchmark, it is enjoying better performance.

Sharpe Portfolio Performance Measure   Sharpe developed a measure to evaluate the performance of portfolios that closely follows his earlier work on the capital asset pricing model (CAPM), dealing specifically with the capital market line (CML).[3]

From our discussion in Chapter 9 of asset pricing models, we saw how the CML is derived. By introducing a risk-free asset, investors can choose between placing funds in the risk-free asset and in risky portfolios along the Markowitz efficient frontier. In essence, investors seek to maximize the slope of the line connecting the risk-free return to the Markowitz efficient frontier, or equivalently, they seek the Markowitz efficient portfolio that allows them to maximize their expected excess return–risk ratio:

$$\textbf{Max (Slope of the Capital Market Line)} = \text{Max}\left(\frac{\textbf{Expected Excess Return}}{\sigma_{\text{port}}} \right)$$

$$= \text{Max}\left(\frac{E(R_{\text{port}} - RFR)}{\sigma_{\text{port}}} \right)$$

The maximum slope occurs at the line drawn from the risk-free rate that is tangent to the efficient frontier. This point of tangency will be the market portfolio. The slope of this line will be

21.6 $$\textbf{Market Portfolio Slope} = \frac{R_M - RFR}{\sigma_M - 0} = \frac{R_M - RFR}{\sigma_M}$$

---

[2]See, for example, Mark M. Carhart, "On Persistence in Mutual Fund Performance," *Journal of Finance* 52, no. 1 (March 1997): 57–82; Kent Daniel, Mark Grinblatt, Sheridan Titman, and Russ Wermers, "Measuring Mutual Fund Performance with Characteristic-Based Benchmarks," *Journal of Finance* 52, no. 3 (July 1997): 1035–1058; and S. P. Kothari and Jerold B. Warner, "Evaluating Mutual Fund Performance," *Journal of Finance* 56, no. 5 (October 2001): 1985–2010.

[3]William F. Sharpe, "Mutual Fund Performance," *Journal of Business* 39, no. 1, part 2 (January 1966): 119–138.

The Sharpe measure for risk–adjusted return is based on this relationship. It is the ratio of the portfolio's actual excess return divided by its standard deviation:

$$\text{Sharpe Measure} = S = \frac{R_{\text{port}} - RFR}{\sigma_{\text{port}}}$$

which represents the slope of the line connecting the risk-free asset and the portfolio under study.

This composite measure of portfolio performance measures the *total risk* of the portfolio by using the standard deviation of returns. Because the numerator is the portfolio's risk premium, this measure indicates the *risk premium return earned per unit of total risk*. In terms of capital market theory, this portfolio performance measure uses total risk to compare portfolios to the CML. Portfolios with Sharpe measures higher than the Sharpe measure for the market portfolio lie above the CML; portfolios with Sharpe measures below those of the market lie below the CML.

Demonstration of composite Sharpe measure. In the following example we compute the Sharpe measure of performance for several portfolios. We will assume that during our period the risk-free rate was 5 percent, the return on the market portfolio was 11 percent, and the standard deviation of the market's annual returns was 20 percent. We will examine the performance of the following portfolios:

Portfolio	Average Annual Rate of Return	Standard Deviation of Return
D	10%	18%
E	14%	22%
F	13%	23%

Using this information, we compute the Sharpe measures for the market and these portfolios as follows:

$$S_M = (11 - 5)/20 = 0.300$$

$$S_D = (10 - 5)/18 = 0.278$$

$$S_E = (14 - 5)/22 = 0.409$$

$$S_F = (13 - 5)/23 = 0.348$$

We see that portfolio D had the lowest risk-adjusted return, or lowest excess return per unit of total risk, and failed to perform as well as the aggregate market portfolio. In contrast, portfolios E and F performed better than the aggregate market; portfolio E had the best risk-adjusted return.

Because we know the return and standard deviation for the market portfolio during this period, we can draw the CML. We can also plot the results for portfolios D, E, and F on this graph, as shown in Exhibit 21.1. Portfolio D plots below the line, showing poor risk-adjusted performance. Portfolios E and F lie above the line, indicating superior risk-adjusted performance.

Treynor Portfolio Performance Measure Treynor recognized that in a completely diversified portfolio, the unique returns for individual stocks should cancel out. His measure of risk-adjusted performance focuses on the portfolio's undiversifiable risk, which we also know

EXHIBIT 21.1   Plot of Performance on the Capital Market Line

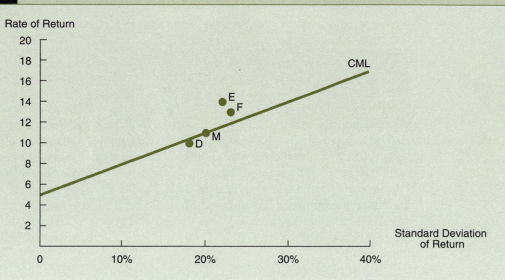

as market risk or systematic risk and is measured by beta (β).[4] The Treynor measure, designated as T, is,

$$T = \frac{R_{port} - RFR}{\beta_{port}}$$

Because the numerator of this ratio, $R_{port} - RFR$, is the risk premium and the denominator is a measure of risk, the total expression indicates the portfolio's *risk premium return per unit of systematic risk.*

We know that beta measures systematic risk. It *implicitly assumes* a completely diversified portfolio, in which case systematic risk is the relevant risk measure.

Because the beta of the market portfolio always equals 1.00, the Treynor measure for the market portfolio reduces to $R_M - RFR$, the market risk premium, which, as we first saw in Chapter 9, equals the slope of the security market line (SML). Therefore, if a portfolio's beta is positive, a portfolio with a T value higher than the market risk premium would plot above the SML, indicating superior risk-adjusted performance; conversely, a portfolio with a T value lower than the market risk premium would plot below the SML, showing poor risk-adjusted performance.

Demonstration of comparative Treynor measures.   Let's assume that during the most recent period the average annual total rate of return (including dividends) on the S&P 500 was 11 percent and the average nominal rate of return on government T-bills was 5 percent. We will evaluate the performance of three equity-portfolio managers:

Portfolio Manager	Average Annual Rate of Return	Beta
W	9%	0.90
X	14%	1.05
Y	13%	1.20

[4]Jack L. Treynor, "How to Rate Management of Investment Funds," *Harvard Business Review* 43, no. 1 (January–February 1965): 63–75.

On the basis of this information, we can compute T values for the market portfolio and for each portfolio manager:

$$T_M = (11 - 5)/1.00 = 6.00$$

$$T_W = (9 - 5)/0.90 = 4.44$$

$$T_X = (14 - 5)/1.05 = 8.57$$

$$T_Y = (13 - 5)/1.20 = 6.67$$

These results indicate that manager W not only ranked the lowest of the three managers in returns but also performed worse than the aggregate market on a risk-adjusted basis. In contrast, both X and Y beat the market portfolio, and manager X performed somewhat better than manager Y on a risk-adjusted basis. In terms of the SML, both of their portfolios plotted above the line, as shown in Exhibit 21.2.

Either poor performance (portfolio return $<$ RFR) or excellent performance with low risk ($\beta < 0$) can yield negative T values. As an example of poor performance, consider manager Z, with a portfolio beta of 0.50 and an average rate of return of 4.00 percent. The T value would be

$$T_Z = \frac{4 - 5}{0.50} = -2.00$$

Obviously, this performance would plot below the SML in Exhibit 21.2.

A portfolio with a *negative* beta and an average rate of return above the risk-free rate of return would likewise have a negative T value. In this case, however, it would indicate

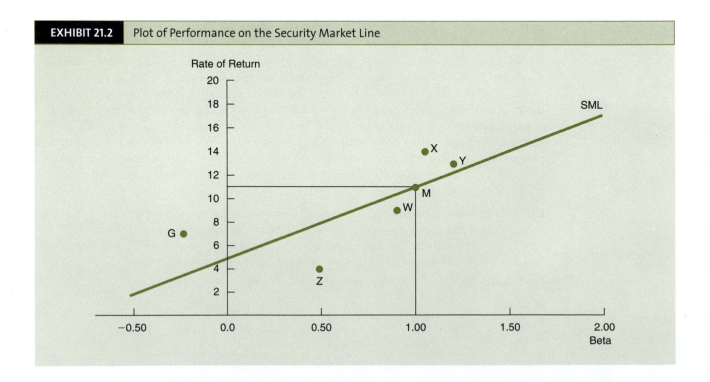

EXHIBIT 21.2 Plot of Performance on the Security Market Line

exemplary performance. As an example, assume portfolio manager G invested heavily in gold mining stocks during a period of great political and economic uncertainty. Because gold typically has a negative correlation with most stocks, this portfolio's beta could be negative. If we examined this portfolio after gold prices increased in value, we might find excellent returns. Assume portfolio G had a beta of -0.20 and yet experienced an average rate of return of 7 percent. The T value would then be

$$T_G = \frac{7 - 5}{-0.20} = -10.0$$

Although the T value is -10.0, these results plot substantially above the SML in Exhibit 21.2.[5]

Information Ratios   Sharpe also suggests a more general performance measure that relates performance to any benchmark for a portfolio.[6]

Using

R_{pt} = the return on a portfolio in period t
R_{Bt} = the return on the benchmark portfolio in period t
D_t = the difference between the portfolio and benchmark $(R_{pt} - R_{Bt})$ in period t
$\overline{D}$ = the average value of D_t over the period being examined, $\overline{D} = \Sigma D_t/n$
σ_D = the standard deviation of the differential return $(R_{pt} - R_{Bt})$ during the period

The general Sharpe ratio (S★) is

$$S^\star = \frac{\overline{D}}{\sigma_D}$$

This ratio indicates the historic average differential return (relative to a specified benchmark) per unit of historic variability of the differential return. Notably, the emphasis is on a differential return relative to a *specific benchmark* that coincides with the objectives of the portfolio.

A ratio such as this is sometimes called an *information ratio*.[7] Instead of using a specific benchmark portfolio, the expected return from a model—such as CAPM or APT—can be used as R_B. If this is the case, the information ratio equals the average alpha divided by the standard error of alpha.

---

[5]Because negative betas can yield T values that give confusing results, it is preferable either to plot the portfolio on an SML graph or to compute the expected return for this portfolio using the SML equation and compare this expected return to the actual return. This comparison will tell us whether the actual return was above or below expectations. For portfolio G, the expected return would be

$$E(R_G) = RFR + \beta_G(R_M - RFR)$$
$$= 5 + (-0.20)(7 - 5)$$
$$= 5 - 0.4$$
$$= 4.60$$

When we compare this expected (required) rate of return of 4.6 percent to the actual return of 7 percent, we see that portfolio manager G has done a superior job.

[6]William F. Sharpe, "The Sharpe Ratio," *Journal of Portfolio Management* 21, no. 1 (Fall 1994): 49–59.

[7]Thomas H. Goodwin, "The Information Ratio," *Financial Analysts Journal* 54, no. 4 (July–August 1998): 34–43.

SCALED RETURNS: RISK-ADJUSTED PERFORMANCE MEASURE

Excess returns and relative ratios result in numbers that are difficult for the average investor to understand; the meaning of a Sharpe ratio of 0.4 or a Jensen's alpha measure of 2.7 are not intuitively clear. To make a return–risk comparison more easily understood, we can adjust the risk of the portfolios to that of the market (or some other benchmark) portfolio and modify their returns accordingly. By examining the adjusted returns, we can easily determine which portfolio offered the best return for its risk exposure and we can easily compare it to the return of the market portfolio. This measure is known as risk-adjusted performance (RAP), sometimes called M^2 or M2 after its developers.[8]

Exhibit 21.3 illustrates how we can risk-adjust returns. Suppose we have two portfolios, the market portfolio M and portfolio A as well as a risk-free asset with return RFR. The historic return to the market portfolio is R_M; historical risk is σ_M. Similarly, portfolio A has an historic average return R_A and risk σ_A. We know from our discussion of the capital market line in Chapter 9 that we can create new portfolios by investing in different combinations of the risk-free asset and portfolio A; these portfolios are represented by the line segment between RFR and portfolio A. We can create portfolios with higher risk–return

| EXHIBIT 21.3 | Graphical Approach to Determining Risk-Adjusted Performance (M^2) |

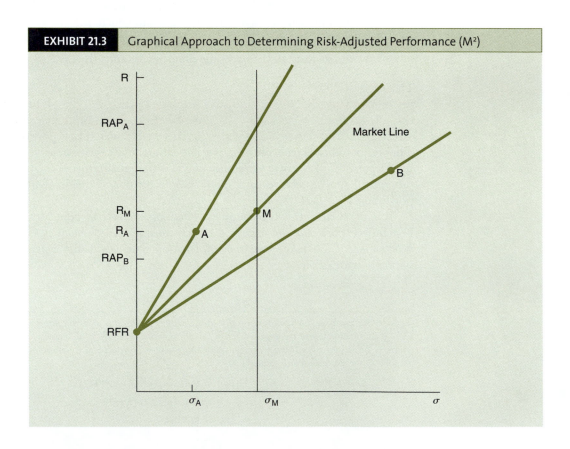

---

[8]See Franco Modigliani and Leah Modigliani, "Risk-Adjusted Performance," *Journal of Portfolio Management* (Winter 1997): 45–54; Leah Modigliani, "The Time for Risk Measurement Is Now," *Morgan Stanley U.S. Investment Research* (February 12, 1997); Leah Modigliani, "Yes, You Can Eat Risk-Adjusted Returns," *Morgan Stanley U.S. Investment Research* (March 17, 1997); Leah Modigliani, "Don't Pick Your Managers By Their Alphas," *Morgan Stanley U.S. Investment Research* (June 3, 1997).

combinations by borrowing at the risk-free rate and investing in portfolio A; these portfolios are indicated by the line segment that continues beyond portfolio A.

Let's extend the line connecting the risk-free asset to portfolio A until it intersects the vertical line at σ_M. We can do this by creating a portfolio with the same risk as the market portfolio by (in this case) borrowing at the risk-free rate and investing in portfolio A. At the point of intersection, a portfolio with the same risk as the market portfolio will have a risk-adjusted performance RAP_A.

Suppose we have a second portfolio, B, with the return and risk levels indicated in Exhibit 21.3. We can adjust the risk of our position by selling part of portfolio B and investing in the risk-free asset until the risk of our position equals that of the market portfolio. The risk-adjusted performance of portfolio B is denoted by RAP_B. The portfolio with the highest RAP is the portfolio that achieves (by borrowing or lending at the risk-free rate) the highest return for any level of risk. The RAP is easily compared to the market's return and is in units that nonexperts can understand.

A portfolio's risk-adjusted performance is computed as

21.7

$$RAP_{port} = RFR + \left(\frac{\sigma_M}{\sigma_{port}}\right) \times (R_{port} - RFR)$$

which can be rewritten as

21.8

$$RAP_{port} = RFR + (\sigma_M) \times S$$

That is, the risk-adjusted performance measure is the risk-free rate plus the excess return per unit of risk (the Sharpe ratio, S) for the portfolio, $[(R_{port} - RFR)/\sigma_{port}]$, scaled by the risk of the market portfolio σ_M. Because of this relationship between risk-adjusted performance (RAP) and the Sharpe ratio (S), they will always place portfolios in the same rank order.

Demonstration of Risk-Adjusted Performance Measure In the following example we compute the RAP measure of performance for several portfolios. As before, we will assume a risk-free rate of 5 percent, a market return of 11 percent, and a standard deviation of market returns of 20 percent. We will examine the performance of the following portfolios:

Portfolio	Average Annual Rate of Return	Standard Deviation of Return
D	10%	18%
E	14%	22%
F	13%	23%

Using equation 21.7, we compute the RAP measures as follows:

$$RAP_M = 5 + (20/20) \times (11 - 5) = 11 \text{ percent}$$

$$RAP_D = 5 + (20/18) \times (10 - 5) = 10.56 \text{ percent}$$

$$RAP_E = 5 + (20/22) \times (14 - 5) = 13.18 \text{ percent}$$

$$RAP_F = 5 + (20/23) \times (13 - 5) = 11.96 \text{ percent}$$

Recall that the Sharpe measures for these portfolios are $S_M = 0.300$; $S_D = 0.278$; $S_E = 0.409$; $S_F = 0.348$. Using equation 21.8, we obtain the same risk-adjusted returns as above.

The D portfolio had the lowest risk-adjusted return and did not perform as well as the market portfolio. In contrast, the risk-adjusted returns for portfolios E and F performed better than the 11 percent earned by the market; portfolio E had the best risk-adjusted return.

This example shows that the numbers and units of the RAP measure are easier to use and are more intuitively clear than those of the Sharpe, Treynor, or Jensen measures.[9]

COMPARING THE POPULAR MEASURES

The Sharpe and RAP portfolio performance measures use the standard deviation of returns as the measure of risk, whereas both the Treynor and Jensen performance measures use beta (systematic risk). The Sharpe measure, therefore, evaluates the portfolio manager on the basis of both rate-of-return performance and diversification. This is an important distinction. If the return on a portfolio and the market portfolio are not perfectly correlated, measures based on systematic risk (beta) may differ from those based on total risk. Some will prefer the Sharpe and RAP measures because of this. However, the Sharpe ratio is difficult for the novice investor to understand, whereas RAP produces a risk-adjusted return number in easily understood percentage points. Therefore, although it will rank portfolios the same as the Sharpe measure, RAP has gained in popularity.

When completely diversified portfolios—that is, portfolios with no unsystematic risk—are being evaluated, the Sharpe, RAP, Treynor, and Jensen measures will agree on how managers should be ranked, from best risk-adjusted performance to the worst. The ranks will agree because the total variance of a completely diversified portfolio is its systematic variance.

But when both diversified and undiversified portfolios are under review, a poorly diversified portfolio could have a high ranking on the basis of the Treynor or Jensen performance measure but a much lower ranking on the basis of the Sharpe performance measure. The difference in ranks occurs because of the difference in diversification.

When we use the Sharpe, RAP, Treynor, and Jensen measures to evaluate the performance of fairly well-diversified portfolios such as broad-market mutual funds, these performance measures will be highly correlated. Studies routinely find their correlations exceeding 0.80.

Benchmark Portfolios

To use benchmark portfolios as an evaluation tool, we must first know what is required of the managers we are evaluating. Portfolio managers face three major requirements:

1. Follow the client's policy statement.
2. Earn above-average returns for a given risk class.
3. Diversify the overall portfolio to eliminate unsystematic risk.

In Chapter 5 we learned that the portfolio manager should assist clients in their understanding of capital market risks and reasonable return expectations. Once the client develops a portfolio policy statement, it is the manager's duty to follow it. A review of the port-

---

[9]As a relatively recent measure of portfolio performance, researchers are finding ways to try to improve on it or modify it. Modigliani herself discusses an "M² for beta" measure that relies on beta rather than standard deviation for the risk measure (Leah Modigliani, "Don't Pick Your Managers By Their Alphas," *Morgan Stanley U.S. Investment Research* [June 3, 1997]). Another method, dubbed the M-3 by its founder, tries to adjust expected portfolio performance to incorporate the correlation between a portfolio and its benchmark (Arun S. Muralidhar, "Risk-Adjusted Performance: The Correlation Correction," *Financial Analysts Journal* 56, no. 5 [September–October 2000]: 63–71). Another adopts the measure to include style differences in a risk-adjusted measure (Angelo Lobosco, "Style/Risk-Adjusted Performance," *Journal of Portfolio Management* [Spring 1999]: 65–68). Older but related measures to RAP are Fama's measures of selectivity and net selectivity. See Eugene F. Fama, "Components of Investment Performance," *Journal of Finance* 27, no. 3 (June 1972): 551–567 and its discussion in Frank K. Reilly and Keith C. Brown, *Investment Analysis and Portfolio Management,* 7th ed. (Mason, OH: South-Western, 2003).

folio's risks, returns, and performance relative to an appropriate benchmark or index can help determine whether the manager has satisfied the first criterion.

A *benchmark portfolio* represents the performance evaluation standard for a portfolio manager. The benchmark portfolio is usually a passive index or portfolio. For example, the benchmark for many actively managed broad equity funds is the S&P 500 index. Portfolio managers earning an active management fee will be evaluated based on whether they are able to add value relative to the benchmark. One reason for the proliferation of indexes over the years (recall the market indexes from Chapter 7) is the need for different types of benchmarks to meet the needs of clients who want to invest funds in equities and bonds both domestically and internationally.

Specialized or customized benchmarks, sometimes called *normal portfolios,* are constructed to evaluate a manager's unique investment style or philosophy (for example, investing in small stocks with high earnings momentum). To use a broad market index rather than a specific benchmark portfolio would imply that the manager lacks an investment style, which is quite unrealistic. Specialized benchmarks allow the client to determine whether the manager is being consistent with his or her stated investment style.

REQUIRED CHARACTERISTICS OF BENCHMARKS

Any useful benchmark should be:

1. *Unambiguous.* The names and weights of securities composing the benchmark are clearly defined.
2. *Investable.* The client can always choose to forgo active management and simply hold the benchmark.
3. *Measurable.* It is possible to calculate the return on the benchmark on a reasonably frequent basis.
4. *Appropriate.* The benchmark is consistent with the manager's investment style or biases; the returns of the actively managed portfolio should be highly correlated with those of the benchmark.
5. *Reflective of current investment opinions.* The manager has current investment knowledge (be it positive, negative, or neutral) of the securities that make up the benchmark.
6. *Specified in advance.* The benchmark is constructed before an evaluation period begins.

If a benchmark does not possess all of these properties, it is ineffective as a management tool. One example of a flawed benchmark is to compare an active manager's performance with that of the median manager (that is, 50 percent of managers did worse, 50 percent did better) from a universe of managers. Such a comparison does not satisfy many of the above-specified characteristics of a benchmark.[10] For example, such a benchmark would be ambiguous, as different managers in the universe may focus on different sets of stocks or sectors. Also, it is hard to frequently measure returns, as the median manager changes over time because of differing relative performances of their portfolios. Such a benchmark is also not investable, because no one knows beforehand who the median manager will be.

BUILDING A BENCHMARK

A benchmark may be a well-known market index, such as the S&P 500, the Russell 2000, or the Merrill Lynch Corporate Bond Index. Alternatively, many clients, or managers who

---

[10]Jeffrey V. Bailey, "Are Manager Universes Acceptable Performance Benchmarks?" *Journal of Portfolio Management* 18, no. 3 (Spring 1992): 9–13. For a general discussion of what to look for in a benchmark, see Jeffrey V. Bailey, "Evaluating Benchmark Quality," *Financial Analysts Journal* 48, no. 3 (May–June 1992): 33–39.

believe they have specialized expertise, require a specialized index. Such an index may be constructed by taking a broad, well-known index and eliminating some issues, adding others, and reweighting it to reflect the manager's specialized expertise. For example, consider the following benchmark:

> The Tuttle Group Index is weighted 90 percent equities, 10 percent ninety-day Treasury bills. The benchmark return on the Treasury bill component is the actual ninety-day Treasury bill return. The equity benchmark is constructed as follows: The equities are based on the S&P 500. Stocks will be deleted from the index if their debt–equity ratios exceed a multiple of 1.5 of their industry mean. Stocks with low earnings growth (those with growth rates in the bottom 10 percent of the S&P 500 stocks) are also omitted. Returns of firms in the equity benchmark will be equally weighted.

This benchmark includes cash reserves because the normal asset allocation is 90 percent stocks, 10 percent cash. It includes stocks in the S&P 500 that lack excessively high financial risk or poor earnings prospects. It is well-known that small stocks have higher historical average returns than large stocks. To reflect this effect, the index is equal-weighted; if value-weighting was used, the performance of the large-cap stocks would swamp that of small-cap stocks. As a result, smaller firms will have a larger proportionate share in this benchmark than in the S&P 500.

To protect the client from a portfolio manager who seeks to earn returns higher than the benchmark's returns by taking on higher levels of risk, the portfolio's investments may be limited in composition, risk, and diversification, as follows:

> Equities not specifically included in the benchmark index may be purchased for the actual portfolio under management. The portfolio's median characteristics of capitalization distribution and P/E ratio should represent the average characteristics of the Tuttle Equity Benchmark over the course of a market cycle. The Tuttle Equity Benchmark has had a historical beta, relative to the S&P 500, of 1.05. The allowable range for the portfolio beta is 0.88 to 1.25. The portfolio returns are expected to have an R^2 (coefficient of determination) in the range of 0.85 to 0.95 when regressed on the returns of the S&P 500.

These constraints prohibit the portfolio manager from "gaming" the benchmark by constructing an actual portfolio that is measurably different from the benchmark. Deviations from these constraints are grounds for the dismissal of the manager unless extenuating circumstances exist.

Note that the Tuttle Group Index includes the six desirable benchmark characteristics. It is unambiguous, because securities that belong in the benchmark are explicitly noted. It is investable, because funds can be placed in a specified passive index of 10 percent Treasury bills and 90 percent equities. Also, its returns are measurable, and it reflects current investment opinions regarding small-stock returns, the disfavor of high financial risk and low-growth stocks. Finally, it was constructed in advance after the manager and client discussed the client's objectives and constraints and together drafted a mutually agreeable policy statement. Should the client determine that the manager's abilities or style are inconsistent with the benchmark, that manager should be replaced with one whose skills and style match the benchmark.

The performance measures we have discussed are only as good as their data input. We need to be careful when computing the rates of return to take proper account of all inflows and outflows. More important, we must use judgment and be patient in the evaluation process. It is not possible to evaluate a portfolio manager on the basis of a quarter or even a year; the evaluation should extend over several years and cover at least a full market cycle. This will show whether the manager's performance differs during rising and declining markets.[11]

---

[11]For a formal presentation related to the importance of the time element, see Mark Kritzman, "How to Detect Skill in Management Performance," *Journal of Portfolio Management* 12, no. 2 (Winter 1986): 16–20. For a more recent study on the difficulty of detecting superior performance, see S. P. Kothari and Jerold B. Warner, "Evaluating Mutual Fund Performance," *Journal of Finance* 56, no. 5 (October 2001): 1985–2010.

THE MARKET PORTFOLIO PROBLEM

Several of the equity portfolio performance measures we have discussed are derived from the CAPM, which assumes the existence of a market portfolio. Theoretically, the market portfolio is an efficient, diversified portfolio that contains all risky assets in the economy, weighted by their market values.

The problem arises in finding a real-world proxy for this theoretical market portfolio. Analysts typically use the S&P 500 index as the proxy because it contains a fairly diversified portfolio of stocks, and the sample is market value weighted. Unfortunately, the S&P 500 index includes *only* common stocks, most of which are listed on the NYSE. It is not a true market portfolio. Notably, it *excludes* many other risky assets that theoretically should be included in the proxy, such as AMEX and Nasdaq stocks, foreign stocks, foreign and domestic bonds, real estate, coins, precious metals, stamps, and antiques.

This lack of completeness is called *benchmark error*.[12] If the proxy for the market portfolio is not a truly efficient portfolio, the SML using this proxy may not be the true SML; the true SML could have a higher slope. In such a case, a portfolio that plotted above the SML derived using a poor benchmark could actually plot below the SML that uses the true market portfolio. An example would be portfolio A in Exhibit 21.4.

A second problem is that the beta derived using this market proxy could differ from that computed using the true market portfolio. For example, if the "true" beta were larger than the beta computed using the proxy, the true position of the portfolio would shift to the right.

Let's examine the impact of the benchmark problem in an environment of global capital markets. In our analysis, we consider what happens to the individual measures of risk (beta) and to the SML when the world equity market is used as the proxy for the market

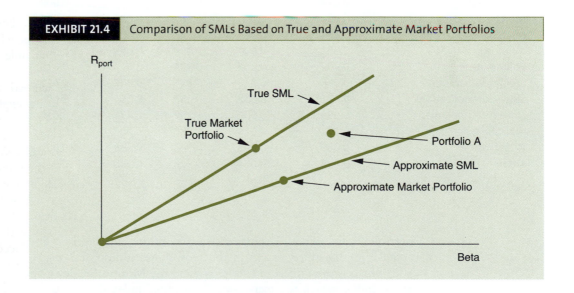

| **EXHIBIT 21.4** | Comparison of SMLs Based on True and Approximate Market Portfolios |

[12]Richard Roll, "A Critique of the Asset Pricing Theory's Tests," *Journal of Financial Economics* 4, no. 4 (March 1977): 129–176; Richard Roll, "Ambiguity When Performance Is Measured by the Securities Market Line," *Journal of Finance* 33, no. 4 (September 1978): 1051–1069; Richard Roll, "Performance Evaluation and Benchmark Error I," *Journal of Portfolio Management* 6, no. 4 (Summer 1980): 5–12; and Richard Roll, "Performance Evaluation and Benchmark Error II," *Journal of Portfolio Management* 7, no. 2 (Winter 1981): 17–22.

EXHIBIT 21.5	Parameters of the Characteristic Line for the Dow Jones Industrials: 1996–2000						
		S&P 500			WORLD		
Stock	Standard Deviation	Intercept	Beta	R^2	Intercept	Beta	R^2
ALCOA	0.113	0.006	1.111	0.210	0.009	1.339	0.240
American Express	0.080	0.010	1.202	0.481	0.015	1.278	0.430
AT&T	0.105	−0.019	1.076	0.228	−0.013	0.990	0.153
Boeing	0.084	0.004	0.566	0.098	0.008	0.487	0.057
Caterpillar	0.095	0.001	0.777	0.144	0.004	0.840	0.133
Citigroup	0.101	0.011	1.503	0.474	0.017	1.563	0.405
Coca Cola	0.090	0.003	0.675	0.121	0.006	0.685	0.099
DuPont	0.081	−0.002	0.765	0.193	0.001	0.836	0.182
Eastman Kodak	0.082	−0.012	0.450	0.064	−0.010	0.515	0.067
Exxon Mobil	0.049	0.008	0.384	0.132	0.010	0.395	0.110
General Electric	0.073	0.008	1.243	0.623	0.013	1.346	0.577
General Motors	0.098	−0.008	1.118	0.282	−0.002	1.098	0.215
Hewlett-Packard	0.131	−0.002	1.465	0.270	0.003	1.728	0.296
Home Depot	0.091	0.015	0.950	0.233	0.017	1.277	0.333
Honeywell International	0.115	0.004	0.972	0.154	0.008	1.043	0.140
IBM	0.097	0.009	1.218	0.336	0.016	1.177	0.248
Intel	0.133	0.013	1.444	0.254	0.021	1.378	0.183
International Paper	0.109	−0.008	1.053	0.202	−0.003	1.100	0.174
J.P. Morgan Chase	0.096	0.000	1.200	0.338	0.005	1.195	0.264
Johnson & Johnson	0.076	0.009	0.653	0.158	0.013	0.537	0.084
McDonald's	0.074	−0.001	0.743	0.218	0.002	0.773	0.186
Merck	0.090	0.014	0.567	0.085	0.018	0.373	0.029
Microsoft	0.134	0.006	1.828	0.401	0.015	1.844	0.322
Minnesota M&M	0.071	0.007	0.430	0.079	0.008	0.492	0.082
Philip Morris	0.097	0.006	0.324	0.024	0.010	0.162	0.005
Procter & Gamble	0.086	0.010	0.355	0.037	0.011	0.385	0.034
SBC Communications	0.081	0.002	0.658	0.143	0.006	0.570	0.084
United Technologies	0.088	0.006	1.299	0.470	0.010	1.535	0.518
Wal-Mart	0.091	0.018	0.880	0.203	0.019	1.169	0.283
Walt Disney	0.089	−0.003	0.940	0.238	0.002	0.889	0.168
Mean	0.093	0.004	0.928	0.230	0.008	0.967	0.203

portfolio.[13] Exhibit 21.5 contains estimates of the characteristic line intercept, slope (beta), and R^2 for the thirty stocks in the Dow Jones Industrial Average (DJIA) using the S&P 500, which is the typical market proxy, and the Morgan Stanley Capital International World Stock Index, which is a market-value-weighted index that contains stocks from around the world. The major differences are reflected in the betas and the R^2 of the regression lines. Specifically, in the majority of cases, beta is *larger* when measured against the World index

---

[13]Frank K. Reilly and Rashid A. Akhtar, "The Benchmark Error Problem with Global Capital Markets," *Journal of Portfolio Management* 22, no. 1 (Fall 1995): 33–52.

than against the S&P 500 index. In fact, the average beta (0.967 versus 0.928) is about 4 percent lower. The effect is also reflected in the R^2, which is often lower with the World index and has an average R^2 (0.230 versus 0.203) 13 percent smaller.

Implications of the Benchmark Problem Several points are significant regarding this benchmark criticism. First, the benchmark problem does *not* negate the value of the CAPM as a *normative* model of equilibrium pricing; the theory is still viable. The problem is one of *measurement* when using the theory to evaluate portfolio performance.

Assuming a measurement problem related to a proxy for the market portfolio, it is necessary to find a better proxy for the market portfolio or to adjust any measure of performance for benchmark errors. Using APT-type factors and characteristic-based benchmarks are one way of alleviating this problem.[14]

Alternatively, we might consider giving greater weight to the Sharpe portfolio performance measure because it does not depend so heavily on the market portfolio. Recall that this performance measure relates excess return to the *standard deviation* of return, that is, to the total risk of the portfolio being evaluated. Also recall that the new Sharpe ratio evaluates performance based on differential return relative to a specified benchmark portfolio, and the risk measure is the standard deviation of this differential return.

Taxable Portfolios and Benchmarking

A practical and difficult issue is how to benchmark portfolios in taxable accounts. Much of the work in benchmarking assumes tax-exempt or tax-deferred portfolios such as those invested by pension funds and in IRA accounts by individuals. But many investors have funds in taxable accounts. Unfortunately, the indexes listed in Chapter 7, which form the basis for most benchmarking studies, are typically examined on a pre-tax basis.

There is a major reason for this: There is no one accepted method of converting a pre-tax return from a benchmark into an after-tax return. After-tax returns depend on the investors' tax situation, which includes their marginal tax rate, when they entered an investment (to determine whether any capital gains and losses are short-term or long-term), and whether there are offsetting capital gains and losses in the overall portfolio.

The after-tax return on a benchmark portfolio depends on two influences. One is the division between the income cash flow generated by the portfolio and the capital gains it generates. The second is how frequently the capital gains are realized. The after-tax return can differ dramatically if the analysis assumes a *capital gains realization rate* of, say, 20 percent (which assumes securities are held an average of five years) or 5 percent (which corresponds to an average holding period of twenty years). Exhibit 21.6 illustrates the effect of these two influences over a twenty-year time horizon. With a 10 percent portfolio pre-tax return, the columns of the table break this down using different combinations of income and capital gains. The rows show the effects of different capital gains realization rates. The effect is dramatic: the after-tax return ranges from 5.5 percent to 9.0 percent annually, based on the assumptions used to construct the after-tax benchmark.

Benchmarking and Portfolio Style

How can we tell if a portfolio manager who claims to follow a certain style adheres to it? Such information is important. An investor who desires to put money into value stocks will not be pleased if he later discovers the portfolio manager was following a growth strategy. We need to identify appropriate benchmarks or indexes with which to judge a portfolio's

---

[14]See, for example, the references listed in footnote 2.

EXHIBIT 21.6	Effect of Capital Gains Realization Rate on After-Tax Return for Various Combinations of Appreciation and Dividend Yield					
	APPRECIATION % + DIVIDEND YIELD % = 10%					
CGRR[a]	**4.0 + 6.0**	**5.0 + 5.0**	**6.0 + 4.0**	**7.5 + 2.5**	**8.0 + 2.0**	**9.8 + 0.2**
5%	6.9%	7.3%	7.6%	8.2%	8.4%	9.0%
10	6.5	6.8	7.2	7.7	7.9	8.5
20	6.1	6.4	6.7	7.2	7.4	7.9
40	5.7	6.0	6.3	6.8	6.9	7.4
60	5.6	5.9	6.2	6.6	6.7	7.2
80	5.5	5.8	6.1	6.5	6.6	7.1

Note: Assumes a 28 percent tax rate.

[a]Capital gains realization rate.

risk and return performance. We are comparing apples to oranges if a small-stock mutual fund's performance is judged against the S&P 500.

Here we focus on two methods for determining a portfolio manager's style. Although the focus of our discussion will be on equities, these methods apply to fixed-income and balanced (containing some equity and some fixed income) portfolios as well.

One means of determining style is to use *returns-based analysis* or *effective mix analysis*, developed by William F. Sharpe.[15] Returns-based analysis uses the historical return pattern of the portfolio in question and compares it to the historical returns of various well-specified indexes. The analysis uses sophisticated quadratic programming techniques to indicate what styles or style combinations were most similar to the portfolio's actual historical returns. Today many pension fund and investment management consultants use software based on Sharpe's technique to identify investment styles and to evaluate manager performance over time.

To illustrate, Exhibit 21.7 shows the asset classes and indexes used in a study of monthly returns of the Fidelity Magellan mutual fund over a 60-month rolling time period. That is, as new monthly returns become available, the new month's data are added to the sixty monthly returns and the oldest observation is dropped. This allows analysts and managers to see how a fund's investment strategy or style changes over time. The exhibit shows shifts in strategy, from small growth to large growth to large value and back to large growth again.

Returns-based style analysis is not without practical difficulties.[16] To be effective, the portfolio under analysis must use well-defined (in terms of existing indexes) styles. In addition, the style indexes used must not be highly correlated with each other; if they are, wildly fluctuating style exposures can result. The style exposures that result may be sensitive to the indexes used in the regressions.

[15]William F. Sharpe, "Asset Allocation: Management Style and Performance Measurement," *Journal of Portfolio Management* (Winter 1992): 7–19.

[16]For a discussion and some examples, see Gerald W. Buetow Jr., Robert R. Johnson, and David E. Runkle, "The Inconsistency of Return-Based Style Analysis," *Journal of Portfolio Management* 26, no. 3 (Spring 2000): 61–77.

| EXHIBIT 21.7 | Rolling Style Analysis for Fidelity Magellan |

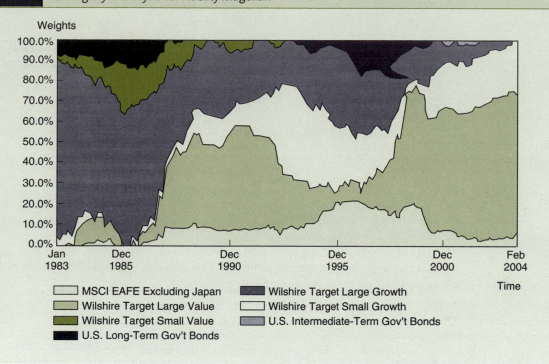

Legend:
- MSCI EAFE Excluding Japan
- Wilshire Target Large Value
- Wilshire Target Small Value
- U.S. Long-Term Gov't Bonds
- Wilshire Target Large Growth
- Wilshire Target Small Growth
- U.S. Intermediate-Term Gov't Bonds

A second method for determining style is to analyze the characteristics of the securities that currently comprise a manager's portfolio. Rather than using historical returns, *characteristic analysis* is based on the belief that the portfolio's current make-up will be a good predictor for the next period's returns.[17]

One such method classifies a portfolio manager into four basic equity styles: value, growth, market-oriented, and small-capitalization. The methodology uses a complex decision-tree approach to classify a portfolio's stocks relative to fundamental characteristics of indexes created by the Frank Russell Company, the consulting firm that developed characteristic analysis. The manager's portfolio is examined on the basis of its small-stock exposure, price–book ratio, dividend yield, price–earnings ratio, and return on equity of its constituent stocks. Finally, Russell's analysts develop a *sector deviation measure* to compare the portfolio's economic sector weightings (consumer, capital goods, technology, and so on) to those of the Russell 3000 index, an overall market index. The results of these analyses are combined to determine the portfolio's style.

Both the characteristic analysis and effective mix approaches have advantages and disadvantages. The detailed characteristic analysis method is likely to be most useful for forecasting a portfolio's near-term future returns, given its current style composition and a set of forecasts for style index returns. It is useful as well for determining whether a manager's

[17]This approach is described in Jon A. Christopherson and Dennis Trittin, "Equity Style Classification System," in *The Handbook of Equity Style Management,* edited by T. Daniel Coggin and Frank J. Fabozzi (New Hope, PA: Frank J. Fabozzi Associates Publishing, 1995), pp. 69–98; and Jon A. Christopherson, "Equity Style Classifications," *Journal of Portfolio Management* (Spring 1995): 32–43.

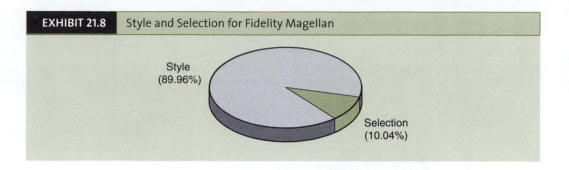

EXHIBIT 21.8 Style and Selection for Fidelity Magellan

Style (89.96%)

Selection (10.04%)

current style is in line with past investing patterns. Sharpe's effective mix method may be the best for the historical evaluation of a manager. Using software to which many consultants and investment managers have access, the effective mix method shows past allocations and trends in a manager's style exposure.

Sharpe's method is also more useful for performance attribution. Using the outcomes of the effective mix analysis, we can construct a benchmark portfolio. We can then do regression analysis using the form of equation 21.9:

21.9
$$\text{Return}_{\text{port}} = \alpha + \beta\,(\text{Return}_{\text{benchmark}})$$

Using regression analysis, we can determine variation in the portfolio's actual returns that can be explained by the passively managed benchmark. The alpha of the regression is Jensen's alpha, which gives us a measure of the manager's ability to earn above-average risk-adjusted returns. The regression results allow us to see what percentage of the managed portfolio's returns were because of style (the R^2 measure or coefficient of determination of the regression) and how much occurred because of stock selection skill $(1 - R^2)$. The pie chart in Exhibit 21.8 shows that these indexes and allocations explain 90 percent of the monthly variation in Magellan's returns. In other words, in terms of performance attribution, 90 percent of the monthly variation in Magellan's returns can be explained by a passive benchmark portfolio composed of the above-specified indexes and percentage allocations. The unexplained variation in Magellan's return, presumably due to stock selection influences, is only 10 percent.

Regardless of how the true style(s) of a manager is determined, the analysis is useful for tying portfolio performance back to the investment policy statement and the target asset allocation of the investor. Style analysis may show that a value fund manager is investing in stocks with growth characteristics, or that a bond manager is chasing higher yields via lower-rated bond issues. These actions can move the overall portfolio far from the target asset mix. Thus, style analysis can assist with a proper allocation of the portfolio assets.

Determining Reasons for Superior (or Inferior) Performance

In addition to examining historical returns, determining style, and adjusting assets for risk, portfolio evaluation also serves in identifying why a manager did better or worse than the benchmark. For example, a manager's superior returns could have been the result of (1) an insightful asset allocation strategy that overweighted an asset class that earned high returns;

(2) investing in undervalued sectors; (3) selecting individual securities that earned above-average returns; or (4) some combination of these. Of course, poor returns can likewise arise from a combination of inappropriate strategies.

A key component of performance attribution is the client's policy statement. Performance attribution begins with the policy statement and the portfolio's policy weights (or normal asset allocation) and benchmark returns. These allow us to determine what the portfolio returns would have been had the manager invested funds according to the normal weights in the benchmark indexes. By comparing this with the portfolio's actual asset weights and actual returns, we can pinpoint the sources of superior or inferior return.

Performance attribution analysis begins with an overall view, focusing on major portfolio decisions that affected returns, and then examines more detailed aspects of how the portfolio was constructed. Because of this, the first step of performance attribution examines the impact of the *asset allocation decision* on portfolio returns. In other words, we seek first to determine the difference in the policy portfolio and actual portfolio returns that occurs because the actual portfolio weights differ from the client's normal policy levels. Specifically, we would compare the policy portfolio returns (assets weighted according to policy, earning the index's returns) and the return on a portfolio that purchased the asset indexes in the same proportion as the actual portfolio weights.

The second phase of the analysis involves determining the impact of *sector and security selection*. In this phase we compare the return components of the actual portfolio (actual weights, actual asset returns) with those of the portfolio invested in the indexes using the actual portfolio weights. This comparison allows us to determine the effect of sector selection and security selection on portfolio returns as it focuses on the difference between portfolio returns versus index returns. For further analysis, we could measure the impact of sector selection by comparing sector weights in the index with the portfolio's sector weightings.

Consider this example. Suppose a portfolio returned 13.4 percent last year and its benchmark portfolio earned 13.0 percent. Why did the portfolio manager earn an extra 0.4 percentage points? Was it because of a change in asset allocation? Security selection choices? Both? Exhibit 21.9 reports the relevant data on the benchmark (policy) portfolio stock and bond allocation, the actual portfolio's allocation, the stock and bond index returns, and the actual returns on the portfolio's stock and bond components. We note that the portfolio had a larger allocation to stocks than its benchmark (70 percent versus 60 percent). The portfolio manager earned less than the index (14 percent versus 15 percent) on the stock portion of the portfolio. The bond portion, however, performed well, beating the index, 12 percent versus 10 percent.

The first step of the evaluation process is to examine the asset allocation decision. Here, we assume the funds were invested in indexes and we compare the return that would have

EXHIBIT 21.9	Return Attribution Analysis		
PORTFOLIO WEIGHTS		**COMPONENT RETURNS**	
Policy Weights	**Actual Weights**	**Index Returns**	**Actual Returns**
60% stock	70% stock	15% stock index	14% stock component
40% bond	30% bond	10% bond index	12% bond component

occurred (a) if the funds were invested using the policy weights and (b) if the funds were invested using the actual weights:

	Stock		Bond
Policy allocation, index returns:	0.6 × 15%	+	0.4 × 10% = 13%
Actual allocation, index returns:	0.7 × 15%	+	0.3 × 10% = 13.5%

We find that the manager earned an extra +0.5 percent return because of a shift in allocation to the equity market during a time period when the equity market outperformed the bond market.

In the second step of the process we seek to determine the role of superior (or inferior) sector or security selection on portfolio returns:

	Stock		Bond
Actual allocation, actual returns:	0.7 × 14%	+	0.3 × 12% = 13.4%
Actual allocation, index returns:	0.7 × 15%	+	0.3 × 10% = 13.5%

Sector/security selection hurt the portfolio's performance; returns were a 0.1 percentage point less than if the manager had invested the funds in the stock and bond indexes. Overall, the manager made a good allocation decision (which increased returns 0.5 percent) but poor sector/security selection (which lowered returns by 0.1 percent).

Evaluating Bond-Portfolio Performance

The environment in the bond market changed dramatically in the 1970s and the 1980s, when interest rates increased dramatically and became more volatile. This new environment created an incentive to trade bonds, and this trend toward more active management led to substantially greater dispersion in the performance by various bond-portfolio managers. In turn, this dispersion in performance created a demand for techniques that would help investors evaluate manager performance.[18]

A prime factor needed to evaluate performance properly is a measure of risk such as the beta coefficient for equities. This is difficult to achieve because a bond's maturity and coupon have a significant effect on the volatility of its prices.

As we have discussed, an appropriate composite risk measure to indicate the relative price volatility for a bond compared to interest rate changes is the bond's *duration*. Using this as a measure of risk, Wagner and Tito derived a bond market line that is similar in concept to the security market line used to evaluate equity performance.[19] Duration simply replaces beta as the risk variable. The bond market line in Exhibit 21.10 is drawn from points defined by returns on Treasury bills to the Lehman Brothers Government–Corporate

---

[18]An overview of this area and a discussion of the historical development is contained in H. Gifford Fong, "Bond Management: Past, Current, and Future," in *The Handbook of Fixed-Income Securities*, 6th ed., edited by Frank J. Fabozzi (New York: McGraw-Hill, 2001).

[19]Wayne H. Wagner and Dennis A. Tito, "Definitive New Measures of Bond Performance and Risk," *Pension World* (May 1977): 17–26; and Dennis A. Tito and Wayne H. Wagner, "Is Your Bond Manager Skillful?" *Pension World* (June 1977): 10–16.

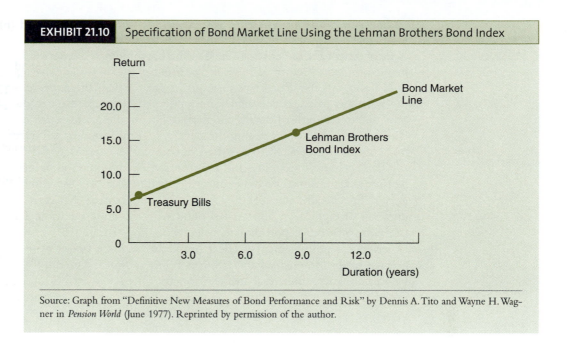

EXHIBIT 21.10   Specification of Bond Market Line Using the Lehman Brothers Bond Index

Source: Graph from "Definitive New Measures of Bond Performance and Risk" by Dennis A. Tito and Wayne H. Wagner in *Pension World* (June 1977). Reprinted by permission of the author.

Bond Index rather than the S&P 500.[20] The Lehman Brothers Index gives the market's average annual rate of return during some common period, and the duration for the index is the value–weighted duration for the individual bonds in the index.

Given the bond market line, this technique divides the portfolio return that differs from the return on the Lehman Brothers Index into four components: (1) a policy effect, (2) a rate anticipation effect, (3) an analysis effect, and (4) a trading effect. When the latter three effects are combined, they are referred to as the *management effect*.

The *policy effect* measures the difference in the expected return for a given portfolio because of a difference in the portfolio's long-term policy duration target compared to that of the Lehman Brothers Index. This assumes that a difference between a portfolio's policy duration and that of the index indicates a decision regarding relative risk. Therefore, given a difference in duration (that is, a difference in interest rate risk), expected returns should be different.

The *interest rate anticipation effect* attempts to measure the differential return from *changing* the duration of the portfolio during this period compared to the portfolio's long-term policy duration. The manager should increase the duration of the portfolio if declining interest rates are expected and reduce the duration if rising interest rates are anticipated. The interest rate anticipation effect is determined by comparing the portfolio's duration over a period to the long-term policy duration of the portfolio. The difference in expected return for these two durations can be determined using the bond market line.

The difference between the *expected* return based on the portfolio's duration and the *actual* return for the portfolio during this period is a combination of an analysis effect and a

---

[20]As you know from the presentation in Chapter 7, it would be equally reasonable to use a comparable bond-market index from Merrill Lynch, Salomon Brothers, or the Ryan Index.

trading effect. The *analysis effect* is the extra return attributable to acquiring bonds that are temporarily mispriced relative to their risk. To measure the analysis effect, we compare the *expected* return for the portfolio held at the beginning of the period (using the bond market line) to the *actual* return of this same portfolio *if it were passively managed* (that is, a buy-and-hold policy). If the actual passive return is greater than the expected return, it implies that the portfolio manager acquired some underpriced issues that became properly priced and provided excess returns during the period. Finally, the *trading effect* occurs due to short-run changes in the portfolio during the period. It is measured by subtracting the analysis effect from the total excess return based on duration.

This technique examines the return based on the duration, which is used as a comprehensive risk measure. The only concern is that *duration does not consider differences in the risk of default*. Specifically, the technique does not differentiate between an AAA bond with a duration of eight years and a BBB bond with the same duration. This could clearly affect the performance. A portfolio manager who invested in BBB bonds, for example, could experience a positive analysis effect simply because the bonds were lower quality than the average quality implicit in the Lehman Brothers Index. The only way to avoid this would be to construct differential market lines for alternative ratings or construct a benchmark line that matches the quality makeup of the portfolio being evaluated.

Investments Online

Mutual fund performance is a matter of public knowledge, but performance for the vast variety of pension funds, endowments, insurance company portfolios, trust portfolios, and other private investment pools may not be public. Investors will have to use the tools discussed in this chapter to evaluate the performance of nonpublic portfolios. Many investor consultants and software firms have proprietary databases and products, and they will sell their services to individual and institutional investors as a means of evaluating portfolio performance. Consultants who evaluate money managers for clients will not offer the proprietary results of that research for free on the Internet. Nonetheless, some sites are helpful in showing applications of the material covered in this chapter.

http://www.styleadvisor.com The Web site of Zephyr Associates Inc. features information about StyleADVISOR. StyleADVISOR is a returns-based style and performance analysis software package. It uses Sharpe's techniques of performance analysis and attribution. Pages offer visitors the chance to learn about StyleADVISOR and to view sample reports, some of whose formats are similar to those shown in this chapter (for example, Exhibits 21.7 and 21.8). Past newsletters are avail-

able for viewing; they give analysis and insights into portfolio performance attribution issues.

http://www.morningstar.com This site allows users to obtain summary reports on funds. These "Quickrank" reports offer information on returns, volatility statistics, Morningstar rating, and MPT (modern portfolio theory) statistics such as alpha and beta. The report gives the fund's style as well, using Morningstar's 3 × 3 style box.

http://www.valueline.com Subscribers can obtain useful mutual fund performance information, including charts, both absolute and relative-to-peer-group return performance, and the fund's style, using Value Line's style box.

http://www.cfainstitute.org The CFA Institute's home page offers a link to information about the CFA Institute Performance Presentation Standards. These are a set of ethical principles and guidelines to help ensure fair representation, full disclosure, and comparability in reported portfolio performance results. The site provides links to resources for training and for library information on the standards.

Summary

- The first major goal of portfolio management is to follow the client's policy statement to meet his or her objectives and satisfy his or her constraints. A second goal is to derive rates of return that equal or exceed the returns on a naively selected portfolio with equal risk. The third goal is to attain complete diversification. An initial step to ensure good client–manager relations and fair manager appraisal is to select or construct an appropriate benchmark portfolio. The performance of the actively managed portfolio will be judged relative to the passive benchmark.

- Several measures have been developed to evaluate equity portfolios in terms of both risk and return (composite measures). The original Sharpe measure indicates the excess return relative to the risk-free return per unit of total risk. The new Sharpe ratio examines the average differential return relative to the portfolio's benchmark divided by the standard deviation of the differential return. The RAP (or M^2) measure is related to the Sharpe measure but is more investor-friendly in its presentation of performance results. The Treynor measure considers the excess return earned per unit of systematic risk. The Jensen alpha also evaluates performance in terms of systematic risk and shows how to determine whether the difference in risk-adjusted performance (good or bad) is statistically significant. Several methods of performance attribution, which examine the impact of asset allocation and selection on a portfolio's returns relative to their benchmark, are also available.

- Studies have challenged the validity of all techniques that assume a market portfolio, which theoretically includes all risky assets, when investigators typically use a proxy such as the S&P 500 that is limited to U.S. common stocks. This criticism does not invalidate the normative asset pricing model, only its application because of measurement problems related to the proxy used for the market portfolio. This benchmark measurement problem is increased in an environment where global investing is the norm and when taxable portfolios are involved.

- The performance of portfolio managers who follow a specific style must be compared to appropriate style benchmarks. Two main techniques help determine a manager's style. Returns-based or effective mix analysis uses quadratic programming to determine what subset and percentage allocations from a group of indexes most closely resembles the portfolio's performance over time. Characteristic analysis examines the characteristics of the securities held in the portfolio to judge the manager's style.

- The evaluation models for bonds typically consider separately the several important decision variables related to bonds: the overall market factor, the impact of maturity–duration decisions, the influence of sector and quality factors, and the impact of individual bond selection.

- Investors need to evaluate their own performance and the performance of hired managers. The various techniques discussed provide theoretically justifiable measures that differ slightly. Although correlation is high among the various measures, *all the measures should be used* because each provides different insights regarding the performance of managers. Finally, a portfolio manager should be evaluated *many times* and *in a variety of market environments* before a final judgment is reached regarding his or her strengths and weaknesses.

QUESTIONS

1. Assuming you are managing your own portfolio, discuss whether you should evaluate your own performance. What would you compare your performance against?
2. What are the three major factors to consider when evaluating a portfolio manager?
3. How can a portfolio manager earn superior risk-adjusted returns?
4. Why is it more difficult to develop a benchmark for a taxable portfolio?
5. How can you measure whether a portfolio is completely diversified? Explain why this measure makes sense.
6. What are the three basic types of portfolio performance measures? Provide one example of each.
7. Define and discuss the Treynor measure of portfolio performance.
8. Define and discuss the original Sharpe measure of portfolio performance.
9. Why is it suggested that an evaluation employ both the Treynor and Sharpe measures of performance? What additional information do we gather when we compare the rankings achieved using the two measures?
10. Define the new Sharpe ratio and discuss how it differs from the original Sharpe measure.
11. What is RAP (or M^2)? How does it differ from the Sharpe measure?

12. What is the information ratio? What information does it provide regarding portfolio performance?

13. Define the Jensen measure of performance and discuss whether it should produce results similar to those from the Treynor or the Sharpe methods.

14. Assuming the proxy used for the market portfolio is not a good proxy, discuss the potential problem with the measurement of portfolio beta. Show by an example the effect on a portfolio evaluation graph if the measured beta is significantly lower than the true beta.

15. Assuming the market proxy is a poor proxy, show an example of the potential impact on the security market line (SML) and demonstrate with an example how a portfolio that was superior relative to the proxy SML line could be inferior when compared to the true SML.

16. Show with a graph the effect global investing should have on the aggregate efficient frontier. Discuss the effect of this on the world SML and individual betas.

17. Why is it important to determine a portfolio manager's style?

18. What is returns–based style analysis? Describe the value of its result to a portfolio manager's client or potential client.

19. What are some of the problems or difficulties that may be faced when using returns–based style analysis?

20. What is characteristic analysis? What advantage(s) does it have over returns–based analysis? What disadvantages?

21. It is contended that the derivation of an appropriate model for evaluating the performance of a bond-portfolio manager is more difficult than an equity-portfolio evaluation model because the former requires more decisions. Discuss some of the specific decisions you must consider when evaluating the performance of a bond-portfolio manager.

22. *CFA Examination Level III*

    Richard Roll, in an article on using the capital asset pricing model (CAPM) to evaluate portfolio performance, indicated that it may not be possible to evaluate portfolio management ability if there is an error in the benchmark used.

    a. In evaluating portfolio performance, describe the general procedure, with emphasis on the benchmark employed. (5 minutes)

    b. Explain what Roll meant by the benchmark error and identify the specific problem with this benchmark. (5 minutes)

    c. Draw a graph that shows how a portfolio that has been judged as superior relative to a "measured" security market line (SML) can be inferior relative to the "true" SML. (10 minutes)

    d. Assume you are informed that a given portfolio manager has been evaluated as superior when com-
    pared to the DJIA, the S&P 500, and the NYSE Composite Index. Explain whether this consensus would make you feel more comfortable regarding the portfolio manager's true ability. (5 minutes)

    e. While conceding the possible problem with benchmark errors as set forth by Roll, some contend this does not mean the CAPM is incorrect but only that there is a measurement problem when implementing the theory. Others contend that because of benchmark errors, the whole technique should be scrapped. Take and defend one of these positions. (5 minutes)

23. *CFA Examination Level III*

    During a quarterly review session, a client of Fixed Income Investors, a pension fund advisory firm, asks Fred Raymond, the portfolio manager for the company's account, if he could provide a more detailed analysis of their portfolio performance than simply total return. Specifically, the client had recently seen a copy of an article on the analysis of bond portfolio returns that attempted to decompose the total return into the following four components:

    a. Yield-to-maturity effect

    b. Interest rate effect

    c. Sector/quality effect

    d. Residual

    Although he does not expect you to be able to provide such an analysis this year, he asks you to explain each of these components to him so he will be better prepared to understand such an analysis when you do it for his company's portfolio next year. Explain each of these components. (20 minutes)

24. What are the attributes of a good benchmark?

25. "If an equity portfolio manager can't do better than the S&P 500 over two or three years, I fire him!" says I. M. Quick, who oversees several external managers of his company's pension fund. Do you agree that Mr. Quick has a good policy? Why or why not?

26. Using the bond market line, is it possible for a manager to have a negative policy effect but a positive interest rate anticipation effect? Can the analysis effect be negative while the trading effect is positive? Explain.

27. *CFA Examination Level III*

    ECB Inc. is a corporate pension fund sponsor. Sloan & Company is ECB's only U.S. equity manager and operates under a mandate that allows Sloan to invest in any U.S. equity. ECB has historically measured the investment performance of Sloan against a "median manager" benchmark. The benchmark performance is derived from a broad universe of U.S. equity managers.

    a. Evaluate ECB's use of the "median manager" approach to measure Sloan's U.S. equity performance.

Justify your response by referencing *each* of *four* characteristics of an effective benchmark. (10 minutes)

As an alternative to the "median manager" approach, ECB's treasurer has suggested using the S&P 500 Index as a benchmark for evaluating Sloan's investment performance.

b. Describe *two* problems with using the S&P 500 Index as an appropriate benchmark for evaluating Sloan's investment performance. (4 minutes)

28. *CFA Examination Level III*

During the annual review of Acme's pension plan, several Trustees questioned Graham about various aspects of performance measurement and risk assessment. In particular, one Trustee asked about the appropriateness of using each of the following benchmarks:

- market index
- benchmark normal portfolio
- median of the manager universe

a. Explain *two* different weaknesses of using *each* of the three benchmarks to measure the performance of a portfolio.
Note: Your response must contain a total of *six* different weaknesses. (6 minutes)

Another Trustee asked how to distinguish among the following performance measures:

- the Sharpe ratio
- the Treynor measure
- Jensen's alpha
  i. Describe how *each* of the three performance measures is calculated.
  ii. State whether *each* measure assumes that the relevant risk is systematic, unsystematic, or total. Explain how *each* measure relates excess return and the relevant risk. (12 minutes)

PROBLEMS

1. Assume that during the past ten-year period the risk-free rate was 6 percent, and three portfolios had the following characteristics:

Portfolio	Return (%)	Beta	σ (%)
A	13	1.10	14
B	11	0.90	10
C	17	1.20	20

Compute the Treynor value for each portfolio, and indicate which portfolio had the best performance. Assume the market return during this period was 12 percent with an 18 percent standard deviation. How did these managers fare relative to the market?

2. Given the standard deviations specified in Problem 1, compute the Sharpe measure of performance for the three portfolios. Is there any difference in the ranking achieved using the Treynor versus the Sharpe measure? Discuss the probable cause.

3. Compute the RAP measure for the portfolios in Problem 1. How do the rankings using the RAP measure compare with those when the Sharpe and Treynor measures are used? Why?

4. Assume that instead of covering ten years, the information in Problem 1 covers only one year. Compute Jensen's alpha measures for each portfolio.

5. The following portfolios are being considered for investment; some statistics for the most recent year are

presented. During this time the risk-free rate was 5 percent.

Portfolio	Return (%)	Beta	σ (%)
P	15	1.0	5
Q	20	1.5	10
R	10	1.6	3
S	17	1.1	6
Market	13	1.0	4

a. Compute the Sharpe measure for each portfolio and the market portfolio.
b. Compute the RAP measure for each portfolio and the market portfolio.
c. Compute the Treynor measure for each portfolio and the market portfolio.
d. Compute the Jensen measure for each portfolio and the market portfolio.
e. Rank the portfolios using each measure.

6. You have decided to undertake an evaluation of the performance of the Cirrus International Fund (CIF) for your Investment Club. You have collected the following data: Return on CIF = 15%; RFR = 5%; beta for CIF is 1.20; market return = 10%.

a. Draw the security market line.
b. Compute a risk-adjusted return measure for CIF. How does CIF compare to the market portfolio?

7. Below are some approximate data on the returns and risks of several assets. Rank them based on their Sharpe and Treynor measures. Which measure provides the most relevant rankings in this case?

Asset	Average Return	Standard Deviation	Beta (Based on the S&P 500)
Small-company stocks	18%	36%	1.34
Large-company stocks	12	21	1.00
Long-term Treasury bonds	9	8	0.70
Intermediate-term Treasury bonds	8	7	0.60
Treasury bills	4	4	0.10

8. Given the data below, what were the actual returns on the portfolios of manager A and manager B? What was the source of the over- or underperformance by managers A and B?

Weights

Manager A	Policy	Actual
	50% stocks	55% stocks
	50% bonds	45% bonds

Returns

Index	Actual
10% stocks	8% stocks
6% bonds	8% bonds

Weights

Manager B	Policy	Actual
	60% stocks	50% stocks
	30% bonds	30% bonds
	10% cash	20% cash

Returns

Index	Actual
−5% stocks	−2% stocks
7% bonds	8% bonds
3% cash	3.5% cash

WEB EXERCISES

1. Go to the Web site of a mutual fund organization (for example, try Vanguard, Fidelity, or T. Rowe Price) and obtain annual (or quarterly) return data for several mutual funds. Using the data available to you on the Web site and the measures discussed in this chapter, which funds are the best performers?
2. Explain how the data on Professor Ken French's personal Web site, *http://mba.tuck.dartmouth.edu/pages/ faculty/ken.french,* might be of interest to an equity-portfolio manager interested in performance evaluation.
3. Find three Web sites that offer performance evaluations of mutual funds. How are their evaluative tools similar? How do they differ?
4. Morningstar's "star" ratings are quite popular in the financial press and in mutual fund advertisements. Explore the Morningstar Web site and report on how the star ratings, which are based on risk-adjusted returns, are developed.

SPREADSHEET EXERCISES

1. Go to the Vanguard Web site and obtain information on the income return and capital return on their Vanguard 500 Index fund. Develop a spreadsheet to compute before-tax and after-tax returns for an investor in the 28 percent income tax bracket. Assume all capital gains are taxed at 20 percent when they are realized. What are the after-tax returns if capital gains are realized every two years? Three years? Four years? Five years? Ten years? What does this show about the sensitivity of after-tax returns to the capital gains realization rate assumption?
2. Develop a spreadsheet that, given the risk-free return, information about the market portfolio, and a portfolio's average return, standard deviation, and beta, will compute its Sharpe, RAP, Treynor, and Jensen's alpha measures. Use it to compute these measures for the following funds. Use the sort function to sort them, from best performing to worst performing, for each of the four measures.

Portfolio	Return (%)	σ (%)	β
ABC	10.1	18.2	1.10
DEF	12.5	22.3	1.25
GHI	8.9	13.8	0.95
RKF	7.2	12.5	0.82
NAE	14.4	24.7	1.43
Market	12.0	20.0	1.00
Risk-free	4.5	0.0	0.00

3. Monthly returns on twenty mutual funds were regressed on returns of the S&P 500. Given the statistical data below, answer the following questions.
   a. Which mutual funds have alphas that are statistically different from zero?
   b. Which mutual funds have beta coefficients that are statistically different from 1.0?
   c. What three mutual funds most closely followed the returns of the S&P 500?

d. Compute the Sharpe, Treynor, and RAP measures for each fund (the "Alpha" column represents Jensen's alpha). Estimate the correlation between the Sharpe, Treynor, RAP, and Jensen measures.

	Alpha	Alpha T Statistic	Alpha Standard Error	Beta	Beta T Statistic	Beta Standard Error	R^2	Arithmetic Mean (%)	Standard Deviation (%)
AIM Constellation A	0.0016	0.1968	0.0083	1.2601	7.6615	0.1645	0.6265	17.478	27.762
American Cent Ultra	0.0014	0.2788	0.005	1.2362	12.4611	0.0992	0.8161	16.995	23.848
Domini Social Equity	−0.0007	−0.4006	0.0018	1.0502	29.1488	0.036	0.9604	12.911	18.662
Dreyfus Growth Opportunity	−0.0059	−2.5378	0.0023	1.0851	23.6461	0.0459	0.9411	7.051	19.484
Fidelity Magellan	0.0013	0.7101	0.0018	1.0603	29.0285	0.0365	0.9601	15.429	18.848
Fidelity Puritan	0.0002	0.0772	0.0022	0.5133	11.7116	0.0438	0.7967	9.519	10.049
Gabelli Asset	0.0024	0.8144	0.003	0.8038	13.6372	0.0589	0.8416	14.625	15.261
Guardian Park Avenue A	−0.002	−0.2698	0.0075	1.1144	7.4243	0.1501	0.6116	11.873	24.829
Janus Venture	0.0071	0.4169	0.017	1.4789	4.359	0.3393	0.3519	25.874	43.493
Lindner Growth and Income	−0.007	−1.7738	0.004	0.4787	6.0696	0.0789	0.5128	0.593	11.679
Merrill Lynch Equity Income A	0.0008	0.1586	0.0053	0.541	5.0802	0.1065	0.4244	10.563	14.545
Morgan Stanley Developing Growth B	0.0075	0.4581	0.0163	1.2846	3.9589	0.3245	0.3093	24.690	40.301
Neuberger Berman Fasciano	−0.0027	−0.5585	0.0049	0.7063	7.2723	0.0971	0.6018	7.650	15.907
Oppenheimer Value A	−0.0082	−1.8268	0.0045	0.9041	10.0867	0.0896	0.744	2.695	18.304
Putnam Fund for Growth & Income A	−0.0034	−0.693	0.005	0.7612	7.7055	0.0988	0.6291	7.250	16.768
Smith Barney Premium Total Return B	−0.0024	−0.8952	0.0027	0.5269	9.8848	0.0533	0.7363	6.551	10.711
T. Rowe Price Growth Stock	0.003	1.108	0.0027	1.0169	18.6307	0.0546	0.9084	17.149	18.594
Value Line Special Situations	0.0101	0.8885	0.0113	1.1877	5.259	0.2258	0.4414	27.020	31.179
Van Kampen Pace A	−0.0043	−3.5839	0.0012	1.0191	43.0623	0.0237	0.9815	8.409	17.920
Vanguard Wellington	0.0004	0.1299	0.0034	0.464	6.8472	0.0678	0.5726	9.435	10.743
S&P 500	0.000			1.000			1.000	13.363	17.422
U.S. Treasury Bill								5.060	

4. The developers of RAP (or M^2) have modified the Treynor measure by developing an "M^2-for-beta" measure. Given what you know about the Treynor measure and the relationship between M^2 and the Sharpe ratio, develop a "M^2-for-beta" measure. Add its calculation to the spreadsheet in the preceding exercise.

5. Develop a spreadsheet to do basic performance attribution evaluation. Solve Problem 8 using your spreadsheet.

6. Use spreadsheets to find the time-weighted rate of return and the dollar-weighted rate of return of the following (see the appendix):
   a. Invest $1,000 at time zero; invest another $5,000 at the end of the first year and again at the end of the second year. The portfolio earns 10 percent during year 1, 15 percent during year 2, and loses 5 percent during year 3.
   b. Invest $5,000 at time zero; invest another $5,000 at the end of the first year, and $1,000 at the end of the second year. The portfolio earns 10 percent during year 1, 15 percent during year 2, and loses 5 percent during year 3.
   c. Invest $10,000 at time zero; no further investments are made. The portfolio returns 10 percent, 5 percent, −8 percent, and 15 percent in the next four years.
   d. Invest $2,000 at time zero, after one year, and after a second year. The portfolio earns 10 percent each year.

REFERENCES

In addition to studies referenced in the footnotes, the following may be of interest:

Coggin, T. Daniel, and Frank J. Fabozzi, eds. *The Handbook of Equity Style Management,* 2nd ed. New Hope, PA: Frank J. Fabozzi Associates Publishing, 1997.

Fabozzi, Frank J., ed. *The Handbook of Fixed-Income Securities,* 6th ed. New York: McGraw-Hill, 2001.

Kahn, Ronald N. "Bond Performance Analysis: A Multi-Factor Approach." *Journal of Portfolio Management* 18, no. 1 (Fall 1991).

Klein, Robert A., and Jess Lederman, eds. *Equity Style Management.* Chicago: Irwin, 1995.

Leibowitz, Martin L., Lawrence Bader, and Stanley Koselman. "Optimal Portfolios Relative to Benchmark Allocations." *Journal of Portfolio Management* 19, no. 4 (Summer 1993).

THOMSON ONE
Business School Edition

1. Evaluating a portfolio's performance may depend on its benchmark. Review the performance of the DJ STOXX index, the MSCI US index (MSUSAML), and a World index from Thomson One: Business School Edition.
   a. How might the performance of a stock be affected when compared to these three indexes?
   b. Using price return data for the past year for General Electric, compute GE's beta and alpha using each of these indexes.
2. Compare the performance of the S&P 1500 composite index to one of its components (S&P 600 small-cap, S&P 400 mid-cap, S&P 500 large-cap).
   a. How might a portfolio's performance be affected if the composite index were used as a benchmark rather than a market-capitalization-based index?
   b. Using price return data for the past year for General Electric, compute GE's beta and alpha using each of these indexes.
3. Compare the performance of the S&P 500 composite index to its two constituent parts: S&P 500 Barra/Growth and S&P 500 Barra/Value.
   a. How might a portfolio's performance be affected if the composite index were used as a benchmark rather than one of the style-based indexes?
   b. Using price return data for the past year for General Electric, compute GE's beta and alpha using each of these indexes.

GLOSSARY

Analysis effect The difference in performance of a bond portfolio from that of a chosen index due to acquisition of temporarily mispriced issues that then move to their correct prices.

Benchmark error An inaccuracy in evaluation of portfolio performance due to poor representation of market performance because of the market indicator series chosen as a proxy for the market portfolio.

Benchmark portfolio A portfolio that represents the performance evaluation standard for a portfolio manager. The benchmark portfolio is usually a passive index or portfolio with an asset allocation equal to that specified in the investor's policy statement.

Capital gains realization rate The net gains or losses realized in a taxable portfolio over a year, expressed as a percentage of the average gains that are available for realizing during the year.

Characteristic analysis Characteristic analysis is based on the belief that the portfolio's current make-up will be a good predictor for the next period's returns. The methodology uses a complex decision-tree approach to classify a portfolio's stocks relative to fundamental characteristics of indexes.

Effective mix analysis *See* returns-based analysis.

Information ratio A ratio that measures the average return in excess of its benchmark divided by the standard deviation of the excess return.

Interest rate anticipation effect The difference in return caused by changing the duration of the portfolio during a period as compared with the portfolio's long-term policy duration.

Management effect A combination of the interest rate anticipation effect, the analysis effect, and the trading effect.

Normal portfolio A specialized or customized benchmark constructed to evaluate a specific manager's investment style or philosophy.

Policy effect The difference in performance of a bond portfolio from that of a chosen index due to differences in duration, which result from a fund's investment policy.

Returns-based analysis Compares the historical return pattern of the portfolio in question to the historical returns of various well-specified indexes. Uses sophisticated quadratic programming techniques to indicate what styles or style combinations were most similar to the portfolio's actual historical returns.

Trading effect The difference in performance of a bond portfolio from that of a chosen index due to short-run changes in the composition of the portfolio.

Computing Portfolio Returns

Before we can evaluate portfolio performance, we need to measure it. In Chapter 2 we learned how to calculate a holding period return (HPR), which equals the change in portfolio value plus income divided by beginning portfolio value, or,

$$\text{HPR} = \frac{(\textbf{Ending Value} - \textbf{Beginning Value}) + \textbf{Income}}{\textbf{Beginning Value}}$$

Depending on the length of the holding period, it is possible to convert the holding period return into an annualized return (if the holding period was less than one year) or an average annual return (if the holding period exceeded one year).

This calculation is not appropriate for many portfolios that experience cash inflows or cash outflows over time, such as a pension fund or mutual fund. The portfolio's ending value may be contaminated by the net effect of the periodic cash flows. We can use two basic approaches to account for intermittent cash flows: the dollar-weighted rate of return or the time-weighted rate of return.

To illustrate how to compute these two measures, we will use the following scenario: at time 0 we invest $1,000 in Unbelievable Mutual Fund (a no-load fund). The fund shares have a NAV of $20, so we are purchasing fifty shares. At time 1, the fund pays a $1 per share income distribution, so we receive $1 × 50 shares or $50 in income. Also, the value of the fund increases by 25 percent to a NAV of $25, which means our holdings are worth $1,300 (50 shares × $25/share NAV + $50 income distribution). The fund has returned 30 percent during this first period.

At time 1 we invest another $1,000 in Unbelievable by purchasing another forty shares ($1,000/$25 NAV). Our total is now ninety shares. At time 2, Unbelievable pays an income distribution of $1 per share (we receive $90) and the NAV has risen another 40 percent to $35. The value of our holdings is now 90 shares × $35 + $90 (income distribution) = $3,240.

What has been our return over this time period? It depends on whether we compute a dollar-weighted rate of return or a time-weighted rate of return.

DOLLAR-WEIGHTED RATE OF RETURN

The dollar-weighted rate of return (DWRR) is simply the internal rate of return on the portfolio's cash flows. It is the rate of return that sets the present value of the cash outflows equal to the present value of the cash inflows. In other words, it is the return earned on the invested funds that allow them to grow to the end-of-period value. To determine the DWRR, our cash outflows to the portfolio were

$1,000 at time 0
$1,000 at time 1

The cash inflows from our investment were

$50 at time 1
$90 at time 2
$3,150 worth of mutual fund shares at time 2

Setting the present values of the inflows and outflows equal to each other, we have

$$\$1,000 + \frac{\$1,000}{1 + r} = \frac{\$50}{1 + r} + \frac{\$90 + \$3,150}{(1 + r)^2}$$

Solving for r, the internal rate of return, or DWRR, is 38.66 percent. Our average annual return over these two periods was 38.66 percent.

TIME-WEIGHTED RATE OF RETURN

The time-weighted rate of return (TWRR) is simply the geometric mean return. We compute the TWRR by finding the product of the holding period returns (which equals $1 + \text{HPR}$) for the n periods of time, raising it to the power of $1/n$, and then subtracting 1 from it:

$$\text{TWRR} = \left[(\text{HPR}_1)(\text{HPR}_2)(\text{HPR}_3) \cdots (\text{HPR}_n) \right]^{1/n} - 1$$

Recall that the history of our Unbelievable investment was

Time	Market Value before Cash Flow	Cash In (Out)	Market Value after Cash Flow	Return
0	$0	$1,000	$1,000	Not applicable
(NAV is $20/share; we purchase 50 shares.)				
1	$1,300	($50) + $1,000	$2,250	$1,300/$1,000 − 1 = 30%
(NAV is now 25% higher, or $25/share; we purchase an additional 40 shares; we now own a total of 90 shares.)				
2	$3,240	($90)	$3,150	$3,240/$2,250 − 1 = 44%

(NAV is $35 per share after the cash payout.)

Thus, the first period's return was 30 percent; the second period's return was 44 percent. The time-weighted rate of return is

$$\text{TWRR} = \left[(1 + 0.30)(1 + 0.44) \right]^{1/2} - 1 = 0.3682$$

or the average annual return is 36.82 percent.

So we have computed our returns two different ways and we have two different answers. The DWRR is 38.66 percent; the TWRR is 36.82 percent. Which of these is the correct return?

WHY THE TIME-WEIGHTED RATE OF RETURN IS SUPERIOR

The TWRR is generally acknowledged as the best way to compute returns; in fact, the portfolio performance standards adopted by the CFA Institute require that returns be computed using the TWRR approach.[21] The TWRR is regarded as the better method because

---

[21] *Performance Presentation Standards* (Charlottesville, VA: CFA Institute, 1999).

it considers only the actual period-by-period portfolio returns. As such, the TWRR has no size bias whereas the dollar-weighted rate of return does.

This size bias was evident in our example. The first period's return was 30 percent; after more funds were invested, the second period's return was 44 percent. The DWRR of 38.66 is higher than the TWRR of 36.82 percent because the fund was larger when it had the higher return in period 2.

We can easily show that, had the periodic returns been reversed, the DWRR would be less than the TWRR since the fund's large 44 percent return would have occurred during a period when less funds were invested in it. The following table represents the cash flows and market values assuming a 44 percent first-period return and a 30 percent second-period return. As before, we assume an annual income distribution of $1 per share and that the initial NAV is $20 per share.

Time	Market Value before Cash Flow	Cash In (Out)	Market Value after Cash Flow	Return
0	$0	$1,000	$1,000	Not applicable
(NAV is $20/share; we purchase 50 shares.)				
1	$1,440	($50) + 1,000	$2,390	$1,440/$1,000 − 1 = 44%
(NAV is now 44 percent higher, or $28.8 per share; we purchase an additional 34.72 shares; we now own a total of 84.72 shares.)				
2	$3,107	($84.72)	$3,022.28	$3,107/$2,390 − 1 = 30%

It is straightforward to see that the TWRR remains the same, at 36.82 percent:

$$\textbf{TWRR} = \left[(1 + 0.44)(1 + 0.30) \right]^{1/2} - 1 = 0.3682$$

Again, the dollar-weighted rate of return is found by equating the present values of the cash inflows and outflows:

$$\$1,000 + \frac{\$1,000}{1 + r} = \frac{\$50}{1 + r} + \frac{\$84.72 + \$3,022.28}{(1 + r)^2}$$

Solving for r, we see that the DWRR is now 35.05 percent. It is lower than the TWRR now because Unbelievable's returns were lower in the second period when the fund size was larger. This illustrates the DWRR's size bias and indicates that using the TWRR generates a more accurate picture of a fund's returns.

For simplicity, our examples here assumed annual cash flows. Real-world managers deal with fund cash inflows and outflows daily that result from dividends, bond coupons, and investor deposits and withdrawals. They must make day-by-day accountings of cash flows and portfolio market values. The time-weighted rate of return is a daily average return; the annual return is derived by compounding the daily return over 365 days.

Once portfolio returns have been measured, they can be compared to those of the benchmark. Portfolio returns should be adjusted for the level of portfolio risk to determine whether higher returns were earned solely because the manager invested in higher-risk securities.

HOW TO BECOME A CFA® CHARTERHOLDER

As mentioned in the section on career opportunities, the professional designation of Chartered Financial Analyst® (CFA®) is becoming a significant requirement for a career in investment analysis and/or portfolio management. For that reason, this section presents the history and objectives of CFA Institute (formerly AIMR) and general guidelines for acquiring the CFA designation. If you are interested in the program, you can write or email CFA Institute for more information.

The CFA examinations were first offered in 1963 by the Institute of Chartered Financial Analysts (ICFA) which was formed in 1959 to enhance the professionalism of those involved in various aspects of the investment decision-making process and to recognize those who achieve a high level of professionalism. The ICFA combined with the Financial Analysts Federation in 1990 to form AIMR. In 2004, the AIMR membership approved a name change to CFA Institute.

The CFA Institute mission is to lead the investment profession globally by setting the highest standards of education, integrity, and professional excellence. As applied to the CFA Program, its focus is:

○ To develop and keep current a "body of knowledge" applicable to the investment decision-making process. The principal components of this knowledge are financial accounting, economics, both debt and equity securities analysis, portfolio management, ethical and professional standards, and quantitative techniques.

○ To administer a study and examination program for eligible candidates, the primary objectives of which are to assist the candidate in mastering and applying the body of knowledge and to test the candidate's competency in the knowledge gained.

○ To award the professional CFA designation to those candidates who have passed three examination levels (encompassing a total of 18 hours of testing over a minimum of $2\frac{1}{2}$ years), who meet stipulated standards of professional conduct, and who otherwise are eligible for membership in CFA Institute.

○ CFA Institute also provides a useful and informative program of continuing education through seminars, publications, and other formats that enable members, candidates, and others in the investment constituency to be more aware of and better utilize the changing and expanding body of knowledge.

○ Importantly, CFA Institute also sponsors and enforces a Code of Ethics and Standards of Professional Conduct that apply to enrolled candidates and to all members.

To enter the CFA Program an applicant must have a bachelor's degree (or the equivalent work experience). An applicant must receive a bachelor's degree no later than December 31 of the current exam year in order to qualify for entrance. To be awarded the CFA charter, a candidate must:

○ Sequentially pass the Level I, Level II, and Level III examinations;

○ Have at least four years of acceptable professional experience working in the investment decision-making process;

○ Join CFA Institute as a member; and

○ Apply concurrently for membership in a CFA Institute Society.

The curriculum of the CFA Program covers:

1. Ethical and Professional Standards
2. Quantitative Methods
3. Economics
4. Financial Statement Analysis
5. Corporate Finance
6. Analysis of Fixed-Income Investments
7. Analysis of Equity Investments
8. Analysis of Derivatives
9. Analysis of Alternative Investments
10. Portfolio Management

Members and candidates are typically employed in the investment field. From 1963 to September 2004, more than 61,000 charters have been awarded. More than 100,000 individuals were enrolled in the 2004 CFA Program. If you are interested in learning more about the CFA Program, CFA Institute has a booklet that describes the program and includes an application form. The address is: CFA Institute, Attn: Information Central, PO Box 3668, Charlottesville, Virginia, 22903, USA. You may also request a booklet by email to info@cfainstitute.org.

CFA INSTITUTE:
THE CODE OF ETHICS AND STANDARDS OF PROFESSIONAL CONDUCT

THE CODE OF ETHICS

Members of CFA Institute shall:

- Act with integrity, competence, dignity, and in ethical manner when dealing with the public, clients, prospects, employers, employees, and fellow members.
- Practice and encourage others to practice in a professional and ethical manner that will reflect credit on members and their profession.
- Strive to maintain and improve their competence and the competence of others in the profession.
- Use reasonable care and exercise independent professional judgment.

STANDARDS OF PROFESSIONAL CONDUCT

Standard I: Fundamental Responsibilities

Members shall:

A. Maintain knowledge of and comply with applicable laws, rules, and regulations (including CFA Institute's Code of Ethics and Standards of Professional Conduct) of any government, governmental agency, regulatory organization, licensing agency, or professional association governing the members' professional activities.

B. Not knowingly participate or assist in any violation of such laws, rules, or regulations.

Standard II: Relationships with and Responsibilities to the Profession

A. **Use of Professional Designation.**

1. CFA Institute members may reference their membership only in a dignified and judicious manner. The use of the reference may be accompanied by an accurate explanation of the requirements that have been met to obtain membership in these organizations.

2. Those who have earned the right to use the Chartered Financial Analyst® designation may use the marks "Chartered Financial Analyst" or "CFA®" and are encouraged to do so, but only in a proper, dignified, and judicious manner. The use of the designation may be accompanied by an accurate explanation of the requirements that have been met to obtain the right to use the designation.

3. Candidates in the CFA Program, as defined in the CFA Institute Bylaws, may reference their participation in the CFA Program, but the reference must clearly state that an individual is a candidate in the CFA Program and cannot imply that the candidate has achieved any type of partial designation.

B. **Professional Misconduct.**

1. Members shall not engage in any professional conduct involving dishonesty, fraud, deceit, or misrepresentation or commit any act that reflects adversely on their honesty, trustworthiness, or professional competence.

2. Members and candidates shall not engage in any conduct or commit any act that compromises the integrity of the CFA designation or the integrity or validity of examinations leading to the award of the right to use the CFA designation.

C. **Prohibition against Plagiarism.** Members shall not copy or use, in substantially the same form as the original, material prepared by another without acknowledging and identifying the name of the author, publisher, or source of each material. Members may use, without acknowledgement, factual information published by recognized financial and statistical reporting services or similar sources.

Standard III: Relationships with and Responsibilities to the Employer

A. **Obligation to Inform Employer of Code and Standards.** Members shall:

1. Inform their employer in writing, through their direct supervisor, that they are obligated to comply with the Code and Standards and are subject to disciplinary sanctions for violations thereof.

2. Deliver a copy of the Code and Standards to their employer if the employer does not have a copy.

B. **Duty to Employer.** Members shall not undertake any independent practice that could result in compensation or other benefit in competition with their employer unless they obtain written consent from both their employer and the persons or entities for whom they undertake independent practice.

C. **Disclosure of Conflicts to Employer.** Members shall:

1. Disclose to their employer all matters, including beneficial ownership of securities or other investments, that reasonably could be expected to interfere with their duty to their employer or ability to make unbiased and objective recommendations.

2. Comply with any prohibitions on activities imposed by their employer if a conflict of interest exists.

D. **Disclosure of Additional Compensation Arrangements.** Members shall disclose to their employer in writing all monetary compensation or other benefits that they receive for their services that are in addition to compensation or benefits conferred by a member's employer.

E. **Responsibilities of Supervisors.** Members with supervisory responsibility, authority, or the ability to influence the conduct of others shall exercise reasonable supervision over those subject to their supervision or authority to prevent any violation of applicable statutes, regulations, or provisions of the Code and Standards. In so doing, members are entitled to rely on reasonable procedures designed to detect and prevent such violations.

Standard IV: Relationships with and Responsibilities to Clients and Prospects

A. **Investment Process.**

A.1 **Reasonable Basis and Representations. Members shall:**

a. Exercise diligence and thoroughness in making investment recommendations or in taking investment actions.

b. Have a reasonable and adequate basis, appointed by appropriate research and investigation, for such recommendations or actions.

c. Make reasonable and diligent efforts to avoid any material misrepresentation in any research report or investment recommendation.

d. Maintain appropriate records to support the reasonableness of such recommendations or actions.

A.2 Research Reports. Members shall:

a. Use reasonable judgment regarding the inclusion or exclusion of relevant factors in research reports.

b. Distinguish between facts and opinions in research reports.

c. Indicate the basic characteristics of the investment involved when preparing for publication a research report that is not directly related to a specific portfolio or client.

A.3 Independence and Objectivity. Members shall use reasonable care and judgment to achieve and maintain independence and objectivity in making investment recommendations or taking investment action.

B. Interactions with Clients and Prospects.

B.1 Fiduciary Duties. In relationships with clients, members shall use particular care in determining applicable fiduciary duty and shall comply with such duty as to those persons and interests to whom the duty is owed. Members must act for the benefit of their clients and place their clients' interests before their own.

B.2 Portfolio Investment Recommendations and Actions. Members shall:

a. Make a reasonable inquiry into a client's financial situation, investment experience, and investment objectives prior to making any investment recommendations and shall update this information as necessary, but no less frequently than annually, to allow the member to adjust their investment recommendations to reflect changed circumstances.

b. Consider the appropriateness and suitability of investment recommendations or actions for each portfolio or client. In determining appropriateness and suitability, members shall consider applicable relevant factors, including the needs and circumstances of the portfolio or client, the basic characteristics of the investment involved, and the basic characteristics of the total portfolio. Members shall not make a recommendation unless they reasonably determine that the recommendation is suitable to the client's financial situation, investment experience, and investment objectives.

c. Distinguish between facts and opinions in the presentation of investment recommendations.

d. Disclose to clients and prospects the basic format and general principles of the investment processes by which securities are selected and portfolios are constructed and shall promptly disclose to clients and prospects any changes that might significantly affect those processes.

B.3 Fair Dealing. Members shall deal fairly and objectively with all clients and prospects when disseminating investment recommendations, disseminating material changes in prior investment recommendations, and taking investment action.

B.4 Priority of Transactions. Transactions for clients and employers shall have priority over transactions in securities or other investments of which a member is the beneficial owner so that such personal transactions do not operate adversely to their clients' or employer's interests. If members make a recommendation regarding the purchase or sale of a security or other investment, they shall give their clients and employer adequate oppor-

tunity to act on the recommendation before acting on their own behalf. For purposes of the Code and Standards, a member is a "beneficial owner" if the member has

a. a direct or indirect pecuniary interest in the securities;

b. the power to vote or direct the voting of the shares of the securities or investments;

c. the power to dispose or direct the disposition of the security or investment.

B.5 Preservation of Confidentiality. Members shall preserve the confidentiality of information communicated by clients, prospects, or employers concerning matters within the scope of the client-member, prospect-member, or employer-member relationship unless the member receives information concerning illegal activities on the part of the client, prospect, or employer.

B.6 Prohibition against Misrepresentation. Members shall not make any statements, orally or in writing, that misrepresent

a. the services that they or their firms are capable of performing;

b. their qualifications or the qualifications of their firm;

c. the member's academic or professional credentials.

Members shall not make or imply, orally or in writing, any assurances or guarantees regarding any investment except to communicate accurate information regarding the terms of the investment instrument and the issuer's obligations under the instrument.

B.7 Disclosure of Conflicts to Clients and Prospects. Members shall disclose to their clients and prospects all matters, including beneficial ownership of securities or other investments, that reasonably could be expected to impair the member's ability to make unbiased and objective recommendations.

B.8 Disclosure of Referral Fees. Members shall disclose to clients and prospects any consideration or benefit received by the member or delivered to others for the recommendation of any services to the client or prospect.

Standard V: Relationships with and Responsibilities to the Investing Public

A. Prohibition against Use of Material Nonpublic Information. Members who possess material nonpublic information related to the value of a security shall not trade or cause others to trade in that security if such trading would breach a duty or if the information was misappropriated or relates to a tender offer. If members receive material nonpublic information in confidence, they shall not breach that confidence by trading or causing others to trade in securities to which such information relates. Members shall make reasonable efforts to achieve public dissemination of material nonpublic information disclosed in breach of a duty.

B. Performance Presentation.

1. Members shall not make any statements, orally or in writing, that misrepresent the investment performance that they or their firms have accomplished or can reasonably be expected to achieve.

2. If members communicate individual or firm performance information directly or indirectly to clients or prospective clients, or in a manner intended to be received by clients or prospective clients, members shall make every reasonable effort to assure that such performance information is a fair, accurate, and complete presentation of such performance.

INTEREST TABLES

TABLE C.1 Present Value of $1: $PVIF = 1/(1 + k)^t$

Period	1%	2%	3%	4%	5%	6%	7%	8%	9%	10%	12%	14%	15%	16%	18%	20%	24%	28%	32%	36%
1	.9901	.9804	.9709	.9615	.9524	.9434	.9346	.9259	.9174	.9091	.8929	.8772	.8696	.8621	.8475	.8333	.8065	.7813	.7576	.7353
2	.9803	.9612	.9426	.9246	.9070	.8900	.8734	.8573	.8417	.8264	.7972	.7695	.7561	.7432	.7182	.6944	.6504	.6104	.5739	.5407
3	.9706	.9423	.9151	.8890	.8638	.8396	.8163	.7938	.7722	.7513	.7118	.6750	.6575	.6407	.6086	.5787	.5245	.4768	.4348	.3975
4	.9610	.9238	.8885	.8548	.8227	.7921	.7629	.7350	.7084	.6830	.6355	.5921	.5718	.5523	.5158	.4823	.4230	.3725	.3294	.2923
5	.9515	.9057	.8626	.8219	.7835	.7473	.7130	.6806	.6499	.6209	.5674	.5194	.4972	.4761	.4371	.4019	.3411	.2910	.2495	.2149
6	.9420	.8880	.8375	.7903	.7462	.7050	.6663	.6302	.5963	.5645	.5066	.4556	.4323	.4104	.3704	.3349	.2751	.2274	.1890	.1580
7	.9327	.8706	.8131	.7599	.7107	.6651	.6227	.5835	.5470	.5132	.4523	.3996	.3759	.3538	.3139	.2791	.2218	.1776	.1432	.1162
8	.9235	.8535	.7894	.7307	.6768	.6274	.5820	.5403	.5019	.4665	.4039	.3506	.3269	.3050	.2660	.2326	.1789	.1388	.1085	.0854
9	.9143	.8368	.7664	.7026	.6446	.5919	.5439	.5002	.4604	.4241	.3606	.3075	.2843	.2630	.2255	.1938	.1443	.1084	.0822	.0628
10	.9053	.8203	.7441	.6756	.6139	.5584	.5083	.4632	.4224	.3855	.3220	.2697	.2472	.2267	.1911	.1615	.1164	.0847	.0623	.0462
11	.8963	.8043	.7224	.6496	.5847	.5268	.4751	.4289	.3875	.3505	.2875	.2366	.2149	.1954	.1619	.1346	.0938	.0662	.0472	.0340
12	.8874	.7885	.7014	.6246	.5568	.4970	.4440	.3971	.3555	.3186	.2567	.2076	.1869	.1685	.1372	.1122	.0757	.0517	.0357	.0250
13	.8787	.7730	.6810	.6006	.5303	.4688	.4150	.3677	.3262	.2897	.2292	.1821	.1625	.1452	.1163	.0935	.0610	.0404	.0271	.0184
14	.8700	.7579	.6611	.5775	.5051	.4423	.3878	.3405	.2992	.2633	.2046	.1597	.1413	.1252	.0985	.0779	.0492	.0316	.0205	.0135
15	.8613	.7430	.6419	.5553	.4810	.4173	.3624	.3152	.2745	.2394	.1827	.1401	.1229	.1079	.0835	.0649	.0397	.0247	.0155	.0099
16	.8528	.7284	.6232	.5339	.4581	.3936	.3387	.2919	.2519	.2176	.1631	.1229	.1069	.0930	.0708	.0541	.0320	.0193	.0118	.0073
17	.8444	.7142	.6050	.5134	.4363	.3714	.3166	.2703	.2311	.1978	.1456	.1078	.0929	.0802	.0600	.0451	.0258	.0150	.0089	.0054
18	.8360	.7002	.5874	.4936	.4155	.3503	.2959	.2502	.2120	.1799	.1300	.0946	.0808	.0691	.0508	.0376	.0208	.0118	.0068	.0039
19	.8277	.6864	.5703	.4746	.3957	.3305	.2765	.2317	.1945	.1635	.1161	.0829	.0703	.0596	.0431	.0313	.0168	.0092	.0051	.0029
20	.8195	.6730	.5537	.4564	.3769	.3118	.2584	.2145	.1784	.1486	.1037	.0728	.0611	.0514	.0365	.0261	.0135	.0072	.0039	.0021
25	.7798	.6095	.4776	.3751	.2953	.2330	.1842	.1460	.1160	.0923	.0588	.0378	.0304	.0245	.0160	.0105	.0046	.0021	.0010	.0005
30	.7419	.5521	.4120	.3083	.2314	.1741	.1314	.0994	.0754	.0573	.0334	.0196	.0151	.0116	.0070	.0042	.0016	.0006	.0002	.0001
40	.6717	.4529	.3066	.2083	.1420	.0972	.0668	.0460	.0318	.0221	.0107	.0053	.0037	.0026	.0013	.0007	.0002	.0001	×	×
50	.6080	.3715	.2281	.1407	.0872	.0543	.0339	.0213	.0134	.0085	.0035	.0014	.0009	.0006	.0003	.0001	×	×	×	×
60	.5504	.3048	.1697	.0951	.0535	.0303	.0173	.0099	.0057	.0033	.0011	.0004	.0002	.0001	×	×	×	×	×	×

*The factor is zero to four decimal places.

TABLE C.2   Present Value of an Annuity of $1 per Period for n Periods:

$$PVIFA = \sum_{t=1}^{n} \frac{1}{(1+k)^t} = \frac{1 - \dfrac{1}{(1+k)^n}}{k}$$

Number of Payments	1%	2%	3%	4%	5%	6%	7%	8%	9%	10%	12%	14%	15%	16%	18%	20%	24%	28%	32%
1	0.9901	0.9804	0.9709	0.9615	0.9524	0.9434	0.9346	0.9259	0.9174	0.9091	0.8929	0.8772	0.8696	0.8621	0.8475	0.8333	0.8065	0.7813	0.7576
2	1.9704	1.9416	1.9135	1.8861	1.8594	1.8334	1.8080	1.7833	1.7591	1.7355	1.6901	1.6467	1.6257	1.6052	1.5656	1.5278	1.4568	1.3916	1.3315
3	2.9410	2.8839	2.8286	2.7751	2.7232	2.6730	2.6243	2.5771	2.5313	2.4869	2.4018	2.3216	2.2832	2.2459	2.1743	2.1065	1.9813	1.8684	1.7663
4	3.9020	3.8077	3.7171	3.6299	3.5460	3.4651	3.3872	3.3121	3.2397	3.1699	3.0373	2.9137	2.8550	2.7982	2.6901	2.5887	2.4043	2.2410	2.0957
5	4.8534	4.7135	4.5797	4.4518	4.3295	4.2124	4.1002	3.9927	3.8897	3.7908	3.6048	3.4331	3.3522	3.2743	3.1272	2.9906	2.7454	2.5320	2.3452
6	5.7955	5.6014	5.4172	5.2421	5.0757	4.9173	4.7665	4.6229	4.4859	4.3553	4.1114	3.8887	3.7845	3.6847	3.4976	3.3255	3.0205	2.7594	2.5342
7	6.7282	6.4720	6.2303	6.0021	5.7864	5.5824	5.3893	5.2064	5.0330	4.8684	4.5638	4.2883	4.1604	4.0386	3.8115	3.6046	3.2423	2.9370	2.6775
8	7.6517	7.3255	7.0197	6.7327	6.4632	6.2098	5.9713	5.7466	5.5348	5.3349	4.9676	4.6389	4.4873	4.3436	4.0776	3.8372	3.4212	3.0758	2.7860
9	8.5660	8.1622	7.7861	7.4353	7.1078	6.8017	6.5152	6.2469	5.9952	5.7590	5.3282	4.9464	4.7716	4.6065	4.3030	4.0310	3.5655	3.1842	2.8681
10	9.4713	8.9826	8.5302	8.1109	7.7217	7.3601	7.0236	6.7101	6.4177	6.1446	5.6502	5.2161	5.0188	4.8332	4.4941	4.1925	3.6819	3.2689	2.9304
11	10.3676	9.7868	9.2526	8.7605	8.3064	7.8869	7.4987	7.1390	6.8052	6.4951	5.9377	5.4527	5.2337	5.0286	4.6560	4.3271	3.7757	3.3351	2.9776
12	11.2551	10.5753	9.9540	9.3851	8.8633	8.3838	7.9427	7.5361	7.1607	6.8137	6.1944	5.6603	5.4206	5.1971	4.7932	4.4392	3.8514	3.3868	3.0133
13	12.1337	11.3484	10.6350	9.9856	9.3936	8.8527	8.3577	7.9038	7.4869	7.1034	6.4235	5.8424	5.5831	5.3423	4.9095	4.5327	3.9124	3.4272	3.0404
14	13.0037	12.1062	11.2961	10.5631	9.8986	9.2950	8.7455	8.2442	7.7862	7.3667	6.6282	6.0021	5.7245	5.4675	5.0081	4.6106	3.9616	3.4587	3.0609
15	13.8651	12.8493	11.9379	11.1184	10.3797	9.7122	9.1079	8.5595	8.0607	7.6061	6.8109	6.1422	5.8474	5.5755	5.0916	4.6755	4.0013	3.4834	3.0764
16	14.7179	13.5777	12.5611	11.6523	10.8378	10.1059	9.4466	8.8514	8.3126	7.8237	6.9740	6.2651	5.9542	5.6685	5.1624	4.7296	4.0333	3.5026	3.0882
17	15.5623	14.2919	13.1661	12.1657	11.2741	10.4773	9.7632	9.1216	8.5436	8.0216	7.1196	6.3729	6.0472	5.7487	5.2223	4.7746	4.0591	3.5177	3.0971
18	16.3983	14.9920	13.7535	12.6593	11.6896	10.8276	10.0591	9.3719	8.7556	8.2014	7.2497	6.4674	6.1280	5.8178	5.2732	4.8122	4.0799	3.5294	3.1039
19	17.2260	15.6785	14.3238	13.1339	12.0853	11.1581	10.3356	9.6036	8.9501	8.3649	7.3658	6.5504	6.1982	5.8775	5.3162	4.8435	4.0967	3.5386	3.1090
20	18.0456	16.3514	14.8775	13.5903	12.4622	11.4699	10.5940	9.8181	9.1285	8.5136	7.4694	6.6231	6.2593	5.9288	5.3527	4.8696	4.1103	3.5458	3.1129
25	22.0232	19.5235	17.4131	15.6221	14.0939	12.7834	11.6536	10.6748	9.8226	9.0770	7.8431	6.8729	6.4641	6.0971	5.4669	4.9476	4.1474	3.5640	3.1220
30	25.8077	22.3965	19.6004	17.2920	15.3725	13.7648	12.4090	11.2578	10.2737	9.4269	8.0552	7.0027	6.5660	6.1772	5.5168	4.9789	4.1601	3.5693	3.1242
40	32.8347	27.3555	23.1148	19.7928	17.1591	15.0463	13.3317	11.9246	10.7574	9.7791	8.2438	7.1050	6.6418	6.2335	5.5482	4.9966	4.1659	3.5712	3.1250
50	39.1961	31.4236	25.7298	21.4822	18.2559	15.7619	13.8007	12.2335	10.9617	9.9148	8.3045	7.1327	6.6605	6.2463	5.5541	4.9995	4.1666	3.5714	3.1250
60	44.9550	34.7609	27.6756	22.6235	18.9293	16.1614	14.0392	12.3766	11.0480	9.9672	8.3240	7.1401	6.6651	6.2402	5.5553	4.9999	4.1667	3.5714	3.1250

TABLE C.3 — Future Value of $1 at the End of n Periods: $FVIF_{k,n} = (1 + k)^n$

Period	1%	2%	3%	4%	5%	6%	7%	8%	9%	10%	12%	14%	15%	16%	18%	20%	24%	28%	32%	36%
1	1.0100	1.0200	1.0300	1.0400	1.0500	1.0600	1.0700	1.0800	1.0900	1.1000	1.1200	1.1400	1.1500	1.1600	1.1800	1.2000	1.2400	1.2800	1.3200	1.3600
2	1.0201	1.0404	1.0609	1.0816	1.1025	1.1236	1.1449	1.1664	1.1881	1.2100	1.2544	1.2996	1.3225	1.3456	1.3924	1.4400	1.5376	1.6384	1.7424	1.8496
3	1.0303	1.0612	1.0927	1.1249	1.1576	1.1910	1.2250	1.2597	1.2950	1.3310	1.4049	1.4815	1.5209	1.5609	1.6430	1.7280	1.9066	2.0972	2.3000	2.5155
4	1.0406	1.0824	1.1255	1.1699	1.2155	1.2625	1.3108	1.3605	1.4116	1.4641	1.5735	1.6890	1.7490	1.8106	1.9388	2.0736	2.3642	2.6844	3.0360	3.4210
5	1.0510	1.1041	1.1593	1.2167	1.2763	1.3382	1.4026	1.4693	1.5386	1.6105	1.7623	1.9254	2.0114	2.1003	2.2878	2.4883	2.9316	3.4360	4.0075	4.6526
6	1.0615	1.1262	1.1941	1.2653	1.3401	1.4185	1.5007	1.5869	1.6771	1.7716	1.9738	2.1950	2.3131	2.4364	2.6996	2.9860	3.6352	4.3980	5.2899	6.3275
7	1.0721	1.1487	1.2299	1.3159	1.4071	1.5036	1.6058	1.7138	1.8280	1.9487	2.2107	2.5023	2.6600	2.8262	3.1855	3.5832	4.5077	5.6295	6.9826	8.6054
8	1.0829	1.1717	1.2668	1.3686	1.4775	1.5938	1.7182	1.8509	1.9926	2.1436	2.4760	2.8526	3.0590	3.2784	3.7589	4.2998	5.5895	7.2058	9.2170	11.703
9	1.0937	1.1951	1.3048	1.4233	1.5513	1.6895	1.8385	1.9990	2.1719	2.3579	2.7731	3.2519	3.5179	3.8030	4.4355	5.1598	6.9310	9.2234	12.166	15.916
10	1.1046	1.2190	1.3439	1.4802	1.6289	1.7908	1.9672	2.1589	2.3674	2.5937	3.1058	3.7072	4.0456	4.4114	5.2338	6.1917	8.5944	11.805	16.059	21.646
11	1.1157	1.2434	1.3842	1.5395	1.7103	1.8983	2.1049	2.3316	2.5804	2.8531	3.4785	4.2262	4.6524	5.1173	6.1759	7.4301	10.657	15.111	21.198	29.439
12	1.1268	1.2682	1.4258	1.6010	1.7959	2.0122	2.2522	2.5182	2.8127	3.1384	3.8960	4.8179	5.3502	5.9360	7.2876	8.9161	13.214	19.342	27.982	40.037
13	1.1381	1.2936	1.4685	1.6651	1.8856	2.1329	2.4098	2.7196	3.0658	3.4523	4.3635	5.4924	6.1528	6.8858	8.5994	10.699	16.386	24.758	36.937	54.451
14	1.1495	1.3195	1.5126	1.7317	1.9799	2.2609	2.5785	2.9372	3.3417	3.7975	4.8871	6.2613	7.0757	7.9875	10.147	12.839	20.319	31.691	48.756	74.053
15	1.1610	1.3459	1.5580	1.8009	2.0789	2.3966	2.7590	3.1722	3.6425	4.1772	5.4736	7.1379	8.1371	9.2655	11.973	15.407	25.195	40.564	64.358	100.71
16	1.1726	1.3728	1.6047	1.8730	2.1829	2.5404	2.9522	3.4259	3.9703	4.5950	6.1304	8.1372	9.3576	10.748	14.129	18.488	31.242	51.923	84.953	136.96
17	1.1843	1.4002	1.6528	1.9479	2.2920	2.6928	3.1588	3.7000	4.3276	5.0545	6.8660	9.2765	10.761	12.467	16.672	22.186	38.740	66.461	112.13	186.27
18	1.1961	1.4282	1.7024	2.0258	2.4066	2.8543	3.3799	3.9960	4.7171	5.5599	7.6900	10.575	12.375	14.462	19.673	26.623	48.038	85.070	148.02	253.33
19	1.2081	1.4568	1.7535	2.1068	2.5270	3.0256	3.6165	4.3157	5.1417	6.1159	8.6128	12.055	14.231	16.776	23.214	31.948	59.567	108.89	195.39	344.53
20	1.2202	1.4859	1.8061	2.1911	2.6533	3.2071	3.8697	4.6610	5.6044	6.7275	9.6463	13.743	16.366	19.460	27.393	38.337	73.864	139.37	257.91	468.57
21	1.2324	1.5157	1.8603	2.2788	2.7860	3.3996	4.1406	5.0338	6.1088	7.4002	10.803	15.667	18.821	22.574	32.323	46.005	91.591	178.40	340.44	637.26
22	1.2477	1.5460	1.9161	2.3699	2.9253	3.6035	4.4304	5.4365	6.6586	8.1403	12.100	17.861	21.644	26.186	38.142	55.206	113.57	228.35	449.39	866.67
23	1.2572	1.5769	1.9736	2.4647	3.0715	3.8197	4.7405	5.8715	7.2579	8.9543	13.552	20.361	24.891	30.376	45.007	66.247	140.83	292.30	593.19	1178.6
24	1.2697	1.6084	2.0328	2.5633	3.2251	4.0489	5.0724	6.3412	7.9111	9.8497	15.178	23.212	28.625	35.236	53.108	79.496	174.63	374.14	783.02	1602.9
25	1.2824	1.6406	2.0938	2.6658	3.3864	4.2919	5.4274	6.8485	8.6231	10.834	17.000	26.461	32.918	40.874	62.668	95.396	216.54	478.90	1033.5	2180.0
26	1.2953	1.6734	2.1566	2.7725	3.5557	4.5494	5.8074	7.3964	9.3992	11.918	19.040	30.166	37.856	47.414	73.948	114.47	268.51	612.99	1364.3	2964.9
27	1.3082	1.7069	2.2213	2.8834	3.7335	4.8223	6.2139	7.9881	10.245	13.110	21.324	34.389	43.535	55.000	87.259	137.37	332.95	784.63	1800.9	4032.2
28	1.3213	1.7410	2.2879	2.9987	3.9201	5.1117	6.6488	8.6271	11.167	14.421	23.883	39.204	50.065	63.800	102.96	164.84	412.86	1004.3	2377.2	5483.8
29	1.3345	1.7758	2.3566	3.1187	4.1161	5.4184	7.1143	9.3173	12.172	15.863	26.749	44.693	57.575	74.008	121.50	197.81	511.95	1285.5	3137.9	7458.0
30	1.3478	1.8114	2.4273	3.2434	4.3219	5.7435	7.6123	10.062	13.267	17.449	29.959	50.950	66.211	85.849	143.37	237.37	634.81	1645.5	4142.0	10143.
40	1.4889	2.2080	3.2620	4.8010	7.0400	10.285	14.974	21.724	31.409	45.259	93.050	188.88	267.86	378.72	750.37	1469.7	5455.9	19426.	66520.	×
50	1.6446	2.6916	4.3839	7.1067	11.467	18.420	29.457	46.901	74.357	117.39	289.00	700.23	1083.6	1670.7	3927.3	9100.4	46890.	×	×	×
60	1.8167	3.2810	5.8916	10.519	18.679	32.987	57.946	101.25	176.03	304.48	897.59	2595.9	4383.9	7370.1	20555.	56347.	×	×	×	×

TABLE C.4   Sum of an Annuity of $1 per Period for *n* Periods:

$$FVIFA_{k,n} = \sum_{t=1}^{n} (1+k)^{t-1} = \frac{(1+k)^n - 1}{k}$$

Number of Periods	1%	2%	3%	4%	5%	6%	7%	8%	9%	10%	12%	14%	15%	16%	18%	20%	24%	28%	32%	36%
1	1.0000	1.0000	1.0000	1.0000	1.0000	1.0000	1.0000	1.0000	1.0000	1.0000	1.0000	1.0000	1.0000	1.0000	1.0000	1.0000	1.0000	1.0000	1.0000	1.0000
2	2.0100	2.0200	2.0300	2.0400	2.0500	2.0600	2.0700	2.0800	2.0900	2.1000	2.1200	2.1400	2.1500	2.1600	2.1800	2.2000	2.2400	2.2800	2.3200	2.3600
3	3.0301	3.0604	3.0909	3.1216	3.1525	3.1836	3.2149	3.2464	3.2781	3.3100	3.3744	3.4396	3.4725	3.5056	3.5724	3.6400	3.7776	3.9184	4.0624	4.2096
4	4.0604	4.1216	4.1836	4.2465	4.3101	4.3746	4.4399	4.5061	4.5731	4.6410	4.7793	4.9211	4.9934	5.0665	5.2154	5.3680	5.6842	6.0156	6.3624	6.7251
5	5.1010	5.2040	5.3091	5.4163	5.5256	5.6371	5.7507	5.8666	5.9847	6.1051	6.3528	6.6101	6.7424	6.8771	7.1542	7.4416	8.0484	8.6999	9.3983	10.146
6	6.1520	6.3081	6.4684	6.6330	6.8019	6.9753	7.1533	7.3359	7.5233	7.7156	8.1152	8.5355	8.7537	8.9775	9.4420	9.9299	10.980	12.135	13.405	14.798
7	7.2135	7.4343	7.6625	7.8983	8.1420	8.3938	8.6540	8.9228	9.2004	9.4872	10.089	10.730	11.066	11.413	12.141	12.915	14.615	16.533	18.695	21.126
8	8.2857	8.5830	8.8923	9.2142	9.5491	9.8975	10.259	10.636	11.028	11.435	12.299	13.232	13.726	14.240	15.327	16.499	19.122	22.163	25.678	29.731
9	9.3685	9.7546	10.159	10.582	11.026	11.491	11.978	12.487	13.021	13.579	14.775	16.085	16.785	17.518	19.085	20.798	24.712	29.369	34.895	41.435
10	10.462	10.949	11.463	12.006	12.577	13.180	13.816	14.486	15.192	15.937	17.548	19.337	20.303	21.321	23.521	25.958	31.643	38.592	47.061	57.351
11	11.566	12.168	12.807	13.486	14.206	14.971	15.783	16.645	17.560	18.531	20.654	23.044	24.349	25.732	28.755	32.150	40.237	50.398	63.121	78.998
12	12.682	13.412	14.192	15.025	15.917	16.869	17.888	18.977	20.140	21.384	24.133	27.270	29.001	30.850	34.931	39.580	50.894	65.510	84.320	108.43
13	13.809	14.680	15.617	16.626	17.713	18.882	20.140	21.495	22.953	24.522	28.029	32.088	34.351	36.786	42.218	48.496	64.109	84.852	112.30	148.47
14	14.947	15.973	17.086	18.291	19.598	21.015	22.550	24.214	26.019	27.975	32.392	37.581	40.504	43.672	50.818	59.195	80.496	109.61	149.23	202.92
15	16.096	17.293	18.598	20.023	21.578	23.276	25.129	27.152	29.360	31.772	37.279	43.842	47.580	51.659	60.965	72.035	100.81	141.30	197.99	276.97
16	17.257	18.639	20.156	21.824	23.657	25.672	27.888	30.324	33.003	35.949	42.753	50.980	55.717	60.925	72.939	87.442	126.01	181.86	262.35	377.69
17	18.430	20.012	21.761	23.697	25.840	28.212	30.840	33.750	36.973	40.544	48.883	59.117	65.075	71.673	87.068	105.93	157.25	233.79	347.30	514.66
18	19.614	21.412	23.414	25.645	28.132	30.905	33.999	37.450	41.301	45.599	55.749	68.394	75.836	84.140	103.74	128.11	195.99	300.25	459.44	700.93
19	20.810	22.840	25.116	27.671	30.539	33.760	37.379	41.446	46.018	51.159	63.439	78.969	88.211	98.603	123.41	154.74	244.03	385.32	607.47	954.27
20	22.019	24.297	26.870	29.778	33.066	36.785	40.995	45.762	51.160	57.275	72.052	91.024	102.44	115.37	146.62	186.68	303.60	494.21	802.86	1298.8
21	23.239	25.783	28.676	31.969	35.719	39.992	44.865	50.422	56.764	64.002	81.698	104.76	118.81	134.84	174.02	225.02	377.46	633.59	1060.7	1767.3
22	24.471	27.299	30.536	34.248	38.505	43.392	49.005	55.456	62.873	71.402	92.502	120.43	137.63	157.41	206.34	271.03	469.05	811.99	1401.2	2404.6
23	25.716	28.845	32.452	36.617	41.430	46.995	53.436	60.893	69.531	79.543	104.60	138.29	159.27	183.60	244.48	326.23	582.62	1040.3	1850.6	3271.3
24	26.973	30.421	34.426	39.082	44.502	50.815	58.176	66.764	76.789	88.497	118.15	158.65	184.16	213.97	289.49	392.48	723.46	1332.6	2443.8	4449.9
25	28.243	32.030	36.459	41.645	47.727	54.864	63.249	73.105	84.700	98.347	133.33	181.87	212.79	249.21	342.60	471.98	898.09	1706.8	3226.8	6052.9
26	29.525	33.670	38.553	44.311	51.113	59.156	68.676	79.954	93.323	109.18	150.33	208.33	245.71	290.08	405.27	567.37	1114.6	2185.7	4260.4	8233.0
27	30.820	35.344	40.709	47.084	54.669	63.705	74.483	87.350	102.72	121.09	169.37	238.49	283.56	337.50	479.22	681.85	1383.1	2798.7	5624.7	11197.9
28	32.129	37.051	42.930	49.967	58.402	68.528	80.697	95.338	112.96	134.20	190.69	272.88	327.10	392.50	566.48	819.22	1716.0	3583.3	7425.6	15230.2
29	33.450	38.792	45.218	52.966	62.322	73.639	87.346	103.96	124.13	148.63	214.58	312.09	377.16	456.30	669.44	984.06	2128.9	4587.6	9802.9	20714.1
30	34.784	40.568	47.575	56.084	66.438	79.058	94.460	113.28	136.30	164.49	241.33	356.78	434.74	530.31	790.94	1181.8	2640.9	5873.2	12940.	28172.2
40	48.886	60.402	75.401	95.025	120.79	154.76	199.63	259.05	337.88	442.59	767.09	1342.0	1779.0	2360.7	4163.2	7343.8	22728.	69377.	×	×
50	64.463	84.579	112.79	152.66	209.34	290.33	406.52	573.76	815.08	1163.9	2400.0	4994.5	7217.7	10435.	21813.	45497.	×	×	×	×
60	81.669	114.05	163.05	237.99	353.58	533.12	813.52	1253.2	1944.7	3034.8	7471.6	18535.	29219.	46057.	×	×	×	×	×	×

*FVIFA > 99,999

STANDARD NORMAL PROBABILITIES

z	0.00	0.01	0.02	0.03	0.04	0.05	0.06	0.07	0.08	0.09
0.0	.5000	.5040	.5080	.5120	.5160	.5199	.5239	.5279	.5219	.5359
0.1	.5398	.5438	.5478	.5517	.5557	.5596	.5636	.5675	.5714	.5753
0.2	.5793	.5832	.5871	.5910	.5948	.5987	.6026	.6064	.6103	.6141
0.3	.6179	.6217	.6255	.6293	.6331	.6368	.6406	.6443	.6480	.6517
0.4	.6554	.6591	.6628	.6664	.6700	.6736	.6772	.6808	.6844	.6879
0.5	.6915	.6950	.6985	.7019	.7054	.7088	.7123	.7157	.7190	.7224
0.6	.7257	.7291	.7324	.7357	.7389	.7422	.7454	.7486	.7517	.7549
0.7	.7580	.7611	.7642	.7673	.7704	.7734	.7764	.7794	.7823	.7852
0.8	.7881	.7910	.7939	.7967	.7995	.8023	.8051	.8078	.8106	.8133
0.9	.8159	.8186	.8212	.8238	.8264	.8289	.8315	.8340	.8365	.8389
1.0	.8413	.8438	.8461	.8485	.8508	.8531	.8554	.8577	.8599	.8621
1.1	.8643	.8665	.8686	.8708	.8729	.8749	.8770	.8790	.8810	.8830
1.2	.8849	.8860	.8888	.8907	.8925	.8943	.8962	.8980	.8997	.9015
1.3	.9032	.9049	.9066	.9082	.9099	.9115	.9131	.9147	.9162	.9177
1.4	.9192	.9207	.9222	.9236	.9251	.9265	.9279	.9292	.9306	.9319
1.5	.9332	.9345	.9357	.9370	.9382	.9394	.9406	.9418	.9429	.9441
1.6	.9452	.9463	.9474	.9484	.9495	.9505	.9515	.9525	.9535	.9545
1.7	.9554	.9564	.9573	.9582	.9591	.9599	.9608	.9616	.9625	.9633
1.8	.9641	.9649	.9656	.9664	.9671	.9678	.9686	.9693	.9699	.9706
1.9	.9713	.9719	.9726	.9732	.9738	.9744	.9750	.9756	.9761	.9767
2.0	.9772	.9778	.9783	.9788	.9793	.9798	.9803	.9808	.9812	.9817
2.1	.9821	.9826	.9830	.9834	.9838	.9842	.9846	.9850	.9854	.9857
2.2	.9861	.9864	.9868	.9871	.9875	.9878	.9881	.9884	.9887	.9890
2.3	.9893	.9896	.9898	.9901	.9904	.9906	.9909	.9911	.9913	.9916
2.4	.9918	.9920	.9922	.9925	.9927	.9929	.9931	.9932	.9934	.9936
2.5	.9938	.9940	.9941	.9943	.9945	.9946	.9948	.9949	.9951	.9952
2.6	.9953	.9955	.9956	.9957	.9959	.9960	.9961	.9962	.9963	.9964
2.7	.9965	.9966	.9967	.9968	.9969	.9970	.9971	.9972	.9973	.9974
2.8	.9974	.9975	.9976	.9977	.9977	.9978	.9979	.9979	.9980	.9981
2.9	.9981	.9982	.9982	.9983	.9984	.9984	.9985	.9985	.9986	.9986
3.0	.9987	.9987	.9987	.9988	.9988	.9989	.9989	.9989	.9990	.9990